MOON HANDBOOKS®
NEW YORK STATE

© CHRISTIANE BIRD

autumn in the Catskills

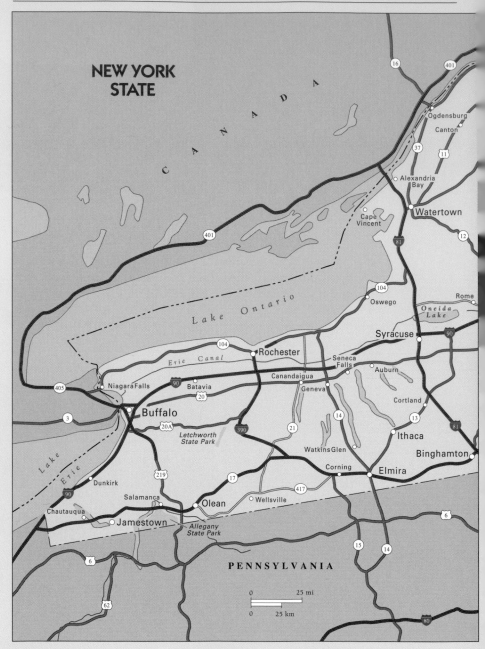

NEW YORK STATE

CANADA

Ogdensburg

Canton

37

11

Alexandria
Bay

401

Cape
Vincent

Watertown

81

12

Lake Ontario

104

Oswego

Rome

Oneida
Lake

16

401

104

Rochester

Erie Canal

Syracuse

90

405

Niagara Falls

90

Batavia

20

Canandaigua

Seneca
Falls

Geneva

Auburn

Cortland

13

81

Buffalo

20A

Letchworth
State Park

390

21

14

Watkins Glen

Ithaca

3

Binghamton

Lake
Erie

219

17

Corning

Elmira

417

6

90

Dunkirk

Salamanca

Olean

Wellsville

15

14

Chautauqua

Jamestown

Allegany
State Park

PENNSYLVANIA

6

62

0   25 mi

0   25 km

80

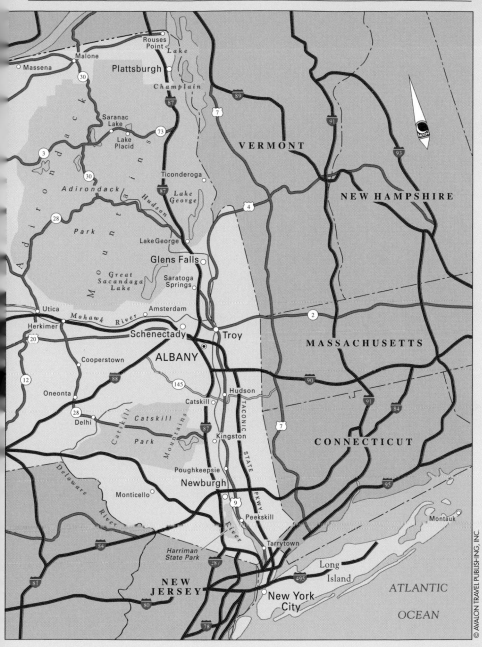

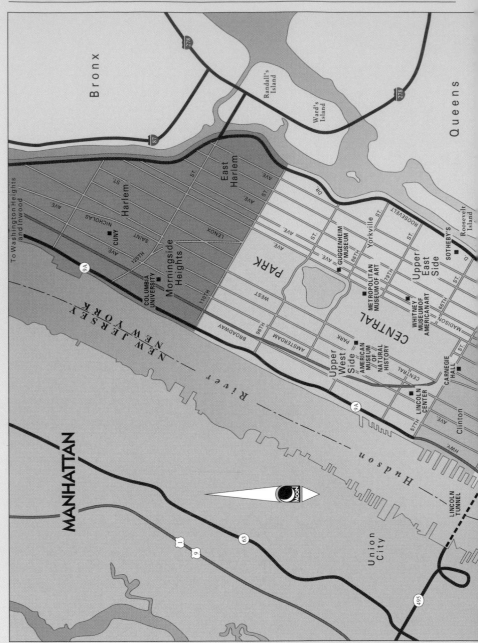

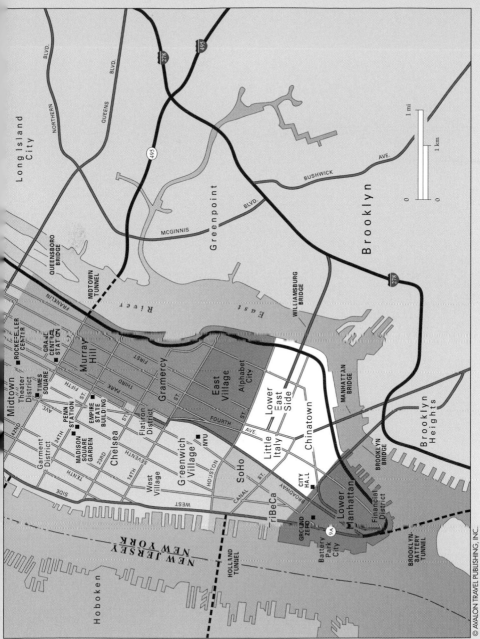

Long Island City

Brooklyn

Greenpoint

BUSHWICK AVE.

MCGINNIS BLVD.

QUEENSBORO BRIDGE

MIDTOWN TUNNEL

FRANKLIN

East River

WILLIAMSBURG BRIDGE

MANHATTAN BRIDGE

Brooklyn Heights

ROCKEFELLER CENTER

GRAND CENTRAL STATION

Murray Hill

Midtown

Theater District

TIMES SQUARE

Gramercy

FIRST

PARK

THIRD

East Village

Alphabet City

Lower East Side

Chinatown

BROOKLYN BRIDGE

FIFTH

42ND

PENN STATION

34TH

EMPIRE STATE BUILDING

Garment District

MADISON SQUARE GARDEN

23RD

Flatiron District

FOURTH

ST.

AVE.

Little Italy

Chelsea

SEVENTH

Greenwich Village

NYU

HOUSTON

SoHo

CITY HALL

14TH

West Village

ST.

BROADWAY

CANAL

Lower Manhattan

Financial District

TENTH

SIDE

WEST

TriBeCa

GROUND ZERO

9A

Battery Park City

BROOKLYN-BATTERY TUNNEL

NEW JERSEY NEW YORK

HOLLAND TUNNEL

Hoboken

1 mi

1 km

0

© AVALON TRAVEL PUBLISHING, INC.

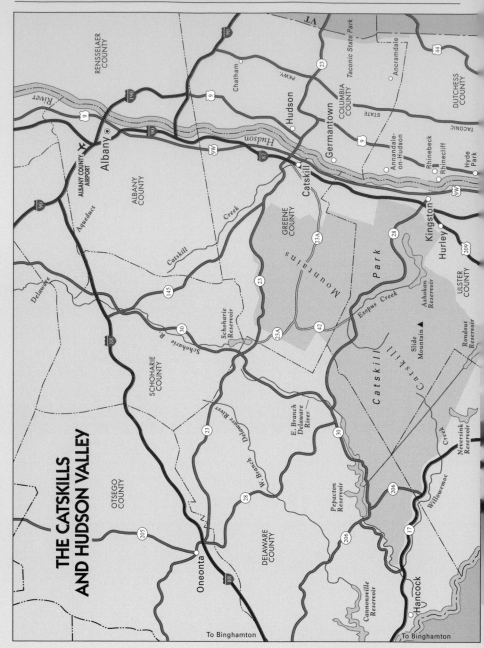

THE CATSKILLS
AND HUDSON VALLEY

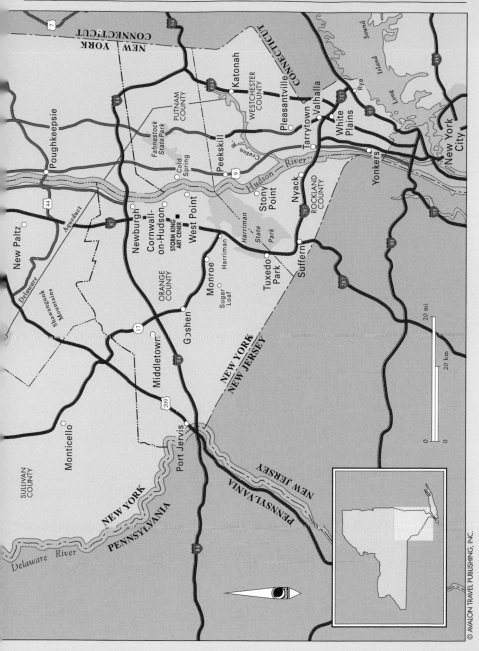

Chrysler Building and Empire State Building, Manhattan

WWW.NYCVISIT.COM

MOON HANDBOOKS®

NEW YORK STATE

THIRD EDITION

CHRISTIANE BIRD

AVALON
TRAVEL

Moon Handbooks New York State
Third Edition

Christiane Bird

Published by:
Avalon Travel Publishing
1400 65th Street, Suite 250
Emeryville, CA 94608, USA
atpfeedback@avalonpub.com
www.moon.com

Please send all comments, corrections,
additions, amendments, and critiques to:
Moon Handbooks New York State
Avalon Travel Publishing
1400 65th Street, Suite 250
Emeryville, CA 94608, USA
atpfeedback@avalonpub.com
www.moon.com

Text © 2003 by Christiane Bird.
Illustrations and maps © 2003 by Avalon Travel Publishing, Inc.
All rights reserved.
Photos and some illustrations are used by permission
and are the property of their original copyright owners.

Printing History
1st edition—1997
3rd edition—May 2003
5 4 3 2 1

ISBN: 1-56691-544-9
ISSN: 1542-6068

Editors: Marisa Solís, Kathryn Ettinger
Series Manager: Kevin McLain
Copy Editor: Jeannie Trizzino
Graphics Coordinator: Susan Snyder
Production Coordinator: Amber Pirker
Cover Designer: Kari Gim
Interior Designers: Amber Pirker, Alvaro Villanueva, Kelly Pendragon
Map Editor: Olivia Solís
Cartographers: Suzanne Service, Naomi Adler Dancis, Kat Kalamaras, Mike Morgenfeld,
   Tim Lohnes
Proofreader: Michael Ferguson
Indexer: Deana Shields

Front cover photo: © Randy Wells

Printed in the U.S.A. by Worzalla
Distributed by Publishers Group West

ABOUT THE AUTHOR
Christiane Bird

© JERRY BROWN

Christiane Bird was born in New York City, but after early childhood, did not live in the Big Apple again until after her graduation from college. In the interim, she got her first taste of exotic travel when her father, a medical doctor, moved the family to Tabriz, Iran, for three years before settling down in the small New England town of Storrs, Connecticut.

When Christiane told her New York City friends that she was writing a guidebook to New York—both city and state—most seemed surprised to hear that there was a state beyond the city. And that, Christiane has found, is a perception shared by many travelers, who don't realize that New York City—as magnificent as it is—is but one small dot on the Empire State map.

One of Christiane's favorite things about New York State is its many quirky, off-the-beaten-track towns that, despite their apparent isolation, nonetheless hold important chapters of civil rights, cultural, and industrial history. Two of her favorite things about New York City are its endless diversity and the unusual quality of its light, most apparent in the late afternoons, when the buildings glow incandescent against a darkening sky.

A graduate of Yale University and former travel writer for the *New York Daily News,* Christiane is also the author of *Moon Handbooks New York City, The Jazz and Blues Lover's Guide to the U.S.,* and *Neither East Nor West: One Woman's Journey Through the Islamic Republic of Iran,* which chronicles her travels back to Iran in 1998. She is currently working on a book about the Kurds.

Contents

SPECIAL TOPICS

MANHATTAN 72

NEW YORK STATE

THE CATSKILLS **387**

CENTRAL NEW YORK **442**

SPECIAL TOPICS

WESTERN NEW YORK **651**

SPECIAL TOPICS

Maps

MAP SYMBOLS

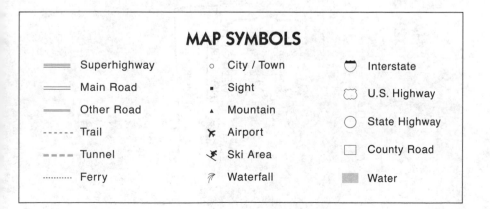

Superhighway		City / Town		Interstate	
Main Road		Sight		U.S. Highway	
Other Road		Mountain		State Highway	
Trail		Airport		County Road	
Tunnel		Ski Area		Water	
Ferry		Waterfall			

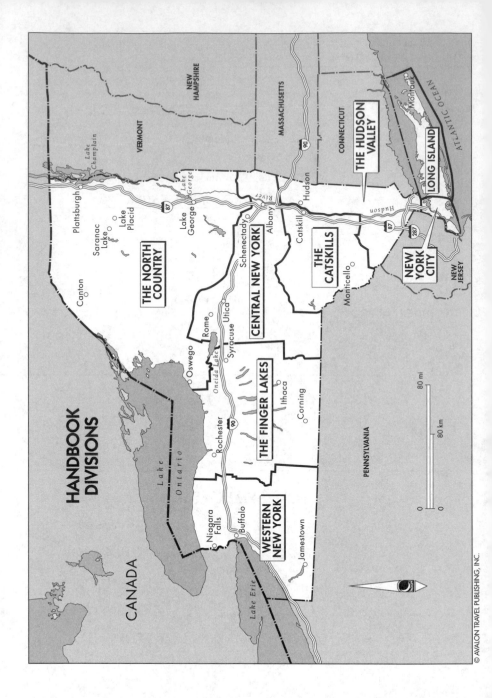

HANDBOOK DIVISIONS

CANADA

Lake Ontario

Lake Erie

Niagara Falls
Buffalo
Jamestown

WESTERN NEW YORK

Rochester

THE FINGER LAKES

Corning
Ithaca

Oswego
Oneida Lake
Syracuse
Utica
Rome

THE NORTH COUNTRY

Canton

Saranac Lake
Lake Placid

Plattsburgh

Lake Champlain

VERMONT

NEW HAMPSHIRE

MASSACHUSETTS

Lake George
Lake George

Schenectady
Albany

CENTRAL NEW YORK

Hudson River

Catskill
Hudson

THE CATSKILLS

Monticello

CONNECTICUT

THE HUDSON VALLEY

Montauk

LONG ISLAND

ATLANTIC OCEAN

NEW YORK CITY

NEW JERSEY

PENNSYLVANIA

Hudson

80 mi
80 km

© AVALON TRAVEL PUBLISHING, INC.

Abbreviations

AYH—American Youth Hostel
B&B—bed-and-breakfast
BYOB—bring your own bottle
d—double occupancy
DEC—Department of Environmental
  Conservation
Ln.—Lane
MAP—Modified American Plan

NYS—New York State
Pkwy.—Parkway
Pl.—Place
pop—population
RV—recreational vehicle
Tnpk.—Turnpike
WW I—World War I
WW II—World War II

Keeping Current

Though we strive to be as accurate as possible, travel information changes rapidly, and various entries in this book may reflect that. A restaurant may have closed or changed its name. Perhaps your motel—mentioned in these pages as an amenable place—proved a nightmare of black velvet Elvis paintings and washcloths posing for bath towels. Or, conversely, maybe you enjoyed that roadside show of tap-dancing chickens and felt it should have been included.

Please send us letters sharing your experiences, corrections, comments, or suggestions.

Moon Handbooks New York State
Avalon Travel Publishing
1400 65th Street, Suite 250
Emeryville, CA 94608, USA
atpfeedback@avalonpub.com

Introduction

The Empire State

New York is not an easy state to get to know or understand. Home to both the largest city in the United States and the largest semi-wilderness area east of the Mississippi, vast acres of farmland and an enormous number of industries, some of the most overeducated people in the world and disturbing pockets of ignorance, New York defies most, if not all, generalizations.

Most discussions of New York State focus on New York City, that alluring "mismanaged ant heap, unfit for human habitation," as historian Kenneth Jackson has called it, located at the mouth of the Hudson River. And yet, the Big Apple is but a smudged dot on the New York State map, occupying far less than one percent of the state's total land mass. Upstate sprawls above the city like a big squashed boot reaching as far north as Canada and almost as far west as Ohio.

Back in the 1800s, upstate New York was nearly as well known to the rest of the country as was New York City. Buffalo, Syracuse, Troy, Schenectady, the Erie Canal, the Catskills, the Adirondacks—back then, upstate meant industrial centers, commerce, transportation, and mountain resorts.

But somewhere in the early to mid-20th century, everything changed. Even as New York City grew larger and larger in the public's consciousness, upstate all

Erie Canal, Fairport, near Rochester

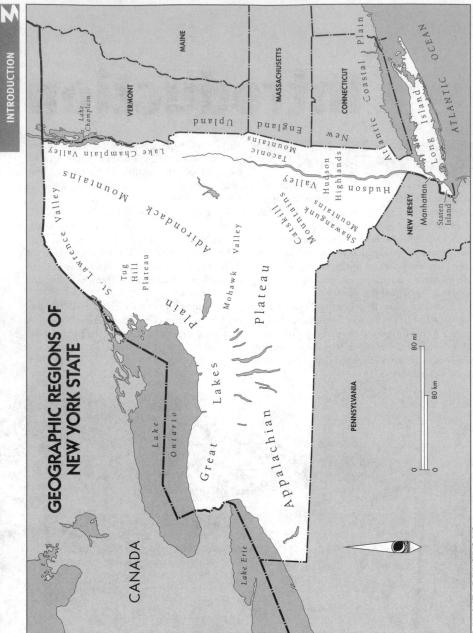

GEOGRAPHIC REGIONS OF
NEW YORK STATE

CANADA

Lake
Ontario

Lake Erie

Great Lakes Plain

St. Lawrence Valley

Tug Hill Plateau

Adirondack Mountains

Lake Champlain

Lake Champlain Valley

Mohawk Valley

Appalachian Plateau

Catskill Mountains

Shawangunk Mountains

Hudson Valley

Taconic Mountains

Hudson Highlands

New England Upland

VERMONT

MAINE

MASSACHUSETTS

CONNECTICUT

NEW JERSEY

PENNSYLVANIA

Manhattan

Staten Island

Long Island

Atlantic Coastal Plain

ATLANTIC OCEAN

80 mi

80 km

0

© AVALON TRAVEL PUBLISHING, INC.

INTRODUCTION

but disappeared. Factories closed, the Erie Canal declined, and the Catskills and Adirondacks went out of style, leaving behind a variegated—and often strikingly beautiful—land that's now virtually unknown to many downstate New Yorkers, let alone the rest of the world.

Today, diversity and sheer size define New York best, both in terms of culture and geography. New York City alone is home to approximately 8 million people, divided into some 200 ethnic groups, while upstate boasts about 12 million more inhabitants, along with 6,000 lakes and ponds, 70,000 miles of rivers and streams, 250 miles of ocean coastline and beach, 150 state parks, and perhaps 1,000 historic sites. New York is one of the oldest states in the union, with landmarks that date back to the 1600s.

Up until the 1960s, New York reigned as the most powerful and populous state in the union. California now holds that position and in 1994, Texas, too, overtook New York in terms of population. Nevertheless, thanks largely to New York City, the Empire State remains the country's business and cultural capital. According to the State Office of Economic Development, New York boasts the 10th largest economy in the world, in a list that includes countries.

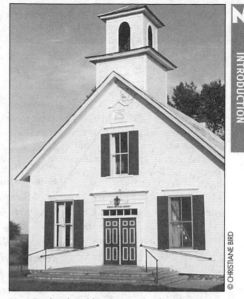

New England architecture arrived early in New York State.

© CHRISTIANE BIRD

A STATE OF IMMIGRANTS

More than any other state, New York is known for its large ethnic populations. As early as 1643, a Jesuit priest visiting the colony reported that among its 500 inhabitants, 18 languages were being spoken.

New York's first European settlers were the Dutch, followed by the English, French, German Protestants, and Scots. African slaves were first brought to the colony in 1626, and the first Jews—fleeing persecution in Spain and Brazil—arrived in Manhattan in the 1650s. By the time of the Revolutionary War, half of the colony's population claimed English descent.

Between 1790 and 1820, New York's population almost quadrupled, due mainly to a huge influx of New Englanders seeking fertile farmland upstate. The Yankees soon greatly outnumbered the older Dutch, French, and German popula-

tions living in the Hudson and Mohawk Valleys, causing much friction and resentment.

The Irish and German Catholics Arrive

Then came the first great wave of Irish and German Catholic immigration. Between 1820 and 1860, New York's population almost tripled, from 1.3 million to 3.8 million. By 1855, the foreign-born comprised almost one-fourth of the state's population and nearly one-half of New York City's population.

The new immigrants arrived in New York City, rather than Boston, Philadelphia, or Virginia, largely because of trade routes. By 1820, New York thrived as a major New World port and the only one with regularly scheduled packet service to Europe. It also had excellent links with the interior and many burgeoning industries. There was no competition from a surplus labor force, as in New England, or from slaves, as in the South.

However, the new immigrants were hardly welcomed with open arms. The older Protestant populations deeply resented the newcomers' Roman

Catholic religion, parochial schools, saloons, and clubs. Setting the precedent for decades of inter-ethnic hostilities to come, they characterized the Irish and German Catholics as morally lax, lazy, ignorant, dirty, and prone to violence.

Post Civil War

The second major wave of U.S. immigration occurred between 1882 and 1924. This time, most of the immigrants came from Southern and Eastern Europe, especially Italy and Poland. Again, the immigrants landed in New York; between 1892 and 1924, 12 million people passed through Ellis Island. Most settled in New York City, but tens of thousands made their way upstate. Utica and Rome became known for their Italian populations, Buffalo for its Italians and Poles, and Binghamton for its Poles and Czechs. Meanwhile, large numbers of Swedes had settled in Jamestown, Irish in Albany, Welsh in Central New York, and French-Canadians in the North Country.

In 1924, strict new immigration laws slowed the influx of foreigners down to a trickle. Simultaneously, black Southerners fleeing from poverty began arriving in New York City. In 1910, Manhattan was home to about 60,000 African Americans; by 1930, that number jumped to 180,000. Tens of thousands more migrated north in the 1940s, '50s, and '60s, attracted by the industries of New York City, Buffalo, Syracuse, and other cities upstate.

Since the lifting of the immigration quotas in 1965, millions more foreigners have entered New York—the greatest wave since the first decade of the 20th century. Over three million foreign-born residents now live in New York State—many from Asia, the Caribbean, Latin America, Russia, and Eastern Europe. Most have settled in New York City, but some live upstate. Rockland County has a large Haitian population; Westchester, a large Japanese one. New

Since the lifting of the immigration quotas in 1965, millions more foreigners have entered New York—the greatest wave since the first decade of the 20th century. Over three million foreign-born residents now live in New York State—many from Asia, the Caribbean, Latin America, Russia, and Eastern Europe.

York State today is home to immigrants from some 180 different countries.

BUSINESSMEN AND FARMERS

If there's one thing New Yorkers historically have had in common, it's a love for making money. Though especially true for New York City, this also applies to the whole state. The Dutch first came to New Amsterdam not to establish settlements but to engage in prosperous trade. They were followed first by frugal New Englanders, and then by hardworking immigrants, all deeply intent on getting ahead. As early as 1795, Talleyrand observed that New York was the best place in the world to make money fast.

Famous New York business tycoons have included John Jay Astor, A. T. Stewart, Cornelius Vanderbilt, J. P. Morgan, and Edward Harriman. John D. Rockefeller, Sr. was born upstate in Moravia, Jay Gould in Roxbury, George Eastman near Rochester, and George Westinghouse in Schoharie County. About one-third of the country's top 500 corporations got their starts in metropolitan New York, while upstate served as the spawning grounds for Eastman Kodak, Bausch & Lomb, Xerox, General Electric, IBM, Endicott-Johnson, and Corning Glass Works, to name but a few.

A counterpoint to New York's many business tycoons has been its many farmers. Up until 1860, agriculture was the state's most important industry, and even today, it plays a major economic role. Farmland represents about 25 percent of the state's total acreage, and annual agricultural sales hover about $2.8 billion. The largest segment, accounting for about half the sales, is dairy; New York ranks third in the nation, behind California and Wisconsin. New York is also known for its superb cheese and apple production.

NEW YORK "FIRSTS"

First school in America (NYC, 1663)

First uniformed police force (NYC, 1693)

First algebra book (NYC, 1730)

First state constitution (April 20, 1777)

First commercial manufacture of ice cream (NYC, 1786)

First dental drill invented (1790)

First turnpike (Albany to Schenectady, 1797)

First insurance company (NYC, 1804)

First steamboat (NYC-Albany, 1807)

Natural gas first used to illuminate village (Fredonia, 1824)

First engineering college (Troy, 1824)

First railroad (Albany to Schenectady, 1831)

First telegraph (1831)

First streetcar (NYC, 1832)

First powered knitting machine operated (Cohoes, 1832)

First photograph taken in United States (NYC, 1839)

First grain elevator (Buffalo, 1840)

First cheese factory (Rome, 1851)

First artificial insemination (NYC, 1866)

First veterinary school (Cornell University, Ithaca, 1868)

First advertising agency (N.W. Ayer and Son, 1869)

First state-designated forest preserve (May 15, 1885)

Birthplace of tennis in United States (Staten Island, 1874)

First practical typewriter manufactured (by Remington, 1874)

First mass-circulation magazine in United States (*McClure's*, 1881)

First tuxedo coat (Tuxedo Park, 1886)

First chartered golf course in United States (Shinnecock Hills Country Club, 1891)

First hydroelectric power plant (1894)

First motion picture (April 23, 1896)

First cancer laboratory (Buffalo, 1898)

First motorcycle (Buffalo, 1900)

First billion-dollar corporation (U.S. Steel, 1901)

First film-pack camera (Rochester, 1903)

First subway operated (NYC, 1904)

First airplane sold commercially (Hammondsport, 1909)

Birthplace of the NAACP (1910)

First Boy Scouts of America troop (Troy, 1911)

First radio station (WABC-FM, October 7, 1921)

First potato chips (Saratoga Springs, 1925)

First artificial heart invented (NYC, 1935)

First television network (NYC and Schenectady, 1940)

First atomic reactor in medical therapy (Brookhaven, 1951)

First sugar-free soft drink (College Point, 1952)

First solar-powered battery (NYC, 1954)

World's first nuclear plant to produce electricity (GE, near Schenectady, 1955)

First solid-state electronic computer (Ilion, 1958)

First Council for the Arts (created by Governor Rockefeller, 1960)

First statewide minimum-wage law (1960)

First bank automatic teller (NYC, 1969)

First corporation to have more than three million stockholders (AT&T, NYC, 1972)

Mario Cuomo, **The New York Idea**

All of which hardly makes up for the fact that since 1900, the Empire State has lost some 200,000 family farms. Less than two percent of New Yorkers still till the soil, on about 32,000 farms. Of those, only 35 percent are commercial operations with annual sales of $50,000 or more; all the others represent hobby or part-time farms. Production in New York State remains high only because efficiency has increased. As elsewhere in the country, a way of life has been lost.

DREAMERS AND REFORMERS

Despite New York's healthy commercial appetite, often bordering on the greedy and the crass, it is also a state of dreamers. Something in the land's silken fields or dark blue twilights seems to bring out all-but-impossible hopes and longings, most destined to go unfulfilled.

From the late 1700s to mid-1800s especially, New York supported an extraordinary number of idealists, reformers, and religious leaders. Mother

Ann Lee founded the first Shaker community near Albany. Joseph Smith founded the Mormon religion in Palmyra. John Humphrey Noyes established the Perfectionist utopian society in Oneida. The Fox Sisters founded the Spiritualist movement near Rochester. Elizabeth Cady Stanton and Susan B. Anthony spearheaded the women's rights movement from Auburn and Rochester. Frederick Douglass, William Seward, and Gerrit Smith helped lead the abolitionist movement from the Finger Lakes.

Some of this idealistic spirit continues into the 21st century. As one of the most progressive states in the union, New York has been the first to institute everything from the first seat belt law and the first acid rain law to the first state-assisted housing program and the first Council on the Arts. New York also consistently spends more than nearly every other state in nearly every social category, from education to hospitals. The Republicans lament this fact every time elections roll around, but for the most part, continue the tradition, even when in power.

UPSTATE VS. DOWNSTATE

How does one encapsulate in one history both upstate and metropolitan New York? Like a massive geological fault, the rivalry between these two sections has ruptured state unity for centuries.

David Maldwyn Ellis,
New York State and City

The antagonism between upstate—a vague term that refers to everything outside New York City, including Long Island—and downstate began as far back as the early 1700s, when upstate farmers and New York City merchants disagreed over taxes and trade regulations. A few decades later, the American Revolution split the regions further when the British captured New York City and held on to it for seven years.

And that was only the beginning. After 1800, the conflict between city and state not only continued but also grew more complex. The more New York City evolved into an economic and cultural capital, the less regard it seemed to have

for the rest of the state. Upstaters—then largely Protestant and native-born—began to eye the metropolis—then largely Catholic and foreign-born—with increasing distrust.

By the late 1800s, the animosity between the two regions had become firmly entrenched. One upstate delegate to the 1894 constitutional convention called New York City "a sewer of ignorance and corruption flowing in . . . from foreign lands." George Templeton Strong of New York City observed in 1905 that "the feeling between this city and the hayseeds that make a livin' by plunderin' it is every bit as bitter as the feelin' between the North and South before the war."

Much of this animosity has its roots in politics. New York City, predominantly Democratic since 1800, runs counter to upstate New York, which has voted Republican since 1856. Nationally, city dwellers tend to vote Democratic, but upstate New York cities usually cast sizeably lower Democratic votes than do most other cities.

Certain recurring issues have divided New York City and State time and again. Among them are representation in the state legislature, allocation of state tax revenues, and state control of the city's finances. The first issue was resolved finally by the Supreme Court in 1964, but the last two—along with countless other, more hidden, agendas—continue to sharply divide the state.

New York City residents claim, with much justification, that they pay far more in taxes than they receive in state aid. Upstate residents claim, also with much justification, that the city's intellectual elites treat them as backcountry fools. Severely aggravating the situation are the regions' markedly different populations. New York City is home to over 80 percent of the state's African Americans and Jews, and to over 90 percent of its Spanish speakers and Asians. Upstate New York is predominantly white.

The state's government is led by an exceptionally strong governor with power over hundreds of appointments, and a legislature comprised of a 61-member Senate and 150-member Assembly. Members of both houses are elected for two-year terms, and each house has standing committees concerned with public policy issues. The governor also appoints nonleg-islative commissions to investigate such prob-lems as education aid and welfare administration. The state's finances are overseen by an indepen-dently elected state comptroller.

On a local level, New York is divided into 62 counties that are further subdivided into towns. The towns, which function as townships do else-where, contain cities and villages, most governed by a mayor and a council. Larger cities such as New York also have a second legislative body, usually called the Board of Estimate.

The Land

Geography has shaped the development of New York State more than any other single factor. Though bordered on the north, south, and east by mountains, lakes, and rivers, the state's central position between the Atlantic and the Great Lakes, along with its flat western terrain, made it a major thoroughfare for early settlers heading West. Highways were established through the Mohawk River basin and Finger Lakes in the late 1700s, followed in 1825 by the Erie Canal. The canal was largely responsible for New York's rise to prominence, and by 1900, four out of five New Yorkers were living along either the Hudson River or the Erie Canal.

Though New York ranks only 30th among the states in terms of area, it is one of the largest states east of the Mississippi and extremely diverse geographically. Mountains, plateaus, lowlands, forests, swamps, lakes, rivers, gorges, and beach-es all make up the state, which was formed main-ly during the last Ice Age. At that time, a continental ice sheet up to two miles thick cov-ered all of New York except southern Long Island and Staten Island, and the extreme southwestern corner of the state.

New York is bounded to the north by the St. Lawrence River and Lake Ontario, to the east by Lake Champlain and the Taconic Mountains, to the southeast by the Atlantic Ocean, to the south by the Delaware River and Allegheny Plateau, and to the west by Lake Erie and the Niagara River. The state's highest point is Mt. Marcy (5,344 feet) in the Adirondack region; its lowest is the Atlantic coastline.

The Hudson River, which originates at Lake Tear of the Clouds atop Mt. Marcy, flows north-south through the eastern end of the state. Run-ning east-west through the center of the state is the Mohawk River, which arises in Oneida Coun-ty, near Rome. Other important rivers include the Genesee and Oswego, which flow northward into Lake Ontario; and the Delaware, Susque-hanna, and Allegheny, which drain the state's southern and western portions.

GEOGRAPHIC DIFFERENCES

The movement of the glaciers left New York with eight distinct geographic areas, all now com-posed largely of farmland, abandoned farmland, or semi-wilderness. Eighty-five percent of New York's population may be urban, but 85 percent of its land is rural.

Atlantic Coastal Plain. Extending from Mass-achusetts to Florida, the Atlantic Coastal Plain takes in Long Island and Staten Island. At 120 miles in length, Long Island is the largest island off the East Coast. Along its southern shore winds a long string of barrier island beaches.

New England Upland. Extending from Penn-sylvania into Connecticut and Massachusetts, the New England Upland encompasses parts of the lower Hudson Valley. Included in its rocky sweep are the island of Manhattan, the Hudson Highlands, and the Taconic Mountains.

Hudson-Mohawk Lowlands. This region flanks the Hudson River from New York City to Albany, then heads west along the Mohawk River. The Hudson River Valley is a thriving area of small towns and fertile farmland. In contrast, along much of the Mohawk River Valley sit aban-doned factories and farms.

Adirondacks. Located in the northeastern section of the state, the semi-wild Adirondacks make up a roughly circular mountainous region about 100 miles wide. To their south and west

REGIONS OF NEW YORK

New York divides into nine distinct regions, and each has something different to offer the traveler.

At New York's southeastern base, wedged between New Jersey, Connecticut, and Long Island, lies **New York City**. By far the state's most popular destination, New York is a vast, dazzling, shape-shifting metropolis that belongs more to the world than it does to the state.

To the east of the city extends thin **Long Island**. Best known for its suburbs and world-class beaches, Long Island is also home to numerous vineyards, turn-of-the-century mansions, and tiny New England–style villages.

To the city's northeast lies the **Hudson Valley**, rich with historic, cultural, and scenic sites. Foremost among them are sumptuous riverfront mansions, outdoor sculpture gardens, the views from the Hudson Highlands, and West Point.

Across from the Hudson Valley rise the romantic, albeit run-down, **Catskill Mountains**. Here you'll find more scenic vistas, the fabled village of Woodstock, excellent day-hiking and fishing, and a plethora of offbeat sights.

In **Central New York** lie Albany, the historic state capital; several dying industrial towns; and Cooperstown, home to the National Baseball Hall of Fame and three other major museums. All around are the lush, forested hills of "Leatherstocking Country."

The **North Country** begins north of Albany in Victorian-era Saratoga Springs, and extends north to the isolated Thousand Islands. In between sprawls Adirondack Park, a mecca for hikers, campers, and canoeists.

West of Central New York laze the long, narrow **Finger Lakes**, flanked by vineyards, stately 19th-century towns, and historic landmarks. To the north is Lake Ontario, a Great Lake, and the friendly, cultured city of Rochester.

Far **Western New York** is home to Buffalo, New York's second largest city, and Niagara Falls, its second most popular tourist attraction. To the south are the dark foothills of the Allegheny Mountains and the all-but-unknown Allegany State Park.

rise gently rolling hills, while to their northeast loom the High Peaks. Hundreds of lakes and streams also characterize the region; best known among them are Lake George and Lake Placid.

St. Lawrence–Lake Champlain Lowland. Situated to the north and east of the Adirondacks, this region of farms, abandoned farms, and semi-wilderness follows the state's borders with Canada and Vermont. In the St. Lawrence River, limestone and sandstone rocks emerge to form the craggy Thousand Islands.

Tug Hill Plateau. The rocky, sparsely populated Tug Hill Plateau is an isolated extension of the Appalachian Plateau. Located at the far western edge of the Adirondacks, this small region receives more snow—over 225 inches a year—than any other area in the United States east of the Rockies.

Appalachian Plateau. The largest land region in New York State, the Appalachian Plateau stretches north from the Pennsylvania border to just south of Lake Ontario. In its center lie the Finger Lakes—glacier-created bodies of water

carved out of broad uplands. To its east are the Catskills, forested peaks ranging from 2,000 to 4,200 feet in height. The northern half of the Appalachian Plateau is a superb agriculture region, producing everything from fruit to hay. The southern half is considerably less fertile, as evidenced by the abandoned farms.

Great Lakes Plain. Excellent farmland extends north from the Appalachian Plateau into the Great Lakes Plain. Created after the Ice Age, as Lakes Ontario and Erie retreated, the plain is characterized by long, oval-shaped hills known as drumlins.

CLIMATE

Late spring, early summer, and early fall are the best times to visit New York City and much of upstate. Temperatures then generally hover in the 70s, and you're more likely to wake up to one of the state's precious cloudless days. Midsummers in New York City and much of upstate tend to be hot and humid; winters are overcast, wet, and cold. In contrast, summer is the best time to visit the more highly elevated regions of the Catskills and Adirondacks.

Average July temperatures range from 77°F in New York City to 64°F in the Adirondacks; average January temperatures range from 33°F on Long Island to 14°F in the Adirondacks. The coldest winters occur in the central Adirondacks and St. Lawrence River Valley, where temperatures often drop below -10°F.

Annual precipitation is 32–45 inches annually, with the Catskills, Long Island, and Tug Hill receiving the most. The typical cloudiness throughout the state results in few completely clear days; New York City averages about 100 inches, Syracuse and Buffalo 72 inches, and Albany 73 inches.

FLORA AND FAUNA

Over half of New York State is blanketed with forests, in which grow over 150 kinds of trees. Among them are a few southern species such as the tulip tree and sweetgum, and far more northern species such as beech, sugar maple, red maple, hickory, ash, cherry, birch, various oaks, white pine, spruce, balsam fir, and hemlock. In the Adirondacks and Catskills, evergreens predominate, while elsewhere in the state, hardwoods are more numerous.

Among the state's most common wildflowers are buttercups, violets, daisies, black-eyed Susans, devil's paintbrush, wild roses, and Queen Anne's lace. Bright specks of alpine flora can be found high on the Adirondack peaks, while woodland flora such as dewdrops and Jack-in-the-pulpits flourish in the forests. Hundreds of species of shrubs, herbs, grasses, ferns, mosses, and lichens also abound throughout the state.

Birdlife in New York runs the gamut from pigeons and common house sparrows—first introduced in North America from Europe in Brooklyn in 1850—to grouse and osprey. Raptors, including bald eagles and peregrine falcons, are making a comeback, while during the migrating season, hundreds of thousands of wild ducks and geese pass through the state.

In New York's fresh waters swim over 90 species of fish, including perch, trout, salmon, walleye, northern pike, and small- and large-mouth bass. Saltwater fish such as bluefish and flounder inhabit the waters off New York City and Long Island, also known for its oysters and clams.

As for mammals, the smaller varieties predominate. Among them are raccoon, skunk, porcupine, weasel, fox, woodchuck, squirrel, and opossum. The most common larger species is the white-tailed deer, but beaver, black bear, and wildcats can also be found in remote areas. Recently reintroduced into the Adirondacks are the elusive moose and lynx.

As elsewhere in the East, New York's flora and fauna have been badly affected by environmental contamination. The Adirondacks and Catskills suffer from acid rain, the Great Lakes from chemical pollution; and solid-waste management is a major problem on Long Island and Staten Island, where New York City folk dump most of their garbage. Oil spills also intermittently blight New York's Atlantic coast, thanks to oil refineries in nearby New Jersey.

On a brighter note, most of New York's rivers flow significantly cleaner today than they did 20 years ago. Back then, the Hudson, St. Lawrence, and Niagara Rivers were heavily polluted with PCBs, petrochemicals, and pesticides. The Clean Water Act of 1972, along with other state laws, has helped to greatly reduce this pollution. Much work remains to be done, but a solid start has been made.

History

EARLY PEOPLES

When the Europeans first arrived in what is now New York State, they found it inhabited by two major tribes. The Algonquins lived near the Atlantic coast and along the Hudson River Valley, while upstate dwelled the five tribes of the Iroquois—the Mohawk, Oneida, Onondaga, Cayuga, and Seneca.

The Algonquins and the Iroquois are contemporary peoples, but archaeologists believe that human beings were living in the New York State region as early as 7,000 B.C. These early "mound people," as they are now known, survived through hunting, fishing, and, later, cultivating corn.

Around 1570, the Iroquois tribes banded together to form the Iroquois League, an advanced confederacy with social laws and government institutions designed to promote peace among its members. Fifty sachems, chosen from the village chiefs, governed the confederacy, and each nation had one vote. In 1722, a sixth nation, the Tuscarora, joined the Iroquois League.

Within a century after the arrival of whites, the Algonquin population was decimated, due largely to virulent European diseases such as measles and smallpox. The Iroquois, however, thrived during initial contact. First the Dutch, and then the French and British, enlisted their help in the profitable fur trade, and cultivated their friendship through gifts and the selling of firearms. During the French and Indian War, the alliance of the Iroquois with the British against the French

NATIVE AMERICAN HISTORIC SITES

Note: For more detailed information on the following sites, refer to the appropriate chapter.

New York City
George Gustav Heye Center, National Museum of the American Indian. A branch of the Smithsonian; some of the finest Native American art and artifacts around.

American Indian Community House Gallery. The only Native American–owned and –operated gallery in New York City; sometimes features historical exhibits.

Long Island
Indian Museum, Southold. A small museum housing one of the country's largest collections of Native American pottery.

Shinnecock Nation Cultural Center and Museum, Southampton. A museum of artifacts past and present; on the Shinnecock Reservation, where a large pow-wow is held Labor Day weekend.

Indian Field, Montauk. A burial ground, whose permanent residents were buried according to ancient custom, in a circle, sitting up.

Central New York
Fenimore House Museum, Cooperstown. Contains the Eugene and Clare Thaw Collection of American Indian Art, perhaps the most important privately owned collection of its kind.

Mohawk-Caughnawaga Museum and Kateri Tekakwitha Memorial Shrine, Fonda. Iroquois artifacts and modern art; an excavated Native American village, and a shrine devoted to the first laywoman in North America to be honored as a "Blessed."

The Noteworthy Indian Museum, Amsterdam. Housed in a snug historic house; over 60,000 artifacts trace the history of Native Americans in the Mohawk Valley.

Iroquois Indian Museum, Howe Caverns. One of the finest Native American museums in the state, with a remarkable collection of contemporary Iroquois art.

Shako:Wi Cultural Center, Oneida. A modern center housing classrooms, a small gift shop, and a small museum dedicated to the Oneida Nation.

was instrumental in allowing England to gain control over North America.

The Iroquois did not fare so well during the American Revolution. Once again allying themselves with the British, they became the object of a ruthless 1779 campaign waged by American generals Clinton and Sullivan. By the time the campaign was over, the Iroquois nation was in ruins. Thousands fled to Canada; others were resettled onto reservations.

EUROPEAN SETTLEMENT

In 1524, the first white man, Giovanni da Verrazano, arrived in what is now New York State by sailing into New York harbor. Verrazano left almost immediately, however, and the land remained undisturbed until 1609, when Henry Hudson, sailing up the river that now bears his name, traveled as far north as Albany. That same year, Samuel de Champlain sailed south from Canada to explore the lake later named after him.

In 1624, the Dutch established Fort Orange, the first European settlement in New York State. Situated at present-day Albany, the fort served primarily as an outpost for the fur trade. One year later, the Dutch established a similar outpost, New Amsterdam, at the foot of Manhattan Island. In exchange for the land, the Dutch governor Peter Minuit paid the Algonquins 60 Dutch guilders—about $24.

The English peacefully took over the Dutch colony in 1664, changing its name from New Amsterdam to New York. The colony remained predominantly Dutch, however, until the end of the century. In 1690, of the estimated 14,000 white settlers in New York, over half were Dutch. Albany and Kingston retained a large Dutch population and much Dutch architecture until well into the 1700s.

The North Country
Six Nations Indian Museum, Onchiota. A fantastic, delirious array of pictographs, paintings, basketwork, beadwork, quillwork, pottery, canoes, masks, drums, and lacrosse sticks—all collected by one man, Ray Fadden.

Akwesasne Museum, Hogansburg. Mohawk medicine masks, wampum belts, carved cradle boards, water drums, modern artwork, basketry, and historic photographs.

The Finger Lakes
Saint Marie Among the Iroquois, Syracuse. Recreates the 17th-century world of the French Jesuits and Iroquois who once lived near Onondaga Lake.

Logan Monument, Fort Hill Cemetery, Auburn. A 57-foot-high obelisk honoring the famed Cayuga orator who was born nearby.

Ganondagan State Historic Site, Victor. The former site of an important Seneca village and palisaded granary; now equipped with historic walking trails and a visitor center.

Owasco Teyetasta (Iroquois Museum), Emerson Park, Auburn. A small collection of Native American artifacts.

Squaw Island, Canandaigua Lake. During General Sullivan's ruthless 1779 campaign, many Seneca women and children escaped slaughter by hiding out here.

Ontario County Courthouse. The Pickering Treaty, which granted whites the right to settle the Great Lakes Basin, was signed here. A plaque commemorates the event; an original copy of the treaty is in the Ontario County Historical Society Museum.

Mary Jemison Grave and Council House, Letchworth State Park. The grave of the "White Woman of the Genesee," and site of the region's last Iroquois council meeting.

Rochester Museum, Rochester. Contains "At the Western Door," a powerful permanent exhibit on the Seneca Nation.

Western New York
Forest Lawn Cemetery, Buffalo. Final resting place of the famed Seneca orator Red Jacket.

Seneca-Iroquois National Museum, Salamanca. A thoughtful, well-laid-out museum covering the history of the Seneca Nation from its pre-history to the present day.

The land-use system in upstate New York developed differently than it did elsewhere in the New World. First, the Dutch established the patroon system, whereby an individual was given a large tract of land in return for bringing over at least 50 settlers to work that land. Then the English set up a similar landlord-tenant system whereby a few men were given enormous manor estates that they rented out in parcels to poor farmers. In some parts of the Hudson Valley and Catskills, remnants of this feudal-like system remained in effect until the 1840s.

REVOLUTION

By the time of the Revolutionary War, New York City had reached a population of 25,000. Albany and Kingston thrived as river ports, and several smaller settlements, including Saratoga and Fort Stanwix, had been established as far north as Lake Champlain and as far west as Rome. Manor estates lined the Hudson River, and Long Island was peppered with productive farm communities.

When rumblings of revolution began, New York at first took a pro-Tory stance. Merchants and manor landlords intent on making money wanted nothing to do with war. "What is the reason that New York must continue to embarrass the Continent?" queried John Adams at one point. As the tensions escalated, however, New Yorkers changed their position and, after 1753, supported the Revolution wholeheartedly.

No state bore the brunt of the war more than New York. The earliest battles were fought in New York City—which remained in British hands throughout the war—and many of the later ones took place upstate. The Americans were badly defeated by the British at Oriskany, near Rome, in 1777. The British were unexpectedly defeated by the Americans at Saratoga, also in 1777. Benedict Arnold

The land-use system in upstate New York developed differently than it did elsewhere in the New World. The Dutch established the patroon system, whereby an individual was given a large tract of land in return for bringing over settlers to work that land. Remnants of this feudal-like system remained in effect until the 1840s.

plotted to betray the Continental Army at West Point in 1780. General Washington declared victory over the British in Newburgh in 1781.

In 1789, Washington was inaugurated as the first president of the United States in Federal Hall on Wall Street, New York City. The city served as the nation's capital until 1790, when the federal government transferred to Philadelphia.

RISE TO POWER

After the war, New York made a rapid recovery. Settlers poured into New York City, the Mohawk River Valley, and the Finger Lakes region, which before the war had been Iroquois territory. Many of the new settlers were Yankees, tired of eking out marginal livings on rocky New England soils. Attracted to New York's fertile farmland, they brought with them their strong work ethic, Protestant religion, and austere architectural styles, many examples of which still stand.

And then, in 1825, came the opening of the Erie Canal. Stretching from the Hudson River to Lake Erie, the canal established the first water route between the East and Midwest. Shipping rates between Buffalo and New York City dropped by 80–90 percent, and hundreds of boats started plying the waters. By 1834, the canal's tolls had more than paid for the entire cost of its $7.7 million construction.

The Erie Canal was the making of New York. It transformed New York City from one of many important colonial centers into the largest metropolis in the New World, and gave rise to virtually every other major city in the state, including Syracuse, Rochester, and Buffalo.

SLAVERY AND CIVIL WAR

Slavery had been a fact of life in New York since 1626, when 11 African slaves were brought to

INTRODUCTION

About 500,000 New Yorkers served in the war, and about 50,000 were killed. The state also contributed much in the way of supplies and weapons.

THE LATE 1800s

The Civil War put a temporary dent in New York's economy, but by the 1880s, it was back in full force. Corporations doubled, tripled, or even quadrupled in size, with a corresponding explosion of activity in commerce, transportation, banking, and, especially, manufacturing fields.

With rapid industrialization came rapid urbanization and the need for a large work force. Immigrants with next to nothing to their names flocked into New York. These changing conditions created many problems throughout the state, including the exploitation of workers, poor health and housing conditions, pollution, a waste of natural resources, and increasing crime.

The larger the cities grew, the greater became the need for improved transportation. Horsecars gave way to streetcars, and by 1900, nearly every city upstate had a streetcar system. The first subway tunnel was built in Manhattan in 1900, but 20 years elapsed before subways connected the island to Brooklyn and the Bronx, both annexed onto New York City in 1898, along with Queens and Staten Island.

BOB RACE

Frederick Douglass

New Amsterdam and forced to work as servants and craftspeople. Before the Revolution, New York had the largest number of slaves of any colony north of Maryland. Most lived in or near New York City.

In 1799, New York passed legislation that freed the children of slaves born after July 4, 1799, after they reached the age of 25 (females) or 28 (males). Slavery wasn't completely abolished, however, until 1827.

Despite this dismal beginning, New York played a critical role in the antislavery movement before and during the Civil War. Many of the country's most ardent abolitionists—including William Seward, Frederick Douglass, Gerrit Smith, and Martin Van Buren—lived upstate, and the Finger Lakes region was regarded as a hotbed of antislavery sentiment. John Brown established a farm for escaped slaves near Lake Placid in 1849, and Underground Railroad stations dotted the state, especially along the Niagara frontier. When escaped slave William "Jerry" McHenry was arrested by federal marshals in Syracuse in 1851, he was promptly rescued by vigilante abolitionists. That rescue, which challenged the Fugitive Slave Act of 1850, was one of the early precipitating events leading up to the Civil War.

"New York is to the nation what the white church spire is to the village—the visible symbol of aspiration and faith, the white plume saying the way is up."

E. B. White

REFORM, DEPRESSION, AND WAR

At the beginning of the 20th century, New York was the most powerful state in the United States. Two-thirds of the nation's leading corporations were headquartered in New York City, and the state as a whole produced one-sixth of the gross national product. Ex-New York governor Theodore Roosevelt had just succeeded President William McKinley—assassinated in Buffalo in 1898—to the White House.

The Progressive Era in politics had begun—it would peak following the tragic 1911 Triangle Shirtwaist factory fire that took the lives

AFRICAN AMERICAN HISTORIC SITES

It goes without saying that you'll find innumerable important African American historic sites in New York City. Sections of Harlem in particular are lined with one landmark after another. Below, find only a few of the highlights.

Elsewhere in the state, major historic African American sites are few and far between. Those that do exist, however, honor figures of enormous importance.

Note: For more detailed information on the following sites, refer to the appropriate chapter.

Harlem
Studio Museum in Harlem. A world-class institution with changing exhibits by such masters as Romare Bearden and Jacob Lawrence.

The Apollo. Perhaps the single most important landmark in the history of African American music.

Malcolm Shabazz Mosque. Where civil rights leader Malcolm X taught in the 1960s.

Schomburg Center. A renowned institution for research in black culture. Includes a spacious art gallery and gift shop.

Abyssinian Baptist Church. The former church of Adam Clayton Powell; one of largest black congregations in the United States.

Striver's Row. Designed by architects McKim, Mead & White; once home to W. C. Handy and Eubie Blake, among numerous others.

Elsewhere in Manhattan
Fraunces Tavern, Lower Manhattan. Many historians believe the original Revolutionary War–era Fraunces Tavern, of which this is a replica, was owned by a black French West Indian.

Former slave market, Lower Manhattan. One of the busiest slave markets of the 1700s once stood on Wall Street.

African Burial Grounds, Lower Manhattan. Only rediscovered in 1991, this graveyard may once have covered nearly six acres and held the remains of 20,000 African Americans.

Charlie Parker Place, East Village. The former abode of the jazz great.

The Outer Boroughs
Weeksville, Crown Heights, Brooklyn. Four wooden houses, once part of a free black community established in the 1840s.

Plymouth Church of the Pilgrims, Brooklyn Heights. The former pulpit of minister Henry Ward Beecher, whose rousing, antislavery sermons helped galvanize the North during the Civil War.

Louis Armstrong house, Corona, Queens. The legendary trumpeter's home from the early 1940s until his death in 1971.

Sandy Ground, Staten Island. One of the oldest free black communities in the United States; settled by African American oystermen.

of 146 workers in downtown Manhattan. Many progressive reforms were propelled through the state legislature by Democrat Al Smith, later one of New York's greatest governors. A self-educated man, born poor on the Lower East Side, Smith helped push through dozens of monumental labor, safety, education, and housing bills.

The Great Depression of 1929 hit New York State especially hard. By 1932 industrial production upstate had fallen by one-third, bread lines filled city blocks, and New York City banks shut down and reopened as soup kitchens.

Enter Franklin Delano Roosevelt. In 1930, as governor of New York, Roosevelt devised a five-point program to help the state cope with the economic disaster. In 1932, elected president of the United States, Roosevelt applied and expanded his New York program into the national New Deal. New Yorkers went back to work on public works projects ranging from transportation to housing. Many were projects envisioned and developed by Robert Moses, the autocratic "master builder" largely responsible for the shape of modern-day New York.

However, like the rest of the nation, New York's greatest boon to post-Depression recovery was WW II. Overnight the state's factories and shipyards thrived anew, producing arms, uniforms, and other items for the war effort.

INTRODUCTION

Long Island
Whaling Museum, Cold Spring Harbor. Includes an exhibit on early African African whalemen; whaling was the first truly integrated industry in America.
African American Museum, Hempstead. One of the only African American museums in the state; changing historical and cultural exhibits.
Joseph Lloyd Manor House, Lloyd Harbor Peninsula, Huntington. Once home to Jupiter Hammon, a slave who became the first published black poet in America.
Sag Harbor. The former port of African American whaling ship captains, some of whose mansions still stand along Main Street.

The Hudson Valley
Villa Lewaro, Tarrytown. The posh former home of Madame C. J. Walker, the country's first African American female millionaire.

The Catskills
Ulster County Courthouse, Kingston. A plaque out front honors abolitionist and evangelist Sojourner Truth, who won a lawsuit here in 1797 that saved her son from slavery.
Hardenberg House, Hurley. Where Sojourner Truth spent the first nine years of her life, as a slave.

The North Country
John Brown Farm State Historic Site, Lake Placid. The site of a farming community for escaped slaves established in 1849 by abolitionists John Brown and Gerrit Smith. Related exhibits in the Lake Placid–North Elba Historical Society Museum.

The Finger Lakes
Jerry Rescue Monument, Syracuse. Honors William "Jerry" McHenry, who successfully escaped from slavery in North Carolina to Syracuse. McHenry was arrested by federal marshals in 1851, only to be freed by vigilante abolitionists a few days later.
Harriet Tubman Home, Auburn. The escaped slave and abolitionist who made 19 trips south, rescuing more than 300 slaves, settled here after the Civil War.
Frederick Douglass Statue and Grave, Rochester. The escaped slave, abolitionist, and writer settled in Rochester in 1847, and published his newspaper here for 17 years. His statue, erected in 1898, was the first in the United States to honor an African American.

Western New York
Stations of the Underground Railroad, the Niagara Frontier. "Stations," marked with sculptures, honor those who helped the many slaves who escaped through this region to Canada.

MODERN TIMES

In 1959 Nelson A. Rockefeller was elected governor of New York. An ambitious man with grand visions, Rockefeller greatly expanded the state university system and built Albany's impressive, futuristic Empire State Plaza. By the time Rockefeller left office in 1973, however, the state budget had grown 400 percent from its 1959 level and the state debt had increased 14 times over.

Additionally, New York was losing thousands of manufacturing jobs, both upstate and in New York City. Social unrest was pervasive, and urban race riots and antiwar demonstrations rocked the state. In 1969 the Woodstock Music and Arts Festival drew young people from all over the country to a dairy farm in the Catskills. In 1971 a deadly uprising at Attica prison left 43 inmates and guards dead.

More jobs were lost throughout the '70s and again in the early '90s as companies moved from the Northeast to the South and West. Many New Yorkers blamed these industrial losses on the state's steep tax rate—among the highest in the nation—but the truth was, and is, that no amount of tax cuts can make New York the state it once was. The emergence of the Pacific Rim, the shift in the nation's demographics, and the rise of a global economy

INTRODUCTION

have irrevocably altered New York's economic position.

Modern-day New York faces its share of problems. Many upstate cities are struggling with population exoduses and rising crime rates, while New York City is still reeling with the aftermath of the September 11, 2001 attacks, when terrorists flew two jets into the World Trade Center towers, taking with them over 3,000 innocent lives. At the same time, it's easy to overestimate the effect of these problems. For New York is nothing if not resilient, and still leads the country in a wide variety of fields, ranging from publishing and the arts to banking and finance.

E. B. White once wrote, "New York is to the nation what the white church spire is to the village—the visible symbol of aspiration and faith, the white plume saying the way is up."

Tarnished or not, the steeple still stands.

On the Road

Recreation

Hiking, Biking, Boating, Skiing

New York boasts some of the finest hiking in the Northeast. Nearly 1,000 miles of trails traverse the Adirondack and Catskill Forest Preserves, while 800 more miles of trails meander through the state parks. Part of the 2,000-mile Appalachian Trail also cuts through New York State.

For free basic information on outdoor activities in the Adirondacks and Catskills, contact the **Department of Environmental Conservation** (DEC), 625 Broadway, Albany, NY 12233; 518/402-9428, www.dec.state.ny.us. The **Adirondack Mountain Club,** 814 Coggins Rd., Lake George, NY 12845, 518/668-4447 or 800/395-8080, www.adk.org, is also a good resource. For a free basic guide to trails in the state parks, contact **New York State Parks,** Empire State Plaza, Albany, NY 12238, www.nysparks.com. For information on the Appalachian Trail, contact the **New York–New Jersey Trail Conference,** 156 Ramapo Valley Rd., Mahwah, NJ 07430, 201/512-9348, www.nynjtc.com; or the **Appalachian Mountain Club,** 5 Tudor City Pl., New York, NY 10017, 212/986-1430, www.amc-ny.org. Recommended regional hiking guidebooks and resources are also listed in chapter introductions throughout this book.

Most cities and parks in New York have bicycle trails. One of the best-known is the 35-mile Mohawk-Hudson Bikeway, which begins in Albany and heads north to Rotterdam Junction along a

Taxicabs are one of the major ways to get around New York City.

WEIRD SIGHTS, STOPS, AND HIGHLIGHTS

Note: For more detailed information on the following sites, refer to the appropriate chapter.

New York City
New York City Police Museum, Financial District: Antique guns, Al Capone's marriage certificate, and "recently acquired contraband weapons."

Pearl River Mart, Chinatown: Paper lanterns, kites, dried herbs, musical instruments; Chinatown's largest department store.

Hells Angels' Headquarters, East Village: Look for the long line of shiny bikes parked out front.

Chess Shop, Greenwich Village: Where the obsessed go to play, at all hours of the day and night.

Leisure Time Bowling, Port Authority Bus Terminal: An old-time bowling alley; one of the last in Manhattan.

Riverbank State Park, Harlem: A state-of-the-art 23-acre park built on top of a sewage treatment plant.

Sideshows by the Sea, Coney Island, Brooklyn: Snake ladies, fire eaters, escape artists, and the Torture King.

New York Panorama, Queens Museum of Art: A scale model of the city, showing virtually every single building in the five boroughs—some 895,000 of them.

Long Island
Wicks Farm and Garden, St. James: Guarded by a looming 25-foot-high witch complete with hooked nose and broomstick.

Sunken Forest, Fire Island: A 300-year-old maritime forest growing below sea level between two lines of dunes.

The Big Duck, Flanders: A 20-foot-high pure white duck with a bright orange bill and eyes made from red Model T headlights.

The Whaling Museum, Sag Harbor: A hodgepodge place housing everything from harpoons and ostrich eggs to needlepoint created by a paralyzed town resident who stitched with her teeth.

The Hudson Valley
Old Dutch Burial Ground, Tarrytown: Washington Irving based many of his characters' names on the names he found on the tombstones here.

Sing Sing Prison, Ossining: One of the state's most infamous prisons, visible (and audible) from a waterfront park.

Somers Circus Museum, Somers: Housed in the former Elephant Hotel, built by "the father of the American circus" who imported the first elephant to the United States in 1796.

Hambletonian's Grave, Chester: Most pacers and trotters racing today trace their lineage back to Hambletonian, who sired 1,331 foals in 24 years.

Wing's Castle, Millbrook: An idiosyncratic "castle" built out of everything from antique barn doors and colored glass to toilet bowl floats and carousel animals.

Old Rhinebeck Aerodrome, Rhinebeck: Where Sir Percy Good Fellow fights the Evil Black Baron for the heart of Trudy Truelove most summer Sunday afternoons.

The Catskills
Opus 40, Woodstock: An environmental sculpture covering six acres of an abandoned bluestone quarry. All created by artist Harvey Fite.

Ukrainian Churches, Lexington and Glen Spey: Two grand Byzantine sanctuaries built of rich brown woods, entirely without nails. Startlingly beautiful, and in the middle of nowhere.

Mahayana Buddhist Temple and Monastery, Cairo: Red-and-gold temples, pavilions, bridges, and pagodas in a woodsy setting.

The village of East Durham: Shamrocks, leprechauns, Irish pubs, and Irish sweaters; nicknamed Ireland's 33rd County.

Siddha Yoga Dham, South Fallsburg: An ashram and the headquarters of a powerful Eastern spiritual movement. Surrounded by brightly colored statues of Hindu gods.

Route 30 around the Pepacton Reservoir: When the waters are low enough, the flooded towns of Pepacton, Shavertown, and Union Grove are still visible.

Central New York
The Big Dog, Albany: A 25-foot-high, four-ton statue of Nipper sits atop the former Victor Company factory.

Uncle Sam's Grave, Troy: The inspiration for the cartoon-figure symbol of the United States was a meatpacker named Sam Wilson.

Herkimer Diamond Mines, Herkimer: Hunt for "diamonds" in the former bed of the Devonian Sea.

Petrified Creatures Museum, Richfield Springs: Dig for ancient fossils in the former bed of the Devonian Sea.

Holy Trinity Russian Orthodox Monastery, Jordanville: Shining golden domes and spires, surrounded by woods and farm country.

The Petrified Forest, Gilboa: Stone stumps from now-extinct seed-bearing fern trees.

The yellow brick road, Chittenango: Built to honor L. Frank Baum, author of *The Wizard of Oz.*

The Mansion House, Oneida: Once home to the Perfectionists, a long-lived Utopian society founded by John Humphrey Noyes.

The six historic Herschell carousels of Binghamton: The cost for a ride is "one piece of litter."

The North Country

Grant Cottage, Wilton: One of the oddest and most moving of house museums, located in the middle of a correctional facility.

Hotel Cambridge, Cambridge: Where pie à la mode was "invented."

New Skete Monastery, Cambridge: A hilltop retreat known for its homemade cheesecake, smoked meats, and German shepherds.

Pember Museum of Natural History, Granville: Hundreds upon hundreds of specimens, all but bursting out of their display cases.

The Shipwreck Preserve, Lake George: A diving preserve containing seven sunken bateaux from the French and Indian War.

Camp Santanoni, Newcomb: A deserted great camp accessible only by hiking five miles in and five miles back out.

Muskie Hall of Fame, Thousand Islands Museum, Clayton: Devoted to the region's most prized fish.

Thousand Islands Inn, Clayton: Where Thousand Islands salad dressing purportedly was invented.

Thousand Islands Park, Wellesley Island: Hundreds of wooden Victorian homes painted in luscious ice cream pastels.

The Finger Lakes

Tipperary Hill, Syracuse: Home to the only upside-down traffic light in the country.

The Three Bears, Ovid: Three red-brick Greek Revival buildings, so nicknamed because of the way they diminish in size.

Wilder Brain Collection, Cornell University, Ithaca: The eight surviving stars of a human brain collection that once numbered over 1,600.

The pure white deer of the Seneca Arms Depot: Visible from Route 96A between Seneca and Cayuga Lakes.

Seneca Lodge, Watkins Glen: A favorite haunt of bow-and-arrow hunters.

Wine & Grape Museum of Greyton H. Taylor, Hammondsport: An eccentric collection assembled by a local rebel turned hero.

Caboose Motel, Avoca: Spend the night in one of five red cabooses, salvaged from a railroad yard.

Birkett Mills Griddle, Penn Yan: One-half of a giant griddle used in 1987 to make the world's largest pancake (28 feet, 1 inch).

William Phelps General Store Museum, Palmyra: A most unusual series of unkept rooms, once inhabited by a village eccentric.

High Falls, Rochester: Towering waterfalls along a gaping gorge that runs right through the heart of downtown.

Western New York

Anchor Bar, Buffalo: Where Buffalo chicken wings were invented.

The grain elevators of Buffalo Harbor: Giant, silolike structures made of poured concrete—mute, monolithic, mysterious.

Pedaling History Bicycle Museum, Orchard Park, Buffalo: The only all-bicycle museum in America.

The Original American Kazoo Company, Eden: Now more a shop than a factory, but one of a kind nonetheless.

Herschell Carousel Factory Museum, North Tonawanda: The plant that once produced hundreds of beloved wooden carousels.

continued on next page

ON THE ROAD

WEIRD SIGHTS, STOPS, AND HIGHLIGHTS (cont'd)

Le Roy House, Le Roy: Includes an exhibit on Jell-O, invented in Le Roy in the early 1900s.

The roque court, Angelica: One of only two places in the country where roque—a game similar to croquet—is still played.

The Block Barn, Cuba: A long, rectangular, and very unusual silver-gray structure with a multileveled roof.

Griffis Sculpture Park, Ashford Hollow: Towering humanoid sculptures frolic atop a hill. Created by artist Larry Griffis.

Lily Dale Assembly, Cassadaga: A spiritualist community; services, lectures, and sessions with clairvoyants.

---

historic canal. Others include the 32-mile Old Erie Canal State Park bikeway just east of Syracuse, and the 60-mile Barge Canal Recreationway in Monroe and Orleans Counties, Western New York. For a free map of the New York State Canalway bicycle trail, contact the **New York State Canal Corporation,** P.O. Box 189, Albany, NY 12201, 800/4CANAL4, www.canals.state.ny.us. Or, visit the New York State Parks website at www.nysparks.com.

Boating enthusiasts can row, paddle, or propel their craft over more than 70,000 miles of rivers and canals, and thousands of lakes and ponds. A free "New York State Boater's Guide" is available through New York State Parks, Marine and Recreational Vehicles, Empire State Plaza, Albany, NY 12238, 518/474-0445, www.nysparks.com/boats. Information on canoeing the 2,800-plus lakes and ponds of the Adirondacks is available through the Department of Environmental Conservation, listed above.

Downhill skiing is a popular activity in the Catskills and Adirondacks. Good cross-country skiing can be found virtually everywhere upstate.

Fishing Licenses

Everyone over age 16 needs a license to fish in New York's fresh waters. You can obtain licenses through local bait shops, sporting goods stores, and town offices, or from a regional office of the **DEC Di-**

History buffs will want to keep an eye out for the state's many Heritage Areas. These are loosely delineated historic areas linked by a common theme, and can include everything from historic homes and neighborhoods to abandoned factories and shipyards.

vision of Fish, Wildlife and Marine Resources; call 518/402-8924 for office locations or more information.

General Upstate Guide

For a free guide to New York's hundreds of visitor attractions, including over 200 state parks, campgrounds, and historic sites, contact the **New York State Division of Tourism,** P.O. Box 2603, Albany, NY 12220, 518/474-4116 or 800/CALL-NYS, www.iloveny.com.

State Heritage Areas

History buffs will want to keep an eye out for the state's many Heritage Areas. These are loosely delineated historic areas linked by a common theme, and can include everything from historic homes and neighborhoods to abandoned factories and shipyards. In the Kingston Heritage Area, the theme is transportation; in Albany, business and finance; in Seneca Falls, reform movements. The Heritage Areas and their visitor centers are described elsewhere in this book.

Entertainment and Events

New York knows how to entertain. From the Broadway theaters of New York City to "The Egg" performing arts center of Albany to the Eastman Theatre of Rochester, the state presents a fantastic array of cultural events year-round. Symphony, opera, jazz, rock, ballet, modern dance, avant-garde theater, performance art—you'll find it all in New York. Even many smaller communities, including those isolated in the Catskills or Adirondacks, often have at least one strong local arts organization.

New York also knows how to party. Special events ranging from county fairs to jazz festivals to ethnic celebrations take place throughout the state year-round. One of the biggest is the New York State Fair, held in Syracuse in late summer.

With the exception of Thanksgiving, Christ-mas, and New Year's Day, most tourist attractions remain open on major holidays. Banks and many businesses close down on New Year's Day (January 1); Martin Luther King Jr.'s Birthday (January 15, usually observed the following Monday); President's Day (the third Monday in February); Memorial Day (the last Monday in May); Independence Day (July 4); Labor Day (the first Monday in September); Veterans Day (November 11); Thanksgiving (the fourth Thursday in November); and Christmas (December 25).

Accommodations and Food

Camping

Excellent campgrounds are located in most of New York's 200-plus state parks. For $13–25 a night, campers are provided with a tent site, table, fire ring, running water, flush toilets, and hot showers; RV hookups are extra. Some of the campgrounds also offer cabins or lean-tos. Only a handful remain open through the winter.

Many of New York's state-run and private campgrounds are described elsewhere in this book, but for a complete list, contact the NYS Division of Tourism, 518/474-4116 or 800/CALL-NYS, www.iloveny.com. Make reservations for all state-operated campsites and cabins by calling 800/456-CAMP.

Youth Hostels and YMCAs

The **Hosteling International–American Youth Hostels** organization offers clean and friendly accommodations for people of all ages. A hostel usually consists of dormitory rooms, kitchen, common room, and sometimes several private rooms available for families. Hosteling International–AYH facilities are located in New York City, Buffalo, New Paltz, Syracuse, Niagara Falls, and Cape Vincent. Overnight rates are $10–20 per person.

You must be a member to stay at many AYH hostels. Annual membership fees are adults $25, seniors $15, youths under 17 $10, and families $35. Membership cards are usually sold on-site or through the AYH national office, P.O. Box 37613, Washington, D.C. 20013-7613, 202/

783-6161. Reservations at all AYH hostels should be made well in advance. Their website is www.hiayh.org.

Other **independent hostels,** similar in price and spirit to those run by AYH, are located in New York City.

The **Young Men's Christian Association** offers inexpensive, but not necessarily especially clean, accommodations in New York City, Syracuse, Buffalo, Tarrytown, and other urban areas throughout the state. For information on New York City's YMCAs, which are co-ed, contact Y's Way, 224 E. 47th St., New York, NY 10017, 212/308-2899. For elsewhere in the state, contact the local tourism information office or YMCA.

Motels and Hotels

Motels offering anywhere from six to 200 rooms abound throughout New York State. Some are independent operations, others belong to nationwide chains. Among the motel chains operating in New York are **Days Inn of America,** 800/325-2525; **Motel 6,** 800/466-8356; **Super 8 Motels,** 800/800-8000; **Red Roof Inns,** 800/733-7663; and **Econo Lodge,** 800/553-2666. All will send a free listing of locations and prices upon request.

Choice Hotels International, 866/446-6900, can help you located a Quality Inn, Comfort Inn, Quality Inn, or Sleep Inn in various locations upstate.

An extraordinary number of hotels, from flea-ridden to ultra-deluxe, are located in New

York City. Other large cities, such as Rochester and Buffalo, also offer a good choice of hotels.

Bed-and-Breakfasts

B&Bs are a popular lodging option in New York State, especially in the Hudson Valley, Cooperstown, Saratoga Springs, Rochester, Ithaca, and eastern Long Island regions. Many are quite expensive, and cater more to city folk looking for pampering than to budget travelers.

Numerous individual B&Bs, and local registries or reservation services, are described elsewhere in this book. Two B&B associations that operate throughout the state are **Empire State B&B Association,** P.O. Box 1020, Canandaigua, NY 14424, www.esbba.com (all regions, including New York City), and **American Country Collection of Bed and Breakfasts,** 1353 Union St., Schenectady, NY 12308, 518/370-4948 or 800/810-4948, www.bandbreservations.com (in the Hudson Valley, Catskills, Adirondacks, and central NY regions only).

> *With 18,000 eating establishments, New York City is a food lover's paradise.*

Food

With 18,000 eating establishments, New York City is a food lover's paradise. Restaurants, cafes, and take-out joints serve a wide variety of international cuisines in a wide variety of price ranges. Other large New York cities and popular tourist regions, such as Saratoga Springs and Cooperstown, also offer a fine selection of restaurants. Buffalo is especially known for its ethnic eateries.

In rural New York, restaurants tend to serve basic American fare. Prices are usually inexpensive to moderate.

Farm Produce

Agriculture is big business in New York, and many farms welcome visitors. Information on the state's hundreds of produce stands, pick-your-own farms, wineries, and farmers' markets can be picked up in local tourism offices listed elsewhere in this book.

Transportation

By Air

Most major U.S. airlines and many foreign carriers offer regularly scheduled flights into New York City's La Guardia, JFK, or Newark International airports. Several major U.S. airlines also offer flights to other cities in the state, including Albany, Rochester, and Buffalo. For more details, consult the regional chapters.

Bargain air fares for international travelers are often available. Most are APEX (advance purchase excursion) fares requiring advance purchase, with minimum and maximum stays. U.S. travelers can benefit from Super Saver fares, booked well in advance, and from the frequent fare wars waged by major airlines.

By Train

Amtrak, 800/USA-RAIL (800/872-7245), offers service between New York City's Pennsylvania Sta-

tion and Niagara Falls, with stops in Croton-Harmon, Poughkeepsie, Rhinecliff, Hudson, Albany-Rensselaer, Schenectady, Amsterdam, Utica, Rome, Syracuse, Rochester, and Buffalo. Amtrak also travels between New York City and Montreal, Canada, making stops in Croton-Harmon, Poughkeepsie, Rhinecliff, Hudson, Albany-Rensselaer, Schenectady, Saratoga Springs, Fort Edward–Glens Falls, Whitehall, Ticonderoga, Port Henry, Westport, Port Kent, Plattsburgh, and Rouses Point.

Metro-North, 212/532-4900 or 800/638-7646, a commuter railroad, offers service between New York City's Grand Central Station and the Hudson Valley region, while the **Long Island Rail Road** (LIRR), 718/217-LIRR or 516/822-LIRR, www.lirr.org, offers service between New York City's Penn Station and Long Island. For more details, consult the Long Island and Hudson Valley chapters.

By Bus

Greyhound, 800/231-2222, www.greyhound.com, offers regular bus service to major cities and popular tourist destinations throughout the state. **Adirondack–Pine Hill Trailways,** 800/225-6815, and **New York Trailways,** 800/295-5555, also service major cities, as well as a variety of rural areas.

By Car

Though New York City is best explored by foot, subway, bus, and taxi, upstate New York is best traversed by car. Outside the downstate metropolitan region, public transportation is limited and infrequent.

I-87 is the principal highway running north-south from New York City to Canada. I-90 is the main highway running east-west, from Buffalo to Albany and Massachusetts.

The statewide speed limit for open highway driving is 65 miles per hour. Speed limits for cities, towns, villages, and smaller roads are considerably slower. It is against the law to drive without using seatbelts in the driver's and front passenger's seats. Unless otherwise stated, a right turn on red is permitted almost everywhere except New York City.

If renting a car, try to do so outside Manhattan. Rates are considerably lower at the airports, in the boroughs, and elsewhere in the state. Major car rental companies operating in New York State include **Avis** (800/331-1212), **Budget** (800/527-0700), **Hertz** (800/654-3131), and **National** (800/328-4567).

Services and Information

For Foreign Visitors

Most foreign visitors entering the United States are required to carry a current passport, a visitor's visa, and proof they intend to leave (a return airplane ticket is usually enough). It's also wise to carry proof of citizenship, such as a driver's license or birth certificate. Canadian citizens entering New York from Canada need only carry proof of residence.

To obtain a U.S. visa, contact the nearest U.S. embassy or consulate. Tourist visas are valid for up to six months; special visas are required to work or study in the United States.

To extend your visa for a maximum of six months, contact the nearest Immigration and Naturalization Service office. To replace a passport lost while in the United States, contact your country's nearest embassy.

Visitors to the United States do not need inoculations unless they are coming from an area known to be suffering from an epidemic such as cholera or yellow fever. Visitors with medical conditions requiring treatment with narcotics or the use of drug paraphernalia such as syringes must carry a valid, signed physician's prescription.

Special Interests

The **Council on International Educational**

Exchange (CIEE), 205 E. 42nd St., New York, NY 10017, 212/822-2600, www.ciee.org, provides information on low-cost travel and work-study programs in the United States, including New York State. The CIEE also sells the International Student Identity Card, good for travel and entertainment discounts.

Help for disabled travelers is available through the **Society for Accessible Travel and Hospitality,** 212/447-7284, www.sath.org, a nationwide, nonprofit membership organization that collects data on travel facilities around the country.

Disabled residents of New York State should apply for the **Access Pass,** which provides free entry to most state parks and recreation areas. For an application, contact Access, State Parks, Albany, NY 12238.

Anyone over age 50 is eligible to join the **American Association of Retired People** (AARP), 601 E St. NW, Washington, D.C. 20049, 202/434-2277 or 800/424-3410, www.aarp.org, which provides its members with hotel, airfare, car rental, sightseeing, and other travel discounts. **Elderhostel,** 11 Avenue de Lafayette, Boston, MA 02110, 617/426-7788, www.elderhostel.org, offers educational tour packages in New York City and State for travelers age 60 and older.

The **Golden Age Program** provides New York

ON THE ROAD

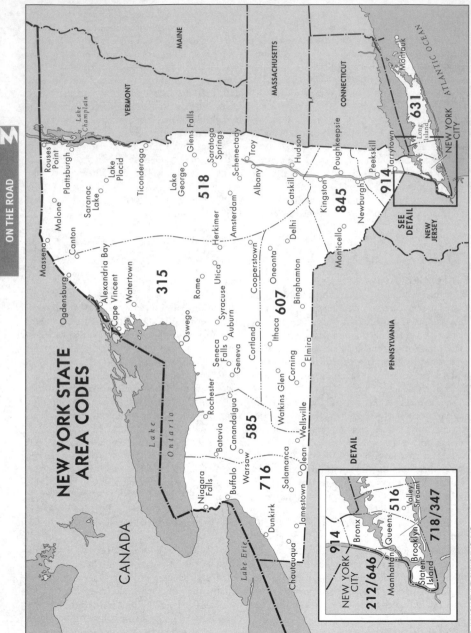

NEW YORK STATE AREA CODES

State residents age 62 or older with free entry to state parks and recreation areas any weekday, excluding holidays. To take advantage of the program, simply present your current driver's license or Non-Driver's Identification Card at the entrance gate.

Business Hours, Shopping, Money

Standard business hours in New York are Mon.–Fri. 9 A.M.–5 P.M. Banks are usually open Mon.–Fri. 9 A.M.–3 P.M., with some branches open Saturday 9 A.M.–1 P.M. Many banks offer 24-hour automated teller service.

Most shops are open Mon.–Sat. from 9 or 10 A.M. to 5 or 6 P.M. Sunday afternoon and evening hours are also common, and many grocery stores and delis remain open 24 hours a day. The state sales tax is 8.25 percent.

With the exception of inexpensive motels and restaurants, credit cards are accepted almost everywhere in the state, and are mandatory for renting cars and most sports equipment. The safest way to bring cash is to carry traveler's checks. American Express traveler's checks are the most widely accepted.

Measurements, Mail, Communication

Like the rest of the United States, New York still eschews the metric system. See the U.S.-Metric Conversion Chart in the back of this book. New York lies within the eastern standard time zone. Daylight saving time, which sets the clocks one hour ahead, goes into effect from the first Sunday in April to the last Sunday in October.

Normal post office hours are Mon.–Fri. 8:30 A.M.–5 P.M., and Saturday 8:30 A.M.–noon. Some post offices are also open late one night a week.

New York State uses an ever-proliferating number of area codes. To obtain a number from directory services, dial 411.

General Information

The best source for general information on New York State is the **New York State Division of Tourism**, P.O. Box 2603, Albany, NY 12220, 800/CALL-NYS or 518/474-4116, www.iloveny.state.ny.us. It publishes a free, 200-page *I*

Love New York guide that's updated annually, as well a wide variety of brochures on specific regions. For an updated calendar of events staged throughout the state, including New York City, call 800/CALL-NYS.

Most regions, cities, and towns also staff their own tourism offices and/or visitor centers. Addresses are listed by location elsewhere in this book.

Excellent maps of New York State are published by the **Automobile Association of America**. The AAA maps are available free to members at any local AAA office. For more information about AAA membership and services in New York, contact the American Automobile Association, 1415 Kellum Pl., Garden City, NY 11530, 516/746-7730 or 212/586-1166.

Rand-McNally and Hagstrom publish excellent street maps of Manhattan and the other New York City boroughs; these are available at most bookstores and many newsstands. The De-Lorme Mapping Company publishes two excellent oversize map books: *New York State Atlas & Gazetteer* and *Upstate New York City Street Maps*.

HEALTH AND SAFETY

Emergencies and Medical Care

Call 911 for any emergency throughout most of New York State. In some isolated areas, the 911 system is only now going into effect; if it's not yet operational, dial 0 (the number zero, not the letter o) for the operator.

Twenty-four-hour health care services are available in clinics and hospital emergency rooms throughout much of the state. To make sure service will be readily provided, carry proof of health care coverage.

City Safety

Though drastically reduced in recent years, crime continues to be a problem in both the Big Apple and other New York cities. Wherever you go, stay alert and use common sense. Carry only small amounts of cash; ignore hustlers and con artists; keep a tight hold on your purse and camera; label and lock your luggage; lock your car; and avoid lonely and unlit stretches, especially after dark.

Outdoor Safety

Before heading into the forests and semi-wilderness areas of New York State, be sure you know where you're going and what you're doing. Check with park officials and other knowledgeable outdoorspeople about trail conditions, weather, water sources, and fire danger. Be sure your equipment is functioning properly, and don't head out alone. If you're an outdoors novice, accompany someone with more experience.

Basic accoutrements for most day-hikes include a small knapsack, hat, sunscreen, lip balm, compass, whistle, insect repellent, multipurpose knife, good hiking boots, layered clothing, food, and an ample water supply. For longer or more demanding hikes, bring a butane lighter or waterproof matches, nylon rope, first-aid kit, "space blanket," extra socks and shoelaces, and a waterproof poncho or large plastic bag.

Lyme Disease

Anyone who spends much time outdoors in New York should be aware of the symptoms of Lyme disease. The bacterium that causes the disease is carried by the deer tick, which is found in brush, meadows, forests, and even lawns. In early stages, the disease is easily treatable with antibiotics, but if left unattended, it can lead to serious neurological, heart, and joint problems.

Many—*but not all*—of those infected develop a red circular rash around the bite location within three days to one month. The rash usually begins with a small red dot that expands to a diameter of one to five inches. The expanded rash may feature a bright red border and a hard, pale center.

The rash is usually accompanied by flulike symptoms. These include fatigue, nausea, vomiting, diarrhea, pain in the muscles and joints, stiff neck, swollen lymph glands, headaches, fevers, chills, sore throat, dry cough, dizziness, sensitivity to the sun, and chest, ear, and/or back pain.

Lyme disease was first identified in Old Lyme, Connecticut, in 1975, and quickly spread throughout New England. It's now one of the fastest growing communicable diseases in New York. If you suspect that you have Lyme disease, contact your doctor immediately.

Prevention: Wear light-colored clothing to make it easier to spot ticks, and long pants and long-sleeved shirts to discourage the beasties. Tuck pants cuffs into socks, and use an insect repellent with a 25–30 percent DEET content around clothing openings and on exposed skin.

Use gloves and tweezers to remove ticks; grasp the tick's head parts as close to your skin as possible and apply slow steady traction. Wash both your hands and the bitten area afterward. Do not attempt to remove ticks by burning them or coating them with anything like nail polish remover or petroleum jelly. If you remove a tick before it has been attached for more than 24 hours, you greatly reduce your risk of infection.

Ticks do not jump, but usually crawl upward until they find exposed skin. Among their favorite dining spots are the back of the neck, the scalp, armpits, the groin area, and the backs of knees. Not all bites result in illness.

If you plan to spend much time outdoors in New York State, you may wish to ask your doctor about the newly developed inoculation for Lyme disease.

New York City

Introduction

History

New York has historically been a city people love to hate. It's dirty, it's dangerous, it's crass, and it's loud. It's cynical, corrupt, cold, and uncomfortable. Worst of all, say out-of-towners, there's something un-American about it. All that pushiness, all that traffic, all those people actually choosing to live in ugly apartment buildings with no green front lawns or white picket fences in sight. This can't be the American Dream, or the United States as our forefathers meant it to be. No—New York may be a fine place to visit, but it's no place to live.

New Yorkers don't disagree. In fact, they'll enthusiastically endorse any negative a visitor comes up with, and add a few of their own. New York's transportation system sucks, its taxes are too high, its real estate prices are exorbitant, and poverty is rampant. The school system is falling apart, the middle class is being forced out, the job market is impossible, and everyone is only out for himself. No, New Yorkers sigh, wearily shaking their heads, New York is no place to live. . . .

But then again—they arch their eyebrows—it is the *only* place to live.

Imagine New York in the early morning, when a pink light bathes the buildings, and the sky turns from black to a shimmering blue. Imagine New York at rush hour when hundreds of thousands of workers whoosh energetically through the subways and streets. Imagine New York at midday, when the air crackles and pops with imagination and ideas and deals in the making. Imagine New York in the evening, when a quiet calm briefly descends and secrets are exchanged in shadow-filled bars and restaurants. And most of all, imagine New York at night, when the brilliant lights

Brooklyn Bridge

beckon, warding off the darkness, and everything seems possible.

There's no other place quite like New York City. Where else can you find teeming sidewalks at most any hour of the day and night? Where else can you meet people of a dozen nationalities in just a few blocks? Where else can you choose from among over 18,000 eating establishments, 150 museums, 400 art galleries, 240 theaters, 50 dance spots, 60 live music spots, 90 institutions of higher learning, and 10,000 shops and boutiques?

Since the terrorist attacks of September 11, 2001, too, the image of the city has changed. In that black hour, when it seemed as if the end of the world was at hand, New Yorkers proved themselves to be extraordinarily heroic, compassionate, generous, resilient, and determined.

John Steinbeck may have said it best. New York "is an ugly city," he wrote, "a dirty city. Its climate is a scandal. Its politics are used to frighten children. Its traffic is madness. Its competition is murderous. But there is one thing about it—once you have lived in New York and it has become your home, no other place is good enough."

New York "is an ugly city," Steinbeck wrote, "a dirty city. Its climate is a scandal. . . . Its traffic is madness. Its competition is murderous. But there is one thing about it—once you have lived in New York and it has become your home, no other place is good enough."

Early New York

New York has always been different. It was the only American colony settled by the Dutch, and the only colony settled for economic rather than religious reasons. Ever since the 1600s, people have come to New York City to make money, and they've never been too scrupulous in making it. They've also never cared much about who does the making. For all its occasional outbursts of ethnic and racial violence, New York has long been a tolerant and heterogeneous city. As early as 1643, a Jesuit priest visiting the colony reported that among its 500 inhabitants, 18 languages were spoken.

New York City's first human inhabitants were the Algonquin Indians. Several subtribes and local groups, including the Reckgawawanc, Canarsee, and Matinecock, once roamed through the area, planting corn and tobacco and hunting bobcat and wild turkey. Their New York was a land of great abundance, filled with verdant forests and meadows, ice blue streams and ponds, plump fish and game. The upper part of Manhattan was rocky and thick with trees, the lower part grassy and rich with fruits and flowers.

In 1524, explorer Giovanni da Verrazano arrived, sailing into New York Harbor on the *Delfina*. "We found a very pleasant situation amongst some steep hills, through which a very large river, deep at its mouth, forced its way to the sea," Verrazano reported to King Francis I of France, financier of the voyage. "Therefore, we took the boat, and entering the river, we found the country on its banks well peopled, the inhabitants being dressed out with feathers of birds of different colors. They came toward us with evident delight, raising loud shouts of admiration. . . ."

However, due to a sudden "violent contrary wind [that] blew in from the sea and forced us to return to our ship," Verrazano never set foot on New York, and King Francis never sent anyone back to explore its "great riches." Not until 1598 did a handful of Dutch traders working summers in Greenland first winter in Manhattan, ensconced in two small forts they built on the southern tip.

Between 1609 and 1611, Englishman Henry Hudson made two voyages to the New World aimed at finding a northwest passage to the Orient. On the first—backed by the Dutch West India Company—Hudson sailed into New York harbor and ventured halfway up the Hudson River before abandoning his quest and returning home. The following year he returned as captain of a British ship. This time he sailed into Hudson Bay, where the ship became icebound. Starving and doubting their captain's navigational abilities, the crew mutinied. They cast Hudson, his son, and several others adrift in a small boat, never to be seen again.

SIGHT-SEEING HIGHLIGHTS

Icons
Empire State Building, Rockefeller Center, Statue of Liberty

Major Museums
American Museum of Natural History, Brooklyn Museum, Cloisters, Cooper-Hewitt National Design Museum, Ellis Island, Frick Collection, Guggenheim Museum, Metropolitan Museum of Art, Museum of Modern Art, National Museum of the American Indian, Studio Museum of Harlem, Whitney Museum

Smaller Museums
American Craft Museum, American Folk Museum, American Museum of the Moving Image, Asia Society and Museum, Dahesh Museum, Edgar Allan Poe Cottage, Forbes Galleries, Jewish Museum, Lower East Side Tenement Museum, Morgan Library, Museum of Chinese in the Americas, Museum of the City of New York, Neue Galerie, New Museum of Contemporary Art, New York Hall of Science, New-York Historical Society, New York City Police Museum, Noguchi Garden Museum, Old Merchant's House

Experiences
Birdwatching in the Ramble, Brooklyn Bridge at twilight, Central Park on the weekends, Chinatown, Coney Island on a summer's day, eating in the East Village, ethnic eats along Ninth Avenue, fortune-tellers throughout the city, Fulton Fish Market before dawn, Hasidic Lee Avenue in Williamsburg (Brooklyn), Italian Arthur Avenue in the Bronx, meandering through the West Village, Mets' and Yankees' games, SoHo on a weekend afternoon, Staten Island Ferry at night, the soul-food restaurants of Harlem, Times Square just before showtime

Views
Socrates Sculpture Park in Long Island City (Queens), the Empire State Building at night, the Admiral George Dewey Promenade at the World Financial Center/Battery Park City, the Promenade in Brooklyn Heights, the sculpture garden atop the Metropolitan Museum of Art

Architecture
Ansonia, Cathedral of St. John the Divine, Chrysler Building, Citicorp Building, City Hall, *Daily News* Building, Dakota, Flatiron Building, Grand Central, Haughwout Building, Jefferson Market Library, Lever House, Morris-Jumel Mansion, New York Public Library, San Remo, Seagram Building, St. Paul's Chapel, Striver's Row, Trinity Church, Woolworth Building

Environments
Bronx Zoo and Botanical Garden, Brooklyn Botanic Garden, Bryant Park, City Island, Conservancy Garden in Central Park, Gramercy Park, New York Aquarium, Washington Square Park, Woodlawn Cemetery

Entertainment
Amateur Night at the Apollo, Broadway plays, free performances in Central Park, jazz in Greenwich Village, poetry readings and Off-Off-Broadway theater in the East Village, the Russian nightclubs of Brighton Beach

Only in New York
Twenty-three acre Riverbank State Park on the roof of a sewage treatment plant in Harlem, justice-of-the-peace weddings in the Municipal Building, model of New York City in the Queens Museum of Art, night court in the Criminal Courts Building, outdoor rollerblading disco at the Central Park Mall, Russian and Turkish Baths in the East Village

Rockefeller Center

Though unsuccessful in his search for a northwest passage, Hudson proved instrumental in drawing Europeans to the New World. His reports to the Dutch West India Company described the area's abundant natural resources—including a wealth of beaver and mink—and soon a group of Dutch merchants established a trading post on lower Manhattan. The Dutch West India Company was run by the foremost traders of the day and was perhaps the greatest business enterprise ever; the company returned an average annual profit of 18 percent over 250 years.

Dutch New York

The Dutch named their new outpost Fort Amsterdam and built a fort on the site of what is now the National Museum of the American Indian (and former U.S. Custom House). In 1626, Peter Minuit was appointed first governor of the tiny colony—population 300—and almost immediately bought Manhattan Island from the Algonquins for trinkets worth about $24. The Algonquins considered it a good deal at the time. Having a different sense of ownership than did the Dutch, they thought they were selling only the right to use Algonquin land, not the land itself.

They would soon find out otherwise. Problems between the Algonquins and the Dutch arose quickly. First, Dutch cattle strayed into Indian cornfields, taking a toll on the crops. Then the Dutch tried to impose a tax on the Indians. In 1643, open warfare broke out. The colony, now known as New Amsterdam, applied to Holland for help, and it arrived in the form of arms and men. By 1645, the Indians were no longer an issue.

Unlike their dour fellow colonizers in New England, the Dutch were a fun-loving, easygoing bunch who had to be constantly reminded by their governors not to play tennis when they should be working and not to drink on Sunday when they should be listening to sermons. Both

In 1626, Peter Minuit bought Manhattan Island from the Algonquins for trinkets worth about $24. The Algonquins considered it a good deal at the time. Having a different sense of ownership than did the Dutch, they thought they were selling only the right to use Algonquin land, not the land itself.

men and women smoked, and as one observer of the day noted, "All drink here from the moment they are able to lick a spoon." In 1644, the Dutch even issued their own Emancipation Proclamation, freeing the black slaves who had arrived in 1625 and 1626, and giving them their own farmland near what is now Greenwich Village. The Dutch themselves were afraid to settle that far north, due to the possibility of Indian attacks.

Dutch control of New York lasted 40 years, with the last and most flamboyant Dutch governor, Peter Stuyvesant, in power 1647–64. Nicknamed "Old Peg Leg," due to a leg lost in battle, Stuyvesant was an arrogant, quick-tempered man with a puritanical streak. He ordered the taverns closed on Sundays and tried to prevent a group of Portuguese Jews from settling in the colony—an action for which he was swiftly reprimanded by his bosses back in Amsterdam.

For all his failings, however, Stuyvesant was responsible for turning the colony into a semblance of a town. He straightened the streets, repaired the fences, and established a night watch. And he was one of the few Dutch colonists who wanted to fight off the English. The rest of the colony didn't much care; the English, who had by this time established a strong presence in New England, had promised the residents of New Amsterdam that if they surrendered, their lives would go on as before. That was just fine with the Dutch merchants. As long as they were making money, it made no difference to them who governed the colony.

Enter and Exit the English

The British took over New Amsterdam in 1664, renaming the city New York after the Duke of York, later crowned King James II. The Dutch system of government was replaced with the British one, but for most of the colonists, life did go on as before. The town continued to prosper and grow, reaching a population of 25,000 in 1750. In the New World, only Philadelphia was bigger.

For the colonists of African heritage, however, life under British rule became increasingly difficult. Slavery was reinstated, and the slave trade encouraged; a slave market was set up on Wall Street. Some black families had their land confiscated; others lost it after passage of a 1712 law prohibiting blacks from inheriting land.

Elsewhere in the colonies, the initial rumblings of the American Revolution began. When word reached New York, the city first took a pro-Tory stance. Merchants intent on making money wanted nothing to do with war. As tensions escalated, however, New Yorkers changed their position. After 1753, they supported the Revolution completely, rioting against the Stamp Act and burning the British lieutenant governor in effigy.

The earliest battles of the Revolution were fought in New York City. Most notable among them was the Battle of Long Island, in which George Washington tried to defend what is now Brooklyn Heights from the British. Washington was trounced, but managed to retreat up Manhattan with a large enough army to continue the war. The battle also taught him an important lesson: He hadn't a prayer of defeating the professional British soldiers head-on and would have to resort to guerrilla tactics.

New York remained in the hands of the British throughout the Revolutionary War and served as an incarceration center. More men perished in the prison ships anchored in Wallabout Bay, just north of Brooklyn, than in all the war's battles combined.

After the war, in 1789, Washington was inaugurated as first president of the United States. The ceremony took place in New York City—in Federal Hall on Wall Street. The city had been designated the fledgling nation's first capital in 1785 and held the honor until 1790, when the federal government was transferred to Philadelphia.

Rise to Power

The years following the Revolution were critical ones for New York City. Between 1790 and 1830, the city gradually transformed itself from one of many important Colonial centers into the largest and wealthiest metropolis in the new republic.

The factors leading to New York's ascendancy were many, but probably the most important was the opening of the Erie Canal in 1825. The hand-dug canal—stretching from the Hudson River to Lake Erie—established a water route to the West, thereby reducing the cost of transporting goods by a whopping 90 percent. Hundreds of thousands of small boats were soon plying the new route, carrying cargo to New York City for transfer onto oceangoing vessels. New York Harbor became one of the world's busiest ports, with grain elevators and warehouses sprouting up all along the docks.

About the same time, New York established the country's first regularly scheduled transatlantic shipping service. Previously, ships had sailed only when their holds were full. This innovation gave the metropolis a competitive edge for decades to come.

Manhattan's famous grid street system was established in 1811. All of the island that had not yet been settled was scored into 12 major avenues—each 100 feet wide—and 155 consecutively numbered streets. Most of the streets were 60 feet wide, but those that intersected the already established Broadway when it crossed an avenue were 100 feet wide. Later, when the subway system was built, stops were placed along many of the wider streets.

In 1842, New York opened the Croton Aqueduct Water System, then the world's largest water system. The $12 million project dammed the Croton River, 40 miles upstate, and brought water into the city through a series of reservoirs and aqueducts. New York thus became one of the first cities in the world to supply all its citizens—even the poorest—with clean fresh water. As a result, outbreaks of cholera and other epidemic diseases were drastically reduced. Today, New York still has one of the world's best water systems.

Slavery and Immigration

Reminiscent of its pre–Revolutionary War ambivalence, New York was slow to take a stand on the issues surrounding the Civil War. As a commercial city conducting lucrative business with the cotton-growing states, it often conveniently turned its back on the cruelties of slavery. In fact, New York State was one of the last of the

Northern states to abolish slavery, only doing so in 1827.

Nonetheless, New York City had an active free black community that by the mid-1800s had established many prominent churches, schools, theaters, and other institutions. Many of the city's middle-class blacks were active in the Underground Railroad—the network of abolitionists who helped fugitive Southern slaves reach freedom in Canada.

The pre–Civil War years also witnessed the influx of the first of the great waves of immigrants that swept into the city between the mid-1800s and the 1920s. From 1840 to 1855, over three million Irish and Germans arrived. Many of the Irish were escaping the potato famines, many of the Germans the failed Revolution of 1848.

When the Civil War began, New York officially supported the Union. But the citizenry remained divided. The city's newest immigrants particularly resented having to fight to free slaves, who might then come north and compete for jobs. In 1863, this deep-rooted discontent led to the Draft Riots, in which 2,000 people were injured or killed.

After the war, the infamous William Marcy "Boss" Tweed came to power in New York City. A tough street fighter, Tweed became America's first "political boss." He never held mayoral office, but he controlled the city from behind the scenes, through the Democratic machine known as Tammany Hall. During Tweed's corrupt reign, from 1866 to 1871, he and his henchmen pocketed as much as $200 million from padded or fraudulent city expenditures and tax improprieties. Eventually indicted, Tweed died in a Ludlow Street jail not far from his birthplace.

All That Glitters

By the late 1800s, New York was in its full glory. In 1892, 1,265 millionaires lived either in the city or its suburbs. In 1895, the city housed nearly 300 companies worth over one million dollars—more than the next six largest cities combined. In 1898, New York annexed Brooklyn, Queens, Staten Island, and the Bronx, thereby increasing its area from 23 to 301 square miles.

The rich and the powerful flocked to New York from all over the country, and the social elite were soon defined as the "Four Hundred"— the maximum number of guests who could squeeze into Mrs. Astor's Fifth Avenue ballroom. Investment bankers such as J. P. Morgan and August Belmont became household names, as did leaders of commerce and industry such as John D. Rockefeller, Andrew Carnegie, and F. W. Woolworth.

New York became the nation's cultural capital as well. Theaters sprang up along Broadway, and the Metropolitan Museum of Art and the Metropolitan Opera opened their doors in 1880 and 1890, respectively. Walt Whitman sang the city's praises in poems such as "Leaves of Grass" and "Crossing Brooklyn Ferry," and Henry James and Edith Wharton reported on the lives of the upper crust in *Washington Square* and *The Age of Innocence*.

But the years surrounding the turn of the century also had a darker side. Between 1880 and 1919, a new wave of more than 17 million immigrants—this time mainly from Southern and Eastern Europe—swept into New York. In his 1890 book, *How the Other Half Lives,* Jacob Riis wrote, "A map of the city, colored to designate nationalities, would show more stripes than on the skin of a zebra, and more colors than any rainbow." Many settled in the Lower East Side, where they worked miserable, low-paying jobs in the garment industry. Overcrowding became a serious problem; by 1900, more than two-thirds of the city's residents were crowded into some 80,000 tenements in Manhattan and Brooklyn. The Lower East Side had a population density of 209,000 people per square mile, equal to that of today's Bombay.

In 1904, Manhattan opened its first subway, long after London (1863) and shortly after Boston (1897). But New York's subway system would soon be distinguished for both its enormous size and its technological innovations. Within a year after opening, New York's subway—then just a single line running up Park Avenue, across 42nd Street, and up Broadway— was carrying over 600,000 passengers per day. By 1937, the city boasted over 700 miles of track handling 4.2 million passengers per day. Today, the subway system still has about 700 miles of track, but it handles only about 3.5 million passengers a day.

Prosperity

After WW I, the United States emerged as a world power, and nowhere was this newfound status more evident than in dazzling New York. Business and manufacturing flourished. The Jazz Age arrived and the liquor flowed. F. Scott Fitzgerald came to town, and Jimmy Walker was elected mayor. A dandified gentleman with a taste for the good life, Walker spent most of his time visiting nightclubs, sporting halls, and showgirls. Thanks to his late-night carousing, he rarely appeared at City Hall before 3 P.M., if at all. "No civilized man," he once said, "goes to bed the same day he wakes up."

The strict new federal immigration laws of 1921 and 1924 slowed the influx of foreigners to a trickle, but Harlem boomed as black Southerners fleeing poverty took refuge in the city. In 1910, Manhattan was home to about 60,000 blacks; by 1930, that number had tripled. Harlem became the center for African American culture, with the Harlem Renaissance attracting writers and intellectuals such as Langston Hughes and W. E. B. DuBois, and jazz clubs and theaters attracting the likes of Duke Ellington and Chick Webb.

All this high living crashed with little warning in October 1929, when the stock market collapsed. Overnight, the gaiety stopped and the Depression began. By 1932, one out of every four New Yorkers was unemployed, and scores of shantytowns called "Hoovervilles" dotted Central Park.

But the city didn't stay down for long. That same year, Fiorello La Guardia was elected mayor. La Guardia—regarded by many historians as the best mayor New York ever had—set about cleaning up corruption, imposing stiff taxes, and obtaining moneys through FDR's New Deal programs. Together with Parks Commissioner Robert Moses, La Guardia embarked on an enormous public works program that transformed the city both physically and economically. The nation's entry into WW II in 1941 also gave New York a much needed economic jolt.

During the war, Columbia University at 116th

ROBERT MOSES, MASTER BUILDER

City Parks Commissioner Robert Moses—part civil servant, part evil genius—was one of the most unusual and controversial figures in New York's history. Though a nonelected official, he wielded enormous political power extending far beyond his office, the city, and even the state.

In power for 44 years (1924–68), Moses conceived of and executed public works costing $27 billion, thereby shaping virtually the entire modern landscape of New York. He was responsible for all but one of the city's major expressways, most of Long Island's parkways and beaches, thousands of public housing units, and over 600 playgrounds and parks. Literally hundreds of major construction projects were completed during his tenure, among them the Henry Hudson, Bronx-Whitestone, Cross Bay, Throgs Neck, Verrazano Narrows, Marine Parkway, and Triborough Bridges; the Brooklyn-Battery Tunnel; Lincoln Center; the New York Coliseum; Shea Stadium; Co-Op City; the United Nations; the giant dams at the St. Lawrence and Niagara Rivers; and both the 1939 and 1964 World's Fairs.

According to biographer Robert Caro, Moses began his career as a visionary idealist yearning to bring about social change but ended it as a power-hungry tyrant who would stop at nothing to achieve his goals. To build his highways, he evicted over 250,000 people and destroyed scores of neighborhoods; the housing he designed for the poor was "bleak, sterile, cheap"; his World's Fairs cost the city hundreds of thousands of dollars; his highways sapped funding for the subways and created the mess of a transportation system New York suffers from today.

Writes Caro in *The Power Broker,* "Robert Moses was America's greatest builder. He was the shaper of the greatest city in the New World. But what did he build? What was the shape into which he pounded the city? . . . It is impossible to say that New York would have been a better city if Robert Moses had never lived. It is possible to say only that it would have been a different city."

Moses died in 1981 at the age of 92.

St. and Broadway was the site of a nuclear experiment conducted by Dr. Robert Oppenheimer. Code-named the "Manhattan Project," the experiment led to the creation of the world's first atomic bomb, dropped on Japan in August 1945.

Post-War Decline

Despite the prosperity brought to New York by WW II, the city reached its economic peak relative to the rest of the country around 1940. Thereafter, certain trends already in effect began to undermine both New York and the entire Northeast. These trends would not become visible for many years, but they were there, slowly eating away.

In 1880, 16 percent of all U.S. production workers lived in the New York Metropolitan Region. By 1900, that figure had fallen to 14 percent, and by 1990, it had fallen to four percent. Between 1956 and 1985, the region lost over 600,000 industrial jobs, most in small, light-industrial businesses such as glass-making and textile manufacturing. Unlike most cities, New York has always been dominated by small businesses. Some of these companies left the city due to demographic shifts towards the South and West, others due to technological changes that allowed them to decentralize. Still others fled from the rising cost of doing business in New York.

During this same period, New York's once-thriving port also declined. The advent of container ships—which require large dockside cranes for loading—spelled its death. New York's old shipyards simply did not have the space needed to maneuver the cranes. In addition, the Brooklyn Naval Yard—a major employer since before the Civil War—closed in 1968.

With these economic shifts came considerable social unrest. The declining number of manufacturing jobs, coupled with continuing in-migration of poor blacks and Puerto Ricans, resulted in racial disturbances and an increase in crime, which frightened the middle class. Between 1950 and 1970, over one million families left the city in the "Great White Flight," further eroding the once-stable tax base.

On the up side, New York's cultural scene was thriving. The Guggenheim Museum opened in 1959, followed by Lincoln Center in the mid-'60s. Broadway was producing one great hit after another—including *My Fair Lady* and *West Side Story*—and the publishing and television industries were booming. "Culture had become a commodity," wrote historian Harold Syrett, "and New Yorkers were its largest producers. Most other Americans had to be content with being consumers."

Fiscal Crisis and Rebound

Things came to a head in 1975. Cultural attractions aside, New York was all but bankrupt. Banks shut off credit, and the city, in desperation, turned to the federal government for help. The famous *Daily News* headline "Ford to City: Drop Dead" caustically summed up Washington's stony response.

The city was temporarily rescued by the Municipal Assistance Corporation, put together by financier Felix Rohatyn and Gov. Hugh Carey to issue city bonds and thereby borrow money. Washington was impressed enough by this effort to finally extend the city a short-term loan of $2.5 billion.

The city's recovery was further aided in 1978 by the election of Mayor Ed Koch. A one-time liberal from the Bronx via Greenwich Village, Koch helped set the city back on track through budget cuts and austerity programs. Brash, shrewd, and outspoken, Koch managed to play the city's various interest groups off one another to the general public's advantage, winning the respect of many New Yorkers in the process. Much of the '80s' construction boom, which included Trump Tower and the World Financial Center, was attributed to his efforts. Unfortunately, so was the city's steadily increasing homeless population.

Koch was reelected twice. But by 1990, the city was fed up with his egotistical style, neglect of the poor, and insensitivity to racial issues. In his stead was elected David Dinkins, the city's first black mayor. The consummate party politician, Dinkins succeeded in implementing several important anticrime programs. But overall, his indecisive governing style did not sit well with most New Yorkers. In 1994, he was defeated by

Rudolph Giuliani, a tough former U.S. attorney who soon surprised the predominantly Democratic city by supporting Democrat Mario Cuomo instead of fellow Republican George Pataki in the 1994 gubernatorial election.

But many later Giuliani decisions did not prove to be as popular. Even while helping to drastically lower the city's crime rates, Giuliani's "quality-of-life" campaign to clean up the streets cracked down on some of the very things that make New York New York—sidewalk vendors and newsstands, for example. Giuliani also paid astonishingly little attention to such major urban problems as homelessness, education, the city's crumbling infrastructure, and race relations.

The New Prosperity

At the end of the 1990s, New York was riding the crest of the bull stock market. Dozens of new businesses, restaurants, bars, and shops were opening up daily, on even the most depressed of blocks. Rents were skyrocketing, while the streets teemed with well-dressed twenty-somethings earning salaries their grandparents never even dreamed of.

At the same time, the chasm between the haves and the have-nots was widening. According to the 1990 census, the mean annual income of the poorest 10 percent of Manhattan families was only about $3,000, while among the upper 10 percent it was nearly $200,000—66 times as high. In contrast, in 1980, the top 10th was only 48 times richer than the poorest 10th, and in 1970, 39 times.

With such statistics, it's not surprising that homelessness was—and continues to be—a major problem. Some estimate the city's homeless population to be close to 300,000. But, ironically, the homeless are no longer visible on most New York streets. They've been swept out into the boroughs and Manhattan's outer edges, to sleep under highways and bridges.

On a more positive note, crime in the city fell dramatically throughout the 1990s. By 1997, according to FBI statistics, New York didn't even make the top-25 list of cities with the highest homicide rates anymore, while crime in the subways had dropped nearly 50 percent between 1990 and 1999.

In addition, New York was—and is—benefiting from yet another enormous influx of immigrants. Many have been steadily arriving since the easing of immigration quotas in 1965; others have come since the end of the Cold War, or following political upheaval in their home countries. Some 90,000 documented immigrants enter the city each year, and one out of every three New Yorkers is foreign born.

These new immigrants are transforming the city. Between 1965 and 1990, the city's Chinese population more than quadrupled, to an estimated 250,000. Since 1989, the Russian presence has exploded from a small group of émigrés to a community of over 100,000. Many of the city's doctors and medical technicians now hail from India, Korea, or the Middle East, while many of its nurses come from the West Indies, Korea, or the Philippines. The Koreans have a corner on the fruit markets, while immigrants from India control the newsstands. Almost half of the city's cab drivers are from India, Pakistan, or Bangladesh; another third are from Eastern Europe and Russia.

More important than statistics, however, is the energy and spirit immigrants bring with them. Into a city that sometimes seems about to topple from the sheer weight of excess sophistication, solipsism, wealth, and hype, the immigrants bring a much-needed freshness. Some might be working menial jobs today, but rest assured that their children won't be working those menial jobs tomorrow. And as the immigrants and their offspring weave their way into the warp and woof of the city's fabric, they revitalize Gotham's brilliance and ensure its future.

The 21st Century

As the ball dropped in Times Square on December 31, 1999, the city seemed poised to enter one of its most prosperous decades ever. In fact, in 2000, the Big Apple even had a budget surplus—unheard of in recent years—leading to tax cuts and multiple new development schemes.

Then came the recession, and the September 11 terrorist attack on the World Trade Center that killed over 3,000 innocent people in a morning that will be forever seared into New York's

THE BOROUGHS: AN OVERVIEW

New York City, official population 8 million, is made up of five boroughs—Manhattan, Brooklyn, Queens, the Bronx, and Staten Island—covering a total of 301 square miles. Only the northernmost borough, the Bronx, sits on the mainland; the rest of the city is spread out over a group of islands in New York Bay, where the Hudson River meets the Atlantic Ocean. Manhattan and Staten Island are islands in their own right. Brooklyn and Queens are on the western tip of Long Island.

Queens is the largest borough in area (118 square miles), followed by Brooklyn (78.5 square miles), Staten Island (61 square miles), the Bronx (43 square miles,) and Manhattan (23 square miles). By population, Brooklyn takes top spot with 2.5 million residents, followed by Queens (2.2 million), Manhattan (1.5 million), the Bronx (1.3 million), and Staten Island (just 443,000).

Between Staten Island and Brooklyn runs the Verrazano Narrows, a strait separating the upper and lower parts of New York Bay. Manhattan lies in upper New York Bay and is separated from the mainland by the East River to the east, the Hudson River to the West, and the Harlem River and Spuyten Duyvil to the northeast. Technically, the East River isn't a river at all, but a strait running between Long Island Sound and New York Bay.

Manhattan

Manhattan is the epicenter of New York City. Its preeminent status is evidenced by the fact that when people speak of "the boroughs," they're usually referring to the *other* boroughs, outside Manhattan.

The island is 12 miles long and three miles wide, and scored by a grid of streets (running east-west) and avenues (running north-south). "Downtown" generally refers to anything south of 14th Street, "Midtown" to addresses between 34th and 59th Streets, and "Uptown" to areas above 59th Street. "Downtown" also translates as hip, bohemian, and avant-garde; "Midtown" as high-rise offices and the corporate world; and "Uptown" as either the sophisticated and the well-heeled, or

the ethnic worlds of the Harlems, depending on whom you're talking to. These shorthand definitions hardly do justice to the island's complexities, but they're true enough to be part of every New Yorker's lexicon.

The East Side encompasses everything east of Fifth Avenue; the West Side, everything to the west. The East Side has the reputation of being stuffier, wealthier, and less interesting than the West, but again, this is a generalization of limited utility.

Brooklyn

A separate city until 1898, Brooklyn boasts its own civic center, cultural institutions, downtown shopping district, and residential neighborhoods. Among its many visitor attractions are the Brooklyn Museum, Brooklyn Botanic Gardens, Brooklyn Academy of Music, New York Aquarium, and Coney Island boardwalk.

Queens

A largely residential borough that many Manhattanites once dismissed as a snore, Queens in now one of the most ethnically diverse sections of the city. Ethnic neighborhoods here include Astoria (Greek), Jackson Heights (Latino), and Flushing (Asian). Flushing Meadows–Corona Park and Shea Stadium are among the borough's biggest attractions.

The Bronx

The Bronx holds some of the city's worst pockets of urban decay, but also the city's biggest parks, including the Bronx Zoo, New York Botanical Garden, Van Cortlandt Park, and Pelham Pay Park. Yankee Stadium's here, too.

Staten Island

Largely residential, Staten Island is the most rural and isolated of the boroughs, and the only one whose residents speak longingly of seceding from New York City. Its major visitor attractions are historic Richmond Town, the Jacques Marchais Museum of Tibetan Art, and the Staten Island ferry.

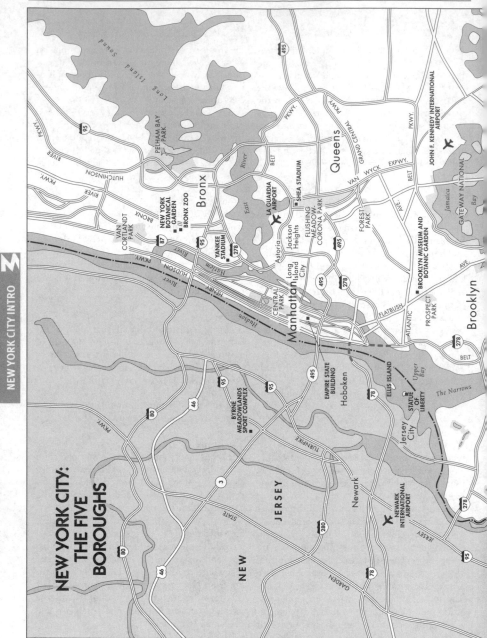

NEW YORK CITY:
THE FIVE
BOROUGHS

NEW JERSEY

Newark

Jersey City

Hoboken

Manhattan

Bronx

Queens

Brooklyn

Long Island Sound

PELHAM BAY PARK

NEW YORK BOTANICAL GARDEN

BRONX ZOO

YANKEE STADIUM

VAN CORTLANDT PARK

LA GUARDIA AIRPORT

SHEA STADIUM

FLUSHING MEADOW CORONA PARK

JOHN F. KENNEDY INTERNATIONAL AIRPORT

GATEWAY NATIONAL

FOREST PARK

BROOKLYN MUSEUM AND BOTANIC GARDEN

PROSPECT PARK

CENTRAL PARK

EMPIRE STATE BUILDING

BYRNE MEADOWLANDS SPORT COMPLEX

ELLIS ISLAND

STATUE OF LIBERTY

NEWARK INTERNATIONAL AIRPORT

Jackson Heights

Astoria

Long Island City

Upper Bay

The Narrows

Jamaica Bay

East River

Hudson River

Harlem River

Bronx River

HUTCHINSON RIVER PKWY

RIVER PKWY

HENRY HUDSON PKWY

VAN WYCK EXPWY.

GRAND CENTRAL PKWY

BELT

FLATBUSH

ATLANTIC

AVE.

PKWY.

TURNPIKE

STATE

GARDEN

JERSEY

PKWY

95

95

87

278

495

495

495

278

78

278

80

46

3

280

78

95

95

278

95

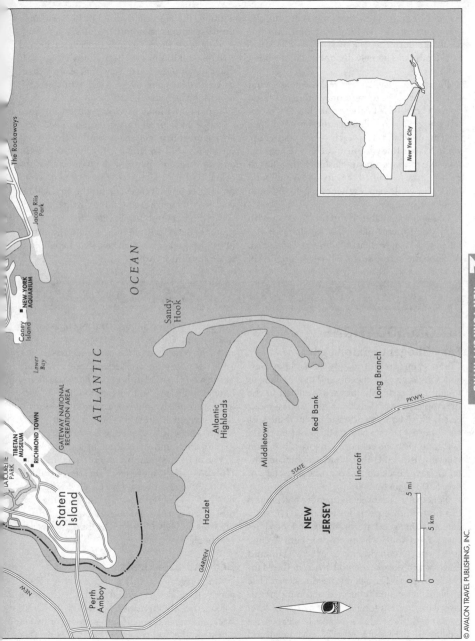

The Rockaways

Jacob Riis
Park

OCEAN

Sandy
Hook

Coney
Island

NEW YORK
AQUARIUM

Lower
Bay

ATLANTIC

Long Branch

PKWY.

Red Bank

Atlantic
Highlands

Middletown

GATEWAY NATIONAL
RECREATION AREA

TIBETAN
MUSEUM

RICHMOND TOWN

LA TOURETTE
PARK

STATE

Staten
Island

Lincroft

Hazlet

NEW
JERSEY

GARDEN

Perth
Amboy

NEW

5 mi

5 km

0

0

New York City

sense of itself. In a few short moments, the city was plunged into death, devastation, and unspeakable horror as one of its biggest architectural landmarks literally disappeared in the blink of an eye.

But even as New Yorkers reeled with grief and fear, they also rose to meet one of the city's finest hours. Thousands of citizens quickly pulled themselves together to volunteer their time, donate their money, and keep each others' spirits up, while Mayor Rudy Giuliani became a hero nationwide for his strong leadership during the crisis. The attacks unified the city—rich and poor, black and white—in a way never before seen in modern times.

Giuliani was unable to run for mayor again in 2001 due to term-limits law and the new Republican Mayor Michael Bloomberg was elected. A billionaire businessman, who many accused of winning the election because of his seemingly limitless coffers, Bloomberg quickly set about dealing with the aftermath of the attacks and reaching out to some of the minority groups that Giuliani shunned. Today, New York seems well on its way back to a recovery, which while perhaps not complete, places the city firmly on the cutting edge of international developments once again.

In the end, for all its concrete and steel, New York is an ephemeral, shape-shifting city—both physically and spiritually. See it in one light and its streets are paved with gold; see it in another, and it's the antechamber to hell. Hold on long enough, however, and the city will reveal to you neither splendor nor decay, but something resembling its eclectic, energetic, rainbow-hued soul, slipping around the corner just in front of you somewhere only to disappear again into the crowds.

Practicalities

ACCOMMODATIONS

From Budget to Extravagant

Cheap sleeps are not readily available in New York City except to students and those willing to rough it. A relatively inexpensive hotel in the Big Apple costs $80–100 a night, while a moderately priced one, with standard "nothing special" rooms, costs $100–200. Room rates did fall along with the economy in early 2001, and following the September 11 attacks, but are now on their way back up and promise an average of over $200 again by 2003.

Nonetheless, relatively inexpensive hotel rooms can be found, especially if you reserve early enough. One good area in which to look is between 23rd and 34th Streets near Fifth Avenue (see From Union Square to Murray Hill and Chelsea and the Garment District, in the Manhattan chapter). Though this is a desolate area late at night, it's centrally located and not particularly dangerous as long as you stay alert. Other good neighborhoods for relatively inexpensive lodging are the Theater District in Midtown and the Upper West Side. Also good options for the budget conscious are bed-and-breakfast inns, hostels, and YMCAs.

At the other end of the economic scale, New York is a glittering wonderland, home to some of the world's grandest hotels. The Plaza, Pierre, Four Seasons, and St. Regis are among the reigning monarchs. Even if you can't afford to stay in these elegant hostelries—and at $350–500 a night, who can?—they're well worth stepping into for afternoon tea, a drink, or just a look-see.

For more information on hotels, contact the **Hotel Association of New York City,** 212/754-6700, www.hany.org. **NYC & Company,** 800/NYC-VISIT or www.nycvisit.com, the city's official convention and visitors' bureau, can also provide you with a free booklet listing more than 140 hotels.

Bed-and-Breakfasts

Though not necessarily cheaper than an inexpensive or moderately priced hotel, a B&B can be a good, friendly alternative. Some New York City B&Bs are the traditional kind—a room or two in a host's home. Others are entire apartments that you'll have completely to yourself. Rooms usually run $90–150/night; apartments $135–250/night. The cheapest B&Bs are in the boroughs. Reservations should be made a few weeks in advance. A number of B&B registries operate in the city. The **Bed and Breakfast Network of New York,** 212/645-8134, has about 400 listings citywide, with single/double rooms starting at $90/night and apartments at $135/night; a three-night minimum is required; weekly rates also available. **All Around the Town,** 212/675-5600 or 800/443-3800, has studio rooms starting at $90/night and apartments starting at $130/night in 300 properties, mostly in Manhattan. A two-night minimum is required, and monthly rates are available.

Run by artists, **CitySonnet** (formerly called West Village Reservations), 212/614-3034, www.citysonnet.com, specializes in Greenwich Village, the East Village, SoHo, and Chelsea, but also has accommodations elsewhere in Manhattan. Rates for a single or double room are $85–155, while apartments run $135–325.

City Lights Bed & Breakfast, 212/737-7049, www.citylightsbandb.com, and **At Home in New York,** 212/956-3125 or 800/692-4262, both match mostly artists and professionals with like-minded hosts. City Lights lists about 400 properties in Manhattan and Brooklyn, while At Home lists about 300, most in Manhattan, but some in Brooklyn, Queens, and Staten Island. Rates for a single/double room are $90–160, while apartments run $135–400. A minimum stay of two nights is required by both registries.

A Hospitality Company, 212/965-1102, www.hospitalityco.com, lists about 200 apartments, most located in Manhattan. Studios run $99–165/night, one-bedroom apartments $125–225, and two-bedroom apartments $275–325.

For longer stays, check out **New York Habitat,** 212/352-0267, www.nyhabitat.com, which offers furnished apartment sublets in all prices and locations throughout the city.

Hostels and YMCAs

New York has an enormous, 620-bed Hosteling International-American Youth Hostel on the Upper West Side, as well as a number of smaller ones scattered throughout the city. Hostels can't be beat for budget travelers willing to live with the communal atmosphere. YMCAs, 800/FIT-YMCA or 212/308-2899, are another alternative for the budget conscious. Rooms should be reserved well in advance—two months, if possible—and rates include use of the athletic facilities.

Getting the Most for Your Money

Before you book, ask about discounts. Almost no one pays full rack rates in New York, and most hotels offer at least a corporate discount. Many business and luxury hotels also offer substantial weekend discounts—as much as a third off regular rates. Off-season or long-term packages are sometimes available as well. A good place to look for discounted packages is in the back pages of the Travel section of the Sunday *New York Times.*

Another option is to use a booking service. These companies buy large blocks of rooms at a discount and pass on the savings (as high as 40 percent) to consumers. Among the best of these companies are **Quikbook,** 800/789-9887 or 212/779-ROOM, www.quikbook.com; **Express Hotel Reservations,** 800/407-3351, www.express-res.com; **Accommodations Express,** 609/391-2100 or 800/444-7666, www.accommodationsexpress.com; **Hotel Reservations Network,** 214/361-7311 or 800/715-7666, www.hoteldiscount.com; and **Central Reservation Service,** 305/408-6100 or 800/555-7555, www.reservation-services.com.

A welcome service offered by NYC & Company is the free **Visitors Hotel Hotline,** 212/582-3352 or 800/846-7666. In operation during the summer and Christmas seasons, the hotline matches visitors with hotels in various locations and price ranges.

Keep in mind that in addition to the room rate, you'll also have to pay a hefty tax. Although New York State finally reduced hotel taxes by five percent in 1994, and New York City by another one percent later that same year, Gotham's hotel tax is still 13.25 percent, plus two dollars.

Be sure to book your accommodations well in advance, especially if you're hoping to stay in an inexpensive hotel. During the early summer and the Christmas holidays in particular, rooms go fast.

The prices quoted in this book are the current rack rates for single and double rooms, but these are subject to frequent change; be sure to check on current rates before booking.

FOOD

New York boasts about 18,000 eating establishments. Some come and go almost overnight, while others have been around for decades. A few rules of thumb: The East Village is an excellent neighborhood for cheap eats and ethnic restaurants; SoHo, TriBeCa, and Columbus Avenue boast lots of trendy spots; and Midtown and the Upper East Side are home to some of the city's most venerable and expensive restaurants.

For coffee and dessert suggestions, see Light Bites under the district headings in the Manhattan chapter. A number of bars in New York are also good spots for casual meals; see Watering Holes and Lounges under the district headings.

SERVICES

Emergencies

Dial 911 for emergency **police, ambulance,** or **fire department** response. For the location of the nearest police precinct, dial 212/374-5000.

Private hospitals with 24-hour emergency rooms include **St. Vincent's Hospital,** Seventh Ave. at 11th St., 212/604-7000; **Beth Israel Medical Center,** First Ave. at 16th St., 212/420-2000; **New York University Medical Center,** First Ave. at 34th St., 212/263-7300; **St. Luke's-Roosevelt Hospital,** Ninth Ave. at 58th St., 212/523-4000; **New York Hospital,** York Ave. at 68th St., 212/746-5454; and **Mount Sinai Hospital,** Fifth Ave. at 100th St., 212/241-6500.

Post Offices

Many post offices are open weekdays 8 A.M.–6 P.M., and Saturday 8 A.M.–1 P.M., but hours vary from branch to branch. The city's main post office on Eighth Avenue at 33rd Street is open 24 hours a day, seven days a week. For general post office information, call 212/967-8585.

Telephones

Public phones in various states of distress are available on many street corners, but when you do find one that works, there's often a queue. In Midtown, hotel phones are a good alternative.

The area code in Manhattan has historically been 212/, while the other boroughs use 718/. Since July 1999, however, Manhattan now has a second area code—646/—while the boroughs now also use 347/. By 2003, it will be necessary to dial all 10 numbers when placing a call.

For **directory assistance** in Manhattan, call 411. For directory assistance in the other boroughs, call 718/555-1212.

Other useful numbers include **time,** 212/976-2828; **weather,** 212/976-1212; and **wake-up calls,** 212/540-WAKE (9253).

Restrooms

Public restrooms can be difficult to find in New York. The city plans to put public toilets on the sidewalks, but at the moment, your best bet is to duck into a major hotel, department store, or public institution such as a library. Restaurants are also worth a try, although they often reserve their facilities for patrons.

Some of the most accessible public restrooms in Manhattan are at Cooper Union (41 Cooper Square, near Third Ave. and 8th St., downstairs), Penn Station (Seventh Ave., between 30th and 32nd Sts.), Grand Central Station (42nd St. and Park Ave.), the New York Public Library (Fifth Ave. and 42nd St., ground and third floors), the GE Building (30 Rockefeller Plaza, concourse level), Citicorp Center (153 Lexington Ave., at 53rd St., lower level), Trump Tower (725 Fifth Ave., at 56th St., downstairs), the 92nd Street Y (1395 Lexington Ave., at 92nd St., ground level), and Mart 125 (260 W. 125th St., near Adam Clayton Powell Jr. Blvd., 2nd Fl., key available at any counter).

Gay and Lesbian Services

Founded in 1983, the **Lesbian, Gay, Bisexual & Transgender Community Center,** 208 W. 13th St., between Seventh and Eighth Aves., 212/620-7310, www.gaycenter.org, works with hundreds of organizations, including Act-Up and GLAAD, and houses the National Museum and Archive of Lesbian and Gay History. Everything from dances to movies is presented here, and free information "Welcome Packets" about the city are available for travelers. The **Gay and Lesbian Switchboard of New York Project,** (212/989-0999, Mon.–Fri. 4 P.M.–midnight and Saturday noon–5 P.M.; website: www.glnh.org), offers peer counseling and information on accommodations, restaurants, and clubs.

Services for the Disabled

New York is a difficult city for visitors with disabilities to navigate, but help is available. One source is the **Mayor's Office for People with Disabilities,** 212/788-2830, which puts out a free Access Guide. Another is **Hospital Audiences, Inc.,** 212/575-7676, which publishes a guide to the city's cultural institutions that includes information on elevators, ramps, Braille signage, services for the hearing impaired, and restroom facilities. For more general information, contact the **Society for the Advancement of Travel for the Handicapped,** 347 Fifth Ave., New York, NY 10016, 212/447-7284, a nationwide, nonprofit membership organization that collects data on travel facilities around the country.

Two hundred of the 500 volunteer "Big Apple Greeters" are specifically trained to help the handicapped enjoy the city. The Big Apple Greeter program, available free to all visitors, matches out-of-towners with New Yorkers eager to share their hometown. The Big Apple Greeters can also provide handicapped visitors with resource lists and answer questions regarding accessibility. For more information, call 212/669-8159.

All of New York's buses are wheelchair accessible, but only a handful of subway stations are. For more information, call New York City Transit, 718/596-8585, and request copies of the free brochures *Accessible Travel* and *Accessible Transfer Points within the NYC Subway.*

INFORMATION
Tourist Information
New York City's **Official Visitor Information Center,** 810 Seventh Ave., at 53rd St., 212/484-

1222, www.nycvisit.com, is open 365 days a year, Mon.–Fri. 8:30 A.M.–6 P.M., Sat.–Sun. 9 A.M.–5 P.M. Maps, hundreds of brochures, and calendars of events are available, while kiosks provide up-to-date information. A downtown **Visitor Information Kiosk,** stands at the southern end of City Hall Park, on the Broadway side; it operates daily 8 A.M.–8 P.M.

When out of town, written information can be ordered by calling **NYC & Company,** the city's tourism marketing organization, at 800/NYC-VISIT or 212/397-8222.

Smaller **visitor information booths** are located at Grand Central Station (42nd St. and Vanderbilt Ave.), and the JFK Airport International Arrivals building.

Publications
New York City has three major daily newspapers—the *New York Times,* the *Daily News,* and the *New York Post.* The *Times* is the country's unofficial paper of record, exhaustively covering the national and international scene. But it also contains good information on happenings around town, especially in its Friday Weekend sections. The Sunday *Times* features an Arts & Leisure section offering extensive listings on events of all sorts, as well as a City section containing imaginative features on various aspects of city life.

You'd be coming away with a skewed view of New York, however, if you didn't also pick up occasional copies of the *Daily News* and the *New York Post.* Both tabloids, with their in-your-face headlines, do a much better job of covering local news than does the *Times.* The *Daily News* is also a good source for crisp, pithy features and reviews of local events. The *New York Post* often revels in sensationalism and right-of-center politics, but its Page Six gossip column is must reading for many New Yorkers, and many of its reviews are excellent. In addition, both papers feature a daily movie schedule, which the *Times* does not.

When it comes to "alternative" papers, the weekly *Village Voice* is the granddaddy. Though best known for its leftist politics, the *Voice's* strongest suit is its cultural coverage and events listings—among the city's most comprehensive.

CITY OF ISLANDS

Manhattan and Staten Islands are not the only islands of New York City. Dotting the rivers and harbor are many little outcroppings of land, some with complex histories. Only a few of these islands are open to the public; others house institutions such as hospitals or prisons, while still others are accessible only to wildlife, including rare birds such as herons, ibis, egrets, and even a few ospreys.

Hart Island

The city's potter's field since 1868, Hart Island is the final resting place of about 750,000 unknown or unwanted bodies. Approximately 2,800 new burials take place each year, and a crew of 15 to 30 prisoners from nearby Rikers Island handles the formalities. The bodies are buried in white-pine coffins made in six standard sizes; the smallest ones are for infants and body parts. New York is one of the only cities in the United States that has a potter's field; most cities cremate their unclaimed dead.

City Island

Known for its numerous seafood restaurants and small boatbuilding industry, City Island is a little piece of nautical New England transported south. See the special topic The Boroughs: An Overview, in the introduction to this chapter.

Rikers Island

Named after its original owner, Abraham Rycken, Rikers Island now houses a number of penal institutions. The largest is the Men's House of Detention, where about 5,000 prisoners are incarcerated. Built in 1935 to replace the old prison on Welfare Island (now called Roosevelt Island), Rikers was once regarded as a model penitentiary. Today it's seriously outmoded and overcrowded.

North Brother Island

Typhoid Mary was once quarantined on this now abandoned island that's become an important nesting ground for rare birds. An infected cook who worked in dozens of kitchens in the days before the nature of communicable diseases was completely understood, Typhoid Mary may have infected hundreds of people. She herself was a carrier who wasn't affected by the disease, and she didn't understand why she had to be quarantined. She fiercely attacked the officials who

tried to confine her and refused to give up her career as a cook. In 1923, after isolating Typhoid Mary in several different hospitals, the city gave her a one-room cottage of her own on North Brother Island. She lived here until 1938, when she died of a stroke at age 70. At the time of her death, she'd spent nearly half her life in confinement.

South Brother Island

Seven-acre South Brother Island is heavily wooded, privately owned, and a favorite nesting site of egrets.

Randalls Island

Like several other islands surrounding Manhattan, Randalls Island has at various times been the site of a potter's field, poorhouse, reform school, and insane asylum. In 1929, the island became the headquarters of the Triborough Bridge and Tunnel Authority, from where controversial City Parks Commissioner Robert Moses once ran his empire. Randalls Island is connected to Wards Island by landfill.

Wards Island

Used as a military base by the British during the Revolutionary War, Wards Island is now home to the Manhattan Psychiatric Center; the Manhattan Children's Treatment Center, which provides care to mentally impaired and disturbed children; and the Firefighters' Training Center.

Mill Rock Island

This one-time pirate's refuge got its name from a tide-powered mill that stood here in the early 1700s. During the War of 1812, a fort was built on the island; in the 1880s, the U.S. Army Corps of Engineers used it as a base to mix the explosives with which they blew up nearby Flood Rock. That explosion is said to have been the biggest ever before the atomic bomb. In 1953, the island was taken over by the Parks Department because Commissioner Moses was worried that a commercial enterprise might erect a billboard there, blocking his views on the way to work.

Roosevelt Island

Today a planned residential community where no cars are allowed, Roosevelt Island was once the site of a grim and nasty penal institution notorious for its innovative tortures, including "cooler" rooms and the "water drop cure." Politician Boss Tweed served time here in 1873, and actress Mae West was imprisoned here for 10 days in 1927, for her scandalous play *Sex*.

Governors Island
Governors Island has been the site of a sheep farm, quarantine station, racetrack, game preserve, the governor's "pleasure house," a Civil War prison for Confederate soldiers, and a U.S. Coast Guard Station. The Coast Guard left in late 1998, however, and the island's future remains uncertain.

Liberty Island
Egg-shaped Liberty Island, where the Statue of Liberty stands, was once known as Bedloe's Island and used as a place of execution. One of the most famous men hung here was Albert E. Hicks, who in 1860 was shanghaied onto a sloop heading for Virginia. Five days later, the boat was discovered—empty—off the coast of New Jersey. Hicks, meanwhile, was sighted around Manhattan flashing wads of money. He was promptly arrested, and eventually confessed to killing the entire crew with an axe. The case attracted the attention of P. T. Barnum, who gave it even more notoriety by buying up Hicks's clothes and putting them on display.

Ellis Island
From 1892 to 1924, Ellis Island was the primary point of entry for immigrants to the United States. The island's main building, fancifully equipped with red-brick towers topped with white domes, now houses a $150-million museum. Its cavernous halls still seem to echo with the voices of the 12 million terrified immigrants who once passed through here.

Hoffman and Swinburne Islands
These two manmade bits of land were constructed as a quarantine station in 1872. On Hoffman once stood the quarantine hospital; on Swinburne, the crematory. The station was abandoned in the 1920s when tough laws restricting immigration were passed. Now the islands are deserted and undeveloped, home to seagulls and cormorants.

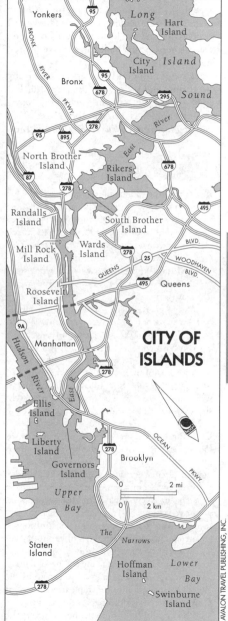

CITY OF ISLANDS

NEW YORK CITY INTRO

This is the paper to browse to find out what's happening where, whether you're interested in foreign films or jazz meets hip hop. The *Voice* is free of charge and can be found in red boxes on street corners, or in bookstores, music stores, clubs, and delis.

Free neighborhood newspapers containing good listings and reviews are also plentiful. The best of these papers, currently giving the *Voice* a run for its money, is the *New York Press.*

Among magazines, *New York, The New Yorker,* and *Time Out New York* cover the city extensively. *New York* is mostly lightweight mainstream patter, with entertaining articles, good reviews, and a solid events listing. *The New Yorker* is renowned for its acerbic, and usually deadly accurate, listings and reviews. *Time Out New York,* founded by the London-based magazine and guidebook company, features excellent round-up articles and a phenomenal listings section—the most comprehensive in the city.

More consciously hip is the monthly *Paper,*

EXPLORING THE BIG APPLE ONLINE

For up-to-the-minute info on where to go, what to do in New York, check out one of these comprehensive online guides, all of which list thousands of events and visitor attractions: **CitySearch NY,** website: www.citysearchnyc.com; *Time Out New York,* website: www.timeoutny.com; **New York Sidewalk,** website: www.newyork.sidewalk.com; and **New York Today,** website: www .nytoday.com.

Another good general source is the official site of New York City's convention and visitors' bureau, run by **NYC & Company,** website: www.nycvisit.com.

City Hall, website: www.nyc.gov, offers a website with lots of interesting links, while the *Village Voice* hosts a site filled with listings at www.villagevoice.com. The *New York Times* website is www.nytimes.com.

For the latest on the New York club scene, visit **Club Planet,** website: www.clubplanet.com, or **Papermag,** papermag.com, run by hip *Paper* magazine. For the latest on galleries, arts events, and other intellectual pursuits, visit **Echo NYC,** website: www.echonyc.com, a.k.a. "the crankiest group in cyberspace." **New York Arts Online,** website: www.nyc-arts.org, also provides extensive arts listings and links to dozens of cultural institutions.

The literate **Mr. Beller's Neighborhood,** website: www.mrbellersneighborhood.com, collects stories from New Yorkers living and dead, famous and obscure, and keys them onto a map of the city. The Algonquin Round Table lives on at **Dot City,** website: www.dorothyparker.nyc.com.

Subway and bus info can be found at the

Metropolitan Transportation Authority website: www.mta.nyc.ny.us. **New York City Subway Resources** covers everything from the history of the IRT, BMT, and IND lines, to subway maps and technical facts at its website: www.nycsubway.org.

Part traditional guide, part eccentric ramblings, **New York City Reference,** website: www.panix .com/clay/nyc, is the place to go to find unusual listings on a wide variety of topics, including advertising, apparel, art, body modification, bookstores, drink, food, health, real estate, utilities, videos, and waste management.

To find great ethnic places to eat, visit **Chowhound** at the website: www.chowhound.com. To find a restaurant by name, cuisine, or neighborhood, visit **Zagat.com** at the website: www.zagat.com.

Radio fans interested in finding a complete guide to local radio stations and daily programming will want to check out **New York Radio Guide,** website: www.nyradioguide.com. Those interested in social affairs, politics, history, and a wide variety of other topics should visit the website: www.gothamgazette.com, the online home of the Citizens Union Foundation.

Get away from the congestion of Midtown by venturing out to the **Gateway National Recreation Area** in Brooklyn, Queens, and Staten Island. A travel guide complete with directions, camping and wildlife information can be found at the website: www.nps.gov/gate. Take a virtual tour of Central Park at **Welcome to Central Park,** website: www.centralpark.org.

which does an especially good job of covering the ever-changing downtown nightlife scene. To find the latest alternative publications, visit **St. Marks Bookshop,** 31 Third Ave., near St. Marks Pl., 212/260-7853.

Budget Tips

New York is an expensive city, but there are ways to keep costs down:
• Stay in hotels a bit off the beaten track. Take advantage of hotel packages.
• Avoid routine purchases in Midtown. You'll get much better values in other parts of the city. Avoid those Midtown restaurants and stores that obviously cater to tourists—their prices are always inflated.
• Eat in ethnic restaurants. They're ubiquitous and often amazingly cheap; the East Village has an especially large supply.
• Watch the papers for free events. Top performers in many artistic disciplines often appear in public plazas or parks, especially during the summer.
• Take advantage of free regularly scheduled activities, such as the tours offered by the New York Stock Exchange, Grand Central Terminal, and the 42nd Street Partnership; and the exhibits presented by the New York Public Library and Harlem's Schomburg Center. Many museums also offer free admission one night a week.
• Walk or take public transportation. New York is a great walking city, and public transportation is excellent.
• Take advantage of discount services. The TKTS booth in Times Square, at 47th St. and Broadway, 212/768-1818, sells half-price orchestra tickets to many Broadway shows.
• Explore the small music clubs that feature unknown performers. In New York, the "unknowns" are often well-known performers in their hometowns, and many small clubs charge little or no cover.

Citypass, 707/256-0490, is a discount pass to seven famous New York City attractions: the Empire State Building, Guggenheim Museum, Whitney Museum of American Art, American Museum of Natural History, Museum of Modern Art, *Intrepid* Sea-Air-Space Museum, and the Circle Line (which offers cruises around Manhattan). Prices are adults $38, youths 13–18 $31. The passes can be purchased at any of the seven sites and are good for nine days from first use.

Tipping

A 15–20 percent tip is customary for waiters and taxi drivers. Hotel bellhops expect $1 a bag, porters $1 for hailing a cab, and room attendants $1 per person per night.

Safety

As in most big cities, crime in New York can be a serious problem. But according to the FBI, New York is one of America's safest large cities. It doesn't even make the top-25 list of cities with the highest homicide rates, and has reported a drop crime every year between 1994 and 2001. Statistically, your chances of being mugged are less than 30,000 to 1. To avoid being that one:
• Act as if you know where you're going, especially when passing through empty neighborhoods. New Yorkers—forever blasé—keep up a brisk, disinterested pace at all times. If you spend too long ogling the sites or looking nervously about, you'll be targeted as an easy mark.
• Don't carry large quantities of cash or large bills, but do carry something; $20 is recommended.
• Ignore hustlers and con artists, especially the three-card monte players and anyone who approaches you with an elaborate sob story.
• Avoid the parks at night, and be extra careful around transportation centers such as the Port Authority and Penn Station.
• Don't carry valuables in lightweight backpacks that can easily be slashed open. Carry handbags close to your body.
• When in rougher neighborhoods, stick to blocks where other people are in sight or at least where cars are passing by. At night, on empty streets, walk near the curb, away from dark overhangs.
• If you're mugged, hand over your valuables immediately—they're not worth dying for.

Travel Seasons

New York has plenty to offer any time of year, but the best times to visit are the spring, early summer, and fall, when temperatures are moderate

COCKROACHES

Much to its residents' dismay, New York is home to four kinds of cockroaches—the brown German, the one- to two-inch-long American, the striped brown-banded, and the stocky Oriental. All are much despised, but it is the German who elicits the foulest expletives, inhabiting dark crevices in kitchens and bathrooms from the dingiest East Village dive to the most luxurious Upper East Side condo.

New Yorkers have sense enough to know that it's impossible to eradicate *Blatella germanica.* The bugs have been around for about 350 million years, after all, and can survive on next to nothing, including salts from tennis shoes, grease spots on a wall from cooking, and starch on postage stamps. In one laboratory experiment, a cockroach colony lived two and a half years without any protein at all. Then, too, a female cockroach needs but one sex act a year to store enough sperm to produce 35,000 more cockroaches.

So instead of eradication, New Yorkers have to content themselves with pest control. In the past, this has meant chemical sprays and fumigations. In today's more environmentally aware times, the most popular methods are bait traps, boric acid, and—the Tokay gecko. This small blue-skinned lizard with orange spots measures between six inches and two feet long, and loves to eat cockroaches. A nocturnal creature, it's rarely seen during the day, but has an odd, distinctive bark that's sometimes heard at night.

BOB RACE

and conducive to exploring the city on foot. Autumns are often especially wonderful, with deep cobalt blue skies and the excitement of a new season in the air. Winters in New York can be bitterly cold (in the 20s, with bone-chilling winds), summers stiflingly hot (in the 90s, with high humidity), and, though both have their charms—there's nothing like Manhattan after a snowfall or during an August thunderstorm—you do take your chances. On the other hand, the best times for inexpensive hotel packages are weekends in July and August and January and February.

GETTING THERE
By Air
New York is serviced by three airports. **John F. Kennedy International Airport** is about 15 miles from Manhattan in Queens. It's the largest of the three and handles primarily international flights. **La Guardia Airport,** also in Queens, is about eight miles from Manhattan and handles primarily domestic flights. **Newark Airport,** across the Hudson River in New Jersey, handles domestic and some international flights. Kennedy is generally the most congested of the three airports, Newark the least.

JFK International Airport is currently in the midst of an extensive redevelopment programs, which can cause delays. By the year 2006, $9 billion will be spent on the airport; improvements will include new roadways, terminals, and parking lots, and a rail line that will link Manhattan with JFK.

Public transportation from the airports into Manhattan and the other boroughs is excellent; call 800/AIR-RIDE for general information.

A **taxi ride** into Manhattan from La Guardia takes 20–30 minutes and costs about $25, including tolls and tip. The ride from Kennedy to Manhattan takes 30–45 minutes and costs a flat fare of $35, plus tolls and tip (when going the other way, from Manhattan to Kennedy, however, the trip is metered and usually costs about $10 more; the $35 Kennedy-to-Manhattan rate may also go up in late 2002). The 45-minute ride from Newark usually runs about $50. Cabs leave from well-marked stands staffed by dispatchers, just outside the flight arrival areas at all airports. Avoid the gypsy cabs near the baggage-claim areas.

New York Airport Service, 212/875-8200, www.nyairportservice.com, offers frequent bus service to and from La Guardia ($10 one-way; $17 round-trip) and Kennedy ($13 one-way;

$23 round-trip). Stops are made near Grand Central Terminal (Park Ave. between 41st and 42nd Sts.), inside the Port Authority Bus Terminal (42nd St. and Eighth Ave.), near Pennsylvania Station (33rd St. and Seventh Ave.), and outside several hotels (call for details).

Olympia Trails, 212/964-6233 or 877/894-9155, www.olympiabus.com, offers frequent bus service between Newark Airport and Manhattan. Buses leave every 15–20 minutes, and make three stops in Manhattan: near Grand Central Station (41st St. and Park Ave.), outside Pennsylvania Station (34th St. and Eighth Ave.), and inside the Port Authority (42nd St. and Eighth Ave.). Tickets cost $11 one-way, $21 round-trip.

SuperShuttle, 212/258-3826 or, outside Manhattan, 800/BLUE VAN (258-3826), www.supershuttle.com, offers pick-up van service from homes and hotels to any of the three area airports. Fares range from $14.50 to $19.50.

By Train

Manhattan has two main railroad stations: **Pennsylvania Station** at 33rd St. and Seventh Ave.; and **Grand Central Station** at 42nd St. and Park Avenue. All **Amtrak** trains arrive and depart from Pennsylvania Station. For information, call 800/872-7245 or visit www.amtrak.com. **New Jersey Transit,** 973/762-5100 or 800/772-2222, www.njtransit.com, and **Long Island Rail Road,** 718/217-5477, www.lirr.org, also offer passenger-train service out of Pennsylvania Station. **Metro-North,** 212/532-4900 or 800/638-7646, www.mnr.org, runs commuter trains to suburban New York and Connecticut from Grand Central. Both stations are well serviced by buses, subways, and taxis.

By Bus

The **Port Authority,** Eighth Ave. between 40th and 42nd Sts., is the world's largest bus terminal, serving both commuter and long-distance travelers. For bus information, call 212/564-8484.

Major bus lines departing from the terminal include **Greyhound,** 800/231-2222, www.greyhound.com, **Peter Pan,** 800/343-9999, www.peterpan.com, and **New Jersey Transit,** 973/762-5100 or 800/772-2222, www.njtransit.com.

By Car

If you must drive into Manhattan, be prepared to pay a steep price for parking at a garage (often $7–12 per hour) or to spend 20 minutes or so looking for street parking. In contrast, street parking in most sections of the boroughs is generally available. When parking on the street, never leave *anything* on the seats; cars are broken into frequently.

GETTING AROUND

Most of Manhattan is laid out in a grid pattern, which makes it easy to find your way around. Avenues run north-south, streets east-west, and most are one way. Fifth Avenue, which more or less marks the center of the city, separates the East and West Sides. Street addresses are labeled accordingly (1 E. 50th Street, 1 W. 50th Street), with the numbers increasing as you head away from Fifth. Broadway, following an old Algonquin trail, cuts through the city on a diagonal.

Streets with ordinals are spelled with numerals (1st Street, 2nd Street, etc.) and Avenues with ordinals are spelled with letters (First Avenue, Second Avenue, etc.) throughout this book, including on maps.

Those neighborhoods not laid out in a numbered grid pattern—essentially everything south of 14th Street—are considerably more difficult to navigate, and it helps to have a good map. The same applies in the other boroughs, where it's also a good idea to get exact directions to your destination before you set out.

If you don't know how to get where you're going, call the New York City Transit Authority at 718/330-1234, between 6 A.M. and 9 P.M., and they'll tell you the best route via subway or bus.

By Subway

Despite their reputation and the constant complaints of commuting New Yorkers, the subways are the easiest and quickest way to get around town. Service is frequent—at least in Manhattan—and the trains run all night.

To ride the subways, you need either tokens—which can be purchased for $1.50 each at booths in the subway stations—or electronic fare cards,

NEW YORK CITY INTRO

known as MetroCards, also for sale at most stations. There has been talk of completely replacing tokens with fare cards but, as of this writing, no final decision has been made. The MetroCards come in two types: pay-per-use cards and unlimited-ride cards. The unlimited-ride cards are an excellent bargain: the one-day pass costs $4; the 7-day pass, $17; and the 30-day pass, $63.

Subway maps are usually posted in each station, and free copies are sometimes available at the token booths. You can also pick up a copy at New York City's Official Visitor Information Center, 810 Seventh Ave. at 53rd St., 212/484-1222.

Three subway lines service the city: The IRT runs north-south on either side of Manhattan; the IND runs along Sixth and Eighth Avenues; and the BMT runs from lower Manhattan to Brooklyn and Queens. The subway lines used most frequently by visitors are the IRT No. 6 train, which makes local stops along the East Side of Manhattan, and the IRT No. 1/9 train, which makes local stops along the West Side. There's also a Grand Central—Times Square Shuttle connecting the east and west sides of the IRT at 42nd Street.

(Note: All of the downtown subway lines, including the IRT No. 1/9 line, which was out of service following the September 11 attacks, are operational. Two new subway lines, the V and the W, have also been recently added—and changes made in the B, D, and Q lines—due to long-term work on the Manhattan Bridge.)

New Yorkers will delight in telling you stories about how dangerous their city's subway system is, but in reality, about 3.5 million passengers travel the 700 miles of track every day without mishap. Still, crime can be a problem and you should take certain precautions. Keep a close eye on your belongings, especially during rush hours when the crush of the crowd makes pickpocketing easy. Don't wear expensive jewelry. Avoid empty or near-empty cars, even during the day when the subways are theoretically the safest. During off hours, wait for your train in the well-lit "Off-Hour" waiting areas near the token booths. When your train comes, sit in the center car, which has a conductor and is usually the most crowded car on the train. Finally, although many New Yorkers

ride the subways at all hours, it's not especially advisable to take them after midnight.

By Bus

Buses run 24 hours a day uptown along Tenth, Eighth, Sixth, Madison, Third, and First Avenues, and downtown along Ninth, Seventh, Fifth, and Second Avenues. East-west crosstown service can be found along 14th, 23rd, 34th, 42nd, 57th, 65th/66th, 79th, 86th, and 96th Streets. Bus stops are usually located every two blocks, and signs or shelters mark the spots.

The fare is $1.50, payable with either exact change, a subway token, or the electronic MetroCard. Free transfers are available between uptown-downtown buses and crosstown buses, enabling you to make any one-way trip in Manhattan on a single fare. Good bus service is also available in the outer boroughs.

By Taxi and Car Service

Another notorious mode of New York City transportation that's nonetheless quite good is the taxi cab. The New York City Taxi and Limousine Commission licenses 11,787 cabs annually, and they're all painted yellow with lighted signs on their roofs. When the sign is lit, the cab is available and may be hailed anywhere. Fares begin at $2 when the meter is started, then jump 30 cents for each additional one-fifth mile and 20 cents for each minute of waiting time. A 50-cent surcharge per ride is added nightly 8 P.M.–6 A.M., and a 15–20 percent tip is the norm.

The nationalities of New York City's cab drivers reflect the fortunes of the world. Nowadays, almost half are from India, Pakistan, or Bangladesh; a few years ago, most were from Eastern Europe or Africa. Since many cab drivers haven't been in the country long, and are behind the wheel after only 40 hours of training, it's best to have patience, an exact address, and a general sense of where you're going before flagging one down. If you have any complaints regarding a driver's service, call the **Taxi and Limousine Commission** at 212/692-8294. The driver's photo and license number are displayed on the dashboard.

In the boroughs, where licensed cabs are few and far between, your best bet is to call one of the many private car services. Ask for recommendations at the place you're visiting or check the Yellow Pages. The services charge a flat rate that's usually reasonable, and pick you up wherever you wish.

By Foot

Walking is by far the best way to see Manhattan and many parts of the boroughs. In Manhattan, figure on needing about a minute for each north-south block, two minutes for each east-west one.

TOURS

No matter where your interests lie—in architecture, ethnic foods, or social history—chances are good you'll find a tour tailor-made for you. Walking tours abound all over the city, especially in the spring and fall, with each one more imaginative than the next ("Famous Murder Sites," "Edith Wharton's New York," "Irish New York"). *Time Out New York* has the best listings; other resources include the weekend editions of the daily papers, *New York,* and *The New Yorker.*

City Tours

One of the best ways to get an overview of the city is to take a **Circle Line** cruise, 212/563-3200, www.circleline.com. The boats leave daily from Pier 83, West 42nd Street, and the Hudson River, April–December. Standard daytime cruises last three hours; "express" and evening cruises last two. The fare is adults $20–24, seniors $17–20, children under 12 $10–12.

On summer nights, **Seaport Music Cruises,** 212/630-8888, offer two-hour excursions around Manhattan featuring live blues, jazz, gospel, and pop bands. Tickets usually cost $15–25. **World Yacht,** 212/630-8100, departing from W. 41st St. at the Hudson, offers three-hour luxury dinner cruises with live entertainment and dancing. Prices start at $73 per person.

Gray Line Tours, 900 8th Ave., near 53rd St., 212/397-2600, www.graylinenewyork.com, offers over 20 different bus tours lasting anywhere from two hours to a full day. Tours are offered year-round, and foreign language tours are available. Prices are $26–75; reduced rates for kids.

LOCATING CROSS STREETS

To find the nearest cross street of an avenue address, drop the last digit of the address number and divide by two. Then, add or subtract the number shown below. (For example, to find the cross street of 666 Fifth Avenue, drop the last 6, divide 66 by 2 which is 33, and add 18 to get 51.)

Ave. A, B, C, D: add 3
First Ave.: add 3
Second Ave.: add 3
Third Ave.: add 10
Fourth Ave.: add 8
Fifth Ave.—
    up to #200: add 13
    up to #400: add 16
    up to #600: add 18
    up to #775: add 20
    #775 to #1286: do not divide by 2, subtract 18
    up to #1500: add 45
    up to #2000: add 24
Sixth Ave.: subtract 12
Seventh Ave.—
    below 110th St.: add 12
    above 110th St.: add 20
Eighth Ave.: add 10
Ninth Ave.: add 13
Tenth Ave.: add 14
Amsterdam Ave.: add 60
Audubon Ave.: add 165
Broadway above 23rd St.: subtract 30
Central Park West: divide full address by 10, add 60
Columbus Ave.: add 60
Convent Ave.: add 127
Lenox Ave.: add 110
Lexington Ave.: add 22
Madison Ave.: add 26
Park Ave.: add 35
Riverside Dr.: divide full address by 10, add 72
St. Nicholas Ave.: add 110
West End Ave.: add 60
York Ave.: add 4

For a spectacular bird's-eye view of the city, try **Liberty Helicopter Tours,** 212/967-4550, or 212/465-8905 for recorded info. Flights leave from the VIP heliport at Twelfth Avenue and West 30th Street. Prices start at $50. Reservations required.

Walking Tours

The **Municipal Art Society,** 457 Madison Ave., near 51st St., 212/935-3960, www.mas.org, runs an extensive series of walking tours almost daily year-round. Most focus on architecture and history; cost is $12–15. The society also offers occasional bus tours.

Big Onion Walking Tours, 212/439-1090, www.bigonion.com, founded by two Columbia University graduate students, offers some of the city's most fun and well-researched tours. Many concentrate on New York's immigrant history and on neighborhoods below 14th Street. Cost is $12.

The 92nd Street Y, 1395 Lexington Ave., at 92nd St., 212/415-5500 or 212/415-5628, www.92ndsty.org, a leading cultural institution, offers many excellent walking and bus tours. They're very popular and must be signed up for weeks in advance. Tours start at $18.

Mainly Manhattan, 212/755-6199, offers three basic tours: "42nd Street Off-Off-Broadway," which explores East 42nd Street from Bryant Park to the United Nations; "New York's West Bank," which is a literary tour of Greenwich Village; and "West Side Story," which explores the Upper West Side from Lincoln Center to the Dakota. Cost is $10.

Uptown, **Harlem Spirituals,** 212/391-0900, www.harlemspirituals.com, specializes in visits to gospel services and soul-food restaurants, as well as historic sites; prices start at $30. **Harlem Heritage Tours,** 212/280-7888, www.harlemheritage.com, offers about 30 different tours, ranging from "jazz nights in Harlem" to gospel walking tours; prices start at $10.

Downtown, the **Lower East Side Tenement Museum,** 90 Orchard Street, between Delancey and Broome, 212/431-0233, www.tenement.org, sponsors walking tours of old immigrant neighborhoods; cost is $9–12. For a hip tour of the East Village and environs, check out **Rock Junket Tours,** 212/696-6578. "Rocker guides" lead participants past legendary rock, punk, and glam sites from the '60s to the present; cost is $20.

Radical Walking Tours, 718/492-0069, specializes in revolutionary and labor history; the cost is $10. **Foods of New York Walking and Tasting Tours,** 212/334-5070, www.foodsofny.com, explores some of the most famous restaurants and food shops in Greenwich Village. Cost is $35, tastings included.

In Crown Heights, Brooklyn, the **Chassidic Discovery Welcome Center,** 305 Kingston Ave., at Eastern Pkwy., 718/953-5244, www.jewishtours.com, offers walking tours of a traditional Hassidic community. Led by members of that community, the tour includes a kosher deli lunch and visits to a synagogue and private mansions. Cost is adults $36, children under 12 $18.

Urban historian **Joyce Gold,** 212/242-5762, www.nyctours.com, who teaches city history at New York University, has been offering walking tours for over 20 years. Her tours usually concentrate on history, architecture, and cultural movements. Cost is $12.

Well worth watching out for are the free nature walks offered in all five boroughs by the **Urban Park Rangers,** 212/360-2774 or 866/NYC-HAWK (information line), www.nyc.gov/parks.

The **Big Apple Greeter** program, 1 Center St. at Chambers St., 212/669-8159, www.bigapplegreeter.org, matches visitors up with enthusiastic volunteers eager to introduce the city to out-of-towners. The service is completely free and especially helpful to the disabled and tourists interested in visiting off-the-beaten-track spots.

Site Tours

Tours are also available at many specific Manhattan visitor attractions, including the Federal Reserve Bank and New York Stock Exchange (Lower Manhattan); Grand Central Station, the United Nations, NBC Studios, and Radio City Music Hall (Midtown); and Gracie Mansion (the Upper East Side). For more information, see the listings for those sites in the corresponding neighborhood sections below.

Entertainment

Excellent entertainment listings can be found in *The New Yorker, New York, New York Free Press,* the *Village Voice,* the Friday and Sunday editions of the *New York Times,* and—especially—*Time Out New York,* which includes hundreds upon hundreds of listings. The *Voice, Time Out,* and *Free Press* do a very good job of covering downtown, while *The New Yorker* is the best source for capsule theater reviews. The most complete daily movie schedules are published by the *Daily News, New York Post, Village Voice,* and *New York Free Press.* For information on the volatile club scene—with its roving DJs, hip hop, soul, and techno parties—pick up *Time Out,* the *Free Press,* or the monthly *Paper.*

Unless stated otherwise, all the venues listed below are in Manhattan.

POPULAR MUSIC VENUES

New York's largest venue is the 19,000-seat **Madison Square Garden,** Seventh Ave. between 31st

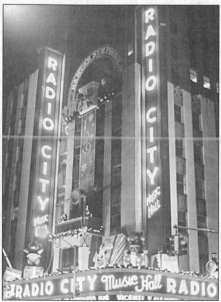

© CHRISTIANE BIRD

Radio City Music Hall

and 33rd Sts., 212/465-MSG1 (212/465-6741), www.thegarden.com. Also home to the city's basketball and hockey teams, it's hardly an atmospheric spot, and usually not worth the very high admission price unless there's someone you've just got to see. The 5,600-seat **Paramount,** a separate venue inside the Garden, is considerably more stylish and comfortable.

The grand, art deco **Radio City Music Hall,** 1260 Sixth Ave., at 50th St., 212/247-4777, www.radiocity.com, sometimes presents popular music acts, as does the legendary **Carnegie Hall,** 154 W. 57th St., at Seventh Ave., 212/247-7800, www.carnegiehall.org. Recently renovated, the atmospheric **Apollo,** 253 W. 125th St., near Adam Clayton Powell Jr. Blvd., 212/749-5838, presents R&B, soul, and rap, while on Wednesday, the famed amateur-night tradition continues. Don't hesitate to venture up here at night—125th Street is always bustling.

The historic **Beacon Theater,** 2124 Broadway, at 74th St., 212/496-7070, is a convivial spot with an eclectic booking policy. Ditto **The Town Hall,** 123 W. 43rd St., between Sixth and Seventh Aves., 212/840-2824, which presents an interesting variety of jazz, world, and traditional music. The **Hammerstein Ballroom,** 311 W. 34th St., between Eighth and Ninth Aves., 212/564-4882, built inside the Unification Church–owned Manhattan Center, features top rock and pop acts.

ROCK, POP, BLUES, AND SOUL

East Village

The granddaddy of New York rock clubs is the ratty, hole-in-the-wall **CBGB & OMFUG,** 315 Bowery, at Bleecker, 212/982-4052, www.cbgb .com, still going strong after more than 20 years. During the 1970s, the battle-scarred CBGB's—short for "Country, Bluegrass, Blues, and Other Music for Uplifting Gormandizers"—was America's cradle of punk rock, home to such later legends as the Talking Heads, Television, and Patti Smith. Nowadays, an average of six fledgling bands are booked nightly; cover, $5–12. Next door is

NEW YORK RADIO STATIONS

FM

WBAI/99.5. Independent station, diverse programming.

WBGO/88.3. Jazz, broadcast from Newark.

WBLS/107.5. Rap, house, soul, hip hop.

WCBS/101. Rock-and-roll oldies and top 40.

WFMU/91.1. Eclectic programming, listener-supported station.

WKCR/89.9. Columbia University's station. First-rate jazz.

WNEW/102.7. Talk.

WNYC/93.9. News and culture.

WPLJ/95.5. Top 40.

WQXR/96.3. Commercial classical music station.

WRKS/98.7. Urban contemporary.

WXRK/92.3. Alternative rock; home to the infamous Howard Stern.

AM

WINS/1010. News around the clock.

WLIB/1190. Caribbean music and black talk station.

WNYC/820. Excellent talk station; NPR's New York outlet.

WOR/710. Interviews and talk programs.

CB's 313 Gallery, 212/677-0455, which concentrates primarily on singer-songwriters.

Brownies, 169 Ave. A, at 10th St., 212/420-8392, is a comfortable, bare-bricked place featuring top local bands, mostly rock, along with the occasional "name"; cover, $3–10. **Lakeside Lounge,** 162 Ave. B, between 10th and 11th Sts., 212/529-8463, often hosts young rock bands and boasts a great blues jukebox.

At the dark, black, down-and-dirty **Continental,** 25 Third Ave., at St. Mark's Pl., 212/529-6924, you'll hear local bands playing alternative, roots rock, punk, or metal; cover, $3–10. The **Acme Underground,** 9 Great Jones St., at Lafayette, 212/677-6963, offers a good PA system and some of the hottest young bands in town; cover $5–10. The laid-back **C-Note,** 157 Ave. C, at 10th St., 212/677-8142, features

mostly singer-songwriters, along with the occasional jazz musician; free.

Just north of the East Village is **Irving Plaza,** 17 Irving Pl., at 15th St., 212/777-6800, an unusual venue with a wide balcony, large dance floor, and elaborate ornamentation left over from its days as a Polish dance hall. Many bigger-name rock and new-music groups play here, along with some reggae, blues, rap, and world bands; cover, $10–30. On the first Sunday of the month, the Swing Dance Society, 212/696-9737, gathers here to dance to the hits of yesteryear; nonmembers welcome.

Lower East Side

Just south of the East Village, on the south side of Houston Street, is the long, dark **Mercury Lounge,** 217 E. Houston, near Essex, 212/260-4700, featuring an antique wooden bar, exposed brick walls, heavy red drapes, and an excellent sound system. Some hip rock and jazz acts play here; cover, $6–15. Owned by the same people who own Mercury Lounge, **Bowery Ballroom,** Delancey St., between the Bowery and Chrystie St., 212/533-2111, is one of the city's few midsize venues. Complete with a balcony, it presents a wide variety of rock, jazz, etc.; cover $5–20.

An excellent place to catch top up-and-coming or favorite local bands is **Arlene Grocery,** 95 Stanton St., between Ludlow and Orchard Sts., 212/358-1633, housed in a former bodega; cover none–$10. Also a local favorite is **Luna Lounge,** 171 Ludlow St., between Houston and Stanton Sts., 212/260-2323, where you'll find a packed bar up front and a snug live music room in back; no cover.

The **Living Room,** 84 Stanton St., at Allen St., 212/533-7235, is a friendly, laid-back lounge featuring mostly singer-songwriter acts, along with the occasional jazz singer; one-drink minimum.

TriBeCa

A downtown hot spot lined with red velvet, **Shine,** 285 W. Broadway, at Canal St., 212/941-0900, offers a mix of local bands, DJs, and the occasional well-known act such as Stevie Nicks; cover $10–20.

Long, high-ceilinged **Tribeca Blues,** 16 Warren St., between Broadway and Church, 212/766-1070, features local blues acts, along with the occasional big name; cover $5–20.

Greenwich Village

One of the city's most venerable music institutions is the big, laid-back **Bottom Line,** 15 W. 4th St., at Mercer, 212/228-6300. Packed with tables, the club has been around since 1974 when Dr. John opened the place, with Stevie Wonder sitting in. Since then, the legendary venue has presented an eclectic array of rock and jazz—everyone from Bruce Springsteen to the Sun Ra Arkestra; cover, $15–25.

Also in the neighborhood are the decades-old **Bitter End,** 147 Bleecker St., at Thompson, 212/673-7030, usually presenting singer-songwriters, and the considerably newer **Lion's Den,** 214 Sullivan St., between Bleecker and W. 3rd St., 212/477-2782, known for rock, reggae and funk; cover at both, $3–10. The low-ceilinged, dark, and intimate **Cafe Wha?,** 115 MacDougal St., near W. 3rd St., 212/254-3706, usually presents rock, R&B, and soul, but Monday nights are Brazilian Nights, with the nine-piece Brazilian Beat band attracting crowds of enthused Brazilian ex-pats.

One of the newer and more interesting venues in town is the **Village Underground,** 130 W. 3rd St., between Sixth Ave. and MacDougal St., 212/777-7745, a laid-back basement space with a long bar to the back, a sunken table area to the front. Roots, jazz, blues, and alternative acts can be heard here, some well-known, some not; cover $8–20.

Also relatively new is **Joe's Pub,** 425 Lafayette St., between Astor Pl. and W. 4th St., 212/539-8770, a snug cabaret housed inside the Public Theater. Named in honor of the theater's founder, Joseph Papp, the upscale spot offers an eclectic line-up ranging from country to world and jazz; cover $12–35.

Terra Blues, 149 Bleecker St., near Thompson, 212/777-7776, is a small upstairs club with picture windows overlooking the street. Most of the bands are local favorites, but better-known acts appear form time to time; cover, $5–10.

Midtown

Posh, state-of-the-art, and all decked out in blue, **B.B. King Blues Club & Grill,** 237 W. 42nd St., between Seventh and Eighth Aves., 212/997-4144, www.bbkingblues.com, sits smack in the heart of heavy-duty tourist territory. Nonetheless, it's an enjoyable venue, with a superb sound system, intimate stage, and excellent menu. Despite its namesake, blues acts are the exception here; most nights feature rock or pop acts; cover $15–40.

Downtime, 251 W. 30th St., near Eighth Ave., 212/695-2747, is a two-tiered music-industry hangout featuring mostly rock and pop during the week, dance parties on the weekend; cover, $5–10. The rustic, peanut-shell-strewn **Rodeo Bar,** attached to the Albuquerque Eats restaurant, 375 Third Ave., at 27th St., 212/683-6500, presents local rock, blues, and country; no cover.

Recently renovated, **Roseland,** 239 W. 52nd St., 212/777-1224, is a grand old '30s-era dance hall now turned dark, pulsating nightclub, complete with two stages and a young crowd; cover, $15–25.

Brooklyn

In Williamsburg, tiny **Pete's Candy Store,** 709 Lorimer St., between First and Richardson Sts., 718/302-3770, tucked into a back room behind a bar, features primarily singer-songwriters. **Ear Wax,** 204 Bedford Ave., between N. 5th and N. 6th Sts., 718/486-3771, is a local hot spot showcasing young rock bands, while **Teddy's Bar and Grill,** 96 Berry St., near N. 8th St., 718/384-9787, is a long-time local favorite bar with live music on weekends.

Also in Williamsburg, the **Galapagos Art Space,** 70 N. 6th St., between Kent and Wythe Ave., 718/782-5188, presents a diverse mix of live music ranging from hip-hop to the Galapagos "house string quartet;" cover $6–12. Cozy **Luxx,** 256 Grand St., between Driggs Ave. and Roebling St., 718/599-1000, is a long thin lounge known for its up-and-coming rock bands, and late-night DJ parties; cover $5–10.

In Fort Greene, above the lobby of the Brooklyn Academy of Music, is the high-ceilinged

BAMcafe, 30 Lafayette Ave., between Flatbush Ave. and Fulton St., 718/636-4100, www.bam .org, offering weekly concerts ranging from cabaret to gospel; cover $10–20.

New Jersey

Many New Yorkers frequent **Maxwell's,** 1039 Washington St. in Hoboken, New Jersey, 201/798-0406. Just a short subway ride from Manhattan, the casual and unpretentious club features top up-and-coming bands, as well as occasional big names; cover $6–15. To reach Hoboken, catch the PATH train, which runs underneath Sixth Avenue, with station stops between Christopher and 34th Streets.

JAZZ AND EXPERIMENTAL

New York is an international center for jazz, and top-caliber musicians can be heard in dozens of top-caliber clubs every night of the week. In general, such first-rate entertainment doesn't come cheap; many of the best clubs charge $15–25 cover, plus a two-drink minimum. Cheaper venues do exist, however, typically booking lesser known but still accomplished acts. You'll find many of New York's jazz clubs in Greenwich Village.

Below Canal Street

Now a New York institution, the quirky, three-story **Knitting Factory,** 74 Leonard St., between Church St. and Broadway, 212/219-3055, www.knittingfactory.com, features four snug performance rooms, all equipped with state-of-the-art sound systems. Best known for its avant-garde jazz, the club also books everything from alternative rock to poetry readings; cover $5–20.

Somewhat similar in booking style to the Knitting Factory is the cavernous, bare-boned **Tonic,** 107 Norfolk St., between Delancey and Rivington Sts., 212/358-7501, www.tonicnyc.com, presenting everything from outsider jazz to klezmer music. Each month, a different artist creates his or her own series, bringing in various groups to perform before a discerning audience of hipsters; cover $5–12.

Avant-garde jazz, computer music, and experimental music of many types are presented

by **Roulette,** 228 W. Broadway, at White St., 212/219-8242, www.roulette.org. The place is not open every night—just when there's a gig—so call in advance; cover $8–10.

Greenwich Village

The oldest and arguably best jazz club in the city is the **Village Vanguard,** 178 Seventh Ave. S, at 11th St., 212/255-4037, www.villagevan-guard.com, a dark, wedge-shaped basement room filled with rickety tables and fading photographs. Established in 1934, the Vanguard has booked all the greats, from Miles Davis and Dinah Washington to Wynton Marsalis and Terence Blanchard; cover, $15–20, plus a two-drink minimum. On Monday nights, the 17-piece Vanguard Jazz Orchestra jams.

Just down the avenue from the Village Vanguard is **Smalls,** 183 W. 10th St., near Seventh Ave., 212/929-7565, www.smallsjazz.com, a young and scrappy club featuring up-and-coming players who jam until dawn. No liquor is served, but there's free food and drink after 2 A.M.; cover, $10.

One avenue over is the pricey **Blue Note,** 131 W. 3rd St., near Sixth Ave., 212/475-8592, www.bluenote.net, the city's premier jazz supper club. A large rectangular place all done up in glitzy blues, the club can seem annoyingly commercial. Come during a late weeknight set when the crowds are small and the intimacy level is high. After midnight, lesser-known players jam for a $5 cover. Otherwise, the cover runs a steep $25–60, plus a $5 minimum.

Also in Greenwich Village is **55 Bar,** 55 Christopher St., near Seventh Ave., 212/929-9883, a convivial hole-in-the-wall with live jazz as well as a great jazz jukebox; cover, $5, with a one-drink minimum. The dark, sardine-can **Arthur's Tavern,** 57 Grove St., near Seventh Ave., 212/675-6879, is another traditional jazz venue; no cover.

On the border between Greenwich Village and East Village lies **Fez Under Time Cafe,** 380 Lafayette St., at Great Jones, 212/533-2680, www.feznyc.com, a dark, low-ceilinged underground joint where one of the city's most unusual jazz events—the gathering of the Mingus Big Band—takes place once a week; cover, $20.

The dark **Zinc Bar,** 90 Houston St., between La Guardia Pl. and Thompson St., 212/477-8337, is a tiny cellar joint showcasing jazz and Latin acts. Superb jazz guitarist Ron Affif is a regular here; cover $5–10.

One of the more unusual venues in town is the second-story **Jazz Gallery,** 290 Hudson St., near Spring St., 212/242-1063. Long and thin, this intimate space features an imaginative array of concert series with titles such as "Heartsong" (jazz vocalists), "Jazz Cubano," and "Strings that Swing" (jazz guitar duos); cover $10–15.

One restaurant with a serious commitment to live jazz is the **Knickerbocker Cafe,** 33 University Pl., at 9th St., 212/228-8490, the steak house where Harry Connick Jr., got his start; no cover.

See also the **Village Underground** and **Bottom Line,** under "Rock, Pop, Blues, and Soul," above.

Midtown

The **Jazz Standard,** 116 E. 27th St., between Park and Lexington Aves., 212/576-2232, is a sleek and upscale basement spot with a friendly wait staff, tasty menu, and excellent sight lines and acoustics. Top names such as David Newman and Greg Osby play here; cover $15–25.

Spiffy **Birdland,** 315 W. 44th St., between Eighth and Ninth Aves., 212/581-3080, www.birdlandjazz.com, offers excellent sight lines, a good dinner menu, and a regular lineup of some of the best big bands in the city, along with top-name individual acts; cover $10–25, with a $10 minimum.

Woody Allen blows clarinet with the **Eddy Davis New Orleans Jazz Band** every Monday at the posh Cafe Carlyle in the Carlyle Hotel, Madison Ave. at 76th St., 212/744-1600. Tickets cost $50. For traditional jazz and swing dancing, stop by the boisterous **Swing 46,** 349 W. 46th St., between Eighth and Ninth Aves., 212/262-9554, www.swing46.com.

Recently relocated to just north of Times Square, **Iridium,** 1650 Broadway, at 51st St., 212/582-2121, is a posh basement spot that features many of the top names in jazz. Guitar legend Les Paul performs on Monday nights; cover $15–30.

Upper West Side

Small, cozy, and easy-going elegant, **Smoke,** 2751 Broadway, between 105th and 106th Sts., 212/864-6662, www.smokejazz.com, is largely a haven for bebop, although avant-garde types play here too; cover $10–12.

Harlem

After years of inactivity, jazz is hot in Harlem again. One not-to-be-missed spot is **St. Nick's Pub,** 773 St. Nicholas Ave., at 149th St., 212/283-9728, a tiny neighborhood joint best known for its smoking Monday-night jam sessions; cover $5, with a two-drink minimum.

More elegant, but not as swinging or as much fun is the vintage art deco **Lenox Lounge,** 288 Lenox Ave., between 124th and 125th Sts., 212/427-0253, where first-class musicians perform on the weekends; cover $8.

For years the only regularly operating jazz club uptown, **Showman's,** 375 W. 125th St., at Eighth Ave., 212/864-8941, is still a convivial club presenting both top acts and local favorites; no cover, two-drink minimum. For more suggestions, see Watering Holes and Lounges in the Harlem and Upper Manhattan chapter.

Brooklyn

The friendly, laid-back **Up Over Jazz Cafe,** 351 Flatbush Ave., at Seventh Ave., Park Slope, 718/398-5413, www.upoverjazz.com, brings top-name jazz to Brooklyn; cover $10–18.

OTHER LIVE MUSIC

SoHo

S.O.B. (short for Sounds of Brazil), 204 Varick St., at Houston, 212/243-4940, www.sobs.com, is a stylish, multiethnic place emphasizing "tropical music," including African, Caribbean, reggae, Latin, and some jazz; cover $8–20. Most of the well-known bands are dance-oriented, and the small dance floor stays packed with beautiful bodies. Tasty Caribbean food is served.

East Village

The **Sidewalk,** 94 Ave. A, at 6th St., 212/473-7373, bills itself as an "anti-folk" club but

UNDERGROUND MUSICIANS

They say that Tony Bennett started his career down under, in the long bleak corridors of the New York subways. In this unlikely concert hall, you might hear the sad, sensuous notes of a Lester Young solo, or the mad, rushing arpeggios of a Bartók concerto. Who knows what future musical genius is now starting out down here?

But playing the New York subways is not as spontaneous as it seems. Since 1985, musicians have had to audition for the choicest spots, and only about 100 of the 300-plus acts that try out each year are granted a license. These musicians are then booked into two-week slots, just as if they were working regular jobs. Many also have other, more traditional gigs, and even a CD or two to their name. Making a living as a musician is tough, even after you've been "discovered."

Not to be completely outdone, independent performers—i.e., those without a license—do still play some of the subway's more out-of-the-way spots. They won that right several years ago when they took the Metropolitan Transportation Authority to court. But they're not allowed to use the small amplifiers popular among their licensed colleagues, and they face constant police harassment.

212/686-1210, is a boisterous pub that hosts Irish bands several nights a week.

O'Lunney's, 12 W. 44th St., between Fifth and Sixth Aves., 212/840-6688, is a casual restaurant with live country-and-western once a week; cover, $3. In an old recording studio is swank **Le Bar Bat,** 311 W. 57th St., between Eighth and Ninth Aves., 212/307-7228, offering a mix of funk, soul, and pop; cover $10–20.

CLASSICAL

Classical music thrives in New York City, especially at the **Lincoln Center for the Performing Arts,** Broadway, between 62nd and 66th Sts., 212/546-2656, www.lincolncenter.org. The center presents an astonishing 3,000 performances a year. On its north side is the 2,700-seat **Avery Fisher Hall,** 212/875-5030, home to the New York Philharmonic (Sept.–May), the Great Performers Series (Oct.–May), the Mostly Mozart Festival (July–Aug.), and the Jazz-at-Lincoln Center Series, run by Wynton Marsalis (Sept.–April). Ticket prices run $20–90, depending on the event. The Philharmonic also opens its rehearsals to the public once a week; tickets are $5. Call for more information.

Just north of Avery Fisher, above 66th Street, is the 1,096-seat **Alice Tully Hall,** 212/875-5050, where the Chamber Music Society of Lincoln Center performs. Tickets run $15–40.

A dozen or so blocks from Lincoln Center is Manhattan's other major classical-music venue, **Carnegie Hall,** Seventh Ave. and 57th St., 212/247-7800, www.carnegiehall.com. Saved from demolition by Isaac Stern and others in the early 1960s, this legendary hall was once home to the New York Philharmonic and remains a favorite spot among musicians of all persuasions. Tickets run $15–90.

The **Miller Theatre at Columbia University,** Broadway at 116th St., 212/854-7799, www.millertheatre.com, offers much contemporary concert music ranging from classical to jazz.

Classical music can also be heard at a number of unusual venues around town. The **Metropolitan Museum of Art,** Fifth Ave. at 82nd St., 212/570-3949, offers a regular series in its

nonetheless features plenty of acoustic types; no cover, one-drink minimum.

Greenwich Village

From the outside, **Gonzalez y Gonzalez,** 625 Broadway, between Bleecker and Houston Sts., 212/473-8787, appears to be just another ho-hum Mexican restaurant, but inside you'll find plenty of first-rate Latin music and a packed dance floor; cover $15–20.

Housed in a creaky old building once belonging to Thomas Paine is **Marie's Crisis Cafe,** 59 Grove St., at Seventh Ave., 212/243-9323, a lively piano bar where a predominantly gay crowd has been gathering to sing show tunes for over 50 years.

Midtown

Paddy Reilly's, 519 Second Ave., at 29th St.,

Grace Rainey Rogers Auditorium, as well as less formal performances in such splendid settings as the Temple of Dundur or the Medieval Sculpture Hall. **Bargemusic,** at Fulton Ferry Landing in Brooklyn, 718/624-4061, is a large barge moored beneath the Brooklyn Bridge, where string quartets are accompanied by glorious views of Manhattan. Those on a tight budget should call or stop by the **Juilliard School,** 60 Lincoln Center Pl., 212/769-7406, where the students and faculty members frequently perform in superb recitals costing little or nothing.

OPERA

On the west side of Lincoln Center is the grand **Metropolitan Opera House,** 212/362-6000, www.metopera.org, home of the Metropolitan Opera Company. A good seat here costs $100 or more, but $20 seats are often available in the upper balcony, along with $12 standing-room spots (bring binoculars).

On the south side of the center is the **New York State Theater,** 212/870-5570, www.nyc-opera.com, where the less exalted New York City Opera performs. Regular tickets run $25–100; $10 standing-room tickets and $15 seats are also usually available (again, bring binoculars).

The tiny **Amato Opera Theater,** 319 Bowery, at Bleecker, 212/228-8200, puts on splendid weekend productions in a creaky turn-of-the-century vaudeville house. The $20 tickets are a great deal but must be reserved well in advance.

CLUBS

Since the mid-1990s, night life in New York has been under siege, due in part to a "quality-of-life" campaign begun by former mayor Rudolph Giuliani and in part to skyrocketing rents. Some long-established clubs have been shuttered; others have been toned down considerably. In their wake has come a new, more modest generation of clubs, which tend to be smaller and more mainstream than were their predecessors.

Some of both New York's older and newer clubs are listed below, but as these can change

overnight, be sure to check local listings before venturing out. A few other general rules:

Nothing really gets going until after midnight, and although arrogant door policies are often in effect, be patient—all but the snootiest of clubs eventually let almost everyone in. Be prepared to be searched at the door and to spend big bucks—in addition to a steep cover, you'll have to shell out about $8 per drink. Admission prices are generally lower during the week than on weekends.

Some of New York's most interesting club events are independent roving parties, which tend to take up residence in one location for six months or so and then move on. To find out the latest on the roving club scene, check the listings in *Time Out New York, Flyer,* or *Paper.*

SoHo and TriBeCa

Part live-music venue and part dance club, **Don Hill's,** 511 Greenwich St., at Spring St., 212/334-1390, hosts some of the best DJs in town, spinning everything from jump-blues to hip hop. Lesbians, gays, and straights frequent the scene, with the crowd changing nightly, according to the music.

Vinyl, 6 Hubert St., near Hudson St., 212/343-1379, is big, dark club best known for its Sunday afternoon dance party, Body & Soul, that packs them in from 3 to 11 P.M.

East Village and Lower East Side

Sapphire, 249 Eldridge St., between Houston and Stanton Sts., 212/777-5153, is one of the older lounges on the Lower East Side, offering hip-hop, R&B, reggae, and disco classics. **Webster Hall,** 125 E. 11th St., near Third Ave., 212/353-1600, is a five-floored extravaganza, often packed with out-of-towners. Each room has a different sound—disco, Latin, hip hop, house, and soul.

West Village

Though not as hot as it once was, **Lotus,** 409 W. 14th St., between Ninth Ave. and Washington St., 212/242-9710, still attracts its share of celebs. Part restaurant and part dance club, the place is sleek and dark with lots of comfortable sitting areas.

Nell's, 246 W. 14th St., between Seventh and

Eighth Aves., 212/675-1567, has been in business for well over a decade now, offering live jazz and dining upstairs, DJs spinning hip-hop, house, and R&B below.

Chelsea

The **Roxy,** 515 W. 18th St., between 10th and 11th Aves., 212/645-5156, once solely a roller-skating rink, is now part roller-disco, part straight dance club. Some nights are gays only, other nights are mixed.

Hip, futuristic **Centro-Fly,** 45 W. 21st St., between Fifth and Sixth Aves., 212/627-7770, www.centro-fly.com, boasts two sound systems and some of the top DJs in town. Food is served in the club's Tapioca Room.

One of the hottest gay bars in town is the recently revamped **Splash Bar New York,** 50 W. 17th St., between Fifth and Sixth Aves., 718/691-0073. It's especially known for its muscle-bound bartenders, and disco scene.

Chic **Cheetah,** 12 W. 21st St., between Fifth and Sixth Aves., 212/206-7770, bills itself as "the fastest club in the world." Inside you'll find golden columns, lots of cheetah prints, a floor-to-ceiling waterfall, and a largely over-30, hetero crowd.

Midtown

Club Shelter, 20 W. 39th St., between Fifth and Sixth Aves., 212/719-4479, offers a mix of DJs spinning everything from house to techno, along with live performances. **Sound Factory,** 618 46th St., between Eleventh and Twelfth Sts., 212/643-0728, a legendary club of the early '90s, has been reborn on the far West Side—without famed DJ Junior Vasquez. The crowd, once streetwise and largely gay, is now mostly white and suburban.

Junior Vasquez has now moved on to host a enormous weekly party called Earth at **Exit,** 610 W. 56th St., between Eleventh and Twelfth Aves., 212/582-8282, a vast venue with a stunning sound system. Other nights at the club are more mundane.

Latin music fans will want to head to **Club New York,** 252 W. 43rd St., between Broadway and Eighth Ave., 212/997-9510, where DJs spin salsa, merengue, hip hop, and pop.

Brooklyn

One of the city's more unusual venues is **Halcyon,** 227 Smith St., between Butler and Douglass Sts., Carroll Gardens, 718/260-9299. A cafe, record store, and lounge by day, it turns into an underground club with a superb sound system at night.

THEATER AND PERFORMANCE ART

Theater productions in New York are listed as "Broadway," "Off-Broadway," and "Off-Off Broadway." The terms do not refer to geographic location, but to theater size and cost of production. "Broadway" shows are the big, expensive kind, playing to audiences of over 500; "Off-Broadway" are smaller shows, playing to audiences of 100–499; and "Off-Off Broadway" are the smallest of all, with audiences of fewer than 100. Broadway productions lean toward the mainstream, and Off-Broadway productions—which began in the 1930s as a rebellion against Broadway values—almost equally so. Off-Off Broadway theater was a 1960s rebellion against the rebellion; its shows are often quirky and experimental.

For information on major shows and ticket availability, call the **NYC/ON STAGE hotline** at 212/768-1818.

Broadway

Attending a Broadway show is a quintessential New York experience. No matter whether the play you see turns out to be a dazzler or a dud, there's nothing quite like hurrying down the neon-splashed streets of Times Square along with thousands of other theatergoers, most of whom always seem to be running late. Among Broadway's many gorgeous, historic venues—most located just off Times Square—are the **Shubert, Booth, Nederlander, Majestic, Belasco,** and **Lyceum.**

Tickets: Full-price tickets to Broadway plays usually run $45–75, although some of the larger theaters offer $15 seats far in the back. Half-price orchestra-seat tickets (about $25, plus a $2.50 service fee) to same-day performances are sold daily at the **TKTS** booth, 212/221-0013, www.tdf.org, located on the triangle formed by

The TKTS booth in Times Square is *the* place for discount tickets.

47th St., Seventh Ave., and Broadway. The booth is open Monday–Saturday 3–8 P.M. for evening performances, Wednesday and Saturday 10 A.M.–2 P.M. for matinees, and Sunday 11 A.M.–2 P.M. for matinees and 11 A.M.–7 P.M. for evening performances. The lines are often very long, but they move quickly. If you don't want to wait, come early, or—surprisingly enough—come late. Your selection will be more limited then, but there's often no wait at all after about 7 P.M.

TKTS also operates a booth in Lower Manhattan at the South Street Seaport, at the corner of John and Front. Here, tickets to evening performances are sold Mon.–Fri. 11 A.M.–5:30 P.M., Saturday 11 A.M.–3:30 P.M., closed Sunday. Tickets to matinee performances are sold 11 A.M.–closing on the day *before* the performance.

Another similarly priced budget option is to pick up the **twofer** ticket coupons that can be found at bookstores, delis, and hotels all over town, as well as at the New York City Official Visitor Information Center, 810 Seventh Ave., at 53rd St. "Twofers" allow you to buy two tickets for the price of one, and they're usually issued for old Broadway shows that have been around forever or are about to close.

Off and Off-Off Broadway

Many Off-Broadway theaters are in the East Village or in Greenwich Village, or along Theater Row on 42nd Street between Ninth and Tenth Avenues. Off-Broadway tickets generally run $20–40, with discounted tickets also available through TKTS. Off-Off Broadway shows, which can cost as little as $7, tend to be produced in theaters below 14th Street. A number of these theaters consistently produce fine theater.

East Village: Foremost among Off-Broadway companies is the **Public Theater,** 425 Lafayette St., near Astor Pl., 212/260-2400, www.publictheater.org, founded by the late Joseph Papp, who also fought long and hard to bring the free **New York Shakespeare Festival** to the city. The Public still puts on two free Shakespeare plays—featuring top actors—every summer in Central Park's Delacorte Theater, near Central Park West and 81st St., 212/539-8750.

Not far from the Public Theater is a bastion of the avant-garde: **La MaMa E.T.C.,** 74A E. 4th St., near Second Ave., 212/475-7710, www.lamama.org. It's a sprawling three-theater complex run by the innovative Ellen Stewart, one of the founders of the Off-Off Broadway movement.

© CHRISTIANE BIRD

NEW YORK CITY INTRO

Theatre for the New City, 155 First Ave., near 11th St., 212/254-1109, presents new and experimental drama, often at very low prices. The **Bouwerie Lane Theater,** 330 Bowery, at Bond St., 212/677-0060, home to the Jean Cocteau Repertory Company, presents the classics in the old German Exchange Bank, built in 1876.

On the Lower East Side, you'll find the **Angel Orensanz Center for the Arts,** 172 Norfolk St., between E. Houston and Stanton Sts., 212/529-7194, a fantastic old synagogue—flying buttresses, lacy stonework—that's now in a state of picturesque decay. The center presents everything from theater and comedy to pop music and community events.

Greenwich Village: The **Circle Repertory Company,** 159 Bleecker St., between Thompson and Sullivan Sts., 212/239-6200, is one of the city's top theater ensembles, committed to presenting five new American dramas each year; playwrights connected to the theater include Lanford Wilson and Terrence McNally. The **Cherry Lane Theater,** 38 Commerce St., near Barrow St., 212/989-6200, is a small, appealing venue founded by Edna St. Vincent Millay and others in 1924. The delightful **Ridiculous Theater Company,** 1 Sheridan Square, near Seventh Ave., 212/691-2271, was founded by the late Charles Ludlam. It's a creaky, downstairs venue that's the irreverent home of parody, farce, and actors in drag.

SoHo: The avant-garde **Performing Garage,** 33 Wooster St., between Grand and Broome, 212/966-3651, is home to the Wooster Group, one of the country's oldest experimental theater companies.

Chelsea and Union Square: The **Atlantic Theater Company,** 336 W. 20th St., between Eighth and Ninth Aves., 212/239-6200, housed in a converted church, is an acting ensemble that grew out of a series of workshops taught by David Mamet and William H. Macy in the mid 1980s. The **Vineyard Theatre,** 108 15th St., just off Union Square, 212/353-3366, www.vineyardtheatre.org, is a nonprofit theater company that focuses on new voices for the New York stage; writers such as Nicky Silver, Brian Friel, and Paula Vogel have premiered works here.

Midtown: Playwrights Horizons, 416 W. 42nd St., near Ninth Ave., 212/279-4200, www.playwrightshorizons.org, produces many plays that eventually move on to Broadway. The **Negro Ensemble Company,** 212/582-5860, founded in 1967, is one of the older African American companies around; it performs in various venues. The **Manhattan Theatre Club,** 131 W. 55th St., between Sixth and Seventh Aves., 212/399-3000, www.manhattantheatreclub.com, presents plays by both new and established playwrights, and sponsors a Writers-in-Performance series, featuring readings by well-known authors.

The newly revamped **Symphony Space,** 2537 Broadway, at 95th St., 212/864-1414, complete with a spiffy bar/cafe and cinema, now features a wide diversity of cultural offerings ranging from live theater to jazz concerts to French cinema.

Performance Art

P.S. 122, 150 First Ave., at 9th St., 212/477-5288, www.ps122.org, housed in a former school, is a mecca for often highly imaginative performance art, as well as a center for avant-garde dance. Other venues regularly presenting performance artists include the **Kitchen,** 512 W. 19th St., between Tenth and Eleventh Aves., 212/255-5793, www.thekitchen.org, a three-story emporium best known for its video series and avant-garde music; the underground Alterknit Room at the **Knitting Factory,** 74 Leonard St., between Church and Broadway, 212/219-3055; **Sidewalk,** 94 Ave. A, at 6th St., 212/473-7373, a restaurant and "anti-folk" club; and **P.S. 1,** 46-01 21st St., Long Island City, 718/784-2084, in Queens. **Exit Art,** 548 Broadway, 212/966-7745, and **HERE,** 145 Sixth Ave., at Dominick St., 212/647-0202, are gallery/performance spaces in SoHo.

The hip **Nuyorican Poets Cafe,** 236 E. 3rd St., between Aves. B and C, 212/505-8183, www.nuyorican.org, is a big, raw, high-ceilinged place best known for its Friday night poetry slams, in which poets compete with one another in front of an opinionated audience. The rest of the week, performance art and literary readings are frequently featured.

DANCE

New York is home to two major ballet companies, several smaller ones, and numerous modern-dance troupes. The **American Ballet Theater,** once directed by Mikhail Baryshnikov, performs at the Metropolitan Opera House in Lincoln Center, 212/362-6000, from May to July; tickets cost $25–130. The **New York City Ballet,** founded by George Balanchine, performs at the New York State Theater in Lincoln Center, 212/870-5570, during the winter and spring; tickets cost $16–85.

Many of the city's other companies perform in three major venues. The gorgeous, Moorish-style **City Center,** 131 W. 55th St., between Sixth and Seventh Aves., 212/581-7907, annually hosts the **Dance Theater of Harlem,** the **Alvin Ailey Dance Company,** the **Paul Taylor Dance Company,** and the **Merce Cunningham Dance Company,** among others; tickets cost $25–75. The more intimate **Joyce Theater,** 175 Eighth Ave., at 19th St., 212/242-0800, www.joyce.org, hosts the **Eliot Feld Ballet** and numerous touring dance troupes. The **Brooklyn Academy of Music** (BAM), 30 Lafayette Ave. in Brooklyn, 718/636-4100, www.bam.org, presents a Next Wave series featuring avant-garde dance companies from New York and around the world.

Two important smaller venues presenting experimental dance are the **Dance Theater Workshop,** 219 W. 19th St., between Seventh and Eighth Aves., 212/924-0077; and **P.S. 122,** 150 First Ave., at 9th St., 212/477-5288. **St. Mark's Church-in-the-Bowery,** 131 E. 10th St., at Second Ave., 212/674-8112, also offers an experimental dance program in its newly renovated main sanctuary.

COMEDY CLUBS

Carolines, 1626 Broadway, at 49th St., 212/757-4100, www.carolines.com, is the glitziest and most expensive club around, booking big-name acts on a regular basis; cover is $15–35, with a two-drink minimum. Another well-established spot is **Dangerfield's,** 1118 First Ave., between 61st and 62nd Sts., 212/593-1650. Opened by comedian Rodney Dangerfield, it showcases new talent and attracts a large tourist crowd; cover is $12–20. **Stand-up NY,** 236 W. 78th St., at Broadway, 212/595-0850, is the sort of place where Robin Williams might drop in unexpectedly; cover $7–12, with a two-drink minimum.

Top New York comics often appear at the dark and cozy **Comedy Cellar,** 117 MacDougal St., between W. 3rd St. and Bleecker, 212/254-3480; cover is $10–12, with a one-drink minimum. **Chicago City Limits,** 1105 First Ave., between 60th and 61st Sts., 212/888-5233, www.chicagocitylimits.com, is also a popular spot, founded in the Windy City but in New York since 1979. One of the city's newest comedy clubs, **Gramercy Comedy Club,** 35 E. 21st St., between Broadway and Park Ave. S, 212/254-5709, is a posh spot that features a regular line-up of mostly TV comedians; cover is $15, with a two-drink minimum.

Among the best of the alternative comedy clubs, where the comics work less traditional material, are laid-back **Luna Lounge,** 171 Ludlow St., between Houston and Stanton Sts., 212/260-2323; and the loft-like, second-story **Surf Reality,** 172 Allen St., between Stanton and Rivington Sts., 212/673-4182, www.surfreality.org; the cover at both ranges up to $10.

CINEMA

As you'd expect, the city boasts a large number of commercial, multiplex theaters, most of which are owned by Cineplex Odeon or Loews. Revival and art-house theaters have died long and torturous deaths over the last decade, until now only a handful remain.

TeleTicket, 212/777-FILM, allows you to reserve movie tickets in advance by charging them over the phone to your credit card. This does avoid disappointment—first-run movies frequently sell out—but a service fee is charged. Tickets can also be purchased at www.moviefone.com and www.fandango.com; service fees are charged.

For independent and foreign films, and retrospectives, the best place in town is the **Film Forum,** 209 W. Houston St., near Sixth Ave.,

212/727-8110, equipped with three screens and a small coffee bar. Lincoln Center's **Walter Reade Theater,** 70 Lincoln Center Plaza at on 65th St., above Alice Tully Hall, between Broadway and Amsterdam, 212/875-5600, www.filmlinc.org is another excellent venue for foreign films and retrospectives, while the **Public Theater,** 425 Lafayette St., near Astor, 212/260-2400, offers an unusual selection of art and experimental film classics.

The **Museum of Modern Art,** now temporarily relocated to Long Island City, Queens (see Queens chapter), features many classic films that are free with museum admission. In Astoria, Queens, the **American Museum of the Moving Image,** 35th Ave. at 36th St., 718/784-0077, has three full-size theaters presenting film in all its forms. Two smaller venues for avant-garde films are the **Anthology Film Archives,** 32 Second Ave., at 2nd St., 212/505-5181; and the **Mil-**lennium Film Workshop,** 66 E. 4th St., near Second Ave., 212/673-0090.

The only truly magnificent movie theater left in Manhattan is the Clearview Ziegfeld, on West 54th Street, between Sixth and Seventh Avenues, which has one of the largest screens in America and a deliciously ornate red-and-gold decor.

The only truly magnificent movie theater left in Manhattan is the **Clearview Ziegfeld,** 141 W. 54th St., between Sixth and Seventh Aves., 212/765-7600, which has one of the largest screens in America and a deliciously ornate red-and-gold decor. Another unusual venue—this one minimalist—is the **Angelika Film Center,** 18 W. Houston St., at Mercer, 212/995-2000, which screens a mix of new and old films to a hip, downtown crowd, and features an extensive cafe.

Sony Lincoln Square & IMAX Theatre, 1992 Broadway, at 68th St., 212/336-5000, is as much a Disneyfied theme park as it is a movie theater. Inside you'll find plenty of neon, classic movie sets, a gift shop selling movie memorabilia, 12 screens presenting first-run features, and an eight-story-high IMAX screen.

Activities

SHOPPING

Sometimes it seems as if all of New York City is one enormous shopping center, with new stores opening up and older ones closing down daily. Nevertheless, certain areas of town are particularly well known for their shops.

Fifth Avenue between 49th and 59th Streets, has long been home to many of the city's most famous and expensive stores, including Saks Fifth Avenue, Bergdorf Goodman's, and Tiffany's. In recent years, tourist meccas such as the Coca-Cola Company and Warner Brothers Studio store have also set up shop here. **Madison Avenue** between 59th and 82nd Streets has many exclusive antique and designer shops. **Herald Square** at 34th Street and Sixth Avenue, and **34th Street** between Fifth and Sixth Avenues feature more moderately priced stores such as Macy's, The Gap, and The Limited.

Columbus Avenue between 66th and 86th Streets offers a large number of stylish clothing stores, as well as gift and home-furnishings shops.

SoHo is known for trendy clothing stores and unusual gift shops, while the **East Village** has some of the most imaginative and reasonably priced stores in town. **Lower Fifth Avenue** below 23rd Street has an eclectic smattering of clothing shops, and the **Lower East Side** is a bargain-hunter's delight, especially for clothing, shoes, and linens.

Some specific areas on which to focus your shopping endeavors are listed below. For further shopping suggestions, see the Shopping entries in the individual neighborhood sections and the Appendix.

Antiques

Many of the city's oldest and most expensive antique stores line Madison Avenue above 59th

© WWW.NYCVISIT.COM

shopping on Fifth Avenue

Street, while 60th Street between Third and Second Avenues is a center for more reasonably priced furnishings.

An eclectic array of antique shops can be found in SoHo along Lafayette and Wooster Streets; and in the West Village, along Bleecker Street west of Christopher. For bargains, try 9th Street in the East Village and the city's flea markets in Chelsea and SoHo.

Cameras and Electronics

Cameras and electronic equipment are available at excellent prices throughout the city, but avoid the tourist traps along Fifth Avenue and 42nd Street, all of which have been "Going Out of Business" for years. The Tuesday editions of the *Daily News* and *New York Times* carry advertisements from electronics retailers. **The Wiz** is a reputable chain with several branches in the city. **J&R,** on Park Row, in Lower Manhattan, has a wide selection. Many camera stores selling new and used equipment, as well as darkroom supplies, are located in Chelsea.

Clothing: New

On the Upper East Side, **Madison Avenue** above

59th Street is home to some of the world's most expensive designer shops. More reasonably priced stores are clustered near Bloomingdale's at **Lexington Avenue and 59th Street.** On the Upper West Side, **Columbus Avenue** between 72nd and 82nd Streets has a large number of boutiques aimed at young professionals.

On **34th Street,** between Fifth and Sixth Avenue, and around **Herald Square** at 34th Street and Sixth Avenue, you'll find one store after another. Most are moderately to inexpensively priced. **Lower Fifth Avenue,** just west of Union Square, features many clothing boutiques catering to young professionals.

SoHo is filled with trendy clothing shops, most along Prince and Spring Streets. Ninth Street between First Avenue and Avenue A, in the **East Village,** and Ludlow Street south of Houston on the **Lower East Side** are home to some of the town's hippest young designers.

Clothing: Vintage and Discount

Most vintage clothing stores are in SoHo, the East Village, and Greenwich Village. **Orchard Street** on the Lower East Side offers many bargain-priced stores carrying both designer goods and casual wear.

Two of the city's largest and best-known stores for discounted designer wear are **Century 21** in Lower Manhattan and **Loehmann's,** in Chelsea and the Bronx. Smaller stores featuring both discounted designer and casual wear include **Daffy's, Bolton's,** and **Hit or Miss;** all have multiple outlets in the city. The best place for really cheap secondhand clothes—some vintage, some not— is **Domsey's** in Brooklyn.

Shoes

Manhattan's two main thoroughfares for shoes are West 8th Street between Fifth and Sixth Avenues in Greenwich Village and West 34th Street between Fifth and Sixth Avenues near Herald Square. The former caters to young fashion mavens with money, the latter to office workers looking for bargains.

Business Hours

In general, most stores are open Monday–Saturday from about 10 A.M. to about 6 P.M., and on Sunday afternoons. Many department stores stay open late on Thursday, and some on Monday as well. Stores in SoHo, the East Village, and along Columbus Avenue keep later hours, often opening at about noon and closing about 8 P.M.

SPORTS AND RECREATION

Baseball

New Yorkers take their baseball seriously, and even if you're not much of a fan, it's worth riding the subway out to Shea or Yankee Stadium just to take in the scene. The season starts in April and runs into October. Tickets are usually available at the box office, at prices ranging $12–55.

Though there's currently much talk of building a new Yankee stadium—perhaps in Manhattan or (gulp) New Jersey—for the moment, the **New York Yankees** still play at 161st St. and River Ave., in the Bronx, 718/293-6000 (box office) or 718/293-4300, www.yankees.com; take the No. 4 train to 161st Street and follow the crowd. Built by a brewery magnate in 1923, the stadium is sometimes called "the house that Ruth built," in honor of the man who hit 60 home runs here in 1927 alone. The **New York Mets** play in more modern and nondescript Shea Stadium, 126th St. at Roosevelt Ave. in Queens, 718/507-METS or 718/507-8499, www.mets.com; take the No. 7 train to Willets Point–Shea Stadium and follow the crowd.

Basketball

The **New York Knicks** play out of Madison Square Garden, Seventh Ave. and 33rd St., 212/465-6741 or 212/465-JUMP (fan line), www.nba.com/knicks, from late fall to late spring. Theoretically, ticket prices start at $25, but that doesn't mean much as the games are usually sold out well in advance.

Football

Both New York teams, the **Giants,** website: www.giants.com, and the **Jets,** play across the river in Giants Stadium, Byrne Meadowlands Sports Complex, East Rutherford, New Jersey, 201/935-3900. Buses to the complex operate out of the Port Authority, 212/564-8484, but since tickets to Giants games are nearly impossible to get (there's a 10-year waiting list) and to Jets games nearly as bad, you'll probably end up staying in the city and watching them on TV.

Hockey

The **New York Rangers,** website: www.newyork rangers.com, play out of Madison Square Garden, Seventh Ave. and 33rd St., from late fall to late spring. For information, call 212/465-6741. The **New York Islanders,** website: www .newyorkislanders.com, play out of Nassau Memorial Coliseum, off Hempstead Turnpike in Uniondale, Long Island, 516/794-4100. Train service to and from the stadium is available on the Long Island Rail Road, 718/217-5477. Tickets to both teams' games run $20–60 and are generally available.

Horse Racing

The city's two racetracks run alternately. **Belmont Park,** Hempstead Tnpk. and Plainfield Ave., Belmont, Long Island, 718/641-4700, is by far the more attractive of the two, with a large grandstand and pond, and red and white geraniums. Races run May–July and September–mid-October, Wednesday–Sunday. (In August, the entire industry migrates up to Saratoga Springs, see the North Country chapter.) To reach Belmont, take the Long Island Rail Road from Pennsylvania Station.

The **Aqueduct Racetrack,** 108th St. and Rockaway Blvd., Jamaica, Queens, 718/641-4700, is a considerably smaller and seedier affair. Built in 1894, it's named for an aqueduct that once ran nearby. Races run late October–early May, Wednesday–Sunday. To reach Aqueduct, take the A or C train to the Aqueduct station.

Grandstand admission at both tracks costs $2, and bets start at $1. Daily programs include explicit instructions on how to place a bet.

Tennis

The **U.S. Open** is held in late August and early September at the U.S. Tennis Association's Tennis Center in Flushing Meadows Park, Queens, 718/760-6200. Tickets, which cost $35–75, go on sale May 31st and sell out quickly.

Bicycling

Although very crowded on nice weekends, one of the best places to ride bikes in New York is Central Park, where bikes can be rented at the **Loeb Boathouse,** near the Fifth Ave. and E. 72nd St. entrance, 212/517-4723. Other rental shops near Central Park include **Metro Bicycles,** 1311 Lexington Ave., at 88th St., 212/427-4450; and the **Pedal Pusher Bicycle Shop,** 1306 Second Ave., between 68th and 69th Sts., 212/288-5592. Rates usually run $7–9 an hour, $28–35 a day, and security deposits are required.

Boating

Paddling about on The Lake in Central Park is a popular pastime. Rowboats can be rented at the **Loeb Boathouse,** 212/517-4723, near the park's Fifth Ave. and E. 72nd St. entrance. Rates are $10 an hour, with a $30 deposit.

Fitness Classes

New York has a plethora of well-equipped health clubs offering a wide variety of fitness classes, but most are closed to visitors. One of the few exceptions is **Crunch,** where you can take a single aerobics or yoga class for about $20. Crunch has branches at 54 E. 13th St., between University and Broadway, 212/475-2018; 162 W. 83rd St., between Columbus and Amsterdam, 212/875-1902; 404 Lafayette St., near E. 4th St., 212/614-0120; and 1109 Second Ave., between 58th and 59th Sts., 212/758-3434.

Single classes costing about $15 each are also offered by **Steps,** 2121 Broadway, at W. 74th, 212/874-2410; and **West 72nd Street Studios,** 131 W. 72nd St., between Broadway and Columbus, 212/799-5433. The **Integral Yoga Institute,** 227 W. 13th St., between Seventh and Eighth Aves., 212/929-0585, offers single yoga classes for about $12.

Day passes are available at the enormous **Sports Center at Chelsea Piers,** Pier 60, 23rd St. at the Hudson River, 212/336-6000, www.chelseapiers.com, where you'll find a quarter-mile indoor track, an Olympic-sized swimming pool, basketball and volleyball courts, a weight room, multiple fitness classes, and an indoor climbing wall. Passes cost $50.

Horseback Riding

Manhattan's oldest and largest riding center is **Claremont Riding Academy,** 173-177 W. 89th St., at Amsterdam, 212/724-5100, which rents horses with English-style saddles to ride in Central Park. The horses are well taken care of, and some are quite spirited. Rates run $50 an hour, and lessons are also available.

Ice Skating

The city's most famous rink, often surrounded by spectators, is the sunken **Rockefeller Center Ice Rink,** Fifth Ave. and 50th St., 212/332-7654, where admission is adults $13–15 and kids under 12 $10; rentals cost $7. The wonderful **Wollman Memorial Rink,** in Central Park near 64th St., 212/439-6900, with its great views of the city skyline, is much more low-key and about half the price. The **Chelsea Piers Sky Rink,** 23rd St. and the Hudson River, 212/336-6100, belongs to the Chelsea Piers sports complex; admission is adults $12, kids under 12 $8.50; skate rental is $5.50.

Indoor Games

Indoor batting cages, basketball courts, in-line skating rinks, a gymnastics center, golf driving range, rock-climbing wall, health club, and spa are just some of the many attractions at the **Chelsea Piers Sports & Entertainment Complex,** 23rd St. at the Hudson River. For general information, call 212/336-6666. Day passes run about $50.

Over the past decade, many spiffy **pool halls** have opened up in Manhattan. Among them are **Chelsea Billiards,** 54 W. 21st St., between Fifth and Sixth Aves., 212/989-0096; **Soho Billiards,** 298 Mulberry St., at Mott, 212/925-3753; and the **Amsterdam Billiard Club,** 344 Amsterdam, near 77th St., 212/496-8180. All have a multitude of tables and keep late hours.

For bowling fans, the **Leisure Time Bowling and Recreation Centre,** at the Port Authority, Eighth Ave. and 42nd St., 212/268-6909, is a well-kept place with 30 lanes and a bar. In Greenwich Village, the recently renovated, 44-lane **Bowlmor Lanes,** 110 University Pl., at 12th St., 212/255-8188, is an old-fashioned spot by day and a hip downtown club by night.

Jogging

New Yorkers jog in all sorts of places in all sorts of weather, but one especially popular route is the track around the **Jacqueline Onassis Reservoir,** in Central Park, where the late former first lady herself often ran. The main entrance is at Fifth Avenue and East 90th Street; one lap is about a mile and a half.

Kayaking

To get an unusual view of Manhattan, explore the Hudson River and New York Harbor by kayak. Because navigating the currents and water traffic is tricky, kayaks cannot be rented for individual use, but you can take a class or tour. **New York Kayak,** Houston St. at West Side Hwy., 212/924-1327, www.nykayak.com, offers beginner to advanced classes, as well as short tours. The **Manhattan Kayak Company,** 23rd St. at West Side Hwy., Pier 63, 212/924-1788, www.manhattankayak.com, also offers beginner to advanced classes, and tours ranging from 90 minutes to eight hours. Call for rates.

To get an unusual view of Manhattan, explore the Hudson River and New York Harbor by kayak. Because navigating the currents and water traffic is tricky, kayaks cannot be rented for individual use, but you can take a class or tour.

EVENTS

New York is a city of parades and festivals, the larger of which are usually announced in the daily papers. Or you can call NYC & Company, New York's tourism marketing organization, at 212/484-1222 or 212/397-8222, or visit their website at www.nycvisit.com. Telephone numbers for smaller or more site-specific events are listed below.

January

On New Year's Day, the intrepid **Arctic Ice Bears** take a dip in the icy waters off Coney Island. Between mid-January and early February, the streets of Chinatown come alive with dragon dances, lion dances, and fireworks celebrating **Chinese New Year.** The two-day **Winter Antiques Show,** in the Seventh Regiment Armory, Park Ave. and 67th St., is a great excuse to see the building's grand, cavernous interior, designed by Stanford White and Louis Tiffany.

February

Black History Month is celebrated throughout the city with a variety of events, including concerts, films, exhibits, and lectures. For two days mid-month, dogs of every imaginable breed strut their stuff at the **Westminster Kennel Club Dog Show,** Madison Square Garden, Seventh Ave. and 33rd St., 212/465-6741. For one week mid-month, the **National Antiques Show** comes to Madison Square Garden.

March

Felines from around the world primp and preen at the two-day **International Cat Show,** Madison Square Garden, Seventh Ave. and 33rd St., 212/465-6741. The 17th marks the date of one of the city's biggest events and the oldest parade in the United States—the **St. Patrick's Day Parade,** first marched in 1752. A bright green stripe runs up Fifth Avenue from 44th to 86th Streets, and Midtown swells with thousands upon thousands of spectators and party animals, many of them teenagers from the suburbs who see the day as an excuse to get falling-down drunk. Meanwhile, throughout the city, Irish taverns celebrate St. Pat's with party favors and green beer, and many New Yorkers—Irish or not—don something green. Smaller St. Patrick's parades are held on Staten Island and in Brooklyn on the weekends before and after the 17th, respectively.

Greek Independence Day is celebrated on the 25th with a more sedate parade on Fifth Avenue. Madison Square Garden blooms with the **New York Flower Show.** At the end of the month, the **Ringling Brothers and Barnum & Bailey Circus** comes to Madison Square Garden for its annual two-month stint; the animals parade into town around midnight through the Queens Midtown Tunnel.

April

On Easter Sunday, citizens show off their spring finery in the **Easter Parade** on Fifth Avenue near St. Patrick's Cathedral (49th Street). This is not an organized event but a sort of free-for-all in which participants dress to the hilt. At the Brooklyn Botanic Garden, the two-day **Cherry Blossom Festival** celebrates both the flower and Asian culture through performances and traditional crafts demonstrations, 718/623-7200.

May

In mid-May, the colorful three-day **Ukrainian Festival** on 7th Street in the East Village, 212/228-0110, commemorates Ukraine's conversion to Christianity. The enormously popular two-day **Ninth Avenue Food Festival,** between 36th and 59th Streets, features delectable edibles from around the world. The **Martin Luther King Jr. Day Parade** is held on Fifth Avenue on or around May 17.

Also mid-month, the city's Norwegian population celebrates its heritage by marching down Brooklyn's Fifth Avenue from 90th to 67th Streets in a **Norwegian Day Parade.** Other ethnic festivals celebrated during the month include the **India Festival,** which often takes place at the South Street Seaport, 212/732-7678; the **Czechoslovak Festival,** held in the city's last beer garden, Bohemian Hall in Astoria, Queens, 718/274-4925; and the **Salute to Israel Parade,** which marks the independence of Israel by marching down Fifth Avenue.

Over Memorial Day weekend, artists of varying talents pack the streets around Washington Square, selling their wares during the **Washington Square Outdoor Art Exhibition,** 212/982-6255. The same exhibition also takes place in the fall.

June

The city's enormous smorgasbord of free, and mostly outdoor, summer festivities begins in June. Events include dance, drama, opera, jazz, pop, and folk music. Among the top series are performances by the **Metropolitan Opera,** 212/362-6000, and the **New York Philharmonic,** 212/875-5709, held in parks throughout the city; the **Central Park SummerStage** series at the bandstand in Central Park, which features everything from dance and poetry to salsa and rock, 212/360-2777, www.summerstage.org; the **Lincoln Center Out-of-Doors** performing arts festival, 212/875-5928; and the **New York Shakespeare Festival** at the Delacorte Theater in Central Park, 212/539-8750.

During the day-long **Museum Mile Festival,** all of the museums on Fifth Avenue from 82nd to 102nd Streets are free to the public, 212/606-2296. The fabulistic **Mermaid Parade,** displaying eye-popping costumes down the boardwalk in Coney Island, is an event not to be missed, 718/372-5159, www.coneyisland.com. The 10-day **Festival of St. Anthony,** on Sullivan Street in Little Italy, is mostly a commercial affair, with booths selling games of chance, pizza, and ices. **Rose Day Weekend,** at the New York Botanical Garden in the Bronx, features tours, lectures, and demonstrations of horticultural crafts, 718/817-8700. In mid-June, Puerto Ricans celebrate their heritage with the boisterous **Puerto Rican Day Parade** on Fifth Avenue. In late June and early July, the 10-day **JVC Jazz Festival** takes place at various concert halls around the city and also offers a few free outdoor events, 212/501-1390, www.festivalproductions.net. Accompanying it is the multi-faceted **New York Jazz Festival,** presenting hundreds of imaginative events; it's sponsored by the Knitting Factory, 212/219-3006, www.jazzfest.com, an eclectic, downtown jazz, etc., club, and a corporate sponsor that changes each year. Late in the month, the **Gay and Lesbian Pride March,** 212/807-7433, www.nycpride.org, heads down Fifth Avenue to Greenwich Village.

July

On the Fourth of July, Macy's lights up the skies with spectacular **fireworks** over either the Hudson or the East River. One of the city's favorite concert series, the **Mostly Mozart Festival** at Lincoln Center, begins mid-month and lasts through August, 212/875-5400. Also at Lincoln Center in July and August is the **Serious Fun Festival,** a series that celebrates the avant-garde performing arts.

Mid-month, the four-day **African Street Festival** offers sports, art, music, and food on Fulton Street in Brooklyn between Schenectady and Utica Avenues. On the second Saturday, during the **Feast of Our Lady of Mt. Carmel** in East Harlem, a statue of Our Lady of Mt. Carmel is carried through the streets as churches ring their bells and street vendors hawk their wares, 212/534-0681. The highlight of the mid-month, week-long **Feast of the Giglio** in Williamsburg, Brooklyn, comes when a platform weighing thousands of pounds and carrying an enormous tower is "danced" through the streets on the shoulders of 250 men, 718/384-0223. On the Saturday closest to the full moon, the **Obon Festival** comes to Riverside Park; featured is a ritual dance with drummers and kimono-clad dancers.

August

Harlem Week, which began as Harlem Day back in 1975, now lasts almost the entire month, and festivities run the gamut from fashion shows, open houses, and sports competitions to concerts, films, and food. Mid-month, Ecuador's independence from Spain is celebrated with an **Ecuadorian Festival** in Flushing Meadows–Corona Park, Queens, 718/520-5900. Also mid-month is the **India Day Parade,** when floats depicting landmark events in India's history parade down Madison Avenue between 34th and 21st Streets. Late in the month, the **U.S. Open Tennis Tournament** comes to Flushing, Queens, 718/760-6200. The **Fringe Festival,** held at various locations in downtown Manhattan, 212/420-8877, showcases up-and-coming talent in theater and performing arts; nearly 200 productions are offered in a two-week period.

September

Over a million spectators gather along Brooklyn's Eastern Parkway every Labor Day to watch the most fantastic of fantastic parades—the **West Indian American Day Carnival.** Steel bands ring out with calypso music, feathered dancers balance on stilts, and West Indians of all ages strut their stuff, many wearing costumes that have taken months to construct, 718/625-1515. Also on Labor Day is **Wigstock,** a take-off on Woodstock performed in drag, which takes place in Tompkins Square Park.

The first Saturday of the month marks the **Brazilian Carnival,** when West 46th Street rocks with the samba, bossa nova, and dancing in the street. Also early in the month is the 10-day **Feast of San Gennaro,** the best-known Italian festival in the city. An effigy of the saint is paraded through the streets, but otherwise the celebration—complete with a small Ferris wheel—is a commercial affair with over 300 vendors.

A second **Washington Square Outdoor Art Exhibit** (see May) takes place early in September. Mid-month is the **"New York Is Book Country"** fest, when over 150 publishers and booksellers set up booths along Fifth Avenue in Midtown. The three-week **New York Film Festival,** previewing some of the ensuing year's finest films, starts mid-September at Alice Tully Hall, Lincoln Center, 212/875-5610; tickets should be ordered well in advance.

Other special events in September include the **Von Steuben Day Parade** on Fifth Avenue, featuring the German Drum and Bugle Corps; and the **African American Day Parade,** held mid-month in Harlem, featuring hundreds of bands. On the last Sunday of September, Koreans celebrate the autumn moon during the splendid **Korean Harvest and Folklore Festival** in Flushing Meadows–Corona Park, Queens, 718/520-5900.

October

On or about October 5, the **Pulaski Parade** on Fifth Avenue salutes Polish heritage. On or about October 9, the **Hispanic Day Parade** celebrates the city's Latinos. And on or about October 12, the popular **Columbus Day Parade** salutes the explorer and his Italian heritage.

The **Blessing of the Animals** is a singular event held at the Cathedral of St. John the Divine, Amsterdam Ave., at 112th St., 212/316-7540 or 212/316-7400, on the feast day of Saint Francis of Assisi. Thousands of New Yorkers bring their animals in for a special mass.

October 31 marks the night of the granddaddy of the city's outrageous parades, the **Greenwich Village Halloween Parade.** Each costume seems more fantastic than the next as the procession wends its way downtown, ending with a party in Washington Square.

November

On the first Sunday of the month, the **New York Marathon** is run through all five boroughs. Early in November, the week-long **National Horse Show** comes to Madison Square Garden, Seventh Ave. and 33rd St., 212/465-6741. On Thanksgiving, the traditional **Macy's Thanksgiving Day Parade** makes its way down Broadway. From just after Thanksgiving well into the New Year, many of the stores in the city deck out their windows for the holidays. Fifth Avenue is especially well decorated; check out Lord & Taylor, between 38th and 39th Streets, and Saks Fifth Avenue, between 49th and 50th Streets.

December

One afternoon in early December, a huge Christmas tree is raised and lighted at Rockefeller Center, behind the skating rink. The **tree-lighting ceremony** is one of the city's signature events, drawing celebrities and dignitaries, tourists and, yes, even cynical native New Yorkers. Also during the month is the lighting of the **Chanukah Menorah** at Grand Army Plaza, Fifth Avenue and 59th Street, and the **Kwanzaa Holiday Expo,** at the Javits Convention Center, 655 W. 34th St., 212/216-2000. **New Year's Eve** is celebrated with events including the traditional dropping of the Big Apple ball from the top of Times Tower, Times Square; a **midnight run** in Central Park; and family-oriented **First Night** events held at various locations throughout the city.

NEW YORK CITY INTRO

Manhattan

To many people, Manhattan *is* New York. On this small island, just 12 miles long by three miles wide, are crowded most of the city's skyscrapers, businesses, museums, theaters, hotels, restaurants, and famous sites. Though by far the smallest of the five boroughs in area, Manhattan is by far the largest in reputation.

Manhattan was settled from south to north, with the first Dutchmen arriving near what is now known as Battery Park in 1500. By 1650, the city had spread northward to include today's Financial District, and by 1800, Greenwich Village was a thriving community. Union Square was established in the early 1900s. The wealthy began moving to the Upper East Side in the late 1800s, and the Dakota—New York's first grand apartment building—went up on the Upper West Side in 1884. Harlem existed as an independent farming community until 1873, when it was annexed to the borough.

Manhattan can be subdivided into a dozen or so large "neighborhoods" or districts, which are then sometimes divided again according to commercial activity or ethnic bent. Each neighborhood is distinct from the rest, and all are worth a visit.

the East River and Manhattan skyline

Lower Manhattan

New York City began down here, on this tip of an island where the Hudson and East Rivers meet. This is where the Dutch West India Company established its first New World outpost, and where Peter Minuit "bought" Manhattan from the Algonquins for the grand sum of $24. This is where George Washington bade farewell to his troops at the end of the Revolutionary War, and where he was inaugurated as the first president of the United States. Here the New York Stock Exchange was born beneath a buttonwood tree, and here over 20 million immigrants entered the country on their way to new and often difficult lives as Americans.

Whispers of this early history still echo throughout Lower Manhattan, in sites tucked away among the glistening towers and stone fortresses of corporate and financial America. In this most compressed of cities, this is the most compressed of neighborhoods. Everything here—the old and the new, the glitzy and the drab—is squeezed together on narrow, crooked streets that seem to belong more to the past than to the present.

Alas, lower Manhattan is also site of the former World Trade Center, whose ghost lingers over everything. Streets down here are emptier than they used to be, and some once-bustling small businesses have closed. However, with the ex-

ception of the World Trade Center site itself, all of downtown Manhattan is now fully accessible, with all subway lines running.

Orientation

Lower Manhattan includes roughly everything south of City Hall. To take in all the sights here in one day would be extremely difficult—a trip to the Statue of Liberty and Ellis Island alone takes about four hours. But since everything's within walking distance of everything else, it's easy to pick out sights that interest you and skip the rest.

Highlights include the Statue of Liberty and Ellis Island boat tour (or the Staten Island Ferry—an excellent way to see the harbor free of charge), Wall Street and the New York Stock Exchange, the National Museum of the American Indian, the Museum of Jewish Heritage, the South Street Seaport/Fulton Fish Market, and the World Trade Center Viewing Platform at the corner of Liberty Street and Broadway. Many area businesses and restaurants are closed weekends, but commercial attractions such as South Street Seaport remain open. Be sure to keep a map handy—it's easy to get lost down here.

During the summer, the **Alliance for Downtown New York,** 212/566-6700, offers free 90-minute Wall Street Walking Tours every Thursday and Saturday at noon. The tours leave from the U.S. Custom House (now the National Museum of the American Indian) at Bowling Green and explores such sites as the New York Stock Exchange, the Federal Reserve Building, and the Stone Street Historic District.

BATTERY PARK, THE STATUE OF LIBERTY, AND BOWLING GREEN

At Manhattan's tip is Battery Park—a gentle, crescent-shaped park filled with curved pathways, statues, and sculptures. Built on landfill, it's lined by the wide **Admiral George Dewey Promenade.** Wooden benches along the Promenade make great places to relax in the sun and enjoy superb harbor views. At the park's south end is the

E. B. WHITE ON NEW YORK CITY

On any person who desires such queer prizes, New York will bestow the gift of loneliness and the gift of privacy. It is this largess that accounts for the presence within the city's wall of a considerable section of the population: for the residents of Manhattan are to a large extent strangers who have pulled up stakes somewhere and come to town, seeking sanctuary or fulfillment or some greater or lesser grail. The capacity to make such dubious gifts is a mysterious quality of New York. It can destroy an individual, or it can fulfill him, depending a good deal on luck.

E. B. White

MANHATTAN

NEIGHBORHOODS: AN OVERVIEW

New York City's neighborhoods are described below, in order from south to north.

Lower Manhattan
Also known as the **Financial District** and **Wall Street,** this is the city's oldest developed area. It's full of historic buildings and towering, glass-sheathed skyscrapers. Near its northern edge is Ground Zero, the site of the former World Trade Center.

Chinatown, Little Italy, and the Lower East Side
Just north of the Financial District, and in startling contrast to it, is an area of low-slung brick buildings housing small apartments and bustling businesses. Chinatown is booming; Little Italy disappearing. The Lower East Side was once home to thousands of Eastern European Jews. It's now mostly Asian and Latino but is still known for its Jewish-owned discount shops.

SoHo and TriBeCa
Short for "**So**uth of **Ho**uston" (a major cross street) and "**Tri**angle **Be**low **Ca**nal," SoHo and TriBeCa were once commercial warehouse districts. SoHo was discovered by artists in the 1970s and is now a trendy hot spot filled with boutiques, restaurants, bars, and galleries. TriBeCa has some of the same, but is considerably less undeveloped.

The East Village
Since the 1960s, the scruffy East Village has been a haven for young artistic types. Despite encroaching gentrification, it's still the best place in the city for cheap coffeehouses, bars, and restaurants. **Alphabet City** is the term used for the eastern section of the East Village, where the avenues take on letter names—A, B, C, and D.

Greenwich Village
For decades a bohemian capital, Greenwich Village today is largely overrun with tourists and teens. Wonderful blocks rich with atmosphere still remain, however, especially in the West Village. West of the West Village is the cobblestoned **Meatpacking District,** once known for its warehouses, now known for its trendy nightlife.

Gramercy Park and Murray Hill
Though primarily quiet and sedate residential neighborhoods, both Gramercy Park and Mur-

---

MANHATTAN

East Coast War Memorial, featuring a giant bronze American eagle by sculptor Albino Manca and granite slabs engraved with the names of WW II casualties. At the north end, half submerged in the harbor, is the **American Merchant Marines Memorial,** an eerie Marisol sculpture of a drowning man reaching up to his comrades. Behind the sculpture is **Pier A,** the last remaining historic pier in New York, built in 1886.

Battery Park is part of "the Battery," the term used for the whole downtown tip of Manhattan. The name comes from the battery of cannons that once stood along Battery Place, on the park's north side. The Dutch erected the cannons to protect Fort Amsterdam, their original settlement, established in 1624–25. The fort was located where the former U.S. Custom House is today.

Castle Clinton

Though not much to look at now, this roofless red sandstone ring near the north end of the promenade was once an American fort protecting the city against the British. When it was built in 1807, it stood on an outcropping of land some 200 feet out in the harbor and could only be reached by drawbridge.

After the War of 1812, the fort was converted into the Castle Garden theater. In 1850, P. T. Barnum made a fortune at the theater by presenting Swedish singer Jenny Lind. Barnum was New York's original impresario and the man who coined the phrase "there's a sucker born every minute." He created such a fervor over Lind—hitherto unknown in America—that tens of thousands turned out to welcome her when she arrived in New York. Six thousand people paid three dollars each—a lot of money at the time—for the privilege of hearing her sing.

From 1855 to 1890, before the establishment of Ellis Island, Castle Clinton served as the Immigrant

ray Hill have their share of history and unusual attractions. Here you'll find **Little India,** centered on Lexington Avenue between 26th and 29th Streets.

Chelsea and the Garment District
Chelsea harbors many lovely residential blocks, a few deserted ones, a large gay community, a dwindling Latino one, and an ever-increasing number of lively restaurants and shops. The **Flatiron District,** centered on the historic Flatiron building on 23rd Street and Fifth Avenue, is also burgeoning with restaurants and shops. The small wholesale **Flower District** is on Sixth Avenue, between 26th and 28th Streets, and the sprawling **Garment District** starts just north of Chelsea.

Midtown
Most of Manhattan's skyscrapers are found in Midtown, along with most of its offices, major hotels, theaters, shops, restaurants, department stores, and visitor attractions. The **Theater District** is on the west side of Midtown and centers on Times Square. The **Diamond District** is on 47th Street between Fifth and Sixth Avenues.

The Upper East Side
For the most part, this is a hushed and elegant neighborhood that's home to some of New York's wealthiest residents. Museums here include the Metropolitan Museum of Art and the Frick Collection.

The Upper West Side
In some parts shabby and genteel, in other parts imposing and ornate, this neighborhood is home to many actors, writers, musicians, dancers, and intellectuals, as well as Lincoln Center and the American Museum of Natural History.

Harlem
Though one of the city's least explored areas, Harlem has much to offer, both in terms of its African American history and its architecture. Highlights include the Apollo Theater and the Studio Museum of Harlem. **Morningside Heights,** home to Columbia University, is on the west edge of Harlem. **East Harlem,** predominantly Hispanic, lies east of Fifth Avenue, and **Washington Heights,** to the north, is home to the medieval Cloisters museum.

Landing Depot. In 1896 it was remodeled into the New York Aquarium. A beloved institution for generations, the aquarium was nonetheless closed in the 1940s due primarily to Parks Commissioner Robert Moses. Some said that Moses closed the aquarium as an act of revenge against the city because it had refused to let him use the park for his proposed Brooklyn-Battery Bridge.

Today, Castle Clinton houses a small bookstore, tourist information center, and ticket booth for the Statue of Liberty and Ellis Island. A small National Park Service museum on the monument's east side chronicles the Castle's history. It's open daily 8:30 A.M.–5 P.M., 212/344-7220. Admission is free.

Statue of Liberty and Ellis Island Immigration Museum

Visible from Battery Park is New York's most famous symbol, the Statue of Liberty. Despite all the clichés, sentimentalities, and ironies attached to the statue, it's still a powerful sight. If nothing else, there's something strangely eloquent about an enormous statue of a woman standing alone above a choppy blue-gray sea.

The Statue of Liberty Enlightening the World, created by sculptor Frédéric-Auguste Bartholdi, was given to the United States by France in the late 1800s. The French people paid for the sculpture largely because they believed in the American cause and wanted to show support. The statue was made in France and shipped to New York in 214 crates. But once here, getting the statue erected proved difficult. In 1876, its right arm, carrying the torch, was set up in Madison Square Park in what was supposed to be a temporary exhibit. The arm sat there for over seven years, however, while its American supporters tried to raise money for the statue's base. Finally, journalist Joseph Pulitzer, himself an immigrant from

MANHATTAN

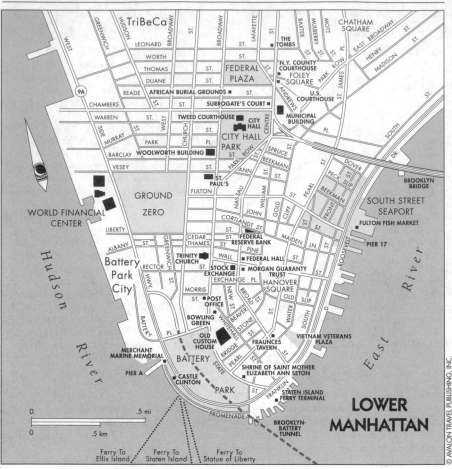

LOWER MANHATTAN

© AVALON TRAVEL PUBLISHING, INC.

Hungary, ran a major campaign in the *New York World* and raised the necessary $100,000. Eighty percent of that money came from contributions of less than a dollar.

On the base of the Statue of Liberty is inscribed the passage from Emma Lazarus's famous poem: "Give me your tired, your poor/Your huddled masses yearning to breathe free. . . ." The statue itself, restored in 1986, stands 151 feet tall and has a three-foot mouth, an eight-foot index finger, and a 25-foot waist. An elevator ascends to the top of the pedestal, but the only way up to the crown from there is via a narrow

spiral staircase. It's a 22-story climb that is decidedly not for the claustrophobic, the very young, or the elderly. Unless you make it over on the first boat, expect long waits to get inside. If you don't have enough patience for the wait, rest assured that the views of Manhattan island from the base—while not bird's eye—are almost as good as those from the crown.

A half mile north of Liberty Island is Ellis Island, the primary point of entry for immigrants to the United States from 1892 to 1924. From a distance, the main building looks like a Byzantine castle, with red-brick towers topped with white domes. Inside, the cavernous halls still seem to echo with the voices of the 12 million immigrants who passed through here.

After a $150-million restoration, the facility's main building opened as a museum in 1990. Powerful black-and-white photographs, taped oral histories, and other exhibits re-create the immigrant experience. Visitors pass through the Baggage Room, the Registry Room, and the physical examination rooms, where those who were ill were marked on the shoulder with chalk and taken to separate quarters where they were treated. Two excellent films are also shown; tickets to the free screenings must be picked up at the information desk upon entering. Outside, across a narrow waterway, stand acres of eerie abandoned red-brick buildings, once also used by the immigration service and now going to seed.

Ferries serve both the Statue of Liberty and Ellis Island on the same trip. The boats leave from the dock near Castle Clinton every half-hour 9 A.M.–3:50 P.M. during peak season, and every 45 minutes 9:30 A.M.–3:15 P.M. the rest of the year. For schedule information, call the Circle Line at 212/269-5755; www.circlelineferry.com. Admission to the monuments is free, but the ferry tickets cost adults $10, seniors $8, children 3–17 $4, under three free. Tickets go on sale at Castle Clinton at 8:30 A.M., and it's best to arrive early to avoid the inevitable long lines. Expect security screening; knapsacks are discouraged.

Staten Island Ferry

Few people—New Yorkers or tourists—ever get around to exploring Staten Island, but nearly everyone rides the free Staten Island ferry, one of the best deals in the city. The views of Manhattan from the harbor are spectacular, especially at twilight when the sunset reflects off a hundred thousand windows, or at night, when the skyline lights up like a carnival midway. The sights inside the ferry are fun as well: New Yorkers of every ethnicity bump up against tourists of every nationality; an ageless shoeshine man toils tirelessly up and down the aisles; young musicians quietly strum guitars.

On your right, as you head toward Staten Island, are Ellis Island and the Statue of Liberty. On your left are Governors Island and the Verrazano-Narrows Bridge. Governors Island, where 1,500 Confederate soldiers were imprisoned during the Civil War, became a U.S. Coast Guard Station in 1966. The Coast Guard left in late 1998, and now the island's future remains up in the air. The city is considering various development projects, including public parks and luxury housing. In the waters far beneath the Verrazano-Narrows Bridge is an odd artificial ledge, made up of the bricks and debris from hundreds upon hundreds of condemned tenement buildings torn down in the 1930s. Informally known as the Doorknob Grounds, the ledge is a spawning area for fish.

The Staten Island ferries, 718/727-2508, www.siferry.com, operate 24 hours a day, leaving from the southern tip of Manhattan every 15 minutes during rush hour, every half-hour during much of the day, and every hour at night.

7 State Street

Across State Street from Battery Park is a lone Federal-style house almost strangled by the buildings towering around it. The house was built around 1800, when State Street was an elegant residential promenade. The columns on its curved wooden porch may have been made from ships' masts. During the Civil War, Union Army officers lived here, where they could keep an eye on their troops camped out in Battery Park.

The house is now the **Shrine of Saint Mother Elizabeth Ann Seton,** 212/269-6865, commemorating the first American-born saint (1774–1821). Once a resident of State Street, Seton was canonized in 1975. Visitors are welcome inside, where a peaceful chapel invites contemplation. Open daily 6:30 A.M.–5 P.M.; Mass on Saturday at 12:15 P.M. and Sunday at 9 A.M. and noon.

New York Unearthed

Just behind the shrine, in the basement of one of the skyscrapers surrounding it, is a small, archaeological museum called New York Unearthed. The museum's actual address is 17 State St., but the entrance is in back, separate from the main building. Inside are pottery shards, Native American

MANHATTAN

artifacts, coins, jewelry, and more, arranged in a time line, as well as a hokey 10-minute video purporting to take you into the bowels of the earth. The museum, 212/748-8628, is run by the South Street Seaport. It's open Mon.–Fri. noon–5 P.M. Admission is free.

National Museum of the American Indian

At State Street and Battery Place is the stunning former U.S. Custom House, a 1907 beaux arts masterpiece designed by Cass Gilbert. Standing on the site of New York's first European settlement, Fort Amsterdam, the Custom House now houses the George Gustav Heye Center of the Smithsonian's National Museum of the American Indian. Opened in late 1994, the center is a precursor to, and will eventually be a branch of, a larger American Indian museum slated to open in Washington, D.C. Inside the center are displays holding some of the country's finest Native American art and artifacts, ranging in date of origin from 3200 B.C. to the 20th century. The maze of galleries surrounds a gorgeous elliptical rotunda lined with Reginald Marsh murals.

Also in the first-class museum are two sophisticated museum shops, a library, and a video room with daily screenings. The Heye Center, 1 Bowling Green, 212/514-3700, www.nmai.si.edu, is open daily 10 A.M.–5 P.M. and Thursday 5–8 P.M. Admission is free.

Don't leave the museum without noticing the anthropomorphized sculptures of the four continents standing out front; under the circumstances, they're more than a little ironic. Designed by Daniel Chester French, who's best known for his Lincoln Monument in Washington, D.C., the sculptures show a personified young "America" of European ancestry holding a sheath of corn in her lap while an American Indian hovers uncertainly behind her. The area in front of the Custom House was also where Peter Minuit closed his $24 deal with the Algonquins.

Bowling Green

The Custom House sits on the southern edge of small, circular Bowling Green, the city's first park. Used initially as a cattle market and then as a parade ground, the park was leased out as a bowling green in 1733 for the fee of one peppercorn per year. A statue of King George III once stood in the park, but irate patriots tore it down on July 9, 1776. Parts of the statue were then melted down "to make musket balls so that his troops will have melted Majesty fired at them"; other parts were found in a swamp in Connecticut as recently as 1972.

Today, all that remains from Bowling Green's Colonial era is its encircling iron fence. Brought from England in 1771, the fence was erected to protect King George's statue and keep out "all the filth and dirt in the neighborhood."

Broadway

Broadway, the city's central and most idiosyncratic avenue, begins at the north end of Bowling Green. Once an Algonquin trail, it runs diagonally the entire length of Manhattan and on up into upstate, where it's known as Albany Post Road. A street of commerce, entertainment, and public ceremony, it's witnessed everything from Washington's first public reading of the Declaration of Independence, to Malcolm X's assassination 189 years later (at the Audubon Ballroom, Broadway and 166th Street).

One of Broadway's southernmost addresses of note is the former **Cunard Building,** at 25 Broadway, now a U.S. post office. Designed by Benjamin Morris in 1921, the building boasts a splendid domed lobby lined with frescoes of sailing ships, mermaids, and maps highlighting the voyages of Leif Eriksson, Sebastian Cabot, Christopher Columbus, and Sir Francis Drake.

Across the street from the Cunard Building is the small **Museum of American Financial History,** 28 Broadway, 212/908-4110. The museum is open Tues.–Sat. 10 A.M.–4 P.M. Admission is $2. "World of Finance" walking tours that include visits to Wall Street and the New York Stock Exchange leave from the museum weekly.

BROAD STREET AREA

Stone Street

About two blocks southeast of Bowling Green (off Broad Street) is Stone Street, a narrow, nondescript lane that in 1658 became the first paved street in Manhattan. Legend has it that the street's resident brewer, Oloff Stephensen Van Cortlandt, had the street paved at the urging of his wife and her friends, who hated the dust raised by the brewery's horses and carts. The job was completed in three years, with most of the work done by African slaves.

Fraunces Tavern

At the corner of Broad and Pearl Streets is the red-brick, yellow-shuttered Fraunces Tavern, a 1907 reconstruction of the historic pub where George Washington bade good-bye to his troops in 1783. During the late 1700s, Samuel Fraunces, whom many historians believe was a black French West Indian, owned Fraunces Tavern. If so, Fraunces, also known as Black Sam, would have been one of the most important African Americans of his day. Following Washington's election to the presidency, Fraunces was appointed steward of the presidential mansion.

Though not especially known for its historical accuracy (no one is really sure what the original Fraunces Tavern looked like), the reconstructed site offers a recently restored taproom/restaurant and informal museum with exhibits on early American history. The taproom/restaurant, 54 Pearl St., 212/968-1776, is open Mon.–Fri. for lunch and dinner, and Saturday for dinner. The museum, 212/425-1778, is open Tues.–Fri. 10 A.M.–5 P.M., Saturday 11 A.M.–4 P.M. Admission is adults $3, students and seniors $2, under seven free.

On the block surrounding the tavern is one of the few surviving groups of 18th- and 19th-century buildings in Lower Manhattan.

Vietnam Veterans' Plaza

One block east of the tavern sits the windswept Vietnam Veterans' Plaza, 55 Water St., where translucent blocks of glass are engraved with the heart-wrenching writings of Vietnam veterans. Worn down by the elements, the engravings are hard to read in more ways than one.

New York City Police Museum

After years of being housed in the Police Academy on East 20th Street, New York's police museum now has a new home, but is still filled with the same fascinating displays. One is devoted to antique firearms, including a palm-size pistol, a long-barreled "game getter," and a .410-caliber cane, circa 1895. Another explains how fingerprints are used in crime detection, and another chronicles New York's mobsters. Al Capone's baptism and marriage certificates are on display, along with his machine guns and 75-diamond belt buckle.

Most intriguing of all is an exhibit entitled "Recently Acquired Contraband Weapons: Youth Gang Weapons." Here you'll see a concrete-filled blackjack, a nail ring with a sharp blade, a dagger disguised as a fountain pen, and a baseball bat with horseshoes attached. The bat's wielder apparently wanted the police to believe that his victim had been kicked to death by a horse.

The museum, 100 Old Slip, between South and Water Sts., 212/480-3100, www.nycpolicemuseum.org, is open Tues.–Sat. 10 A.M.–5 P.M. Admission is free.

Hanover Square

A few blocks north of Fraunces Tavern, where Pearl Street meets William Street, is Hanover Square. Today the square is just a small park with a few benches, but it once stood at the heart of a fine residential district whose most notorious resident was the Scotsman William Kidd. Captain Kidd, as he is more commonly known, was a privateer commissioned by the British crown to capture pirate ships. He was hanged in England in 1701 for murdering his gunner. Hanover Square was also where William Bradshaw published the city's first newspaper, the *New York Gazette*, in 1725.

On the square's south side is a handsome dark-brown Italianate building with a blue awning. Known as the India House, it's been the home of Hanover Bank (1851–54) and the N.Y. Cotton Exchange (1870–85). Today it houses **Harry's at Hanover Square,** 1 Hanover Square, 212/425-3412, a clubby steak house for Wall Streeters.

Delmonico's

One block west of Hanover Square, at 56 Beaver St., is the former Delmonico's building, perched

MANHATTAN

on a triangular plot of land between two narrow streets. New York's premier restaurant for generations, Delmonico's almost single-handedly changed America's eating habits. Before Delmonico's, the city's only eateries were grimy boardinghouses and rough-and-ready taverns, serving what Charles Dickens called "piles of indigestible matter." Then in 1827, a family of Swiss restaurateurs introduced to America the idea of fresh food served in a clean environment. It was a welcome innovation and Delmonico's took off. For 96 years, nearly everyone who was anyone ate here or at other locations later established farther uptown. Boss Tweed, Lillian Russell, Diamond Jim Brady, Jenny Lind, and Oscar Wilde—all were among the restaurant's patrons. The original Delmonico's restaurants shut down in 1923; the current version opened in 1998.

WALL STREET

One block north of Hanover Square, Pearl Street bumps into that most famous of New York thoroughfares: Wall Street. Before heading west toward the canyon of financial buildings, look right, towards the East River, where the city's slave market once stood. Established by the British in the late 1600s to accommodate the Royal African Company's growing human cargo, this was once the busiest slave market outside of Charleston, South Carolina. In the early 1700s, nearly 20 percent of New York City's inhabitants were slaves, and it was here they were examined and sold to the highest bidder.

The wall for which Wall Street was named was erected by the Dutch in 1653 to defend the city against an expected attack by the British (Britain and the Netherlands were at war at that time). All able-bodied men were called upon to dig a ditch from river to river and "prepare jointly the stakes and rails." The attack never did come, and the British tore down the wall in 1699.

If you've never seen it before, Wall Street will probably seem surprisingly narrow, dark, and short. Surrounded by towering edifices that block out the sun most of the day, the street stretches only about a third of a mile before bumping into the lacy, Gothic spires of Trinity Church.

The Regent Wall Street and Morgan Guaranty Trust

At 55 Wall St. is an impressive landmark building—now the Regent Wall Street hotel (see Accommodations, below)—lined with double tiers of Ionic and Corinthian columns. The Ionic ones were hauled here from Quincy, Massachusetts, by 40 teams of oxen. Built in 1842, the building was originally the Merchants' Exchange, while from 1863 to 1899, it served as the U.S. Customs House.

At 23 Wall St. is the Morgan Guaranty Trust building, erected by J. P. Morgan in 1913. About halfway down the length of the building are the pockmarks left by a 1920 explosion that killed 33 people and injured 400 others. The bomb—strapped to a driverless horse cart—may have been the work of anarchists intent upon attacking J. P. and capitalism, but nothing was proven one way or another.

Federal Hall National Memorial

Across the street from Morgan Guaranty Trust is the Federal Hall Memorial, 26 Wall St., at Broad,

© CHRISTIANE BIRD

looking down Wall Street to Trinity Church

MANHATTAN

A DYING CANOPY OF GREEN

Street trees in New York City have always had a tough time of it. Their soil pits are often too compacted, their rooting spaces are tight, and their water supply is sporadic. They also have to put up with interminable indignities, including pollution, vandalism, dog urine, and the occasional gash inflicted by a passing car or bus.

In recent years, however, thanks largely to budget cuts, things have gone from bad to worse. Though the exact number of trees in New York is unknown, the Parks Department estimates that since the mid-1980s, the city's tree population has declined from around 700,000 to 500,000. Some 15,000 to 20,000 trees die each year, while only 9,000 new ones are planted. Norway maples and Callery pear trees, the most prevalent of the streets' 50-odd species, have been especially hard hit.

212/825-6888. The fine Greek Revival building, fronted by a wide set of stairs, makes a perfect perch for watching the Wall Streeters and fellow tourists go by. Beside the stairs is a bronze statue of George Washington, who took his inaugural oath of office here in 1789. Back then, the English City Hall stood on this site, and Washington, dressed in a plain brown suit, spoke to the crowds from the building's second-story balcony.

The English City Hall also witnessed the 1735 libel trial of John Pete Zenger, publisher of the *Weekly Journal.* Zenger's acquittal established a precedent for freedom of the press, a concept later incorporated into the Bill of Rights.

Inside today's Federal Hall—which was built in 1842, well after these historic events—are several small exhibits. One exhibit commemorates Washington's inauguration; the Bible that he used to take his oath of office is on display.

The Federal Hall Memorial is open Mon.–Fri. 9 A.M.–5 P.M. Admission is free.

New York Stock Exchange

Just south of Federal Hall Memorial, the enormous building resembling a Roman temple is the New York Stock Exchange, 20 Broad St., 212/656-

5168, www.nyse.com. As a plaque on the building reads, the Exchange was founded in 1792 when a group of 24 brokers drew up a trading agreement beneath a buttonwood tree on Wall Street.

For all its grandeur, the Exchange has seen a lot of less-than-admirable human behavior in its day. In the 1860s, financial titans Jay Gould, Jim Fish, and Daniel Drew—with the help of bribed New York legislators—manipulated the market so that they could wrest control of the Erie Railroad from Cornelius "Commodore" Vanderbilt. In 1869, Gould and Fisk again used their financial wiles to try to corner the gold market; their effort failed, but it led to a 10-year panic that caused thousands of businesses to fail and the doors of the Exchange to close. In 1901, the struggle between J. P. Morgan and E. H. Harriman for control of Northern Pacific Railway led to another market collapse and nationwide panic. And in our own day, Ivan Boesky and Michael Milken got their 15 minutes of infamy and time behind bars for securities violations.

Not surprisingly, tours of the Exchange don't delve into these sordid details. Instead, they begin with a series of bland exhibits describing how the stock market works. Then visitors are herded into a glassed-in balcony viewing area from which they can watch the frenzy of the trading floor below. A recorded voice explains what's going on as the traders rush to and fro, but it's not particularly illuminating or insightful. Even the Crash of 1929 is glossed over as a day of "reckless speculation" that, due to increased regulation, could never happen again.

Free tickets to the Exchange are given out weekdays, 9 A.M.–3:30 P.M., on a first-come, first-served basis.

Trinity Church

Trinity Church, at Wall St. and Broadway, 212/602-0872, is one of the oldest and wealthiest churches in Manhattan. The present building—the third Trinity Church to be built on the site—was designed by architect Richard Upjohn in 1846.

Up until 1892, Trinity was the city's tallest building, thanks to its 264-foot tower from which visitors could view the sea. The Gothic Revival church also boasts one of the first stained-glass windows installed in America.

Inside, a small museum documents this and other aspects of Trinity's history. Not to be found in the museum's chronology is the fact that during the 1800s, Trinity—which owned all the land west of Broadway between Fulton and Christopher Streets—was the un-Christianlike slumlord of nearly 500 tenement buildings. The tenements were finally razed in the early 1900s, due to embarrassing publicity.

Trinity is surrounded by a pretty cemetery where some of New York's most illustrious early residents are buried. Among them are Alexander Hamilton, the first secretary of the treasury; Robert Fulton, inventor of the steamship; and Charlotte Temple, whose seduction and abandonment by a British officer was romanticized in a popular novel of the day, *A Tale of Truth* by Susanna Rowson. Trinity Church is open Mon.–Fri. 7 A.M.–6 P.M., Sat.–Sun. 7 A.M.–4 P.M. The church's museum is open Mon.–Fri. 9–11:45 A.M. and 1–3:45 P.M., Saturday 10 A.M.–3:45 P.M., and Sunday 1–3:45 P.M.

North to Liberty Street

Across the street from Trinity Church is **Irving Trust Company,** 1 Wall Street. Known for its lush art deco lobby done up in red, orange, and gold mosaics, the 1932 building is well worth a quick look.

One block north of Trinity, at 120 Broadway, stands the massive, light gray **Equitable Building,** which shoots straight up for 40 stories, darkening all the streets around it. Though nothing special to look at, the building did New York and the entire country an enormous favor; its heavy presence led to the nation's first zoning laws in 1916. The laws required that new buildings over a certain height be designed with tiered setbacks to let more light down into the streets. Hence, the wedding-cake look characteristic of many New York skyscrapers.

At 140 Broadway, in front of **Marine Midland Bank** (designed by Skidmore, Owings & Merrill), is a wide, empty plaza with the huge, 28-by-28-by-28-foot *Red Cube* at its center. The creation of sculptor Isamu Noguchi, the cube is so large

that a building permit was required before it could be erected.

Just east of Marine Midland Bank and visible down Cedar Street, is *Group of Four Trees,* a sculpture by Jean Dubuffet. Beside the sculpture is a sunken garden with meteoritelike sculptures designed by Noguchi; behind it is **Chase Manhattan Bank.** Completed in 1961, the bank was the first big office building built in the financial district after WW II. It helped spur the area's rapid development in the late 1960s.

Federal Reserve Bank of New York

This massive, fortresslike structure of dark limestone fills an entire city block and safeguards one of the world's largest accumulations of gold—over 10,000 tons. Built in the style of an Italian Renaissance palace, the Federal Reserve is a "bank for banks," where cash reserves are stored. In addition, nearly 80 foreign countries keep gold bullion here, in thick-walled vaults five stories underground. As international fortunes change, the bars are simply moved from one country's pile to the next. Most of the gold was deposited here during WW II—when many European countries needed a safe storage site—and hasn't left the building since.

Tours of the Fed include an informative video and a look at the vaults. Some of the gold bars are reddish due to their copper content; some are especially shiny due to their silver content; and all seem fake, looking more like giant bricks of candy than precious metal. No one has ever attempted to rob the Fed, but if someone should, the entire building shuts down in 31 seconds. The guards are tested on their shooting ability monthly, and there's a shooting range in the building (not open to the public).

The Federal Reserve Bank is at 33 Liberty St., between Nassau and Liberty, 212/720-6130, www.ny.frb.org. The free one-hour tours are offered Mon.–Fri. 9:30 A.M.–2:30 P.M., and reservations must be made at least one week in advance.

GROUND ZERO AND ENVIRONS

Though no longer extant, the twin, 110-story towers of Minoru Yamasaki's World Trade Center—

once bounded by Church, West, Vesey, and Liberty Streets—still seem to hover over downtown Manhattan, and all of New York. Erected between 1966 and 1970 by the New York and New Jersey Port Authority, the 1,350-foot-high towers were among the first modern skyscrapers built with weight-bearing walls instead of the steel frame construction popular since the late 1800s.

Entering the World Trade Center complex from the east on Church Street, visitors would climb a wide set of steps onto Tobin Plaza, where it was hard not to feel overwhelmed. The plaza was so stark, and the towers so tall, that human beings seemed insignificant—which was just one of the many complaints about the complex initially voiced by everyone from architectural critics to office workers. The complex is sterile, people would say, it's boring, and it doesn't fit in with the rest of downtown. All those objections were valid, and yet, when you sat down near the plaza's fountain, and looked up, up, up, the sight was startling—that anything manmade could be so tall.

In the end, the World Trade Center stood for just 28 years, during which time New Yorkers grew accustomed to them. Their sleek self-containment, their shimmering prosperity, their constant reassuring presence. . . . New York didn't know what it had until it was gone.

The cleanup of Ground Zero, as the former World Trade Center site become known, was completed in June 2002. Proposals for an overall design of the 16-acre area, complete with a memorial, were unveiled the following month, but as of this writing, no final plans for the site have been adopted.

A 16-foot-high **World Trade Center Viewing Platform** is at the intersection of Liberty Street and Broadway; tickets for the platform, required for months following the disaster, are no longer necessary.

World Financial Center and Battery Park City

Across the street from where No. 6 World Trade Center (the U.S. Customs House) once stood, is the World Financial Center, designed by Cesar Pelli and Associates. Though badly damaged during the September 11 attacks, the Center has since been restored to its former self: a glittering complex of ultramodern office towers, complete with first-class shops and restaurants, a pleasant outdoor plaza, and the **Winter Garden**—a splendid glass-domed public space with enormous palm trees imported from the Mojave Desert. Both the plaza and the Winter Garden overlook the Hudson River, and the Winter Garden is the site of frequent free concerts. Call 212/945-0505 for information.

Stretching from the World Financial Center south to Battery Park City is a breezy esplanade and park offering great river views. Along the way are playful sculptures, inviting benches, and pockets of green. Residential Battery Park City, however, is a disappointment. Largely built on landfill excavated during construction of the WTC towers, it's glitzy and sterile, with little to interest the visitor.

The esplanade and park also run north of the World Financial Center, to what is known as the **North Lawn,** filled with sunbathers and ball players during the summer. The park officially ends at Chamber Street but still further north, the shoreline and piers are slowly being developed into what will become the **Hudson River Park.**

Skyscraper Museum

Scheduled to open in early 2003, the Skyscraper Museum, 212/968-1961, www.skyscraper.com, will be located at the southern tip of Battery Park City, in the same building as the new Ritz-Carlton Hotel. The museum will focus on the history of New York's most famous icons.

Museum of Jewish Heritage

Overlooking the Hudson River is a freestanding hexagon—symbolic of the Star of David—housing the new $21.5 million Museum of Jewish Heritage. Opened in 1997, and now undergoing a major expansion, it features thousands of moving photographs, cultural artifacts, and archival films documenting both the inconceivable inhumanity of the Holocaust and the resilience of the Jewish community. The museum, 18 First Pl., at Battery Pl., Battery Park City, 212/968-1800, www.mjhnyc.org, is open Sun.–Wed., 10 A.M.–5:45 P.M., Thursday 10 A.M.–8 P.M., and

Friday 10 A.M.–3 P.M. Admission is adults $7, students and seniors $5, under 5 free. Last tickets sold one hour before closing.

Fulton Street

Extending east from Ground Zero is a short, narrow street filled with discount clothing stores and cheap eateries. The street is named after Robert Fulton, who invented the steamship in 1807 and started a ferry service between Manhattan and Brooklyn in 1814. Each of Fulton's ferries could accommodate 200 passengers and numerous horses and wagons, and could cross the river in eight minutes. At the east end of Fulton Street, where it meets the East River, is the site of the old ferry terminal—now the Fulton Fish Market.

St. Paul's Chapel

On Broadway at Fulton Street is St. Paul's Chapel, 212/602-0874, dedicated in 1766. It's one of Manhattan's oldest buildings and the only one built by the British. Designed by Thomas McBean, the Georgian church is surprisingly light inside, with pale pink and blue walls, white trim, and cut-glass chandeliers. A coronet atop the pulpit is thought to be the only emblem of British nobility in New York surviving in its original place.

George Washington worshiped at St. Paul's, in a pew on the north aisle now marked with an oil painting of the Great Seal of the United States. The church was also a central place of solace for emergency workers toiling at the World Trade Center site following the September 11 attacks. Behind the chapel is a pretty 18th-century cemetery.

St. Paul's is open Mon.–Sat. 9 A.M.–3 P.M., Sunday 7 A.M.–3 P.M. Free classical music concerts are presented most Mondays at noon; call 212/602-0768 for details.

SOUTH STREET SEAPORT

Fulton Street meets the East River at South Street Seaport, one of the city's oldest and most historic areas. A thriving port during the 19th century, the seaport went into a steep decline in the 20th. In the early 1980s, the Rouse Company took over the place and filled it with commercial enterprises, restaurants, and shops. A surprising number of these enterprises went out of business in the early to mid 1990s, but today, the Seaport is once more on the upswing, renting out vacancies and attracting about 10 million visitors a year.

The Seaport's historic sites are scattered throughout the 11-block district. Many of the sites are free, but to get into the Seaport's three galleries and 19th-century sailing ships—or to join a walking tour—you'll need to purchase a ticket at the **Seaport Museum's Visitor Center** and ticket booth, 12 Fulton St., at South St. and Pier 16, 212/732-7678 or 212/748-8600, www.southstseaport.org. The center is open daily 10 A.M.–5 P.M., with extended hours in summer, closed Tuesdays in winter; tickets are adults $6, seniors $5, students $4, and children $3.

Schermerhorn Row is the heart of the Seaport. Built in 1812, it's made up of pretty, Federal-style buildings that once housed warehouses and accounting offices. Around back, at 171 John St., is the **A. A. Low Building,** an elegant 1850 hall used as a countinghouse during the China trade. The building now houses **Norway Galleries,** showcasing changing maritime exhibits. Next door is the **Children's Center,** 165 John St., with hands-on exhibits for kids, while down the street is the **Boat Building Shop,** John and South Sts., where boatwrights build and restore small wooden vessels.

Just beyond Schermerhorn Row are Piers 15 and 16, where a number of historic sailing ships are moored. The *Pioneer* is an 1885 schooner that cruises the harbor in summer; the *Peking* is a 1911 four-masted ship housing exhibits on maritime life. Not to be missed aboard the *Peking* is a fascinating documentary film about the ship's early journeys around stormy Cape Horn.

Also docked at Pier 16 are the modern boats of **Seaport Music Cruises,** 212/630-8888. The boats offer live blues, Latin, and jazz music cruises during the summer months; tickets cost $15–25.

Water Street

Many of the Seaport's other historic sites are along Water Street. The **Museum Gallery,** 213

Water St., specializes in exhibits on New York City history. Next door is **Bowne & Co., Stationers,** 211 Water St., a working 19th-century print shop. Down the street, between Beekman Street and Peck's Slip, is the **Seaman's Church Institute,** a large brick structure whose top floor resembles the hull of a steamship. Still in operation as a philanthropic society, the Seamen's Church once provided a safe haven for sailors who would all too often be shanghaied out of the regular boardinghouses. At 273 Water St. is one of Manhattan's oldest buildings, dating to the 1770s. The now-neglected structure once housed **Sportsmen's Hall,** a place known for its "rat pits" where rats were pitted against bull terriers.

Fulton Fish Market

The best part of South Street Seaport is the Fulton Fish Market, where the best time to visit is about 4 A.M. That's when you'll see enormous tuna carcasses being carved into steaks, big piles of shiny flat fish getting dumped into vats, basketfuls of crabs scrabbling over each other, and burly Italian fishmongers wrangling with their wholesalers. But even if you get here later in the morning, you'll still get a sense of what this boisterous, smelly, fishy place is all about.

Adjacent to Pier 17, the Fulton Market dates back to at least 1822, when vendors selling everything from fish to meat to produce set up their stalls here. By 1834, the messy fish dealers had been exiled to their own shed on the water, behind which floated vats filled with live fish. Use of these vats was discontinued in the early 1900s because of the East River's pollution. Today, ironically enough, most of the market's fish is trucked or flown in.

Up until recently, the fish market was largely controlled by organized crime. A 1995 crackdown by Mayor Giuliani, however, apparently dispersed such influences to the winds. "We say family down here," one fishmonger recently told the *Daily News.* "Brothers, sisters, sons. There are no gangsters here."

Note: Due to new, more stringent government regulations regarding the refrigeration of fish, the Fulton Fish Market, 212/487-8476, will be moving to Hunts Point in the Bronx in 2004.

AROUND CITY HALL

Woolworth Building

The Woolworth, 233 Broadway, between Barclay and Park Pl., stands at the edge of City Hall Park. Its glistening white walls and green copper roofs are probably best seen from a distance, where they can be appreciated in all their elegant 800-foot glory. But up close, the 1913 Cass Gilbert extravaganza is also a visual feast. Craggy-faced gargoyles peer down at you from the detailed Gothic exterior, while mosaic-covered ceilings grace the lobby. One lobby caricature shows the architect on the run, hugging a model of the building; another shows Frank Woolworth, king of the discount stores, counting out his nickels and dimes.

Woolworth, a farmer's son, began as a salesman earning $8 a week. By the time he built his $13.5 million headquarters here, however, he was able to pay for it in cash. Completed in 1913, "the Cathedral of Commerce" was the world's tallest building when it opened. President Wilson did the inaugural honors via telegraph from Washington, by pressing a button that illuminated the building's 80,000 lightbulbs.

Park Row and Newspapering

The diagonal street across from the Woolworth Building is Park Row, once the center of New York's newspaper industry. From the 1850s well into the 1920s, as many as 12 papers were published here, including Joseph Pulitzer's *New York World,* Horace Greeley's *New York Tribune,* Charles Anderson Dana's *New York Sun,* and the *New York Times.* The original home of the *Times,* 41 Park Row, still stands.

Tributes to newspapering still dot the immediate area. A statue of Benjamin Franklin stands at the corner of Park Row and Spruce Street. A statue of Horace Greeley—abolitionist, feminist, and coiner of the phrase "Go West, young man"—presides over the northeast quadrant of City Hall Park. The former 20th-century headquarters of the *New York Sun* is at the corner of Broadway and Chambers Street, where a bronze clock still reads, "The Sun It Shines for All." This building was also once home to the nation's

MANHATTAN

first department store, founded by A. T. Stewart in 1846. Initially ridiculed for the department-store concept, Stewart later became one of America's richest men.

City Hall Park

This busy park was once a cow pasture, then a gathering place for Revolutionary-era political meetings. Now it's the site of City Hall, one of the finest Federal-style buildings in New York. Inside the surprisingly small building is an unusual circular staircase that hangs with no visible signs of support. Open to the public are the Rotunda and the Governor's Room, which is lined with portraits by John Trumbull.

Visitors are welcome Mon.–Fri. 10 A.M.–3 P.M. For more information, call the Mayor's Office at 212/788-3000; www.nyc.gov.

A new **Visitor Information Kiosk** now stands at the southern tip of City Hall Park, on the Broadway sidewalk. The eight-foot-high octagon dispenses information, primarily about downtown New York, daily 8:00 A.M.–8:00 P.M.

Tweed Courthouse

Behind City Hall, at 52 Chambers St., is Tweed Courthouse. The building was named for William Marcy "Boss" Tweed, the corrupt Tammany Hall official who embezzled millions of dollars from the city. The courthouse was Tweed's most notorious project. It was projected to cost the city $250,000, but ultimately cost over $13 million thanks to exorbitant bills submitted by Tweed-controlled contractors. For just three tables and 40 chairs, the city paid $179,729. For carpets, $350,000. For brooms, $41,190. And then there were the gaudy courthouse thermometers—11 of them, each five feet long and one foot wide, with cheap paper fronts. Their cost: $7,500.

The Tweed Ring was exposed in 1871, the same year the building was completed. The "Boss" was tried in his own courthouse and sentenced to 12 years in prison for fraud, but the Court of Appeals reduced that sentence to one year on a legal technicality. In 1875, Tweed was arrested again on other charges of theft. While in prison awaiting trial, he escaped to Spain. There he had the bad luck to be recognized from a

THE "GREAT NEGRO PLOT"

The tragic "Great Negro Plot" of 1741, which resulted in 33 needless deaths, was supposedly hatched in a seedy Irish pub in Lower Manhattan. Hughson's Tavern, once located on Broadway near today's City Hall Park, had an unsavory reputation as a gathering place for sailors and prostitutes. After several mysterious fires erupted in the city, Mary Burton—an indentured servant working at the tavern—testified in court that the fires had been set by slaves who met with her employers at the bar. They were plotting to burn the entire city, she said, free all slaves, declare Hughson king, and divide the white women among the black men. On the basis of Burton's testimony alone, the Hughsons, their daughter, a prostitute, and four slaves were found guilty and hanged or burned at the stake.

But Burton's conspiracy charges didn't end there. Over the next few months, she began to point her finger wildly in all directions. Hysteria gripped the city as she accused first one slave and then another, then identified a white schoolteacher as the mastermind behind the plot. Only after she had accused several other white men in even more prominent positions did the judge declare it time to have "a little relaxation from this intricate pursuit." But by then, for many, it was far too late. Sixteen blacks and four whites had been hung, 13 blacks had been burned at the stake, and 70 blacks had been deported.

Thomas Nast caricature, and soon was returned to the Ludlow Street jail. He died there on April 12, 1878, at the age of 55.

Half-empty for years, the three-story Tweed Courthouse was recently renovated, and its lobby is notable for its WPA murals. The renovation fueled the Tweed legend; it was discovered that the supposedly solid-brass elevators the city paid for are merely brass plated.

The courthouse is now home to the city's Board of Education.

North of City Hall Park

At the north end of City Hall Park is the **Surrogate's Court and Hall of Records,** 31 Chambers

St., at Centre—a glorious, ostentatious building in the traditional beaux arts style. To its east is the skyscraping 1913 **Municipal Building,** designed by McKim, Mead & White. The building houses many city offices, including those of the justice of the peace, where as many as 14,000 couples are married every year. Photographers and flower vendors mill about the lobby, eager to help the happy couples celebrate their new status.

Brooklyn Bridge

South of the Municipal Building is the entrance ramp to one of the city's most spectacular sights, the Brooklyn Bridge. Nothing can compare to walking over this soaring span—intricate as a spider's web—with the roar of the traffic below you, the lights of Manhattan behind, and the mysteries of Brooklyn ahead. The best time to cross is at sunset, when the rays of the sun reflect off the steel cables and wires.

Design of the bridge was begun by John A. Roebling and completed by his son, Washington. Construction took 14 years, and the bridge finally opened in 1883. The world's first steel suspension bridge, it was built largely by Irish immigrants working for 12 ½ cents an hour.

From the beginning, the bridge's construction was plagued with tragedy. Only three weeks after the city approved the elder Roebling's plans, his foot was crushed by the Fulton Ferry. He died of gangrene a few weeks later. His son, then age 32, took over the project, but soon fell prey to caisson disease—known today as the bends. At the time, the dangers of rapid decompression were not yet understood, and Roebling and his employees spent hours working in the caissons (huge upside-down boxes filled with compressed air) far beneath the river. In the end, as many as 110 workers may have suffered or died from the disease.

When Roebling became too sick to work on site, he supervised the project from his Brooklyn Heights apartment, watching via telescope. His wife Emily became his emissary, carrying messages between Roebling and his foremen. By the time the bridge was finished, Emily was an engineer in her own right. A plaque in her honor can be found on the bridge, near the Brooklyn side.

Tragedy at the bridge didn't end with its completion. On the day of the grand opening, some 20,000 people crowded onto the span. Someone panicked, and in the resulting stampede, 12 people were killed. Future New York governor Al Smith, watching from the shore, said that the blue sky was suddenly filled with hats and umbrellas fluttering down into the river.

Next came the publicity stunts. In 1884, P. T. Barnum led 24 elephants across the bridge to prove that it was safe. In 1886, a stuntman named Steve Brodie "jumped" off the bridge. Some said he never actually took the plunge, that a dummy was used in his stead. But Brodie nonetheless became a celebrity, living off his stunt for the rest of his life. He lectured, appeared in museums, and opened a saloon that became a tourist attraction. To "pull a Brodie" still means to have pulled off an impossible feat.

African Burial Grounds

On the east side of Broadway, about one block north of City Hall Park (between Reade and Duane), is a new office building with an interesting history. In 1991, when workers were first digging the building's foundation, they unearthed one of the most exciting archaeological discoveries in Manhattan in recent decades—the African Burial Grounds.

This centuries-old boneyard dates to about 1755. At that time, blacks were not allowed to join the city's churches and so were buried outside the city limits. Scholars studying old city maps believe that the graveyard may once have covered nearly six acres and held the remains of 20,000 free and enslaved African Americans.

After the discovery of the graveyard, the new office building's site was adjusted, and more scholarly digging began. Excavating about 14,000 square feet, archaeologists discovered about 390 bodies, all buried east to west, with their heads toward Africa. Many were buried with seashells, and some in the remnants of British uniforms. During the Revolutionary War, the British offered freedom to any slave who joined in their cause.

A plaque and enclosed field of green now mark the excavation site near the corner of Elk and Duane Streets.

Foley Square

Just north and slightly east of City Hall Park is another government hub, this one dominated by two imposing courthouses and lots of criss-crossing traffic. The neoclassical **U.S. Courthouse,** designed by Cass Gilbert in 1936, is the building with the incongruous 32-story tower on top. Facing it is the 1926 **New York County Courthouse,** the inside rotunda of which is covered with worn WPA murals depicting "Law Through the Ages." Both buildings are open to the public, and if you've a hankering to see a trial, ask the guards at the doors which rooms are in session.

Foley Square is named after Thomas Foley, a Tammany Hall politician who conducted business out of his saloon—the last one of which was located in today's square. Foley was said to have had a soft heart. Above one of his saloons he kept a dozen beds for derelicts, whom he also fed for free. And he once borrowed over $100,000 to help the bankrupt husband of an old neighbor.

The Tombs

One block north of Foley Square, at 100 Centre St., is the forbidding New York Criminal Courts Building, an imposing gray hulk that makes even the innocent feel guilty. On one side of its columns are inscribed the stern words, "Where Law Ends There Tyranny Begins"; on the other, the daunting "Only the Just Man Enjoys Peace of Mind."

Both prison and courthouse, the Criminal Courts Building works around the clock in its disheartening, seemingly futile attempt to cope with the city's staggeringly high arrest load. Inside, Room 130 is the site of **Night Court,** a depressing yet eerily fascinating place where arraignments take place after hours. Night court is open to the public.

The building's lugubrious nickname, the "Tombs," actually refers to its 1835 predecessor, which stood about a block away. Built in a sort of recessed pit in an Egyptian Revival style, the first Tombs was designed to hold only about 350 prisoners, but often had a population exceeding several thousand. Officially, only prison officials and politicians were invited to witness the Tomb's frequent hangings, but the public would crowd onto the roofs of nearby buildings to join in the fun.

SHOPPING

Located directly across the street from Ground Zero, **Century 21,** 22 Cortlandt St., near Broadway, 212/227-9092, was shuttered for months after the attacks, but has since reopened at its old site. One of the city's largest and oldest discount clothing stores, it features designer wear and an especially good men's department.

Once just a record store, **J&R,** 23 Park Row and adjoining buildings, between Ann and Beekman Sts., near City Hall, 212/238-9000 or 800/221-8180, has branched out over the years to become a long row of shops selling every conceivable electronic device, including audio equipment, TVs, computers, and appliances. And, oh yes, they still sell recordings, too.

ACCOMMODATIONS

$100–150

At the **Cosmopolitan Hotel,** 95 West Broadway, at Chambers St., 212/566-1900 or 888/895-9400, www.cosmohotel.com, you'll find simple but clean rooms furnished with red carpeting, white furniture, comfortable beds, and ceiling fans. Though nothing special, the hotel does offer both an excellent location (within easy walking distance of TriBeCa, Chinatown, SoHo, and the Financial District) and reasonable rates; $119 s, $149 d.

$150–250

Near the South Street Seaport is **Manhattan Seaport Suites,** 129 Front St., near Wall St., 212/742-0003. The lobby is worn and the furnishings are nondescript, but the suites are relatively large and equipped with kitchenettes; $109 s, $175 d, $205–245 for a one-bedroom suite that accommodates four.

Designed mostly for businesspeople, the **Holiday Inn Wall Street,** 15 Gold St., at Platt St., 212/232-7700 or 800/HOLIDAY, www.HolidayInnWSD.com, offers small basic rooms equipped with high-speed Internet access, eight-foot-long desks and unlimited offices supplies. $169–319 s or d, $500–800 for suites; good weekend packages often available.

$250 and up

Wall Street's first and only hotel, the **Regent Wall Street,** 55 Wall St., between Hanover and William, 212/845-8600 or 800/545-4000, www.regenthotels.com, is housed in a historic 1842 building that was once home to the Merchants' Exchange. Built around a vast ballroom, with 60-foot-high Corinthian columns and marble walls, it offers luxuriously appointed rooms equipped with all the amenities. $335–525 s or d; $225–450 on the weekends.

One of the newest hotels in town, and located just north of the former World Trade Center site, the ultra-luxurious **Ritz-Carlton New York, Battery Park,** 2 West St., at Battery Pl., 212/344-0800, www.ritz-carlton.com, opened just five months after the September 11 attacks. Views from its upper floors are fantastic, while inside, you'll find the ultimate in deluxe accommodations, including goose-down pillows, original artwork by New York–based artists, and the services of a "water sommelier" (who'll offer you the choice of mineral waters). $425–625 s or d.

FOOD

American

At the foot of Brooklyn Bridge is Manhattan's oldest restaurant building, said to date back to 1794. It's now home to the casual, atmospheric **Bridge Cafe,** 279 Water St., near Dover, 212/227-3344, serving lots of seafood and a popular brunch; average entrée $18. Recently renovated, historic **Fraunces Tavern,** 54 Pearl St., at Broad St., 212/269-0144, offers solid American fare; average entrée $20. Spiffy **Delmonico's,** 56 Beaver St., at William St., 212/509-1144, with its elegant high ceilings and chandeliers, offers a mix of the innovative and the old-fashioned. Menu items range from sirloin buffalo steak to lobster Newburg; average entrée $27.

French

A downtown branch of acclaimed midtown bistro run by chef-turned-author Anthony Bourdain (author of *Kitchen Confidential,*), **Les Halles Downtown,** 15 John St., between Broadway and Nassau, 212/285-8585, is heralded for its "Amer-

GOT LUNCH?

During the 1992 Democratic Convention, some of the city's top restaurants—including the "21" Club, Lutece, and Four Seasons—celebrated the extravaganza by offering a $19.92 prix fixe luncheon. The program proved so popular that it's been repeated every summer since, with the luncheons' cost increasing one cent each year. In 2002, for example, nearly 200 top restaurants offered the $20.02 prix fixe lunch during the last week in June, with about 50 extending the program throughout the summer. It's a great way to sample the city's poshest eateries. Contact NYC & Company, the city's convention and visitors bureau, 212/397-9222, www.nycvisit.com, for details.

ican beef, French style" and lively atmosphere; average entrée $19.

Italian

The elegant, Old World **Ecco,** 124 Chambers St., between W. Broadway and Church, 212/227-7074, is a Northern Italian favorite situated in a cozy setting; average entrée $20.

Seafood

Once a hole-in-the-wall waterside bar, **Jeremy's Ale House,** 254 Front St., near Dover, 212/964-3537, is still best known for its pints, but it also offers simple fish dishes, burgers, and its trademark—fish and chips; average entrée $8.

Light Bites

Both the Statue of Liberty and Ellis Island have decent, albeit overpriced, cafeterias.

For scrumptious Argentine take-out, including over a dozen types of empanadas, stop by **Ruben's Empanadas,** 15 Bridge St., between Broad and Whitehead, 212/509-3825; empanadas, $3.

Near City Hall is **Ellen's Cafe,** 270 Broadway, at Chambers, 212/962-1257, an upscale coffee shop frequented by politicians. Ellen's is owned by Ellen Hart Sturm, a former Miss Subways whose face once graced placards on the IRT, BMT, and IND lines.

MANHATTAN

Chinatown, Little Italy, and the Lower East Side

No region of New York has been home to more immigrants than the East Side between the Brooklyn Bridge and Houston Street. Various ethnic groups have lived here over the years, including the Irish, Germans, and freed blacks in the mid-1800s; and the Chinese, Italians, and especially the Jews in the late 1800s and early 1900s. Around the turn of the century, over 700 people per acre lived on the Lower East Side, making it the second most crowded place in the world, after Bombay.

Today the district is still home to small enclaves of Jews and Italians, but it is the Asian population that has exploded. And a number of Latinos and West Africans have also moved in. On an island quickly becoming homogenized by white-collar professionals, this is one of the few districts left where you can see and feel the immigrant vibrancy that once characterized much of Manhattan. Jewish delis bump up against Spanish bodegas; West African grocery stores stand next to Chinese restaurants.

Orientation

Chinatown, Little Italy, and parts of the Lower East Side are the sorts of neighborhoods where you can have a great time wandering haphazardly about, going nowhere in particular. Especially in traditional Chinatown, the streets teem with jostling crowds and exotic markets. Chinatown's central street is Mott, just below Canal. What's left of Little Italy is centered along Mulberry Street just north of Canal. Orchard Street, lined with discount clothing shops, is the best place to get the flavor of the Lower East Side.

Chinatown can be visited at any time; afternoons and evenings are best for Little Italy. Orchard Street shops are at their liveliest on Sunday afternoon, but for serious shopping, go during the week. Don't visit the Lower East Side on Saturday, when many shops close for the Jewish Sabbath. All three neighborhoods are close to each other, though the easternmost sections of the Lower East Side are a hike.

CHINATOWN

The Chinese didn't begin arriving in New York until the late 1870s. Many were former transcontinental railroad workers who came to escape the violent persecution they were encountering on the West Coast. But they weren't exactly welcomed on the East Coast either. Pushed out of a wide variety of occupations, they were forced to enter low-status service work—part of the reason they established so many laundries.

Then came the Exclusion Acts of 1882, 1888, 1902, and 1924. Those acts prohibited further Chinese immigration—including the families of those who were already here—and denied Chinese the right to become American citizens. Chinatown became a "bachelor society" almost devoid of women and children. The Exclusion Acts were repealed in 1943, but even then only 105 Chinese per year were allowed to enter the country.

As a result, Chinatown was for many years just a small enclave contained in the six blocks between the Bowery and Mulberry, Canal and Worth Streets (now known as "traditional Chinatown"). Not until 1965, when racial quotas for immigration were abolished, could the Chinese establish a true community here. Since then, Manhattan's Chinese population has grown to an estimated 100,000.

This enormous new influx has created tension. In the last decade especially, strains have developed between the established Cantonese community and the latest group of immigrants, the Fujianese, who come from Fujian Province on the southern coast of mainland China. Many of the Fujianese are here illegally, having been smuggled in on overcrowded vessels, and they work desperately at meager wages to pay back their exorbitant $30,000–50,000 smuggling fees.

Chinatown has also witnessed the rebirth of the nonunion garment factory. New York's garment manufacturers began moving into Chinatown in the 1970s, when it became apparent that it was less expensive to produce clothing here than in Asia or the Caribbean. Look up

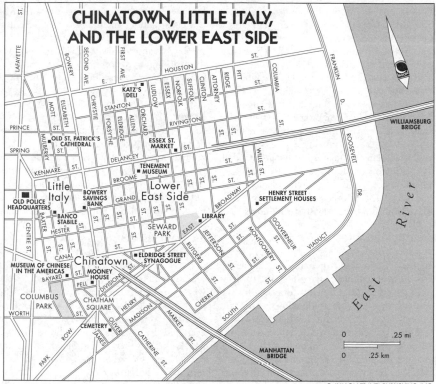

CHINATOWN, LITTLE ITALY, AND THE LOWER EAST SIDE

© AVALON TRAVEL PUBLISHING, INC.

MANHATTAN

from many streets, especially on the fringes of Chinatown, and you'll see clouds of steam escaping from third-story sweatshops. Also note the bright red sheets of paper plastered on buildings here and there—help wanted posters for the garment industry.

Chatham Square/Kim Lau Square

At the southeastern entrance to traditional Chinatown, where 10 streets meet (!), is Chatham Square, also known as Kim Lau Square. The first name comes from the Earl of Chatham, William Pitt, an Englishman who supported American opposition to the Stamp Act. The second comes from the Kim Lau Memorial Arch in the middle of the square. Erected in 1962 in memory of the Chinese-Americans who died in WW II, the arch is named after Lt. Kim Lau.

Lieutenant Lau was flying a training mission over a residential district when his plane developed engine trouble. He ordered the rest of the crew to bail safely out while he stayed with the plane, guiding it away from city streets and crashing to his death in the ocean.

To the east side of the square at Division Street is Confucius Plaza, where a statue of the philosopher is dwarfed by a high-rise apartment building—one of the few new buildings in Chinatown.

First Shearith Israel Cemetery

Slightly south of Chatham Square along St. James Place is a small cemetery dating back to 1683—the oldest artifact in New York City. Buried here in the "Jew Burying Ground" are 18 Revolutionary War–era soldiers and patriots, and the first American-born rabbi. Like the

African Burial Grounds farther downtown (see Around City Hall under Lower Manhattan, above), this cemetery was once well outside the city limits, and funeral parties had to be escorted here under armed guard.

By the time the 23 Jews who later established this cemetery arrived in Manhattan in 1654, they had already been thrown out of Spain and Brazil. Dutch governor Peter Stuyvesant didn't want them here either, but when he wrote to the Dutch West India Company, asking permission to throw them out, he was firmly reprimanded. First of all, his employers replied, we're a corporation, and these Jewish merchants and traders can help us make money; secondly, we have a number of important Jewish stockholders.

Nearby Churches

Just south of the cemetery on St. James Place is the pretty **St. James Church,** built in 1827 for an Irish Roman Catholic congregation. Former New York governor Al Smith was born nearby and received what little formal education he had at the church's Hall of St. James School next door. Around the corner on Oliver Street is the **Mariner's Temple Church,** built in 1844. Originally a mission for sailors and derelicts, the Mariner's Temple is now home to a largely Asian-American congregation and a powerful African American gospel choir.

Fujianese East Broadway

Before heading west into traditional Chinatown, you might want to head northeast along East Broadway to the Manhattan Bridge. The bridge once served as a dividing line between the area's Chinese and Jewish neighborhoods, but is now in the center of the new Fujianese community. In a three-block circumference around the bridge, you'll find Fujianese rice-noodle shops, herbal medicine shops, outdoor markets, and hair salons. Many of these businesses have the word "Fu"—meaning "lucky"—in their names, but thus far at least, things are noticeably scruffier and poorer here than in traditional Chinatown.

At the corner of East Broadway, Eldridge, Division, and Market Streets are dozens of employment agencies where undocumented

Fujianese men linger, hoping for work. Most will eventually be hired at low-level restaurant jobs paying $800–1200 a month for a 70-hour work week, and most will use all but a fraction of their earnings to pay off the smugglers, or "snake-heads," who got them into the country in the first place.

Doyers Street

Returning to Chatham Square, cross over to the odd elbow-shaped street just to the north. Some say that more people have died at this "Bloody Angle"—a *New York Post*–coined nickname—than at any other intersection in America.

For much of the 1900s, Doyers Street was the battleground of the Hip Sing and On Leong tongs. Similar to criminal gangs, the tongs fought for control of the opium trade and gambling racket. The On Leongs were the more powerful of the two tongs at first. But then, around 1900, a man named Mock Duck appeared. A loner who wore chain mail and a silver-dollar belt buckle, he liked to psych out his enemies by squatting in the middle of the street, closing his eyes, and firing his guns in all directions. With Mock Duck as their leader, the Hip Sings took over Pell and Doyers Streets, and the On Leongs retreated to Mott.

The tong wars continued off and on through at least the 1940s, with vestiges continuing into the present day. Nearby Pell Street is still the headquarters of the Hip Sing Business Association. As recently as 1992, members of the Flying Dragons—a youth gang said to be controlled by Hip Sing—could be found loitering on the street. Crackdowns from police have changed that during the last decade, although as far as the visitor is concerned, it hardly matters. Its drug trafficking notwithstanding, Chinatown has long been one of the city's safest neighborhoods.

During the 1890s, one of the favorite pastimes of some Caucasians was to go "slumming" in Chinatown. The more hardcore visited the then-legal opium dens—often just darkened rooms with mattresses—while the more mainstream signed up for expensive tours given by a man named Chuck Connors. Connors—a lively character who is said to have coined such phrases as "the real thing" and "oh, good night"— liked to terrify his tourists by pointing to innocent passersby and saying they were axe murderers or drug lords.

One of the stops on Connors's tour was **5-7 Doyers,** where he would stage a mock kidnapping, and rescue, of one of his tourists. The Chinese eventually threw Connors out of Chinatown for giving them a bad name, and in the early 1900s, 5-7 Doyers became the first Chinese theater in New York.

Today, the section of Doyers south of the Bloody Angle often feels gray and deserted, as if filled with ghosts from its violent past. The section north of the angle, however, is lined with busy barber and beauty shops.

Pell Street

Even more barber and beauty shops are situated along Pell Street, which accounts for its nickname, Haircut Street. Many of these small establishments have an old-fashioned feel, with candy-striped barbershop poles rotating out front.

At 16 Pell St. is the headquarters of the **Hip Sing Business Association,** housed in a red-and-gold building with a green awning. A few doors down, at 4 Pell St. is a **Buddhist Temple,** here for the benefit of the tourist trade. Bus tours come to the temple; most worshipping Chinese do not. The more authentic Buddhist temples are modest affairs, hidden well away from prying eyes.

Edward Mooney House

At 18 Bowery, at the corner of Pell St., stands the oldest dwelling in New York, built in 1785 by a butcher and amateur racehorse-breeder named Edward Mooney. The building was used as a private residence until the 1820s; after that, it became a tavern, store, hotel, pool parlor, restaurant, Chinese club room, and bank.

Church of the Transfiguration

The church at 25 Mott St. is one of the oldest in New York, built by the English Lutheran Church in 1801 and sold to the Roman Catholic Church of the Transfiguration in 1853. Over the years, it has helped many immigrants adjust to life in the New World. First those immigrants were pri-

marily Irish, then Italian, then Chinese. The future Cardinal Hayes was educated here, Mother Cabrini ministered here, and Jimmy Durante— whose dad was a Mott Street barber—worshipped here. Today, the church offers services in Cantonese, Mandarin, and English.

North on Mott Street

Mott is the oldest Chinese-inhabited street in the city. A man named Ah Ken moved in here in 1858, and New York's first Chinese grocery store, Wo Kee, opened here in 1878.

Chu Shing, 12 Mott St., 212/227-0279, is an antique shop that was once the office of the Chinese Revolutionary Dr. Sun Yat-sen (1866–1925). Sun Yat-sen is sometimes referred to as the "father of modern China."

At **41 Mott St.** is a tall white building marked with large golden Chinese characters, and topped by the only remaining wooden pagoda-roof in Chinatown; such roofs were outlawed in the early 1900s as fire hazards. The **Chinese Community Centre,** 62 Mott St., is run by the Chinese Consolidated Benevolent Association (CCBA). The CCBA was established in 1883 by wealthy merchants who spoke English and served as unofficial "mayors" for the neighborhood. These merchants were exempt from the Exclusion Acts and were allowed to bring their families into the country. Today, the CCBA is closely aligned with the Taiwan government.

The **Eastern States Buddhist Temple of America,** 64 Mott St., 212/966-6229, is another temple aimed primarily at tourists, with $1 fortunes for sale near the front. Yet here you'll also find many Chinese, resting on the wooden pews after a hard afternoon's shopping. Some buy joss (incense) sticks, which they place at a pretty altar covered with golden Buddhas and offerings of fresh fruit.

Near where Mott meets Canal is the intricate but somewhat crooked **Golden Dragon** neon sign, "famous" for lighting up on both sides.

Museum of Chinese in the Americas

Recently renovated, the small but fascinating Museum of Chinese in the Americas, 70 Mulberry St., at Bayard, 2nd Fl., 212/619-4785, centers around a permanent exhibit entitled "Where Is Home?" Encased in a large structure reminiscent of a glowing lantern, the exhibit features personal stories, photographs, mementos, and poetry culled from 16 years of research in the Chinese community. Among the topics explored are women's roles, religion, the Chinese laundry, and the bachelor society.

The museum is on the second floor of an 1891 red-brick building that was once a school. On sale in the project's bookstore is an excellent "Chinatown Historical Map & Guide" ($4), which provides insights into the neighborhood's history, as well as tips on what to order in Chinese restaurants, where to shop, and what to buy. The bookstore also carries about 80 other titles by or about Asian-Americans.

Hours are Tues.–Sat. noon–5 P.M.; admission adults $3, students and seniors $1, children under 12 free. The museum also sponsors occasional walking tours. As you enter or leave the museum, keep an eye out for flyers; this is the best place in the city to find out about Asian-American cultural events.

Columbus Park

On Mulberry Street, a half-block south of the museum, is Chinatown's only park, created in the late 1890s through the heroic efforts of Jacob Riis and other early social reformers. Before the park was constructed, Riis—then working as police reporter—called this dilapidated stretch of the city "the worst pigsty of all"; he reported a stabbing or shooting here at least every week. To get an idea of what living conditions in this then-Italian neighborhood were like, take a look at the "rear tenements" on Mulberry Street, just below Bayard. These tenements were built *in between* two rows of other tenements, and most of their rooms had no windows or airshafts.

FROM POND TO SLUM

Collect Pond—early Manhattan's largest body of water—once covered a large chunk of Chinatown between present-day Franklin and Worth, and Lafayette and Baxter Streets. Though full of fish when the Dutch arrived, the pond was nearly exhausted by the mid-1700s. Then, around 1800, the city began filling it in with mounds of dirt and garbage; by 1807, a 15-foot-high pile of nasty-smelling refuse towered in its middle. Finally, in 1808, the city built a canal to drain the pond into the sea. That paved-over canal later became Canal Street.

Though advised against it, developers started building on the newly drained land without waiting for it to settle. The new homes were no sooner completed than they began to crack and tilt. No one with money would move in, and the area quickly evolved into Manhattan's first and arguably most notorious slum ever—Five Points. Named after the five streets that once intersected where Columbus Park is today, the neighborhood housed over 40,000 people in less than half a square mile. Most of its residents were desperate immigrants earning $1 a day and freed blacks earning even less. Local lore had it that policemen were afraid to enter the area except in squads of 10, and some said that at least one murder a day was committed there.

Wrote Charles Dickens in 1842, after his ill-fated trip to New York (he hated everything about it): "What place is this, to which the squalid street conducts us? A kind of square of leprous houses . . . reeking everywhere with dirt and filth. . . . See how the rotten beams are tumbling down, and how the patched and broken windows seem to scowl dimly, like eyes that have been hurt in drunken frays."

Desperate living conditions gave rise to dangerous gangs, among them the Forty Thieves, the Dead Rabbits ("dead" meant "best," "rabbit" meant "tough guy"), the Plug Uglies, and the Shirt Tails. The latter, as might be expected, wore their shirts outside their pants, while the Plug Uglies wore big plug hats stuffed with leather and wool. The gangs' weapons of choice were clubs, bats, and hobnail boots.

Recent scholarship indicates, however, that Five Points had another side to it. In 1996, archaeologists examining remnants concluded that the neighborhood had also been home to a large, family-oriented population.

Though more concrete than greenery, Columbus Park is usually filled with Chinese kids at play and old women gossiping under rice-paper umbrellas. On the weekends, Chinese fortune-tellers often set up shop.

Mulberry Street

At the southernmost end of Mulberry across from the park is a row of funeral parlors that many Chinese who dabble in gambling go out of their way to avoid. No use courting bad luck. Heading north on Mulberry Street to Canal Street, you'll pass some of the many outdoor markets that crowd the streets of Chinatown. These oft-mobbed stands sell everything from baby shrimp to Chinese broccoli at bargain prices. Yet the storeowners in traditional Chinatown—where the demand for space is ferocious—pay more rent per square foot than do the owners of Tiffany & Co. in Midtown.

Canal Street

You'll find it all on this most remarkable of streets—fruits and vegetables, plastic toys, burglar alarms, car stereos, art supplies, Asian banks, and hordes and hordes of people. It's easy to spend hours here just meandering about, soaking it all in.

Most overwhelming at first are the fish stores near Baxter Street, where enormous piles of fish seem to stare balefully at you as you pass by. Live carp, bass, eel, crabs—they're all here, some shipped in from as far away as Hong Kong, some from the Fulton Fish Market just down the street.

Next you'll notice the enormous number of banks. At the intersection of Mott and Canal Streets alone stand four behemoths: Chase, Chemical, Abacus, and United Orient. Some say that banks in Chinatown now outnumber restaurants, and although that seems hard to believe, the banks' presence is indicative of the enormous investments from Hong Kong, Taiwan, and China that have flooded New York in recent years. In keeping with Chinese tradition—which puts a high value on savings—the banks in Chinatown stay open evenings and weekends. Employees in some branches speak seven dialects.

Shopping

Some of Chinatown's oldest stores are on Mott Street. **Quong Yuen Shing,** 32 Mott St., 212/962-6280, is a small 1890s store filled with ceramic dishes, figurines, and beautiful wood-and-glass cabinets. Also on Mott are the **Kam Tat Trading Co.,** 54 Mott St., one of the many herb shops in Chinatown, and the **Ten Ren Tea & Ginseng Co.,** 75 Mott St., near Canal, 212/349-2286, a spiffy and very friendly store selling dozens of exotic teas.

Near the north end of Columbus Park is **Ping's Dried Beef,** 58 Mulberry St., 212/732-0850, a dark and uninviting store that's been in Chinatown for over 20 years. The well-known shop uses an original recipe from a school in Guangzhou (Canton) to preserve its products. Besides dried beef, the store sells pork and liver sausages, pressed duck, and Chinese bacon. The narrow **Chinese American Trading Company,** 91 Mulberry St., 212/267-5224, stocks cooking utensils, dishes, and other Chinese products, while the modern emporium **Kam Man Food Products,** 200 Canal St., between Mott and Mulberry Sts., 212/571-0330, stocks a large selection of Chinese, Thai, and other Asian foods, along with cooking utensils.

Soon to relocate from 277 Canal St. to 477 Broadway (between Broome and Grand Streets), **Pearl River Mart,** 212/431-4770 is Chinatown's largest department store and a fascinating place to explore. On sale are Chinese musical instruments, paper lanterns, kites, dried herbs, clothing, and lots of merchandise from the People's Republic.

On Canal near West Broadway, you'll run into a stretch of odd, informal stores selling a combination of hardware, industrial ware, machine parts, and junk. Boxes of *stuff* line the sidewalks, and unless you're a mechanic of some kind, you'll probably have a hard time figuring out what's what. On the south side of Canal is the venerable **Pearl Paint Company,** 308 Canal St., near Broadway, 212/431-7932. The grand five-story emporium is the world's largest art and graphics discount center, with more than 100 clerks on duty at all times.

Accommodations

$100–150: The **Holiday Inn Downtown,** 138 Lafayette St., at Howard, 212/966-8898 or

MANHATTAN

800/HOLIDAY, offers a modern second-story lobby accessible by escalator, 223 nondescript rooms, and an on-site Chinese restaurant. Despite the location, most of the guests are occidental; $139–169 s or d, with packages sometimes available.

Food and Drink

Chinatown is home to over 300 restaurants serving various cuisines including Hunan, Szechuan, Shanghai, Cantonese, Vietnamese, and Thai. You can't go wrong with most of the restaurants here, especially those catering to a large Asian clientele. All are inexpensive to moderately priced, with the average entrée less than $10 unless otherwise noted.

Chinese: Two good choices on Mott Street are **Wong Kee,** 113 Mott, near Hester, 212/966-1160, serving consistently fresh Cantonese food, and **Tai Hong Lau,** 70 Mott, near Bayard, 212/219-1431, offering unusual Hong Kong–style cuisine and cheap dim sum. Bustling **Joe's Shanghai,** 9 Pell St., between Bowery and Mott St., 212/233-8888, features some of the best and freshest food in Chinatown (with another branch in Flushing, Queens) and is especially famous for its "soup dumplings"—a mouthful of soup *inside* the dough; average entrée $12.

The modern, bilevel extravaganza known as the **Nice Restaurant,** 35 E. Broadway, near Catherine, 212/406-9510, offers fresh Hong Kong–style Chinese cuisine and dim sum. One of the best noodle shops in the neighborhood is **New Chao Chow,** 111 Mott, between Canal and Hester, 212/226-2590, a hole-in-the-wall spot where you may be asked to share a table.

Other Asian Fare: Fresh and healthy Vietnamese fare is the specialty at the unassuming **Nha Trang,** 87 Baxter St., between Bayard and Canal, 212/233-5948. Some of the city's best Thai food can be found at **Thailand Restaurant,** 106 Bayard St., at Baxter, 212/349-3132; average entrée $15.

Dim Sum: Chinatown is home to a number of cavernous, gaily decorated restaurants serving dim sum from mid-morning until late afternoon, and fixed-priced banquets thereafter. The latter usually cater to groups of eight or more, so if you come at night, bring lots of friends. One of the largest and best of these eateries is **Golden Unicorn,** 18 E. Broadway, at Catherine, 212/941-0911, where waiters use walkie-talkies to communicate—arrive early, as there's often a long wait. Another good choice is the sleek **Dim Sum Go Go,** 5 E. Broadway, at Chatham Sq., 212/732-0797, a relatively new eatery that has acquired a near-instant following. **HSF,** 46 Bowery, near Canal, 212/374-1319, is a good place for beginners as it's one of the few dim sum restaurants in Chinatown where explanations of the dishes are available in English.

Treats: Chinatown is also filled with bakeries. Some are big and modern, others are holes-in-the-wall with atmosphere in spades. One of the oldest is the creaky, 70-year-old **Nom Wah Tea Parlor,** 13 Doyers St., near Pell, 212/962-6047. Near where Pell meets Mott is Nom Wah's antithesis, the cheery **May May Bakery,** 35 Pell St., 212/267-0733. Try the moon cakes, almond cookies, "cow ears" (chips of fried dough), or pork buns. Also, don't miss the **Chinatown Ice Cream Factory,** 65 Bayard St., near Mott, 212/608-4170, where you can buy every flavor of ice cream from ginger to mango.

Watering Holes: On the northern edge of Chinatown you'll find **Double Happiness,** 173 Mott St., between Broome and Grande Sts., 212/941-1282, a hip basement bar that's always packed with young urbanites. Just above the bar is its sibling, the tiny **Wyanoka,** 212/941-8757, serving an eclectic menu; average entrée $15.

LITTLE ITALY

In contrast to Chinatown, Little Italy is but a shadow of its former self. The Italian population here reached its zenith between 1890 and 1924. Today only about 10 percent of the neighborhood's residents are of Italian ancestry, and the heart of its dining and shopping district has shrunk to just three short blocks. Even on those blocks, the buildings tend to be owned by Asian-Americans, who—knowing a good thing when they see it—rent to Italian-Americans on the understanding that the buildings be used to perpetuate the tourist trade.

Despite all of this, little pockets of the Italian community can still be found here and there throughout downtown. This is especially evident during warm weather when older Italian women dressed in black set up folding chairs along Mott Street, in sections of Greenwich Village around Sullivan Street, and in SoHo east of Lafayette.

Mulberry Street

Most of what is left of Little Italy is along Mulberry Street just above Canal Street. Here, Italian restaurants and cafes line the street, with tables and striped umbrellas set out in warm weather. It's all very touristy, but it's also a lot of fun, with mustachioed waiters gesticulating wildly like caricatures of themselves, and lots and lots of bright, garish colors.

Not far from the intersection of Canal St., at 109 Mulberry St., is the **Church of the Most Precious Blood,** its pretty courtyard often filled with birds. Though usually shuttered and empty, the church is the center of the feast of San Gennaro, held for 10 days around September 19. San Gennaro is the patron saint of Naples, and his blood—kept in a church in his home city—is said to turn to liquid on his feast day. During the festival, the streets of Little Italy are filled with bright lights, tacky games of chance, and food stands, very few of which sell Italian food.

Umberto's Clam House

On April 7, 1972, at 5:20 A.M., gangster "Crazy" Joe Gallo was shot to death in an Italian fishhouse at 129 Mulberry Street. The reputed leader of organized crime, and the man thought to be responsible for two of the mob's most famous hits—Albert Anastasia in 1957 and Joe Colombo in 1971—Gallo had been out celebrating his 43rd birthday with his new bride and 10-year-old stepdaughter.

The Gallo party arrived at Umberto's a little after 4 A.M. and sat in the back, with Joey facing the door, naturally. But his vigilance wasn't enough. A balding man wearing a tweed overcoat stepped in through the rear and fired more than a dozen shots at Gallo. While everyone else hit the floor, he staggered out into the street and fell down dead.

Bullet marks were still visible on Umberto's stainless steel kitchen door until the restaurant closed in early 1997. The police never arrested anyone for the shooting, but they believe that Gallo was killed by followers of Joe Colombo, intent upon revenge.

Banco Stabile

On the corner of Mulberry and Grand Streets stands the 1865 Banco Stabile. In the early 1900s, about 70 percent of all Italian immigrants prepaid their tickets to and from the United States through this Italian bank. These immigrants were sometimes called "Birds of Passage," because they spent half the year working in the New York garment industry, the other half in Italy, planting and harvesting the vineyards. Since an immigrant was charged a $25 tax if he or she returned home before three years were up, these Birds of Passage often traveled without papers—hence the slur "wop."

Old St. Patrick's Cathedral

On Mott near Prince Street, on the fringes of SoHo, is Old St. Patrick's Cathedral. The predecessor to the famous St. Patrick's Cathedral on Fifth Avenue, this 1809 Gothic structure was once the cathedral of the see of New York. Behind the church is a walled cemetery (usually locked) where Pierre Toussaint is buried. Toussaint was a Haitian born into slavery who later became the first black American candidate for sainthood.

Around the corner from the cathedral is the unusual **Elizabeth Street Garden,** 210 Elizabeth St., 212/941-4800, filled with enormous pieces of weathered statuary. The outdoor sculpture garden is maintained by the gallery across the way.

Shopping

Across from the Banco Stabile is the city's mother lode of great Italian food stores, including the **Italian Food Center,** 186 Grand St., 212/925-2954, stocked with a wide variety of wares; **Alleva Dairy,** 188 Grand St., 212/226-7990, said to sell two tons of cheese a week; and **Piemonte Ravioli,** 190 Grand St., 212/226-0475, known for its homemade pasta. Also at the corner is **Rossi & Co.,** 191 Grand St., 212/966-6640, a

MANHATTAN

variety store where you can buy everything from a Mussolini T-shirt to opera CDs.

Though becoming increasingly Chinese, Mott Street north of Canal Street still holds a number of traditional Italian shops. For Italian cheese, try **DiPalo's Fine Foods** 206 Grand St., at Mott, 212/226-1033. For excellent breads, head for **Parisi Bakery,** 198 Mott St., 212/226-6378.

Food

Though Little Italy is generally *not* the place to go for good Italian food, it does hold some bargain-priced eateries, cheery cafes, and a few noteworthy dinner houses.

The friendly, old-fashioned **Da Nico,** 164 Mulberry St., between Grand and Broome, 212/343-1212, with a garden out back, specializes in excellent coal-oven pizza and savory roasted meats and fish; average entrée $12. Homey **Benito I,** 174 Mulberry St., between Grand and Broome, 212/226-9171, serves good, traditional Sicilian food; average entrée $11.

One of Little Italy's best restaurants is **Il Cortile,** 125 Mulberry St., near Hester, 212/226-6060, a multi-roomed spot with brick walls and an indoor garden, specializing in Northern Italian cuisine; average entrée $19. Also very good is **Taormina,** 147 Mulberry St., between Hester and Grand, 212/219-1007, once former mobster John Gotti's favorite spot; average entrée $18.

For an afternoon snack, try the cozy, tile-floored **Cafe Roma,** 385 Broome St., at Mulberry, 212/226-8413, a wonderful espresso-and-pastry cafe that was once a hangout for opera singers. Another good choice is the flashy **Ferrara's,** 195 Grand St., near Mulberry, 212/226-6150.

Watering Holes and Lounges

Onieal's Grand Street Bar, 174 Grand St., between Mulberry and Court Sts., 212/941-9119. In the 1940s, *Daily News* photographer Arthur Felig, better known as Weegee, hung out here while waiting to follow police sirens to nasty crime scenes. Nowadays, the clientele tends to be younger, trendier, more sheltered, and more upscale.

Mare Chiaro, 176 Mulberry St., near Broome, 212/226-9345, is an out-of-time, *Godfather*-esque bar where, as one journalist commented not long

ago, you might find the owner dancing in his underwear or the proprietress smoking a cigar.

THE BOWERY

Heading east, you'll bump into one of the city's most famous thoroughfares—the gray, neglected Bowery. Though long associated with alcoholism and abject poverty, the Bowery has a long and singular history that predates New York.

Named after the Dutch word for farm *(bouwerie),* the street was first an Indian path, then a trail leading to Peter Stuyvesant's farm in what is now the East Village. Later in the 18th century, the Bowery became part of the Boston Post Road and was lined with a number of fine homes and estates, as well as roadside taverns. George Washington often drank at the Bullshead Tavern, 146 Bowery, since torn down.

By the mid-1800s, the Bowery had become a glittering strip of lowbrow theaters where rowdy audiences roared out their laughter or jeers. Extravagant productions were the order of the day, with dozens of horses or full-rigged ships often appearing on stage. The Bowery Amphitheater (37 Bowery) presented the nation's first blackface minstrel show, while the National Theater (104 Bowery) produced a long serial play about a mythic street fighter named Mose. Mose could lift streetcars off their tracks, blow wind into ships' sails, and jump from Manhattan to Brooklyn in a single bound.

Around 1880, the Bowery began changing again. Cheap boardinghouses, gin mills, missions, and brothels began replacing the theaters, and the down-and-out began replacing the working class. Crime became rampant, and the street slowly slid into poverty and despair. By 1907, an estimated 25,000 homeless men were living in the flophouses and missions here. (The Bowery has always been the province of men: In 1907, 115 stores on the Bowery sold menswear; none carried women's apparel.)

The Bowery continued to be known as a haven for the down-and-out until well into the 1960s, but today, all the bars are gone and only one or two flophouses remain. The Bowery's adjoining streets above Houston Street are rapidly becom-

HORSEPOWERED POLLUTION IN THE 1800s

New York today may not seem like the cleanest of cities, but before you voice a complaint, consider the way it was back in the late 1800s. Back then, the 120,000-some horses in the city left about 1,300 tons of manure a day on the streets. The city employed only a handful of street cleaners, and "that foul aliment" was allowed to accumulate in huge piles, breeding "pestilential vapours" and millions of flies. In addition, whenever one of the poor, overworked horses expired, it was simply left to rot by the side of the road. In 1880 alone, New York City removed 15,000 dead horses from its streets.

Reported *Harper's Weekly* on February 26, 1881: "The condition of the streets of New York during the present winter has been frightful beyond all precedent even for the dirtiest city in the U.S. . . . The thaw that followed aggravated the evil, and today the city lies ankle-deep in liquid filth through which the pedestrians are obliged to wade and flounder. There is no such thing as picking one's way, for with a few exceptions, one spot is as bad as another and everybody plunges in and ploughs through it without regard to the consequences."

ing gentrified, while the Bowery above Canal Street is becoming part of Chinatown.

The Bowery around Broome Street is the city's lighting district, filled with shops selling lamps and lampshades of every conceivable variety. Farther north, around Rivington Street, is the kitchen-supplies district, where restaurants come to buy silverware, utensils, and the like.

At the corner of the Bowery and Grand Street is **Bowery Savings Bank,** a grand building with a magnificent domed interior and glass skylight. The building was designed by McKim, Mead & White in 1894. At the corner of the Bowery and Hester Street is a giant, swirling 1977 mural—complete with a dragon, gambler, and man with a wok—entitled "Wall of Respect for the Working People of Chinatown."

THE LOWER EAST SIDE

East of the Bowery is the Lower East Side, where a once-thriving Jewish community has dwindled away. In 1892, some 75 percent of New York's Jews lived here; by 1916, that figure had dropped to 23 percent. Today, the figure is less than one percent. Only about 10,000 Jewish residents remain here; most of the neighborhood's population is now Puerto Rican or Asian. Nonetheless, many older Jews in other parts of the city still regard today's windswept and largely abandoned Lower East Side as a sort of spiritual center, coming here to shop for religious articles or to eat a

kosher meal. Yiddish signs still dot the streets; Orthodox Jews dressed in traditional clothes still own many of the stores.

The Jewish people began arriving on the Lower East Side in the late 1800s, many finding work either as peddlers or in the garment industry. Sweatshops—so named because their stoves had to be kept on at all times to heat the flatirons—sprang up throughout the neighborhood, employing both on-premises laborers and outside workers who took enormous piles of piecework home with them to sew by candlelight. Children were often employed along with adults, the pay was extremely low (about $12.50 a week in 1905), and suicide was not uncommon.

Nonetheless, the Lower East Side possessed extraordinary vitality and intellectual life. Many actors, artists, and writers came out of the neighborhood, including Eddie Cantor, Fannie Bryce, Al Jolson, Jacob Epstein, and Abraham Cahan. Writes Michael Gold in *Jews Without Money:* "I can never forget the East Side street where I lived as a boy. . . . Always these faces at the tenement window. The street never failed them. It was an immense excitement. It never slept. It roared like a sea. It exploded like firecrackers. . . . Excitement, dirt, fighting, chaos! . . . The noise was always in my ears. Even in sleep I could hear it; I can hear it now."

Delancey and Allen Streets

The Lower East Side's major east-west cross-street

MANHATTAN

is Delancey. Once bustling with people and peddlers, this wide thoroughfare is now primarily an entrance ramp to the Williamsburg Bridge. Cheap clothing stores and fast-food joints still line it in spots, but like so many streets on the Lower East Side, it has an abandoned, underpopulated feel. As you head east on Delancey, you'll pass over Allen Street, another wide, scruffy boulevard. In the late 1800s, it was notorious for its "creep houses"—brothels equipped with sliding panels so that thieves could slip in and rob customers.

Orchard Street

For decades, this major shopping strip was jammed with pushcarts selling fruits, vegetables, knishes, bagels, hardware, and work clothes. Often the first stop for immigrants after Ellis Island, it was known for cut-rate bargains. Many of the city's most successful retailers, including Brooks Brothers, got their starts here. Today, Orchard Street is still known for bargains. On a sunny Sunday afternoon, its sidewalks teem with shoppers and shopkeepers, who spread out their merchandise on outdoor tables and racks. Most of the stores sell clothing—both designer goods and casual wear—and linens, with the stores below Delancey somewhat more upscale than the ones above. Be prepared to bargain.

Lower East Side Tenement Museum

This museum re-creating early immigrant life is housed in an 1863 tenement building at 97 Orchard St., between Delancey and Broome, 212/431-0233, www.tenement.org. It's a deliberately dark and oppressive place; the building originally had no windows, except in front, and no indoor plumbing. Declared illegal in 1935, it was sealed up and forgotten about until 1988, when historians looking for a structurally unaltered tenement building stumbled upon it.

Today, the museum's ground floor is devoted to temporary exhibits, while the upstairs rooms have been left more or less as they were when the house was occupied. Still eerily visible on one wall are the scribblings of an early garment worker, listing the numbers of skirts, dresses, and "jackets #2" he or she had cut or sewn.

Tours are the only way to see the museum,

and it's a good idea to book early, as they often sell out. Tours are offered Tues.–Sat.; call for details. Tickets can be purchased via the website: www.ticketweb.com or by calling 800/965-4827. Tour prices are adults $9, seniors and students $7.

Across the street from the museum is **Gallery 90,** 90 Orchard St., which serves as an informal visitor center. It also holds a wonderful miniature model of an inhabited tenement building, and is open Tues.–Sun. 11 A.M.–5:30 P.M.

The museum also sponsors walking tours of the area.

Eldridge Street Synagogue

About four blocks south of the Tenement Museum, at 12 Eldridge St., between Division and Canal, is the 1886 Eldridge Street Synagogue. The first synagogue in New York built by Eastern European Jews, it's a large and startlingly elaborate building with beautifully carved wooden doors. Due to a dwindling congregation, the main sanctuary was sealed in the 1930s and not entered again for 40 years. In the early 1990s, restoration work began, and the synagogue now houses the **Eldridge Street Project,** 212/219-0903, www.eldridgestreet.org, an exhibition space. Tours of the synagogue are offered Sunday 11 A.M.–3 P.M. on the hour, and Tuesday and Thursday at 11:30 A.M. and 2:30 P.M. Rates are adults $5, seniors and students $3.

Across the street from the synagogue are excellent examples of the early "Old Law" tenement buildings that were erected in the city between 1879 and 1901. Laid out in a dumbbell shape—their facades and backs bumping up against each other with just a one-foot-wide air shaft in between—these apartments had virtually no light and only one bathroom per floor, to be shared by about 30 people. In 1901, a new building code improved these conditions somewhat, but by that time, some 1,196 dumbbell tenements had already been built on the Lower East Side.

Jewish East Broadway

Heading east, at 175 E. Broadway, at Rutgers, you'll come to the former headquarters of the Yiddish *Jewish Daily Forward.* Founded in 1897 and edited by Abraham Cahan, the *For-*

ward published writers such as Isaac Bashevis Singer and Sholom Aleichem, as well as a famous popular column called the Bintel Brief (Bundle of Letters). This column, responding to letters from readers, offered advice on everything from what to do about children who ridiculed the Old Country to how to cure the common cold.

The *Jewish Daily Forward* is still being published uptown, but its old headquarters is now home to various Chinese associations. A barely visible sign up top reads Forverts, while a much more visible one above the door reads Jesus Saves in Chinese. **Seward Park Library,** 192 E. Broadway, and the **Educational Alliance,** 197 E. Broadway, both contributed significantly to the success of Jews in the New World. The library had an enormous selection of Yiddish books and a rooftop reading garden built to accommodate its thousands of book-hungry immigrant readers. The Alliance served as a sort of settlement house where the uptown German Jews, often embarrassed by the peasant habits of their newly arrived kinspeople, helped to "Americanize" them.

Between Jefferson and Montgomery Streets are a number of small storefront synagogues, many with Yiddish signs out front. Most of these small Orthodox congregations are Hasidic.

Henry Street

At 263-267 Henry St., east of Montgomery St., stand the attractive red-brick **Henry Street Settlement Houses,** founded by Lillian Wald in 1827. Wald was an important social reformer, credited with starting both the school nurse and school lunch programs. She built her houses here largely because many tenement buildings once stood across the street. Then, as now, the houses functioned as a neighborhood safety net, offering a wide range of social services aimed at children, young mothers, and the elderly.

Next door to the settlement houses is a bright red, meticulously kept firehouse—**Engine Co. 15,** where William Marcy "Boss" Tweed got his start. Another block east is **St. Augustus Church,** where

> *"If you live in New York, even if you're Catholic, you're Jewish."*
>
> *Lenny Bruce*

Tweed supposedly watched his mother's funeral from the balcony while on the run from the law.

Shopping

Orchard Street holds a number of popular stores, among them **Forman's,** 82 Orchard St. (with branches at 78 Orchard and 94 Orchard), 212/228-2500, selling discounted women's designer clothes. For more information on shopping in the area, stop by the **Orchard Street Shopping District Center,** 261 Broome St., between Orchard and Allen, 212/226-9010, open daily 10 A.M.–4 P.M. Free shopping tours are often offered on Sunday.

Clotheshorses might want to stroll down **Ludlow Street,** just off Houston Street, where some of the city's younger and more outrageous fashion designers have set up shop. On **Essex Street** are numerous small Jewish stores selling religious books and supplies such as yarmulkes, *talith* (prayer shawls), and menorahs.

Food Shops

The legendary **Guss' Pickles,** once a boisterous storefront selling sour, half-sour, and hot pickles in huge outdoor plastic vats, has temporarily relocated to the Lower East Side Tenement Museum, 97 Orchard St., between Broome and Delancey Sts.; call 212/431-0233 for updated information. Guss is also famed for its sauerkraut, horseradish, and pickled tomatoes and watermelon rinds.

Just off Essex are **Gertel's,** 53 Hester St., 212/982-3250, the area's major bakery; **Kadouri & Sons,** 51 Hester St., 212/677-5441, a Middle Eastern shop selling a wide variety of spices; and **Kossar's Bialystoker Kuchen Bakery,** 367 Grand St., 212/473-4810, famed for its fresh onion and garlic bialys and bagels.

On Essex between Delancey and Rivington is the indoor **Essex Street Market.** Created in the 1930s after Mayor La Guardia banned pushcarts from the streets, it's now run-down but worth a quick look.

Another thoroughfare lined with some wonderful old Jewish shops is Rivington Street. At **Streit's Matzoth Company,** 150 Rivington St.,

MANHATTAN

© CHRISTIANE BIRD

Fresh bialys are a favorite on the Lower East Side.

212/475-7000, you can sometimes see the flat breads being made. West of Essex is **Economy Candy,** 108 Rivington St., 212/254-1531, an unassuming store selling great marzipan and halvah along with kosher marshmallows and huge bags of nuts.

The dividing line between the Lower East Side and the East Village is Houston (HOW-ston) Street, home to the famous Katz's Deli (205 E. Houston, at Ludlow), as well as to several traditional food shops. **Russ & Daughters,** 179 E. Houston, between Allen and Orchard, 212/475-4880, is a bustling place filled with smoked fish and dried fruits, all arranged in neat rows; while **Yonah Schimmel's,** 137 E. Houston St., between First and Second Aves., 212/477-2858, is a rickety old storefront selling some of the best knishes in New York. Visible across the street from these shops, on the rooftop of 250 E. Houston, is a 15-foot statue of Lenin, his hand raised to the sky. Toppled by an angry crowd in Moscow in 1991, the statue was transported here by an art collector in 1993.

Accommodations

Under $50: Popular with students and backpackers, the **Bowery's Whitehouse Hotel of** New York, 340 Bowery, between Second and Third Aves., 212/477-5623, is part flophouse, part hostel. Built in 1917 for railroad workers, it still houses about 50 permanent residents. Rooms are basic but clean and safe; $35–60 s or d.

$100–200: A five-minute walk east of SoHo is **Off-SoHo Suites,** 11 Rivington St., between Chrystie and the Bowery, 212/979-9808 or 800/OFF-SOHO, www.offsoho.com, a clean and friendly budget hotel featuring large, homey suites with kitchenettes and marble bathtubs (these are subject to being shared with the suite next door). Adjoining the narrow, mirror-lined lobby is a spartan cafe done up in gray and white, and a 24-hour self-service laundry room; $119 s or d with shared bath; $209 s or d with private bath; suites accommodating four, $160–189.

Food and Watering Holes

The Lower East Side is famous for its Jewish delicatessens. The granddaddy among them is **Katz's,** 205 Houston St., at Ludlow, 212/254-2246, a huge, cafeteria-style place where you take a number at the door; overhead hang WW II–era signs reading Send a salami to your boy in the Army; average sandwich $8. The sit-down **Ratner's,** 138 Delancey St., between Norfolk and Suffolk, 212/677-5588, is a longtime favorite best known for its blintzes, egg creams, prune danishes, and brusque waiters (average entrée $12), but as of this writing, alas, it seems in danger of closing; call before you go.

One of the neighborhood's newer eateries is **Oliva,** 161 E. Houston St., at Allen St., 212/228-4143, specializing in tasty Basque fare. Pitchers of sangria are set up on the bar and a wide range of seafood tapas are on the menu; average entrée $16. Also a newcomer is **Paladar,** 161 Ludlow St., between Houston and Stanton Sts., 212/473-3535, a funky Cuban joint serving spicy sea bass and other favorite dishes; average entrée $12.

Watering Holes: Ludlow, Stanton, and Clinton Streets are the hub of the hip Lower East Side nightlife, where you'll find lots of laid-back bars and lounges, some holes-in-the-wall, others more upscale. One of the oldest is **Max Fish,** 178 Ludlow St., between Houston and Stanton Sts., 212/529-3959, a long, comfortable watering hole drawing an artsy crowd. Once a coffee bar, the snug **Lotus Club,** 35 Clinton St., at Stanton, 212/253-1144, now offers a full bar and limited menu. Scruffy **Arlene Grocery,** 95 Stanton St., between Ludlow and Orchard Sts., 212/358-1633, presents up-and-coming local bands, often for no cover.

A little farther east is **Lansky Lounge & Grill,** 104 Norfolk St., between Delancey and Rivington Sts., 212/677-9489, named after the Jewish gangster who used to eat next door at Ratner's. Now a trendy lounge, Lansky's entrance is unmarked.

SoHo and TriBeCa

SoHo—short for **So**uth of **Ho**uston—is the city's trendiest neighborhood. Within its 25 upscale blocks, bounded by Houston and Canal Streets, Lafayette Street and West Broadway, glitter hundreds of galleries, museums, restaurants, bars, and, especially, shops.

Once a quiet residential suburb, SoHo began developing in the early- to mid-1800s, when a number of expensive hotels opened up, along with brothels and dance halls. By the 1870s, however, most of this activity had moved to more fashionable digs uptown, leaving SoHo to turn to the industrial sector. Foundries, factories, warehouses, and sweatshops sprang up all over the district. Frequent fires started by machinery sparks soon gave the district the nickname, "Hell's Hundred Acres."

The factories flourished until the mid-1900s. By the 1960s, most of them were gone and artists began moving in. Attracted to the area by its low rents and high-ceilinged spaces—perfect for studios—they illegally converted the commercial buildings into living spaces, secretly adding plumbing and adequate heating. Soon thereafter, the art galleries began arriving, and then the shops and restaurants. Almost overnight, SoHo became fashionable again, so much so that the artists who started it all could no longer afford the high rents.

The gallery owners held on for a decade or so longer, but in the last few years, they, too, have been moving out in alarming numbers. Most have resettled in Chelsea, and a few on 57th Street, while their old spaces have been converted into upscale boutiques and restaurants. Some fine galleries do still remain, however, and art lovers will still find much to interest them in the neighborhood.

Besides, in the end, SoHo's cast-iron build-

ings—many freshly painted—remain its greatest treasure. Originally envisioned as a cheap way to imitate elaborate stone buildings, the cast-iron facades were prefabricated in a variety of styles—including Italian Renaissance, French Second Empire, and Classical Greek—and bolted onto iron-frame structures. An American invention, the cast-iron building was erected primarily in New York, with SoHo boasting the largest collection.

Orientation

SoHo is the perfect neighborhood for just wandering about—it's compact and filled with sights. **Broadway and West Broadway** are the main thoroughfares. West Broadway, originally built to help ease Broadway's traffic congestion, is lined with some of the most prestigious addresses in SoHo. Every weekend its sidewalks swell with hordes of fashionable people—many of them European—and artists hawking their wares. At the north end of the street, near Houston, and again farther south, near Grand, are numerous inviting, albeit pricey, restaurants, offering outdoor tables in good weather.

Prince and Spring Streets hold an enormous array of upscale shops, galleries, restaurants, and bars, along with a few old spots predating the SoHo scene. The intersections of Prince and Spring Streets with West Broadway could be called the heart of modern-day SoHo. West of West Broadway, and east of Lafayette Street, Prince Street takes on its older Italian feel. Children play in the street and old women gossip on the stoops as the smell of fresh-baked bread wafts up and down the street.

To get the full effect of SoHo, come on a weekend afternoon—when the streets are jammed

MANHATTAN

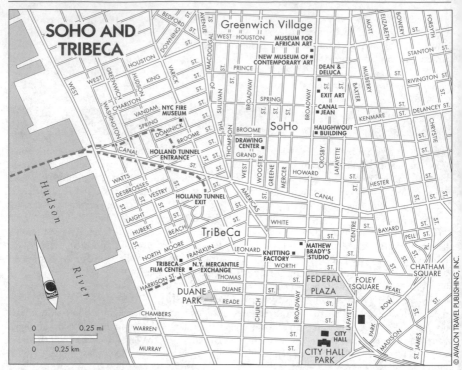

with beautiful people—or at night, when hip bars and restaurants—both upscale and down—attract the high life.

For up-to-date information on goings-on in SoHo, check out the SoHo Partnership website: www.sohonyc.org.

ARCHITECTURE

Many of SoHo's finest cast-iron gems can be found along Broadway. Foremost among them is the Italianate **Haughwout Building,** 488 Broadway, at Broome. The magnificent edifice is five stories tall and nine bays wide on the Broadway side, and sports 92 windows all flanked by Corinthian columns. Built for a merchant who once provided china to the White House, the store was the first in the city to install a passenger elevator.

Farther north is the magnificent **Singer Building,** 561 Broadway, designed by the innovative architect Ernest Flagg in 1904. It's decked out with red terra cotta panels, delicate wrought-iron detailing, and large plate-glass windows. Also be sure to note the glorious maroon-and-white facade of **575 Broadway.**

For a glimpse of what all of SoHo looked like before the trendy shops and art galleries moved in, head down to the lower end of dark, narrow Greene Street. Many of the cast-iron buildings here are still equipped with their old loading platforms, built waist-high so that horse-drawn wagons could pull right up and unload. At 28 and 30 Greene, below Grand, is the so-called **"Queen of Greene Street,"** an ornate Second Empire building painted pale gray. On the southwest corner of Greene and Broome is the once-elegant **Gunther Building,** 469 Broome St., now in dire need of a facelift.

Charlton-King-Vandam Historic District

Just west of Sixth Avenue, this three-block district including Charlton, King, and Vandam Streets was once home to Richmond Hill, a fine mansion built on a crest overlooking the Hudson. George Washington established his headquarters here during part of the Revolutionary War, and later, Vice Pres. John Adams and his wife Abigail took up residence. In 1793, Aaron Burr bought the place and entertained lavishly up until his notorious duel with Alexander Hamilton in 1804. After the duel he was indicted for murder and fled to Philadelphia.

In 1817, his career in ruins, Burr sold Richmond Hill to John Jacob Astor, who moved the mansion (which was eventually demolished) and leveled off the crest. Speculators then built the lovely rows of Federal-style houses that still line the streets today. The best preserved street is Charlton.

MUSEUMS

Art Museums

Heading south down Broadway from Houston Street, you'll come to is the **Museum for African Art,** 593 Broadway, between Houston and Prince Sts., 212/966-1313, which presents excellent changing exhibits on Africa's ancient and tribal cultures. The museum, done up in deep yellows and blue-greens, was designed by architect Maya Lin. Up front is an interesting gift shop. Hours are Tues.–Fri. 10:30 A.M.–5:30 P.M., Sat.–Sun. noon–6 P.M. Admission is adults $5; students, seniors, and children $2.50. Free on Sunday.

On the same block is the spacious **New Museum of Contemporary Art,** 583 Broadway, 212/219-1222, www.newmuseum.org, one of the oldest, best-known, and most controversial exhibition spaces in SoHo. Founded in 1976 by Marcia Tucker, a former curator of the Whitney Museum, who's now moved on to other pastures, the museum has historically presented experimental, conceptual, and often risky shows by contemporary artists from all over the world. Nowadays, it's taking a somewhat less provocative approach, but still presents the unexpected. Hours are Tues.–Sun. noon–6 P.M. and Thursday 6 P.M.–8 P.M. Suggested admission is adults $6; students, artists, and seniors $3. Free for children under 12, and for everyone Thursday 6–8 P.M.

Alas, if you're looking for the Guggenheim Museum SoHo, once located at the corner of Broadway and Prince (575 Broadway), it closed in November 2000, after nine years of existence.

Children's Museum of the Arts, 182 Lafayette St., between Broome and Grand Sts., 212/274-0986, is a hands-on experimental museum designed to expose kids to the visual and performing arts. In the "Artist's Studio," youngsters can try their hand at sand painting, origami, sculpture, and beadwork. The museum is open Wed.–Sun. noon–5 P.M. Admission is $5 per person; seniors over 65 and children under 12 months, free.

New York City Fire Museum

Technically outside of SoHo to the west is the New York City Fire Museum, 278 Spring St., between Varick and Hudson, 212/691-1303, www.nycfiremuseum.org. Housed in an actual firehouse that was active up until 1959, the museum is staffed by ex-firefighters. It's filled with intriguing items, including a 1790 hand pump, a lifesaving net (which

MANHATTAN

The New York City Fire Museum was once a functioning fire station.

"caught you 75 percent of the time"), gorgeous 19th-century fire carriages, engraved lanterns, evocative photographs, helmets and uniforms, and wooden buckets. New to the museum is an exhibit on the firefighters' courageous work following the World Trade Center attacks.

The firefighters love to talk to visitors—they'll give you a personalized tour filled with anecdotes if they're not too busy. The museum is open Tues.–Sat. 10 A.M.–5 P.M. and Sunday 10 A.M.–4 P.M. Suggested admission is adults $4; students $2; children under 12, $1.

ART GALLERIES AND ALTERNATIVE SPACES

Below, find a sampling of SoHo's art galleries and alternative exhibition spaces, most of which are open Tues.–Sat. from about noon to about 6 P.M. To find out about others, or about who's exhibiting where, pick up a copy of the *Art Now Gallery Guide,* available at many bookstores and galleries. Other especially good sources for listings are *Time Out New York* and the Friday Weekend section of the *New York Times.*

Wooster Street

Drawing, sculpture, photography, and film are among the art forms exhibited at **American Fine Arts,** 22 Wooster St., between Canal and Grand Sts., 212/941-0401, currently one of the most interesting galleries in SoHo. Multimedia artist Mark Dion is a regular here.

The **Drawing Center,** 35 Wooster, between Broome and Grand Sts., 212/219-2166, www.drawingcenter.org, an airy, first-rate exhibition hall dedicated to drawing as a major art form. Hours are Tues.–Fri. 10 A.M.–6 P.M., Saturday 11 A.M.–6 P.M.; admission is by donation.

Howard Greenberg & 292 Gallery, 120 Wooster St., between Prince and Spring Sts., 212/334-0010, focuses on well-known 20th-century photographers such as Berenice Abbott and Robert Frank.

Greene Street

Run by a German expatriate, **David Zwirner,** 43 Greene St., between Broome and Grand Sts.,

212/966-9074, exhibits a cutting-edge selection of both New York and international artists. At 38 Greene St., near Broome, is the **Artist's Space,** 212/226-3970, www.artistsspace.org, an alternative arts space that has focused on emerging artists since 1973.

Mercer Street

Long a mainstay in SoHo, **Ronald Feldman Fine Arts,** 31 Mercer St., between Grand and Canal, 212/226-3232, is especially known for its avant-garde installations.

Broadway

The **Nolan/Eckman Gallery,** 560 Broadway, 212/925-6190, is a small but prestigious space usually dedicated to works on paper. Two superb contemporary photography galleries are **Ariel Meyerowitz,** 580 Broadway, between Houston and Prince Sts., 212/625-3434, and **Janet Borden,** 560 Broadway, at Prince St., 212/431-0166.

Exit Art/The First World, 548 Broadway, between Prince and Spring, 2nd Fl., 212/966-7745, is a 17,000-square-foot alternative space that holds two exhibit areas, a cafe, store, and performance space. Shows tend to be experimental and focus on both new and established artists.

SHOPPING

Most SoHo stores are open from about noon to about 8 P.M.

Antiques and Furnishings

SoHo is known for its upscale home furnishings stores. **Portico Home,** 72 Spring St., between Broadway and Lafayette St., 212/941-7800, is the place to go for country chic, while **Moss,** 146-150 Greene St., at Houston, 212/226-2190, is a spacious emporium devoted to modern design. **Wyeth,** 315 Spring St., at Greenwich St., 212/243-3661, sells fine vintage furniture from the 20th century.

Recently relocated out of SoHo and into TriBeCa is **Urban Archaeology,** 143 Franklin St., between Hudson and Varick Sts., 212/431-4646, specializing in artifacts from demolished buildings.

Clothing and Accessories

SoHo abounds with chic designer stores. Among them are **Agnes B.,** 76 Greene St., between Prince and Spring St., 212/925-4649; **Anna Sui,** 113 Greene St., between Prince and Spring Sts., 212/941-8406; **Marc Jacobs,** 163 Mercer St., between Houston and Prince Sts., 212/343-1490; **Betsey Johnson,** 138 Wooster St., between Houston and Prince Sts., 212/995-5048; and **Prada,** 575 Broadway at Prince St., 212/334-8888.

Heading east on Prince Street from West Broadway, you'll pass a number of more affordable clothing stores, including **French Connection,** 435 W. Broadway, at Prince, 212/219-1197, and **Phat Farm,** 129 Prince St., 212/533-7428, selling the hid-hop couture of impresario Richard Simmons. On the west side of West Broadway is **Stella Dallas,** 218 Thompson St., between Prince and Houston, 212/674-0447, specializing in the '40s look.

Alice Underground, 481 Broadway, between Broome and Grand, 212/431-9067, sells vintage clothing at relatively reasonable prices; styles range from Victorian to funk. **What Comes Around Goes Around,** 351 West Broadway, near Broome, 212/343-9303, houses over 60,00 vintage designer items, as well as denim and military threads. **Amy Chan,** 247 Mulberry St., between Prince and Spring Sts., 212/966-3417, sells imaginative handbags made of silks, feathers, and more. Hats galore are to be found at the **Hat Shop,** 120 Thompson St., between Prince and Spring Sts., 212/219-1445.

One of the neighborhood's oldest and most beloved of stores is **Canal Jean,** 504 Broadway, 212/226-1130. This cavernous warehouse, housed in a classic cast-iron building, offers an enormous, jumbled selection of bargain-priced jeans, T-shirts, and vintage coats.

Gifts and Toys

The irrepressible **Pop Shop,** 292 Lafayette St., between Houston and Prince Sts., 212/219-2784, sells T-shirts, posters, hats, refrigerator magnets, inflatable baby dolls, jigsaw puzzles, and more, all designed by the late artist Keith Haring. One of the city's most wonderful toy stores is **Enchanted Forest,** 85 Mercer St., just south of Spring, 212/925-6677. Made up to look like a magical

rain forest, the store attracts as many adults as children. **After the Rain,** a long-time SoHo store specializing in kaleidoscopes, has recently merged with the Enchanted Forest.

Stationery and Cards

Kate's Paperie, in the Singer Building, 561 Broadway, at Prince, 212/941-9816, is an upscale stationery shop filled with handmade paper products. A good selection of art postcards are available at **Untitled,** 159 Prince St., near W. Broadway, 212/982-2088.

Other Shops

Evolution Nature Store, 120 Spring St., between Greene and Mercer, 212/343-1114, is an odd natural history store where you can pick up a giraffe skull or wild boar tusk. **Broadway Panhandler,** 477 Broome St., between Wooster and Greene, 212/966-3434, sells discounted cookware. **Vesuvio,** 160 Prince St., 212/925-8248, is a 70-odd-year-old Italian bakery with dozens of round loaves of bread in its window.

TRIBECA

If you follow West Broadway south out of SoHo and over Canal Street, you'll enter TriBeCa. Looking west from Canal, you can see the entrance to the **Holland Tunnel,** often backed up with traffic at the end of the day. TriBeCa, short for **Tri**angle **Be**low **Ca**nal, encompasses about 40 blocks between Canal, Chambers, West, and Church Streets. The district is often considered a second-tier SoHo, with plenty of fashionable restaurants, galleries, and cast-iron treasures. Yet large sections of TriBeCa remain empty and windswept, filled with half-deserted buildings and quiet blocks. TriBeCa's character is different than SoHo's—much of it still feels like industrialized, 19th-century New York.

Like SoHo, TriBeCa's main thoroughfares are Broadway and West Broadway, though some of its best unrestored cast-iron buildings are on side streets, especially White Street.

West Broadway Art

Soho Photo Gallery, 15 White St., at W. Broadway, 212/226-8571, is a cooperative

MANHATTAN

photography gallery showcasing the works of its 100-plus members; hours are Fri.–Sun. 1–6 P.M., Thursday 6–8 P.M.

Mathew Brady's Studio

The scruffy, five-story, cast-iron building at 359 Broadway, at Franklin, once housed the photographic studios of Mathew Brady. The famed 19th-century photographer, best known for his photos of Lincoln and the Civil War, began his career in 1844, only five years after the daguerreotype was invented. In 1861, Lincoln said of him, "Brady and the Cooper Union speech made me president of the United States." Nonetheless, Brady went bankrupt in 1873 and died a pauper. A faint sign advertising his studio can still be seen high up on the south wall.

TriBeCa Film Center

At the corner of Greenwich and Franklin Streets is TriBeCa Film Center, housed in the landmark 1905 Martinson Coffee Company warehouse. The center was started in 1989 by actor and director Robert DeNiro, who wanted to create a site where filmmakers could conduct meetings, screen films, and talk business over lunch.

The center's **TriBeCa Grill** is usually filled with more celebrity watchers than celebrities, but the famous do occasionally turn up here. Upstairs, off-limits to the public, are screening and business rooms, the headquarters of Miramax Films, and the New York offices of Stephen Spielberg and Ron Howard, among others.

Harrison Street and Duane Park

At Greenwich and Harrison Streets are the **Harrison Houses,** a lovely group of nine restored Federal-style homes. Several were designed by John McComb Jr., New York's first architect. East of the houses, at the northwest corner of Harrison and Hudson Streets, is the former **New York Mercantile Exchange,** a five-story brick building with gables and a tower. At the turn of the century, $15,000 worth of eggs would change hands in an hour on the building's trading floor. TriBeCa is still the city's distribution center for eggs, cheese, and butter; a few remaining wholesalers can be found around Duane Park, one block south.

ACCOMMODATIONS

$150–250

A banal HoJo's in the heart of trendy SoHo? It seems like a contradiction in concepts, but the new **Howard Johnson Express Inn–SoHo,** 135 E. Houston St., at Forsyth St., 212/358-8844, is a welcome reasonably-priced addition to the hyper-expensive neighborhood. $129–289 s or d.

$250 and up

SoHo's first hotel since the 1800s, the 370-room **SoHo Grand,** 310 W. Broadway, at Grand, 212/965-3000 or 800/965-3000, www.sohogrand.com, opened in summer 1996. Sleekly done up in industrial metals, oversized lamps, columns, and sofas in its lobby, the hotel has become a chic, minimalist haven for well-heeled fashionables and Europeans. The custom-designed guest rooms feature muted grays, while adjoining the lobby is a classy, high-ceilinged bar; $279–389 s, $329–549 d.

The SoHo Grand's sister hotel, the **TriBeCa Grand,** 2 Sixth Ave., between Church and White Sts., 212/519-6600 or 800/965-3000, www.tribecagrand.com, was the first hotel to open in the triangle below Canal Street. Noisier, less stylish, and less spacious than its big sister, the TriBeCa features a large and trendy bar lobby area that's always mobbed. Getting a good night's sleep seems like an afterthought here; $239–429 s or d.

Opening about two years after the SoHo Grand, **The Mercer,** 147 Mercer St., at Prince, 212/966-6060 or 888/918-6060, is a stylish spot, located smack in the middle of SoHo. Each of its 75 understated rooms is done up in furniture made of exotic African woods and features a large bathroom; $345–395 s, $375–525 d.

FOOD

American

Though now a bit worn, the **Moondance Diner,** 80 Sixth Ave., at Grand, 212/226-1191, is a classic New York spot, offering gourmet sandwiches and the like; average entrée $9. **Jerry's,** 101 Prince St., between Mercer and Greene, 212/966-9464, is an upscale diner with red leather booths and an eclectic menu; average entrée $14. The light and airy **Spring Street Natural,** 62 Spring St., at Lafayette, 212/966-0290, features lots of plants, big windows, and solid vegetarian fare; average entrée $13.

The snug **Cub Room,** 131 Sullivan St., near Prince, 212/677-4100, is sleek yet comfortable, with an interesting menu and a large classy bar area opening onto the street; average entrée $22. Adjoining the Cub Room's main restaurant is a moderately priced cafe; average entrée $13. **Zoe,** 90 Prince St., between Broadway and Mercer, 212/966-6722, is a handsome and popular spot known for its open kitchen and California-style cuisine; average entrée $21. Robert DeNiro's brick-walled **TriBeCa Grill,** 375 Greenwich St., at Franklin, 212/941-3900, may attract hordes of celebrity watchers, but the food and service are nonetheless surprisingly good; average entrée $24.

Asian

In TriBeCa, the simple **Thai House Cafe,** 151 Hudson St., at Hubert, 212/334-1085, is especially good for weekday lunch, when specials are served; average entrée $11. **Clay,** 202 Mott St., at Spring, 212/625-1105, is an appealing, minimalist spot serving unusual Korean fare, such as fried tofu stuffed with eggplant; average entrée $14.

Reserve months in advance to get a seat at **Nobu,** 105 Hudson St., at Franklin St., 212/219-0500, arguably the most famous Japanese restaurant (with Peruvian touches) in America. Partly owned by Robert DeNiro, and a favorite among celebrities, the sleek eatery offers lots of innovative fare created by acclaimed chef Nobu Matsuhisa; average small dish $15. If you have no reservation, check out **Next Door Nobu,** where you may have to wait (they accept no reservations), but the food and ambience are similar, and the prices not quite so high.

French Bistros

SoHo is home to a number of popular bistros that double as late-night hot spots.

Lucky Strike, 59 Grand St., between Wooster and W. Broadway, 212/941-0479, was one of the first of these downtown joints. It's been

around for years now, but still attracts a lively crowd, especially after midnight when the young, the beautiful, and the hopeful gather to exchange glances; average entrée $13.

A longtime favorite among night-crawlers is the chic, art deco **Odeon,** 145 W. Broadway, at Thomas, 212/233-0507, serving consistently good food in a lively, downtown setting; average entrée $19. The dark and stylish **Raoul's,** 180 Prince St., between Sullivan and Thompson, 212/966-3518, is a downtown mecca and with good reason; the food and ambience are top-notch; average entrée $23.

Tiny, cozy **Le Pescadou,** 16 King St., at Sixth Ave., 212/924-3434, specializes in fresh fish, and attracts a loyal following; average entrée $19.

Eclectic

Famed chef/restaurateur David Bouley's latest creation is **Danube,** 30 Hudson St., between Duane and Reade Sts., 212/791-3771, an intimate, romantic, over-the-top spot serving Viennese classics—Tyrolean wine soup, Wiener schnitzel; average entrée $35. Housed in the landmark Mercantile Exchange Building, is **Chanterelle,** 2 Harrison St., near Hudson, 212/966-6960, a cool, ultra-elegant eatery serving nouvelle cuisine to an art-world crowd; prix fixe dinners $75–89.

Balthazar, 80 Spring St., between Crosby and Broadway, 212/965-1414, is a large, bustling brasserie that serves an eclectic cuisine and draws a sleek, celebrity-studded crowd; average entrée $24.

Other Ethnic

The homey **Lupe's East L.A. Kitchen,** 110 Sixth Ave., at Watts, 212/966-1326 serves first-rate east L.A.–style Mexican food in a simple setting; average entrée $9. Dark **Cafe Noir,** 32 Grand St., at Thompson, 212/431-7910, offers spicy French-Moroccan cuisine, served tapas-style; up front is a narrow bar, often crowded with young Europeans; average entrée $14.

Friendly newcomer **Ideya,** 349 W. Broadway, between Broome and Grand Sts., 212/625-1441, specializes in Caribbean fare, served to a Brazilian beat; average entrée $18.

Filled with comfortable booths, **Brother's Barbeque,** 225 Varick St., near W. Houston, 212/727-2775, is a large and casual joint serving tasty ribs, barbecued chicken, and all the Southern trimmings; average entrée $12.

Light Bites

At the north end of SoHo you'll find **Kelley & Ping,** 127 Greene St., between Prince and Houston, 212/228-1212, a simple but excellent combination Asian grocery shop and noodle parlor. At the south end of SoHo is the cozy **Cupping Room Cafe,** 359 W. Broadway, near Broome, 212/925-2898, especially good for afternoon snacks. Many New Yorkers go out of their way to visit **Eileen's Special Cheesecake,** 15 Cleveland Pl., near Lafayette St., just below Spring, 212/966-5585 (take-out only). For some of the best crepes in town, check out snug, tin-tabled **Palacinka,** 28 Grand St., between Sixth Ave. and Thompson St., 212/625-0362; average crepe $8.

Watering Holes and Lounges

The classic bar in SoHo is **Fanelli's,** 94 Prince St., at Mercer, 212/226-9412, an 1876 pub complete with beveled glass doors, tiled floors, and heavy dark wood. In the back are worn wooden tables where passable bar food is served.

Though not as trendy as it once was, the **Merc Bar,** 151 Mercer St., near Houston, 212/966-2727, done up in sleek, modernized Adirondackiana, still attracts a lively crowd. The **Broome Street Bar,** 363 W. Broadway, at Broome, 212/925-2086, is a SoHo mainstay, with a long bar up front and a casual dining area in back. On the Eastern fringe of SoHo is **Milano's,** 51 Houston St., between Mulberry and Mott, 212/226-8632, a long, narrow dive with a good jukebox.

Classic TriBeCa bars include **Puffy's Tavern,** 81 Hudson St., at Harrison, 212/766-9159, a one-time artists' hangout that now attracts everyone from bankers and bikers to police and firefighters (this was a central hangout after the September 11, 2001 attacks), and **Walker's,** 16 N. Moore St., at Varick, 212/941-0142, an 1890s saloon that serves tasty pub grub and Guinness on tap. The **Raccoon Lodge,** 59 Warren St., between Church and W. Broadway, 212/766-9656, is a big, scruffy place with a good pool table.

The **Church Lounge,** in the TriBeCa Grand Hotel, 2 Sixth Ave., between Church and White Sts., 212/519-6677, is an enormous bar-lobby that is always filled with downtown revelers. Of the restaurants listed above, the **Cub Room, Lucky Strike, La Jumelle, Cafe Noir,** and **Raoul's,** all have lively bar scenes. The bar at the **SoHo Grand Hotel** also draws a crowd.

The East Village

Musicians in post-punk, artists in retro, and pouty young fashionables in vinyl and faux fur—such are some of the types you'll find in the East Village. But it'd be a mistake to think that the neighborhood is only the province of the young and flamboyant. Over the last few decades, each generation has left a number of its own nonconformists in this gray, eclectic, and well-worn part of town.

For much of its existence, the East Village was simply an extension of the Lower East Side. Though favored by the well-to-do in the mid-1800s, by the turn of the century most of its residents were German Lutheran immigrants. By WW I, those Germans had been replaced by Poles, Ukrainians, Greeks, Jews, and Russians—some of whom still live in the neighborhood. Not long thereafter, a sizeable Latino population moved in, settling in the easternmost stretches. They, too, are still here.

In the 1950s, artists, writers, radicals, and counterculturists began arriving. Many were fleeing the rising rents in Greenwich Village, and they transformed the East Village into a distinct neighborhood with a character all its own. First on the scene were artists such as Willem de Kooning, Paul Georges, and Joan Mitchell, followed quickly by writers such as Norman Mailer, W. H. Auden, and Allen Ginsberg. Next came the beatniks, and then the hippies and the yippies, the

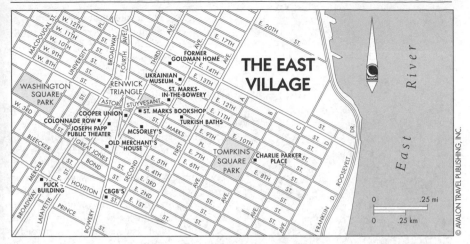

THE EAST VILLAGE

rock groups and the punk musicians, the artists and the fashion designers.

Only in the early 1980s did the East Village begin to gentrify. Young professionals moved in, bringing with them upscale restaurants and shops. This trend slowed during the recession of the late 1980s, but has since returned full force, with pricey new establishments threatening to force out the neighborhood's once-trademark hole-in-the-wall joints. Still, the East Village has not completely succumbed and offers a heady mix between the cutting edge and the mainstream. Performance artists and community activists rub shoulders with tourists and businesspeople. Owners of hip boutiques share sidewalk space with the homeless. Drug dealers skulk outside the doors of trendy restaurants.

Nightlife is a key component of East Village character. The neighborhood is home to scores of restaurants and bars, along with fly-by-night music clubs and performance spaces.

Orientation

The East Village encompasses everything east of Fourth Avenue between East Houston and 14th Streets. Some blocks are crowded with business establishments, others with dull, crumbling buildings. East of First Avenue, the avenues take on lettered names—A, B, C, and D; this area is also known as Loisaida (a phonetic

corruption of Lower East Side) or Alphabet City. Avenues A, B, and much of C have been gentrified, but parts of C and D have many rough spots and are best avoided unless you have a specific address in mind. The most interesting streets for aimless wandering are First and Second Avenues, Avenue A, St. Mark's Place, and 7th and 9th Streets.

ALONG SECOND AVENUE
St. Mark's-in-the-Bowery

Historic St. Mark's Church, 131 E. 10th St., at Second Ave., stands near the former site of Peter Stuyvesant's farm. Its hodgepodge of architectural styles includes a 1799 base, an 1828 Greek Revival steeple, and an 1854 cast-iron Italianate porch.

Buried in the bricked-in graveyard surrounding the church is "Petrus Stuyvesant" himself, the last and most colorful of the Dutch governors. By all accounts a crusty, often forbidding man, Stuyvesant spent the last of his years stomping around his farm on his wooden leg.

Some say Stuyvesant's ghost still haunts the graveyard. A tapping noise, like that made by the famous leg, has been heard from deep inside his tomb, and an angry wraith, resembling the dead man, has been seen limping around among the headstones. Several times, the church bells

© CHRISTIANE BIRD

Behind St. Mark's-in-the-Bowery is a graveyard where the city's last Dutch governor, Peter Stuyvesant, is buried.

have supposedly tolled without being touched by human hands.

Also once buried in St. Mark's cemetery was Alexander Stewart, the founder of the modern department store. But in 1878, body snatchers dug up his body—buried 12 feet down under three heavy slabs—and held it for ransom. Two years went by before Stewart's widow, worth millions, finally coughed up $20,000 for her husband's remains. The corpse was reburied in Garden City, an early planned suburb on Long Island that Stewart had financed. His new tomb was equipped with a burglar alarm.

Today, St. Mark's is known primarily for its poetry readings, performing-arts presentations, and leftist politics. In the 1950s, Beat poets gave frequent readings here and, until his death in April 1997, Allen Ginsberg was a fixture. An annual poetry fest is held on New Year's Day.

The interior of the church is open Mon.–Fri. 9 A.M.–4 P.M., Sunday 9 A.M.–1 P.M. For information, call 212/674-6377 (parish office), 212/674-0910 (poetry project), or 212/674-8112 (dance project).

Renwick Triangle

A half-block west of St. Mark's on 10th Street is Renwick Triangle, which holds 16 gorgeous Italianate brownstones designed by the then-young architect James Renwick. Renwick also designed St. Patrick's Cathedral on Fifth Avenue and Grace Church on Broadway. Just up from Renwick Triangle, at 21 Stuyvesant St., is the elegant, red-brick **Stuyvesant-Fish Residence,** which the great-grandson of Peter Stuyvesant built as a wedding present for his daughter Elizabeth.

Emma Goldman's Home

At 208 E. 13th St., between Second and Third Aves., is a six-story apartment building that was once a gathering place for radicals and intellectuals. Anarchist Emma Goldman lived here from 1903 to 1913, making it one of the most permanent of the many addresses she occupied in the East Village and Lower East Side. Goldman was frequently evicted because of her politics.

While living here, Goldman began publishing her journal, *Mother Earth,* named after "the nourisher of man, man freed and unhindered in his access to the free earth!" In 1906, her former lover Alexander Berkman took up a troubled residence with her. Berkman had just been released after serving a 14-year prison term for the attempted assassination of industrialist Henry Clay Frick, and had a hard time readjusting to day-to-day life. Goldman had assisted him in plotting the murder.

South on Second Avenue

From the turn-of-the-century through the 1930s, Second Avenue between 14th Street and Houston was lined with lively Yiddish theaters. All are now gone, but the movie theater at the corner of 12th Street was once the **Yiddish Art Theatre,** and still boasts a magnificently restored domed ceiling.

On the same block as the theater is the tiny

Ukrainian Museum, 203 Second Ave., 212/228-0110. Though of limited appeal, the museum does house a nice collection of embroidered clothing and *pysanky* (elaborately dyed Easter eggs), as well as changing exhibits and a small gift shop. It's open Wed.–Sun. 1–5 P.M.

At the southeast corner of 10th St. is **Second Avenue Deli,** its sidewalk studded with the names of stars of the Yiddish theater. Across the street, between 9th St. and St. Mark's Pl., are two grand terra cotta buildings from the 1880s: **Stuyvesant Polyclinic,** 137 Second Ave.; and **Ottendorfer Library,** 135 Second Avenue. The Ottendorfer, its facade adorned with miniature books, globes, and sage old owls, was the first building in the city built specifically for use as a public library.

Bill Graham's famous **Fillmore East** once rocked the corner of Second Avenue and 6th Street. Over the years, the theater hosted everyone from Janis Joplin and Jimi Hendrix to Jefferson Airplane and The Doors. In 1994, the city renamed the corner "Bill Graham's Way," in honor of the rock-and-roll promoter, who died in a helicopter crash in 1991.

The Gershwin Family

The second floor of the well-kept red brick building at 91 Second Ave., between 5th and 6th Sts., was an early home of the Gershwin family. George was 12 and Ira was 14 when they moved in. While living here, Mrs. Gershwin bought the family its first piano, which was hoisted into the apartment through a window. No sooner had it arrived than George sat down at the keys and began teaching himself to play. Six years later, he published his first song.

Murder on Second Avenue

The building at 79 Second Ave. once housed the BiniBon restaurant, site of a famous murder that had an interesting prologue. When Norman Mailer was writing *The Executioner's Song,* he befriended an inmate named Jack Henry Abbott. Abbott, in prison for robbery and murder, had written a series of letters to the author about life behind bars. Mailer loved Abbott's letters, and turned them over to Random House, who published them in 1978 under the title *In The Belly of the Beast.* With Mailer's help, Abbott was paroled three years early. He came to New York, where he was interviewed by *Good Morning America* and feted by the intelligentsia. Then, on July 17, 1981, in the BiniBon restaurant, a waiter named Richard Adan told Abbott that the restaurant's restroom was for employees only. Enraged, Abbott stabbed him to death and fled. He was then sent back in prison, to serve a 15-year sentence.

AROUND ST. MARK'S PLACE

Raucous and run-down in spots, outrageously entertaining in others, St. Mark's is the heart of the East Village. Punked-out artists and rock musicians, students and tourists, drug dealers and the down-and-out, all jostle each other, while the stores on either side sell everything from gourmet pretzels to frightening-looking leather goods. To get the full effect of the craziness, come after 10 P.M. on a weekend night.

In the 19th century, St. Mark's was a fashionable street with elegant residences set back from the sidewalks. Author James Fenimore Cooper lived at 6 St. Mark's Pl. for a while, and several Eastern European social clubs were headquartered here.

St. Mark's is at its raunchiest between Second and Third Avenues. One of its noisiest addresses is the **community center,** 23 St. Mark's Pl., the stairs of which are always draped with black-leathered people—both young and middle-aged. The building once housed the Dom, a huge dance hall and bar where Andy Warhol presented "The Exploding Plastic Inevitable," starring Lou Reed and the Velvet Underground. The rock club called the Electric Circus also occupied the site for a number of years.

W. H. Auden's Digs

Between First and Second Avenues, St. Mark's becomes residential. Poet W. H. Auden lived in a fourth-floor apartment at 77 St. Mark's Pl. from 1953 to 1972. A plaque by the door commemorates the man and quotes the line: "If total affection cannot be, let the more loving one be me." In contrast to those noble sentiments, Auden lived in considerable filth, amidst piles of dirty plates and a cockroach population reputedly so large that the walls of his apartment appeared to be moving.

In 1917, in the basement of this same building, the revolutionary newspaper *Novy Mir* was published. One of its contributors was Leon Trotsky, in town for a few months before returning home to Russia in time for the Bolshevik Revolution.

Tompkins Square Park
This small park bounded by East 7th and East 10th Streets, and Avenues A and B, was the scene of a violent confrontation over a decade ago. During the 1980s, the park was a squalid haven for the homeless as well as a marketplace for drugs. One hot August night in 1988, a dozen cops on horseback rode in to shut the park down. The homeless and their advocates protested in a four-hour-long riot that left at least 50 people injured. Acts of police brutality were recorded on video by a local artist, and 121 people filed complaints against the police department.

Rioting took place again the following summer and the summer after that. Finally in 1991, amid much local protest, Mayor Dinkins padlocked the park for renovations. Today, Tompkins Square is quiet and well kept, with playgrounds, benches, and a dog run . . . as well as a midnight curfew and a marked police presence.

As the park has become more gentrified, so has Avenue A. Once considered the fringe of East Village, the thoroughfare is now home to a mix of hole-in-the-wall bars and upscale restaurants.

The *General Slocum* Memorial
At the north end of the park is a small weathered statue of a boy and girl looking at a steamboat. The statue is a memorial to the disastrous *General Slocum* fire, which took place on board an excursion boat in the East River on June 15, 1904. Some 1,300 German Lutherans, en route to their annual picnic, died when the boat exploded near a dangerous passage known as Hell Gate. The remaining German community, which lived near the park, was so devastated

that they abandoned the neighborhood. Many moved uptown into the East 80s.

Charlie Parker Place
In 1951, jazz great Charlie Parker moved into 151 Ave. B, a small, solid building on the east side of Tompkins Square Park. With him were his girlfriend, Chan, and her daughter, Kim. "I like the people around here," he said once to biographer Robert Reisner. "They don't give you no hype."

While here, Parker kept his life middle-class and respectable, greeting Chan's relatives in a suit and tie, and taking walks in the park with Kim. Later, Chan said that if it hadn't been for his talent, race, and drug addiction, Charlie could have lived out his days on Avenue B as a "happy square."

The city renamed this block Charlie Parker Place in 1993.

Little Ukraine
Some dub 7th Street between Second and Third Avenues "Little Ukraine," and it's true that the Ukrainian community here is thriving. But for the tourist, there's not much to see. **Surma,** 11 E. 7th St., 212/477-0729, is a Ukrainian shop selling books, records, and crafts. Across from it is **St. George's Ukrainian Catholic Church,** a large domed church built in 1977. Every May, the church puts on a splendid Ukrainian festival, featuring traditional foods and crafts.

McSorley's Old Ale House
At 15 E. 7th St. stands the famed McSorley's Old Ale House, 212/473-9148, established in 1854. Engineer Peter Cooper once drank here, as did *The New Yorker* writer Joseph Mitchell, who wrote of the alehouse in his book, *McSorley's Wonderful Saloon.* McSorley's only opened its doors to women in the early 1970s, and then only under court order.

Outside, you'll see barrels and an aging green-and-gold sign. Inside, the pub sports a potbellied stove, old gas lamps, a carved mahogany bar, and pressed tin ceilings. Memorabilia collected by old John McSorley hangs everywhere, but the old neighborhood drinking crowd is gone, replaced primarily by boisterous twenty-something

McSorley's Old Ale House was a male-only preserve clear up until the early 1970s.

males. The best time to come is at lunch, when you can take a look around while munching on a plowman's lunch of bread and cheese. Ale is the only beverage served, and it comes two glasses at a time, light or dark.

THE BOWERY AND ASTOR PLACE

Playing the Bowery

At 315 Bowery, at Bleecker, stands the famed, hole-in-the-wall nightclub known as **CBGB & OMFUG** (short for Country, Blue Grass, Blues and Other Music For Uplifting Gourmandizers), 212/982-4052. Here in the 1970s flourished an underground rock scene of the kind that seems impossible today. The club opened in 1974 with Richard Hell, bass player for the group Television (the nation's "first psychosexual rock group"). That set the tone for years to come. Everyone played here, including the Ramones, Patti Smith, and David Byrne. The club endures to this day.

Next door to CBGB's is the tiny, ornate **Amato Opera Theater,** 319 Bowery, 212/228-8200, which during the 19th century was a vaudeville

stage. Across the street is the **Bouwerie Lane Theater,** 330 Bowery, 212/677-0060—now home to the Jean Cocteau Repertory—housed in an elaborate cast-iron building that was once home to the German Exchange Bank.

McGurk's Suicide Hall

On the east side of the Bowery, just below East 1st Street, is the shell of a four-story building that once housed McGurk's, a hangout for sailors and longshoremen during the late 19th century. The establishment was nicknamed "Suicide Hall" because of the many prostitutes who killed themselves here. McGurk's was also known for its headwaiter, Short-Change Charley (who used knockout drops on his rougher customers), as well as its no-nonsense bouncer, Eat-'Em-Up Jack McManus.

Merchant's House Museum

The classic Greek Revival home at 29 E. 4th St., just west of the Bowery, was once one of many elegant residences lining this block. Today it's the Merchant's House Museum, 212/777-1089, www.merchantshouse.com. Inside, the house is furnished exactly as it was in 1835 when

© CHRISTIANE BIRD

CBGB's, East Village

merchant Seabury Tredwell and his family lived here. On display are the family's entire belongings, including the framed diplomas of the Tredwell daughters and trunks filled with sumptuous satin clothes. On the second floor is a secret trapdoor that may once have led to an underground tunnel. The museum is open Thurs.– Mon. 1–5 P.M. Admission is adults $5, students and seniors $3, children under 12 free.

The Public Theater

Two blocks north of the Old Merchant's House stands an imposing, columned building with colorful banners beckoning out front. Once the Astor Library, this is now the Public Theater, 425 Lafayette St., 212/260-2400, www.publictheater.org, founded by Joseph Papp.

Until his death in 1991, Papp was one of America's most important theater producers. Best known as founder of the New York Shakespeare Festival, he was also the man who first produced *Hair, A Chorus Line,* and 15 other plays that later moved to Broadway.

Today, the Public is home to five stages, a coffee bar, and a cabaret space called Joe's Pub. The theater is now under the direction of George C. Wolfe, who first brought Tony Kushner's *Angels in America* to New York.

Astor Place

Adjoining the Public Theater is a windy, disjointed plaza centering on the "Alamo," a big black cube by artist Bernard Rosenthal. Precariously balanced on one corner, the cube is sup-

JOHN JACOB ASTOR

Both the Astor Library and Astor Place were named after John Jacob Astor, once the richest man in the United States. A poor German immigrant with an obsessive passion for money, Astor made his fortune first in the fur trade and then in the New York real estate market. On his deathbed he was reportedly so weak that he was fed on breast milk—thought to be extra nutritious—and tossed in a blanket 10 minutes a day for exercise. Nonetheless, money was still foremost in his mind and one day as he was being tossed, he urged one of his rent agents to collect from an impoverished widow. The man pleaded with him—saying that the widow needed more time—but Astor would not hear of an excuse. Eventually the agent went to Astor's son, who gave him the money. "There," said the dying Astor as the agent handed him the overdue rent, "I told you she would pay if you went to the right way to work with her."

posed to rotate when pushed, but that's easier said than done. The plaza also holds a cast-iron reproduction of one of the original subway kiosks that once stood all over the city.

No longer standing is the highbrow Astor Place Opera House, which once lorded over the west side of the plaza. In 1849, the Opera House's management sparked the bloody Astor Place riots by hiring English actor George Macready rather than Irish-American actor Edwin Forrest to play Hamlet. When Forrest's loyal, working-class Irish fans heard the news, they took to the plaza in protest. A crowd of 12,000 gathered, and the police—then a private organization paid by the wealthy—appeared. They opened fire, killing about 30 people and wounding about 120 others.

Cooper Union

The largest brownstone in New York City is Cooper Union, located in the triangle between Astor Place and Third and Fourth Avenues. The 1859 building was financed by Peter Cooper, a remarkable engineer who—among many other things—made a fortune in the iron industry, designed the first American locomotive, invented gelatin and a self-rocking cradle, and helped develop Morse's telegraph. The son of a poor storekeeper, Cooper built his Union to house a free school of practical arts and sciences. Still in operation today, Cooper Union was also the first coeducational, racially integrated school in the country.

Downstairs inside Cooper Union is the Great Hall, where Abraham Lincoln made his famous "Might makes right" speech that won him the Republican presidential nomination in 1860. Abolitionists Henry Ward Beecher, Frederick Douglass, and William Cullen Bryant also spoke here, as did every president following Lincoln up through Woodrow Wilson, and Bill Clinton.

A statue of Peter Cooper stands on the building's south side. Across the street, at 36 Cooper Sq., are the offices of the *Village Voice,* founded in 1955.

SHOPPING

Books and Newspapers

One of the city's best bookstores, **St. Mark's Bookshop** is no longer on its namesake street but just around the corner at 31 Third Ave., at

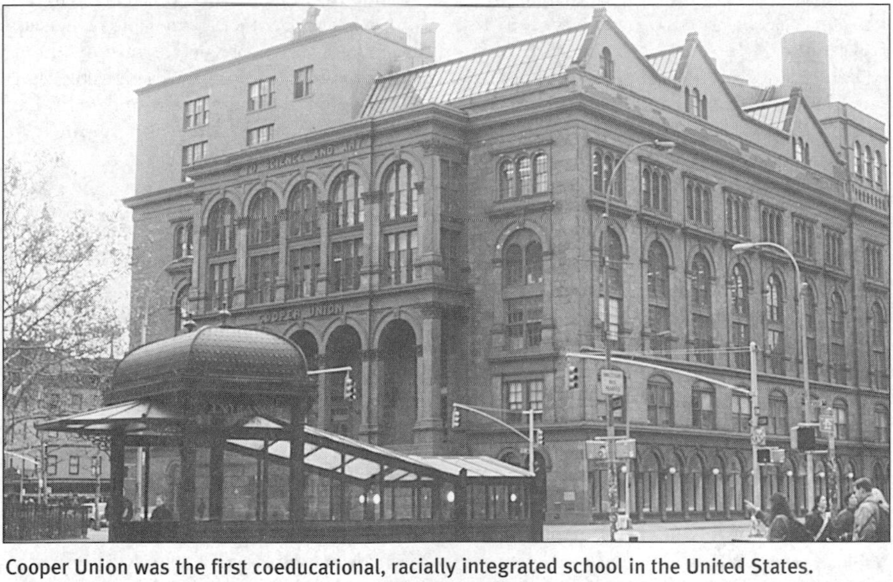

© CHRISTIANE BIRD

© CHRISTIANE BIRD

MANHATTAN

Cooper Union was the first coeducational, racially integrated school in the United States.

Stuyvesant St., 212/260-7853. Open daily until midnight, the store has an especially fine selection of fiction and alternative publications.

On the southwest corner of Second Ave. and St. Mark's Pl. is **Gem Spa** newsstand, a dilapidated joint famous for egg creams. Made of very cold milk, seltzer water, and chocolate syrup, egg creams were once a staple in this part of town.

Clothes

Love Saves the Day, 119 Second Ave., at 7th St., 212/228-3802, is the stuffed-to-the-rafters secondhand clothing (etc.) store where Rosanna Arquette bought her jacket in the movie *Desperately Seeking Susan*. **Trash and Vaudeville,** 4 St. Mark's Pl., 212/982-3590, is an over-the-top spot selling everything from studded halter tops to rock-and-roll gear from the 1960s. **Screaming Mimi's,** 382 Lafayette St., near E. 4th St., 212/677-6464, is known for '50s-, '60s-, and '70s-era duds.

Crafts and Gifts

The bright and colorful **Back from Guatemala,** 306 E. 6th St., between First and Second Aves., 212/260-7010, is filled with ethnic clothing, jewelry, masks, and crafts, mostly from Central America. For eclectic gifts, try **Howdy Do Toy Collectibles,** 72 E. 7th St., 212/979-1618; **Mostly Bali,** 324 E. 9th St., 212/777-9049; or **Dinosaur Hill,** 306 E. 9th St., 212/473-5850—three unusual shops selling exactly what their names imply. For offbeat souvenirs and postcards, step into **Alphabets,** 115 Ave. A., between St. Mark's Pl. and 7th St., 212/475-7250.

Health and Beauty

The traditional **Tenth Street Russian and Turkish Baths,** 268 E. 10th St., between First Ave. and Ave. A, 212/473-8806, is filled with saunas, steam rooms, and massage rooms. At one time, many such establishments existed in the East Village, but this is the last one left. Some days are coed, others for men or women only.

The 1851 **Kiehl's,** 109 Third Ave., near 13th St., 212/677-3171, is an old-fashioned chemist's where you can buy a full line of natural, handmade beauty products.

Music and Art

Sounds, 20 St. Mark's Pl., between Second and Third Aves., 212/677-3444, is stocked with a good selection of alternative music and used CDs. **Fat Beats,** 406 Sixth Ave., 212/673-3883, carries a mix of new hip hop, reggae, and breakbeat vinyl. **Footlight Records,** 113 E. 12th St., between Third and Fourth Aves., 212/533-1572, carries a good selection of show tunes, jazz, and used CDs. **Finyl Vinyl,** 204 E. 6th St., near Second Ave., 212/533-8007, features records from the '30s to the '70s.

American Indian Community House Gallery, 708 Broadway, 2nd Fl., 212/598-0100, www.aich.org, is the city's only Native American-owned and -operated gallery. Hours are Tues.–Sun. noon–6 P.M.

Other Shops of Interest

Surma, 11 E. 7th St., between Second and Third Aves., 212/477-0729, is a Ukrainian shop selling books, records, and crafts. **Jam Paper and Envelope,** 111 Third Ave., near 13th St., 212/473-6666, stocks a wide array of budget-priced stationery.

East of Second Avenue, **9th Street** is lined with one tiny, eccentric, and often highly unusual shop after another. Names and ownerships change frequently; for sale are antiques, home furnishings, vintage clothing, fashions by young designers, books, pottery, herbs, and crafts. East of Second Avenue, **7th Street** and **Avenue A** are also good streets for shopping.

FOOD

American

The informal **Life Cafe,** 343 E. 10th St., at Ave. B, 212/477-8791, is a neighborhood stand-by offering vegetarian and Tex-Mex fare; average main course $7. Also an East Village mainstay, **7A,** 109 Ave. A, at 7th St., 212/673-6583, has a nice selection of salads, sandwiches, and more substantial entrées; average main course $9. **Miracle Grill,** 112 First Ave., at 7th St., 212/254-2353, offers tasty Southwestern cuisine and a scruffy but romantic garden; average entrée $12. American food is served with Mediterranean flair at the upscale **Five Points,** 31 Great Jones St., between the Bowery and Lafayette St., 212/253-5700, where the menu changes nightly; average entrée $20.

Asian
Mingala Burmese Restaurant, 21 E. 7th St., near Third Ave., 212/529-3656, serves good food in a comfortable setting adorned with Burmese handicrafts; average main course $9.

An excellent new addition to the neighborhood, **Cyclo,** 203 First Ave., between 12th and 13th Sts., 212/673-3957, serves fresh, tasty Vietnamese fare in an airy setting; average entrée $12. **Iso,** 175 Second Ave., at 11th St., 212/777-0361, offers first-rate sushi along with imaginative Japanese dishes—come early, as the lines are often long; average entrée $14. The simple **Shabu Tatsu,** 216 E. 10th St., between First and Second Aves., 212/477-2972, is an oft-crowded cook-it-yourself Japanese barbecue place; average entrée $14.

Eastern European
The East Village has traditionally been known for its cheap, Eastern European eateries, where the average main course costs $6–8. Two legendary Second Avenue spots are **Second Avenue Deli,** 156 Second Ave., at 10th St., 212/677-0606, a classic Jewish delicatessen serving great pastrami and corned beef sandwiches, and **Veselka,** 144 Second Ave., at 9th St., 212/228-9682, the place to go for borscht, pierogi, and scrumptious poppy-seed cake. **Odessa,** 119 Ave. A, between 7th and 8th Sts., 212/253-1470, is a good spot for heaping platters of Ukrainian food, while **Christine's,** 208 First Ave., at 12th St., 212/254-2474, serves classic Polish fare.

Eclectic
The sprawling **Yaffa Cafe,** 97 St. Mark's Pl., near First Ave., 212/674-9302, serves a little bit of everything. The food's only fair, but the funky, artsy garden out back is delightful; average main course $6. The friendly **Two Boots,** 37 Ave. A, between 2nd and 3rd Sts., 212/505-2276, serves first-rate pizza and other spicy fare from the lands shaped like "Two Boots"—Italy and Louisiana; average pizza or main course $9. **Time Cafe,** 380 Lafayette St., at

Great Jones St., 212/533-7000, attracts a sleek neighborhood clientele with its varied menu and Moroccan-styled bar; average entrée $13.

Indian
The East Village is also known for its Indian restaurants, most of which lie along the south side of 6th Street between First and Second Avenues. The lines waiting to get into these restaurants can be long, and many require that you BYOB. Average main course is about $8. One of the best of the group is the **Sonargaow Exotic Indian Restaurant,** 328 E. 6th St., 212/677-8876, where the chicken and lamb dishes are especially good. Other solid, though somewhat more expensive, choices (average entrée $13) are **Mitali,** 334 6th St., 212/533-2508, which is also the oldest Indian restaurant on the block, and **Haveli,** 100 Second Ave., 212/982-0533, a more upscale spot located around the corner.

Italian
Always packed with hipsters and foodies alike is tiny **Frank,** 88 Second Ave., between 5th and 6th Sts., 212/420-0202, serving "country Italian" food in a simple setting; average entrée $13. Cheery, old-fashioned **Lanza,** 168 First Ave., between 10th and 11th Sts., 212/674-7014, is a popular eatery decorated with bright oil paintings of Italy. Out back is a pleasant garden; average entrée $13. **John's,** 302 E. 12th St., near Second Ave., 212/475-9531, serves huge portions of Southern Italian food in a dark, romantic setting complete with wine bottles draped with candle wax; average entrée $13.

Seafood
Often jammed with a young, bustling crowd, **Cucina di Pesce,** 87 E. 4th St., between Second and Third Aves., 212/260-6800, serves good pasta and seafood at cheap prices; average entrée $11. The upscale **Pisces,** 95 Ave. A, at 6th St., 212/260-6660, offers unusual seafood dishes, as well as outdoor tables in good weather; average entrée $15.

Southern/Cajun
First-rate Cajun food is the specialty at the tiny,

jumpin' **Great Jones Cafe,** 54 Great Jones St., between Bowery and Lafayette, 212/674-9304, which turns into a hip hangout after midnight; average main course $9. The enormous **Acme Bar & Grill,** 9 Great Jones St., between Broadway and Lafayette, 212/420-1934, offers Southern eats and a boisterous late-night drinking crowd; average main course $9.

Vegetarian

Still going strong after all these years is **Angelika Kitchen,** 300 E. 12th St., between First and Second Aves., 212/228-2909, serving the best vegan fare in the city; average entrée $10. Another good choice for vegetarians is the newish **Kate's Joint,** 58 Ave. B, between 4th and 5th Sts., 212/777-7059; average entrée $8.

Other Ethnic

Laid-back **Tsampa,** 212 E. 9th St., between Second and Third Aves., 212/614-3226, is a new Tibetan restaurant that's already acquired an enthusiastic following; average entrée $12. Step down three steps into cozy **Jules,** 65 St. Mark's Pl., between First and Second Aves., 212/477-5560, a lively French bistro often presenting jazz quartets; average entrée $16.

The stylish and very popular **First,** 87 First Ave., at 5th St., 212/674-3823, lined with burnished steel and comfy gray booths, serves an eclectic international fare that's part Asian, part Mexican, part Italian, and part French; average entrée $17. Lively, square-shaped **Boca Chica,** 13 First Ave., at 1st St., 212/473-0108, offers imaginative Latin dishes, along with tasty cocktails; average entrée $12.

Light Bites

One of the oldest and largest pastry shops in the East Village is the century-old **Veniero's,** 342 E. 11th St., near First Ave., 212/674-7070, featuring classic Italian treats. Across First Avenue is **De Robertis,** 176 First Ave., at 11th St., 212/674-7137, a cheery Italian shop with a handful of tables and wonderful window displays.

Watering Holes and Lounges

The large and friendly **Telephone Bar & Grill,** 149 Second Ave., between 9th and 10th Sts., 212/529-5000, sports bright red English-style phone booths out front. **KGB,** 85 E. 4th St., between Second and Third Aves., 212/505-3360, is a former speakeasy now filled with eclectic Soviet souvenirs and lovely wooden furniture. Especially popular among writers and editors, it hosts frequent readings and literary get-togethers. The intimate, tiled **WCOU,** First Ave. and 7th St., 212/254-4317, is a good place for a quiet drink.

Holiday Cocktail Lounge, 75 St. Mark's Pl., near First Ave., 212/777-9637, is a classic East Village dive where white-haired Ukrainian bartenders serve cheap drinks to surly old poets and cynical young musicians. Also a classic is **Vazac's,** 108 Ave. B, at 7th St., 212/473-8840, or "7B," equipped with a horseshoe-shaped bar that's been featured in a number of movies, including *Crocodile Dundee* and *The Victim.* **McSorley's Old Ale House,** 15 E. 7th St., between Second and Third Aves., 212/473-9148, is one of New York's oldest bars, but its callow fraternity crowd—drinking as much as they can as quickly as they can—makes it a place to avoid.

Though also an upscale restaurant, the sleek retro-hip **Bowery Bar,** 358 Bowery, at 4th St., 212/475-2220, straight out of the '50s, is especially known for its back room bar and garden, usually packed with beautiful people. The elegant **Temple Bar,** 332 Lafayette St., between Bleecker and Houston, 212/925-4242, is a lush hideaway with Oriental rugs and expensive drinks; it claims to have re-introduced the martini to the world in the early 1990s.

Inside the Time Cafe restaurant is **Fez,** 380 Lafayette St., at Great Jones St., 212/533-2680, an upscale Moroccan-style bar sporting exotic fabrics and tile. Over on rapidly gentrifying Avenue C is **C-Note,** 157 Ave. C, at 10th St., 212/677-8142, presenting an interesting mix of live jazz, Latin, folk rock, and poetry readings.

Among gay bars, **Meow Mix,** 269 Houston St., at Suffolk St., 212/254-0688, is a funky lesbian hangout that hosts many theme parties and all-women bands. The oft-crowded **Wonder**

Bar, 505 E. 6th St., at Ave. B, 212/777-9105, caters to both men and women, with DJs spinning the classics.

A number of East Village restaurants mentioned above, including **Great Jones Cafe,** and **Acme Bar & Grill,** also have lively bar scenes. See also the Entertainment section in the Introduction.

Greenwich Village

It's easy to knock Greenwich Village. Once a hotbed of radical and artistic activity, its narrow winding streets now sometimes seem too tame, its restored buildings too cute, its shops and boutiques too artsy and out of sync with sleek, modern times. Only the well-to-do can afford to live here now, and nearly all the dingy old dives have gone safely commercial and mainstream. Worst of all, the streets are always filled with busloads of tourists and bands of roving teenagers looking for wild, sinful times.

And yet—Greenwich Village cannot be dismissed that easily. For all its patina of tourism and well-fed complacency, it still has a bohemian soul lurking somewhere underneath. You can feel it sometimes in the old jazz clubs, or in Washington Square on a windy afternoon, or in the faces of some of the older residents, who saw it all happen, not so long ago.

History

Once an Algonquin settlement, Greenwich Village was settled by Dutch tobacco farmers in the late 1600s and by English landowners in the early- to mid-1700s. By the 1790s, however, the large estates were breaking up as many New Yorkers came north to escape the yellow-fever epidemics in Lower Manhattan. During the epidemics, the city erected barricades along Chambers Street to prevent people from returning to the infected areas, and Greenwich Village started filling up with stores, banks, and other businesses.

Over the next few decades, as the city spread north along Broadway, Greenwich Village turned into a low-rent backwater that attracted immigrants. First came the Irish in the 1850s, then the African Americans after the Civil War, and the Italians in the 1890s.

Around 1910, artists and writers also discov-ered the low rents, and soon the area was teeming with artistic and political activity. Max Eastman founded his radical paper, *The Masses;* tea rooms, literary bars, and basement poetry clubs sprouted up; and theater groups flourished. Among the Village residents during this period were Eugene O'Neill, Edna St. Vincent Millay, Bette Davis, Sherwood Anderson, Theodore Dreiser, John Dos Passos, and e. e. cummings. Greenwich Village's tolerance of "the Third Sex," as gays and lesbians were discreetly called, also dates from this period.

In the 1960s, folk clubs, antiwar rallies, and the civil rights movement brought to the Village another wave of new settlers, including Bob Dylan and Jimi Hendrix, Abbie Hoffman and Jerry Rubin. In 1969, the Village's Stonewall Riots marked the beginning of the national gay-rights movement.

Orientation

Greenwich Village stretches from Houston Street north to 14th Street, and from Fourth Avenue west to the Hudson River. The neighborhood west of Seventh Avenue is generally referred to as the West Village. Nearly every street has something interesting to offer, and you can't go wrong just wandering about. Be sure to bring a map, however—there's no grid system here and even the locals get confused. First-time visitors will probably want to concentrate on Washington Square and on Bleecker, Christopher, and Bedford Streets.

Touring is best here in afternoon and early evening, but it's also well worth returning at night, especially if you're interested in jazz. The Village holds many of the city's top jazz clubs, including the Village Vanguard—arguably the best jazz joint in New York (see Jazz under Entertainment in the Introduction).

MANHATTAN

WASHINGTON SQUARE AND THE SOUTH VILLAGE

Though nothing special to look at, Washington Square Park is the heart of the Village. On a sunny day you'll find everyone here, from kids hotdogging on skateboards and students strumming guitars, to die-hard Hare Krishnas spreading the word and old men taking in the sun. At the park's southwest corner are stone chess tables where the click-clack of the pieces never seems to stop; at the northwest end is the dog run, where dogs of every conceivable shape and size dash madly to and fro.

Once marshland, the eight-acre park was purchased by the city near the end of the 18th century to be used as a potter's field. During the yellow fever epidemic of 1797, at least 660 people were buried here; in 1965, a Con Ed excavation unearthed a sealed tomb containing 25 skeletons that date back to that time. In the late 1700s, the park was used as a public hanging ground, with many of the doomed coming from the state penitentiary that once stood above Christopher Street at the Hudson River. Physical evidence of those days still exists: in the park's extreme northwest corner is an enormous tree bearing the sign, The Hangman's Elm. According to the *New York Times,* the sign is accurate.

In 1826, the square was turned into a parade ground. But the heavy artillery on display sometimes sank into the graves below, so the following year, the parade ground was turned into a park. Elegant townhouses went up all around, and by the 1830s, Washington Square was considered to be the city's most fashionable residential neighborhood.

New York University (NYU) erected its first building on the park in 1837, and now occupies much of the park's periphery. Most of the old townhouses have been replaced by institutional buildings; the genteel old families, by students.

Washington Square Arch

The park's biggest landmark is the marble arch marking the north entrance. Eighty-six feet tall, the arch replaces a temporary wooden one erected in 1889 to commemorate the centennial of

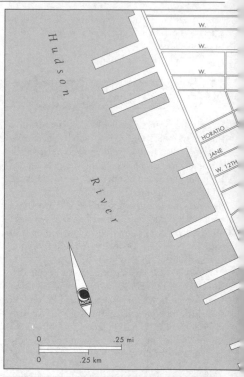

Washington Square Arch

© CHRISTIANE BIRD

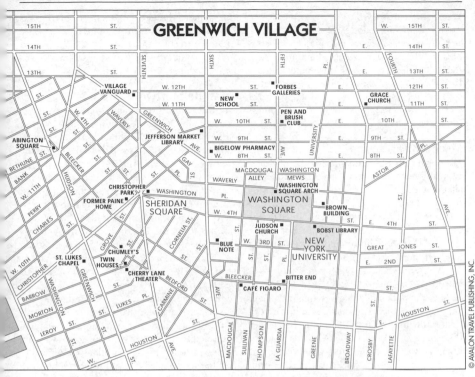

GREENWICH VILLAGE

George Washington's inauguration. Citizens liked the wooden arch so much that they decided to have it remade in marble. The designer was architect Stanford White, and the sculptor was A. Stirling Calder (father of famous mobile sculptor Alexander Calder).

In 1916, a group of Villagers led by a woman named Gertrude Drick climbed a now-sealed staircase inside the arch to read a Greenwich Village declaration of independence, which proclaimed that the neighborhood was seceding from the rest of the city. Among Drick's party were artists John Sloan and Marcel Duchamp. The group partied until dawn by the light of red Chinese lanterns. Prior to this, Drick had already established herself as a bit of an eccentric by passing out black-bordered calling cards wherever she went. The cards bore the single word, Woe; when asked why, Drick would reply, "Because woe is me."

Washington Square North

The beautiful red-brick Greek Revival townhouses on the north side of Washington Square date back to the early 1830s. The house at 1 Washington Square North was home, at different times, to novelists Edith Wharton and Henry James, who once described the neighborhood as "the ideal of quiet and of genteel retirement." James was born in 1843 just off Washington Square at 21 Washington Pl., and he set his novel *Washington Square* at his grandmother's house, 19 Washington Square North. Neither of these two buildings still stands.

The painter Edward Hopper lived at 3 Washington Square North—once known as the "Studio Building"—from 1913 until his death in 1967. Other notables claiming this address at one time or another included painter Rockwell Kent, literary critic Edmund Wilson, and writer John Dos Passos, who started his novel *Manhattan Transfer* in this building in 1922.

MANHATTAN

Washington Mews

Just north of Washington Square North, off University Place to the east, runs a picturesque cobblestone alley lined with stucco buildings. Once stables for the residents of Washington Square Park, Washington Mews is now a row of highly coveted homes and NYU buildings. Political journalist Walter Lippman lived at 50 Washington Mews from 1923 to 1926.

MacDougal Alley

Just north of Washington Square Park, off MacDougal Street to the west, is another picturesque alleyway, this one full of crooked houses, old-fashioned street lamps, and birdhouses. The building at the rear of the alley (No. 19) was once the studio of Gertrude Vanderbilt Whitney, the heiress, sculptor, and art patron who founded the Whitney Museum of Art.

Washington Square South

Most of the buildings along Washington Square South belong to NYU. One outstanding exception is **Judson Memorial Church,** the amber Romanesque bell tower of which lends an air of European elegance to the park. Architect Stanford White designed the 1888 church. Today the church is known for its political activism and arts-oriented congregation.

Before being replaced by the NYU student center, 61 Washington Square South was known as the "House of Genius." Numerous writers lived there over the years, including Willa Cather, Stephen Crane, John Dos Passos, Theodore Dreiser, O. Henry, and Eugene O'Neill. Before being replaced by NYU Law School, 43 Washington Square South was home to Marxist journalist John Reed. While living there, Reed married Louise Bryant, and in 1917, they traveled to Russia to witness the Bolshevik Revolution first-hand.

At 70 Washington Square South is NYU's **Elmer Bobst Library,** an enormous red-granite building. Just behind it is the I. M. Pei apartment complex, **Washington Square Village.**

To reduce costs, many of the NYU buildings erected during the 1830s were made of stone cut by convicts in Sing Sing. When members of the Stone-Cutters Guild heard of this arrangement, they paraded through the park in one of the city's first demonstrations of organized labor. The Stone-Cutters Riot, as it was later called, lasted four days, ending only when the National Guard was called in.

Triangle Shirtwaist Fire

Another important event in labor history is recorded by a plaque mounted high on the Brown Building, 29 Washington Pl., at Greene, just east of the park. It was in this building, on the afternoon of March 25, 1911, that 146 garment workers—mostly young Italian and Jewish women—lost their lives in a tragic fire. The women were working for the Triangle Shirtwaist factory, then located on the building's top three floors. When the fire broke out, the workers found their one exit door bolted on the outside by a management intent on keeping them from leaving early. Some of the women burned to death; most jumped to it.

Incredible though it may seem today, the fire wasn't particularly severe as fires in those days went. But it generated much publicity—largely because the women had gone on strike two years before to protest their poor working conditions—and led to the enactment of the city's first fire and safety codes. The Triangle Shirtwaist Company was indicted, but acquitted, of all responsibility for the tragedy.

West 3rd Street

One block south of Washington Park is West 3rd Street, once the epicenter of the folk world. **Gerde's Folk City,** the famed club where Bob Dylan, Phil Ochs, Tom Paxton, and many others got their starts, was located at 130 West 3rd Street. The address now belongs to a bar called the Kettle of Fish. Across the street is the city's premier jazz supper club, the pricey **Blue Note,** 131 W. 3rd St., 212/475-8592.

Bleecker East of Sixth Avenue

Two blocks south of Washington Park is Bleecker Street. Also once known for its vibrant folk music and jazz scene, this part of Bleecker now looks bedraggled and worn, especially in the early morning when it's still strewn with garbage left behind by the previous night's revelers. Even worse are weekend nights, when the place teems with a raucous bridge-and-tunnel crowd (as New Yorkers so charitably dub anyone who's from the boroughs or suburbs) wandering from club to club.

Still, Bleecker Street should be seen. At Bleecker and La Guardia Place is the **Bitter End,** 212/673-7030, a legendary folk-music club where groups such as Peter, Paul and Mary once performed. Once 158-160 Bleecker St. was home to the **Village Gate,** a sprawling basement club where big names such as Miles Davis, Charles Mingus, B. B. King, and Tito Puente once played; now it's a CVS pharmacy. In 1895, a young Theodore Dreiser lived upstairs at this address in what was then the flea-bitten Mills House. Beds in the 1,500-room hotel went for 25 cents a night.

For information on Bleecker Street west of Sixth Avenue, see Bleecker West of Sixth Avenue under West to Hudson Street, below.

MacDougal Street

The old **San Remo** bar, where literary giants such as James Baldwin and James Agee hung out, once stood at 93 MacDougal St., at Bleecker. Also a regular at the San Remo was poet Maxwell Bodenheim, who wrote, "Greenwich Village is the Coney Island of the soul."

Heading north on MacDougal, you'll pass a myriad of small funky jewelry and T-shirt shops, storefront falafel stands, and old reliable Italian restaurants. At the corner of MacDougal and Minetta Lane is the **Minetta Tavern,** 113 MacDougal St., 212/475-3850, the interior of which is lined with wonderful murals of early Village life and memorabilia from one of its most famous patrons, Joe Gould. As profiled by Joseph Mitchell in the *The New Yorker,* Gould was a Harvard-educated bohemian who spent his life prowling the city streets in search of material for his 11-million-word opus, the *Oral History of Our Times.* He was friendly with many literary types, including Malcolm Cowley, William Carlos Williams, and e. e. cummings (who wrote a poem about Gould), and he cadged free drinks from one and all while expounding eloquently on his tome. But when he died in an insane asylum in 1958, only a few of his supposed hundreds of notebooks were found, and those were more or less unpublishable.

Pretty, narrow **Minetta Lane** is named for Minetta Brook, which once ran from Madison Park through the Village to the Hudson, and still runs underground here. New Amsterdam's first free black farmers began homesteading along this brook in the 1640s, on land given them by the Dutch.

Provincetown Playhouse, 133 MacDougal St., got its start back in 1915, when a group of Villagers vacationing on Cape Cod produced one-act plays on their porch. Eugene O'Neill was the group's most famous member, and most of his work from 1916 through the 1920s was produced here first. Recently restored, the Provincetown now functions as an education performance space for young audiences, young playwrights, and community groups performing O'Neill's work.

NORTH TO 14TH STREET

8th Street

To the immediate north of Washington Park runs 8th Street. Once a highlight of Greenwich Village, 8th Street is now best known for its impossible number of shoe stores, grungy boutiques, and cheap food joints. The street hit rock bottom in terms of atmosphere in 1994–95, but residents are now working to clean the place up and progress has been made.

Eighth Street has been a Village tourist attraction since the late 1940s, when straight couples came to dance at the Bon Soir or the Village Barn, and gay men hung out at a bar called Mary's. In 1970, Jimi Hendrix brought attention to the street when he built his splendid **Electric Lady Studios,** shaped like a giant guitar, into a row of brownstones at 52 W. 8th. Hendrix recorded some 600 hours of tapes at his studio, but he died the following September—from inhalation of vomit following barbiturate intoxication—before anything was released.

The building at 5 W. 8th St. was once the **Marlton Hotel,** where nightclub comedian Lenny Bruce stayed during his highly publicized obscenity trial in 1964. Arrested for an "obscene" performance at the Cafe Au Go Go on Bleecker Street, he was eventually found innocent. He died less than two years later in Hollywood.

Across the street from the old Marlton, in what is now the New York Studio School, was the first home of the **Whitney Museum of American Art.** Gertrude Vanderbilt Whitney founded the museum in 1931, with her own collection of over 500 works by artists such as Edward Hopper, Joseph Stella, Charles Demuth, Thomas Hart Benton, and Isamu Noguchi. The museum was in this pinkish art deco building for almost 20 years before moving uptown.

Grace Church

If you continue east on 8th Street to the shopping mecca of Lower Broadway, then look north, you'll see that Broadway takes an enormous swerve to the left at 11th Street. That's because in 1847, a stubborn old farmer named Hendrick Brevoort refused to let the city's new grid street system cut through his property. It would have meant the death of his beloved gardens and his favorite elm tree.

At the curve today stands **Grace Church,** a lovely, lacy, Gothic Revival cathedral built by Brevoort's son-in-law James Renwick. Then a young construction engineer who had never studied architecture, Renwick entered a contest for the church's design, and won.

On February 10, 1863, Gen. Tom Thumb and Lavinia Warren Bumpus were married at the church, much to the chagrin of many of its parishioners who regarded the P. T. Barnum–planned stunt as beneath the church's dignity. Nonetheless, when the wedding took place, over 1,200 of these same parishioners pushed and shoved and climbed up on the pews to get a better view of the little people.

Lower Fifth Avenue

Fifth Avenue begins at Washington Square Park. One block north, at the southwest corner of Fifth Ave. and 8th St., stands the lovely, art deco **1 Fifth.** During the 1920s, a women's political group called the "A Club" met here. The club's eclectic membership included Rose O'Neill, who later invented the Kewpie doll, and Frances Perkins, who later served as secretary of labor under Franklin Delano Roosevelt.

Other venerable clubs are still based in the area. The **Pen and Brush Club,** 16 E. 10th St., at Fifth Ave., is the oldest professional-women's organization in the United States, founded in 1893. The **Salmagundi Club,** 57 Fifth Ave., near 11th St., is the nation's oldest artists' club, founded in 1870.

The streets between Fifth and Sixth Avenues in this part of town are among the prettiest in the city; 9th, 10th, and 11th Streets in particular are lined with one gorgeous brownstone after another, many with colorful window boxes out front.

Poet Marianne Moore lived at 35 W. 9th St. from 1966 until her death in 1971 at the age of 84. Mark Twain lived at 14 W. 10th St. from 1900 to 1901. He was famous by then and subjected to a constant stream of strangers filing by his door, asking for autographs and handshakes. Dashiell Hammett was living at 28 W. 10th St. in 1951 when he was sent to prison for 22 weeks for refusing to testify about the Civil Rights Congress, a leftist organization of which he was a member.

The Weathermen Blow-Up

At 18 W. 11th St. is a handsome 19th-century townhouse with an oddly modern, triangular front of red brick and glass. That's because on March 6, 1970, the radical group the Weathermen accidentally blew off the front part of the building while concocting bombs in the basement. Three Weathermen died in the accident, but Cathlyn Wilkerson—whose parents owned the building—and her friend Kathy Boudin escaped and vanished. Wilkerson turned herself in 10 years later and served 11 months in prison for negligent homicide. Boudin was captured in 1981 in connection with a Brinks armored-truck holdup in which three people were killed. She was sentenced to 20 years to life.

Forbes Magazine Galleries

On the ground floor of the Forbes Building are the Forbes Magazine Galleries, 62 Fifth Ave., near 12th St., 212/206-5548. The museum is best known for its fabulous collection of Fabergé eggs—perfect in their miniature beauty—but you'll also find much else of interest. Highlights include over 500 toy boats, 12,000 toy soldiers, lots of historical documents, and a weird and wacky trophy section called the "Mortality of Immortality." Everything was collected by idiosyncratic media tycoon Malcolm Forbes, and the whole place feels like the giant playhouse of a precocious kid.

The galleries are open Tues.–Wed., Fri.–Sat. 10 A.M.–4 P.M. Though only 900 tickets are handed out a day, there's usually no problem getting in. Tickets are free.

New School

One block west of the Forbes Building is the New School for Social Research, 66 W. 12th St., 212/229-5600, an adult educational institution known for its excellent social sciences department and eclectic course offerings. Worth a quick look is the school's impressive lobby mural, *The Coming Together of the Races,* by Mexican artist José Clemente Orozco.

Sixth Avenue

Near the northwest corner of Sixth Avenue and 10th Street are two unusual residential courtyards, cut off from the streets by iron gates. The utilitarian **Milligan Place,** off Sixth Avenue just north of 10th Street, was built in 1852, supposedly to house the waiters of the Brevoort Hotel. The more picturesque **Patchin Place,** off 10th Street just west of Sixth Avenue, comes from the same time period and the same architect, Aaron Patchin.

Poet e. e. cummings once owned 4 Patchin Pl., living there from 1923 until his death in 1962. During much of that same time, writer Djuna Barnes rented a tiny apartment at 5 Patchin Place. Legend has it that cummings used to stand below the then-elderly Barnes's window every morning and shout up, "Djuna, are you dead yet?" As fate would have it, cummings died first.

Jefferson Market Library

Reigning over Sixth Avenue and 10th Street are the Gothic turrets and towers of Jefferson Market Library. Designed by Frederick Clarke Withers and Calvert Vaux in 1876, the stunning maroon and white building was originally a courthouse

© CHRISTIANE BIRD

Originally a courthouse, Jefferson Market Library is a grand showcase of Gothic architectural features.

and part of a complex that also included a jail, firehouse, and market. The jail was later replaced by the Women's House of Detention, where jazz great Billie Holiday was once imprisoned for the possession of marijuana. The market's former site is now a community garden bursting with color in the spring.

WEST TO HUDSON STREET

West to Waverly Place

Heading west of Sixth Avenue on Christopher Street to Waverly Place, you'll pass a picturesque elbow-shaped street on the left lined with 1840s row houses. Originally a stable alley, **Gay Street** was later home to African Americans, many of whom worked as servants for the families on Washington Square. Waverly Place was named after Sir Walter Scott's best-selling novel, *Waverley.*

At the intersection of Christopher, Waverly,

MANHATTAN

and Grove is an odd, three-sided building called the **Northern Dispensary.** When it was built in 1831, it was one of the city's first free hospitals and was then at the city's northernmost edge—hence the name. Edgar Allan Poe was treated here for a cold in 1837.

Just around the corner to the north, at 193 Waverly Pl., is anthropologist Margaret Mead's old residence. A single mother, Mead lived with her daughter in this handsome four-story townhouse from 1955 to 1966.

Christopher Park/Sheridan Square

Just west of the dispensary, at Christopher Street and Seventh Avenue South, is scruffy Christopher Park, often mistaken for Sheridan Square. The latter is just southeast of Christopher Park at the triangle where Washington Place, Barrow, Grove, and West 4th Streets meet. The confusion is understandable—Christopher Park is more central and marked by a statue of Gen. Philip Sheridan. Sheridan was a Union general best remembered for the unfortunate, often misquoted, line, "The only good Indians I saw were dead."

Next to the general is a George Segal sculpture depicting two gay couples—one male and standing, the other female and sitting on a bench. Erected in 1991, the statue commemorates the Stonewall Riots, which took place across the street at the Stonewall Inn on June 27, 1969. (The original Stonewall Inn was at 51 Christopher St. and is now gone; the bar called Stonewall at 53 Christopher is just a namesake.)

The night began with what the cops later said was a routine raid of a bar that was serving alcohol without a liquor license. But the gay men inside the Stonewall didn't see it that way. All too used to being unfairly harassed by the police, they resisted arrest. Friends in neighboring bars called out their support, and beer bottles began to fly. Eventually, 13 protestors were arrested, but that was almost beside the point. More significantly, the riots marked the first time that gays had collectively engaged in civil disobedience. The next night, an even bigger group of protestors gathered; the modern gay-rights movement had begun.

At night, and especially on the weekends,

Sheridan Square and the adjoining blocks of Seventh Avenue South swell with out-of-towners and visitors of all types—young and middle-aged, gay and straight, white and black. Many popular bars and music clubs (see Watering Holes and Lounges under Food, below) are located in the immediate area.

Thomas Paine's Home

Across the street from Christopher Park, at 59 Grove St., is the former home of Thomas Paine, the Revolutionary War–era author of *Common Sense, The Crisis,* and *The Rights of Man.* It was Paine who wrote the famous words, "These are the times that try men's souls."

Born to Quaker parents in England, Paine immigrated to the United States in 1774 and served in the Revolutionary army. He moved into this house in 1808, at the age of 71. By then Paine was a difficult and crusty man, and also an atheist—a fact his straight-laced neighbors could not forgive. Upon his death in 1809, only six mourners attended his funeral and his request to be buried in a Quaker graveyard was denied.

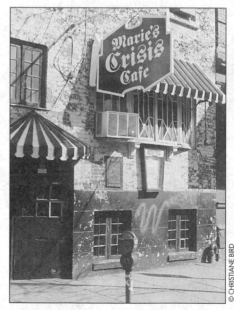

© CHRISTIANE BIRD

Thomas Paine's old home is now a gay piano bar.

Paine's house—marked with a plaque—is now a venerable gay piano bar called **Marie's Crisis Cafe,** 212/243-9323, named partly as a tribute to Paine.

Bleecker West of Sixth Avenue

Bleecker Street west of Sixth Avenue is much different than Bleecker Street to the east. Between Sixth and Seventh Avenues, the thoroughfare is lined with old-fashioned food shops that hark back to the days when this was a largely Italian neighborhood. Between Seventh and Eighth Avenue are numerous gift and antique shops, many of them quite expensive (see Shopping, below), along with a flock of trendy new boutiques—**Yamak, Sleek, Blush,** and **Verve.**

Bleecker ends at **Abingdon Square** at Eighth Avenue. Continuing farther west on either Bethune or West 12th Street, you'll come to **Gansevoort Meat Market,** at the north end of the meatpacking district. Once largely deserted by day, and a magnet for transvestites and the ultrahip by night, the neighborhood has recently morphed into Manhattan's newest hot spot, and is acquiring an ever-growing number of bustling restaurants, clubs, and boutiques.

Christopher Street

Built along a path that the Algonquins once used to carry lobsters and oysters inland from a cove on the Hudson, Christopher Street was a working-class address for most of its modern existence. For years, longshoremen working the nearby Hudson River piers lived here with their families. But long before Stonewall, the street also had a thriving, underground gay nightlife. Gay bars such as the Colony operated as early as the 1940s. And by the early 1970s, the street's gay nightlife had become known around the world.

Christopher Street is still the center of gay New York, but this is changing. Because gays no longer feel as shunned by the rest of the city as they once did, they're moving into other neighborhoods—most notably Chelsea. At the same time, straight tourists—who no longer feel as threatened by gay life—are taking good looks around. "Sometimes I feel like this is kind of

like a gay Jurassic Park," one gay Christopher Street habitué recently told the *New York Times.*

Walking west on Christopher from Seventh Ave., you'll pass provocatively named leather and clothing shops such as Boyz, Leather Man, and Oh Boy. West of Hudson Street, outside tourist territory, are many of Christopher Street's rougher gay bars.

Bedford Street

One of the prettiest and oldest areas in the Village is centered on Bedford Street, just south of Christopher. Much of the property around here once belonged to Aaron Burr; his former coach house is now a bar and restaurant called **One If By Land, Two If By Sea.** It's at 17 Barrow St., near Seventh Ave., 212/228-0822.

At 102 Bedford is a small building known as **Twin Peaks** because of its two odd, very steep roofs. The roofs were the brainchild of designer Clifford Daily, who built the 1926 additions onto the formerly ordinary 1830 house because he felt that "the Village is growing into a desert of mediocrity with nothing of inspiration."

Right next to Twin Peaks, at 17 Grove St., at Bedford, is a lovely wooden clapboard house. Built in 1822 by William Hyde, a window-sash maker, it's still superbly well preserved.

At 77 Bedford, at the corner of Commerce St., is the oldest existing house in the Village, the 1799 **Isaacs-Hendricks House.** At 75 ½ Bedford is the so-called **Narrowest House in New York.** Though not much to look at, it was poet Edna St. Vincent Millay's home in the 1920s.

Commerce Street

One of the shortest streets in the city is Commerce, which runs a graceful arch from Seventh Avenue South to Barrow Street. At the curve is the **Cherry Lane Theater,** 38 Commerce St., 212/989-2020, founded by Edna St. Vincent Millay and others in 1924. Experimental in nature at first, the Cherry Lane is now an off-Broadway theater with an excellent reputation.

At 39 and 41 Commerce St., where Commerce meets Barrow, are two delightful **Twin Houses,** separated by a shared garden. Legend has it they were built by a sea captain for his two feuding daughters; the more mundane land records say they were built by a local milk merchant.

Hudson Street and Grove Court

Just north of where Barrow meets Hudson is the **Church of St. Luke-in-the-Fields,** 479-487 Hudson. Once literally surrounded by fields, the church was built in 1821 as an uptown chapel of Wall Street's Trinity Church. Author Bret Harte lived in St. Luke's Parish House as a boy in the 1840s.

Directly across the street from St. Luke's, on Grove Street, is Grove Court, a picturesque little courtyard lined with white shutters. Built in 1854 for workers, the courtyard was not always as serene as it is today. Among its early nicknames were "Mixed Ale Alley" and "Pig's Alley."

St. Luke's Place

Heading south on Hudson Street you'll come to St. Luke's Place, a picturesque 1850s block lined with Italianate row houses on one side, St. Luke's Park on the other. The charming but corrupt Jimmy Walker, mayor of New York City from 1926 to 1933, once lived at 6 St. Luke's Pl.; two "lamps of honor" mark the spot. Other former residents of the street include Sherwood Anderson, who lived at No. 12 in 1923; Theodore Dreiser, who began *An American Tragedy* while living at No. 16 in 1922–23; and Marianne Moore, who lived at No. 14 with her mother in the earliest years of her career, 1918–29.

SHOPPING

Antiques

Bleecker Street is known for antique stores. Among them are old stand-bys such as **Old Japan, Inc.,** 382 Bleecker St., 212/633-0922, and **Susan Parrish,** 390 Bleecker St., 212/645-5020, selling American country and folk. At 506 Hudson St., near Christopher, is **Uplift Lighting,** 212/929-3632, specializing in art deco fixtures. Along **Broadway between Union Square and 8th Street,** find a good half-dozen antique furniture shops, some of which cater only to wholesalers.

Art and Crafts

Russian Arts, 451 Sixth Ave., near W. 10th St., 212/242-5946, specializes in Russian crafts and artifacts.

Books

Oscar Wilde Memorial Bookshop, 15 Christopher St., near Sixth Ave., 212/255-8097, was established in 1967, and is said to be the world's oldest gay bookstore. **Three Lives & Co.,** 154 W. 10th St., between Sixth and Seventh Aves., 212/741-2069, is one of the city's top literary bookstores, and hosts frequent readings by well-known authors.

Other independent Village bookstores of note include **Biography Bookshop,** 400 Bleecker St., at 11th St., 212/807-8655, specializing in biographies, memoirs, and letters; the literary **Shakespeare & Co.,** 716 Broadway, 212/529-1330; and **East West Books,** 78 Fifth Ave., at 14th St., 212/243-5994, specializing in Eastern and New Age philosophy books. Chain stores include **Barnes & Noble,** Sixth Ave. and 8th St., 212/674-8780, and **Tower Books,** 383 Lafayette St., 212/228-5100, open daily until midnight.

Clothing

Vintage clothing stores abound in Greenwich Village. **Star Struck,** 43 Greenwich Ave., near W. 10th St., 212/691-5357, carries a good selection of old coats, and creaky **Antique Boutique,** 712 Broadway, near Astor, 212/460-8830, is a great emporium selling everything from vintage cocktail dresses to leather jackets.

Andy's Chee-Pees, 691 Broadway, near W. 4th St., 212/420-5980; and **Cheap Jack's,** 841 Broadway, near 12th St., 212/777-9564, both offer heaps of *stuff*. You might find some gems, but you'll have to dig.

More up-to-date styles are offered by **Urban Outfitters,** 360 Sixth Ave., near Waverly, 212/677-9350, a trendy store featuring natural-fabric fashions for both men and women, along with home furnishings and gifts. Over-the-top **Patricia Field,** 10 E. 8th St., near Fifth Ave., 212/254-1699, is the place to go for outré fashion and clubwear.

Along **8th Street** is a mother lode of shoe shops.

Games and Fun Stuff

The famed **Chess Shop,** 230 Thompson St.,

just south of W. 3rd St., 212/475-9580, may sell all sorts of chessboards and pieces, but more importantly, endless chess games are always in session. Players of all levels are welcome. **Game Show,** 474 Sixth Ave., between 11th and 12th Sts., 212/633-6328, is well stocked with games for all ages. **Classic Toys,** 218 Sullivan St., 212/674-4434, is a fun and unusual spot, specializing in old and new toys and miniature figures; children, sophisticate collectors, and the general public are all welcome.

Gourmet Treats

Balducci's, 424 Sixth Ave., at 9th St., 212/673-2600, is a legendary Village food shop selling gourmet treats of every conceivable variety. On Bleecker Street, between Sixth and Seventh Avenues, are **Murray's Cheese Shop,** 257 Bleecker St., 212/243-3289, selling cheeses from around the world; **A. Zito & Sons,** 259 Bleecker St., 212/929-6139, Frank Sinatra's favorite bakery; **Faicco's Pork Store,** 260 Bleecker St., 212/243-1974, especially known for its homemade sausages; and the **Bleecker Street Pastry Shop,** 245 Bleecker St., 212/242-4959.

McNulty's Tea and Coffee, 109 Christopher, near Bedford, 212/242-5351, is an aromatic

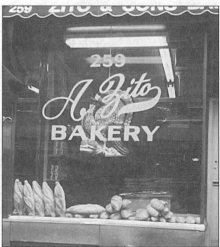

© CHRISTIANE BIRD

Bleecker Street's A. Zito & Sons was Frank Sinatra's favorite bakery.

haven over 100 years old. **Li-Lac Chocolates,** 120 Christopher, 212/242-7374, sells luscious homemade sweets.

Music

Tower Records, 692 Broadway, at E. 4th St., 212/505-1500, offers an overwhelming array of recordings from rock to classical to everything in between. The store opened in 1983 and was largely responsible for transforming this one-time no-man's-land between the two villages into a distinct shopping strip. Tower is open until midnight every night, and **Tower Video** and **Tower Books,** both at 383 Lafayette St., 212/505-1500 and 212/228-5100, respectively, are directly behind the main store. **Revolver Records,** 45 W. 8th St., near Sixth Ave., 212/982-6760, carries lots of rock and is the premier bootleg shop in town. **Bleecker Bob's,** 118 W. Third St., near MacDougal, 212/475-9677, an old Village favorite, is now something of a tourist trap.

Other Shops

More Bleecker Street stores include the nationally renowned **Matt Umanov Guitar Store,** 273 Bleecker St., between Sixth and Seventh Aves., 212/675-2157; and **Aphrodisia,** 264 Bleecker St., 212/989-6440, stocked with an enormous number of herbs, oils, and New Age remedies. **Condomania,** 351 Bleecker St., near Christopher, 212/691-9442, is the place for condoms and erotica.

Bigelow Pharmacy, 414 Sixth Ave., 212/533-2700, is New York's oldest continuously operating pharmacy; the official historic landmark was established in 1838, and still sports its original oak fittings and gaslight fixtures. **Star Magic,** 745 Broadway, near 8th St., 212/228-7770, with branches all over the city, sells a fascinating selection of space-age gifts, including science kits, mobiles, prisms, kaleidoscopes, and books.

ACCOMMODATIONS

$50–100

Stepping into the beaux arts **Larchmont Hotel,** 27 W. 11th St., between Fifth and Sixth Aves.,

212/989-9333, www.larchmonthotel.com, is like stepping into a private home. Umbrellas are standing in the tiled foyer; someone is asleep on the loveseat in the tiny lobby. A much-needed addition to Greenwich Village, the Larchmont offers 77 attractive rooms with rattan furnishings, good lighting, and clean, shared bathrooms down the hall. $70–90 s, $90–115 d; includes continental breakfast.

$100–150

Though small, the lobby of the family-owned **Washington Square Hotel,** 103 Waverly Pl., between MacDougal St. and Sixth Ave., 212/777-9515 or 800/222-0418, www.washingtonsquarehotel.com, is stunning—all black and white tiles, lacy iron grillwork, gilded adornments, and Audubon prints. The rooms aren't anything special, but they're not bad either, and neither is CIII, a stylish on-site restaurant lined with jazzy paintings. Combine all this with moderate prices and a terrific location, just off Washington Square, and you have a good bargain. $126–145 s, $150–160 d; includes continental breakfast.

FOOD

American

One of the best places for a burger is the **Corner Bistro,** 331 W. 4th St., at Jane and Eighth Ave., 212/242-9502, a dark pub with creaky wooden booths and an excellent jazz jukebox; burger $6. The casual **Cornelia Street Cafe,** 29 Cornelia St., between Bleecker and W. 4th St., 212/989-9318, presents poetry readings and jazz concerts in its big downstairs room, with open-air dining upstairs during the summer; average entrée $13.

Anglers & Writers, 420 Hudson St., at St. Luke's Pl., 212/675-0810, specializes in homemade foods, country charm, and books and fishing paraphernalia a la Hemingway; average entrée $14. Warm, posh **Grange Hall,** 50 Commerce St., near Hudson, 212/924-5246, features a wonderful Depression-era mural, polished wooden booths, and an imaginative menu filled with updated American classics; average entrée $16.

One of the city's top restaurants is the sleek and fashionable **Gotham Bar and Grill,** 12 E. 12th St., near Fifth Ave., 212/620-4020, winner of numerous awards for both its design and food; average entrée $30. For steaks in an old-fashioned setting, try the **Old Homestead,** 56 Ninth Ave., near 14th St., 212/242-9040, a classic eatery with a huge brown-and-white cow above its door; average entrée $28.

French/Continental

In the meatpacking district, find **Pastis,** 9 Ninth Ave., at Little 12th St., 212/929-4844, an airy, ultra-hip bistro complete with excellent food, beautiful people, and reasonable prices; average entrée $15. Not far away is the 24-hour bistro/diner **Florent,** 69 Gansevoort St., between Greenwich and Washington, 212/989-5779, a pioneering eatery in the district and longstanding hipster fave; average main dish, $14. Low-key, low-ceilinged **Cafe Loup,** 105 W. 13th St., near Sixth Ave., 212/255-4746, is a Village institution serving a wide range of excellent French fare; average entrée $18.

Italian

The city's best pizzeria is **John's,** 278 Bleecker St., near Seventh Ave., 212/243-1680. Its New York–style pies are thin, crispy, and low on grease; sold by the whole pie only, no slices. Expect long lines unless you come during the off-hours; medium pizza $10. **Arturo's,** 106 W. Houston St., at Thompson, 212/677-3820, also serves good pizza, and is especially popular among students and young professionals; large pizza $12.

Friendly, elegant **Cent'Anni,** 50 Carmine St., between Bleecker and Bedford, 212/989-9494, is a modern trattoria serving a wide range of fresh Tuscan dishes; average entrée $18. A longtime favorite among connoisseurs of Italian food is comfortable, brick-walled **Il Mulino,** 86 W. 3rd St., between Thompson and Sullivan, 212/673-3783, serving traditional Abruzzese fare; average entrée $25.

Latin/Caribbean

Recently renovated **Caribe,** 117 Perry St., at Greenwich, 212/255-9191, is a friendly slice of the Caribbean transported to the West Village;

average entrée $11. The cheery, upscale **Mi Cocina,** 57 Jane St., at Hudson, 212/627-8273, serves authentic Mexican food in a simple, brick-walled setting; average entrée $16.

Southern

For many years the tiny, diner-like **Pink Teacup,** 42 Grove St., near Seventh Ave., 212/807-6755, was one of downtown's only soul food restaurants. Brunch, featuring pancakes, biscuits, and grits, is especially good; average main dish $10.

Other Ethnic

Stylish **Tangerine,** 228 W. 10th St., between Bleecker and Hudson, 212/463-8585, serves up first-rate Thai food—try the purple-blossom appetizers; average entrée $15. For some of the freshest sushi in town, step into **Japonica,** 100 University Pl., at 12th St., 212/243-7752, a long-time Village favorite; average entrée $17. Dark, old-fashioned **El Faro,** 823 Greenwich St., between Horatio and Jane, 212/929-8210, is a bit worn but still known for its tasty Spanish cuisine; average entrée $15.

Airy, laid-back **Gus' Place,** 149 Waverly Pl., near Sixth Ave., 212/645-8511, serves Greek and Mediterranean food; average main dish $17. New to the meatpacking district is **Meet,** 71-73 Gansevoort St., at Washington St., 212/242-0990, housed in a former meat freezer now equipped with an illuminated catwalk and onyx bar. On the menu is Mediterranean-American fare; average entrée $24.

Light Bites

Pane & Cioccolato, 10 Waverly Pl., at Mercer St., 212/473-3944, is a friendly coffee shop just east of Washington Square. **Mamoun's Falafel,** 119 MacDougal St., between Bleecker and W. 3rd Sts., 212/674-8685, offers good, cheap takeout.

Bleecker and MacDougal Streets are known for their many Italian coffee and pastry shops. Among the best are **Cafe Dante,** 79 MacDougal St., 212/982-5275, and **Caffé Reggio,** 119 MacDougal St., 212/475-9557. **French Roast,** 78 W. 11th St., at Sixth Ave., 212/533-2233, is a popular spot serving both sandwiches and desserts. **Tea and Sympathy,** 108 Greenwich Ave., at 13th St., 212/807-8329, features a British-style afternoon tea.

Watering Holes and Lounges

Sturdy old **White Horse Tavern,** 567 Hudson St., at 11th St., 212/243-9260, was once a writer's hangout; Dylan Thomas drank himself to death here. Now the tavern caters mostly to a collegiate crowd. Outdoor picnic tables are set up in summer.

Chumley's, 86 Bedford St., between Barrow and Grove, 212/675-4449, is an old speakeasy/restaurant where writers John Dos Passos and Theodore Dreiser once drank. It's unmarked, but not hard to find. The big, worn **Cedar Tavern,** 82 University Pl., between 11th and 12th Sts., 212/741-9754, was once frequented by Jackson Pollock and other abstract expressionists. It's still a good place for a beer, but avoid the food.

To the west, the **Art Bar,** 52 Eighth Ave., near Horatio, 212/727-0244, is downtown grunge in front, aging Victorian parlor in back. **Automatic Slim's,** 733 Washington St., at Bank, 212/645-8660, is a tiny, high-ceilinged joint with blues posters on the walls, and Cajun fare on the menu.

In the Gansevoort Meat Market, find the raucous, testosterone-filled **Hogs & Heifers,** 859 Washington St., near Gansevoort St., 212/929-0655, its crowds spilling out onto the streets. **Hell,** 59 Gansevoort St., between Greenwich and Washington Sts., 212/727-1666, is a velvet-draped spot complete with chandeliers and lots of comfortable seating areas. Decked out as its name implies, the **APT,** 419 W. 13th St., near Ninth Ave., 212/414-4245, offers the chance to hear up-and-coming DJs in an intimate setting. **Gaslight,** 400 W. 14th at Ninth Ave., 212/807-8444, is an old neighborhood-style bar with tile floors and doors that open onto the street in good weather.

Among gay bars, the low-key **Stonewall,** 53 Christopher St., near Seventh Ave. S, 212/463-0950, is named after the landmark (see above). Across the street sprawls the **Monster,** 80 Grove St., 212/924-3558, featuring a drag cabaret. Two popular lesbian bars, drawing largely professional crowds, are **Henrietta Hudson,** 438 Hudson St., at Morton, 212/924-3347; and

Crazy Nanny's, 21 Seventh Ave. S, at Leroy, 212/366-6312.

Among the restaurants mentioned above, the

Corner Bistro, Grange Hall, Pastis, and **Florent** all have lively late-night scenes. See also Entertainment in the Introduction.

From Union Square to Murray Hill

The East Side between 14th and 42nd Streets is mostly residential, and lacks both the history of Lower Manhattan and the energy of the Villages. But it does have a considerable quiet charm and a number of quirky attractions sandwiched between the brownstones and apartment buildings.

Various neighborhoods make up this section of the East Side. **Union Square** begins at 14th Street and Broadway. **Madison Square,** which replaced Union Square as the city's commercial and theater center in the late 1800s, begins at 23rd Street and Broadway. East of those two neighborhoods is **Gramercy Park,** a residential square centered at 20th Street and Irving Place. **Murray Hill** lies between Madison and Third Avenues, and 34th and 42nd Streets. It's a well-heeled neighborhood named for Quaker Robert Murray, who owned all the land in the area during the Revolutionary War era. Legend has it that Murray's wife, Mary Lindley, helped George Washington win the war by detaining the British officers for tea while the Americans escaped up the West Side to Harlem Heights.

In recent years, it has become fashionable to refer to the area around the Flatiron building at 23rd Street and Fifth Avenue as the **Flatiron District.** No one seems to be sure exactly what this area encompasses, but it takes in slices of the Union and Madison Square areas, as well as a hunk of Chelsea to the west.

UNION SQUARE

Just over a decade ago, this small green square between 14th and 17th Streets, immediately east of Broadway, was dirty and neglected—a haven for drug dealers and petty criminals. Many of its buildings were deteriorating, others were abandoned.

Today the square has been transformed into a bustling urban center complete with sleek mega-

stores, upscale restaurants, fashionable bars, and a farmers' **Greenmarket,** 212/477-3220, operating on Monday, Wednesday, Friday, and Saturday mornings.

Laid out as a park in 1815, Union Square was first the province of prominent local families such as the Roosevelts, who lived nearby. Then in the mid-1800s, the city's entertainment and commercial industries moved in. The famous Academy of Music started up on 14th Street, and department stores went up all along Broadway from 8th to 23rd Streets. This commercialism was short lived, however. By 1900 both the theaters and the shops had moved uptown, to Madison Square at 23rd Street, and Union Square had become home to garment factories and immigrant workers. Many of the fine old homes were converted into tenement buildings.

From the 1910s until after WW II, Union Square was a center for political demonstrations. Socialists, communists, and the Wobblies (members of the Industrial Workers of the World) protested here, while many left-wing organizations had headquarters on or near the square. One of the most dramatic protests took place on August 22, 1927, the night anarchists Nicola Sacco and Bartolomeo Vanzetti were executed. The police had machine guns mounted on a roof overlooking the square, but the demonstration remained peaceful.

Andy Warhol's Factory

The sixth floor of the narrow Moorish-accented building at 33 Union Square W, between 16th and 17th Streets, was once home to Andy Warhol's Factory, frequented by the likes of Lou Reed, John Cale, and Nico of the Velvet Underground; Truman Capote; and John Lennon. Here Warhol made many of his underground films, including *Blow Job, Flesh,* and *I, Man,* featuring a woman named Valerie Solanas.

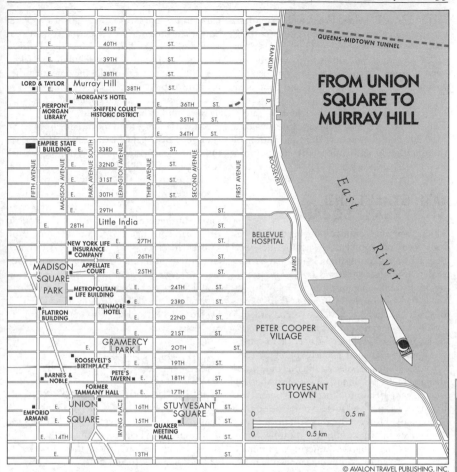

FROM UNION SQUARE TO MURRAY HILL

© AVALON TRAVEL PUBLISHING, INC.

Solanas went on to found SCUM, or the Society for Cutting Up Men. As she wrote in her manifesto, "there remains to civic-minded, responsible, thrill-seeking females only to overthrow the government . . . and destroy the male sex." One day in June 1968, Solanas went by the Factory to see Warhol. He was on the phone, but she waited patiently until he got off and then shot him four times in the chest. At the hospital, Warhol was declared clinically dead, yet he managed to survive. Solanas turned herself in but was declared incompetent to stand trial. Nonetheless, she pleaded guilty and served two years in prison.

Tammany Hall

Today, the red-brick building at 100 E. 17th St. houses the New York Film Academy, where filmmakers learn their craft. But it was once Tammany Hall, the headquarters of the city's Democratic machine. Though today's building dates to 1928, it was in an earlier Tammany Hall, located farther downtown, that William Marcy "Boss" Tweed and his cronies hatched their greedy schemes, eventually robbing the city of up to $200 million.

It was also in an earlier Tammany Hall that Richard Croker, the most powerful Democratic boss after Tweed, helped invent a more modern get-rich-quick scheme: honest graft. Croker's colleague George Washington Plunkitt described the concept best when he wrote, without any sense of irony: "There's the biggest kind of a difference between political looters and politicians who make a fortune out of politics by keepin' their eyes wide open." At the height of his career, Croker, who never held political office, owned a $180,000 house, an upstate farm, and a string of thoroughbreds—all supposedly earned on a $25,000-a-year salary.

14TH STREET AND STUYVESANT SQUARE

Throughout much of this century, 14th Street has had a seedy reputation as a haven for hucksters, peep shows, and porn shops. Even as far back as the late 1800s, the street was a center for prostitution. In 1892, anarchist Emma Goldman, inspired by Dostoyevsky's *Crime and Punishment,* tried her hand at streetwalking here in order to earn the money she and her lover needed to assassinate industrialist Henry Clay Frick. Goldman was none too adept at her self-appointed task. Only after hours of walking did one older gentleman finally buy her a drink, and then he slipped her $10 and told her to go home. "You haven't got it, that's all there is to it," he said.

Some of this seedy quality still hovers over 14th Street, but it's steadily disappearing. Shiny new stores and a movie theater now dominate the southern end of Union Square, while many other new shops have opened nearby.

West of Union Square in what is technically considered Chelsea, 14th Street is crammed with discount stores catering to a largely Hispanic clientele. For years, these stores have been frenetic with activity, but recently, they, too, have started to lose their vitality. See the wig stores, plastic toy vendors, and clerks sitting on ladders—shouting out the day's bargains—while you still can.

Stuyvesant Square

Between 15th and 17th Streets, and Second and Third Avenues, is a small, somewhat neglected park, once part of Dutch governor Peter Stuyvesant's farm. On the park's west side, at 15th Street, is the **Friends' Meeting House,** a lovely red-brick Greek Revival building. Back in the 1800s, in order to obtain the quiet that they needed for their meetings, the Friends used to spread six inches of tanbark on the street to muffle the sound of horses' hooves.

Across the street from the meeting house is **St. George's Episcopal Church,** 209 E. 16th St., an impressive Romanesque Revival complex. It's sometimes called "J. P. Morgan's church" because the wealthy financier worshipped here. Also once affiliated with St. George's was baritone soloist Harry T. Burleigh. Born the son of slaves, Burleigh helped popularize the African American spiritual. People would come from all over the city to hear him sing. Burleigh also composed more than 300 songs, and helped Czech composer Antonin Dvorak adapt traditional black melodies into his *New World Symphony.* Dvorak lived nearby at 327 E. 17th St. from 1892 to 1895; his statue stands in Stuyvesant Park.

IRVING PLACE TO GRAMERCY PARK
Washington Irving's "Home"

Though the plaque on the pretty building at 40 Irving Pl., at 17th St., states that Washington Irving once lived here, he never actually did. The street was named after the author, however, as was the high school across the street, which sports a grim bust of Irving out front.

It is to Washington Irving that we owe our impressions of Dutch New York. Irving immortalized the fat, loll-about burghermeisters and their bossy, red-cheeked wives in his satiric 1821 tome, *A History of New-York, from the beginning of the World to the end of the Dutch Dynasty: Containing, among many surprising and curious matters, The Unutterable Ponderings of Walter The Doubter, The Disastrous Project of William The Testy, and The Chivalric Achievements of Peter The Headstrong, The Three Dutch Governors of New-Amsterdam: Being the only authentic history of the times that ever hath been published.*

Pete's Tavern

Founded in 1864, Pete's Tavern, 129 E. 18th St., at Irving Pl., 212/473-7676, bills itself as the city's oldest bar. The creaky joint was once a favorite hangout of short-story writer O. Henry, who lived across the street at 55 Irving Place. Henry—whose real name was William Sydney Porter—had previously served time in Texas for embezzlement. Supposedly he wrote his famous short story, "The Gift of the Magi," in a booth at the back. Pete's is open for lunch and dinner, but go for the atmosphere and drink, not the food.

Gramercy Park

At the north end of Irving Place, between 20th and 21st Streets, is Gramercy Park, bought and laid out in 1831 by lawyer and real estate developer Samuel Ruggles. As fashionable today as it was back then, the park consists of both stately buildings and an enclosed green to which only the residents have access. Outsiders have to con-

© CHRISTIANE BIRD

Short-story writer O. Henry made Pete's Tavern a home away from home.

E. B. WHITE ON NEW YORK CITY NEIGHBORHOODS

Life in New York follows the neighborhood pattern. The city is literally a composite of tens of thousands of tiny neighborhood units. There are, of course, the big districts and big units: Chelsea and Murray Hill and Gramercy. . . . But the curious thing about New York is that each large geographical unit is composed of countless small neighborhoods. Each neighborhood is virtually self-sufficient. Usually it is no more than two or three blocks long and a couple of blocks wide. Each area is a city within a city within a city. Thus, no matter where you live in New York, you will find within a block or two a grocery store, a barbershop, a newsstand. . . .

E. B. White

tent themselves with peering in through an eight-foot-high iron fence.

At 3 and 4 Gramercy Park W are two somber 1840 brownstones sharing an ornate cast-iron veranda. Actor John Garfield was residing here in 1952, when he died in his sleep at the age of 39. At 34 Gramercy Park E is a turreted red-brick building that was probably the city's first housing cooperative. Famous residents here over the years have included actors James Cagney and Margaret Hamilton. The building boasts one of the city's few remaining birdcage elevators. At 36 Gramercy Park E is a Gothic apartment house guarded by two near-life-size silver-plated knights. Actor John Barrymore lived here with his first wife in the mid-1920s.

In 1925, John Steinbeck lived in a small, dingy room on the sixth floor of 38 Gramercy Park North. He'd been working as a reporter for the *New York World*, but got fired. After that he holed up in his room, living on sardines and crackers and writing around the clock. Also on the north side is the genteel **Gramercy Park Hotel,** 2 Lexington Avenue. Humphrey Bogart lived in the hotel in 1926, just after marrying his first wife, and critic Edmund Wilson lived here with novelist Mary McCarthy in the early 1940s. Writer S. J. Perelman died in his apartment in the hotel in 1979, at the age of 75.

MANHATTAN

Gramercy Park South

The square's most impressive buildings stand on the south side. At 15 Gramercy Park S is the **National Arts Club,** a formidable Gothic Revival brownstone that was once home to New York governor Samuel Tilden. Tilden is best remembered as the man who lost the 1876 presidency to Rutherford Hayes by only one electoral vote. But he was also responsible for Boss Tweed's downfall. After Tweed was arrested, Tilden had steel doors installed in his windows and an escape tunnel dug to 19th Street in case of repercussions. The building became the National Arts Club in 1906. Club members have included George Bellows, Alfred Stieglitz, and Frederic Remington.

Across the street at 16 Gramercy Park S is the **Players Club,** an extravagant, columned building with large flags out front. The building was purchased by the great thespian Edwin Booth in 1888, who turned it into a home for a group of actors. The brother of Lincoln-assassin John Wilkes Booth, Edwin Booth ironically was the president's favorite actor. After the assassination, Edwin holed himself up in the club and refused to come out. A crowd of thousands gathered in Gramercy Park to show him their support. Today, a statue of Booth playing Hamlet stands in the park, facing his former home. Recent members of the Players Club have included Laurence Olivier and Frank Sinatra.

Kenmore Hotel

A few blocks north of Gramercy Park is the old Kenmore Hotel, 145 E. 23rd St., at Lexington, where young writer Nathanael West worked as night manager in 1927–28. West spent his nights reading the classics and entertaining his friends, who included Dashiell Hammett and S. J. Perelman.

The hotel stands on the former site of the building where writer Stephen Crane lived in 1893, sharing a small studio with three friends. The four were so poor that they only had enough clothes for one of them to look for work at a time. Crane worked on *The Red Badge of Courage* while living there.

In 1994, federal agents seized the Kenmore— by then a dilapidated, crime-infested residence— and arrested 18 people in one of the city's largest drug busts ever. Today, the building has been cleaned up and converted into studio apartments for low-income single adults.

BROADWAY AND LOWER FIFTH AVENUE

During the late 1800s, the stretch of Broadway between 8th and 23rd Streets, and especially between Union and Madison Squares, was known as **Ladies Mile** because of the many fashionable department stores located there. The original stores themselves are now long gone, but their elaborate cast-iron building facades remain, with two of the finest examples standing opposite each other on Broadway just south of 20th Street. On the east side, at 900 Broadway, is an 1887 McKim, Mead & White creation notable for its lovely brickwork; on the west side, at 901 Broadway, is the former home of Lord & Taylor, cast in a deluxe French Second Empire style. At 881-887 Broadway, at the southwest corner of 19th Street, stands the former Arnold Constable Dry Goods Store, topped with an immense mansard roof.

Running alongside Broadway is lower Fifth Avenue, which like many other parts of the Flatiron District was gray and neglected from the 1960s through the 1980s. Then, in the early- to mid-1980s, publishing and advertising companies looking to escape exorbitant midtown rents began moving in, and trendy shops soon followed.

Theodore Roosevelt's Birthplace

The handsome four-story brownstone at 28 E. 20th St., near Broadway, is an exact replica of Theodore Roosevelt's birthplace. It was rebuilt by Roosevelt's family and friends just after his death in 1919 and only a few years after the original building was torn down in 1916. Now a museum, it's filled with thousands of engrossing photographs and the world's largest collection of Roosevelt memorabilia, including TR's christening dress, his parents' wedding clothes, and much original furniture.

During a tour of the house, you'll learn that the first American Roosevelts came to Manhattan from Holland in the 1640s, and made their fortune in the glass import trade. Theodore was born in this house in 1858, and grew up a sickly, asthmatic child. In addition to his political achievements, he also spent years in North Dakota raising cattle, served as New York's first police commissioner, led the Rough Riders at San Juan Hill, wrote over 50 books, shot game in Africa for the Smithsonian, and raised a large family. "No president has ever enjoyed himself as much as I," he once said.

The birthplace, 212/260-1616, is open Mon.–Fri. 9 A.M.–5 P.M. Admission is $3. Tours are given on the hour.

Flatiron Building

Where Fifth Avenue and the Ladies Mile meet 23rd Street is one of Manhattan's most famous and idiosyncratic landmarks. The Flatiron Building, more formally known as the Fuller Building, was designed by Chicago architect Daniel H. Burnham in 1902. Its nickname comes from its narrow triangular shape, only six feet wide at the northern end. H. G. Wells once described it as a "prow . . . ploughing up through the traffic of Broadway and Fifth Avenue in the afternoon light." The portrayal is apt.

Gusty winds often swirl around the Flatiron's northern end, where men used to gather to watch the billowing skirts of the lady shoppers. Policemen shooed the men away, giving rise to the old expression, "23 skiddoo."

Madison Square

Between 23rd and 26th Streets, and Fifth and Madison Avenues, is Madison Square. Once a marsh, potter's field, and parade ground, the square became fashionable in the mid-1800s. In those days, expensive hotels stood along its west side, the old Madison Square Garden stood to the north, and the Statue of Liberty's torch-bearing right arm stood in the center of the square, awaiting funding for the monument's base. Today all those buildings—and the arm—are gone, but other graceful structures have taken their place. A statue of William Henry Seward, the U.S. senator and secretary of state best remembered for purchasing Alaska from Russia, guards the southwest entrance.

THE STANFORD WHITE SCANDAL

New York's first Madison Square Garden, built in 1890 and demolished in 1925, once stood where the New York Life Insurance Company stands today. Designed by architect Stanford White, the sports arena was a sumptuous affair, complete with turrets, towers, and a revolving golden statue of Diana on top. In addition, the building housed an upscale restaurant, theater, and roof garden, and it was in the roof garden that Stanford White was murdered by the husband of his former mistress, Evelyn Nesbit.

A pretty chorus girl from Pittsburgh, Nesbit was only 16 when White fell in love with her and took her to his studio. Already well known for his philandering, he had love nests all over town, including one at 22 W. 24th St. (the building still stands), which he had lined with mirrors and hung with a red velvet swing. He liked his girlfriends to swing in the nude above him while he watched from the bed.

Nesbit, intent on finding a rich husband, soon left White, and in 1905 married millionaire Harry Kendall Thaw. But Thaw seemed obsessed with White, asking her about him again and again, until the evening of June 25, 1906, when they were all in the roof garden together. Then he pulled out a gun and shot White three times in the back of the head.

Thaw was found unfit to stand trial, due to what his lawyer called "dementia Americana," a mental disease supposedly afflicting husbands trying to defend their wives' honor. Thaw was sent to an insane asylum instead, where he stayed until 1915. Nesbit, divorced, starred in a silent film about the scandal (called *The Girl in the Red Velvet Swing*), and joined a traveling cabaret show. Later, she became a heroin addict and worked in a Panamanian brothel. She died in 1966.

On the park's east side along Madison Avenue, are several impressive buildings. Between 23rd and 25th Streets is the 1932 **Metropolitan Life Insurance Company,** an enormous art deco building made of limestone that seems to change color with the day. On the north corner of 25th Street is the 1900 **Appellate Division of the**

New York State Supreme Court, covered with an impossible number of marble sculptures. Taking up the whole block between 26th and 27th Streets is the New York Life Insurance Company, an elaborate 1898 wedding-cake extravaganza designed by Cass Gilbert, the architect of the Woolworth Building.

LITTLE INDIA

Though now much smaller than the rapidly growing Indian communities in Queens, Little India—centered on Lexington Avenue between 27th and 29th Streets—is still frequented by women in saris doing their weekly shopping. The area offers some excellent Indian restaurants and food shops, a few Indian music-and-video stores, and a dwindling number of shops selling sari silks.

MURRAY HILL

Morgan Library

This elegant neoclassic gem, 29 E. 36th St., at Madison Ave., 212/685-0610, www.morganlibrary.org, was designed by McKim, Mead & White in 1906 as John Pierpont Morgan's personal library and art gallery. Now a museum, it retains its original elaborately carved wooden ceilings, medieval tapestries, renaissance paintings, and domed rotunda.

At the heart of the museum's collection are Morgan's priceless illuminated manuscripts and Old Master drawings. Compelling traveling exhibitions—ranging from illustration to photography—are often on display as well. In recent years, the museum has doubled its exhibit space and opened a glass-enclosed garden court where classical-music concerts are sometimes presented. The museum also offers a very pleasant cafe and a gift shop stocked with unusual books and gifts.

Hours are Tues.–Thurs. 10:30 A.M.–5 P.M., Friday 10:30 A.M.–8 P.M., Saturday 10:30 A.M.–6 P.M., Sunday noon–6 P.M. Suggested admission is adults $8, students $6, children under 12 free.

Notable Residences

Many of the streets in Murray Hill have their share of fashionable residences. Two addresses especially worth looking out for are the ornate mansion at 233 Madison Ave., at 37th St., now the Polish Consulate; and 148 E. 40th St., now a converted carriage house. Also of prime interest is the Sniffen Court Historic District, 150-158 E. 36th St., between Lexington and Third Avenues. Built in the mid-1850s by a man named John Sniffen, the 10 brick carriage houses are all delightfully converted and preserved.

Scandinavia House

The stylish new Scandinavia House: The Nordic Center in America, 58 Park Ave., between 37th and 38th Sts., 212/779-3587, features exhibits, films, concerts and more, all focusing on the five Scandinavian countries—Denmark, Finland, Iceland, Norway, and Sweden. Hours are Tues.–Sat. 11 A.M.–5 P.M. Suggested donation is adults $3, seniors and students $2.

SHOPPING

Books

Two blocks south of Union Square is Strand Book Store, 828 Broadway, at 12th St., 212/473-1452. By far the city's largest secondhand bookstore, it claims to stock some two million books on eight miles of shelves. Some New Yorkers seem to spend their entire lives here, browsing, browsing, browsing. The store is open until 10 P.M. every evening. Across the street is Forbidden Planet, 840 Broadway, 212/473-1576, a gold mine for science fiction lovers, selling books, comic books, games, and more.

Manhattan's oldest Barnes & Noble store, in operation decades before the current crop of megastores, is located at 105 Fifth Ave., at 18th St., 212/807-0099; the Barnes & Noble, flagship is now at 33 E. 17th St., between Broadway and Park Ave. S, 212/253-0810. Travel lovers should stop by the Complete Traveller Bookstore, 199 Madison Ave., at 35th St., 212/685-9007.

Clothing

Fifth Avenue between 23rd and 14th Streets is the place to shop for clothes in this area. Anthropologie, 85 Fifth Ave., 212/627-5885, offers

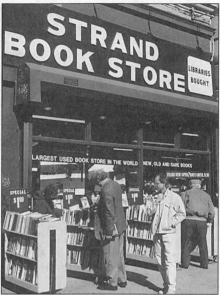

© CHRISTIANE BIRD

The city's largest used bookstore, the Strand boasts some two million volumes on miles of shelves.

an interesting mix of ethnic-influenced urban wear. **Bebe,** 100 Fifth Ave., at 15th St., 212/675-2323, offers hip urban styles, some sleek, some frilly. **Emporio Armani,** 110 Fifth Ave., at 16th St., 212/727-3240, is an expensive designer showroom. **Daffy's,** 111 Fifth Ave., at 18th St., 212/529-4477; and **Bolton's,** 4 E. 34th St., near Fifth Ave., 212/684-3750, are known for discounted designer fashions, while **Ann Taylor, Banana Republic, Nine West,** the **Gap, Kenneth Cole,** and **J. Crew** all also have outlets along the avenue.

Food Shops

In Little India, a number of food stores waft their luscious smells out onto the street. Foremost among them is the venerable **Kalustyan's,** 123 Lexington Ave., 212/685-3451. The first store to import Indian foodstuffs into the city, the bustling shop sells everything from homemade *labne* yogurt to Afghan naan bread to stuffed pita pockets to go. **Foods of India,** 121 Lexing-

ton Ave., 212/683-4419, carries an especially good supply of cooking utensils.

Other Shops

The beguiling **ABC Carpet and Home,** 888 Broadway, at 19th St., 212/473-3000, arranged more like a luxurious living room than a shop, sells everything from painted country furniture to French antiques. **Fishs Eddy,** 889 Broadway, at 19th St., 212/420-9020, is known for its bargain-priced china. **Paragon Sporting Goods,** 867 Broadway, at 18th, 212/255-8036, is the city's top sporting-goods department store.

The **Wiz** is a reputable chain of electronics stores with a large branch at 17 Union Square W, at 15th St., 212/741-9500. The **Compleat Strategist,** 11 E. 33rd St., near Fifth Ave., 212/685-3880, sells games for players of all persuasions.

ACCOMMODATIONS

Under $50

A bunk in a dorm-style room at the irrepressible **Gershwin** (see $100–150, below) goes for $40 a night. Some dormitory rooms accommodate four people, others eight. The shared bathrooms are reasonably clean.

$50–100

As its brochure notes, the cheap and cheerful **Carlton Arms,** 160 E. 25th St., at Third Ave., 212/679-0680, is not for everyone. Artists' murals cover most of the walls but otherwise, the décor and furnishings are minimal, and the bathrooms are not particularly clean. Still, this can be a fun place to stay for the exuberant and the young. $70 s and $80 d with shared bath, $85 s and $100 d with private one.

Hotel 17, 225 E. 17th St., between Second and Third Aves., 212/475-2845, bills itself as "New York's most notorious night-time drama." The hostelry of choice among club hoppers and drag queens, Hotel 17 offers such over-the-top amenities as rooftop fashion shows. Meanwhile, the rooms are as basic as it gets. $60–80 s, $80–120 d.

More hostel than hotel, the friendly **Murray Hill Inn,** 143 E. 30th St., between Lexington and Third Ave., 212/683-6900 or 888/996-6376, www.murrayhillinn.com, located on a quiet residential street, offers 50 small but clean rooms at budget rates. All rooms have cable TV and daily maid service. $60–75 s with shared bath; $75–85 d with shared bath, $95–120 s or d with private bath. The Inn has a second location, the **Union Square Inn,** 209 E. 14th St., between Second and Third Aves., 212/614-0500, where rates are somewhat higher.

$100–150

The high-spirited **Gershwin Hotel,** 7 E. 27th St., between Fifth and Madison, 212/545-8000, aswirl with artwork and young budget travelers from around the world, is a sort of cheaper, more modern version of the classic Chelsea Hotel (see Chelsea and the Garment District, below). Here you'll find a lobby brimming with color, no-frills rooms of all shapes and sizes, a gallery with changing exhibits, and a rooftop bar in summer. Private room rates are $99–149 s, d, or t.

Considerably quieter and smaller is **Hotel 31,** 120 E. 31st St., between Park and Lexington Ave., 212/685-3060. Once a private men's hotel, the late 18th-century townhouse offers small but adequate rooms, many of which share bathrooms; $90 s or d with shared bath, $125 s or d with private bath.

Hotel Grand Union, 34 E. 32nd St., between Madison and Park, 212/683-5890, offers clean, basic rooms, a restful environment, and a friendly staff. $110–130 s or d.

$150–250

The **Carlton,** 22 E. 29th St., at Madison Ave., 212/532-4100 or 800/542-1502, a striking beaux arts edifice partially built of rose-colored brick. The large, well-kept lobby gleams with polished windows, mirrors, and brass; rooms are attractive and well kept. Adjoining the lobby is a small cafe. $139–189 s, $149–199 d.

The new, nautical **Park Avenue South,** 122 E. 28th St., between Lexington and Park Ave., 212/448-0888, housed in a 1906 building, offers 143 tidy rooms complete with art deco furnishings, an open-air lounge, business center, and excellent restaurant, the Black Duck (see Food, below); $189–260 d.

The **Gramercy Park Hotel,** 2 Lexington Ave., at 21st St., 212/475-4320 or 800/221-4083, www.gramercyparkhotel.com, may be more than a bit worn, but it still has a gracious old–New York feel. The rooms are large and airy, and downstairs reigns a '50s-era cocktail lounge that attracts all ages. The hotel is a favorite among publishing types and rock musicians. $145 s, $160 d.

$250 and up

At the stylish hot spot, **W Union Square,** 201 Park Ave. S, at 17th St., 212/253-9119, you'll find well-appointed rooms filled with ultra-comfortable furnishings and a lively lobby-bar filled with beautiful people; $249–459 s or d.

Housed behind a discreet gray facade with huge dark windows that allow insiders to see out but prevents outsiders from seeing in is the posh **Morgans,** 237 Madison Ave., at 38th St., 212/686-0300. Started up by Ian Schrager of Studio 54 fame, the place is so hip, it doesn't even hang a sign out front. Not surprisingly, rooms are sleek and luxurious; $240–300 s, $255–335 d.

The atmospheric opposite of Morgans is charming **Shelburne Murray Hill,** 303 Lexington Ave., at 37th St., 212/689-5200 or 800/ME-SUITE. Downstairs, find an attractive lobby filled with baroque antiques, and an especially helpful staff. Upstairs, find very spacious suites with two double beds and well-equipped kitchens, making this good value for money. The blue and gold furnishings are plush, yet comfortable; suites from $260.

FOOD

American and Barbecue

America, 9 E. 18th St., between Fifth Ave. and Broadway, 212/505-2110, is a huge, cheery hangar of a place serving an astonishing array of mouthwatering foods from the 50 states; average main dish $13. **Albuquerque Eats,** 375 Third Ave., at 27th St., 212/683-6500, specializes in Tex-Mex fare, moderately priced; average entrée $10.

Danny Meyer's latest creation, the big, high-ceilinged **Blue Smoke,** 116 E. 27th St., between Park Ave. S and Lexington Ave., 212/447-7733, is the ultimate take on an urban barbecue joint. There's a spiffy jukebox to one side, a bar stocked with 30 varieties of bourbon to the other, and one of the best jazz clubs in town downstairs (the Jazz Standard). Average entrée $18.

The playful, high-ceilinged **Mesa Grill,** 102 Fifth Ave., at 15th St., 212/807-7400, offers first-rate Southwestern delights; average entrée $25. Younger sibling to the tried-and-true Union Square Cafe (see Eclectic, below), the swank, retro **Gramercy Tavern,** 42 E. 20th St., 212/477-0777, offers prix fixe dinners in the back room ($65) and a la carte dishes in the swish bar room up front.

Asian

Sam's Noodles, 411 Third Ave., at 29th St., 212/213-2288, offers a tasty array of noodle dishes from various parts of Asia; average main dish $8. Next door to the Irving Plaza, a music club, is the **Galaxy,** 15 Irving Pl., at 15th St., 212/777-3631, an intimate hot spot bestrewn with tiny ceiling lights. On the menu is a wide variety of Asian-influenced fare; average entrée $9.

Well-lit, blond wood **Tatany,** 380 Third Ave., between 27th and 28th Sts., 212/686-1871, serves excellent sushi, reasonably priced; average entrée $14. Posh, new **TanDa,** 331 Park Ave. S, between 24th and 25th Sts., 212/253-8400, named after a Vietnamese poet, has been winning kudos for both its design and Asian-inflected fare; average entrée $23.

Eclectic

A longtime favorite among restaurant critics and New Yorkers alike is Danny Meyer's **Union Square Cafe,** 21 E. 16th St., near Fifth Ave., 212/243-4020, a gracious and hospitable place serving an imaginative mix of Italian, French, and American cuisine; average entrée $25. New to the neighborhood is the **Black Duck** at the Park Avenue South Hotel, 122 E. 28th St., between Lexington and Park Ave. S, 212/448-0888, serving "Pan-Atlantic bistro fare," which translates into such dishes as sesame-seared tuna, pepper-encrusted Long Island duck, and char-grilled filet mignon; average entrée $19.

French

Chef/author Anthony Bourdain's **Les Halles,** 411 Park Ave. S, between 28th and 29th Sts., 212/679-4111, is a boisterous French bistro and

Park Bistro, sister restaurant to Les Halles across the street

butcher shop with meats hanging in the windows. Directly across the street is its quieter but still bustling sister restaurant, **Park Bistro,** 414 Park Ave. S, between 28th and 29th Sts., 212/689-1360. Both serve good, authentic fare; average main course at both $19.

Indian

Tasty Indian fast food can be picked up at **Curry in a Hurry,** 119 Lexington Ave., at 28th St., 212/683-0900, housed in a bright turquoise building; average main course $6. Another good choice is **Joy of India,** 127 E. 28th St., 212/685-0808, a spic-and-span cafeteria-style eatery always crowded with Indians; average entrée $6.

Muriya, 129 E. 27th St., near Lexington Ave., 212/689-7925, specializes in Mughali fare; average entrée $12. For vegetarian dishes from southern India, try the stylish **Mavalli Palace,** 46 E. 29th St., 212/679-5535; average entrée $11.

Seafood

Housed in a stunning former bank building with lots of white marble and red lamps is the popular **Blue Water Grill,** 31 Union Square W, at 16th St., 212/675-9500, serving fresh seafood; average entrée $19.

Southern/Latin/Caribbean

For tasty Southern fare, try **Live Bait,** 14 E. 23rd St., between Broadway and Madison Ave., 212/353-2400, a comfortable dive with a long, scruffy bar; average entrée $10. Even after 10 years, the **Coffee Shop,** 29 Union Square W, at 16th St., 212/243-7969, is still a fashionable hot spot serving Brazilian-accented food; average main course $11. During the summer, a sidewalk dining cafe opens up.

Lola, 30 W. 22nd St., between Fifth and Sixth Aves., 212/675-6700, offers spicy Caribbean food in a colorful, sophisticated setting, and a popular gospel brunch on Sunday; average entrée $19. Festive **Patria,** 250 Park Ave. S, at 20th St., 212/777-6211, offers nouveau Latin American fare in a sleek, high-ceilinged setting; average entrée $25.

Other Ethnic

One of the city's few Turkish restaurants is the two-tiered, red-and-gilt **Turkish Kitchen,** 386 Third Ave., between 27th and 28th Sts., 212/679-6633; average entrée $14. Terry Brennan's cavernous **Artisanal,** 2 Park Ave., at 32nd St., 212/725-8585, is a stylish French brasserie serving over 160 kinds of wine by the glass and an enormous number of *fromage*-based dishes, including a 100-cheese fondue; average entrée $21.

Light Bites

Union Square area: City Bakery, 3 W. 18th St., near Fifth Ave., 212/366-1414, is a good place for simple gourmet lunches and baked goods, while **Friend of a Farmer,** 77 Irving Pl., between 18th and 19th Sts., 212/477-2188, serves hearty soups and sandwiches.

Fifth and Sixth Aves.: Eisenberg's, 174 Fifth Ave., near 22nd St., 212/675-5096, is one of the few old-time sandwich shops left in the city.

Farther Uptown: Sarge's, 548 Third Ave., near 36th St., 212/679-0442, is the best-known deli in the area. **Chez Laurence,** 245 Madison Ave., at 38th St., 212/683-0284, is a good spot for sandwiches and dessert.

Watering Holes and Lounges

One of the most stunning historic bars around is the **Old Town,** 45 E. 18th St., between Broadway and Park Ave. S, 212/529-6732, complete with high ceilings, mosaic floors, and a gorgeous back bar. Upstairs is a casual dining room serving passable food. Open in the summer only is **Luna Park,** a lively bar-cafe on the northern end of Union Square Park.

Near Union Square is **119,** 119 E. 15th St., near Irving Pl., 212/995-5904, a comfortable dive with a pool table in front, dart boards in back, and a handful of creaky booths in between. The historic **Pete's Tavern,** 129 E. 18th St., at Irving Pl., 212/473-7676, is somewhat touristy, but soaked in the ale of time (see above).

The genteel **Gramercy Park Hotel,** 2 Lexington Ave., at 21st St., 212/475-4320, offers a cozy, worn-around-the-edges cocktail lounge that seems frozen in the '50s. The Irish **Connie**

Doolan's, 354 Third Ave., at 25th St., 212/532-1978, features roomy booths, a boisterous bar, and tasty pub food.

Among the restaurants mentioned above,

Galaxy, Live Bait, and the **Coffee Shop** all have late-night bar scenes. Adjoining Albuquerque Eats is the **Rodeo Bar,** presenting free live bands nightly.

Chelsea and the Garment District

The West Side between 14th and 42nd Streets is not the most tourist-oriented of neighborhoods. Part residential, part industrial, this section of the city has no major public spaces. But it does have a solid, gritty feel and its share of one-of-a-kind attractions, including cutting-edge arts organizations and the Empire State Building.

Chelsea, roughly stretching between 14th and 28th Streets, Sixth Avenue and the Hudson River, is one big residential neighborhood, made up of brownstones, row houses, tenements, and apartment buildings. Most of the area was once owned by Capt. Thomas Clarke, whose grandson, Clement Charles Clarke, laid out a residential district here in the early 1800s. Clement Charles was also a scholar who wrote the *Compendious Lexicon of the Hebrew Language* and the famous poem beginning, "'Twas the night before Christmas."

Chelsea began to change character in the mid-1800s, when the Hudson River Railroad was built along Eleventh Avenue. With the railroad came breweries, slaughterhouses, warehouses, and immigrant laborers desperate for work. Most of the earliest immigrants were Irish. They were followed by Greeks, who clustered around Eighth Avenue, and Hispanics, many of whom still live in the area. Meanwhile, the eastern section of Chelsea retained a more genteel character, becoming a theater district in the 1870s and 1880s, and a short-lived center for the movie industry around the time of WW I.

Today, Chelsea is in a state of flux. Though still middle- and working-class in some parts, it is now also home to affluent professionals and a large gay population, drawn to the area by its tranquility and relatively moderate rents. Trendy stores and restaurants have moved in, along with advertising and publishing companies. East of Seventh Avenue, Chelsea is considered part of the Flatiron District (see introduction to From Union Square to Murray Hill, above).

Chelsea ends and the historic Garment District begins somewhere around 28th Street, where the streets change from residential to commercial. The heart of today's Garment District is farther north, however, around Seventh Avenue and 35th Street. Chelsea can be visited at almost any hour, while weekdays are the best time to roam the Garment District.

Back in the late 1800s, all of this area was known as the Tenderloin, or "Satan's Circus," and it was filled with brothels, saloons, clip joints, dance halls, and raucous restaurants. As a song from the period went:

*Lobsters! Rarebits! Plenty of Pilsener beer
Plenty of girls to help you drink the best
of cheer
Dark girls, blonde girls, and never a one
that's true
You get them all in the Tenderloin when
the clock strikes two.*

CHELSEA WEST

West 20th Street
One of Chelsea's prettiest blocks is West 20th Street between Eighth and Ninth Avenues. The house with the curved bay windows at 402 W. 20th St. was designed by Charles Gilbert in 1897. At 404 W. 20th St. you'll find the area's earliest Greek Revival house, while at 406-418 W. 20th is Cushman Row—a group of charming brick houses named after its developer, dry-goods merchant Don Alonzo Cushman.

In 1951, Jack Kerouac lived at 454 W. 20th St., near Tenth Ave., while writing his novel *On the Road.* He wrote most of the book in about 20 days, typing almost nonstop at his kitchen table

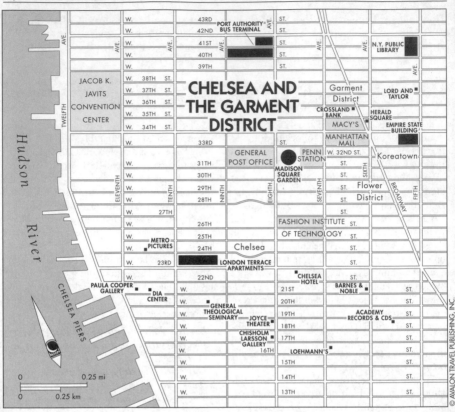

while a roll of paper fed continuously into his typewriter. The roll eliminated the need for the time-consuming task of putting individual sheets of paper into the machine.

Other especially pretty residential streets in Chelsea are West 21st and West 22nd Streets between Eighth and Tenth Avenues.

General Theological Seminary

The block bounded by Ninth and Tenth Avenues between 20th and 21st Streets is home to the General Theological Seminary, a peaceful, campuslike enclave of ivy-draped buildings that look as if they belong more in rural England than in urban New York. Charles Clement Moore, who taught Hebrew and Greek here, donated the land on which the seminary stands.

Most of the seminary's Gothic buildings were built in the late 1800s.

In the center of the seminary complex is a square that can be entered through the modern brick building on Ninth Avenue. Most of the buildings within are closed to the public, but you can visit the **Chapel of the Good Shepherd,** marked by a 161-foot tower.

Dia Center for the Arts

Another "alternative" arts center in Chelsea is the Dia Center, 548 W. 22nd St., between Tenth and Eleventh Aves., 212/989-5566. Founded in 1974 to support a select group of artists working outside the mainstream, the foundation has a major exhibition space at this address. The foundation also operates a second major exhibit space across

THE CHELSEA PIERS

The largest gymnastics facility in the state, the largest rock-climbing wall in the northeast, the longest indoor running track in the world, a huge fitness center, a golf driving range, an ice-skating rink, a full-service marina, restaurants, and a 1.2-mile public esplanade all opened at the Chelsea Piers in the fall of 1995. The piers date back to 1910 when they served as "the most extensive and complete steamship terminal in this country," as the *Times* once put it. But they fell into disuse and disrepair with the building of the Midtown piers and the coming of transatlantic jet travel. The recent rehab project cost over $60 million.

To reach the Chelsea Piers, head west on 23rd Street to the Hudson River. For more information, call 212/336-6666.

the street. Hours are Wed.–Sun. noon–6 P.M. Admission is adults $6, students and seniors $3, children under 10 free.

Galleries

Over the last few years, West Chelsea has rapidly metamorphosed into the new SoHo. Dozens of galleries—including some of the most prestigious names in town—have moved into the neighborhood, turning it from a rather nondescript area into one of New York's most exciting places. Even if you have little interest in contemporary art, it's worth visiting some of the exhibition spaces for their architectural exuberance alone.

Among the many galleries that can now be found in West Chelsea are the famed **Paula Cooper Gallery,** 534 W. 21st St., between Tenth and Eleventh Aves., 212/255-1105, whose clients include such heavyweights as Jonathan Borofsky, Carl Andre, and Elizabeth Murray; and **Metro Pictures,** 519 W. 24th St., between Tenth and Eleventh Aves., 212/206-7100, which exhibits such names as Cindy Sherman and Robert Longo. The renowned **Barbara Gladstone,** specializing in painting, sculpture, and photography by established artists, is now located at 515 W. 24th St., between Tenth and Eleventh Aves., 212/206-9300, while **Sean Kelly,** the British ex-

patriate who focuses on conceptual art is at 528 W. 29th St., between 10th and Eleventh Aves., 212/239-1181.

Max Protetch Gallery, 511 W. 22nd St., between Tenth and Eleventh Aves., 212/633-6999, hosts much contemporary artwork from around the world, and many architectural installations. Young, smart, visionary, and offbeat are some of the adjectives used to describe the American and European artists who exhibit at the **Anton Kern Gallery,** 532 W. 20th St., between Tenth and Eleventh Aves., 212/965-1706, owned by the son of the German artist Georg Baselitz.

PaceWildenstein, 534 W. 25th St., between Tenth and Eleventh Aves., 212/929-7000, is the downtown branch of the famed uptown gallery and features works by the likes of Sol LeWitt and Julian Schnabel. The enormous **Gagosian Chelsea,** 555 W. 24th St., between Tenth and Eleventh Aves., 212/741-1111, is also the downtown branch of an uptown institution, this one dedicated to artists such as Andy Warhol, Richard Serra, and David Salle.

A bit farther downtown, **Alexander and Bonin,** 132 Tenth Ave., between 18th and 19th Sts., 212/367-7474, is a long, thin gallery focusing on contemporary painting, photography, and works on paper. **Sperone Westwater,** 415 W. 13th St., between Ninth and Tenth Aves., 212/431-3685, is known for exhibiting modern Italian painters such as Sandro Chia and Francesco Clemente.

To find out about other galleries, or about who's exhibiting where, pick up a copy of the *Art Now Gallery Guide,* available in many bookstores and galleries. Or check magazine or Sunday newspaper listings.

Chelsea Hotel

With its deep maroon paint job accented by numerous black gables, chimneys, and ornate cast-iron balconies, the Chelsea Hotel, 222 W. 23rd St., between Seventh and Eighth Aves., 212/243-3700, is a West Side landmark. One of the city's first cooperative apartment buildings when it opened in 1884, the Chelsea became a hotel in 1905 and almost immediately began attracting writers, many of whom took up residence.

MANHATTAN

© CHRISTIANE BIRD

Over the years, the Chelsea Hotel has been home to an extraordinary range of personalities, from Arthur Miller to Sid Vicious.

Plaques at the door honor Dylan Thomas, Thomas Wolfe, Brendan Behan, Arthur Miller, and Mark Twain, while others who've lived here include Edgar Lee Masters, Eugene O'Neill, Tennessee Williams, Vladimir Nabokov, Mary McCarthy, and Nelson Algren.

Arthur Miller lived at the Chelsea from 1962 to 1968, while writing *After the Fall*. Arthur C. Clarke lived here on and off for years, and wrote *2001: A Space Odyssey* in his 10th-floor apartment. And William S. Burroughs wrote *Naked Lunch* here.

The hotel has also attracted an extraordinary number of actors, painters, photographers, musicians, and film producers over the years, among them Sarah Bernhardt, Jackson Pollock, Willem de Kooning, Larry Rivers, Jane Fonda, Robert Mapplethorpe, Milos Forman, and Peter Brook. Andy Warhol filmed part of his movie *Chelsea Girls* here

in 1966, and musician Virgil Thompson lived on the hotel's ninth floor for over 40 years.

In the late 1960s, the Chelsea became a favorite stopover for rock stars passing through town. Among those who overnighted were Janis Joplin, Jimi Hendrix, the Grateful Dead, the Mamas and the Papas, Leonard Cohen, and Patti Smith. Bob Dylan wrote *Sad-Eyed Lady of the Lowlands* while staying at the Chelsea.

But perhaps the hotel's most notorious couple was Sid Vicious, lead singer for the Sex Pistols, and his girlfriend Nancy Spungen. The two were living here in 1978 when Nancy was found in her negligee beneath the bathroom sink, stabbed to death with a hunting knife. Vicious was indicted for the murder but died of a heroin overdose before he could stand trial. Alex Cox documented the events in his film *Sid and Nancy,* part of which was shot at the Chelsea. The hotel has since gotten rid of Room 100, where the murder was committed.

Artists, tourists, and well-heeled pseudobohemians still live and stay at the Chelsea, whose lobby is hung floor-to-ceiling with artwork by present and former tenants. The rooms are relatively big and reasonably priced, but the place is well worn and without amenities.

CHELSEA EAST
Sixth Avenue

A continuation of the Ladies Mile (see Broadway and Lower Fifth Avenue under From Union Square to Murray Hill, above), Sixth Avenue between 17th and 23rd Streets is flanked by impressive cast-iron buildings, considerably larger than the ones on Broadway. Dirty and underused until the early 1990s, the buildings now house several new megastores. At night their brightly lit facades cast mysterious shadows onto the street.

Today's Man, 625 Sixth Ave., between 18th and 19th Sts., was once B. Altman's, built in the 1870s. Across the street, at 620 Sixth Ave., where Bed Bath and Beyond is today, once housed Siegel-Cooper, the world's largest store when it opened in the late 1890s. Farther north at 655 Sixth Ave., between 20th and 21st Sts., is an especially lovely building equipped with columned

MANHATTAN

turrets at either end and an immense, inscribed pediment. It was once home to the Hugh O'Neill Store, a dry goods emporium. Another unusual Sixth Avenue address is 47 W. 20th St., a Gothic-style church designed in 1846 by architect Richard Upjohn. For years, the church housed the nightclub **Limelight,** now closed.

Center for Jewish History

The new Center for Jewish History, 15 W. 16th St., between Fifth and Sixth Aves., 212/294-8301, www.cjh.org, brings the American Jewish Historical Society, the American Sephardic Federation, the Leo Baeck Institute, the Yeshiva University Museum, and the YIVO Institute for Jewish Research together under one roof. The Center's library provides access to a vast collection of archival materials, while the galleries feature a wide range of exhibits on Jewish culture and history.

Of special interest to visitors is the **Yeshiva University Museum,** formerly located on the Yeshiva University campus at 155th Street. Now considerably more accessible to the general public, the museum houses an impressive collection of art and religious objects, including detailed models of 10 historic synagogues from around the world (including the 1763 Touro Synagogue of Newport, Rhode Island, which is the nation's oldest synagogue). Also on site is an inviting cafe and spiffy auditorium where films, lectures, and other special events are presented.

Tours of the center are offered Tuesday and Thursday at 2 P.M.; cost is adults $6, seniors and students $3. The Yeshiva University Museum is open Tues.–Wed. and Sunday, 11 A.M.–5 P.M., and Thursday 11 A.M.–8 P.M. Admission is adults $6, seniors and students $4.

Flower District

In the early morning, the area around 28th Street and Sixth Avenue is all abustle with flowers of red, orange, blue, purple, yellow, and white. Later in the day, the stores cater to the retail market, setting up small forests of green along the sidewalks.

The city's wholesale Flower District may be small, but it's been centered on these streets since about 1870, when Long Island growers brought their flowers to the foot of E. 34th St. at the East River. Recently, rising rents have been threatening to drive the market elsewhere, but thus far, the vendors have managed to hold their own.

Fashion Institute of Technology

On Seventh Avenue between 26th and 28th Streets is a gray, boxy complex of buildings known as F.I.T. *The* school in the city for young fashion designers, the institute often features unusual exhibits that are open to the public. When an exhibit is up, the galleries at the Shirley Goodman Resource Center, southwest corner of Seventh Ave. at 27th St., 212/217-5800, are open Tues.–Fri. 10 A.M.–8 P.M., Saturday 10 A.M.–5 P.M. Admission is free.

Penn Station and Vicinity

On Seventh Avenue at 32nd Street is the entrance to the ugly underground Pennsylvania Station, topped with the equally ugly Madison Square Garden. There's no reason to visit either place unless you're taking a train, have tickets to a game, or want to take a look at Maya Lin's "Eclipsed Time" clock, installed in 1994 on the station's lower level. Lin is the architect who, as a 21-year-old undergraduate at Yale in 1980, created the winning design for the Vietnam Veterans Memorial in Washington, D.C. She spent five years working on the Penn Station project, and her sculpture, hovering in the ceiling above commuters' heads, looks like a glowing flying saucer with numerals etched along its edges. Time is marked by a slowly moving shadow.

West of Penn Station, on Eighth Avenue between 31st and 33rd Streets, is the glorious, block-long **General Post Office,** or James A. Farley Building, designed by McKim, Mead & White in 1913. Lined with tall Corinthian columns, the post office is all that the train station is not, and it is now being converted to become the new hub for Amtrak; the $484 million project is scheduled for completion in 2003. The original Penn Station, located where the present Madison Square Garden is now, was also designed by McKim, Mead & White, and was said to have been their masterpiece. Its demolition in 1968 spawned the birth of today's landmark-preservation movement.

MANHATTAN

THE GARMENT DISTRICT

Centering on Seventh Avenue in the mid-30s is the Garment District, now sporting the more tony "Fashion Center" label. Once stretching roughly between Fifth and Ninth Avenues, 25th and 42nd Streets, the district—like the American garment industry itself—has shrunk considerably in recent years. Now it reaches only between 34th and 42nd Streets, and is currently being threatened by real estate developers and rising rents. Nonetheless, for now, this is still the country's largest clothing-manufacturing district and constitutes an important part of New York's economy. About $10 billion a year in clothing is designed, cut, and sewn here. In the Fashion Center are 450 buildings with 5,000 fashion-trade tenants, including 4,500 factories.

The garment industry moved to Seventh Avenue from the Lower East Side around the time of WW I. It's always been predominantly Jewishrun, but the labor force has become increasingly Hispanic and Asian. Traditionally, the southern part of the district was devoted to the fur industry, the area around 34th Street to children's clothing, and the area north of 36th Street to women's apparel.

Visiting the Garment District on a weekday morning you'll see long lines of double-parked trucks, brawny men wheeling clothing racks, and young fashion assistants hustling to and fro with large boxes and bags. The industry's showrooms are closed to the public, but you can get a good sense of the place just by wandering the streets. Especially interesting are the many millinery, trimming, and fabric outlets—most catering to the trade only—along 37th and 38th Streets.

A long-overdue monument honoring the industry's thousands of workers stands in front of 555 Seventh Ave. at 39th Street. Cast in bronze by artist Judith Weller in 1984, *The Garment Worker* was sponsored by several dozen companies in the area, and depicts a Jewish tailor at his sewing machine.

Macy's and Herald Square

"The World's Largest Department Store" dominates Herald Square, a small gray triangle of land where Sixth Ave., Broadway, and 34th St. intersect. In the middle of the square stands a memorial to the *New York Herald,* once published here.

Macy's—rescued from bankruptcy in 1994 by its merger with Federated Department Stores—boasts about 170 departments stocking half a million items, from sneakers to bed linens, furs to baked goods. Ten stories high and a full block wide, the store was founded in 1858 by Rowland Hussey Macy, a Quaker from Nantucket. Macy went to sea at the age of 15 and returned four years later with $500 and, legend has it, a red star tattooed on his hand—now Macy's logo. Six times Macy tried to establish a shop, and six times he failed. Then he started Macy's.

One block south of Macy's, where its arch rival Gimbel's once stood, is a 90-store complex known as **Manhattan Mall.** Built largely of glass, it's equipped with playful glass elevators and pink and green lights.

Just north of Herald Square, where Broadway meets 36th Street, is **Crossland Bank.** Though nothing special to look at from the outside, the building's interior is an astonishing visual delight, with a graceful elliptical lobby and oval skylight. South of Herald Square, below 34th Street, is another gray triangle of land holding a statue of journalist Horace Greeley. Surrounding Greeley is a small park, usually filled with pigeons and the down-and-out.

Empire State Building

One of the world's most famous buildings, this landmark at 350 Fifth Ave., at 34th St., is best visited at night, when the city lights lie strewn at your feet. There are fewer visitors then, too, and it's easy to imagine yourself back in the early 1930s, just after the Empire State went up. The building was erected during the Depression in an astonishing 14 months, at the rate of 4 ½ stories a week.

For years, the art deco Empire State, built on the former site of the Waldorf-Astoria hotel, was the world's tallest building. That's no longer true, yet the Empire State—extensively renovated in 1993—remains the quintessential skyscraper. The landmark holds 73 elevators, 6,500 windows, 3,500 miles of telephone and telegraph

© CHRISTIANE BIRD

No longer the tallest building on the planet, the Empire State Building is still the world's quintessential skyscraper.

wire, 1,860 steps, and two observation decks, one on the 86th floor, the other on the 102nd.

In 1933, Irma Eberhardt became the first person to commit suicide by jumping off the Empire State. That same year, the classic film *King Kong* was made, showing a giant ape climbing up the skyscraper. In 1945, a B-25 bomber smacked into the building's 79th floor, killing 14 people. And in 1986, two parachutists jumped from the 86th floor to land safely on Fifth Avenue. Also, in case you're wondering, pennies thrown off the Empire State *cannot* kill passersby walking below, but they can cause severe burns.

The Empire State Building's observation decks, 212/736-3100, www.esbnyc.com, are open daily 10 A.M.–midnight. Tickets are sold until 11:15 P.M. on the concourse level, one floor below the main lobby. Admission is adults $9, seniors $7, children 5–12 $4, children under five free.

Also in the Empire State Building is **Skyride,**

212/279-9777, a virtual-reality flight that takes viewers over, under, and through New York. Introduced in 1995, the 7.5-minute journey takes place in a theater built with a hydraulic floor that rises, falls, and banks left and right to match the on-screen action. Tickets are adults $11.50, children and seniors $8.50. Open daily 10 A.M.–10 P.M.

Koreatown

In recent years, the two blocks between Fifth Avenue and Broadway on 32nd and 33rd Streets have become packed with Korean bars, restaurants, bookstores, and health and beauty shops. For the most part, these new enterprises cater to Koreans, not tourists, but if you want to check out a shop or restaurant, chances are you'll be welcome. Most of the signs are in Korean.

SHOPPING
Books and Music

Housed in a renovated cast-iron building along Sixth Avenue is a **Barnes & Noble** megastore, 675 Sixth Ave., between 21st and 22nd Sts., 212/727-1227. It features frequent readings, a cafe, and many comfortable chairs, and is open until 11 P.M. nightly. **Revolution Books,** 9 W. 19th St., 212/691-3345, the country's largest radical bookstore, harks back to Union Square's inflammatory Sacco-and-Vanzetti days. **Books of Wonder,** 16 W. 18th St., 212/989-3270, is a great children's bookstore.

Between Fifth and Sixth Avenues, find **Academy Records and CDs,** 12 W. 18th St., 212/242-3000, selling used classical and jazz recordings. **Skyline Books and Records,** 13 W. 18th St., 212/759-5463, specializes in used books, while J&R Music World operates the **Jazz Record Center** at 236 W. 26th St., 8th Fl., 212/675-4480.

Clothes

Loehmann's, the Bronx emporium known for its discounted designer wear, now has a branch at 101 Seventh Ave., at 16th St., 212/352-0856. **Reminiscence,** 50 W. 23rd St., near Sixth Ave., 212/243-2292, is the place to go for reasonably priced retrowear.

MANHATTAN

Along 34th Street between Fifth and Sixth Avenues are shops, shops, and more shops, most selling clothing and shoes. Some are branches of national stores such as **The Gap, The Limited,** and **Benetton.** Others are discount emporiums.

On Fifth Avenue is New York's largest and oldest hat store, the **J.J. Hat Center,** 310 Fifth Ave., at 32nd St., 212/239-4368. Established in 1911, J.J.'s stocks over 15,000 men's hats, including fedoras, Stetsons, homburgs, and caps.

Department Stores

King of the department stores is **Macy's** (see Macy's and Herald Square under The Garment District, above), 151 34th St., at Sixth Ave., 212/695-4400. A few blocks farther northeast is **Lord & Taylor,** 424 Fifth Ave., at 38th St., 212/391-3344, a comfortable midsize store that may not be as glamorous as some, but still carries a first-rate selection. One of the store's most gracious touches is the free coffee, served in a silver pot, that it offers to shoppers who arrive before the place opens at 10 A.M.

Garment District Retailers

Most of the Garment District shops are wholesale only. Some of the stores that sell retail are **Margola,** 48 W. 37th St., between Fifth and Sixth Aves., 212/695-1115, offering glass beads, rhinestones, and trinkets; **Cinderella Trimmings & Ribbons,** 60 W. 38th St., 212/840-0644, specializing in feathers and bridal veils; **Manny's Millinery Supply,** 26 W. 38th St., 212/840-2235, selling hats and notions; and **M&J Buttons,** 1008 Sixth Ave., 212/391-6200, offering beads, buttons, lace, and feathers.

Flea Markets

Though much smaller now than it once was, thanks to real estate development, the empty lot along Sixth Avenue between 25th and 26th Streets still hosts an enormous outdoor market, the **Annex Antique Fair and Flea Market,** 212/243-5343, every weekend, as it has for over 30 years ago. The market is currently open Sat.–Sun., 9 A.M.–5 P.M.

The Annex's success led to the establishment of several nearby indoor markets. Run by the same people who run the Annex is the **Garage,** 112 W. 25th St., a former parking garage with about 125 vendors. Next door is the 12-floor **Chelsea Antiques Building,** 110 W. 25th St., 212/929-0909 (open daily), while to the east is **Markus Galleries,** 30 W. 26th St., 212/242-2228 (open Tues.–Sun.).

Other Shops

Chisholm Larsson Gallery, 145 Eighth Ave., at 17th St., 212/741-1703, specializes in European travel and product posters. Recently relocated from Greenwich Village, **Abracadabra,** 19 W. 21st St., near Fifth Ave., 212/627-5194, features an enormous number of rubber Halloween masks and wacky gag gifts.

ACCOMMODATIONS

$50–100

Themed rooms are a main attraction at the **Chelsea Star Hotel,** 300 W. 30th St., at Eighth Ave., 212/244-7827, where you can choose to sleep in guestrooms paying tribute to the likes of Shakespeare, Cleopatra, Star Trek, Esther Williams, Betty Boop, Madonna (the hotel was one of her first NYC homes), and about a dozen others. The place is a bit grungy, but that's part of its charm. Up top is a roof deck. Rates are $33 per person for a dorm room, $70–90 d with shared bath, $130–170 d for suite with private bath.

$100–150

Once the home of *Life* magazine, the beaux arts **Herald Square Hotel,** 19 W. 31st St., between Fifth and Sixth Aves., 212/279-4017 or 800/727-1888, boasts a lovely facade complete with lacy iron fretwork and a plump, gilded cherub reading the magazine. Rooms are small and dark, but adequate, and the shared baths are reasonably clean. $65 s or d with shared bath, $115–140 s or d with private bath, $150 t with private bath, $160 q with private bath.

Just east of the Herald Square is another beaux arts hostelry—the **Hotel Wolcott,** 4 W. 31st St., near Fifth Ave., 212/268-2900. Its elaborate but well-worn lobby is packed with marble columns, enormous mirrors, and shiny chandeliers—all contrasting strangely with the room's utilitarian furnishings and the harried staff at the front desk. Rooms are small but adequate; $75 s or d with shared bath; $100–120 with private bath.

Housed in side-by-side townhouses is the friendly 13-room **Chelsea Inn,** 46 W. 17th St., between Fifth and Sixth Aves., 212/645-8989, sporting 18-foot-high ceilings. Some of the rooms have semi-private baths, some private, and all are equipped with small refrigerators. $109–129 d.

A European-style hostelry for budget travelers, the **Chelsea Lodge,** 318 W. 20th St., between Eighth and Ninth Aves., 212/243-4499, www.chelsealodge.com, is housed in a historic brownstone featuring 22 guest rooms and several suites. $90–110 s or d with shared bath, $135–155 s or d with private bath.

The **Best Western Manhattan Hotel,** 17 W. 32nd St., between Fifth and Sixth Aves., 212/736-1600 or 800/567-7720, is more imaginatively designed than its name might imply. In the busy lobby, find neo-art deco decor in black and white; upstairs, find well-kept rooms designed in "airy Central Park," "sophisticated Fifth Avenue," and "trendy SoHo" themes. Adjoining the lobby is a Korean restaurant—in keeping with surrounding Koreatown. $109–169 s, $119–179 d.

Also in Koreatown find the **Red Roof Inn,** 6 W. 32nd St., between Fifth Ave. and Broadway, 212/643-7100 or 800/RED-ROOF, an excellent value for money. Surprisingly stylish, the inn offers small but clean rooms and a 24-hour fitness center; $110–250 s or d.

$150–250

One of the city's most historic hotels is the **Chelsea Hotel,** 222 W. 23rd St., between Seventh and Eighth Aves., 212/243-3700, www.chelseahotel.com, once home to everyone from Dylan Thomas to Sid Vicious (see Chelsea Hotel under Chelsea West, above). Nowadays, the Chelsea is neither particularly clean nor particularly cheap, but it does have atmosphere. Offbeat, bohemian, and chic in its own faded way, it offers thick walls, many rooms with kitchenettes, a friendly staff, and excellent people-watching. In the basement is a trendy cocktail lounge, Serena. $150–265 s or d.

Down the block from the Chelsea is the

Chelsea Savoy Hotel, 204 W. 23rd St., at Seventh Ave., 212/929-9353, offering 90 moderately sized rooms done up in dark floral greens and woods. The decor is nothing special, but everything's very clean. This is also one of the only hotels in Chelsea. $145–180 s or d.

A good choice in the Midtown area is the spiffy, neo-art deco **Metro,** 45 W. 35th St., between Fifth and Sixth Aves., 212/947-2500 or 800/356-3870. Built in 1901, the hotel offers 175 comfortable guest rooms and a large sitting room, where complimentary coffee is served throughout the day. On the top floor is an exercise room and rooftop terrace, where drinks are served in summer. $165–195 s or d; includes continental breakfast.

Hostel

The **Chelsea Center,** 313 W. 29th St., between Eighth and Ninth Aves., 212/643-0214, www.chelseacenterhostel.com, is a small, friendly hostel with dorm-style accommodations and a garden out back. All rooms share bathrooms; $30 per person.

FOOD

American

Though somewhat overpriced, the **Empire Diner,** 210 Tenth Ave., at 22nd St., 212/243-2736, is a stylish, art deco original well worth visiting; open 24 hours; average main dish $11. **Chelsea Commons,** 242 Tenth Ave., near 24th St., 212/929-9424, is a creaky tavern with solid bar food, an old-fashioned bar, and an outdoor garden. Live music sometimes adds spice; average main course $8.

A tiny gem of a hideaway, serving just a handful of entrées, is the subterranean **Alley's End,** 311 W. 17th St., between Eighth and Ninth Aves., 212/627-8899; average entrée $14. For a taste of late 19th-century New York, visit **Keens Steakhouse,** 72 W. 36th St., between Fifth and Sixth Aves., 212/947-3636, an atmospheric multi-roomed pub with a crackling fireplace in winter; average entrée $18.

French

The charming **Gascogne,** 158 Eighth Ave., near 18th St., 212/675-6564, specializes in the hearty foods of southern France. In summer, a secluded garden opens up; average entrée $18.

Italian

Da Umberto, 107 W. 17th St., near Sixth Ave., 212/989-0303, is a classy, albeit noisy, spot acclaimed for its Northern Italian fare, Italian wines, and well-dressed crowd; average entrée $23.

Korean

The spotless, narrow **Gam Mee Ok,** 43 W. 32nd St., between Fifth and Sixth Aves., 212/695-4113, filled with artwork, is one of Koreatown's top restaurants; average entrée $11. The lovely **Hangawi,** 10 E. 23rd St., 212/213-0077, is the place to go for vegetarian dishes, including pancakes and "porridges"—warm sweetened vegetable purees; average dish $15.

Latin/Caribbean

La Taza De Oro, 96 Eighth Ave., between 14th and 15th Sts., 212/243-9946, is a tiny luncheonette serving authentic Puerto Rican food; average main dish $7. For hearty Cuban-Chinese fare, try hole-in-the-wall **La Chinita Linda,** 166 Eighth Ave., between 18th and 19th Sts., 212/633-1791; average main dish $6.

    Bachue Cafe, 36 W. 21st St., between Fifth and Sixth Aves., 212/229-0870, is a newcomer specializing in Colombian cuisine; average entrée $12. Good Mexican fare can be found at the bustling **Rocking Horse Mexican Cafe,** 182 Eighth Ave., between 19th and 20th Sts., 212/463-9511; average entrée $13.

    Colorful, festive **Negril,** 362 W. 23rd St. between Eighth and Ninth Aves., 212/807-6411, serves spicy Caribbean fare in a lively setting; average entrée $14. The tiny, cheerful **Bright Food Shop,** 216 Eighth Ave., at 21st St., 212/243-4433, offers unusual Mexican-Asian cuisine; average entrée $9.

Other Ethnic

Cool, sophisticated **Periyali,** 35 W. 20th St., between Fifth and Sixth Aves., 212/463-7890, is acclaimed for its authentic Greek fare; average entrée $23.

Watering Holes and Lounges

Merchants, N.Y., 112 Seventh Ave., at 17th St., 212/366-7267, is a stylish bar with a sidewalk cafe in summer and a crackling fireplace in winter; on the menu are gourmet sandwiches, salads, and desserts. Trendy **Ciel Rouge,** 176 Seventh Ave., near 20th St., 212/929-5542, is the place to go for first-rate *caipirinhas,* served with appetizers from Brazil. Martinis are the specialty of the house at **Serena,** a subterranean club located in the basement of the Chelsea Hotel, 222 W. 23rd St., between Seventh and Eighth Aves., 212/255-4646. A lively outdoor bar called **Metro Grill** can be found atop the Metro hotel, 45 W. 35th St., between Fifth and Sixth Ave., 212/947-2500.

    The well-worn **Peter McManus,** 152 Seventh Ave., at 19th St., 212/929-9691, still attracts some long-time regulars as well as young professionals; juicy burgers are served at the big, rickety booths in back. Sleek, chic **G,** 223 W. 19th St., between Seventh and Eighth Aves., 212/929-1085, is an ultra-popular gay bar/lounge centered on a steel circular bar in front and a juice bar in the back. **Chelsea Commons** (see American, above) has a lively bar scene.

Midtown

Rush, rush, rush. Sometimes all the people in the world seem to be elbowing their way through here. Most of Manhattan's skyscrapers are in Midtown, along with most of its offices, major hotels, theaters, famous shops and restaurants, and many visitor attractions. If you have time to visit only one part of Manhattan, you should probably make Midtown the part you visit.

Fifth Avenue is the heart of Midtown, the artery to which all other addresses relate. Though nothing more than a line on a map as late as 1811, Fifth Avenue was the city's most fashionable address by the time of the Civil War. The Astors, Vanderbilts, and many other wealthy families all had homes along it, leading *Leslie's Weekly,* a popular magazine of the day, to comment that Fifth Avenue "has upon it 340 residences, all of the finer class, except for a few shanties near the Park. It may safely be said that of these 340 houses, not one costs less than $20,000."

Fifth Avenue began to turn commercial in the early 1900s. Today, its Midtown stretch is almost entirely lined with shops and office buildings. In the lower 40s and upper 30s, these shops tend to be tourist traps selling discounted electronic gadgetry and junky souvenirs; in the upper 40s and 50s stand the upscale boutiques and department stores for which the avenue is famous.

As in other parts of the city, Fifth Avenue is also the dividing line between the wealthier, more established East Side and the scruffier, more fly-by-night West Side. In Midtown on the East Side are a plethora of expensive office buildings and posh residences, along with such institutions as the Waldorf-Astoria and the United Nations. Immediately west of Fifth Avenue are more of the same—including Rockefeller Center and the Plaza Hotel. But continue west past Sixth Avenue, and things get a bit more disheveled. Here, you'll find Times Square and the once notorious neighborhood of Hell's Kitchen, now also known as Clinton.

To see Midtown at its frenzied best, you should tour during the week. However, most of the visitor attractions are also open on weekends. With the exception of Times Square, much of Midtown shuts up tight after business hours. First-time visitors will probably want to make stops at Grand Central Station, Times Square, Rockefeller Center, and Fifth Avenue between 50th and 59th Streets.

EAST 42ND STREET AND VICINITY

Grand Central Station

Having just completed a $200-million renovation, Grand Central Station, on 42nd Street between Vanderbilt and Lexington, is one of New York's most glorious buildings. To step inside its vast 125-foot-high concourse—with glassed-in catwalks, grand staircases, and vaulted, star-studded, aquamarine ceiling—is to be transported back to a more romantic era when women wore hoop skirts and men wore top hats.

Completed in 1913 by the design firms of Reed & Stem and Warren & Wetmore, Grand

historic Grand Central Station

MANHATTAN

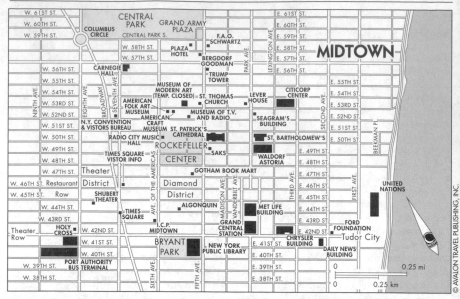

Central Station is a city within a city. Beaux arts eclectic on the outside, early 20th-century modern on the inside, it houses innumerable new shops and newsstands, several bars and restaurants, and a library devoted to railroading (open by appointment only). Also here, but off-limits to the public, are a shooting range and a rooftop tennis court. Adjoining the station are 27 miles of track that loop and stretch beneath Park Avenue as far north as 50th Street, and seven stories of tunnels containing electric power facilities, water and gas mains, sewage pipes, steam, and rats.

In its heyday, Grand Central was the terminus for two major railroads: the New York Central, and the New York, New Haven, and Hartford lines. Trains with romantic names such as the Empire State Express and Super Chief rolled in daily. A theater in the station screened newsreels, and CBS broadcast from the roof. Today, Grand Central Station is but a shadow of its former self. Only about 500 commuter trains arrive and depart daily (all long-distance trains use Penn Station).

To get the best view of Grand Central, take the escalators up to the balconies on the north side. From here, you can watch the foot traffic criss-crossing beneath you in seemingly choreographed style, while listening to the musicians who frequently perform by the east wall.

Adjoining Grand Central to the north, via the escalators, is the wide, 59-story Met Life Building, still known among many New Yorkers by its former name, the Pan Am Building. In its lobby is one of the city's best newsstands.

Fascinating one-hour tours of the terminal are conducted every Wednesday by the Municipal Art Society, 212/935-3960, www.mas.org. Groups meet at 12:30 P.M. at the information booth in the center of the concourse. Donations are appreciated.

Vanderbilt Avenue and Nathan Hale

The short street between 42nd and 47th Streets along the west side of Grand Central is named after Commodore Cornelius Vanderbilt (1794–1877), the man responsible for building Grand Central Station. Born working class, Vanderbilt began accumulating his fortune at the age of 16 when he started ferrying passengers between his native Staten Island and Manhattan. Gradually, he transformed that simple service into a large fleet of transatlantic steamships and, later in life, switched to railroading.

On an outside wall of the Yale Club at Vanderbilt Avenue and 44th Street is a plaque honoring Nathan Hale, the Revolutionary War hero hanged by the British for spying. The blond, blue-eyed, twenty-something Hale—a Yale grad—was caught in Brooklyn on September 21, 1776, and was executed just east of here (see Beekman Place, below).

Around Grand Central

Just across 42nd Street from Grand Central is the **Philip Morris Building,** 120 Park Ave., which houses an atrium and a branch of the **Whitney Museum of American Art at Philip Morris,** 917/663-2453. The museum is open Mon.–Fri. 11 A.M.–6 P.M., Thursday 11 A.M.–7:30 P.M. Admission is free.

At 110 E. 42nd is an impressive, Romanesque building that once housed the **Bowery Savings Bank** and now houses a special events venue owned by the Cipriani restaurant family. Designed by York & Sawyer in 1923, the building boasts a vast lobby filled with mosaic floors, marble columns, and huge pendant lamps. At 122 E. 42nd is the equally handsome **Chanin Building,** a 1929 art deco treasure done up in bronze and marble. The lobby is filled with bas-reliefs depicting the City of Opportunity, where a man of poor beginnings rises to a position of wealth and power.

Next to Grand Central is the glitzy **Grand Hyatt,** 109 E. 42nd, built on the shell of the old Commodore Hotel. In 1920, the Commodore was temporary home to Scott and Zelda Fitzgerald. Newly married, they moved in here after being kicked out of the nearby Biltmore Hotel for disturbing the other guests. But things didn't go well at the Commodore, either. When the Fitzgeralds spent half an hour spinning in the revolving door and generally creating a ruckus, they were asked to leave.

Free tours of historic East 42nd Street are offered by the Grand Central Partnership Business Improvement District, 212/697-1245. The tours leave from the Philip Morris Building, Fridays at 12:30 P.M.

The Chrysler Building and East

At the northeast corner of 42nd Street and Lexington Avenue stands the stunning Chrysler Building, a 1930 art deco masterpiece. Financed by Walter Chrysler, the towering building is a tribute to the automobile age. Winged gargoyles shaped like hood ornaments, and brick designs taken from wheels and hubcaps lead the eye up to a gleaming, stainless steel spire. At night, the concentric circles of the spire light up, tripping the city with a touch of the light fantastic.

Another block east, at 220 E. 42nd St., is the **Daily News Building,** a soaring art deco skyscraper designed by Raymood Hood in 1930. The *Daily News* left for cheaper digs (at 450 W. 33rd St.) in 1995, but the huge, slowly revolving globe in the building's lobby remains. Used in the *Superman* movie remakes of the 1980s, the globe is delightfully out-of-date, depicting countries that haven't existed in years.

Down the street from the News is the **Ford Foundation** building, 320 E. 42nd St., which has a lush three-story indoor garden enclosed by walls and ceilings of glass. Visitors are welcome to wander along the garden's meandering paths, surrounded by plants and trees. The garden lacks benches, however; to rest your weary peds, you'll have to trudge another half block east to **Tudor City.** Head up the stone staircases on either side of 42nd Street near First Avenue to reach the self-contained community with its 3,000 apartments, hotel, and small park. Tudor City's buildings—brick with Gothic touches—all face inward, with limited views of the river. That's because back in the 1920s, an ugly, foul-smelling slaughterhouse was situated below.

United Nations Plaza

Extending from 42nd to 48th Streets and from First Avenue to FDR Drive is the windswept United Nations Plaza, where the flags of the nearly 200 member nations flap noisily in the breeze. Legally, the United Nations isn't part of New York at all but is international territory. The U.N. has its own post office, postage stamps, and uniformed security force.

Built in 1948, on 18 acres bought and donated by J. D. Rockefeller Jr., the United Nations complex is made up of three buildings. The vertical greenish glass slab is the Secretariat Building, housing many offices. The low-slung horizontal

THE DRAFT RIOTS

One of the bloodiest riots in U.S. history began at the corner of Third Avenue and 46th Street during the Civil War. By the time the riots were over, nearly 100,000 people had rampaged through the streets, 18 blacks had been lynched, as many as 2,000 other people had been injured or killed, and innumerable buildings had been destroyed.

The riots began on the hot morning of July 12, 1863, when the first draft lottery in U.S. history was held at an enrollment office then located here. A large crowd looked on as names of local men were selected at random to join the Union army. Most of the unlucky "winners" were poor Irish laborers; the rich had already bought their way out of military service by paying the government $300 (the equivalent of one year's wages for the poorer men). The laborers weren't too keen on the idea of risking life and limb to free Southern slaves, who might then come north and compete for work.

As the names were being called, someone fiercely yelled out, "I ain't going!" and a few moments later an enraged crowd attacked the Union Army office, destroying it and the draft lottery wheel. From there, the crowd swarmed through the streets, gaining momentum and more followers as it went. The city's 800-man police force stood by helplessly as the mob overran the city's arsenal, burned down mansions, and looted stores. The protesters chased down the police chief and beat him unconscious; attacked the Colored Orphans Asylum on Fifth Avenue at West 43rd Street, killing one child as 250 others escaped out the back door; and strung up black boys along the trees of Bleecker Street, then a black residential district.

Finally, on July 15, Lincoln sent in troops—badly needed in the war itself—and the riots were quelled. Afterward, the lottery was quietly forgotten.

edifice is the Conference Building, and the dramatic white building with concave sides is the General Assembly.

Only the General Assembly Building is open to the public; to see it, you must join one of the scheduled 45-minute tours. English-language tours, 212/963-7713, www.un.org, leave daily every 30 minutes 9:30 A.M.–4:45 P.M. The tours take you past much wonderful art donated by member nations, and into the General Assembly Hall and Security Council Chamber. If meetings are in session, you can listen in on simultaneous interpretation in six languages.

The United Nations' visitor entrance is at 46th Street and First Avenue. Tour fees are adults $8.50, senior citizens $7, students $6, children in grades 1–8 $5, children under age five not admitted. The basement holds a gift shop selling handicrafts from around the world; the Delegates Dining Room, 212/963-7626, is open to visitors for lunch during the week. A delicious buffet is offered; reserve well in advance.

Just north of the General Assembly building are peaceful and surprisingly underutilized gardens filled with interesting sculptures, donated to the U.N. by member nations. The gardens have splendid views of the East River and are a good place to catch some sun on a summer's day.

Beekman Place

At the north end of the U.N. Plaza, just east of where 49th Street meets First Avenue, is Beekman Place, a tony residential avenue lined with townhouses and private parks. It's named for the Beekman family, whose mansion—Mount Pleasant—once stood here. The British commandeered Mount Pleasant during the Revolutionary War, using the mansion as their headquarters. Nathan Hale was tried as a spy in the greenhouse and hanged in the nearby orchard. A fresco depicting his trial and death is in the Hale House, 440 East 51st Street.

The great American songwriter, Irving Berlin, lived at 17 Beekman Pl. for over three decades; a plaque marks the spot. Greta Garbo lived at 2 Beekman Pl. during the 1930s, Billy Rose at 33 Beekman Pl. in the 1940s.

Sparks Steak House

On December16, 1985, mob boss Paul Castellano and his driver Thomas Bilotti were gunned down outside this modern Midtown eatery at 210 E. 46th St., near Second Avenue. As they climbed out of their car, both were shot six times by a hit squad armed with walkie-talkies and semiautomatics. "Dapper Don" John Gotti—so named because of his predilection for double-breasted silk suits and floral print ties—was convicted of ordering the murders and sent to jail in 1992. He died there of cancer in 2002.

TIMES SQUARE AND HELL'S KITCHEN

Simultaneously New York's glitziest and seediest symbol, Times Square centers around the intersection of Broadway and Seventh Avenue between 42nd and 48th Streets. Not really a square at all, but rather two elongated triangles, it is named after the *New York Times*, which was once located in the white Times Tower building where Broadway, Seventh Avenue, and 42nd Street meet. (The *Times* is now around the corner at 229 W. 43rd Street.) It is from Times Tower that the illuminated ball drops every December 31, ushering in the New Year.

Before 1904, when the *New York Times* moved in, Times Square was known as Longacre Square. The center of the horse business in a city then largely dependent upon four-footed transportation, the square was lined with horse exchanges, carriage factories, stables, and blacksmith shops. Not until the 1910s did Times Square become a bona fide theater district; not until the 1960s did it become known for its thriving sex industry.

Times Square's biggest year for theatrical productions was 1927–28, when 257 shows were mounted at 71 theaters. The sex industry peaked here in the early 1970s with an estimated 150 sex joints and porn shops. The man most responsible for turning the area into a porno-amusement park was Martin Hodas, the Peep Show King. Hodas first introduced the coin-operated viewing booth to Times Square in the late '70s. At the height of his career, he was said to have been grossing $13 million annually.

Times Square has been much cleaned up in recent years, thanks largely to the efforts of the Times Square Business Improvement District—a nonprofit organization formed of the area's business and community leaders. Almost all of the old porn shops have been closed down and the three-card-monte games broken up. Police and private security officers patrol the streets 24 hours a day.

All this has not come without a price. A number of fine old movie theaters were destroyed along with the porn shops, to be replaced by sterile glass-sheathed office buildings and hotels. And without the denizens of the night—evicted from their traditional haunts—Times Square is rapidly losing much of its character.

Two things that could help protect Times Square from a bland future are its street performers—each one more inventive than the next—and its neon signs. The lights start to burn at dusk, hinting at the magic yet to come, and by night, the streets are ablaze with huge panels of red, green, yellow, blue, and white. Except for the Las Vegas Strip, no other place in America boasts more neon lights.

The main entrance to the Times Square Visitor Center, 1560 Broadway, is on Seventh Avenue between 46th and 47th Streets. It's open daily 8 A.M.–8 P.M., and the staff is multilingual. Free and very enjoyable walking tours of the area, led by actors, leave from the center on Fridays at noon; call 212/869-1890 for more information.

Theater District

Most of the Broadway theaters are not on Broadway at all, but on the side streets surrounding Times Square. The area is home to 37 legitimate theaters, 22 of which are city landmarks. West 44th and 45th Streets between Seventh and Eighth Avenues are especially rich blocks; here you'll find the **Shubert,** the **Helen Hayes,** the **Booth,** the **Majestic,** the **Minskoff,** and several more.

Next to the Shubert, connecting 44th and 45th Streets, is **Shubert Alley,** where unemployed performers once waited, hoping for a part. Today, a souvenir shop selling theater memorabilia is located here. Across the street from the Shubert is the legendary **Sardi's** restaurant, 234 W. 44th St., its walls lined with caricatures.

Once frequented by theater folks, Sardi's now attracts mostly tourists, but is still a fun and lively place serving a varied international cuisine.

West 42nd Street

During the last five years, big changes have come to West 42nd Street, especially between Seventh and Eighth Avenues. For years a center for porn movies, this most historic of theatrical streets has regained some of its former turn-of-the-century glory.

Nine historic theaters, many of which have been restored, line the block. The Victory, 207 W. 42nd St., opened by Oscar Hammerstein in 1900, is now the **New Victory,** specializing in programming for young people. The **New Amsterdam,** 214 W. 42nd, once home to the Ziegfeld Follies, is now owned by Disney. On its docket are both movies and plays, while next door is the splashy **Disney Store,** 210 W. 42nd Street.

Also on 42nd Street is **Madame Tussaud's New York,** 234 W. 42nd St., between Seventh and Eighth Aves., 800/246-8872, www.madame-tussauds.com, where you'll find waxy renditions of famous New Yorkers, past and present. Hours are Sun.–Thurs. 10 A.M.–6 P.M., Fri.–Sat. 10 A.M.–8 P.M. Admission is adults $19.95, seniors $17.95, children 4–12 $15.95.

Port Authority and West

Between 40th and 42nd Streets, Eighth and Ninth Avenues, is the Port Authority Bus Terminal, also much cleaned up in recent years but still no place to linger voluntarily. To the rear of the terminal's second floor is the well-kept, '50s-era **Leisure Time Bowling,** 212/268-6909, one of the only bowling alleys left in Manhattan.

Across the street from the Port Authority is the 1870 **Church of the Holy Cross,** 333 W. 42nd St., studded with windows and mosaics designed by Louis Comfort Tiffany. Father Francis Duffy, chaplain of the "Fighting Irish" 69th Division during WW I, became pastor of the church in 1921 and helped break up the area's notorious Hell's Kitchen gangs (see below). Much beloved by theater people, Duffy is honored with a statue in Times Square, across from the statue of George M. Cohan.

Down the block is the former **McGraw-Hill** building, 330 W. 42nd Street. This blue-green art deco tower was designed by Raymond Hood as a complement to his *Daily News* skyscraper at the eastern end of the street.

Between Ninth and Tenth Avenues, 42nd Street is known as **Theater Row** because of the its Off-Broadway theaters. Among them are the **Harold Clurman Theatre,** 412 W. 42nd St., and **Playwrights Horizon,** 416 W. 42nd Street.

Hell's Kitchen

Up until a few years ago, the whole area west of Eighth Avenue between 23rd and 59th Streets was usually referred to as Hell's Kitchen. During the late 1800s and much of the 1900s, this seedy part of town was gangland territory, home to such rival groups as the Gophers, the Gorillas, the Hudson Dusters, and more recently, the Westies. The Westies were still in business up until 1987 when former gang member Mickey Featherstone, arrested for murder, testified against his former colleagues in exchange for immunity.

Today, many civic-improvement types prefer to call the northern part of Hell's Kitchen "Clinton," in recognition of the extensive cleanup efforts made here in recent years. Though still home to plenty of crumbling tenements and shady characters, Clinton is slowly becoming gentrified, especially around Ninth Avenue.

For foodies, Ninth Avenue between 37th and 54th Streets is nirvana. One tiny, often disheveled, ethnic food shop or restaurant follows another in an update of the old pushcart market that flourished here around the turn of the century. Every May, the whole avenue celebrates with a gigantic two-day **Ninth Avenue Food Festival** that draws thousands of people from all over the city.

Intrepid Sea-Air-Space Museum

Docked at Pier 86, on the far western edge of Manhattan, is the *Intrepid,* W. 46th St., at 12 Ave., 212/245-0072, www.intrepidmuseum.org. A former WW II aircraft carrier now devoted to military history, the museum houses lots of audio visuals and hands-on exhibits, most designed to appeal to kids. The decks are strewn with small aircraft and space capsules; permanent exhibits explore the mysteries of satellite communication and ship design; special exhibits focus on such subjects as women pilots and Charles Lindbergh. Open May 1–Sept. 30, Mon.–Fri. 10 A.M.–5 P.M., Sat.–Sun. 10 A.M.–7 P.M.; Oct. 1–April 30, Wed.–Sun. 10 A.M.–4 P.M. Admission is adults $13; veterans, senior citizens, and students 12–17 $9; children 6–11 $6, children under 6 $2.

BRYANT PARK TO THE DIAMOND DISTRICT

New York Public Library

Filling two blocks of Fifth Avenue between 40th and 42nd Streets, this lavish beaux arts building houses one of the world's top five research libraries. The library's vast collection of over nine million books and 21 million other objects occupies some 88 miles of shelves above ground and 84 miles below.

Designed by Carrere & Hastings, and completed in 1911, the library occupies the former site of Croton Reservoir, a huge 150-million-gallon granite water tank that stood here from 1842 to 1900. The promenade that once encircled the top of the reservoir was a popular place from which to take in the local sights.

Libraries aren't usually worth touring, but the New York Public Library is an exception. On the main floor is an elaborate entrance hall with a vaulted ceiling and wide sweeping staircases. Behind the entrance hall is **Gottesman Hall,** where unusual exhibits on such subjects as illustrator Charles Addams or photographer Berenice Abbott are displayed.

Big as a football field, and sumptuous as the lobby of a luxury hotel, the recently restored Main Reading Room on the third floor is the library's highlight. Books are ordered via a pneumatic tube system that sucks call slips down into the bowels of the stacks, while overhead float pastel murals of satyrs, cherubs, and clouds. Also on the third floor is the Map Room—where the U.S. Army planned the invasion of North Africa during WW II—and the Science and Technology Room, where Chester Carlson invented Xerox and Edwin Land invented the Polaroid camera.

© CHRISTIANE BIRD

Patience (or it might be Fortitude) reposes on the steps of the New York Public Library.

The stone lions lounging on the library's front steps were originally named "Leo Astor" and "Leo Lenox," after the library's founders John Jacob Astor and James Lenox. Later, in the 1930s, Mayor La Guardia dubbed the felines "Patience" and "Fortitude"—qualities he felt New York would need to survive the Depression. A popular saying of that time had it that the lions roared whenever a virgin passed by, but no one's mentioned that bit of folklore in years.

Free tours of the library are given Mon.–Sat. at 11 A.M. and 2 P.M. For exhibit information, call 212/869-8089.

Bryant Park

Just behind the library is Bryant Park, filled with pretty flower beds, gravel paths, a stylish indoor-outdoor restaurant, and lots of benches that are usually packed with office workers at lunchtime. The park is named after poet and journalist William Cullen Bryant, a great proponent of parks and one of the people most responsible for the creation of Central Park.

International Center of Photography

Heading north one block, you'll find the largely subterranean International Center of Photography,

MANHATTAN

1133 Sixth Ave., at 43rd St., 212/860-0000, www.icp.org. Once an offshoot of its parent institution on E. 94th St., the Sixth Avenue location now houses the center's entire operations, including spacious exhibit areas, a school, library, and bookshop. Founded in 1974 by Cornell Capa, Robert Capa's brother (Robert Capa was a photojournalist killed in Vietnam), the center presents many of the city's most important contemporary photography exhibits. Hours are Tues.–Thurs. 10 A.M.–5 P.M., Friday 10 A.M.–8 P.M., Sat.–Sun. 10 A.M.–6 P.M. Suggested donation is adults $8, students and seniors $6.

The Algonquin and Vicinity

At the famed old Algonquin Hotel, 59 W. 44th St., between Fifth and Sixth Aves., Dorothy Parker and friends assembled in the 1920s at a round table in the Rose Room. Notable residents have included editor H. L. Mencken, who stayed here in 1914 while starting up the magazine *The Smart Set* with George Nathan; writer James Thurber, who lived here for long periods in the 1930s and 1950s; and actor Douglas Fairbanks who, while living here from 1907 to 1915, did gymnastics on the roof. Today the venerable Algonquin remains cozy and old-fashioned.

Across the street from the Algonquin are the former editorial offices of *The New Yorker*, 5 W. 45th St. (now housed in the Condé Nast building in Times Square); and the 1898 **Royalton Hotel,** 44 W. 44th St., transformed by Ian Schrager of Studio 54 fame into a sleek, artsy, and very expensive hostelry. Next door to the Algonquin is the **Iroquois Hotel,** 49 W. 44th St., where James Dean lived as a young actor in 1951. The first thing friends saw upon entering Dean's apartment was the shadow of a hangman's noose, created by a small model of a gallows that Dean had backlit.

Diamond District

Continuing north, you'll come to the Diamond District, West 47th Street between Fifth and Sixth Avenues, where an estimated $400 million in gems is exchanged daily. Many—but far from all—of the dealers and cutters of the 2,500 companies crammed into this block are Hasidic

Jews, identifiable by their long beards, earlocks, and black frock coats. As has long been their tradition, the Hasidim often negotiate their biggest deals in back rooms or out on the sidewalks, but efforts are being made to make the block more user-friendly. New streetlights have been installed and a marketing campaign now woos tourists to the block.

Dahesh Museum

One block north of the Diamond District is the compact Dahesh Museum, an unusual institution dedicated to 19th and early 20th century European academic art. The museum is named after a Lebanese writer and philosopher who acquired many of the works in the museum's collection. The changing exhibits cover a surprisingly wide range, from Middle Eastern pen-and-ink drawings to French landscapes. The museum, 601 Fifth Ave., at 48th St., 212/759-0606, www.daheshmuseum.org, is open Tues.–Sat., 11 A.M.–6 P.M. Admission is free.

ROCKEFELLER CENTER AND VICINITY

The area between 48th and 51st Streets, and Fifth and Sixth Avenues, was once a notorious red-light district. Today it's occupied by New York's most famous city within a city, Rockefeller Center. Built by John D. Rockefeller during the height of the Depression, the magnificent art deco complex is comprised of 19 buildings, connected by plazas and underground passageways. Throughout the year, thousands of tourists and New Yorkers, street performers and the homeless, congregate here daily.

Rockefeller called upon his international contacts to sponsor the center, which helps account for its international feel. On the Fifth Avenue side, between 49th and 50th Streets, the wryly named **Channel Gardens** separate the **British Empire Building** to the north from **La Maison Française** to the south. Lovely friezes adorn both buildings' facades, while their ground floors are filled with international shops and tourism offices. The center's once unique art deco basement has, alas, recently been transformed into an upscale shopping center.

The Channel Gardens lead to the sunken **Lower Plaza** at the heart of the complex. This plaza offers an outdoor restaurant in summer, an ice-skating rink in winter, and great people-watching year-round. All around the plaza are towering flagpoles bearing brightly colored banners flapping in the wind, while at one end lounges an ungainly gilded Prometheus. At Christmastime, the famous Rockefeller tree is erected directly behind him.

Just west of Lower Plaza is **30 Rockefeller Plaza,** a wonderful, 70-story art deco skyscraper designed by Raymond Hood. Still known as the RCA building—though its correct name these days is the GE building—it features a bearded bas relief of *Genius* above its door. Inside the lobby is a rather bland mural, *American Progress,* painted by Jose Maria Sert to replace a much more controversial one by Diego Rivera. Commissioned by Rockefeller to create the original artwork, Rivera chose to depict Lenin and the proletariat taking over industry while important plutocrats were being eaten away by syphilis. Not surprisingly, that was too much for Rockefeller, and he had it replaced.

Also in 30 Rockefeller Plaza are the **NBC Studios,** 212/664-3700, www.nbc.com, where you can peer through the *Today* show studio window or take a tour. Lasting about one hour, the tours leave from the **New York Experience Store** every 30 minutes Mon.–Sat. 8:30 A.M.–5:30 P.M. and Sunday 9:30 A.M.–4:30 P.M. Tickets cost adults $17.50, children 6–16 and seniors $15; children under six not permitted. Reservations recommended.

Guided tours of Rockefeller Center also leave from the New York Experience Store Mon.–Sat. 9 A.M.–4 P.M. and Sunday 10 A.M.–4 P.M. Cost is adults $10, children 6–16 and seniors $8.

Radio City Music Hall

Despite, or perhaps because of, its dated feel, this art deco landmark at the corner of Sixth Avenue and 50th Street has been bringing them back for generations. An over-the-top creation with a stage as wide as a city block, it's the world's largest indoor theater.

Part of Rockefeller Center, the Music Hall was largely created by impresario Samuel Lionel Rothafel, nicknamed Roxy. Born in a Lower East Side tenement, Roxy began his career by showing movies in the back room of a bar. From that humble beginning, he soon rose to become a major power in show business, producing radio shows and plays, and managing a string of theaters including the sumptuous Roxy which once stood in Times Square.

Roxy had a hand in designing the Music Hall; the magnificent, egg-shaped, 6,200-seat auditorium is said to be based on an idea he had while sailing on an ocean liner at dawn. The proscenium arch, painted with multicolored rays, represents the sun, while the carpet adorned with art deco fish represents the sea. Roxy also equipped his theater with all the latest technology of the day, including four elevators for the raising and lowering of scenery, machines capable of creating rain and steam, and the Mighty Wurlitzer, an organ loud enough to be heard in the subway below.

Though the Music Hall has hosted many unusual performers over the years—including elephants and horses—its most famous are the Rockettes. Chorus girls all between five feet four inches and five feet seven inches in height, the Rockettes once appeared nightly. Now they kick and strut their stuff only during the Music Hall's two-month-long Christmas show.

One-hour backstage tours of the Music Hall, 212/247-4777, www.radiocity.com, are offered Mon.–Fri. 10 A.M.–5 P.M., Sat.–Sun. noon–5 P.M.; call for winter hours. Tours cost adults $17, children under 12 $10.

Two Fifth Avenue Churches

On Fifth Avenue between 50th and 51st Streets is **St. Patrick's Cathedral,** the largest Roman Catholic cathedral in the United States. Designed by James Renwick, this elaborate Gothic creation with its soaring towers and lovely rose window took 21 years to build, replacing the old St. Pat's in Little Italy in 1879. Its grandeur attests to the success of New York's Irish Catholic immigrants who, at the time the church was being built, were largely shunned by the city's predominantly Protestant upper classes. Back then,

MANHATTAN

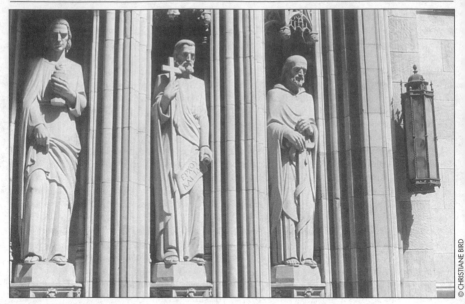

statuary at St. Thomas Church

© CHRISTIANE BIRD

some snooty upper crusts even went out of their way not to cross in front of the cathedral.

Kitty-corner to St. Pat's, at the corner of 53rd Street, is another famous New York church, the Protestant Episcopal **St. Thomas Church,** completed in 1914. A French Gothic gem known for its lovely stonework and stained glass, the church has long been a favorite site for society weddings. St. Thomas has a wonderful choir that can be heard on Sunday mornings or daily at evensong. Call 212/757-7013 for more information.

52nd Street

Back in the 1930s and '40s, more great musicians congregated on 52nd Street between Fifth and Sixth Avenues than anyplace else in the world, before or since. Art Tatum, Billie Holiday, Coleman Hawkins, Oran "Hot Lips" Page, Roy Eldridge, Teddy Wilson, Fats Waller, Erroll Garner, Mary Lou Williams, Dizzy Gillespie, Charlie Parker, Miles Davis, Sarah Vaughan, Count Basie, Woody Herman, Buddy Rich, Dave Tough, George Shearing—all were here.

The magic began just after Prohibition when

New York's jazz epicenter began shifting from Harlem to downtown. "The Street" at that time was lined with dark and smoky speakeasies, all housed in dilapidated brownstones with tiny vestibules, long bars, pressed-tin ceilings, and water-stained walls.

The first music club to open on 52nd Street was the Onyx, later dubbed the Cradle of Swing. Then came the Famous Door, named for the door inscribed with autographs that sat on a small platform near the bar; the Downbeat, where Dizzy Gillespie often played; and the Three Deuces, a regular gig for Erroll Garner. The Street's most famous club, Birdland—named after Charlie Parker—was not actually on 52nd St. at all, but around the corner at 1674 Broadway, in a building that still stands.

The Street began to decline after WW II, and today all but one of the brownstones have been torn down, replaced by modern skyscrapers. The only reminders of the past are the street signs reading "Swing Street," and the sidewalk plaques embedded near Sixth Avenue that honor some of the jazz greats.

The one brownstone that *does* remain is the upscale **"21" Club,** 21 W. 52nd St., 212/582-7200. The restaurant is marked by a line of miniature cast-iron jockeys out front.

Museum of Television and Radio

This shiny museum at 25 W. 52nd St., between Fifth and Sixth Aves., 212/621-6800, www.mtr.org, was founded by William Paley and designed by Philip Johnson. Here you can watch your favorite old TV show, listen to a classic radio broadcast, or research pop-culture subjects such as '50s sitcoms or beer commercials. In the museum for your listening and viewing pleasure are 96 semiprivate radio and television consoles, two large theaters, and two screening rooms. The museum also offers more traditional exhibits on such topics as animation and costume design.

The museum is open Tues.–Wed. and Sat.–Sun. noon–6 P.M., Thursday noon–8 P.M., Friday noon–9 P.M. If you're interested in using one of the consoles on the weekend, it's advisable to come early. Admission is adults $6, students $4, seniors and children under 13 $3.

American Craft Museum

Directly across the street from MoMA (which is closed for renovation), this museum, 40 W. 53rd St., 212/956-3535, is engaged in an ambitious decade-long exhibit series tracing the history of American crafts. Exquisite textiles, ceramics, glasswork, and other crafts are on display, but unfortunately, the exhibits often seem to be more geared toward experts than the general public. Still, if you've any interest in crafts, the museum and its unique gift shop are well worth a look.

Hours are Tues.–Sun. 10 A.M.–6 P.M. and Thursday 6–8 P.M. Admission is adults $8, students and seniors $5, children under 12 free; Thursday 6–8 P.M. pay as you wish.

American Folk Art Museum

Recently relocated to 53rd Street from its old digs directly across from Lincoln Center, the stunning American Folk Art Museum, 45 W. 53rd St., between Fifth and Sixth Aves., 212/977-7170, www.folkartmuseum.org, designed by New York architects Tom Williams and Billy Tsien, has increased its size four-fold. Now housed in an airy eight-story building—complete with an auditorium, gift shop, and cafe—the museum exhibits a wide range of folk art, including quilts, toys, weather vanes, samplers, paintings, sculpture, handmade furniture, and the like. Temporary exhibits often focus on the work of individual self-taught artists.

Hours are Tues.–Sun. 10 A.M.–6 P.M., and Friday 10 A.M.–8 P.M. Admission is adults $9, seniors and students $5, under 12 free.

(The museum's former location, 2 Lincoln Sq., Columbus Ave. between 65th and 66th Sts., 212/595-9533, now functions as a branch. Hours are Tues.–Sun. 11 A.M.–7:30 P.M. Suggested donation $3.)

Rock's Demise

Poor Nelson Rockefeller met his inopportune death in the gorgeous family townhouse at 13 W. 54th St. at 11:15 P.M. on January 26, 1979. At first, an official spokesperson tried to claim that the 71-year-old former New York governor had died an hour earlier in his nearby office. But as the truth emerged, it turned out that Rocky had not only died at home, but had also suffered his fatal heart attack while in the company of his attractive, 25-year-old assistant, Megan Marshack. Marshack had been dressed in a black evening gown.

Happy Rockefeller had her husband's body cremated the day after his death; Marshack has never spoken publicly about her last night with Rocky.

ART ON THE MOVE

The **Museum of Modern Art (MoMA)** has closed up shop at 11 West 53rd Street until 2005 for a $650-million renovation and expansion which will double its exhibition space. In the interim, the museum is being housed in a former Staples factory building in Queens. For more information on the new **MoMA QNS,** 45-20 33rd St., off Queens Blvd., see Long Island City in the Queens section of the Outer Boroughs chapter. The museum can still be reached at 212/708-9400, www.moma.org.

MANHATTAN

THE EAST 50s

Villard Houses/New York Palace Hotel

On Madison Avenue between 49th and 50th Streets are the Villard Houses, a group of six Italianate brownstones now incorporated into the New York Palace Hotel. Built for railroad magnate Henry Villard in 1886 by McKim, Mead & White, the houses center around a courtyard, with the glitzy glass hotel tower rising behind. It's incongruous, but the old houses have been well restored. Especially wonderful are two sweeping staircases and the Gold Room, built to resemble the music room of an Italian Renaissance palace.

Appropriately, the north wing of the Villard Houses serves as the **Urban Center,** of the **Municipal Art Society,** 457 Madison Ave., 212/935-3960, an organization dedicated to historic preservation and urban planning. The center holds an excellent bookstore and exhibition halls where temporary shows on the city's history and architecture are mounted. Hours are Mon.–Wed. and Fri.–Sat. 11 A.M.–5 P.M. Admission is free.

Waldorf-Astoria

At 301 Park Ave., between 49th and 50th Sts., is the extravagant Waldorf-Astoria Hotel. When rebuilt on this location in 1931 (the original stood at 34th St. and Fifth Ave.), it was the world's tallest, most lavish hotel, with 2,200 rooms, 2,700 telephones, and 16 elevators, one of which was big enough to take a limousine up to the ballroom for the annual automobile exhibition.

Now a Hilton hotel catering to a largely business clientele, the Waldorf has lost its exclusive edge but is still well worth a look. Recently restored, it features a lobby filled with marble, bronze, and wood, and a giant 1893 clock built for the Chicago Columbian Exposition.

Looking south from the Waldorf, you'll see Park Avenue swerve to both sides around a white beaux arts building with a splendid gold roof. Known as the **Helmsley Building,** the 1929 edifice is especially lovely at night, when its lit roof serves as a beacon for the Upper East Side.

One of the owners of the building, Leona Helmsley—wife of real estate kingpin Harry Helmsley—was convicted of tax evasion in 1989 and sentenced to four years in prison. New York had a field day with her trial, with the tabloids dubbing her the "Queen of Mean," the TV stations gleefully reporting her every indiscretion, and the public rubbing their hands over her downfall. There's no doubt that Leona did deserve her nickname—this is a woman who once said, "I don't pay taxes. The little people pay taxes." But the ferocity of the attack upon her was hardly New York's finest hour.

All of this section of Park Avenue was once an open railroad yard, and the tracks leading to Grand Central still run beneath it. The avenue itself is actually just a thin skin of metal and pavement, held up and together with planks, while the buildings on either side stand on stilts wedged between the tracks. Sometimes, as the cars whisk past, you can hear the avenue clanking.

St. Bartholomew's

On Park Avenue between 50th and 51st Streets is the romantic Romanesque dome of St. Bartholomew's Church, looking oddly dwarfish compared to the towering General Electric Building behind it. The church was designed by architect Stanford White. Inside, an elaborate mosaic ceiling depicts the story of creation.

Two Architectural Landmarks

The **Seagram's Building,** on the east side of Park Avenue between 52nd and 53rd Streets, was designed in 1958 by Ludwig Mies van Der Rohe and Philip Johnson. It was unusual at the time for its spare, streamlined construction, and its wide, wide plaza. Still considered one of New York's finest skyscrapers, it's home to the famed **Four Seasons Restaurant.**

On the west side of Park Avenue between 53rd and 54th Streets is the **Lever House,** designed by Skidmore, Owings & Merrill in 1952. It was the city's first glass-encased office tower and was used as a model by dozens of other architects. Today, the Lever House doesn't look all that unusual, but back in the 1950s, surrounded by heavy stone apartment buildings, it was as alien as a spaceship.

Citicorp Center and Vicinity

The gleaming skyscraper with the strange sloping roof at Lexington Avenue and 54th Street is the Citicorp Center, built in 1978. On its lower level is an indoor courtyard filled with tables and chairs, and surrounded by stores and gourmet takeout eateries.

Also in the Citicorp Center is **St. Peter's Lutheran Church,** 212/935-2200, a big, modern sanctuary with towering ceilings. Nicknamed the "jazz church" because of its ministrations to the jazz community, St. Peter's hosts frequent jazz events, including Sunday afternoon jazz vespers, occasional Sunday evening jazz concerts, and free Wednesday noontime concerts.

Kitty-corner to St. Peter's, at Lexington Avenue and 55th Street, is **Central Synagogue.** Designed in 1872 by Henry Fernbach, the first Jewish architect in New York, it's the oldest synagogue in continual use in the state.

Meanwhile, on a more frivolous note, it was at the northwest corner of Lexington Avenue and East 52nd Street that a draft from a subway vent blew up Marilyn Monroe's skirt in *The Seven Year Itch.* The now-famed scene took place in front of the since demolished Trans Lux theater, but the subway vent is still there.

Sony Wonder Technology Lab

On Madison Avenue between 55th and 56th Streets is the Sony Building, the soaring atrium of which houses several gourmet takeout shops and something called the Sony Wonder Technology Lab. Part giant advertisement, part electronics amusement park, the four-story "lab" is packed with dozens of high-tech video games, along with a sound board and editing console where you can play at producing CDs and videos of Sony recording artists. The lab, 212/833-8100, is open Tues.–Sat. 10 A.M.–6 P.M., Sunday noon–6 P.M. Admission is free.

Trump Tower

At Fifth Avenue and 56th Street stands Trump Tower, a glittering rose-and-gilt edifice with its own nexus of shops. Open daily 8 A.M.–10 P.M. (the building; shop hours vary), Trump Tower boasts a skinny cascading waterfall, far too much brass, and a multitude of glitzy escalators.

BIG APPLE ATRIUMS

Scattered throughout Midtown are numerous hidden atriums and courtyards that offer a welcome respite from the madding crowds. Some of these free public spaces are landscaped with plants and waterfalls, while others hold restaurants and shops.

The atriums of the **Ford Foundation,** 320 E. 42nd St.; the **Sony Building,** Madison Ave. at 55th St.; and **Citicorp Center,** Lexington Ave. at 54th St., are covered elsewhere in this chapter. Also noteworthy are the atriums at **Olympic Tower,** Fifth Ave. and 51st St., filled with inviting benches and a waterfall; the **IBM Garden Plaza,** Madison Ave. at 56th St., equipped with tables and chairs, towering bamboo trees, and a refreshment kiosk; and **Equitable Center,** 787 Seventh Ave., between 51st and 52nd Sts., which features many shops and restaurants, along with stunning artwork by Roy Lichtenstein, Thomas Hart Benton, and others.

57TH STREET AND THE PLAZA

57th Street

Like 42nd Street, 57th Street is one of the city's major east-west thoroughfares and one that changes character as it heads crosstown. To the east, 57th is the poshest of areas, with some of the city's most expensive boutiques and art galleries. To the west, the street becomes sort of an outdoor theme park for adults.

Among the most famous galleries on 57th Street are **PaceWildenstein,** 32 E. 57th St., 212/421-3292, which represents such heavyweights as Picasso, Louise Nevelson, and Julian Schnabel; and the **Marlborough,** 40 W. 57th, 212/541-4900, representing such artists as Larry Rivers and Francis Bacon. **Marian Goodman,** 24 W. 57th, 212/977-7160, specializes in contemporary European artists, while **Artemis Greenberg Van Doren,** 730 Fifth Ave., at 57th St., 212/445-0444, represents primarily American

SIDEWALK FORTUNES

Mrs. Crystal will read your entire life without asking a single question." "Mrs. Lisa tells—past—present—future." "Thousands of people who have been CROSSED, HAVE SPELLS, CAN'T HOLD MONEY, WANT LUCK, WANT THEIR LOVED ONES BACK, WANT TO STOP NATURE PROBLEMS or WANT TO GET RID OF STRANGE SICKNESS . . . are amazed at the results gotten by MRS. STELLA."

Walk the streets of Manhattan for any length of time and chances are good a silent dark-haired man will hand you a flyer printed with promises similar to these. Follow the flyer's advice, and you'll probably find yourself in a small storefront where a woman dressed in long flowing garments sits next to a crystal ball. In the back, children and cats hover.

Though not as plentiful as they once were, unlicensed and unregulated fortune-tellers dot the streets of Manhattan. Many are Gypsies—or Roma, as they preferred to be called—who've immigrated here from Eastern Europe. Others are "professional" astrologers, psychics, and New Age spiritualists. The former usually charge around $10 to read your palm or the tarot cards; the latter charge $20–50 and up, and advertise in the Yellow Pages.

---

artists, both established and up-and-coming. The **Mary Boone Gallery,** once a fixture on the SoHo scene, is now located both in Chelsea and at 745 Fifth Ave., between 57th and 58th Sts., 212/752-2929. Come here to view the works of David Salle, Eric Fischl, Barbara Kruger, and Bryan Hunt, to name but a few.

To find out about other galleries, or about who's exhibiting where, pick up a copy of the *Art Now Gallery Guide,* available at many bookstores and galleries. Or check magazine or Sunday newspaper listings.

As for that theme park, the fun begins at Sixth Avenue. On Sixth Ave. one block south of 57th St. is the glitzy **Harley Davidson Cafe,** 1370 Sixth Ave., 212/245-6000, adorned with motorbikes and leather jackets. On 57th St. just north of Sixth Ave. is the **Jekyll and Hyde Club,** 1409 Sixth Ave., 212/541-9517, decked out with sinking bar stools and talking corpses. On 57th St. proper are the **Brooklyn Diner USA,** 212 W. 57th St., 212/977-2280, serving enormous platters of home-style cooking; and the **Hard Rock Cafe,** 221 W. 57th St., between Broadway and Seventh Ave., 212/489-6565, bejeweled with shiny guitars and gold records.

Another address to watch for on West 57th is **Carnegie Hall,** W. 57th St. at Seventh Ave., 212/247-7800, www.carnegiehall.org. The dean of concert halls since its completion in 1891, Carnegie Hall was originally built by An-drew Carnegie as a home for the Oratorio Society, of which he was then president.

The Plaza

Just west of Fifth Avenue between 58th and 59th Streets stands the famed Plaza Hotel, still one of New York's loveliest buildings. Designed by

the Plaza Hotel, built in the French Renaissance style

© CHRISTIANE BIRD

Henry Hardenbergh in 1907, it's built in a French Renaissance style, with lots of dormers, high roofs, and rounded corners. In 1988, the hotel was bought and extensively renovated by real-estate mogul Donald Trump and his then-wife Ivana.

The **Palm Court,** in the hotel's lobby, is decorated with white marble columns, small tea tables, and fresh flowers. In the back is the comfortable **Oak Bar,** paneled in heavy wood. Both are ridiculously expensive and frequented by hordes of people, but are nevertheless excellent spots in which to get a taste of old New York.

The hotel stands on the edge of Grand Army Plaza, home of the ornate Pulitzer Memorial Fountain. To the north is Central Park, and a gathering place for the **horse-drawn hansoms** that clip-clop their way throughout this part of town. No New Yorker ever rides these things, but many visitors love them; rates are $40 for about twenty minutes. For more information, call the Manhattan Carriage Company at 212/664-1149.

SHOPPING
Books, Newspapers, Maps
Tucked in between the glittering jewelry stores in the Diamond District is one of the city's most historic bookstores, the **Gotham Book Mart,** 41 W. 47th St., between Fifth and Sixth Aves., 212/719-4448. The store was established in 1920 by Frances Steloff, who was an early supporter of such writers as James Joyce, Henry Miller, and T. S. Eliot.

Urban Center Books, 457 Madison Ave., between 50th and 51st Sts., 212/935-3595, specializes in books on architecture and urban design. **Barnes & Noble,** operates a branch at 600 Fifth Ave., at 48th St., 212/765-0590. The classy, wood-paneled **Rizzoli,** 31 W. 57th St., 212/759-2424, stocks an especially fine collection of art and photography books.

Mysterious Book Shop, 129 W. 56th St., between Sixth and Seventh Aves., 212/765-0900, sells hardcover, paperback, new, and used. The **Argosy,** 116 E. 59th St., between Park and Lexington Aves., 212/753-4455, carries an excellent selection of used books.

Hagstrom Map and Travel Center, 57 W. 43rd St., between Fifth and Sixth Aves., 212/398-1222, stocks an impossible number of maps. The **Rand McNally Map & Travel Store,** 150 E. 52nd St., between Lexington and Third Aves., 212/758-7488, also stocks a good selection of maps, along with travel guides and travel accessories.

Department Stores
Lots of fun for both shopping and browsing is **Saks Fifth Avenue,** 611 Fifth Ave., between 49th and 50th Sts., 212/753-4000, a wonderfully plush store with high-quality merchandise. **Henri Bendel,** 712 Fifth Ave., between 55th and 56th Sts., 212/247-1100, is frequented by the very rich and the very thin. **Bergdorf Goodman,** 754 Fifth Ave., 212/753-7300, between 57th and 58th Sts., is a favorite among wealthy socialites.

The Japanese department store, **Takashimaya,** 693 Fifth Ave., near 54th St., 212/350-0100, is an elegant mansionlike place that feels more like a museum than a store, and does indeed present frequent art exhibits. Cheap, cheerful, and trendy, the Swedish department store **H&M,** 640 Fifth Ave., at 51st St., 212/489-0390, opened in 2000 to a rave reception; other branches are located at 558 Broadway at Prince St. (212/343-2722) and 1328 Broadway at 34th St. (646/473-1165).

Food Shops
At the lower end of Ninth Avenue food-shopping stretch, around 40th St., are **Manganaro's,** 488 and 492 Ninth Ave., 212/563-5331 and 212/947-7325, an 1893 Italian grocery store that also sells six-foot-long hero sandwiches; and **Ninth Avenue Cheese Market,** 615 Ninth Ave., 212/397-4700 selling dozens of varieties. The **International Grocery and Meat Market,** 543 Ninth Ave., 212/279-5514, is a spic-and-span shop run by two Greek brothers.

Around 45th Street are the 1908 **Empire Coffee & Tea Company,** 592 Ninth Ave., 212/586-1717, one of the oldest gourmet coffee shops in town; and **Poseidon Bakery,** 629 Ninth Ave., 212/757-6173, a Greek shop that has been hand-rolling phyllo dough for about 75 years.

Everything at **Amy's Bread,** 672 Ninth Ave., near 47th St., 212/977-2670, is homemade.

Health and Beauty

Two of the city's oldest and most respected salons are **Elizabeth Arden,** 691 Fifth Ave., between 54th and 55th Sts., 212/546-0200; and **Georgette Klinger,** 501 Madison Ave., between 52nd and 53rd Sts., 212/838-3200.

At **Osaka Health Center,** 50 W. 56th St., between Fifth and Sixth Aves., 212/956-3422, masseurs can knead your knots or walk on your back. **Caswell-Massey,** 518 Lexington Ave., at 48th St., 212/755-2254, is Manhattan's oldest apothecary. The wood-paneled den dates back to 1752 and claims to have sold George Washington his shaving cream.

Jewelry

The well-known **Cartier's** is at 2 E. 52nd St., at Fifth Ave., 212/753-0111, but if you're in the market for jewelry, you'll probably be much happier just up the street at **Tiffany's,** 727 Fifth Ave., at 56th St., 212/755-8000. In Truman Capote's *Breakfast at Tiffany's,* character Holly Golightly opines, "Nothing bad can ever happen to you at Tiffany's," and she may be right. The store is as classy as Cartier's, but much friendlier.

Music and Musical Instruments

Just east of Broadway on West 48th Street is a row of top-notch musical-instrument stores, including **Sam Ash,** 160 W. 48th St., 212/719-2299; **Manny's,** 156 W. 48th St., 212/819-0576; and the **International Woodwind & Brass Center,** 174 W. 48th St., 212/840-7165. **Colony Records,** 1619 Broadway, at 49th St., 212/265-2050, is the largest provider of sheet music in New York City. **Steinway & Sons,** 109 W. 57th St., between Sixth and Seventh Aves., 212/246-1100, is a lovely, old-fashioned piano showroom.

The three-tiered **Virgin Mega Store,** 1540 Broadway, between 45th and 46th Sts., 212/921-1020, bills itself as "the largest music and entertainment store in the world." Inside find more than a million CDs, 7,400 film titles on laserdisc, and 20,000 videotapes and DVDs. Also on site are a bookstore and a cafe.

Souvenirs and Sneakers

Near 56th Street is a strange new addition to Fifth Avenue—the **Coca-Cola Company,** 711 Fifth Ave., 212/355-5475. Always packed with tourists, this seems to be the place to go to get those essential Coca-Cola bottles, mugs, postcards, and socks.

Homage to the almighty sneaker is paid at **Niketown,** 6 E. 57th St., at Fifth Ave., 212/891-6453, a sleek gray emporium built in neo-art deco style. As many as 30,000 people a day are said to pass through this five-story shrine, which sits on prime Manhattan real estate. Inside, you'll find not only Nike sneakers and clothing, but also multiple aquariums, a recreated Town Square, a short film, and museum-style cases displaying Nike sneakers once worn by such stars as Michael Jordan.

Toys and Games

Across the street from the Plaza Hotel is **F.A.O. Schwarz,** 767 Fifth Ave., at 58th St., 212/644-9400, a vast, highly imaginative, and expensive toy emporium that's as much fun for adults as it is for kids. The new **Toys "R" Us,** 800/869-7787, 1514 Broadway, at 44th St., in Times Square is said to be the largest toy store in the world. Inside, find a 60-foot-fall Ferris wheel, along with three floors of toys and games.

Other Shops

Manhattan Art & Antiques Center, 1050 Second Ave., just south of 57th St., 212/355-4400, houses about 100 small antique shops. **Hammacher-Schlemmer,** 147 E. 57th St., near Lexington, 212/421-9000, and at other Midtown locations, features the world's most imaginative and expensive high-tech gadgets.

ACCOMMODATIONS

$100–150: East Side

One of the better deals in the city is **Pickwick Arms,** 230 E. 51st St., between Third and Second Aves., 212/355-0300 or 800/742-5945, www.pickwickarms.com, on a quiet block that's nonetheless near everything. The Pickwick's rooms are small but comfortable, and there's a sundeck on the roof. The cheapest single rooms share bathrooms. $75–110 s, $135–195 d.

Another option for budget travelers in Midtown is the **Habitat Hotel,** 130 E. 57th St., at Lexington Ave., 212/753-8841 or 800/255-0482, www.stayinny.com, housed in the old Allerton Hotel, a longtime residence for women. Rooms feature a single twin-sized bed or two adjacent twin-sized beds, and are clean and adequate. $85 s with shared bath, $95 d with shared bath, $125–145 s or d with private bath.

$100–150: West Side

A theater hotel since 1904, the small **Portland Square Hotel,** 132 W. 47th St., between Sixth and Seventh Aves., 212/382-0600, is a good choice for budget travelers. The rooms are spartan but adequate and clean, and the shared bathrooms only somewhat grungy. Photographs of Broadway in the '20s and '30s line the utilitarian lobby and hallways; young James Cagney was once a resident here. $65 s or d with shared bath; $110 s with private bath, $125 d with private bath.

The **Comfort Inn Midtown,** 129 W. 46th St., 212/221-2600, is nothing special, but its lobby is inviting and its small rooms clean and comfortable. $89–125 s or d.

Two good options in the Theater District are the **Broadway Inn,** 264 W. 46 St., at Eighth Ave., 212/997-9200 or 800/826-6300, www .broadwayinn.com, and the **Mayfair,** 242 W. 49th St., between Broadway and Eighth Ave., 212/586-0300 or 800/55-MAYFAIR. Both are very attractive, spanking clean, friendly, and reasonably priced.

The Broadway Inn offers 45 basic rooms appointed in greens and grays and an airy, second-floor lobby filled with potted plants, inviting chairs, and well-stocked bookshelves; $95–165 s or d, continental breakfast included. The Mayfair offers a classy lobby lined with warm woods and historic photographs from the Museum of the City of New York. The 78 rooms vary widely in size, but all are equipped with mahogany furnishings; some also have marble baths. $120–160 s, $130–190 d.

Farther north is the clean and comfortable **Westpark,** 6 Columbus Circle, near 58th St.,

between Eighth and Ninth Aves., 212/246-6440 or 800/248-6440. The lobby here is somewhat worn, but the small rooms are well kept; those overlooking Central Park cost extra. $105–115 s, $125–145 d. Similar in style, albeit more loudly floral in its decor, is the **Park Savoy,** 158 W. 58th St., between Sixth and Seventh Aves., 212/245-5755; $95–145 s or d, the cheaper rooms share baths.

$150–250: East Side

After years spent as a sleazy fleabag, the historic **Roosevelt Hotel,** 45 E. 45th St., at Madison, 212/661-9600 or 888/TEDDY-NY, www.theroo-seveltotel.com, has been completely renovated to the tune of $65 million. The bustling 1920s lobby features tall fluted columns, lots of marble, and fresh flowers; the rooms are quite comfortable as well. $149–289 s or d.

The family-run **Fitzpatrick Manhattan Hotel,** 687 Lexington Ave., between 56th and 57th Sts., 212/355-0100 or 800/367-7701, www.fitzpatrickhotels.com, is a friendly Irish hostelry all done up in green. Upstairs are 92 comfortable rooms and suites, and downstairs is Fitzer's, serving up authentic Irish fare. $199–305 s or d.

$150–250: West Side

An excellent choice for families during the summer is the 367-room **Days Hotel Midtown,** 790 Eighth Ave., at 49th St., 212/581-7000 or 800/572-6232, thanks largely to the rooftop swimming pool. The hotel also offers babysitting services, on-site parking, a lobby restaurant, and adequate rooms. $145 s, $160 d, packages available.

One of the largest hotels in New York is the 1,000-room **Edison,** 228 W. 47th St., near Eighth Ave., 212/840-5000 or 800/637-7070, www.edisonhotelnyc.com. Most notable for its striking art deco lobby lined with murals of the 1920s Yankees, the Cotton Club, construction workers, and more, the hotel also offers clean, good-sized rooms. Adjoining the lobby is a hair salon, two restaurants, and a cafe popular among young actors. $150 s, $170 d.

Across from the famed Plaza Hotel is the

Wyndham, 42 W. 58th St., near Fifth Ave., 212/753-3500, www.wyndham.com, a spacious old hostelry with a cozy, low-ceilinged lobby, and rooms airily decorated with lots of flowered wallpaper, upholstery, and chintz. The owners designed the place themselves and live on the premises, which helps account for the hotel's easygoing, old-fashioned feel. Many of the guests are actors in town for Broadway runs. $140–155 s, $150–165 d; reserve well in advance.

Filled with eclectic touches, the sleek **Paramount,** 235 W. 46th St., near Eighth Ave., 212/764-5500 or 800/225-7474, www.ianschragerhotels.com, is a fun place to stay. Created by Ian Schrager of Studio 54 fame, it features a darkened lobby filled with lollipop-colored chairs and a big-checked rug, and, in the rooms, beds slung close to the floor and stainless steel sinks shaped like ice cream cones. A second-story restaurant wraps around the lobby, and the hotel's Whiskey Bar is a popular late-night spot. $145–195 s, $220–285 d.

$250 and up: East Side

No two rooms are alike at the **Roger Smith,** 501 Lexington Ave., at 47th St., 212/755-1400 or 800/445-0277, www.rogersmith.com. The atmosphere-infused hotel was once a worn haven for graying businessmen but is now a jazzy retreat complete with several art galleries, a gift shop selling arts and crafts, and a long, narrow restaurant painted with a floor-to-ceiling mural. The rooms are tastefully furnished; live jazz is sometimes presented. $265–280 s or d.

The **Drake Swissôtel,** 440 Park Ave., at 56th St., 212/421-0900 or 800/372-5369, is a lovely hostelry, managed to perfection in impeccable Swiss style. The lobby gleams with marble and polished glass; the rooms are spacious and airy, with separate sitting areas and oversized desks. In back of the lobby is the Drake Bar and Cafe, serving Swiss, European, and American specialties. $275–305 s, $285–355 d.

The European-styled **Hotel Elysée,** 60 E. 54th St., between Madison and Park Aves., 212/753-1066 or 800/535-9733, is furnished in dark woods, plush carpets, and Oriental antiques. Most of the rooms have Italian marble bathrooms, and adjoining the lobby is the classy Monkey Bar, its walls covered with murals. Among the famous residents who once lived in the Elysee were Joe DiMaggio, Tallulah Bankhead, and Tennessee Williams. $285–325 s or d; continental breakfast included.

Though now catering largely to a business clientele, the famed **Waldorf-Astoria,** 301 Park Ave., between 49th and 50th Sts., 212/355-3000 or 800/WALDORF, www.waldorf.com, nonetheless continues to beckon with opulence and romance. Surrounding the newly renovated art deco lobby are glittering stores selling jewelry, antiques, and rare books. Downstairs is Peacock Alley, an elegant cafe with a piano that once belonged to Cole Porter. Upstairs are 1,120 rooms in varying shapes and sizes, and numerous conference rooms. $275–400 s, $325–425 d.

Step into the lobby of the minimalist I. M. Pei–designed **Four Seasons New York,** 57 E. 57th St., between Madison and Park Aves., 212/758-5700 or 800/332-3442, www.fourseasons.com, and you feel as if you're about to request an audience with the king. The reception desk is just so big and far away—up two flights of stairs—and you're so small. Once you get used to it, however, the place feels grand. Designed with earth tones, a muted skylight, and octagonal columns, it offers an understated restaurant to one side, a lounge to the other. The guest rooms are the largest in New York (600 square feet), and come equipped with all things state-of-the-art, including bathtubs that fill in 60 seconds. Alas, all this futuristic luxury does not come cheap. $495–675 s, $545–710 d.

One of the city's most opulent hostelries is the **St. Regis Hotel,** 2 E. 55th St., at Fifth Ave., 212/753-4500 or 800/759-7550, built by John Jacob Astor in 1904. Filled with marble, crystal, and gold leaf, the St. Regis underwent a $100 million restoration several years ago and now offers every conceivable amenity—as well it should, given the prices. $495–605 s or d.

$250 and up: West Side

With only 120 rooms, the stylish **Gorham,** 136 W. 55th St., between Sixth and Seventh Aves., 212/245-1800, www.gorhamhotel.com, offers a personalized European ambience. Downstairs, find a warm lobby paneled in bird's-eye maple; upstairs find contemporary Italian design–style rooms complete with kitchenettes. A cheery breakfast room overlooks the historic City Center across the street. $225–380 s or d.

The **Mansfield,** 12 W. 44th St., between Fifth and Sixth Aves., 212/944-6050 or 877/847-4444, www.boutiquehg.com, was built in 1904 as a residence for well-to-do bachelors. Now a gleaming 123-room hotel, it features gorgeous woodwork, a 12-story oval staircase, and rooms equipped with everything from Victorian sleigh beds to etched glass French doors. Complimentary cappuccino is offered throughout the day, and a complimentary after-theater dessert buffet is served every evening. $265 s, $285 d; includes continental breakfast.

Still deliciously old-fashioned, with lots of wood paneling and brocaded chairs, is the 1902 **Algonquin,** 59 W. 44th St., between Fifth and Sixth Aves., 212/840-6800 or 800/555-8000, www.camberleyhotels.com. Each floor has a different color scheme, and the inviting rooms offer plump beds, comfy armchairs, and bathrooms equipped with plenty of amenities. Downstairs, where Dorothy Parker and friends once met (see The Algonquin and Vicinity, above), are several snug lounges perfect for afternoon tea, cocktails, or aperitifs. $269–389 s or d.

The **Royalton,** 44 W. 44th St., near Fifth Ave., 212/869-4400, www.ianschragerhotels.com, is another hip Ian Schrager creation, designed by Philippe Starck. Its long, tunnel-like lobby is lined with shiny black elevators to one side, a step-down sitting area to the other. Chairs are draped in white cloth; a posh restaurant caters to media types in the back. The rooms feature fireplaces and playful round bathtubs. $355–390 s, $370–425 d.

The **Plaza,** 768 Fifth Ave., at 59th St., 212/759-3000 or 800/759-3000, www.fairmont.com, one of New York's best-known hotels, was nicely restored by the Trumps in the late 1980s. The rooms come in all shapes and sizes and are furnished with both period antiques and reproductions. Some rooms offer grand four-poster beds, others marble fireplaces and crystal chandeliers. $275–575 s or d.

YWCA

The centrally located **Vanderbilt YWCA,** 224 E. 47th St., between Third and Second Aves., 212/756-9600, www.ymcanyc.org, is a good bet for budget travelers. Open to both men and women, it offers small, clean rooms with shared baths. $70 s, $86 d. Reserve well in advance.

FOOD

Note: If you're planning to eat in the Theater District before a show, make reservations or give yourself plenty of time. Many restaurants are packed between 6:30 and 8 P.M.

American

Popular **Virgil's Real BBQ,** 152 W. 44th St., between Broadway and Sixth Ave., 212/921-9494, serves up enormous portions of spare ribs, smoked brisket, and the like in a bustling, two-story setting; average main course $13. The **Carnegie Deli,** 854 Seventh Ave., near 54th St., 212/757-2245, is a New York City landmark, famous for enormous overstuffed deli sandwiches. Similar in style is **Stage Deli,** 834 Seventh Ave., between 53rd and 54th Sts., 212/245-7850, the Carnegie's major competitor. Average sandwich at both, $11.

In the Theater District, you'll find the newly revamped **West Bank Cafe,** 407 W. 42nd St., near Ninth Ave., 212/695-6909, an airy, friendly spot that attracts many actors; average entrée $16. **Joe Allen,** 326 W. 46th St., near Eighth Ave., 212/581-6464, is a classic, well-known pub with a celebrity-studded clientele, but the service can be rude; average entrée $15.

The recently renovated **Rock Center Cafe,** 20 W. 50th St., 212/332-7620, serves American-style food in a superb setting overlooking the skating rink at Rockefeller Center. Be sure to make reservations if you want to go for lunch; average entrée $18. Behind the New York Public Library, overlooking Bryant Park, are the **Bryant Park Grill** and the **Bryant Park Cafe,** 25 W. 42nd St., 212/840-6500. Both serve imaginative American fare in a handsome, airy setting, but the grill is somewhat more formal. In summer, a rooftop terrace opens up. Average entrée $18.

MANHATTAN

© CHRISTIANE BIRD

the Carnegie Deli, renowned for its overstuffed sandwiches

Asian

Bustling **Ollie's Noodle Shop,** 200B W. 44th St., near Broadway, 212/921-5988, offers a wide variety of noodle and dumpling dishes, for an average price of $8. A long-time favorite among vegetarians is **Zen Palate,** 663 Ninth Ave., at 46th St., 212/582-1669, known for its imaginative Asian-influenced fare; average entrée $13.

One of the best Chinese restaurants in the city is **Shun Lee Palace,** 155 E. 55th St., between Lexington and Third Aves., 212/371-8844, featuring gourmet fare in an elegant yet friendly setting; average entrée $22. Two excellent Japanese restaurants are the classic **Hatsuhana,** 17 E. 48th St., between Fifth and Madison Aves., 212/355-3345; and stylish **Sushisay,** 38 E. 51st St., near Madison Ave., 212/755-1780, which some say serves the best sushi in Manhattan. Average entrée at both, $22.

French/Continental

A budget traveler's lifesaver, **La Bonne Soupe,** 48 W. 55th St., between Fifth and Sixth Aves., 212/586-7650, serves hearty soups with bread, salad, dessert, and wine for about $10. **Chez**

Josephine, 414 W. 42nd St., near Ninth Ave., 212/594-1925, is a charming, low-lit French/Southern bistro run by one of Josephine Baker's adopted French children; average entrée $17. The food at **Cafe Un, Deux, Trois,** 123 W. 44th St., between Sixth and Seventh Aves., 212/354-4148, is nothing special, but the restaurant's towering columns, gilt-edge mirrors, and lively clientele make it great fun nonetheless; average entrée $15.

Though now under new ownership, **Lutece,** 249 E. 50th St., near Second Ave., 212/752-2225, is still New York's top classic French restaurant. Prix fixe only: lunch $38, dinner $65. **La Côte Basque,** 60 W. 55th St., between Fifth and Sixth Aves., 212/688-6525, immortalized in Truman Capote's unfinished *Unanswered Prayers,* is another classic bastion of French haute cuisine. Prix fixe only: lunch $36, dinner $68.

Indian

The sophisticated **Dawat,** 210 E. 58th St., near Third Ave., 212/355-7555, is considered to be one of the city's best Indian restaurants; average entrée $18. Exotic **Nirvana,** 30 Central Park

S, between Fifth and Sixth Aves., 212/486-5700, may be a touristy spot, but you can't beat its spectacular views of Central Park; average entrée $20.

Italian

Just north of Grand Central in the Met Life Building, 200 Park Ave., is **Cucina & Co.**, 212/682-2700, an Italian-accented eatery serving gourmet sandwiches, salads, pastas, and baked goods; average main course $10. The sprawling, noisy **Carmine's**, 200 W. 44th St., between Broadway and Eighth Ave., 212/221-3800, serves huge portions of Southern Italian food, family style; average main course $14.

Near Carnegie Hall is the stylish **Trattoria dell'Arte**, 900 Seventh Ave., between 56th and 57th Sts., 212/245-9800, featuring tasty pastas and thin-crust pizzas; average main course $20. **Barbetta's**, 321 W. 46th St., between Eighth and Ninth Aves., 212/246-9171, is a classy spot housed in a townhouse with a romantic garden out back; average entrée $24.

Latin

Several Brazilian restaurants are found on West 45th and 46th Streets between Fifth and Seventh Avenues. The two-story **Cabana Carioca**, 123 W. 45th St., near Seventh Ave., 212/581-8088, painted with vibrant tropical scenes, is tops for decor and generous portions, but the service can be rude; average entrée $14. The decor at **Ipanema**, 13 W. 46th St., between Fifth and Sixth Aves., 212/730-5848, is considerably more sedate, but the food is tasty and the service first-rate; average entrée $15.

Russian

Now that the famed Russian Tea Room, reopened in 1999 for a short three-year run, has closed down once again, the city's reigning extravagant Russian eatery is the **Firebird**, 365 W. 46th St., between Eighth and Ninth Aves., 212/586-0244. Housed in two posh brownstones, the Firebird resembles a prerevolutionary St. Petersburg mansion, complete with paintings, objets d'art, antiques, crystal, and authentic cuisine; average entrée $24.

Seafood

For a classic New York lunch, eat at Grand Central Station's **Oyster Bar**, 42nd St. and Park Ave., lower level, 212/490-6650, complete with red-checked tablecloths and a vaulted ceiling. On the menu in the restaurant is a wide variety of fish dishes, priced at about $25. Adjoining the main restaurant is a cheaper counter area, where dishes average about $12. Closed weekends. The plush and highly acclaimed **Le Bernardin**, 155 W. 51st St., between Sixth and Seventh Aves., 212/554-1515, is a French restaurant that specializes in fresh seafood; prix fixe lunch $45, dinner $77.

Steakhouses

Along with the recent renovation of Grand Central Terminal has come **Michael Jordan's—The Steak House NYC**, located on the West Balcony of the Terminal, 23 Vanderbilt Ave., at 43rd St., 212/655-2300. The popular spot serves humongous portions and some of the best French fries in the city; average entrée $30.

Other steakhouse favorites are the traditional, clubby **Smith & Wollensky**, 797 Third Ave., at 49th St., 212/753-1530, sporting a wood-and-brass decor; and **Sparks Steak House**, 210 E. 46th St., near Third Ave., 212/687-4855. The average entrée at both, $28.

Other Ethnic

Ninth Avenue between 42nd and 59th Streets is lined with one ethnic restaurant after another. Among them is the **Afghan Kebab House**, 764 Ninth Ave., between 51st and 52nd Sts., 212/307-1612, serving succulent kebabs in exotic surroundings (average entrée $9), and airy, well-lit **Uncle Nick's**, 747 Ninth Ave., between 50th and 51st Sts., 212/245-7992, one of Manhattan's few Greek restaurants (average entrée $12). Low-key **Taprobane**, 234 W. 56th St., near Broadway, 212/333-4203, is one of the city's only Sri Lankan restaurants; average entrée $10.

The sophisticated, streamlined **B. Smith's**, 320 W. 46th St., between Eighth and Ninth Aves., 212/315-1100, serves first-rate Southern-accented food. Its host is supermodel Barbara Smith; average entrée $18.

Light Bites

During warm weather, both Bryant Park (between 40th and 42nd Streets, Fifth and Sixth Avenues) and the steps of the New York Public Library are good spots for lunch. Nearby vendors sell everything from hot dogs to gourmet fare. Grazers might want to head over to Ninth Avenue and nibble their way through its many food shops (see Shopping, above). Be sure to include a dessert stop at **Cupcake Cafe,** 522 Ninth Ave., at 39th St., 212/465-1530, known for its baked goods. And don't forget the pretzel and chestnut vendors along Fifth Avenue—they're as New York as it gets.

Watering Holes and Lounges

For a bird's-eye view of New York at night, Midtown is the neighborhood. The cozy **Top of the Tower** at the Beekman Tower Hotel, 3 Mitchell Pl., off First Ave. at 49th St., 212/355-7300, offers an art deco lounge and an outdoor terrace open in summer. For a drink in the city's only revolving bar, overlooking Times Square, take an elevator to the top of the glitzy **Marriott Marquis,** 1535 Broadway, at 45th St., 212/398-1900.

Back on ground level, near the Theater District is the elegant, wood-paneled **Algonquin Hotel,** 59 W. 44th St., between Fifth and Sixth Aves., 212/840-6800, offering several bars and lounges. The bar at the swank **Royalton Hotel,** 44 W. 44th St., between Fifth and Sixth Aves., 212/869-4400, offers expensive drinks in a sleek, muted setting. The **Bryant Park Cafe,** 25 W. 42nd St., 212/840-6500, is at its liveliest at cocktail hour.

Newly reopened in restored Grand Central Terminal is the **Campbell Apartment,** 15 Vanderbilt Ave., at 43rd St., 212/953-0409, once the private office of railroad trustee John Campbell. Designed to resemble a 13th-century Florentine palazzo, the bar offers expensive drinks in an intimate setting.

Farther north, in the post-modern Four Seasons Hotel, is the **Fifty Seven Fifty Seven Bar,** 57 E. 57th St., between Madison and Park Aves., 212/758-5700, serving 15 different kinds of oversized martinis. Drinks at the posh St. Regis Hotel's **King Cole Bar and Lounge,** 2 E. 55th St., at Fifth Ave., 212/753-4500, don't come cheap, but the room's beautifully restored mural makes it all worthwhile. In the Plaza Hotel is the famed **Oak Bar,** Fifth Ave. and 59th St., 212/546-5200, a plush but pricey spot, always filled with tourists.

Nearby, find **Mickey Mantle's,** 42 Central Park S, between Fifth and Sixth Aves., 212/688-7777, the city's best-known sports bar, although many sports fans regard the new-ish **ESPN Zone,** 4 Times Square Plaza, 212/921-3776, as the best sports bar in town. **P.J. Clarke's,** 915 Third Ave., at 55th St., 212/759-1650, is an out-of-time saloon sporting brass railings, worn wood, and sawdust on the floor. Featured in the 1945 movie *The Lost Weekend,* P.J.'s also serves overpriced burgers and sandwiches.

Ninth Avenue is home to a number of lounges and bars. Among them are **Otis,** 754 Ninth Ave., between 50th and 51st Sts., 212/246-4417, a comfortable bar-restaurant with exposed brick walls and stamped tin ceilings, and **Rudy's Bar & Grill,** 627 Ninth Ave., between 44th and 45th Sts., 212/974-9169, where the booths have seen better days and hot dogs are free with a drink purchase.

The Upper East Side

Since the turn of the century, the Upper East Side has been associated with wealth. Everyone from Andrew Carnegie to Gloria Vanderbilt, from Henry Clay Frick to Franklin Delano Roosevelt has resided in this hushed, exclusive neighborhood. Here you'll find so many mansions and brownstones, clubs and penthouses, that at times the neighborhood resembles an open-air museum.

The wealthy began arriving on the Upper East Side in the late 1800s as an ever-encroaching business tide forced them off the Midtown stretches of Fifth Avenue. But the real turning point came in 1905, when steel magnate Andrew Carnegie built his mansion on Fifth Avenue at 91st Street. Soon thereafter, one industrialist after another followed suit, until the stretch of Fifth Avenue facing Central Park became known as "Millionaire's Row." Many of these mansions have since been converted into museums and cultural institutions.

But the Upper East Side is not only about the wealthy. It's also about more ordinary folk, who—as elsewhere in Manhattan—settled closer to the river. At one time, Madison, Park, and Lexington Avenues were basically middle-class, while the area east of Lexington was working-class and home to recent immigrants. Yorkville, a hamlet established in the 1790s between what are now 83rd and 88th Streets, had an especially large German population.

Today, these sections of the Upper East Side are slowly becoming gentrified, but many remnants of their earlier days still exist, especially east of Lexington Avenue and north of 86th Street. Here, the streets can get as funky and eclectic as anywhere else in town.

Stretching roughly from 59th to 100th Street, Fifth Avenue to the East River, the Upper East Side's long residential blocks are pleasant for strolling. Most of the sights and shops are along the north-south avenues rather than the east-west side streets. Madison Avenue is known all over the world for its upscale shops. Many are designer boutiques, astronomically priced, but a few more moderate establishments are found here and there.

First-time visitors will probably want to walk up Fifth Avenue to the Metropolitan, and then perhaps visit Central Park or stroll back downtown along Madison Avenue.

UP FIFTH AND MADISON AVENUES

The Pierre
One of the most famous and elegant hostelries in New York is the Pierre, at the northeast corner of Fifth Avenue and 61st Street. A favorite among monarchs and presidents, the Pierre has also been home to heiress Barbara Hutton, writer John O'Hara, then-married actors Robert Taylor and Barbara Stanwyck, and writer Dashiell Hammett. Hammett began his book *The Thin Man* here in 1932, but that same year—having run up a tab he couldn't pay—he disguised himself and left the hotel without settling his bill.

The Pierre was also the site of one of the greatest jewel heists ever. On January 2, 1972, at 4 A.M., four thieves dressed in tuxedos arrived at the hotel in a chauffeur-driven limousine. The security guard, suspecting nothing, let them in. Once inside, the thieves whipped out guns, tied up 21 hotel employees and guests, and made off with $8 million in jewelry, cash, and securities. The only evidence the thieves left behind were the rubber noses they'd dropped on the lobby floor. Nevertheless, within a week, with the help of an informant, the police tracked the robbers down. All were arrested and sentenced, but according to Paul Schwartzman and Rob Polner, writing in *New York Notorious,* it's believed that several million dollars' worth of jewels were never recovered.

Al Smith's Residence
Former New York governor and 1928 Democratic presidential candidate Al Smith lived at 820 Fifth Ave., between 63rd and 64th Sts., from the early 1930s until his death in 1944. A great animal lover, Smith often spent his afternoons across the street at the Central Park Zoo (now the Central Park Wildlife Center).

MANHATTAN

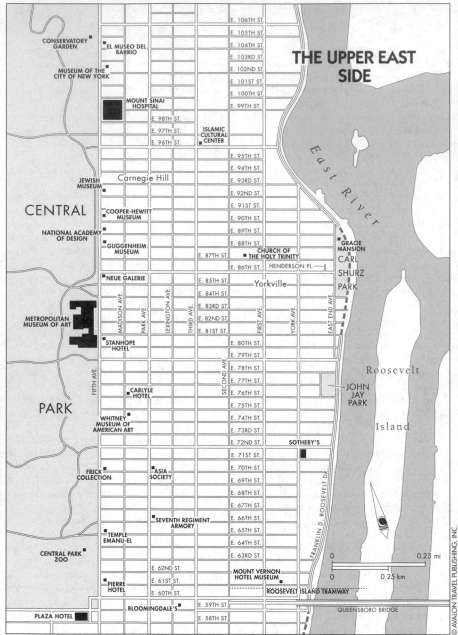

MANHATTAN

CONSERVATORY GARDEN
EL MUSEO DEL BARRIO
MUSEUM OF THE CITY OF NEW YORK
MOUNT SINAI HOSPITAL
ISLAMIC CULTURAL CENTER

E. 106TH ST.
E. 105TH ST.
E. 104TH ST.
E. 103RD ST.
E. 102ND ST.
E. 101ST ST.
E. 100TH ST.
E. 99TH ST.
E. 98TH ST.
E. 97TH ST.
E. 96TH ST.

THE UPPER EAST SIDE

East River

E. 95TH ST.
E. 94TH ST.
E. 93RD ST.
E. 92ND ST.
E. 91ST ST.
E. 90TH ST.
E. 89TH ST.
E. 88TH ST.
E. 87TH ST.
E. 86TH ST.
E. 85TH ST.
E. 84TH ST.
E. 83RD ST.
E. 82ND ST.
E. 81ST ST.
E. 80TH ST.
E. 79TH ST.
E. 78TH ST.
E. 77TH ST.
E. 76TH ST.
E. 75TH ST.
E. 74TH ST.
E. 73RD ST.
E. 72ND ST.
E. 71ST ST.
E. 70TH ST.
E. 69TH ST.
E. 68TH ST.
E. 67TH ST.
E. 66TH ST.
E. 65TH ST.
E. 64TH ST.
E. 63RD ST.
E. 62ND ST.
E. 61ST ST.
E. 60TH ST.
E. 59TH ST.
E. 58TH ST.

JEWISH MUSEUM
Carnegie Hill
COOPER-HEWITT MUSEUM
NATIONAL ACADEMY OF DESIGN
GUGGENHEIM MUSEUM
CHURCH OF THE HOLY TRINITY
HENDERSON PL.
GRACIE MANSION
CARL SHURZ PARK

CENTRAL

NEUE GALERIE
Yorkville

METROPOLITAN MUSEUM OF ART

MADISON AVE.
PARK AVE.
LEXINGTON AVE.
THIRD AVE.
FIRST AVE.
YORK AVE.
EAST END AVE.
SECOND AVE.
FIFTH AVE.

STANHOPE HOTEL

Roosevelt

CARLYLE HOTEL
JOHN JAY PARK

PARK

WHITNEY MUSEUM OF AMERICAN ART

Island

SOTHEBY'S

FRICK COLLECTION
ASIA SOCIETY

SEVENTH REGIMENT ARMORY

FRANKLIN D. ROOSEVELT DR.

TEMPLE EMANU-EL

CENTRAL PARK ZOO

MOUNT VERNON HOTEL MUSEUM

PIERRE HOTEL

ROOSEVELT ISLAND TRAMWAY

BLOOMINGDALE'S

QUEENSBORO BRIDGE

PLAZA HOTEL

0   0.25 mi
0   0.25 km

City Parks Commissioner Robert Moses was a close friend and political ally of Al Smith's. In 1934, with great fanfare, Moses had the old city zoo renovated, largely as a favor to his friend. Moses also arranged for Smith to be appointed the zoo's night superintendent, which meant that he was given a key. As Robert Caro describes it in *The Power Broker,* the doormen at No. 820 became accustomed to seeing Smith—a paunchy figure often wearing a big brown derby—walk out the front door in the evenings, cross Fifth Avenue, and disappear down the steps of the darkened zoo, not to reappear for hours.

Temple Emanu-El

The world's largest Reform synagogue is the imposing Temple Emanu-El at 1 East 65th Street. It's built in a mix of Moorish and Romanesque styles to symbolize the joining of Eastern and Western cultures. Inside, the temple is overwhelmingly large and dark, with a bronze-grilled ark containing the Torah, and blue-and-gold mosaics by artist Hildreth Meiere. The temple is open Sun.–Thurs. 10 A.M.–5 P.M., Saturday noon–5 P.M. Organ recitals are presented Friday at 5 P.M.

Frick Collection

Now a museum, the former home of industrialist Henry Clay Frick, 1 E. 70th St., is one of the city's most beautiful residences. It's a classic 1914 mansion built around a courtyard and an exquisite European art collection. Every room is hung with masterpieces—by Breughel, El Greco, Hogarth, Vermeer, Rembrandt, Turner, and others—yet the place maintains a private, homey feel.

The Frick's most famous room is the Fragonard Room, where all four walls are covered with *The Progress of Love,* painted by French artist Jean-Honoré Fragonard. The panels were originally commissioned by Louis XV for his lover, Mme. du Barry.

Despite his impeccable taste, Frick was reputedly one of the nastiest of the early American capitalists. A pioneer in the coke and steel industries, he repeatedly used violence to break up labor unions, at one time sending in 300 thugs who provoked a riot in which 14 people were killed. It was shortly after this incident that young anarchist Alexander Berkman—Emma Goldman's lover—tried to assassinate Frick in his office. Frick was badly wounded but survived. Berkman was sentenced to 14 years in jail.

The Frick, 212/288-0700, www.frick.org, is open Tues.–Sat. 10 A.M.–6 P.M., Friday 6–9 P.M., Sunday 1–6 P.M. Admission is adults $10, students and seniors $5, children under 10 not admitted.

Famous Area Residents

In the late 1950s, actress **Joan Crawford** lived with her husband, Pepsi-Cola tycoon Al Steele, in a penthouse apartment at 2 E. 70th St., directly across the street from the Frick. The couple spent over $1 million redoing their apartment, but when it was finished, according to Crawford's adopted daughter Christina, writing in *Mommie Dearest,* "There was something barren about it. . . . Everything was new and modern and plastic. Even the flowers and plants were plastic. . . . There were plastic covers on all the upholstered furniture. . . . All the windows were sealed."

The notorious gambler **Arnold Rothstein,** best known as the man who fixed the World Series of 1919, spent the last years of his life at 912 Fifth Avenue. He was living here in November 1928 when he was murdered for refusing to pay a $320,000 poker debt.

Actress and businesswoman **Gloria Swanson** lived in the large apartment building at 920 Fifth Ave., at 73rd St., from 1938 until her death in 1983. While living here, she made a magnificent comeback in Billy Wilder's 1950 movie *Sunset Boulevard,* started a cosmetics company, and hosted one of the world's first weekly television talk shows.

The apartment building at 23 E. 74th St. was once a residential hotel called the Volney. Writer **Dorothy Parker** lived here during the last 15 years of her life; she was discovered in her apartment, dead of a heart attack, on June 7, 1967.

Whitney Museum of American Art

The boxy gray building with the wedge-shaped front at the corner of Madison Avenue and 75th Street is the Whitney Museum of American Art, designed by Marcel Breuer in 1966. Recently

MANHATTAN

THE FINE CRIME OF JAYWALKING

Jaywalking has long been a favorite sport among New Yorkers, and out-of-towners are welcome to join in. As Sig Spaeth wrote in his 1926 essay, "The Advantages of Jay Walking," there's nothing quite as fine as sneaking across the street *just in time:*

"Visitors to New York will find that both exercise and excitement may be had at a minimum of expense through the simple practice of jaywalking. With only a little experience, they may actually compete on even terms with the native New Yorker. . . .

"One of the first things to be learned is the proper time to start across the street. It is not considered sporting to do this while traffic is standing still. Wait for the policeman's whistle, which is the signal that the cross-current is about to begin. But if you are a stickler for etiquette, take the first step only after the sound of shifting gears has been heard on both sides of the street.

"If you get across after that, without having to stop in the middle [or without getting hit], you are credited with a perfect score."

Nowadays, the game is played not with policemen's whistles but with Don't Walk signs. These usually blink between 10 and 14 times before the traffic starts, and it's perfectly safe to saunter across during the first five blinks. Much more sporting, however, as Spaeth would agree, is to hurry over during the last two or three, or, even better, dash across in those few seconds just after the blinking has stopped and before the traffic has begun. Note: Several signs on Fifth Avenue blink only five times.

controversial "Biennial" show, presented every two years to showcase the latest works of contemporary American artists. The next biennial will be held in the year 2004.

The Whitney, 945 Madison Ave., 212/570-3676, www.whitney.org, is open Tues.–Thurs. and Sat.–Sun. 11 A.M.–6 P.M., Friday 1–9 P.M. Admission is adults $10, students and seniors $8; free to children under 12 and to everyone Friday 6–9 P.M.

Carlyle Hotel

One of New York's most elegant hotels is the Carlyle, 35 E. 76th St. near Madison Avenue. President Truman stayed here whenever he was in town, and President Kennedy had a duplex suite on the hotel's 34th floor. Kennedy reportedly often brought an incognito Marilyn Monroe back to the hotel with him when his wife was not in town.

The understated Carlyle is also known for its **Cafe Carlyle,** where high society's favorite jazzman, Bobby Short, has been playing for close to 30 years. He performs two stints annually, one in the spring, the other in the fall.

THE METROPOLITAN MUSEUM OF ART AND VICINITY
The Met

One of the world's greatest museums is the Metropolitan Museum of Art, on the east side of Central Park at Fifth Avenue and 82nd Street. Housed behind an imposing beaux arts facade designed by Robert Morris Hunt, the museum boasts collections of almost everything from Egyptian sarcophagi to modern American paintings.

Equally important, the museum's exhibitions are well edited and well viewed. This is not an elite or stuffy institution. On weekends, the place takes on a carnival air as jugglers, acrobats, vendors, and mimes hawk their talents and wares on the museum's wide staircase out front. And even early on weekday mornings, the museum's grand marble halls echo with excited whispers.

Founded in 1870, the Met centers around the Great Hall, a vast entrance room with an imposing staircase leading to the second floor. From

renovated and enlarged, the museum offers plenty to see but not enough to overwhelm.

Most of the museum's shows are temporary and feature the work of one 20th-century American artist. Past shows have focused on Edward Hopper, Maurice Prendergast, Jasper Johns, Isamu Noguchi, and Jacques Basquiat, to name just a few. Founded in Greenwich Village by Gertrude Vanderbilt Whitney in 1930 (see Greenwich Village, above), the museum is also known for its superb permanent collection and its

© CHRISTIANE BIRD

the peerless Met—to be visited time and again

the hall, the Met spreads out over about 1.5 million square feet. Other impressive statistics: the Met houses over two million works of art; has 19 curatorial departments; is visited by more than four million people a year; has an annual operating budget of about $80 million; and employs over 2,000 paid workers and 600 volunteers.

To do the Met justice takes a number of visits, so the best approach is to study the floor plan and decide what interests you most. Free orientation tours leave from the information booth in the Great Hall every half-hour or so.

The Met's European Paintings galleries—some 20 rooms' worth—house a whole roomful of Rembrandts, five of the fewer than 40 known Vermeers, a rich collection of Hals and Van Dyck, and works by Breughel, Rubens, Botticelli, El Greco, Goya, and others. The best way to view these galleries is to go through them in numerical order; otherwise, it's easy to get disoriented.

Right next door to the European Paintings galleries are two galleries holding 19th-century European paintings and sculpture. Here, painters such as Corot, Courbet, Manet, Monet, and Cézanne all have entire rooms devoted to them,

while van Gogh, Gauguin, Seurat, Pissarro, and Renoir are also well represented.

Three sides of the Met's original building are flanked by modern glass wings that contrast beautifully with the old limestone edifice. At the back is the arrowhead-shaped Robert Lehman Collection, which houses an impressive collection of Old Masters and 19th-century French painters. On the south side are the Rockefeller and Acheson Wings. The Rockefeller Wing is named after Michael C. Rockefeller, the son of the late vice president who disappeared while on a research expedition in New Guinea. Many of the items on display were collected during Rockefeller's earlier expeditions, and they're mind-boggling works ranging from intricately carved 100-foot-long canoes to towering musical instruments made of hollowed logs. The Lila Acheson Wing is devoted to 20th-century art, and though the Met has historically *not* been the place to see modern art, this has recently begun to change, thanks to scores of recent acquisitions of works by the likes of Picasso, Matisse, and Georges Braque. Also, don't miss the sculpture garden on the Acheson roof. The views from here are terrific.

On the north side are the Sackler and American Wings. The Sackler Wing houses the low-lit, 15th-century-B.C. Temple of Dendur, carved in faded hieroglyphics. The American Wing has its own private courtyard, framed by Tiffany windows; exhaustive galleries of decorative arts; and many fine paintings by the likes of Gilbert Stuart, Thomas Eakins, John Singer Sargent, Mary Cassatt, and James Whistler.

Other important stops in the Met include the Egyptian department, housing the largest collection of Egyptian art outside Egypt; the Islamic art collection, one of the world's finest; the new South and Southeast Asian art collection; and, of course, the museum's many superb temporary exhibits. Finally, too, if you have the time or are weary of concentrated viewing, it's well worth just roaming around the museum to see what treasures you might stumble across. One of the most winsome is the 16th-century Spanish patio, a small and peaceful inner courtyard near the grand staircase.

The Met has one of the city's best gift shops,

MANHATTAN

but the same cannot be said for its noisy cafeteria and separate sit-down restaurant. Be prepared for long waits and high prices.

If possible, avoid the Met on weekends, when it can get exceedingly crowded. Come on a weekday morning instead, or on a Friday or Saturday evening when the candlelit Great Hall Balcony Bar is open and a jazz or classical quintet performs.

The Met, 1000 Fifth Ave., at 82nd St., 212/535-7710, www.metmuseum.org, is open Tues.–Thurs., Sunday 9:30 A.M.–5:15 P.M., Fri.–Sat. 9:30 A.M.–8:45 P.M. Suggested admission is adults $10, students and seniors $5, children under 12 free.

Stanhope Hotel

Directly across from the Met, at the southeast corner of 81st Street and Fifth Avenue, is the Stanhope, an ornate luxury hotel filled with Louis XVI furnishings and Baccarat chandeliers. In summer, the hotel's restaurant spills out into a sidewalk cafe that's expensive but perfect for peoplewatching.

Jazz musician Charlie Parker died in the hotel apartment of Baroness "Nica" de Koenigswarter on March 12, 1955, while watching jugglers on the "Tommy Dorsey Show." The eccentric baroness, who was a friend and patron of many jazz musicians, had called a doctor upon Bird's arrival three days earlier, and he had warned her that the musician could die at any time.

Parker was only 34 when he died, but his death certificate estimated his age to be 53. Drugs and alcohol had so ravaged his body that he seemed much older.

Frank E. Campbell Funeral Home

The small building at 1076 Madison Ave., at 81st St., is the funeral home of the rich and famous. Rudolph Valentino started the trend in 1926, followed by Montgomery Clift, James Cagney, Joan Crawford, John Garfield, and Tommy Dorsey.

Judy Garland's funeral was also held at the Campbell Home. Her daughter Liza Minnelli, wanting to keep things upbeat, insisted that the rooms be decorated in yellow—Judy's favorite color—and that the mourners wear "anything but black." Before the funeral, about 22,000 fans filed past the glass-topped, blue-velvet-lined casket, many clutching portable record and tape players that played Judy's greatest hits.

CARNEGIE HILL AND VICINITY

The area bounded roughly by 86th and 98th Sts. and by Fifth and Park Aves. is known as Carnegie Hill, one of the city's wealthiest districts. Several important museums line Fifth Avenue here, while the side streets hold a treasure trove of sights.

Neue Galerie

One of the newest museums in town is the Neue Galerie, 1048 Fifth Ave., at 86th St., 212/628-6200, www.neuegalerie.org, devoted solely to the fine and decorative arts of Germany and Austria from the first half of the 20th century. Housed in a renovated beaux arts mansion, the museum includes a large collection of works by Gustav Klimt and Egon Schiele, a bookstore, design shop, and the smart Cafe Sabarsky, where you can indulge in Viennese coffee and a piece of Sacher torte.

The museum is open Mon. and Fri.–Sat. 11 A.M.–7 P.M. and Sunday 1–6 P.M. Admission is adults $10, seniors and students $7, children 12–16 must be accompanied by an adult, children under 12 not admitted.

Guggenheim Museum

The Solomon R. Guggenheim Museum, 1071 Fifth Ave., at 89th St., 212/423-3500, www.guggenheim.org, first opened its doors in 1959, and immediately met with considerable controversy. The city's only Frank Lloyd Wright-designed building, it was compared to everything from a snail to a toilet bowl. Nowadays it's hard to see what the fuss was about. From the outside, the circular building seems as permanent a part of Fifth Avenue as the neoclassic buildings that surround it, while from the inside, the multileveled spirals of the main galleries seem almost staid. To show how times have changed, the museum was even declared a New York City landmark in 1989—the youngest building ever to be so honored.

The main galleries of the Guggenheim are

usually devoted to a temporary exhibition of a major modern artist or group of artists. Most of the exhibits start at the top, then curve their way slowly downward through a series of bays linked by a circular ramp.

Abutting the main galleries to the north is a small rotunda housing the Justin K. Thannhauser Collection. Works by Picasso, Rousseau, van Gogh, Cézanne, Modigliani, and Seurat, to name but a few, are on permanent display, and they're a stunning group, not to be missed.

Also abutting the main galleries is a glistening 10-story tower, which, upon its completion in 1992, doubled the museum's exhibition space. Lit by skylights, the tower looks out over the Central Park reservoir and boasts an outdoor sculpture garden open in fair weather.

The Guggenheim is open Sun.–Wed. 9 A.M.– 6 P.M., Fri.–Sat. 9 A.M.–8 P.M. Admission is adults $15, students and seniors $12, children under 12 free, voluntary donation Friday 6–8 P.M.

National Academy of Design

The musty National Academy, 1083 Fifth Ave., between 89th and 90th Sts., 212/369-4880, www.nationalacademy.org, is one of the country's oldest art institutions. It was founded in 1825 by artists Thomas Cole, Rembrandt Peale, Samuel Morse, and others. Today, 425 contemporary artists, elected by their peers, are members of the Academy, which also owns a large collection of 19th- and 20th-century American art.

A selection of work from the permanent collection is always on display, along with loan exhibitions. The museum itself is also an eyeful; it's housed in a stately turn-of-the-century mansion donated to the Academy by sculptor Anna Hyatt Huntington.

Hours are Wed.–Thurs. and Sat.–Sun. noon– 5 P.M., Friday 10 A.M.–8 P.M. Admission is adults $8, students and senior citizens $4.50, free to children under 16; voluntary donation Friday 5–8 P.M.

Cooper-Hewitt National Design Museum

A branch of the Smithsonian Institution dedicated to design and the decorative arts, the Cooper-Hewitt, 2 E. 91st St., 212/849-8400, www

.si.edu/ndm, concentrates on such subjects as textiles, metalwork, wallpaper, ceramics, furniture, and architectural design. But half the story is the building itself; the museum occupies a 64-room mansion built by industrialist Andrew Carnegie after his marriage at the ripe old age of 51.

Carnegie was a Scottish immigrant who began his career as a bobbin boy in a cotton factory. By the time he built this mansion, he was one of the world's richest men, head of an empire that included steamship and railroad lines, and iron, coal, and steel companies.

The magnificent 1901 building is a delight to wander through. Built by Babb, Cook & Willard in a heavy Georgian style, the mansion incorporated all the advanced technologies of its day, including air-conditioning, central heating, and the first passenger elevator in a private home. The plush interior boasts dark wood paneling, an imposing carved staircase, and chandeliers. Out back is a romantic garden, where concerts are sometimes presented, while on the ground floor is an unusual gift shop where you can buy such things as handmade birdhouses and reproduction Victorian toys.

The museum is open Tuesday 10 A.M.–9 P.M., Wed.–Sat. 10 A.M.–5 P.M., and Sunday noon– 5 P.M. Admission is adults $8, students and seniors $5, free to children under 12.

Jewish Museum

Housed in a magnificent French Gothic mansion once belonging to businessman Felix Warburg, the newly restored Jewish Museum, 1109 Fifth Ave., at 92nd St., 212/423-3200, is the nation's largest Jewish-culture museum. Spread over three floors and a basement are top-notch, changing exhibits on such subjects as "The Dreyfus Affair," or "Jews and African Americans," as well as an outstanding permanent collection of ceremonial objects and cultural artifacts. Among the latter are an ancient Israelite altar; part of a 16th-century Persian synagogue wall; and a collection of Torah cases.

The museum is open Sunday 10 A.M.–5:45 P.M., Mon.–Wed. 11 A.M.–5:45 P.M., Thursday 11 A.M.– 8 P.M., Friday 11 A.M.–3 P.M., closed Saturday. Admission is adults $8, students and seniors $5.50,

MANHATTAN

free to children under 12, and free to everyone Thursday 5–8 P.M.

Exploring the Side Streets

On Park Avenue at 92nd Street is a towering Louise Nevelson sculpture called *Night Presence.* The views from here are splendid, stretching all the way down to the gold-topped Helmsley Building at 46th Street.

At 56 E. 93rd St. stands a gorgeous white limestone mansion with a curving facade. Erected in 1932, the 45-room edifice was once home to theatrical producer Billy Rose, who lived here until his death in 1965. Today, the building houses one of the city's most chic and expensive rehab centers, the **Smithers Alcohol and Drug Treatment Center.** Among those who've sought treatment here have been Truman Capote, John Cheever, Joan Kennedy, Dwight "Doc" Gooden, and Darryl Strawberry.

At 75 E. 93rd St. is the **Russian Orthodox Church Outside Russia,** housed in the former mansion of banker George Baker. In Baker's day, a private railroad line ran directly beneath the house to Grand Central.

Just a few blocks farther north is a second Russian sanctuary—the **Russian Orthodox Cathedral of St. Nicholas,** 15 East 97th Street. With its five onion domes, gold crosses, and red, yellow, and blue tiles, it's a strange and exotic interloper in this conservative neighborhood.

Museum of the City of New York

The renovated, neo-Georgian building on Fifth Avenue between 103rd and 104th Streets houses the one-of-a-kind Museum of the City of New York, 212/534-1672, www.mcny.com. Inside this eclectic establishment, find a vast collection of paintings and photographs, maps and prints, furniture and clothing, Broadway memorabilia and old model ships—all telling the story of New York City.

The museum also features imaginative temporary exhibits. Recent examples include exhibitions on Duke Ellington, New York City mayors, photographer Jessie Tarbox Beals, and stickball. On the museum's ground floor is a delightful gift shop.

Hours are Wed.–Sat. 10 A.M.–5 P.M. and Sunday noon–5 P.M. Suggested donation is adults $7; students, seniors and children $4; families $12. The museum also sponsors occasional walking tours.

El Museo del Barrio

A community museum dedicated to the art and culture of Puerto Rico and Latin America, El Museo del Barrio, 1230 Fifth Ave., between 104th and 105th Sts., 212/831-7272, www.elmuseo.org, presents both contemporary and historical exhibits. Just a few blocks from Spanish Harlem, it was founded in an elementary school classroom over 25 years ago, and continues to work closely with local residents. Most of its exhibits are temporary; on permanent display is a superb collection of *santos de palo,* or carved wooden saints. The museum is open Wed.–Sun. 11 A.M.–5 P.M. Suggested admission is adults $7, seniors $3, children under 12 free.

Note: One block north of El Museo at 105th Street is the lovely **Conservatory Garden,** a sometimes overlooked nook of Central Park most easily entered from Fifth Avenue (see Central Park and the Upper West Side, below).

Islamic Cultural Center

At the corner of 96th Street and Third Avenue is a surprising sight—a modern, gold-domed mosque, built off the axis, facing Mecca. Beside it is a tall skinny minaret from which taped calls-to-prayer are broadcast five times a day.

Largely subsidized by the government of Kuwait, the $17-million mosque was designed in 1988 by an Islamic architect working for the very American company of Skidmore, Owens, & Merrill. Inside, the mosque is a tranquil oasis—all pale greens and blues, with an enormous carpet covered with geometric shapes. About 1,000 men can be accommodated here; the women worship upstairs on the mezzanine level, where they're out of sight.

On Friday, the mosque is surrounded by a sea of cabs, as Indo-Pakistani, Moroccan, Egyptian, and Arab drivers come from all over the city for the most important service of the week. Smaller services are held on Sundays.

Visitors are welcome to visit the mosque,

212/722-5234, or to attend the Sunday service, but it's best to call in advance.

Marx Brothers' Residence

Groucho (Julius), Harpo (Adolf), and Chico (Leonard) Marx grew up in a small apartment at 179 E. 93rd St., between Lexington and Third Aves., where they lived with seven other family members from 1895 to 1910. In those days, this block was part of a poor Jewish neighborhood sandwiched between an Irish neighborhood to the north and a German one to the south.

The Marxes moved out in 1910 because Minnie Marx, the brothers' mother, decided that the family vaudeville act would do better in Chicago than it had in New York. The Marxes didn't return to live permanently in New York until the 1920s. By then they were famous.

PARK AND LEXINGTON AVENUES

The sights below are arranged from north to south.

The Asia Society

First-rate exhibits, concerts, films, and lectures on various aspects of Asian culture and history are always on the docket at the recently revamped Asia Society, 725 Park Ave., at 70th St., 212/517-2742, www.asiasociety.org. Inside the modern red-granite building, you'll find a slim atrium, undulating staircase, and extensive book and gift shop.

The Asia Society is open Tues.–Thurs. and Sat.–Sun. 11 A.M.–6 P.M., Friday 11 A.M.–9 P.M. Admission is adults $7, students and seniors $5; free admission Friday 6–9 P.M.

Seventh Regiment Armory

Between Park and Lexington Avenues, 66th and 67th Streets, is an odd sight—an enormous castlelike armory with crenellated towers and iron-studded wooden doors. Inside are long dark corridors, a drill hall, and ornate rooms designed by Louis Tiffany. Large-scale events such as a winter antiques show and a spring crafts show have historically been held here.

Jimmy Walker's Uptown Abode

Jimmy Walker, the flamboyant gentleman mayor of New York from 1925 to 1932, lived in a suite at the charming Mayfair Hotel, 610 Park Ave., at 65th St., during the last four years of his term. By then he had already left his wife for showgirl Betty Compton. While living here, Walker was forced to resign from office, largely because he was unable to explain how $1 million had mysteriously appeared in his bank account. Immediately thereafter, under a cloud of suspicion, he left for Europe, where he married Compton and lived for the next three years. When he returned to New York, however, his loyal public welcomed him back with open arms, and he was appointed chairman of the garment industry by his old political foe, Fiorello La Guardia. When Walker died on November 18, 1946, hundreds of people tried to see him at the hospital, while thousands more jammed the hospital's telephone lines.

CARL SCHURZ PARK AND VICINITY

This small, idyllic park with meandering walkways and wonderful views stretches between 84th and 90th Streets, East End Avenue and the East River. The park is named for a German-American politician and soldier who campaigned for Abraham Lincoln, served as a brigadier general in the Civil War, and was appointed secretary of the interior under Pres. Rutherford Hayes.

From the park southward extends **John H. Finley Walk,** a pleasant pedestrian walkway built above FDR Drive. The brainchild of City Parks Commissioner Robert Moses, the walk was named after a *New York Times* editor who enjoyed walking around Manhattan Island, a distance of 32 miles.

Gracie Mansion

At the north end of the park, at East End Avenue and 88th Street, is New York City's mayoral mansion, 212/570-4751, a pretty wooden house sitting on a small rise. It was built in 1799 as the country home of merchant Archibald Gracie, who once entertained such luminaries as Alexander Hamilton and Washington Irving here. The

City of New York appropriated the mansion in 1896 for back taxes, but it wasn't until 1942 that it became the official mayoral residence. New York is one of the nation's only cities with a mayor's mansion; the house is filled with lovely period pieces, and the guides are brimming with interesting anecdotes.

From Gracie Mansion you have a good view of choppy **Hell Gate,** a treacherous stretch of the East River. Hundreds of wrecks are believed to lie beneath its waters, including a Revolutionary War frigate that went down in 1780 carrying an estimated $500 million in gold and silver coins. The money was meant to be payroll for the British troops stationed in America. Spanning Hell Gate is the Triborough Bridge and, north of that, Hell Gate Arch, which carries railroad tracks.

Tours of Gracie Mansion take place late March–mid-November by appointment only; call for details.

Henderson Place

On the north side of 86th Street between East End and York Avenue is a small residential alley lined with 24 quaint Queen Anne–style townhouses. The houses were developed by John Jacob Astor and were once part of his country estate.

In 1944, literary critic Edmund Wilson, his wife novelist Mary McCarthy, and their young son lived at 14 Henderson Place. In the 1950s, actors Lynn Fontanne and Alfred Lunt were Henderson Place residents.

Yorkville

Once home to a large German and Hungarian population, Yorkville is now an eclectic neighborhood filled with everything from tacky shops to luxury apartment buildings. The ethnic communities have disappeared, save for a few leftover businesses still in operation here and there.

Just off wide and scruffy 86th Street are **Schaller & Weber,** 1654 Second Ave., 212/879-3047, a 1937 butcher shop that will mail sausages anywhere in the world; and the **Elk Candy Company,** 1628 Second Ave., 212/585-2303, known for its old-fashioned marzipan. Nearby is **Glaser's Bake Shop,** 1670 First Ave., between 87th and 88th Sts., 212/289-2562, where the *linzer torte* is a local favorite.

The traditional Hungarian **Yorkville Packing House,** 1560 Second Ave., at 81st St., 212/628-5147, sells veal and pork sausage made with plenty of paprika. One of the last of the many Hungarian restaurants that once thrived in Yorkville is **Mocca Restaurant,** 1588 Second Ave., between 81st and 82nd Sts., 212/734-6470.

LOWER YORK AVENUE AND ROOSEVELT ISLAND

Dead Ringers

The twin gynecologists upon whose life story David Cronenberg's movie *Dead Ringers* was based once lived in an apartment building at 450 E. 63rd St., between York Ave. and FDR Drive. Born two minutes apart, Stewart and Cyril Marcus did everything together. They attended the same college and medical school, were captains in the army, held prestigious jobs at New York Hospital, and ran a very successful joint practice on East 72nd Street. Women came from all over the country to consult them about fertility problems, and sometimes the doctors switched patients without telling anyone.

The Drs. Marcus also shared an addiction to barbiturates. In 1975, their decomposed bodies were found in this building, surrounded by half-eaten sandwiches and empty bottles of pills. The city's medical examiner determined that they were killed by withdrawal from the drugs they'd been taking.

Mount Vernon Hotel Museum and Garden

Formerly known as the Abigail Adams Smith Museum, the Mount Vernon Hotel, 421 E. 61st St., between First and York Aves., 212/838-6878, is the sixth-oldest building in Manhattan. The 1799 edifice sits apart from hurly-burly city life, on a small hill behind a stone wall not far from the East River. It was originally intended to be the carriage house for the country estate of Pres. John Adams's daughter, but due to financial difficulties, she never moved in.

The carriage house then became part of the

Mount Vernon Hotel, which catered to New Yorkers who wanted a day in the country; back then, Uptown was predominantly rural. "Come bathe and sail in the East River," ran the early advertisements.

Today, the nine-room museum is full of period furnishings and paintings, including one that shows East 61st Street as it once was, complete with meadows, sailboats, and a bathing dock. Out back is a pleasant garden where puppet shows and other performances are sometimes presented. The museum is open Tues.–Sun. 11 A.M.–4 P.M. Admission is adults $4, students and seniors $3, children under 12 free.

Roosevelt Island

Swinging high above the east end of 60th Street is one of Manhattan's more incongruous sights— the Roosevelt Island cable car. The ride lasts four minutes, costs $1.50 one way, offers great views of the Upper East Side and the East River, and sets you down in one of New York's stranger neighborhoods, Roosevelt Island.

Eerily quiet and empty after the hubbub of Manhattan, Roosevelt Island is a planned residential community where no private cars are allowed. Designed by Philip Johnson and John Burgee, it was built in the 1970s as an "Instant City." In addition to about 3,200 units of mixed-income housing, the community has its own schools and stores, several hospitals, and a promenade with good views of Manhattan.

Roosevelt Island was once known as Blackwell's Island, named after its original owner, Robert Blackwell. Blackwell built the farmhouse that still stands today just north of the tram station. In 1828, the city bought the island and turned it into a penal institution for petty criminals. A grim and nasty place, it was notorious for frequent riots and innovative tortures, including "cooler" rooms and the "water drop cure." Politician Boss Tweed served time there in 1873, and actress Mae West spent 10 days behind bars in 1927 for her notorious play *Sex*. Others incarcerated on the island included anarchist Emma Goldman and birth control advocate Ethel Byrne.

During the 1800s, a poorhouse, a pavilion for the insane, and several hospitals were added

Roosevelt Island cable car

to the island, which in 1921 was renamed Welfare Island. These institutions were also notorious for their inhumane conditions, and were eventually exposed by Charles Dickens and Nellie Bly. Today, the remains of the insane pavilion—a haunting octagonal structure of gray stone—still stand near the island's north end. Also at the north end is a 50-foot-high stone lighthouse, designed by James Renwick, who also designed St. Patrick's Cathedral on Fifth Avenue.

The Roosevelt Island tram station is at the corner of Second Avenue and 60th Street. Maps of the island are available at the ticket booth. Call 212/832-4540 for information about special events on the island.

SHOPPING

Books

The enormous **Barnes & Noble** megastore at 1280 Lexington Ave., at 86th St., 212/423-9900, features endless aisles of books along with comfortable armchairs and an upscale cafe. It's open until 11 P.M. weeknights, 7 P.M. on Sunday.

Kitchen Arts & Letters, 1435 Lexington Ave., near 93rd St., 212/876-5550, stocks an astonishing array of cookbooks.

Clothing

Among the many upscale clothing stores you'll find on Madison Avenue are **Polo Ralph Lauren,** 650 Madison, at 60th St., 212/318-7000; **Yves St. Laurent,** 855 Madison, near 71st St., 212/988-3821; and **Issey Miyake,** 992 Madison, near 78th St., 212/439-7822.

Across from Bloomingdale's are many moderately priced clothing shops, including the **Levi Store,** 750 Lexington Ave., at 60th St., 212/826-5957, a huge warehouse selling jeans in all colors, sizes, and styles. For $65, the store will also custom tailor a pair of women's jeans in their 512 cut. **Second Chance Consignment Shop,** 1109 Lexington Ave., 2nd Fl., 212/744-6041, is the place to go for secondhand couture. **Tracey Tooker Hats,** 1211 Lexington Ave., near 83rd St., 212/472-9603, sells an imaginative array of handmade hats.

Department Stores

Once a bargain basement, **Bloomingdale's,** 1000 Third Ave., at 60th St., 212/705-2000, is now one of New York's most glamorous department stores. It's well worth a browse, even if you're not planning to buy. **Barney's New York,** 660 Madison Ave., at 61st St., 212/826-8900, carries fashionable and expensive clothing for men and women.

Gourmet Goodies

The **Elk Candy Company,** 1628 Second Ave., near 86th St., 212/585-2303, is known for old-fashioned marzipan. **Schaller & Weber,** 1654 Second Ave., 212/879-3047, is a 1937 German butcher shop that will mail sausages anywhere in the world.

Toys, Games, and Gifts

A Bear's Place, 789 Lexington Ave., at 61st St., 212/826-6465, sells a whole menagerie of stuffed animals. **Big City Kite Company,** 1210 Lexington Ave., at 82nd St., 212/472-2623, offers kites in all shapes and sizes. **Game Show,** 1240 Lexington Ave., between 83rd and 84th Sts., 212/472-8011, carries games galore; **Star Magic,** 1256 Lexington Ave., between 84th and 85th Sts., 212/988-0300, is known for "space-age gifts."

Other Stores

Over a half-dozen **antique stores** are on 60th Street between Third and Second Avenues. Nearby is **Things Japanese,** 127 E. 60th St., 2nd Fl., between Lexington and Park Aves., 212/371-4661, offering antiques, kimonos, and folk art in a variety of price ranges. **Lalique,** 712 Madison Ave., at 63rd St., 212/355-6550, is renowned for its crystal and glass.

ACCOMMODATIONS

$100–150

One of the best bargains in the neighborhood is a building on **E. 93rd,** between Fifth and Madison Avenue, 212/472-2000, filled with nothing but B&Bs. All the rooms are large and equipped with a queen-sized bed, microwave, and toaster oven, while the ones in back overlook a garden. $120 s or d.

$250 and up

Downstairs at the small and stylish **Franklin,** 164 E. 87th St., between Lexington and Third Aves., 212/369-1000, www.boutiquehg.com, is a tiny streamlined lobby done up in black and burnished steel with mirrors and fresh flowers. Upstairs are 53 cozy guest rooms featuring beds with billowing canopies, cherrywood furnishings, and a fresh rose at each bedside. $249–269 s or d; includes continental breakfast, and espresso and cappuccino all day.

A few blocks north of the Franklin is one of its sister hotels, the Victorian **Hotel Wales,** 1295 Madison Ave., between 92nd and 93rd Sts., 212/876-6000 (another hotel in the group is the Mansfield in Midtown). Small and old-fashioned in flavor, the Wales centers around a dark green lobby hung with illustrations from the story of Puss and Boots. A worn marble staircase in back leads to 92 guest rooms; next door is Sarabeth's Kitchen, known for its baked goods. $265–285 s, $285–305 d; includes continental breakfast, and espresso and cappuccino all day.

The sturdy, red brick **Barbizon Hotel,** 140 E. 63rd St., at Lexington Ave., 212/838-5700 or 800/223-1020, was once an old-fashioned hostelry catering exclusively to women; men were only allowed in the public rooms downstairs. In the late '80s, however, the hotel was completely revamped and now caters to both sexes. The low-ceilinged lobby sports vaguely Oriental decor; guest rooms are newly renovated, with lots of blond wood. Adjoining the hotel is the upscale Equinox health club, which guests can use for free. $260–320 s or d.

First-class service and unerring good taste have made the **Carlyle Hotel**, 35 E. 76th St., at Madison Ave., 212/744-1600 or 800/227-5737, www.thecarlyle.com, one of the city's top hotels ever since it opened, in 1930 (see Up Fifth and Madison Avenues, above). The airy, spacious rooms are equipped with every conceivable amenity, while downstairs, the Cafe Carlyle is home to Bobby Short and other superb jazz musicians. $475–700 s or d.

The Mark, 25 E. 77th St., near Madison Ave., 212/744-4300 or 800/843-6275, www.themarkhotel.com, is small, stylish, and very elegant, with a neoclassical Italian look. In the lobby, gleaming marble floors reflect sumptuous vases overflowing with fresh flowers. The Mark's Bar offers plenty of cozy nooks and crannies; the guest rooms are large and comfortably furnished. $495–600 s, $525–630 d; weekend packages often available, continental breakfast included.

A magnificent slice of the Old World can be found at the **Pierre Hotel**, Fifth Ave. at 61st St., 212/838-8000 or 800/PIERRE4 (see Up Fifth and Madison Avenues, above), www.fourseasons.com/pierre. The stunning lobby is adorned with chandeliers, fresh flowers, silks, and damasks, while the guest rooms are lavishly furnished with antiques. A good way to sample the Pierre, even if you can't afford to stay, is to stop in at the baroque-styled Rotunda for an elegant afternoon tea. $425–590 s, $475–630 d.

YMHA

The **YMHA (de Hirsch Residence at the 92nd Street Y)**, 1395 Lexington Ave., at 92nd St., 212/415-5650 or 800/858-4692, offers dorm-style rooms for nightly and monthly rates. The rooms are clean, and you can attend the Y's many cultural events—including concerts and literary readings—at discounted rates. $49 s, $98 d; one

month rates start at $945 (with shared bath). Reserve well in advance.

FOOD

American

Open for breakfast, lunch, and dinner is the **Barking Dog Luncheonette**, 1678 Third Ave., at 94th St., 212/831-1800, a cheery place with good soups, sandwiches, and simple entrées; average main course $8. Adjoining the Hotel Wales is **Sarabeth's Kitchen**, 1295 Madison Ave., between 92nd and 93rd Sts., 212/410-7335, serving homemade American food in a lace and floral setting; average main course $14. **Pig Heaven,** 1540 Second Ave., between 80th and 81st Sts., 212/744-4333, specializes in all things porcine—including spicy pigs' ears; average entrée $14.

Asian

A good, reliable Thai restaurant is the unpretentious **Sala Thai,** 1718 Second Ave., between 89th and 90th Sts., 212/410-5557; average entrée $12. Despite its Italian sounding name, **Baluchi's,** 1565 Second Ave., at 81st St., 212/288-4810, is strictly Asian/Indian and named after Baluchistan, the region that stretches from Iran to Pakistan. On the menu are lots of lamb, eggplant, and spicy dishes; average entrée $12. Spicy, delicious Korean food is the specialty of classy **Emo's,** 1564 Second Ave., between 81st and 82nd Sts., 212/628-8699.

French

Chic sleek **Le Bilboquet**, 25 E. 63rd St., between Madison and Park Aves., 212/751-3036, is a bit snooty, but the food is fine; average entrée $20. **Daniel,** 60 E. 65th St., between Madison and Park Aves., 212/288-0033, wins kudos from food critics all over Manhattan for its superb French cuisine, discerning wine list, and impeccable décor; prix fixe dinner $85–150.

Italian

Caffé Grazie, 26 E. 84th St., between Fifth and Madison Aves., 212/717-4407, conveniently located near the Met (average entrée $14) and **Caffé Buon Gusto,** 236 E. 77th St., between

MANHATTAN

Third and Second Aves., 212/535-6884, a solid neighborhood spot (average entrée $11) are good choices for pasta and other basic entrées. The chic bistro **Paper Moon Milano,** 39 E. 58th St., between Madison and Park Aves., 212/758-8600, may be pricey, but it's also very satisfying, with beautifully presented Northern Italian fare; average entrée $19. Next door is a more moderately priced cafe.

Other Ethnic

One of the last of the many Hungarian restaurants that once thrived in this neighborhood is **Mocca Restaurant,** 1588 Second Ave., between 81st and 82nd Sts., 212/734-6470; average entrée $12. Good Persian food can be found at the cheerful **Persepolis,** 1423 Second Ave., between 74th and 75th Sts., 212/535-1100, offering succulent kabobs, unusual stews, and sour cherry rice; average entrée $13. **Rosa Mexicano,** 1063 First Ave., at 58th St., 212/753-7407, is an unusual haute-Mexican restaurant serving fresh, flavorful food that draws large crowds; average entrée $20.

Light Bites

Near the Metropolitan is **Nectar,** 1090 Madison Ave., near 81st St., 212/772-0916, a standard but reliable coffee shop. **E.A.T.,** 1064 Madison Ave., between 80th and 81st Sts., 212/772-0022, is a pricey gourmet-food shop and cafe.

Lexington Candy Shop, 1226 Lexington Ave., at 83rd St., 212/288-0057, is an old-fashioned luncheonette founded in 1925. Greenwich Village's first-rate **John's Pizzeria** has an uptown location at 408 E. 64th St., near First Ave., 212/935-2895.

For German bakeshops, see Yorkville under Carl Schurz Park and Vicinity, above.

Watering Holes and Lounges

An institution in this part of town are **J.G. Melon,** 1291 Third Ave., at 74th St., 212/744-0585, a friendly saloon that also serves great burgers. The famed **Elaine's,** the celebrity hangout and Italian restaurant, is at 1703 Second Ave., between 88th and 89th Sts., 212/534-8103, and sports a crowded bar that's especially worth a visit if you've just got to spot *someone.* For class, stop into the dark and gracious **Bemelmans Bar,** in the posh Hotel Carlyle, 35 E. 76th St., at Madison Ave., 212/744-1600.

The Upper East Side is also home to a number of singles bars that come and go with the seasons. Among them is the **Cocktail Room,** 334 E. 73rd St., between First and Second Aves., 212/988-6100, specializing in tall tropical drinks. One bar that has been around for awhile is **Merchants NY,** 1125 First Ave., at 62nd St., 212/832-1551, a sleek and stylish place with a polished semicircular bar, lots of small tables with flickering candles, and a good bar menu.

Among neighborhood hangouts, **Rathbones,** 1702 Second Ave., near 88th St., 212/369-7361, is a large, creaky tavern with heavy wooden tables and sawdust-covered floors. The laid-back **Kinsale Tavern,** 1672 Third Ave., at 94th St., 212/348-4370, an Irish pub, attracts everyone from clerical workers to politicians. Near the Met you'll find the well-worn, step-down **Madison Pub,** 1043 Madison Ave., between 79th and 80th Sts., no phone, known for its good burgers and jukebox filled with Bing Crosby, Frank Sinatra, and cohorts.

Central Park and the Upper West Side

A mix of ornate 19th-century landmarks, solid pre–WW II apartment buildings, and well-worn tenements, the Upper West Side is primarily a residential district. Unlike the Upper East Side with its upper-crust traditions, the Upper West Side is known for its feisty liberal politics, love of culture, and upper-middle class, including an especially large quotient of doctors, lawyers, writers, actors, musicians, dancers, and intellectuals.

Up until the late 19th century, the Upper West Side was called the Bloomingdale district, named after the Dutch word for "vale of flowers." Washington Irving once described the area as "a sweet rural valley, beautiful with many a bright flower, refreshed by many a pure streamlet, and enlived here and there by a delectable little Dutch cottage."

The district began developing in the late 1800s with the building of the Dakota, a grand apartment house. Prior to the Dakota, most middle-class and wealthy Americans regarded the apartment-house concept as too "French"—i.e., risqué and common. All those strangers rubbing shoulders together in communal hallways. The lavish appointments of the Dakota quickly changed that attitude.

The Upper West Side received its second seismic shift in the late 1960s when Lincoln Center displaced the sprawling, largely poor neighborhood of San Juan Hill. As the poorer people were forced out, the wealthier ones moved in, and the area became more and more fashionable—a process that is continuing today throughout the Upper West Side.

The best streets for wandering are Broadway and Columbus Avenue, both lined with a multitude of shops. In comparison, the streets running from east to west tend to be quiet and almost exclusively residential.

Central Park lies between Fifth and Eighth Avenues, 59th and 110th Streets. The two gracious avenues lining it to the south and west are called Central Park South (a continuation of 59th Street) and Central Park West (a continuation of Eighth Avenue), respectively.

Weekends are the best time to visit Central Park; any time is a good time to tour the Upper West Side. First-time visitors will probably want to check out the southern end of Central Park, Lincoln Center, and the American Museum of Natural History, and take a stroll along Columbus or Broadway.

CENTRAL PARK

Between the Upper East and the Upper West Sides lies that most glorious of New York institutions, Central Park. Without this vast, rolling estate of green—the lungs of the city—life in New York would become unbearable. Despite the highly publicized crimes that occasionally occur here, Central Park is where New Yorkers go to escape cramped apartments, roaring traffic, and an endless cityscape of concrete and steel.

The Central Park, as it was once known, was the brainchild of poet turned newspaper editor William Cullen Bryant. Worried that the city was being smothered by block after block of relentless building, Bryant first called for the park's creation in the July 3, 1844, edition of his *Evening Post*. Landscape architect Andrew Jackson Downing and a number of politicians soon added their voices to Bryant's plea. Together, they hammered away at city government for 12 years until finally, in 1856, the city bought most of what is now the park for $5 million. The land at that time was ugly and desolate, filled with scrawny trees and rocky outcroppings, but it was also home to several small villages, established by groups of squatters. Among them was Seneca Village, an early African American settlement whose existence was only rediscovered in 1996; it and all other villages were destroyed in the building of the park.

Frederick Law Olmsted and Calvert Vaux were the visionary landscape architects who turned Bryant's Central Park dream into reality. As Olmsted saw it, the park had two functions. One was to provide a place for the contemplation of nature. The other was to create a social mixing

MANHATTAN

INFORMATION, PLEASE

For up-to-date information on Central Park, stop by the **Visitor Information Center,** 212/794-6564, in the Dairy building in the center of the park just south of the 65th Street Transverse. The center features a small exhibit area and a gift shop, where you can buy a pocket map filled with wonderful details about the park, past and present ($4). The center is open Tuesday–Sunday 10 A.M.–5 P.M., and runs a special events hotline at 212/360-3456.

Other groups also sponsor walks in the park. The **Urban Park Rangers,** 212/360-1406 or 866/NYC-HAWKS (events hotline), offer free weekend environmental walking tours; their website is www.nyc.gov/parks. The **New York City Audubon Society,** 212/691-7483, sponsors bird walks through the Ramble—one of the top 10 birding spots in the country—in the spring, summer, and fall.

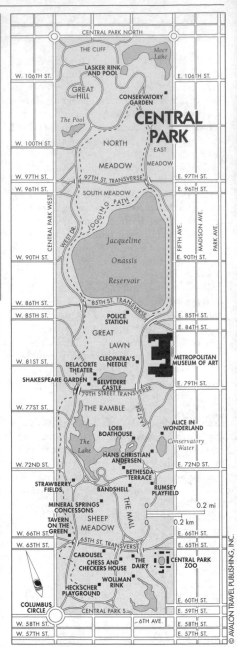

bowl where the haves and have-nots could pass each other every day, providing an opportunity for the poor to become inspired by the rich.

Entirely man-made—with every bush, tree, and rock planned—the park took 20 years to complete. By the time it was finished, workers had shifted 10 million cartloads of dirt, imported a half-million cubic yards of topsoil, and planted four to five million trees. Central Park was such an immediate and overwhelming success that it led to a park movement across the United States and the world.

Central Park is 2.5 miles long and a half mile wide, and covers about 843 acres. Though not the largest open space in New York City—several parks in the boroughs are bigger—it is the most used, with 15–20 million day visitors annually. Walking through the park is like walking through some gigantic carnival site. You'll see scantily clad in-line skaters, svelte bicyclists, oblivious lovers, sports-crazed kids, cough-racked beggars, cashmere-clad matrons, professional dogwalkers with multiple canines in tow, and scruffy musicians playing everything from rock to rap. Every size, shape, color, and make of humanity is here. Central Park is too big to cover in a day, so the best approach is to just dip into it here and there, combining a visit to the Met, for example, with a stop at the model-boat pond, or a visit to the Plaza with a stop at the Central Park Wildlife Center. Most of the visitor attractions are in the southern half of the park, although the northern reaches have recently been restored and rediscovered. On the weekends, most of the park is safe (though keep your eyes open when visiting the Ramble and some northern areas), but during the week, it's best to stick to well-populated areas. Avoid the park completely at night. If you get lost during your visit, just find a lamppost—each is marked with the number of the nearest street.

South of 65th Street

Entering Central Park at Fifth Avenue and 59th Street, through what is known as **Scholar's Gate,** you'll soon come to the delightful **Central Park Wildlife Center,** 212/861-6030. Completely overhauled in 1988, this small gem groups its animals by climatic zones; especially fun is Polar Circle, where polar bears prowl and penguins promenade in a snowy clime behind thick glass. The center is open daily 10 A.M.–4:30 P.M., with longer hours in summer. Admission is adults

$3.50, seniors $1.25, children 3–12 50 cents, under three free.

Above the arch at the wildlife center's northeast end is **Delacorte Clock,** where every hour a parade of bronze animals marches around playing nursery tunes. The clock was a gift to the city from philanthropist George Delacorte, who also gave the park the Alice in Wonderland statue at Conservatory Water and the open-air Delacorte Theater at the Great Lawn. Ironically, Mr. Delacorte and his wife, then ages 92 and 66, respectively, were mugged in the park one morning in 1985. The thieves got away with Mr. Delacorte's wallet and Mrs. Delacorte's $5,500 mink coat. That incident might have discouraged a lesser man, but Delacorte simply said, "I've walked five miles in the park every day of my life. This will not stop me." He kept walking in the park until his death in 1991 at age 98.

Just across East Drive from the wildlife center is **Wollman Rink,** 212/396-1010, packed in winter with exuberant ice skaters of all ages. In summer, Wollman becomes a roller rink and miniature golf course. Admission is adults $5.50, children under 12 $3.50.

North of the rink is the octagonal **Chess and**

chess in Central Park—the perennial pursuit (this game is circa 1946)

Checkers House, complete with 24 concrete game boards outside and 10 tables inside. Free playing pieces for the boards can be picked up with a photo ID in the nearby **Dairy** building, which also houses the **Visitors' Information Center.** Dating back to the park's earliest days, the Dairy was once an actual working dairy selling glasses of fresh milk. The cows were kept in a pasture where the Wollman Rink is now.

Directly west of the Dairy are the gay colors and the 58 beautifully carved horses of the **Carousel,** 212/879-0244, built in 1908. The carousel operates daily 10 A.M.–4:30 P.M., extended hours in summer, weather permitting. Just south of the Carousel is **Heckscher Playground,** with five softball diamonds, handball courts, horseshoes, and a puppet theater.

The sunken transverse road running from East 65th Street to West 66th Street is one of four such roads in the park (the others are at 79th, 85th, and 97th Streets). These roads were one of Olmsted's most brilliant innovations. Dynamited out of bedrock, they allow cars and buses to pass below the level of the park, while pedestrians pass on bridges above. This makes it possible, in Olmsted's words, for even "the most timid and nervous to go on foot to any district of the park."

65th Street to 72nd Street

Heading a bit farther north and west, you'll come to **Tavern-on-the-Green,** 212/873-3200, a glittering extravaganza of a restaurant on the edge of the park near 67th Street and Central Park West. Built to resemble a deluxe Victorian cottage, the over-the-top Tavern is packed to the bursting point with brass, glass, mirrors, chandeliers, thousands upon thousands of tiny lights, and, of course, tourists. It's all very festive, especially in the late afternoons when it takes on a fairy-tale air.

The Tavern-on-the-Green borders **Sheep Meadow,** a huge expanse of lawn covered with thousands of semiclad sun-worshippers in warm weather. Real sheep grazed here until 1934 when

> *Central Park is entirely man-made—every bush, tree, and rock is planned. By the time it was finished, workers had shifted 10 million cartloads of dirt, imported a half-million cubic yards of topsoil, and planted millions of trees.*

Parks Commissioner Robert Moses got rid of them. By then, the sheep were so inbred that many were malformed.

East of Sheep's Meadow is the **Mall,** a promenade lined with trees and busts of famous men. This quarter-mile avenue was once a parade ground for the elite, who cruised up and down in the late afternoons, courting and showing off their fancy carriages. Today, the Mall is frequented by in-line skaters, especially on the weekends when an impromptu blading party regularly takes place. Then, seemingly hundreds of lithe, muscular skaters dressed in tight, bright spandex, twist and turn, jump and flex, 'round and 'round as a DJ blasts out music from a big black box.

North of the Mall is the bandshell at **Rumsey Playfield,** where a first-rate series of free outdoor concerts is presented every summer by **SummerStage,** 212/360-CPSS (212/360-2777), www.summerstage.org. Past performers have ranged from blueswoman Ruth Brown to the Erick Hawkins Dance Company.

72nd Street to 79th Street

Bethesda Terrace, just north of the bandshell and the 72nd Street Transverse, is one of the park's grandest sights. The wide, brick-paved plaza centers around an ornate fountain featuring a statue called *Angel of the Waters* by Emma Stebbins. Surrounding the plaza is a semicircle of tiered steps where you can sit and listen to the street musicians who perform here in warm weather. Lapping at the north end of the terrace is **The Lake,** a peaceful spot usually crowded with splish-splashing rowboats. These boats can be rented at the nearby **Loeb Boathouse,** 212/517-4723, daily 10 A.M.–dusk. The cost is $10 per hour, with a $30 deposit. Also at the boathouse is a bike-rental shop.

West of Bethesda Terrace is **Strawberry Fields,** which Yoko Ono had landscaped into a Garden of Peace as a memorial to her husband John Lennon (see The Dakota under Central Park

West, below). Just inside the garden's wall at 72nd Street is a circular Italian-marble mosaic spelling out the word *Imagine*. Fans gather here in especially large numbers every October 9 and December 8 to commemorate Lennon's birth and death, and a few regulars can almost always be found here.

East of Bethesda Terrace is the **Conservatory Water,** better known to New Yorkers as the model-boat pond. The pond is often dotted with miniature boats, most radio-controlled. During warm weather, a model-boat regatta is held on Saturday mornings.

Near the model-boat pond are two of the park's most famous statues: *Alice in Wonderland*, by Jose de Creefts, perches on a mushroom to the north, while *Hans Christian Andersen*, by Georg Lober, sits with his Ugly Duckling to the west. Both statues are usually covered with adoring children, playing, climbing, and posing for photographs. Storytellers often perform at the Hans Christian Andersen statue on Saturday mornings.

West of the model-boat pond and north of The Lake is the 38-acre **Ramble,** a near wild place crisscrossed with meandering footpaths. Far removed from city life, the Ramble is a favorite spot among birdwatchers; on a typical morning, about 15 kinds of warblers and 35 other species can be seen. It's also a prime haunt for gay men on the make, and condoms litter the woods. It's best not to visit the Ramble alone.

79th Street to 97th Street

North of the Ramble is the Gothic Revival **Belvedere Castle,** designed in 1858 by Calvert Vaux. Situated atop Vista Rock, one of the park's highest spots, the castle offers bird's-eye views from its top floor. Downstairs is the **Central Park Learning Center.** The castle is open during daylight hours; admission is free.

Near the castle are the bedraggled **Shakespeare Garden,** filled with plants and flowers mentioned in the playwright's work, and the **Delacorte Theater,** where a free **New York Shakespeare Festival,** 212/539-8750 or 212/539-8500, is produced every summer. Two plays are usually featured, each running about a month. The free tickets for each day's show are handed out beginning at 6:15 P.M. the same day, and people start lining up for the tickets in the early afternoon.

Abutting the Delacorte Theater is the dry and often dusty **Great Lawn,** where yet more free events are held in summer. Tens of thousands of New Yorkers spread out their blankets and picnic baskets on the lawn when the New York Philharmonic and the Metropolitan Opera Company perform here. At other times, the Great Lawn hosts innumerable softball, soccer, football, field hockey, and Frisbee games.

At the southeastern edge of the Great Lawn, just behind the Metropolitan Museum of Art, is **Cleopatra's Needle.** The 200-ton granite obelisk was rolled here on cannonballs in 1880. It was once engraved with hieroglyphics, but those have been almost completely worn away by pollution and the elements.

North of the Great Lawn is Central Park Reservoir, now known as **Jacqueline Onassis Reservoir** because the former first lady used to jog around its 1.58-mile perimeter. This is the city's most popular jogging course; Dustin Hoffman even jogged here in *Marathon Man*. The reservoir holds about a billion gallons of water, most of which comes via aqueduct from the Catskills.

North of 97th Street

The northernmost section of Central Park, between 97th and 110th Streets, is often overlooked by locals and out-of-towners alike, but holds a number of unusual gems. As Frederick Law Olmsted originally intended, the park here becomes rugged and wild, filled with secret waterfalls, craggy cliffs, and—at 105th Street near Fifth Avenue—the lovely, formal **Conservatory Garden.** Actually three gardens in one, the Conservatory was restored in the mid-1980s and now blooms from late spring through early fall. Its most popular spot is the Secret Garden, named after Frances Hodgson Burnett's classic book. A statue of the book's two central characters—Mary and Dickon—stands at the garden's center.

Just above the Conservatory is 11-acre **Meer Lake,** surrounded by bald cypress trees, flowering shrubs, and wetlands. Up until about five years ago, this lake—like much of the park above 97th

Street—was avoided by New Yorkers fearful of crime. But since the early 1990s, the Central Park Conservancy has been pouring millions of dollars into the area, and it's been vastly improved. Meer Lake is now stocked with some 50,000 bluegill, largemouth bass, and catfish, and has become a favorite fishing grounds for youngsters who are given free poles and told to go fish.

On the edge of Meer Lake is the **Charles A. Dana Discovery Center.** The center houses natural history exhibits and offers free hands-on science programs.

LINCOLN CENTER AND VICINITY

Columbus Circle

Now in the midst of redevelopment, this gray, windswept circle is marked by a constant rush of traffic and a tiny statue of Columbus perched atop an 80-foot column. On the south side stands a white, vaguely Islamic-style building originally designed by Edward Durrell Stone to house the art collection of A&P heir Huntington Hartford. Considered an architectural fiasco when it opened in 1965, the building is now just another New York anomaly. Empty for the last few years, it is now being renovated to become the new home of the American Craft Museum (see American Craft Museum, Midtown).

It was at Columbus Circle that Mafia boss Joe Colombo was gunned down on June 28, 1971. Colombo, who always claimed to be just a simple real estate salesman from South Brooklyn, had formed the Italian American Civil Rights League earlier in the year. On that June day, he sponsored an Italian Unity Day at Columbus Circle. Thousands showed up for the antidiscrimination rally, but before things could get properly underway, a young man wearing press credentials shot Colombo in the face and head. Colombo was rushed to the hospital, but ended up permanently and almost totally paralyzed. He died of a stroke seven years later. Investigators believe that Joe Gallo, Colombo's archrival, was responsible for the hit; Gallo didn't last too much longer himself (see Umberto's Clam House under Little Italy in Chinatown, Little Italy, and the Lower East Side, above).

On the north side of the circle is the glitzy **Trump International Hotel and Tower,** while to the west, the $1.7 billion **Columbus Centre** is going up. Once the site of the New York Coliseum (since torn down), the center will house AOL Time Warner's headquarters on its lower floors and **Jazz at Lincoln Center,** 212/258-9800, www.jazzatlincolncenter.org, up above. Also in the complex will be a Mandarin Oriental Hotel and plenty of shops. The development is expected to be completed in the fall of 2003, but Jazz at Lincoln Center won't move in until the fall of 2004.

Lincoln Center

On the west side of Broadway between 62nd and 66th Streets is the famed Lincoln Center for the Performing Arts, 212/LINCOLN, www.lincolncenter.org, which presents about 3,000 performances each year. Centering on a circular fountain and a wide marble plaza, the 14-acre complex always seems to be filled with well-dressed concertgoers scurrying to get to their seats on time, and pastel-clad sightseers swinging their legs as they sit on the fountain's rim.

Completed in 1969, Lincoln Center was another Robert Moses project. The center aroused much controversy when it was built, due to its displacement of San Juan Hill—a neighborhood named in honor of the black veterans of the Spanish-American War who once lived there. When construction began, over 7,000 families were thrown out of their apartments and, despite city government assurances to the contrary, received little or no relocation assistance. Most resettled in Harlem and the Bronx.

Lincoln Center consists of three major theaters and an assortment of related buildings. **Avery Fisher Hall,** 212/875-5030, on the plaza's north side, is where the New York Philharmonic performs, and where most of the larger classical-music and jazz concerts are presented. The **Metropolitan Opera House,** 212/362-6000, on the plaza's west side, is the center's most ornate building, graced with sparkling multistoried windows and two vivid murals by Marc Chagall. The **New York State Theater,** 212/870-5570, on the plaza's south side, is home to the New York City Opera and the New York City Ballet.

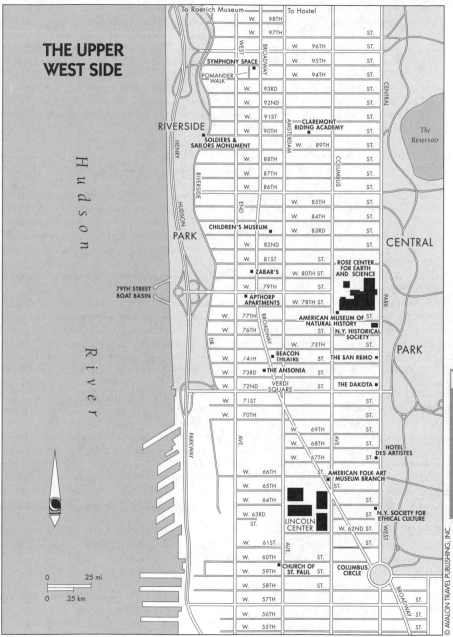

THE UPPER
WEST SIDE

Hudson
River

79TH STREET
BOAT BASIN

To Roerich Museum
To Hostel

W. 98TH
W. 97TH ST.
W. 96TH ST.
W. 95TH ST.
W. 94TH ST.

SYMPHONY SPACE
POMANDER WALK

W. 93RD ST.
W. 92ND ST.
W. 91ST ST.
W. 90TH ST.

RIVERSIDE

CLAREMONT
RIDING ACADEMY

SOLDIERS &
SAILORS MONUMENT

W. 89TH

W. 88TH ST.
W. 87TH ST.
W. 86TH ST.
W. 85TH ST.
W. 84TH ST.

PARK

CHILDREN'S MUSEUM

W. 83RD ST.
W. 82ND ST.
W. 81ST ST.

ZABAR'S

W. 80TH ST.
W. 79TH

APTHORP
APARTMENTS

W. 78TH ST.

W. 77TH
AMERICAN MUSEUM OF
NATURAL HISTORY

W. 76TH
N.Y. HISTORICAL
SOCIETY

W. 75TH

W. 74TH
BEACON
THEATRE

THE SAN REMO

W. 73RD
THE ANSONIA

W. 72ND
VERDI
SQUARE

THE DAKOTA

W. 71ST ST.
W. 70TH ST.

W. 69TH
W. 68TH
W. 67TH

HOTEL
DES ARTISTES

W. 66TH

AMERICAN FOLK ART
MUSEUM BRANCH

W. 65TH
W. 64TH
W. 63RD
ST.

LINCOLN
CENTER

N.Y. SOCIETY FOR
ETHICAL CULTURE

W. 62ND ST.

W. 61ST ST.
W. 60TH ST.
W. 59TH

CHURCH OF
ST. PAUL

COLUMBUS
CIRCLE

W. 58TH ST.
W. 57TH ST.
W. 56TH ST.
W. 55TH ST.

ROSE CENTER
FOR EARTH
AND SCIENCE

CENTRAL

PARK

The
Reservoir

MANHATTAN

0   .25 mi
0   .25 km

MOON

© AVALON TRAVEL PUBLISHING, INC.

Lincoln Center extends to the northwest just beyond Avery Fisher Hall. Here are located the **Vivian Beaumont Theater,** 212/362-7600, which stages Broadway plays and musicals; and the **Lincoln Center Library for the Performing Arts,** 212/870-1630, which stores a vast collection of sheet music and recordings, and presents frequent exhibits on the performing arts.

Ho-hum tours of Lincoln Center leave daily from the concourse level; call 212/875-5350 for information. More interesting tours of the Metropolitan Opera House, 212/769-7020, are also offered. In July and August, the Lincoln Center Festival, 212/875-5928, takes place in and around the arts complex. In late July and early August, **Midsummer Night Swing,** 212/875-5766, offers dancing to live bands on the plaza beneath the stars.

Columbus Avenue

Actually an extension of Ninth Avenue, Columbus Avenue begins just north of the branch of the American Folk Art Museum at 66th Street (see American Folk Art Museum, Midtown) and is packed cheek-by-jowl with shops and restaurants. Just north of Lincoln Center, find numerous coffee bars, ice cream shops, and restaurants. Then around 71st Street begin the clothing and specialty stores.

Hotel des Artistes

At 1 W. 67th St. stands the renowned Hotel des Artistes, its elaborate interior bursting with plush furnishings, dark wooden beams, and mildly erotic murals by Howard Chandler Christy. Originally built to accommodate artists, the 1915 hotel was soon too expensive for anyone but the well-to-do. Famous residents have included Rudoph Valentino, Noel Coward, Norman Rockwell, Isadora Duncan, and former New York mayor John Lindsay. On the building's ground floor is the romantic and pricey **Cafe des Artistes,** 212/877-3500, the setting and filming location of Louis Malle's 1981 film, *My Dinner with Andre.*

James Dean's Apartment

After leaving the Hotel Iroquois (see Bryant Park to the Diamond District under Midtown, above),

Dean settled into a tiny room with a bathroom down the hall at 19 West 68th Street. He was living here when he left for Hollywood in 1954 to shoot his first major film, *East of Eden,* and he returned here in 1955 for what would prove to be an unhappy visit home. According to friends, he was cranky and ill at ease, and blew up at his former girlfriend when she refused to take any money out of his suitcase full of cash. Dean left New York soon thereafter, and died in a car crash nine months later.

CENTRAL PARK WEST

Many of the Upper West Side's most impressive buildings stand sentinel along Central Park West (CPW). Just south of the Hotel des Artistes are the splendid art deco **Century Apartments,** 25 CPW, between 62nd and 63rd Sts.; and **55 CPW,** at 65th Street. Ethel Merman lived in the Century Apartments in the 1930s; Sigourney Weaver's character lived at 55 CPW in *Ghostbusters.*

At the southwest corner of 70th Street is the synagogue of the **Congregation Shearith Israel,** 99 CPW. The nation's oldest Jewish congregation, the Shearith Israel, or "remnant of Israel," dates to 1654 when the first Jewish refugees arrived in the New World after escaping the Spanish Inquisition. Their graveyard near Chinatown is New York City's oldest artifact.

On the southwest corner of 72nd Street and Central Park West is the twin-towered art deco **Majestic,** one of the city's most luxurious apartment houses. Movie director Elia Kazan and entertainer Milton Berle once lived here, along with gangsters Frank Costello, Meyer Lansky, and Lucky Luciano. Costello was shot in the Majestic's lobby on May 2, 1957, but survived the attack and continued to peacefully reside in his penthouse apartment with his wife, their poodle, and Doberman pinscher until he died of natural causes in 1973.

The Dakota

On the northwest corner of 72nd Street and Central Park West is the avenue's most famous apartment building—the Dakota. Built in 1884, the Dakota was financed by Edward Clark, heir to the

© CHRISTIANE BIRD

the grand Dakota apartment building, where innumerable celebrities have lived and outside which John Lennon was murdered in 1980

Singer Sewing Machine fortune. At the time of its construction, the building stood so far north of the rest of Manhattan that it was said to be as remote as Dakota. Clark liked that idea, and had the architect, Henry Hardenburgh, add ears of corn and an Indian's head above the entrance.

Built of light-colored brick, the Dakota resembles a European chateau. A dry moat topped with a cast-iron fence surrounds the building, and a porter in a sentry box guards the front door.

The Dakota's roster of famous tenants may be the most impressive in the city. Among those who've lived here are Lauren Bacall, Judy Holliday, Jack Palance, Roberta Flack, Fannie Hurst, Jose Ferrer, Rosemary Clooney, John Lennon, Yoko Ono, Gilda Radner, and William Henry Pratt, a.k.a. Boris Karloff. Legend has it that on Halloween, the kids in the building were too afraid of Karloff to take any of the trick-or-treat candy he left outside his door.

John Lennon was murdered outside the Dakota on December 8, 1980. His assassin, Mark David Chapman (whose *Double Fantasy* album

Lennon had autographed only six hours earlier), jumped out of the shadows as the star returned home and shot him four times in the back and chest. By the time the cops arrived, Chapman was leaning against the side of the Dakota reading *Catcher in the Rye*. "Please don't hurt me," he said as he was arrested.

Directly across from the Dakota in Central Park is **Strawberry Fields,** the teardrop-shaped acre of land that Yoko Ono had landscaped in her husband's memory.

San Remo

Two blocks north of the Dakota at 74th Street is another famous Upper West Side residence, the mammoth twin-towered **San Remo Apartments,** 145-146 CPW. Home at various times to Dustin Hoffman, Mary Tyler Moore, Raquel Welch, Donald Sutherland, Paul Simon, Tony Randall, and Diane Keaton, the San Remo is also where the legendary actress Rita Hayworth lived at the sad end of her life. A victim of Alzheimer's disease, Hayworth needed nurses round the clock. Up until her death in 1987, a single rose arrived for her daily, sent by her old friend, Glenn Ford.

New-York Historical Society

After a shaky last few years, in which it seemed as if a lack of capital might force a permanent closing, the New-York Historical Society has come back with a roar. Founded in 1806, it was one of the country's first cultural institutions, and now boasts a brand new 17,000-square-foot gallery space. On permanent display are such artifacts as George Washington's Valley Forge cot and exhibits such as Kid City, where kids can learn more about New York circa 1901. Temporary exhibits focus all aspects of the city's history, from immigrant groups to board games.

The society, 2 W. 77th St., at CPW, 212/873-3400, www.nyhistory.org, is open Tues.–Sun. 10 A.M.–5 P.M. Admission is adults $5, children and seniors $3, children under 12 free.

American Museum of Natural History

Though long one of the city's greatest museums, justifiably famous for its breathtaking dioramas, the American Museum of Natural History, CPW

MANHATTAN

at 79th St., 212/769-5100, www.amnh.org, has traditionally been a rather chaotic and musty affair. In 1996, however, the museum—always crowded with hundreds of shouting, shoving, enthusiastic kids—quietly entered the modern era, refurbishing old galleries and introducing new, state-of-the-art exhibitions.

At the heart of the museum's collections are its approximately 100 dinosaur specimens, nearly 85 percent of which are real fossils. Housed beneath soaring windows and ceilings in the renovated Theodore Roosevelt Memorial Hall, the dinosaurs are mounted in dramatic poses, just as they might have appeared millions of years ago while hunting, climbing trees, rearing up, or running. The most amazing skeleton of all is that of a skinny, 50-foot-high barosaurus arching its angry neck high into the dome as it protects its young from the much smaller allosaurus. The collection's smallest artifact is a tiny, fossilized dinosaur embryo, unearthed in the Gobi Desert in 1993.

Other highlights of the museum—which owns about 37 million specimens—include the African Mammals wing, featuring seven furious stampeding elephants; the recently expanded Hall of Human Biology and Evolution, where a holographic "Visible Woman" struts her circulatory stuff; and the brand-new Hall of Primitive Vertebrates, which traces the evolution of the first animals with backbones. Also, be sure to visit at least one of the museum's several gift shops, which are packed with unusual items from around the world.

Adjoining the museum is the **Hayden Planetarium,** which reopened in February 2000, following an extensive, three-year overhaul. Now part of the **Rose Center for Earth and Space,** the new planetarium centers on a state-of-the-art Zeiss sky projector that has more than 30 motors controlled by 45 computers. It is capable of projecting 9,100 stars as viewed from earth, the planets, and beyond.

The museum is open Sun.–Thurs. 10 A.M.–5:45 P.M. and Fri.–Sat. 10 A.M.–8:45 P.M. Suggested admission is adults $10, students and seniors $7.50, children under 12 $6. Call for planetarium hours and prices.

BROADWAY AND AMSTERDAM

At the busy intersection of 72nd Street and Broadway is **Verdi Square,** complete with a statue of composer Giuseppe Verdi, erected in 1906. Though much cleaned up in recent years, this small triangle of green was once known as Needle Park. At one point, 25 percent of New York's heroin addicts were believed to live within a few blocks of here; the 1971 movie *Panic in Needle Park* was filmed here. Immediately across from Verdi Square is one of the only original subway kiosks still left in the city. Built to look like a Dutch cottage, the structure (now undergoing a $53 million renovation) dates back to 1904, when the IRT first reached the Upper West Side.

Of Murder and Madams

At 250 W. 72nd St., between Broadway and West End, once stood Tweed's, the tavern where schoolteacher Roseanne Quinn met psychopath John Wayne Williams on New Year's Eve, 1973. The pair were strangers when they met, but they danced and partied for hours and then crossed the street to Quinn's apartment at 253 W. 72nd St., where Williams stabbed Quinn to death. That killing became the inspiration for Judith Rossner's book, *Looking for Mr. Goodbar,* later made into a movie starring Diane Keaton and Richard Gere. Williams was eventually arrested; he killed himself in jail.

Yet another infamous New York address is two blocks north at 307 W. 74th St., between West End and Riverside. This solid, innocuous-looking brownstone is where the Mayflower Madam, Sydney Biddle Barrows, conducted her $1-million-a-year prostitution ring from 1979 to 1984. The daughter of blue bloods listed in the Social Register, Barrows never served time for running her 300-woman service; instead she copped a plea and paid a mere $5,000 fine. That light sentencing probably had something to do with her "black book" listing the names of her rich and famous clients, who were *very* interested in keeping the case from going to trial. Barrows has since gone on to write several best-selling books, and runs seminars teaching women "call girl secrets that work."

The Ansonia

From 72nd Street north, Broadway is a mix of ornate old apartment buildings, specialty food stores, and dingy, hole-in-the-wall shops. At the northwest corner of Broadway and 73rd Street is the extraordinary, though now somewhat worn, beaux arts Ansonia. Covered with towers, mansard roofs, balconies, and gargoyles, this opulent building had all the state-of-the-art amenities of its day when it opened in 1903, including electric stoves, air-conditioning, freezers, a pneumatic tube system for delivering messages, two swimming pools, a lobby fountain complete with playful seals, and a roof garden inhabited by a bear.

The building also had incredibly thick walls, which meant that its rooms were among the most soundproof in the city. This feature attracted many famous musicians to take up residence, including Enrico Caruso, Igor Stravinsky, Arturo Toscanini, Enzio Pinza, and Lily Pons. Theatrical impresario Florenz Ziegfeld moved into the building as well, living with his wife on one floor and keeping a mistress on another.

Members of the 1919 Chicago White Sox were staying at the Ansonia when they conspired to fix the World Series that year. Babe Ruth moved into the building in 1920 when he joined the New York Yankees, and stayed until 1929. Entertainer Bette Midler got her start in a gay spa that occupied the Ansonia's basement in the early 1960s. Some of this history is chronicled in an informal exhibit in the Ansonia's lobby.

Children's Museum of Manhattan

The bright and cheery Children's Museum, 212 W. 83rd St., between Broadway and Amsterdam Ave., 212/721-1223, www.cmom.org, is full of hands-on exhibits for kids ages 2–10. Here, children can draw and paint, learn crafts, play at being newscasters, listen to stories, or just explore one of the ever-changing play areas. The museum is open Wed.–Sun. 10 A.M.–5 P.M. Admission is $6, free to children up to age one.

Amsterdam Avenue

Though it lacks the foot traffic of Broadway and the cachet of Columbus, Amsterdam Avenue—running parallel between the two—has a scruffy

appeal. Home to a mix of neighborhood stores and Spanish bodegas, boisterous bars, and trendy restaurants, it attracts a multicultural crowd, especially at night when the avenue comes alive.

WEST END AND RIVERSIDE

Heading west of Broadway anywhere between 72nd and 106th Streets, you'll come first to West End Avenue and then to Riverside Drive, two peaceful residential thoroughfares. West End Avenue is straight and very wide, filled with one big boxy red-brick apartment building after another. Riverside Drive is more exclusive and curvaceous, lined with a mix of mansions, townhouses, and smart apartment buildings.

Many well-known people have lived on or just off these two streets. Marlon Brando was living with his mother and two sisters at 270 West End Ave., at 73rd St., when he was a young actor appearing in the Broadway play *I Remember Mama*. George Gershwin was living at 33 Riverside Dr., at 75th St., when he finished writing *Porgy and Bess*. Babe Ruth lived at 100 Riverside Dr., at 83rd St., from 1942 until 1948, when he died of throat cancer at age 53. Spencer Tracy resided at 790 West End Ave., between 98th and 99th Sts., while studying at the American Academy of Dramatic Arts.

Miles Davis bought the handsome red townhouse—once a Russian Orthodox church—at 312 W. 77th St., between West End and Riverside, in the early 1960s. He had a gym and music room installed in the basement, and recorded many important albums while living here, including *In a Silent Way* and *Bitches Brew*. Davis sold the place in the early 1980s, when he and Cicely Tyson started living together.

In 1918, William Randolph Hearst bought the multimillion-dollar home at 331 Riverside Dr., at 105th St., for his mistress, musical comedy star Marion Davies. He then spent another cool million redecorating it for her. Ironically, the lovely beaux arts building today houses the Buddhist Academy of the Jodo Shinshu sect.

Pomander Walk

Tucked between Broadway and West End Avenue on 94th Street is Pomander Walk, a tiny

MANHATTAN

Tudor street blocked off by iron gates. Built in 1921 to resemble the set of a hit play of that same name, the street has been home to a number of celebrities over the years, including Humphrey Bogart, Rosalind Russell, and Lillian and Dorothy Gish. In 1986, Woody Allen set several scenes from *Hannah and Her Sisters* here.

Humphrey Bogart was born not far away from Pomander Walk at 245 W. 103rd St., just east of West End Ave., in 1899. The son of a surgeon and a magazine illustrator, Bogart—unlike the tough-guy characters he would later play—grew up in an upper middle-class world. He attended fashionable private schools, including Phillips Academy in Andover, Massachusetts (from which he was expelled for "excessive high spirits"), then joined the Navy. He took up acting in his mid-20s.

Riverside Park and the Boat Basin

Riverside Drive abuts Riverside Park, a long and narrow sloping slice of green that stretches from 72nd to 153rd Street along the Hudson River. Designed in the 1870s by Frederick Law Olmsted and Calvert Vaux, the park is a pleasant, though well worn, place with glorious views of the Hudson.

Near the south end of the park is the low-key, somewhat neglected **79th Street Boat Basin,** where a number of houseboats are docked. Go by here on a weekday morning and you'll see Federal Express making deliveries just as if this were any other street.

Nicholas Roerich Museum

This odd little museum at 319 W. 107th St., near Riverside Dr., 212/864-7752, www.roerich.org, is dedicated to Nicholas Roerich—artist, philosopher, scientist, and humanitarian. Born in Russia in 1874, Roerich painted over 6,000 paintings, wrote over 30 books, conducted extensive archaeological research in Russia and Central Asia, and authored the Roerich Pact, an agreement for international protection that was signed by the heads of 21 nations, including Pres. Franklin D. Roosevelt.

Visiting the Roerich Museum is a bit like visiting the home of a family friend. Upon ringing a buzzer, you enter a cozy house complete with a piano, fireplaces, Oriental vases, and dozens upon dozens of bright paintings hung willy-nilly along the walls and staircase well. No one grunts much more than a hello, and you are free to wander about as you please.

The museum is open Tues.–Sun. 2–5 P.M. Admission is by donation.

SHOPPING
Books and Music

Applause Theatre Books, 211 W. 71st St., just west of Broadway, 212/496-7511, specializes in drama. **Gryphon Bookshop,** 2246 Broadway, at 80th St., 212/362-0706, is a good shop for secondhand books and records. The **Barnes & Noble** megastore at 2289 Broadway, between 82nd and 83rd Sts., 212/362-8835, features a cafe and frequent readings. **Murder Ink,** 2486 Broadway, between 92nd and 93rd Sts., 212/362-8905, sells mysteries new and old.

Tower Records, 1961 Broadway, at 66th St., 212/799-2500, stocks a huge inventory of recordings, and features a music-video computer that lets you preview songs before buying. The store is open until midnight daily. **Gryphon Records,** 233 W. 72nd St., between Broadway and West End, 212/874-1588, is a collector's paradise selling many rare recordings.

Clothing

Many chain clothing stores such as **J. Crew, Banana Republic** and **The Gap** are located along Columbus Avenue. Designer **Laura Ashley** has a store at 398 Columbus Ave., at 79th St., 212/496-5110. **Off Broadway,** 139 W. 72nd St., off Broadway, 212/724-6713, sells secondhand clothes once worn by stars.

Food Shops

Zabar's, 2245 Broadway, at 80th St., 212/787-2000, is the city's most beloved food store. Dating back to the 1930s, when it moved to Broadway from Brooklyn, Zabar's sells over 10,000 pounds of coffee, 10 tons of cheese, and 1,000 pounds of salmon a week, not to mention pots and pans, microwave ovens, vacuum cleaners, and the like. Some 10,000 customers are said to pass through its friendly portals on a Saturday afternoon. The best time to come is week-days before 5 P.M.

Citarella's, 2135 Broadway, at 75th St., 212/874-0383, is a fish market known for its window displays.

Other Shops

La Belle Époque, 280 Columbus Ave., near 73rd St., 212/362-1770, specializes in French posters of the 1890s and 1900s.

Maxilla & Mandible, 451 Columbus Ave., near 81st St., 212/724-6173, offers a most unusual assortment of skulls, skeletons, bones, teeth, beetles, butterflies, seashells, and fossils.

Flea Markets

An indoor/outdoor flea market is held every Sunday 10 A.M.–5:30 P.M. at P.S. 44, on Columbus Avenue between 76th and 77th Streets.

ACCOMMODATIONS

$50–100

Entering the cheerful **Malibu Studios Hotel,** 2688 Broadway, at 103rd St., 212/222-2954 or 800/647-2227, www.malibuhotelnyc.com, is like entering a giant swimming pool. The hallways are painted a bright aqua blue with a bubble and wave motif, while stenciled palm trees adorn the lobby. Rooms are basic but clean, and most share bathrooms. Free passes to nightclubs are often available. $79 s or d with shared bath, $129 s or d with private bath.

The stark, red brick **Riverside Tower Hotel,** 80 Riverside Drive, at 80th St., 212/877-5200 or 800/724-3136, is not much to look at, but its rooms are serviceable and clean. Many feature great views of the Hudson River; downstairs is a sunny lobby furnished in rattan. $95 s, $100–110 d.

$150–250

Country Inn the City, W. 77th St., between Broadway and West End Ave., 212/580-4183, www.countryinnthecity.com, is a lovely landmark townhouse with four bed-and-breakfast units, all equipped with a large bedroom, sitting area, and antiques. $170 s or d.

The friendly **Hotel Beacon,** 2130 Broadway, at 75th St., 212/787-1100 or 800/572-4969, offers good value for the money. Its rooms are large and attractive and equipped with two double beds and kitchenettes. The lobby gleams with black-and-white marble and brass. $180–225 s or d.

Though now more pricey than it once was, the well-maintained **Excelsior,** 45 W. 81st St., between CPW and Columbus Ave., 212/362-9200 or 800/368-4575, has been a favorite among budget travelers for decades. Its handsome, step-down lobby is adorned with dark woods, mirrors, and wrought iron; $139–229 s or d.

The comfortable, 365-room **Mayflower,** 15 Central Park West, at 61st St., 212/265-0060, www.mayflowerhotel.com, is an Upper West Side institution, known for both its Old World charm and great views of Central Park. It's especially popular among musicians, opera singers, and ballet dancers, all in town to perform at Lincoln Center. $185–205 s, $200–260 d. Rooms with park views cost extra.

The stylish **On the Ave Hotel,** 2178 Broadway, at 77th St., 212/362-1100 or 800/509-7598, www.ontheave-nyc.com, is a welcome new addition to the Upper West Side. Rooms feature canopied beds, original artwork, and industrial-style bathrooms. $200–280 s or d.

Hostel, YMCA

One of the cheapest places to stay in New York is the **Hosteling International New York,** 891 Amsterdam Ave., between 103rd and 104th Sts., 212/932-2300. www.hinewyork.org. Occupying a block-long landmark building designed by Richard Morris Hunt, this hostel is the nation's largest, with 90 clean, dorm-style rooms each sleeping four to eight in bunk beds, as well as some family rooms. Also on the premises are kitchens, lounges, coin-operated laundry machines, and a garden. The hostel's only real drawback is its off-the-beaten-track location.

You must be a Hosteling International–American Youth Hostel member to stay in the hostel, and reservations should be made two to three months in advance. Rates are $29–35 per person for dorm rooms, $120 for a family room, and $135 for a private room with bath. Hosteling

MANHATTAN

International–American Youth Hostel annual membership fees are adults $25, seniors $15, youth under 18 $10, and families $35; call 202/783-6161 for more information, or visit www.hiayh.org.

West Side YMCA, 5 W. 63rd St., near CPW, 212/875-4100, www.ymcanyc.org, offers many small rooms with shared bath for $80 s, 90 d, and a few slightly larger rooms with private baths for $130 s or d. The rooms themselves are quite clean, but the shared bathrooms and halls are a bit grungy. Reserve well in advance.

Jazz on the Park, 36 W. 106th St., between Central Park West and Manhattan Ave., 212/932-1600, www.jazzhostel.com, offers small basic rooms and a basement lounge that features live jazz and hip hop on the weekends. $27–35 per person for dorm rooms, $68 d for private room.

FOOD

American

Tasty homemade soups and breads are the specialties at **Popover Cafe,** 551 Amsterdam Ave., between 86th and 87th Sts., 212/595-8555; average main dish $10. **Good Enough to Eat,** 483 Amsterdam Ave., near 80th St., 212/496-0163, serves hearty brunches; average main dish $11. The long-time, no-frills, neighborhood institution **Barney Greengrass,** 541 Amsterdam Ave., between 86th and 87th Sts., 212/724-4707, offers traditional bagels and lox; average main dish $9.

Located directly across from Lincoln Center, the **Saloon,** 1920 Broadway, at 64th St., 212/874-1500, is an enormous restaurant with an enormous menu and outdoor tables perfectly suited for people-watching; average entrée $13.

In Central Park, the sleek, upscale **Boat House,** on East Dr., near 72nd St., 212/517-2233, serves grilled meats and fish, salads, and sandwiches on a patio overlooking the lake; average dinner entrée $19. A traditional New York favorite for celebrating graduations and the like is the festive **Tavern-on-the-Green,** CPW and 67th St., 212/873-3200, ablaze with mirrors, chandeliers, and 350,000 lightbulbs. The menu features imaginative American and continental cuisine; average entrée $27.

Asian

The popular **Empire Szechuan Gourmet,** 2574 Broadway, at 97th St., 212/663-6004, is one of a reliable chain; average entrée $10. **Jo-An Japanese,** 2707 Broadway, between 103rd and 104th Sts., 212/678-2103, is a homey family-run restaurant with a menu ranging from teriyaki to sushi; average entrée $12. The **Limeleaf,** 2799 Broadway, at 108th St., 212/864-5000, serves tasty Thai and seafood dishes; average entrée $12.

French

Housed in the turn-of-the-century Hotel des Artistes is **Cafe des Artistes,** 1 W. 67th St., at CPW, 212/877-3500, a plush and romantic belle époque spot known for its superb French food and naked nymphs cavorting on the walls; average entrée $30. The art deco **Cafe Luxembourg,** 200 W. 70th St., near Amsterdam Ave., 212/873-7411, is sister restaurant to the Odeon downtown. Still a hot spot after all these years, it offers an excellent menu, zinc bar, rattan chairs, and a lively late-night scene; average entrée $21.

Italian

The streamlined **Isola,** 485 Columbus Ave., between 83rd and 84th Sts., 212/362-7400, serves tasty Northern Italian fare cooked in a wood-burning oven; average entrée $14. **Meridiana,** 2756 Broadway, between 105th and 106th Sts., 212/222-4453, is a friendly place with good food, slow service, and a relaxing outdoor garden; average entrée $11.

Latin/Caribbean

The hole-in-the-wall **La Caridad,** 2199 Broadway, at 78th St., 212/874-2780, is the best of the Cuban-Chinese restaurants in this part of town—just look at the long line of cab drivers out front; average main dish $7. The no-frills **Cafe con Leche,** 424 Amsterdam Ave., at 80th St., 212/595-7000, and 726 Amsterdam Ave., between 95th and 96th Sts., 212/678-7000, is a modern Latin diner with first-rate beans and rice; average main dish $9.

Popular **Gabriela's,** 685 Amsterdam Ave., at 93rd St., 212/961-0574, and 311 Amsterdam Ave., at 75th St., 212/875-8532, offers authentic

Mexican cooking in an inviting spot accented with desert murals. The cheese-and-spinach-stuffed eggplant and *posole* (traditional Mexican stew) are especially good; average entrée $12.

Elegant yet laid-back **Calle Ocho,** 446 Columbus Ave., between 81st and 82nd Sts., 212/873-5025, offers Nuevo Latino cuisine to an enthusiastic following; average entrée $20.

Soul/Southern

The stylish **Shark Bar,** 307 Amsterdam Ave., between 74th and 75th Sts., 212/874-8500, is part soul-food restaurant, part hip late-night hangout; average entrée $16.

Other Ethnic

Tiny **Awash,** 947 Amsterdam Ave., between 106th and 107th Sts., 212/961-1416, is one of the best of the Ethiopian restaurants that dot the Upper West Side; average entrée $10. For tasty Middle Eastern fare, along with live jazz and a classy circular bar, try **Cleopatra's Needle,** 2485 Broadway, between 92nd and 93rd Sts., 212/769-6969; average entrée $12. At the **World Cafe,** 201 Columbus Ave., at 69th St., 212/799-8090, you can sample an eclectic mix of dishes from around the world; average main course $10.

Light Bites

In Central Park, food vendors set up shop in various locations, including near Central Park Wildlife Center and Bethesda Terrace, and in the Mineral Springs Pavilion just north of Sheep Meadow. An outdoor cafe and snack bar abut the model-boat pond.

A number of outdoor/indoor cafes are near Lincoln Center. Most are crowded and over-priced, but they're all excellent for peoplewatching. Among them is the tiny **Opera Expresso Cafe,** 1928 Broadway, near 64th St., 212/799-3050. During warm weather, a pricey outdoor cafe operates near Lincoln Center's fountain.

Cafe Mozart, 154 W. 70th St., near Broadway, 212/595-9797, serves especially good desserts. Funky **Gray's Papaya,** 2090 Broadway, at 72nd St., 212/799-0243, sells some of the city's best cheap hot dogs—to be eaten standing up.

Watering Holes and Lounges

Time Out, 349 Amsterdam Ave., between 76th and 77th Sts., 212/362-5400, is a popular sports bar. For punk rock millennium-style, head over to the **Ding Dong Lounge,** 929 Columbus Ave., between 105th and 106th Sts., 212/663-2600. The uptown version of the **Raccoon Lodge,** 480 Amsterdam Ave., at 83rd St., 212/874-9984, re-creates the laid-back pleasures of the downtown original. The friendly **Dive Bar,** 732 Amsterdam Ave., at 96th St., 212/749-4358 and **Dive 75,** 101 W. 75th St., at Columbus, 212/362 7518 are all decked out in aquatic themes.

At the often-packed **Boat Basin Cafe,** 79th St. at the Hudson River, 212/496-5542, you can watch the boating life along the Hudson River.

Two popular Irish pubs are the rowdy **Dublin House,** 225 W. 79th St., between Broadway and Amsterdam Ave., 212/874-9528, which boasts a good jukebox; and the more low-key **Emerald Inn,** 205 Columbus Ave., near 70th St., 212/874-8840.

Among the restaurants mentioned above, Cafe Luxembourg and the Shark Bar both have late-night bar scenes.

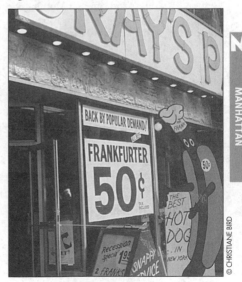

Gray's Papaya makes no secret of its trademark cheap eats.

Harlem and Upper Manhattan

Stretching roughly from 110th to 168th Streets, between the Harlem and Hudson Rivers, Harlem is one of the city's most historic and least understood neighborhoods. Often written off as a crime-infested no-man's-land, it's actually a diverse place, with many streets that are well-worn rather than raw, and a landscape studded with an impressive number of elegant brownstones and churches. Harlem has more than its share of crime and poverty, but it also has many attractions, and is currently on the upswing. Middle-class New Yorkers—black and white—are moving back in, and property values are rising, to the loud lament of the locals. Former president Bill Clinton also brought much attention to the neighborhood when he opened his post–White House office here (at 55 W. 125th St.).

The area is divided into West/Central Harlem—composed mostly of African Americans—and East Harlem, home to many Latinos and a smaller number of Italians. West of Morningside Park between 110th and 125th Streets is **Morningside Heights,** where Columbia University is located; to the north of 155th Street is **Washington Heights,** home to the Cloisters. Harlem and the Heights are considerably hillier than the rest of Manhattan; here you'll find steep streets, gentle valleys, and magnificent bluffs overlooking the Hudson.

History

Established as Niew Haarlem in 1658, Harlem remained a quiet farming community until 1837. Then the Harlem Railroad arrived, bringing with it hundreds of new settlers. In 1873, the village was annexed to the city, and by the early 1900s, it was an affluent white suburb.

In 1901, the IRT subway was extended along Lenox Avenue and wealthy speculators, seeing the chance to make millions, built row after row of attractive townhouses. But they overextended themselves, and sales were slow. When a black realtor offered to fill the empty buildings with black tenants, the developers jumped at the chance. Fearing racial changes, the neighborhood's white residents fled.

During the 1920s and '30s, Harlem was the country's African American cultural center. The Harlem Renaissance bloomed, attracting writers and intellectuals such as Langston Hughes and W. E. B. DuBois, while the streets were jammed with jazz clubs, theaters, dance halls,

LANGSTON HUGHES ON HARLEM

Harlem, like a Picasso painting in his Cubistic period. Harlem—Southern Harlem—the Carolinas, Georgia, Florida—looking for the Promised Land—and ending up in the subway at morning rush time—headed downtown. West Indian Harlem—warm rambunctious sassy remembering Marcus Garvey. Haitian Harlem, Cuban Harlem, little pockets of tropical dreams in alien tongues. Magnet Harlem, pulling an Arthur Schomburg from Puerto Rico, pulling an Arna Bontemps all the way from California, a Nora Holt from way out West, an E. Simms Campbell from St. Louis, likewise a Josephine Baker, a Charles S. Johnson from Virginia, an A. Philip Randolph from Florida, a Roy Wilkins from Minnesota, an Alta Douglas from Kansas. Melting-pot Harlem—Harlem of honey and chocolate and caramel and rum and vinegar and lemon and lime and gall. Dusky dream Harlem rumbling into a nightmare tunnel where the subway from the Bronx keeps right on downtown, where the money from the nightclubs goes right back downtown, where the jazz is drained to Broadway, whence Josephine goes to Paris, Robeson to London, Jean Toomer to a Quaker Meeting House, Garvey to the Atlanta Federal Penitentiary, and Wallace Thurman to his grave; but Duke Ellington to fame and fortune, Lena Horne to Broadway, and Buck Clayton to China.

Langston Hughes,
"My Early Days in Harlem"

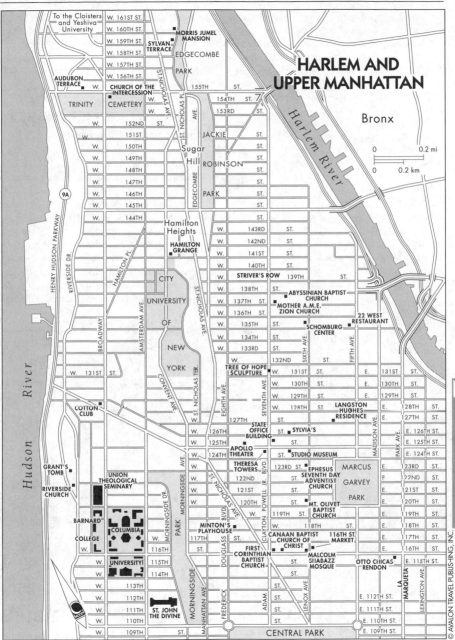

HARLEM AND UPPER MANHATTAN

and speakeasies. Duke Ellington played at the Cotton Club, Chick Webb at the Savoy.

Harlem lost much of this vibrancy during and after the Depression, when poverty began taking a stronger hold. In the '60s, however, civil rights leaders Malcolm X, Stokely Carmichael, and others turned the neighborhood into a mecca for black consciousness.

Today, Harlem, for all its continuing problems with poverty and drugs, is in the midst of what many are calling a Second Renaissance. Some middle-class residents have moved back in, tourism is returning, and there's a growing citywide awareness of the need to preserve the neighborhood's historic and cultural landmarks. Blocks are being rehabilitated, new jazz joints are flourishing, and more businesses are opening up, especially around 125th Street. The newish **Harlem USA Mall,** complete with the area's first Disney Store and The Gap, stands not far from the recently renovated Apollo.

Orientation

Though Harlem has a notorious reputation for crime, much of it can safely be explored on foot. The areas around 116th Street, 125th Street, and the Schomburg Center, especially, are always crowded with people. It's still best to stick to the main and populated streets, however, and avoid the parks completely. If you're white, you may encounter some hostility, but then, too, you'll also encounter much friendliness.

The following list of sights begins near Columbia University, then heads east (cross on 110th or 125th Streets; don't go through Morningside Park) to the Lenox Ave.–116th Street area. Next comes a foray into *El Barrio,* or Spanish Harlem, followed by an exploration of 125th Street, and a zigzagging route uptown. Subway directions are included to the more distant sights.

In Harlem, many of the numbered avenues take on proper names. Sixth Avenue becomes Lenox Avenue or Malcolm X Boulevard; Seventh Avenue becomes Adam Clayton Powell Jr. Boulevard (ACP Blvd.); and Eighth Avenue becomes Frederick Douglass Boulevard.

First-time visitors should be sure to visit the Cathedral of St. John the Divine, 116th Street, 125th Street, the Studio Museum in Harlem, the Apollo, and the Morris-Jumel Mansion. Organized tours are also a good way to see Harlem the first time around (see Tours in the New York City introduction).

COLUMBIA UNIVERSITY AREA
Cathedral of St. John the Divine

The world's largest Gothic cathedral is on Amsterdam Ave. at W. 112th St., 212/316-7540, www.stjohndivine.org. Said to be large enough to fit both Notre Dame and Chartres inside, it accommodates some 10,000 people and is still under construction. Scheduled completion date, *if* enough money becomes available: 2050.

Begun in 1892, the cathedral's imposing but still towerless facade is covered with stone carvings and bronze sculptures. Inside, it's a vast and cavernous space with endless rows of seats, many floor inscriptions ("Live all you can; it's a mistake

The Cathedral of St. John the Divine will not be completed before the year 2050.

© CHRISTIANE BIRD

not to."—Henry James; "Out of space—out of time."—Edgar Allan Poe), and several chapels housing changing exhibits. To the rear is an excellent gift shop—destroyed by fire in late 2001, but now operational again—while out back is a workshop where you can see stonemasons at work. Immediately south of the cathedral is its Peace Fountain, lined with an odd and whimsical mix of figures and animals, many of them sculpted by schoolchildren.

In addition to its regular services, the cathedral stages concerts and special events. One of the most wonderful is the Blessing of the Animals, held every October on Saint Francis of Assisi's feast day. The event draws thousands of New Yorkers into the church with a hodgepodge of animals in tow.

The cathedral is open Mon.–Sat. 7 A.M.–6 P.M., Sunday 7 A.M.–8:30 P.M. Tours are given Tues.–Sat. at 11 A.M., Sunday at 1 P.M.; cost is $3.

Columbia University and Vicinity

The campus of Columbia University stretches from West 114th Street to West 120th Street, between Amsterdam Avenue and Broadway, www.columbia.edu. Founded as King's College in 1754, it educated some of the country's earliest leaders, including Alexander Hamilton—the first secretary of the treasury—and John Jay, first chief justice of the U.S. Supreme Court. Free tours are given year-round; call 212/854-4900 for more information.

Across Broadway from Columbia is **Barnard College,** 212/854-5262, founded in 1899 by Frederick A. P. Barnard, a former president of Columbia and a champion of higher education for women. The college is especially well known for its anthropology department; among its alumni are Margaret Mead and Zora Neale Hurston.

North of Columbia are three more prestigious educational institutions. **Teachers College,** where John Dewey once taught, is on the east side of Broadway between 120th and 121st Streets; **Union Theological Seminary,** known for its liberal thought and social activism, is on the west side between 120th and 122nd Streets; and the **Jewish Theological Seminary**—with a light burning in its tower in remembrance of the Holocaust victims—is at the northeast corner of 122nd Street and Broadway.

Grant's Tomb

High on a bluff overlooking the Hudson is General Grant's National Memorial, 122nd St. and Riverside Dr., 212/666-1640, an imposing mausoleum where the former president and his wife are buried. The site is run by the National Park Service.

Hours are daily 9 A.M.–5 P.M. Admission is free.

Riverside Church

Next door to Grant's Tomb is the Gothic-inspired Riverside Church, 490 Riverside Dr., between 120th and 122nd Sts., 212/870-6700. Built in the 1920s, the church is home to an impressive 74-bell carillon, donated to the church by the Rockefeller family. The carillon's 20-ton bell is the world's largest; the carillon's smallest bell weighs only 10 pounds. The carillon tower, offering grand views of upper Manhattan, is generally open to visitors Tues.–Sat. 11 A.M.–4 P.M. and Sunday 12:15–4 P.M., but it's best to call in advance. Admission is $1.

RANDOLPH SQUARE AREA
Minton's Playhouse

One of the greatest revolutions in jazz was spawned in a neighborhood club run by one-time bandleader Teddy Hill in the Cecil Hotel, 210 W. 118th St., just west of St. Nicholas Avenue. Hill hired a house band that included pianist Thelonious Monk and drummer Kenny Clarke, and soon the small, dark place was packed every night with talent eager to jam. Dizzy Gillespie, Charlie Parker, Charlie Christian, and Max Roach were among the regulars who came here to experiment with a brand-new style of jazz that came to be called bebop. Still hanging in the back of the club is a striking mural depicting four musicians, two of whom have been identified as Tony Scott and Charlie Christian.

For years, plans have been in the works to restore Minton's—now on the National Register of Historic Places. But the project, once backed by

MANHATTAN

Robert DeNiro and his restaurateur partner Drew Nieporent, has stalled, due to investors are wary of signing onto this $3.1 million project.

Today, the renovated Cecil Hotel houses apartments for the elderly. It sits on the edge of **A. Phillip Randolph Square,** at the intersection of ACP Blvd., St. Nicholas Ave., and 117th Street. Randolph organized the Brotherhood of Sleeping Car Porters, and in 1941 persuaded President Roosevelt to establish the Fair Employment Practices Commission which made it possible for blacks to work in defense jobs.

Two Baptist Churches

At the corner of Adam Clayton Powell Jr. Boulevard and 116th Street is **First Corinthian Baptist Church,** a playful building covered with a multitude of colored tiles. The building was once the Regent Theater, completed in 1913 as the city's first deluxe movie palace. Before that, movies had been shown in storefronts or tiny vaudeville theaters. In its heyday, the Regent had its own eight-piece orchestra, pipe organ, uniformed ushers, and printed programs.

Just east of the First Corinthian is **Canaan Baptist Church of Christ,** 132 W. 116th St., 212/866-0301, known for its high-spirited gospel choirs. Call ahead for service times.

Malcolm Shabazz Mosque

The silver-domed mosque topped with a star and a crescent at 102 W. 116th St., at Lenox Ave., 212/662-2200, is named after civil-rights leader Malcolm X, who taught here in the 1960s just before his break with the Black Muslims. After his death, the mosque was firebombed.

On the busy block surrounding the mosque are the **Malcolm Shabazz Harlem Market** (see Shopping, below), a hodgepodge of small Muslim-run businesses, and the **Shabazz Restaurant.** Established by Malcolm X, the restaurant was once famous for its bean pies and health food. Today, it's under different ownership, and a sign reads, "Shabazz Fried Chicken—The Name You Can Trust."

EL BARRIO

Heading farther east on 116th Street, you'll come to the heart of Spanish Harlem, a lively area filled with discount clothing stores, toy shops, beauty and wig salons, storefront churches, bakeries selling towering wedding cakes, pet stores selling homing pigeons, botanicas, ice cream vendors, and the sounds of salsa.

Composed of a motley array of buildings—you'll find few fine churches or brownstones here—East Harlem has been run-down ever since the late 1800s, when it attracted large numbers of recent German, Scandinavian, Italian, and Irish immigrants. The Hispanics, most of whom are Puerto Rican, Cuban, and Dominican, began moving here in the 1920s, with the largest influx arriving just after WW II.

At Park Avenue between 116th and 111th Streets is **La Marqueta,** a large indoor market selling fruits and vegetables, meats and poultry. Here you can pick up Puerto Rican specialties such as beef tripe, conches, plantains, and papayas.

International Salsa Museum

Located in the back of a neighborhood stationery shop, the International Salsa Museum, 2127 Third Ave., at 116th St., 212/289-1368, www.intlsalsamuseum.homestead.com, is a friendly spot dedicated to Latin music. On display are musical instruments, photographs, record covers, and personal mementos, and musicians from the neighborhood—some well known, some not—often stop by to shoot the breeze with visitors.

The museum is open Sat.–Sun. noon–7 P.M. Suggested donation is $2.

LENOX AVENUE CHURCHES

Heading north on Lenox from the Malcolm Shabazz Mosque, you'll pass one enormous church after another, along with a number of grand old funeral homes. At W. 120th St. is the 1907 **Mt. Olivet Baptist Church,** originally one of New York's most elegant synagogues. At W. 122nd St. is the 1888 **St. Martin's,** a Romanesque church known for its carillon and stained-glass windows. At W. 123rd St. is the

1887 **Ephesus Seventh Day Adventist Church,** notable for its lofty spire.

125TH STREET

The heart of Harlem is 125th Street, always alive with vibrant colors, sights, and sounds. As the neighborhood's main commercial drag for decades, 125th Street has had many ups and downs. It's currently riding an optimistic wave, with more businesses in operation here today than at any other time in recent history. The street is also home to three major Harlem landmarks—the Studio Museum in Harlem, the Theresa, and the Apollo.

Just south of 125th Street, on Fifth Avenue, is **Marcus Garvey Park,** lined with elegant brownstones, some of which are open to the public several times a year. For more information, call the Mount Morris Park Community Improvement Association at 212/369-4241.

Studio Museum in Harlem

The Studio Museum, 144 W. 125th St., between Lenox Ave. and ACP Blvd., 212/864-4500, www.studiomuseuminharlem.org, was founded in 1968 in a small factory loft. Today, it's a first-class institution spread over several well-lit floors of a turn-of-the-century building. The "principal center for the study of Black art in America," its permanent display features works by such masters as Romare Bearden, James Van-DerZee, and Jacob Lawrence.

The Studio is also known for excellent temporary exhibits, showcasing both world-renowned and emerging artists, and its lively lecture, concert, and performance series. A tempting gift shop is on the ground floor.

Hours are Wed.–Thurs. noon–6 P.M., Friday noon–8 P.M., Sat.–Sun. 10 A.M.–6 P.M. Admission is adults $5, students and seniors $3, children under 12 $1. Free first Saturday of each month.

Note: Art lovers may also want to head one block north and several blocks west of the museum to visit **The Project,** 427 W. 126th St., between Morningside and Amsterdam Aves., 212/662-8610, one of the best of Harlem's new art galleries.

Theresa Hotel

The glistening white-brick Theresa, 2090 ACP Blvd., at 125th St., was once Harlem's largest and most famous hotel. Among the notables who stayed here were musicians Lena Horne, Jimi Hendrix, Dizzy Gillespie, Lester Young, Milt Hinton, and Andy Kirk (who managed the place in the late 1950s). Boxer Joe Louis stayed here as well.

In 1960, Cuban leader Fidel Castro and his 85-member entourage checked into the Theresa after checking out of a downtown hotel due to what Castro considered to be poor treatment. Castro was in town to deliver an address to the United Nations, and while he was staying at the Theresa, thousands of demonstrators and Soviet leader Nikita Khrushchev stopped by to show their support.

The Theresa is now an office building. In 1990, Nelson Mandela, then the leader of the South African antiapartheid movement, held a huge rally outside the hotel's doors to celebrate his release from prison.

The Apollo

Perhaps the single most important landmark in the history of African American music, the recently renovated Apollo, 253 W. 125th St., between ACP and Frederick Douglass Blvds., 212/749-5838, has hosted nearly every major jazz, blues, R&B, and soul artist to come along. Bessie Smith, Ella Fitzgerald, Billie Holiday, Duke Ellington, Louis Armstrong, Count Basie, Fats Waller, Ray Charles, James Brown, The Ink Spots, Mahalia Jackson, Aretha Franklin, Diana Ross, Al Green, Gladys Knight, and Michael Jackson all played the Apollo, and the list could go on and on. It is said that when a teenage Elvis Presley first came to New York, the one place he wanted to see was the Apollo. The same was later said of the Beatles.

Originally built in 1913, the Apollo was once Hurtig & Seamon's New Burlesque Theatre, known for presenting vaudeville to a Harlem that was then predominantly white. Back in those days, the best seats in the house cost a whopping $1.65.

By 1935, the neighborhood's racial mix had

MANHATTAN

shifted, and the two-balconied theater, capable of seating 2,000, became famous for its Amateur Nights. Lena Horne was one of the unfortunate ones—the audience booed and threw pennies at her, driving her off the stage.

The Apollo was closed down in the late 1970s. In the early 1980s, Percy Sutton—a NAACP official and cofounder of the Inner City Broadcasting Corp.—bought the abandoned building, which at that time was flooded and full of rats. After a several-million-dollar renovation, the theater was opened once again. Another renovation is now in the works; among the fundraisers is former President Clinton, who also has an office just down the block.

Now a nonprofit enterprise, the Apollo continues to present a variety of entertainment, including a Wednesday amateur night. In the lobby is a small exhibit on the theater's early history, and tours are offered; call 212/531-5337 for details.

The Apollo has hosted nearly every major jazz, blues, R&B, and soul artist to come along since the 1930s.

© CHRISTIANE BIRD

NORTH TO 135TH STREET

Langston Hughes Residence

The famed Harlem Renaissance author and poet lived in the three-story, Italianate brownstone at 20 E. 127th St., between Lenox and Fifth Aves., for the last 20 years of his life. This is the only residence that Hughes, who died in 1967, occupied for any length of time. The block is now called Langston Hughes Place.

Tree of Hope Sculpture

The rusting steel sculpture standing in the middle of Adam Clayton Powell Jr. Blvd. at 131st St. marks the spot where the Tree of Hope once grew. The Tree—whose bark passersby rubbed for good luck—had originally stood on the side of the street, but when the avenue was widened, Bill "Bojangles" Robinson had it moved and replanted in the street's midway. His nearby plaque reads: "You wanted a tree of hope and here it is. Best Wishes."

You'd never know it now, but this intersection was once one of the hottest spots in Harlem. Known as "The Corner," it was home to numerous jazz clubs and dance halls, including Connie's Inn, the Band Box, the Barbeque, and the Hoofers' Club. "This wasn't just one more of them busy street crossings, with a poolroom for a hangout. Uh, uh," writes Mezz Mezzrow in *Really the Blues.* "On The Corner in Harlem you stood with your jaws swinging wide open while all there is to this crazy world, the whole frantic works, strutted by."

Liberation Book Shop

This most famed of Harlem bookstores, originally a 125th Street landmark, was later located at 421 Lenox Ave., at 131st St. for many years. Founded by Lewis Michaux, the store was a favorite gathering spot for decades, and had one of the largest selections of African American, African, and Caribbean books in New York. Malcolm X once bought much of his reading matter here. The store closed down in 2000.

22 West Restaurant

Another favorite Malcolm X hangout was the informal 22 West Restaurant, 22 W. 135th St., near Fifth Ave., 212/862-7770. Today a red-cushioned booth in the back, where he usually sat, bears a plaque reading: "El Hajj Malek El Shabazz (Malcolm X) . . . Always face the door—Watching my back!"

The Schomburg Center

The Schomburg Center for Research in Black Culture, 515 Lenox Ave., at 135th St., 212/491-2200, is a world-renowned institution founded by Arthur A. Schomburg, a Puerto Rican of African descent who as a child was told that the Negro had no history. Scholars come from all over the world to consult the extensive collections of this branch of the New York Public Library, housed in a modern brick and glass building.

For the sightseer, however, the center's most interesting attraction is its adjacent exhibition area, where a wide array of changing exhibits is presented. In the back, too, is an excellent book and gift shop.

The Schomburg's galleries and shop are open Mon.–Wed. noon–8 P.M., Thurs.–Sat. 10 A.M.–6 P.M. Admission is free.

Directly across the street from the Schomburg is **Harlem Hospital,** where two exquisite Depression-era murals by African American artists can be found. In the 136th Street lobby is Charles Alston's *Magic of Medicine,* while in the 135th Street lobby is Vertis Hayes's eight-paneled panorama of black history. The murals were originally rejected by the hospital's white administrator because they contained "too much Negro subject matter."

Harlem YMCA

The Harlem YMCA, 180 W. 135th St., between Lenox Ave. and ACP Blvd., was an important gathering spot for artists, writers, and entertainers during the Harlem Renaissance. Writers Langston Hughes and Ralph Ellison lived here temporarily, and Paul Robeson began his acting career here.

CENTRAL AND UPPER HARLEM

Mother A.M.E. Zion Church

The impressive neo-Gothic Mother A.M.E. Zion Church, 140 W. 137th St., between Lenox Ave.

and ACP Blvd., was New York City's first church organized by and for blacks. It was founded in 1796—originally downtown at 156 Church St.—with money donated by a former slave. The current church was designed by the noted African American architect George Washington Foster Jr.

Also known as the "Freedom Church" because of its connection to the Underground Railroad, the church has had many famous members, including Harriet Tubman, Frederick Douglass, Paul Robeson, and a woman named Isabella. One Sunday morning, Isabella, already highly respected by her community, announced during the service that she wanted to be called Sojourner Truth—"Sojourner because I am a wanderer, Truth because God is truth."

Abyssinian Baptist Church

One of Harlem's most famous addresses is the impressive Abyssinian Baptist Church, 132 W. 138th St., near ACP Blvd., 212/862-7474. It was founded in 1801 when a few members of the First Baptist Church refused to accept that church's racially segregated seating policy. The Abyssinian now has one of the country's largest black congregations.

Two of the church's most famous leaders were the Adam Clayton Powells—Sr. and Jr. The flamboyant Powell Jr. was also the first black U.S. congressman from an Eastern state, and he did much to empower the black community before being charged with misconduct and failing to win reelection. The church houses a small memorial room honoring both Powells.

The Reverend Dr. Calvin Butts is the Abyssinian's current pastor, and he continues the church's activist tradition. Services, complete with gospel music, are held Sunday at 9 A.M. and 11 A.M. Visitors are welcome; arrive early to get a seat. During the week, the church is open Mon.–Fri. 9 A.M.–5 P.M.

Striver's Row

Just down the street from the Abyssinian church are two famous blocks, located on 138th and 139th Streets between Adam Clayton Powell Jr. and Frederick Douglass Boulevards. Built in 1891 by developer David King, the blocks—

MANHATTAN

GOSPEL

Hallelujah! Gospel is thriving in New York, especially in Harlem and Brooklyn, where Baptist churches rock every Sunday morning with voices praising the Lord. Respectful visitors are welcome; call ahead for service times, and arrive early, as seats go fast.

The best known church in Harlem is the **Abyssinian Baptist Church,** 132 W. 138th St., 212/862-7474, whose powerful choir and pastor, Calvin Butts, have been attracting tourists for decades. But the Abyssinian is just the beginning.

Two blocks away stands the small 1918 **New Mount Zion Baptist Church,** 171 W. 140th St., 212/283-0788, where the energetic Pastor Carl Washington, Jr., leads a rollicking call-and-response service every Sunday. Further downtown is the famed **Mount Neboh Baptist Church,** 1883 Seventh Ave., at 114th St., 212/866-7880, whose mighty Mass Choir has performed all over the world.

At the **Greater Refuge Temple,** 2081 Adam Clayton Powell Jr. Blvd., at 124th St., 212/866-1700, popular gospel shows are put on every third Sunday of the month by the church's all-male choir. The **Canaan Baptist Church of Christ,** 132 W. 116th St., 212/866-0301, is also known for its high-spirited gospel services.

Many of Harlem's gospel churches are frequented by tourists, most of them foreign and arriving by the busload. **Harlem Spirituals,** 690 Eighth Ave., between 43rd and 44th Sts., 212/391-0900, is one tour company that specializes in gospel-oriented tours, often combined with a soul-food lunch.

If you'd like to escape your fellow tourists, head out to Brooklyn. One of the best-known churches there is the **Brooklyn Tabernacle,** 290 Flatbush Ave., near Prospect Pl., 718/783-0942, where the astonishing Brooklyn Tabernacle Choir puts on an ecstatic show. Much less well-known, but friendly and intimate, is the **Concord Baptist Church of Christ,** 833 Gardner C. Taylor Blvd., between Putnam Ave. and Madison St., Bedford-Stuyvesant, 718/622-1818, home to several small but soulful choirs.

lined with 158 four-story buildings—were designed by three sets of architects, with McKim, Mead & White designing the most impressive, northernmost row. The blocks acquired their nickname when they became the preferred address of early ambitious blacks. They continue to be immaculately kept, with service alleys running behind and flower boxes out front. Among the rich and famous who've lived here are W. C. Handy, Eubie Blake, and Stepin Fetchit.

Hamilton Heights

A few blocks northwest of Striver's Row is **Hamilton Grange,** 287 Convent Ave., between 141st and 142nd Sts., a Federal-style mansion where Alexander Hamilton lived before being killed in a duel by Aaron Burr. In 1889, the Grange was moved to this site, where it sits—looking uncomfortably squeezed—on a narrow plot between two other buildings.

The Grange, now managed by the National Park Service, is closed due to structural problems and isn't scheduled to reopen any time soon. There's talk it may be moved again, this time to a park or other more accessible site.

Above Hamilton Grange is Hamilton Heights, stretching from 142nd to 145th Streets between Amsterdam and St. Nicholas Avenues. Once part of Hamilton's estate, this historic district is filled with grand mansions and elegant brownstones.

Looking south from the Grange, you can see the impressive, neo-Gothic spires of the **City College,** 212/650-7000, a branch of the City University of New York, centering on Convent Avenue between 130th and 135th Streets. The college was founded as a free academy for qualified city students in 1849. Though no longer free, it still offers relatively inexpensive tuition (about $2,500 a year). The original quad has recently been restored.

Sugar Hill

Just north of Hamilton Heights is Sugar Hill, stretching from 143rd to 156th Streets between St. Nicholas and Edgecombe Avenues. Built on a steep incline, Sugar Hill is another affluent residential area that's long been known for its "sweet life."

The great jazz artist Duke Ellington lived at

ONLY IN NEW YORK!

It's one of the oddest sites in the city: a gorgeous, 23-acre park built on top of a sewage treatment plant. To the north is the glistening expanse of the George Washington Bridge; to the south, the skyline of Manhattan; down below, a cluster of sludge storage, settling, and aeration tanks.

Located on the Hudson River between 137th and 145th Streets, Riverbank State Park, 212/694-3600, is one of the best equipped parks in the city, attracting residents from all over New York. Within its spic-and-span confines—blanketed with an emerald-green synthetic turf—are baseball and football fields, a 400-meter track, three swimming pools (one Olympic size), four tennis courts, four basketball courts, four handball courts, four playgrounds, an ice-skating rink, picnic areas, a cultural center, a bike path, a community garden, and 700 trees. On a busy weekend day, as many as 15,000 to 20,000 people come here to relax.

The park was conceived in 1968, when the sewage treatment plant originally planned for West 72nd Street was bumped up to Harlem, due to influential Upper West Side residents. Harlem's rage was so great that the city promised it a park in return. The $1.3 billion North River Water Pollution Control Plant was completed in 1986; the $129 million park, in 1994.

When the sewage treatment plant first opened, residents complained bitterly about its smell. Since then, about $20 million has been spent on odor control. While the problem has not been eradicated, at least it's rarely noticeable within the confines of the park itself.

935 St. Nicholas Ave., near 156th St., from 1939 to 1961, and the handsome building has since been placed on the National Register of Historic Places in his honor. While living here, Ellington performed at the Cotton Club, wrote many of his most famous compositions, and premiered his controversial "Black, Brown, and Beige"—which he called a "tone parallel to the history of the American Negro"—at Carnegie Hall.

Future Supreme Court justice Thurgood Marshall, scholar W. E. B. Du Bois, and civil rights leader Roy Wilkins all once lived at 409 Edgecombe Ave., at 155th St., a worn-looking apartment house with a commanding view of the valley below. Declared a city landmark in 1993, the 13-story building was also home to many other members of the black elite from the 1930s through the 1950s.

New to the neighborhood is the **Sugar Hill Arts Center,** 3658 Broadway, at 151st St., 212/491-5890, offering four galleries that showcase the work of up-and-coming New York–based artists. The center also features a roof garden and sculpture garden.

Morris-Jumel Mansion

This big white gem of a mansion on W. 160th St. and Edgecombe Ave., 212/923-8008, sits in a small, lush park. Manhattan's last remaining Colonial residence, it was built in 1765 as a country home for British colonel Roger Morris. The house once offered excellent views of both the Hudson and East Rivers (now obstructed by other buildings), and served as a temporary headquarters for George Washington during the Revolutionary War.

Several decades following the war, the house was purchased by Stephen Jumel, a wealthy French wine merchant. His wife, Mme. Jumel, was said to have been a manipulative, scheming ex-prostitute from Providence, Rhode Island, who let her husband die of neglect after he was seriously wounded in a carriage accident. His death made her one of America's richest women, and she then married Aaron Burr, with whom she had a tempestuous relationship. She continued to live in the mansion until her death in 1865 at the age of 93, and her ghost is said to haunt the place.

Some of the furnishings in the house are original, others are period pieces. The handsome octagonal dining room to the rear is where Washington hosted a famous dinner, attended by Hamilton, Madison, and Jefferson.

Immediately west of Morris-Jumel is **Sylvan Terrace.** Once the carriage drive to the mansion, this short cobblestone street is now lined with

MANHATTAN

historic wooden row houses and is one of the city's most idyllic spots.

The mansion is open Wed.–Sun 10 A.M.–4 P.M. Admission is adults $3, students and seniors $2.

Audubon Terrace

This monumental marble terrace is often dishearteningly empty, especially since its most famous one-time resident, the Museum of the American Indian, moved to the former U.S. Custom House (see Battery Park and the Statue of Liberty under Lower Manhattan). Still here are the **Hispanic Society of America,** the **American Numismatic Society,** and the **American Academy & Institute of Arts and Letters,** but they're seldom visited thanks to the terrace's off-the-beaten-track location on Broadway between 155th and 156th Streets.

Visitors who do venture up this far, however, will find themselves in a historic spot, with an impressive array of beaux arts buildings to the south, and a plaza filled with friezes and statuary to the north. All of this land was once part of ornithologist John James Audubon's estate; the terrace was built later, in 1904.

Easternmost of the plaza's three museums is the dark and somber Hispanic Society. Mansionlike in feel, it houses a number of paintings by Goya, Velasquez, and El Greco, along with heavy Spanish furnishings, porcelain, and mosaics. The Hispanic Society, 212/926-2234, is open Tues.–Sat. 10 A.M.–4:30 P.M. and Sunday 1–4 P.M. Admission is by donation.

Next door in the American Numismatic Society, you'll find coins dating back to Greek, Roman, Renaissance, and Colonial times, and pick up all sorts of odd tidbits, such as the fact that Marco Polo was the first to tell the Western World about the Chinese invention of paper money. The American Numismatic Society, 212/234-3130, is open Tues.–Fri. 9 A.M.–4:30 P.M. Admission is free.

The American Academy & Institute of Arts and Letters honors 250 American writers, painters, composers, sculptors, and architects. The Academy is only open when presenting exhibits, of which there are about three a year. Call 212/368-5900 for schedule information.

To reach Audubon Terrace, take either the No. 1 train to 157th Street and Broadway, or take the B train to 155th Street near Amsterdam Avenue and walk two blocks west.

Church of the Intercession

Just south of Audubon Terrace is the enormous, Gothic Revival Church of the Intercession, surrounded by idyllic **Trinity Cemetery.** Both look as if they belong more in the English countryside than they do in Harlem.

Trinity Cemetery is owned by Trinity Church (see Wall Street under Lower Manhattan), and is the final resting place of numerous famous New Yorkers, including John James Audubon (whose gravestone is covered with carved animals and birds). The cemetery is open daily 9 A.M.–4:30 P.M.; long-robed priests can sometimes be seen strolling the grounds. The gate to the eastern section is near the church; the gate to the western section is on 155th Street near Riverside Drive.

MANHATTAN'S NORTHERN TIP

Yeshiva University

Founded in 1886 and enrolling more than 7,000 students, this is the oldest and largest Jewish university in the Western Hemisphere. The main building is a startling sight—it's built in a Moorish-Byzantine style with numerous tiles, turrets, minarets, domes, and arches.

Up until recently, the university's main attraction for visitors was its **Yeshiva University Museum,** but that is now located downtown at the Center for Jewish History, 15 W. 16th St., between Fifth and Sixth Aves., 212/294-8330 (see Chelsea).

The university, 212/960-5400, is on Amsterdam Ave. between 183rd and 187th Sts.; take the No. 1 train to 181st or 191st Street.

The Cloisters and Fort Tyron Park

High on a hill at the northern tip of Manhattan is the Cloisters, 212/923-3700, www.met-museum.org, a magical "medieval monastery" with wonderful views of the Hudson. Financed in 1938 by John D. Rockefeller, the Cloisters house the Metropolitan Museum of Art's medieval col-

© CHRISTIANE BIRD

serenity in a Cloisters courtyard

lections. Incorporated into the building are the actual remains of four medieval cloisters—transported here from Europe—along with a reconstructed chapter house and exhibition galleries.

The museum's most prized possessions are its 16th-century Unicorn Tapestries, hung in a darkened room all their own. Six of the seven priceless tapestries are complete, and they tell the story of the "Hunt of the Unicorn" in rich, astonishing detail. The series begins with the "Start of the Hunt" and ends with the "Unicorn in Captivity"—that famous image of the mythical creature in a round, wooden corral with a tree in the center.

Surrounding the museum are the flowering plants and trees, walkways, and benches of Fort Tyron Park, designed by Frederick Law Olmsted Jr., son of the man who designed Central Park. Near the park's south end is a plaque marking the site of the fort where the Americans were defeated on November 16, 1776. After that defeat, the British renamed the site Fort Tyron in honor of the last British governor of New York.

A visit to the Cloisters takes the better part of the day. It's best to go in warm weather so you can wander the grounds, which offer wonderful views of the Hudson. Hours are March–Oct.,

Tues.–Sun. 9:30 A.M.–5:15 P.M.; Nov.–Feb., Tues.–Sun. 9:30 A.M.–4:45 P.M. Suggested admission is adults $10, students and seniors $5, children under 12 free, but you may pay what you wish; ticket includes free admission to the Met. To reach the Cloisters, take the A train to 190th St.–Overlook Terrace. Exit by elevator, then catch the M4 bus or walk 15 minutes through Fort Tyron park to the museum.

SHOPPING
Botanicas
Otto Chicas Rendon, 60 E. 116th St., between Madison and Park Aves., 212/289-0378, is the city's oldest and best-known botanica, selling everything from crystal balls to herbs and love potions. Founded in 1945, the store has been so successful that it now sells wholesale to botanicas around the country, and manufactures Catholic saints, *orishas* (Cuban Santería gods), and perfumes with names such as "Chinese Floor Wash" and "Run Devil Run."

Other smaller botanicas near 116th Street are **El Congo,** 1787 Lexington Ave., between 110th and 111th Sts., 212/860-3921, carrying a good selection of books, miracle beads, and dried herbs; and **Paco's Botanica,** 1864 Lexington Ave., at 115th St., 212/427-0820, a spic-and-span shop with lots of religious statues wrapped in plastic.

Music
Rainbow Music Shop, 102 W. 125th St., just west of Lenox Ave., 212/864-5262, is an old neighborhood favorite selling a terrific selection of R&B and gospel, along with some jazz and blues.

Vendor Markets
On 116th Street between Lenox and Fifth Avenues is the **Malcolm Shabazz Harlem Market,** 212/987-8131, where dozens of vendors sell T-shirts, Kente cloth, African art, wool skullcaps, Gambian drums, women's hair twists, down coats, and CDs. Prices range from about $5 for the skullcaps to about $100 for the down coats, and many of the shoppers are European.

Mart 125, 260 W. 125th St., 212/316-3340, between ACP and Frederick Douglass Blvds., is a large indoor shopping center with four food courts and about 40 shops selling African art, jewelry, clothing, food, music, and books. Individual shop hours vary, but the Mart itself is open Mon.–Sat. 10 A.M.–8 P.M. and Sunday noon–5 P.M.

ACCOMMODATIONS
Hostels and Dorms
The small **Sugar Hill International House,** 722 St. Nicholas Ave., at 146th St., 212/926-7030, and its larger sister, the **Blue Rabbit International House,** 730 St. Nicholas Ave., 212/491-3892, offer both dorm-style and private rooms. Rates per person are $25–30; a passport is required of all guests, including U.S. citizens. At the **New York Uptown International Hostel,** 239 Lenox Ave., at 122nd St., 212/666-0559, beds are available in small, clean dorm rooms sleeping four to six for $20 a night. Affiliated with the Uptown Hostel is the **New York Bed and Breakfast,** 134 W. 119th St., near Lenox Ave., 212/666-0559, offering private rooms for $60–65, double occupancy.

The **International House of New York,** 500 Riverside Drive, at W. 122nd St., 212/316-8473 or 212/316-8436, is primarily in the business of renting rooms to Columbia University graduate students and visiting scholars. In the summer, however, when occupancy rates are low, single student rooms are available to the general public for $50 s. Guest suites are also available; $115–125 a night.

Bed-and-Breakfast
The new **Urban Jem Guesthouse,** 2005 Fifth Ave., near 125th St., 212/831-6029, www.urbanjem.com, is housed in one of Harlem's charming historic brownstones. Accommodations include two studio apartments with private kitchen and bath, a one-bedroom suite, and two furnished rooms with semi-private bath and kitchen. Regular jazz performances take place in the parlor. $90–130 s or d with a minimum 2-night stay.

FOOD
Southern/Soul
M&G Soul Food Diner, 383 W. 125th St., between St. Nicholas and Morningside Aves., 212/864-7326, is an excellent spot for fried chicken; average main dish, $8. **Miss Maude's Spoonbread Too,** 547 Lenox Ave., between 137th and 138th Sts., 212/690-3100, serves up heaping portions of tasty Southern dishes, as does its sister restaurant, **Miss Mamie's Spoonbread Too,** 366 W. 110th St., between Manhattan and Columbus Aves., 212/865-6744; average main dish at both, $11.

The legendary **Sylvia's,** 328 Lenox Ave., between 126th and 127th Sts., 212/996-0660, has been expanding over the years, and attracting tourists by the busload. The food's still fine but the atmosphere is not what it once was; average entrée $12. **Copeland's,** 549 W. 145th St., between Broadway and Amsterdam, 212/234-2357, is the soul food restaurant of choice among politicians and businesspeople, and a popular gospel brunch is offered on Sundays; average entrée $12.

Some of the best fried chicken and grits to be found anywhere in the city are on the menu at **Charles' Southern Style Kitchen,** 2837 Eighth

Ave., near 152nd St., 212/926-4313; average entrée $10.

Housed in a gorgeous 1880s townhouse is newcomer **Sugar Hill Bistro,** 458 W. 145th St., between Amsterdam and Convent Aves., 212/491-5505, offering a sophisticated Southern cuisine, live jazz, gospel brunches, and a back patio; entrées range $17–30.

Caribbean and African

The **Jamaican Hot Pot,** 2260 Seventh Ave., at 133rd St., 212/491-5270, offers mouthwatering curried goat stews, oxtail soups, and the like; average main dish $9. **Obaa Koryoe,** 3143 Broadway, near 125th St., 212/316-2950, serves West African *fufu* and other mash-based foods—to be eaten with fingers only, please; average main dish $10.

Italian

Patsy's Pizzeria, 2287 First Ave., between 117th and 118th Sts., 212/534-9783, was the country's first coal-stoked brick-oven pizzeria. A Frank Sinatra favorite, it was established in 1932; average pizza $10. To get into tiny **Rao's,** 455 E. 114th St., near Pleasant, 212/722-6709, you have to book about three months in advance. The Rao family has been serving fine home cooking in this former Dutch saloon since 1896; average entrée $25.

Light Bites

Near Columbia University, the sprawling **West End,** 2911 Broadway, between 113th and 114th Sts., 212/662-8830, was once a favorite haunt of Jack Kerouac and Allen Ginsberg. It still offers cheap pitchers of beer and a standard bar menu. **Tom's,** 2880 Broadway, near 112th St., 212/864-6137, is best known for its appearance on *Seinfeld* (used in the exterior shot of all the diner scenes)

and milk shakes. The traditional **Hungarian Pastry Shop,** 1030 Amsterdam Ave., near 111th St., 212/866-4230, sells mouthwatering strudel and other sweet treats.

Georgie's Pastry Shop, 50 W. 125th, between Fifth and Lenox Aves., 212/831-0722, is a tiny joint known for tasty donuts and sweet-potato pies. **Wimp's Bakery,** 29 W. 125th, between Fifth and Lenox Aves., 212/410-2296, is a modern spot also serving excellent sweet-potato pies, banana puddings, and the like.

Watering Holes and Jazz Joints

The casual, low-ceilinged **West End,** 2911 Broadway, between 113th and 114th Sts., 212/662-8830, has long been a favorite watering hole among Columbia University students and professors.

After years of quietude, the joints of Harlem are jumpin' again. One of the hottest spots is **St. Nick's Pub,** 773 St. Nicholas Ave., at 149th St., 212/283-9728, best known for its Monday-night jam sessions; cover $5–8. The vintage art deco **Lenox Lounge,** 288 Lenox Ave., between 124th and 125th Sts., 212/427-0253, beckons with comfy semicircular banquettes, gorgeous light fixtures shaped like fins, and first-class musicians on the weekends; cover $15, plus $5 minimum. **Showman's,** 375 W. 125th St., at Eighth Ave., 212/864-8941, for years the only regularly operating jazz club uptown, is still home to music lovers and tap dancers, as well as tour buses; no cover, two-drink minimum.

The **Cotton Club,** 656 W. 125th St., off Riverside Dr., 212/663-7980, is an upscale art deco room with upscale prices that draws plenty of tour buses for its Sunday gospel brunch; jazz is also featured Thurs.–Sat.; $35 for music cover and all-you-can-eat buffet.

MANHATTAN

The Outer Boroughs

Manhattan offers so much to see and do that few visitors—or Manhattanites, for that matter—ever make it to the outer boroughs, where most New Yorkers actually live. Those who do venture outside Manhattan, however, will find in the other boroughs a number of one-of-a-kind sights and an astounding ethnic stew, made up of Italians, Poles, Russians, Chinese, Japanese, Koreans, Thais, Indians, West Indians, West Africans, Latin Americans, Greeks, Orthodox Jews, and African Americans. Most of these neighborhoods don't have "visitor attractions" in the usual sense of the term, but they do have excellent restaurants and food shops, and are an easy way to experience another culture, if only for an afternoon.

The boroughs also offer great views of Manhattan—Brooklyn Heights and Long Island City are two especially good spots—and wide-open outdoor spaces. Prospect Park and Coney Island in Brooklyn, Flushing Meadows–Corona Park in Queens, the Bronx Zoo and Botanical Gardens in the Bronx, and the Staten Island Greenbelt are all unique places offering a welcome respite from the frenzy of Manhattan.

Orientation

Because the boroughs are so vast and geographically confusing, the sections below are divided into manageable chunks—all easily accessible by subway from Manhattan. First-time visitors

Wave Hill

might want to ride the Staten Island ferry, or visit Brooklyn Heights or Coney Island in Brooklyn, Astoria or Jackson Heights in Queens, or the Bronx Zoo in the Bronx.

Brooklyn

Up until 1898, Brooklyn was a city in its own right, separate from New York. It had its own city hall, central park, downtown shops, museums, theaters, beaches, botanical garden, and zoo—all of which helps account for its fierce sense of identity and pride. Of all the boroughs, Brooklyn is the most individualistic, the most mythic, and the most complex.

Brooklyn is: Walt Whitman, Coney Island, the Brooklyn Dodgers, the Brooklyn Bridge, Mae West, Nathan's Famous, Bazooka bubble gum, Lena Horne, John Travolta, Jackie Gleason, the Brooklyn Navy Yards, Mickey Rooney, Topps baseball cards, Pete Hamill, Barbra Streisand, Prospect Park, Chock Full o' Nuts, Junior's cheesecake, Spike Lee. Brooklyn is also "the borough of churches" and the borough of ethnic neighborhoods. In total, 93 ethnic groups call Brooklyn home, among them Hasidic Jews, West Indians, Latin Americans, Russians, Poles, Scandinavians, Asians, Italians, Middle Easterners, and Irish.

History

The largest borough in population (2.5 million) and the second largest in area (78.5 square miles), Brooklyn was first inhabited by the Carnarsie Indians. In 1607, Henry Hudson landed briefly on Coney Island, and a few years later, the Dutch began establishing farms. The first battle after the Declaration of Independence—the Battle of Long Island—was fought in Brooklyn. The colonists lost, but Washington and his troops retreated with enough strength to continue the fight.

After the Revolution, Brooklyn began to boom. Its deep waters were developed into a major shipping port, and in 1814, Robert Fulton's ferry service connected the borough to Manhattan, strengthening its ties of commerce even more. By the end of the 19th century, Brooklyn was plump and prosperous, home to one million residents and countless flourishing industries.

That's when the borough made what journalist Pete Hamill calls the "Big Mistake," signing an 1898 agreement that annexed it to New York City. The annexation was probably inevitable, however, as the Brooklyn Bridge had opened up 16 years before, and the two cities' economies were becoming more and more entwined.

After WW II, Brooklyn's fortunes began to go downhill. The Brooklyn Navy Yards—for nearly a century one of the borough's largest employers—closed down, and the borough's famed newspaper, the *Brooklyn Eagle*, went out of business. Some neighborhoods lost their middle class to the suburbs, and—worst of all—the Brooklyn Dodgers moved to Los Angeles, just two years after winning the World Series for the first time in 1955. Large sections of the borough began to have a bombed-out, abandoned look.

Today, Brooklyn is on the rebound. Although poverty is still a major problem in some areas, neighborhoods such as Park Slope and Fort Greene—which as recently as the 1970s were considered marginal—are now home to large numbers of professionals, attracted by the areas' brownstones and relatively low rents. Other neighborhoods such as Greenpoint and Brighton Beach have witnessed the influx of thousands of energetic new immigrants.

Neighborhoods

The sheer number of neighborhoods in Brooklyn is dizzying. Immediately south of Manhattan are Brooklyn Heights, Cobble Hill, Carroll Gardens, Boerum Hill, and Fort Greene, while directly east are Williamsburg and Greenpoint. Farther out, to the south, are Red Hook, Sunset Park, Borough Park, Bay Ridge, Bensonhurst, Coney Island, and Brighton Beach, while to the southeast are Park Slope, Crown Heights, Bedford-Stuyvesant, Bushwick, Flatbush, Brownsville, East New York, Canarsie, and Sheepshead Bay.

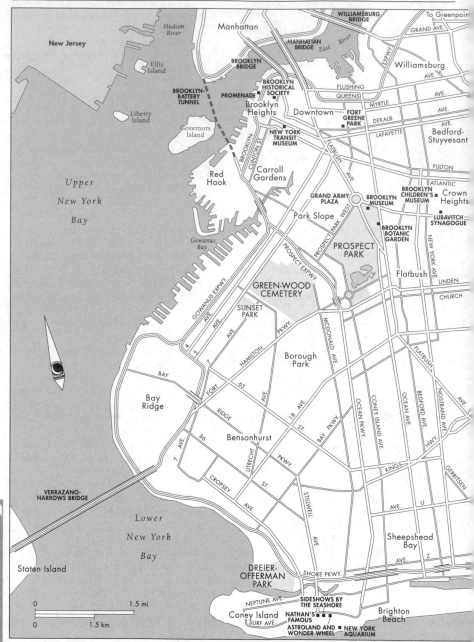

New Jersey

Hudson River

Manhattan

WILLIAMSBURG BRIDGE

To Greenpoin

GRAND AVE.

MANHATTAN BRIDGE

East River

Ellis Island

BROOKLYN BRIDGE

Williamsburg

AVE.

FLUSHING

BROOKLYN HISTORICAL SOCIETY

QUEENS

MYRTLE

AVE.

Liberty Island

BROOKLYN-BATTERY TUNNEL

PROMENADE

Brooklyn Heights

Downtown

FORT GREENE PARK

DEKALB

AVE.

Governors Island

NEW YORK TRANSIT MUSEUM

LAFAYETTE

Bedford-Stuyvesant

FULTON

Upper New York Bay

Red Hook

Carroll Gardens

GRAND ARMY PLAZA

BROOKLYN MUSEUM

BROOKLYN CHILDREN'S MUSEUM

ATLANTIC

Crown Heights

Park Slope

LUBAVITCH SYNAGOGUE

Gowanus Bay

BROOKLYN BOTANIC GARDEN

PROSPECT PARK

Flatbush

GREEN-WOOD CEMETERY

LINDEN

CHURCH

SUNSET PARK

Borough Park

MOON

BAY

Bay Ridge

FORT

RIDGE

65

18 AVE.

Bensonhurst

86

UTRECHT ST

PKWY

OCEAN PKWY.

CONEY ISLAND AVE.

OCEAN AVE.

BEDFORD AVE.

NOSTRAND AVE.

CROPSEY

ST

KINGS

GERRITSEN

VERRAZANO-NARROWS BRIDGE

STILLWELL

Lower New York Bay

AVE.

U

Sheepshead Bay

AVE.

Z

Staten Island

SHORE PKWY.

DREIER-OFFERMAN PARK

SIDESHOWS BY THE SEASHORE

NEPTUNE AVE.

Coney Island

SURF AVE.

NATHAN'S FAMOUS

ASTROLAND AND WONDER WHEEL

NEW YORK AQUARIUM

Brighton Beach

0   1.5 mi

0   1.5 km

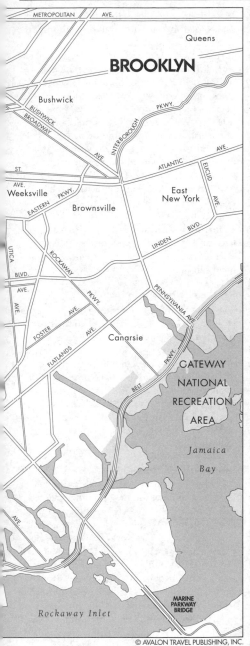

METROPOLITAN AVE.

Queens

BROOKLYN

Bushwick

PKWY.

BUSHWICK
BROADWAY

INTERBOROUGH

AVE.

AVE.

ATLANTIC

EUCLID

ST.

AVE.

Weeksville   PKWY.

East
New York

AVE.

EASTERN

Brownsville

BLVD.

LINDEN

UTICA

ROCKAWAY

BLVD.

AVE.

PKWY.

PENNSYLVANIA AVE.

AVE.

FOSTER

AVE.

AVE.

Canarsie

PKWY

FLATLANDS

GATEWAY

BELT

NATIONAL

RECREATION

AREA

Jamaica

Bay

AVE.

MARINE
PARKWAY
BRIDGE

Rockaway Inlet

© AVALON TRAVEL PUBLISHING, INC.

General Information

For information on special events, or to obtain a visitors guide, contact **Brooklyn Information & Culture Inc.,** 718/855-7882, www.brooklynx.org.

BROOKLYN HEIGHTS AND VICINITY

Quiet, tree-lined streets; dignified, perfectly preserved brownstones; well-dressed parents out playing with their apple-cheeked kids—such is the refined genteel atmosphere of Brooklyn Heights, one of New York City's prettiest neighborhoods. Manhattanites even deign to visit here, largely because of the **Promenade** that runs along the district's western edge, offering magnificent, bluff-high views of the skyline, the harbor, and the Brooklyn Bridge.

Used as a refuge by Gen. Washington and his troops after an early defeat in the Revolutionary War, Brooklyn Heights became the country's first suburb when Robert Fulton started up his ferry service in the early 1800s. Soon thereafter, wealthy Brooklyn Heights landowners—many of them bankers commuting to Wall Street—divided their property into standard building lots, and the neighborhood filled up with brownstones and churches.

Much of the pleasure of visiting Brooklyn Heights lies in simply wandering its idyllic streets. Orange, Pineapple, Clark, Pierrepont, and Montague Street will all take you down to the Promenade, which blooms profusely with flowers during warm weather. Washington Roebling, builder of the Brooklyn Bridge, once lived at the north end of the Promenade, where he could watch the project's progress by telescope from his invalid's bed. Montague Street is Brooklyn Heights' main commercial thoroughfare, where you'll find most of the neighborhood's restaurants, bars, and shops. During warm weather, many of these establishments set up tables on the street, giving it a vaguely European air.

From Manhattan, by far the best way to get to Brooklyn is to walk over the Brooklyn Bridge, then cross through Cadman Plaza Park to the Heights. By subway, take the A train to High Street, or the No. 2 or 3 to Clark Street.

© CHRISTIANE BIRD

walking across the Brooklyn Bridge

You can also take the No. 4 to Borough Hall and walk west.

Historic Buildings

At the corner of Clark and Henry Streets is the 1885 **St. George Hotel.** (If you take the No. 2 or 3 train to Brooklyn Heights, you'll arrive in the hotel's basement and take a strangely quiet ride on a big freight elevator to street level.) A neighborhood landmark, the St. George was once New York City's largest hotel, with 2,632 rooms and a fabled swimming pool lined with mirrors. The building fell on hard times in the 1970s and 1980s but has since been transformed into student housing.

Two blocks from the St. George, on Orange Street between Henry and Hicks Streets, is the red-brick **Plymouth Church of the Pilgrims.** In the Civil War era, this church was famous all over America, thanks to minister Henry Ward Beecher's rousing antislavery sermons. A statue honoring Beecher—brother of Harriet Beecher Stowe—stands in the church's garden; inside is a marker indicating the pew at which Abraham Lincoln sat when he visited.

The Rev. Henry Beecher lived around the corner from his church at 22 Willow St., where he was accused of having an adulterous affair with a

Mrs. Tilton, who sang in the church choir. Beecher was tried and acquitted, but his authority was never the same thereafter.

At 57 Willow St. is a fine 1824 house, crafted with dormers, steeply pitched roofs, and carved stone lintels. Farther south, the basement apartment of 70 Willow St. was once home to Truman Capote, who wrote *In Cold Blood* while living here. At 108-112 Willow St. are excellent examples of the elaborate Queen Anne architectural style, while superb red-brick Federal-style houses, complete with black doors and window frames, can be found at 155, 157, and 159 Willow.

Pierrepont Street is lined with some of the biggest and most playful residences in Brooklyn Heights. At 82 Pierrepont is a giant turreted affair initially built as a private mansion and later used as a hotel, whorehouse, residence hall for Franciscan brothers, and, finally, an apartment building.

Historical Museum

The pretty, terra cotta building at 128 Pierrepont St., at Clinton St., is home to the **Brooklyn Historical Society,** 718/222-4111, www .brooklynhistory.org. Both library and museum, the society is currently undergoing restoration and is scheduled to reopen in spring 2003. Exhibits will focus on such Brooklyn subjects as the Brooklyn Navy Yard, the Dodgers, Coney Island, and the borough's many ethnic communities. The society also sponsors occasional walking tours.

Jehovah's Witnesses

Brooklyn Heights is dotted with a number of large, institutional-looking buildings painted a pale mustard yellow—a sign that they're owned by the Jehovah's Witnesses. The fundamentalist religious sect bases its world headquarters here, publishing numerous books and brochures out of the former Squibb factory—marked with the watchtower logo—just north of the Brooklyn Bridge. The Jehovah's Witnesses have over 20 residences in Brooklyn, including one Residence Hall at 124 Columbia Heights and the Bethel Home at 79-99 Willow St.; the Jehovah's Witnesses Library is at 119 Columbia Heights.

Fulton Ferry Historic District

At the extreme northern end of Brooklyn Heights, almost beneath the Brooklyn Bridge, is the Fulton Ferry Historic District, which centers around Old Fulton Street and a clutch of historic buildings. One of these, the medieval-looking **Eagle Warehouse,** 28 Old Fulton St., is now a co-op building. Near the entrance is a plaque honoring Walt Whitman and the *Brooklyn Eagle,* which was published on this site from 1841 to 1892. Whitman served as the newspaper's editor until he was fired for his stand against slavery.

Atlantic Avenue

Brooklyn Heights ends at Atlantic Avenue, a wide, gray boulevard known for its Arab restaurants and shops. The Middle Eastern community began settling here back in the days when Brooklyn was a bustling seaport. While the thoroughfare is not as lively as it once was, the block between Court and Clinton Street is still lined with Arab-run businesses. Atlantic Avenue is also known for its quirky antique shops. (see Shopping, below).

Cobble Hill and Carroll Gardens

South of Atlantic Avenue, between Henry and Hoyt Streets, is Cobble Hill. Though not as classy as Brooklyn Heights, Cobble Hill has its share of pretty brownstones and red-brick family homes, most dating from the 19th century. Particularly interesting here are **Clinton Street,** great for strolling; and **Verandah Place,** just off Clinton south of Congress, a peaceful mews filled with renovated carriage houses. Architect Robert Upjohn once lived at 296 Clinton, while Thomas Wolfe once resided at 40 Verandah Place.

Below DeGraw Street, Cobble Hill turns into Carroll Gardens, an older Italian neighborhood. **Court Street,** flanked with food shops, is the main thoroughfare here, while the side streets are home to neat brownstones and gardens, many dotted with religious statues.

Entertainment

Bargemusic, foot of Fulton St., at Water St., 718/624-4061, www.bargemusic.org, is a converted barge now serving as a wood-paneled concert venue for chamber music and jazz; cover $15–25. The barge also offers great views of Manhattan.

In summer, the soaring, sepulchral **Anchorage,** situated inside the four-story structure that anchors the Brooklyn Bridge, between Hicks and Old Fulton Sts. at the East River, 212/206-6674, www.creativetime.org, presents some of the most avant-garde shows in town.

Shopping

Food shops on Atlantic Avenue include the tiny **Damascus Breads,** 195 Atlantic Ave., 718/625-7070, selling freshly baked pita bread; and the large, well-stocked **Sahadi Importing Company,** 187-189 Atlantic Ave., 718/624-4550, offering dried fruits and grains, olives, feta cheese, stuffed grape leaves, and the like.

Horseman Antiques, 351 Atlantic Ave., 718/596-1048, is a four-floor emporium specializing in furniture from the early 1900s. **In the Days of Old, Limited,** 357 Atlantic Ave., 718/858-4233, specializes in late Victorian furnishings.

In the Cobble Hill area is **Bookcourt,** 163 Court St., 718/875-3677, Brooklyn's best bookstore. Among Carroll Gardens' food shops are **Esposito's,** 357 Court St., 718/875-6863, known for its fresh sausage; and **Caputo's Bakery,** 329 Court St., 718/875-6871, selling crusty semolina breads and Italian pastries.

Accommodations

In Carroll Gardens, find the **Angelique Bed & Breakfast,** 405 Union St., between Hoyt and Smith Sts., 718/852-8406, a brownstone offering four snug rooms decked out in Victorian antiques. $75 s, $125 d.

Food and Drink

For tasty blintzes, pierogi, and thick French toast, head to **Teresa's,** 80 Montague St., 718/797-3996, a neighborhood institution for over a decade; average main dish $7. Also still going strong for over a decade is cozy **Henry's End,** 44 Henry St., 718/834-1776; on the menu are such exotic dishes as antelope and elk, average entrée $18.

Down at the waterfront is the famed **River Cafe,** 1 Water St., 718/522-5200, an upscale and expensive eatery offering imaginative American cuisine and marvelous views of Manhattan; prix fixe dinner, $70–80. It's also possible to come just for a drink.

For Middle Eastern cuisine, try **Tripoli,** 154 Atlantic Ave., 718/596-5800, with a three-masted sailing ship painted on its huge windows; average entrée $14. Down the block is bustling **La Bouillabaisse,** 145 Atlantic Ave., 718/522-8275, a first-rate fish bistro; average entrée $18. The **Waterfront Ale House,** 136 Atlantic Ave., 718/522-3794, is a favorite local watering hole known for its happy hours and burgers.

In Carroll Gardens, the **Grocery,** 288 Smith St., between Sackett and Union Sts., 212/596-3335, is a tiny popular spot serving creative New American fare. Out back is a garden; average entrée $19. Charming **Patois,** 255 Smith St., between Douglass and Degraw Sts., Carroll Gardens, 718/855-1535, offers tasty bistro food and a garden as well; average entrée $16.

The oddball **Halcyon,** 227 Smith St., between Butler and Douglass Sts., Carroll Gardens, 718/260-9299, is part underground club, part lounge, part record store, and part coffee bar. During the day it attracts parents and their kids, while at night, hipsters flock in to hear top DJs spin their magic on a superb sound system.

DOWNTOWN AND FORT GREENE

Adjacent to genteel Brooklyn Heights is scrappy downtown Brooklyn, home to a number of imposing government buildings that hark back to the days when Brooklyn was a city in its own right. The Greek Revival **Borough Hall,** at the

FORT GREENE RENAISSANCE

Harlem's not the only center for African American culture in town. Ever since the late 1980s, Fort Greene has been attracting an influx of young professionals, two-thirds of them African American, and the population has now reached a critical mass. The neighborhood boasts a clutch of new restaurants, bars, and shops, making it a destination in its own right, even for jaded Manhattanites.

Among the neighborhood's more unusual attractions is **Madiba,** 195 DeKalb Ave., at Carlton Ave., 718/855-9190, the city's only South African restaurant, made up to look like a *shebeen,* one of that country's illegal township bars. On the menu are a wide range of unusual dishes, including *bunny chow,* a half loaf of bread that's been hollowed out, filled with lamb and vegetables, and topped with sliced bananas and grated coconut; average entrée $15.

Just down the street reigns **Loulou,** 222 DeKalb Ave., 718/246-0633, an ultra-romantic spot filled with candles and cozy tables. The cuisine here is from Brittany—scallops in vermouth sauce, grilled portobello mushrooms, seared cod; average entrée $17. The **Cambodia Restaurant,** 87 S. Elliot Pl., between Lafayette Ave. and Fulton St., 718/858-3262, serves an interesting cuisine that's similar to Vietnamese; average main dish $7.

Butta' Cup Lounge, 271 DeKalb Ave., 718/522-1669, is an inviting, bilevel watering hole housed in a townhouse with an garden terrace and hypnotic DJ sounds. Two-story **Two Steps Down,** 240 DeKalb Ave., between Clermont and Vanderbilt Aves., 718/399-2020, offers live comedy, jazz, and a laid-back bar.

Indigo Books & Cafe, 672 Fulton St., between S. Oxford St. and S. Portland Ave., 718/488-5934, offers a good selection of African American, Latino, Caribbean, and European authors. Exposed brick walls, roomy couches, a relaxing garden, and frequent literary events make this a place to linger.

For shoppers, there's **Ashanti Origins,** 59 Lafayette Ave., at Fulton St., 718/855-1006, where West African and European design come together in elegant home furnishings. The **Downtown Showroom,** 659 Fulton St., between Ashland and Rockwell Pls., 718/222-9262, run by young fashion designers, is the place to go for retro clothing designs. **Carol's Daughter,** 1 S. Elliott Pl., at DeKalb Ave., 718/596-1862, is a holistic body shop selling lotions, soaps, moisturizers, and the like, in all colors and flavors.

intersection of Joralemon, Fulton, and Court Sts., was once Brooklyn's City Hall and still houses government offices. The Romanesque Revival **Brooklyn General Post Office,** 271 Cadman Pl. E, once handled all of the city's mail. To reach downtown Brooklyn from Manhattan, take the No. 2, 3, or 4 train to Borough Hall.

New York Transit Museum

Two blocks southwest of Borough Hall is the New York Transit Museum, downstairs at the northwest corner of Schermerhorn St. and Boerum Pl., 718/243-3060, www.mta.info/museum. Appropriately housed in a former subway station, the museum is currently being restored and is scheduled to reopen in early 2003. In the meantime, the museum is continuing to present exhibits in its smaller gallery in Grand Central Station, 42nd St. at Park Ave., adjacent to the station's master's office just off the main concourse, 212/878-0160.

Fulton Mall

Just east of Borough Hall along Fulton Street is the pedestrians-only Fulton Mall. Built in the 1960s to help revive a dying downtown, the mall is a lively place crowded with mainstream and discount stores, street vendors, and multiethnic crowds.

Fort Greene

Immediately east of downtown Brooklyn lies Fort Greene, named after Nathanael Greene, an American general in the Revolutionary War. Filled with rows of renovated brownstones, Fort Greene is one of the city's most racially integrated middle-class communities, as well as one of its more artistic. Many jazz musicians, including Terence Blanchard and Cassandra Wilson, call this district home, along with many artists, writers, filmmakers, and directors. For years, the neighborhood's most famous resident was Spike Lee, whose production company, 40 Acres and a Mule, was headquartered in renovated Firehouse No. 256 on DeKalb Avenue. Fort Greene also boasts a plethora of new restaurants, bars, and shops.

On DeKalb Avenue between St. Edwards Street and Washington Park is hilly **Fort Greene Park,** designed by Frederick Law Olmsted. In the center of the park is the towering granite **Prison Ship Martyrs Monument.** The monument pays tribute to the thousands of American men who lost their lives in the British prison ships anchored nearby during the Revolutionary War. Though a little-known chapter in American history, more men perished in those horrific vessels than in all the war's battles and campaigns combined; enough bones washed up after the war to indicate that as many as 11,000 may have died. Their bones are now buried in a crypt beneath the monument.

Fort Greene is also home to the **Brooklyn Academy of Music,** 30 Lafayette Ave., at Atlantic and Flatbush, 718/636-4100, www.bam.org, a.k.a. BAM, a world-famous institution that's especially known for its avant-garde productions. Thanks to a relatively new $18 million restoration, BAM now also offers several small movie theaters presenting mostly foreign and art films, and the inviting BAMcafé, which serves everything from simple sandwiches to full-fledged entrées.

A neighborhood landmark is the 1929 **Williamsburg Savings Bank,** 1 Hanson Pl., at Flatbush, the tallest building in Brooklyn.

Accommodations

In downtown Brooklyn is the **Awesome Bed & Breakast,** 136 Lawrence St., between Fulton and Willoughby Sts., 718/858-4859, where you'll find eight well-appointed theme rooms with names such as Ancient Madagascar. The B&B is one stop from Manhattan on the No. 4 or 5 train. $79–110 s or d.

Also in downtown Brooklyn is the **New York Marriott Brooklyn Hotel,** 333 Adams St., 718/246-7000, www.marriott.com. With 365 brand new rooms, all priced about 20 percent less than they'd be in Manhattan, the hostelry offers good value for money. $170–230 s or d during the week; about a third off on weekends.

Food

Two of Brooklyn's best-known eateries are on or just off the Fulton Mall. **Gage & Tollner,** 372 Fulton St., at Jay St., near the mall's center, 718/875-5181, is a classic turn-of-the-century restaurant—perhaps the oldest in the city—filled with dark woods, gilt-edged mirrors, and gaslight fixtures; average entrée $18. **Junior's,** 386 Flatbush Ave., at DeKalb, 718/852-5257, is a sprawling, well-lit place, famed all over the city and beyond for its smooth, rich cheesecake, sold for about $5 a slice, along with burgers, etc.

Near the Transit Museum is the old-fashioned **Queen,** 84 Court St., near Livingston, 718/596-5955, a first-rate Italian restaurant favored by the courthouse crowd; average entrée $15.

For Fort Greene restaurants, see special topic, Fort Greene Renaissance.

WILLIAMSBURG

North of Fort Greene lies Williamsburg, home to a community of about 40,000 Satmarer Hasidim, a strict orthodox Jewish sect originally from Hungary. Men dress in long black coats with wide-brimmed hats, and sport full beards and earlocks, while women wear long skirts and sleeves, and if married, cover their heads with wigs and scarves. Although first settled by middle-class Irish and Germans, Williamsburg became predominantly Jewish in the early 1900s after the Williamsburg Bridge was completed. The bridge connected Brooklyn to Manhattan's then-hugely-overpopulated Lower East Side, and working-class Jews fled to Williamsburg by the thousands. Though most have since moved on to more suburban pastures, the Satmar remain. From Manhattan, take the J train to Marcy Avenue and walk south to Lee Avenue.

The Hasidim are centered along **Lee Avenue,** which is lined with shops selling everything from religious articles to timers that will automatically operate electrical appliances on the Sabbath. On **Bedford Avenue,** paralleling Lee, are many sturdy turn-of-the-century mansions; check out 505 Bedford, once a casino, and 559 Bedford, covered with turrets and elaborate friezes.

Also in Williamsburg are sizeable Italian and Puerto Rican communities, and a steadily growing enclave of ex-Manhattanite artists, attracted to the area by its low rents and abandoned industrial spaces. Most of the artists live about 15 blocks north of Lee Avenue near **Bedford Av-**

enue. Here you'll find a clutch of inexpensive restaurants, shops, and bars, and a number of galleries, including **Momenta Art,** 72 Berry St., at N. 10th St., 718/218-8058, and **Pierogi 2000,** 167 N. 9th St., near Bedford, 718/599-2144.

To reach the area directly from Manhattan, take the L train to the Bedford Avenue stop.

Italian Festival

Every July, Williamsburg is the site of a 12-day Italian festival centering on Our Lady of Mount Carmel Church, 275 N. 8th St., near Havemeyer, 718/384-0223. The highlight of the festival is the Dance of the Giglio, when a towering metallic structure weighing thousands of pounds is "danced" through the streets on the shoulders of about 120 men.

Food and Drink

The famed 1887 **Peter Luger Steak House,** 178 Broadway, near Driggs, 718/387-7400, is an expensive, no-frills, century-old steak house featuring enormous cuts of meat and crusty waiters who seem as old as time. It's just a short cab ride from Manhattan across the Williamsburg Bridge; average entrée $28.

Farther north, try **Vera Cruz,** 195 Bedford Ave., near N. 6th St., 718/599-7914, for cheap and tasty Mexican food, a lively bar scene, Latin music, and an outdoor garden in summer; average entrée $10. Across the street is popular **Planet Thailand,** 133 N. Bedford Ave., near Berry St., 718/599-5758, serving cheap and tasty Thai; average entrée $10. Tiny **La Brunette,** 300 N. 6th St., between Havemeyer and Meeker Sts., 718/384-5800, offers a mix of French and Caribbean fare; average entrée $14.

Watering Holes and Lounges

Near Bedford Avenue rocks **Teddy's Bar and Grill,** 96 Berry St., near N. 8th St., 718/384-9787, a long-time local favorite bar with live music on weekends.

The **Galapagos Art Space,** 70 N. 6th St., between Kent and Wythe Ave., 718/782-5188, offers two separate spaces. The 125-capacity back room presents a diverse mix of live music ranging from hip-hop to the Galapagos "house string quartet," while the front room is a popular hangout filled with tall tables and stools.

Warm, cozy **Luxx,** 256 Grand St., between Driggs Ave. and Roebling St., 718/599-1000, is a long, thin lounge known for its vinyl-covered couches, up-and-coming rock bands, and late-night DJ parties. Tiny 19th-century **Pete's Candy Store,** 709 Lorimer St., between Frost and Richardson Sts., 718/302-3770, complete with a curved ceiling, presents lots of local singer-songwriters and the occasional jazz band.

GREENPOINT

The birthplace of Mae West, Greenpoint was once a prime industrial center. Shipbuilding plants and oil refineries were located along its shoreline, while publishing, porcelain, and glass manufacturing companies were farther inland. Today, most of Greenpoint's industries have been abandoned, but the scruffy neighborhood is still very much alive, thanks mostly to its Polish community—the largest in New York. The Poles first came to Greenpoint in the late 19th century to work in the factories and are continuing to arrive today, post–Cold War. Many Italians and Irish also live in the area. From Manhattan, take the L train to Lorimer St. and transfer to the G train heading north. Get off at Greenpoint Avenue.

Polish Greenpoint's commercial center is **Manhattan Avenue.** Here, you'll find a smattering of Polish butcher shops, bakeries, and grocery stores, along with standard American shops. Numerous Polish shops are also found along **Nassau Street.** Try **W. Nassau Meat Market,** 915 Manhattan Ave., between Greenpoint and Kent, 718/389-6149, for kielbasa and stuffed cabbage.

Historic Buildings

Largely residential, Greenpoint is filled with historic brick row houses interspersed with modern aluminum-sided ones. Many of the prettiest brick buildings are between Manhattan and Franklin Avenues, Java and Calyer Streets. On Kent Street between Manhattan and Franklin is the Gothic **Elias Greek Rite Church,** along with several pretty Italianate houses. On the corner of Manhattan and Calyer is the 1908 **Green-**

point Savings Bank, which began here and now has branches citywide.

Two other interesting churches in Greenpoint are the ornate **St. Stanislaus Kostka Church,** 607 Humboldt St., at Driggs, where Polish masses are held daily; and the stunning, onion-domed **Russian Orthodox Cathedral of the Transfiguration,** 228 N. 12th St., at Driggs, 718/387-1964, which boasts a wooden screen with icons painted by the Kiev Orthodox Monastery of the Caves, open Sunday morning only.

Warsaw at the Polish National Home

This former community center, 261 Driggs Ave., at Eckford St., 718/387-5252, complete with lavish paintings and mirrors, is now one of the more unusual rock-and-roll clubs in town. The 1,000-capacity hall often features such mid-size bands as Patti Smith, Blonde Redhead, and the New Pornographers, while out front is a restaurant serving Polish fare. Cover $10–20.

PROSPECT PARK AND VICINITY

Three of Brooklyn's finest attractions—the Brooklyn Museum of Art, the Brooklyn Botanic Garden, and Prospect Park—are all within a few minutes' walk of each other here, while next door is one of the borough's most historic residential districts, Park Slope. After Brooklyn Heights, Park Slope is the neighborhood of choice among ex-Manhattanites. Here you'll find many young professionals strolling about with dogs and kids, along with a decreasing number of older families who've lived in the area for generations. From Manhattan, take the No. 2 or 3 train to Eastern Parkway.

Brooklyn Museum of Art

The lovely beaux arts Brooklyn Museum, 200 Eastern Pkwy., at Washington, 718/638-5000, www.brooklynart.org, was designed by McKim, Mead & White in 1897. Though one of the world's largest museums, it's always lived in the shadow of its mighty cousin across the river—the Metropolitan Museum of Art. But the Brooklyn Museum is very different from the Met or any other Manhattan art museum. It's usually quieter and less crowded. And more importantly, it stages some of the more unusual shows in town, among them major retrospectives by African American artists such as Romare Bearden and Jacob Lawrence, and women artists such as Elizabeth Murray and Louise Bourgeois.

Like the Metropolitan, the Brooklyn Museum's collections span virtually the entire history of art. Highlights include extensive Egyptian holdings, an excellent Native American collection, and a major permanent collection of contemporary art. Most of these contemporary pieces are housed in the light and airy West Wing. The museum also sponsors a lively jazz and blues concert series, and has one of the city's most eclectic gift shops, filled with reasonably priced handicrafts from around the world.

The museum is open Wed.–Fri. 10 A.M.–5 P.M., Sat.–Sun. 11 A.M.–6 P.M. Also open the first Saturday of each month 6–11 P.M. for an evening of special events. Suggested admission is adults $6, students $3, seniors $1.50, children under 12 free.

Brooklyn Botanic Garden

Next door to the Brooklyn Museum is the Brooklyn Botanic Garden, 1000 Washington Ave., 718/623-7200, www.bbg.org, another unusual and much beloved Brooklyn institution. Though considerably smaller than the world-famous botanical gardens in the Bronx, the Brooklyn gardens are in many ways more conducive to visit. Spread out over 50 carefully designed acres are a rose garden, a children's garden, a Japanese scholar's garden, and a garden for the blind, complete with Braille signs. The Steinhardt Conservatory houses tropical and desert plants, along with the country's largest collection of bonsai. The best time to visit is May, when the cherry blossoms burst forth, all pink and white froth.

Hours are April–Sept., Tues.–Fri. 8 A.M.–6 P.M., Sat.–Sun. 10 A.M.–6 P.M.; Oct.–March, Tues.–Fri. 8 A.M.–4:30 P.M., Sat.–Sun. 10 A.M.–4:30 P.M. Admission is adults $3, students and seniors $1.50. Free to kids under 16, and to all on Tuesday and on Saturday 10 A.M.–noon.

Prospect Park

Behind the Brooklyn Museum and the Brooklyn Botanic Garden is enormous Prospect Park—

525 acres of forests and meadows, lakes and streams. Prospect Park was designed by Frederick Law Olmsted and Calvert Vaux, who also designed Central Park. The two men considered this to be their masterpiece. Considerably wilder than Central Park, Prospect Park creates the illusion of being in the country.

The main entrance is at **Grand Army Plaza,** just up from the Brooklyn Museum at the intersection of Eastern Parkway, Flatbush Avenue, and Prospect Park West. In the center of the plaza, surrounded by an ever-present rush of traffic, is a towering triumphal arch honoring the Union soldiers of the Civil War.

Immediately inside the main entrance is the park's most glorious sight—Long Meadow. Stretching over a mile, this gently rolling lawn is lined on both sides with lush trees that completely hide the cityscape. During warm weather, the meadow attracts West Indian cricket players; in winter, the cross-country skiers come out.

East of Long Meadow are an 18th-century **carousel;** a wooden Dutch farmhouse known

Grand Army Plaza, a monument to the Union soldiers of the Civil War, guards the main entrance to Prospect Park.

as **Lefferts Homestead;** and the **Prospect Park Wildlife Center,** 450 Flatbush Ave., which houses about 45 species in enclosures resembling their natural habitats. The zoo, 718/399-7339, is open April–Oct., Mon.–Fri. 10 A.M.–5 P.M., Sat.–Sun. 10 A.M.–5:30 P.M.; Nov.–March, daily 10 A.M.–4:30 P.M. Admission is adults $2.50, seniors $1.25, children 3–12 50 cents, children under three free.

Other attractions in the park include the odd, usually locked **Friends' Cemetery,** where Montgomery Clift and his mother are buried; **Wollman Rink,** open for skating in winter; and **Prospect Lake,** a shimmering expanse of blue at the park's south end.

Like Central Park, Prospect Park is generally safe but has its share of crime. It's not advisable to explore isolated areas alone or to enter the park after dark.

Maps are situated at the entrances and on signposts throughout the park. For more information about the park or its many special events, call 718/965-8999 or visit the website: www.prospectpark.org.

Park Slope

West of Prospect Park and south of Grand Army Plaza is Park Slope. Once known as the "Gold Coast," the area is home to one of the country's largest concentrations of Victorian brownstones. Park Slope fell on hard times after WW II, but has been on the upswing since the 1970s.

The main commercial thoroughfares are **7th and 5th Avenues,** while most of the neighborhood's prettiest brownstones are on the side streets between Prospect Park and 6th Avenue. **Carroll Street** and **Montgomery Place** are especially worth a gander. The **Montauk Club,** 25 8th Ave., at Lincoln, is one of Park Slope's finest old buildings. It's an eclectic Venetian palace lined with a frieze depicting the history of Long Island's Montauk Indians.

Mobster **Al Capone** grew up in a two-story brick house at 38 Garfield Place. He moved here with his family in 1907, when he was eight years old, and used to hang out at a pool hall down the block at 20 Garfield Place. As a teenager, Capone ran with a group of mobsters-in-training known as

the James Street gang. He fled to Chicago in 1919 when he became a suspect in a murder case.

Green-Wood Cemetery

About 10 blocks south of Prospect Park reigns the 478-acre Green-Wood Cemetery, 25th St. at 5th Ave., Sunset Park, 718/768-7300, www.green-wood.com, a glorious expanse of green filled with mausoleums, monuments, and New York City history. Tammany Hall's William "Boss" Tweed is buried here, along with architect Stanford White.

The cemetery is open daily 8 A.M.–4 P.M., and maps are available for $3 at the gate. To reach the cemetery, take the M, N, or R train to 25th Street.

Accommodations

Brooklyn offers a number of charming B&Bs. Among them is **Bed & Breakfast on the Park,** 113 Prospect Park West, between 6th and 7th Sts., 718/499-6115, a spacious home overlooking Prospect Park. All seven guestroom come equipped with oriental rugs and comfortable beds; $125–250 s or d. The turn-of-the-century **Foy House Bed & Breakfast,** 819 Carroll St., between 8th Ave., and Prospect Park West, Park Slope, 718/636-1492, is an attractive brownstone offering three cozy bedrooms and a garden apartment. $89–150 d.

In nearby Bedford-Stuyvesant, find the **Akwaaba Mansion,** 347 MacDonough St., between Stuyvesant and Lewis Aves., 718/455-5968, www.akwaaba.com. This grand 18-room stone edifice, sitting on a peaceful tree-lined street, offers four luxurious guestrooms, each with a different theme. $120–150 s or d.

Across the street from the mansion is the **Akwaaba Cafe,** which serves Southern dishes and Afro-diaspora specialties.

To find other B&Bs in Brooklyn, consult the directories listed under Accommodations in the Introduction chapter.

Food

Cousin John's, 70 7th Ave., between Berkeley and Lincoln, 718/622-7333, offers light fare and wonderful baked goods. **Red Hot Szechuan,** 347 7th Ave., at 10th St., 718/369-0700, is a

THE OUTER BOROUGHS

neighborhood favorite, serving especially good vegetarian dishes; average entrée $8.

Stylish **Max & Moritz,** 426A 7th Ave., between 14th and 15th Sts., 718/499-5557, is a friendly, bustling bistro serving imaginative contemporary American cuisine; average entrée $16. Newcomer **Rosewater,** 787 Union St., at 6th Ave., 718/783-3800, offers innovative American dishes in a lively setting that includes sidewalk seating in summer; average entrée $17.

On 5th Avenue, you'll find some of the neighborhood's best restaurants, including **Al Di Lá,** 248 5th Ave., at Carroll St., 718/783-4565, which specializes in Northern Italian fare; average entrée $15. **Cucina,** 256 5th Ave., near Garfield, 718/230-0711, serves first-rate Tuscan fare in a sophisticated setting; average entrée $18.

Watering Holes and Lounges

Once primarily a gay cafe, the **Rising Cafe,** 186 5th Ave., at Sackett St., 718/789-6340, has recently morphed into a comfortable neighborhood lounge complete with an eclectic music booking policy. One night you'll hear singer-songwriters, another night a jazz band; cover $5–10. At the local dive **Great Lakes,** 284 5th Ave., at 1st St., 718/499-3710, you'll find lots of indie rock on the jukebox and live local bands on Sunday and Monday. **Bar Reis,** 375A 5th Ave., between 5th and 6th Sts., 718/832-5716, is the place to go for live jazz and torch singers; out back is an inviting garden.

CROWN HEIGHTS

The name Crown Heights was invented by real estate agents in the 1920s to attract residents to what was supposed to be a brand new residential area. In reality, Crown Heights is made up of bits and pieces of five older Brooklyn neighborhoods—Bedford, Stuyvesant (now known as one district, Bedford-Stuyvesant, or Bed-Stuy), Brownsville, East New York, and Prospect Heights. From Manhattan, take the No. 3 train to Kingston Avenue.

Today, Crown Heights is best known for its two very distinct ethnic communities: the West Indians—mostly Haitians and Jamaicans—and the Lubavitch Hasidim, who comprise about

nine percent of the neighborhood's population. Crown Heights also houses a sizeable African American population and a small Asian one.

The neighborhood made the headlines in the 1990s due to racial tensions between the Lubavitch and the neighborhood's black populations. In 1991, a young black boy was killed by a careening car driven by a Hasidic man, touching off racial riots and the slaying of a Hasidic scholar, Yankel Rosenbaum. Reverberations from those riots are still being felt today.

The Lubavitch Hasidim

Like the Hasidim of Williamsburg (see above), the Lubavitch trace their roots to Eastern Europe. The men dress in dark suits and hats, while the women keep their collarbones, elbows, and knees covered. Unlike some Hasidim, however, the Lubavitch make use of modern technology. Until his death in 1994, the Rebbe Menachen Schneerson, the community's spiritual leader, used email to send his sermons to the approximately 1,600 other Lubavitch communities worldwide.

The center of the Lubavitch community is Kingston Avenue, between Eastern Parkway and Empire Boulevard. Here you'll find food shops and stores selling religious articles such as prayer shawls and yarmulkes.

At the corner of Kingston Avenue and Eastern Parkway is the **Lubavitch synagogue,** where members of the community pray, meditate, and chant the liturgy at all times of day. Women sit upstairs behind a glassed-off partition, while men sit downstairs on long, plain wooden benches. Many wear black-and-white prayer shawls.

Visitors are welcome at the synagogue and in the stores, but the best way to visit is to take one of the tours offered Sundays at noon by the Chassidic Discovery Center, 305 Kingston Ave., 718/953-5244, www.jewishtours.com. The tours include a short talk on the history and beliefs of the Lubavitch, followed by visits to the synagogue, the World Headquarters where religious artifacts are on display, the *mikvah* (a spiritual bathhouse), and lunch at a kosher deli.

The West Indians

The West Indians first began arriving in Crown

Heights in the 1920s, attracted by the neighborhood's many solid one- and two-family homes. Many were members of an aspiring middle class and were soon opening up small businesses. This influx dwindled in the 1950s due to strict immigration quotas, but soared again after 1965 when the laws were loosened up.

Today, the West Indian community is centered along Nostrand and Utica Avenues north of Eastern Parkway. Nostrand is three blocks west of Kingston Avenue; Utica is four blocks east. On both streets, you'll find a smattering of restaurants and bakeries, grocery stores and hair-braiding shops, storefront churches, and music, music, music. Bearded Rastas in brightly colored caps sell tapes of everything from reggae to country, while schoolchildren dressed in plaid skirts and jackets saunter by with armloads of books.

Brooklyn Children's Museum

Founded in 1899, this cheery place at 145 Brooklyn Ave., at St. Marks Ave., 718/735-4432, www.brooklynkids.org, was the world's first children's museum, and still attracts families from all over the city. Most of the exhibits are hands-on and interactive, and highlights include a liquid light show, a working windmill, a greenhouse, and an artificial set of lungs and larynx that can be made to "sing." The museum is open Wed.–Fri. 2–5 P.M. and Sat.–Sun. 10 A.M.–5 P.M. Suggested admission is $4 per person.

Weeksville

On a small knoll not far from Utica Avenue stand the Weeksville Houses, 1698-1708 Bergen St., 718/756-5250. Also known as the Hunterfly Road Houses, these four proud wooden-frame structures are all that's left of Weeksville, a free black community established here in the 1840s. Weeksville was forgotten by the world until 1968, when historian James Hurley, knowing that the community had existed here someplace, flew over the site by helicopter and noticed an oddly placed lane that didn't quite jibe with the modern grid system.

Today, the restored Weeksville houses tell their story through photographs, maps, artifacts, and videos. Some of the community's earliest residents included Dr. Susan Smith McKinney-Steward, who was the nation's third black female physician; and Maj. Martin Delaney, the grandson of an enslaved West African prince, who was active in the Underground Railroad. The community was named after James Weeks, who purchased the land in 1838 from the Lefferts family.

Free tours by appointment only.

Shopping and Food

Straker's Calypso Record World, 242 Utica Ave., near St. Johns, 718/756-0040, is the place to buy hard-to-find Caribbean records and tapes. **Dewar's,** 807 Nostrand Ave., near President, 718/773-8403, is a favorite family restaurant serving traditional West Indian fare.

FROM CONEY ISLAND TO SHEEPSHEAD BAY

If you've only got time to make one stop in Brooklyn, Coney Island/Brighton Beach should be it. Though no longer the amusement center it once was, there's something about this windy, run-down place—with its magnificent boardwalk, rusting rides, tawdry snack stands, buoyant Russian community, and hordes of summertime sunbathers—that's quintessential New York. Which is not to say that Coney Island isn't also a poor and sometimes desperate place—many parts of it are, especially in winter when most of the pleasure seekers are gone.

From Manhattan, take the B, D, or F train to Coney Island/Stillwell Avenue. It's a long subway ride out, and you'll wind up on the elevated tracks above scrappy Surf Avenue. One block west are the beach and boardwalk—crowded to the bursting point on hot summer days, pleasantly empty the rest of the time. Old Russian women sit gossiping beneath big black umbrellas, young boys run fishing lines off the piers, joggers kick up sand on the wide expanse of beach.

History

Named *Konijn Eiland* (Rabbit Island) by the Dutch, Coney Island remained uninhabited until the early 1800s, when several resorts for the rich were built. After the Civil War, the railroad opened the area to the masses, and the honky-tonk days and nights began. Saloons, gambling dens, boxing rings, and racetracks soon packed the place, to be followed by three enclosed parks, or "small cities of pleasure," called Steeplechase, Luna Park, and Dreamland.

But it was the building of the subway in 1920 that really transformed Coney Island; for just a five-cent fare, almost everyone could escape the oppression of the city for a day, and Coney Island grew and grew. New technologies led to the invention of the Ferris wheel and the roller coaster, and in 1923, the 80-foot-wide boardwalk was built.

Coney Island was magical. It seemed nothing could dull its shine. But Dreamland burned down in 1911, and Luna Park went up in flames in the 1940s. Next came the rise of the automobile, the flight to the suburbs, and the invention of a new kind of midway—a tamed, sanitized place known as Disneyland. Steeplechase Park closed in 1966, leaving only a remnant of itself behind.

Astroland and Wonder Wheel

That remnant is today called the **Astroland Amusement Park.** It's on the boardwalk at 1000 Surf Ave., around W. 10th St., 718/372-0275. Inside find the **Cyclone,** a classic 1920s roller coaster built on an old wooden frame that shakes and clatters as the cars shoot by. Enthusiasts consider the 60-mile-an-hour Cyclone—declared a city landmark in 1988—to be one of the country's best roller coasters. Also in the park are about 20 modern rides and plenty of honky-tonk video arcades and game booths. The park is open weekends in spring and daily in summer noon–midnight.

Adjoining Astroland is the **Wonder Wheel,** a regal 1920s Ferris wheel offering fairy-tale views of Manhattan, especially at night. The wheel is open weekends in spring and daily in summer noon–midnight.

Nathan's Famous

On the island side of the amusement park, at the corner of Surf and Stillwell Aves., is Nathan's Famous, 718/946-2202. Nathan's was started in 1916 by Nathan Handwerker, a sometime em-ployee of Charles Feltman. Feltman is said to have "invented" the hot dog by his simple act of putting a wiener inside a bun. Handwerker undersold his boss's fare by a nickel, and so secured his place in entrepreneurial history. Nowadays, on a busy summer weekend, the stand-up eatery sells as many as 50,000 hot dogs, 20,000 orders of French fries, and 500 gallons of lemonade.

Half Moon Hotel

Though torn down in 1996, the legendary Half Moon Hotel once stood on the boardwalk at 29th Street. Here, mobster and star witness for the prosecution Abe "Kid Twist" Reles jumped, fell, or was pushed out of a sixth-floor window while supposedly under police protection. Reles was to have testified against his boss, Albert Anastasia of Murder, Inc., but, despite the half-dozen cops guarding him day and night, he was found dead in the alleyway on the morning of November 12, 1941. The cops claimed to have found a white sheet attached to a wire hanging out of the Kid's window, but the fact that his body landed 20 feet from the wall made the suicide theory unlikely.

Across Surf Avenue north of the old Half Moon site, stand Coney Island's bleak housing projects. Located about as far away from jobs as it's possible to get, the soulless brick buildings, with their familiar problems of poverty, drugs, and violence, are among the city's worst examples of urban planning.

Sideshows by the Seashore

Heading east on the boardwalk from the amusement park, you'll soon come to the brightly painted storefront of "Sideshows By The Seashore," 1208 Surf Ave., at W. 12th St., 718/372-5159, www.coneyisland.com. A fierce-looking tattooed man lounges by the door, while inside is a mad-cap scene crowded with Snake Ladies, the Fire Eater, Human Blockheads, the Elastic Lady, Escape Artists, and the Torture King. It's all a sort of shrine to the way Coney Island used to be, run by a group of actors and performance artists, many from the East Village.

Started in 1985 by a Yale Drama School graduate named Dick Zigun, the nonprofit Sideshows also presents a whimsical, not-to-be-missed Mermaid Parade every June, a Tattoo Festival in late summer, and alternative rock-and-roll bands on summer nights.

Summer hours are Friday 2–9 P.M., Sat.–Sun. 1 P.M.–midnight; call for other times of the year. Admission is adults $5, children $3. Next door to the theater you'll find a small museum of Coney Island memorabilia and a souvenir shop.

New York Aquarium for Wildlife Conservation

Between the boardwalk and Surf Ave. at W. 8th St. is the delightful New York Aquarium for Wildlife Conservation, 718/265-FISH, www.wsc.org/nyaquarium. The thoroughly up-to-date place contains close to 4,000 residents, including walruses, beluga whales, sharks, stingrays, sea otters, and electric eels. In summer, dolphin and sea lion shows are featured daily, and an outdoor exhibit allows children to handle horseshoe crabs, sea urchins, starfish, and the like.

The aquarium is open daily 10 A.M.–4:30 P.M., with extended hours in summer. Admission is adults $11, seniors and children under 12 $7, children under two free.

Brighton Beach

Next door to Coney Island, and spilling over into it, is Brighton Beach. For many years home to a small and aging Russian Jewish community, Brighton Beach has been exploding with new life ever since the end of the Cold War. Over 100,000 Russians have settled in New York since 1989—some with green cards, others without—and about 75 percent of them have moved to Brooklyn. Stroll the streets and boardwalk here and you'll see old women in babushkas, middle-aged men and women in drab socialist dress, and teenagers courting a hipness that is half East, half West. Many of the store signs speak of Russia—Vladimir's Unisex, Rasputin, the Stolichny Deli—as do the smells and the music.

With all this tremendous new life have come new tensions. An organized Russian crime ring has entered the drug trade, bringing with it murder and extortion. Much distrust also exists between the Russian populace—who grew up learning to evade officialdom—and the New York City authorities.

Not that any of this affects the visitor. Step off the boardwalk onto **Brighton Beach Avenue,** and you'll find many friendly Russian shops, restaurants, and nightclubs. See Shopping, below.

Sheepshead Bay

If you continue walking 20 minutes down Brighton Beach Avenue to Brighton 11th Street to Emmons Avenue (or take the B or D train one stop), you'll come to Sheepshead Bay. A tiny New England-like port inhabited by a large number of retirees, the place is full of fishing boats and yachts, seafood restaurants, and tackle shops. Fishing boats can be rented by the half-day; expect to pay about $15 per adult, with discounts for kids under 12.

Shopping

Of the Brighton Beach food shops, **M&I International,** 249 Brighton Beach Ave., 718/615-1011, is the best. The bright and modern two-story emporium is stocked with an enormous array of cheeses, fresh breads, sausages, smoked fish, and—of course—caviar and borscht.

For a classic knish, stop into the 50-odd-year-old **Mrs. Stahl's Knishery,** 1001 Brighton Beach Ave., 718/648-0210.

Every day between 9 A.M. and 5 P.M., the **Coney Island Flea Market,** 1231 Surf Ave., between Stillwell Ave. and W. 8th St., is open for business, with cluttered booths selling everything from rugs to records.

Entertainment

Brighton Beach is famous for its over-the-top, Las Vegas–style Russian nightclubs where the music is fast and loud and the vodka flows nonstop. Two favorite spots are the glamorous **Rasputin,** 2670 Coney Island Ave., at Ave. X, 718/332-8333, complete with a balcony and oft-packed dance floor; and the more intimate **Primorski,** 282-B Brighton Beach Ave., 718/891-3111, which also serves an excellent, relatively inexpensive lunch. Evenings at these restaurants don't come cheap; plan on spending about $50 per person for dinner and entertainment. Reservations are a must.

THE OUTER BOROUGHS

Other Restaurants

Not far from the Boardwalk in Coney Island is **Gargiulo's,** 2911 W. 15th St., between Mermaid and Surf Aves., 718/266-4891, a longtime neighborhood favorite serving huge portions of Italian food; average entrée $14. For crisp-crusted pizza, check out **Totonno Pizzeria Napolitano,** 1524 Neptune Ave., between W. 15th and W. 16th Sts., 718/372-8606. Reopened in 1996 in Sheepshead Bay is the enormous **Lundy Brothers,** 1901 Emmons Ave., at Ocean Ave., 718/743-0022, a legendary seafood restaurant that had been closed for 17 years. Food-wise, the new eatery does not measure up to the old, but the place still has a nostalgic charm; average entrée $16.

Queens

Until recently, Queens was widely regarded as a snore. This was where the complacent everyman lived, in a row house exactly like his neighbor's. Queens was home to Archie Bunker and hundreds of thousands of others like him. Queens was mediocrity. Queens was suburbia. Queens was boring, boring, boring.

Whether or not this was ever really true, it certainly isn't so today. New York's largest borough now boasts some of the city's biggest and most vibrant ethnic neighborhoods, as well as some architectural and cultural gems that are just beginning to be appreciated. Queens is also where Louis Armstrong, Will Rogers, Jackie Robinson, and Jack Kerouac all once lived; where the early movie industry was headquartered; and where the wealthy once summered, on grand estates in Bayside or on the then-pristine beaches of the Rockaways.

Named for Queen Catherine of Braganza, the wife of England's Charles II, Queens was first settled in the 17th century. An important agricultural center supplying Manhattan, it was annexed to New York City in 1898. Western Queens began developing in the mid-1800s, but it wasn't until the building of the Long Island Rail Road in 1910 that the borough really boomed. Then, apartment houses and private homes sprang up all over, and thousands of New Yorkers moved out into the "country."

Neighborhoods

Like Brooklyn, Queens is composed of many distinct neighborhoods. Nearest Manhattan are Long Island City and Astoria, while scattered throughout the borough are seven planned neighborhoods built around parks. Noteworthy among these "Seven Sisters," as they're known, are Richmond Hill, filled with shingled Victorian homes and the dense Forest Park; Kew Gardens, a 1910s neo-Tudor community; Forest Hills Gardens, splendidly landscaped by Frederick Law Olmsted; and Sunnyside Gardens, a 1920s utopian community still studied today as a model of middle-income housing.

Elsewhere in Queens, Forest Hills has a large Bukharan Jewish population, while many middle-class African Americans reside in Jamaica, St. Albans, and Corona. Flushing is nicknamed Little Asia; Jackson Heights has large Latin American and Indian communities; and Elmhurst is home to many Thais. Thousands of new Irish immigrants have settled in Woodside.

At the southern end of Queens is Howard Beach, now associated in many New Yorkers' minds with racism and violence. In 1986, at 12:30 A.M., 23-year-old Michael Griffith's Buick broke down on an isolated stretch of Cross Bay Boulevard. He and his two companions walked into predominantly Italian Howard Beach to get help, and stopped in a pizza parlor looking for a pay phone. They were told there was none, but because they were hungry, they ordered slices and sat down. A few moments later, two cops stopped by to check out an anonymous 911 complaint about "three suspicious black males." When the threesome left the restaurant, they were attacked by a dozen white men wielding

> *"You know, the more they knock New York, the bigger it gets."*
>
> **Will Rogers**

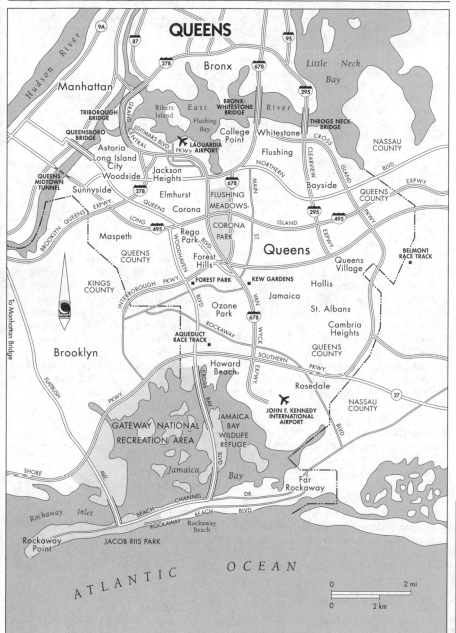

THE OUTER BOROUGHS

© AVALON TRAVEL PUBLISHING, INC.

WHERE THE WILD THINGS ARE

At the far southern end of Queens is the Jamaica Bay Wildlife Refuge, where over 300 species of birds, 80 types of fish, and dozens of kinds of reptiles and amphibians live. It seems amazing that wildlife can flourish here. JFK Airport is directly across the bay, and all around the refuge, traffic—both ground and air—drones on incessantly. Still, the refuge is on the Atlantic flyway, and well worth a visit during the autumn and spring. The refuge is open daily 8:30 A.M.–5 P.M.; call 718/318-4340 for more information and directions by either car or public transportation. Or write Gateway National Recreation Area, Floyd Bennett Field, Bldg. 69, Brooklyn, NY 11234.

baseball bats. Griffith and his cousin ran to escape, but as Griffith crossed the Belt Parkway, he was struck by a car and killed. One year later, three members of the Howard Beach gang were sentenced to 15–30 years in prison.

South of Howard Beach stretches **Jamaica Bay** and the 10-mile-long **Rockaway peninsula.** Once a playground for the rich and then for the middle class, the Rockaways are now sadly abandoned, a dumping ground for the city's poor.

A Note on Addresses

Theoretically, Queens is laid out according to a grid system. The streets run north-south, from 1st Street, paralleling the East River, to 250th Street, at the borough's eastern end. Similarly, the avenues run east-west, with the lowest numbered addresses to the north and the highest numbered to the south. Addresses are supposedly coded with their nearest cross-street or avenue: 28-13 23rd Ave., for example, should mean that the building is at No. 13 23rd Avenue near 28th Street. But things don't always work out that neatly. When in doubt, it's best to call ahead.

Addresses below are listed with their closest cross-street when it's different from the one stated in the address.

LONG ISLAND CITY

Directly east of the Queensboro Bridge lies Long Island City. Though largely a dreary industrial area filled with windowless factory buildings, Long Island City has in the last decade become home to a cutting-edge artistic community. That fact went largely unnoticed by the general public until June 2002, when the Museum of Modern Art opened its temporary quarters here (see the special topics on MoMA QNS, next page, and Art on the Move, in the Rockefeller Center section of the Manhattan chapter). Suddenly, the neighborhood is in the news, with some predicting that it will soon become another Williamsburg (the once-tired Brooklyn neighborhood now revitalized by young urban professionals).

From Manhattan, to reach the Museum of Modern Art in Queens (dubbed MoMA QNS), take the No. 7 local train to 33rd Street/Queens Boulevard; the museum is located directly across the boulevard. To reach P.S. 1, take the No. 7 train to 45th Road/Court House Square, or the E or F train to 23rd Street. To reach the Noguchi Museum, take the N train to the Broadway station in Queens.

Also, on the weekends, a free **Queens Art Link,** 212/708-9750, www.queensartlink.org, travels to all three institutions and the American Museum of the Moving Image (see Astoria, below). The shuttle service leaves from the Manhattan MoMA building, 11 W. 53rd St., between 5th and 6th Aves., Sat.–Sun. every hour between 10 A.M.–4 P.M.

Noguchi Museum and Socrates Sculpture Park

The austere Isamu Noguchi Garden Museum, 32-37 Vernon Blvd., at 33rd Rd., 718/204-7088, www.noguchi.org, housed in the late sculptor's former studio, is closed for renovation until Spring 2004. In the meantime, the museum is operating a temporary exhibit space in Sunnyside, Queens, at 36th St. and 43rd Ave. The temporary space is open Thurs.–Fri. 10 A.M.–5 P.M., Sat.–Sun. 11 A.M.–6 P.M., and Monday 10 A.M.–5 P.M. Suggested donation is adults $5, seniors and students $2.50. Call for directions and exhibit details.

A few blocks north of the Noguchi Museum is

the delightful Socrates Sculpture Park, 31-29 Vernon Blvd., at Broadway, 718/956-1819. Dotted with huge outdoor sculptures—most of them colorful and playful, a few dark and forbidding—the park is the brainchild of artist Mark di Suvero. For 10 years, di Suvero and other area artists worked to turn the once-garbage-strewn lot into a bona fide park. The city officially recognized their efforts in 1994, and the site is now part of New York's park system. The park offers great views of Manhattan and is open daily 9 A.M.–sunset. Free.

P.S. 1 Contemporary Art Center

After a three-year renovation, P.S. 1 reopened in the fall of 1997 to enthusiastic reviews. New York's premier center for art on the cutting edge, acquired by the Museum of Modern Art in 1999, P.S. 1 specializes in the avant-garde, conceptual, and experimental. Housed in a four-story building that was once a public school, it offers artwork in all sorts of nooks and crannies—stairwells, basements, holes in the floor—as well as in large galleries. Bold graphics mark the museum's entrance, while art ranging from painting and sculpture to video and installation is inside. Two or

three shows are usually featured at once, and traveling international shows are showcased as well. On the first floor is an inviting cafe.

P.S. 1, 22-25 Jackson Ave., at 46th St., 718/784-2084, www.ps1.org, is open Wed.–Sun, noon–6 P.M. Suggested donation is adults $5, seniors and students $2.50.

Other Galleries

Long Island City is also home to a number of other interesting art centers. Among them are the Maya Lin–designed **SculptureCenter,** 44-19 Purves St., 718/361-1750, which features three exhibition galleries, **L.I.C.K. Ltd. Fine Art,** 46-44 11th St., 718/937-3080, and the **Dorsky Gallery,** 11th St. at 45th Ave., 718/937-6317. All are clustered around P.S. 1.

Food

Near P.S. 1, find **Manducatis,** 13-27 Jackson Ave., 718/729-4602, known for its classic Italian food, and **Manetta's,** 10-76 Jackson Ave., 718/786-6171, which serves brick-oven pizza to a bustling lunchtime crowd. Near MoMA QNS is **Hemsin,** 39-17 Queens Blvd., 718/937-1715,

MUSEUM OF MODERN ART IN QUEENS (MOMA QNS)

Painted a deep blue, with bits and pieces of the museum's logo peppering its roof, the Museum of Modern Art in Queens (MoMA QNS) is hard to miss, especially if you're arriving by subway, which travels above ground here. Now housed in a former Swingline factory building, redesigned by architect Michael Maltzan, MoMA will make its home in Queens until 2005.

The museum's temporary quarters are smaller than its old home, with just 25,000 square feet of gallery space and a 50-seat cafe. But a vital part of the museum's permanent collection of paintings and sculpture is on view, and the exhibit's smaller size is an advantage in some ways, as it's easier to take in.

The museum's lobby is alive with flickering films and videos, while elsewhere, white serpentine ramps contrast with polished gray cement floors. The museum has moveable white walls and no windows, giving it an industrial loft-like feel.

One of the world's foremost museums of modern art, MoMA opened in 1929, shortly after the crash of the stock market. The museum's collection includes over 100,000 paintings, sculptures, drawings, prints, and photographs, and some 10,000 films and four million film stills. Among its many famous holdings are Cezanne's *The Bather,* van Gogh's *Starry Night,* Rousseau's *The Sleeping Gypsy,* Magritte's *The Empire of Light,* Hopper's *Gas,* Rothko's *Red, Brown and Black,* de Chirico's *The Song of Love,* Picasso's *Les Demoiselles d'Avignon,* and Monet's *Water Lilies.*

MoMA QNS hosts its first blockbuster show, a Picasso-Matisse exhibit, in 2003.

MoMA QNS, 45-20 33rd St., at Queens Blvd., 212/708-9400, www.moma.org, is open Thurs.–Mon. 10 A.M.–5 P.M., and to 7:45 P.M. on Friday. Admission is adults $12, seniors and students $8.50, children under 12 free.

THE OUTER BOROUGHS

offering tasty Turkish fare, and **Blooms,** 41-06 Queens Blvd., 718/706-1000, one of the area's many Irish pubs.

The romantic and expensive **Water's Edge,** East River at 44th Dr., 718/482-0033, offers imaginative American fare and great views of the skyline. Complimentary water shuttle service from Manhattan's East 34th Street pier is offered starting at 6 P.M.; average entrée $27.

ASTORIA

Not far from Long Island City is Astoria, one of the oldest settlements in Queens. It was developed in 1839 by John Jacob Astor, who built it up into a thriving shipping port. Later, in the 1920s and 1930s, the neighborhood was the center of the movie-making business on the East Coast; Astoria Movie Studios produced such legendary stars as Rudolf Valentino and Gloria Swanson. Astoria today is a stable and well-kept working- and middle-class community with the largest concentration of Greeks outside of Greece. From Manhattan, to reach the Greek community, take the N train to 30th Avenue. To reach the American Museum of the Moving Image, take the R or G train to Steinway Street and walk south to 35th Avenue.

After the easing of immigration quotas in 1965, Astoria's Greek population expanded exponentially; today it's estimated to be about 80,000. The earliest of these immigrants began arriving in the late 1920s and promptly built **St. Demetrios Greek Orthodox Church,** a magnificent domed structure at 31st Street and 30th Drive. Another gorgeous Greek Orthodox church is **St. Irene's,** 36-25 23rd Ave., which features an altar adorned with red-and-gold peacocks.

Along **30th Avenue** between 31st and Steinway Streets, several wonderful food shops sell imported olive oils, feta cheese, and the like, while Greek pastry shops beckon with outdoor tables. **Titan Supermarket,** 25-56 31st St., between 25th and 30th Aves., 718/626-7771, is an especially popular stop stocking grape leaves, olives, olive oils, thick Greek yogurt, and much more. On **Broadway,** you'll find numerous Greek bakeries, as well as butcher shops

advertising baby pigs, baby lambs, and baby goats. Also in Astoria are many Pakistani, Italian, and Latino food shops, restaurants, and retail businesses.

American Museum of the Moving Image

Not far from the Greek community, at 34-12 36th St., is the site of the former Astoria Movie Studios. The studios were renovated and reopened in the late 1970s, and are now known as the **Kaufman-Astoria Studios.** Among the many movies and television shows that have been completely or partially produced here are *The Wiz, The Verdict, The World According to Garp,* and *The Cosby Show.*

Also here is the American Museum of the Moving Image, 36-01 35th Ave., 718/784-0077, www.ammi.org, which traces the history of movies and television. The museum houses over 70,000 artifacts covering all aspects of the film industry—from make-up to fan magazines—and features hands-on exhibits in which visitors can create their own animated films, design soundtracks, and the like. The museum also boasts an excellent screening program; call in advance to find out what's playing. The museum is open Tues.–Fri. noon–5 P.M. and Sat.–Sun. 11 A.M.–6 P.M. Admission is adults $8.50, seniors $5.50, students and children 5–18 $4.50, children under four free.

Steinway Piano Factory

At the Steinway Piano Factory, Steinway Pl., between 19th Ave. and 38th St., 718/721-2600, www.steinway.com, you can watch skilled artisans assemble the famed musical instruments and tune them in soundproof rooms. The four-hour tours are free but must be reserved well in advance.

Shopping

Some Greek food shops to look for are **Mediterranean Foods,** 30-12 34th St., 718/728-6166, in business for over 20 years; and **Titan Supermarket,** 25-56 31st St., 718/626-7771, a supermarket lined with barrels of olives and other pickled foodstuffs.

Food and Entertainment

Near the American Museum of the Moving Image is **Cafe Bar,** 32-90 36th St., 718/204-5273, an artsy cafe-bar featuring Mediterranean-style food and a laid-back bar scene in the evenings; average entrée $11.

Among the area's many Greek restaurants, informal **Telly's Taverna,** 28-13 23rd Ave., between 28th and 29th Sts., 718/728-9056, offers especially delicious grilled lamb dishes and an outdoor garden in summer; average entrée $14. For excellent fish dishes, prepared Greek-style, try the no-frills **Elias Corner,** 24-02 31st St., 718/932-1510; average entrée $13. **Taverna Vraka,** 23-15 31st St., between 23rd and 24th Aves., 718/721-3007, is a glitzy place that has been attracting celebrities for over 20 years; average entrée $15. **Uncle George's,** 33-19 Broadway, at 34th St., 718/626-0593, is a bright, 24-hour spot that's one of the neighborhood's favorite restaurants; average main course $8.

Live Greek music and dancing are often featured at upscale restaurants such as the Taverna Vraka on the weekends. Flyers announcing the events are posted in shop windows and on telephone poles.

JACKSON HEIGHTS

Nicknamed the "cornfield of Queens" in the early 1900s, Jackson Heights began developing in the 1910s and 1920s. Large blocks of attractive apartment houses were constructed, many featuring pretty courtyards and gardens, fireplaces, and high ceilings. Ironically, given Jackson Heights' multicultural make-up today, developers advertised it as a "restricted garden residential section," meaning Jews, blacks, and even Catholics need not apply.

Jackson Heights began turning from gardens to concrete around the time of WW II, when nearby **La Guardia Airport** was constructed. In the 1940s and 1950s, the Irish and Italians moved in, and in the 1960s, the first Latinos began arriving. Most of the latter were Argentinians fleeing an unstable government, and Cubans fleeing Castro. From Manhattan, take the No. 7 train to 82nd Street and exit onto Roosevelt Avenue.

Ethnic Jackson Heights

Today, Jackson Heights is still home to a few Irish, Italians, Argentinians, and Cubans, but its largest ethnic group is Colombian. Walk north or south on Roosevelt Avenue and you'll see newsstands selling Colombian newspapers, bakeries selling Colombian cakes and coffees, and stores selling Colombian videos. Residents even call the area Chapinero, after the Bogotá suburb. Jackson Heights is also home to a sizeable Indian population, centered around 74th Street, and to smaller Peruvian, Uruguayan, Filipino, and Thai communities.

Historic Jackson Heights

To get a sense of what life was like in Jackson Heights when it was a "restricted garden residential district," head northwest of Roosevelt Avenue to 37th or 35th Avenue between 78th and 88th Streets. This area was declared a historic district in 1994 and holds many fine apartment buildings adorned with griffins, columns, and arches. Many share lush communal gardens.

Food

Two excellent Colombian restaurants are **La Pequeña Colombia,** 83-27 Roosevelt Ave., 718/478-6528; and **Tierras Colombianas,** 82-18 Roosevelt Ave., 718/426-8868, both casual spots serving heaping platters of food; average entrée $9. For tasty Bolivian food, try **Nostalgias,** 85-09 Northern Blvd., 718/533-9120; average entrée $9. **Crazy Chicken,** 78-07 Roosevelt Ave., 718/779-6711, and other locations, barbecues some of the juiciest chickens in town for about $6.

The **Jackson Diner,** 37-47 74th St., 718/672-1232, is a favorite Indian eatery among New Yorkers in the know; average entrée $9. Another popular Indian spot is **Shaheen Sweets,** 72-09 Broadway, 718/639-4791; average main dish $6.

FLUSHING MEADOWS–CORONA PARK

Today, Flushing Meadows is a peaceful green oasis attracting families, couples, and kids. But back in the early 1900s, it was a towering, reeking garbage dump that smoldered by day and glowed

THE OUTER BOROUGHS

at night. One hundred ten railroad carloads of Brooklyn's refuse were dumped here daily, providing succulent meals for hordes of rats "big enough to wear saddles," as one observer put it. F. Scott Fitzgerald, writing in *The Great Gatsby*, described the place as "a valley of ashes—a fantastic farm where ashes grow like wheat into ridges and hills and grotesque gardens. . . ."

Enter Robert Moses, city parks commissioner. Moses, looking at the noxious heap, saw not an irredeemable wasteland but a potential park. In 1934, he directed the removal of some 50 million cubic tons of garbage. Thereafter began the construction of the 1939 World's Fair, followed 25 years later by the construction of the 1964 World's Fair. Both extravaganzas were largely created through Moses' sheer force of will, and both ended up costing the city and its backers millions of dollars.

Remains of the fairs still dot the 1,225-acre park. Most conspicuous is the 1964 **Unisphere,** a shining 140-foot-high, 380-ton hollow globe sitting in the middle of a pretty fountain. All around the fountain circle rollerbladers, kids on tricycles, and couples out for a stroll.

Flushing Meadows–Corona Park is also known for its U.S.T.A. National Tennis Center, where the U.S. Open Tennis Tournament is held each year. Other park attractions include a miniature golf course, several playgrounds, a botanical garden, two lakes, a marina, and a turn-of-the-century carousel. Signs are posted at intersections throughout the park pointing the way to attractions, and free tours are frequently offered by the Queens Urban Park Rangers, 718/217-6034. Across the street is the huge, 55,000-seat **Shea Stadium,** home to the New York Mets. From Manhattan, take the No. 7 train to Willets Point/Shea Stadium and follow the signs. A visit to the park can easily be combined with a visit to Jackson Heights (above) or Flushing (below), as all are located along Roosevelt Avenue.

Queens Museum of Art

Next to the Unisphere is the Queens Museum of Art, 718/592-9700, www.queensmuse.org, housed in what was the New York City pavilion at both the 1939 and the 1964 World's Fairs. Renovated in the late 1990s to the tune of $15 million, the museum presents first-rate temporary exhibitions and houses an unusual permanent exhibit—the New York Panorama. First showcased at the 1964 fair, the panorama is a scale model of the city, showing every single building and house in the five boroughs—some 895,000 of them, built of plastic and wood. One of Moses' pet projects, the panorama was originally intended to be a serious tool for urban planners but now feels more like a nostalgic work of art. The model is constantly being updated, with over 60,000 changes at last count.

The museum is open Tues.–Fri. 10 A.M.–5 P.M., Sat.–Sun. noon–5 P.M. Suggested admission is adults $5, seniors and students $2.50, children under five free.

Queens Zoo

About a five-minute walk north of the Queens Museum, over the Grand Central Parkway (take the bridge just west of the museum, next to the ice rink) is the Queens Zoo, 53-51 111th St., 718/271-7761, www.queenszoo.org. Operated by the Wildlife Conservation Society (which also runs the Central Park and Prospect Park zoos), the state-of-the-art center is devoted to North American wildlife, including mountain lions, bison, bobcats, coyotes, bears, and Roosevelt elk. Hours are Mon.–Fri. 10 A.M.–5 P.M. and Sat.–Sun. 10 A.M.–5:30 P.M.; the last tickets are sold one-half hour before closing. Admission is adults $2.50, senior citizens $1.25, children 3–12 50 cents, and children under three free.

New York Hall of Science

West of the zoo is the New York Hall of Science, 47-01 111th St., 718/699-0005, www.nyhallsci.org, ranked as one of the country's top 10 science museums. Housed in a dramatic, undulating building—another odd leftover from the 1964 World's Fair—the museum is packed with hands-on exhibits. Among them are a distorted room that makes people appear to shrink or grow, and an enlarged drop of water showing microscopic organisms going about their daily lives. Out back is a large Science Playground, where kids can learn about the laws of physics. The museum is open July 1–Aug. 31, Monday 9:30 A.M.–2 P.M.,

Tues.–Fri. 9:30 A.M.–5 P.M., Sat.–Sun. 10:30 A.M.–6 P.M.; Sept. 1–June 30, closed Monday, Tues.–Wed. 9:30 A.M.–2 P.M., Thur.–Sun. 9:30 A.M.–5 P.M. Admission is adults $7.50, seniors and children under 12 $5; free Wed.–Thurs. 2–5 P.M., except during July–August.

Corona

A few minutes south of the Hall of Science, in the small community of Corona, is the **Lemon Ice King,** 52-02 108th St., 718/699-5133, known throughout the city for selling the best Italian ices *anywhere.* The Ice King, Ben Faremo, has been making his sweets from real fruit since 1944, and flavors range from cantaloupe to peanut butter. The shop is open daily 10 A.M.–10 P.M. from Memorial Day to Labor Day; call for hours the rest of the year. To reach the Ice King from the Hall of Science, walk south on 111th Street to 51st Avenue and turn right. Continue to 108th Street.

Corona was once home to **Louis Armstrong,** who lived in a red-brick building at 34-56 107th St. from the early 1940s until his death in 1971. Tales are often told of how the jazz giant used to sit on his front steps with his trumpet and entertain the neighborhood kids, some of whom came by with horns of their own. The Armstrong home is now on the National Register of Historic Places. It's owned by Queens College, which hopes to turn it into a museum. Armstrong is buried in **Flushing Cemetery,** 163-06 46th Ave., 718/359-0100; on his tombstone is a sculpture of a trumpet draped in cloth.

The **Louis Armstrong Archives,** Queens College, 65-30 Kissena Blvd., between Melbourne and Reeves Aves., 718/997-3670, www.satchmo.net, hosts frequent exhibits and occasional concerts. Call for more information and an update on the Armstrong house museum.

FLUSHING

From Manhattan, take the No. 7 train to Main Street, the end of the line.

Asian Flushing

Once a Dutch town known as Vlissingen, and later a popular resort for the wealthy, Flushing is now home to one of the city's largest Asian communities. Before their arrival in the late 1970s, the middle-class area was beginning to go downhill. Today, however, Flushing is a vibrant place packed with a hodgepodge of Asian billboards, shops, and restaurants.

Asian Flushing is roughly bordered by Northern Boulevard to the north, Sanford Avenue to the south, College Point Boulevard to the west, and Union Street to the east. **Main and Union Streets** are the most active thoroughfares, with the Korean community centering on Union, and the Chinese and Indian communities on the northern and southern stretches of Main, respectively.

Historic Flushing

Buildings dating back to Dutch and Colonial times still stand in Flushing. At the corner of 37th Ave. and Bowne St. is the **Bowne House,** 37-01 Bowne St., 718/359-0528, a small wooden building used for illegal Quaker meetings in the 1660s. Upon learning of these meetings, Dutch governor Peter Stuyvesant—who had banned the Quaker sect—had John Bowne put in prison and whipped. Bowne appealed his case before the more tolerant Dutch West India Company in Amsterdam and was acquitted. The company's ruling became a precedent for America's Bill of Rights.

Inside, the Bowne house is filled with furnishings belonging to many generations of Bownes, the only family who ever lived here. The house is currently closed for renovation until 2006.

Around the corner from the Bowne house is the **Friends Meeting House,** 137-16 Northern Blvd., between Main and Union Sts., where the Quakers met in the centuries following the Bowne decision. This dark, shingled building has been in continuous use since 1719, making it New York City's oldest house of worship. Tours of the meetinghouse are usually offered on the first Sunday of every month; call 718/358-9636 for more information.

Also nearby is the **Kingsland House,** 143-35 37th Ave., 718/939-0647. Built in 1785 in the English shingle–style, the building is now home to the Queens Historical Society, which presents frequent exhibits and offers walking tours of various Queens neighborhoods. Hours are Mon.–Fri. 9 A.M.–5 P.M. Tours are offered Tuesday, Thursday, and Sat.–Sun. 2:30–4:30 P.M. Cost is $3.

Hindu Temple of New York

A good 15-minute walk from the Main Street subway station is one of the more unusual sights in Flushing—the pale blue Hindu Temple of New York, 45-57 Bowne St., at Holly Ave., 718/460-8484. Tucked between two simple residences, the ornate temple was built in 1977 at a cost of nearly a million dollars. Crafts specialists were flown in from India to create the temple's rich detail.

Food

Two good Chinese bakeries to keep an eye out for are **Maria's Bakery,** 41-42 Main St., 718/358-8878, and **Tai Pan Bakery,** 135-20 Roosevelt Ave., 718/461-8668. Try a chestnut tart or an egg custard.

Everyone orders the special at the informal **Joe's Shanghai,** 136-21 37th Ave., near Main, 718/539-3838—e.g., dome-shaped "soup" dumplings filled with a rich crab or pork broth; average main dish $9. For some of the tastiest Malaysian food in town, try the exotic **Penang,** 38-04 Prince St., one block from Main, 718/321-2078, where popular dishes include *roti canai,* or flatbread served with chicken, potatoes, and broth, and *Penang rojak,* a mix of cucumber, pineapple, zucchini, tofu, and shrimp paste; average dish $12. Extravagant **Kum Gang San,** 138-28 Northern Blvd., 718/461-0909, filled with waterfalls, offers delicious Korean food seven days a week, 24 hours a day; average entrée $15.

The Bronx

The Bronx is a borough of extremes. Home to such great New York institutions as the Bronx Zoo, the New York Botanical Garden, and Yankee Stadium, it has also long stood as a symbol of urban decay. In 1981, the movie *Fort Apache, The Bronx* was filmed here; in 1987, Tom Wolfe set his novel *Bonfire of the Vanities* here. Horrific stories involving murders, arson, drug warlords, and children killing children come out of here daily, while images of the borough's burnt-out walk-ups and rubble-strewn lots have been seared into the national consciousness.

But the biggest story in the Bronx in the last decade is that things are actually looking up. Since 1986, more than $1 billion in public funds has been spent on the South Bronx—where most of the decay has taken place. At least 20,000 apartments have been refurbished and more than 3,000 new houses built. Charlotte Street, whose devastation Pres. Jimmy Carter drew attention to in 1977, is now lined with single-family homes surrounded by white picket fences—a strangely surreal sight in an otherwise still-blighted neighborhood. Big retail stores such as Bradlees and Pathmark are moving back in, and the borough recently opened its first new mall in decades. Though drugs, arson, and murder continue to plague the Bronx, the place is in better shape now than it's been in for years.

Of course, even at its worst, the Bronx was never as bad as its reputation. The urban devastation has been confined largely to the South Bronx, and even there, safe and stable pockets have always existed. Meanwhile, elsewhere in the borough flourish many large and pleasant residential neighborhoods, most working- and middle-class (City Island, Co-Op City, Norwood), a few quite exclusive (Riverdale, Fieldston). Most notably of all, the Bronx also boasts over 5,800 acres of parks.

For more information on the Bronx, contact the **Bronx Tourism Council,** 198 E. 161st St., Suite 201, Bronx, NY 10451, 718/590-3518, www.ilovethebornx.com.

Of course, even at its worst, the Bronx was never as bad as its reputation.

History

The Bronx is New York City's second smallest borough both in size and population, and it's

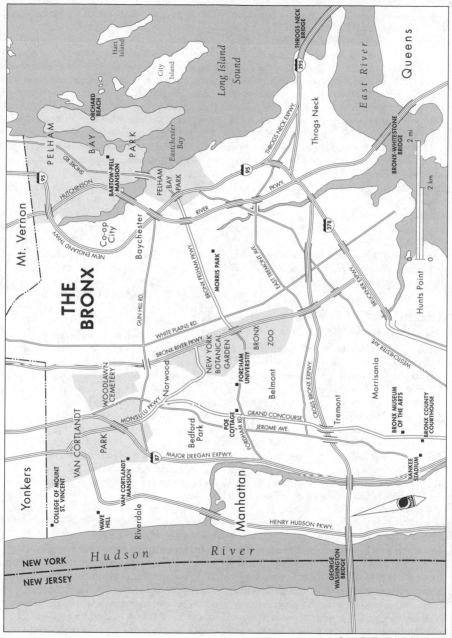

© AVALON TRAVEL PUBLISHING, INC.

the only one attached to the mainland. Purchased from the Algonquins by the Dutch West India Company in 1639, it was first settled in 1644 by a Scandinavian named Jonas Bronck. The area soon became known as "The Broncks," and remained a peaceful rural community up until the late 1800s. Then the 3rd Avenue Elevated Railway arrived, bringing with it thousands of European immigrants. By 1900, the borough's population had soared to over 200,000.

Many consider the 1920s through the early 1950s to be the golden era of the Bronx. That's when the borough was filled with many tightly knit ethnic neighborhoods, each with its own vibrant community life. The arrival of the affordable automobile, however, soon allowed many of the Bronx's more affluent residents to move to Long Island or Westchester. And in 1950, Robert Moses' six-lane Cross-Bronx Expressway was constructed, destroying a number of the borough's most stable neighborhoods.

THE BRONX ZOO AND BOTANICAL GARDEN

Though the zoo and botanical garden are next door to each other, to visit both in one day would require much fortitude, as both are very large. It's smarter to opt for one, and perhaps combine it with a meal or coffee and dessert on Arthur Avenue. The botanical garden is at its best in May and June. From Manhattan, to reach the zoo, take the No. 2 train to Pelham Parkway and walk west. Or, take a Liberty Lines express bus; call 718/652-8400 for details. To reach the botanical garden, take the No. 4 or D train to Bedford Park Boulevard and walk a half-dozen or so long blocks east.

The Bronx Zoo

One of the most beloved of New York institutions is the enormous Bronx Zoo, Fordham Rd. and Bronx River Pkwy., 718/367-1010, www.bronx-zoo.org, where New Yorkers have been spending weekends with their families for generations. It's among the world's largest and most important zoos, housing over 4,000 animals, many of which roam relatively freely in large landscaped habitats.

The Bronx Zoo was one of the world's first wildlife centers to adopt this technique.

Among the 250-acre zoo's most popular attractions is its Wild Asia Express, a monorail ride above a 38-acre savanna inhabited by elephants, antelope, Siberian tigers, rhinos, and many different kinds of deer. In the World of Birds, centered around a towering waterfall, about 100 species flit freely from tree to tree. In the World of Darkness, low lights make it possible to see nocturnal animals at their most active; included in this exhibit is the world's largest collection of captive bats.

Except in winter, the zoo is open Mon.–Fri. 10 A.M.–5 P.M., Sat.–Sun. 10 A.M.–5:30 P.M.; admission is adults $11, seniors $7, children 2–12 $6, free for children under two and for everyone on Wednesday. In winter the zoo is open daily 10 A.M.–4:30 P.M. and admission fees are reduced.

New York Botanical Garden

Just north of the zoo is the 250-acre New York Botanical Garden, Southern Blvd. and 200th St., 718/817-8700, www.nybg.org. Made up of both the cultivated and the wild, the park contains dozens of constituent gardens such as a rose garden and an herb garden, an arboretum, a hemlock forest, and—best of all—the enormous, shimmering, Victorian-style Enid Haupt Conservatory. Here, you'll find over 100 varieties of palms, tropical plants, desert flora, and ferns, and changing seasonal exhibits. The 1902 conservatory, with its 11 glass pavilions and many reflecting pools, was inspired by Kew Gardens in London and is the largest building of its type in America.

New to the garden as of 1999 is the Everett Children's Adventure Garden. This indoor-outdoor museum features lots of hands-on exhibits about the natural world for kids.

The garden is open April–Oct., Tues.–Sun. 10 A.M.–6 P.M.; Nov.–March, Tues.–Sun. 10 A.M.–4 P.M. Admission to the grounds is adults $3; seniors and students $2; children 2–12 $1; and free for everyone on Wednesday. Admission to the Enid Haupt Conservatory is adults $5, seniors and students $4, children 2–12 $3. Admission to the Everett Garden is adults $4, seniors and students $3, children 2–12 $2; hours are Tues.–Fri. 1–4 P.M. and Sat.–Sun. 10 A.M.–4 P.M.

Belmont

Just west of Bronx Zoo is the Italian community of Belmont, one of the city's older and more established ethnic neighborhoods. A stable and middle-class haven just north of the South Bronx, Belmont is chock-a-block with Italian restaurants, pastry shops, bakeries, butcher shops, poultry stores, and food markets, most of which are along **Arthur Avenue** or **187th Street.** This friendly neighborhood of spic-and-span streets and small backyard shrines has a warm, old-fashioned feel.

To reach Belmont from the zoo, walk west seven long blocks, or catch the Bx22 bus on East Fordham Road. From the garden, walk south through the campus of Fordham University.

Food Shops

At the heart of Belmont is the indoor **Arthur Avenue Retail Market,** 2344 Arthur Ave., at 187th St., 718/295-5033, where some of the city's freshest and cheapest fruits and vegetables can be found, along with fresh mozzarella, ravioli cutters, and espresso machines. Just up the street are **Madonia Brothers Bakery,** 2348 Arthur Ave., 718/295-5573, selling mouth-watering crusty bread, and **Biancardi's,** 2350 Arthur Ave., 718/733-4058, selling whole baby lambs and goats (no place for the squeamish). Down the street is the **Calabria Pork Store,** 2338 Arthur Ave., 718/367-5145, its ceiling densely hung with meats and sausages, and **Randazzo's Fish Market,** 2327 Arthur Ave., 718/367-4139, piled high with crab, sole, scrod, and the like. In warm weather, Randazzo's operates a raw seafood bar out front.

Food

A number of pastry shops and cafes are on 187th Street. **DeLillo's Pastry Shop,** 606 187th St., 718/367-8198, serves both pastries and homemade gelato and spumoni. **Egidio,** 622 187th St., 718/295-6077, is renowned for its miniature pastries.

Mario's, 2342 Arthur Ave., between 184th and 185th Sts., 718/584-1188, serves huge portions of Southern Italian food, and may be Bel-

mont's best-known, though not necessarily best, restaurant; it was featured in the film *The Godfather;* average entrée $16. **Dominick's,** 2335 Arthur Ave., at 187th St., 718/733-2807, has some of the neighborhood's best food, served family style at long tables covered with red tablecloths; average entrée $11. Good pizza joints can also be found all along Arthur Avenue.

POE COTTAGE AND THE GRAND CONCOURSE

From Manhattan, take the No. 4 train to Kingsbridge Road/Jerome Avenue and walk three blocks east to the Grand Concourse, or take the D train to Kingsbridge Road.

Poe Cottage

Run by the Bronx Historical Society, the Poe Cottage is at the corner of the Grand Concourse and East Kingsbridge Rd., 718/881-8900, www.bronxhistoricalsociety.org. Today, it seems inconceivable that this tiny white cottage surrounded by well-worn buildings and pothole-filled streets was once an isolated farmhouse. But in 1846, writer Edgar Allan Poe moved in here with his wife, Virginia, in hopes that the country air would cure her tuberculosis. When Poe wrote his famous poem "Annabel Lee," beginning "It was many and many a year ago/In a kingdom by the sea/That a maiden there lived whom you may know/By the name of Annabel Lee," it was his wife and the Bronx that he was talking about.

The cottage is a simple place with a large kitchen and sitting room downstairs and Poe's old cramped office and bedroom upstairs. A short video covers the highlights of Poe's life, leaving out many of the more controversial aspects (such as his serious drinking problem) and focusing on what the couple's lives were like while they were here. At that time, they were suffering from extreme poverty and often survived by foraging in the fields for dandelions and other edible plants. They had no money for fuel, and spent many winter days as well as nights bundled up in blankets.

After Virginia's death, in January 1847, Poe stayed on in the cottage for a few more years.

THE OUTER BOROUGHS

His mental and physical health—already poor—continued to deteriorate, and in 1849, on his way to Richmond, Virginia, he disappeared in Baltimore. When he was found a few days later, he was delirious. He died shortly thereafter.

Hours are Saturday 10 A.M.–4 P.M. and Sunday 1–5 P.M.; closed in January. Suggested admission is adults $3, seniors and students $2.

The Grand Concourse

Outside Poe Cottage runs the Grand Concourse, once one of the city's most glamorous boulevards, now a windswept and run-down thoroughfare. During the late 1920s and 1930s, the avenue was known as the "Jewish 5th Avenue." One of the country's first controlled-access parkways, it featured separate lanes for carriages, cyclists, and pedestrians, and was lined with one stunning art deco building after another.

Heading south on the Grand Concourse from Poe Cottage, you'll soon come to **Fordham Road,** an incredibly crowded street packed with all races and creeds of humans, hundreds of honking cars and noxious buses, and innumerable street vendors and discount stores. Two blocks farther south, at 2417 Grand Concourse, stands the former **Loew's Paradise,** designed in 1929 by John Eberson, the "Father of the Atmospheric Theater." Though not much to look at from the outside, the Paradise once featured an extravagant interior filled with baroque balconies, classical statues, a vast domed ceiling with blinking constellations, and a machine that could move clouds across the sky. In 1981, the theater was converted into a four-screen complex, and its interior painted bright green. Today it stands abandoned; preservationists are pushing to get it restored.

Other points of interest are farther south on the Grand Concourse, but since it's a long and not particularly pleasant trek to some of them, you'd best catch a Bx1 bus.

Bronx Museum of the Arts

At 165th Street is the Bronx Museum of the Arts, 1040 Grand Concourse, 718/681-6000, featuring changing contemporary art exhibits and a good permanent collection of works by Romare Bearden. The museum's hours are Wednesday noon–9 P.M., Thurs.–Sun. noon–6 P.M. Suggested admission is adults $3, students and seniors $2, children under 12 free.

Architectural Highlights

One of the grandest buildings along the Grand Concourse is the 1924 **Andrew Freedman Home,** located just north of the Bronx Museum of Art between McClennan and 166th Streets. Built by millionaire Andrew Freedman, this handsome stone edifice is now a home for the elderly.

Other art deco buildings to look out for further south on the Grand Concourse include **888 Grand Concourse,** designed in 1937 by Emery Roth, who also designed many of the buildings along Central Park West; the **Bronx County Courthouse,** 851 Grand Concourse, the immediate environs of which are not nearly as dangerous as Tom Wolfe described in his novel *Bonfire of the Vanities;* and the **Bronx General Post Office,** 558 Grand Concourse.

Nightlife

The hot spot in the Bronx is **Jimmy's Bronx Cafe,** 281 W. Fordham Rd., between Broadway and Cedar Ave., 718/329-2000. Run by the charming Jimmy Rodriguez, the club attracts partygoers from all over the city, especially on its weekend salsa nights. The club also serves tasty Caribbean fare; average entrée $18.

NORTHWEST BRONX

Woodlawn Cemetery

Filled with lush rolling hills, shady trees, meandering walkways, and a shimmering sky-blue lake, Woodlawn dates back to the 19th century. In that era, cemeteries were thought of as places to talk to God and commune with nature. Precursors to today's parks, they were also major tourist attractions, described in great detail in guidebooks, and so crowded on weekends that traffic controllers had to be stationed at the main intersections.

Few people think of Woodlawn as anything but a cemetery anymore, but it's still a fun place to explore. Many once-prominent New Yorkers are buried here. From Manhattan, take the No. 4 train to Woodlawn, the end of the line.

One of the park's most ornate mausoleums, just inside the main gate, belongs to Oliver Hazard Perry Belmont, financier and horse lover. Belmont, who apparently thought very highly of himself, designed his final resting place after the St. Hubert Chapel in Amboise, France, where Leonardo da Vinci is buried. Also near the main gate is the fine Ionic temple where the unscrupulous financier Jay Gould was buried in 1892. The railroad speculator was so hated that stock in his empire *rose* more than two points on the day he died.

Herman Melville's grave is a more modest affair. The author of *Moby Dick* died poverty-stricken in 1891, near the Gansevoort meat market, where he had worked as a customs official. He's buried beside his wife under a tall oak tree. On his tombstone are carved an unrolled scroll and a quill pen.

Duke Ellington also rests beneath a large tree, less than 10 yards away from the shiny black granite tombstone of Sir Miles Davis. Cemetery officials say the proximity of the two jazz greats' graves is purely coincidental.

One of the strangest epitaphs in the cemetery can be found on the tombstone of one George Spenser, who died in 1909. It reads: "Lost life by stab in falling on ink eraser, evading six young women trying to give him birthday kisses in office of Metropolitan Life Building."

Woodlawn Cemetery, 718/920-0500, is open daily 8:30 A.M.–5 P.M. A free map with grave locations is available at the office near the main gate. The office is closed on Sunday.

Van Cortlandt House Museum and Park

A charming 18th-century mansion, all but untouched by the vagaries of time, sits in Van Cortlandt Park in the northernmost section of the Bronx. Still surrounded by woods and fields (now used as ball fields), the recently restored stone house was built in 1748 by wealthy landowner Frederick Van Cortlandt. It's furnished with antiques—some of which belonged to the Van Cortlandt family—and a number of interesting paintings, including a portrait of John Jacob Astor by Gilbert Stuart.

George Washington stayed in the mansion on and off during the Revolutionary War, using the

west parlor as his office. During the late 1700s and early 1800s, about 17 slaves lived here as well, most sleeping in cramped quarters on the third floor.

The Van Cortlandt house, 718/543-3344, is open Tues.–Fri. 10 A.M.–3 P.M. and Sat.–Sun. 11 A.M.–4 P.M. Admission is adults $2, students and seniors $1.50. From Manhattan, take the No. 1 or 9 train to 242nd Street/Van Cortlandt Park. The mansion is in the park's southern end, near Broadway.

Surrounding the mansion is hilly Van Cortlandt Park, which at two miles square is the city's third largest park. Its serenity is marred, however, by the three major parkways (the Henry Hudson, the Major Deegan, and the Monsulu) that run through it. At the park's east end are the remains of the Croton Aqueduct, now a favorite path for runners. To the west, near the mansion, are the park's Parade Grounds, which attract cricket- and rugby-playing West Indians on weekends. For more information about the park, call 718/430-1890.

Wave Hill

Wave Hill, an estate perched on bluffs high above the Hudson in the wealthy community of Riverdale, boasts many fine gardens and greenhouses, breathtaking views, and a pretty 1844 Greek Revival mansion. Theodore Roosevelt, Mark Twain, and Arturo Toscanini all once lived in this lovely oasis, now serving as a city park. In summer, frequent dance and music events are presented here—most of them outdoors.

When Mark Twain leased Wave Hill from 1901 to 1903, he set up a treehouse parlor in the branches of a chestnut tree on the lawn. Of winter at the estate he wrote, "I believe we have the noblest roaring blasts here I have ever known on land; they sing their hoarse song through the big tree-tops with a splendid energy that thrills me and stirs me and uplifts me and makes me want to live always."

Just west of the mansion is Abrons Woodland, 10 acres of woods and meadows currently being replanted with native plants. A trail meanders through the woodland, and signs along the way explain the project's progress.

Wave Hill, 718/549-3200, is open May–Oct., Tues.–Sun. 9 A.M.–5:30 P.M. and Oct.–May Tues.–Sun. 9 A.M.–4:30 P.M. Admission May–Nov., Wed.–Sun., is adults $4, students and seniors $2, children under six free; free to all on Tuesday, and Saturday 9 A.M.–noon. From Manhattan, take a Metro-North train, 212/532-4900, from Grand Central to the Riverdale Station at 254th Street, and walk southeast and uphill to Wave Hill's entrance at the intersection of Independence Avenue and 249th Street. Or, take the A train to 231st Street, then board the Bx7 or Bx10 bus. Take it to 252nd Street, walk across the parkway bridge, and head left to 249th Street. Liberty Lines, 212/652-8400, also offers express bus service from Manhattan to 252nd Street.

Discount Clothing

One of New York City's best-known stores for discounted designer wear is **Loehmann's,** a warehouse-type affair at Broadway and 236th St., 718/543-6420.

CITY ISLAND AND PELHAM BAY PARK

City Island is one of New York City's oddest communities, a sailors' haven that fancies itself part of New England. "Welcome to New York City's Nautical Community, 1645," reads the sign arching over the bridge leading from the mainland. And then you're there, on a narrow strip of land lined with boatyards, tiny clapboard houses, and bustling seafood restaurants attracting the tourist trade.

Back in the 1700s, the inhabitants of City Island hoped to develop a port that would rival New York's. Obviously their plan failed, but the community has been home to a number of thriving industries, including a solar salt works (in the 1830s), an oystering industry (in the mid-1800s), and—most importantly—a shipbuilding industry that continues to this day. Several America's Cup yachts were built here.

City Island has only one real street—City Island Avenue. But some of its side roads, which are only a few blocks long, are pretty and worth a

gander. To reach the island from Manhattan, take the No. 6 train to Pelham Bay Park, the last stop, and catch the Bx12 (summer only) or Bx29 bus to City Island. The trip is time-consuming, so budget a full day if possible.

The "Tyrone" House

At 21 Tier Street, on the north side of City Island Avenue, is a charming shingled house with a turret, gazebo, and stone fence. The house was used as the Tyrone family's residence in the 1962 film version of Eugene O'Neill's *Long Day's Journey Into Night,* starring Katharine Hepburn.

Accommodations and Food

One of the most unusual places to stay in New York City is **Le Refuge Inn,** 620 City Island Ave., at Cross St., 718/885-2478, www.lerefugeinn.com, a French auberge and restaurant housed in a 19th-century Victorian house. Rooms cost $65 s with a shared bath, $85 d with a shared bath, $142 d with a private bath; two-night minimum on weekends. Continental breakfast included; the prix fixe dinners cost $50.

City Island restaurants run the gamut from simple diners to elaborate (and expensive) old-fashioned affairs with nautical themes and plush booths. The rambling **Johnny's Reef Restaurant,** 2 City Island Ave., 718/885-2086, at the far end of the island, is a local favorite, offering huge portions of fried fish cafeteria-style, along with great views of the Sound; average main dish, $10. More sedate and also very good is the moderately priced **Crab Shanty,** 361 City Island Ave., 718/885-1810.

Orchard Beach

Just north of City Island, on the Manhattan side of the bridge, is Orchard Beach, another one of City Parks Commissioner Robert Moses' creations. Laid out in a semicircle lined with a broad walkway and colonnaded bathhouses, Orchard Beach is in dire need of renovation. But it's a pleasure to walk along nonetheless, especially in spring or fall, when it's marvelously empty.

From the beach looking east, you have good views of small Rat Island, once a shelter for yellow fever victims, later an artists' colony; and, farther east, Hart Island, the city's potter's field since 1868. From the southern end of the beach looking west, you can see some of the 35 massive towers of Co-Op City, the country's largest co-op housing project. The complex houses 15,372 apartments, seven schools, three shopping centers, five baseball diamonds, and over 55,000 mostly working- and middle-class people.

Pelham Bay Park

Orchard Beach is part of Pelham Bay Park, the largest park in New York City. Within its 2,118 acres are salt marshes, forests, lagoons, meadows, and seashore, along with ball fields, golf courses, tennis courts, and, incongruously, a police shooting range. Some parts of the park are exquisitely beautiful—reminiscent of the Maine coast—but many others are seriously neglected.

The park's foremost historical attraction is the 1836 **Bartow-Pell Mansion,** on Shore Road about a mile from the Pelham Bay Park subway (in summer, take the Bx12 bus), 718/885-1461, www.bartowpellmansionmuseum.org. The gray stone, Greek Revival mansion is filled with carved woodwork and surrounded by formal gardens. Hours are Wednesday, Sat.–Sun. noon–4 P.M.; the garden is open Tues.–Sun. 8:30 A.M.–4:30 P.M. Admission to the house is adults $2.50, seniors and students $1.25, free to children under 12 and to all on the first Sunday of the month. Admission to the gardens is also free.

Pelham Bay Park is the site where Anne Hutchinson—a Puritan religious leader expelled by the Massachusetts Bay Colony for her liberal views—settled with her children and followers in 1638. Five years later, their settlement was attacked by Indians, and everyone but Hutchinson's youngest daughter was killed. The Hutchinson River, which splits Pelham Bay Park, is named after Anne Hutchinson.

For more information on Pelham Bay Park, call 718/430-1890. Free maps of the park can be picked up at the Ranger Nature Center near the Bruckner Boulevard and Wilkinson Avenue entrance.

Staten Island

Staten Island is difficult to explore. Buses run much less frequently than they do elsewhere in New York City and have more ground to cover, making travel between destinations a time-consuming business. Travel by car can also be frustrating, as many of the streets are poorly marked.

One way to get an overall sense of the island is to take a Staten Island Rapid Transit (SIRT) train from St. George in the north to Tottenville in the south. The 14.3-mile journey passes through such typical residential communities as New Dorp, Bay Terrace, and Great Kills, before terminating in Tottenville, a well-worn town of narrow tree-lined streets and Victorian houses.

From Manhattan, take the ferry from Battery Park to the northern end of Staten Island, where buses fan out to cover the island. The SIRT trains also begin at the ferry terminal. For information on events and help with travel directions, contact the Staten Island Chamber of Commerce at 718/727-1900, www.sichamber.com.

The Forgotten Borough

Sometimes dubbed "the forgotten borough," Staten Island is different from the rest of New York City. Significantly more rural and suburban than the other boroughs, it's also predominantly white, politically conservative, and working- to middle-class. As the *New York Times* put it in one article, "Staten Island is the land of Kiwanis Clubs and big gas guzzlers for sale on small front lawns, and guys who don't split the checks with their dates, and girls who wear high heels to the grocery store and marry young."

All of which means that Staten Island frequently feels estranged from the rest of the city—and periodically threatens to secede. The last time was in 1993 when the issue was put to a public vote; the referendum was enthusiastically passed, but its implementation remains doubtful, as numerous legal and political obstacles have yet to be hurdled.

Yet Staten Island, pop. 443,000, is considerably more complex than these facts might imply. On

THE OUTER BOROUGHS

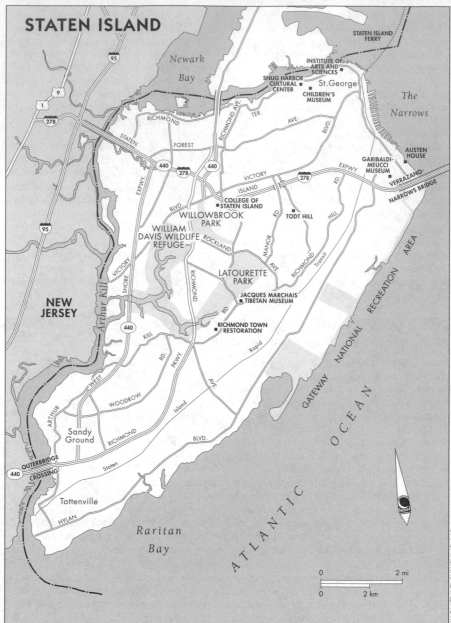

STATEN ISLAND

STATEN ISLAND FERRY

Newark Bay

INSTITUTE OF ARTS AND SCIENCES

SNUG HARBOR CULTURAL CENTER

St. George

CHILDREN'S MUSEUM

RICHMOND TER.

RICHMOND AVE.

AVE.

BLVD.

The Narrows

AUSTEN HOUSE

STATEN

FOREST

VICTORY

GARIBALDI-MEUCCI MUSEUM

EXPWY.

VERRAZANO-NARROWS BRIDGE

440

278

440

ISLAND

COLLEGE OF STATEN ISLAND

BLVD.

RD.

TODT HILL

HILL

WILLOWBROOK PARK

WILLIAM DAVIS WILDLIFE REFUGE

ROCKLAND

MANOR AVE.

RICHMOND

Transit

NATIONAL

RECREATION

AREA

95

VICTORY

SHORE

RICHMOND

LATOURETTE PARK

RD.

JACQUES MARCHAIS TIBETAN MUSEUM

Rapid

GATEWAY

NEW JERSEY

Arthur Kill

440

KILL

RICHMOND TOWN RESTORATION

PKWY.

WEST

ARTHUR

WOODROW

Island

AVE.

ATLANTIC OCEAN

Sandy Ground

RICHMOND

BLVD.

OUTERBRIDGE CROSSING

440

Staten

HYLAN

Tottenville

Raritan Bay

ATLANTIC

0   2 mi

0   2 km

MOON

the one hand, it provides Manhattan with 65,000 daily commuters, has some of the city's most polluted waters, and was long home to the city's largest garbage dump—finally closed in the year 2002, only to be temporarily reopened to accept rubble from the World Trade Center. On the other, the borough holds an annual county fair with bed races and ribbons for the best home-grown vegetables, and boasts over 1,800 acres of protected forests and seashore. Staten Island has also been the favored retreat of Mafia bosses for generations.

History

Fourteen miles long by seven miles wide, Staten Island is a hilly place made up largely of bedrock. Originally settled by Native Americans who successfully fought off the Dutch until 1661, it became a military camp for the British during the Revolutionary War. The borough remained predominantly agricultural throughout the 1800s, and was still largely undeveloped in 1964 when the Verrazano-Narrows Bridge opened. The bridge connected the island to the rest of the city for the first time, bringing with it new industry, residents, and crime. Many Staten Islanders still blame the bridge for many of the island's current problems, and divide life into "Before the Bridge" and "After the Bridge."

Before the Bridge, Staten Island was almost exclusively white, and yet it has a surprisingly interesting African American history. During the Revolutionary War, when the British controlled New York, three British soldiers attacked a black Staten Islander named Bill Richmond. A strong man with considerable boxing talent, Richmond managed to hold them off. Later, the Duke of Northumberland—who was a big boxing fan—heard of the incident and brought Richmond to London, where he became a major sports figure. Richmond also trained Tom Molineaux, who was America's first unofficial black heavyweight boxing champion.

Then too, during and just after the Civil War, many black Southerners settled in the southwestern corner of Staten Island, where they established the community of **Sandy Ground,** one of the country's oldest free black communities.

Several homes belonging to these early settlers still stand, and the town's history is being preserved by the Sandy Ground Historical Society, 718/317-5796.

NORTHERN STATEN ISLAND

The Ferry

The Staten Island Ferry is the borough's biggest attraction—3.5 million tourists ride it every year, but very few actually disembark on Staten Island. The views the ferry offers of the harbor and Manhattan are spectacular, especially in the early evening and at night. The ferry lands in the scruffy little hillside town of St. George, the oldest and most urban section of Staten Island.

Staten Island Institute of Arts & Sciences

Two blocks from the ferry terminal is Staten Island Institute of Arts & Sciences, 75 Staten Island Pl., 718/727-1135. Founded in 1881, the institute features small but well-done changing exhibits on the arts, natural sciences, and culture of the borough, and offers occasional walking tours. Hours are Mon.–Sat. 9 A.M.–5 P.M., Sunday 1–5 P.M. Suggested admission is adults $2.50, students and seniors $1.50.

Snug Harbor Cultural Center

About 1.5 miles east of the ferry terminal is Snug Harbor, 1000 Richmond Terrace, 718/448-2500, www.snug-harbor.org, an odd complex of historic buildings with a decidedly institutional feel. Once a maritime hospital and home for retired sailors, Snug Harbor is now a National Historic Landmark District slowly being transformed into an arts center. Much work still needs to be done on the sprawling estate filled with Greek Revival, beaux arts, and Italianate architecture, but the place has a spooky grandeur. Its highlight is a restored 1833 building featuring a soaring gallery adorned with stained glass and ceiling murals. The building now holds the **Newhouse Center for Contemporary Art,** open Wed.–Sun. 11 A.M.–5 P.M. Suggested admission is $2.

Adjoining Snug Harbor is the 80-acre **Staten Island Botanical Garden,** 718/442-3645, a historic Victorian landscape made up of wood-lands, natural ponds, and formal gardens. The **Chinese Scholar's Garden,** opened in 1999 after 14 years in the planning, was designed by China's foremost authority on classical gardens and is the only one of its kind in America. It includes a lotus pond, Billowing Pine Court, and Court of Uncommon Reeds.

Snug Harbor is open during daylight hours. Admission to the general complex is free, and free tours are offered on summer weekends. Admission to the Chinese Scholar's Garden, open Tues.–Sun. 10 A.M.–5 P.M. is $5. From the ferry terminal, take the S40 bus; the ride takes about 15 minutes.

Staten Island Children's Museum

The third component of Snug Harbor is the Staten Island Children's Museum, 718/448-6557, which draws families from all over the city. Among the most popular of its many hands-on exhibits are its simulated radio and TV stations. The museum is open Tues.–Sun. noon–5 P.M. Admission is $5, free for kids under one.

Alice Austen House

Several miles southwest of St. George is a pretty gabled house, 2 Hylan Blvd., 718/816-4506, that was once home to photographer Alice Austen. A contemporary of Jacob Riis, Austen never worked professionally but took pho-tographs just "for fun." Between 1884 and 1932 she produced more than 8,000 photos, which comprise one of the finest extant pictorial records of turn-of-the-century American life.

Austen lived in her 17th-century cottage from the age of two to the age of 70, when she was forced out due to poverty. Crippled with arthritis, she moved into the poorhouse. There she was "discovered" by an editor of *Life* mag-azine, who wanted to publish her work. She was then moved into a private nursing home, and lived to see her photographs published to much acclaim.

A visit to the Austen house begins with a short documentary film, narrated by Helen Hayes. The house has been restored to the way it was in Austen's day and is full of Victoriana

clutter. One room houses a gallery which mounts changing exhibits of Austen's and other photographers' work. Outside is a wonderful view of the harbor.

The house is open Thurs.–Sun. noon–5 P.M.; closed January–February. Suggested admission is $2. From the ferry terminal, take the S51 bus; the ride takes 15 minutes.

Garibaldi-Meucci Museum

Not far from the Austen House is the Garibaldi-Meucci Museum, 420 Tompkins Ave., at Chest-nut Ave., 718/442-1608. The museum is housed in the former home of Antonio Meucci, the Ital-ian-American inventor who developed the first working model of the telephone in 1857. Though kudos for the invention went to Alexan-der Graham Bell throughout Meucci's lifetime, Meucci was declared the first inventor of the telephone by the Supreme Court in 1886.

Meucci also offered his home as a refuge to Italian expatriate hero Giuseppe Garibaldi, who lived here in 1850 while recuperating from ill health. During that time, the two men support-ed themselves by hunting, fishing, and making candles in the backyard. Later, Garibaldi returned to Italy, where he and his followers succeeded in establishing Italy as a nation.

Today, Meucci's simple white home is a low-key, special-interest kind of place, filled with letters, photos, and memorabilia documenting the lives of both men. The house is open Tues.–Sun. 1–4:30 P.M. Suggested donation $3. From the ferry terminal, take the S78 bus; the ride takes 15 minutes.

CENTRAL STATEN ISLAND
Todt Hill

Just off Richmond Road south of the Staten Is-land Expressway rises the rocky hump of Todt Hill, an exclusive residential neighborhood filled with rambling estates and white, columned man-sions. Francis Ford Coppola turned one of them into the Corleone family estate for his film *The Godfather;* it's at 110 and 120 Longfellow Rd., at the end of a tree-lined dead-end street. Todt Hill is best reached and explored by car.

STATEN ISLAND NATURE PRESERVE

Smack in the middle of Staten Island is the Greenbelt, a 2,500-acre nature preserve made up of contiguous woodlands, wetlands, and open fields, along with a golf course and a few historic sites. Though surrounded by development, the Greenbelt is a favorite stop for migratory birds on the Atlantic flyway. It also supports one of the most diverse floras in the northeast, thanks to a wide variety of soils deposited by the Wisconsin glacier about 10,000 years ago. In the Greenbelt's upland hills, the soil covers an uncommon serpentinite bedrock found only a few places in the world. When exposed to the elements, the bedrock weathers to a light gray-green.

Two major hiking trails traverse the Greenbelt. One is the 8.5-mile Blue Trail (17 miles roundtrip), marked with blue dots, which runs east-west from the College of Staten Island to the William Davis Wildlife Refuge. Highlights along the way include Deer Park, which lies on the slopes of the highest point along the Atlantic coastline between Maine and Florida; Reed's Basket Willow Swamp, often filled with blooming wildflowers; and High Rock Park, where outcroppings of the serpentinite bedrock can be seen. To reach the College of Staten Island from the ferry terminal, take the S66 bus. The trail begins on Milford Drive and is marked by a sign.

The other trail is the four-mile White Trail (eight miles roundtrip), marked with white dots, which begins at High Rock Park and runs north to Willowbrook Park. Highlights along the way include Bucks Hollow, notable for its wetlands, and the steep Egbertville Ravine. To reach the trail, take the S74 bus to the corner of Richmond Road and Rockland Avenue. Walk two blocks on Rockland to Nevada Avenue and turn right up the hill to the park's entrance and visitor center. Maps are available at the visitor center on weekends; on weekdays, stop by the Greenbelt's administration office at 200 Nevada Avenue.

Other, shorter trails also traverse the Greenbelt. For more information, call 718/667-2165.

Jacques Marchais Museum of Tibetan Art

Perched on a steep hill farther south, off Richmond Hill Rd., is the Tibetan Museum, 338 Lighthouse Ave., at Windsor, 718/987-3500, www.tibetanmuseum.com. The museum was created by Jacqueline Norman Klauber, who adopted the alias Jacques Marchais to promote her career as a New York art dealer. Fascinated with Tibetan figurines from childhood (her great-grandfather had brought some home from his travels), she spent her adult years collecting Asian art. In the 1940s, she built this personalized museum, which was designed to resemble a Buddhist temple.

The Marchais Center houses the biggest collection of Tibetan art in the Western world, but is still quite small, contained in just one high-ceilinged room and a rectangular garden. Highlights include a series of brightly colored masks, and a large collection of golden *thangkas,* or religious images, lined up at a red-and-gold altar. A garden out back offers distant views of the bay, and a gift shop sells a nice selection of books and crafts.

The Marchais Center is usually open April–Nov., Wed.–Sun. 1–5 P.M.; Dec.–March, Wed.–Fri. 1–5 P.M., but double check before you make the long trek out here. Admission is adults $5, students and senior citizens $3, children $1. From the ferry terminal, take the S74 bus; the ride takes about 35 minutes.

Historic Richmond Town

Just a few minutes' walk from the Tibetan Museum is Richmond Town, 441 Clarke Ave., at Patrick's Pl., 718/351-1611, a 30-acre complex filled with 29 historic buildings, seven of which are open to the public. Most have been moved here from elsewhere on the island, and they line up neatly along several streets that come alive in summer with craftspeople and guides in period dress.

Richmond Town sits on the site of an early Dutch settlement and interprets three centuries of daily life. The oldest building is the 1695 Voorlezer's House (a *voorlezer* was a lay minister and teacher); one of the newest is the New

© CHRISTIANE BIRD

a historic Richmond Town building

Dorp Railroad Station, complete with a Queen Anne–style porch and gables. Other interesting buildings include a two-story jail, tinsmith shop, general store, carriage "manufactory," gift shop, cafe, and visitor center with changing exhibitions.

Richmond Town is usually open July–Aug., Wed.–Sat. 10 A.M.–5 P.M. and Sunday 1–5 P.M.; Sept.–June, Wed.–Sun. 1–5 P.M., but it's best to call ahead. Admission is adults $4; students, seniors, and children 6–18 $2.50; children under

six free. From the ferry terminal, take the S74 bus; the ride takes about 40 minutes.

Accommodation

Within walking distance of the Staten Island ferry terminal is the **Stanbrook Manor English Bed & Breakfast,** 396 Van Duzer St., between Beach and Wright St., 718/273-7365. This charming old stone house offers eight small but cozy guestrooms, each decked out in a different floral motif. $69 s or d.

New York State

Long Island

Introduction

Long, thin Long Island stretches east from Manhattan for about 120 miles. The largest island on the East Coast, Long Island is a jumbled mix of ugly suburbs, magnificent estates, congested highways, pristine nature preserves, sanitized shopping malls, one-stoplight villages, glitzy corporate headquarters, and some of the finest white-sand beaches in the world.

At the westernmost end of the island are the New York City boroughs of Brooklyn and Queens, so in common parlance, Long Island begins at the Queens-Nassau County border. East of there, the island is divided into two counties: Nassau and Suffolk. At 252 square miles, Nassau is about one-fourth the size of Suffolk but is considerably more populated, holding half of Long Island's 2.6 million people. Nassau is quintessential suburbia, the birthplace of the single-family-home bedroom community.

Suffolk County has its share of suburbanization as well. Remarkably though, given its proximity to New York City, much of it is still farmland, dunes, and beach. The farther east you travel, the more

Stony Brook Grist Mill

the island resembles its Algonquin name, *Paumanok*, said to mean "the island with its breast long drawn out and laid against the sea."

THE LAND

Long Island's shape has often been compared to a whale. Its western bulk, never much more than 20 miles wide, splits at the 80-mile point into two curving spits of land, or "flukes," most commonly referred to as the North and South Forks.

The island was once an extension of a barren plain that stretched east from the Alleghenies. But about 15 million years ago, two glaciers moving southward dug out the deep valley that is now Long Island Sound and severed the island from the mainland. The glacier also cut hundreds of notches into the north shore, forming the coves, bays, and peninsulas seen there today. Furthermore, as the glacier melted, its waters ran south, flooding a huge meadow—now the Great South Bay and its neighboring waters—and creating low sand bars that became the foundation of today's miles-long barrier beach.

HISTORY

The Algonquins

The earliest Long Islanders were the Algonquins. Before the arrival of the whites, 13 Algonquin tribes inhabited the island. Along the south shore, from west to east, were the Canarsees, the Rockaways, the Merricks, the Massapeaques, the Secatogues, the Unkechaugs, the Shinnecocks, and the Montauks. Along the north shore from west to east were the Matinecocks, the Nissequogues, the Setaukets, and the Corchauges. The Manhassets inhabited Shelter Island. Many of the island's villages, harbors, and bays are named for these early peoples.

The Algonquins lived in wigwams made of bark and grass. They fished in coastal waters, harvested quahog clams (producing much of the wampum used by the Northeastern Indians from the shells), and grew such crops as corn, pumpkin, melon, and tobacco. According to one settler's journal, "they were a tall proud and handsome people with grace of walk, active of body carried

straight as arrows. Hair and skin was carefully looked after . . . [they] saved their copper skin by use of oyl of fishes, eagle fat, and raccoon grease rubbed over their bodies. . . ."

The Montauk chief, Wyandanch, was the grand sachem of the Long Island tribes, and he befriended the white settlers who began arriving in the 1640s. Ninicraft, the chief of the Narragansetts who lived across the sound, tried to enlist Wyandanch's help in killing off the whites in 1652. When Wyandanch refused, the Narragansetts opened a war on the Montauks and nearly destroyed them.

Within a century after the arrival of the Dutch and English, only about 400 Indians remained on Long Island. Most had died of diseases introduced by the Europeans, and those who survived were subject to innumerable indignities. In 1759, the Indians had to beg for the right to cut firewood, and in 1778, the New York State superintendent of Indian affairs had to instruct the citizens of Montauk to honor Indian fishing rights granted under earlier agreements.

Today, a small Algonquin community of about 400 Shinnecocks still lives on the Shinnecock Reservation near Southampton. Each Labor Day weekend, they proudly celebrate their heritage with a three-day pow-wow that attracts Native Americans from across the country.

F. SCOTT FITZGERALD ON LONG ISLAND

And as the moon rose higher the inessential houses began to melt away until gradually I became aware of the old island here that flowered once for Dutch sailors' eyes—a fresh, green breast of the new world. Its vanished trees . . . had once pandered in whispers to the last and greatest of all human dreams; for a transitory enchanted moment man must have held his breath in the presence of this continent, compelled into an aesthetic contemplation he neither understood nor desired, face to face for the last time in history with something commensurate to his capacity for wonder.

F. Scott Fitzgerald,
The Great Gatsby

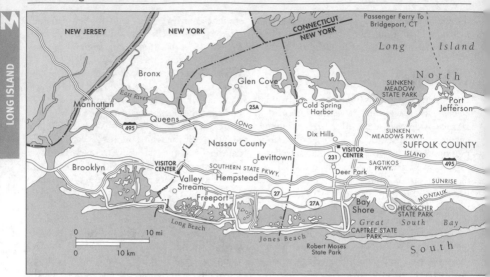

Farming and Fishing

The Dutch were the first to arrive on Long Island, settling in southern Brooklyn in 1636. They were quickly followed by the English, who settled in Southold and Southampton (on the North and South Forks, respectively) in 1640. Unlike many settlers elsewhere in Colonial America, the new Long Islanders had it easy. The land around them was flat, rich, and easy to cultivate; the sea was brimming with seafood and shellfish. Soon dozens of small communities were flourishing both along the coast and inland.

During the Revolutionary War, Long Island was occupied by the British, and many settlers chose to flee rather than remain under the king's rule. But after the war, the island prospered once again. Cattle ranching (in Montauk) and whaling (in Cold Spring Harbor, Sag Harbor, and Greenport) joined farming and fishing as the island's most important industries. In the mid-1800s, the Long Island Rail Road was built, allowing for easier transport of goods. As a result, agriculture became big business on the island. To this day, Suffolk County remains one of New York's most productive farming regions, yielding bountiful harvests of fruits and vegetables.

Long Island's fishing industry has not fared as well. As Long Island native Peter Matthiessen writes in *Men's Lives,* a highly acclaimed account of the island's fisherfolk, "In recent decades, most fishing families have been forced to sell off land that had been in the family for generations. Those who are left subsist in the last poor corner of a community in which they were once the leading citizens." Much of this decline, not surprisingly, is due to suburbanization and its accompanying pollution. But as if that weren't bad enough, writes Matthiessen, powerful sportsmen's organizations with much political clout have also been successful in limiting the commercial fisherman's harvest of certain game fish.

The dwindling number of fisherfolk who remain on Long Island live much the way their ancestors did: "Moving at daybreak on back roads, the fishermen go their traditional way down to the sea. They are tough, resourceful, self-respecting, and also (some say) hidebound and cranky, too independent to organize for their own survival. Yet even their critics must acknowledge a gritty spirit that was once more highly valued in this country than it is today."

Suburbanization and Modern Woes

If few people connect Long Island with fishing or

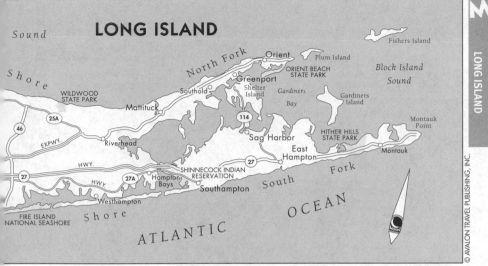

even farming any more, almost everyone connects it with suburbia. Long Island is the archetypal American suburb.

Early suburbs began springing up in western Nassau County in the 1920s. But the island's real transformation came with the onset of WW II, when factories producing aircraft and specialized weapons systems turned Long Island into an important manufacturing center. After the war, Long Island continued as an industrial hub, and large housing tracts were built to accommodate the returning GIs. The most famous of these tracts was Levittown, where one developer built 17,447 homes almost overnight (see Central Nassau County under the South Shore, below). Between 1950 and 1960, Long Island's population doubled from 670,000 to 1.3 million, and between 1960 and 1980 it doubled again.

The island's suburban explosion has not been without its negative consequences. Nassau and Suffolk Counties combined now have one of the highest rates of AIDS of any suburban area in the United States, a homeless population estimated at 40,000, and one of the highest infant mortality rates among black babies in the state. Local governments originally set up to serve a suburban middle class are ill-equipped to deal

with such urban-style malaise, and for the first time in modern history, people have been moving away from Long Island.

Fortunately, none of this affects the tourist much. And despite its problems, Long Island is a unique and complex place that becomes more and more interesting the closer you look. The North Shore boasts a number of impressive museum-mansions and untouched nature preserves; the South Shore is lined with unparalleled white-sand beaches. Both the North and South Forks, with their historic villages and windswept shores, are astonishingly beautiful, and remind you of a central fact that's curiously easy to forget: this really is an island, with an idiosyncratic culture very different from that of the mainland.

GETTING AROUND
Orientation
Long Island can be divided into four sections: the North Shore, the North Fork, the South Shore, and the South Fork. Each section can be explored in a day or so, depending on how many stops you make, or can be combined into one long loop that begins and ends in New York City. If you do make the 120-mile trip from Manhattan

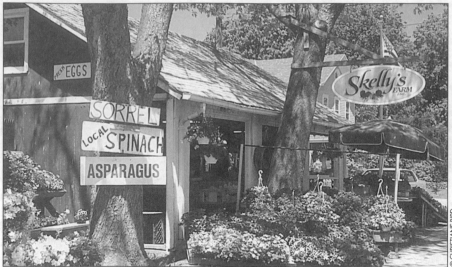

© CHRISTIANE BIRD

one of Long Island's numerous roadside produce stands

to either the North or South Fork, you'll probably want to overnight there at least one night.

For many visitors, Long Island's beaches are its biggest attraction. The most spectacular shores are along the southern coast, where white sands and dunes stretch out for an incredible, all-but-unbroken 123 miles. Among the best south-coast bathing spots are Jones Beach, Robert Moses State Park, Fire Island National Seashore, the East Hampton beaches, and Hither Hills State Park.

Most of the beaches along the northern coast front the gentle waters of Long Island Sound, and are small and pebbly. White-sand exceptions are the beaches at Sunken Meadow State Park, Wildwood State Park, and Orient Beach State Park. Orient Beach is located at the far eastern tip of the North Fork and faces the waters of Gardiners Bay.

Beaches aside, both the North Shore and the South and North Forks have much to offer the visitor. The North Shore is home to many of Long Island's 75 museums, as well as private mansions and nature preserves. The jet-setting South Fork boasts the fashionable Hamptons, interesting historic sites, and a glittering social scene. The more rural North Fork holds yet more historic sites, picturesque harbors and bays, and a flourishing wine industry.

Transportation

The best way to explore Long Island is by car. Among the major west-east thoroughfares are Routes 25 and 25A to the north; the Long Island Expressway (LIE), or I-495, in the middle of the island; and the Sunrise Highway/Route 27 and the older Montauk Highway (Route 27A and 80) to the south. The Southern State Parkway also traverses the South Shore, but ends mid-island, at Heckscher State Park.

Keep in mind that traffic on Long Island can be horrific, and it'll probably take you longer than you expect to get where you're going. Avoid the Long Island Expressway altogether during rush hour and on summer Friday afternoons, when thousands of Manhattanites head for the Hamptons.

It's also possible to reach many Long Island communities from Manhattan via the **Long Island Rail Road,** 718/217-LIRR or 516/822-5477. Fares are reasonable and taxis are usually available at the other end. During the summer, the LIRR offers special packages to such destinations as Jones Beach, Captree State Park, and Long Beach; call for information.

RECREATION AND EVENTS

Touring Farms and Vineyards

Against all odds, much of eastern Long Island is still devoted to agriculture, and **produce stands** and **pick-your-own farms** are everywhere. Over the last 20 years, **wineries** have been flourishing as well, especially on the North Fork. Lists and maps can be picked up in the visitor information centers.

Events

Though festivals and fairs take place on Long Island year-round, summer is by far the best time to catch something special. Here are a few highlights:

June: During the **Blessing of the Fleet,** 631/668-2428, hundreds of fishing vessels and pleasure craft sail to Montauk Harbor to receive a prayer for a safe season.

July: The annual **Croquet Tournament,** 631/323-2480, takes place at the Oysterponds Historical Society in Orient. Classical music concerts are presented during the **Hampton Summerfest,** 631/725-0011 or 631/725-0894, held in the Old Whalers' Church in Sag Harbor.

August: Riverhead's annual two-day **Polish Town Street Fair and Polka Festival,** 631/727-7600, comes complete with kielbasa, funnel cakes, and folk dancers. East Hampton celebrates summer with its famed **Guild Hall Clothesline Art Sale,** 631/324-0806. Watch the local papers for the popular **Annual Shelter Island Heights Firemen's Chicken Barbecue,** 631/749-0399.

September: Over 25 tribes participate in the **Shinnecock Pow Wow,** 631/283-6143, held at

LONG ISLAND HIGHLIGHTS

The North Shore
Nassau County Museum of Art, Roslyn
Sea Cliff village
Old Westbury Gardens, Old Westbury
Sagamore Hill, Oyster Bay
Whaling Museum, Cold Spring Harbor
Old Bethpage Village, Old Bethpage
Walt Whitman Birthplace, Huntington
The drive to Lloyd Neck
Caumsett State Historic Park, Lloyd Neck
Vanderbilt Museum, Centerport
Northport village
Long Island Museum of Art, History, and
Carriages, Stony Brook
Three Village Inn, Stony Brook

The North Fork and Shelter Island
Briermere Farms, Riverhead
The drive to New Suffolk
Cutchogue village
Wineries near Cutchogue and Peconic
Horton Point Lighthouse, Southold
Downtown Greenport
Orient village
Orient Beach State Park, Orient

Mashomack Preserve, Shelter Island
Ram's Head Inn, Shelter Island

The South Shore
Jones Beach; Fire Island beaches
Ehrhardts Clam House, Freeport
African American Museum, Hempstead
Cradle of Aviation Museum, Garden City
Sunken Forest, Fire Island
Bayard Cutting Arboretum, Oakdale
Long Island Maritime Museum, West Sayville

The South Fork
Beaches, beaches, beaches
Parrish Art Museum, Southampton
East Hampton village
The port of Sag Harbor
Lobster Roll (a.k.a. Lunch), Amagansett
Mill-Garth Country Inn, Amagansett
Pollock-Krasner House, Springs
Whalewatching cruises, Montauk
Montauk Lighthouse, Montauk
Indian Field, Montauk
Hither Hills State Park, Montauk
Gurney's Inn & Spa, Montauk

Shinnecock Reservation over Labor Day weekend. The **Historic Sag Harbor Weekend,** 631/725-0778, features special tours of historic sites and whaling-boat races.

VISITOR SERVICES

The **Long Island Convention and Visitors Bureau** (LICVB) operates three **Visitor Information Centers.** One is on the eastbound side of the Long Island Expressway (LIE), or I-495, between Exits 51 and 52 in Deer Park; the second is on the eastbound side of the Southern State Parkway between Exits 13 and 14 at Valley Stream; and the third is in the Tanger Outlet Center, Tanger Drive, Riverhead. All are open Memorial Day–Labor Day, daily 9 A.M.–5 P.M.; the Tanger Outlet Center location is open year-round. Information on Long Island can also be obtained year-round by contacting the main LICVB office at 330 Motor Pkwy., Suite 203, Hauppauge, NY 11788, 631/951-3440 or 877/FUN-ON-LI, www.licvb.com.

For more information on any of the state parks or campgrounds mentioned below, visit www.nysparks.com.

The North Shore

In its stretch nearest New York City, the North Shore is a densely packed suburbia, stuffed to the bursting point with single-family homes, shopping malls, and highways and byways so thick with traffic you'll want to scream. Yet even here, once you get off the main roads up into the peninsulas, you'll find a number of wonderful historic sites and nature preserves.

The farther east you travel along the North Shore, the more rural it gets. Around Oyster Bay, the traffic thins out considerably, and by the time you reach Centerport—located less than 20 miles from the Queens-Nassau border— you've left the city far behind.

Route 25A, also known as Northern Boulevard and North Hempstead Turnpike in Nassau County, is the northernmost major route that traverses Long Island, and the best one to use for unhurried exploring. Running parallel to it to the south is the Long Island Expressway (LIE), or I-495, which is the quicker route (except during rush hour) and therefore good to use when driving directly to a specific site.

GREAT NECK AND PORT WASHINGTON PENINSULAS

Heading into Long Island on congested Route 25A, you'll immediately cut across the bases of two large peninsulas, Great Neck and Port Washington. F. Scott Fitzgerald and his wife Zelda once lived at 6 Gateway Dr., Great Neck, and it was on these two thick thumbs of land that he modeled his West and East Eggs of *The Great Gatsby.*

Many opulent estates such as the ones Fitzgerald describes in his novel are still scattered along the so-called **Gold Coast,** which stretches 30 miles between Great Neck and Eatons Neck. Most were built in the early 20th century by captains of industry and commerce such as J. P. Morgan, F. W. Woolworth, Louis Tiffany, and Henri Bendel. At one time, there were some 600–700 mansions here; today—due to fire, demolition, and subdivision—only about 200 remain. About half of these are still privately owned, and most of the others have been converted into schools, religious retreats, and country clubs. Only a handful of the estates are open to the public (see the special topic, The Gold Coast at a Glance).

American Merchant Marine Museum

Turning off onto the Great Neck peninsula on Bay View Avenue, you'll soon come to Kings Point and the American Merchant Marine Museum, situated on the campus of the U.S. Merchant Marine Academy. The academy's grounds offer good views of Throgs Neck Bridge, the marinas of City Island, and the Bronx. The museum showcases such oddities as models of well known passenger liners, the wooden wheel of "Old Ironsides" (the USS *Constitution*), and a life-size model of a cargo ship, used to train students during WW II.

THE GOLD COAST AT A GLANCE

Stretching between Great Neck and Eatons Neck, the so-called Gold Coast was once home to hundreds of opulent estates: French chateaus, English castles, Italian palazzos, and the like. Most were built in the early 20th century by such prominent families as the Vanderbilts, Astors, Morgans, Woolworths, Tiffanys, and Chryslers.

Today, only about 200 of these mansions still exist. Most were killed off by the Great Depression, fire, demolition, and subdivision. And of the mansions that do remain, only a handful are easily accessible to the general public. Among them are: **Wiley Hall** at the U.S. Merchant Museum Academy, Kings Point

Castlegould and **Falaise** at Sands Point Preserve, near Port Washington

Nassau County Museum of Art, Roslyn

Westbury House at Old Westbury Gardens, Old Westbury

Coe Hall at Planting Fields Arboretum, Oyster Bay

Eagle's Nest at the Suffolk County Vanderbilt Museum, Centerport

To find out more about the history of the Gold Coast, visit the fledgling **Museum of Long Island's Gold Coast,** Coindre Hall, Huntington. Housed in what was once the estate of George McKesson Brown, heir to a pharmaceutical fortune, the museum is very much a project in the making, as the mansion—originally known as West Neck Farm—is gradually being restored. Free tours of Coindre Hall can be arranged by calling Splashes of Hope, a nonprofit group housed in the mansion, at 631/424-8230.

To reach the museum, at the foot of Steamboat Rd., 516/773-5515, www.usmma.edu, take Bay View Ave. to West Shore Rd., and watch for signs. Hours are Tues.–Fri. 10 A.M.–3 P.M., Sat.–Sun. 1–4:30 P.M. Admission is $1.

Manhasset

Near where the bases of the Great Neck and Port Washington peninsulas meet is the sprawling suburban town of Manhasset, one of the oldest communities on the North Shore. During the 1800s, it was the site of Success, a flourishing community made up of free blacks, former slaves, and Matinecock Indians. The Indians had inhabited the area before the arrival of the Dutch and English, and many intermarried with the Africans brought to Manhasset by white landowners.

Following the abolition of slavery in New York in 1827, more black families arrived in Manhasset, some buying land along Valley Road. In 1833, the community built the **A.M.E. Zion Church** on Community Drive, and in 1867, "Institution u.s.a.," the first free black school in Nassau County. Today, most of Success has been obliterated by suburbia, but the church and its cemetery still stand.

Manhasset's current claim to fame is its **Miracle Mile,** a shopping strip of upscale stores—

Bonwit Teller, Polo/Ralph Lauren, etc.—that stretches along Route 25A between Community Drive and Port Washington Boulevard.

Port Washington

The attractive town of Port Washington, on its namesake peninsula, is built on a hill overlooking Manhasset Bay. Here you'll find a spiffy mural that stretches from the end of Main Street to the waterfront, and the **Polish-American Museum,** 16 Bellview Ave., at Main St., 516/883-6542. Small and informal, the museum focuses on well-known Poles and Polish-Americans, including Copernicus, Frédéric Chopin, Marie Curie, Pope John Paul II, and Gen. Thaddeus Kosciuszko, whose namesake bridge straddles Brooklyn and Queens. Also in the museum are examples of traditional dress and a small art gallery. Hours are Tues.–Fri. 10 A.M.–4 P.M., Sat.–Sun. by appointment. Admission is by donation.

For a small town, Port Washington has many good restaurants. **Louie's Oyster Bar & Grill,** 395 Main St., next to the town dock, 516/883-4242, offers great views of Manhasset Bay; average entrée $16. For Indian food that's reasonably priced, try the friendly, pleasant **Diwan,** 37 Shore Rd., 516/767-7878; average entrée $11. Tasty coal-over pizza is the specialty of the house at

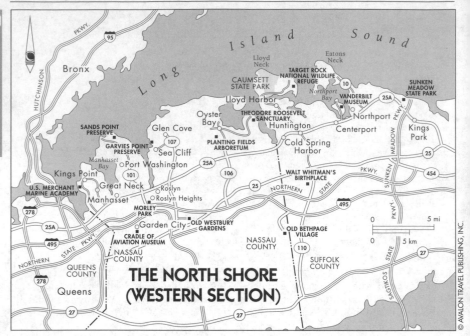

THE NORTH SHORE
(WESTERN SECTION)

© AVALON TRAVEL PUBLISHING, INC.

Salvatore's Coal-Fired Brick Oven Pizza, 124 Shore Rd., 516/883-8457; average pie $10. **Chez Noelle,** 34 Willowdale Ave., 516/883-3191, is an upscale French restaurant serving both classic and modern dishes that draws raves from the locals; entrées range from $26 to $30.

Sands Point Preserve

Just beyond Port Washington at the tip of the peninsula is the idyllic 216-acre Sands Point Preserve, filled with woods and shoreline, ball fields and nature trails, great views of the Sound and several castle-like buildings. One of these, **Castlegould,** distinguished by its enormous crenellated top, now houses a small visitor center and natural history museum.

Sands Point was originally developed by railroad heir Howard Gould, and later purchased by the Guggenheims. Between the two families, they built three mansions: the immense Tudorstyle **Hempstead House,** the much smaller **Mille Fleures,** and the Norman-style chateau, **Falaise** (French for cliff). Both Falaise and Hempstead

House are open to the public. At Falaise—perched on a cliff overlooking the Sound—you'll find Guggenheim's purple Cadillac, parked next to the station wagon that once belonged to his good friend Charles Lindbergh. At Hempstead House, you'll find a fine collection of Wedgwood ceramics.

To reach the preserve, 95 Middleneck Rd., continue north on Rte. 101 (which turns into Middleneck Rd.) and watch for signs. The preserve, 516/571-7900, is open year-round, Tues.–Sun. 10 A.M.–5 P.M. Admission is $2. Guided tours of Falaise are offered May 1–Oct. 31, Wed.–Sun. noon–3 P.M. Tour fees are $5 adults and children over 10, $4 seniors; children under 10 not admitted. Guided tours of Hempstead House are offered May 1–Oct. 31, Fri.–Sun. 12:30–4 P.M.; cost is $2 per person.

ROSLYN

Though now surrounded by congested highways and upscale shops, Roslyn still lays claim to

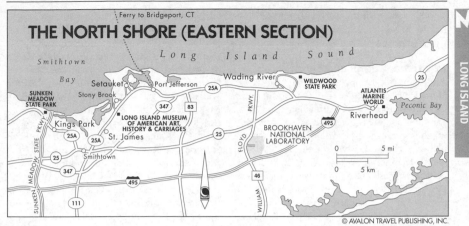

THE NORTH SHORE (EASTERN SECTION)

Ferry to Bridgeport, CT

Long Island Sound

Smithtown Bay

Setauket · Port Jefferson · 25A · Wading River · WILDWOOD STATE PARK · 25

SUNKEN MEADOW STATE PARK · Stony Brook · ATLANTIS MARINE WORLD · Peconic Bay

347 · 83 · PKWY

LONG ISLAND MUSEUM OF AMERICAN ART, HISTORY & CARRIAGES · 495 · Riverhead

Kings Park · St. James · 25 · BROOKHAVEN NATIONAL LABORATORY

25A · 25A · FLOYD

25 · Smithtown · 0 · 5 mi

347 · 0 · 5 km

495 · 46

111 · WILLIAM

© AVALON TRAVEL PUBLISHING, INC.

LONG ISLAND

a small, historic, and attractive downtown. Many of the buildings along its short but friendly Main Street predate the Civil War, giving the place a low-key, old-fashioned feel. For more information on the area's history, contact the Roslyn Landmark Society, 516/625-4363, www.historicroslyn.org.

During the mid-1800s, Roslyn was home to William Cullen Bryant, the poet and newspaper editor who was largely responsible for the creation of Central Park. Bryant is buried in Roslyn Cemetery, and many of his papers are housed in the Bryant Library, 2 Paper Mill Rd., 516/621-2240. The library was established in 1878, making it the oldest such facility still in operation on Long Island.

Nassau County Museum of Art

At the northern end of Roslyn is the Nassau County Museum of Art, Long Island's largest art museum. Occupying the 145-acre former Frick estate, the museum grounds boast about 30 stunning outdoor sculptures by the likes of Roy Lichtenstein and Richard Serra, and a few formal gardens. Inside the mansion house are first-rate temporary exhibits, a small bookshop, and a cafe. In an adjacent annex are 100 miniature rooms depicting living environments from the 18th century to the present.

The museum, 516/484-9337, www.nassaumuseum.com, is located on Museum Dr. off

Rte. 25A (Northern Blvd.), between Roslyn Rd. and Glen Cove Road. Hours are Tues.–Sun. 11 A.M.–5 P.M. Admission to the museum buildings is adults $6; seniors $5, students and children over 5 $4. Admission to the gardens and sculpture garden is free.

Morley's "Knothole"

Another literary figure connected with Roslyn is Christopher Morley, the poet, essayist, and novelist who compiled the entirely new 11th edition of *Bartlett's Familiar Quotations,* published in 1937. For this monumental task, as Morley later wrote in the book's preface, he built himself "a pine-wood cabin, as aloofly jungled as a Long Island suburb would permit, to consort with the shade of John Bartlett."

This simple cabin, known as the Knothole, now sits in Christopher Morley Park, where it looks oddly rustic and out of time. Operated by the Nassau County Department of Parks, 516/571-8113, it's been recently recently restored and is worth a look, if only for its "dymaxion bathroom." One of only two such bathrooms created by the inventive Buckminster Fuller, it's molded from a single piece of metal, with all the usual facilities—including a wash basin, toilet, and bathtub—welded in. The bathroom had to be transported to Roslyn via a special truck and was loaded into the cabin by crane. Open Sunday 1–5 P.M.

Christopher Morley Park is at 500 Searington Rd. in Roslyn Heights, which is just south of Roslyn proper.

Accommodations and Food

The plain, comfortable **Gold Coast Inn,** 1053 Northern Blvd., 516/627-2460, is nothing special, but the rooms are quite adequate and clean, and rates are a reasonable $89–101 d. Within walking distance of historic Main Street is the plush and elegant **Roslyn Claremont,** 1221 Old Northern Blvd., 516/625-2700 or 800/626-9005, www.roslynclaremonthotel.com, a European-styled hotel offering 77 well-appointed guest rooms, all done in deep roses and greens, and a small health club ($209–275 d). Adjoining the lobby is the charming **Christina's,** an intimate and romantic spot serving global cuisine; average entrée $23.

The old-fashioned **George Washington Manor,** 1305 Old Northern Blvd., 516/621-1200, is housed in a Colonial-era mansion where George Washington once ate breakfast. Specialties include Yankee pot roast, chicken pot pie, and seafood; entrées are $16–27.

The plain and simple **Chicken Shish Kebab,** 92 Mineola Ave., 516/621-6828, one block from the post office in Roslyn Heights, is a local favorite, serving delicious Greek and Middle Eastern specialties; average entrée $9. The charming **Friend of a Farmer,** 1382 Old Northern Blvd. (Main St.), 516/625-3808, housed in a rustic barn overlooking a duck pond offers plenty of hearty sandwiches, soups, and salads, along with more substantial traditional American dishes and scrumptious baked goods; average main dish $9.

SEA CLIFF AND GARVIES POINT

Perched high on bluffs overlooking Hempstead Harbor is Sea Cliff, a charming, off-the-beaten-path village filled with wooden Victorian homes. Some are in dire need of a facelift, but most are well kept and well adorned with fanciful turrets, wide front porches, and gingerbread eaves. Many of the best of these houses are located along Sea Cliff Avenue, Central Avenue, and Glen Avenue. At 95 10th St., near Sea Cliff Ave., is the **Sea**

Cliff Village Museum, filled with early 20th-century photographs of village life. Back then, Sea Cliff was a popular resort, and the photographs show the marvelous old hotels and dressed-to-the-hilt summer vacationers arriving via ferry. Walking-tour maps of the village are available here. The museum, 516/671-0090, www.seacliff.org, is open Sat.–Sun. 2–5 P.M.; closed in August and September.

On Carpenter Avenue, north of 8th Avenue, is **St. Seraphim Russian Orthodox Church,** a small white sanctuary with an onion dome. Russians have been settling in Sea Cliff since 1917, and constitute a large segment of the town's population.

For more information on the historic town, contact the Roslyn Landmark Society, 516/625-4363, www.historicroslyn.org.

Just north of Sea Cliff, in Glen Cove, is **Garvies Point Preserve,** a 62-acre plot of land overlooking Long Island Sound. Five miles of nature trails meander through the preserve, and a small museum focuses on local archaeology and geology. The preserve, 50 Barry Dr., 516/571-8010, is open daily 8:30 A.M.–dusk; admission is free. The museum is open Tues.–Sun. 10 A.M.–4 P.M.; admission is adults $2, children $1.

To reach Sea Cliff from Route 25A, take Glen Cove Road or Route 107 north, and turn left onto Sea Cliff Avenue. To reach Garvies Point from Sea Cliff, continue on Glen Cove Road north and look for Barry Drive or signs.

Food

A long-time favorite lunch spot in Sea Cliff is the cozy **Once Upon a Moose,** 304 Sea Cliff Ave., 516/676-9304, across the street from the Village Complex. Sandwiches start at $9. **Joanne's Gourmet Pizza & Pasta,** 500 Glen Cove Ave., 516/671-7222, housed in small cottage, offers homemade cooking with lots of fresh vegetables; average entrée $14.

OLD WESTBURY GARDENS

A few miles beyond Roslyn, near the Long Island Expressway, stands one of Long Island's most sumptuous mansions, now known as Old

Westbury. Built in 1906 in a palatial Charles II style, this grand edifice was once home to John S. Phipps and his wife Margarita Grace, heirs to steel and shipping fortunes.

The mansion is magnificently furnished with 18th-century antiques, but it's the 88 acres of formal gardens out front and back that draw the crowds. Considered to be the finest English gardens in the United States, Old Westbury's grounds are filled with tree-lined walks, grand allées, ponds, statuary, architectural "follies," and hundreds of species of plants, including historic varieties and new hybrids. Among the highlights are the Lake Walk leading to the Temple of Love, the Rainbow Garden planted with flowers of all colors, and the Ghost Walk, flanked with dark, forbidding-looking hemlock trees and bronze peacocks.

The mansion and gardens, 71 Old Westbury Rd., 516/333-0048, www.oldwestburygardens.org, are open mid-May–Dec., Wed.–Mon. 10 A.M.– 5 P.M. (no admission after 4 P.M.); to avoid the crowds, come during the week. Admission is adults $10, seniors $8, and children $5. To reach the gardens from the LIE, take Exit 39 S.

OYSTER BAY

In the mid-1700s, both the English and the Dutch inhabited picturesque Oyster Bay, which accounts for the fact that the place has two main streets just a block apart. East Main Street was once controlled by the Dutch, West Main Street by the English. To reach Oyster Bay from Route 25A, head north on Route 106.

Raynham Hall

At 20 W. Main St. is Raynham Hall, 516/922-6808, www.raynhamhallmuseum.com, once the home of prosperous Revolutionary War–era merchant Samuel Townsend. Townsend was a suspected Tory, but his son was George Washington's chief spy in New York City. When the war broke out, Raynham Hall was confiscated by the British and used as headquarters for the Queens Rangers. Townsend's daughter Sally remained in the house, however. There she overheard the British discussing Benedict Arnold's planned betrayal of West Point and conveyed that information to the colonists. The house is open Tues.–Sun. 1–5 P.M. Admission is adults $3, students and seniors $2, children under six free.

Sagamore Hill

On the outskirts of Oyster Bay is Sagamore, a rambling hilltop estate that was once the summer home of Theodore Roosevelt. The former president of the United States, assistant secretary of the Navy, governor of New York State, police chief of New York City, and author of 30-odd books came here with his wife and six children to indulge in the "strenuous life"—i.e., hiking, swimming, playing tennis, and horseback riding. Roosevelt never forgot his public duties while living here, however; out front is a wide porch with its railing removed so that he could more easily address the crowds who often assembled to hear him speak.

Sagamore is now operated by the National Park Service, and rangers conduct frequent tours through the dark, creaky, antique-filled house. The guides offer numerous anecdotes about the former president, but what's most striking about the house is its enormous number of preserved animal parts. There's the rhinoceros-foot inkwell, the elephant-foot wastepaper basket, the chair made of moose antlers, chimes made out of elephant tusks, the bearskin rug given to Roosevelt by Admiral Perry, and, of course, scores and scores of mounted animal heads, most shot by Roosevelt. Upstairs there's even a taxidermy room where the former president taught his son how to stuff animals at the tender age of seven.

The grounds of Sagamore are sleepy and serene, overhung with the boughs of huge trees. Near the entrance is a windmill, its arms weathered a silvery gray, while out back are stables, an icehouse, and the Old Orchard House, filled with exhibits documenting Roosevelt's life. A short film is also screened here.

Sagamore Hill, 20 Sagamore Rd., off Cove Rd., 516/922-4788, www.nps.gov/sahi, is open daily in summer, 9 A.M.–5 P.M.; Oct.–April, Wed.–Sun. 9 A.M.–5 P.M. Admission is adults $5, children under 16 free, and it's best to

hilltop estate Sagamore Hill, former residence of Theodore Roosevelt

© CHRISTIANE BIRD

arrive early on summer weekends. To get there from downtown Oyster Bay, head east on East Main Street to Cove Road and follow the signs.

Theodore Roosevelt Sanctuary

Across the street from Sagamore is the 12-acre Theodore Roosevelt Sanctuary. Now owned by the National Audubon Society, the refuge is planted with trees, shrubs, and vines specifically chosen to attract birds. A small visitor center near the entrance features exhibits on the area's wildlife and on Roosevelt's extensive involvement in the then-new conservation movement. The sanctuary, 134 Cove Rd., 516/922-3200, is open daily 9 A.M.–4:30 P.M.; the visitor center is open Mon.–Fri. 9 A.M.–4:30 P.M., Sat.–Sun. 1–4:30 P.M. Admission is free. Adjoining the refuge is **Young's Cemetery,** where Roosevelt is buried.

Planting Fields Arboretum

West of Oyster Bay, on Planting Fields Road, is Planting Fields Arboretum State Historic Park, a lush affair on the former estate of insurance executive William Robertson Coe. Some 160 acres here are planted with ornamental trees and shrubs, while about 200 other acres are preserved

in their natural state. Also on the grounds are two enormous greenhouses infused with intoxicating colors and fragrances. The Main Greenhouse is devoted to orchids, ferns, cacti, begonias, bromeliads, and "economic plants" (bananas, citrus trees, etc.), while the second greenhouse is devoted exclusively to camellias.

At the heart of Planting Fields is **Coe Hall,** a Tudor Revival stone mansion. The 1918 house is furnished with European antiques to give it the feel of an old English country manor.

The arboretum, 516/922-9200, www.plantingfields.org, is open year-round, daily 9 A.M.–5 P.M. Admission to the grounds is free but parking is $7 in summer. Coe Hall, 516/922-9210, is open daily 12:30–3:30 P.M. House tours cost adults $5, seniors $3.50, and children 7–12 $2.

Accommodations and Food

The **East Norwich Inn,** 6321 Northern Blvd. (Rte. 25A) at Rte. 106, 516/922-1500, is a pleasant, upscale motel offering comfortable rooms with double beds ($120 s, $135 d).

In downtown Oyster Bay, you'll find the boisterous **Canterbury Ales Oyster Bar & Grill,** 46 Audrey Ave., 516/922-3614, specializing in its namesake—direct from Oyster Bay, of course. Also on the menu is everything from sandwiches to lobster; average main dish $11. Hungry book lovers will want to stop into the historic **Book Mart Cafe,** 1 E. Main St., 516/922-0036, where an eclectic menu is served in a quaint bookshop; average lunch entrée $11.

For a more elaborate meal, head north to Bayville, where **Pier 1,** 33 Bayville Ave., 516/628-2153, serves fresh seafood in a beautiful setting overlooking the Sound; average entrée $22. Or head to the snug and elegant **Mill River Inn,** 160 Mill River Rd., 516/922-7768, one of the North Shore's best fine-dining restaurants featuring innovative American fare and a small but excellent wine list; average entrée $28.

COLD SPRING HARBOR

Cold Spring Harbor is now a small tourist village holding a few shops and galleries, several historic buildings, and two interesting museums. But during the mid-1800s, the village was a busy whaling port. Its main street—now Route 25A— was called Bedlam Street for the cacophony of foreign languages heard there. The village's taverns were full of exotic objects that sailors had brought back from all ends of the earth. And on the village's outskirts was Bungtown, a small settlement where barrels for whale oil were made. Today, only the boats bobbing in the harbor recall the port's rich and adventurous past.

Whaling Museum

The centerpiece of today's village is the Whaling Museum, a small and friendly institution founded in 1936. Exhibits in the trim, whitewashed building include a large collection of scrimshaw (the folk art of whalers), a fully rigged whale boat, huge iron caldrons used to process whale blubber, thousands of journals and letters, and a great collection of historical photographs.

In the museum you'll learn that Cold Spring Harbor was once the 27th largest whaling port in the world, and that whaling was the first racially integrated American industry. As early as the 1810s and 1820s, white and black seamen, captains, shipbuilders, and ship owners were work-

ing alongside each other. One boat, the *Industry,* out of Nantucket, Massachusetts, was captained and crewed entirely by African Americans.

The museum, 25 Main St. (Rte. 25A), 631/367-3418, www.cshwhalingmuseum.org, is open year-round, Tues.–Sun. 11 A.M.–5 P.M., and on Monday as well in summer. Admission is adults $3, seniors $2, and children 6–12 $1.50, children under six free.

Dolan DNA Learning Center

Just down the street from the Whaling Museum is a large red-brick building that houses the DNA Learning Center, "the world's first biotechnology museum." As the educational arm of the Cold Spring Harbor Laboratory, the museum presents changing exhibits on such subjects as the use of DNA testing in criminal cases. Though the exhibits are aimed at children, the subject is new and complex enough to interest adults as well. The center also presents frequent screenings of *Long Island Discovery,* a 28-minute video show that's a good introduction to the island's history and heritage. Call for showtimes. The center, 334 Main St., 516/367-5170, website: vector.cshl.org, is open Mon.–Fri. 10 A.M.–4 P.M., Saturday noon–4 P.M. Admission is free.

SPLIA Gallery

At 161 Main St. at Shore Rd. is a small but first-rate gallery, 631/692-4664, operated by the Society for the Preservation of Long Island Antiquities, a nonprofit organization. Changing exhibits trace the island's social and cultural history, while next door is an excellent bookstore stocked with unusual books about Long Island. Hours are May–Oct., Tues.–Sun. 11:30 A.M.–4:30 P.M.; Nov.–Dec., Fri.–Sun. 11 A.M.–4 P.M.; and Jan.–Apr., Sat.–Sun. 11 A.M.–4 P.M.

Cold Spring Harbor Fish Hatchery and Aquarium

A few miles south of the village center is New York's oldest fish hatchery, established in 1883. As recently as the early 1970s, this small plant produced about 100,000 brook trout a year, to be shipped upstate to stock the waters of the Adirondacks and the Catskills.

The hatchery suspended such mammoth operations in 1979, following the construction of larger facilities upstate, but it still operates as an educational institution and is a good place to view aquatic life. A half-dozen pools teem with hundreds of thousands of growing trout—all swimming together in one direction at one moment, switching to another the next. You'll also see a hatch house where the eggs are incubated, and a warm-water pond stocked with bass, bowfin, catfish, carp, bluegill, pumpkinseed, perch, eel, and redhorse sucker. In the turtle pond doze dozens of varieties of turtles—some young and tender, others old and hoary—while in the aquarium building there are about 30 species of freshwater fish native to New York State.

The hatchery, Rte. 25A, 516/692-6768, www.cshfha.org, is open daily 10 A.M.–5 P.M. Admission is adults $3.50, seniors and children 5–12 $1.75, children under five free.

Food

The cozy, old-fashioned **Wyland's Country Cafe,** 55 Main St., 631/692-5655, is the place to go for tasty sandwiches, salads, and homemade baked goods; average main dish $7. More elaborate, French-influenced fare is offered by **Inn on the Harbor,** 105 Harbor Rd. (Rte. 25A), 631/367-3166, housed in a romantic setting overlooking the Sound; average entrée $18.

OLD BETHPAGE VILLAGE RESTORATION

About 10 miles south of Cold Spring Harbor is Old Bethpage Village, a restored 19th-century village filled with craftspeople and interpreters in period dress. Spread out over the restoration's 200-odd acres are a blacksmith shop, a general store, a hat shop, a tavern, a working farm stocked with plenty of farm animals, and about 20 other pre–Civil War buildings, most of which have been moved here from other locations on the island. The village endeavors to reenact rural Long Island life from 1830 to 1860.

Each time you visit Old Bethpage, you'll see something different. Come in December and you'll witness a 19th-century Christmas. Come in May and you'll spot Union soldiers training in the fields. Come in August, and baseball games, played according to 1860 rules, will be in progress. Wrote the *Long Island Democrat* on July 20, 1858: "It is only a few years that the game of base ball has been considered of much account. . . . But now we have daily accounts of spirited contests in this healthy and exhilarating game, from almost every section of the country." The village also has an excellent museum shop, filled with handmade gifts, reproduction antiques, and unusual books.

Old Bethpage Village, 516/572-8400, is located at Round Swamp Road. From the LIE (I-495), take Exit 48 heading south and follow the signs. The village is open March–Oct., Wed.–Sun. 10 A.M.–5 P.M.; November, Wed.–Fri. 10 A.M.–4 P.M.; call for December hours; closed January–February. Admission is adults $6, seniors and children 5–12 $4, children under five free.

Camping is available nearby at the 64-site **Battle Row Campground,** 1 Claremont Rd., 516/572-8690; open April–November. Basic nightly rates $7–15; a children's area and recreation building is on site.

HUNTINGTON

Though Huntington is now principally a tidy suburban community with the usual contingency of well-heeled commuters and shops, evidence of its vibrant Colonial past can still be spotted here and there. The 1750 **Conklin Farmhouse,** 2 High St., once housed four generations of Conklins, and is now a historic museum furnished in a mix of Colonial, Federal, and Victorian styles. The 1795 Federal-style **Kissam House,** 434 Park Ave., was once home to an early family of physicians. Both houses are run by the Huntington Historical Society, 631/427-7045, and are open to the public; call for hours.

Also downtown is the **Heckscher Museum of Art,** 2 Prime Ave. at Rte. 25A, 631/351-3250, www.heckscher.org, which houses a small but excellent collection of American and European painting and sculpture. The museum's array of 19th-century American landscapes is especially noteworthy. Hours year-round are Tues.–Fri. 10 A.M.–5 P.M. and Sat.–Sun. 1–5 P.M.; in summer, the museum is also open Thurs.–Sat. 5–8:30 P.M. Suggested donation is adults $5, seniors $3, and children $1.

Walt Whitman Birthplace State Historic Park

A few miles south of Huntington proper stands the clapboard farmhouse where Walt Whitman was born. Driving here on multi-lane highways, past an enormous shopping mall named in his honor, it's hard not to shudder at what's become of the bard's beloved Long Island.

For all the congestion surrounding it, however, the Walt Whitman House itself sits in serene isolation behind a tall hedge. Stepping into its snug, sunny hall is like stepping into a well-crafted poem. Whitman's father built this house, and everything within it is meticulously designed and constructed—from hand-hewn beams held together with wooden pegs, to innovative storage closets built into the fireplace walls.

Whitman only lived here until he was five, when his family moved to Brooklyn. But he came back to Long Island as a young man to teach school, and the museum does a good job of chronicling his entire life. A short movie covers the highlights of his career, while upstairs and in the brand-new interpretive center next door are exhibit rooms filled with his papers, early editions of *Leaves of Grass*, and his schoolmaster's desk. The interpretative center also houses a nice-sized library, gift shop, and classrooms for its educational programs.

To reach the Whitman House from Huntington, take Route 110 south and watch for Old Walt Whitman Road (not to be confused with Walt Whitman Road, which is another name for Route 110 south of Jericho Turnpike)—it's on the right about a half mile south of Jericho Turnpike. The house, 246 Old Walt Whitman Rd., Huntington Station, 631/427-5240, is open Monday and Wed.–Fri. 11 A.M.–4 P.M. and Sat.–Sun. noon–5 P.M.; closed Monday in winter. Admission is adults $3, seniors and students $2, and children 7–12 $1. A Whitman poem entitled "To Rich Givers" is posted by the door: "What you give me I cheerfully accept/A little sustenance, a hut and garden, a little money as I rendezvous with my poems."

Other Whitman Sites

Other sites connected with Walt Whitman are located throughout the West Hills region. Some are buildings, others are hills or hollows through which the poet liked to meander on his frequent trips back to the village of his birth. Ask at the Walt Whitman Birthplace for a copy of the booklet and trail map outlining these sites.

Accommodations

The largest full-service hotel in Suffolk County, the **Melville Marriott,** 1350 Old Walt Whitman Rd., Melville, 631/423-1600, offers a glass-enclosed lobby, 370 rooms, indoor pool, fitness center, business center, and restaurant ($159–219 d).

Food

Huntington has many good restaurants. For Greek food, or fresh fish, try the popular **Mediterranean Snack Bar,** 360 New York Ave., 631/423-8982, where everything from the souvlaki dishes to soft-shell crabs are served with a Greek salad; average entrée $14.

Tortilla Grill, 335 New York Ave., 631/423-4141, specializes in fresh tortillas, quesadillas, and "fajitas by the pound"; average main course $9. **Jonathan's,** 15 Wall St., 631/549-0055, is a classy bistro serving eclectic Italian fare, including a wide range of pastas; pasta dishes average $15, other entrées slightly higher. The lively **Brasserie 345,** 345 Main St., 631/673-8084, offers innovative French-American fare; average entrée $16.

LLOYD NECK PENINSULA

The drive north of Huntington to the Lloyd Neck peninsula is exquisite, especially on a late spring day when the trees and grasslands are a pale lime green and the bay is a biting cobalt blue. The narrow, winding roads are flanked by low wooden-rail fences that suddenly give way to vistas of choppy seas specked with sailboats.

Joseph Lloyd Manor House

Nearing the peninsula on West Neck and Lloyd Harbor Roads, you'll pass by the Joseph Lloyd Manor House, an imposing white Colonial home overlooking the waters of Lloyd Harbor. Built in 1766 to replace the first Lloyd manor house built in 1711, the house is filled with antiques and fine, hand-carved woodwork, while out back is a formal garden.

The house was once home to Jupiter Hammon, a slave who became the first published black poet in America. Hammon was taught to read in the manor's school and was allowed to use his master's library. His owners encouraged him to learn, and he published his first poem, "An Evening Thought," in 1760 at the age of 49. Later, at age 75, he wrote "An Address to the Negroes in the State of New York," in which he pointed out the irony of the American Revolution. That address may have been the impetus for New York State's 1799 law freeing slaves born after July 4, 1799, after they reached the age of 25 (females) or 28 (males).

Now run by the Society for the Preservation of Long Island Antiquities, the Joseph Lloyd Manor House, 1 Lloyd Lane Rd., at Lloyd Harbor Rd., 631/692-4664, is currently open only Memorial Day–Columbus Day, Sunday 1–5 P.M., but hours may be extended in summer. Admission is adults $3, seniors and children under 12 $1.50.

Caumsett State Historic Park

Occupying most of the Lloyd Neck peninsula is wild Caumsett State Historic Park. No motor vehicles are allowed here, and no visitor facilities are available. To explore, you park your car in a wide grassy lot and then hike through meadows filled with wildflowers or along paths and dirt roads shrouded by tall, leafy trees.

One side of the 1,500-acre park abuts Long Island Sound and sports a pebbly beach from which anglers cast their lines. The beach—one of the few wild public beaches on the North Shore—is an easy, two-mile walk from the parking lot. Near the beach is a salt marsh that's excellent for birdwatching.

On another side of the park is a complex of buildings constructed in the 1920s by Marshall Field III, the grandson of the founder of the department store. Caumsett State Historic Park was once Field's estate. He built it to be self-sufficient, complete with its own electricity, dairy, and veg-

etable farm. The buildings are not open to the public; some of the fields are still being cultivated.

Caumsett State Historic Park, 37 Lloyd Harbor Rd., off West Neck Rd., 631/423-1770, is open daily sunrise–sunset. Parking is $7 in summer, and free maps are available at the gate.

Target Rock National Wildlife Refuge

Just east of Caumsett, on Target Rock Road off Lloyd Harbor Road, is Target Rock National Wildlife Refuge. The refuge is laced with nature trails, and is especially interesting in May when an enormous number of warblers stop over during their spring migration. The refuge is also known for its rhododendron and azalea gardens. Target Rock, 631/271-2409, is open daily sunrise–sunset. Parking is $4 in summer.

NORTHPORT AND VICINITY

One of the prettiest undiscovered towns along the North Shore is Northport, just off Route 10. The downtown centers around a picturesque marina with a shoreside park and bandstand, and an old-fashioned Main Street lined with shops and 19th-century homes. Recreational boaters frequent Northport, but it is still blessedly free of commercialism and tourist kitsch.

Once known as Cowharbor, Northport was purchased by the English from the Matinecock Indians in 1656. By the early 1800s, the village had become an important shipbuilding center; 170 vessels were constructed here between 1820 and 1884. In the early 1900s, Northport was a summer resort "known as one of the most healthful in the State and famous for the fine views from its wooded slopes," according to one guidebook of the day.

Much of this history is chronicled in the redbrick **Northport Historical Society Museum,** 215 Main St., 631/757-9859, www.northporthistorical.org. The museum, which is relatively large for such a small town, is open Tues.–Sun. 1–4:30 P.M. Admission is by donation.

Suffolk County Vanderbilt Museum and Planetarium

In Centerport, just west of Northport, is the Vanderbilt Museum, a storybook Spanish Baroque mansion built in the 1910s by William K. Vanderbilt II, the great-grandson of Commodore Vanderbilt. Two huge black eagles that once sat atop Grand Central Station mark the estate's entrance, while inside the 24-room mansion are such odd treasures as suits of armor, Napoleon's bed and desk, and a Spanish Moroccan dining room with a hand-painted ceiling. The views of Northport Bay from the mansion would be superb, but for the three white-and-red-striped towers of a power plant across the way.

Vanderbilt, who lived at his Eagle's Nest estate during the summers only, was an eccentric who liked to disguise himself and go into town to drink with the locals. A man of many interests, he was especially fascinated with marinelife and collected hundreds of specimens which he housed in his own enormous **Marine Museum.** Still located on the estate's grounds, the museum is now a musty affair stuffed with fishes, Egyptian mummies, and shrunken heads.

When Vanderbilt died, he willed his estate to the people of Suffolk County "for the education and enjoyment of the public." In 1971, the **Vanderbilt Planetarium** was added to the estate's grounds. One of the country's largest planetariums, the facility puts on sky shows filled with more than 11,000 stars.

The museums and planetarium, 631/854-5555, www.vanderbiltmuseum.org, are at 180 Little Neck Rd. off Rte. 25A; watch for signs. Hours year-round are Tues.–Sun. noon–5 P.M.; call for possible extended hours in summer. Admission is adults $8, seniors and students $6, and children $4. Tickets to a sky show at the planetarium are an additional $3; children under six not admitted.

Eatons Neck

North of town on Route 10 is a long, skinny spit leading to windswept Eatons Neck. Along one side is a pebbly beach frequented by fisherfolk; along the other is Northport Bay, often filled with pleasure craft. All around are the blue, blue waters of the sea. Though it can get crowded during the summer, Eatons Neck is more often a lonely spot good for strolling or birdwatching in the early morning or evening.

Food

In Northport, **La Casa,** 445 Waterside Ave., 516/757-7720, is a good pizza/pasta joint with a great view of the Sound; average pie $11. **Show Win,** 325 Fort Salonga Rd., 631/261-6622, offers some of the best sushi rolls on Long Island; on the menu are almost 50 different kinds. For traditional German cuisine, try **Pumpernickel's,** 640 Main St., 631/757-7959; average entrée $15, served with soup or salad.

EAST TO ST. JAMES
Sunken Meadow State Park

The main attraction at the popular, 1,266-acre Sunken Meadow State Park is a mile-long beach, often packed in summer with thousands of sun worshippers baking, swimming, napping, and playing. Also within the park are three golf courses, lots of hiking trails, a salt marsh, a boardwalk, and bathhouses, and a small museum with exhibits on Long Island's natural history. A free map to the park is available at the entrance; lifeguards are on duty Memorial Day–Labor Day.

The Long Island Greenbelt Trail runs the 34-mile width of Long Island from Heckscher State Park to Sunken Meadow (see Long Island Greenbelt Trail under Bay Shore and Vicinity for more information).

Sunken Meadow, 631/269-4333, is at the intersection of Rte. 25A and Sunken Meadow Pkwy. near Kings Park. The park is open daily sunrise–sunset. Parking is $7 in summer.

St. James

Continuing east on Route 25A, through the large, traffic-clogged town of Smithtown, you'll soon come to tiny St. James, whose biggest claim to fame is the **St. James General Store,** 516 Moriches Rd., at Harbor Hill Rd., 631/862-8333. Listed with the National Register of Historic Places and used continuously since 1857, the store is a creaky, hodgepodge affair stuffed to the bursting point with old-fashioned candy, scented soaps, homemade jellies, historic postcards, and the like. Standing sentinel out front is a wooden cigar-store Indian. Hours are March–Dec., daily 10 A.M.–5 P.M.; Jan.–Feb., Wed.–Sun. 10 A.M.–5 P.M.

Also in St. James is the 50-year-old, family-owned **Wicks Farm and Garden,** 445 North Country Rd. (Rte. 25A), 631/584-5727. At 200 acres, Wicks is one of the larger produce farms dotting Suffolk County, and is unique in one respect—looming over its greenhouses is a black-caped 25-foot-high witch, her crooked nose and broomstick outlined against the sky. It's not to be missed by lovers of roadside architecture.

STONY BROOK

Built on a hill sloping down to the water is the restored 18th-century village of Stony Brook. Though a popular tourist destination, complete with shopping malls and an ultraclean feel, Stony Brook has managed to retain much of its rural character and is an enjoyable town in which to meander.

Much of Stony Brook's charm is due to a man named Ward Melville, owner of the Thom McAn shoe company. Back in the 1940s, Melville—concerned about encroaching suburbia—had the village rebuilt along historical lines while at the same time successfully fighting for strict zoning codes. He even paid for much of the re-building himself.

Along Main Street in the middle of town are the harbor and Village Center, where well-marked signs point the way to shops and historic sites. To one side is an old **U.S. post office,** equipped with a mechanical eagle that flaps its wings every hour on the hour. To the other side is the **Three Village Inn,** 150 Main St., built in 1751. Once the home of Capt. Jonas Smith—Long Island's first millionaire—the rambling white house is now a first-class historic inn and restaurant.

Beyond the post office is the unusual **All Souls' Episcopal Church,** built by architect Stanford White in 1889. Pitched on the steep slope of a small hill, the tiny church—complete with zig-zagging steps and a narrow steeple—has a fairy-tale quality, as if it were built for elves.

Continue walking a few blocks past the church to wide, dark Mill Pond, and you'll come to the gray-shingled **Grist Mill,** Harbor Rd. off Main St., 631/751-2244. Built in 1751, the mill has been restored and still grinds corn. Hours are

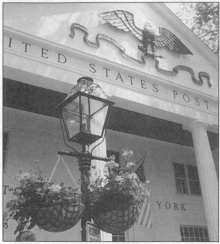

the post office on Main Street in Stony Brook

June–Aug., Wed.–Sun. noon–4:30 P.M.; April–May and Sept.–Dec., Sat.–Sun. noon–4:30 P.M. Admission is adults $2, children $1.

Walking-tour maps of Stony Brook are available in the Three Village Inn, in many of the stores, and at the Ward Melville Heritage Center, 111 Main St., 631/751-2244, www.stony-brookvillage.com, a few doors down from the post office.

Long Island Museum of American Art, History, and Carriages

Formerly known as the Museums at Stony Brook, this nine-acre complex on the outskirts of town focuses on American history and art. Foremost among its museum buildings is the renowned Carriage House, which contains about 90 horse-drawn vehicles ranging from hand-painted coaches and fire-fighting equipment to elaborate sleighs and a very rare Roma wagon. Roma wagons seldom survive because of the Roma custom of burying all a person's possessions after his or her death—even wagons.

Meanwhile, in the Art Museum, you'll find both changing exhibits and an enjoyable collection of works by William Sidney Mount, a 19th-century painter from Stony Brook who depicted rural Long Island life. The Bayman's Art Gallery of history features a large collection of hand-carved antique decoys and 15 miniature period rooms.

Here and there throughout the complex are a number of restored 19th-century buildings moved here from nearby. Among them are a blacksmith's shop, a barn, and a one-room schoolhouse. The museum, 1208 Rte. 25A, 631/751-0066, www.longislandmuseum.org, is open Wed.–Sun. noon–5 P.M. Admission is adults $4, seniors $3, students and children 6–17 $2, children under six free.

Accommodations and Food

The lovely **Three Village Inn,** 150 Main St., 631/751-0555, offers period antiques, fireplaces, ceiling beams, and plenty of Colonial atmosphere in a setting overlooking the water. Some of the rooms are housed in the historic, white-clapboard main building; others in an attractive modern wing where the rooms are quite spacious and equipped with many amenities ($179 d). An adjoining restaurant specializes in old-fashioned American dishes such as New England lobster pie and clam chowder, served by waiters in Colonial garb; average entrée $18.

A good choice for families with children is the family-style **Brook House,** in the Village Center, off Main St., 631/751-4617, serving everything from burgers and sandwiches ($6–8) to dinner entrées such as steak and chicken ($13–15). Not far from the Long Island Museum is the **Village Bistro,** 766 Rte. 25A, 631/941-0430, offering innovative global-American fare; average entrée $14.

SETAUKET

Along with St. James and Stony Brook, Setauket is one of the communities historically referred to as the "Three Villages." All are filled with shady winding roads, historic homes, meadows dusted with wildflowers, and peaceful ponds.

During the Revolutionary War, the Three Villages served as a center of espionage for George Washington. Members of the Setauket Spy Ring, as it later came to be known, were recruited by a friend of Nathan Hale's who was from Setauket. The ring's function was to warn Washington of enemy ships entering the Sound. One of the patriot spies was a housewife named Anna Strong, whose clothesline was used to send messages.

Strong's house no longer stands, but you can get

Three Village Inn

a sense of early Long Island life at the **Thompson House,** 93 N. Country Rd., 631/692-4664, now owned by the Society for the Preservation of Long Island Antiquities. Built circa 1770, the gray-shingled saltbox contains a fine collection of early island furniture. Out back is a Colonial herb garden and the Thompson family cemetery. Hours are Memorial Day–Columbus Day, Sat.–Sun. 1–5 P.M. Admission is adults $3, seniors and children $1.50.

PORT JEFFERSON

Another harbor town, located just beyond Stony Brook, is Port Jefferson. Once a thriving ship-building community, and then home to several lace factories and gravel pits, Port Jefferson today caters mostly to the tourist trade. It has a rawer and more windswept feel than does Stony Brook. Witness the town's many visiting Harleys—Port

Witness Port Jeff's many visiting Harleys—the town has long been a favorite stop among touring motorcyclists.

Jeff has long been a favorite stop among touring motorcyclists.

Downtown offers several small tourist-oriented malls as well as some interesting one-of-a-kind shops, including **Good Times Bookshop,** 150 E. Main St., 631/928-2664, carrying about 20,000 scarce and out-of-print titles; and **Village Chairs & Wares,** 402 Main St., 631/331-5791, which specializes in handmade reproduction chairs and tables.

Also downtown are a number of historic homes. Most are privately owned, but one that is open to the public is the **Mather House Museum,** Prospect and High Sts., 631/473-2665. Inside is an eclectic collection of 19th-century garments, Native American artifacts, model boats, and antiques. Out back are herb gardens, a marine barn, and a crafts house. The museum is open May–Labor Day, Sat.–Sun. 1–4 P.M.; July–Aug., Tues.–Wed. 1–4 P.M. Admission is $2.

THE PINE BARRENS

Much of the eastern end of Long Island, from just east of Port Jefferson to Hampton Bays, is covered by a 100,000-acre pine barren wilderness. Five times larger than the size of Manhattan, and one-thirteenth the size of Long Island, it sits over what is said to be the purest underground drinking water supply in the state. In its scruffy wooded growth, dominated by pitch pine and scrub oak, are several rare plant and animal species, including unusual stands of dwarf pine.

For many years, the pine barrens were at the center of an intense environmental debate that pitted conservationists against builders and local government officials. In 1989, an environmental group, the Long Island Pine Barrens Society, sued Suffolk County for approving building projects in the wilderness area without studying the environmental impact. The New York State Court ruled that no study was required but said that the state needed to draw up a plan to protect the area. A Central Pine Barrens Joint Policy and Planning Commission was created, and in 1994, they proposed establishing a 53,000-acre core area where building would be banned, surrounded by a 47,000-acre area open to controlled development.

The plan became law in July 1995—a major environmental victory. The Pine Barrens are now New York's third forest preserve, following the Adirondacks and the Catskills.

To access a five-mile trail that leads through the pine barrens, head south of the Riverhead Traffic Circle on Route 104 for about two miles and watch for signs. The trail should be avoided during the hunting season, October–February. For more information, contact the Long Island Pine Barrens Society, P.O. Box 429, Manorville, NY 11949, 631/369-3300. Or, stop by the Pine Barrens Trail Information Center, 631/369-9768, a quarter-mile north of the Long Island Expressway Exit 70 in Manorville. The center is open Memorial Day–Columbus Day, Fri.–Mon., 9 A.M.–5 P.M.

The ferry to Bridgeport, Connecticut, leaves from the Port Jefferson docks; call 631/473-0286 for schedules and information.

For brochures and a map of the village, stop into the **Port Jefferson Chamber of Commerce,** 118 W. Broadway (Rte. 25A), 631/473-1414, www.portjeffchamber.com. The chamber is open year-round, Mon.–Fri. 10 A.M.–4 P.M.; and Memorial Day–Sept., Sat.–Sun. noon–4 P.M.

Accommodations and Food

The large and always bustling **Danford's on the Sound,** 25 E. Broadway, 631/928-5200, www.danfords.com, serves as a de facto anchor for downtown Port Jefferson. Most of the rooms have balconies and views of the water ($219 d, with breakfast). The inn's restaurant serves first-rate but pricey seafood and contemporary American fare. During warm weather, an outside deck is opened up; average dinner entrée $22.

B&B fans might want to check into the **Holly Berry Bed & Breakfast,** 415 West Broadway (Rte. 25A), 631/331-3123, housed in an 1800s farmhouse on a hill above Port Jeff; $95–125 d.

The casual, laid-back **Village Way,** 106 Main St., 631/928-3395, is a good place for simple seafood and sandwiches; average entrée $9. For basic, reasonably priced Japanese fare, try **Hana,** 21 Oakland Ave., 631/473-9264; average entrée $13. Spanish seafood cuisine is the specialty of **Costa de España,** 9 Trader's Cove, 631/331-5363; try the paella with lobster; average entrée $15.

EAST TO WADING RIVER

East of Port Jefferson, the North Shore becomes flatter and more rural. Fruit and vegetable farms replace suburban lawns, small empty roads replace congested highways. Pale green fields and lumbering farm vehicles are everywhere.

Brookhaven National Laboratory

South of Wading River, in the center of Long Island, lies the enormous Brookhaven National Laboratory (BNL), one of the country's leading scientific research centers. Scientists at BNL have studied everything from the mysteries of DNA to the health effects of industrial chemicals, but the place is best known for its research into particle physics and the peacetime use of nuclear science.

Spread out over 5,265 acres and 350 buildings along the William Floyd Parkway, BNL employs about 3,300 people and attracts an almost equal number of visiting scientists and students each year. Brookhaven is also famed for its four "big machines"—the Alternating Gradient Synchrotron, the High Flux Beam Reactor, the National Synchrotron Light Source, and the Scanning Transmission Electron Microscope—all housed in enormous, airplane-size hangars.

Though BNL is usually closed to the general public, guided tours of its laboratory are offered on Sunday 10 A.M.–3 P.M. in July and August (except July 4th weekend). The tours are free and include a science show and tour of a different scientific department each week. For more information, call the Public Affairs Office at 631/344-4049, www.pubafbnl.gov. To reach the main entrance from Route 25A, head south on the William Floyd Parkway and watch for signs. From the LIE, take Exit 68 and head north about a mile and a half.

Wildwood State Park

Northeast of Wading River, off Route 25A along Hulse Landing Road, is Wildwood State Park. Surrounded by farm country, Wildwood is blissfully empty during the off-season, but crowded during the summer. Within its 737 acres are nearly a mile and a half of beach, 10 miles of hiking trails, bathhouses, picnic areas, ball fields, refreshment stands, and a 322-site campground (basic overnight rates $13–18). The park, 631/929-4314, is open daily sunrise–sunset. Parking in summer is $7. The campground is open April–November. Reservations are essential for summer weekends; call 800/456-CAMP.

RIVERHEAD

Riverhead lies on the shores of Peconic Bay, right between the North and South Forks. The Suffolk County seat since 1727, Riverhead was once a thriving commercial center that benefited from the area's many farms. In more recent years, it has suffered its share of economic depression, but is now experiencing something of a renaissance, thanks in large part to its spiffy new aquarium, the Atlantis Marine World. The downtown is also home to a number of lovely old brick buildings, while its revitalized waterfront is a pleasant place for a summer stroll.

For maps and other information, stop into the **Riverhead Chamber of Commerce,** 542 E. Main Rd., 631/727-7600, www.riverheadli.com. Hours year-round are Mon.–Fri. 10 A.M.–4 P.M., and Memorial Day–Labor Day, Saturday 10 A.M.–noon.

Atlantis Marine World

One of Long Island's newest attractions, this large, state-of-the-art aquarium houses everything from native Long Island fishes to moray eels, Pacific octopuses, piranhas, stingrays, and seals. Near the entrance reigns an impressive figure of Poseidon, king of the sea, while further on is a large live coral reef—aswirl with brilliantly colored tropical fish—an underwater cavern that's home to over a dozen sharks, and about 80 other exhibits. Visitors can also embark on a simulated submarine dive and take in a seal show.

The aquarium was built around the **Riverhead Foundation for Marine Research,** which also maintains several exhibits on site. Among them is a center for rehabilitating injured seals, sea turtles, and other marinelife, and a touch-tank where children can handle starfish, crabs, snails, and small fish.

The aquarium, 431 E. Main St., 631/208-9200, www.atlantismarineworld.com, is open daily Memorial Day–Labor Day 9 A.M.–6 P.M., and Labor Day–Memorial Day 9 A.M.–5 P.M. Admission is adults $12.60, seniors $10, children 3–11 $10, under 3 free.

Riverhead Foundation for Marine Research

Adjoining Atlantis Marine World is the Riverhead Foundation, 428 E. Main St., 631/369-9840, www.riverheadfoundation.org, which still houses a number of educational exhibits that are separate from the aquarium. The foundation also offers seal-watching cruises that depart from Point Lookout on the South Shore (see Freeport) and specimen-gathering cruises along the Peconic River and Flanders Bay (visitors help marine specialists gather the specimens).

The center is open July–Labor Day daily 10 A.M.–5 P.M.; after Labor Day, Sat.–Sun. 10 A.M.–5 P.M.

Suffolk County Historical Society

At the other end of Main Street is the Suffolk County Historical Society, 300 W. Main St. (Rte. 25), 631/727-2881. An excellent place in which to get a sense of Suffolk County's past, this large, rambling museum is filled with eclectic treasures. Among them are a good-size collection of Indian artifacts, Colonial furniture and ceramics, some nice examples of early crafts, and an excellent bookstore. The museum is open year-round, Tues.–Sat. 12:30–4:30 P.M. Admission by donation.

Recreation

Where East and West Main Streets meet is **Riverhead Village Pier,** an attractive, parklike place where the *Peconic River Lady* docks. The boat, 631/369-3700, offers lunch and dinner cruises of Peconic Bay.

West of town is **Splish Splash,** 2549 Middle Country Rd., 631/727-3600, a 40-acre water theme park with a wave pool, 16 water slides, four kiddie pools, a kiddie car wash, and tube rides. The park is open weekends and holidays mid-May–mid-June, and daily mid-June–Labor Day, 10 A.M.–5 P.M. Admission is adults $27, children under 48 inches $20, children under three years free. Parking is $7. To reach Splish Splash directly from the LIE, take Exit 72 and watch for signs.

The North Fork and Shelter Island

The North Fork is: fertile farms, rolling vineyards, pebble-strewn beaches, one-stoplight towns, white-steepled churches, Colonial saltboxes, village greens. Like the better-known South Fork across Great Peconic Bay, the North Fork was first settled in 1640 by colonists from New England, and that heritage flavors everything, from the look of the villages to the independent mindset of the people. Unlike the South Fork, the North Fork is still predominantly rural, with only a handful of tourist hotels and "attractions." This is changing—wealthy outsiders are buying up land at an alarming rate. But for the moment at least, the North Fork is still sleepy, friendly, and unpretentious.

You can easily explore the North Fork in a day or even an afternoon, although the area is so achingly beautiful—especially near the windswept beaches of Orient Point—that it's well worth lingering a while longer. Highlights include the historic villages of Cutchogue, Southold, and Orient, the bustling harbor town of Greenport, and four-mile-long Orient Beach. In addition, the region has developed a first-rate reputation for its wine. Most of the area's dozen or so vineyards are located in the vicinity of Cutchogue and are open to the public for tastings and tours.

For the most part, accommodation options on the North Fork are limited to simple, inviting beachfront resort motels and B&Bs. Shelter Island has several historic inns. As in other shore areas, rates tend to be on the high side in season (usually Memorial Day–Labor Day), very reasonable the rest of the year. Two- or three-night minimum stays are often required in summer, especially on weekends.

Getting There

The quickest way to reach the 30-mile-long North Fork, located about two hours from Manhattan, is to take the Long Island Expressway (LIE), or I-495, to Riverhead. From there, two major roads traverse the North Fork. Route 25 to the south is the more popular route and can get congested on summer weekends. Sound Avenue/Route 48 to the north offers a good alternative.

The North Fork can also be reached by train and bus, although transportation once you arrive is problematic unless you're content to stay in one place or bike. The **Long Island Rail Road,** 718/217-5477 or 516/822-5477, runs several trains daily between Manhattan and Greenport. The **Sunrise Express,** 631/477-1200 or 800/527-7709, offers bus service between Manhattan and various North Fork villages.

Several ferries operate between Connecticut and Long Island. The **Cross Sound Ferry,** 631/323-2525 or 860/443-5281, www.longis-landferry.com, travels between New London, Connecticut, and Orient Point. The **Bridge-port/Point Jefferson Ferry,** 631/473-0286, lands you in Port Jefferson, an easy hour's drive to the west of the North Fork.

SOUND AVENUE SIGHTS

Heading east onto the North Fork via the northern route of Sound Avenue (which soon becomes Route 48), you'll immediately come to **Brier-mere Farms,** 631/722-3931, Sound Ave. at Rte. 105. Especially well known for its homemade pies, Briermere features about 15 different varieties on any given day, ranging from the standard blueberry and peach to the more unusual blackberry apple and strawberry rhubarb.

Entering Wine Country reads a sign, and almost immediately you'll spy **Palmer Vineyards,** 108 Sound Ave., 631/722-WINE. It's the westernmost of the Long Island vineyards, and one of the largest, attracting close to 500 visitors on a typical summer's day. Palmer offers self-guided tours, a tasting room made up to look like a snug English pub, and an outdoor deck overlooking its vineyards. Hours are daily 11 A.M.–5 P.M.

Near the intersection of Sound Avenue and Herricks Lane is the **Hallockville Museum Farm and Folklife Center,** 6038 Sound Ave. (Rte. 48), 631/298-5292, a 102-acre farm that was owned by the Hallock family for over 200 years. Now a museum listed on the National Register of Historic Places, Hallockville centers around a

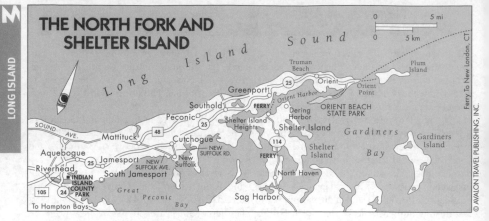

THE NORTH FORK AND SHELTER ISLAND

1765 homestead, a large barn, a shoemaker's shop, and a smokehouse, along with a few still-cultivated potato fields and a pretty apple orchard. The shoemaker's shop, filled with old-fashioned tools of the trade and shoes in various stages of completion, is especially interesting. In it, Capt. Zachariah Hallock made over 1,700 pairs of shoes between the years 1771 and 1820. Hallockville is open year-round Wed.–Sat. noon–4 P.M. Admission is adults $5, children $4. During the spring, summer, and autumn, the museum stages frequent crafts demonstrations, festivals (including a popular pumpkin festival in October), and workshops.

ROUTE 25 TO CUTCHOGUE

Heading onto the North Fork via the southern route—Route 25, also known as Main Road in many spots—you'll pass one pretty little town after another. **Aquebogue** and **Jamesport** are dotted with small stores and a number of good lunch spots. The **Modern Snack Bar,** 628 Main Rd. (Rte. 25), Aquebogue, 631/722-3655, is a family-style roadside diner that has been offering home cooking since 1950; average main dish $8. The **Jamesport Country Kitchen,** 1601 Main Rd. (Rte. 25) in the center of Jamesport, 631/722-3537, specializes in North Fork produce and wine. Everything is fresh, with entrées ranging from burgers to grilled salmon. The place can get packed in summer, and reservations are recommended; average dinner entrée $13.

New Suffolk

Well worth the short detour is New Suffolk Avenue, leading south off Route 25 at Mattituck to New Suffolk. To the left are lime-green wetlands, specked with osprey nests; to the right, the shimmering blue and white waters of Great Peconic Bay. New Suffolk itself is a sleepy place equipped with a tiny post office, a wide beach, and several simple lunch shacks. Back in the 1800s, however, New Suffolk—then known as Robin's Island Neck—was a busy port, and in 1899–1900, the U.S. Navy tested its first commissioned submarine here.

Cutchogue

One of the prettiest of the North Fork hamlets is Cutchogue, filled with white churches, leafy trees, and weathered, shingled homes. The town—named after the Indian word for "principal place"—centers around the village green, in the middle of which are clustered a group of historic wooden buildings, moved here from nearby.

By far the most interesting of the group is the **Old House,** which dates back to 1649. Dark and very cozy inside, it's outfitted with all the luxuries of its day, including wooden paneling, leaded glass windows, and a fluted chimney. The house was "lost" for close to 100 years, but was rediscovered in the 1930s by a WPA worker who noticed its unusual chimney.

Next to the Old House is the **Old Schoolhouse Museum,** built in 1840, and the **Wickham Farmhouse,** equipped with furniture and farm implements from the early 1700s. Across the street is the **Village Library,** Main Rd. (Rte. 25), housed in a lovely New England–style Congregational church. The church was built in 1862 because of a schism within the Presbyterian church. The Presbyterian minister was an ardent abolitionist who preached against slavery week after week until the church elders got tired of it and threw him out. The minister then gathered his followers together and built the Congregational church.

With the exception of the library, the historic buildings on the green are run by the Cutchogue-New Suffolk Historical Council, 631/734-7122. The buildings are open July–Aug., Sat.–Mon. 1–4 P.M.; call for hours the rest of the year. Admission is adults $1.50, children 50 cents.

A few minutes' walk from the village green is the vintage, chrome-laden **Cutchogue Diner,** Main Rd. (Rte. 25), 631/734-9056. Especially good are the pancakes and meatloaf; average main meal $7. Also nearby is **Braun's Seafood,** Main Rd. (Rte. 25), 631/734-6700, where you can purchase clam pies, an East End specialty (these can't be eaten on the spot; they must be cooked).

For excellent French cuisine, check out the **Wild Goose,** 4805 Depot Lane, 631/734-4145, one of the North Fork's top restaurants; average entrée $24.

WINE COUNTRY

Cutchogue—along with Peconic, just down the road—is the center of Long Island's wine-producing country. Unless otherwise noted, most of the wineries are open for tastings daily 11 A.M.–5 P.M. Tours can usually be arranged by appointment.

Off Route 25 east of Cutchogue are **Peconic Bay Vineyard,** 631/734-7361, which produces an especially fine chardonnay; **Bedell Cellars,** 631/734-7537, a small but highly regarded winery that has won a number of awards; and **Pugliese Vineyards,** 631/734-4057, which features a lovely collection of hand-painted bottles

containing a chardonnay, blanc de blanc champagne, cabernet sauvignon, and merlot.

Along Route 25 closer to Peconic is the 300-acre **Pindar Vineyards,** 631/734-6200, the largest vineyard on the island. Over 20 different wines are produced here annually, and tours run continuously throughout the day. As many as 3,500 people might stop by on a fine summer's weekend (open daily 11 A.M.–6 P.M.). Also popular is the nearby **Lenz Winery,** Rte. 25, 631/734-6010, a 60-acre vineyard with a striking modern main building.

To the north, along Route 48 in Cutchogue, are **Castello di Borghese-Hargrave Vineyard,** 631/734-5111, the oldest vineyard on the island, founded in 1973 (open daily 11 A.M.–5 P.M., closed Mondays Jan.–March); and **Bidwell Vineyards,** 631/734-5200.

Another winery, **Palmer Vineyards,** is farther west along Sound Avenue (see Sound Avenue Sights, above).

SOUTHOLD AND VICINITY

Settled in 1640, Southold is one of the oldest communities in New York State. The earliest white settlers to arrive here came from New Haven, Connecticut.

Southold Historical Society Museum

Standing testimony to the town's long past is a sleepy museum complex smack in the middle of the low-key downtown. Among many historic buildings here are the weathered 1750 **Thomas Moore House,** the lavishly furnished Victorian **Currie-Bell House,** and the lovely, hand-hewn **Pine Neck Barn.** Also on the museum grounds are a working blacksmith shop, a buttery, and a millinery filled with a wonderful assortment of 19th- and early 20th-century hats.

A map and more information about the museum complex can be picked up in the 19th-century **Prince Building,** Main Rd. (Rte. 25), where the Southold Historical Society is headquartered; 631/765-5500. Also in the building is the **Museum Shop,** which sells an imaginative selection of gifts and antiques. The complex is open July–Labor Day, Wednesday, Saturday, Sunday

1–4 P.M. Admission is $2. The museum shop is open weekdays 9:30 A.M.–2:30 P.M.

Horton Point Lighthouse

Just north of downtown is the striking Horton Point Lighthouse, which stands high on a bluff at the end of Lighthouse Road. The first lighthouse on this site was commissioned by George Washington in 1790. The current lighthouse was built in 1857 and is still operational. Painted in stark white and surrounded by rhododendrons, the building overlooks Long Island Sound and a lonely stretch of beach.

Tours of the lighthouse, 631/765-5500 (weekdays 9:30 A.M.–2:30 P.M.) or 631/765-2101 (summer weekends), take visitors through the keeper's quarters and the working light tower. Downstairs is a small museum filled with artifacts, paintings, and "treasures" from sunken ships. The lighthouse/museum is open Memorial Day–Columbus Day, weekends 11:30 A.M.–4 P.M. Suggested donation is adults $2, children free.

Other Sites

East of downtown, at 1080 Main Bayview Rd., is the **Southold Indian Museum,** 631/765-5577. Run by the Long Island chapter of the New York State Archeological Association, the museum houses an extensive array of Algonquin artifacts, including one of the country's largest collections of Native American pottery (from 3000 B.C. to Colonial times), arrowheads, and spears. Hours are July–Aug., Sat.–Sun. 1:30–4:30 P.M.; Sunday 1:30–4:30 P.M. the rest of the year. Suggested donation is adults $1, children 25 cents.

Ironically enough, directly across from the Indian Museum you'll find the **Custer Institute,** 631/765-2626. The institute actually has nothing to do with Native American history. Instead, it's a membership organization that presents films and lectures on the arts and sciences, along with stargazing sessions at its astronomical observatory, equipped with a three-meter radio telescope and various refractors. Call for hours and more information.

Accommodations

Housed in a Victorian farmhouse with several fireplaces, three guest rooms, and lots of antiques is the **Home Port Bed & Breakfast,** 2500 Peconic Ln., in nearby Peconic, 631/765-1435,

Horton Point Lighthouse

© CHRISTIANE BIRD

www.northfork.com/homeport. The home is owned by a family whose ancestors arrived on the North Fork in 1640, and they have plenty of stories to tell about Long Island's fast-disappearing fishing way of life ($98–108 d; the two cheaper rooms share a bath).

Basic but adequate accommodations are offered by the 15-room **Southold Beach Motel** on North Rd. (Rte. 48) one mile north of the village, 631/765-2233. It fronts the beach and is open June–September ($75–120 d).

GREENPORT

The principal commercial center on the North Fork is the bustling town of Greenport, laid out in neat squares that slope down to the harbor. The main streets are lined with an interesting hodgepodge of restaurants and shops—some tourist-oriented, some not—while the harbor is always full of fishing boats and pleasure craft.

Greenport has been a boating community since before the Revolutionary War. In the 1700s, cargo ships from the West Indies docked here to unload molasses and rum. Later, the port became a center for whaling and the oyster trade. Even today, an estimated two-thirds of Greenport's population earns its living from boats and related industries.

Until the late 1800s, traveling via Greenport was the quickest route between New York and Boston. This became especially true after the Long Island Rail Road came to Greenport in 1844. The overland route through Connecticut back then had bumpy roads and few bridges crossing the numerous rivers, so travelers took the train to Greenport and boarded steamers that arrived in Boston the next day. On board was much wining and dining, dancing and gambling.

Most of Greenport's activity centers around its harbor. At the end of Main St. is Claudio's Restaurant (see below) and **Preston's Outfitters,** Main St. Wharf, 631/477-1990, a not-to-be-missed barn of a store where you can buy everything from rope and paint to paintings and Top-Sider shoes. Preston's was established in 1883.

Docked just outside Preston's is the *Mary E.,* 631/477-8966, a historic 53-foot schooner that

offers scenic cruises of the bay. The cruises last two and a half hours and cost adults $25, children under 12 $12.50.

Information
The **North Fork Tourist Information Center,** 631/477-1383, www.northfork.org, is located about a mile west of downtown Greenport, on Main Road (Route 25) just east of Chapel Lane. The center is open July–Aug., daily 10 A.M.–4 P.M.; Sept.–Oct., Fri.–Mon. 10 A.M.–4 P.M., and weekends April–June. Information can also be found at the website: www.greenport.org.

Museums
The **East End Seaport Maritime Museum,** end of 3rd St., 631/477-0004 or 631/477-2100, www.eastendseaport.org, is loaded with artifacts from the fishing and boatbuilding industries, and features interesting changing exhibits on such subjects as women and the sea, and yacht racing. Hours are Memorial Day–Labor Day, Tues.–Sun. 10 A.M.–5 P.M.; call for hours the rest of the year. Suggested donation is adults $2, children $1.

Railroad buffs will want to visit the **Railroad Museum of Long Island,** 440 4th St., 631/477-0439 or 631/727-7920. Housed in what was once a freight station, the museum traces the history of railroading on the island and features a 20-foot model of the Greenport freight yard as it looked in 1955. Hours are Memorial Day–Columbus Day, Sat.–Sun. noon–4 P.M., and by appointment. Admission is adults $1, children 50 cents.

Camping and Accommodations
Camping is available at the 150-site **Eastern Long Island Kampground,** 690 Queen St., 631/477-0022, open April–November. The basic nightly rate is $24, and on site are a camp store, laundry facility, and children's playground.

The main building at the **Townsend Manor Inn,** 714 Main St., 631/477-2000, is a historic 1835 Greek Revival house complete with a restaurant, old-fashioned cocktail lounge, and cozy living room. Guest rooms are located in several modern additions, and in between is a pool ($105–185 d in summer; $75–125 d off-season; open year-round).

The elegant **Bartlett House,** 503 Front St., 631/477-0371, www.greenport.com/bartlett, is a 1908 Victorian mansion complete with stained glass windows and a wide front porch. Each of the nine rooms is different, but they all have private baths and many antiques ($125–215 d in summer, with full breakfast included; about $110 d off-season).

Along the beach in the Greenport area, you'll find the '50s-era **Silver Sands Motel,** Rte. 25 at Silvermere Rd., 631/477-0011, www.silver-sands-motel.com, painted bright pink and blue ($90–110 d), and the small and friendly **Sunset Motel,** 62005 Rte. 48, 631/477-1776 ($80–100 d). Also on the beach is the very, very long **Sound View Inn,** North Rd. (Rte. 48), 631/477-1910, www.soundviewinn.com, where all the rooms here have balconies, and some have kitchenettes. On the grounds are tennis courts and a pool, and live bands play in the cocktail lounge on summer weekends ($115–140 d in mid-summer; $80–95 d in early June and September). All three motels are open June–September.

Food

Dominating the harbor area is **Claudio's,** 111 Main St., 631/477-0627, a huge and rambling seafood restaurant; average entrée $20. First established by a Portuguese sailor in 1870, Claudio's bills itself as the "oldest same family owned restaurant in the United States." Inside is much heavy carved wood, stained glass, and an enormous bar brought to the restaurant by barge from a New York City hotel in 1885. Claudio's also runs the first-rate and considerably less expensive **Claudio's Clam Bar and Wharf,** 631/477-1889, which features live bands on summer weekends; average main dish $11.

In the Brewer Yacht Yard, find the new **Antares Cafe,** 2530 Manhasset Ave., 631/477-8839, which has been drawing raves for its New American cuisine; average entrée $17. **Aldo's,** 103-5 Front St., 631/477-1699, is a tiny, casual bistro serving breakfast, lunch, and dinner. Fresh breads are featured for breakfast; French/Mediterranean peasant food for lunch and dinner. Bring your own wine; average dinner entrée $14.

For a light bite, step into the lovely, high-ceilinged **Greenport Tea Company,** 119A Main St., 631/477-8744, where tea is served in china cups from vintage tea pots. Also on the menu are clam pie, scones, and finger sandwiches.

ORIENT

At the far, far end of the North Fork is Orient, one of the most glorious spots on the island. Only a few buildings dot this narrow windswept piece of land. Instead you'll find osprey nests, gentle beaches, and a tiny historical town.

In the 1930s, the WPA guide described the village of Orient in terms that still apply today: "The little weathered shingle houses, few more than one-and-a-half stories high, sit primly behind picket fences. In sun or storm the Atlantic winds roll in. . . ."

To reach Orient proper, you cross a narrow isthmus. To the left are crescent-shaped Truman Beach and Long Island Sound; to the right, Orient Harbor and Gardiners Bay.

The town centers around an old-fashioned post office and the **Orient Country Store,** Village Ln., 631-323-2580. The former is still equipped with turn-of-the-century stamp windows, while the latter sells sandwiches at bargain prices.

Historical Sites

At the end of Village Lane is the **Oysterponds Historical Society,** a group of seven well-preserved historic buildings. The **Webb House** is a pre–Revolutionary War inn, while the **Village House** is a 19th-century home containing much memorabilia from the 1800s. Back then, Orient was a popular resort with two big hotels. First-rate temporary exhibits are showcased in the **Schoolhouse Building,** the only building open year-round.

Oysterponds, 1555 Village Ln., 631/323-2480, is open July 4–Labor Day, Thursday and Sat.–Sun. 2–5 P.M.; by appointment the rest of the year. Admission is adults $3, children 50 cents.

If you continue down Village Lane to King Street and turn onto Narrow Avenue, you'll come to an early slaves' burial ground, where 20 slaves are buried along with another branch of the Tuthill family—Dr. Seth Tuthill and his wife

GUIDES TO PRESERVES

The South Fork–Shelter Island Chapter of the Nature Conservancy, 631/329-7689, publishes a detailed "Preserve Guide" filled with information about their refuges. Copies can be ordered by sending $8, plus $1 for shipping, to the Nature Conservancy, South Fork–Shelter Island Chapter, P.O. Box 5125, East Hampton, NY 11937, or by stopping at one of the **Book Hampton** stores on the Main Streets of East Hampton, Southampton, and Sag Harbor.

The Nature Conservancy also puts out *Walks in Nature's Empire,* a comprehensive guide to all its preserves in New York State. The guide is published by the Countryman Press, costs $15, and can be obtained in bookstores or by calling 800/245-4151.

Maria. "It was [the Tuthills'] wish that they be buried with their former slaves" reads a plaque near the cemetery, which occupies a pretty spot overlooking the sea.

Orient Point and Beach

A few miles beyond Orient, at the very tip of the North Fork, is Orient Point, where ferries dock on their way to and from New London, Connecticut. Abutting the point is Orient Beach State Park, N. County Rd., off Rte. 25, 631/323-2440, one of the finest beaches on Long Island. Stretching west over a long finger of land, the 357-acre park features endless miles of white, ocean-washed sands. It's especially popular among birdwatchers and nature-lovers. Facilities include a bathhouse, refreshment stand, horseshoe court, and hiking trails. Lifeguards are on duty from late June to Labor Day.

The park is open daily sunrise to sunset. Parking in summer is $7.

From Orient Point and the park, you have a good view of **Gardiners Island.** Privately owned by the Gardiner family for over three centuries, the island was given to Lion Gardiner by King Charles I of England in 1639. Lion Gardiner was an engineer, diplomat, and statesman whose daughter, Elizabeth, was the first English child born in New York State. Gardiner was also in-

strumental in rescuing the daughter of Montauk chief Wyandanch after she'd been kidnapped by the warring Narragansett tribe.

Today Gardiners Island is the only known English land grant of its kind in the United States that remains in the hands of its original family. On its premises—which are strictly off-limits to the public—stand a manor house, windmill, and farm.

SHELTER ISLAND

In the middle of the bay between the North and South Forks is Shelter Island, a quiet retreat of wooded hills, uncrowded beaches, and expensive vacation homes, some of which date back to the Victorian era. Shelter Island has an exclusive air about it, due partly to its moneyed population, partly to the fact that it can be reached only by ferry. The high cost of the very short ferry rides—$7–8 one-way—also helps keep out the hoi polloi.

The island's first European resident was Nathaniel Sylvester, one of four businessmen who bought the island in 1651. Thanks to Sylvester, the island subsequently became a haven for Quakers fleeing persecution in Massachusetts. Sylvester gave the Quakers shelter and allowed them to practice their religion.

Sights

For the day visitor, Shelter Island has few especially compelling attractions, but it is the sort of place that's fun to explore without any particular destination in mind. Many of the roads wander past sun-splashed meadows and bays, dark woods and historic homes. Near the North Ferry dock is **Shelter Island Heights,** filled with steep streets and Victorian-era gingerbread cottages. Across the bay from the Heights is **Dering Harbor,** boasting a number of impressive mansions along the Shore Road. Dering Harbor is the smallest incorporated village in New York State, holding just 32 houses and 28 year-round residents (some homes are occupied only in the summer, when the population swells to 90).

History buffs might also want to stop at **Havens House,** 16 South Ferry Rd. (Rte. 114), 631/749-0025, a 1743 home on the National

Register of Historic Places. The five-room house, run by the Shelter Island Historical Society, is outfitted with period furnishings and features a nice collection of antique dolls and toys. Hours are June–Sept., Fri.–Sun. 11 A.M.–3 P.M. Admission is by donation.

Mashomack Preserve

Shelter Island does have one major treasure— Mashomack Preserve, operated by the Nature Conservancy. Occupying nearly a third of the island, the preserve spreads out over 2,000-plus acres of oak woodlands, marshes, freshwater ponds, tidal creeks, and shoreline. Within its confines is one of the East Coast's largest concentrations of nesting osprey, along with everything from ibis and hummingbirds to harbor seals and terrapins. Nature trails and hikes ranging 1.5 to 11 miles in length meander through the preserve.

The preserve, 79 S. Ferry Rd., 631/749-1001, is open Wed.–Mon., 9 A.M.–5 P.M. Suggested donation is adults $3, children $1.50 cents; maps and brochures are provided. The entrance to the preserve is located about a mile from the South Ferry dock.

Accommodations and Food

Built on bluffs overlooking Coecles Inlet on Shelter Island is the 1929 **Ram's Head Inn,** Ram Island Dr., 631/749-0811, www.shelter-islandinns.com, boasting its own private beach, small boats, tennis court, exercise room, and

restaurant. Out front is a wide porch complete with wicker furniture, and out back there's an inviting terrace that's used for dining in summer. Most of the 17 rooms are filled with lots of light and simple antiques. The cheaper rooms share bathrooms and a continental breakfast is included in the room rates ($135–315 d in summer; about a third less off-season). Lunch and dinner is served in an elegant, high-ceilinged room hung with oil paintings; average dinner entrée $18. On summer Sunday nights, small jazz groups perform.

In Shelter Island Heights is the friendly, turn-of-the-century **House on Chase Creek,** 3 Locust Ave., 631/749-4379, www.chasecreek.com. The B&B offers three comfortable guest rooms ($125–200 d summer; $95–105 d off-season).

Ferry Information

To reach Shelter Island from the North Fork, take the North Ferry, 631/749-0139, which leaves from Route 114 at the foot of 3rd Street in Greenport. From the South Fork, take the South Ferry, 631/749-1200, which leaves from Route 114 in North Haven, about three miles north of Sag Harbor. Both ferries operate every 10 or 15 minutes from about 6 A.M. to about midnight, and cost $7–8 one-way for a car and driver, plus $1 for each additional passenger. Considerably less expensive roundtrip tickets to and from Greenport or to and from North Haven are available ($8–10) but cannot be applied to a trip that combines the two ferry services.

The South Shore

Like the North Shore, the South Shore is unbearably congested near New York City. Unlike the North Shore, the South Shore has few isolated peninsulas or moneyed ex-estates to escape to. Much of the South Shore is composed of bumper-to-bumper working- and middle-class communities.

What the South Shore does have, however, just off its coast, is a long line of barrier islands lined with beaches, beaches, beaches. The South Shore is home to some of the longest, widest, whitest beaches in the world, stretching out for miles and miles against the pounding surf of the Atlantic. Nearest the city are Lido Beach, Long Beach, and the famed Jones Beach, followed by the beaches of Fire Island, and the beaches of the South Fork.

FREEPORT

Heading into Nassau County on the Sunrise Highway (Route 27), you'll soon come to Freeport, a bustling fishing and boating community that's the largest town on the South Shore. Freeport's most famous native son was Guy Lombardo, and a long avenue named in his honor runs through downtown.

Freeport's main visitor attraction is its recently revitalized "Nautical Mile," located along the **Woodcleft Canal,** bordered by a street of the same name. Much of Freeport was built on landfill, and Woodcleft is one of seven or eight canals in town. Along it, you'll find lots of new shops, many selling arts and crafts, and a plethora of seafood restaurants, as well as fishing boats sporting signs advertising "Halfday Flounder" and "Blues AM." On summer evenings, music beckons from outdoor bars while party boats set sail for dinner and moonlight cruises.

The Nautical Mile is also home to the **South Street Seaport Museum Long Island Marine Education Center,** 202 Woodcleft Ave., 516/771-0399. On display here is everything from ship models and fishing lures to a racing hy-droplane that once belonged to Guy Lombardo. The center is open year-round Tues.–Fri. 11 A.M.–4 P.M., Sat.–Sun 1–5 P.M. Admission is adults $2, children under 12 free.

For more information on Freeport, contact the **Freeport Chamber of Commerce,** 300 Woodcleft Ave., 516/223-8840, www.freeport-ny.com. For more information on sportfishing, call the **Freeport Boatmen's Association** at 516/378-4838.

Seal-Watching Cruises

In the fall, the **Riverhead Foundation for Marine Research,** 631/369-9840, www.riverhead-foundation.org, offers seal-watching cruises that leave from Point Lookout, south of Freeport near Jones and Lido Beaches. Rates are adults $20, children $15.

Accommodations and Food

Just north of Jones Beach is **Freeport Motor Inn and Boatel,** 445 S. Main St., 516/623-9100, a good, clean choice ($95–100 d). Incidentally, this is where much of the Amy Fisher–Joey Buttafuoco boondoggle took place.

According to many locals, one of the best seafood eateries in town is the casual, weatherbeaten **Ehrhart's Clam House,** 239 Woodcleft Canal, 516/623-3521, specializing in steamers and chowder. Average main dish $8.

One of the best restaurants along the Nautical Mile is **Hudson & McCoy,** 340 Woodcleft Ave., 516/868-3411, serving both seafood and steaks; average entrée $18. A family favorite, located at the very end of the canal, is **Schooner,** 436 Woodcleft Ave., 516/378-7575; average entrée $14.

In Baldwin, a few miles west of Freeport, is **Raay-Nor's Cabin,** 550 Sunrise Hwy., 516/223-4886, which has been serving up fried chicken, yams, and corn fritters since 1932. Housed in a block-long log cabin, Raay-Nor's is decked out with wooden tables, red booths, and chicken-shaped lamps; average entrée $13.

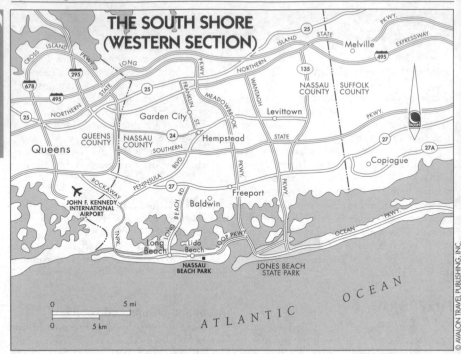

THE SOUTH SHORE (WESTERN SECTION)

© AVALON TRAVEL PUBLISHING, INC.

JONES BEACH AND VICINITY

The most famous beach in the New York City metropolitan region is Jones Beach, just 25 miles from midtown Manhattan. Though packed cheek-to-jowl on a hot summer's day, the beach is so magnificent—its white sands stretching out for well over five miles—that it still manages to impress. And talk about good peoplewatching. . . .

Jones Beach is also more than just a beach. Another one of Robert Moses' many creations, his goal here was to transform a sandbar off a windswept reef into the finest public beach in America. He largely succeeded, in an engineering feat that took two years to complete. Finished in 1929, the beach boasts an enormous number of well-worn but first-class facilities, including two lovely art deco bathhouses, wading and Olympic-size pools, ball fields, pitch-and-putt golf, shuffleboard courts, basketball courts, picnic areas, refreshment stands, an excellent restaurant, a wide weathered boardwalk, and a

200-foot-high water tower shaped like an obelisk. Also at the beach is the **Jones Beach Theater,** 516/221-1000, which presents big-name acts in summer.

Jones Beach, Ocean State Pkwy., south of Wantagh, 516/785-1600, is open year-round, sunrise–sunset, but lifeguards are on duty only Memorial Day–Labor Day. Parking is $7 in summer, but there's no fee to use the beach.

To reach Jones Beach, take the Wantagh State or Meadowbrook State Parkways south off the Sunrise Highway (Route 27), and watch for signs. Traffic can be horrendous in summer, so if you're coming from New York City, consider taking the Long Island Rail Road, 718/217-5477. The train travels to Freeport, where shuttlebuses operate to and from the beach.

West of Jones Beach are several smaller beaches—including Long Beach and Lido Beach—that are fun to explore. To reach these often less-crowded locales, take the Meadowbrook State Parkway to the Loop Parkway. In Lido

BAY HOUSES

If you pay close attention while driving along the Wantagh, Meadowbrook, or Loop Parkways linking Jones Beach and Point Lookout to the mainland, you'll spot a number of small cottages perched on platforms and surrounded by marshland and water. At one time, there were hundreds of such bay houses, as they are called, in the Town of Hempstead. Now there are only 32.

The building of the bay houses began back in the early 1700s when the island's farmers, needing hay for their cattle, hired their neighbors the baymen to row out to remote marshlands and bring back hay for their animals. The journey often took several hours each way, so it wasn't long before the baymen began building shacks in which to overnight. At first, these shacks were crude affairs. But as the years went by, the baymen developed them into cozy cabins that they could also use for recreation and for the planting and harvesting of oysters and clams.

In the early 1900s, recreational fishermen discovered the South Shore and the bay houses developed yet another purpose: bait stations. Then, a decade or two later, Prohibition arrived. Some baymen, writes folklorist Nancy Solomon in her book *On the Bay,* "played an indispensable role in rum running, smuggling, via their bay houses, illegal booze from large cargo ships off shore to hotels. . . ."

All this history was almost lost in 1993, when the baymen's lease on their bay houses—last renewed by the Town of Hempstead in 1965—ran out. The town government had voted to have the houses destroyed, but Solomon's book, together with the efforts of the South Shore Bayhouse Owners' Association, convinced the town board of the homes' historic value. Their leases have since been extended virtually indefinitely.

Although the bay houses can be seen from the parkways, the best way to view them is by boat. The charter fishing boats that run out of Freeport pass close by.

Approximately 50 other bay houses are located in Suffolk County opposite Captree State Park near Captree Island, Sexton Island, and Havermeyer Island.

Beach is the 74-site **Nassau Beach Park Campground,** Lido Blvd., 516/571-7724, open April–Oct.; basic nightly fees are $15–25 and reservations are highly recommended throughout summer.

CENTRAL NASSAU COUNTY

Heading into Long Island on Southern State Parkway, you'll pass one of the state's only African American museums and two historic residential communities. Neither of the latter are tourist attractions in the traditional sense, but both have played an interesting role in America's suburban development.

African American Museum

On a scruffy main drag in sprawling downtown Hempstead is the African American Museum, a small but very active institution where the exhibits change every 8–10 weeks. Most of the exhibits are arts or history oriented, and range in style from locally produced shows to traveling Smithsonian productions. Subjects covered in the past have included the role of African Americans in the Civil War, and contemporary black Long Island artists.

The museum, 110 N. Franklin St., 516/572-0730, is open Thurs.–Sat. 10 A.M.–4:45 P.M., Sunday 1–4:45 P.M., and Wednesday 6–9 P.M. Admission is free.

Garden City

Just north of Hempstead is Garden City, a ritzy residential enclave that was one of America's first planned communities. Filled with broad avenues, elegant homes, and a plethora of parks, Garden City was developed by Alexander Stewart, a Scottish immigrant who'd made a fortune by opening the world's first department store—Stewart's—in 1846 in New York City.

Stewart built his suburb for the elite, but instead of selling his homes, he rented them out at then-exorbitant rates of between $250 and $1,000 a year. The wealthy did not cotton to the idea of renting, nor to Stewart's rigorous screening process. By the 1890s, after two decades, only 30 of the city's 60 houses had been rented. Only after the houses were put up for sale did Garden City become a success.

Stewart died in 1876 and was originally buried in New York City, in the cemetery of St. Mark's-in-the-Bowery. In one of the odder incidents in New York City history, his corpse was stolen for ransom (see East Village in the New York City chapter). After his widow bought it back, she had it reburied beneath Garden City's imposing **Cathedral of the Incarnation,** which still stands on Cathedral Avenue at 6th Street. Stewart's new grave was equipped with a burglar alarm.

The poshest hotel in Long Island is the world-class **Garden City Hotel,** 45 7th St., 516/747-3000, featuring a gleaming, marble-filled lobby, luxurious rooms with all the amenities, a health spa, a piano lounge, several restaurants, and a shopping arcade ($250–350 d; packages available).

The exciting new **Cradle of Aviation Museum** is only one of several museums that will eventually be housed at **Mitchel Center** on the outskirts of Garden City. (See the special topic Garden City's Museum Row.)

Levittown

Another important landmark in American sub-urban history is Levittown, transformed from potato fields into 17,447 inexpensive ranch homes by developer William Levitt in 1949. The largest housing development ever created by a single builder, Levittown was the American Dream come true for the working class, as well as the butt of countless jokes about "ticky tacky houses" all looking just the same.

Levittown was originally built exclusively for GIs returning from WW II, but was later opened up to the general public. Each pre-assembled house was built in 27 steps in five days, and each had a living room, two bedrooms, a kitchen and bath, an attic, washing machine, barbecue grill, and television set. The cost to young families was $60 a month, no money down.

In the end, the individuality and imagination of Levittown's residents foiled many of the community's detractors. Drive down the streets here today and you'll be hard-pressed to find any house that closely resembles another. Some owners have added rooms and second floors, others have changed the facades or added driveways.

To reach Levittown from Hempstead, head east on Hempstead Turnpike (Route 24).

Cradle of Aviation Museum

COURTESY OF CRADLE OF AVIATION MUSEUM

GARDEN CITY'S MUSEUM ROW

After years of quiescence, Garden City is suddenly exploding onto the cultural scene with an ambitious new museum row, housed in the hangars of a former airfield called Mitchel Center. At the heart the new project is the enormous **Cradle of Aviation Museum,** 1 Davis Ave., off Charles Lindbergh Blvd., 516/572-0411, www.cradleofaviation.org, which opened in May 2001. In the atrium here, biplanes and fighter planes seem to soar up above, while all around are dozens of rare aircraft documenting the history of flight. Many major aviation events took place on Long Island, including Charles Lindbergh's 1927 nonstop transatlantic flight, which departed from nearby Roosevelt Field (now a shopping mall). Also in the museum are Long Island's first IMAX theater and the Red Planet Cafe, designed to look like a 21st century Mars space base.

The museum is open daily 9:30 A.M.–5 P.M. Museum admission is adults $6, children $5; IMAX tickets cost adults $8.50, children $6.

The long-established **Long Island Children's Museum,** 11 Davis Ave., off Charles Lindbergh Blvd., 516/222-0207, www.licm.org, has also recently relocated into Mitchel Center. Here, you'll find numerous hands-on exhibits for kids of all ages. Build a skyscraper, be a musician, or climb a two-story play tower. Open Wed.–Sun., 10 A.M.–5 P.M. Admission is $8 for adults and children over age one, $7 for seniors.

Other Mitchel Center projects scheduled to open in the next few years include a **Nassau County Firefighters Museum & Safety Center,** a science museum, and an events plaza centered on the complex's historic **Nunley's Carousel.**

Directions: To reach Mitchel Center from the Northern State Parkway, take Exit 31A south to the Meadowbrook Parkway. Get off at Exit M4 and go to Charles Lindbergh Boulevard. From the Southern State Parkway, take Exit 22 and go north on the Meadowbrook Parkway to Exit M4 and Charles Lindbergh Blvd.

FIRE ISLAND

Fire Island is a long skinny stick of land stretching 32 miles parallel to Long Island's south shore. It's a near-mythic place known for both its party atmosphere and its wilderness. Four distinct visitor areas and 17 resort communities make up the island, but it's all part of the National Seashore system. No cars are allowed on most of Fire Island, where park rangers administer a number of the magnificent white sand beaches.

One note of caution: Fire Island has abundant poison ivy and a large deer tick population. A tick bite can cause Lyme disease; small posters describing precautions and symptoms are posted all over the island. As long as you stick to the beaches and boardwalks, however, or wear long pants when exploring the grasses and woodlands, you shouldn't have a problem (see Health and Safety under Information and Services in the main Introduction).

Free and excellent maps of Fire Island are available at the various interpretive centers mentioned below, or from the **Fire Island National Seashore Headquarters,** 120 Laurel St., Patchogue, NY 11772, 631/289-4810, www.nps.gov/fiis. Other helpful websites are www.fireisland.com, www.fireislandbeaches.com, and www.barrierbeaches.com.

Robert Moses State Park

At Fire Island's westernmost end is the 1,000-acre Robert Moses State Park, off Robert Moses Causeway, 631/669-0449, one of only two sections of the island that you can drive to. A public beach since 1898, the popular park feels like a smaller, less crowded version of Jones Beach. Run by the National Seashore, it's equipped with bathhouses, shops, snack bars, and pitch-and-putt golf. Lifeguards are on duty Memorial Day–Labor Day; parking in summer is $7. The park is open daily sunrise–sunset.

At the western end of the park is the black-and-white-striped **Fire Island Lighthouse,** 631/661-4876, first built in 1827 to help put an end to the many shipwrecks that had occurred here. The current lighthouse dates back to 1858, and at its base is a visitor center with historical

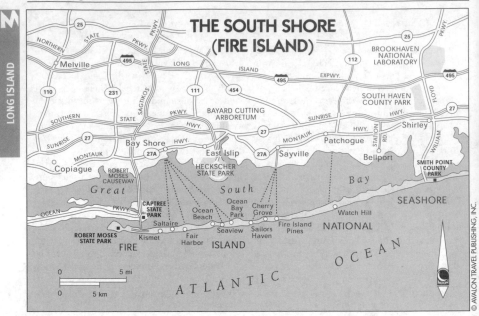

THE SOUTH SHORE
(FIRE ISLAND)

© AVALON TRAVEL PUBLISHING, INC.

exhibits. The center is open July–Labor Day, daily 9 A.M.–5 P.M.; call for hours in the spring and fall. Tower tours must be reserved in advance and cost adults $4, seniors and children 5–11 $4. Touring the lighthouse is not for everyone: it's a 0.7-mile walk across the dunes.

To reach the park, take the Robert Moses Causeway off the Sunrise Highway (Route 27) or the Southern State Parkway.

Sailors Haven

For the day visitor, one of the island's most interesting beaches is Sailors Haven, reached via ferry from Sayville. Sailors Haven is part wild beach and boardwalk, part dunes and grasses, and part **Sunken Forest**—a scrappy 300-year-old maritime forest located below sea level between two lines of sand dunes. A weathered gray boardwalk leads from the ferry dock through the 40-acre forest lush with oak, maple, red cedar, sour gum, and holly trees, as well as sassafras, bayberry, inkberry, catbrier, cinnamon fern, and cattail. Due to the island's strong winds and salty air, none of the trees can grow taller than the dunes, even though

beneath their roots fresh water extends as deep as 40 yards. This fresh water, essential to the forest's existence, occurs because the island's annual rainfall exceeds its annual evaporation.

Sailors Haven, run by the Fire Island National Seashore, is well equipped with attractive bathhouses, a snack bar, a gift shop, and an interpretive center. Lifeguards are on duty Memorial Day–Labor Day. Ferries operated by the Sayville Ferry Service, 631/589-8980, www.sayvilleferry.com, leave from River Road May–November. Roundtrip tickets cost adults $9, children $5,

Watch Hill

Another National Seashore visitor center, similar to but larger than the one at Sailors Haven, is located at Watch Hill, at the eastern end of Fire Island. Remote and lonely in feel, Watch Hill is filled with windswept dunes and a largely unpopulated beach, while adjacent to it is a seven-mile National Wilderness Area that visitors are welcome to explore. Fall and spring are especially good times to come, as Fire Island is on the Atlantic flyway, a major avian migratory route.

At the center of Watch Hill are bathhouses, snack bar, nature trail, and interpretive center, along with a yacht basin and grocery store. Also on site is the 25-site **Watch Hill Campground,** 631/597-6633, open May–October. Reservations are necessary and there's a maximum stay of four nights.

Ferries operated by the Davis Park Ferry Co., 631/475-1665, leave from West and Division Streets, Patchogue, May–November. Roundtrip tickets cost adults $12, children $7.

Smith Point County Park

East of Watch Hill and its adjacent National Wilderness Area is another beach park accessible by car. Like Robert Moses Park, Smith Point Park has plenty of bathhouses and concession stands, and attracts large crowds on summer weekends. A 146-site campground here is open year-round (reservations recommended in summer). Technically speaking, the park is not part of the National Seashore, but since it's located next to **Smith Point West,** which *is,* and both are lined with the same wide and wonderful beach, it all feels the same. Smith Point West also has a National Seashore visitor center and self-guiding nature trail.

Smith Point County Park, 631/852-1315, and Smith Point West, 631/281-3010, are at the southern end of the William Floyd Pkwy., off the Sunrise Highway (Route 27). Parking during the summer is $10. Basic nightly camping fees are $13–26.

William Floyd Estate

As you drive down William Floyd Parkway to and from Smith Point, you'll pass by signs for the William Floyd Estate. Floyd was one of the signers of the Declaration of Independence. After his death, his family's estate grew to include over 600 acres of forests and meadows, along with a grand 25-room mansion and 12 outbuildings. The estate remained in the Floyd family's hands until 1977, when Cornelia Floyd Nichols signed it over to the National Park Service one year before her death.

As incongruous as it sounds, the Floyd Estate, 245 Park Dr., 631/399-2030, is now part of the Fire Island National Seashore, and is open to the public. House tours are offered Memorial Day–Oct., Fri.–Sun. 11 A.M.–4:30 P.M. and the grounds are open Jan.–Oct., Sat.–Sun. 9 A.M.–dusk. Admission is free.

LONG ISLAND

© CHRISTIANE BIRD

the wide, wonderful beach at Smith Point County Park

Resort Communities

Fire Island wasn't declared a National Seashore until 1964, by which time 17 resort communities—some dating back to the turn of the century—had already been established. These communities were allowed to remain, as long as they didn't grow beyond their designated boundaries. Today they are popular vacation spots, especially among Manhattanites.

Each Fire Island community has its own distinct character. **Cherry Grove** and **Fire Island Pines** are the island's two gay retreats; **Kismet** and **Fair Harbor** attract a large singles crowd; **Saltaire** and **Seaview** cater primarily to well-heeled families.

Most of these communities are not designed for the casual visitor. Their vacationers tend to rent or share houses—usually for the entire summer—and often arrive via hired water taxi. Most of these communities also do not offer bathhouses or other public facilities.

Two communities that *do* welcome day-trippers and overnight visitors are **Ocean Beach** and **Ocean Bay Park.** Ocean Beach attracts many families, Ocean Bay Park many singles. Both are friendly, middle-class communities equipped with public facilities and serviced by Fire Island Ferries in Bay Shore, 631/665-3600. Roundtrip tickets cost adults $12, children $6.

Cherry Grove is another good spot for the casual visitor. Older, smaller, less expensive, and more exuberant than its sister community, the Pines, it centers around the **Cherry Grove Beach Hotel,** which always teems with a gay crowd—talking, drinking, and partying. Cherry Grove is serviced by the Sayville Ferry Co., 631/589-8980, which leaves from River Rd., Sayville, May–November. Roundtrip tickets cost adults $11, children $6.

Accommodations

One of the few hotels on Fire Island is the simple but comfortable **Fire Island Hotel and Resort,** 25 Cayuga Park, Ocean Bay Park, 631/583-8000, housed in converted U.S. Coast Guard buildings. The hotel caters primarily to families, but rooms go very fast—reserve well in advance. Rates in summer range from $134 d midweek to $1,100 d for a three-night weekend stay; rates drop 25–50 percent in June and September. Another good choice is the comfortable, air-conditioned, 1940s-era **Cleggs Hotel,** 478 Bayberry Walk, Ocean Beach, 631/583-5399 ($110 d midweek, $320 d for the weekend).

The **Grove Hotel,** Ocean Walk, Cherry Grove, 631/597-6600, www.grovehotel.com, caters to the gay community. Summer rates for a clean, basic room here are $70–160 d midweek and $470–790 d for a two-night weekend stay; rates drop significantly in May, June, and September; closed Oct.–April.

For a more comprehensive list of hotels on Fire Island, go to the website: www.fireislandcc.org.

BAY SHORE AND VICINITY

Several of the Fire Island ferries leave from the town of Bay Shore. Once a popular resort community—and still surrounded by a number of large and very wealthy estates—Bay Shore has more recently been stricken with urban blight, and feels tired and run-down.

The ferry docks at the foot of Maple Avenue, and on summer days, beachgoers stream down the thoroughfare, armed with coolers, beach chairs, and umbrellas. Few stop at the **Gibson/Mack/Holt House,** 22 Maple Ave., no phone, but the very attractive historical home is well worth a look. Several rooms have been restored to their original 1820 condition, while others house memorabilia from the town's turn-of-the-century heyday. The house is run by the Bay Shore Historical Society and was restored almost entirely by volunteers. Summer hours are Sat.–Sun. 2–4 P.M. Admission is by donation.

Day Cruises

Hour-and-a-half sightseeing cruises around Great South Bay offered by **South Bay Cruises,** 631/321-9005, July 4–Labor Day. The cruises leave from the Bayshore Marina at the foot of Clinton Avenue, and cost adults $10, seniors and children $8. Lunch and dinner cruises are offered aboard the *Lauren Kristy* **Paddlewheeler,** at rates starting at $35 (for lunch) and $45 (dinner).

Heckscher State Park

East of Bay Shore is 1,500-acre Heckscher State Park, the protected bay waters of which make it an especially good place for families. Facilities include three beaches, a pool, bathhouses, boat ramps, refreshment stands, nature trails, and a 69-site campground open May–September. Reservations at the campground are highly recommended in summer; call 800/456-CAMP; basic campsite rates are $15.

The park is off Heckscher State Parkway in East Islip, 631/581-2100. It's open sunrise–sunset, and parking in summer is $7.

Long Island Greenbelt Trail

Also in Heckscher State Park is the trailhead of the Long Island Greenbelt Trail, which runs the 34-mile width of Long Island to Sunken Meadow State Park on the North Shore. The trail follows the Connetquot and Nissequogue River valleys through wetlands, pine barrens, and forest, past virtually every form of wildlife indigenous to the island. For more information on the trail or guided hikes, contact Long Island Greenbelt Trail Conference, Inc., P.O. Box 5636, Hauppauge, NY 11788; 631/360-0753, www.hike-li.com. Or, stop into the Conference's office at the northern end of Blydenburgh County Park, Veterans Highway, Smithtown.

Bayard Cutting Arboretum

One of the greatest estates along the South Shore is the Bayard Cutting Arboretum, once owned by railroad magnate William Bayard Cutting. The 690-acre estate was designed by Frederick Law Olmsted, the famed landscape architect who also designed New York City's Central Park.

The arboretum centers around a dark baronial Tudor mansion. Inside are a few natural history exhibits and a snack bar, but the place feels oddly empty. Perhaps that's because compared to the estate's glorious grounds, the mansion seems almost an afterthought.

Just outside the mansion is an enormous and verdant lawn, stretching 600 feet down to the Connetquot River. On either side are huge old black oak trees, spreading out their leafy boughs, while all around are various gardens—the azalea

garden, the rhododendron garden, the lilac garden, the holly garden.

Parts of the arboretum are much less lush than others, due to the devastation wrought by Hurricane Gloria in 1985. An estimated 1,000 trees were lost during that storm, including about 20 of Long Island's oldest trees and 80 of the 120 major species originally planted by Mr. Cutting in the "Pinetum." Younger trees have since been planted in their stead, but it'll be many years before they reach their predecessors' 70–90-foot heights.

The arboretum, 466 Montauk Hwy. in Oakdale, 631/581-1002, is open Tues.–Sun. 10 A.M.–sunset. Parking in summer is $7.

Long Island Maritime Museum

The laid-back Long Island Maritime Museum occupies an idyllic spot overlooking Great South Bay. Housed in shipshape buildings, the museum boasts the largest collection of small craft in Long Island. On display are everything from oyster vessels and sailboats to ice scooters and clam boats.

Also at the museum are a historic oyster house and an 1890s' bayman's cottage, both of which were moved here from elsewhere on the island. The oyster house holds an extensive exhibit on the harvesting of shellfish, while next door is a working boat shop where volunteers build new boats and restore old ones.

The Maritime Museum, 86 West Ave., off Montauk Hwy. in West Sayville, 631/854-4974, is open Mon.–Sat. 10 A.M.–4 P.M., Sunday noon–4 P.M. Admission is adults $4, seniors and children $2.

Food

The **Bay Shack,** at the end of Maple Ave. in Bay Shore (no phone), serves great clam chowder, lobster rolls, and other seafood to ferry passengers. Opposite the train station is the tiny **Siam Lotus,** 1664 Union Blvd., 631/968-8196, serving first-rate Thai food in a cramped but friendly setting; average entrée $11.

EAST TO HAMPTON BAYS

Turning south off Sunrise Highway onto Montauk Highway around Sayville or Patchogue will save you time and take you past a number of

LONG ISLAND

LONG ISLAND

SUBURBAN NIGHTMARES

Serial killers. Kidnappers. Wife slayers. Jealous lovers. In the late 1980s and 1990s, once-somnolent Long Island was the setting for one bizarre and tragic crime after another. You couldn't make this stuff up if you tried.

Garden City: On December 7, 1993, Colin Ferguson opens fire on the Long Island Rail Road, killing six commuters and wounding 19 others. Remorseless, he attributes his crime to "black rage," and serves as his own ranting lawyer, even demanding that Pres. Bill Clinton and then-New York governor Mario Cuomo take the stand.

East Meadow: On June 28, 1993, Joel Rifkin confesses to the serial killing of 17 women, most of them young prostitutes. No one had previously suspected the 34-year-old landscaper of any wrongdoing; he'd lived quietly in a middle-class suburb with his mother and sister. A bumper sticker on his car read "Sticks and stones may break my bones but whips and chains excite me."

Bay Shore: On January 13, 1993, contractor John Esposito is arrested for kidnapping 10-year-old Katie Beers. A friend of Beers's family, Esposito had chained Katie around the neck and imprisoned her for 16 days in a six-by-seven-foot dungeon that he'd secretly built beneath his garage.

Katie was then sent to live with a foster family and is said to be doing well.

Massapequa: On May 19, 1992, jealous 17-year-old Amy Fisher shoots and badly wounds Mary Jo Buttafuoco in front of her home. Fisher is having an affair with Mary Jo's husband, autobody shop owner and former weightlifting champ Joey Buttafuoco. Fisher is sentenced to 5-to-15. One year later, Joey—wearing his trademark snakeskin boots—pleads guilty to having sex with Amy when she was underage; Mary Jo stands by her man. Fisher is released in May 1999 and is now working as a journalist.

Bayport: On December 17, 1990, prominent physician Robert Reza flies home from a medical convention in Washington, D.C., shoots and kills his wife Marilyn, and then flies back to the conference to establish an alibi. Reza is having an affair with the organist at his church—the same organist who later plays Marilyn's three favorite hymns at her memorial service.

And as if that weren't enough—**Lindenhurst:** On November 13, 1987, nurse Richard Angelo is arrested for having injected four patients with lethal doses of muscle relaxant; the "Angel of Death" had hoped to revive his patients and be hailed as a hero.

pretty villages, including Bellport, the Moriches, Westhampton, Quogue, East Quogue, and Hampton Bays.

Kid Stuff

Just north of Moriches in Manorville are two popular kids' attractions. The largest is **Long Island Game Farm,** where children can feed baby lambs and pigs, pet barnyard animals and deer, and watch tiger and elephant shows. Also at the park are bears, zebras, buffalo, camels, and monkeys; an antique carousel; an 1860s' train, and amusement rides. The park, on Chapman Blvd., about 1.5 miles north of County Road 111, 631/878-6644, www.ligfwildlife.com, is open Memorial Day–Columbus Day, daily 10 A.M.–5 P.M. Admission is adults $14, children 2–11 and seniors $12. To reach the park from Montauk Highway, take Chapman Boulevard north about five miles.

Similar to the game farm, but smaller and best for very small children, is **Animal Farm Petting Zoo,** where kids can feed and pet rabbits, cows, sheep, and goats, and watch burros, monkeys, kangaroos, and deer. The zoo, 184A Wading River Rd., 631/878-1785, is open April–Oct., daily 10 A.M.–5 P.M. Admission is adults $12, seniors and children 2–16 $10, children under two free. To reach the zoo from Montauk Highway, take Wading River Road north three miles.

Quogue

One of the prettiest villages along Montauk Highway is Quogue, a tiny place filled with big old shingled homes and wide empty streets. On its outskirts is the **Old School House Museum,** Quogue St. E, 631/653-4111, a local history museum housed in a pristine 1822 schoolhouse;

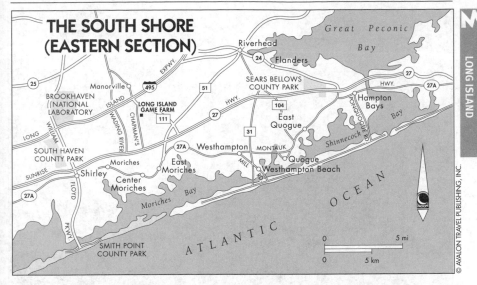

THE SOUTH SHORE
(EASTERN SECTION)

hours are July–Aug., Wednesday and Friday 3–5 P.M., and Saturday 10 A.M.–noon.

Not far away is the 200-acre **Quogue Wildlife Refuge,** Old Main and Old Country Rds., 631/653-4771, filled with ponds, swamps, freshwater bogs, pine barrens, and nature trails. Also on site is a Distressed Wildlife Complex where injured birds and other animals are rehabilitated. Trails are open daily sunrise–sunset. The visitor center is open Tues.–Thurs. 1–4 P.M., Sat.–Sun. 11 A.M.–4 P.M. Admission is free.

In the center of town is the **Inn at Quogue,** 52 Quogue St., 631/653-6560, www.innat quogue.com, housed in both a 200-year-old inn and several modern buildings. The inn's 70 rooms, many of which were renovated by a consultant for Ralph Lauren, vary considerably in style (from historic to upscale motel) and in price ($175–395 d).

Also at the inn is the **Inn at Quogue Restaurant,** 52 Quogue St., 631/653-6800, serving a New World cuisine; average entrée $26, with a less expensive menu available at the bar.

The Big Duck

Before heading onto the South Fork, lovers of roadside architecture *must* take a detour north for a look at the Big Duck. Sitting all by itself by the side of the road, the pure white bird—with its orange bill and bright red eyes made from Model-T taillights—looks like a simple child's drawing come to life. The only giveaway that something else is afoot is the dark outline of a door just beneath the duck's throat.

The 20-foot-high Big Duck was built in 1931 by an ambitious duck-raising farmer who hoped to attract more customers. Ducks were big business on Long Island at that time; in 1939 there were 90 duck farms in Quogue alone. Most raised White Pekin (Peking) ducks—prized for their tender meat—which had first been imported from China to Long Island in the 1870s.

Today the Big Duck is a shop run by Friends for Long Island's Heritage, a nonprofit group working to preserve Long Island's past. On sale are lots of duck collectibles—duck books, duck T-shirts, duck coffee mugs, and the like—along with postcards and books on roadside architecture.

The Big Duck, 631/852-8292 or 631/854-4970, is on Rte. 24 in Flanders, at the entrance to Sears Bellows County Park. It's open May 1–Labor Day, daily 10 A.M.–5 P.M.; Labor Day–Dec., Fri.–Sun. 10 A.M.–5 P.M.; closed Jan.–April.

© CHRISTIANE BIRD

Built in 1931, the Big Duck today houses a nonprofit shop whose proceeds support preservation of Long Island history.

Hampton Bays

Bowen's by the Bays, 177 W. Montauk Hwy., 631/728-1158, offers both standard motel rooms and cottages with one- or two-bedrooms. On the grounds are a pool, lighted tennis courts, and playground ($119–179 d in summer; about 20 percent less off-season).

The 70-site **Sears Bellows County Park,** 63 Bellows Pond Rd., 631/852-8290, is open May–September. Basic nightly fees are $13–23, and reservations are recommended on summer weekends.

For good, basic seafood in a lively setting overlooking the water, try **Oakland's Restaurant & Marina,** Dune Rd., on Shinnecock Inlet, 631/728-6900; average entrée $17. Casual **JT's Place,** 26 Montauk Hwy., Hampton Bays, 631/723-2626 serves everything from seafood to baby back ribs; average entrée $15.

The South Fork

The South Fork is New York City's playground. The rich and the influential, the middle-class and the obscure—all flock here during the summer to rent weathered cottages, poke around in picture-perfect towns, indulge in fast-paced nightlife, and, most of all, explore the beaches. Like the South Shore, the South Fork is home to some of the world's most magnificent beaches, and they're considerably less crowded here than they are near the city.

But the South Fork also has a culture all its own that has nothing to do with tourists. Farmers and, to a lesser extent, fishermen continue to practice their livelihoods here just as they have for hundreds of years. Humble potato fields butt up against million-dollar second homes, fishing boats share harbors with pleasure craft.

The South Fork is also often referred to as the Hamptons. Several of the Hamptons (Westhampton Beach, Quogue, Hampton Bays) are actually west of the South Fork, but when people speak of the "Hamptons," they're generally referring to those towns east of Shinnecock Canal.

History

The South Fork was first inhabited by the Algonquins and first settled by the English, who arrived in Southampton from Lynn, Massachusetts, in 1640—the same year the settlers from New Haven arrived in Southold on the North Fork. Much of their reason for coming was the fact that the Indians made wampum on the island. Wampum could be exchanged for valuable beaver and other furs, and the English wanted to get access to the beads—made from clams and other shells—before the Dutch.

As elsewhere on Long Island, the Algonquins welcomed the English. In a matter of decades, English villages were flourishing. Most featured New England–style village greens surrounded by white-steepled churches and Colonial saltboxes. Many of these early buildings still exist today.

Tourists started arriving on the South Fork in the 1800s. Residents opened their homes to the visitors and by the 1850s, the local press was reporting that all rooms in East Hampton were fully booked, at $7 a night. Shortly thereafter, Southampton started building hotels to accommodate its guests. In 1895, the railroad arrived, marking the beginning of the end of sleepy village life.

Recreation and Entertainment

Since much of the terrain on the South Fork is relatively flat, **bicycling** is a popular activity, and bike rental companies are located in most of the villages. **Sailboats, windsurfing boards,** and **canoes** for exploring the area's ponds can also be rented. Inquire at the local chambers of commerce.

The South Fork is noted for its nightlife, which runs the gamut from casual bars to discos. In general, things get going as late out here as they do in major urban centers—say 11 P.M.—and don't shut down until 2 A.M. or even 4 A.M. on weekends.

Lodging Information

As in many other resort areas, peak-season accommodations in the Hamptons don't come cheap. Peak season rates usually apply from mid-June through Labor Day, but this varies from property to property. Minimum two- or three-night stays are often required, especially on weekends and holidays. During the off-season, rates drop dramatically.

Along the beach near Montauk, you'll find many simple family-style resort motels, moderately priced. Rates listed below are for double rooms, but most places also offer family packages. Meanwhile, historic inns and B&Bs are plentiful throughout the region, with East Hampton laying claim to an especially large number. Most of

> *The South Fork is New York City's playground, but it also has a culture all its own that has nothing to do with tourists. Farmers and fishermen continue to practice their livelihoods here just as they have for hundreds of years.*

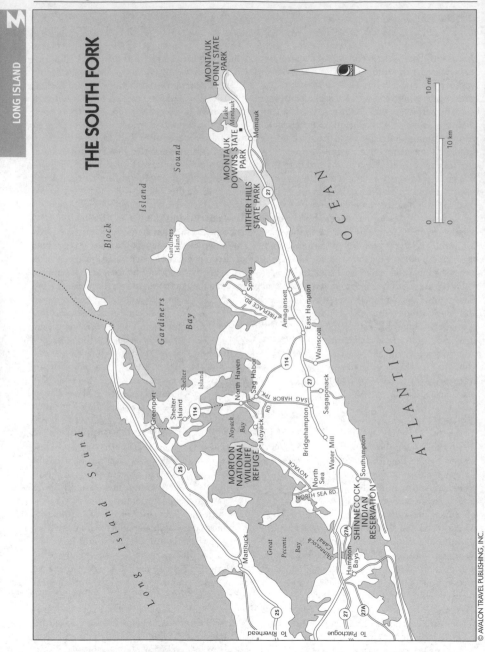

THE SOUTH FORK

the resort motels are closed in winter; most of the inns and B&Bs are open year-round.

Getting There

From Manhattan, the quickest way to drive to the South Fork is to take the Long Island Expressway (LIE), or I-495, to Route 111 to Route 27 (the Sunrise Highway, which later becomes the Montauk Highway). Traffic is often bumper-to-bumper on a summer Friday afternoon or Saturday morning, so avoid going out on the weekend, if possible. The drive from Manhattan to East Hampton can take anywhere from two and a half to four hours, depending on traffic.

Once you get onto the South Fork, the two-lane Montauk Highway is the only road that runs all the way from Southampton to Montauk. It, too, often gets unbearably congested, but there is no alternative route.

The South Fork can also be reached via public transportation. The **Long Island Rail Road,** 718/217-5477 (New York), 516/822-5477 (Nassau County), or 631/231-5477 (Suffolk County), operates between Manhattan and Montauk, running numerous trains on summer weekends. A popular bus company servicing the Hamptons is **Hampton Jitney,** 631/283-4600 or 800/936-0440 (New York metro area) or 800/327-0732 (outside New York metro area). Taxi service is available in most of the villages.

Beach Parking

Although all South Fork beaches are open to the public, parking can be a major problem. Many village and town beaches require parking permits, which usually cost nonresidents around $100 (good for the entire summer). However, a number of excellent public beaches have daily parking fees; the best of these are Atlantic Beach in Amagansett, the Main Beach in East Hampton, and the beach at Hither Hills State Park in Montauk. Many hotels and motels also offer low-cost day-parking passes to their guests; be sure to inquire when you book.

Parking illegally is not a good idea; rules are strictly enforced, and you will be ticketed with a heavy fine or towed away. Most parking rules apply during the summer only. The rest of the year, you can park most anywhere you like.

SOUTHAMPTON

The oldest of the Hamptons villages is Southampton, a pristine and deceptively simple-looking town attracting a high quotient of socialites and the nouveaux riches. The downtown is just a few blocks long, but it's lined with leafy trees, posh boutiques, and expensive cars—Jaguars are especially well represented. All around town are winding wooded lanes dotted with splashy second homes, most of which are protected from prying eyes by tall privet hedges.

Settled in 1640, Southampton was first called Conscience Point, but its name was later changed to honor the Earl of Southampton. North of the village at the end of North Sea Road is a huge boulder with a brass plaque marking the spot where the English first landed.

The town centers around the intersection of Main Street and Job's Lane. Walking maps and brochures can be picked up at the **Southampton Chamber of Commerce,** 76 Main St., 631/283-0402, www.southamptonchamber.com. Hours are Mon.–Fri. 10 A.M.–4 P.M. year-round, and also summer weekends 11 A.M.–3 P.M. More information on the South Fork can also be obtained by visiting these websites: www.hamptontravelguide.com and www.thehamptons.com.

Old Halsey House

The oldest building in Southampton is also the oldest wooden frame house in the state. It's the 1648 Old Halsey House, a tiny gray cottage sitting primly on South Main Street, oblivious to the modern world. Built by one of the town's original settlers, the homestead is still in excellent condition and is furnished with a nice collection of 17th- and 18th-century antiques. Behind the homestead is a small herb garden and a pretty apple orchard. The Halsey House, S. Main St., a half mile from the Job's Ln. and Main St. intersection, 631/283-2494, is open July–Columbus Day, Fri.–Sat. 11 A.M.–4 P.M., Sunday 1–5 P.M. Admission is adults $3, seniors $2, and children $1.

Southampton Historical Museum

Also downtown is the Southampton Historical Museum, 17 Meeting House Ln. (an extension of Job's Ln.), 631/283-2494 or 631/283-1612 (off-season), which centers around a snug Greek Revival home built by a whaling captain in 1843. Inside the home are period furnishings and clothing, along with a Shinnecock Indian exhibit and Revolutionary War artifacts. Out back is a compact collection of historical buildings, including a one-room schoolhouse, carriage shed, blacksmith's shop, carpenter's shop, drug store, cobbler and harness shop, and barn filled with whaling equipment. The museum is open June–Sept., Tues.–Sat. 11 A.M.–5 P.M., Sunday 1–5 P.M. Admission is adults $3, seniors $2, and children $1.

Parrish Art Museum

Founded in 1898 by a wealthy summer resident, the Parrish Art Museum, 25 Job's Lane, 631/283-2118, houses a notable collection of 19th- and 20th-century American art. William Merritt Chase and Fairfield Porter, both of whom spent much time in the area, are especially well represented. Out back you'll find an arboretum and a sculpture garden shaded by rare trees. In summer, the museum presents many lectures, concerts, films, and other special events, some of which take place in the garden. The museum is open Mon.–Sat. 11 A.M.–5 P.M., Sunday 1–5 P.M.; closed Tues.–Wed. in the off-season. Admission is adults $5, seniors and students $3, children under 12 free.

Beaches

Southampton's main public beach is **Cooper Neck Beach,** at the end of Cooper Neck Lane, where parking fees hover around an unfriendly $20. No parking permit is required at the often uncrowded **Old Town Beach,** at the end of Old Town Road. There are only about 30 parking spaces, however, and no facilities.

Shinnecock Reservation

Just west of town, the Shinnecock Reservation is home to about 400 Native Americans and the new **Shinnecock Nation Cultural Center and Museum,** Montauk Hwy. at West Gate Rd.,

631/287-4923. Only opened in 2001, after a decade of fund-raising, the museum showcases historic birchbark canoes and farm implements, jewelry, beadwork, basketry, weavings, murals, and totems by contemporary Shinnecock artist David Bunn Martine. An interesting video and historical photos are also featured. Hours are Saturday 11 A.M.–4 P.M., and Sunday in summer, or by appointment. Admission is adults $5, seniors and children $3.

Visitors are also welcome to attend the annual three-day **Shinnecock Pow Wow,** held on Labor Day weekend. This major event attracts Native Americans and other visitors from all over the country. Traditional dances, foods, and arts and crafts are featured.

Accommodations

The pleasant 90-room **Southampton Inn,** 91 Hill St., at First Neck Ln., 631/283-6500, offers a pool, tennis courts, a bustling bar, and live entertainment with dancing on summer weekends ($195–235 d). The considerably smaller, 30-room **Bayberry Inn of the Hamptons,** 281 County Rd. 39A, 631/283-4220, also has a pool and accepts pets ($195–225 d).

For a more historic stay, check out the 70-room **Village Latch Inn,** 101 Hill St., 631/283-2160, which was once an annex to the then-famous Irving Hotel (since burned down) across the street. Tall hedges frame the mansion's green-shuttered front, while outside are a swimming pool and tennis courts. Many of the rooms have refrigerators and some have private patios (summer weekend rates start at $295 d, with a three-night minimum, weekdays at $175 d).

Food

The **Golden Pear,** 99 Main St., 631/283-8900, a gourmet cafe, offers homemade baked goods, sandwiches, and pasta. It's an especially good place for brunch or lunch, but also serves dinner; average main dish $9. Fresh storefront tapas are for sale at **La Tasca Espanola,** 48 Jagger Lane, 631/287-6814; average tapa $7. For takeout, try the **Village Gourmet & Cheese Shop,** 11 Main St., 631/283-6949, which sells a nice selection of sandwiches and salads.

More serious meals can be had at **Le Chef,** 75 Job's Ln., 631/283-8581, a winsome French restaurant with surprisingly reasonable prices. The prix fixe $21.75 dinner menu includes about a dozen appetizers (crab cakes, lobster bisque) and a dozen entrées (grilled tuna, veal chops), and is offered every night of the week.

Basilico, 10 Windmill Ln., 631/283-7987, has long been a popular hot spot, serving Northern Italian fare in an airy, high-ceilinged setting. The menu ranges from sophisticated pastas and pizzas to a wide variety of fresh fish; average entrée $24. The trendy but casual **75 Main,** 75 Main St., 631/283-7575, features a large spiffy bar area up front and a restaurant in back. On the menu is innovative international fare; average entrée $18. Refined, imaginative Thai cuisine is the specialty of the blond-wood-and-wicker **QA Thai Bistro,** 129 Noyac Rd., 631/204-0007, where dishes range from green-curry salmon to drunken noodles with basil and red pepper; average entrée $20.

Nightlife

Still going strong after many years is **Conscience Point,** 1976 N. Sea Rd., 631/204-0600, a snazzy dance club that keeps reinventing itself. With an outdoor terrace and newly redecorated dance floor, it draws a high quotient of models and celebrities.

The party happy **Life at Tavern,** 125 Tuckahoe Lane, 631/287-2125, offers DJs spinning mostly house music and hip hop. Rollicking **Buckley's Irish Pub,** 76 Job's Ln., 631/283-4316, hosts a DJ on Saturdays, live Irish music on Sundays.

WATER MILL AND BRIDGEHAMPTON

A few miles east of Southampton is the small village of Water Mill, named for the big gristmill near the town center. The village's first gristmill was built in 1644; this one dates to 1800 and now operates as the **Water Mill Museum.** Open to the public in summer, the mill still grinds corn and wheat with its all-wooden gears, shafts, and wheel. The ground meal and flour are for sale. Also at the museum are various arts-oriented exhibits and events.

The museum, Old Mill Rd., off Rte. 27, 631/726-4625, is open Memorial Day–Sept., Thurs.–Mon. 11 A.M.–5 P.M. Admission is adults $3, seniors $2.50, children free.

A few miles east of Water Mill is Bridgehampton, named for a small bridge that was built over Sagg Pond in 1686. During the 1800s, Bridgehampton was known for helping distressed ships at sea. The first headquarters of the Life Saving Service of Long Island was founded here in 1878; it merged with the Coast Guard in 1915.

Today, Bridgehampton is another picture-perfect town. Big red-brick buildings line its Main Street, along with a number of antique shops. Among the latter is **Ruby Beets Antiques,** Poxybogue Rd. at Montauk Hwy., 631/537-2802, an 1850s' farmhouse packed with everything from painted furniture to vintage fabrics.

Food

Sit indoors or outdoors at trendy **Bobby Van's,** 2393 Main St., 631/537-0590, a place to see and be seen—once frequented by the literati, now by celebs. On the menu is classic steakhouse fare; average entrée $25–30.

EAST HAMPTON

At the center of the South Fork and the Hamptons lies East Hampton, an Old Money stronghold now better known for its hordes of famed artists and writers, actors and directors, publishers and media moguls, and more ordinary folk. East Hampton has been a center for successful "creative types" since the 1870s, when artists William Merritt Chase, Childe Hassam, and others summered here.

In the late 1970s, the now-defunct *Saturday Evening Post* ran a contest asking readers to vote for the most beautiful town in America. East Hampton won, and it's not hard to see why. Even more than Southampton, East Hampton is an idyllic New England village that seems to have stepped out of time. Everywhere are perfect Colonial homes, emerald-green lawns, and white picket fences. Nothing seems quite real, but who cares? What could possibly go wrong in a world such as this.

Hook Windmill stands at the eastern end of East Hampton's Main Street.

A pond, a village green, and the **Old Burying Ground** split Main Street at the western end, while at the eastern end, in isolated splendor on a plush lawn, stands the weathered **Hook Windmill.** Between these two landmarks lie most of the town's shops, restaurants, and historic sites, all of which can be explored on foot. To catch a glimpse of the area's many posh summer homes, take a drive along Ocean Avenue or Lily Pond Lane.

Like elsewhere in the Hamptons, traffic in East Hampton is horrific at the height of the summer. Park as soon as you can; lots with limited two-hour parking are located just off Main Street, while long-term lots are located off Lumber and Gingerbread Lanes.

The **East Hampton Chamber of Commerce,** 4 Main St., 631/324-0362, www .easthamptonchamber.com, is well stocked with brochures and maps. Hours in season are Mon.–Sat. 10 A.M.–4 P.M.; call for hours off-season. The **East Hampton Historical Society,** 101 Main St., 631/324-6850, www .easthamptonhistory.org, sponsors downtown and cemetery **walking tours** in the summer and fall. Many are led by guides dressed in Colonial garb.

Historic James Lane

At the western end of the village are the Town Pond—once a watering hole for East Hampton's cattle—and the snug **Home Sweet Home,** a nicely restored 1650 saltbox that was the boyhood home of John Howard Payne, composer of the song "Home Sweet Home." Inside the house is a good collection of English ceramics and early American furniture, while out back are a windmill and garden.

The Payne home, 14 James Ln., 631/324-0713, is open May–Sept., Mon.–Sat. 10 A.M.–4 P.M., Sunday 2–4 P.M.; call for off-season hours. Admission is adults $4, children $2.

Next door to Payne's old residence is a complex of restored weathered buildings known as the **Mulford Farm.** Owned by the same family from 1712 to 1944, the four-acre homestead—still in its original site—includes a farmhouse, barn, garden, and several outbuildings. In summer, costumed guides lead narrated tours through the farm.

Among the many Mulfords who once lived on the homestead was a stubborn Colonial whaler named Samuel. Samuel didn't like anyone telling him what to do, so when a New York governor levied a tax on the whale trade, Samuel headed to London to complain to the king. No one would let him into the palace, but one day, after his pocket was picked while he was waiting outside, Samuel had a brainstorm. Returning to his inn, he sewed several fishhooks into his pockets and went back to the palace. Soon he heard a curse from a would-be thief and called over a guard, who marched the pickpocket off to jail. The event was written up in the papers, Mulford got his audience with the king, and the whale tax was lifted.

The farm, 10 James Ln., 631/324-6850, is open July 4–Labor Day, Thurs.–Mon. 11 A.M.–4 P.M.; Labor Day–Columbus Day, Sat.–Sun. 11 A.M.–4 P.M. Admission is adults $4, seniors and children $2.

Historic Main Street

Just east of James Lane stands **Clinton Academy,** 151 Main St., 631/324-1850, a large wood-and-brick building dating back to the late 1700s.

The first prep school in the state and one of the first coed schools in the country, the academy sent many of its students on to Harvard, Princeton, and Yale. Today it's a historical museum filled with furniture, clothing, photographs, and the like. Out back is a wildflower garden.

Next to the Clinton Academy is the **Town House,** an elfin, one-room schoolhouse containing a potbellied stove, old school desks, books, slates, and quill pens. The building also once served as the town hall. Both the Clinton Academy and the Town House are open July 4–Labor Day, Sat.–Sun. 1–5 P.M. Admission is adults $5, seniors and children $2.

At the other end of Main Street reigns the 1806 **Hook Windmill,** the best surviving example of the many windmills that once dotted the South Fork (11 still stand but most are not open to the public). It was built by Nathaniel Dominy V, an innovative designer who included several then-unheard-of labor-saving devices—including a grain elevator—in his remarkably efficient mill.

The windmill is open July–Aug., Fri.–Sun. 2–4 P.M., and is run by volunteer guides, one of whom is the great-great-great-grandson of Nathaniel Dominy V and now a grandfather himself. For more information, call Home Sweet Home at 631/324-0713.

Guild Hall

Across the street from Clinton Academy is Guild Hall, 158 Main St., 631/324-0806, www.guildhall.org, one of the premier art institutions on Long Island. Inside its three large galleries are temporary exhibits featuring top contemporary artists such as Jackson Pollock, Willem de Kooning, and Larry Rivers. Also part of Guild Hall is **John Drew Theatre,** which presents dance, theater, and music events, along with literary readings by some of the famed authors who summer in the Hamptons. Every August, the **Clothesline Art Sale** features work by both established and emerging artists. Guild Hall is open mid-June–Labor Day, Mon.–Sat. 11 A.M.–5 P.M., Sunday noon–5 P.M.; Labor Day–mid-June, Wed.–Sat. 11 A.M.–5 P.M., Sunday noon–5 P.M. Suggested admission is adults $5, seniors $4, students $3.50.

Shopping

Most of East Hampton's upscale shops are along Main Street or Newtown Lane. Some are branches of Manhattan stores, others independent boutiques.

A number of commercial art galleries are also located along Main Street and Newtown Lane. Among them is **Giraffics,** 79A Newtown Ln., 631/329-0803, which specializes in graphics and prints.

Quite different in feel from the upscale shops is the oddly old-fashioned **Ladies Village Improvement Society,** 95 Main St., 631/324-1220, which runs a year-round secondhand shop in an aging mansion. The society was founded in 1895 in order to beautify the town's parks and gardens; the shop—featuring books, clothes, dishware, and antiques—helps pay for their work. It's open April–Dec., Tues.–Sat. 10 A.M.–5 P.M.; Jan.–March, Fri.–Sat. 10 A.M.–5 P.M.

Beaches

In summer, the gorgeous **Main Beach** at the end of Ocean Avenue comes equipped with bathhouses, lifeguards, concession stands, and a large crowd; parking is $18 a day. All the other beaches in East Hampton are usually less crowded, but require a parking permit. These beaches include the family-oriented **Georgica Beach** at the end of Apaquogue Road, and **Two Mile Hollow** at the end of Two Mile Hollow Road. Georgica, surrounded by ritzy estates, has showers and restrooms; Two Mile Hollow is in the middle of a nature sanctuary and has no facilities.

Camping and Accommodations

Camping is available at the 190-site **Cedar Point County Park,** Cedar Point Rd., off Alewife Brook Rd., 631/852-7620. The campgrounds are open May–Sept., and reservations are highly recommended. Basic campsite rates are $13–23.

The **East Hampton House,** 226 Pantigo Rd., 631/329-3000, is a comfortable motor lodge offering rooms with efficiency kitchens, a pool, and tennis courts ($135–200 d).

Among the more moderately priced inns in this expensive town is the **Bassett House Inn,** 128 Montauk Hwy., 631/324-6127. Built in the

1830s, it features 12 guest rooms, all uniquely outfitted with antiques ($175–275 d). The laid-back and private **Country Place,** 29 Hands Creek Rd., 631/324-4125, www.webhampton.com/the-countryplace, is a modern B&B with four guest rooms surrounded by trees, lawn, and a goldfish pond ($195 d in summer, $105 d off-season).

The cozy, old-fashioned, and very lovely **Maidstone Arms,** 207 Main St., 631/324-5006, www.maidstonearms.com, overlooks the village green. Outside is a breezy patio and porch, while inside, unusual antiques decorate the 16 rooms and three cottages ($290–340 d). Also on site is the romantic, Old-World **Maidstone Arms Restaurant,** 631/324-5494, which serves innovative American fare; average entrée $28.

Among the oldest of hostelries on the South Fork is **Hedges Inn,** 74 James Ln., 631/324-7100. Built by one of the town's founding families, with sections dating back to the mid-1700s, the inn features 11 nicely restored rooms ($275–375 d in summer, $175–300 d off-season). On the ground floor is the romantic **James Lane Cafe,** serving first-rate American fare; average entrée $24.

Another historic spot is **Huntting Inn,** 94 Main St., 631/324-0410, which dates back to the Revolutionary War. All 19 rooms—each one different from the next—have been thoroughly modernized but still contain plenty of antiques ($275–375 d in summer, $200–250 d off-season; rates include continental breakfast). The bustling **Palm Restaurant,** 631/324-0411, a branch of the ritzy New York steakhouse, adjoins the inn; average entrée $30. The Palm's website, www.thepalm.com, contains information about both the restaurant and the inn.

Food

For pricey gourmet takeout, try the **Barefoot Contessa,** 46 Newtown Ln., 631/324-0240, which offers a tempting array of prepared foods, along with lots of cheeses, breads and baked goods. Great deli sandwiches can be had at **Dreesen's Excelsior Market,** 33 Newtown Ln., 631/324-0465, a family-owned business established in 1920.

For casual dining, **The Grill,** 29 Newtown Ln.,

631/324-6300, offers both sidewalk dining and comfortable booths in back; menu choices range from burgers and salads to steaks and grilled fish; average dinner entrée $14. **Nicole's,** 100 Montauk Hwy., 631/324-3939, is a friendly restaurant and pub serving seafood pie and 10 kinds of draft beer. For first-rate Southwestern fare, including smoked ribs and crusty pizza, try **Santa Fe Junction,** 8 Fresno Pl., 631/324-8700; average entrée $16. **Bostwick's Seafood Grill,** 39 Gann Rd., 631/324-1111, is a festive place that offers wonderful views of the ocean; average entrée $16.

Not surprisingly, East Hampton also has its share of posh eateries where getting a reservation is no mean feat. One long-time hot spot is the airy and elegant **Della Femina,** 99 N. Main St., 631/329-6666, serving innovative American and Italian fare; average entrée $28. Another good spot for people-watching is **Nick & Toni's,** 136 N. Main St., 631/324-3550, featuring Tuscan cuisine in a sophisticated yet casual setting; average entrée $28. Newcomer **1770 House,** 143 Main St., 631/324-1770, is an elegant spot serving seasonal American cuisine; average main course $29. For other, more classic dining suggestions, see Accommodations, above.

SAG HARBOR

Driving north from East Hampton along Route 114, through lush and fertile farm country, you'll soon come to the old whaling port of Sag Harbor. During its heyday, Sag Harbor was a bustling and bawdy commercial town, and some of that lively atmosphere—so different from the elegance of the Hamptons—still lingers.

Sag Harbor is a good town to explore on foot. Lower Main Street is filled with shops and restaurants, while upper Main and the side streets hold dozens of wooden 19th-century homes and huge old trees. At the foot of Main Street is the weather-beaten 1,000-foot Long Wharf, which offers close-up views of the harbor.

Plentiful parking is available near the waterfront, especially between Main and Meadow Streets. Traffic usually doesn't get as congested here as it does in the Hamptons, but it can still be daunting.

Information

The **Sag Harbor Chamber of Commerce,** 55 Main St., 631/725-0011, www.sagharborchamber.com, runs an information center in the old windmill at the entrance to Long Wharf; it's open July–Aug., daily 9 A.M.–5 P.M. During the rest of the year, contact the chamber by phone or mail. **Sag Harbor Express,** website: www.sagharboronline.com, is also a good resource.

The Society for the Preservation of Long Island Antiquities, 631/692-4664, publishes a succinct **walking-tour map** of historic Sag Harbor sites inside their brochure on the Custom House (see below).

History

The Algonquins once lived in a village called Wegwagonock at the foot of the Sag Harbor hill. The village was known for producing wampum, which was exported throughout New England, New York, and New Jersey. Many pieces of shell can still be found in the area.

The first white settlers arrived in the harbor around 1730 and quickly turned it into a seaport. In 1753, the town's first wharf was built, and in 1760, its first whaling ships set out. The colonists had learned about whaling from the Algonquins, who taught them how to drive whales onto the beach and use the blubber for food and oil. For many years, the colonists gave the fins and tails of the whales they caught to the Indians, who used the parts in religious ceremonies.

In 1797, Sag Harbor became the first official port of entry in New York State. By 1839, it boasted a 31-boat whaling fleet, making it the world's third-largest whaling port. In town were over 80 thriving businesses, including coopers, boat builders, tool makers, and rope makers, as well as taverns and brothels. A ship anchored offshore served as a jail for drunken sailors. Lower Main Street was lined with rum-sellers; upper Main with the fashionable homes of ship captains, a number of whom were African American. Whaling was the first truly integrated industry in America, which helps account for the fact that you'll see far more black residents in Sag Harbor than in the rest of the Hamptons.

Sag Harbor's high spirits did not go overlooked by writers. The port makes a number of appearances in Herman Melville's *Moby Dick* and in the works of James Fenimore Cooper. Cooper—married to the daughter of a local—lived in Sag Harbor from 1819 to 1823, and wrote part of his first novel, *Precaution,* while working as an agent for a whaling company. One of the characters in his Natty Bumppo series, Long Tom Coffin, was modeled on Sag Harbor's Capt. David Hand.

Sag Harbor's heyday was short-lived, however. Whaling began to decline in the mid-1800s, as petroleum products began replacing oil. By 1849, the town had only two whalers left. The last voyage of a Sag Harbor whaler took place in 1871, and in 1913, the town was decommissioned as a port. Sag Harbor then went into a sleepy hibernation until the tourism boom of the 1980s began.

Sag Harbor Whaling and Historical Museum

One of the finest buildings in town is the elegant Greek Revival Sag Harbor Whaling and Historical Museum, the entrance of which is marked with tall Corinthian columns and the gleaming jawbones of a right whale. The mansion was built in 1845 by architect Minard Lafever for whaling-ship owner Benjamin Huntting.

Inside is an endless hodgepodge of jumbled exhibits—some absolutely fascinating, others looking suspiciously like junk—which makes exploring the museum a lot of fun. Poking around here is rather like poking around in a treasure-filled attic. On display you'll find everything from wooden boats and tools used by whalers to ostrich eggs and the needlework of a Miss Fannie Tunison, an 1800s Sag Harbor resident who was paralyzed except for her lips and tongue.

The museum, 200 Main St., at Garden St., 631/725-0770, www.sagharborwhalingmuseum.org, is open May–Oct., Mon.–Sat. 10 A.M.–5 P.M., Sunday 1–5 P.M. Admission is adults $3, senior citizens $2, children 6–13 $1, children under six free.

Old Custom House

Around the corner from the Whaling Museum is the 18th-century house where customs inspector Henry Packer Dering lived for three decades, beginning in 1789. Dering's job was to record all the goods entering the harbor and collect entry taxes. He used the front room of his house as an office; the room is equipped with wooden window shields that he shut whenever he wanted to count money. Dering also raised nine children in the Custom House, and some of the family's original furnishings still remain in the building.

The house, Garden St., 631/725-0250 or 631/692-4664 (off-season), is open Memorial Day–June and Sept.–Oct., Sat.–Sun. 10 A.M.–5 P.M.; July–Aug., Tues.–Sun. 10 A.M.–5 P.M. Admission is adults $3, seniors and children under 12 $1.50.

Other Historic Sites

All along Main Street near the Custom House stand impressive **sea captains' houses,** while on Union St., at Church St., is the **Old Whalers' Church,** 631/725-0894. Designed in 1844 by Minard Lafever, the church is built in an unusual Egyptian Revival style, and has a soaring interior where concerts are frequently presented.

Shopping

Most of Sag Harbor's shops and boutiques are located along Main Street. The **Sag Harbor Variety Store,** 45 Main St., 631/725-9706, is an old-fashioned five-and-dime with two cigar-store Indians out front and lots of odds and ends for sale inside.

Wildlife Refuge

About four miles west of Sag Harbor on Noyack Road is 187-acre **Elizabeth Morton National Wildlife Refuge,** 631/286-0485. The refuge overlooks Peconic and Noyack Bays, and features sandy and rocky beaches, wooded bluffs, ponds, and nature trails. It's also a nesting stop for the endangered piping plover. The refuge is open daily sunrise–sunset, but much of the beach is closed from April to mid-August. Parking is $4.

Accommodations

On the edge of downtown is the **Sag Harbor Inn,** W. Water St., 631/725-2949, www.sagharborinn.com, a modern, two-story hotel with about 40 clean, spacious rooms, many of which have balconies overlooking the harbor ($185–355 d in summer; about one-third less off-season). **Baron's Cove Inn,** 31 W. Water St., 631/725-2100, www.baronscove.com is an upscale resort motel with its own marina. All the rooms have kitchenettes, and some have private balconies overlooking the water (about $175–350 d in summer; $105–135 d off-season).

In the heart of the village is its classiest hostelry, the 1846 **American Hotel,** 25 Main St., 631/725-3535, www.theamericanhotel.com, a fine restored inn built of red brick with a white porch out front. Upstairs are eight guest rooms done up in Victorian antiques ($195–325 d); downstairs is an acclaimed restaurant.

Food

Provisions, Bay St., at Division St. (Rte. 114), 631/725-3636, is a homely but homey natural-foods shop and restaurant; average main dish $7. Lively **La Super Rica,** Main and Bay Sts., 631/725-3388, specializes in Mexican dishes made with healthy ingredients, and giant-sized margaritas. Not surprisingly, it's a favorite with the young and trendy; average entrée $13.

For great views of the yacht basin while dining, check out the **Dockside Bar & Grill,** 26 Bay St., 631/725-7100, serving lots of seafood, along with other American favorites; average entrée $15. Also offering great views is **B. Smith's,** Long Wharf at Bay Street, 631/725-5858, owned by Barbara Smith, former model and expert on African American cuisine. Specialties here include hickory ribs, roast chicken, and fresh fish, all served with Long Island wines; average entrée $19.

Il Capuccino Ristorante, 30 Madison St., 631/725-2747, serves delicious Northern Italian fare in a rambling yet somehow cozy old wooden building filled with red-checked tablecloths and Chianti bottles; average entrée $17. For superb Thai cuisine, check out the classy **Phao,** 62 Main St., 631/725-0055; average entrée $18.

The classic spot for dining in Sag Harbor is the red-brick **American Hotel,** 25 Main St., 631/725-3535, which despite its name has a European feel. The restaurant has won numerous awards for its 46-page wine list; the cuisine is French-American; average entrée $26.

AMAGANSETT

Small, picturesque Amagansett (pop. 2,180) takes its name from the Algonquin word for "place of good waters." Indians traveling between East Hampton and Montauk often stopped here for fresh water; a monument and plaque on Bluff Road mark the spot.

The East Hampton settlers bought Amagansett from the Indians in 1670, and by 1700 the village was bustling. But Amagansett's growth was cut short by the Revolutionary War, when many of its residents fled to Connecticut to escape British rule. The village never really recovered from that exodus. By 1843, the settlement had dwindled to fewer than 50 houses, and it's not much larger today.

Miss Amelia's Cottage

At the intersection of Montauk Highway and Windmill Lane stands a snug Colonial home built in 1725. Miss Mary Amelia Schellinger lived here between 1841 and 1930, and a look inside her house—still furnished with many of her belongings—gives visitors a good sense of what life on the South Fork was like back then. Behind the cottage is the **Roy K. Lester Carriage Museum,** which contains about 30 restored carriages, including a surrey with a fringe on top.

Run by the Amagansett Historical Association, 631/267-3020, the cottage is open late June–Sept., Fri.–Sun. 10–4 P.M. Suggested donation is adults $3, children $1.

East Hampton Marine Museum

On Bluff Road on the outskirts of town is the long and creaky East Hampton Town Marine Museum, filled with artifacts relating to whaling, fishing, and the sea. On the first floor are boats and more boats, along with an exhibit on shipwrecks; upstairs are exhibits on shellfish harvesting, haul seining, scalloping, ice fishing, harpooning, and whaling. The museum also offers great views of the dunes and the Atlantic, and out back are boats for children to play in.

The museum, 631/267-6544 or 631/324-6850, is open daily July 4–Labor Day, 10 A.M.–5 P.M. Admission is adults $4, seniors and children under

13 $2. To reach the museum from Montauk Highway, turn south onto Atlantic Avenue. Watch for Bluff Road and turn right.

Beaches

At the end of **Atlantic Avenue** is a wide and wonderful public beach. Equipped with lifeguards and an elaborate concession stand, the beach was once known as "asparagus beach" because it attracted bunches of singles who stood together watching everyone else. Now it attracts a more mixed crowd. Parking is $12.

Accommodations

The midsize **Ocean Colony Beach and Tennis Club,** Montauk Hwy. four miles east of the village center, 631/267-3130, offers a private beach, pool, and tennis courts. Accommodations range from studios to two-bedroom cottages, and all rooms have kitchenettes ($220–295 d in summer, $110–150 d off-season).

Mill-Garth Country Inn, 23 Windmill Ln., 631/267-3757, parts of which date back to 1840, is a romantic and eclectic B&B composed of cozy cottages and studio rooms clustered around small patios. Lush vegetation and wicker furniture are everywhere, and the beach is about a half mile away ($225–350 d in summer, $165–230 d off-season; hearty continental breakfast included).

Food

Amagansett's most popular restaurant is the **Lobster Roll,** 1980 Montauk Hwy., between Amagansett and Montauk, 631/267-3740. Also known as "Lunch" because of the huge sign it sports out front, the place is a modern roadside diner serving fresh, no-frills seafood; average main dish $11. Popular with the locals is **Gordon's,** Main St., 631/267-3010, an elegant, low-key spot known for its excellent fresh seafood and enormous wine list; average entrée $19.

On Main Street in the village center is the very popular **Amagansett Farmers Market,** 631/267-3894. Open seven days a week, the market sells everything from fresh produce and cheese to sandwiches and baked goods, and includes a coffee bar.

© CHRISTIANE BIRD

In Amagansett, no-frills seafood diner The Lobster Roll is also known simply as "Lunch," for some reason.

Nightlife

The oldest and most beloved of nightspots on the South Fork is **Stephen Talkhouse,** 161 Main St., 631/267-3117, where first-rate musicians—everyone from Bob Dylan to Billy Joel—have been playing for decades. The place was established in 1932 and has a nice laid-back feel, with worn wooden tables and a friendly wait staff. The kitchen remains open until 3 A.M., making it a good spot for a late-night snack.

SPRINGS

At first, there doesn't seem to be any reason to visit this out-of-the-way spot, located at the intersection of Fireplace Road and Old Stone Highway, north of Amagansett. The place has no downtown, and no real stores or parking lots.

But Springs—a village of winding roads overhung with dark scrub pines—actually carries quite a cache. Painters Jackson Pollock and Lee Krasner, husband and wife, bought a house here in 1945, and soon thereafter, numerous other artists followed suit. Today the village continues to be recognized as a vital artistic center.

Springs is also home to a tightly knit community of farmers and fisherfolk. Long isolated from the rest of the world, the community developed its own dialect—complete with the vowel pronunciations of post–Elizabethan England—still spoken by some of the older villagers today.

Art Sites

The unassuming 19th-century farmhouse where Pollock and Krasner lived, at 830 Fireplace Rd., is now open to the public. Known today as the **Pollock-Krasner House and Study Center,** it houses the artists' collection of Victorian furniture, books, and jazz records. Out back is a creaky barn—complete with a paint-spattered floor—where Pollock created many of his greatest works. Also on site is a collection of photographs documenting the lives of the two painters.

The house, 631/324-4929, is open May–Oct., Thurs.–Sat. 11–4 P.M., by appointment only. Admission is $5.

On Accabonac Road, not far from Pollock's old residence, is **Green River Cemetery,** which has recently become one of the Hamptons' odder tourist attractions. Pollock, who died in a car accident in 1956, is buried in the cemetery, beneath a boulder marked with an engraving of his signature. Since his death, numerous other personages—including artist Stuart Davis, poet Frank O'Hara, and art critic Harold Rosenberg—have also chosen to be buried in Green River, also beneath engravings of their signatures. As a result, carloads of visitors often drop by to show their respects, sometimes leaving tributes such as paintbrushes behind.

All this doesn't make the locals very happy. The cemetery is small, and the villagers worry that there won't be room left for them when their time comes. Some of the outsiders buried here—such as Davis—never even lived in Springs.

The cemetery, surrounded by a white fence, is located on Accabonac Road, just south of Old Stone Highway.

Wildlife Refuge

The **Merrill Lake Sanctuary,** run by the Nature Conservancy, is an easily accessible salt marsh especially good for birdwatching. Ospreys nest here in late June and early July. The sanctuary, 631/329-7689, is located off Fireplace Rd., near Hog Creek Rd., and is open daily sunrise–sunset. A self-guiding trail leads through the refuge. Admission is free.

MONTAUK

I stand on some mighty eagle's beak,
Eastward the sea absorbing, viewing,
(Nothing but sea and sky)
The tossing waves, the foam, the ships in the
distance
The wild unrest, the snowy, curling caps—
that inbound urge and urge of waves,
Seeking the shore forever.

Walt Whitman, "Montauk Point"

From Amagansett to Montauk is a drive of only about 10 miles, but the landscape changes dramatically along the way. Near Amagansett, the South Fork still feels like a well-tended region of small towns and farms; near Montauk, the terrain becomes windswept, barren, and wild. Despite all the tourists who flock here in summer,

Montauk basically remains an isolated fishing village surrounded by dunes and sandy beach. Commercial deep-sea fishing is big business here.

Montauk proper centers around a circular green with a weathered gazebo. On one side of the green, known as the Village Plaza, is an eight-story office building—by far the largest structure in town—and **White's,** 631/668-2994, a creaky old variety store where you can buy everything from postcards and sunglasses to small appliances and 14-carat-gold jewelry.

The **Montauk Chamber of Commerce,** Main St., at the Village Plaza, 631/668-2428, www.montaukchamber.com, is well stocked with brochures and maps. Hours are May–Oct., Mon.–Sat. 10 A.M.–5 P.M.; call for off-season hours. Parking is usually available in the lots along Main Street or on the side streets.

North of Montauk proper is **Montauk Harbor,** always teeming with fishing and pleasure craft. The drive to the Harbor passes cornflower-blue Lake Montauk, while the harbor itself is home to a number of restaurants. Every June, the harbor hosts the festive **Blessing of the Fleet,** in which hundreds of boats (some owned by celebs such as Billy Joel) receive prayers for a safe season.

Montauk comes as a welcome respite after the heady, moneyed land of the Hamptons. Though it, too, now has its share of trendy hot spots, Montauk's main attraction remains the sea and shore.

History

Some 15,000 years ago, Montauk—Algonquin for "hilly land" or "island country"—was an island unto itself, separate from Long Island. Not until relatively recently in its geologic history did it become connected to the mainland.

The earliest white settlers arrived in the area in the mid-1600s, but didn't settle in Montauk for another 150 years. Instead they used the spit of land as a summer pasture for their sheep and cattle, thus making Montauk the country's oldest cattle ranch.

To house the keepers of their cattle, as well the hunters who came to Montauk for its abundant game, the English built three houses. The First House was destroyed by fire, but the **Second House** and **Third House,** originally built in

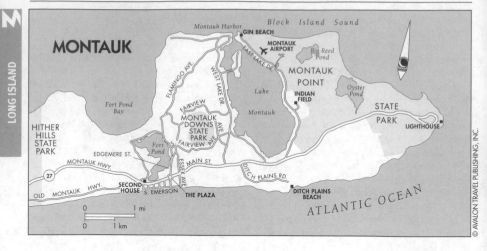

1746 and 1747, respectively, still stand and function as small historical museums.

In 1898, Theodore Roosevelt and his Rough Riders, along with close to 30,000 other men who had fought in the Spanish-American War, used Montauk as a quarantine station. Many of the soldiers had contracted infectious diseases during the war, and they recuperated on Montauk. In WW I, the area was home to a naval aviation base built to house dirigibles and hydroplanes; in WW II, it was home to a torpedo testing range.

In 1926, developer Carl Graham Fisher bought up most of Montauk in hopes of turning it into a sort of "Miami Beach of the North." Fisher built the village center and office tower that still stand today, along with a Tudor-style luxury hotel called Montauk Manor (now condos) at the top of North Fairview Avenue. Unfortunately, Fisher went bankrupt in the Crash of 1929 and his office tower stood vacant for over 50 years. Not until the 1980s did Montauk boom into a popular vacation spot.

Second House Museum

The oldest building in Montauk is a dark and long-ceilinged affair, first built in 1746 and rebuilt in 1797. Inside you'll find period furniture and artifacts, along with small, casual exhibits on various aspects of Montauk's history.

One of the most interesting displays concerns Samson Occom, a Monhegan Indian born in Connecticut. Occom came to Montauk in 1744 after converting to Christianity. He married a Montauk woman and became a noted preacher, as well as the author of several hymns still sung today. Together with two white ministers, Occum went to England in the 1760s to raise money for indigent Indians. The earl of Dartmouth was so impressed with Occum's powerful preaching that he donated £10,000 to the cause. Back in America, however, the white ministers took over administration of the funds—which they used to found Dartmouth College in 1769. Occum withdrew from village life, a disillusioned, discouraged man.

The house, Second House Rd., 631/668-5340, just off Montauk Hwy. (Rte. 27) immediately west of the village, is open July 4–Columbus Day, Thurs.–Tues. 10 A.M.–4 P.M., Memorial Day–June, Sat.–Sun. 10 A.M.–4 P.M. Admission is adults $2, children $1.

Third House

The Third House, first built in 1749 and rebuilt in 1806, is a big, rambling affair several times the size of the Second House. Set in the middle of what is now **Theodore Roosevelt County Park,** it was used by Teddy Roosevelt and his Rough Riders in 1898, and currently functions as the park headquarters. In the house is a small exhibit on Roosevelt and his troops, along with early Montauk artifacts.

The house, Theodore Roosevelt County Park, off Rte. 27 two and a half miles east of village center, 631/852-7878, is open Memorial Day–Labor Day, Wed.–Sun. 10 A.M.–5 P.M. Admission is free.

Indian Field

A much more interesting spot connected with Montauk's Native Americans is the peaceful, oddly spiritual Indian Field, now surrounded by homes at the end of Pocahontas Lane, off East Lake Drive. The last piece of land owned by the Montauks on Long Island, Indian Field is a burial ground. According to ancient custom, the Indians were buried here in a sitting position, in a circle relative to one another. Each grave is marked with a rough fieldstone.

The cemetery's largest and only engraved stone belongs to Stephen Pharaoh, better known as Stephen Talkhouse, who died in 1879. A whaler, Civil War soldier, and the last of the Montauk sachems, Talkhouse was also a famous walker who charged 25 cents to carry a letter from Montauk to East Hampton. Talkhouse's long legs enabled him to make the 35-mile roundtrip journey in a day.

Beaches and Parks

About three miles west of Montauk, bordering Napeague Harbor, is **Hither Hills State Park.**

Home to the only official public beach in Montauk where you can park without a permit, Hither Hills has a bathhouse, general store, picnic area, and 165 very popular campsites. The park is also laced with hiking trails leading into isolated dunes, far from humankind. The dunes offer wonderful views of ocean and bay.

Hither Hills, 631/668-2554, Old Montauk Hwy., about three miles west of the village center, is open mid-April–November. Lifeguards are on duty during the summer, when parking is $7 a day.

An unofficial public beach borders the village's center. Just park in the village, walk south down South Essex Street at the end of town, and you're there. Don't expect any facilities, however.

Two other beaches in Montauk are **Ditch Plains,** near the village's center off Ditch Plains Road; and **Gin Beach,** north of town at the end of East Lake Drive. Ditch Plains is known for great surfing, Gin Beach for its wide empty sands and good fishing. Both require parking permits.

North of Montauk is **Montauk Downs State Park,** S. Fairview Ave. about one mile east of the village center, 631/668-5000, offering tennis courts, a swimming pool, and a golf course, all of which are open to the public. Montauk Downs is open April–December.

Six miles east of Montauk, at the tip of the South Fork and end of Montauk Hwy., is **Montauk Point State Park,** 631/668-5000, a lonely

THE MONTAUK CATTLE DRIVE

For over 250 years, from 1661 to 1926, cattle and sheep were driven onto Montauk in the spring and off again in the fall. Most were owned by farmers in East Hampton village or Amagansett, but some may have come from as far as Patchogue, a good two days' ride away. Depending on the year, anywhere from 1,000 to 3,000 cattle were pastured on Montauk. The farmers kept their animals apart with ear marks, which they registered with the town office.

The cattle's first stop was the green at the west end of East Hampton, where they were "baited" or fed; hence the street name, Baiting Hollow Road.

They were then funneled through Amagansett's wide main street and onto the isthmus.

A Mrs. Elizabeth Cartwright, born in the mid-1800s, once recounted the excitement of those so-called Cattle Days for the *East Hampton Star:* "The family was astir long before daylight; East Hampton street was noisy with cattle lowing, men and boys on horseback, one herd after another going slowly by. . . . It was a busy time on Montauk the day before, preparing batches of bread, milkpans of pork and beans, dripping pans of roast veal, home-cured ham, pickles, coffee and pie, for sixty or more men."

and very windy spot overlooking the sea. Throughout the park are hiking and biking trails. It's open year-round; parking in the summer is $7.

Montauk Lighthouse

Within Montauk Point State Park, but not officially a part of it, is the still-operating Montauk Lighthouse, one of the most popular visitor attractions on Long Island. The striped black-and-white structure was commissioned by George Washington in 1792 and has been protecting vessels traveling the transatlantic trade route ever since. At one time, the lighthouse burned whale oil. Today it's automated and no longer requires a keeper. The Coast Guard still runs the technical end of the lighthouse but leases the building to the Montauk Historical Society, which operates it as a museum. On display are the keeper's quarters, lots of lighthouse memorabilia, and an extensive collection of lenses. Visitors can also climb up into the tower for a grand view of the ocean.

The lighthouse, Montauk Point State Park, end of Montauk Hwy., 631/668-2544, www.montauklighthouse.com, is open mid-June–Labor Day, daily 10:30 A.M.–6 P.M.; call for hours in the spring and fall. Admission is adults $6, seniors $5, children 6–11 $4; babies and children under 41 inches tall are not allowed in the tower.

Recreation

The nation's oldest cattle ranch, established in 1658, is **Deep Hollow Ranch,** Montauk Hwy. three miles east of village center, 631/668-2744. Today a center for horseback riding, the ranch offers guided trail rides through 4,000 acres of parklands, pastures, and beach, along with pony rides, family barbecues, and riding lessons. Rates for the standard one-and-one-half hour beach and trail ride is $60.

Sportfishing is one of Montauk's major attractions. "Party boats" take out large groups of anglers daily. To sign on, call **Lazybones in Montauk,** 631/668-5671; **Viking Fishing Fleet,** 631/668-5700, www.vikingfleet.com; or **Marlin V,** 631/668-2818. The Viking Fleet also offers **whalewatching** cruises departing from the Montauk Harbor in July and August.

Camping and Resort Motels

About 165 campsites are available at **Hither Hills State Park,** Old Montauk Hwy. about three miles west of the village center, 631/668-2554, between mid-April and November. Reservations are necessary: in July and August, the sites can be reserved for a week only, and during the rest of the season they can be reserved for a week or more only. To make a reservation, call 800/456-CAMP; sites cost $24 a night.

Among the many resort motels you'll find in and near Montauk is the clean and friendly **Atlantic Terrace,** 21 Surfside Pl., 631/668-2050, conveniently located right on the ocean and three blocks from downtown ($175–249 d in summer, $95–155 d off-season). One half mile west of the village is **Breakers at the Ocean,** Old Montauk Hwy., 631/668-2525, which offers motel rooms, studios, and cottages, all of which face the beach ($160 d in summer, $95 d off-season). The newly renovated **Royal Atlantic Beach Resort,** 126 S. Edgemere St. at Montauk Hwy., 631/668-5103, offers a variety of accommodations as well, including studios, one-bedroom suites, and "two-story luxury beach houses"; all have kitchenettes and private terraces ($185–235 d in summer, $95–125 d off-season).

Inns, Condos, and Bed-and-Breakfasts

The easygoing **Shepherd's Neck Inn,** 90 Second House Rd., 631/668-2105, is a long, white, half-timbered building that looks like a modern Swiss chalet. Out back are five lush acres, a swimming pool, tennis courts, and putting green; inside is a restaurant specializing in fresh seafood and vegetables ($120–240 d in summer, $90–130 d off-season; packages available).

On the edge of Montauk village, by the beach, is the modern, gray-shingled **Surf Club,** S. Essex St. and Surfside Ave., 631/668-3800, a condominium resort that also rents spiffy one- and two-bedroom duplexes. The condos are built around an attractive pool ($295–535/unit in summer; about a third less off-season).

Peri's, 206 Essex St., 631/668-1394, is an unusual B&B housed in a historic Carl Fisher Tudor home of stucco walls and half-timber beams. The three imaginatively designed guest rooms are all done up differently: one to evoke dreams of the tropics, another of Morocco, and a third of Paris ($220–295 d).

Now over 60 years old, Montauk's grande dame is **Gurney's Inn Resort & Spa,** 290 Old Montauk Hwy., 631/668-2345, www.gurneysweb.com. The inn is perched on a bluff overlooking the ocean and has a rustic, old-fashioned feel. Heavy wooden furniture fills the main lodge, while along the beach are new and very spacious guest rooms filled with amenities. Gurney's also features a full-service restaurant serving continental fare and state-of-the-art spa that are open to the public. Among the many treatments the spa offers are salt baths, thalasso baths (underwater massage with jets of water), facials, and herbal wraps ($310–400 d in summer, including a full breakfast and dinner; $250–330 d off-season; special packages and spa packages are available).

Food and Drink

Mr. John's Pancake & Steak House, Main St. in the village center, 631/668-2383, serves an especially good breakfast, featuring seven kinds of pancakes, waffles, and crepes; average main dish $8. The **Naturally Good Foods & Cafe,** S. Etna and S. Essex Sts., 631/668-9030, is a small, unassuming natural foods store that also serves breakfast and lunch; average main dish $7. For an all-you-can-eat Sunday brunch, visit **Surfside Inn,** 685 Montauk Hwy., 631/668-5958.

Shagwong, Main St., 631/668-3050, caters to Montauk's large Irish population. On the menu is plenty of good pub grub (average entrée $13), but the place is really best known for its lively nightlife, and is packed year round with people drinking pints at the bar.

Now over 50 years old is bustling **Gosman's Dock,** West Lake Dr. at the Harbor, 631/668-2549. A Montauk institution, this enormous dockside restaurant has three dining rooms, all of which overlook the harbor, and serves consistently fresh fare; average entrée $17.

Also overlooking Montauk Harbor, but from a different vantage point, is **Dave's Grill,** 468 Flamingo Rd., 631/668-9190, a classy diner specializing in grilled fish. During the summer, there's often a long wait, but it's worth it; average entrée $18. For innovative American fare, elegant, romantic **Caswell's,** 17 S. Edison St., 631/668-0303, is a good choice; average entrée $18.

The Hudson Valley

Introduction

As hard as it is to believe, to the immediate north of honking, teeming, steaming New York City lies some of the most splendid scenery in the Northeast. The visual feast begins at the edge of the Bronx, where for a 21-mile stretch the blue-gray Palisade cliffs drop precipitously into the Hudson River. Farther north and to the west sprawl the scrappy Ramapo Mountains, while to the east you'll glimpse the long, dark, silent reservoirs of New York City's water system. Midway up the Valley begin the Hudson Highlands, an extension of the Appalachian Mountains made up of steep cliffs, craggy bluffs, and brooding blue-black peaks. Lush, loamy farmland, heavy with fruits and vegetables, characterizes the regions to the east, west, and north of the Highlands.

Along with its seductive landscape, the Hudson Valley lays claim to dozens of major historic sites, ranging from Revolutionary War battlefields to grand river estates; it also offers first-rate cultural institutions, offbeat museums, gourmet restaurants, and glorious state parks.

To fully explore the Hudson Valley region would take at least a week, but you can see a lot on day or weekend trips. Easily accessible from New York City, the area sights are closely spaced; to drive from Manhattan to the northern reaches of the Valley takes less than three hours.

fall in the Hudson Valley

Albany, the state capital, guards the northern end of the Hudson Valley. The Catskill Mountains lie to the northeast of the Hudson Highlands.

THE LAND

The Hudson River

Most of the Hudson River isn't a river at all but an estuary, or arm of the sea; ocean tides run as far north as Albany. The Algonquin Indians, recognizing this natural phenomenon, called the Hudson "Muhheahkantuck," or "the river that flows both ways." To put it another way, most of the Hudson, which narrows at Bear Mountain into a deep gorge, is a fjord. The only other fjord in the northeast is in Maine.

The Hudson, which is navigable as far north as Albany, begins at Lake Tear in the Clouds atop Mt. Marcy in the Adirondacks. Only 315 miles long from its source to New York Harbor, it varies in width from two feet to three and a half miles, and in depth from a few inches to 216 feet. The Hudson's widest point is at Haverstraw Bay, its deepest is between Newburgh and West Point.

The river was first formed about 75 million years ago. The land around it rose, and the river began cutting a course between the Catskill and Taconic Mountains down to the Atlantic. Later, during the Ice Age—when the sea level was lower than it is today—the Hudson flowed on beyond present-day New York Harbor through about 120 miles of Continental Shelf. The sea then rose, but the river kept on flowing.

When European settlers first arrived in New York, they found the banks of the Hudson— like all the Northeast—lined with primeval forest. The trees were of gargantuan size, with foliage so dense there was virtually no undergrowth. By

THE HUDSON VALLEY

HUDSON VALLEY HIGHLIGHTS

Westchester County
Hudson River Museum, Yonkers
Cropsey House, Hastings-on-Hudson
Tarrytown's historic mansions
Tarrytown House, Tarrytown
Crabtree's Kittle House, Chappaqua
Caramoor Center, Katonah
Hammond Museum and Garden, North Salem
Donald M. Kendall Sculpture Gardens at Pepsico,
    Purchase
Rye Playland, Rye

Rockland County
Nyack village
Piermont village
Turning Point, a music club, Piermont
DeWint House, Tappan
Harriman and Bear Mountain State Parks
Bear Mountain Inn, Bear Mountain

Orange and Putnam Counties
U.S. Military Academy, West Point
Constitution Island, West Point
Storm King Highway
Washington's Headquarters, Newburgh
Mill House, Marlboro

Storm King Art Center, Mountainville
Museum Village, Monroe
Harness Racing Museum, Goshen
Bear Mountain Bridge, near Garrison
Boscobel Restoration, Garrison
Cold Spring village

Dutchess County
Vassar Art Gallery, Poughkeepsie
Innisfree Garden, Millbrook
Wing's Castle, Millbrook
Roosevelt homes, Hyde Park
CIA restaurants, Hyde Park
Rhinebeck village
Montgomery Place, Annandale-on-Hudson

Columbia County
Clermont, Germantown
Lake Taghkanic and Taconic State Parks
Rodgers Book Barn, Hillsdale
Antique stores, Warren Street, Hudson
Olana, Hudson
American Museum of Firefighting, Hudson
Kinderhook village
Shaker Museum and Library, Old Chatham

the mid 1800s, most of those trees were gone, cleared away for agriculture. Then came the Industrial Revolution, and cities, towns, and factories sprang up all along the river, bringing with them increasingly toxic levels of pollution. By the early 1970s, the Hudson had become, in the words of one local newspaper, a "flowing cesspool that was the shame of the Empire State."

Today, thanks largely to the Clean Water Act of 1972, the Hudson is a much cleaner place. Towns no longer spew untreated sewage into its waters, and factories have significantly reduced their chemical discharge. Much work remains to be done, but the Hudson is now regarded as a "recovering" river with an "improving" environmental condition.

Geology

The New York Metropolitan Region, which includes most of the Hudson Valley, is one of the world's most geologically diverse areas. Over the past millions of years, as geologist Christopher J. Schuberth writes in the *New York Walk Book,* it has been subjected to "an unprecedented barrage of one dynamic geologic process after another," including "submergence beneath marginal seas; sedimentation and crustal subsidence; volcanism; mountain-building; metamorphism and plutonism; more mountain-building; long-term and deep erosion. . . ."

Ahem! What all this amounts to, in layperson's terms, is an extremely varied terrain that can be divided into five distinct geological subregions: (1) the flat Atlantic Coastal Plain, once submerged beneath the Atlantic (Rockland County); (2) the New England Upland, which dates back to Precambrian times and includes both relatively flat terrain and the imposing peaks of Bear Mountain and Storm King (Westchester, Orange, Putnam, and Rockland Counties); (3) the Newark Basin, made up largely of red sandstone and the igneous bluestone of the Palisade cliffs (Rockland County); (4) the Folded Appalachians, composed of horizontal layers from ancient seas (Orange, Dutchess, and Columbia Counties); and (5) the Appalachian Plateau, a broad terrain of conglomerate, sandstone, and shale (Ulster and Greene Counties).

What this also amounts to is a surprising number of mountains in a region that is otherwise flat. Through the center of the Valley, in an area known as the Hudson Highlands, run the Appalachians. On the Rockland-Orange border are the Ramapos. West of the Ramapos is Schunemunk Mountain. In Columbia County are the Taconics. On the western edge of Valley, and covered in the Catskills chapter, are the Shawangunks and Catskills.

Flora and Fauna

The Hudson Valley region supports a wide variety of flora and fauna, best seen in the state parks. Among the best parks for wildlife are Harriman State Park in Rockland/Orange Counties, Fahnestock State Park in Putnam County, and Taconic State Park in Columbia County. The Constitution Marsh Sanctuary in Putnam County features a 300-foot boardwalk for the observation of wetland life.

Most of the Hudson Valley's woodlands are composed of second-growth hardwood forest. The most common deciduous trees are oak,

a small sampling of the Hudson Valley's abundant agricultural output

maple, hickory, ash, tulip, beech, sour gum, and sweet gum; evergreens include cedar, spruce, hemlock, balsam, and pine. Among the shrubs are laurel, rhododendron, witch hazel, wild azalea, sweet pepper bush, alder, blueberry, and sumac.

The region's animal life includes 39 species of mammals, 24 species of reptiles, and 246 species of birds—94 species of which nest in the area. Among the mammals most frequently seen are deer, raccoons, woodchucks, and squirrels. Present in much smaller numbers are otters, mink, beavers, and wildcats.

In the lower Hudson River are over 200 species of both saltwater and freshwater fish, including American shad, striped bass, black bass, and sturgeon. The estuary is an excellent nursery, especially for shad, striped bass, crayfish, and yellow perch.

HISTORY

Early History

Before the arrival of Europeans, the banks of the Hudson River were inhabited by the Algonquins, a group of linguistically related tribes who once controlled most of the Atlantic seaboard from Maine to the Carolinas. On the west bank, just north of Manhattan, lived the Lenapes, which included the Munsees and the Tappans, while on the east bank lived the Manhattans and the Wappingers. Further north, between today's Albany and Lake Champlain, lived the strongest of all the Algonquin tribes, the Mohicans.

A handsome and peaceful people, the Algonquins survived through hunting, fishing, and agriculture. They built canoes out of single large trees, and planted fields of corn and pumpkin. Too easygoing and loosely organized to be victorious in war, the Algonquins lived in fear of their fierce neighbors to the north, the Mohawks.

European Settlement

The first European to set eyes on the Hudson was Giovanni da Verrazano, who explored the coast of North America for France in 1524. But it was Henry Hudson, looking for a route to the Orient in 1609, who sailed the river as far north as Albany and put it on the Western map.

Most of Hudson Valley's early European set-

tlers were poor tenants recruited by the Dutch patroons, or shareholders of the Dutch West India Company. The patroons had received huge tracts of land in exchange for establishing settlements of 50 people or more, and they lured tenants to the New World with promises of wealth and an easier life. But with one major exception—the ruthlessly run Rensselaerswyck, near Albany (see Albany in the chapter on Central New York)—the system was a dismal failure.

The English took over the Dutch colony in 1664, and soon replaced the patroon system with a similar system of their own. "Manor lords" built great estates along the Hudson and brought tenants north to work them. Predominant among these early lords was Frederick Philipse, who once owned all the riverfront between Yonkers and the Croton River.

During the Revolutionary War, the Hudson Valley played a prominent role. Major battles were fought near White Plains, Stony Point, Bear Mountain, and Saratoga farther north. Benedict Arnold's plot to betray West Point was foiled by the capture of the British spy, Maj. John Andre, at Tarrytown. General Washington declared the Continental Army's victory over the British from his headquarters in Newburgh in 1781, and it was here, too, that he first received what he later called an "offer of a crown." He turned the suggestion down "with abhorrence," paving the way for the establishment of today's democratic system.

Prosperity

After the war, the fertile valley began to develop into a thriving agricultural community, shipping many of its products south to New York City. This prosperity grew even greater after 1825, when the building of the Erie Canal opened up the nation's first trade route to the west. The canal helped turn New York City, and by extension the Hudson Valley, into the most important metropolitan region in the new republic.

As New Yorkers grew more wealthy, more great estates were built along the Hudson, especially in the region between Yonkers and Peekskill. The newly rich wished to prove to their more established counterparts in Europe that they, too, were a sophisticated and cultured bunch who enjoyed living in baronial style, surrounded by luxury.

The coming of the railroad in the mid-1800s allowed the middle and working classes to move up the Hudson as well. For the first time, it was no longer necessary for people to live within streetcar distance of their jobs—they could commute. Small villages sprang up along the railroad lines; the suburban era was born.

At the same time, the railroad brought with it dozens of riverfront factories manufacturing everything from shoes to ball bearings, textiles to elevators. The factories attracted large numbers of Italian, Irish, and Eastern European immigrants, many of whose descendants still live in the Valley today.

Modern Times

Then, in the mid-1900s, the Valley's luck began to change. Factories closed down due to changes in industrial demands. Small farms went bankrupt due to increasing operating costs and competition from large farms. Urban renewal knocked the guts out of some once-thriving cities. The woes of modern society—pollution, poverty, crime—spread.

Somehow, though, the Hudson Valley took it all in stride, and today the region remains one of the most interesting in the state. Small farmers live next door to commuters and second-home owners; recent immigrants from the Caribbean or Central America share counties, if not villages, with high-powered New York City executives. Some of the river towns remain scruffy and forlorn, but others have been nicely restored.

GETTING AROUND

Orientation

As with other New Yorkers, the people of the Hudson Valley don't think by region, they think by county, and everything they tell you will be phrased accordingly. Hyde Park is not in the Hudson Valley, it's in Dutchess County; to get to West Point from Nyack, you don't just travel north on Route 9 W, you cross over from Rockland County to Orange County. Anyone would think you were traveling between foreign countries, and each county does indeed have its own distinct character.

Depending on how you count, the Hudson Valley encompasses all or part of 10 different counties: Westchester, Rockland, Putnam, Orange, Dutchess, Columbia, Ulster, Greene, Albany, and Rensselaer. Since much of Ulster and most of Greene lie in the Catskills, however, and most of Albany and Rensselaer in Central New York, they are not included in this chapter. Keep in mind though, that Ulster and Greene Counties—home to Kingston, New Paltz, Woodstock, and Saugerties—are just a short drive across the Hudson from Dutchess and Columbia Counties, respectively.

Westchester and Rockland are the counties closest to New York City and are, not surprisingly, the most suburban. Dutchess and Orange Counties have the most to offer in terms of developed visitor attractions. Much of Columbia County is still farmland and is astonishingly beautiful. Putnam County is best known for its charming river towns and many lakes and reservoirs.

Top destinations for first-time visitors include Tarrytown (Westchester), Hyde Park (Dutchess), West Point and Storm King Art Center (Orange), Nyack (Rockland), Cold Spring (Putnam), Hudson (Columbia), plus the Columbia County countryside.

Transportation

The easiest way to explore the Hudson Valley is by car. However, many towns along the east bank of the Hudson River and some in Westchester's Harlem Valley (including Rye, North White Plains, Pleasantville, and Katonah) and Orange County (including Tuxedo, Harriman, and Middletown) are serviced by **Metro-North Commuter Railroad,** 212/532-4900 or 800/638-7646, which leaves out of Grand Central Station (Park Ave. and 42nd St. in Manhattan). Roundtrip fares are reasonable, and taxis are usually available at the villages' railroad stations. **Amtrak,** 212/582-6875 or 800/872-7245, provides rail service between New York City and Rhinecliff, Hudson, and points further north.

If traveling up the Hudson River valley by train, be sure to sit on the left-hand side of the car.

The railroad hugs the eastern shoreline and offers spectacular views.

Adirondack–Pine Hill Trailways, 212/967-2900 or 800/225-6815; and **Shortline Bus,** 212/736-4700 or 800/631-8405, offer daily bus service between the Port Authority Bus Terminal (41st St. and 8th Ave., Manhattan) and many Hudson Valley communities.

In addition to flying into New York City, travelers can also opt to fly into the Albany County Airport, located at the northern end of the Hudson Valley. Among the major airlines flying into Albany are **American,** 800/433-7300, **Delta,** 800/221-1212, **Northwest,** 800/225-2525, and **United,** 800/241-6522.

RECREATION

Rail and River Tours

The **Metro-North One Day Getaways** program, leaving from New York City's Grand Central Station, offers a variety of day trips via rail throughout the Hudson Valley Region; call Metro-North at 212/532-4900 or 800/638-7646.

A number of cruise options are listed under the various recreation headings below. For travel directly upriver from Manhattan, **NY Waterway,** 800/533-3779, offers Sleepy Hollow Cruise and Kykuit Cruise tour packages that include admission to the Tarrytown-area estates of Sunnyside and Kykuit, respectively.

Fishing

The Hudson River—part fresh water, part salt water—is home to a remarkable variety of fish, including American shad and striped bass. Brochures and guides to fishing throughout the region can be picked up at tourism offices. Fishing licenses are mandatory for everyone over age 16 and can be obtained in sporting goods stores, bait shops, and town offices.

Hiking and Other Outdoor Activities

A number of good day-hikes can be found throughout the Hudson Valley, especially in Harriman and Bear Mountain State Parks and in the Hudson Highlands region. Individual parks can usually provide you with basic information on their hiking

trails, but more serious hikers will want to contact the **New York–New Jersey Trail Conference,** 156 Ramapo Valley Rd., Mahwah, NJ 07430, 201/512-9348, www.nynjtc.com. The conference publishes *Harriman Trails* and "East Hudson Trails" (a map set), among many other things, and operates an excellent **Park Visitor Center** off the Palisades Interstate Parkway (see Bear Mountain State Park under Rockland County, below).

Two excellent books cover hiking in the region. One is the classic *New York Walk Book,* published by the New York–New Jersey Trail Conference. Another is *Fifty Hikes in the Hudson Valley* by Peter Kick, Barbara McMartin, and James M. Long (Backcountry Press).

The Hudson Valley region also offers a wide variety of other outdoor activities, including **hot-air ballooning, horseback riding, canoeing, biking,** and **golf.** For more information, inquire at local tourism offices.

Touring Farms and Vineyards

Much of the Hudson Valley is still devoted to agriculture, and produce stands and pick-your-own farms are everywhere. Lists and maps are available at visitor information centers.

The Hudson Valley wineries do not yet have the reputation of the Finger Lakes or Long Island wineries, but they're getting there. For a free brochure and map of the area's vineyards, call Hudson Valley Tourism at 800/232-4782.

VISITOR SERVICES

Each county has its own tourist information centers; addresses are listed under the individual counties below. If you'd like general information sent to you, contact Hudson Valley Tourism, P.O. Box 284, Salt Point, NY 12578, 800/232-4782. For online information on the region, visit the "Enjoy Hudson Valley" website: www.enjoyhv.com.

For more information on any of the New York State parks or historic sites described below, visit the website: www.nysparks.com.

Hudson Valley, 845/485-7844, www.hudsonvalleymagazine.com, is a glossy monthly with informative articles on the region. It's available at area newsstands for $3.95.

Westchester County

Westchester County is considerably more complex than it seems at first sight. While partly a bland land of posh suburbs and glitzy corporate headquarters, it also holds Revolutionary War history, grand estates, a stretch of the Hudson River, and a large number of parks.

Most of Westchester County south of I-287 is densely suburban. This is where you'll find such legendary wealthy communities as Scarsdale and Rye, the gritty cities of Yonkers and Mt. Vernon, and a growing number of ethnic communities.

North of I-287, Westchester begins to take on a whole different feel. Well-tended suburbs gradually give ground to an increasing number of trees, reservoirs, and lakes. Already by mid-county, you'll find bona fide historic villages, complete with New England-like churches and greens. And by the time you get to the northeasternmost section of the county, you're in a rural land of winding back roads, horse farms, and Old Moneyed estates. Northern Westchester has remained relatively undeveloped because it's largely owned by New York City, which began acquiring land and building reservoirs for its water supply here in the mid-1800s.

And then there are the towns and villages along the Hudson River, which have a character all their own. Commuter towns since the late 1800s, many center around a railroad station and one main street. Meanwhile, on their outskirts—carefully hidden from prying eyes—stand dozens of grand, turn-of-the-century estates, only a few of which are open to the public.

First-time visitors to the county will probably want to concentrate on the Hudson River towns and villages. To explore them by car, follow Route 9, or Broadway, which is an extension of Manhattan's Broadway. To reach Route 9 from Manhattan, take the West Side Highway (Route 9A) north and watch for signs.

Information

For more information, contact the **Westchester Country Visitors Bureau,** 222 Mamaroneck Ave., White Plains, NY 10605, 914/995-8500 or 800/833-9282, www.westchestergov.com/tourism. Hours are Mon.–Fri. 9 A.M.–5 P.M.

YONKERS

Yonkers, on the Hudson just north of New York City, takes its name from *youncker* (young nobleman) Adriaen Van Der Donck, who first acquired it from the Dutch West India Company in the early 1600s. With a population of about 200,000, Yonkers is actually the fourth largest city in New York State, but it functions primarily as a sort of scruffy extension of its much larger neighbor to the south.

Originally a Lenape Indian village known as Nappeckamack, Yonkers became an important manufacturing center in the second half of the 19th century. Among its chief products were textiles, carpets, patent medicines, insulated wire and cable, and elevators. Inventor Elisha G. Otis settled in Yonkers in 1852 and introduced the first "perpendicular stairway" in 1853. These factories—most of which are now long gone—attracted large numbers of Irish, Scotch, German, Polish, Hungarian, Italian, and Armenian immigrants, some of whose descendants still live in the area.

Hudson River Museum

Today, the town's biggest visitor attraction is the Hudson River Museum, partially housed in an impressive stone mansion overlooking the Hudson. Built by financier John Bond Trevor in 1876, Glenview Mansion is still outfitted with its original Victorian furnishings and art. Next door is a large, modern museum wing that presents first-rate exhibits on everything from regional flora and fauna to Hudson River history. Also at the museum are the exuberant Red Grooms Bookstores—both the first complete "environmental sculpture" designed by the artist (in 1977) and an actual bookstore—and the Andrus Planetarium, equipped with a Zeiss star machine. Every July and/or August, the museum hosts a **summer concert series.**

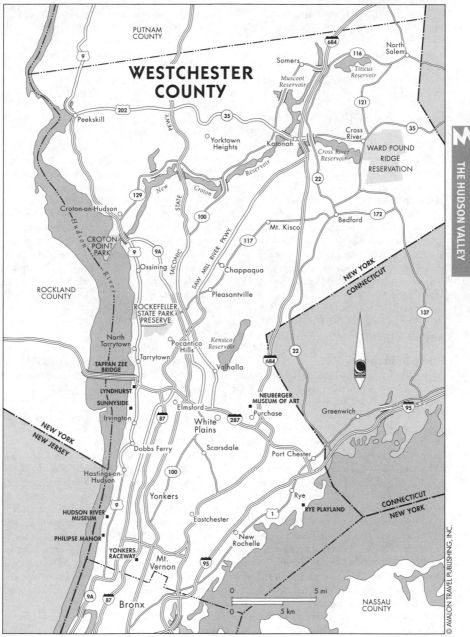

WESTCHESTER
COUNTY

PUTNAM
COUNTY

Peekskill

Yorktown
Heights

Somers

Muscoot
Reservoir

North
Salem

Titicus
Reservoir

Cross
River

WARD POUND
RIDGE
RESERVATION

Katonah

Cross River
Reservoir

Croton-on-Hudson

CROTON
POINT
PARK

Ossining

Mt. Kisco

Bedford

Chappaqua

Pleasantville

ROCKLAND
COUNTY

Hudson River

ROCKEFELLER
STATE PARK
PRESERVE

North
Tarrytown

Pocantico
Hills

Kensico
Reservoir

TAPPAN ZEE
BRIDGE

Tarrytown

Valhalla

LYNDHURST

SUNNYSIDE

Irvington

Elmsford

White
Plains

NEUBERGER
MUSEUM OF ART

Purchase

Greenwich

NEW YORK
NEW JERSEY

Dobbs Ferry

Scarsdale

Port Chester

Hastings-on-
Hudson

Yonkers

Rye

HUDSON RIVER
MUSEUM

Eastchester

RYE PLAYLAND

CONNECTICUT
NEW YORK

PHILIPSE MANOR

New
Rochelle

YONKERS
RACEWAY

Mt.
Vernon

Bronx

NASSAU
COUNTY

NEW YORK
CONNECTICUT

0   5 mi

0   5 km

THE HUDSON VALLEY

© AVALON TRAVEL PUBLISHING, INC.

The museum, 511 Warburton Ave., 914/963-4550, www.hrm.org, is at the north end of town; watch for signs on Route 9. Hours are Wed.–Sun. noon–5 P.M. and Friday 5–9 P.M. Admission is adults $5, seniors and children under 12 $3. Planetarium shows cost adults $5, seniors and children $3.

Untermyer Park

About a mile north of the Hudson River Museum, also overlooking the Hudson, is Untermyer Park. Once the garden of a long-gone mansion owned by lawyer Samuel Untermyer, the park is a beautifully landscaped but somewhat neglected place filled with opulent architecture. Inside its high brick walls are an amphitheater with Ionic columns, a classical Greek temple, reflecting pools lined with mosaics, and looming octagonal towers. Untermyer is one of the few gardens in America designed in the grand beaux arts–style; it is on the National Register of Historic Places.

The park, 914/377-6450, is on N. Broadway (Rte. 9) just south of Odell Avenue. It's open daily and admission is free.

Philipse Manor Hall

A few miles south of the Hudson River Museum, next door to a sad, well-worn park where the unemployed aimlessly linger, is the grand Philipse Manor Hall. The manor was originally built in the 1680s for Dutchman Frederick Philipse, who first came to New York to work as a carpenter for Gov. Peter Stuyvesant. Through his own skills and a strategic marriage, Philipse soon rose to become one of the most powerful men in the Hudson Valley. By the end of his life, he owned a 52,000-acre estate that covered virtually all of today's Westchester County.

Philipse was also a prominent Loyalist and one of the 200-plus Colonial New Yorkers who signed the Declaration of Dependence, swearing allegiance to King George III shortly after those 56 other Americans signed the Declaration of Independence.

Much of this history is on display in the manor hall, which also features elaborate rococo ceilings created out of papier mâché, an excellent collection of American portraits by Gilbert Stuart and others, and local history exhibits.

The manor, 29 Warburton Ave., at Dock St., 914/965-4027, www.philipsmanorfriends.org, is open April–Oct., Wed.–Sat. noon–5 P.M. and Sunday 1–4 P.M., and by appointment off-season. Suggested admission adults $3, seniors and students $2.

Yonkers Raceway

At run-down Yonkers Raceway, nighttime harness racing can be seen year-round. The smallest of the metropolitan-area tracks, Yonkers was first built in 1898 and was long known as the "poor man's racecourse." In fact, one of its earliest owners, chain store magnate James Butler, liked to pretend that he was actually poor. He once declined to play golf with John D. Rockefeller, Sr.—calling it a rich man's game—and rode around town in a rickety, out-of-date automobile. The raceway is at the intersection of Yonkers and Central Aves., off I-87 between Exits 2 and 4, 914/968-4200.

Food

The **Hudson River Museum Cafe,** 511 Warburton Ave., 914/963-4550, serves a good lunch in a setting overlooking the Hudson; average sandwich $6.

THREE RIVER TOWNS

Hastings-on-Hudson

Heading north from Yonkers on Route 9, you'll soon come to the tidy residential community of Hastings-on-Hudson. Like Yonkers, Hastings began to grow after the construction of the Hudson River Railroad in 1849. Famed newspaperman Horace Greeley was one of the town's earliest resident commuters. In 1862, a drunken mob, blaming Greeley for inciting the draft riots in New York City (see Midtown in the Manhattan chapter), started down from Ossining to blow up his house, but fortunately lost its resolve somewhere along the way.

Nineteenth-century Hastings was also home to Johannus Stalton, an eccentric button maker who may have been the model for Washington

Irving's Rip Van Winkle. In the early 20th century, the small town was known for its factories producing chemicals, copper, paving-blocks, and—during WW I—mustard gas.

Another prominent Hastings resident was Hudson River School painter Jasper Francis Cropsey, whose former home at 49 Washington Ave., 914/478-1372, is still standing and open to the public weekdays by appointment only. Located on the slopes of a steep hill overlooking the Hudson, the yellow Gothic-style **Cropsey House** contains about 100 of his luminous works, hung here and there throughout the house. Especially wonderful is the artist's former studio, an enormous wood-paneled room the walls of which are packed from floor to ceiling with canvases of all shapes and sizes.

Receiving raves from the locals is **Buffet de la Gare,** 155 Southside Ave., 914/478-1671, which serves classic French fare in an intimate setting; dinner entrées $21–31.

Dobbs Ferry

Route 9 continues north to Dobbs Ferry, another commuter community, this one named after Jeremiah Dobbs who in 1698 hollowed out a log to ferry passengers back and forth across the Hudson River. During the Revolutionary War, Benedict Arnold meant to betray West Point to Major Andre in Dobbs Ferry, but Andre was captured in Tarrytown before Arnold could get to him. Later, in the late 1800s and early 1900s, many Italians, imported into the country to build the great Hudson estates and the Croton Reservoir System, settled in Dobbs Ferry because it reminded them of the hill towns from which they had come. Due partly to these Italian immigrants, and partly to its long history, Dobbs Ferry has an interesting variety of architectural styles.

Dining options in town include the **Louisiana Cajun Cafe,** 25 Cedar St., 914/674-0706, where you'll find tasty cajun and creole dishes, and a

Most of the Hudson River isn't a river at all but an estuary, or arm of the sea; ocean tides run as far north as Albany. The Algonquin Indians, recognizing this natural phenomenon, called the Hudson "Muhheahkantuck," or "the river that flows both ways."

Dixieland jazz band on Saturday night; average entrée $14. The **Chart House,** foot of High St., near the railroad station, 914/693-4130, serves a wide selection of seafood dishes, along with steak and chicken. What makes the place unusual, however, are its superb views of the Hudson, Tappan Zee Bridge, and distant New York City; entrées average $15–30.

Irvington

Beyond Dobbs Ferry is the fashionable suburb of Irvington, where sections of Route 9 are lined with imposing stone walls. Named for Washington Irving, who once lived next door in Tarrytown, Irvington has been home to a number of famous people, including artist Albert Bierstadt and businesswoman Madame C. J. Walker.

Walker, the country's first African American female millionaire, was the daughter of former slaves who made her fortune by selling hair and beauty products. She began her career in 1905 in St. Louis, selling a patented hair straightener door to door. By 1910, she had earned enough money to open up the Madame C. J. Walker factory and laboratories in Indianapolis, Indiana. A woman of many interests and talents, Walker also founded a beauty school, established a center for black intellectuals, organized numerous social-welfare clubs, and was a leader in community affairs.

Walker's former home, an ornate brick mansion called **Villa Lewaro,** is located on North Broadway (Route 9) just north of Fargo Lane. Designed in 1917 by the first black architect of New York State, Ventner Woodson Tandy, the 34-room home is still privately owned but can be glimpsed from the road. In Walker's day, the Italian Renaissance mansion boasted a Gold Room—its ceilings trimmed with gold leaf—and a $25,000 organ that chimed on the quarter-hour and piped music throughout the house.

Walker's close friend Enrico Caruso came up with the name for the villa. It's an acronym of sorts gleaned from the name of Walker's daughter, Lelia Walker Robinson. Lelia later went on to establish the Dark Tower, a famous nightclub in Harlem. Upon her death in 1951, Villa Lewaro was left to the NAACP. Prohibitive upkeep expenses kept them from accepting the bequest, however, and the house was sold at auction.

Dining options in town include the **River City Grill**, 6 S. Broadway, 914/591-2033, serving eclectic American fare; average entrée $20.

TARRYTOWN AND SLEEPY HOLLOW

The most popular visitor destinations along Route 9 in Westchester are Tarrytown and Sleepy Hollow, formerly known as North Tarrytown. Despite being busy commuter villages, the towns are also home to four major historic sites (Sunnyside, Lyndhurst, Philipsburg Manor, and Kykuit) and a handful of smaller ones. Washington Irving once quipped that the name Tar-

GREAT RIVER ESTATES

Westchester County

Philipse Manor Hall, Yonkers: The oldest of the Hudson River estates, originally built for Dutchman Frederick Philipse in the 1680s. The grounds are no more, but the house is nicely restored.

Sunnyside, Tarrytown: Writer Washington Irving's former abode, a fairytale-like place "as full of angles and corners as an old cocked hat."

Lyndhurst, Tarrytown: Financier Jay Gould's magnificent Gothic Revival estate, designed by the great Alexander Jackson Davis in 1838.

Philipsburg Manor, Tarrytown: A carefully reconstructed 17th- and 18th-century manor house complete with costumed guides and a working gristmill. Especially good for kids.

Kykuit, Tarrytown: The former Rockefeller estate, famed for its magnificent grounds and collection of modern art. Only opened to the public in 1994.

Van Cortlandt Manor, Croton-on-Hudson: A lovely 18th-century stone-and-clapboard house that's half-English, half-Dutch. Not as well known as the Tarrytown mansions and therefore a good place to visit on summer weekends.

Putnam County

Boscobel, Garrison: An elegant, early 19th-century mansion that features an extraordinary collection of decorative arts from the Federal period. Outside are great views of Constitution Marsh.

Dutchess County

Locust Grove, Poughkeepsie: A romantic octagonal villa that was once the summer home of artist-

scientist-philosopher Samuel Morse, inventor of the telegraph. One of the smaller estates.

Roosevelt Estates, Hyde Park: Perhaps the most interesting of the Hudson River estates. Springwood, FDR's former home, is a deeply personal place; adjoining it is a first-rate library-museum. Nearby is Eleanor Roosevelt's equally personal Val-Kill. All three should be visited together.

Vanderbilt Mansion, Hyde Park: The most extravagant of the Hudson River estates, built in a posh beaux arts–style by McKim, Mead & White. Go here to drool over lavish furnishings, gold-leaf ceilings, Flemish tapestries, and the like.

Mills Mansion, Staatsburg: A vast, 65-room mansion on a hill, now in the midst of a much-needed restoration. Edith Wharton based the Trenor estate in *The House of Mirth* on Mills.

Wilderstein, Rhinebeck: A playful all-wooden Queen Anne mansion set on grounds designed by Calvert Vaux. One of the smaller estates.

Montgomery Place, Annandale-on-Hudson: Perhaps the loveliest of the river estates, with every line of the classical mansion, every inch of the romantic grounds perfectly in place. First built in 1802, remodeled in the 1860s by Alexander Jackson Davis.

Columbia County

Clermont, Germantown: A grand mansion, with an especially fine front lawn lined with black locust trees.

Olana, Hudson: Perched high on a hill is this eccentric Persian-style castle, built by Hudson River School painter Frederic Church in 1870.

rytown came from the early Dutch farmers' tendency to linger too long at the village tavern. But most historians agree that "tarry" is a corruption of *tarwe,* the Dutch word for wheat.

Sunnyside, Philipsburg Manor, and Kykuit, along with the historic Union Church of Pocantico Hills, are all operated by **Historic Hudson Valley,** an educational institution founded by John D. Rockefeller. The organization began back in 1937 when Philipsburg Manor was in danger of being torn down. Rockefeller bought it just in time; a few years later, in 1945, he did the same for Sunnyside. Today, Historic Hudson Valley also owns and operates the Union Church of Pocantico Hills (Tarrytown) and Van Cortlandt Manor (Croton-on-Hudson) in Westchester County, and Montgomery Place (Annandale-on-Hudson) in Dutchess County. All are well worth visiting. For general information, call 914/631-8200 or 800/448-4007, at www.hudsonvalley.org. Sunnyside and Kykuit may also be visited on one-day boat tours that leave from Manhattan; see Rail and River Tours in the introduction to this chapter.

Tarrytown is located at one of the Hudson River's widest points, the Tappan Zee. *Zee* means sea in Dutch, and the Tappan were an Algonquin tribe. Across the Tappan Zee runs the exquisite Tappan Zee Bridge, its graceful silver lines glinting in the sun.

For more information on Tarrytown and Sleepy Hollow, contact the **Sleepy Hollow Chamber of Commerce,** 80 S. Broadway, Tarrytown, NY 10591, 914/631-1705, www.sleepyhollowchamber.com.

Sunnyside

One of Tarrytown's earliest commuters was Washington Irving. In 1835 he moved into an old village farmhouse where he felt he could find the quiet he needed for his work, yet still be within easy reach of New York City. Almost immediately upon moving into his new abode, Irving began remodeling it, adding gables, dormers, and towers until the place was, as he described it, "as full of angles and corners as an old cocked hat."

Today the 17-room, wisteria-draped Sunnyside is open to the public. It's a charming, fairytale-like place, complete with costumed guides, a landscaped garden and pond, and a bevy of swans. Much of Irving's furniture, including his desk and old woodstove, is still in the house, along with many of his books. Just below Sunnyside runs the Hudson River Railroad, which Irving allowed to be built through his property on the condition that it stop to pick him up whenever he wanted.

Sunnyside, end of Sunnyside Ln., off Rte. 9 at the southern end of Tarrytown, 914/591-8763 or 800/448-4007, is open April–Dec., Wed.–Mon. 10 A.M.–5 P.M. The house tour costs adults $9, seniors $8, and students 6–17 $5; a grounds pass is $4.

Lyndhurst

Less than a mile north of Sunnyside is Lyndhurst, a magnificent Gothic Revival mansion designed by Alexander Jackson Davis in 1838. Originally built for William Paulding, a former New York City mayor, Lyndhurst was later owned by the unscrupulous financier Jay Gould. Among Gould's many questionable acts were his attempt to corner the gold market, which resulted in the disastrous panic of Black Friday, September 24, 1869, and his engineering of a deal that ruined his former business associate, Cyrus W. Field. Not surprisingly, none of this history is discussed at the site.

Covered with gables and chimneys, turrets and towers, Lyndhurst from the outside is a magical and mysterious place. Inside, however, it feels cold and dour, with much of the Goulds' heavy furnishings and art collection still in place. The mansion was in the possession of the family until 1961, when daughter Anna Gould deeded it to the National Trust.

Surrounding the mansion are 67 delightful though well-worn acres, complete with formal gardens, a children's playhouse, a bowling alley, nature paths, and spectacular views of the Hudson. Don't miss the romantic ruins of an enormous greenhouse, the 14 rooms of which once housed a renowned orchid collection.

Lyndhurst, 635 S. Broadway (Rte. 9), 914/631-4481, www.lyndhurst.org, is open May–Oct., Tues.–Sun. 10 A.M.–5 P.M.; Nov.–April, Sat.–Sun. 10 A.M.–5 P.M. Admission is adults $10, seniors

$9, students 6–17 $4. In summer, concerts are often held on the grounds on Saturday evening.

Tarrytown Village Sights

North of Lyndhurst is the compact but often congested village of Tarrytown, where on September 23, 1780, the town's residents captured Maj. John Andre, a British spy who had conspired with Benedict Arnold to betray West Point. A Captors Monument in Patriots' Park commemorates the event, but today Tarrytown is better known for its eclectic mix of corporate executives and blue-collar workers, neighborhood taverns and antique shops. Most of the latter are located along Main Street, a sleepy, old-fashioned thoroughfare that slopes gently down to the river.

The **Historical Society of the Tarrytowns,** 1 Grove St., 914/631-8374, offers eight rooms of exhibits tracing the area's history. One room is devoted to the capture of Major Andre. The Society is open Tues.–Thurs. and Saturday 2–4 P.M.; admission is by donation.

Old Dutch Church and Burying Ground

Continuing north a few miles, you'll come to Sleepy Hollow and the Old Dutch Church, at the corner of Broadway (Route 9) and Pierson Street. Dating back to 1685, it's believed to be the oldest church in continuous use in New York State. Except for its thick walls, little of the structure is original. The church, 914/631-1123, can be toured by appointment.

Surrounding the church is a romantic old Dutch cemetery that early settlers believed was haunted by a headless Hessian ghost. That local tale later became the inspiration for Washington Irving's *The Legend of Sleepy Hollow;* Irving took many of his characters' names from the cemetery's tombstones.

Adjacent to the old Dutch cemetery is the newer **Sleepy Hollow Cemetery,** 430 N. Broadway, a large, scenic, and peaceful place where Washington Irving, Andrew Carnegie, William Rockefeller, and other early movers and shakers are buried. Irving's grave is in a gardenlike family plot surrounded by about 50 other graves.

Philipsburg Manor

Across the street from the Old Dutch Church is Philipsburg Manor, a carefully reconstructed 17th- and 18th-century manor house, complete with a working gristmill and small farm. Once owned by Frederick Philipse of Yonkers, the estate is now usually jammed with tour buses and groups of schoolkids. Costumed guides describe life in Colonial times as visitors pass through a number of buildings, including a simple stone house, the gristmill, and a Dutch barn.

The Manor, 381 N. Broadway (Rte. 9), 914/ 631-3992 or 800/448-4007, is open April–Dec., Wed.–Mon. 10 A.M.–5 P.M. Admission is adults $9, seniors $8, and students 5–17 $5, so unless you're especially interested in Colonial history, or are traveling with kids, you'll probably be happier visiting the more unusual Sunnyside, Lyndhurst, or Kykuit.

Kykuit

Just northeast of Sleepy Hollow is the elite little village of Pocantico Hills, where Kykuit (KYE-cut) is located. Only opened to the public in 1994, Kykuit—Dutch for lookout—was built in 1908 by John D. Rockefeller, Sr. The house served as the weekend home for three generations of the Rockefeller family.

Compared to many of the estates along the Hudson, the beaux arts Kykuit is a relatively modest affair, done up in 18th- and 19th-century antiques. In fact, the house tour that leads through the main rooms of the first floor doesn't become especially interesting until it descends to Nelson Rockefeller's astonishing subterranean art gallery, filled with over 100 works by such modern masters as Picasso, Motherwell, Warhol, and Léger.

Even more wonderful are Kykuit's 87 acres of meticulously landscaped grounds, offering glorious views of the Hudson and Palisades. The gardens—complete with boxwood hedges, romantic arbors, and linden allées—are whimsically dotted with yet more masterpieces of modern art, including sculptures by Gaston Lachaise, Aristide Maillol, and Alexander Calder.

Kykuit, 914/631-9491 or 800/448-4007, can be visited only on two-hour escorted tours, which leave from Philipsburg Manor, 381 N. Broadway

(Rte. 9). Hours are April–Oct., Wed.–Mon. 10 A.M.–5 P.M. Reservations are not required; same-day tickets are given out on a first-come, first-served basis beginning at 9 A.M. Tickets cost adults $20; seniors, students and children over 12 $17.

Union Church of Pocantico Hills

A sleeper of a visitor attraction is the serene Union Church of Pocantico Hills in the center of Pocantico Hills. Inside are nine stunning stained-glass windows by Marc Chagall and a luminous rose window by Henri Matisse. The Chagall windows depict biblical scenes. The Matisse window—a leafy swirl of green, yellow, and blue—was the final work completed by the artist before his death.

The church, Bedford Rd. (Rte. 448), 914/631-8200 or 800/448-4007, is open to visitors for tours Apr.–Dec., Monday and Wed.–Sat. 11 A.M.–5 P.M. and Sunday 2–5 P.M. Tour cost is $3. Concerts are often presented on Sunday afternoon. Church events sometimes preempt visitor hours.

Rockefeller State Park Preserve

Once part of the Rockefeller estate, this well-kept 750-acre preserve is filled with meadows and woodlands, a small lake, and over 14 miles of mostly level carriage and walking paths. Maps are available at the entrance. The preserve is located northeast of North Tarrytown, just off Route 117. Watch for signs. It's open daily dawn to dusk.

Accommodations

One of the most romantic hideaways in Westchester County is the **Castle at Tarrytown Relais Chateaux,** 400 Benedict Ave., 914/631-1980, www.castleattarrytown.com or www.relais-chateaux.com. Perched on a hill overlooking the Hudson, this authentic castle with its 75-foot-high main tower was built around the turn of the century by the son of a Civil war general. Now a luxury establishment run by Swiss hoteliers, it offers 24 deluxe guest rooms and six luxury suites, four with working fireplaces. On the premises is the Equus restaurant (see Food, below). $285 d and up.

Also scoring high in the romance department is the regal **Dolce Tarrytown House Executive Conference Center,** E. Sunnyside Ln., Tarry-

town, 914/591-8200 or 800/553-8118, www .dolce.com. It's housed in two pristine 19th-century estates; one a Greek Revival mansion once owned by B&O Railroad executive Thomas King, the other a sprawling crenellated "castle" that belonged to tobacco heiress Mary Duke Biddle. Together, the estates boast lavish gardens, a well-equipped health club, a bowling alley, a billiard room, and jogging tracks. Individual travelers may feel a bit out of place here, as most of the guests are conference attendees, but rates are a surprisingly reasonable $159–219 d.

The modern **Tarrytown Courtyard,** 475 White Plains Rd., 914/631-1122, operated by Marriott, offers 140 rooms surrounding a pleasant pool and scenic courtyard. A cafe is on the premises ($129–169 d; weekend packages often available).

Food

Horsefeathers, 94 N. Broadway, 914/631-6606, is a cozy local institution, serving up home-style lunches and dinners ranging from simple sandwiches to filet mignon; average dinner entrée $16. The **Santa Fe,** 5 Main St., 914/332-4452, is a small but very popular spot specializing in make-your-own tacos, quesadillas, and—especially—fajitas (including shark); entrées are $9–15.

Serving both Portuguese and Brazilian fare is the casual **Caravela,** 53 N. Broadway, 914/631-1863. Brazilian music play softly in the background while broiled sardines, shrimp mango, charbroiled codfish, seafood stew, and other tasty dishes are served (entrées cost $15–23).

The ultra-romantic **Equus Restaurant** at the Castle at Tarrytown (see Accommodations, above), 914/631-3646, is spread out over several elegant rooms and an enclosed terrace that offers great views of the Hudson. On the menu is innovative French cuisine; the prix fixe lunch costs $35 and the prix fixe dinner, $64.

PLEASANTVILLE AND VICINITY

Usonia

Usonia is a unique residential community, laid out in the 1940s by Frank Lloyd Wright, who also designed three of the 48 homes. An acronym for the United States of North America, with an extra "i" thrown in, Usonia was designed to be an ideal housing enclave for the "average U.S. citizen," meaning the houses were affordable.

Tucked into wooded hills, Usonia is still an idyllic spot. The homes are built of wood and stone, with large windows and low rooflines to blend into the land. Two of the houses designed by Wright are on Orchard Brook Drive just off Usonia Road; the third—and best—is located at the end of Usonia Road. All are easily recognizable as Wright's work, and though privately owned, can be clearly viewed from the road.

To reach Usonia from Route 117, turn off onto Route 141. Bear left onto Bear Ridge Road and follow it to Usonia Road.

Accommodations and Food

Smack in the middle of the county is one of Westchester's more unusual lodgings, the 12-bedroom **Crabtree's Kittle House,** 11 Kittle Rd., off Rte. 117, Chappaqua, 914/666-8044, www.kittlehouse.com. Now over 200 years old, the building has been a carriage house, roadhouse, girls' school, guest house for the Mount Kisco Little Theater, restaurant, and inn. Henry Fonda and Tallulah Bankhead were among the actors who once overnighted here ($127 s, $147 d, includes continental breakfast).

Attached to the inn is a restaurant where lunch is served Mon.–Fri., brunch on Sunday, and dinner daily. The eclectic menu includes a mix of innovative Italian, French, Asian, and American dishes, and live jazz is often offered on the weekends. Dinner entrées $17–32.

For first-rate Spanish food, including tasty paella and gazpacho, check out **La Camelia,** 234 N. Bedford Rd., 914/666-2466, housed in a 150-year-old building in nearby Mount Kisco. Dinner entrées $18–25.

OSSINING

The next large village north of North Tarrytown is Ossining, a once-prosperous river town that has fallen on harder times. Ossining was known as Sing Sing until 1901, when the villagers grew tired of hearing jokes that linked their hometown with the state prison.

Sing Sing prison—original inspiration for the colloquial phrase, "to send up the river"—was built in Ossining in 1825–28 by a group of prisoners transported south from Auburn State Prison in the Finger Lakes region. The shackled prisoners toiled in the village's marble quarries to build their new home, and lived under what was then known as the "Auburn system"—silent group labor by day, solitary confinement by night.

When the prison was finished, things got even worse. Sing Sing became known as the "House of Fear," largely because of its tyrannical warden who often complained that he couldn't find keepers who were ruthless enough. The inmates were punished for laughing, talking, or making any sort of noise. Flogging and torture were routine. Reform didn't come until much later in the century.

Also noteworthy in town is the 1840 Croton Aqueduct, built to carry water across Kill Brook. Its two tiers of arches run right through town center near the intersection of Routes 9 and 133.

Exhibits on Ossining's prison history and the building of the Croton Aqueduct are on display at the **Ossining Heritage Area Visitor Center,** located inside the Ossining Community Building. The center also features two excellent films and publishes free walking-tour maps to the village. The center, 95 Broadway (Rte. 9), 914/941-3189, near the intersection of Rte. 133, on the river side, is open Mon.–Sat. 10 A.M.–4 P.M. Admission is free.

Not far from the center are the blackened ruins of the original prison destroyed in the early 1940s, and the massive walls of today's Sing Sing, which continues to operate as a maximum security prison housing more than 2,000 prisoners. The prison is just barely visible from **Lewis Engle Waterfront Park,** on the Hudson at Westerly Road, where you can sometimes hear the sounds of bells, clanking doors, and voices coming from within the prison walls.

Teatown Lake Reservation

A few miles northeast of Ossining, peaceful 650-acre Teatown Lake Reservation, 914/762-2912, www.teatown.org, holds a shimmering blue lake, hiking trails, an interpretive museum in two Colonial buildings, and wildflowers galore (over 200 species) in the spring, summer, and fall. Most of the flowers grow on an isolated two-acre island in the middle of the park, which is accessible only a few times a week by tour ($3 per person; reservations required). The interpretive center is open Tues.–Sat. 9 A.M.–5 P.M., Sunday 1–5 P.M.; admission is free. The grounds are open daily, dawn to dusk. To reach the reservation from Ossining, take Route 9 to 1600 Spring Valley Road.

CROTON-ON-HUDSON

Originally settled in the 1800s by the Irish and Italian stonemasons and laborers who were building the Croton Reservoir, Croton-on-Hudson is still a small and homey, working- and middle-class village. Its one fashionable period came around the time of WW I, when writer Max Eastman, poet Edna St. Vincent Millay, radical John Reed, and other Greenwich Village artists and intellectuals—looking to escape city life—acquired land in the hills overlooking the town. This bohemian influx caused great excitement among the locals, who were appalled by the sight of women wearing shorts, smoking cigarettes, and other modern behavior.

Croton Point Park

At the southern end of the village, off Rte. 9, is Croton Point Park, 914/271-3293, occupying a beak-shaped peninsula jutting out into the Hudson. Equipped with playgrounds, campgrounds, and a sandy beach, the park is often crowded but offers superb views of the Hudson. Hours are 8 A.M.–dusk; May–Sept., a steep $8 parking fee is charged to nonresidents of Westchester County.

Van Cortlandt Manor

Just east of Croton Point Park is the 18th-century Van Cortlandt Manor, another splendid estate owned by Historic Hudson Valley (see

THE HUDSON VALLEY

THE CROTON RESERVOIR SYSTEM

One of the most important events in New York City history occurred in June 1842, when the first water from manmade Lake Croton in Ossining flowed south along 32 miles of aqueduct into a giant reservoir at 42nd Street and 5th Avenue, Manhattan. Hundreds of church bells and a 38-gun salute rang out as the reservoir filled up with 150 million gallons of water. Then, and arguably still now, the Croton reservoir system (now greatly augmented with Catskill waters) provided New York with the best water system in the world; its creation allowed the city to escape the devastating 19th-century plagues of cholera and fire.

Although Lake Croton—made by damming the Croton River—was big, it wasn't big enough. In 1892, a new dam was begun just outside Ossining. Hundreds of homes were relocated and thousands of Italian stonemasons imported to construct what would become, 17 years later, the second-largest piece of hand-hewn masonry in the world. At 297 feet high and 2,168 feet long, the dam is said to have used as much stone as was used to build the Great Pyramid in Egypt.

Hiking the Old Croton Aqueduct

Westchester's portion of the Old Croton Aqueduct, shut down in 1955, is now a 26-mile-long linear state park popular with hikers and cross-country skiers. Throughout the park, the walkway is wide, level, and grassy, and half-ruined stone ventilation shafts jut up at one-mile intervals.

The trail begins on the east side of the New Croton Dam (closed to visitors) in Croton-on-Hudson, where it passes through a wooded area of pine, oak, and hemlock. In spring, the area is rife with dogwood and mountain laurel.

If you pick up the trail farther south, between Tarrytown and the Hudson River Museum in north Yonkers, you'll pass a number of historic churches and 19th-century estates, and get great views of the Hudson. One easy access point is located just opposite the Hudson River Museum.

For a free guide to hiking along the old aqueduct, contact the Friends of the Old Croton Aqueduct, 15 Walnut St., Dobbs Ferry, NY 10522; 914/693-5259. The organization also publishes a more elaborate history and guide available for $5.25.

Tarrytown and Sleepy Hollow, above). Oloff Van Cortlandt arrived in this county in 1638, and his son, Stephanus Van Cortlandt, became the first native-born mayor of New York City. The Van Cortlandt family once owned 87,000 acres of land stretching from Croton all the way east to Connecticut. They were staunch supporters of the Revolution, and among their many famous guests were Generals Washington and Lafayette.

The deed to the Van Cortlandts' property still hangs in the house, along with interesting family portraits. Also on display are period furnishings and a working kitchen where guides concoct Colonial recipes. Outside, a long, brick-paved walk flanked with flower beds leads to a restored 18th-century inn.

The manor, S. Riverside Ave., off Rte. 9, 914/271-8981 or 800/448-4007, is open April–Dec., Wed.–Mon. 10 A.M.–5 P.M. Admission is adults $9, seniors $8, students 6–17 $5.

NORTHEASTERN WESTCHESTER

Katonah

About 10 miles east of the Hudson River, where Route 35 meets I-684, is the well-heeled, picturesque village of Katonah. On broad, tree-lined Bedford Street alone are 55 historic homes, all part of an area that's on the National Register of Historic Places.

And therein lies a tale. The homes were moved here between 1895 and 1897 when the original village of Katonah, located a half mile away, was flooded to create Cross River Reservoir. That event is known locally as "the Inundation" or "the Move."

Katonah Avenue, running parallel to Bedford, is also lined with Victorian-era buildings that were moved from the old village. Among them are the creaky, old-fashioned **Charles Department Store,** 914/232-5200, still operated by descendants of the original owners.

Museum Mile

Route 22 just outside Katonah is known as Museum Mile because of the three major cultural institutions found there. Most famous among them is the **Caramoor Center for Music and the Arts,**

website: www.caramoor.org. An overgrown and romantic estate built in the 1930s by financier Walter Tower Rosen, Caramoor presents a highly acclaimed outdoor **music festival** every summer, featuring many top names in classical music and opera and a few top names in jazz.

But Caramoor, originally built by Rosen to house his outstanding art collection, is well worth visiting at other times as well. The fascinating main house, now known as the House Museum, was created by combining entire rooms from historic European buildings and surrounding them with a Mediterranean-styled shell. One of the bedrooms comes from a 1678 French chateau; the exquisite music room was originally part of a 16th-century Italian villa. Meanwhile, all around the house are sunbaked courtyards and deserted gardens strewn with weathering statuary.

The house museum, Girdle Ridge Rd., off Rte. 22, 914/232-5035, is open May–Oct., Wed.–Sun. 1 A.M.–4 P.M.; Nov.–April by appointment. Admission is adults $7, children under 16 free. The music festival runs late June–August. Tickets are $15–45, and reservations are recommended; box office, 914/232-1252.

Down the street from Caramoor is **John Jay Homestead.** Jay was president of the Continental Congress, first chief justice of the U.S. Supreme Court, and co-author of both the Federalist Papers and the Treaty of Paris (which ended the American Revolution). He retired here after leaving public office in 1801. The large wooden house with purple shutters and an inviting veranda is filled with period antiques and memorabilia that will appeal mostly to serious history buffs. Surrounding the house are landscaped gardens and a peaceful 900-acre farm.

The homestead, 400 Rte. 22, 914/232-5651, is open April–Oct., Wed.–Sat. 10 A.M.–4 P.M., Sunday noon–4 P.M.; call for winter hours. The grounds are open year-round. Admission is adults $3, seniors $2, children 5–11 $1.

Just north of John Jay's former home is the small but exceedingly lovely **Katonah Museum of Art,** Rte. 22 at Jay St., 914/232-9555, www.katonah-museum.org. Designed by Edward Larrabee Barnes, the museum features unusual temporary exhibits by major contemporary artists such as Milton Avery and Mark Rothko. Hours are Tues.–Fri. and Sunday 1–5 P.M., Saturday 10 A.M.–5 P.M., with extended hours in summer. Admission is free.

Somers

The main reason to visit tiny Somers, located about five miles north of Katonah, is the oddball **Somers Circus Museum,** housed on the top floor of the former Elephant Hotel. This once-elegant hostelry—now used for town offices—was built in 1825 by one Hachaliah Bailey, "the father of the American circus." Bailey made his fortune by importing the first elephant to the United States in 1796. For years he traveled up and down the East Coast showcasing his prized possession, whom he called Old Bet. He later expanded his business to include other exotic animals. Hachaliah's younger distant relative, James A. Bailey, perhaps inspired by the older man's example, later became one of the founders of the famed Barnum & Bailey Circus.

The walls of the somewhat musty museum, run by the Somers Historical Society, are covered with early circus posters and broadsides, while the main exhibit is a miniature of a three-ring circus with its canvas top removed. In the display cases are Old Bet's trappings—an elephant prod, the chain that kept the elephant from wandering—and a hodgepodge of memorabilia from dozens of other circuses.

To reach Somers from Katonah, take Route 35 to Route 100 north. The museum, intersection of Rts. 100 and 202, 914/277-4977, is only open Thursday 2–4 P.M., and the 2nd and 4th Sunday of each summer month, or by appointment. Admission is by donation.

On the way to Somers, you'll pass the vast, dark **Muscoot Reservoir,** part of the New York City water system. On Rte. 100 about one mile south of the Rte. 35 intersection is **Muscoot Farm,** 914/232-7118, an interpretive 1920s farm run by the county. Primarily of interest to kids, the 777-acre farm includes a dairy barn, horse barn, duck pond, pig pen, plenty of farm animals, and nature trails. It's open daily 10 A.M.–4 P.M.; summer daily 10 A.M.–6 P.M. Admission is free.

North Salem

If you travel east from Somers on Route 116, you'll come to North Salem, a rustic but moneyed one-stoplight burg surrounded by horse farms (the village is said to have more horses than people), wooded hills, and Titicus Reservoir. North Salem also boasts the Golden's Bridge Hounds, the only hunt club left in Westchester County. During the hunting season, the club's 70-odd members ride to the hounds on the golf courses surrounding the village as often as three times a week.

On a hill overlooking North Salem is the unusual **Hammond Museum and Japanese Stroll Garden.** Established by Natalie Hays Hammond in 1957, the place bills itself as a "cross-cultural center" for Eastern and Western arts. Inside the museum are changing exhibits on such subjects as antique Japanese fans and watercolors, while outside are meticulously designed Japanese gardens. Among the 15 different small landscapes—where everything means something—are the Waterfall Garden, the Azalea Garden, the Fruit Garden, and the Zen Garden.

Hammond was the daughter of John Hays Hammond, the mining engineer who discovered and developed the long-lost King Solomon Mines in South Africa. She traveled the world as a child, became engaged eight times but never married, and worked as a Broadway set and costume designer, an author, a miniaturist, and a needlepoint artist.

The museum, 914/669-5033, www.hammondmuseum.org, is at the top of Deveau Rd. off June Rd., a quarter-mile north of Rte. 116. Hours are May–Sept., Wed.–Sat. noon–4 P.M.; July–Aug. also open Sunday 11 A.M.–3 P.M.; Oct.–April, by appointment. Admission is adults $4, seniors and students $3.

Cross River

A few miles east of Katonah, where Rts. 35 and 121 meet, is 4,700-acre **Ward Pound Ridge Reservation,** 914/864-7317, the largest park in Westchester County. Laced with 35 miles of good, fairly rugged hiking trails, the park also features two rivers for fishing and a small **Trailside Nature Museum.** Trail maps are available at the museum. Year-round camping under lean-tos is available. Reservations are recommended and a two-night stay is required. No tents or trailers are allowed.

The park is open daily 8 A.M.–dusk; May–Sept., a $8 parking fee is charged to nonresidents of Westchester County. The museum, near the park entrance, is open Wed.–Sun. 10 A.M.–4 P.M.; admission is included in the park fee.

Shoppers might like to stop at nearby **Yellow Monkey Village**, on Rte. 35 just east of the Rte. 121 intersection in Cross River, 914/763-5848, an attractive collection of shops housed in reproduction 18th-century buildings. The shops sell everything from English antiques and Portuguese pottery to cooking utensils and silk flowers; open Tues.–Sunday.

Bedford

A few miles south of Katonah, where Route 22 meets Routes 121 and 172, is Bedford, another picture-perfect village. Here, pristine white 19th-century homes cluster around a village green, along with a carpenter-Gothic Presbyterian church and a nicely restored 1787 Court House—the oldest public building in Westchester County.

On a plaque in front of the Court House is printed a walking tour of the village. Take the tour and you'll pass the 1681 Old Burying Ground, as well as a general store, post office, and library that date back to the early 1800s. On Court Road just off the green is a row of shops selling antiques, clothing, and gifts.

Food

The romantic outdoor **Silk Tree Cafe** at the Hammond Museum, top of Deveau Rd., Salem, 914/669-6777, is an excellent place for lunch. It's open May–Sept., Wed.–Sat., and reservations are recommended; average main dish $9.

Situated in wooded seclusion on an estate that once belonged to J. P. Morgan is **Le Chateau**, junction of Rts. 35 and 123, South Salem, 914/533-6631. On the menu is innovative French fare; average entrée $28. Also in the area is the highly acclaimed **Auberge Maxime**, junction of Rts. 116 and 121, North Salem, 914/669-5450, which specializes in classical French cuisine

and is especially noted for its duck, prepared in a multitude of ways; average entrée $27.

SOUTHEASTERN WESTCHESTER
White Plains and Vicinity

Unless you're interested in shopping malls, there's not much reason to visit sprawling, suburban White Plains. Despite an appealing downtown, the city is an often-congested place with its share of urban problems. One of the city's most frequented malls is downtown on Post Road; others can be found along Central Avenue between White Plains and Scarsdale. The newest mall in the area is the **Westchester** on South Broadway, which houses about 150 upscale shops such as Neiman-Marcus and Nordstrom's.

The red, white, and chrome **City Limits Diner**, 200 Central Ave. at Rte. 119, 914/686-9000, may be the best reason to visit White Plains; when it opened in 1994, it won an AIA award for what *Esquire* called its "three-hundred seat homage to neon." On the menu are both traditional diner fare and gourmet treats.

In adjacent North White Plains, tucked away on the scruffy backside of town, you'll find a seldom-visited museum that was **Washington's headquarters** during the 1776 Battle of White Plains. Inside the dark and cool farmhouse—with its uneven floors and thick stone walls—are the chair and table that Washington once used, and an enormous boot that supposedly belonged to the general. The museum, 140 Virginia Rd., near N. Broadway, 914/949-1236, is open by appointment only. Not far away is **Battle Hill**, where the famed battle took place. To reach the museum from I-287, take Exit 6, head left past four stoplights to Virginia Road, and turn left again.

In nearby **Valhalla**, June brings the **Clearwater Hudson River Revival**, Westchester Community College, 75 Grasslands Rd., 800/677-5667. The festival offers music, dancing, and storytelling in one of the biggest annual events in the Hudson Valley.

Purchase

Despite its bland appearance, the wealthy community of Purchase is home to two remarkable cultural sites. The **Neuberger Museum,** on the campus of the State University of New York, is a first-rate art museum with an outstanding collection of modern works by such masters as Georgia O'Keeffe, Jackson Pollock, Henry Moore, Frank Stella, Mark Rothko, Edward Hopper, and—especially—Milton Avery. Avery was the favorite painter of the museum's founder, Roy Neuberger, and 20 of his canvases are on display.

The museum, 735 Anderson Hill Rd., 914/251-6100, www.neuberger.org, is open Tues.–Fri. 10 A.M.–4 P.M., Sat.–Sun. 11 A.M.–5 P.M. Admission is adults $4, seniors and students $2, children under 12 free.

Just down the street from the Neuberger are the **Donald M. Kendall Sculpture Gardens at PepsiCo.** Here at the corporate headquarters of the Pepsi-Cola company is an impressive outdoor sculpture garden filled with works by Alexander Calder, Jean Dubuffet, George Segal, Claes Oldenburg, and many others. Over 40 works are on display, scattered over carefully landscaped grounds complete with dramatic fountains. A path winds through the area, and a map is available at the entrance. The gardens, 700 Anderson Hill Rd., 914/253-2000, are open daily 9 A.M.–dusk; admission is free.

To reach either the museum or the gardens from I-684, take the State University of New York exit and follow the signs.

Rye

A sprawling suburban town located on Long Island Sound, Rye dates back to the 1660s when it was a notable stopping place on the old Post Road between New York and Boston. Then, as now, the town centered around Purchase Street, which today is lined with trees and sleepy **antique shops.**

The **Square House Museum,** 1 Purchase St., is housed in a 1760 farmhouse/tavern that once hosted everyone from Generals Washington and Lafayette to John and Samuel Adams. Later, the building served as a municipal hall, barbershop, and medical office. Tours of the museum, 914/967-7588, are offered Tues.–Fri. 1:30–3:30 P.M., call for Saturday hours. Admission is

by donation. To reach the museum from Port Chester, take Route 1 south to Purchase Street. From I-95 heading north, take Exit 20.

At the southern end of Rye is the wonderful **Rye Playland.** Built in 1928 as the nation's first amusement park, this dreamy art deco refuge still boasts its original green-and-cream buildings and a number of original rides, including the Carousel, the Derby Racer, the Old Mill boat ride, and the wooden Dragon Coaster. Also in the park are about 40 other rides, a crescent-shaped beach with a weathered boardwalk, an Olympic-size pool, and a lake where rowboats can be rented.

Most of the rides at Playland, end of Playland Pkwy., 914/813-7000, www.ryeplayland.org, are open May–Labor Day; midsummer hours are Tues.–Sun. noon–11 P.M. Admission is free, parking is $5–7. Major rides cost $2.50–5, kiddie rides cost $2.50. To reach Playland from downtown Rye, head east on Playland Parkway. From I-95, take Exit 19.

Paine Cottage

On the outskirts of New Rochelle stands the Thomas Paine Cottage, a quaint little saltbox beside a rocky brook. Paine was the Revolutionary War–era author of *The Age of Reason* and *The Rights of Man,* and he lived here and in New York City (see Greenwich Village in the Manhattan chapter) during the last years of his life.

Inside the house are Paine's chair and desk, and the old Franklin stove that was given to him by Benjamin Franklin. A letter of introduction from Franklin that helped Paine get his first writing job hangs on the wall. Also in the house are handsome handmade quilts and period antiques.

The cottage, 983 North Ave., 914/632-5376, www.thomaspaine.org, is open May–Oct., Fri.–Sun. 2–5 P.M. Suggested donation is adults $3, children $1. Across from the cottage is the Thomas Paine Memorial House, which contains more Revolutionary War–era exhibits. To reach the cottage from Rye, head south on Route 1 to North Avenue.

Rockland County

Rockland County is named for the great outcroppings of rock that tower over the Hudson River at the northern end of the county. At only 176 square miles, Rockland is one of the smallest counties in the state. Just 33 miles northwest of New York City, it holds a predictable share of nondescript suburbs, congested highways, and glass-sheathed corporate headquarters. But a closer look reveals a rich tapestry of historic river towns, Revolutionary War sites, and growing ethnic communities. Due largely to the preservation efforts of its concerned citizenry, Rockland is about 30 percent green. Two of Hudson Valley's biggest state parks—Bear Mountain and Harriman—straddle the Rockland/Orange County border here.

During WW II, Rockland was home to Camp Shanks, one of the two largest Army ports of embarkation on the East Coast. About 1.3 million troops passed through here on their way to North Africa and England. Today Camp Shanks, now known as Shanks Village, is the largest veterans housing complex in the country. It's located in the southeastern part of the county, between Tappan and Blauvelt.

First-time visitors will probably want to concentrate on the historic river towns of Nyack and Tappan, and on Harriman and Bear Mountain State Parks.

Information

For more information, contact **Rockland County Tourism,** 18 New Hempstead Rd., New City, NY 10956, 845/353-5533 or 800/295-5723, www.rockland.org, is open Mon.–Fri. 8 A.M.–4 P.M. The tourism office also operates an events hotline at the same number.

NYACK

First inhabited by the Nyack Indians, Nyack was settled by Dutch farmers in the mid-1600s and became home to thriving shipping, boatbuilding, shoe- and cigar-manufacturing industries in the 1800s. The village fell into decline after the De-

pression, but in the 1970s, it was reborn as an antiques and arts-and-crafts center. Today, almost all of Nyack's quaint Victorian downtown has been restored, while homes of the rich and famous perch on the steep wooded hills surrounding the village. Famous residents here have included Edward Hopper, Ben Hecht, Carson McCullers, Helen Hayes, Jonathan Demme, Ellen Burstyn, Harvey Keitel, and Toni Morrison.

To reach Nyack from New York City, take the Palisades Parkway north to Exit 4 and follow Route 9W north. To reach Nyack from Westchester County, take I-287 to Exit 10 and follow signs.

Edward Hopper House

The birthplace and home of painter Edward Hopper (1882–1967) is a two-story clapboard house on North Broadway. The son of a prosperous dry-goods merchant, Hopper grew up in Nyack and held title to the house until his death, even though he left the village in 1910 to live in New York City. Hopper is buried in Nyack's Oak Hill Cemetery.

The rooms of the Hopper House are wonderfully evocative—filled with a clean white light reminiscent of the artist's work. Unfortunately, only a small section of one room is devoted to Hopper's art. Most of the house is a gallery showcasing the work of local artists, while out back is a picturesque garden where concerts are sometimes presented.

The house, 82 N. Broadway, 845/358-0774, www.edwardhopperhouseartcenter.org, is open Thurs.–Sun. noon–5 P.M. Admission is by donation.

Pretty Penny

Continuing up North Broadway to the district known as Upper Nyack, you'll pass a number of grand Victorian estates. Helen Hayes once lived with her husband, playwright Charles MacArthur, at 233 N. Broadway, a white house with a widow's walk that she called "Pretty Penny."

In 1939, during the Depression, Hayes and MacArthur commissioned a portrait of their

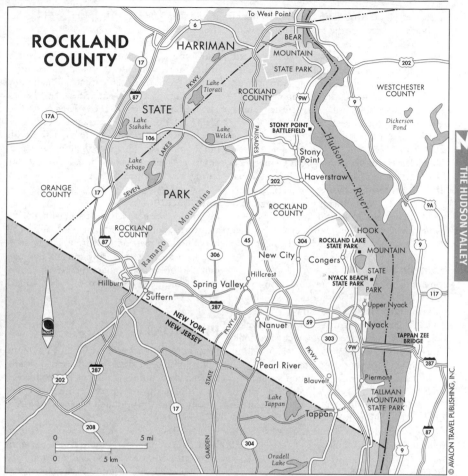

THE HUDSON VALLEY

house from a resentful Edward Hopper. Hopper took the work because he needed it, but he disdained working on commission as it reminded him of the days when he'd been forced to hire himself out as a commercial illustrator.

Recalled Hayes in 1981, "As a performer I just shriveled under the heat of this disapproval. I backed into a corner and there I stayed in the dark, lost . . . really, I was utterly unnerved by this man."

Today, Hopper's remarkable portrait, *Pretty Penny*, hangs in the Smith College Museum of Art.

Parks and Recreation

Right in town, the riverfront **Memorial Park,** off Main Street, offers great views of the Hudson. Two miles farther north is **Nyack Beach State Park,** off North Broadway, a riverfront stretch offering hiking, fishing, picnicking, and more great views. Trails lead from here to **Rockland Lake State Park,** which centers on a small lake just off Route 9W in Congers. Both state parks, 845/268-3020, are open daily dawn–dusk, and $8 parking fees apply May–October.

At the steep northern end of North Broadway

you'll find **Hook Mountain State Park,** offering bird's-eye views of the Hudson, along with hiking and biking trails. Once a favorite campground among Native Americans, the park is said to be haunted by the Guardian of the Mountain, a Native American medicine man who appears every September during the full moon to chant the ancient harvest festival. A hawk watch is held in the park every spring and fall.

Entertainment

The **Helen Hayes Performing Arts Center,** 123 Main St., 845/358-6333, is a 700-seat center that presents first-rate theater, concerts, lectures, and dance. Living, rollicking **O'Donoghue's,** 66 Main St., 845/358-0180, is a local pub favorite, where you're bound to hear many a tale; live Irish bands perform on Monday night.

Shopping

Most of the village's shops are found along Main Street (Route 59) and South Broadway. Among them are **Hand of the Craftsman,** 5 S. Broadway, 845/358-3366, offering kaleidoscopes, kaleidoscopes, kaleidoscopes, and the **Pickwick Book Store,** 8 S. Broadway, 845/358-9126, selling new and old books and art postcards.

Nyack also hosts many street fairs and festivals. Three of the biggest, all featuring about 200 vendors, are the Art, Craft & Antiques Dealers' Fairs, usually held on the third Sunday of May, July, and October. Call 845/353-6981 for more information.

Accommodations

Several motels are located on the outskirts of town. At the junction of Rte. 59 and Waldron Rd., you'll find the **Super 8 Nyack,** 845/353-3880 ($69–99 d). At the junction of Rts. 303 and 59 is the **Nyack Motor Lodge,** 845/358-4100 ($65–80 d).

Food

Nyack is filled with eateries of all styles and price ranges. Among the inexpensive spots, simple, casual **Strawberry Place,** 72 S. Broadway, 845/358-9511, is a local favorite that's especially good for breakfast. **Temptations,** 80 ½ Main

St., 845/353-3355, is the place to go for ice cream and desserts.

Among moderately priced restaurants, the **Hudson House,** 134 Main St., 845/353-1355, housed in an historic firehouse, is a good choice, offering an eclectic American cuisine and patio dining in summer; average entrée $15. For the best Thai food in town, try the cheery **King & I,** 91-93 Main St., 845/353-4208; average entrée $14.

In nearby West Nyack, find the **Clarksville Inn,** 1 Strawtown Rd., 845/358-8899, serving innovative American cuisine in a historic 1850s setting; average entrée $16.

Information

In summer, when Nyack is overrun with tourists, an **information booth** operates daily at the corner of Main Street and Broadway. The booth is also open weekends in spring and fall. For year-round information, contact the Nyack Chamber of Commerce, P.O. Box 677, NY 10960, 845/353-2221.

PIERMONT

Just south of Nyack is the village of Piermont, which in its heyday was a bustling commercial center at the terminus of the Erie Railroad. Today it's a quieter, less touristy version of Nyack. Woody Allen filmed much of *The Purple Rose of Cairo* here in 1983.

Most of the village's shops and art galleries are located on or just off Piermont Avenue. Among them are **Boondocks,** 490 Piermont Ave., 845/365-2221, an "environmental marketplace" selling rainforest kits and the like; and **Piermont Flywheel Gallery,** 220 Ash St., 845/365-6411, which features the work of its 24 co-owners, all artists and sculptors.

In the center of town is **Piermont Pier,** which extends out into the river about a mile. Built by Chinese immigrants to allow the railroad easier access to Hudson River ships, the pier was used as a point of debarkation for troops leaving Camp Shanks during WW II (see chapter Introduction). Now, the pier is delightfully overgrown with cottonwoods, poplars, and goldenrod. From along its length you'll have unobstructed views of the Tappan Zee bridge and **Piermont Marsh,** a 950-acre wetland and bird sanctuary.

If you're interested in actually visiting Piermont Marsh, enter **Tallman Mountain State Park** just south of the pier and follow the bike path to the shore. The preserve, covered with wildflowers in the spring, is one of the most important fish-breeding areas along the Hudson and an excellent birdwatching spot. The marsh and state park, 845/359-0544, are open daily dawn–dusk, and there's a $5 parking fee in summer.

Architecture buffs might want to photocopy the detailed **walking guide** to Piermont on file at the Piermont Library, 153 Hudson Terrace, 845/359-4595. The guide points out that many buildings in town were built in the late 1800s with "Plans by Mail"—early pre-fab kits that came with pre-cut boards and hardware in the Queen Anne, Revival, and Federal styles.

Food

A number of restaurants are located along Piermont Avenue. Classiest among them is **Xavier's of Piermont,** 506 Piermont Ave., 845/359-7007, a highly acclaimed fine dining establishment serving contemporary American fare. The prix fixe dinner costs $60, and the chef's tasting menu costs $80 (across the river in Garrison is the original Xavier's). Next door is the informal but trendy **Freelance Cafe and Wine Bar,** 506 Piermont Ave., 845/365-3250, serving an eclectic, innovative cuisine with Asian, French, and Italian influences; average entrée $20.

For a simpler meal, head over to **Pasta Amore,** 200 Ash St., 845/365-1911, where you'll find a wide variety of pasta dishes; average entrée $14. Or, try the **Sidewalk Cafe,** 482 Piermont Ave., 845/359-7007, serving American food with Southwestern accents; average entrée $15.

Nightlife

One of the Hudson Valley's oldest and best music clubs is the **Turning Point,** 468 Piermont Ave., 845/359-1089, www.turningpoint.com. Low-ceilinged and filled with dark wood, the club presents mostly folk and folk-rock, along with some jazz and blues. Among those who've performed here in recent years are Marshall Cren-

shaw and the Dirty Dozen Brass Band. Tickets run $12–25. A favorite among both locals and visitors, the club also serves a moderately priced lunch and dinner. Dishes range from angel-hair pasta to sliced duck; average dinner entrée $15.

TAPPAN

To the west of Piermont is the historic town of Tappan, the first town in New York State to establish an official historic district. Its Main Street is flanked with many nicely restored 18th- and 19th-century buildings, and in the center of town is a village green that once held public stocks and a whipping post.

Revolutionary War Sites

Tappan is also associated with both the beginning and the end of the planned betrayal of West Point by Benedict Arnold and British major John Andre during the Revolutionary War. It was in the DeWint House on Livingston Avenue that Washington entrusted West Point to Arnold, and it was in the Mabie House on Main Street that Andre—after his capture in Tarrytown— was imprisoned before being hanged.

Both buildings are still standing and open to the public. The **DeWint House,** 20 Livingston Ave., 845/359-1359, is now a bona fide museum holding Washington memorabilia, artifacts regarding Masonic history, and information about the Andre trial. Washington was headquartered here in 1780 and 1783, and was a Mason for 47 years. On the day of Andre's execution, Gen. Washington closed the shutters to his room. The house is open daily 10 A.M.–4 P.M. and is stocked with free walking guides to Tappan.

The Mabie House is now better known as the **Old '76 House,** 110 Main St., 845/359-5476, and is a dark, low-ceilinged establishment that has functioned as a tavern and restaurant since 1800. Andre's former bedroom is now a dining room.

Also connected with Andre is the **Andre Monument** on Old Tappan Road at Andre Hill Road. Here, a large crowd of spectators, held back by 500 infantrymen, watched Andre's execution on October 2, 1780. Only upon seeing the hangman's noose did Andre realize that his request to be shot as a soldier, rather than hung as a spy, was not to be granted. Impatient with his slow-moving hangman—a sympathetic fellow prisoner—Andre placed the noose around his own neck and the handkerchief around his own eyes. "All I request of you gentlemen," he said before the final signal was given, "is that you bear witness to the world that I die like a brave man."

Camp Shanks WWII Museum

The old processing center for the 1.3 million soldiers who were shipped from the Piermont Point to Normandy during WWII has been turned into a small museum. Inside the recreated barracks, find exhibits and memorabilia documenting military life, along with a camp model and vintage training films. The museum, at the junction of Rts. 303 and 340, Orangeburg, between Tappen and Blauvelt, 845/638-5244, is open Memorial Day–Labor Day, Sat.–Sun. 10 A.M.–3 P.M.

Food

The **Old '76 House,** 110 Main St., 845/359-5476, complete with exposed beams, Dutch tiles, and fireplaces, specializes in traditional Ameri-

can fare for lunch and dinner. A jazz vocalist or pianists often performs on the weekend; average dinner entrée $17. **Giulio's,** 154 Washington St., 845/359-3657, is a Tappan institution that's been serving Italian cuisine in an incongruous Victorian setting for over 20 years; average entrée $17.

Mongolian barbecue is the specialty of the house at the new **Khan's Mongolian Garden,** 588 Rte. 303, Blauvelt, 845/359-8004, where diners choose their preferred fresh protein (beef, lamb, chicken, tofu, shrimp), vegetables, and sauces from a buffet table before handing them over to be cooked. Minced lamb dumplings and delicious soups are on the menu, too; the buffet lunch—including appetizers, soup, buffet, and dessert—costs about $15,

CENTRAL ROCKLAND COUNTY

Along Route 304

Two towns on Route 304 are worth a mention. North of I-87/287 is **New City,** where history buffs will want to visit the first-rate **Historical Society of Rockland County,** 20 Zukor Rd., off New Main St., 845/634-9629,

The Old '76 House, which once served as jail for Benedict Arnold's British co-conspirator, Major John Andre, has been a tavern and restaurant for more than a century.

www.RocklandHistory.org. Housed in both a modern building and a restored 1832 Dutch farmhouse, the museum offers early 19th-century furniture, textiles, and prints; Lenape Indian exhibits; historic toys and dolls; open-hearth cooking demonstrations; and temporary exhibits of local artists. Hours are Tues.– Sun. 1–5 P.M. Admission is adults $4, children under 12 $2.

South of I-87/287 on Rte. 304 is **Pearl River,** where you'll find the county's poshest hostelry: the five-story **Pearl River Hilton,** 500 Veterans Memorial Dr., 845/735-9000. The 150-room hotel, all done up in pastels and light woods, is built to resemble a giant modern chateau ($199–329 d with weekend packages often available).

Spring Valley and Vicinity

Once a resort destination to which city dwellers flocked to escape the summer heat, Spring Valley began to boom after the building of Tappan Zee bridge. During the 1960s, many working- and middle-class families, including large numbers of Hasidim, moved here. In more recent years, thousands of new immigrants, mainly from Haiti, Jamaica, Guatemala, and El Salvador, have moved in.

These new immigrants have brought to Spring Valley a new energy and cosmopolitan flavor, especially along **North Main Street,** where you'll find lots of small Haitian shops and grocery stores. Rockland County's Haitian community, estimated to number between 17,000 and 25,000, is the largest non-urban Haitian community in the United States.

Also in Spring Valley is the **Rockland Center for Holocaust Studies.** Unique to the New York City region, the center's two-room exhibit hall begins with pre-war European life, documents the horrors of the ghettos and concentration camps, and commemorates the courage of the Holocaust survivors, a number of whom settled in Rockland County. The center, 17 S. Madison Ave., 845/356-2700, also sponsors temporary exhibits, lectures, and films. Hours are Sept.–June, Sun.–Thurs. noon–4 P.M.; July–Aug., Tues.–Thurs. noon–4 P.M. Admission is free.

THE RAMAPO MOUNTAINS

Continuing west on I-87/287, you'll pass through a nondescript region of corporate headquarters before coming to the craggy foothills of the Ramapo Mountains. At nearly 600 million years old, the Precambrian Ramapos—which spill over into New Jersey—are one of the oldest land masses in North America. At one time, their slopes—now eroded and dotted with erratics left during the Ice Age—constituted a mountain system as grand as the Rockies.

In New York, most of the Ramapos fall within two very popular state parks—Harriman and Bear Mountain (see below). The parks were created largely through the efforts of Mrs. E. H. Harriman, widow of the railroad tycoon Edward Harriman and mother of the late statesman W. Averell Harriman. When the state proposed building a prison at Bear Mountain in 1908, Mrs. Harriman offered to give the Palisades Interstate Park Commission 10,000 acres in return for dropping the project. The proposal was accepted and since then the parks have been significantly enlarged through other gifts and purchases.

Harriman State Park

Straddling Rockland and Orange Counties is Harriman State Park, a 46,000-acre preserve that is considerably less developed than its better-known neighbor to the north, Bear Mountain State Park. Through the heart of Harriman runs **Seven Lakes Drive,** which hugs the shores of only a small portion of the many bodies of water to be found in this preserve. Two of the most spectacular of these are crystal-clear **Lake Tiorati** and **Lake Sebago.** Ironically, their Indian names—bestowed upon them by white men eager to create a romantic atmosphere—are not local, but rather names that come from Western tribes. Both of the large, manmade lakes have swimming beaches.

About 200 miles of **marked trails** loop through Harriman and its neighbor, Bear Mountain. Basic information on some of these trails can be picked up at the headquarters of the Palisades Interstate Park Commission, Bear Mt., Rte. 9 W, 845/786-2701. For detailed information and

THE RAMAPOUGH PEOPLE

In the foothills of the Ramapo Mountains live the Ramapough people, who trace their mixed ancestry to Munsee Indians, early freed blacks and escaped slaves, and the Dutch. Most of the 3,000 or so Ramapoughs live in or near **Hillburn,** a small town just south of Harriman State Park, and in Ringwood and Mahwah, New Jersey.

The first permanent residents of the Ramapos were the Munsees, a subgroup of the Algonquins who moved into the area after being displaced from the lowlands by the Europeans around 1700. The Munsees were joined by early settlers—both black and white—around 1750. Many of the settlers came to the area to escape discrimination or the law, or to achieve a level of independence impossible in more settled communities.

Living on the fringes of developing America, the Ramapoughs survived by hunting, subsistence farming, and selling crafts, fruits, and berries door to door. Treated as outcasts throughout much of the 19th and 20th centuries, they were the subject of much local gossip and lore. Many disparagingly called them the "Jackson Whites" and "Jackson Blacks" in reference to a trader who allegedly furnished hundreds of white and black prostitutes

for His Majesty's troops in Manhattan during the Revolution. After the war, so the story goes, the prostitutes were driven out of New York City and into the Ramapos.

Only since WW II and the influx of new residents have local attitudes regarding the Ramapoughs started to change. In fact, during the past few decades, several civic groups composed of both the mountain people and their neighbors have been actively working to improve community relations.

Since 1980, too, the Ramapough people have been petitioning the federal government to acknowledge them as a legitimate American Indian tribe. So far, that recognition—which would bring many benefits, including housing and health care—has been withheld. The government says that the Ramapoughs have not conclusively proven their Indian heritage. However, the group has been recognized by the State of New Jersey, New York State, and numerous other Indian tribes. And with or without federal recognition, the Ramapoughs continue to practice many of their Indian traditions. They divide themselves into three clans—the Turtle, Deer, and Fox—elect a chief and council, and carry tribal identity cards.

maps, contact the **New York–New Jersey Trail Conference,** 156 Ramapo Valley Rd., Mahwah, NJ 07430, 201/512-9348, www.nynjtc.com. The park also offers an excellent, 200-site **campground** where basic rates start at $15; call 800/456-CAMP for reservations.

Harriman is open daily 8:30 A.M.–dusk. From May to October, parking is $7. Seven Lakes Drive can be most easily accessed via I-87, Route 17, or the Palisades Parkway.

Just south of the park, on a mountaintop near Hillburn, is **Mount Fuji,** Rte. 17, 845/357-4270, a big, glitzy Japanese steakhouse offering great views of the valley below; entrées range from $19–37. Nearby Suffern is the site of a large **Native American Festival,** 845/353-5533, usually held in late October. On the western border of the park are the Clove Furnace Historic Site, Tuxedo Park, and Sterling Forest (see

Southern Orange County, under Orange and Putnam Counties, below).

Bear Mountain State Park

When New Yorkers think about getting out of the city for a day-hike, they think about Bear Mountain—one of the most popular recreational areas in the region. Abutting Harriman to the north, the park offers dramatic views of the Hudson River and—on the clearest of days—the New York City skyscrapers. Because Bear Mountain can get very crowded on weekends, it's best to come during the week. This is also no place for the outdoors purist; almost every inch of the 5,000-acre park has been trodden over many times.

To hike to the top of Bear Mountain and back takes three to four hours. For those who prefer to drive to the summit, **Perkins Memorial Drive** offers stunning overlooks and historic markers that tell of the Revolutionary War battles that took place here. Legend has it that Hessian Lake was named for the many dead Hessian soldiers whose bodies were weighted and dumped into the lake after the battle of Fort Clinton. The fort's ruins are nearby.

Though overrun with crowds on summer weekends, the rustic **Bear Mountain Inn,** Rte. 9 W, 845/786-2731, is a charming spot, now over 80 years old. The inn's 61 rooms are divided among the Main Inn, four small stone lodges, and the Overlook, a hotel with 24 rooms near Hessian Lake. Come on a weekday in fall and you'll have the place to yourself ($89–99 d).

Also in the inn are an inexpensive cafeteria and a restaurant serving standard American fare (average entrée $14). Other attractions include the **Trailside Museum and Wildlife Center,** ball fields, a swimming pool, and an ice-skating rink.

Bear Mountain State Park, Palisades Pkwy. and Rte. 9 W, 845/786-2701, is open daily 8:30 A.M.–dusk. A $7 per vehicle use fee is charged daily May–Sept. and weekends the rest of the year. Perkins Drive is open March–October. The museum and inn are open daily year-round; museum hours are 9 A.M.–5 P.M. To reach Bear Mountain from the south, take Palisades Parkway or Route 9W. From Harriman State Park, head northeast on Seven Lakes Drive. An excellent **Park Visitor Information Center,** 845/786-5003, equipped with many books and maps

about New York State, is located between exits 16 and 17 off the Palisades Parkway.

STONY POINT

South of Bear Mountain is **Stony Point Battlefield,** Park Rd., off Rte. 9 W, 845/786-2521, where the British army that was threatening West Point was based in the summer of 1779. Stony Point was captured by the Americans in a daring midnight raid led by Gen. "Mad" Anthony Wayne. A tour of the battlefield takes visitors through a small interpretive museum, past the ruins of the British fortifications, and past the oldest lighthouse on the Hudson River. All around is lots of beautiful countryside. The site is open April–Oct., Wed.–Sat. 10 A.M.–5 P.M., Sunday 1–5 P.M. Parking is $7.

The town of Stony Point is also the home of **Penguin Repertory Company,** Cricket Town Rd., 845/786-2873, a nonprofit professional acting troupe that presents plays and readings in a converted 1880s barn. Before the show, you might want to grab a bite at **Annie's Restaurant,** 149 Rte. 9 W, 845/942-1011. Since 1952, motorists have been coming to this drive-in, which serves its fast food in paper plates shaped like Chevy convertibles. According to the manager, the eatery attracts lots of bikers and soap-opera stars. Bruce Springsteen is also a fan.

Orange and Putnam Counties

Eastern Orange County is one of the most popular tourist destinations in the Hudson Valley, and it shows. You'll see more signs directing you towards visitor attractions here than in most of the region, and more tourist-oriented shops. Most visitors head first to the justifiably popular West Point, perched on cliffs overlooking the Hudson, and then to the important Revolutionary War sites near Newburgh or the spectacular Storm King Art Center—surely one of the most beautiful outdoor sculpture parks in the world. Afterward, though, many get trapped in the Central Valley region, where the sprawling Woodbury Common Factory Outlets and the extremely commercial Brother-

hood Winery act as magnets to dollars, checkbooks, charge cards, and loose change.

In contrast, the western part of Orange County is still largely rural farm country. In the laidback county seat of Goshen is a unique museum dedicated to trotters, pacers, and harness racing. Near Pine Island is the "black dirt" or "drowned lands" farming region dotted with produce stands and pick-your-own farms. At the southeastern end of the county, straddling the Rockland border, are the adjoining Bear Mountain and Harriman State Parks.

Putnam County, located directly across the Hudson River from Orange, is also full of quiet

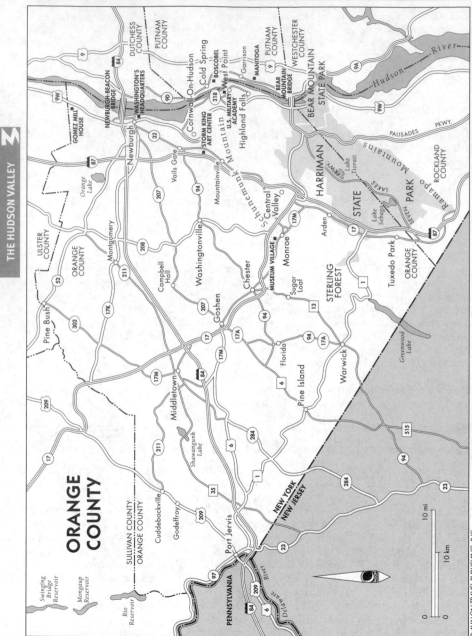

small towns. Along its riverbank are the Victorian village of Cold Spring and a splendid Federal-style mansion known as Boscobel. And eastern Putnam County holds acres upon acres of lakes and reservoirs. Like northeastern Westchester County, much of Putnam County (two-thirds to be exact) is part of New York City's watershed system, which has helped to preserve its rural character. The **Appalachian Trail** cuts through both Orange and Putnam Counties; call the Palisades Interstate Park Commission, 845/786-2701, for more information.

First-time visitors will probably want to concentrate on West Point and Storm King Mountain in Orange County, and on Cold Spring and Garrison in Putnam County.

Information

For more information on Orange County, contact the **Orange County Division of Tourism,** 30 Matthews St., Goshen, NY 10924, 845/291-2136 or 800/762-8687), www.orangetourism.org. A **visitor information booth** is located at Woodbury Common, Rte. 32, Central Valley (at Exit 16 off I-87), 845/928-6840. Both are open Mon.–Fri. 10 A.M.–5 P.M. For more information on Putnam Country, contact the **Putnam County Visitors Bureau,** 110 Old Rte. 6, Bldg. 3, Carmel, NY 10512, 845/225-0381 or 800/470-4854, www.visitputnam.org.

For more information on any of the state parks, campgrounds, or historic sites described below, visit the website: www.nysparks.org.

WEST POINT

The Hudson Valley between Dunderberg Mountain to the south and Storm King Mountain to the north is known as the **Hudson Highlands.** Along this 15-mile stretch, the Hudson River, narrowing and deepening, cuts through the Appalachian Mountain Range, creating a spectacular rocky gorge.

About halfway up this stretch, where the river takes a sharp turn, is a rocky outcropping known as West Point. With its strategic views of both sides of the river, it's easy to see why it was such an important stronghold during the Revolutionary War.

On West Point today sits the country's oldest and best-known **U.S. Military Academy,** website: www.usma.edu, authorized by Congress in 1802. About 4,400 cadets are enrolled here each year. Graduates have included Generals Grant, Lee, Pershing, MacArthur, and Eisenhower; misfits have included James Whistler and Edgar Allan Poe.

Near the Thayer Gate entrance to the Gothic, fortresslike academy is a giant **visitor center,** Rte. 218, 845/938-2638. The center stocks informative brochures and maps, and screens a short movie about the cadets' lives. It's open daily 9 A.M.–4:45 P.M.

Next door to the visitor center is the **West Point Museum,** Rte. 218, 845/938-2203, filled with a wide and fascinating array of exhibits on military history. Here you'll find everything from a Stone Age axe to weapons used in Vietnam and the Gulf War; dioramas of famous battles fought between the 16th and 20th centuries; the letter that Einstein wrote to President Roosevelt urging him to begin research on the uses of plutonium; and a pistol that once belonged to Adolf Hitler. One philosophical panel, simply entitled "Reflections," includes quotes by famous military leaders throughout history—from Thucydides to Eisenhower. The museum is open daily 10:30 A.M.–4:15 P.M. Admission is free.

Since the September 11 attacks, the academy can only be visited via escorted tours, which leave throughout the day, except during special events such as football games (call the visitor center for exact tour departure hours). Highlights include the **Cadet Chapel,** lined with lovely stained-glass windows donated by graduated classes; the **Plain,** where the cadets march out in formation at precisely 12:20 P.M. every day; and **Trophy Point,** where you'll find unforgettable views of the blue-gray Hudson. Also at the point are captured trophies of war and links of the "Great Chain" that the patriots once stretched across the river here to prevent the passage of British ships.

Constitution Island

One of the more unusual spots at West Point is Constitution Island, accessible only by boat. Strategically important during the Revolution, the

THE HUDSON VALLEY

island later became the home of Susan and Anna Warner, two 19th-century writers who also taught Bible classes at West Point. Susan was the author of the popular 1850 novel *The Wide, Wide World;* Anna was best known for writing the words to the hymn "Jesus Loves Me."

The sisters lived in the **Warner House,** a 17-room Victorian mansion built on the island by their father in 1836. One wall of the mansion dates back to Revolutionary War days, and the whole house is furnished more or less as it was when the sisters lived here.

The house, 845/446-8676, www.constitutionisland.org, is open June–Oct., Wednesday and Thursday afternoons. A boat leaves from West Point's South Dock; advance reservations are required. Cost is adults $8, seniors and students $7, children under five $4.

Recreation and Entertainment

Hudson Highland Cruises, 845/534-7245, offers cruises of the Hudson that leave from the West Point's South Dock and West Haverstraw May–October. Call for details.

Though best known for its military band concerts, the **Eisenhower Hall Theatre** on the West Point campus, 845/938-4159, also features other events from time to time, including modern dance and classical music.

Accommodations and Food

On the academy grounds just outside Thayer Gate off Route 218 stands the big, gray, castlelike **Hotel Thayer,** 845/446-4731 or 800/247-5047, which recently completed a $50 million expansion and renovation. Most of the hotel's rooms reopened in summer 1999, and are somewhat bigger, as well as considerably brighter and more welcoming than before. The lobby and restaurant, however, remain basically the same, and are still outfitted with their trademark marble floors and iron chandeliers. Outside is a pleasant terrace overlooking the Hudson. The upscale restaurant serves traditional American and Continental cuisine ($170–220 d; average dinner entrée $20).

South of the Academy in Highland Falls, you'll find the simple but adequate **West Point** motel, 361 Main St., 845/446-4180 ($80–98 d).

CORNWALL-ON-HUDSON

From West Point north to the tidy village of Cornwall-on-Hudson runs the **Storm King Highway** (Route 218), a twisting, narrow roadway that hugs the cliffs of the Hudson River gorge, offering stunning views of the landscape below. It's a particularly fine drive in fall, when the hills are ablaze with maroon, bright red, orange, and yellow.

Museum of the Hudson Highlands

Cornwall's Museum of the Hudson Highlands, founded by a group of teenagers in 1959, is one of the oldest environmental museums in the country. The high schoolers began what was then thought of as a temporary display in a room in the Town Hall, where they exhibited specimens of plants, animals, and rocks.

Today, the museum is considerably larger but still retains a hands-on, down-to-earth feel. In the natural history wing are re-created regional habitats filled with live turtles, reptiles, ferrets, and the like. In an adjacent gallery hang the works of local artists.

The museum also recently acquired Kenridge Farm, a 174-acre historic horse farm, which it is converting into a major environmental institute. Open to the public are the farm's self-guided nature trails, a historic sheep trail, meadows, wooded areas, and a gallery. Many special programs and activities also take place here; call for details.

To reach the museum, at The Boulevard, off Payson Rd., 845/534-7781, www.museumhudsonhighlands.org, take Route 218 to Payson Road and follow the signs. Museum hours are Fri.–Sat. 10 A.M.–5 P.M., Sunday 1–5 P.M. The trails at Kenridge Farm are open daily dawn–dusk, and its gallery is open Sat.–Sun. noon–4 P.M. Suggested donation at either location $2.

Accommodations and Food

The supremely luxurious **Cromwell Manor,** Angola Rd., 845/534-7136, www.cromwellmanor.com, is an elegant 1820s B&B with 13 guest rooms, some equipped with working fireplaces, Jacuzzis, or steam rooms. On the National Register of Historic Places, the manor is situated on a seven-acre estate surrounded by mountains and has its own formal gardens and croquet courts ($165–370 d).

Along the twisting, turning highway between West Point and Cornwall-on-Hudson is the **Hudson Street Cafe,** 237 Hudson St., 845/534-2335, a good place for breakfast and lunch; average main dish $8. The **Painter's Tavern,** 266 Hudson St., 845/534-2109, offers an eclectic array of sandwiches and burgers, salads and pasta, along with some Mexican specialties. The walls are hung with works by local artists; average dinner entrée $12.

NEWBURGH AND VICINITY

North of Cornwall-on-Hudson, Route 9 W leads to the small city of Newburgh. Once a thriving whaling port and later an important factory town manufacturing everything from lawn mowers to handbags, Newburgh spent much of the late 20th century in a very sorry state. Many of its buildings were boarded up, and residents joked that the place was so untouchable they couldn't even get the county legislature to build a toxic dump here, let alone something more desirable. More recently, however, Newburgh has been benefiting from a downtown renewal plan, and boasts a revitalized waterfront, Newburgh Landing, that is flush with restaurants and shops. Come on a summer's evening and you'll find lots of strollers here. Newburgh is also home to some interesting historic sites.

Washington's Headquarters State Historic Site

At the far edge of downtown, on bluffs overlooking the Hudson, is Washington's headquarters, where the general spent the last six months of the war while his officers and troops waited farther south. It was from this headquarters—originally a farmhouse built by the Hasbrouck family—that Washington issued a victorious order for a "cessation of hostilities," bringing about an end to the Revolutionary War on April 19, 1783.

Now run by the National Park Service, Washington's headquarters has been restored to reflect his stay, and the place has a very personal feel. Its small, whitewashed rooms are simply furnished with cots, bedrolls, firearms, and facsimiles of Washington's account books, along with the desk he once used. The general remained in the house

THE HUDSON VALLEY

Newburgh Landing

for about a year after the war ended, waiting for the British to leave New York. During much of that time, he was restless and bored, and resentful of the public demands upon his time.

Surrounding the house are a wide lawn and high stone wall. At the entrance is an excellent visitor center featuring exhibits and films, while near the bluffs is a 53-foot Tower of Victory, built to commemorate the 100th anniversary of the war's end.

The headquarters, 84 Liberty St., 845/562-1195, is open April–Oct., Wed.–Sat. 10 A.M.–5 P.M., Sunday 1–5 P.M. Admission is adults $3, seniors $2, children 5–12 $1.

Crawford House

While in Newburgh, history buffs might also want to stop into the 1830 David Crawford House, located just a few blocks from Washington's headquarters at 189 Montgomery St., 845/561-2585. The home of the Historical Society of Newburgh, the house is filled with period antiques, Hudson Valley paintings, and an intriguing series of photo exhibits that document Newburgh's more prosperous days. The house is open June–Oct., Sunday 1–4 P.M. or by appointment. Donations are welcome.

Other Nearby Revolutionary War Sites

After visiting Washington's Headquarters, Revolutionary War buffs often head south a few miles to **Knox's Headquarters.** Originally home to the Ellison family, the attractive stone house served as headquarters for Generals Henry Knox, Horatio Gates, and Nathanael Greene at various times during the Revolutionary War, and has been restored to look the way it did back then. Behind the house is the **Jane Colden Native Plant Sanctuary,** filled with wildflowers; Colden was the country's first woman botanist.

A mile or two northwest of Knox's headquarters is the **New Windsor Cantonment,** where Washington's 7,000 troops, accompanied by some 500 women and children, waited out the last months of the war. There they lived in log huts during a long, hard winter—a situation that almost led to rebellion. At that time, peace negotiations had stalled

and some of the officers began circulating what became known as the Newburgh Addresses, proposing a mutiny. Washington eventually succeeded in diffusing the tensions.

Today's cantonment re-creates the lives of the Continental Army's soldiers and camp followers. Inside the visitor center are two floors of exhibits and a slide show. Outside, a military drill complete with the firing of muskets and cannons is staged every afternoon.

Knox's headquarters, Forge Hill Rd., Vails Gate, 845/561-5498, is open Memorial Day–Labor Day, Wednesday and Sunday 1–5 P.M., or by appointment; the New Windsor Cantonment, Temple Hill Rd. (Rte. 300), New Windsor, 845/561-1765, is open April–Oct., Wed.–Sat. 10 A.M.–5 P.M., Sunday 1–5 P.M. Admission at both sites is adults $3, seniors $2, and children under 12 $1. To reach Knox's headquarters from Newburgh, take Route 94 south to Forge Hill Road. To reach the cantonment, continue on Route 94 to Temple Hill Road (Route 300) and head north.

Gomez Mill House

Four miles north of Newburgh is the 1714 Mill House—the oldest extant house of a Jewish family in the nation. Continuously occupied for more than 275 years, the Mill House has been home to fur traders, merchants, Revolutionary War soldiers, farmers, artisans, and statesmen.

The house was originally built by Louis Moses Gomez, who bought 6,000 acres along the Hudson after fleeing the Spanish Inquisition. Several Indian paths converged on his property, and Native Americans once gathered near his home to hold ceremonial rites. In the early 20th century, Dard Hunter, a renowned craftsperson and paper maker, lived in the house.

The house, Mill House Rd., off Rte. 9 W, Marlboro, 914/236-3126, www.gomez.org, is open April–Oct., Wed.–Sun. 10 A.M.–4 P.M.; tours are offered. Admission is adults $3, children under 12 free.

River Cruises

Hudson River Adventures, 845/782-0685, www.prideofthehudson.com, offers narrated two-hour river cruises leaving from Newburgh

Landing, May–October. Call for details; reservations required.

Food

Commodore's, 482 Broadway, 845/561-3960, is an old-fashioned ice cream parlor that's also a good spot for a simple lunch. The place is famous for its handmade chocolates.

Yobo's, 1297 Union Ave., 845/564-3848, serves a wide variety of dishes from China, Korea, Indonesia, and other Asian countries in a man-made atmosphere of babbling brooks and waterfalls. It was voted as serving the region's Best Sushi in a recent Hudson Valley magazine readers poll; average entrée $14.

Voted best Italian restaurant in the same poll is **Il Cena'Colo,** 152 Rte. 52, 845/564-4494, which serves Tuscan-style fare. Among the tasty specials are oyster stew, fried baby artichokes, Dover sole with orange juice, and gnocchi with venison sauce; average entrée $16.

Friendly **C. D. Driscoll's,** 1100 Union Ave., 845/566-1300, features primarily American cuisine, along with some Mexican dishes, and live bands on fall weekend nights; average entrée $15.

In downtown Marlboro, near the Gomez Mill House just north of the Orange-Ulster county border, is the lively **Raccoon Saloon,** 1330 Main St. (Rte. 9 W), 845/236-7872. On the menu in this lively joint is an enormous selection of burgers and beers; average burger $7.

STORM KING ART CENTER AND VICINITY

One of Hudson Valley's most astonishing sights is Storm King Art Center, a breathtakingly beautiful sculpture park built on a hilltop. About 120 permanent works and many more temporary ones are scattered over jade-green lawns and wheat-blond fields, while in the distance are the dusk blue Shawangunks. Nearly every major post–WW II sculptor is represented here—Alexander Calder, Henry Moore, Louise Nevelson, Isamu Noguchi, and Richard Serra among them. A map to the 400-acre park and its sculptures is available at the gate. In the center of the park stands an imperial Norman-style building

THE BATTLE FOR STORM KING MOUNTAIN

An important chapter in the history of the environmental movement was played out in the 1960s over Storm King Mountain, a magnificent blue-black peak that architectural historian Vincent Scully once called a "dome of living granite, swelling with animal power."

The chapter began in 1963 when Consolidated Edison Co. of New York filed for a license to build a hydroelectric plant at the mountain's base. It was to be the largest hydroelectric plant in the world, generating 2,000 kilowatts of power. A 40-foot-wide tunnel would have to be blasted through the heart of Storm King, a 300-foot-deep cut made across its face, 200 acres of forest appropriated, and a 15-story powerhouse built. Once completed, the plant would need six billion gallons of water a day to operate.

When the plan was made public, citizens were outraged. Not only would the plant destroy the area's natural beauty, but it would also seriously harm recreational and commercial fishing as far south as Long Island. An environmental group called the Scenic Hudson Preservation Conference quickly mobilized the protests and brought the case to court.

Much to the industrialists' surprise, in December 1965, the U.S. Court of Appeals ruled for the people against Con Ed. That historic decision marked the first time that ordinary citizens successfully brought suit against a commercial developer. The case has since been cited as precedent in dozens of other environmental cases.

that was originally the home of lawyer Vermont Hatch. The stone mansion now houses temporary exhibits and a small cafe open weekends.

Storm King, Old Pleasant Hill Road in Mountainville, is off Route 32, a couple of miles south of Vails Gate, 845/534-3115, www.stormking.org. It's open April–Nov., daily 11 A.M.–5:30 P.M. Admission is adults $9, seniors $7, students $5; free for children under 5.

Washingtonville

Take Route 20 to Route 94 west of the Storm King Art Center about five miles if you must go to **Brotherhood Winery.** The place bills itself as "America's Oldest Winery, est. 1839," but be that as it may, it's an exceedingly commercial place selling wines that are mediocre at best. The wine-tasting tours cost a steep $5, and the grounds are crowded with tourist shops and a bandstand where "special events" are staged.

The winery, 35 North St., off Rts. 94 and 208, 845/496-9101, www.wines.com/brotherhood, is open May–Oct., daily noon–5 P.M.; Nov.–April, Sat.–Sun. noon–5 P.M.

A much more interesting destination in Washingtonville is the **Moffat Library,** 6 W. Main St., 845/496-5483. Built in 1887, the library has six Tiffany windows, is on the National Register of Historic Places, and features local history exhibits. Open Mon.–Fri. 10 A.M.–5 P.M., Saturday 10 A.M.–4 P.M., Sunday 1–4 P.M.

Accommodations

Offering excellent views of Storm King Mountain is the **Storm King Lodge,** 100 Pleasant Hill Rd., 845/534-9421, www.stormkinglodge.com. Housed in a converted carriage house, the lodge offers four cozy guest rooms, two of which have private fireplaces; $150–175 d.

SOUTHERN ORANGE COUNTY

Central Valley

Just north of the junction of I-87 and Route 17 is the town of Central Valley and **Woodbury Common,** Rte. 32, 845/928-4000, a factory-outlet complex that attracts busloads of tourists. The complex houses over 150 shops, including Calvin Klein, Donna Karan, and Jones New York, as well as a number of restaurants. It's open daily year-round. To reach it from I-87, take Exit 16 (Route 32); the complex is immediately off the exit.

One and one-half miles north of Woodbury Common is **Gasho of Japan,** Rte. 32, 845/928-2277, a big touristy spot that nonetheless serves tasty Japanese food, cooked at your table. The restaurant is housed in a centuries-old Japanese farmhouse that was transported here from Japan; average entrée $18.

Route 17 South

South of Central Valley, Route 17 runs along the western edge of Harriman State Park (see the Ramapo Mountains under Rockland County, above). Before it was a state park, Harriman was mining country, and its mountains are still pocked with mine shafts and foundries. A small museum documenting the area's mining history now stands at the **Clove Furnace Historic Site,** Clove Furnace Rd., in Arden, off Route 17. The museum, run by the Orange County Historical Society, 845/351-4696, is open Mon.–Fri. 8 A.M.–4:30 P.M.; closed 12:30–1 P.M. Admission is free.

Just behind the museum is a romantic, ivy-covered conference center known as the **Arden House.** The house was the residential estate of the Harriman family until 1972. Local lore has it that Edward Harriman built his mansion on this mountain site because he'd been shunned by the exclusive nearby community of Tuxedo Park, and wanted his wife to be able to look down on it daily.

> *It was in Tuxedo Park that the formal dinner jacket of the same name was first introduced.*

Continuing south on Route 17, you'll come to the junction of Route 17A (heading west) and Route 106 (heading east). Route 106 leads into Harriman State Park and the Seven Lakes Drive. Traveling west on Route 17A about two miles will bring you to the dark, quiet woods of **Sterling Forest State Park,** most of which was only acquired by the state in the late 1990s. The park is best known for the popular **New York Renaissance Festival** that is presented here weekends from August through mid-September. During the festival, which annually attracts about 175,000 visitors, knights in shining armor joust on horseback, minstrels strum love songs, a human chess game is played, and Shakespearean plays are staged. Plenty of food and drink are also on hand.

Sterling Forest is open dawn to dusk. Tickets for the Renaissance Festival, 914/351-5171 (after June 1), www.renfair.com, cost adults $17, and children 5–12 $7. A special Short Line leaves for the festival from Port Authority terminal, Manhattan, 212/736-4700 or 800/631-8405.

Farther south on Route 17, you can catch a glimpse of **Tuxedo Park.** Watch for a high stone wall and romantic gatehouse on the right. The residential community was designed in the 1880s as a millionaires' refuge and is filled with large turreted mansions. Etiquette maven Emily Post lived here for many years, and it was in Tuxedo Park that the formal dinner jacket of the same name was first introduced.

Monroe

West of Central Valley is Monroe, where you'll find one of the largest museums in America devoted to everyday folk arts. **Museum Village** is a reconstructed settlement composed of about 35 historic buildings moved here from elsewhere. Self-guided tours take visitors past costumed guides who pound out horseshoes, churn butter, operate a printing press, and otherwise engage in activities of the preindustrial age. The village also hosts many special events, including square dancing, magic shows, and the largest **Civil War encampment** in the Northeast, reenacted every Labor Day weekend.

Museum Village, 130 Museum Village Rd., off Rte. 17M off Rte. 17 (Exit 129), 845/782-8247, www.museumvillage.org, is open July–Aug., Tues.–Fri. 10 A.M.–5 P.M., Sat.–Sun. 10 A.M.–5 P.M.; call for spring and fall hours. Admission is adults $8, seniors $6, and children 3–15 $5.

Also in Monroe is the **Ananda Ashram,** Sapphire Rd., 845/782-5575, a 100-acre retreat-resort run by the Yoga Society of New York. On the grounds are nature trails, a lake, and an outdoor pool. The basic rate for dormitory-style accommodations is $55–60 per night night; included are three meals, *satsangs,* lectures, cultural programs, and one yoga or tai chi class a day. Semiprivate rooms are also available, or you can opt to visit the ashram as a day visitor and partake of one of the meals, lectures, or classes for a small fee (about $9).

Sugar Loaf Village

Back in the 18th century, this village at the base of Sugar Loaf Mountain was filled with artisans who sold their handmade goods to local farmers. By 1900, however, the Industrial Revolution had all but put an end to this tradition.

Enter the 1960s and a sudden explosion of interest in crafts. A few local residents decided to revive their heritage and today, Sugar Loaf bustles with dozens of shops selling everything from rag dolls to woodcarvings. Some of the shops are sophisticated galleries; others are dishearteningly commercial.

Most of the shops are open Tues.–Sun. 9 A.M.–5 P.M. To reach Sugar Loaf Village from Monroe, take Route 17 west to Route 13 (Exit 127) and travel south a few miles. For more information, call the **Sugar Loaf Chamber of Commerce** at 845/469-9181.

A good stop for lunch is the **Barnsider Tavern,** King's Hwy., 845/469-9810, offering burgers, salads, and simple entrées in a taproom setting; average main dish $8.

The **Sugar Loaf Village B&B,** Pine Hill Rd., 845/469-2717, is a 100-year-old renovated home with three guest rooms, one located in a private carriage house ($140–160 d).

GOSHEN AND VICINITY

Named after the biblical land known for its fertile soil, Goshen was once a major dairy center. The first milk shipped into New York City came from this area, and Goshen butter was famous. The town has been the Orange County seat since 1798.

Historic Buildings

Numerous historic buildings line the village's sleepy streets. Most interesting among them is the yellow-brick 1841 **Orange County Courthouse,** 101 Main Street. Local legend has it that the abnormally large skull of outlaw Claudius Smith is encased in the courthouse's cornerstone. Smith was hanged on Goshen's village green.

Also of interest, especially if you find it open, is **St. James Episcopal Church,** on Church Street near Park Place. Designed by Richard Upjohn in 1803, the church features windows made in the Tiffany studios and an altar designed by Cass Gilbert.

COWBOY OF THE RAMAPOS

As befits an ancient mountain range, the Ramapos have their share of legend and lore. Most pervasive is the story of the "Cowboy of the Ramapos," Claudius Smith. Around the time of the Revolution, Smith led a group of outlaws who stole horses and cattle from local farmers to sell to the British. Smith was also said to have tortured old men and women out of their life savings, and to have ambushed supply trains en route to Gen. Washington. After each raid, Smith and his outlaws hid out in caves in the Ramapos, where the authorities had little chance of tracking them down.

Known for his irrepressible high spirits, Smith seemed invincible until October 1777, when he murdered patriot Nathaniel Strong at his family homestead. That brutal act caused Gov. George Clinton to put a $1,200 bounty on Smith's head, and the outlaw was subsequently captured and hanged in Goshen, Orange County, on January 22, 1779.

New York's eminent folklorist Harold W. Thompson writes of Smith's last day in *New York State Folktales, Legends, and Ballads:* "Dressed in a handsome suit of broadcloth with silver buttons, the tall outlaw had made his last graceful bows to former neighbors when he was addressed by an elderly person who elbowed his way to the scaffold. 'Mr. Smith, Mr. Smith,' he called, 'where shall I find those deeds and other papers that you—er—*had* from me?' Smith turned his gaze. . . . 'Mr. Young,' he said, 'this is no time to talk about papers. Meet me in the next world, and I'll tell you about them.'"

Legend also has it that Smith's abnormally large skull is encased in the cornerstone of the Old Courthouse in Goshen.

Harness Racing Museum and Hall of Fame

In addition to its dairies, Goshen is best known for being the "Cradle of the Trotter"; it was once home to the most important harness-racing track in the country. "In July and August," stated one guidebook of the 1930s, "the near-by roads are daily congested with horse lovers; it is hard to find rooms in the town and many people have to eat at the lunch counters that cluster near the tracks."

Those days are now long gone, but their history lives on in the Harness Racing Museum and Hall of Fame, a large and sophisticated affair with exhibits on virtually every aspect of harness racing. Among the displays are restored stalls complete with horse replicas; nearly 200 trotting prints by Currier and Ives; famous racing silks, sulkies, and wagons; and an impressive Hall of the Immortals devoted to yesteryear's champions.

The museum, 240 Main St., 845/294-6330, www.harnessmuseum.com, is open daily 10 A.M.–6 P.M. Admission is adults $7.50, seniors $6.50, children 6–15 $3.50, under 6 free.

Just behind the museum is the **Historic Track,** the only sports facility in the United States that's a National Historic Landmark. The track, which dates back to the 1830s, is now used primarily for training purposes, but the Grand Circuit races are still held here once a year on Fourth of July weekend.

Hambletonian's Grave

Almost all trotters and pacers racing today trace their lineage back to Hambletonian, a colt born in Sugar Loaf on May 5, 1849. Though "extremely ugly" and never a racehorse himself, Hambletonian sired 1,331 foals in 24 years, many of whom went on to become racing champions. In fact, Hambletonian's sons' bloodlines were so strong that they eventually eliminated all other horse families.

Hambletonian's grave is located six miles east of Goshen in Chester, on Hambletonian Avenue off Route 94; watch for signs. As the local literature reads, "a tall shaft marks the spot."

Events

A highlight of Goshen's calendar is the Fourth of July **Great American Weekend,** 845/291-2136, featuring harness racing, concerts, and sidewalk sales. The 10-day **Orange County Fair,** 845/343-4826, comes to the Middletown fairgrounds in late July.

Camping and Accommodations

Campers can head south of town to the 160-site **Black Bear Campground,** 197 Wheeler Rd.,

© CHRISTIANE BIRD

harness racers in Goshen, "the Cradle of the Trotter"

THE HUDSON VALLEY

off Rte. 94 in the town of Florida, 845/851-7717. The basic site rate is $27.

For travelers who prefer motels, a **Days Inn,** 845/374-2411, is located just outside town at the junction of Rts. 17M and 6 ($79–89 d).

Food

Catherine's, 153 W. Main St., 845/294-8707, housed in a historic 1869 building, is a congenial spot for lunch or dinner, and serves especially good pasta; average dinner entrée $11.

THE DROWNED LANDS

County Route 6, not to be confused with U.S. Route 6, heads southwest out of Goshen into the fertile "black dirt" region. Over 10,000 acres are under cultivation here, and although a variety of produce is grown, onions—New York's most successful vegetable crop—are particularly popular. The region's unofficial capital is the village of Pine Island.

"Black dirt" is actually a highly organic soil, scientifically known by the unscientific name of "muck," that was deposited here about 10,000 years ago by glacial lakes. Orange County has the second-largest concentration of muck in the

United States, second only to the Everglades in Florida. The Orange County muck was inaccessible until about 100 years ago when impoverished Polish, German, and Italian immigrants drained the swamps for farmland.

Scattered throughout the region are farmstands and more farmstands. Right next to one is the **Ye Jolly Onion Inn,** Rte. 517, Pulaski Hwy. and County Road 1, 845/258-4277, which serves onions every which way; average entrée $10. Every August, the Drowned Lands' farmers host the popular **Orange County Onion Harvest Festival,** 845/291-2136, in Goshen.

Just east of the black-dirt region in Warwick, the **Peach Grove Inn,** 205 Rte. 17A, 914/986-7411, www.peachgroveinn.net, offers rooms in a restored 1850 Greek Revival home that sits on the site of a former peach grove overlooking a 200-acre farm. The owner, an antiques dealer for years, has decorated the premises with handsome Victorian furniture, while all the rooms feature tall canopy beds topped with fluffy eiderdowns ($120–150 d).

GARRISON

If you head south from West Point, rather than north to Newburgh, on Routes 218 and 9W, you'll come to the small and graceful **Bear Mountain Bridge,** once the world's longest suspension bridge. The bridge offers great views of the Bear Mountain Gorge as it heads across the Hudson to **Putnam County** and Route 9D. About four miles north on Route 9D is the village of Garrison.

Take the turnoff to **Garrison Landing,** and you'll find yourself in a small parklike area by the riverfront. Nearby is a 19th-century gazebo used in the filming of *Hello Dolly,* an old stone railroad station, and the **Garrison Art Center,** 845/424-3960, www.garrisonartcenter.org. The center presents exhibits and special events, including an arts-and-crafts fair in August and auctions in May and October. When there's an exhibit, daily hours are noon–5 P.M. Admission is free.

Boscobel Restoration

Just north of Garrison proper is an elegant, early 19th-century mansion known as Boscobel, or "beautiful wood." Standing high on bluffs overlooking the Hudson, the historic house features an extraordinary collection of decorative arts from the Federal period.

Much of the collection was assembled by the home's extravagant original owner, States Morris Dyckman, who wanted Boscobel to have the finest of everything. He even told his more frugal wife that the house would be their "last sacrifice to Folly." The house is filled with a graceful assortment of china, silver, and New York–made furniture, along with more idiosyncratic treasures such as a hand-carved staircase, a brightly colored 1800 rocking horse, a 1790 set of *Encyclopedia Britannica,* and a few Benjamin West paintings. Outside are gardens bursting with orchids and roses, as well as an orangery and an herb garden.

Incredibly, Boscobel was almost destroyed by a wrecker's ball in the 1950s. Only at the last moment were enough funds raised to purchase the house and transport it piece by piece to its current location.

Boscobel, Rte. 9D about one mile north of Garrison, 845/265-3638, www.boscobel.org, is open April–Oct., Wed.–Mon. 10 A.M.–5 P.M. (last tour at 4:15 P.M.); Nov.–Dec., March, Wed.–Mon. 10 A.M.–4 P.M. (last tour at 3:15 P.M.). Admission to the house and grounds is adults $8, seniors $7,

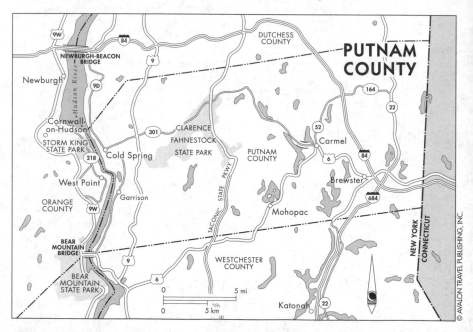

THE HUDSON VALLEY

© CHRISTIANE BIRD

Almost destroyed in the 1950s, the 19th-century mansion Boscobel now peacefully overlooks the Hudson just south of Garrison.

children 6–14 $5. Admission to the grounds only is adults $5, children $3.

Constitution Marsh

Boscobel looks out over Constitution Marsh Sanctuary, a 207-acre tidal marsh managed by the National Audubon Society. A self-guiding nature trail and boardwalk run through the preserve, while at river's edge is a visitor center. The sanctuary is rich with birds—194 species have been spotted—and wildflowers.

Also in the preserve are canals created around the turn of the century by farmers who hoped to use the marshlands to grow rice. Once a day at high tide, from May through early October, the Audubon Society runs guided canoe trips through these canals. The trips are free but are enormously popular, and reservations must be made weeks in advance.

The marsh, 845/265-2601, is located on Indian Brook Rd. off Rte. 9D, about a quarter-mile south of Boscobel. The grounds are open year-round, Tues.–Sun. 9 A.M.–dusk; the visitor center is open May–Oct., Tues.–Sun. 9 A.M.–5 P.M. Admission is free.

Manitoga

South of Garrison off Route 9D—watch closely for signs—is the idiosyncratic Manitoga. Created by industrial designer Russel Wright over a period of about three decades beginning in 1947, Manitoga is designed to, as the artist put it, "bring to American culture an intimacy with nature." Throughout the center run three hiking trails that Wright carefully manipulated to their best natural effect. Not surprisingly, some parts are reminiscent of a Japanese garden; others are considerably wilder, filled with wildflowers and steep ravines.

Also at Manitoga is Wright's glass-walled home, **Dragon Rock,** built on the edge of a small quarry. Wright rerouted a waterfall to turn the quarry into a sleepy pond.

The trails at Manitoga, off Rte. 9D, 845/424-3812, are open April–Nov., daily 10 A.M.–4 P.M. Dragon Rock house tours are offered about once a month; advance registration is required. Suggested donation is adults $4, seniors and children under 12 $2.

Graymoor

Due east of Manitoga off Rte. 9 is Graymoor,

845/424-3671, a monastery of the Franciscan Friars of the Atonement. Built by the Episcopal Church in 1898, the monastery is perched high on a hill with magnificent views of the Hudson Valley. On the grounds are shrines, chapels, and Stations of the Cross. The grounds are open to the public daily 9 A.M.–dusk. To reach Graymoor from Manitoga, located just a few miles away, take Route 9D north to Route 403 south to Route 9 south.

Accommodations and Food

Though best known for its gourmet restaurant, the **Bird & Bottle Inn,** Old Albany Post Rd. (Rte. 9 just east of the village), 914/424-3000, also features a handful of snug guest rooms complete with canopied beds and working fireplaces. The inn dates back to 1761, when it was a major stagecoach stop between New York City and Albany ($210–260 d, with breakfast and a $37 dinner credit per person). The inn's acclaimed restaurant offers traditional American and continental fare. Meals are served by candlelight, and there's a crackling fire in cold weather. Four-course prix fixe dinners start at $39.

For pasta and pizza, stop into the popular, family-run **Papa John's,** Rte. 9, 845/265-3344, frequented by locals; average pie $11. One of the top restaurants in the region is **Xaviar's,** Rte. 9D just south of the Rte. 403 intersection, 845/424-4228. Housed in a country-club setting, Xaviar's features innovative American fare also served by candlelight. The prix fixe dinners cost $85; served Fri.–Sat. only. The prix fixe Sunday brunch costs $40.

COLD SPRING

Legend has it that the quaint village of Cold Spring was first named by George Washington after he took a sip of the local waters. The village didn't flourish, however, until the 1800s when the federal government created an iron foundry here. Around the same time, tourists traveling by steamboat first discovered the glories of the Hudson Valley. Cold Spring, with the granite dome of Storm King Mountain looming across the way, was a favorite overnight stop.

Today, much of Cold Spring still dates back to its Victorian heyday. Throughout the area are a number of old inns, while along Main Street are restored 19th-century buildings housing attractive antique and gift shops. Among them is the well-stocked **Salmagundi Books,** 66 Main St., 845/265-4058. Walking tours of the village are frequently offered on Sunday afternoon by the Putnam County Historical Society and Foundry School Museum (see below).

At the foot of Main Street is the Hudson River, but you can't get there without first detouring south, under the Metro-North train tracks (a sign marks the way). Once at the shore, you'll find a gazebo and plaza jutting into the river and offering outstanding views.

Foundry School Museum

Originally a school for children of the Irish immigrants employed by Cold Spring's foundry, this small 1820 building is now a local history museum run by the Putnam County Historical Society. Inside are a re-created foundry room, school room, country store, and country kitchen, along with a dugout canoe, horse-drawn sleigh, and historic photographs. The museum, 63 Chestnut St., 845/265-4010, is open March–Dec., Tues.–Thurs. 10 A.M.–4 P.M., Sat.–Sun. 2–5 P.M. Admission is free.

Accommodations

Smack on the banks of the Hudson, with magnificent views of Storm King Mountain, is the boxy **Hudson House Inn,** 2 Main St., 845/265-9355, www.thehudsonhouseinn.com, the second-oldest continuously operating inn in New York. Built in 1832 to house steamboat passengers, the inn features 15 renovated guest rooms furnished with antiques ($140–225 d, includes continental breakfast). On site is a pleasant restaurant serving lunch and dinner.

The charming **Pig Hill B&B,** 73 Main St., 914/265-9247, is housed in a brick Georgian townhouse with antiques for sale. Six of the nine guest rooms have a fireplace or wood stove, and four have private baths. Out back is a terraced garden ($120–170 d).

Food

The friendly **Cold Spring Depot,** 1 Depot Sq., 845/265-2305, is a casual joint housed in an old railroad station; average main dish $7. The **Foundry Cafe,** 55 Main St., 845/265-4504, specializes in naturally healthy foods and regional American cooking. On the menu are lots of soups, home-baked goods, and grain dishes (average main dish $7); next door is a gourmet health-food store.

On the shores of the Hudson River you'll find the sprawling **Northgate at Dockside Harbor,** 1 North St., 845/265-5555, serving fresh seafood, steaks, and regional American cuisine. In summer, an outdoor dining area opens up, and many tables—both indoors and outdoors—have great views of the river; average entrée $18. Nearby is the historic **Hudson House Restaurant,** 845/265-9355 (see Accommodations, above), also serving fresh seafood and regional American cuisine in a setting that overlooks the Hudson; average entrée $18.

One of the village's most upscale spots is the **Plumbush Inn,** Rte. 9D about one mile south of the village center, 845/265-3904, housed in a building that dates back to 1867. Here you'll dine by candlelight in a lush Victorian dining room complete with working fireplaces and dark wood paneling. Prix fixe dinners from $32.50.

EASTERN PUTNAM COUNTY

Clarence Fahnestock State Park

Fahnestock State Park spreads out over 12,000 acres of Putnam Valley. It's crisscrossed with a number of hiking trails, including the Appalachian Trail, and offers lakes (boat rentals available), swimming beaches, fishing ponds, and an extensive performing-arts program. An 86-site campground is open May–October; for reservations (recommended), call 800/456-CAMP. Admission to the park, off Rte. 301, east of Taconic State Pkwy. in Carmel, 845/225-7207, is free; maps are available at the entrance. During the summer, a $6 parking fee is charged at the beach.

Southeast Museum

This idiosyncratic museum in the small village of Brewster is full of oddities. Housed in the 1896 Old Town Hall, it contains a large collection of minerals from local mines, early artifacts from the Harlem Railroad Line, and an assortment of early memorabilia from the Borden condensed-milk factory. Gail Brewster began producing condensed milk here in the 1850s. He hit upon the idea while sailing home from England, when he longed for a glass of fresh milk. The town's other famous resident was Rex Stout, creator of the orchid-loving detective Nero Wolfe and his sidekick Archie Goldwin.

The museum, 67 Main St., 845/279-7500, www.southeastmuseum.org, is open Tues.–Fri. noon–4 P.M., Sat.–Sun. 1–4 P.M.; closed January–March. Admission is by donation.

Food

One of the few old-fashioned drive-ins left in the region is the ever-popular **Red Rooster Diner,** Rte. 22, two miles northeast of Brewster, 845/279-8046, always crowded with families and enthused kids. On the grounds, you'll also find a miniature golf course.

Dutchess County

Named for England's Duchess of York, who was later crowned Queen Mary, Dutchess County lies in the center of the Hudson Valley and feels much like its hub. Most of the grand riverfront estates for which the area is famous are located here, as are Vassar and Bard Colleges, the historic town of Rhinebeck, the Culinary Institute of America, and a plethora of country villages, pick-your-own farms, public gardens, and excellent restaurants and lodgings. Over two million people visit Dutchess every year.

The historic museum-estates are all in a 20-mile riverfront stretch between Hyde Park in the center of the county and Clermont just over the border to the north. In 1990, this stretch was declared a National Historic Landmark District—the second largest such district in the United States. It contains some 2,000 buildings, only a handful of which are open to the public. These include Franklin Delano Roosevelt's home (Springwood), the Vanderbilt Mansion, Mills Mansion, Wilderstein, Montgomery Place, and Clermont.

Of these, FDR's estate is by far the most personal and popular, and can be combined with a visit to Val-Kill, Eleanor Roosevelt's retreat. Between the two homes and the nearby FDR Library and museum, you'll come away with a good sense of both the Roosevelts and the times in which they lived. Of the other museum-estates, the Vanderbilt Mansion is the most lavish, Montgomery Place the most beautiful, Mills Mansion the most cavernous, Clermont the most elegant, and Wilderstein—just recently opened to the public on a regular basis—the smallest and least known.

South of Hyde Park are the river cities of Beacon and Poughkeepsie. Both have fallen on hard times, yet have interesting historic and cultural sites to offer; Beacon is also home to a mammoth new Dia Art Foundation museum. A few miles east of Route 9, the expansive rural countryside is dotted with small villages, wineries, produce stands, and horse farms. The entire Hudson Valley is a major horse-breeding area,

with about half of its 100 horse farms located in Dutchess County.

First-time visitors will probably want to concentrate on Hyde Park and Rhinebeck.

Information

For general information on the county, contact the **Dutchess County Tourism Promotion Agency,** 3 Neptune Rd., Poughkeepsie, NY 12601; 845/463-4000 or 800/445-3131, www.dutchess-tourism.com. The agency is open Mon.–Fri. 9 A.M.–5 P.M.

BEACON

Once a bustling manufacturing town best known for its brick and hat factories, Beacon today, like many towns along the Hudson, feels worn out and run-down. Many of its 19th-century buildings are boarded up or covered with dust. Nonetheless, the town has character and was used as the setting for the relatively recent movie *Nobody's Fool,* starring Paul Newman. A number of **antique stores** can be found along Main Street between Tioronda Avenue and Route 52. **Mount Beacon** towers over the city and has played an important role in the town's history. During the Revolutionary War, the colonists set signal fires on the summit to warn their compatriots of British troop movements. During the early 1900s, a casino serviced by a funicular sat atop the mountain—the tracks are still visible today.

Exciting new changes are also underway in Beacon, thanks largely to the arrival of a Dia Art Foundation museum, expected to open in spring 2003.

Two Historic Houses

One of the oldest houses in the county is the **Madam Brett Homestead,** a graceful stone estate built in 1708 by Catheryna and Robert Brett. After the death of her husband by drowning, Mme. Brett succeeded in establishing the region's first thriving business venture—the Frankfort Storehouse and Mill. The locals used to joke,

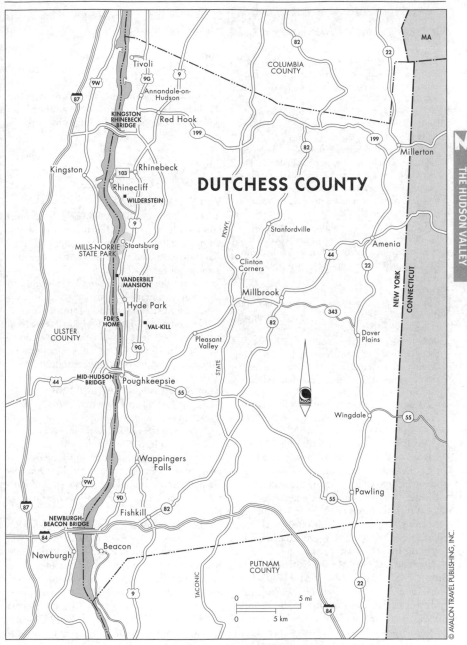

THE HUDSON VALLEY

ART BY THE RIVERSIDE

In the spring of 2003, the Dia Art Foundation, an innovative arts institution based in New York City, plans to open a major new museum in Beacon, New York. To be housed in a 300,000-square-foot former printing plant, the new museum will showcase Dia's permanent collection. Among the works to be displayed will be Andy Warhol's 1979 *Shadows*, composed of 102 paintings; Richard Serra's monumental Torqued Ellipses series; a large-scale sculpture by Walter De Maria; a series of fluorescent light works by Dan Flavin; and Agnes Martin's 1999 suite of paintings *Innocent Love*, created specifically for the Beacon museum.

The new museum building, donated to the Dia Art Foundation by International Paper, has been redesigned by artist Robert Irwin, who has filled the former factory with open and well-lit galleries. Outside are gardens and flowering fruit trees.

The new museum is a five-minute walk from the Metro-North train station and is expected to draw about 50,000 visitors a year. The town of Beacon is already gearing up for the fun, and has several development projects in the works, including the revitalization of Beacon Landing. Hopes are to turn the former junk yard and train yard into a waterfront park, complete with a walkway, restaurant, inn, shops, and ferry dock.

"All roads lead to Mme. Brett's mill." During the Revolutionary War, the Brett homestead may have been used for the storage of military supplies, and Catheryna's granddaughter entertained Generals Washington and Lafayette here.

Now owned by the Daughters of the American Revolution, the homestead, 50 Van Nydeck Ave., 845/831-6533, is open May–Dec., the first Sunday of the month, or by appointment.

Not far away is the **Mount Gulian Historic Site,** 145 Sterling St., 845/831-8172, where you'll learn about the Dutch, Native American, and African American culture of the Revolutionary War–era Hudson Valley. Costumed guides conduct tours. Open April–Oct., Wed.–Fri. and Sunday 1–5 P.M.; Nov.–Dec.,

Wednesday and Sunday 1–5 P.M. Admission is adults $5, children $3.

Food

"The meeting and eating spot of Beacon" is **Quinn's,** 330 Main St., 914/831-8065, an old-fashioned town cafe with a big American flag outside and great homemade bread, meat loaf, potato soup, and rice pudding inside; average main dish $8.

FISHKILL AND WAPPINGERS FALLS

Van Wyck Homestead

A few miles east of Beacon is a Dutch Colonial home built in 1732 by Cornelius Van Wyck. During the Revolution, the homestead was used as a courtroom and is believed to have been the inspiration for James Fenimore Cooper's *The Spy.* Today, the building houses a museum filled with Revolutionary War artifacts and furnishings. Costumed guides conduct tours.

The homestead, junction of Rte. 9 and I-84, 845/896-9560, is open Memorial Day–Columbus Day, Sat.–Sun. 1–4 P.M. or by appointment. Admission is adults $2, children under 12 $1.

Recreation and Entertainment

The Class A **Hudson Valley Renegades,** website: www.hvrenegades.com, minor league baseball team came to the Fishkill-Wappingers Falls area in 1994, and have been packing them in ever since. The season runs from mid-June to early September. Home games are played in Dutchess Stadium, north of Fishkill on Route 9D. For directions and game times, call the stadium at 845/838-0094.

The area also offers a number of other fun activities for various ages. In Fishkill, the kids will go for **Splashdown Family Water Park,** 2200 Rte. 9, 845/896-5468, which features three large water slides, a kiddie slide, bumper boats, and miniature golf. In nearby Wappingers Falls, their parents might prefer the **County Players Falls Theatre,** 15 W. Main St., 845/297-9821, a solid community theater presenting traditional Broadway fare.

Food

In Wappingers Falls, you'll find the lively **La Fonda Del Sol,** 100 Old Rte. 9, 845/297-5044, which serves a wide variety of Mexican and Tex-Mex dishes; average entrée $11. Downstairs is **La Cantina,** featuring DJs most nights of the week. The **Cornerstone Restaurant,** junction of Rts. 9 and 52, 845/896-8050, is an airy, plant-filled spot serving traditional German fare; average entrée $12.

POUGHKEEPSIE

The seat of Dutchess County, Poughkeepsie was founded in 1683 and was designated the state capital in 1777. From the mid-1800s through the mid-1900s, the town was a major industrial center, serving as homebase for IBM after WW II. But the latter decades of the 20th century were not kind to Poughkeepsie. First, many of the factories closed down. Then urban renewal ravaged the city, replacing 19th-century brick buildings with stingy, low-slung edifices. Finally, in the 1990s, IBM laid off thousands upon thousands of employees.

Today, much of downtown Poughkeepsie—Wappinger Indian for reed-covered lodge by the little water place—feels depressed. Its long Main Street, climbing up a steep slope from the Hudson River, is lined with a desolate Main Mall, boarded-up storefronts, and the lingering unemployed. Through the center of town run multilaned roadways—silent reminders of the fact that people can't get out of here fast enough. Meanwhile, glistening shopping malls surround the city, siphoning off whatever downtown retail business is left. Nevertheless, Poughkeepsie is a tough-minded city with a tough-minded citizenry, and one suspects that it won't stay down for long.

> *Built by a handful of volunteers,* **Clearwater** *has been sailing and bringing with it a message of environmental urgency since 1969. The Poughkeepsie-based vessel has been instrumental in helping to clean up the Hudson.*

Downtown Culture

Near the river and railroad station, where Union and Academy Streets intersect Main and Mill,

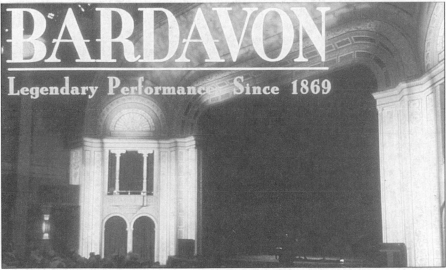

Bardavon 1869 Opera House

are two bustling, restored **historic districts** filled with shops, pubs, and restaurants. Just up the hill from the restored historic district near the railroad station is the **Cunneen-Hackett Cultural Center,** 9 and 12 Vassar St., 845/471-1221. The center occupies two handsome Italianate buildings that were built in the 1880s by the nephews of Matthew Vassar, the Poughkeepsie brewer who founded Vassar College. No. 9, once used as a home for the aged, now houses offices and a small art gallery. No. 12, once an educational institute, is home to an exquisite Victorian auditorium—complete with gold-cushioned seats and stained-glass windows—where plays, concerts, and films are frequently presented. The center's gallery is free and open Mon.–Fri. 9 A.M.–5 P.M.; call for theater information.

East of the center is Poughkeepsie's premier cultural gem, the **Bardavon 1869 Opera House,** 35 Market St., 845/473-2072, www.bardavon.org. One of the oldest theaters in the country, the Bardavon was almost destroyed during urban renewal but has since been restored to its original splendor.

History buffs can head for the **Clinton House** and the **Glebe House,** junction of Main and North Sts., 845/471-1630, www.pojonews.com, where the Dutchess County Historical Society presents exhibits on the area's history. The two 18th-century buildings served as the center of New York State government in 1777. The Clinton House is open Tues.–Fri. 10 A.M.–3 P.M.; the Glebe House is open by appointment. Admission is free.

The *Clearwater*

Poughkeepsie is home to the sloop *Clearwater,* 112 Market St., 845/454-7673, www.clearwater.org, which often docks downtown at the newly restored Main Street pier. Built by a handful of river-loving volunteers, *Clearwater* has been sailing the Hudson since 1969, bringing with it a message of environmental urgency. The vessel has been instrumental in helping to clean up the Hudson, and is the impetus behind the popular, three-day **Clearwater Festival,** 800/677-5667, held at Westchester Community College every June.

Locust Grove, the Samuel Morse Historic Site

Immediately south of Poughkeepsie's downtown is Locust Grove, a romantic octagonal villa that was once the summer home of artist-scientist-philosopher Samuel Morse, inventor of the telegraph. Morse bought his home in 1847 when he was already a widower in his fifties. With the help of renowned landscape architect Alexander Jackson Davis, he transformed it into a Tuscan-styled estate complete with a four-story tower, skylit billiard room, and extensive gardens. Throughout the house are paintings by Morse, John James Audubon, and other of the inventor's contemporaries, while in the basement is a collection of telegraphs.

Locust Grove overlooks the Hudson and the adjoining **Young Memorial Wildlife Sanctuary,** a 145-acre preserve laced with short hiking trails. The preserve is especially beautiful in spring, when it's filled with wildflowers. Concerts are occasionally presented on the grounds in summer.

Locust Grove, 370 South Rd. (Rte. 9), 845/454-4500, www.morsehistoricsite.org, is open May–Nov., daily 10 A.M.–4 P.M. (last tour begins at 3:15 P.M.); March–April and December by appointment. Admission is adults $5, seniors $4, children under 12 $2. Grounds open daily 8 A.M.–dusk.

Vassar College and Art Gallery

At the southeastern edge of town is Vassar College, founded as a women's college in 1861 by the brewer Matthew Vassar, at the instigation of his friend Samuel Morse. Considered a risky experiment at the time, Vassar today—now coeducational—is recognized as one of the best colleges in the country.

Surrounding much of the campus are towering stone walls with arched gates. Inside is the 1865 Main Building—reputedly designed in such a way that it could be converted into a brewery should the educational experiment fail—and a Norman-style chapel with five Tiffany windows. One of the windows depicts Elena Lucrezia Cornaro Piscopia, the first woman to receive a doctorate (from the University of Padua in 1678). Near the main gate stands the Frances Lehman

Loeb Art Center, designed by Cesar Pelli. Vassar was the first college in the country to have its own art gallery, and today owns more than 12,500 works ranging in origin from ancient Egypt to modern-day New York. Especially strong are the collections of Hudson River landscape paintings (a founding gift from Matthew Vassar), Old Master prints by Dürer and Rembrandt, and contemporary European and American art.

The art center, 124 Raymond Ave., off Rte. 44/55, 845/437-5632, http://fllac.vassar.edu, is open Tues.–Sat. 10 A.M.–5 P.M., Sunday 1–5 P.M. Admission is free.

Springside

Also connected with Matthew Vassar is the "ornamental farm" he used as a summer home. Saved from destruction by a group of concerned citizens in 1990, Springside—now a National Historic Landmark—is the only remaining domestic commission of Andrew Jackson Downing, the brilliant 19th-century landscape architect.

Due largely to neglect and vandalism, all but one of the small buildings that once dotted Springside are now gone, but the grounds are being restored. Gentle rolling hills and rounded shrubbery contrast with rocky outcroppings and gnarled tree trunks.

Maps of Springside, on Academy Street just west of Route 9, are usually available at the entrance.

Entertainment

The county's premier performing arts venue is the historic **Bardavon 1869 Opera House** (see above), presenting everything from top-caliber opera to serious drama. Two small but interesting professional theater groups connected with Vassar College are the **New Day Repertory Co.,** 845/485-7399; and the **Powerhouse Theatre,** 845/437-7235.

For live music, stop into **The Chance,** 6 Crannel St., 845/471-1966, where nationally known artists playing everything from country to R&B perform. The **Mid-Hudson Civic Center,** Civic Center Plaza, along Main St. between Market and Garden Sts., 845/454-5800, sometimes presents big-name touring rock groups.

The weekend editio[...] *Journal* contain good en[...]

Accommodations

One of the nicest places[...] is the classy **Inn at the** [...] Rd., 914/462-5770, w[...] which overlooks Wappingers Creek on the outskirts of town. The rooms are handsomely outfitted in contemporary European and country styles, and a substantial breakfast is included in the room rates ($170–205 d).

Downtown you'll find the attractive, upscale **Poughkeepsie Grand Hotel,** 40 Civic Center Plaza, 845/485-5300, www.pokgrand.com, one of the few hostelries in the immediate area to offer a health club ($99–149 d, full American breakfast included). On the outskirts of town is a 115-room **Econo Lodge,** 418 South Rd., 845/452-6600 ($79–109 d).

Food

For tasty baked goods and sandwiches in the historic districts, try **Cafe Aurora,** 145 Mill St., 845/454-1900, or **Mill Street Market,** 195 Mill St., 845/454-4647. Both are simple, friendly places serving fresh foods for under $10.

Overlooking the Hudson is **River Station,** 1 Water St., at Main, 845/452-9207, serving everything from sandwiches and burgers to steak and fresh fish. Established in 1866, River Station is the oldest food-and-drink establishment in Poughkeepsie; average dinner entrée $17. Also overlooking the Hudson is the **Brass Anchor,** 31 River Point Rd., just north of the bridge, 845/452-3232; on the menu is American Continental fare, with lots of seafood specials and a good choice of vegetarian dishes; dinner entrées $18–30.

Drawing raves from the locals is the newish **Haymaker,** 718 Dutchess Tnpk., 845/486-9454, serving regional American cuisine; average entrée $15. For Cajun-Creole fare, try **Spanky's,** 85 Main St., 845/485-2294, a lively and casual downtown spot. On the menu is everything from gumbos to jambalayas; average entrée $14.

Outside town, you'll find the cozy, elegant **Le Pavillon,** 230 Salt Point Tnpk., 845/473-2525. Housed in a 200-year-old farmhouse, this classic

...aurant serves much game and fresh ...andlelight; average entrée $27.

MILLBROOK AND VICINITY

About 12 miles northeast of Poughkeepsie on Route 44 is sleepy yet moneyed Millbrook, surrounded by large estates and horse farms. Though it seems hard to believe today—in this village of pricey antique stores and gift shops—Timothy Leary once ran his League for Spiritual Discovery out of the old Danheim estate on Franklin Avenue. The estate, located about a mile from the village green, is recognizable by its large stone gatehouse built in Bavarian style. Others who've made Millbrook their home in more recent years are Mary Tyler Moore, Daryl Hall, Liam Neeson, and Natasha Richardson.

Innisfree Garden

Landscaped around a small glacial lake just outside Millbrook is a serene 200-acre sanctuary that its founders, painter Walter Beck and his wife Marion, called a "cup garden." Designed according to Eastern principles, the garden is actually a series of many little gardens, each arranged to draw attention to one especially beautiful object at its center. One of these small gardens focuses on a lotus pool, another on a group of "purple smoke trees," a third on a hillside cave. On a spit of land jutting out into the lake are the Dragon, the Turtle, and the Owl—three large rocks standing sentinel over the preserve.

Despite the gardens' careful design, it has a wild and natural feel. Spreading out over a series of small hills and dales, dappled by sunlight, it features many isolated spots where visitors can dreamily linger.

Innisfree, Tyrell Rd., one mile off Rte. 44 west of Millbrook, 845/677-8000, is open May–Oct., Wed.–Fri. 10 A.M.–4 P.M., Sat.–Sun. 11 A.M.–5 P.M. Admission is $3 on weekdays, $4 on weekends for everyone over age 6.

Mary Flagler Cary Arboretum

A few miles west of Millbrook is a 1,900-acre

Innisfree Garden

preserve that's home to both the Flagler Cary Arboretum and the **Institute of Ecosystem Studies,** website: www.ecostudies.org. The arboretum is open to the public, but much of the institute and its grounds—where ecological research is being conducted—is not. Both are connected to the prestigious New York Botanical Garden in New York City.

Visitors to the arboretum must stop first at the Gifford House Visitor and Education Center to pick up a visitor permit, information, and maps. Directly behind the center are the perennial gardens, filled with over 1,000 species of plants. Among these gardens is a daffodil bed with 12 kinds of daffodils, a poisonous plants bed, an ornamental grass bed, and a garden specifically planted to attract butterflies. Surrounding the gardens are roads and short hiking trails that lead past meadows, fern glens, and pine and hemlock forests.

The arboretum, Rte. 44A, just off Rte. 44, 845/677-5359, is open May–Sept., Mon.–Sat. 9 A.M.–6 P.M., Sunday 1–6 P.M.; Oct.–April, Mon.–Sat. 9 A.M.–4 P.M., Sunday 1–4 P.M. Admission is free.

Wing's Castle

One of the oddest sites in the Hudson Valley is the whimsical Wing's Castle, set atop a rolling, lime-green hill with a panoramic view of the Hudson Valley. Built by Peter and Toni Wing and family, the castle is a 20-odd-year-old work-in-progress, lovingly put together out of everything from antique barn doors to toilet bowl floats. Much of its stone came from abandoned railroad bridges.

It all began in the late 1960s when Peter, just back from Vietnam, and his wife Toni needed a place to live. They owned a piece of land, but had only $1,100 between them. The solution? They'd build the place themselves, out of salvaged materials; never mind the fact that they had no construction experience whatsoever.

Everyone told them it couldn't be done, but today the castle stands, quirky and proud. Each part is designed in a different style—Asian, Tibetan, Germanic, French—and it all works beautifully, with bits of colored fiberglass winking in the

walls and a water-filled moat leading to an inviting hot tub. Inside is a hodgepodge collection of military artifacts, carousel animals, Native American arts, and the Wings' personal possessions.

Though a private house, Wing's Castle, 717 Bangall Rd., off Rte. 44 northeast of Millbrook, 845/677-9085, is open for tours Memorial Day–Christmas, Wed.–Sun. noon–4:30 P.M. The fees—adults $7, children $5—may seem a bit steep, but consider it a tribute to the power of imagination.

Area Wineries

Spread out over 50 acres just below Wing's Castle is **Millbrook Vineyards,** junction of Wing Rd. and the Shunpike (Rte. 57), 845/677-8383 or 800/662-9463, www.millbrookwine.com. Tours and tastings are offered daily noon–5 P.M. Millbrook is especially known for its chardonnay, but it also produces a pinot noir, merlot, and several other wines.

About 10 miles northeast of Millbrook is the award-winning **Cascade Mountain Winery and Restaurant,** Flint Hill Rd., Amenia, 845/373-9021, www.cascademt.com, where self-guided tours and tastings are offered Thurs.–Sun. 11 A.M.–6 P.M. or by appointment. Also on the premises is a chalet-style restaurant open for lunch Thurs.–Sun. and dinner Saturday (average lunch entrée $9; closed Jan.–Feb.). To reach the winery, take Route 44 east to Cascade Mountain Road to Flint Hill Road.

Camping and Accommodations

Camping in the area is available at **Wilcox Memorial Park,** on Rte. 199, just off the Taconic Pkwy. in Stanfordville, 845/758-6100. The park offers 40 sites for $10–20 each; open May–September.

The refreshingly down-to-earth **A Cat in Your Lap,** junction of Rts. 82 and 343, 845/677-3051, is a B&B housed in a gracious 1840s farmhouse ($85 d in the main house; $120 d for the studios in the barn).

In Salt Point, you'll find the unusual **Mill at Bloomvale Falls,** junction of Rts. 82 and 13, 845/266-4234, which occupies an 18th-century stone mill that's on the National Register

THE HUDSON VALLEY

COURTESY OF DUTCHESS COUNTY TOURISM

Cascade Mountain Winery and Restaurant

of Historic Places. Three of its four guest rooms overlook a waterfall, while surrounding the mill are 24 acres for hiking, fishing, and canoeing. Call for rates.

Food

The vintage, stainless-steel **Millbrook Diner,** Franklin Ave., in the village center, 845/677-5319, serves dependable diner fare and especially good breakfasts; average main dish $7.

Foremost among the area's more serious eateries is **Allyn's,** Rte. 44 midway between Millbrook and Amenia, 845/677-5888, which always offers a few regional specialties along with more general innovative American fare; average entrée $20. Next door is a moderately priced cafe decorated with a long mural of Millbrook; average entrée $14.

SOUTH ALONG ROUTE 22

Eight miles east of Milbrook, Route 44 joins Route 22. Heading south from the junction you'll come to **Dover Plains,** where you'll find the charming **Old Drover's Inn,** Old Rte. 22, near Duncan Hill Rd., 914/832-9311, www.old-droversinn.com, named after the cattle drovers who once roared through here on their way to New York City. Now a member of the exclusive Relais & Chateaux group, the inn dates back to the 18th century, and features all the amenities, including working fireplaces in three of its four guest rooms and plenty of antiques. The inn is as known for its fine dining as it is for its accommodations, and serves an innovative American/Continental cuisine ($150–230 d midweek with breakfast; $320–425 d weekends, with breakfast and dinner; average entrée $24).

Continuing south on Route 22 another eight miles brings you to **Wingdale,** presided over by a 30-foot-high Big Chair. Here at **Webatuck Craft Village,** artisans demonstrate their skills—furniture making, weaving, glassblowing, and the like. The "village," spread out along Webatuck Rd. off Rte. 55, 845/832-6601, is open Wed.–Sat. 10 A.M.–4 P.M., Sunday noon–5 P.M. An art gallery and cafe are also on site.

Still farther south is **Pawling,** home of the **Towne Crier Cafe,** 62 Rte. 22, 845/855-1300, one of the region's top live music venues. Featured is everything from folk to jazz, blues to world music; performers in the past have included Clarence Gatemouth Brown, New Riders of the Purple Sage, and Larry Coryell.

HYDE PARK AND VICINITY

The most popular visitor destination in Dutchess County is Hyde Park, once home to Franklin Delano Roosevelt, Eleanor Roosevelt, and a branch of the Vanderbilt family. Despite its blue-blood ancestry, the sprawling village is a down-scale affair filled with aging shopping malls, tour buses, traffic jams, and motels named after the village's famous former residents.

One of the most popular stops for antique lovers in the area is the **Hyde Park Antiques Center,** 544 Albany Post Rd. (Rte. 9), 845/229-8200.

FDR's Home and Library

Franklin Delano Roosevelt was born and grew up in Springwood, a low-lying Georgian-style mansion along the Hudson. Later, he and his wife Eleanor raised their five children here, while Franklin rose through the political ranks. In 1928, he was elected governor of New York; in 1932, president of the United States.

FDR's home has been restored to look much like it did during his presidential days, and has a very intimate feel. In the living room are the leash and blanket of his dog Fala; in the "snuggery" are furnishings once belonging to his domineering mother, Sara Delano Roosevelt; in his office are the books and magazines he was reading during his last visit here in March 1945.

Of equal interest is the next-door Franklin D. Roosevelt Library and Museum, which houses an excellent series of exhibits on the family and their times. Here you'll find everything from FDR's christening dress and early political speeches to Eleanor's diary entries describing the enormous pain she felt upon learning of her husband's extramarital affairs.

Springwood, 511 Albany Post Rd. (Rte. 9), 845/229-9115, www.nps.gov/hofr, is usually open daily 9 A.M.–5 P.M., but during the winter months, it's best to call ahead. The museum, 800/FDR-VISIT (800/337-8474), is open daily 9 A.M.–5 P.M. year round. A combined admission ticket to the home and museum is adults

$10, children under 17 free; admission to grounds free.

Val-Kill

By 1924, Eleanor Roosevelt had had enough of both her husband's political cronies and her mother-in-law. She built a weekend retreat for herself two miles east of the family estate, and moved there permanently after FDR's death in 1945.

Surrounded by fields and woodlands, Val-Kill—a.k.a., the Eleanor Roosevelt National Historic Site—is a simple and rustic place that, compared to Springwood, attracts relatively few visitors. The former First Lady's tastes were delightfully unassuming; she used regular china, set up card tables for extra guests at Christmas, and hung family photographs helter-skelter over the cottage's rough-hewn walls. Nonetheless, it was in this simple setting that Mrs. Roosevelt drafted the U.N. Declaration of Human Rights and entertained important world leaders such as Nikita Khrushchev, Haile Selassie, Adlai Stevenson, and John F. Kennedy. A photograph of a 40-something JFK and a 70-something Eleanor is prominently displayed in the living room.

Val-Kill, Rte. 9G, off Rte. 9, 845/229-9115, www.nps.gov/elro, is open Memorial Day–Labor Day., daily 9 A.M.–5 P.M.; call for off-season hours. Closed January–February. House tours cost adults $5, children under 17 free; admission to grounds free.

Vanderbilt Mansion

Two miles north of the relatively modest Roosevelt homes is the ultra-extravagant Vanderbilt Mansion National Historic Site, built in a posh beaux arts style complete with lavish furnishings, gold-leaf ceilings, Flemish tapestries, and hand-painted lampshades. Built in 1899 by Frederick and Louise Vanderbilt, the mansion—designed by McKim, Mead & White—cost what was then a whopping $2.5 million. Nonetheless, it was the smallest of the Vanderbilt estates and was used only in spring and fall.

Next door to the mansion are extensive formal gardens and a coach house in which the Vanderbilts housed six limousines that were always at their guests' disposal. From the gardens

COURTESY OF DUTCHESS COUNTY TOURISM

Vanderbilt Mansion

are glorious views of the Hudson, with the smoky Shawangunk Mountains rising behind.

The mansion, Rte. 9, 845/229-9115, www .nps.gov/vama, is open daily 9 A.M.–5 P.M. House tours cost adults $8, children under 17 free; admission to the grounds is free.

Hugging the riverbank between the Vanderbilt Mansion and the Roosevelt homes is the **Hyde Park Trail,** an 8.5-mile system of easy hiking trails, well marked by white-and-green signs. Maps of the trails can be picked up at all three historic homes.

Mills Mansion and Park

In Staatsburg, about five miles north of the Vanderbilt mansion, reigns Mills Mansion. Compared to the other exceedingly well-preserved estates along the Hudson, this vast 65-room hilltop hideout seems weary and forlorn. Friends of the mansion expect this to change, however, when the current renovation is complete.

In the meantime, Mills Mansion is still open to visitors, and there's something refreshing about touring a mansion-museum that's not quite finished. Guides take you through cavernous rooms plush with Louis XIV, XV, and XVI furnishings, past halls where craftspeople are busy at restoration work. The most beautiful room is the long, long dining room, flanked with Flemish tapestries and large windows overlooking the Hudson.

Parts of Mills Mansion date back to 1825, but most of the house was built in 1896 by McKim, Mead & White. Named after its original owner, financier Ogden Mills, the mansion was frequented by Edith Wharton, who used it as the model for the Trenor estate, Bellomont, in *The House of Mirth.*

Surrounding Mills Mansion is **Mills-Norrie State Park,** a 1,000-acre preserve with a marina, campground, small environmental museum, and two nine-hole golf courses. Scenic hiking trails run along the west side of the park, overlooking the Hudson. The 55-site campground is open May–October. Reservations are highly recommended; call 800/456-CAMP. A basic site costs $13.

Mills Mansion, Old Post Rd., off Rte. 9, 845/889-8851, is open April–Labor Day, Wed.–Sat. 10 A.M.–5 P.M., Sunday noon–5 P.M.; Labor Day–Oct., Wed.–Sun. noon–5 P.M. Admission is adults $3, seniors $2, children under 12 $1. Mills-Norrie State Park, 845/889-4646, is open daily dawn–dusk.

THE HUDSON VALLEY

Culinary Institute of America

A half mile south of Hyde Park proper is Culinary Institute of America (CIA), the nation's most prestigious cooking school, founded in 1946. Housed in a former Jesuit seminary overlooking the Hudson, the institute trains about 1,850 students at a time, in a 21-month program that includes courses in everything from pork butchering to purchasing. Between classes, the students hurry about campus dressed in traditional white chefs' tunics and white-and-gray checked pants.

The CIA, 433 Albany Post Rd. (Rte. 9), 845/452-9600, www.ciachef.edu, is open daily and visitors are welcome to stroll the grounds, browse in the well-stocked **James Beard Bookstore,** or eat in the four first-rate, student-staffed restaurants (see Food, below), open by reservation only.

Accommodations

Directly across from the Vanderbilt Mansion is the comfortable **Journey Inn Bed & Breakfast,** 1 Sherwood Pl., 845/229-8972, www.journeyinn.com, filled with antiques and memorabilia. The inn offers three guest rooms and two master suites ($95–155 d).

Hyde Park has an abundance of decent budget motels, many of which cater to families and tour groups. Among them are **Village Square, A Country Inn,** 531 Albany Post Rd. (Rte. 9), 845/229-7141 ($55–60 d); **Golden Manor Motel,** Rte. 9 across from FDR's home, 845/229-2157 ($55–65 d), and the **Roosevelt Inn,** 616 Albany Post Rd. (Rte. 9), 845/229-2443 ($65–95 d).

Food

Hyde Park's best restaurants are in the CIA, Rte. 9 at the southern end of town, 845/471-6608, www.ciachef.edu, but you must plan well in advance, as reservations go fast. Each of the four restaurants has its own distinct style. The most casual is **St. Andrew's Cafe,** which offers well-balanced meals featuring everything from wood-fired pizza to beef tenderloin; average dinner, $35. The most elegant is the award-winning **Escoffier Restaurant,** offering classic French cuisine; average dinner, $50–60. In between are **Caterina de Medici,** featuring contemporary and traditional Italian specialties (average dinner $30–45); and the **American Bounty Restaurant,** dedicated to regional American dishes (average dinner, $45–50). Jackets and reservations are required in all rooms.

THE HUDSON VALLEY

Culinary Institute of America

RHINEBECK

Continuing north along Route 9, you'll come to the picturesque village of Rhinebeck, the shady streets of which are lined with restored Victorian buildings. Rhinebeck was first settled in 1686 by Dutch immigrants and has been home to five illustrious Hudson Valley families—the Beekmans, Livingstons, Astors, Montgomerys, and Schuylers.

Downtown

In the center of town is **Beekman Arms,** 4 Mill St. (Rte. 9), 845/876-7077. Built in 1766, it's said to be the oldest inn in continuous operation in America. Everyone from George Washington and Aaron Burr to William Jennings Bryan and FDR once ate or slept at the Beekman. Even if you're not planning to do so yourself, the place is definitely worth a look. Inside are low ceilings, heavy beams, wide floorboards, walk-in fireplaces, and benches dating back to the Revolutionary War.

Next door to the Beekman Arms is a tiny **U.S. post office,** built in 1939 as a replica of the first home built in Rhinebeck. Inside are artifacts from the original building along with murals depicting the town's history.

Across the street from the post office stands the **Dutch Reformed Church,** designed by Robert Upjohn in 1808. Next to the church is a picturesque graveyard with tombstones that date back to the 1700s.

Rhinebeck today is known for its antique stores, restaurants, and galleries, many of which are located along Route 9 or Market Street. One popular site is the **Beekman Arms Antique Market,** 411 Mill St. (Rte. 9), 845/876-3477, which houses 30 vendors.

Tucked in between the newer stores are two creaky village institutions: the **Rhinebeck Department Store,** 1 E. Market St., 845/876-5500; and **A.L. Stickles Five and Dime,** 13 E. Market St., 845/876-3206. Both are veritable time capsules from the 1940s.

The **Rhinebeck Chamber of Commerce,** 845/876-4778, operates a visitor information booth on Mill St. (Rte. 9) diagonally across from the Beekman Arms. Hours are Mon.–Sat.

10 A.M.–4 P.M.; some Sundays noon–4 P.M. Taped visitor information can also be obtained by calling their main number.

Old Rhinebeck Aerodrome

Most summer Sundays at the storybook Old Rhinebeck Aerodrome, Sir Percy Good Fellow climbs into his biplane to fight the Evil Black Baron for the heart of Trudy Truelove. Cheering the adversaries on as the rotary engines roar and the castor oil burns are the excitable Madame Fifi, the dashing Pierre Loop-da-Loop, and a crowd of late-20th-century citizens who have donned WW I–era hats and scarves, dresses, and coats at the gate.

Appearances to the contrary, this charming aerodrome—holding a hodgepodge of hand-painted signs and rickety hangars—is a serious place. On its grounds are about 75 historic airplanes dating back to the early 1900s. Among them are a 1911 Curtiss D, a 1929 Sopwith Camel, and a 1908 Voison whose double canvas wings, light as gossamer, resemble those of a giant dragonfly. Summer Saturdays feature an air show reenacting historic flights.

The aerodrome, 845/758-8610, www.oldrhinebeck.org, is located about three miles north of Rhinebeck at 42 Stone Church Rd., off Rte. 9. It's open as a museum June–Oct., daily 10 A.M.–5 P.M.; admission is adults $6, children $2. The air shows take place June–Oct., Sat.–Sun. 2–4 P.M.; tickets are adults $12, children $5, and include museum admission. After the shows, flights in a 1929 open-cockpit biplane are offered; cost is $40 for 15 minutes.

Wilderstein

This playful all-wooden Queen Anne mansion—sporting dormers, gables, and a magnificent five-story tower—sits in the middle of a 19th-century estate designed by Calvert Vaux, one of the two men who designed Central Park. Inside the 1852 house are lavish interiors by J. B. Tiffany; outside are 40 acres of meadows and woods, drives and trails offering great views of the Hudson. *Wilderstein* means "wild man's stone" and was named after an Indian petroglyph found on the property.

Wilderstein, Morton Rd., off Rte. 9 south of

COURTESY OF DUTCHESS COUNTY TOURISM

Wilderstein

Rhinebeck, 845/876-4818, www.wilderstein.org, is open May–Oct., Thurs.–Sun. noon–4 P.M., or by appointment. A one-hour tour is adults $6, students under 17 free; admission to the grounds is free. A complimentary tea is served to visitors at 3 P.M.

Omega Institute

Hidden away in the hills southeast of Rhinebeck is an adult learning center reminiscent of a kids' summer camp. Guests sleep in cabins, go swimming in a lake, and eat meals together in a cavernous community hall. At any one time, up to 450 students are enrolled in courses ranging from spiritual studies and holistic health (the center's core offerings) to gospel music and creative writing.

Omega, founded in 1977, is no place for day visitors, but many of its 200-odd workshops take place over a single weekend. Tuition for a weekend seminar is usually about $195; room and board for the two days is an additional $140–190.

For a free catalog, contact the Omega Institute, 260 Lake Dr., Rhinebeck, NY 12572-3212; 800/944-1001.

Accommodations

The famed **Beekman Arms,** 4 Mill St. (Rte. 9), 845/876-7077, www.beekmanarms.com, is an inn that has expanded in recent years to include a cluster of about 10 small buildings. Rooms in the historic main building have plenty of atmosphere but are small ($95–105 d); those in the handsome, American Gothic **Delamater Inn** are the most splendid and popular ($99–140 d). Rooms in the other buildings cost $95–140 d.

B&B fans will find many good choices in the area. In the heart of the town is the Gothic Victorian **Gables at Rhinebeck,** 6358 Mill St., 845/876-7577, www.gablesbnb.com. Once owned by two eccentric sisters who shared the house with a huge doll collection, the home now offers three recently renovated guest rooms and an inviting porch. A complimentary afternoon tea with lemonade and scones is served ($140–180 d).

On the outskirts of town, surrounded by fields and woodlands, is the delightful **Whistle Wood Farm,** 11 Pells Rd., 845/876-6838, www.whistlewood.com. Both a working horse farm and a friendly B&B, the Whistle Wood boasts a Jacuzzi, decks overlooking the corral, and plenty of in-room amenities ($105–225 d).

Motels in town include the tiny, eight-room **Rhinebeck Motel,** 117 Rte. 9, 845/876-5900 ($65–79 d); and the family-owned **Rhinebeck Village Inn,** 6 Rte. 9, 845/876-7000 ($68–84 d). Both are clean and friendly.

Food

A good place for burgers and fries, sandwiches and salads is **Foster's Coach House Tavern,** 22 Montgomery St., 845/876-8052. Housed in an actual former coach house, Foster's is filled with wacky horse paraphernalia, including horseshoes, a horse carriage that's now a telephone booth, and mock horse stalls; average main dish $9.

Schemmy's, 19 E. Market St., 845/876-6215, is a genuine old-fashioned ice cream parlor that also serves tasty soups, sandwiches, salads, and simple entrées; average main dish $8. At the energetic **Rolling Rock Cafe,** 46 Rte. 9, 845/876-7655, you can choose from an enormous menu ranging from pizza and pasta to steak and Cajun chicken; average entrée $13. The simply decorated **Mughal Raj,** 110 Rte. 9 S, 845/876-4696, serves first-rate Indian food (average entrée $14), while the upscale **China**

Rose, 100 Shatzell Ave., 845/876-7442, is a Chinese restaurant with a patio overlooking the Hudson (average entrée $15).

The most famous, albeit overrated, restaurant in town is the **Beekman 1766 Tavern,** 4 Mill St. (Rte. 9), 845/871-1766. Decorated with everything from powder horns to historic maps, the tavern serves hearty American fare with an emphasis on regional foods; average entrée $23. Local favorite **Le Petit Bistro,** 8 E. Market St., 845/876-7400, is a classy yet casual bistro offering tasty French cuisine; average entrée $18.

Entertainment and Events

Upstate Films, 26 Montgomery St. (Rte. 9 in the center of Rhinebeck), 845/876-2515, is a revival movie theater screening foreign, independent, and documentary films, along with the classics. The new **Center for the Performing Arts at Rhinebeck,** Rte. 308, 845/876-3080, open June–Sept., offers theater, childrens' shows, concerts, jazz under the stars, and other events.

Rhinebeck's **Dutchess County Fairgrounds,** Rte. 9 north of the village, 845/876-4001, hosts a number of events throughout the year. Among them are an **Antiques Fair** in May, **crafts fairs** in June and October, and the five-day **Dutchess County Fair** in late July or early August. The latter is the largest county fair in the Hudson Valley.

NORTH OF RHINEBECK

About a mile west of Rhinebeck is County Road 103, or the old **River Road,** a short scenic drive that'll take you past grand estates and luscious river vistas. Just north of Rhinebeck on River Road is **Ferncliff,** once the estate of William Astor, now a nursing home; and **Ferncliff Forest,** a 192-acre preserve with nature trails, ponds, and an observation tower. Parking for the forest is at the intersection of County Road 103 and Mt. Rutsen Road. Farther north, at the intersection of Route 199, is **Rokeby,** a working family farm originally built in 1811 by Revolutionary War general John Armstrong and his wife.

Red Hook

If you make a short detour off the River Road on Route 199, you'll come to Red Hook, another attractive village with its share of antique shops and historic buildings. Among the latter are **Elmendorph Inn,** which dates back to the mid-1700s, and the **Octagonal House,** which now houses the Red Hook Library.

The real reason to make a stop here, however, is the wonderful old **Village Diner,** 39 N. Broadway, 845/758-6232, open for breakfast, lunch, and dinner. Built in 1927, the art deco eatery—listed on the state's historic register—is still family-owned and operated. Try the homemade doughnuts, soups, and/or egg creams.

Within walking distance of the downtown is the **Grand Dutchess Bed and Breakfast,** 50 N. Broadway, 845/758-5818, www.grand-dutchess.com, a Victorian Italianate mansion offering six guest rooms, four with private bath ($95–155 d). Also a popular choice among B&B fans is the Federal-style **Red Hook Inn,** 845/758-8445, www.theredhookinn.com, complete with a cozy fireside bar ($135–250 d).

The Hudson Valley region in general has been a supplier of cut flowers since Victorian times, and Dutchess County in particular was once the violet and anemone capital of the world. One of the oldest nurseries still around is **F. W. Battenfeld's & Sons,** 845/758-8018, on Rte. 199 just outside Red Hook. The best time to visit is Oct.–May, when the anemones are in bloom. Also of note near Red Hook is the large, family-owned **Greig Farm,** on Pitcher Ln., just west of Rte. 9, 845/758-1234, where you can pick your own apples, pumpkins, peaches, and berries. Grieg's also features a produce market, greenhouse, and herb gardens.

Annandale-on-Hudson

Back on the old River Road, in Annandale-on-Hudson, is **Montgomery Place,** one of the loveliest mansions along the Hudson. This quiet, 1802 Federal-style gem was remodeled in the 1860s by the famed Alexander Jackson Davis, and every line of the classical structure, every inch of the romantic grounds seems perfectly in its place. From the mansion's circular, columned portico are stunning views of the Hudson and the Catskills beyond.

For almost 200 years, Montgomery Place was home to the prominent Livingston family. One early Livingston was a noted patriot, another served as secretary of state under Pres. Andrew Jackson. Members of the family continued to live in the house until the 1980s, and it is still almost entirely furnished with their treasures.

Surrounding Montgomery Place are landscaped grounds laced with walking trails. Just outside the estate's gates are its still-thriving **Montgomery Place Orchards,** 845/758-6338, where you can pick your own fruits and berries June–October. The orchards also operate a farm stand at the junction of Routes 9G and 199.

Montgomery Place, River Rd., 845/758-5461 or 914/631-8200, www.hudsonvalley.org, three miles north of Rhinebeck, can also be reached by taking Route 9G to Annandale Road to River Road. Hours are April–Oct., Wed.–Mon. 10 A.M.– 5 P.M., Nov.–Dec., Sat.–Sun. 10 A.M.–4 P.M. Admission to the house is adults $7, seniors $6, students 6–17 $4. A grounds pass is $4.

Abutting Montgomery Place in Annandale-on-Hudson is **Bard College,** Rte. 9G at Annandale Road, 845/758-6822, www.bard.edu. Once owned by Columbia University in New York City, Bard is now an independent institution known for its creative arts programs. The two-week **Bard Music Festival** in August, 845/758-7410, focuses on the work of a different major classical composer each year.

On campus are two historic Hudson River estate houses, Blithewood and Ward Manor, now used as the Admissions Building and Levy Economic Institute, respectively. Changing art exhibits are also presented at the **Avery Art Center.**

Tivoli

If you continue north of Annandale-on-Hudson on Route 9G to Route 78 and head west, you'll come to the hamlet of Tivoli. Henry Hudson is thought to have anchored offshore here in 1609, and nearby Crugers Island may once have been an important meeting ground for the local Wappinger and upstate Iroquois Indians.

In Tivoli, you'll find one of the area's most popular restaurants—the boisterous **Santa Fe,** 52 Broadway, 845/757-4100, offering authentic Southwestern and Mexican food. In summer, a small outdoor dining area opens up upstairs; average entrée $14. Also a favorite is the more low-key **Stoney Creek,** 76 Broadway, 845/757-4117, which serves contemporary American fare using local organic produce in a rustic setting; average entrée $15. For tasty sushi in a relaxed setting, try **Osaka,** 74 Broadway, 845/757-5055; average entrée $14.

Columbia County

Though it lacks the drama of the mountainous Hudson Highlands, Columbia may be the most beautiful of the Hudson Valley counties. Rolling, forested hills give way to fields of silvery grain dotted with maroon silos and barns, which in turn give way to historic hamlets centered around village greens and white-steepled churches. Columbia, still highly dependent on agriculture, is also one of the least developed and visited of the Hudson Valley counties.

Columbia's only city, and its county seat, is Hudson, once a major whaling port. Originally settled by a group of seafaring Quakers from Nantucket and Martha's Vineyard, Hudson today is an architectural treasure trove in the process of being restored, as well as an antiques center. On its outskirts are two unusual attractions: Olana, a Persian-styled castle built by the painter Frederic Church; and the largest fire-fighting museum in the United States, filled with hundreds of surprisingly beautiful artifacts.

South of Hudson are Clermont—the furthest north of the grand Hudson Valley estates—and two glorious parks, Lake Taghkanic State Park and Taconic State Park. To the northeast are the picturesque villages of Kinderhook, the Chathams, and New Lebanon. Kinderhook was once home to Pres. Martin Van Buren, whose former home is open to the public. The Chathams and New Lebanon were the sites of early Shaker settlements.

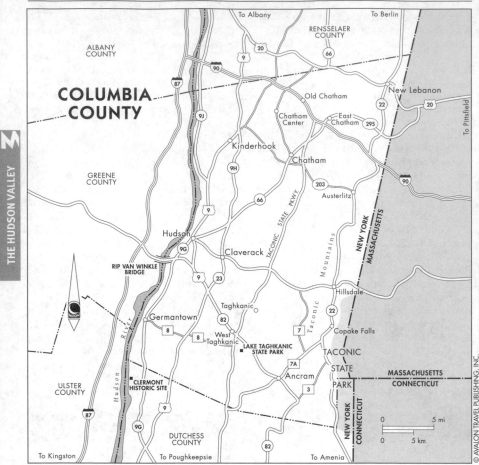

COLUMBIA COUNTY

ALBANY COUNTY

To Albany

To Berlin

RENSSELAER COUNTY

20

9

66

New Lebanon

90

Old Chatham

22

20

87

9J

Chatham Center

East Chatham

295

To Pittsfield

Kinderhook

9H

Chatham

GREENE COUNTY

203

Austerlitz

90

66

9

Hudson

9G

Claverack

RIP VAN WINKLE BRIDGE

9

23

Hillsdale

Taghkanic

22

Germantown

82

7

Copake Falls

8

8

West Taghkanic

LAKE TAGHKANIC STATE PARK

TACONIC STATE PARK

7A

Ancram

MASSACHUSETTS CONNECTICUT

ULSTER COUNTY

CLERMONT HISTORIC SITE

3

87

9

NEW YORK CONNECTICUT

0   5 mi

0   5 km

9G

DUTCHESS COUNTY

82

To Kingston

To Poughkeepsie

To Amenia

TACONIC STATE PKWY

Taconic   Mountains

NEW YORK   MASSACHUSETTS

Hudson River

MOON

© AVALON TRAVEL PUBLISHING, INC.

One other town is worth a mention for music-lovers. Ancramdale is home to a peerless four-day **Bluegrass Festival,** which comes to town for four days in mid-July, 888/946-8495. www.greyfoxbluegrass.com.

Almost every road in Columbia County is a scenic drive, but byways particularly worth exploring include Route 9H north of Hudson, and Routes 82 and 22 in the southern and western parts of the county. The five-mile stretch of Route 11 between Routes 23 and 27 near Taghkanic was declared a **National Beautiful Highway** in the late 1960s.

Information

For more information on Columbia County, contact Columbia County Tourism, 401 State St., Hudson, NY 12534, 518/828-3375 or 800/724-1846, www.columbiacountyny.com; or the Columbia County Chamber of Commerce, 507 Warren St., Hudson, NY 12534, 518/828-4417. Both offices are open Mon.–Fri. 8 A.M.–4 P.M.

SOUTHERN COLUMBIA COUNTY
Clermont State Historic Site

Just north of the Dutchess County border is Clermont, a grand historic estate that was once home to seven generations of the Livingston family. The Georgian manse sits on the edge of a wide lawn lined with enormous black locust trees. Views from the estate are superb; down below is the Hudson River, and in the distance are the high Catskill Mountains peaks that inspired the estate's name (*Clermont* is French for clear mountain).

The 35-room mansion holds many of the Livingstons' heirlooms, including period furniture and family portraits by Gilbert Stuart and others. Robert R. Livingston (1746–1813) was arguably the most famous of the clan. He administered the first oath of office to George Washington, helped draft the Declaration of Independence, and served as minister to France under Thomas Jefferson.

The landscaped grounds include a Lilac Walk (in bloom in May), formal gardens, and many acres of fields, forests, and wetlands laced with carriage paths and hiking trails. Each August, a **croquet tournament** is held here. On the front lawn near the river is a plaque honoring inventor Robert Fulton whose steamboat, the *Clermont,* first traveled up the Hudson from New York City to Albany in August 1807. Fulton was a good friend of Robert R. Livingston and married one of his cousins.

Clermont, 518/537-4240, www.friendsof-clermont.org, is located on Woods Rd., off Rte. 9G, near Germantown. The house is open April 1–Oct. 31, Tues.–Sun. 11 A.M.–5 P.M.; call for off-season hours. The grounds are open daily 8:30 A.M.–dusk. Admission is adults $3, seniors $2, children $1.

Lake Taghkanic State Park

To the east of Clermont, amid rolling hills, is a pristine state park centering around cool, blue Lake Taghkanic, a 1,569-acre body of water ringed with bathing beaches and boat launches. Hiking trails climb small peaks to offer splendid views of the valley below. Also in the park are 60 campsites, picnic areas, a boat-rental shop, ball field, and fitness trail.

The park, 518/851-3631, is off Rte. 82 just east of the Taconic State Parkway. From May to September, a $7 parking fee is charged. Camping facilities are open May–Oct., and reservations are highly recommended; call 800/456-CAMP. The basic site rate is $14.

West Taghkanic

Not far from Lake Taghkanic State Park is the simple but adequate **Taghkanic Motel,** 1011

a classic diner in West Taghkanic

Rte. 82 at the Taconic State Pkwy., 518/851-9006 ($68–75 d). At the classic **West Taghkanic Diner,** Rte. 82, 518/851-7117, the red, neon-lit profile of an Indian chief greets motorists as they turn off the Taconic State Pkwy.; average main dish $7.

Taconic State Park

Not to be confused with Lake Taghkanic State Park is the much larger Taconic State Park, another lovely preserve. It's on the New York–Massachusetts border amid the Taconic Mountains, a small range that extends northward into Vermont. In the 5,000-acre park are two separate recreation areas—Rudd Pond and Copake Falls—featuring hiking trails, bathing beaches, 112 campsites, boat rentals, picnic areas, and playgrounds. The Copake Falls area also offers trout fishing.

The park's greatest attraction is Bash-Bish Glen, where Bash-Bish Brook cascades down a striking series of waterfalls. A craggy outcropping known as Eagle Cliff stands at the top of the cataract; local legend has it that several Indians once fell to their deaths over its edge. Among them was a woman named Bash Bish, after whom the brook was named. Her spirit is said to still inhabit the area. Also nearby is an ice-cold, 40-foot-deep quarry pool with a kiddie pool next door.

The park, 518/329-3993, is on Rte. 344, off Rte. 22, near Copake Falls. In summer there's a $7 parking fee. The camping facilities are open May–Oct., and reservations are highly recommended; call 800/456-CAMP. A basic site costs $14.

Copake Falls and Vicinity

On the edge of Taconic State Park is the serene little hamlet of Copake Falls, centered around a handful of historic wooden buildings and a small traffic circle with a historic four-faced clock. At the intersection of Route 344 and Miles Road stands the **Roeliff-Jansen Historical Society Museum,** 518/329-2376, housed in a striking white former church. On permanent display are exhibits on southern Columbia County—once a flourishing iron district. The museum is open the last weekend of June–Labor Day, Sat.–Sun. 2–4 P.M. Admission is by donation.

One of the county's most popular weekend events, attracting everyone from farmers to second-home owners, is the **Copake Country Auction,** held in Copake on Saturday nights. Watch for advertisements in the *Independent,* a Columbia County paper that comes out on Monday and Thursday.

Hillsdale

Winter brings skiers to Hillsdale's **Catamount Ski Area,** Breezy Hill Rd., off Rte. 23, Hillsdale, 518/325-3200. The small ski resort offers 24 slopes and trails, along with a laid-back atmosphere that makes it especially good for families.

The creaky and near-legendary **Rodgers Book Barn,** Rodman Rd., off West End Rd., off Rte. 23, 518/325-3610, is filled with books, books, and more books—over 50,000 titles, all secondhand. They're housed in a two-story barn with lots of nooks and crannies. The barn is open Thurs.–Mon. noon–6 P.M.; call for winter hours.

The comfortable **Swiss Hutte,** Breezy Hill Rd., off Rte. 23, 518/325-3333, www.swisshutte.com, sits in the middle of the Catamount ski area, overlooking the slopes. On site is a cozy wood-paneled bar and separate dining room that serve Swiss-American fare ($120 d; bar dishes $5–18, restaurant entrées $20–28).

For good regional American cuisine or wood-fired pizza, try the **Hillsdale House,** Rte. 23 in the village center, 518/325-7111; average entrée $13. One of the best restaurants in Columbia County is **Aubergine,** junction of Rts. 22 and 23, 518/325-3412. Housed in a 1783 brick Colonial home, the restaurant serves French-American fare that changes according to what fresh produce is available. Open for dinner only; average entrée $26.

HUDSON

Hudson is one of the most interesting towns along its namesake river. The town is part gentrifying tourist territory, part 19th-century boomtown now down on its luck. Handsome antique stores and sophisticated ex-Manhattanites live side-by-side with weathered Victorian buildings and proud descendants of African American whalers, struggling to make ends meet.

History

The Dutch began arriving in Hudson, then known as Claverack Landing, in the 17th century. But the town wasn't really settled until the 1780s, when a group of seafaring New Englanders—seeking a harbor safe from British attack—discovered the area's deep waters and steep bluffs. They purchased the land in 1783 and by the following spring, several families had arrived and built homes.

Many of the new settlers were Quakers who made a pact to either remain in Hudson permanently or sell their property to others "at first cost, without interest." They carefully designed their new city to be a shipping center, complete with straight main streets, a shipyard, wharves, and warehouses. On April 22, 1785, Hudson received the third city charter granted in New York State, and by 1790, 25 schooners—most in the whaling and sealing business—were registered in the city. Forty-one liquor licenses had

also been granted, and a red-light district flourished. In 1797, Hudson missed becoming the capital of New York State by one vote.

By the mid 1800s, however, the whaling industry had all but disappeared, and Hudson began a transformation into a small industrial city. The coming of the railroads in the late 1840s enabled the area's existing gristmills, tanneries, and breweries to flourish, and new knitting and cotton mills, brick yards and car-wheel works to be built. Business boomed until the early 1900s, when industrial demands changed and Hudson began a slow decline that hit rock bottom in the 1960s and '70s. The city was rediscovered in the 1980s, largely by second-home owners, and is now being slowly restored.

Historic Warren Street

A detailed walking guide to the city can be picked up at **Columbia County Tourism,** 401 State St., 518/828-3375, www.columbiacountrny.org, or the **Columbia County Chamber of Commerce,** 507 Warren St., 518/828-4417; both are open Mon.–Fri. 8 A.M.–4 P.M. The

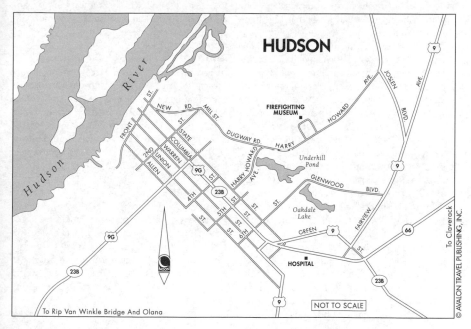

Hudson's Warren Street is a walkable exhibit of varied historic architecture.

© CHRISTIANE BIRD

guide is divided into two leisurely walks, each about an hour and a half long, that highlight the city's architecture.

Even if you don't formally set off on a walking tour, you'll be struck by how many historic buildings—in many different architectural styles—have survived here. Along several blocks of Warren Street alone are a Greek Revival mansion with a "widow's walk" that once belonged to a whaling captain (No. 32), a Federal-style brick house with "eyebrow" windows (No. 102), a Queen Anne clapboard house with attractive trim (No. 114), a rare Adam-style house with an ornamental marble frieze (No. 116), and about 30 other noteworthy buildings.

The 1811 **Robert Jenkins House,** 113 Warren St., 518/828-9764, is open to the public. Built by an early mayor of Hudson, the building now houses a local history museum. Exhibits include paintings by several lesser-known Hudson River School artists; the jawbone of a whale; the "three-star flag from General Grant's headquarters and his personal table"; and other curious odds and ends. The house is open July–Aug., Sun.–Mon. 1–3 P.M., or by appointment. Admission is adults $3, seniors $2, children under 12 free.

Antiques

In recent years, Warren Street has become a mecca for antiques lovers; dozens of stores of varying quality are located here, most between 5th and 7th Streets. Among them are the **Hudson Antiques Center,** 536 Warren St., 518/828-9920, housing about 20 dealers; and **Theron Ware,** 548 Warren St., 518/828-9744, specializing in classic Americana.

The Parade

If you follow Warren Street all the way down to Front Street, you'll come to the Parade, or Promenade Hill Park, which dates back to the town's founding. Situated on bluffs overlooking the Hudson, the park is sadly run-down but offers splendid views of the river, the Catskills, and the lovely, still functioning Hudson-Athens Lighthouse, built in 1874.

To get an even better look at the lighthouse,

which sits by itself on a tiny island, cross over the romantic Rip Van Winkle Bridge to Greene County and head up Route 385 to Athens (see Greene County in the Catskills chapter). The road hugs the shore, and the lighthouse feels close enough to touch.

Olana State Historic Site

Perched high on a hill just south of Hudson is an eccentric, Persian-style castle built in 1870 by landscape artist Frederic Church, with the help of architect Calvert Vaux. Church was then at the height of his career and had just returned from a trip to the Middle East, a land with which he had fallen in love.

A tour of Olana begins in the formal greeting room, which is hung with a good dozen paintings, including one by Church's teacher and the founder of the Hudson River School, Thomas Cole. Here, a guide explains that one of the largest contributions the Hudson River School made to America was its portrayal of the wilderness as something approachable and worth preserving; before, it had been regarded as hostile and dangerous. One of Church's most famous paintings, a portrayal of Niagara Falls,

was used to spearhead a movement to save the falls from destruction.

Throughout the castle, painted in deep blues, reds, and yellows, are romantic arched doorways, wide-open windows, stenciled Persian lettering, and plush Persian rugs. Every room is filled with unique and exotic objects carefully picked out by the artist, who one critic said had the "best taste of his time." Each room also houses a number of Church's majestic, luminous canvases, while the dining room is an amazing picture gallery hung floor to ceiling with hundreds of canvases from the 16th to 18th centuries.

Olana, off Rte. 9G, just south of the Rip Van Winkle Bridge, 518/828-0135, www.olana.org, is open May–Labor Day, Wed.–Sun. 10 A.M.–5 P.M.; Labor Day–Nov., Wed.–Sun. noon–4 P.M. Admission is adults $3, seniors $2, children 5–12 $1.

American Museum of Firefighting

This delightful spit-and-polish hall boasts the nation's largest collection of fire-fighting equipment and related paraphernalia, including dozens of exquisite old horse-drawn fire carriages, many equipped with fairy-tale finery. Several carriages

HUDSON'S STREET OF SIN

As sleepy as the small town of Hudson seems today, it once had a nationwide reputation for vice. For a century or so before 1950, a dozen or more houses of ill repute lined Diamond Street (now known as Columbia Street). Alongside them stood illegal horserooms, gambling parlors, floating craps games, and hole-in-the-wall taverns and bars.

No one knows exactly when the illicit businesses began, but by 1840, local citizens were complaining about the "riotous gatherings" on Diamond Street. During Prohibition, the street was a favorite haunt of gangster Legs Diamond and friends, while in the 1940s, it was so popular that out-of-towners arriving by the carloads had a hard time finding parking spots. "Columbia Street was famous as a well-managed, sensual shopping center where even the most discriminating could find what they wanted," writes Bruce Edward Hall in *Diamond Street:*

The Story of the Little Town with the Big Red Light District (Black Dome Press, 1994). "American servicemen at bases around the globe found their familiarity with [Hudson] a common bond."

Many of the most popular bordellos on Columbia Street lay between 3rd and 4th Streets—a stretch known as "The Block." During the 1930s, for example, Madam Mae Healy was at No.328, Dottie Pierson at No.342, and Daisy Rawley at No.358. Evelyn White's brothel at No.320 boasted walls lined with velvet, while the Mansion House at No.332 was a three-storied extravaganza with an enormous bar and bartenders named "Burger Baby" and "Woofing Sam."

Columbia Street was padlocked for good in the 1950s, and today the once-teeming thoroughfare is just a nondescript section of the truck route. Few driving by suspect its notorious past.

sport engraved lanterns and velvet-covered seats. One even has silver- and gold-plated hubcaps.

Part of the museum's charm is its location on the grounds of New York's retirement home for volunteer firemen. You'll see the retirees hanging out on the porch as you drive up, and you'll meet them as you tour the museum. From them you'll learn that 80 percent of New York State's firefighters are still volunteers, a fact that poses a serious problem as the demands of firefighting are not compatible with busy modern-day lives.

The museum, 518/828-7695 or 800/479-7695, is at 125 Harry Howard Ave., off Rte. 9 just north of Rte. 23B. It's open daily 9 A.M.–4:30 P.M.; admission is free.

Claverack

Take Route 23B east out of Hudson and you'll come to the historic village of Claverack, where the proud 1786 **Old Hudson County Courthouse** stands at the junction of Route 23B and Old Lane. Here in 1805, Alexander Hamilton argued for the retrial of Hudson newspaper publisher Harry Roswell, who had been found guilty of libeling President Jefferson. "I contend," said Hamilton, "for the liberty of publishing truth with good motives and for justifiable ends, even though it reflects on government, magistrates or private persons." The court was divided in its decision, but in 1805, New York's state legislature enacted Hamilton's principles into law. On Route 9H just north of the old courthouse is the serene 1767 **Reformed Dutch Church,** built of weathered red brick.

Accommodations

The recently restored **St. Charles Hotel,** 16-18 Park Pl., 518/822-9900, www.stcharleshotel.com, built in the late 1800s, offers comfortable rooms at reasonable rates. Downstairs is a popular taproom and two restaurants ($79–109 d).

On Rte. 9 about 10 miles south of downtown Hudson is the inviting **Inn at Blue Stores,** 518/537-4277, www.innatbluestores.com, a Spanish-style B&B outfitted with tile roofs and stucco walls. Situated on a farm, the inn includes a pool and veranda. All for room have king-size beds and two have private baths ($125–225 d).

Food

Brandow's, 340 Warren St., 518/822-8938, is a popular cafe and bakery serving gourmet sandwiches, salads, pastas, and baked good, along with fresh juices and fancy coffees.

Housed in a restored brick building is the **Paramount Grill,** 225 Warren St., 518/828-4548. A good choice for either lunch or dinner, it offers everything from sandwiches and salads to grilled lamb chops and spicy Cajun shrimp; average dinner entrée $14. For an eclectic international menu featuring everything from spicy Spanish dishes to buffalo and grilled fish, try the **Charleston,** 517 Warren St., 518/828-4990; average entrée $17.

KINDERHOOK

The charming village of Kinderhook, or "children's corner," was first settled by the Dutch—a fact reflected in the town's neat tree-lined streets, historic wooden buildings, and laid-back atmosphere. The village's most famous native son was Martin Van Buren, and signs directing visitors to the former president's birth site, home, and gravesite are everywhere. It is to Van Buren, nicknamed "Old Kinderhook," that we owe the expression "O.K."

To reach Kinderhook from Hudson, take Route 9 north about 10 miles.

Lindenwald

Martin Van Buren, a tavern owner's son who rose to hold the highest office in the land, spent the last 21 years of his life in this large yellow house surrounded by linden trees. Before Van Buren bought the property in 1839, Washington Irving had often visited here, sometimes even tutoring the former residents' children.

A visit to the Martin Van Buren National Historic Site begins with a short film on the "Little Magician" (Van Buren was only five feet six inches), who avidly supported Jeffersonian democracy, served as vice-president under Andrew Jackson, and—probably his most important contribution to history—established the country's independent treasury. In his day, Van Buren was regarded as a cool and competent diplomat who operated most effectively behind the scenes, "row[ing] to his object with muffled oars."

Van Buren settled into his retirement home after his defeat for re-election in 1841, and soon set about remodeling the place. In the sitting room, all done up in elegant gold and light blue, is a fine collection of musical instruments; in the banquet room is a magnificent French wallpaper mural depicting the landscape of the hunt. The room is kept dark at all times to preserve the mural, which can only be viewed by flashlight.

Lindenwald, Rte. 9H south of the village center, 518/758-9689, www.nps.gov/mava, is open May–Oct., daily 9 A.M.–4 P.M.; Nov.–Dec., Sun.–Sun. 9 A.M.–4 P.M. Admission is adults $3, families $7.

Luykas Van Alen House

Also on Route 9H, just north of Lindenwald, is the Luykas Van Alen House, a lovingly restored 1737 Dutch farmhouse complete with a steeply pitched roof, wide chimneys, Delft tile, and sturdy furnishings. If the place looks familiar, it's because it was used in Martin Scorsese's film *The Age of Innocence,* based on the Edith Wharton novel.

In front of the farmhouse is a dark and peaceful pond that's home to several swans, while to one side is the one-roomed **Ichabod Crane School House.** Washington Irving apparently based his famous character on a schoolteacher from Kinderhook; the building has been restored to look as it did in the 1920s.

Both buildings are operated by the Columbia Historical Society, 518/758-9265, www.berk .com/cchs, and are open Memorial Day–Labor Day, Thurs.–Sat. 11 A.M.–5 P.M., Sunday 1–5 P.M. Admission is adults $3, seniors $2, children under 12 free.

Other Historic Sites

In downtown Kinderhook, by the village green, is the 1820 **James Vanderpoel House.** Vanderpoel—a contemporary of Martin Van Buren—was a prominent attorney, state assemblyman, and judge. The house is an excellent example of Federal-style architecture and contains an interesting collection of period furnishings and paintings by early area artists.

The house, 16 Broad St., 518/758-9265, www .berk.com/cchs, is open Memorial Day–Labor Day, Thurs.–Sat. 11 A.M.–5 P.M., Sunday 1–5 P.M. Admission is adults $3, seniors $2, children under 12 free. Combination tickets with the Van Alen House are also available; adults $5, seniors $3.

Next door to the former Vanderpoel home are the **General John Burgoyne House,** where the British prisoner of war was entertained on the night of October 22, 1777 while being taken from the Battle of Saratoga to Boston; and the **Benedict Arnold House,** where the American general was brought after being wounded in the 1777 Battle of Bemis Heights. Both of these houses are private residences but are marked with historic plaques.

Also downtown is the **Columbia County Museum,** 5 Albany Ave., 518/758-9265, www .berk.com/cchs, which features changing exhibits on the history and culture of the county. Hours are May–Oct., Mon.–Fri. 10 A.M.–4 P.M. and Saturday 1–5 P.M.; Dec.–April, Monday, Wednesday, Friday 10 A.M.–4 P.M. Admission is free.

Shopping

Kinderhook centers around a village green lined with shops. At one end is the well-stocked **Blackwood and Brouwer Booksellers Ltd.,** 7 Hudson St., 518/758-1232, where summer story hours, author breakfasts, readings, and book-signings are regularly offered. At the other end of the green is the creaky, old-fashioned **Fisher's O.K. Rock Shop,** 2 Chatham St., 518/758-7657, selling minerals, fossils, jewelry, and gifts made from polished rock.

Kinderhook also has its share of antique shops. One of the biggest is the **Kinderhook Antiques Center,** 518/758-7939, housed in an old dairy barn on Route 9H several miles south of the green.

Accommodations

Housed in a classic 1900s home surrounded by flowering gardens and an inviting side porch is the **Kinderhook B&B,** 67 Broad St., 518/758-1850, www.berk.com/kinderhookbandb. The three air-conditioned guest rooms are smartly outfitted with country antiques, and offer comfortable featherbeds. One reader has written in, however, to

384 The Hudson Valley

complain of faulty air conditioning and bad smells. Breakfast is a multi-course feast ($89–139 d).

Food

The idiosyncratic, log cabin **Carolina House,** 59 Broad St., 518/758-1669—a local favorite that attracts diners from miles around. On the menu is such hearty Southern fare as baby-back ribs, Southern-fried chicken, catfish, crab cakes, biscuits, and pecan pie; average entrée $15.

THE CHATHAMS

To the east of Kinderhook, in a countryside of rolling hills and horse farms, are the Chathams—the Village of Chatham, Chatham Center, East Chatham, North Chatham, and Old Chatham. Old Chatham, settled in 1758, is little more than a crossroads, but it's home to the **Old Chatham Country Store,** Rte. 13 and the Old Albany Tnpk., 518/794-7151, where you can buy everything from homemade muffins to gardening tools.

Farther south is the Chathams' commercial hub, the Village of Chatham. During the late 1800s, over 100 trains a day passed through here on their way to Albany or Boston. The streets are still lined with Italianate brick storefronts dating back to that era. In the village center you'll find **Chatham Booksellers,** 27 Main St., 518/392-3005; the old **Crandell Theatre,** Main St., 518/392-3331, where movie tickets still cost $3.50; and a number of attractive gift shops. On the outskirts of town is one of the state's top summer-stock playhouses, the **Mac-Haydn Theatre,** 1925 Rte. 203, 518/392-9292.

Near East Chatham, on Black Bridge Rd. (Rte. 295), is **Librarium Second Hand Books,** 518/392-5209, a homey book barn with over 35,000 used titles. In summer, the store is open Fri.–Mon.; in winter, Sat.–Sun., or by appointment or chance.

Shaker Museum and Library

Off a narrow county road outside Old Chatham is the Shaker Museum, dedicated to the history and culture of the Protestant sectarians who emigrated from England to the United States in the 1770s. Named for their tendency to dance and

sway during worship, the Shakers were known for their industry, thrift, and celibate lifestyle. They constructed everything they needed with a great deal of thought and care, and to this day, Shaker-designed items are highly valued for their simplicity and grace. As the Shakers themselves put it, "Anything may, with strict propriety, be called perfect which perfectly answers the purpose for which it was designed."

The Shaker Museum is not a particularly friendly place—you get the feeling you're intruding on hallowed scholars' ground here—but it does house the country's largest collection of Shaker handiwork. Spread out over 24 galleries in several buildings are many fine examples of the oval boxes and baskets, clean-lined cabinets and chairs, and ingenious crafts and tools for which the sect is famous. It is to the Shakers that we owe the invention of the flat broom, clothespin, circular saw, screw propeller, turbine water wheel, cut nails, and water-repellent fabric.

The museum, 88 Shaker Museum Rd., off County Road 13, 518/794-9100, www.shaker-museumandlibrary.org, is open May–Oct., Wed.–Mon. 10 A.M.–5 P.M. Admission is adults $8, seniors $6, children 8–17 $4. A small cafe and bookshop are also on the premises.

Entertainment and Events

Chatham celebrates the Fourth of July with a **Strawberry Shortcake Breakfast and Flag-Making Festival** at the Shaker Museum, 88 Shaker Museum Rd., 518/794-9100. The **Columbia County Fair,** 518/828-3375, comes to the Chatham fairgrounds, the junction of Routes 66 and 203, over Labor Day weekend. It's the nation's oldest continuously running county fair.

Camping and Accommodations

Camping is available in nearby Austerlitz at **Woodland Hills Campground,** 86 Fog Hill Rd., 518/392-3557, with 200 sites open May–October. The basic site rate is $18.

Between Chatham and Chatham Center, budget travelers will find the **Chatham Travel Lodge,** Rte. 295 and Taconic State Pkwy., 518/392-4066 ($59–89 d). East of East Chatham, near the Massachusetts border, is the **Inn at Shaker Mill**

THE SHAKERS

History

The Shaker religious movement began in England in 1758, under the leadership of a woman who would later be known as Mother Ann Lee. Lee was originally a Quaker, but instead of worshipping quietly as did her fellow congregants, she would fall into a religious ecstasy, whirling and trembling and "shaking" off evil.

In 1762, Lee married and had four children, all of whom died in infancy following difficult births. Lee saw this as a judgment from God and began to avoid all sexual relations with her husband. Shortly thereafter, she had a conversion—"My soul broke forth to God," she said—and ventured forth to spread the word. Central to her preachings was the philosophy that men and women should live apart from one another.

Before long, Lee was thrown in jail for her radical ideas, and there she had a vision that told her to go to America. In the spring of 1774, she and eight followers (including her husband, from whom she had already separated) set sail, to eventually settle in Watervliet, near Albany (see the chapter on Central New York).

The Shakers slowly gained converts, and by 1794 they had established 11 communities throughout New York and New England. At their peak in the 1850s, the sect had about 6,000 members from Maine to Kentucky. One of their settlements, Sabbathday Lake, Maine, is still a living, working Shaker community open to the public in summer (207/926-4597). "Are you worried about dying out?" one of their members was asked recently. "Nay! Not unless God and Christ and Eternal verities are failing," was the answer.

Beliefs and Lifestyle

Among the basic tenets of Shakerism are celibacy, separation from the world, communal sharing of goods, confessions of sins, equality of the sexes, and pacifism. Children come into the community through the conversion of their parents, or through adoption.

During their heyday, the Shakers were organized into "families" of about 50 members who lived in a home with separate doorways, stairs, and sleeping quarters for the sexes. The "brothers" and "sisters" would only come together for daily meditation, meals—which would be eaten in silence—Sunday worship services, and occasional "union meetings." During the latter, the brothers and sisters would sit facing each other a few feet apart, and converse or sing.

The children lived separately from the adults in a Girls' House and Boys' House. School was held for the girls during the summer and for the boys in winter.

Each family had its own gardens, crops, livestock, and workshops. The sisters did the cooking, cleaning, washing, spinning, weaving, and gardening, while the brothers tended to the heavier farmwork and manufactured products such as chairs, brooms, and oval boxes to sell to the outside world. The Shakers also raised a wide variety of medicinal herbs which they marketed through pharmaceutical companies.

While the Shakers shunned the material culture of modern society, they were not opposed to new ideas, and were frequently ahead of their time in farming and sanitation practices. Many had running water and electricity long before their more worldly neighbors. As early as 1910, many were buying automobiles—to be used, of course, for Shaker business, not personal pleasure.

Hancock Shaker Village

In Massachusetts, not far from Columbia County, is the most interesting Shaker site in the area, the Hancock Shaker Village. This superbly restored living-history museum is comprised of 20 buildings set on 1,200 acres. Craftspeople are at work during the day and candlelight dinners are served on Saturday evenings. The village's finest building is its Round Barn, erected in 1826, which permitted one man working in the center of the building to feed and water the cattle with a minimum of motion.

Hancock Village, Rts. 20 and 41, five miles west of Pittsfield, Massachusetts, 413/443-0188, www.hancockshakervillage.org, is open May–Oct., daily 9:30 A.M.–5 P.M., April and November 10 A.M.–3 P.M. The dinners must be reserved well in advance.

Farm, 42 Cherry Ln., off Rte. 22, Canaan, 518/ 794-9345, www.shakermillfarminn.com. Spartan yet comfortable, the inn is housed in a restored Shaker gristmill surrounded by woodlands. Meals are family-style ($50–70 per person with breakfast, packages available).

Food

In Chatham is the popular **Chatham Bakery and Coffee Shoppe,** 1 Church St., 518/392-3411, a family-run institution known for its baked goods and burgers served on homemade bread.

NEW LEBANON

Mount Lebanon Shaker Village

A community of Shakers once lived to the east of Old Chatham in the Mt. Lebanon Shaker Village. Twenty-four original village buildings still stand. Many are leased to the Darrow School— a prep school that has occupied this site since the 1930s—but four others have been restored and are open to the public. Still others are in the process of being restored, and will be open in years to come.

Near the entrance to the village, in the former wash house, is a visitor center where you can watch a short slide show and view exhibits on the community's early leaders. Foremost among them was Elder Frederick Evans, an intellectual who published his autobiography in the *Atlantic Monthly* and corresponded with Leo Tolstoy.

Also open to the public are a granary, now being used as a gift house and workshop for reproduction furniture; a plant nursery and herb garden; and the brethren's workshop, which once housed a seed shop, printer's shop, and shoe-making shop. Otherwise, visitors have to content themselves with strolling the peaceful grounds and imagining the community as it was when several thousand Shakers lived here.

The village, Shaker Rd., off Rte. 20, 518/794-9500, is open mid-June–Oct., Fri.–Sun. 10 A.M.– 5 P.M. Admission is adults $5, seniors $4.50, children 6–12 $2, families $10.

Abode of the Message

Within easy walking distance of the Mt. Lebanon village, on Shaker Road just beyond Chairfactory Road, is a modern-day spiritual community known as the Abode of the Message. A Sufi community founded in 1975 by Pir Vilayat Inayat Kahn, the Abode spreads out over 430 acres, includes seven original Shaker buildings and an organic farm, and is home to about 50 adults and 15 children. The community devotes itself to worship, "harmonizing with the forces of nature," and spreading the Sufi teachings.

Day visitors are welcome at the **Wisdom's Child Bookstore,** which stocks a wide range of spiritual titles (open Mon.–Sat. 10 A.M.–5 P.M. and Sunday 1–4 P.M.), and at some of the weekly worship services. The Abode also offers various seminars and retreats that are open to the public. For more information, contact the Abode at 518/794-8095 (general info) or 518/794-8181 (the bookshop), www.theabode.net.

Stock Car Racing

On summer Saturday nights, the bleachers are always filled with families and fans at the **Lebanon Valley Raceway,** Rte. 20, just west of West Lebanon, 518/794-9606, www.lebanonvalley.com. Racing season runs April–October.

The Catskills

Introduction

The dense, dark, smoke-blue Catskill Mountains, crowded together to the west of the Hudson, are a strangely enigmatic place. They're not particularly high or particularly grand—the tallest peak is only about 4,200 feet—and they're certainly not remote. Yet the Catskills possess an oddly evocative wildness and solitude. Stepping into them is like stepping into an ancient woodcut, carved to illustrate a dark fairy tale. No wonder Rip Van Winkle met a mysterious "company of odd-looking personages playing at ninepins" here, and drank of their large flagons to fall into a 20-year sleep.

The Catskills have had a remarkable influ-ence on the American imagination. They were the first American landscape to be romanticized in literature and art; author Washington Irving and later the painters of the Hudson River School discovered the beauty of the region's gorges and waterfalls, crags and cliffs, and brought it to the public eye in their works. By the mid-1800s, the primeval Catskills—filled with both impenetrable shadows and luminous shafts of light—had come to symbolize the New World wilderness.

A very popular vacation destination from the mid-1800s well into the mid-1900s, the Catskills are now regarded as a largely second-class resort. Worn-out and shabby in many places, with forlorn houses clinging tenuously to the roadsides, the area feels old-fashioned, passed-over, forgotten.

autumn in the Catskills

As Roland Van Zandt writes in *The Catskill Mountain House,* "Over all the region, side by side with the life of the present and infusing that life with its own deep poignancy, lies the heady atmosphere of decay."

To the romantic, this only adds to the Catskills' appeal. Driving through the region, you'll pass everything from heart-stopping mountain vistas and picturesque villages to listing barns and boarded-up hotels. Scruffy yoga retreats sit next door to famed Jewish megaresorts; garish amusement parks are located just down the street from abandoned family farms.

The Catskills are also on the cusp of a rebirth. Due largely to a recent influx of second-home owners and ex-urbanites, sophisticated restaurants and B&Bs now pop up in unexpected places, and the region boasts a strong arts scene. Evolving as well is a greater appreciation of the area's considerable diversity. The Catskills are not just about mountains and resorts. Small museums and historic attractions can be found everywhere, along with creaky general stores, weekly country auctions, scenic recreational areas, excellent canoeing and day-hiking, and some of the best trout fishing in the world.

THE LAND

Mountains

Geologically speaking, the Catskill Mountains are not mountains at all but an uplifted section of the Allegheny Plateau that was once the floor of a shallow sea. During the Middle- and Late-Devonian and Carboniferous periods, that seabed—made up largely of shales and sandstones—was heaved upwards to an elevation of 5,000–6,000 feet, forming the Catskills. Since then, the plateau has eroded, leaving peaks that range 3,000–4,200 feet in height; one unusual characteristic of the Catskills is their near uniform elevation, seldom found in true mountain ranges. Also unlike other ranges, here you'll see little bare rock, and few flat ledges or exposed cliffs.

The Catskills boast 34 peaks and ridges with elevations over 3,500 feet, and about 65 others with elevations over 3,000 feet. Between these peaks are sharp divides, ravines, and valleys, all

WASHINGTON IRVING ON THE CATSKILLS

Whoever has made a voyage up the Hudson must remember the Kaatskill Mountains. They are a dismembered branch of the great Appalachian family, and are seen away to the West of the river, swelling up to a noble height and lording it over the surrounding country. Every change of season, every change of weather, indeed, every hour of the day, produces some change in the magic hues and shades of these mountains. . . . When the weather is fair and settled, they are clothed in blue and purple, and print their bold outlines on the clear evening sky; but sometimes, when the rest of the landscape is cloudless, they will gather a hood of gray vapors about their summits, which, in the last rays of the setting sun, will glow and light up like a crown of glory.

Washington Irving,
Rip Van Winkle

created by the many rivers and streams that continue to erode the region today.

Marking the eastern edge of the Catskills is a steep, clifflike escarpment known as the Great Wall of Manitou. To the west, the slopes are gentler, and eventually taper off altogether.

A second, much smaller mountain range, the Shawangunks, lies at the southwestern edge of Ulster County. Formed during the Silurian Age and therefore much older than the Catskills, the Shawangunks are composed primarily of limestone and quartz conglomerate. Thick, jointed strata form cliffs several hundred feet high, making the Shawangunks a favorite among rock-climbers.

Waterways

Two major river systems drain most of the Catskills: the Hudson-Mohawk and the Delaware. Principal tributaries of the Hudson-Mohawk include the Schoharie River, Catskill Creek, Kaaterskill Creek, and the Esopus. The headwaters of both the West and East Branch of the Delaware River begin in Delaware County; principal tributaries include Beaver Kill, Willowemoc Creek, and Mongaup Creek.

Since 1828, when the Delaware & Hudson

Canal was built, the Catskills have also been known for their manmade waterways. Today, two main reservoir and aqueduct systems network through the region. The older Catskill Reservoir System, begun in 1909, includes Ashokan Reservoir, Schoharie Reservoir, and the Catskill Aqueduct. Powered by gravity, the mostly surface-level aqueduct passes 1,400 feet beneath the Hudson River to flow into Kensico Reservoir in Westchester County. There the water is chlorinated and sent another 17 miles downstream to Yonkers, where it's distributed to Manhattan and Brooklyn. The total length of the Catskill Aqueduct is 120 miles.

The Delaware Reservoir and Aqueduct System was built in the 1930s, when it became painfully apparent that the Catskill System was no longer large enough to satisfy New York City's ever-increasing water needs. The system is composed of the enormous 18.5-mile-long Pepacton Reservoir; the smaller Rondout, Neversink, and Cannonsville Reservoirs; and the Delaware Aqueduct.

Flora and Fauna

Before the Catskills were decimated by the tanning and logging industries in the 1800s, they were covered with hemlock, beech, chestnut, and sugar maple. Today, like much of the Northeast, the Catskills forests are predominantly oak and hickory, although some hemlock, beech, and sugar maple have returned in second growth. Other common species include red maple, sassafras, white pine, and pitch pine. Fir and spruce flourish at higher elevations.

The Catskills are high enough to support above-timberline alpine flora, but little is found. Wildflowers that flourish on the lower slopes include violets, starflowers, trilliums, adder's tongues, Jack-in-the-pulpits, Indian pipes, mayapples, and milkweed.

The largest mammals inhabiting the Catskills are the white-tailed deer, raccoon, red fox, porcupine, opossum, woodchuck, cottontail rabbit, and occasional black bear. Some of the more common reptiles and amphibians include toads, frogs, salamanders, and turtles, as well as garter, Eastern hognose, and green snakes.

Songbirds such as the black-capped chick-adee, cedar waxwing, pine warbler, ovenbird, and scarlet tanager can be spotted throughout the Catskills; waterfowl such as mallards, wood ducks, and Canada geese often dot the lakes. Along the Upper Delaware River in southern Sullivan County, rare birds such as ospreys, egrets, and great blue herons sometimes put in an appearance, although turkey vultures, hawks, and owls are much more common. Southern Sullivan County also supports the largest winter population of bald eagles in the northeastern United States. About 200 bald eagles flying south from New England and Canada spend their winters on reservoirs here.

HISTORY

Early History

Prehistoric humans may have occupied the area near the town of Catskill as early as 10,000 B.C., but the region's recorded history doesn't begin until about A.D. 1300. At that point, the Lenape Indians were living along the Delaware River in today's southern Sullivan County, and the Esopus Indians had settled along Esopus Creek near Kingston. Few Native Americans actually lived up in the mountains, but many used the heights as hunting grounds.

The Hardenbergh Tract

The area's first European residents were Dutch and French Huguenots, who settled in eastern Ulster County near the Hudson River in the mid-1600s. There they established the early villages of Kingston, Hurley, and New Paltz. The English followed close behind, but in 1708, a patent of almost two million acres, covering most of the Catskill region, was granted to one Johannis Hardenbergh by the English governor Lord Cornbury. That tract, as Arthur Adams writes in *The Catskills,* "hung like a cloud over the Catskills for almost a hundred years and did much to hamper settlement." Not surprisingly, many colonists passed by the Catskills to settle farther west where they could own their own land.

The Hardenbergh Tract was eventually sold to other large landholding families, but they, too, continued to collect rents. In 1844–45, the

DEFINING THE CATSKILLS

The Dutch-derived word "Catskills," probably named for the wildcats who once roamed the region (*kaat* for cat, *kill* for stream), means different things to different people at different times. The most obvious definition would seem to be the one that refers to the Catskill Mountains. But these are primarily located only in northern Ulster and Greene Counties, and most people use the word Catskills to refer to a far bigger region.

A second definition refers to Catskill State Park, which encompasses about 900 square miles and includes both private lands and the state-owned Catskill Forest Preserve, established in 1894 to protect the area's remaining forests. The park extends over parts of all four counties, but is again primarily located in northern Ulster and Greene Counties. Since Catskill State Park, unlike most state parks, does encompass both public and private lands, don't come here expecting to find an isolated preserve such as the Grand Canyon—you'll be disappointed.

A broader, more general definition of the Catskills, and the one used by most travel guides, including this one, encompasses both the state park and its surrounding foothills and resorts. This area is three to four times the size of the park alone, and includes some sections that have nothing to do with either mountains or forests.

Yet a fourth definition of the Catskills refers only to Sullivan County's so-called "Borscht Belt," a string of Jewish megaresorts where many famous comedians and entertainers got their starts. Many of these resorts (none of which, by the way, are located in the mountains) have shut down in recent years. Yet they still represent "the Catskills" for many vacationers.

Commercial Development

Canals, turnpikes, and railroads began penetrating the Catskills in the early- to mid-1800s, and the area soon developed a solid agricultural and industrial base. Products such as maple syrup, hops, vegetables, grain, milk, butter, eggs, and honey were produced to ship south to New York City, while gristmills, sawmills, and small factories sprang up along the Hudson.

It was the tanning industry, however, that soon dominated and all but destroyed the Catskills. Before the automobile age, leather for saddles and harnesses was in great demand. To cure the hides required tannin, best obtained from the bark of hemlock trees. Because an enormous amount of bark was needed to extract a small amount of tannin, it made economic sense to bring the hides to the hemlocks. Vast tanneries filled with clanking machinery and stinking vats set up shop all over the mountains, while sweat-drenched horses pulled wagons loaded with hides up the mountainsides. Millions of trees were cut down only for their bark and then left behind to rot. As soon as one area's hemlock supply was exhausted, the tanneries moved on to another, until virtually the entire hemlock forest was gone. The tanneries then turned to the oak trees.

Catskill Preserve

Finally, in the 1880s, New York State woke up. Citizens concerned with the similar depletion of the Adirondacks banded together to fight for the creation of a forest preserve. Most people supported a preserve either for aesthetic reasons or because they were avid hunters or anglers. The business community, on the other hand, feared that the denuded slopes would cause New York Harbor to fill with silt and the Erie Canal to dry up. Largely due to the influence of the latter group, the state legislature passed the Forest Preserve Act in 1885, and made it an amendment to the state constitution in 1894. From then on, the lands of both the Adirondacks and the Catskills were "to be forever kept as wild forest lands."

Resorts

Starting in the late 1820s, artists Thomas Cole, Asher Durant, and others of the Hudson River

tenant-farmers' long-smoldering resentments finally broke out in the Anti-Rent Wars. Tenants dressed as Indians resisted rent collectors, and riots ensued. An undersheriff was killed, several men were sentenced to death or life imprisonment, and martial law was declared. Only in 1852, with the election of a new governor and state legislators, were pardons issued and the feudal land system declared illegal.

School began painting the romantic Catskills landscape. Their work was unlike anything the American public had ever seen, and it created an overnight sensation. Before long, everyone wanted to visit the mountains for themselves.

Although stagecoach inns and boardinghouses had existed in the Catskills in the late 1700s and early 1800s, the first real resort here was the Catskill Mountain House. Built in 1823 by a group of Catskill businessmen, the Catskill Mountain House was America's first great mountain resort.

Erected high atop the clifflike Great Wall of Manitou, near Kaaterskill Falls in Greene County, the early Mountain House had only 10 rooms and attracted mostly hunters, anglers, and the Hudson River School artists. But the resort quickly expanded as word of its magnificent view spread; by 1845 it had 50 rooms, and by the 1880s more than 300. Thirteen mammoth Corinthian columns marched across its front facade, while to the rear were wings upon wings. The hotel could be seen for miles around—"a small white cloud in the midst of the heavens," as one guest put it—and everyone who was anyone came to stay. Among the guests were Ulysses S. Grant, William Tecumseh Sherman, Jenny Lind, Thomas Nast, Mark Twain, Henry James, and Oscar Wilde.

Dozens upon dozens of other hostelries soon opened in the area. Some were luxurious affairs, as grand as the Mountain House; others were just rustic lodges. By the mid-1800s, six trains a day were leaving New York City for the Catskills, bringing an estimated 300,000 guests annually.

The popularity of the Catskills began to decline in the 1920s; the advent of the automobile had given Americans a much wider choice of vacation destinations. As the traditional resorts began to shut down, however, Sullivan County was discovered by Jewish immigrants living in New York City. In the decades that followed, dozens of inexpensive boardinghouses and luxurious megaresorts went up, and an elaborate entertainment circuit flourished, featuring comedians, singers, and big bands. Among the most famous of these resorts were Flagler's, Grossinger's, and the Concord, which is still in operation today.

GETTING AROUND

Orientation

All of the Catskills' 10 highest peaks are situated in northern Ulster and Greene Counties. Smaller mountains and much dairy country can be found in Delaware County, while Sullivan County is comparatively flat. Southern Ulster County lies squarely in the Hudson Valley.

First-time visitors will probably want to concentrate on the dramatic scenery of northern Ulster and Greene Counties, but if you have time, try to visit the eastern half of Delaware County and the Upper Delaware region of Sullivan County as well. The landscape in both these areas is lovely and all but unspoiled.

Transportation

The only real way to explore the Catskills is by car; sights are often far apart. But public transportation can get you into the area if you don't have your own vehicle.

Adirondack–Pine Hill Trailways, 212/967-2900 or 800/225-6815, offers regular bus service to sections of Ulster, Greene, and Delaware Counties, including Kingston, Woodstock, Catskill, and Delhi. Monticello, Liberty, and other towns in Sullivan County are served by **Shortline,** 212/736-4700 or 800/631-8405.

Traveling up the east bank of the Hudson just across from the Catskills are **Metro-North Commuter Railroad,** 212/532-4900 or 800/638-7646; and **Amtrak,** 212/582-6875 or 800/872-7245. Metro-North leaves out of Grand Central Station (Park Ave. and 42nd St., Manhattan) and travels as far north as Poughkeepsie. Amtrak leaves out of Pennsylvania Station (33rd St. and Seventh Ave., Manhattan) and makes stops in Poughkeepsie, Rhinebeck, and Hudson.

The closest large airport is the Albany County Airport, located about an hour north of the Catskills. Among the major airlines flying into Albany are **American,** 800/433-7300; **Delta,** 800/221-1212; **Northwest,** 800/225-2525; and **United,** 800/241-6522.

THE CATSKILLS

RECREATION

Fishing

Fishing in the Catskills is legendary. Numerous world-famous trout streams—including the Beaverkill, Willowemoc, Esopus, Schoharie, and Catskill—are located here, along with six reservoirs and the Hudson River. Brochures and guides to Catskill fishing can be picked up at tourist centers.

Hiking

More than 200 miles of hiking trails, leading to the summits of over 20 peaks, weave through Catskill Forest Preserve. Surprisingly, unlike the overhiked Adirondack trails, most of these are underused.

The trails are maintained by the **Department of Environmental Conservation** (DEC), 625 Broadway, Albany, NY 12233, 518/402-9428, www.dec.state.ny.us, which offers free trail maps. The DEC maps are badly photocopied, however, and the accompanying information is sketchy. You're better off contacting the **New York–New Jersey Trail Conference,** 156 Ramapo Valley Rd., Mahwah, NJ 07430, 201/512-9348, www.nynjtc.com. The conference publishes the excellent "Catskill Trails" five-map set and "Shawangunk Trails" four-map set.

A few popular day-hikes in Ulster and Greene Counties are outlined below. For more detailed information and suggestions on many other hikes, pick up a copy of the first-rate *Fifty Hikes in the Hudson Valley* by Kick, McMartin, and Long. The book includes a good section on the Catskills and is available in area bookstores or by contacting Countryman Press, 800/245-4151.

CATSKILLS HIGHLIGHTS

Ulster County
Huguenot Street, New Paltz
Mohonk Mountain House, New Paltz
Minnewaska State Park, New Paltz
Historic Stockade, Kingston
Woodstock
Opus 40, Saugerties
Lodge at Catskill Corners
Route 28A around Ashokan Reservoir
Tubing on Esopus Creek

Greene County
Route 23A, Palenville to Haines Falls
Escarpment Trail, off Route 23A
Ukrainian Catholic Church, Lexington
Lexington Hotel, Lexington
Prattsville village
Route 23, East Windham to Cairo
Point Lookout Inn, East Windham
Mahayana Buddhist Temple and Monastery, Cairo
The all-Irish village of East Durham
Winter Clove Inn, Round Top
Bronck Museum, Coxsackie

Sullivan County
Siddha Yoga Dham, South Fallsburg
Trout fishing on the Willowemoc, Roscoe
Fly Fishing Center, Livingston Manor
The back roads of DeBruce
The village of Jeffersonville
Max Yasgur's former farm, Bethel
Driving, canoeing, or camping along the Upper
   Delaware River
Bald eagles in winter
Narrowsburg village

Delaware County
Margaretville
Route 6, Margaretville to Andes
Andes Hotel, Andes
Round Barn, Halcottsville
Roxbury village
Burroughs Memorial Field, Roxbury
Delaware County Historical Association
   Museum, Delhi
Taxidermy shops, Delhi
Hanford Mills, East Meredith
West Kortright Centre, East Meredith
Robert's Auction, Fleischmanns

VISITOR SERVICES

To have general information mailed to you, contact the **Catskill Association for Tourism Services** (CATS), P.O. Box 449, Catskill, NY 12414, 888/856-2287, www.catskillregion today.com. Each ⬛ tourist information c⬛ listed below.

For more information on any ⬛ State parks or historic sites described⬛ the website: www.nysparks.com.

Ulster County

Ulster is a county with a split personality. To the south are towns and farmland that sit squarely in the Hudson Valley. To the north and northwest are the Catskills. In the valley, the land is neat, the residents flush. But in the Catskills, all is poorer and much more wild.

Southern Ulster is notable for its many pre-Revolutionary stone houses, built by early Dutch and French Huguenot settlers. Most of these houses have been nicely restored; the largest clusters are in New Paltz—where an entire historic street functions as an indoor/outdoor museum—and Hurley. Also in the south are the stunning white escarpments of the Shawangunk (SHON-gum) Mountains, a range formed some 100 million years before the Catskills. Perched atop the Shawangunks are the famed Mohonk Mountain House—a 19th-century resort—and Minnewaska State Park, which harbors several glacial lakes.

Midway up the county on the Hudson is Kingston, a large and interesting town with an attractive historic district. North of Kingston are the legendary mountain villages of Woodstock and Saugerties, still inhabited largely by artists and artisans. Northwest of Kingston begins Catskill Park and Forest Preserve, where you'll find the enormous Ashokan Reservoir, marvelous scenic drives, excellent hiking trails, and the highest peak in the Catskills—Slide Mountain.

"So fine and free from animosity and greed has been the life of the people of New Paltz that previous to 1873 no lawyer ever found a permanent residence here."

The eastern half of Ulster County is well populated, thanks largely to the presence of the New York State Thruway (I-87). In the mountainous west, however, towns shrink into hamlets and highways into two-lane roads.

First-time visitors will probably want to concentrate on New Paltz, the Shawangunks, Woodstock and Saugerties, and on the drive west along Route 28.

Information

For more information, contact **Ulster County Tourism,** County Office Bldg., P.O. Box 1800, Kingston, NY 12401, 845/340-3566 or 800/342-5826, www.co.ulster.ny.us; hours are Mon.–Fri. 9 A.M.–5 P.M. The county also staffs a summer **visitor information center** off the New York State Thruway (I-87), Exit 19, Kingston, 845/340-3766.

NEW PALTZ

Between the Hudson River and the Shawangunk Mountains lies the small town of New Paltz. New Paltz was founded in 1677 by a group of French Huguenot Protestants who came to the New World seeking religious freedom.

The Huguenots first settled just north of New Paltz, in Kingston and Hurley. But in June 1663, the area's Esopus Indians raided the two small settlements, kidnapping 45 women and children. The Indians held the Huguenots hostage, demanding the return of 20 Esopus braves who had been captured by whites and shipped to Curaçao as slaves.

But in early September, a Huguenot search party found and freed the hostages. While embracing his family, one member of the party—Louis DuBois—noticed the fertile land around

THE CATSKILLS

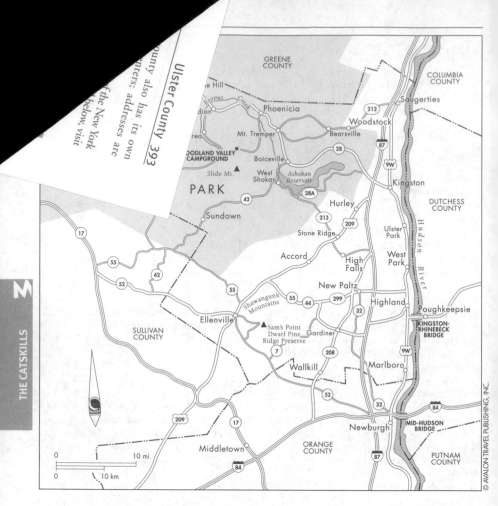

ounty also has its own
nters; addresses are
f the New York
below visit

THE CATSKILLS

© AVALON TRAVEL PUBLISHING, INC.

him. He returned in 1677 with 11 others to buy and patent a 33,000-acre tract of land. The next year, the 12 families moved in and established a small settlement along what is now known as **Huguenot Street.**

The new town was governed by a kind of corporation called the Duzine, referring to the 12 partners. That arrangement continued until well after the Revolution, by special permission of the New York State legislature. The system apparently worked well; one later commentator wrote, "So fine and free from animosity and greed has been the life of the people of New Paltz that previous to 1873 no lawyer ever found a permanent residence here."

Today, the center of New Paltz lies just east of historic Huguenot Street, along Chestnut and Main Streets. Here, you'll find a clutch of attractive stores and restaurants. The town's biggest annual event is the **Ulster County Fair,** held on the county fairgrounds in early August.

To reach New Paltz from I-87, take Exit 18 and head west on Route 299, which becomes Main Street. For more information on the town, contact the **New Paltz Chamber of Commerce,** 124 Main St., 845/255-0243, www.newpaltz

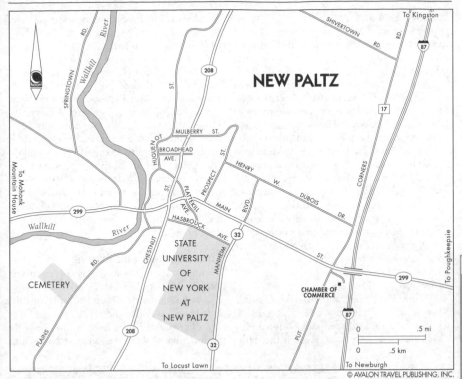

NEW PALTZ

© AVALON TRAVEL PUBLISHING, INC.

chamber.org. Hours are Mon.–Fri. 9 A.M.–5 P.M., Sat.–Sun. 10 A.M.–3 P.M.

Huguenot Street

Just off the hubbub of Main Street is Huguenot Street, "the oldest street in America with its original buildings." It's now a National Historic Landmark. Along its cool and shady time-ripened blocks stand six stone houses built between 1692 and 1890, as well as a French church and cemetery, a library, museum, and gift shop.

All official walking tours of the street, led by knowledgeable guides, begin at the Deyo Hall Visitor Center, 6 Broadhead Ave., just off Huguenot Street. A small museum there documents the street's history. The tours then proceed past the 1692 Abraham Hasbrouck House—once the village's social center—and the 1698 Bevier-Elting House, equipped with an unusual overhang that allowed the residents to work

outside in bad weather. The most interesting house, however, is the Jean Hasbrouck House, which contains much original woodwork and a beautiful "jambless" fireplace. Downstairs are rooms that once served as a tavern and general store, while upstairs are many period furnishings, including a "senility cradle" used for the old and infirm.

Huguenot is run by the Huguenot Historical Society, which includes among its members many descendants of the original families. The society offers walking tours of the street May–Oct., Tues.–Sun. 10 A.M.–5 P.M., with the last tour leaving at 4 P.M. Cost is adults $8, seniors $7, children $3. Admission to Deyo Hall and its museum is free.

For more information, contact the Huguenot Historical Society, 18 Broadhead Ave., New Paltz, NY 12561; 845/255-1889 (tours) or 845/255-1660 (office), www.hhs-newpaltz.org.

Locust Lawn and Vicinity

Four miles south of New Paltz on Route 32 are yet more historic sites administered by the Huguenot Historical Society. Most important among them is Locust Lawn, 400 Rte. 32, an elegant Federal-style mansion built by Revolutionary War hero Col. Josiah Hasbrouck in 1814. After the war, the colonel became one of the wealthiest men in Ulster County. He filled his home with fine period furniture, magnificent china, and paintings by the likes of Ammi Phillips and John Vanderlyn.

Down the road from Locust Lawn is the considerably more rustic **Terwilliger House,** 1400 Rte. 32, built in 1738. A wonderful example of Huguenot and Dutch architecture combined, the stone-and-wood cottage features a wide central hallway, long sloping roof, and creaky front porch.

Call the Huguenot Historical Society, 845/255-1889, for site hours and admission fees.

Wineries

Wine enthusiasts might want to stop into **Adair Vineyards,** 75 Allhusen Rd., 845/255-1377, which centers on a 200-year-old National Historic Landmark dairy barn, painted the tradi-tional red and white. The tasting room is located in the old hayloft. Open daily for tastings May–Nov., noon–6 P.M.

Or, head east to **Route 9 W,** which hugs the shores of the Hudson River. Many small wineries, well marked with signs, are located all along the route between West Park and Marlboro. Most famous among them is **Benmarl Winery,** 156 Highland Ave., Marlboro, 845/236-4265, www.benmarl.com. First planted as a vineyard in the late 16th century, Benmarl sits on a hilltop with great views of the river. The winery produces a number of award-winning varietals, including chardonnays and cabernets. An on-site art gallery showcases the work of owner Mark Miller, a widely published magazine illustrator. Open daily noon–5 P.M.

Entertainment and Events

Though now primarily a casual restaurant, **P&G's,** 91 Main St., 845/255-6161, began as a dancehall in the 1900s and still presents live local bands on Friday and Saturday night.

Concerts and plays are often on tap at the **State University of New York at New Paltz,**

A BOOKWORM'S PARADISE

Ulster County boasts a high number of unusual bookstores, ranging from creaky used-book emporiums to modern independent shops. Looking for that out-of-print 19th-century novel, unusual art book, or obscure tome about New York State? Chances are good you'll find it here.

In Kingston reigns one of the region's best-known shops, **Alternative Books,** 35 N. Front St., 845/331-5439, which has long been a lively gathering place for local artists and writers. The shop's stock of over 20,000 used books includes a large poetry selection, modern first editions, journals, and art books. Also in Kingston is **Three Geese in Flight Books,** 275 Fair St., 845/338-2358, perhaps the only store in the country specializing in Celtic mythology and Arthurian legend; and **Pages Past,** 103 Tammany St., 845/339-6484, known for its selection of used general interest, regional, and children's books.

Not far away in Ashokan sprawls **Editions,** Rte. 28, 845/657-7000, a used-book emporium with an 8-foot-high chart at the front listing all the store's categories. In the 10 quiet rooms here, filled with lots of nooks and crannies perfect for hiding out, you'll find over 60,000 titles.

Two good modern independent bookshops are New Paltz's **Ariel Books,** 3 Plattekill Ave., 845/255-8041, and Woodstock's **Golden Notebook,** 25-29 Tinker St., 845/679-8000. Also in New Paltz is **Barner Books,** 69 Main St., 845/255-2635, barnerbook@aol.com, a barn of a used-book shop where newly arrived volumes sit piled up in boxes. Barner Books also conducts a brisk Internet business, ferreting out obscure titles for clients from all over the world. Not far from Woodstock is **Hope Farm Press Press and Booktrader,** 252 Main St., Saugerties, 845/246-3522, specializing in history, genealogy, and New York State.

Rte. 32, just south of New Paltz, one mile west of I-87, 845/257-3880. **Unison Arts,** 68 Mountain Rest Rd., 845/255-1559, presents an interesting series of concerts (blues, folk, world music) in various venues around town.

The first-rate **Woodstock-New Paltz Arts & Crafts Fair** comes to the Ulster County Fairgrounds, Libertyville Rd., off Rte. 299, twice a year, first on Memorial Day weekend and again on Labor Day weekend. Call 845/340-3566 for more information.

Accommodations

The most popular resort in New Paltz is the Mohonk Mountain House, about five miles northwest of downtown, in the Shawangunks (see below). East of town in Highland is the family-oriented **Rocking Horse Ranch,** 600 Rte. 44/55, 845/691-2927 or 800/647-2624, www.rhranch.com, a family-owned resort and dude ranch. The Rocking Horse sits beside a lake and features both indoor and outdoor pools, saunas, tennis courts, scheduled activities for kids, nighttime entertainment, and trail rides. In the winter, the ranch offers cross-country skiing, ice skating, snowshoeing, and sleigh rides. A two-night high season package costs $345 per adult/double, which includes use of all facilities, instruction, entertainment, day care for children, breakfast and dinner; each child is an additional $165.

In Wallkill, between Walden and New Paltz on Rte. 208, is the 1740 **Audrey's Farmhouse,** 2188 Brunswick Rd., 845/895-3440. The B&B offers comfortable guest rooms with featherbeds, a swimming pool, library, and splendid views of the Shawangunks ($95–120 d).

Motels in town include a **Days Inn,** 601 Main St., 845/883-7373 ($79–99 d); and **Econo Lodge,** 530 Main St., 845/255-6200 ($69–99 d).

Food

With its outdoor cafe and homemade treats, the **Bakery,** 13A N. Front St., 845/255-8840, is a good spot for breakfast or lunch; average main dish $7. Situated in a small shopping mall is the **Main Course,** 232 Main St., 845/255-2600, serving healthy contemporary American fare for lunch and dinner; average dinner entrée $13.

The **Loft,** 46 Main St., 845/255-1426, cooks up first-rate innovative American fare ranging from pastas to grilled Gulf shrimp to duck breast topped with an orange sauce; average entrée $15.

Serious diners might want to check out the **Ristorante Locust Tree,** 215 Huguenot St., 845/255-7888, housed in a cozy 18th-century stone-and-wood house. The candlelit restaurant specializes in European-Italian fare, and its menu changes daily; entrées $17–26.

THE SHAWANGUNKS

Just west of New Paltz rise the Shawangunk Mountains, a tilted ridge of translucent quartz conglomerate cemented into sedimentary rock. One-tenth the age of the earth, the Shawangunks are often mistakenly assumed to be an extension of the Catskills. They're actually a distinct range, separated from the Catskills by Rondout Valley.

Over the Shawangunks' narrow range, dotted with five glacier-carved lakes, a man named Tom Quick once roamed. Legend has it that Quick— "The Avenger of the Delaware"—killed more than 100 Indians singlehandedly during his lifetime. According to one tale, Quick was deep in the woods one day, splitting rails, when six armed warriors appeared and asked to be taken to Tom Quick. He agreed to do so if they would first help him finish his work. Grinning at his insolence, the Indians lined up, three to each side of the log. They grabbed hold of the log and prepared to pull its sides apart, expecting Quick to drive his wedge in deeper. But Quick knocked the wedge out instead and the log snapped shut, catching all six Indians by their fingers. Quick then dispatched the unfortunates with his ax. Some time later, a historian of the day visited the spot and verified the presence of six sets of bleached bones.

Climbing the Gunks

The Shawangunks' steep escarpments make them a favorite haunt of rock climbers. The oldest rock-climbing guide service and school in the Shawangunks is **High Angle Adventures,** 178 Hardenburgh Rd., Ulster Park, NY 12487; 845/658-9811. Beginners are welcome; group size is limited to three.

THE CATSKILLS

Mohonk Mountain House and Preserve

High in the heart of the Shawangunks is Mohonk Mountain House, an enormous castlelike affair on the edge of a deep blue glacial lake. Built by Quaker twins Albert and Alfred Smiley in 1870, Mohonk is the last of the magnificent resort hotels that once lined the Hudson. In its heyday, the Mountain House hosted a long line of distinguished guests, including Presidents Hayes, Taft, and Wilson. Albert Smiley was deeply concerned about the welfare of the American Indian, and from 1883 to 1916, numerous important Friends of the Indian conferences were held at the Mountain House.

From a distance, Mohonk is an ultra-romantic place, bursting with gables and chimneys, turrets and towers. Up close, however, the romance dims. The lodgelike interior is packed to the rafters with people, people, people, constantly to-ing and fro-ing. A beehive of activities is scheduled throughout the day, and you can't even set foot on the grounds without first having your credentials checked.

Nonetheless, Mohonk is well worth a visit. Reserve a spot for a $35 prix fixe lunch (845/256-2056), or hike the adjacent 5,600-acre preserve. Twenty-eight miles of trails and 22 miles of carriage roads crisscross the preserve, and from its highest point, you can see six states. Hikers must purchase day passes at the Preserve Visitor Center next door to the resort, or from a patrolling ranger. Cost is adults $8, children under 12 free; trail maps are provided. The passes do not permit access to the Mountain House or its facilities, which include a lakefront beach and a nine-hole golf course.

If you decide to spend the night, you'll pay $315–670 d, which includes three meals and afternoon tea. About a third of the rooms have working fireplaces; the rest have balconies.

To reach Mohonk from New Paltz, head west a half mile on Rte. 299 (Main St.) and watch for signs for the turnoff on the right. For more information about the Mountain House, Lake Mohonk, New Paltz, NY 12561, call 845/255-1000 or 800/772-6646, www.mohonk.com. For more information about the preserve, call 845/255-0919 or visit www.mohonkpreserve.org.

Minnewaska State Park

If the idea of spending $8 per person to hike the Mohonk Mountain House preserve sounds a bit steep, head farther west through fertile farmland to Minnewaska State Park. Also located high in the spectacular Shawangunks, the park is filled with panoramic views, hiking trails, paved carriage roads, waterfalls, and lakes—all available for a $6 parking fee in summer and on weekends, free on weekdays the rest of the year.

Near the center of the park is deep-blue **Lake Minnewaska**—Iroquois for floating waters—surrounded by white sandstone cliffs. The lake was created during the Ice Age when a glacier sliding by pulled out a hunk of soft sandstone.

On Lake Minnewaska is a sandy beach area where swimming is permitted, but if you like your bathing more secluded, hike the three-mile trail to **Lake Awosting.** This mile-long lake can only be reached on foot and is an idyllic spot surrounded by dark, piney woods.

To reach the park from New Paltz, take Rte. 299 west to Rts. 44/55 and turn right, up the mountain. The park, 845/255-0752, is open daily 9 A.M.–dusk, except during severe winter weather.

After a day at the park, you might want to stop into the **Mountain Brauhaus,** intersection of Rts. 299 and 44/55, Gardiner, 845/255-9766, for a frothy mug of German beer or favorite German dishes such as *rouladen* and *kassler rippchen*. The roadhouse sits at the base of a cliff formation of the Shawangunks, and offers spectacular views; average dinner entrée $14.

Just minutes away from the Minnewaska State Park is the new but already quite popular **Minnewaska Lodge,** Rte. 44/55, 845/255-1203, www.minnewaskalodge.com. Catering to outdoorsy types, the 26-room lodge features rooms with cathedral ceilings and decks overlooking the Gunks, along with Mission-style furniture, picture windows, and a wood-burning stove ($115–275 d).

Ellenville

Southwest of Minnewaska State Park, where Rte. 209 meets Rte. 52, is the village of Ellenville. Located at the western base of the Shawangunks, Ellenville has traditionally been known for its

Jewish boardinghouses and megaresorts. Most of these are gone now, but still in town are many fine Colonial and Greek Revival buildings, and a few remaining kosher shops and restaurants. Among them is **Cohen's Bakery,** 89 Center St., 845/647-7620, famed locally for first-rate raisin-pumpernickel bread.

The best of the old-fashioned megaresorts still in Ellenville is the **Nevele Grand Resort,** Nevele Rd., off Rte. 209, 1.5 miles south of town, 845/647-6000 or 800/647-6000, www.nevele.com. Features here include an 18-hole golf course, five swimming pools, 18 tennis courts, riding trails, and a private lake. Many of the resort's activities are family oriented, and in summer there's a day camp program for kids. Daily rates, including three meals, are $125–179 per adult d; packages and children's rates are available.

The Ellenville area also has a reputation for good hang-gliding. **Mountain Wings Hang Gliding Center,** 150 Canal St., 845/647-3377, www.flightschool.net, rents equipment and offers introductory one-day hang-gliding courses.

Sam's Point Dwarf Pine Ridge Preserve

For years, Ellenville's biggest visitor attraction was Ice Caves Mountain, a sort of natural history theme park perched on a mountaintop just outside town. The park, which had a wonderful 1950s feel, was centered on the caves, which were created 330 million years ago as cold-trapping fissures and still contain ice year round. But as of 1997, alas, the caves were closed due to safety concerns, and the mountain is now a preserve managed by the Nature Conservancy.

Truth be told, however, the mysterious caves weren't ever all that exciting. Much more interesting was—and is—the mile-long hike around "bottomless" Lake Maratanza. The lake sits so high atop the mountain that it seems as if it will surely slop over, and great views are all around. The highest lookout here and in all the Shawangunks is 2,255-foot Sam's Point, named after one Sam Gonsales. As the story goes, Gonsales jumped from the outcropping to escape from Indians, all the while knowing that a thick clump of hemlocks 40 feet below would

break his fall. The ploy worked, and he lived to tell the tale.

The preserve, 845/647-7989, Sam's Point Rd., off Rte. 52 south of Ellenville, is open for hiking May–Oct., Sat.–Sun. 10 A.M.–6 P.M. A $5 parking fee is charged and maps are available at the entrance.

NORTH ON ROUTE 209

Today's 209 closely parallels Old Route 209, reputedly the oldest highway in America. Originally known as the Old Mine Road, the old route ran between the copper mines near Pahaquarry, New Jersey, and Kingston on the Hudson, and was built sometime in the early 1600s. Many old homes and markers commemorating Indian raids are situated along Old Route 209, which runs concurrently with today's route in many places.

Accord

Heading north on Route 209 out of Minnewaska State Park, you'll soon come to the small village of Accord. Shortly after the Revolution, this then-unnamed hamlet was in need of a post office. A resident wrote to the post office department in Washington, D.C., suggesting that the settlement be called Discord because the townspeople couldn't agree on a name. The department did authorize an office, but optimistically changed the name.

Though there's not much to see in Accord, railroad buffs will want to take a look at the **Accord Train Station,** Rte. 209 in the village center, an attractive maroon depot built in 1902 for the Ontario & Western Railroad.

High Falls and Vicinity

About six miles north of Accord (take Route 209 north to Route 213 east) is High Falls, where the **D&H Canal Museum** tells the story of the Delaware & Hudson Canal. Built in the 1820s, the canal was originally intended to facilitate the shipment of coal from the mines of Pennsylvania to the factories of New York. Later it was used to ship cement made in the High Falls area to New York City, to be used in bridges and skyscrapers.

In the museum are dioramas of the canal;

working models of locks; and maps, photos, and artifacts that document the canal's many boomtowns. The museum, Mohonk Rd. off Rte. 213, 845/687-9311, www.canalmuseum.org, is open Memorial Day–Labor Day, Thurs.–Sat., Monday 11 A.M.–5 P.M., Sunday 1–5 P.M. In May, September, and October it's open Saturday 11 A.M.–5 P.M., Sunday 1–5 P.M. Admission is adults $3, children $1.

At the museum, you can pick up a copy of the **Five Locks Walk** self-guided-tour pamphlet, which will lead you past historic canal locks, the ruins of a "suspension aqueduct" built by John Roebling (who later built the Brooklyn Bridge), and the Central Hudson Canal Park. The park offers great views of the falls that once powered the village's cement mills, and at one end are the ruins of the once-formidable Norton Cement Company.

Overlooking Lock 16 is the **DePuy Canal House,** Rte. 213, 845/687-7700, built in 1797 by Simeon DePuy. Once an inn, the two-story building is now a renowned four-star restaurant serving innovative American cuisine in an intimate, historic setting complete with fireplaces, steep staircases, and wide floorboards. Multicourse prix fixe meals are a popular choice here; $60 for four courses, $75 for seven. For a simpler meal, try the **Egg's Nest,** Rte. 213, 845/687-7255, an eccentric spot offering tasty sandwiches and soups (average main dish $7) or the **Northern Spy Cafe,** Rte. 213, 845/687-7295, which serves everything from burgers to Thai chicken with ginger; entrées $8–18.

A variety of interesting shops can be found along Route 213 in the village center. Among them is the **Bird Watcher's Country Store,** 845/687-9410, selling "everything for the wild bird lover."

Stone Ridge

Bed-and-breakfast fans have two excellent choices in Stone Ridge. **Bakers',** 24 Old King's Hwy., 845/687-9795, www.bakersbandb.com, occupies a 1780 stone farmhouse furnished with period antiques and a fireplace. All six guest rooms have private baths, and breakfast is served on a deck overlooking the Shawangunks ($98–138 d).

The **Inn at Stone Ridge/Hasbrouck House,** Rte. 209 just outside the village, 845/687-0736, www.inatstoneridge.com, is an elegant 18th-century Colonial mansion. It offers 10 guest rooms, an antique billiard room, 40 acres of gardens and woods, and a lake ($195–445 d). The inn's cozy, full-service restaurant, **Milliways,** serves American regional fare and three local draft beers; average entrée $18.

Hurley

Just off Route 209 on the outskirts of Kingston lies a small village of about 25 meticulously restored stone cottages similar to those found in New Paltz. Almost all are private residences open to the public only on **Hurley Stone House Day** (held the second Saturday in July), but they're still interesting to view from afar.

Hurley dates back to 1651, when French Huguenots built wooden homes along Esopus Creek. The settlers didn't treat the local Esopus Indians as well as they might have, and in 1663, the Indians retaliated by burning down the Huguenot settlement. Six years later, the settlers rebuilt—this time in stone.

Informative self-guided walking tours of Hurley can be picked up at the post office at the town's entrance, or at the Hurley Library or Elmendorf House, both on Main Street. A plaque with a town map also stands in front of the library.

The **Elmendorf House,** built in the late 1600s, is believed to be the oldest house in Hurley. Known as the Half-Moon Tavern in Revolutionary days, it now houses a small museum. Out back is a picturesque cemetery with gravestones dating to 1715. The museum, 845/338-1661, is open May–Oct., Saturday 10 A.M.–4 P.M., Sunday 1–4 P.M.

Also on Main Street are the **Jan Van Deusen House,** which served as the temporary capital of New York State after Kingston was burned by the British in 1777, and the **Polly Crispell Cottage,** equipped with a "witch catcher," or set of iron spikes set into the chimney. Just west of Main Street is the **Hardenberg House,** where abolitionist and evangelist Sojourner Truth, born a slave in Ulster County, spent the first 11 years of her life.

© CHRISTIANE BIRD

THE CATSKILLS

a stone house in Hurley, built by the Dutch in the late 1600s

In addition to the Stone House Festival, the other big event in Hurley is the **Corn and Craft Festival,** held each August. The festival features a hundred crafts booths plus lots of sweet corn and chowder. For more information, call the Hurley Heritage Society at 845/338-1661, www.hurleyheritagesociety.org. Signs to Hurley are located along Route 209.

KINGSTON

The small and attractive city of Kingston centers on a peaceful, tree-lined historic district known as the Stockade. A few miles away, down by the Hudson, is the city's equally pleasant harbor, Rondout Landing. There you'll find more nicely restored buildings, along with historic vessels and tour boats (see Recreation, below).

Kingston was first settled by the Dutch in 1652, making it the third oldest settlement—after Albany and New York City—in the state. In 1777, the town served as state capital; in the early 1800s, it was known for its boat-building and cement industries. Remnants of these can still be seen at Rondout Landing. The landing is also the end-

point of the Delaware & Hudson Canal. Built in 1828 to help transport coal from Pennsylvania to the Hudson River, the canal turned Kingston from a sleepy port into a major commercial center.

Informative **visitor centers** are located in the Stockade, 308 Clinton Ave., 845/331-9506, and at Rondout Landing, 20 Broadway, 845/331-7517, www.ci.kingston.ny.us. Summer hours are Mon.–Sat. 11 A.M.–5 P.M., Sunday 1–5 P.M.; call for hours the rest of the year. Or, contact the **Kingston Chamber of Commerce,** 1 Albany Ave., Kingston, NY 12401; 845/338-5100, www.ulsterchamber.org. Kingston is one of New York's 16 State Heritage Areas, which are loosely delineated historic parks that have played major roles in the state's development. Each area is dedicated to a different theme; in Kingston, the theme is transportation.

To reach Kingston from the New York State Thruway, take Exit 19. From Hurley, continue north on Route 209.

Historic Stockade Area

In 1658, hostilities broke out between the new Dutch settlers and the Esopus Indians, prompting

Gov. Peter Stuyvesant to come up from Manhattan to oversee the building of a stockade. The settlers moved their homes inside the 13-foot-high stockade walls, and no Esopus were allowed in after dark.

By 1700, the stockade itself was gone, but the site continued to function as the village center. Over the next 200 years, many of Kingston's most important buildings were erected here. Today the eight-block district is lined with shady trees, inviting shops and restaurants, and historic sites.

The district centers around the **Old Dutch Church,** corner of Main and Wall Streets, designed in 1852 by Minard Lafever. The Renaissance Revival–style church features an especially graceful steeple and a vaulted ceiling reminiscent of Christopher Wren.

Around the corner from the church stands the **Ulster County Courthouse,** 285 Wall St., built in 1818. A plaque out front honors Sojourner Truth, who was born a slave in Ulster County in 1797 (see Hurley under North on Route 209, above). In this courthouse on November 26, 1883, Truth won a lawsuit that saved her son from slavery in Alabama. It was the first such case ever won by a black parent.

At the northeastern corner of the Stockade you'll find the ivy-covered **Senate House State Historic Site,** 296 Fair St., off Clinton St., the meeting place of the first New York State Senate. Inside the former Dutch home, which can only be seen by guided tour, are a restored kitchen, bedrooms, and the parlor where the 24-member Senate met in 1777 to ratify the first New York State Constitution.

Connected to the house is a museum with exhibits on early Kingston and an interesting collection of paintings by John Vanderlyn, one of America's first landscape painters. Vanderlyn painted the enormous *Landing of Columbus* that hangs in the Capitol rotunda, and his work attracted the interest of such notables as Aaron Burr and Napoleon. Nonetheless, he lived most of his life in penury and died of starvation in his Kingston apartment.

The Senate House and museum, 845/338-2786, are open mid-April–Oct., Wed.–Sat. 10 A.M.–5 P.M., Sunday 1–5 P.M.; off-season by appointment. Admission is adults $3, seniors $2, children 5–12 $1. Tours of the house begin in the museum.

A self-guided walking tour of the Stockade and about 30 other buildings can be picked up at the visitor centers. Many of the area's shops and restaurants are located along Wall, John, and North Front Streets.

Rondout Landing

To reach the harbor area from the Stockade, take Broadway downtown and descend a long, gentle hill. Once a bustling area of boatyards and factories, the landing is now a sleepy semicircle of historic buildings in various stages of restoration.

At the far end of the landing is the small and friendly **Hudson River Maritime Museum,** 1 Rondout Landing, 845/338-0071, www.ulster.net/~hrmm, which features temporary exhibits on various aspects of Hudson River life. Exhibits in the past have covered such themes as sunken ships, WW II ships, and tourism in the Catskills. Out back, on permanent display, are several historic vessels including an 1898 steam tug; next door is a wooden-boat restoration shop. The museum is open May–Oct., daily 11 A.M.–5 P.M.; November, Fri.–Sun. noon–5 P.M. Admission is adults $4, seniors and children 5–12 $3.

From the Maritime Museum, you can take a 10-minute boat ride to **Rondout Lighthouse.** The largest of the Hudson River lighthouses, the building sits alone on a manmade island and has been restored to look as it did in the 1950s when the lighthouse keeper lived there. Tickets for the boat and lighthouse include admission to the museum, and cost adults $8, seniors $7, children 5–12 $5.

Across from the Maritime Museum is the **Trolley Museum,** 89 E. Strand St., 845/331-3399. There you'll find a nice collection of antique trolleys, as well as kids excitedly waiting to take the short trolley ride around Rondout Creek. Museum hours are Memorial Day–Columbus Day, Sat.–Sun. noon–5 P.M. Admission is adults $3, seniors and children $2.

Recreation

Paralleling Route 28 west of Kingston is the Esopus River, long known for its **trout fishing;** major access points are marked with brown-and-yellow signs. Holders of reservoir permits can fish in Ashokan Reservoir (take Route 28A west of town).

Kingston's Rondout Landing is home port to **Hudson River Cruises,** 845/255-6515 or 800/843-7472, www.hudsonrivercruises.com, which offers some of the best cruises to be found on the Hudson. Among their offerings are sightseeing, music, and dinner cruises aboard the roomy *Rip Van Winkle.* The cruises run May–Oct. and operate daily during the height of the summer.

Entertainment

On the National Register of Historic Places is the 1927 **Ulster Performing Arts Center,** 601 Broadway, 845/339-6088, www.upac.org, a former vaudeville theater that now features Broadway shows, concerts, dance, and children's productions. **New York Conservatory for the Arts,** 120 Schildknecht Rd., 845/339-4340, offers musicals, dramas, and comedies in a cabaret setting.

Camping and Accommodations

Near town is **Hidden Valley Lake,** a 50-site campground at 290 Whiteport Rd., off Rte. 32, 845/338-4616. It's open year-round and offers both campsites and cabins. A basic campsite rate is $20.

Kingston's upscale **Holiday Inn,** 503 Washington Ave., 845/338-0400 or 800/HOLIDAY, boasts over 200 nicely decorated rooms and an enormous indoor recreation center with indoor-outdoor pools, a fitness center, a sauna, and video games ($129–159 d; packages available). Not far from Rondout Landing is the secluded, turn-of-the-century **Rondout B&B,** 88 W. Chester St., 845/331-2369, www.rondoutbandb.com, surrounded by large porches and filled with local artwork. Rates range from $75 s with shared bath to $115 d with private bath.

Food

Deising's, 109-117 N. Front St., 845/338-7503, is both an excellent bakery and a coffee shop known for its tasty soups and sandwiches; average main dish $7. A local favorite is the lively **Armadillo Bar & Grill,** 97 Abeel St., 845/339-1550, which specializes in Southwestern and

New World cuisine; average dinner entrée $13. **Portobello,** Fair and John Sts., 845/338-3000, specializes in fresh pasta and Northern Italian dishes; average entrée $14.

SAUGERTIES

About 15 miles north of Kingston, where Route 212 meets Route 9 W, is Saugerties, a friendly, small town filled with turn-of-the-century brick buildings. Saugerties was once a river port known for its packet trade and racing steamers. Most famous among them was the *Mary Powell,* the fastest ship on the Hudson between 1861 and 1885.

Shopping

Downtown Saugerties is full of antique shops, most of which are located along Main and Partition Streets. Some are serious affairs, others sell what looks suspiciously like junk. One of the largest emporiums is the **Saugerties Antique Center & Annex,** 220 Main St., 845/246-8234, which houses about 25 dealers. A guide to the town's antique stores can be picked up in many local shops.

The **Hope Farm Press & Bookshop,** 252 Main St., 845/246-3522, www.hopefarm.com, specializes in history, genealogy, and regional books. Open by appointment only is the **O. Shale Hill Farm & Herb Gardens,** 6856 Hommelville Rd., off Rte. 32, 845/246-6982, which sells dried herbs and flowers.

Opus 40

Between Saugerties and Woodstock is one of the most unusual spots in Ulster County, an environmental sculpture known as Opus 40. Created by artist Harvey Fite over a period of 37 years, Opus 40 covers more than six acres of an abandoned bluestone quarry. Its pools and fountains, sculptures and walkways, all center around a towering blue-gray monolith reminiscent of the mysterious Stonehenge. Behind rises the dark crest of Overlook Mountain.

Fite, a professor at Bard College, created his monumental work using traditional quarrier's tools. Adjacent to the site is the **Quarryman's Museum,** itself a work of art. The museum is filled with hammers and screws, chains and wagon wheels—everything arranged according to size and shape. A seven-minute video on the site is also featured.

To reach Opus 40 from Saugerties, take Route 212 west to Sickles Road, turn left, and watch *very* carefully for Fite Road on the right. Opus 40, 7480 Fite Rd., 845/246-3400, www.opus40.org, is open Memorial Day–Oct., Friday, some Saturdays, and Sunday, noon–5 P.M. Admission is adults $6, students and senior citizens $5, children 6–12 $3.

Recreation, Entertainment, and Events
Sawkill Creek near Route 375 is known as an excellent spot for **trout fishing.**

In summer, well-known jazz, folk, and classical players are occasionally featured at **Opus 40** (see above), which *Rolling Stone* once called, "the best outdoor concert venue in the Northeast."

In September, Saugerties celebrates everyone's favorite odorous herb with the **Hudson Valley Garlic Festival,** 845/340-3566, featuring cooking demonstrations, food lectures, entertainment, crafts, and food.

Camping and Accommodations
The largest campground in Saugerties is the **Rip Van Winkle,** 14 Robinson St., off Blue Mountain Rd., 845/246-8334, offering 170 sites May–Sept.; basic sites cost $25–29. Somewhat smaller is the **Saugerties-Woodstock KOA,** 7227 Rte. 212, 845/246-4089, offering 100 sites and camping cabins April–Oct.; basic sites cost $25–38. Among the motels in town is a **Comfort Inn,** 2790 Rte. 32, 845/246-1565 ($69–95 d).

Lighthouse B&B
One of the most unusual B&Bs in upstate New York is the **Lighthouse B&B,** 168 Lighthouse Dr., 845/247-0656, where guests can watch boats pass by on the Hudson from their second-story rooms. The bathroom is on the third floor. And from the parking lot, it's a 10-minute walk to the lighthouse; $160 d.

Food
Receiving raves from the locals is the **New World Home Cooking Co.,** 1411 Rte. 212, 845/246-0900, a "funky world cuisine cafe" offering a wide variety of dishes with Asian, Creole, Cajun, and Caribbean influences; average entrée $14. For fine Northern Italian dining, check out the casually elegant **Emiliani Ristorante,** 147 Ulster Ave., 845/246-6169; average entrée $16.

The chic yet casual **Cafe Tamayo,** 89 Partition St., 914/246-9371, is housed in an attractive 1864 brick building complete with ceiling fans. On the menu is sophisticated—and highly acclaimed—contemporary fare; average entrée $17.

WOODSTOCK AND VICINITY
The famed arts colony of Woodstock is still a picturesque and unusual spot, inhabited by an idiosyncratic bunch of artists and craftspeople, individualists and ne'er-do-wells. But the place is usually so overrun with tourists that it's hard to tell.

Woodstock the town dates back to the 1700s, but Woodstock the arts colony dates back to 1902, when a wealthy Englishman, free thinker, and lover of the arts named Ralph Radcliffe Whitehead came here to set up an arts-and-crafts community. A student of John Ruskin who railed against the evils of the Industrial Revolution, Whitehead envisioned his colony as living apart from the modern world, surrounded by scenic splendor, and supporting itself with its arts and crafts.

With two partners, Whitehead bought 1,300 acres and built a small village, Byrdcliffe, just above Woodstock. A few years later one of his followers, poet Hervey White, became fed up with Whitehead's authoritarian demands and started up a second arts community, Maverick, on the south side of town. Then, in 1906, the Art Students League of New York City arrived, opening a summer school in Woodstock's downtown. The village thronged with ever-increasing numbers of painters, potters, weavers, poets, dancers, musicians, novelists, hangers-on, and tourists eager to "see the artists."

In the late 1940s, folk singers Pete Seeger, Joan Baez, and Peter, Paul & Mary discovered Woodstock, and in the 1960s, Bob Dylan moved in, buying a farm on an isolated mountaintop. The town's first recording studio was built, and a series of small concerts, the Woodstock

ETHNIC RETREATS

Ever since the 1930s, '40s, and '50s, the Catskills—and especially Sullivan County—have been renowned for their enormous Jewish resorts. Many famous entertainers, including Milton Berle and Henny Youngman, have helped spread images of the Jewish Catskills all over the world.

Yet the Catskills have long been home to a wide variety of other ethnic groups as well. Germans, Italians, Eastern Europeans, Irish, Greeks, Armenians, African Americans, Spanish Americans, Russians, Koreans, Chinese—all have had, or continue to have, resorts in the Catskills.

"What's especially interesting," says Linda Norris, former director of the Delaware County Historical Association Museum, "is that everyone says they come to the Catskills because it reminds them of home."

The first immigrants to vacation in the Catskills in large numbers were Jews from Germany and Eastern Europe. Arriving during the 1880s, long before the Sullivan County resorts were built, the immigrants flocked to boardinghouses in northern Ulster and Greene Counties. Not always welcome at traditional resorts—one ad for the Hotel Lawrence read, "No Bar. No consumptives or Hebrews"—the Jews soon developed hostelries of their own. One of the first all-Jewish resort towns was Fleischmanns, named after its founder, the yeast magnate from Cincinnati.

In the early 1900s, the Jews were joined by Irish and German Catholics—all looking to escape the stifling heat of New York City. Then came the Italians, the Spanish Americans, and the Armenians. By the time of the Depression, people were joking not only about the Catskills' "Borscht Belt," but also about its "Bocce Belt," "Cuchifrito Circuit," and "Yogurt Belt." And still, the region's diversity continued to grow—by the 1940s, a good two dozen ethnic groups had established resorts here.

The Spanish Americans tended to congregate near Plattekill, the Germans near Roundtop, the Ukrainians near East Jewett, the Poles near Ellenville and New Kingston, the Irish near East Durham, the Greeks near Windham, the African Americans near Otisville, and the Italians near Hunter, Tannersville, and Cairo. Today, most of these towns—almost all of which are located in Greene County—have only a few vestiges of their ethnic heritage left, usually in the form of a resort, church, and restaurant or two.

One enormous exception is East Durham, where dozens of Irish-run resorts and bars crowd the main street, and the Irish brogue lilts over everything. East Durham had all but died by the late 1970s, when cheap airline flights to Ireland lured vacationers abroad. But the town has recently come to life again, thanks to a new wave of Irish immigrants.

Plattekill, once the resort of choice of wealthy Spanish Americans, now caters to large numbers of Puerto Ricans and others from the Caribbean and Central America. Interestingly enough, the Puerto Ricans first came to the Catskills as entertainers playing the mambo for sophisticated crowds. Now they're back on their own terms, having purchased a number of resorts and dance halls that are favorite destinations for social clubs coming up from New York, Beacon, and Newburgh.

African Americans have never vacationed in the Catskills in great numbers, but several black resorts were established in southwestern Ulster County in the early- to mid-1900s. One of the most famous of these was the Peg Leg Bates Country Club in Kerhonkson, founded by the entertainer in 1951 largely because although he often entertained in the Catskills, no hotel would allow him to stay overnight. Still in operation today, the Peg Leg Bates Country Club is now run by a Jamaican-American couple.

Not surprisingly, given current immigration trends, the latest ethnic groups to discover the Catskills are the Koreans, Chinese, and Russians. The Russians favor the bungalows of Sullivan County; the Chinese have taken over several former Italian resorts in Greene County; and the Koreans now own several former Jewish resorts near Monticello and Liberty. One Korean businessman has even purchased Grossinger's, once the quintessential Jewish Catskills resort.

THE CATSKILLS

Soundoffs, was staged. The Soundoffs were the immediate forerunner of the legendary 1969 Woodstock Music Festival that took place in Bethel, 60 miles away (see Sullivan County, below). The concert organizers wanted to hold the event closer to home, but Woodstock had no open space large enough, and last-minute ordinances imposed by nervous officials prevented the concert from taking place in nearby Saugerties as originally planned.

Downtown

For all its renown, Woodstock remains a small village, population about 6,000. Its main thoroughfare is **Tinker Street,** which according to legend is named after a tinker's wagon that sank into the mud here one fine spring day.

Where Tinker Street meets Rock City and Mill House Roads is the **village green,** often filled with teenagers wearing the tie-dyed T-shirts and long granny dresses of their parents' generation. Nearby is the Millstream, immortalized in Tell Taylor's classic song, "Down By the Old Millstream."

Dozens of small shops, galleries, and restaurants—many of them too cute for their own good—crowd the streets of Woodstock. Among the oldest is the **Woodstock Artists Association,** 28 Tinker St., 845/679-2940, which has been exhibiting the works of area artists since 1920 (open Thurs.–Mon. noon–5 P.M.). Among the newest is the **Center for Photography,** 59 Tinker St., 845/679-9957, www.cpw.org, which offers excellent exhibits, along with classes, lectures, and workshops (open Wed.–Sun. noon–5 P.M.). The **Golden Notebook,** 29 Tinker St., 845/679-8000, is a good bookstore.

The **Woodstock Chamber of Commerce,** 845/679-6234, www.woodstock-online.com, on Rock City Rd. near the village green, is open Thurs.–Mon. noon–6 P.M.; closed in winter. Parking is available in the municipal lots on Rock City Road and Tannery Brook Road. For taped information on lodging and dining, call 845/679-8025.

Two miles west of Woodstock is the hamlet of **Bearsville,** which has a long contemporary music history, with people like Bob Dylan recording in the music studios here.

Overlook Mountain

Looming behind Woodstock is Overlook Mountain, the summit of which offers splendid views of the valley and river below. To reach the mountain from town, take Rock City Road to Meads Mountain Road; the trailhead is opposite **Karma Triyana Dharmachakra,** 845/679-5906, www.kagyu.org, a Tibetan Buddhist monastery. In its shrine room, which is open to visitors Sat.–Sun. 1:30–3:30 P.M., is a 13-foot-high statue of the Buddha, which was used by Martin Scorsese in his film *Kundun,* about the life of the Dalai Lama.

The two-mile walk to the top of the mountain follows an old roadbed, is of easy-to-moderate difficulty, and takes about an hour. Along the way you'll pass the ruins of the Overlook Mountain House, once a popular resort that was anchored to the mountain by strong cables to keep it from being blown away. Plaques tell of the resort's fascinating history.

At the top of the mountain are picnic tables and a closed lookout tower.

Entertainment

The **Maverick Concerts** are a famed musical event, founded in 1916 by poet Hervey White. The oldest chamber-music series in the country, the concerts are staged in a small hand-hewn auditorium that seats only 400, but the music can also be heard from the surrounding hillsides. The series runs late July–early Sept., and features world-renowned musicians. The auditorium is on Maverick Road, off Route 375. For more information call 845/679-8217 or visit the website: www.maverickconcerts.org.

Since 2000, Woodstock has been home to the **Woodstock Film Festival,** website: www.woodstockfilmfestival.com.

In Bearsville is the excellent **Bearsville Theater,** Rte. 212, 845/679-4406 or 845/679-7303, which presents original drama throughout the summer. Now housed in the historic 1902 Byrdcliffe art colony is the **Woodstock Guild,** 34 Tinker St., 845/679-2079, www.woodstockguild.org, a multiarts center featuring performance art, theater, and film.

To find out more about what's going on in the

area, check the *Woodstock Times* and the *Catskill Mountain News*. Or listen to WDST, FM 100.1.

Accommodations

Downtown you'll find the attractive **Woodstock Inn on the Millstream,** 38 Tannery Brook Rd., 845/679-8211 or 800/697-8211, www.woodstock-inn-ny.com, an upscale motel equipped with both standard rooms and efficiency units ($99–159 d, with breakfast; two night minimum on summer weekends). A swimming hole is nearby. Also downtown, the comfortable **Twin Gables,** 73 Tinker St., 845/679-9479, www.twingableswoodstockny.com, has functioned as a homey, affordable guesthouse since the 1940s. The nine guest rooms are all nicely furnished; some share baths ($64–104 d).

The elegant **Woodstock Country Inn,** 27 Cooper Lake Rd., 845/679-9380, www.woodstockcountryinn.com, offers four guest rooms, all filled with antiques. There is also an outdoor pool and great views of the mountains ($150–265 d).

Food

For lunch, try **Bluestone Country Foods,** 54H Tinker St., 845/679-5656, offering a good selection of vegetarian dishes, salads, and naturally sweetened desserts; average main dish $7. Overlooking the golf course is the snug **Blue Mountain Bistro,** Rte. 212 and Glasco Tnpk., 845/679-8519, serving an imaginative French Mediterranean cuisine. In summer, there's dining on a deck overlooking a stream and live jazz on Saturday nights. Open for dinner only; average entrée $16.

On the road to nearby Bearsville, you'll find the brightly colored **Gypsy Wolf Cantina,** Rte. 212, 845/679-9563, a lively and popular Mexican cafe; average entrée $14. In Bearsville itself, next to the Bearsville Theater, is a whole complex of good restaurants. Oldest among them is the streamside **Bear Cafe,** Rte. 212, 845/679-5555, housed in a modern barn-like building with a big, comfortable bar. On the menu is imaginative American fare ranging from blackened chicken to grilled fish; average dinner entrée $18. Next door to the Bear Cafe is **Little Bear,** 845/679-8899, serving first-rate Chinese food; average entrée $10.

WEST ON ROUTE 28

Route 28 heads out of Kingston into the heart of **Catskill State Park and Catskill Forest Preserve.** Just past Boiceville, the land turns wooded, wild, and wonderful, with mountains rising to the left and right. Five of the Catskills' highest peaks are located in Ulster County.

Near the entrance to the park begins the 12-mile-long **Ashokan Reservoir.** Built between 1909 and 1919, despite fierce local opposition, the reservoir displaced eight communities, 2,600 graves, 64 miles of road, and 11 miles of railroad.

Around the reservoir, which is not visible from Route 28, runs Route 28A, a marvelous **scenic drive** that skirts Ashokan Dam, fountains, and a picnic area. Peaks rising to 3,000 feet surround the western end.

To either side of Route 28 are small, wistful villages that were once major resort destinations but now aren't much more than clutches of well-worn buildings, huddled together against the modern world. The original Route 28 once ran through their centers; the modern route bypasses them completely.

Route 28 provides access to several excellent hiking trails and scenic drives, while near the county border is Belleayre Mountain, a state-owned ski resort. Beyond Belleayre, Route 28 continues into Delaware County, where you'll find yet more forgotten resort towns, along with lush dairy country and a number of interesting cultural centers.

Boiceville

On the outskirts of Boiceville is **Onteora, the Mountain House,** 96 Piney Point Rd., 845/657-6233, www.onteora.com, a noteworthy B&B. Onteora sits high on a mountaintop overlooking Catskill Park. Once the posh retreat of mayonnaise mogul Richard Hellman, the home features 15-foot-high picture windows, cathedral ceilings, and a huge stone fireplace. The guest rooms are on the small side and all but one share a bath, but the views are magnificent ($195–240 d).

The very popular **Bread Alone Bakery & Cafe,** Rte. 28, 845/657-3328, offers lots of great fresh bread—all baked in a wood-fired oven—along with sandwiches, pastries, and coffees.

Mount Tremper

One of the newer—and weirder—attractions in the Catskills is **Catskills Corners Marketplace** on Rte. 28, 845/688-2451 or 888/303-3936, www.catskillcorners.com. Here you'll find everything from shops to a spa, along with the world's largest kaleidoscope, housed in a former grain silo painted with blue sky, white clouds, and a pair of honey-colored eyes. Inside the 60-foot-tall tower, visitors provided with headrests stare straight up into a myriad of images that are multiplied by 254 facets covering about 45 feet. Shows on American history are presented.

Also in the complex are shops selling kaleidoscopes, furniture, books, wines, and gifts; the family-oriented Spotted Dog Restaurant; the **Catamount Cafe,** serving "international farmhouse cuisine" in a setting overlooking the Esopus River (average entrée $15); the luxurious **Lodge at Catskill Corners,** 845/688-2828, all done up in Adirondack decor ($190–300 d); and the ultra-luxurious **Emerson Inn & Spa,** 146 Mt. Pleasant Rd., a full-treatment spa complete with a pool, fitness facilities, and posh guestrooms and suites.

Catskill Corners is open year-round Wed.–Mon. 10 A.M.–7 P.M. and on Tuesday July 4–Columbus

Day. A basic ticket costs adults $10, juniors $8, and families of four or more $9 per person.

Victorian **La Dutchess Anne Inn,** Rte. 212, off Rte. 28, near Wittenberg Rd., 845/688-5329, www.ladutchessanne.com, built in 1850 as a Norwegian guesthouse, is both an inviting B&B and a very popular French restaurant, run by a French-born owner. Perched on a small hill surrounded by woodlands, the inn offers about a dozen guest rooms, many of which share bathrooms, and a wide, lovely veranda ($90–150 d). The comfortable dining room serves classic French favorites such as assorted pâtés, escargot, and scallops Provençal, and offers a French and American wine list (average entrée $19).

Nearby is the popular **Kenneth L. Wilson Campground,** County Road 40, one mile off Rte. 28, 845/679-7020. Reservations here should be made well in advance; call 800/456-CAMP. Campsite prices start at $12.

Also in Mount Tremper is the luminous **Catskill Rose,** Rte. 212, 845/688-7100, whose front door is framed with pink neon and whose pale blue walls are strung with tiny white lights. To one side is an art deco bar glowing blue, to another a clutch of dining tables. On the menu is classic French cuisine, prepared by a husband and wife team; average entrée $15.

Phoenicia

One of the largest and most prosperous of the villages along Route 28 is Phoenicia, known for its trout fishing, kayaking, and tubing—all done on nearby Esopus Creek. From May to September, floating down the creek on huge black inner tubes is one of the county's most popular "sports." Many of the tube-rental shops are located in Phoenicia. Among them are **Town Tinker,** Bridge St., 845/688-5553, and **FS Tube and Raft Rental,** 4 Church St., 845/688-7633. Both are just off Route 28 at the town's entrance.

Besides outfitter shops, Phoenicia's Main Street holds turn-of-the-century wooden homes, wide porches, creaky gift shops, and general stores. At one end of town, housed in the old railroad station, is the **Empire State Railway Museum,** which documents the history of the five different railroads that serviced the Catskills between the late 1860s and

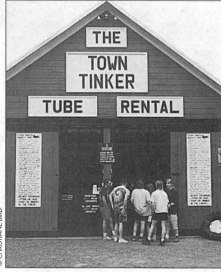

© CHRISTIANE BIRD

Town Tinker

the 1940s. Out back is a 2-8-0 steam locomotive and a classic 1913 Pullman dining car. The museum, far eastern end of Main St., 845/688-7501, www.esrm.com, is open Memorial Day–Columbus Day, Sat.–Sun. 11 A.M.–4 P.M. Suggested donation is adults $3, seniors $2, and children $1.

Between the railroad museum and the nearby village of Mt. Pleasant runs the **Catskill Mountain Railroad,** 845/688-7400, www.catskillmtrailroad.com. The scenic rides hug the banks of Esopus Creek, Memorial Day–Labor Day, Sat.–Sun. 11 A.M.–5 P.M.; Labor Day–mid Oct., Sat.–Sun. noon–4 P.M. Roundtrip rates are adults $7, children 4–12 $4.

Brio's, Main St., 845/688-5370, is a good, dependable luncheonette; average main dish $6. And "everyone goes" to **Sweet Sue's,** also on Main St., 845/688-7852, especially for brunch. On the menu are well over a dozen pancake dishes, along with eggs and sandwiches; average main dish $7.

Woodland Valley Recreation

Off Route 28 one mile west of Phoenicia, Woodland Valley Road turns off to the left and leads through Woodland Valley, one of the deepest and most romantic valleys in the Catskills. Four miles in, the road comes to a parking lot at **Woodland Valley State Campground,** 166 Woodland Valley Rd., 845/688-7647. Reservations at this state campground should be made well in advance; call 800/456-CAMP; basic campsites cost $10.

Also here is a well-marked trail that takes hikers to the top of Wittenberg Mountain. The 3.4-mile, 2,800-foot ascent takes about three hours. It's steep near the beginning and again near the top, but only of moderate difficulty most of the way. The spectacular view from the summit—one of the best in the Catskills—encompasses almost all of Ashokan Reservoir.

From Wittenberg Mountain, a short narrow trail leads via a connecting ridge to Cornell Mountain, which offers good views of Slide Mountain, the highest peak in the Catskills. The hike from Wittenberg to Cornell takes about 30 minutes.

Big Indian

Farther west on Route 28 lies the hamlet of Big Indian, named after a seven-foot-tall Indian

named Winnisook. Legend has it that young Gertrude, a farmer's daughter, fell in love with Winnisook but was forced by her father to marry a man named Joe Bundy. Lovelorn, she ran away, found Winnisook and lived happily with him and his people for seven years.

Then one day, Joe Bundy, out looking for cattle raiders, came across Winnisook and shot him. Before dying, the Big Indian took refuge in a hollow tree where he was discovered, still standing, by Gertrude. She had him buried nearby and lived by the tree for the rest of her life.

In Big Indian begins Route 47, a **scenic drive** among the finest in Ulster County. Take it up a steep hill, past several gorgeous mountain vistas, to Oliverea, a small resort village (see below). The road then descends five miles to Winnisook Lake and then another nine miles through an expansive valley with more spectacular views. From there, you can either retrace your steps or continue on to Route 42, which will circle back up through Sundown and West Shokan—ringed all around by mountains—to Route 28. The entire circuit is about 60 miles.

Dining options along Route 28 in the hamlet include **L'Auberge Du Canard,** 845/254-4646, a friendly French restaurant housed in a cheery wooden building with geraniums out front. Duck dishes are the specialty of the house; average entrée $18. Connected with L'Auberge Du Canard is **Luke's Grill,** a casual French restaurant where children are welcome; average entrée $13.

Oliverea

High on the mountainous slopes of Oliverea is the Indian-run **Mountain Gate Lodge,** 212 McKinley Hollow Rd., 845/254-6000 or 800/733-0344, www.mountaingatelodge.com. The attractive upscale motel offers an outdoor pool, colorful flower gardens, and the **Mountain Gate Indian Restaurant,** where smells of curry waft out of the door; average entrée $12. The lodge is surrounded by woodlands, and lots of good hiking is nearby ($69–99 d).

Pine Hill and Highmount

One of the most economical places to stay in all the Catskills is the friendly **Belleayre Hostel**

and Cabins, 15 Hostel Dr., off Main St., P.O. Box J, Pine Hill, 845/254-4200, www.belleayre-hostel.com, which has recently undergone a major renovation. The establishment now offers a bunkhouse with two revamped bunk rooms and dining hall, three private rooms, three one-room efficiencies, and five three-room cottages. The cost for a bunk is $15, the private rooms are $40, the efficiencies are $60–75, and the cottages are $125–160. Hostelers should bring their own linens and towels. Also in Pine Hill is the old-fashioned **Pine Hill Arms,** Main St., 845/254-4012, which features a beautiful old bar, and live music on some weekends.

Good downhill skiing can be found at New York State–owned **Belleayre Mountain Ski Area,** Belleayre Rd., off Rte. 28 in Highmount, 845/254-5600 or 800/431-4555 (lodging info), and 800/942-6904 (snow phone and events line), www.belleayre.com. On the upper mountain—elevation 3,365 feet—are 16 trails for intermediate or expert skiers; on the lower mountain are beginner and intermediate slopes. The vertical drop is 1,404 feet, and the longest run is over a mile. During the off-season, you can hike or take a chairlift to the summit, which offers sweeping views of the valley below. On Columbus Day weekend, the popular **Belleayre Mountain Fall Festival** takes place on the upper slopes, featuring crafts, entertainment, food, and more great views.

Greene County

Many of the Catskills' highest peaks and longest waterfalls are in Greene County, making it an especially pretty region to explore. It was in Greene County, after all, near the village of Palenville, that Rip Van Winkle supposedly fell into his deep, 20-year slumber, waking to find his fowling-piece rusted, his trusty dog Wolf gone, Dame Van Winkle departed to another world, and his son full-grown into a carbon copy of his younger self.

At the eastern edge of the county, along the Hudson, are Catskill—the county seat, lined with historic buildings in various stages of repair—and Coxsackie, home of the preeminent Bronck Museum. Most of the county's points of interest are farther west, however, in the spectacular mountains. There you'll find scenic drives, good day-hikes, ski centers, amusement parks, and odd, quirky sites—a Ukrainian church built without nails, a Buddhist temple, an all-Irish village.

The downside of Greene County is that some areas are highly commercialized and tawdry looking, especially in the off-season. Tourism is big business here, with about 640,000 tourists—including a half-million skiers—visiting each year. Full-time residents number only about 45,100.

Routes 23 and 23A are the most important east-west routes in the region and offer two of the most scenic drives, through the heart of the Catskills' high peaks. First-time visitors will probably want to concentrate on these two routes and perhaps hike part of the Escarpment Trail near Kaaterskill Falls.

Information

The **Greene County Promotion Department,** P.O. Box 527, Catskill, NY 12414, 518/943-3223 or 800/355-CATS, www.greene-ny.com, operates an information center off the New York State Thruway/I-87, Exit 21, in Catskill. The center is open daily year-round 9 A.M.–4 P.M., with extended hours in summer. After hours, travelers can consult the center's outside information kiosk and use its phone to make free calls to various accommodations and attractions.

For information on arts events throughout the region, contact the **Greene County Council on the Arts** at 518/943-3400.

CATSKILL AND VICINITY

Catskill, the Greene County seat, sits on the sloping banks of the Hudson at the mouth of Catskill Creek. The natural harbor here helped the town grow steadily after its founding in the late 1600s. By the early 1900s, Catskill was the prosperous home of numerous small knitting factories, brickyards, and distilleries.

During Prohibition, the town was known for

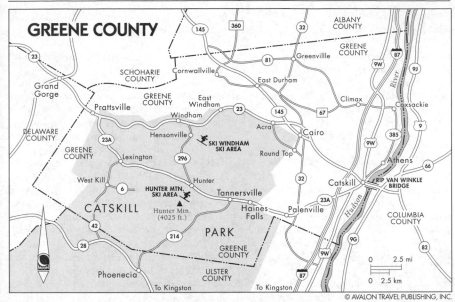

GREENE COUNTY

© AVALON TRAVEL PUBLISHING, INC.

THE CATSKILLS

its "retailers of liquid damnation." Catskill applejack was brewed in the hills surrounding town and buried in jugs whenever the law came around. The lucrative moonshine trade coupled with the inaccessible hills made Catskill a favorite haunt of New York City gangsters Legs Diamond and Vincent Coll. Diamond was once tried in the **Greene County Courthouse,** an imposing neoclassical building that still stands at the corner of Main and Bridge Streets.

Today, the town feels well worn around the edges, but retains a distinct charm. Besides the courthouse, **Main Street** showcases one big wooden building after another, many housing friendly old-fashioned businesses. **Catskill Gallery,** 398 Main St., 518/943-3400, presents exhibits, concerts, readings, and plays throughout the year. The gallery—run by the Greene County Council on the Arts—is open Tues.–Fri. 10 A.M.–4 P.M., Saturday noon–4 P.M. Running parallel to Main Street is **Spring Street,** a treasure trove of Victorian homes.

Thomas Cole House

The father of the Hudson River School, Thomas

Cole, lived in Catskill much of his adult life. Born in England in 1801, Cole came to New York City in 1818. He taught himself to paint landscapes, and in 1825 took his first sketching trip up the Hudson. The group of works he produced on that trip won him instant recognition.

Cole painted dramatic vistas of unspoiled wilderness and picturesque scenery. A deeply religious man and a lover of Romantic poetry, he regarded nature as, in his own words, "a fitting place to speak to God."

The former Cole home, Cedar Grove, is a big yellow-and-white affair with a beautiful veranda overlooking the Hudson. Recently renovated, the house features exhibits on Cole and his family, other Hudson River artists such as Frederic Church, and the Catskills. Also on display are a few small works by Cole, and memorabilia such as his paint box and Bible. Out back is Cole's old studio, housed in what were once slave quarters.

The Thomas Cole house, 218 Spring St., 518/731-6490, www.thomascole.org, is open Memorial Day–Columbus Day, Fri.–Sat. 10 A.M.– 4 P.M. and Sunday 1–5 P.M. Admission is adults $4, children under 12 free.

Food

The old-fashioned **Bell's Coffee Shop,** 387 Main St., 518/943-4070, offers a dependable breakfast and lunch; average main dish $5. Although the steak and seafood dishes at the **Point,** 7 Main St., 518/943-5352, aren't anything special, its views of the Hudson are terrific, especially in summer when an outdoor patio is opened up; average dinner entrée $15.

Athens

About four miles north of Catskill on Route 385 is the attractive village of Athens, first settled by the Dutch in 1686. At one time or another, the town has been a center for brickmaking, shipbuilding, ice harvesting, and even mushroom-growing (after the advent of mechanical refrigeration, the abandoned icehouses were found to be ideal for the growth of fungi).

Today Athens feels like a smaller and sleepier version of Catskill. Its streets, too, are lined with big old wooden buildings, many of them from the Victorian age, and the village hovers on an economic edge between neglect and gentrification. Route 385 just south of Athens parallels the Hudson at water level, offering splendid views of both the river and the 1874 Hudson-Athens lighthouse.

Smack on the shores of the Hudson downtown is the upscale **Stewart House Restaurant and Bistro,** 2 N. Water St., 518/945-1357, housed in a Victorian-era building. To one side is a formal dining room where full dinners are served, to the other a more casual bistro. On the menu is contemporary American fare (average dinner entrée $18; average bistro fare $11).

Catskill Game Farm

Heading west out of Catskill on Route 23A, you'll soon bump into Route 32, where you'll find the widely promoted Catskill Game Farm. A much more sophisticated operation than its name implies, the "farm" is really a shaded, well-kept zoo housing over 2,000 animals, including lions, tigers, elephants, giraffes, zebras, and bears. What makes it especially nice, however, is its huge petting area where visitors can wander among llamas and deer. You can buy packets of food to offer the grown animals, or go to the nursery and feed baby lambs and piglets by baby bottle. Also in the park are amusement rides, a small train, and play areas.

© CHRISTIANE BIRD

Along Route 32, the Catskill Game Farm is more sophisticated and better kept than it at first appears.

The game farm, 400 Game Farm Rd., off Rte. 32, Catskill, 518/678-9595, www.catskillgamefarm.com, is open May–Oct., daily 9 A.M.–5 P.M. Admission is adults $15.95, children 4–11 $11.95. Be forewarned that many things inside cost extra; the train ride is $1, the animal food costs between 75 cents and $2.75.

Camping and Accommodations

Campers can pitch their tents at the 50-site **Catskill Campground,** 79 Castle Rd., off Rte. 32, 518/678-5873; a basic site costs $16. A good motel along Route 32 is the clean and comfortable **Red Ranch,** 4555 Rte. 32, 518/678-3380 or 800/962-4560, www.redranchmotel.com, which offers 39 rooms (many with kitchenettes), a pool, and a playground ($58–78 d).

WEST ON ROUTE 23A

Some of the most dramatic scenery in the Catskills lies west of Route 32 on Route 23A. For about four miles, between Palenville and Haines Falls, the road winds steeply up and up nearly 1,500 feet, past craggy cliffs and rocky streams, forested walls and outstanding views. The incline continues at a gentler angle between Haines Falls and Hunter, then levels out to run through the narrow valley of Schoharie Creek.

Not to be missed is the view from the Catskill Mountain House site, just east of Haines Falls. The site can be reached by hiking the Escarpment Trail or by driving into North-South Lakes Campground and walking a few hundred yards to the edge of the Great Wall of Manitou, a steep escarpment. From here, the whole world seems to lie at your feet. Straight ahead, in the distance, are the gray-blue Taconic and Berkshire Mountains; below is the Hudson, shrunk to a slim silver line.

The view is perhaps best described in James Fenimore Cooper's *The Pioneers,* one of his Natty Bumppo tales: "'What see you when you get there?' asked Edwards. 'Creation!' said Natty, . . . 'all creation, lad.'"

Palenville

A good hostelry for families is the bustling **Catskill Mountain Lodge,** Rte. 32A, between Rts. 32 and 23A, 518/678-3101, www.catskillmtnlodge.com, located in an attractive rustic spot complete with outdoor pools, a playground, and a game room ($70–125 d).

Kaaterskill Falls

Off Route 23A about three miles west of Palenville are Kaaterskill Falls, marked with a sign and roadside parking lot. At 260 feet (compared to Niagara's 167 feet), these are the highest waterfalls in the state. During the Romantic Age, everyone from Thomas Cole and Asher Durand to James Fenimore Cooper and William Cullen Bryant were inspired by this long glittering torrent falling from pool to pool to pool. The falls were portrayed in countless paintings, illustrations, and poems until they became an icon for the American wilderness. Near the top of the falls once stood the Catskill Mountain House, the nation's first mountain resort (see chapter Introduction).

To reach the lower basin of Kaaterskill Falls, follow the well-marked trail on the north side of Route 23A. The hike, which begins at Bastion Falls, takes less than an hour roundtrip, and

CATTERSKILL FALLS

Midst greens and shades the Catterskill leaps
From cliffs where the wood-flower clings;

All summer he moistens his verdant steeps
With the sweet light spray of the
    mountain-springs,

And he shakes the woods on the mountain-side,
When they drip with the rains of the
    autumn-tide.

But when, in the forest bare and old,
The blast of December calls,

He builds, in the starlight clear and cold,
A palace of ice where his torrent falls,

With turret, and arch, and fretwork fair,
And pillars blue as the summer air. . . .
    William Cullen Bryant

THE CATSKILLS

although there are a few steep spots, the trail is mostly level.

Escarpment Trail

One of the most unusual hikes in the Catskills is the Escarpment Trail, which stretches 24 miles between Route 23A in Haines Falls and Route 23 in East Windham without crossing a single highway. Parts of the trail have been used for more than 150 years, as initials and dates carved along its ledges attest.

To access the popular section of the Escarpment Trail that leads past the former site of the Catskill Mountain House, continue about two miles past the Kaaterskill Falls parking area and take the first right onto County Road 18, following signs to North-South Lakes Campground. At the end of this four-mile road, just before the campground, turn right onto Scutt Road, where you'll find a parking area and a blue-marked trail.

Follow the trail through a forested area, past Spruce Creek and a four-way intersection, toward Layman Monument and Sunset Rock. Soon after the intersection, the trail skirts along the top of the Great Wall of Manitou. The terrain here is fairly level and all along the way are overlooks offering magnificent views. Near the Layman Monument—erected to honor a firefighter who lost his life here in 1900—you can see Kaaterskill Clove ("clove" comes from the Dutch word for gorge), with Hunter Mountain in the background. From Sunset Rock and Inspiration Point, distant Kaaterskill Creek and the Hudson River lie like ribbons at your feet.

About a mile and a half past Inspiration Point is a red-marked cutoff trail leading to the site of the former Catskill Mountain House. Take this shorter trail, or continue on the more scenic blue trail past Split and Boulder Rocks. Either way, within 20–30 minutes you'll reach the large open ledge upon which the famed resort once stood. An informative plaque marks the spot.

To hike from the parking lot to the Catskill Mountain House site takes about an hour and a half. From there, you can return the way you came or take the park service road back to the parking lot.

North-South Lakes

If you're short on time, or would rather not hike, you can reach the former Catskill Mountain House site directly by entering the 219-site North-South Lakes Campground and driving to the end of the service road. The short trail that leads to the site is located at the far end of the parking lot.

The North-South Lakes are the focus of a popular state-owned recreation area. Facilities include two long pristine lakes, ringed by deciduous trees that erupt with fiery color in the fall, a sandy beach, bathhouses, and many hiking trails. Rowboats can be rented, and fishing is good.

According to legend, North and South Lakes are the two eyes of a great reclining giant, Onteora; the nearby Lake Creek is his tears. South Lake, formerly known as Sylvan Lake, was one of Thomas Cole's favorite subjects. He painted his well-known "Lake With Dead Trees" and "Catskill Lake" here. During the reign of the Catskill Mountain House, the lake was used for evening festivities and canoe parties, and was frequently lit with Japanese lanterns.

North-South Lakes is off County Road 18, Haines Falls, 518/589-5058. Admission is $5–7 per vehicle. Open May–Nov., daily 9 A.M.–dusk. Reservations at the campground, which closes in October, should be made well in advance; call 800/456-CAMP; basic sites cost $16.

Tannersville

Part scruffy mountain village, part cheery tourist town, Tannersville—named for its once extensive tanning industry—is now home to a few shops and cafes, several inns and B&Bs, and a surprisingly large number of tattoo parlors. Especially elaborate work is done by a man named Bruce Bart; even if you're not in the market, you might want to stop into his friendly shop on Main Street, in the village center, 518/589-5069, to take a look at his impressive portfolio.

The very popular **Eggery Inn,** County Road 16, off Rte. 23A, 518/589-5363, www.eggeryinn.com, has been accommodating guests since 1900. The inn features a wood-burning Franklin stove, heavy oak bar, wraparound porch, and spectacular views of the Catskills ($100–125 d, with breakfast). Another favorite lodging is the nearby **Redcoat's Country Inn & Restaurant,** Dale Ln. off Elka Park Rd. (see Outlying Enclaves, below), 518/589-9858, www.redcoatsonline.com, an English-styled inn housed in an attractive 1850s' farmhouse ($85–135 d, with breakfast). Attached is a cozy restaurant serving Continental fare; open for dinner on weekends only, entrées range $12–28.

In the village center, you'll find **Maggie's Krooked Cafe,** Main St., 518/589-6101, offering home-cooked specialties such as pancakes and fried shrimp in beer batter (average main dish $8). **Last Chance Antique and Cheese Cafe,** Main St., 518/589-6424, is a combination store/cafe featuring overstuffed sandwiches, homemade soups, cheeses, and chocolates.

Outlying Enclaves

From Tannersville, a short detour north along scenic Rte. 23C leads past the elegant homes of **Onteora Park.** Founded by Frances Thurber in 1883, Onteora was a posh summer colony with its own golf course and private lake. Many of its residents were patrons of the arts who encouraged creative types such as Mark Twain and Antonin Dvorak to summer here. In 1927, author Hamlin Garland attended one of the community's exclusive functions and afterwards wrote, "Luxury such as this may be debilitating." Onteora Park is still off-limits to the public, and can only be glimpsed from the road.

South of Tannersville off Elka Park Road is **Elka Park,** another exclusive residential community, this one founded by the German-American Liederkranz Society of New York. It, too, is still off-limits to the public.

Hunter

Known first for its tannery and then for its chair factory, Hunter is now a small, blue-collar ski town. Behind it rises the trail-carved wall of Hunter Mountain Ski Area, while along Main Street stand lodges and restaurants, many done up in ersatz Swiss motif. During the off-season, a good half of these establishments seem shut down and the village takes on a scruffy, neglected feel.

In summer, anglers can be found **trout fishing** in Schoharie Creek along Route 23A, while hik-

ers take to the slopes of Hunter Mountain (see Hunter Mountain Hiking, below). The 24-site **Devil's Tombstone Campground** is four miles south of town on Rte. 214, 845/688-7160. The state-run campground is open Memorial Day–Labor Day; reservations should be made well in advance by calling 800/456-CAMP; basic sites start at $10.

The most charming hostelry in town is the recently restored **Fairlawn Inn,** Main St., 518/263-5025, www.fairlawninn.com. This three-story Victorian hostelry offers 12 attractive bedrooms—complete with brass beds—wraparound porches, and a stunning central staircase ($85–100 d).

The modern **Scribner Hollow Lodge,** Main St. (Rte. 23A), just east of Hunter Mountain, 518/263-4211 or 800/395-4683, www.scribnerhollow.com, is a full-service hostelry with an outdoor pool, an unusual indoor grotto, saunas, and fireplaces. Each of the 38 rooms is furnished differently, and artwork is everywhere ($105–255 per person d, with breakfast and dinner; $25 less without meals). Adjoining the lobby is **Prospect Restaurant,** offering fine continental cuisine and scenic vistas; average entrée $15. The restaurant is open for dinner daily during the ski season, and Friday–Sunday only the rest of the year.

Also in the village is **Hunter Inn,** Main St. (Rte. 23A), 518/263-3777, www.hunterinn.com, offering upscale motel rooms. The inn caters mostly to skiers but is open during the summer as well; $85–125 d.

Hunter Mountain Ski Area

Hunter Mountain Ski Area, off Route 23A in the heart of the village, 518/263-4223 (general info), 800/FOR-SNOW (ski conditions) or 800/875-4641 (lodging info), www.huntermtn.com, is the Catskills' best-known ski center and one of its biggest businesses. In winter, boisterous New York City folk flock here by the thousands to ski its crowded slopes. The three-mountain complex offers 49 trails, 15 lifts and tows, and 100 percent snowmaking capability.

In summer, the **Hunter Mountain Festivals** are staged here. Regulars in the series include the German Festival, Oktoberfest, the Harvest

Festival, and the International Celtic Festival, during which dozens of sturdy men in kilts march down the mountainside. The festivals kick off early in July and run through October. For more information, call 518/263-4223.

Throughout the off-season, the **Hunter Mountain Sky Ride,** the longest chairlift in the Catskills, travels to the mountain's summit on the weekends. Open year-round is the resort's small **Ski Museum,** which documents the history of the sport with antiques, mementos, and photographs; open Mon.–Fri. 10 A.M.–5 P.M., free admission.

Lexington

Continuing west on Route 23A, you'll pass through the nondescript hamlets of South Jewett and Jewett Center before coming to the startlingly beautiful **St. John the Baptist Ukrainian Catholic Church,** Rte. 23A just east of Lexington, 518/263-3862. The church was built in 1962 in memory of the Ukrainians killed by the Communists in WW II. The entire edifice—with its rich brown cedar shingles, onion domes, and steeply pitched roofs—was constructed without nails in the traditional Ukrainian manner. The interior features a stunning hand-carved altar, along with an array of beautiful woodcarvings and icons.

On Saturday evenings in July and August, classical chamber music concerts and Ukrainian crafts workshops are often featured in St. John's adjacent *Grazhda,* or community center. Call for schedule information.

One of the best lodging deals in the region is the creaky old **Lexington Hotel,** Rte. 42, at Rte. 23A, 518/989-6463. Built around the turn of the century, the Lexington once catered to an exclusively Ukrainian clientele but now draws anyone looking for a bargain ($27 per person, with breakfast). Out front is a porch lined with rocking chairs; indoors are spartan but clean rooms, all of which share baths. On Saturday nights, the hotel's simple, no-frills restaurant offers a hearty Ukrainian-American buffet.

Hunter Mountain Hiking

A number of good, well-marked hiking trails lace the area around Hunter Mountain. Many start at the back of the mountain on Old Spruceton Road. To get there, continue west on Route 23A past the Ukrainian church and turn left onto Route 42 south. Continue to the hamlet of Westkill, turn east onto County Road 6, and follow it six miles through pastoral Spruceton Valley. At the end, after the road has become dirt, are two parking lots with trailheads.

The main trail leading to Hunter's summit is of moderate difficulty, covers 7.2 miles roundtrip, and takes about six to seven hours. Along the way is a mile-long spur leading to **Colonel's Chair,** a northern protuberance of the mountain supposedly resembling a giant armchair. The chair was named after Col. William Edwards, an early tanner who made his fortune decimating the area's hemlock forest, and then unceremoniously pulled out. It was Edwards who first put Hunter—then known as Edwardsville—on the map.

One of the easiest hikes in the Catskills, leading to Diamond Notch Falls, also begins at the parking lots. The gently inclining trail is about a mile long and runs alongside West Kill Creek. Wildflowers and birds are abundant. At the end of the trail is a small but forceful 15-foot waterfall.

For more information on hiking Hunter Mountain, stop into the main Hunter Mountain ski lodge, off Rte. 23A in Hunter, 518/263-4223. The lodge is open daily 10 A.M.–5 P.M.

PRATTSVILLE

On Route 23, just west of the Route 23A intersection, is the tidy village of Prattsville—one of the first planned communities in New York State. Prattsville began in 1824 when a man named Col. Zadock Pratt came to what was then known as Schoharie Kill to establish "the largest tannery in the world." Pratt not only succeeded in establishing his tannery—which over 20 years tanned more than a million hides and cleared over 10,000 acres of hemlock—but also built an elaborate village.

First, the "Colonel" widened Main Street and built 100 handsome Greek Revival houses and stores along it. Then he lined the street with 1,000 elm, maple, and hickory trees, and laid slate sidewalks. Next, he built four textile factories, three gristmills, five schools, three churches, and several hotels. In 1843—on his 53rd birthday—he opened his own bank and had currency printed with his image upon it.

For all of this, Pratt—who once said that he had come to "live with the people, not on them"—became a folk hero in his own time, and is still remembered with a great deal of affection. Many of his buildings and trees still stand along Main Street.

Zadock Pratt Museum

Pratt's former home has been turned into a museum holding everything from pictures of his wives (he had five, including two pairs of sisters) to documents from the years he spent as a U.S. Congressman (he never missed a single session). The museum, at the west end of Main St., 518/299-3395, www.prattmuseum.com, is open Memorial Day–Columbus Day, Wed.–Sun. 1–5 P.M. or by appointment. Admission is adults $2, children 12 and under $1.

Pratt Rock

In addition to his many accomplishments, Pratt was also an eccentric who liked to play practical jokes, compete in contests of strength and skill (at age 36, he beat all challengers in the running broad jump), and judge a man's character by the look of his hands. Evidence of Pratt's eccentricity can be found on the outskirts of the village, where he had a small park with rock sculptures built into the mountainside. The sculptures, painted white, tell the story of Pratt's life through symbols—a horse, a hemlock tree, the bust of his son who died in the Civil War.

Also in the park is a half-completed stone coffin. Pratt wanted to be buried in the park as well, but the rock proved too hard and he was buried conventionally, in the Prattsville Cemetery. Pratt Rock, off Rte. 23 at the entrance to the village, 518/299-3395, is open year-round.

EAST ALONG ROUTE 23

Ashland

Heading back east along Route 23, you'll pass a wide and wonderful waterfall on the right known as **Red Falls.** At its base is a deep, dark swimming hole. From the waterfall, Route 23 winds through the hamlet of Ashland. The area is popular with anglers who try their luck in **Batavia Kill.**

On a woodsy back road several miles off Rte. 23 is the secluded 1870 **Ashland Farmhouse,**

© CHRISTIANE BIRD

Pratt Rock

W. Settlement Rd., 518/734-3358. The B&B boasts its own stocked trout pond, grassy fields, hot tub, wood-burning stove, and four comfortable guest rooms ($60–70 d).

Windham

Route 23 continues past Ashland to the bustling ski resort village of Windham. More upscale than Hunter, Windham attracts a largely professional crowd and is filled with Greek Revival buildings, ski lodges, resorts, and restaurants.

Ski Windham, the Catskills' second largest ski resort, C.D. Ln., off South St., one mile from Rte. 23, is considerably smaller than Hunter Mountain, but it's also less hectic. The resort offers 33 trails, a 3,050-foot summit, and 97 percent snowmaking capability. For more information, call 518/734-4300 or 800/SKI-WINDHAM, www.skiwindham.com.

In a rural setting on the outskirts of town is the **Albergo Allegria B&B,** Rte. 296, off Rte. 23, a half mile east of Windham, 518/734-5560, www.AlbergoUSA.com, a charming Victorian manor house that feels more like an inn than a B&B. Upstairs are 16 guest rooms all nicely done up in period antiques, while downstairs is a comfortable lounge with overstuffed couches and a fireplace. All of the rooms have cable TV and phones (weekdays $75–189 d, weekends $99–209 d).

Campers can pitch their tents at **White Birches,** Nauvoo Rd., off Rte. 23, 518/734-3266, a well-kept campground offering 100 campsites and hiking, swimming, and fishing in a spring-fed lake year-round. Sites cost $20–25.

For a hearty breakfast or lunch, or a glass of Guinness in the village center, try **Jimmy O'Connor's Windham Mountain Inn,** South St., 518/734-4270, a lively Irish pub. The homey **Michael's,** on nearby Main St., 518/734-9862, serves breakfast all day, along with sandwiches, burgers, homemade soups, and Greek specialties. An average main dish at both eateries averages about $6.

One of the top-rated restaurants in Greene County is elegant **La Griglia,** now relocated into the Christman Windham House, Rte. 23, 518/733-4230. Open in winter and for dinner only, the restaurant serves Northern Italian fare made with fresh herbs; average entrée $18. Also in town is **La Griglia Cafe,** Church St., 518/734-4499 or 518/734-6100, featuring freshly baked pies, cakes, and breads.

One final note: As you leave Windham on Route 23, look out for an enormous **woodpile** on the left, just beyond the Police Anchor Camp. One year the pile was stacked into the shape of a six-car railroad train; the next, it was shaped into a small house. The woodpile is the creation of artist Alec Alberti, who began the project as a teenager and creates something different every year.

East to Cairo

Between East Windham and Cairo (KAY-ro), Route 23 turns from scenic to spectacular as it traverses the big wide slopes of Windham High Peak, Burnt Knob, and Acra Point. The expansive Helderberg Valley opens up below, while in the distance are the Green Mountains of Vermont and the White Mountains of New Hampshire.

A scenic overlook is located midway, or you can stop for a meal or a drink at the comfortable **Point Lookout Inn and Victorian Rose Restaurant,** Rte. 23, East Windham, 518/734-3381, www.pointlookoutinn.com, about two miles east of the overlook. The modern and casual hostelry overlooking five states serves everything from salads and sandwiches to pasta and steaks (average dinner entrée $16). Fourteen simple, nicely appointed lodge rooms with private baths are also available ($80–155 d), while on the grounds are hot tubs and nature trails.

At Acra, you can continue east directly into Cairo, or loop south through the community of **Round Top,** once known for its German resorts—one to two of which are still in operation. The hamlet's foremost accommodation, however, is the wonderful old **Winter Clove Inn,** Winter Clove Rd., off Rte. 32, 518/622-

Variously nicknamed Ireland's 33rd County, the Irish Catskills, or the Irish Alps, East Durham and environs have been an Irish resort since the late 1800s.

3267, www.wintercloveinn.com, a big white Colonial sitting on a hillside. Owned by the same family since 1830, the Winter Clove has its own swimming pools, tennis courts, nine-hole golf course, hiking trails, and bowling alley. Outside is a big wide porch lined with an array of wicker rocking chairs; inside are 50 spacious rooms filled with flowered wallpaper and antiques ($95 a day per person including all meals, or $75 a day with breakfast only).

Buddhist Temple

Just beyond the scrappy town of Cairo, off Route 23B, is Ira Vail Road and signs that will lead you to the Mahayana Buddhist Temple and Monastery, 518/622-3619. The retreat of the Eastern States Buddhist Temple of America, based in New York City, the red-and-gold enclave sits in a peaceful woodsy area at the end of a dirt road. Not far from the red-gated entrance is the serene Lake of Fortune and Longevity and the Pagoda of Jade Buddha. To one side are the Grand Buddha Hall and several smaller temples. To the other are the plainer buildings of the monastery.

A plaque at the entrance to the Grand Hall tells the story of the Yings, who immigrated to the United States from China in 1955, only to find no organized Buddhist temple in New York. Seven years later they founded the first, at 64 Mott St. in New York City's Chinatown, and soon thereafter built the Mahayana retreat.

Inside the Grand Hall is an altar laden with three golden Buddhas, fruit, and flowers. Two monks in orange robes sit against one wall, while tourists wander about. The retreat, open daily 7 A.M.–7 P.M., actively welcomes visitors, as the many unobtrusive donation boxes and explanatory signs attest.

Don't leave the Mahayana retreat without visiting the fascinating Five Hundred Arhats Hall. Here, 500 golden Buddhas, each one different from the next, sit in a darkened room lit only with small spotlights.

EAST DURHAM AND VICINITY

On Route 145, about five miles northwest of Cairo, is the remarkable village of East Durham.

The Mahayana Buddhist Temple is a retreat of the Eastern States Buddhist Temple of America.

© CHRISTIANE BIRD

THE CATSKILLS

At first, nothing seems too out of the ordinary in this scenic spot surrounding by rolling hills, but then you start to notice one shamrock after another, one green building after another, one Irish name after another. O'Sullivan, Kelly, Mc-Grath, McGuire, O'Connor, McLaughlin, Ryan, O'Shea. Ethnic resorts may be dying out elsewhere in the Catskills, but someone forgot to inform East Durham.

Variously nicknamed Ireland's 33rd County, the Irish Catskills, or the Irish Alps, East Durham and environs have been an Irish resort since the late 1800s, when immigrants living in New York City escaped the summer heat by coming up here to the hills that reminded them of home. With the advent of cheap flights to Ireland in the 1970s, much of this tourist trade died down. But it's recently skyrocketed again thanks to a new wave of Irish immigrants to New York.

Irish American Heritage Museum
In the center of town is the first-rate Irish American Heritage Museum, Rte. 145, 518/634-7497, housed in an 1850s farmhouse with lots of airy gallery space. Established in 1990, the museum documents the history of the Irish in the United States though a series of changing exhibits on such subjects as Irish immigration and Irish music. Also on tap are frequent concerts, lectures, and readings, some of which take place next door in the **Irish Cultural & Sports Centre.** Inside the museum is a good bookshop.

The museum is open Memorial Day–late Sept., Fri.–Sun. noon–4 P.M., or by appointment. Admission is adults $3.50, seniors and children $2.

Guaranteed Irish
Another unique stop in the village center is Guaranteed Irish, Rte. 145, 518/634-2392, "the largest Irish import store in the United States." Inside this sprawling building you'll find everything from Irish sweaters and china leprechauns to an excellent selection of Irish music and literature. Most everyone who shops here seems to have at least a touch of Irish brogue, so even if you don't intend to buy, it's great fun just to listen. The store is open daily April–Dec.; weekends only January–March.

Durham Center Museum
Two miles west of East Durham on Route 145 is the idiosyncratic Durham Center Museum, housed in a turn-of-the-century schoolhouse. The museum was begun in 1945 by Durham resident and amateur paleobotanist Vernon Haskins. An enthusiast of nature and history, Haskins had an ever-growing collection of *stuff* that his friends kept asking to see until finally he opened up this small museum.

Today, the old schoolhouse is packed with everything from fossils and minerals to Indian artifacts, items made at local foundries, war relics, seashells, rare bottles, toys, sand from around the world, Victorian Rogers Group sculptures, and "unusual office and dentist equipment" such as early typewriters and a foot-powered dentist drill. The staff is all volunteer, and Vernon's daughter still helps run the place.

The museum, 518/239-4313, is open June–Aug., Wed.–Thurs. and Sat.–Sun. 1–4 P.M. Suggested donation is adults $2, children under 12 50 cents.

Zoom Flume
Also west of East Durham is a popular water park. Partially created out of natural stone formations, Zoom Flume features two 300-foot water slides, a "river" for tube floating, 10,000-gallon-a-minute "rapids," bumper boats, a pool, a game area, nature trails, and scenic overlooks. The place is clean and well-kept.

Zoom Flume, Shady Glen Rd., off Rte. 145, 518/239-4559 or 800/888-3586, www.zoom-flume.com, is open July–Labor Day, daily 10 A.M.–6 P.M.; June, Sat.–Sun. 10 A.M.–5 P.M. Admission is adults $17.95; children seven and under $14.95.

Adjoining the park is the **Country Place Resort,** 518/239-4559 or 800/888-3586, www.thecountryplace.com, a 20-room, family-oriented hostelry offering budget packages. A two-night package for two adults starts at $204, including breakfast, dinner, and a one-day ticket to Zoom Flume.

Entertainment and Events
The town's **Irish Cultural & Sports Centre,** Rte. 145 in the village center, 518/634-2286,

presents theater, music, dance, and sporting events. Irish music can also be heard at many of the casual, fly-by-night pubs along Route 145, or the more formal lounges situated in the village's resorts. Two resorts with extensive concert schedules are the **Fern Cliff House,** Rte. 67A, off Rte. 145, 518/634-7424, and **Gavin's Golden Hill Resort,** Golden Hill Rd., off Rte. 145, 518/634-2582.

The popular **East Durham Irish Festival,** 518/634-2286, featuring Irish bands, bagpipes, and dancers, takes place over Memorial Day weekend.

Accommodations and Food

The **Hull-O Farm,** Cochrane Rd., 518/239-6950, www.hull-o.com, is a working farm with two private guest houses and a pond stocked with bass. Guests are welcome to help feed the calves and milk the cows, and or take a hayride ($110 per adult per night; children discounted by age). The **Shamrock House,** Rte. 145 in the village center, 518/634-2897, www.shamrockhouse.com, owned by the Kellegher family since 1938, is a well-kept motel with a restaurant, pub, and live Irish music on weekends ($110–140 d with breakfast and dinner). Decidedly non-Irish, but very popular nonetheless, is the casual **Hans & Gretel's,** Rte. 145 at the east end of the village, 518/634-2512, serving everything from sandwiches to sauerbraten; average main dish $10.

GREENVILLE TO COXSACKIE

Greenville

About five miles northeast of East Durham is the picture-perfect, New England–style village of Greenville, centered around the Victorian **Greenville Arms 1889 Inn,** South St., at Rte. 32, 518/966-5219, www.greenvillearms.com. Built as a private residence by William Vanderbilt in 1889, the retreat now features 12 guest rooms and one suite, all equipped with private baths and furnished with fine antiques. Out back are the swimming pool and flower gardens ($115–195 d, includes full country breakfast).

At the southern end of the village is the pristine **Sunny Hill Resort & Golf Resort,** Sunny

Hill Rd., off Rte. 32, 518/634-7642, www.sunnyhill.com, featuring an 18-hole golf course, outdoor pool, private lake with boating and fishing, and lots of ball fields. The resort is especially popular among golf enthusiasts, but is a good place for families as well. A wide variety of packages are available; during the summer, almost all rooms are booked by the week. Summer rates start at about $120 per person per night, and include three meals. The resort is closed October 15–May 15.

Coxsackie

Heading southeast from Greenville on Route 81, you'll pass through the hamlets of Surprise and Climax—both not much more than intersections in the road. (Climax's name sign is nowhere in sight, by the by, perhaps because its residents got tired of the inevitable jokes.) Soon you'll come to the town of Coxsackie (COOK-sackie) and the Bronck Museum.

Coxsackie, first settled by Pieter Bronck in 1661, was the site of the signing of the 1775 Coxsackie Declaration, a local precursor to the national Declaration of Independence. Today, the town is a sprawling industrialized place that's home to granite works and valve-manufacturing plants.

Bronck Museum

One of the most important museums in the Catskills is the Bronck Museum, a complex of Dutch Colonial dwellings and 19th-century barns that was operated as a working farm by eight generations of the Bronck family. The oldest building, a 1663 stone house, contains an Indian lookout loft and lots of local textiles, looms, and spinning wheels. Next door is the 1738 Brick House, now used to display various household items, glass and silver, and an interesting collection of paintings by artists such as Frederic Church, Thomas Cole, and Ammi Phillips.

Outside you'll find a kitchen in its own tiny cottage, and three barns, each representing a different era. The squat Dutch barn is equipped with heavy, blackened beams; the 13-sided Liberty barn is built around a central pole; and the Victorian-house barn is filled with period carriages and wagons. Behind the barns, offering yet a different insight into the past, are the family and slave cemeteries. The family cemetery is enclosed by a big white fence; the slave cemetery is haphazardly scattered over a knoll by a stream.

The museum, Pieter Bronck Rd., off Rte. 9 W four miles south of Coxsackie, 518/731-6490 or 518/731-8862, is run by the Greene County Historical Society, www.gchistory.org. Hours are Memorial Day–Oct. 15, Tues.–Sat. 10 A.M.– 4 P.M., Sunday 1–5 P.M. Admission is adults $4, seniors $3.50, students ages 12–15 $2, children 5–11 $1, under five free. From I-87, take Exit 21B and head south.

Sullivan County

None of the Catskill Mountains and only a sliver of the Catskill Preserve lies in Sullivan County, and yet for many, Sullivan County *is* the Catskills. That's largely because in the years following WW II, the county became known for its megaresorts, many catering to a Jewish clientele. Most of these luxury retreats boasted their own private golf courses, lakes, indoor/outdoor pools, riding stables, ice rinks, ski slopes, and health clubs, and offered packed activities schedules and three gargantuan meals daily, and live entertainment nightly. The resorts also made Sullivan County the cradle of the Catskill comedian—the heart of the so-called "Borscht Belt." Henny Youngman, Moss Hart, Jerry Lewis, Joan Rivers, Milton Berle, Mel Brooks—all cut their teeth in Sullivan County.

"It was all there," remembered Tom E. Pray in a recent issue of a local publication, the *Catskill-Delaware,* "hundreds of resorts, big and small bungalow colonies, *heimisheplatz* boardinghouses, wall-to-wall people in Monticello, Liberty, South Fallsburg, Wurtsboro, the Manor, Roscoe and points in between . . . with no end of places to go, things to do."

Those days are now long gone, and Sullivan County has yet to recover. A few megaresorts remain, most notably the 1,200-room Concord, now being restyled into a convention center, and the 400-room Kutsher's. But the trend today is away from the big and back to the small—a fact that the county still hasn't accepted. Much of Sullivan—especially in the eastern section where most of the resorts once operated—seems to be holding its breath, waiting for the good old days to return. And in the meantime, new and far less lucrative retreats such as ashrams and health spas have sprouted up between the abandoned resorts.

The northern and southern sections of Sullivan County are very different in feel from the resort-based east. To the north are the dense quiet woods of the Catskill Preserve and some of the world's best **trout fishing.** The two most famous streams, producing prize-winning trout each year, are the Beaverkill and the Willowemoc; for a daily report on fishing conditions along them April 1–July 1, call 607/498-5350.

To the south is the often strangely overlooked Upper Delaware Scenic and Recreational River, a marvelously undeveloped region offering great scenic vistas, canoeing, and tubing. The Delaware is a Class I river with "few or no obstructions" and attracts many canoeists, kayakers, and inner tube-ists, as well as fisherfolk. Outfitters along the river can provide you with paddling tips, or you can pick up information in the **National Park Service Center,** 41 Main St., in Narrowsburg, 845/252-3947. For a recorded report on river conditions, call the Park Service at 845/252-7100.

Sullivan County also boasts a large number of lakes, several nature preserves, good campgrounds, and a handful of still-thriving family farms. In Bethel's farm country is a large marker commemorating the Woodstock Music Festival that took place here in 1969.

First-time visitors will probably want to visit the Woodstock Festival site and the Upper Delaware, or else just explore back roads.

Information

The **Sullivan County Visitors Association** has an office in the County Government Center, 100 North St., Monticello, NY 12701, 845/794-3000, ext. 5010, or 800/882-CATS, www.scva.net. Hours are Mon.–Fri. 9 A.M.–5 P.M.

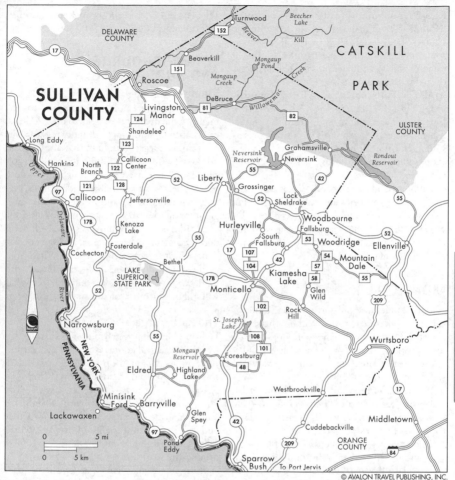

© AVALON TRAVEL PUBLISHING, INC.

In July and August, and weekends in the spring and fall, the office maintains an **information booth** in Rock Hill, Exit 109 off Route 17. **Information Cabooses** are also located in Livingston Manor and Roscoe, Exits 96 and 94 off Route 17, respectively, during the fishing season.

WURTSBORO AND VICINITY

Heading into the heart of Sullivan County is Route 17, also known as the **Quickway.** Once the main artery leading from New York City to

the Borscht Belt—a distance of only 90 miles—Rte. 17 is dotted with scrappy billboards in various stages of neglect. Here and there are outlet shops and roadside food stops, while in the distance rise layers upon layers of mountainous green.

Just over the Orange-Sullivan County border is the village of Wurtsboro, centering around a wide main street flanked with lumbering wooden buildings and American flags. The town was named after the brothers Maurice and William Wurts, who built the D&H Canal. Wurtsboro today is best known for **Wurtsboro Airport,**

Rte. 209, about two miles north of town, 845/888-2791, the oldest soaring center in the United States (established in 1927). Demonstration rides over the Shawangunks last 15–20 minutes and cost $40 per person. The airport is open daily 8:30 A.M.–5 P.M.

Also in Wurtsboro is **Canal Towne Emporium,** Sullivan and Hudson Sts., 845/888-2100. Billing itself as a country store from the 1840s, Canal Towne has won awards for historic preservation. But it's still basically an upscale tourist shop, selling candles, cards, toys, handcrafted items, and furniture.

For homemade baked goods, soups, and daily specials made with herbs and vegetables grown in their garden, stop into the **Potager,** 116 Sullivan St., 845/888-4086. The simple cafe is housed in a century-old church that also sells antique cupboards and garden accessories.

MONTICELLO

About 12 miles west of Wurtsboro on Route 17 is Monticello, the county seat and unofficial capital of the Borscht Belt. The town does boast a few historic buildings—most notably the **Sullivan County Courthouse**—but is mostly unsightly tourist-oriented sprawl.

At the western end of town is **Monticello Raceway,** Exit 104 off Rte. 17B, 845/794-4100, www.monticelloraceway.com, boasting one of the fastest harness-racing tracks in the country. Racing and pari-mutuel betting take place here year-round. On weekends during July and August, a giant **flea market,** featuring about 150 vendors, sets up shop.

Accommodations

One of the last of the county's megaresorts is **Kutsher's Country Club,** Kutsher Rd., off Rte. 42, Monticello, 845/794-6000 or 800/431-1273, www.kutshers.com. Owned by the Kutshers since 1907, the resort is a modern, family-oriented affair with its own lake, 18-hole golf course, indoor and outdoor pools, health club, and full activities program for children and adults. Daily rates, which include three meals, are $98–169 per person d; packages avail-

able. Also in Monticello is an **Econo Lodge,** 190 Broadway, 845/794-8800 ($60–75 d).

TO WOODBOURNE AND HURLEYVILLE

Kiamesha Lake

Now undergoing a multiyear renovation is the mighty **Concord,** Concord Rd., 845/794-4000, www.concordresort.com, once one of the Catskills' most famous megaresorts. In the past the Concord boasted 1,200 rooms, 3,000 acres, three golf courses, 40 tennis courts, indoor and outdoor pools, a health club, horseback riding trails, big-name entertainment, and a full activities program for all ages. At the moment, however, the Concord is open on a limited basis as a golf resort only (two-night packages start at $320 per person double, including three days of golf). When Concord reopens in the year 2004, it will cater primarily to conventioners, but individual travelers will still be welcome; call for more information.

The Fallsburgs

Fallsburg and South Fallsburg are surrounded by both beautiful countryside and disheartening poverty. Boarded-up buildings pockmark the landscape, and the unemployed linger on village street corners. There's a sense of glory gone by, and a sense of waiting. Notable in Fallsburg is the **Country Store,** Pleasant Valley and Old Brickman Rds., 845/436-5352, which sells Native American crafts and folk arts from around the world.

More interesting than what's *in* the towns is what's outside them. The region is a spiritual mecca for a diversity of religious sects. On the back roads surrounding the Fallsburgs are many Hasidic bungalows, and the Hasidim are often out walking, their black frock coats and long dresses flapping in the wind. Just north of Fallsburg is the **Sivananda Ashram Yoga Ranch** (see Woodbourne, following), and just outside South Fallsburg is the ashram of the **Siddha Yoga Dham of America Foundation (SYDA),** a low-slung complex of white-washed buildings hidden behind a high wall. With tens of thousands of followers, 550 meditation centers, and 10 ashrams, SYDA is one of the most popular Eastern spiritual movements in the world.

On a typical summer weekend, the South Fallsburg ashram attracts thousands of visitors. Most come to attend a two-day "Intensive"—a sort of spiritual initiation seminar—or to stop into the bookstore. And today's devotees are no longer the spaced-out flower children of the '60s generation; instead, most are young professionals and/or serious students of Eastern meditation. Among the many celebrities who've been attracted to SYDA over the years are Jerry Brown, John Denver, Diana Ross, Isabella Rossellini, Don Johnson, and Melanie Griffith.

For the casual visitor, the South Fallsburg ashram is an intriguing place to visit. Outside are the grounds, dotted with Hindu gods and the "pavilion," where special ceremonies are held; inside are institution-like halls and meeting rooms, their air thick with an overpoweringly sweet incense. A few very American-looking men and women dressed in orange robes and saris stroll about, while blown-up photographs of the Foundation's beatific guru, Chidvilasananda, are everywhere. As a day visitor, you may be questioned at the gate, but generally speaking, outsiders are welcome to look around—and enroll in the classes and seminars, if interested.

To reach the site from Main Street (Route 42) in South Fallsburg, take the road by the movie theater and bear immediately left at the fork onto Laurel Avenue. Continue 2.5 miles to a flashing red light and turn left onto Brickman Road. The ashram is located about 200 feet down on the right, and the Maneesh Gifts and Bookstore is a few hundred yards beyond that. For more information, or to enroll in a seminar, contact the SYDA Foundation, P.O. Box 600, South Fallsburg, NY 12779; 845/434-2000, www.sydayoga.org.

Woodbourne

At the entrance to **Sivananda Ashram Yoga Ranch,** Budd Rd., off Rte. 52, 845/434-9242 or 845/436-6492, www.sivananda.org/ranch, stands a huge multicolored arch reading "Health is Wealth. Peace of Mind is Happiness. Yoga Shows the Way." Beyond is a motley collection of super-friendly people with red dots on their foreheads,

and an equally motley collection of buildings housing dorm rooms, a greenhouse, and a lovely octagonal meditation room. Visitors are welcome to stop by for a meal ($8) or yoga class ($8) or to spend the weekend. The daily ashram schedule begins at 6 A.M. with meditation and chants and ends at 11 P.M. with lights out. Attendance is required at all *satsangs* and yoga classes. Rates for shared rooms are $50–55 per person, or you can camp for $35–40 per person; meals and classes are included. A day rate that includes all meals and many classes but no accommodations is $35. If you do wish to visit, it's best to call ahead.

Hurleyville and Vicinity

In tiny Hurleyville, on Route 104 between Monticello and Route 52, are a number of antique shops and the **Sullivan County Museum, Art and Cultural Center.** Inside the center is a small gallery of local art and an interesting historical museum. Among the exhibits is one explaining the tanning process, and another containing one of the largest collections of vintage clothing in the state. Though only a few dozen articles are on display at any one time, several hundred pieces are in the collection, including a wide assortment of lavender, blue, brown, and even black wedding dresses. It wasn't until the turn of the century that white became de rigueur.

Also in the center is the **Frederick A. Cook Society Room.** Born in Sullivan County, Cook was a physician, anthropologist, and explorer who—according to his admirers—got to the North Pole before its generally recognized discoverer, Adm. Robert Peary. Documents and artifacts supporting this thesis fill the room; "Frederick Albert Cook is the most defamed man in Arctic history," reads one quote from an eminent polar scientist.

The center, 265 Main St. (Rte. 104), 845/434-8044, www.sullivancountyhistory.org, is open Wed.–Sat. 10 A.M.–4:30 P.M., Sunday 1–4:30 P.M. Suggested donation is $2.

LIBERTY

Continuing north on Route 17 another 12 miles, you'll come to Liberty, the second unofficial capital of the Borscht Belt. Though the town has little to offer in the way of tourist attractions, lining North Main Street are a number of pretty historic buildings, including the Gothic Revival Town Hall and a Greek Revival Methodist church. Along Main and Chestnut Streets are numerous antique shops; watch the papers for the popular **Liberty Antique Warehouse Auctions,** scheduled regularly throughout the year.

NORTHERN SULLIVAN COUNTY

The northernmost sliver of Sullivan County belongs to the Catskill Forest Preserve, and you can see the difference from the rest of the county immediately. Though still far from mountainous, the land here is much more woodsy and wild. It's laced with narrow winding roads, lakes, and reservoirs, with nary a megaresort in sight.

Neversink

Heading east out of Liberty on Route 55, you'll come to the hamlet of Neversink, primarily a debarkation point for anglers trying their luck on scenic, 1,472-acre **Neversink Reservoir.** The hamlet is also home to the no-nonsense **New Age Health Spa,** Rte. 55, 845/985-7601, www.newagehealthspa.com. A stay at the spa includes three low-calorie meals daily, along with fitness classes, hikes, lectures, and the use of a pool, sauna, steam room, and weight room. No smoking, alcoholic beverages, caffeine, drugs, or artificial sweeteners are allowed, and colonics are encouraged. All-inclusive rates for a clean and comfortable room, shared by three people, start at $174 per day.

Grahamsville

Farther northeast is Grahamsville, featuring a small **National Historic District.** The district sits on a hill overlooking the hamlet, and holds Greek Revival, Gothic Revival, and Italianate residences, and a Greek Revival church.

On Five Dave Road about five miles northeast of Grahamsville's center is a dramatic National Natural Landmark known as **Kalonymus Escarpment.** Formed out of an enormous stone left behind by a glacier, the cliff was dedicated in 1982 to the memory of Kalonymus, a Sicilian Jew who

rescued the Holy Roman Emperor Otto II during battle in 982. The dedication came about thanks to the Zuckerman family—local residents who are descendants of the Kalonymus family.

DeBruce

West of Grahamsville and Neversink Reservoir is the hamlet of DeBruce, dotted with a number of big abandoned homes that must once have been very fine. DeBruce sits on the banks of Willowemoc Creek, where fisherfolk often cast their lines.

DeBruce is most easily reached by taking narrow, woodsy Route 81/82 northeast out of Livingston Manor, but you could also opt to take the even narrower and woodsier network of roads that leads from Grahamsville to DeBruce. Just be prepared to get lost.

Along DeBruce Road just east of the hamlet, you'll find the **Willowemoc Covered Bridge,** which was built in Livingston Manor in 1860 and cut in half in 1913 to be moved to its present site. Along Mongaup Road several miles north of the hamlet is the **Catskill State Fish Hatchery,** 845/439-4328. This is a serious industrial operation that raises more than one million trout annually for distribution throughout New York State. The tanks aren't always full, however, so you might want to call ahead. Hours are June–Oct., Mon.–Fri. 8:30 A.M.–4:30 P.M., Sat.–Sun. 8:30 A.M.–noon. Admission is free.

Accommodations in DeBruce are provided by the spacious, turn-of-the-century **DeBruce Country Inn,** 286A DeBruce Rd., 845/439-3900, www.debrucecountryinn.com. The inn is within the Catskill Forest Preserve on the banks of the Willowemoc, and each of its 15 rooms is decorated differently ($100–125 per person per night, includes dinner). The adjoining restaurant, **Ianine's,** is an airy and attractive spot specializing in healthy American-European fare. It's open to the public for dinner Friday and Saturday only; average entrée $20. The inn is closed mid-December–spring.

Camping is available nearby at the 160-site **Mongaup Pond Campground,** Mongaup Pond Rd., three miles north of DeBruce, 845/439-4233, which offers lake swimming, lifeguards, boat rentals, and hiking. Call 800/456-CAMP for reservations; a basic site costs $14.

© CHRISTIANE BIRD

a covered bridge near Livingston Manor

Livingston Manor

Livingston Manor, on the banks of the Willowemoc just off the Quickway, is a rustic sportsman's village best known for its superb trout fishing, although deer hunters also frequent the area in fall. Fly-fishing classes are offered by the **Enchanted Circle Fly Fishing School,** Box 163, Old Rte. 17, Livingston Manor, NY 12758, 607/498-5791.

Downtown Livingston Manor consists of little more than a bridge, a row of practical-looking shops, one or two gift stores, and **Wagon Wheel Junction,** a roadside park with two small working waterwheels. By one of the wheels is a plaque quoting the Fisherman's Prayer: "God grant that I may live to fish until my dying day, And when it comes to my last cast I then most humbly pray, When in the Lord's safe landing net I'm peacefully asleep, Then in His mercy I be judged good enough to keep."

On Lewbeach Road (Route 151) five miles north of Livingston Manor is the 1860 **Livingston Manor Covered Bridge,** one of the few existing covered bridges built in the lattice-truss style. Beside it is a newly constructed park and picnic area, and nearby is the 80-site **Covered Bridge**

Campsite, 58 Conklin Hill Rd., 845/439-5093. A basic site costs $26.

Country Peddler Auctions take place at various venues in the Livingston Manor region throughout the year. Watch the papers for announcements; the viewing usually starts at 3 P.M., the auction at 6 P.M.

The simple 24-room **Willowemoc Motel,** 1 Bruce Rd., 845/439-4220 ($40–55 d), caters primarily to anglers. The rustic, 75-year-old **Lanza's—A Country Inn,** 913 Shandelee Rd., 845/439-5070, www.lanzascountryinn.com, is a rambling, eight-guest room affair ($89–129 d). Downstairs is a creaky 75-year-old taproom and a greenhouse-style dining room serving American, Italian, and continental fare.

Beaverkill and Lewbeach

Continuing up Lewbeach Road (Route 152) from Livingston Manor, you'll enter Catskill Park and soon come to the hamlets of Beaverkill and Lewbeach. In Beaverkill is the state-run **Beaverkill Campground,** Lewbeach Rd., 845/439-4281. The 97-site campground on 62 wooded acres offers river swimming, lifeguards, and fishing; for reservations, call 800/456-CAMP; site rates are $12.

In Lewbeach is **Wulff School of Fly Fishing,** Beaverkill Rd., 914/439-4060, which offers weekend trout fishing and fly casting workshops May–June. Run by Joan Wulff, a championship fisher woman and author, the school is set on 100 acres and includes a private stretch of the Beaverkill River.

Catskill Fly Fishing Center

Appropriately situated about midway between Livingston Manor and Roscoe (a.k.a. Trout Town U.S.A.) is a state-of-the-art museum and cultural center of which area residents are most proud. And rightfully so. The Catskill Fly Fishing Center, started up by a group of local fisherfolk in 1981 and considerably expanded in 1994, does an excellent job of documenting the history of fly-fishing in the United States.

On display in the museum are hundreds of meticulously crafted flies, along with rods, reels (some dating back to 1850), historic photos, and other artifacts. To the uninitiated, that might sound boring, but don't pass judgment until you see the bumble puppy, midge, quill gordon, wet spider, cow dung, red ant, silver doctor, picket pin, spectral spider . . . Fly tying is a bona fide folk art, and each fly is an intricate affair, individually designed and named. At one time, flies were made out of feathers and furs; today, the material is usually synthetic.

Also at the center are "hands-on" exhibits of fly-fishing tackle, fly-tying demonstrations, lectures, and fly-tying classes for beginners. In front of the center runs the Willowemoc, usually lined with hip-booted fisherfolk casting their lines.

The center, 5447 Old Rte. 17, Livingston Manor, 845/439-4810, www.cffcm.org, is open April–Oct., daily 8 A.M.–5 P.M.; Nov.–March, Mon.–Fri. 10 A.M.–1 P.M. Admission is adults $3, children $1.

Roscoe

Trout Town U.S.A. is considerably larger and more sophisticated than Livingston Manor, but its raison d'être is the same. It was at **Junction Pool,** just west of Roscoe where the Willowemoc and Beaverkill meet, that American fly-fishing was first developed.

Downtown Roscoe's attractive wooden buildings house everything from restaurants to sports stores. At the western end of town is the **Roscoe O&W Railway Museum,** Railroad Ave., 607/498-5500, housed in a red caboose that also serves as a visitor information center. Roscoe was once the summer terminus of the Ontario & Western Railway. Museum hours are June–Oct., Sat.–Sun. 11 A.M.–3 P.M.; extended hours in July and August. Admission is free.

A number of expert fly tyers still live and work in Roscoe. Among them is Mary Dette, whose parents started an early fly-tying business back in 1928. Among anglers, the Dette name is known around the world.

Most days, Mary Dette can be found sitting in the front room of her big white house, tying flies. Most of the flies she ties are the traditional kind, made of natural materials. She says she makes too many different kinds to count. Once she gets down to the actual tying—as opposed to the assembling and cutting of materials—each fly only takes her about five minutes. Since the flies sell for a mere $2.15 to $4 each, she has to be quick.

Lots of amateur tiers, some from as far away as Italy and France, stop by Dette's house to watch her work. If you're interested doing the same, inquire at the Catskill Fly Fishing Center.

The **Reynolds House Inn,** Rte. 17 in the village center, 607/498-4422, www.reynoldshouse-inn.com, built by the present owner's great, great "Uncle Billy" Reynolds as a tourist home in 1902, features eight airy guest rooms nicely done up in period furniture, a cozy piano parlor, and a commodious wraparound porch. Out back is a modern 11-room extension known as the **Hendrix Motel** (rates at both are $60–110 d).

Restaurants in town include the enormous and very modern **Roscoe Diner,** Rte. 17 at the entrance to the village, 607/498-4405, a local favorite serving breakfast, lunch, and dinner until midnight; average main dish $8.

WESTERN SULLIVAN COUNTY

Apple Pond Farm

Heading south from Roscoe on narrow, winding Route 124, you'll come to the **Apple Pond Farm-**

ing Center, Hahn Rd., Callicoon Center, 845/482-4764, www.applepondfarm.com, a working organic farm operated by horse power. Open to the public by pre-reserved guided tour only, this is the sort of place where you'll see demonstrations of sheepherding, spinning, beekeeping, and the like. Of special interest to kids are the rides in a covered wagon or sleigh; also on-site is a gift shop and three-bedroom guest cottage that's available for rent ($325 for a summer weekend). Tours are available year-round and cost $30 for groups of 2–5.

Jeffersonville

Where Route 128 meets Route 52 is Jeffersonville, a very attractive village of boxy Victorian buildings and wide shady streets. Originally founded by German immigrants, Jeffersonville is now home to many artists and craftspeople, and several arts-oriented shops are located along Main Street.

The gracious **Griffin House,** 178 Maple Ave. in the village center, 845/482-3371, www.griffin-house.com, was built in 1895 by 10 master carpenters working in American chestnut. Exquisite woodwork is everywhere, along with fine antiques, plush rugs, and floor-length lace curtains ($130–150 d). The **Sunrise House B&B,** 845/482-3778, is a restored 100-year-old farmhouse set on 45 acres; guest rooms are attractively appointed and outside is a wraparound porch; $100–150 d. **Ted's Restaurant,** Main St., 845/482-4242, a local favorite, is a friendly spot where you can order both excellent Turkish cuisine and more standard American fare; average main dish $9.

Kenoza Lake

Route 52 continues further south through green rolling hills to Kenoza Lake, where you'll find **Stone Arch Bridge Historic Park,** a quiet retreat centering around a graceful three-arched stone bridge. The only bridge of its kind in the United States, the structure was built in 1872 by two Swiss-German stonemasons working with hand-cut local stone. Plaques in the park tell the story of the bridge and of a murder that took place here in 1882. A local farmer, believing that his brother-in-law had put a hex on him, convinced his son that in order for the curse to be lift-

ed, the man had to be killed. The son complied with his father's wishes and dumped the body near the bridge. The case gained great notoriety in its day and is one of the few hex murders on record; the brother-in-law's ghost is said to still haunt the park.

Bethel

From Route 52, head east on Route 17B, through mile after mile of scenic farm country. Just when the land is at its prettiest, you've come to Bethel, where the famed Woodstock Music Festival took place on Max Yasgur's farm in 1969 (see Woodstock and Vicinity under Ulster County, above).

The former Yasgur farm is off Hurd Road. Signs off Route 17B point the way to an enormous lime-green field sloping down to borders of dark green trees. A horizontal stone marker near the road reads: "This is the original site of the Woodstock Music and Arts Fair held on Aug. 15, 16, 17, 1969." The marker was erected by the farm's former owners, the Gelish family, and goes on to list the festival's many "on-site performers": Richie Havens, Arlo Guthrie, Joan Baez, Joe Cocker, Ravi Shankar, Santana, Janis Joplin. . . .

In 1996, the Woodstock site was purchased by Alan Gerry, a Sullivan Country native and pioneer in the cable-TV industry, who added the landscaped grounds and parking area that now surround the marker. Also in the works is a $40-million performing arts center that will feature both classical and popular music. Plans call for the center to be up and running in late 2004 or 2005.

Not far from the Woodstock site is the popular **Woodstock On-the-Lake Campground,** Hurd Rd., 845/583-6210, featuring 150 sites, a 100-acre fishing lake, pool, boat rentals, ball fields, and nature trails. A basic campsite costs $28, and cabins are available for rent as well.

Back on Route 17B, just east of Hurd Road, you'll find **Bethel Country Store and Pizza,** 845/583-6425, a genuine, old-fashioned general store with an attached pizza parlor; and **Woodstock Emporium,** 845/583-5238, selling everything from Woodstock bumper stickers and posters to original programs. You can pick up a good takeout sandwich, too.

THE CATSKILLS

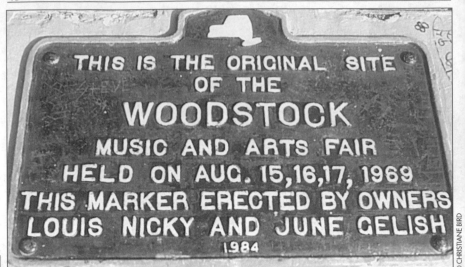

© CHRISTIANE BIRD

Woodstock plaque

South of the stores is the exquisite **Lake Superior State Park,** Dr. Duggan Rd., off Rte. 17B, 845/794-3000, ext. 5002, an all-but-untouched recreation area open for swimming, picnicking, boating, and fishing. The park is open year-round, but the beach and boat rentals are open Memorial Day–June, Sat.–Sun. 9 A.M.–dusk; and July–Labor Day, daily 9 A.M.–dusk. Admission in summer is $6 for nonresidents; the rest of the year it's free for everyone.

ALONG THE DELAWARE

The drive along the wide, gentle Delaware River, which runs across the southern and western borders of Sullivan County up into Delaware County, is one of the most glorious sights in the region. About 73 miles in length, this portion of the Delaware is known as the **Upper Delaware Scenic and Recreational River,** as opposed to the lower, much-less-scenic Delaware which runs between Port Jervis and Delaware Bay.

Meandering South from Monticello

The most interesting way to get to Route 97, which parallels the Delaware, is to take Route 102 out of Monticello. About eight miles down the woodsy back road you'll come to County Road 108 on the right. This road leads to the secluded **Inn at Lake Joseph,** 400 St. Joseph Rd. (County Road 108), off Rte. 42, Forestburgh, NY 12777, 845/791-9506, www.lakejoseph.com, which was once owned by the Roman Catholic Church and used as a retreat for Cardinals Spellman and Hayes. A Queen Anne–style Victorian mansion, the inn sits on the shores of a 250-acre lake and is surrounded by thousands of acres of wildlife preserve. Inside are 10 posh bedrooms equipped with canopy beds and Persian rugs; outside are opportunities for swimming, fishing, boating, tennis, hiking, and cross-country skiing in winter. Rates are $158–385 d, including breakfast, a buffet lunch, and use of all facilities.

Continuing past Road 108 you'll soon come to the dark **Stephen Crane Pond** on the right, where the author of *The Red Badge of Courage* lived with his brother Edmund during several summers in the early 1890s. Crane may have written one of his lesser-known novels, *The Third Violet,* while living here. The Crane cottage is no longer standing, but a plaque marks the spot.

Forestburgh to Glen Spey

About a mile beyond Crane Pond is a T-inter-section, where County Road 48 leads west into Forestburgh. Here, the **Forestburgh Playhouse & Tavern,** County Road 43, just past the Route 42 intersection, 845/794-1194, housed in a re-stored barn, features first-rate drama in the sum-mer, cabaret/buffet in the spring and fall.

Continuing west from Forestburgh, the road (County Road 43) takes a bend south just past the hamlet of Fowlerville. Here gleams **Mongaup Reservoir,** where hundreds of bald eagles spend the winter. The best way to find out about where and how to see the birds is to contact the **Eagle Institute,** 845/557-6162, www.eagleinstitute.org.

Continuing south toward the Delaware River, the next junction is at Glen Spey. Just south of the hamlet on County Road 41 stands the gorgeous, mottled brown **St. Volodymr Ukrainian Church,** built entirely without nails. Even bigger than the Ukrainian church in Lexington (see Greene County, above), the Byzantine, onion-domed St. Volodymr looks as if it belongs in a Russian fairy tale. Also not far away, on the right side of Coun-ty Road 41, are the equally incongruous golden domes of St. Peter and Paul Church.

East to Sparrow Bush

Heading east on Route 97, you'll climb a steep hill to **Hawk's Nest,** an excellent overlook of-fering panoramic views of the river. From Pond Eddy to Hawk's Nest is about five miles. **Hawks Nest Cafe,** Rte. 97, 845/856-9909, offers a menu ranging from sandwiches to seafood platters; av-erage main dish $9.

West to Barryville

Heading west from Pond Eddy on Route 97, you'll pass one lovely river vista after another. On both sides of the river are lush, rolling hills, covered with low-growing forest. Most of the land along the Delaware is privately owned but is protected through local zoning and the coordi-nation of federal, state, and local laws.

The Delaware and its banks are feeding grounds for muskrat, mink, raccoon, and beaver. At dawn and dusk, white-tailed deer can often be seen, while every so often one of the region's black bears puts in an appearance. The river's

Near Glen Spey, St. Volodymr Ukrainian Church is built entirely without nails.

© CHRISTIANE BIRD

THE CATSKILLS

WATCHING BALD EAGLES

After being nearly extinct for years, the bald eagle has returned to the United States, with the largest groups of eagles in the northeast to be found wintering around the Upper Delaware River. The eagles migrate here primarily from Canada and are attracted by the area's large amount of open fresh water. Here, our feathered friends can eat their fill of fresh fish and then relax on large tracts of undisturbed land, including about 12,000 state-owned acres managed strictly for the eagles.

The peak season for viewing the national bird is January through March, when several hundred usually winter in the area. For more information about the eagles and the best way to view them, contact the nonprofit **Eagle Institute,** P.O. Box 182, Barryville, NY 12719; 914/557-6162, www.eagleinstitute.org. During the winter, as many as 15 institute-trained volunteers are on site, guiding group tours, helping individual birders, and monitoring the eagles' activity. The Sullivan County Visitors Association also has maps, eagle-viewing sites, and tips on eagle etiquette on its website, www.scva.net. To reach the Upper Delaware directly from New York City takes about two hours.

most common birds are turkey vultures, hawks, and owls, but bald eagles, ospreys, and great blue herons also inhabit the area.

Canoe outfitters in Barryville are numerous. Oldest among them is **Kittatinny Canoes,** Rte. 97, 845/557-6213 or 800/356-2852; it also rents rafts, inner tubes, and kayaks. Younger operations include **Cedar Rapids Kayak & Canoe Outfitters,** Rte. 97, 914/557-6158; and **Indian Head Canoes,** Rte. 97, 845/557-8777 or 800/874-BOAT.

Campgrounds along Route 97 include **Kittatinny Campground,** 845/557-8611 or 800/356-2852, which offers 250 wooded acres, 330 campsites, a stocked trout stream, and a camp store; and **Indian Head Campground,** 845/557-8777 or 800/874-2628. Both are connected to their respective canoe rental companies.

The highlight of Barryville's events calendar is mid-July's **Annual Pow-Wow,** organized by the Indian League of the Americas, 845/794-3000, ext. 5010. The pow-wow features much dancing and crafts.

Eldred and Vicinity

Detouring north about five miles from Barryville on Route 55, you'll come to **Eldred Preserve,** 1040 Rte. 55, 845/557-8316, www.eldredpreserve.com. Spread over 3,000 acres, the preserve includes woodlands, wetlands, ponds, and lakes. Nature trails run through the park, and boats can be rented. Eldred attracts large numbers of hunters and anglers, so you won't be surprised to also find a tackle shop, sporting-clay range, and trout pools. The preserve is open daily until 6 P.M. in summer (8 P.M. on weekends), and Mon.–Fri. off-season.

Overlooking the preserve is **Eldred Preserve Motel and Restaurant,** 1040 Rte. 55, 845/557-8316 or 800/557-FISH, which offers 20 rooms ($85–95 d), trout and bass fishing, boat rentals, tennis courts, and nature trails. A restaurant specializing in variations on a theme of trout is on the premises (average entrée $16), as is a coffee shop.

Minisink Ford

Back on Route 97, about four miles west of Barryville is a cluster of visitor attractions that includes **Minisink Battleground Park.** The Battle of Minisink, the Upper Delaware's only major Revolutionary War skirmish, was fought on these heights on July 22, 1779. It began after an alliance of Iroquois Indians and Tories under the leadership of Mohawk Chieftain Joseph Brant burned the settlement of Minisink. A hastily assembled Colonial militia unit attempted to strike back at Brant's forces. The Colonials were defeated, but many on both sides were killed in what was one of the bloodiest battles of the war.

In today's 57-acre park are an interpretive center with displays on both the battle and local flora and fauna. Brochures describing the park's four easy hiking trails can be picked up at the center.

The park, Rte. 97, 845/794-3000, ext. 5002, is open daily mid-May–mid-October, dawn–dusk. Admission is free.

Opposite the entrance to Minisink Battleground Park is **Roebling's Aqueduct,** now a lonely highway toll bridge and the oldest extant wire suspension bridge in the United States. Built in 1848 by John Roebling, of Brooklyn Bridge fame, the aqueduct was originally designed to carry canal boats traveling the Delaware & Hudson Canal over the Delaware River.

Next to Roebling's bridge stands the **Bridge,** Rte. 97, 845/557-6088, a simple restaurant serving homemade American fare for lunch and dinner; average main dish $9.

Zane Grey Museum

Roebling's bridge leads across the river to Pennsylvania and the Zane Grey Museum, also run by the Upper Delaware National Park Service. The museum was once home to the Father of the Western Novel, whose best-known work, *Riders of the Purple Sage,* is still considered one of the finest Western novels ever written.

As a young aspiring writer who had trained to be a dentist, Grey left his practice in 1905 to move to Lackawaxen. Here he met his future wife, Lina Elise Roth, who encouraged him to pursue a full-time writing career and provided him with financial backing until he published his first book in 1910.

Today's museum is filled with Grey memorabilia, including fishing trophies and mementos from his trips west. Grey first discovered his subject matter during a journey to the Grand Canyon in 1907.

The museum is on Scenic Drive, Lackawaxen, PA, a half mile from the bridge, 570/685-4871. Call for hours and admission fees.

Narrowsburg

Eleven miles northwest of Minisink Ford is Narrowsburg, a delightful river town whose curving, narrow Main Street is crowded with well-kept wooden buildings dating back to the turn of the century. Here you'll find several attractive restaurants, the newspaper offices of the *River Reporter,* and the grand old 1894 Arlington Hotel.

The Arlington, 41 Main St., is listed on the National Register of Historic Places. It no longer functions as a hotel, but is home to the **Delaware Valley Arts Alliance,** 845/252-7576, and the **National Park Service Center,** 845/252-3947. The Arts Alliance operates a small art gallery

open year-round, Tues.–Sat. 10 A.M.–4 P.M. The National Park Center is stocked with free brochures and includes an excellent bookstore. It's open Memorial Day–Labor Day, Sat.–Sun. 9 A.M.–4:30 P.M. Even when the center is closed, a box with brochures can be found by the door.

The creaky 1840 **Narrowsburg Inn,** 176 N. Bridge St. (Rte. 52), 914/252-3998, is one block from the river. The oldest inn in the county, and the third oldest in the state, it's a bit worn around the edges, and some of the rooms share baths, but at $54 d, who's to complain?

Fort Delaware Museum of Colonial History

A replica of the small Connecticut Yankee settlement that once stood on this site (1755–85), the Fort Delaware Museum is surrounded by thick stockade walls built of logs. Inside are three sturdy settler's cabins, an armory, meetinghouse, blacksmith shop, and animal pens; outside are a small garden and the public stocks once used to discipline miscreants. Friendly costumed guides demonstrate such arts as candle making, weaving, and musket and cannon firing.

The museum, Rte. 97 just north of Narrowsburg, 845/252-6660 or 845/794-3000, ext. 3066, is open late June–Labor Day, daily 10 A.M.–5 P.M.; and Memorial Day–late June, Sat.–Sun. 10 A.M.–5 P.M. Admission is adults $5, children 6–16 $3.

North to Delaware County

North of Narrowsburg, the idyllic countryside continues as Route 97 passes through the villages of Cochecton and Callicoon, Hankins, and Long Eddy. Cochecton, or place of red stone hills, was once an important Indian settlement. Downtown Callicoon features a number of attractive restaurants, including the friendly **Callicoon Depot,** Main St., 914/887-5324, a good spot for lunch; average main dish $6. Considerably more upscale is the **1906 Restaurant,** Main St., 845/887-1906, which serves regional American fare and much game, including buffalo and ostrich; average entrée $17. Upstairs is a cabaret offering live music on the weekends.

Also in Callicoon is the indoor **Callicoon Flea Market,** Main St., 845/887-5411, open Thurs.–Mon. in summer.

The Upper Delaware Scenic and Recreational River ends just upriver near Hancock in Delaware County.

Delaware County

On the western slopes of the Catskills lies Delaware County, a seductive land of small peaks and valleys, picturesque villages and dairy farms. The third largest county in New York State, Delaware is about the size of Rhode Island, and has a gentle, settled quality that's unlike the rest of the Catskills. Though traditionally the region's least "discovered" county, Delaware has recently been attracting more and more tourists and second-home owners. At the same time, its dairy industry—long the economic mainstay of the community—has changed enormously, with the number of family-run farms shrinking from about 1,200 in 1970 to about 300 today.

Both the East and West Branches of the Delaware River begin in the northeastern part of the county—the West Branch in Stamford, the East Branch in Grand Gorge—and traverse the county before joining forces at Hancock. Delaware County boasts more than 750 miles of streams and rivers in all, along with about 11,000 acres of reservoirs. As you'd imagine, canoeing is popular, particularly in the southwestern section of the county. And the entire region attracts many hunters and anglers. For excellent trout fishing, try the Beaverkill, or the East and West Branches of the Delaware. Pepacton Reservoir is also a popular fishing spot.

Delaware County has several interesting museums, a vibrant arts scene, and a few major towns. The county's biggest attraction, however, is its countryside. Back roads lead past farm stands and general stores, covered bridges and Victorian boardinghouses, dark blue reservoirs and stunning mountain vistas. The eastern half of the county holds most of the county's points of interest, as well as two especially pretty villages: Margaretville and Roxbury.

Among the most popular events in Delaware County—attracting hordes of residents and visitors

alike—are auctions. Some are weekly affairs, others special events, and most advertise in the local paper, *The Reporter.* Look for popular auctions in Fleischmanns, Bovina, and Hamden.

Information

The **Delaware County Chamber of Commerce** is at 114 Main St., Delhi, NY 13753; 607/746-2281 or 800/642-4443, www.delawarecounty.org. Hours are Mon.–Fri. 9 A.M.–5 P.M.

FLEISCHMANNS

Just over the Ulster-Delaware border off Route 28 is the long main street that comprises most of the village of Fleischmanns. Once a major resort town lined with "stores and establishments for refreshment and amusement," as one guidebook put it, Fleischmanns today feels weary and run-down, though not without charm. Worn turn-of-the-century wooden buildings are everywhere.

One of the first Jewish enclaves in the Catskills, Fleischmanns was named after Cincinnati yeast-and-distilling magnate Charles F. Fleischmann, who bought 60 acres here in 1883. He and a group of relatives then proceeded to build a luxurious summer settlement, filling their homes with costly furniture, rugs, and works of art. A local band was hired to perform at the railroad station whenever the Fleischmanns arrived (via their private railroad cars), and famous professional ballplayers were hired to play on the Fleischmanns' private baseball diamond. That baseball field, once the most elegant in all the Catskills, is now part of the Village Park.

For more on the town's history, stop into the **Museum of Memories,** Main St., behind the Skene Memorial Library, 800/724-7910. The museum is usually open summer weekends; call for hours.

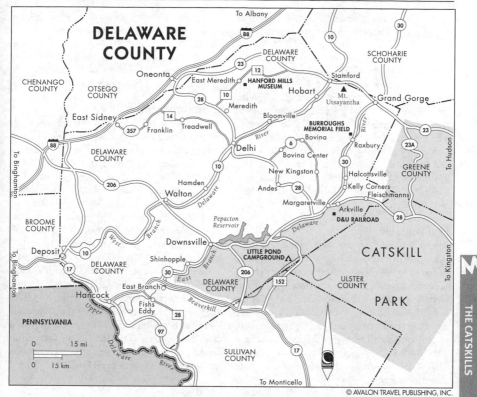

© AVALON TRAVEL PUBLISHING, INC.

Auction House

Taking place most Saturday nights at 7 P.M. is the popular **Roberts' Auction,** Main St., 914/254-4490, selling everything from antiques to junk. Signs on the walls read Think Before Buying, No Refunds, and Pay Out Back, as auctioneer Eddie Roberts barks out orders to one and all.

Accommodations and Food

Scottish-run **Highland Fling Inn,** Main St., 914/254-5650, is spread out over two Victorian homes and six summer cottages ($65–75 d, with breakfast). Two time winner of the Catskill Service Award, the **River Run B&B,** Main St., 845/254-4884, www.catskill.net/riverrun, originally built as a summer retreat for a wealthy businessman, offers eight attractive guest rooms and two apartment suites where children and

pets are welcome ($70–165 d). A good motel in town is the **Northland Motel,** Depot St., 845/254-5125 ($72 d). It's especially popular in winter, thanks to the nearby Belleayre Ski Center in Ulster County, but is open year round.

La Cabana, Main St., 845/254-4966, is a popular Mexican restaurant, but is usually open on the weekends and for dinner only; average entrée $10.

ARKVILLE
Delaware & Ulster Railroad

A few miles west of Fleischmanns in the village of Arkville is a popular family attraction, the Delaware & Ulster Railroad, Route 28 in the village center, 914/586-3877 or 800/225-4132, www.durr.org. A 12-mile excursion onboard this vintage steam-powered line, earlier known as the Ulster & Delaware, takes passengers to the nearby hamlet of Halcottsville and back. Along the way is lots of scenic countryside.

At one time, the U&D—nicknamed the "up and down" because of all the hills it had to climb—was a major transportation route into the Catskills. The journey north brought trainloads of tourists; the journey south took milk down to Kingston where it was shipped to New York City.

Today's sightseeing train operates every weekend Memorial Day–Oct., and also Wed.–Fri. July–Labor Day. Trains depart at 11 A.M., 1 P.M., and 3 P.M. Tickets are adults $7–10, children 3–11 $5–6.

Erpf House

Several nonprofit cultural organizations are headquartered in this big white building on a hill, Route 28 in the village center. Most of the center is devoted to offices, but the downstairs Erpf Gallery features local artwork and a display on environmental concerns. This is also a good place to pick up information on cultural events taking place throughout Delaware County. The center, 845/586-2611, www.catskillcenter.org, is open Mon.–Fri. 9 A.M.–5 P.M., and Sunday noon–5 P.M., closed Saturday.

MARGARETVILLE AND VICINITY

Heading west out of Arkville on Route 28, you'll pass a flea market that operates on weekends only, spring through fall, and several antique shops, before coming to the compact village of Margaretville, nestled into a valley between Pakatakan Mountain to the south and Kettle Hill to the north. For a great view of the area, take Walnut Street up the hill to Margaretville Mountain Road.

Along Main Street are a number of attractive shops and restaurants, and the Binnekill Square mini-mall, where you'll find an information booth staffed on summer weekends only. Otherwise, call the Greater Margaretville Chamber of Commerce at 845/586-3300 or 800/586-3303, www.margaretville.org.

Just west of Margaretville on Route 28 is the Old Stone Church, built in 1920. Beyond, on the left, is Route 30, which skirts around long, skinny Pepacton Reservoir all the way to Downsville. When the waters are low enough, you can still see some of the roads and bridges that once belonged to the now-flooded towns of Arena, Pepacton, Shavertown, and Union Grove.

Accommodations

For the most part, Delaware County is not resort country. One exception is the full-service Hanah Country Club, Rte. 30 about two miles northeast of the village, 854/586-2100 or 800/752-6494, www.hanahcountryclub.com, which caters mostly to golf enthusiasts. Features include a health club, tennis courts, and a restaurant. Daily rates for a standard double room without golf or meals start at $65; a one-night/two-days-of-golf package with one breakfast and one dinner start at $114 per person double. The resort is closed Oct. 15–April 15.

Another good option is Margaretville Mountain Inn, Margaretville Mountain Rd. about a half mile north of the village center, 845/586-3933, www.margaretvillelodging.com, a restored Victorian boardinghouse with great views of the valley below. Each of the five guest rooms is furnished differently, and out front is an inviting porch ($75–85 d, with breakfast).

Food

The Inn Between, Rte. 28 just east of the village, 845/586-4265, is a restaurant and cafe serving breakfast, lunch, and dinner. Outside is a deck; average dinner entrée $13. For more serious dining, try Binnekill Square, in the mini-mall of the same name, Main St., 845/586-4884. The Square specializes in American and Swiss cuisine, and offers a deck overlooking a small stream; average entrée $16.

ANDES AND ROUTE 6

Route 28 continues past Margaretville about eight miles to the mountain-high village of Andes. Along the way, you'll pass through some lovely mountainous countryside, shaded with heavy growth.

Near Andes occurred the climax of the 1845 Anti-Rent War, which brought about the end of the feudal land system in New York. That year, when an undersheriff attemped to evict a farmer for unpaid rent, the farmer's neighbors turned on the lawman and fatally shot him. Martial law was declared, and two men were sentenced to be hanged. However, the succeeding governor issued pardons, and in 1852, the state legislature declared the feudal land system illegal.

In Andes today stand a number of historic wooden buildings, including the striking red-and-white **Andes Fire Hall,** Main St. (Rte. 28). If you're interested in baskets, stop into **Paisley's Country Gallery,** Main St. (Rte. 28), 914/676-3533, which carries an interesting collection from around the world.

Just outside town is **Bobcat Ski Center,** Gladstone Hollow Rd., 914/676-3143, offering 18 trails and slopes. Special events such as antique shows and a lumberjack festival are held here during the summer.

In the center of town is the venerable **Andes Hotel,** Main St. (Rte. 28), 845/676-4408, www.andeshotel.com—a village institution. Rooms at the family-run hotel rent for $50 d, and there's also a comfortable restaurant and a laid-back bar in the main building. Both are favorite local hangouts.

Route 6

Narrow, meandering Route 6 detours off Route 28 north of Margaretville through the hamlets of **New Kingston, Bovina,** and **Bovina Center.** All along the way are steeply pitched hills and valleys, sprawling dairy farms, and a great mountain vista. In Bovina is **Russell's,** Main St., 607/832-4242, a country store that's been in the same family for generations. From April through November, the popular **McIntosh Auction,** 607/832-4829, takes place in the Bovina Creamery, Main St., every Saturday evening at 6:30 P.M. It's a good idea to arrive early, as seats go fast.

In Bovina Center you'll find the 1840 **Country House B&B,** Bramley Mt. Rd., off Rte. 6, 607/832-4371, www.catskill.net/jwburns, which has a fireplace, porch, nearby streams, and three comfortable guest rooms with private baths ($75–80 d).

NORTH ON ROUTE 30

Halcottsville

Several miles northeast of Margaretville on Route 30 is the splendid golden-brown **Round Barn,** 845/586-3326, surrounded by an overgrown

© CHRISTIANE BIRD

backroad barns near Bovina

THE CATSKILLS

field. The reconstructed 1899 barn is the site of a farmer's market, held here on Saturday throughout the summer. Just past the barn on the left is Lake Wawaka—a pond often filled with ducks and geese—and the hamlet of Halcottsville. Here, you'll find the Carriage House, Main St., 607/326-7992, housed in a 100-year-old home owned by the builder's granddaughter ($90 d).

Roxbury

Continue another six miles farther north on Route 30, and you'll come to the elegant town of Roxbury, built around a long Main Street flanked with stately white homes and big shady trees. Much of the town's moneyed ambience is due to the Gould family.

Future financier Jay Gould was born the son of a struggling farmer on the outskirts of Roxbury in 1836. At age 16, he began working in the village store, carefully saving his money until he had enough to invest in a small tannery, on which he made a handsome profit. From there, Gould turned to railroading. By 1880—thanks to some heavy-duty scheming—he controlled one-tenth of the country's rail systems. Then, in 1869, he tried to corner the gold market, causing a disastrous stock-market crash.

Gould had many idiosyncrasies, such as taking his personal cow with him whenever he traveled. He returned to Roxbury frequently throughout his lifetime. After his death in 1892, his daughter Helen served as the town philanthropist. Many of the Gould family retainers and servants also retired to Roxbury.

One of the town's landmarks is the 1892 Jay Gould Memorial Reformed Church, an impressive gray stone building with Tiffany windows located at the north end of Main Street. Built in memory of Jay Gould by his children, the church is only open on Sunday mornings. Behind it is a compact park with stone picnic tables and well-kept walkways leading up the hillside.

Also in downtown Roxbury is the Roxbury Arts Center, Vega Mountain Rd., 607/326-7908, www.roxburyny.com. Inside you'll find a small gallery showcasing the work of Catskill artists; the offices of the Roxbury Arts Group; and a performance space where a wide variety of cultural events—including concerts, dance, and folk arts—are presented throughout the year. The gallery is open Mon.–Fri. 9 A.M.–4 P.M., Saturday 1–4 P.M. Admission is free.

Burroughs Memorial Field

Roxbury's other famous native son—a man about as different in temperament from Gould as it's possible to get—is writer and naturalist John Burroughs. Born in 1837, one year after Gould, Burroughs was as well known in his day as his contemporary and kindred spirit Henry David Thoreau. The author of 27 books that sold over 1.5 million copies, Burroughs was also a good friend of Walt Whitman, Teddy Roosevelt, John Muir, Henry Ford, and Thomas Edison.

During the last years of his life, Burroughs lived in Woodchuck Lodge, a simple frame house that still stands on the outskirts of town, overlooking wide fields and the blue Catskill hills. By the roadside is an interesting series of plaques outlining Burrough's life and work, while nearby is his grave and Boyhood Rock, upon which he used to sit and dream.

To reach Burroughs Memorial Field, Hardscrabble Rd., take Route 30 north out of Roxbury about two miles to Hardscrabble Road and watch for signs. The field is open daily dawn–dusk; the lodge is currently closed.

Grand Gorge

Beyond Roxbury, Route 30 continues north to Grand Gorge where the East Branch of the Delaware begins. Here, the road squeezes through a scenic pass between high rugged hills before heading out of Delaware County into Schoharie County. In the center of Grand Gorge, the Colonial Inn, Prattsville Rd., 607/588-6122, features both standard motel rooms and guest rooms housed in a historic 1832 residence ($65–75 d).

WEST ON ROUTE 10

Eight miles northwest of Grand Gorge, Route 23 intersects Route 10, which follows the valley of the West Branch of the Delaware. Legend has it that a lumber camp once operating in the valley boasted an excellent but temperamental and strong-willed cook. When her cat was killed by one of the lumberjacks, she not only knocked the man out cold, but also punished the whole crew by serving them her pet cooked in a meat pie.

Stamford

Route 10 enters the county at Stamford, a charming old town filled with grand white homes and former boardinghouses. Stamford was also once home to one of the most luxurious resorts in the Catskills, the Hotel Habana, which catered exclusively to wealthy Cubans and South Americans.

During the summer, an imaginative array of music concerts are held in the historic **Rexmere Hotel,** now the Frank W. Cyr Center, Main Street. Sponsored by the Friends of Music of Stamford, New York, www.friendsmusic.org, the concerts have ranged in the past from a birthday tribute to Chopin to klezmer music. Local art exhibits are also usually on display in the old hotel, which is open Mon.–Fri. 8 A.M.–5 P.M.

Jelly Belly's, Main St., 607/652-7384, formerly known as Nicole's, serves up huge platters of diner fare. The homemade pancakes and waffles are especially good; average main dish $7.

Just outside Stamford is **Mount Utsayantha,** named after a beautiful Mohawk princess who fell in love with a Sioux brave. Indian taboo barred the intertribal marriage, and Utsayantha jumped into a lake and drowned. Her grief-stricken father had her buried on the mountaintop, where a marker supposedly still stands. Mountain Avenue, off Route 23 east of town, leads to the top of Utsayantha, but be forewarned that the way is twisting and steep. At the summit you'll find an old fire tower and spectacular views; a hiking trail also leads to the top.

DELHI

One of the largest villages in Delaware County, Delhi (DEL-high) is an attractive place, built around a historic courthouse square lined with Greek- and Gothic Revival buildings. The square was once featured on the cover of the *Saturday Evening Post.*

Delhi received its name back in the 1780s, when some of its more facetious residents suggested that their settlement be named after its most prominent citizen, state legislator Ebenezer Foote. Foote's nickname was the Great Mogul; Delhi was named for Delhi, India, the capital of the real Great Mogul.

North of town in **Meredith,** summers come alive during the **Honest Brook Music Festival,** 607/746-2281, featuring chamber and recital music. The festival takes place in July and August, in a preserved barn off Route 28.

Delaware County Historical Association Museum

This museum is divided into two parts. One is a gallery hall featuring first-rate changing exhibits on such imaginative topics as ethnic resorts, family farms, and the Anti-Rent wars. The other is a complex of nicely restored historic buildings.

At the center of the complex is the 1797 Gideon Frisbee House, a Federal-style residence that at one time or another served as a tavern, inn, post office, and community meeting house. Each room is furnished to reflect a different era—from Colonial days to the early 1900s—thereby showing how technology has changed the way we live.

Other historic buildings on the 60-acre site include the 1860 Amos Wood Gunshop, outfitted with an old woodstove and antique guns, and the turn-of-the-century Husted Hollow Schoolhouse. In the schoolhouse are dozens of tiny wooden desks and quotes from local residents who once studied here. Also at the museum are a library and an excellent gift shop selling local handicrafts and regional history books.

The museum is on Rte. 10, two miles north of Delhi, 607/746-3849. Hours are Memorial Day–Labor Day, Tues.–Sun. 11 A.M.–4 P.M.; Labor Day–Oct. 15, Sat.–Sun. 11 A.M.–4:30 P.M. Admission is adults $3, children $1.50.

Taxidermy

It's hardly for everyone, but taxidermy is a flourishing art in Delaware County; several award-winning taxidermists are located in the Delhi area. Inside their shops you'll find mounts of fish and animals—some available for purchase—as

THE CATSKILLS

well as pelts and leather goods. Among the shops are **Borow's Taxidermy,** Rte. 28 three miles northwest of Delhi, 607/746-2560; and **Perkins Taxidermy,** Arbor Hill Rd., off Rte. 28 south of Delhi, 607/746-3205.

EAST MEREDITH
Hanford Mills
Heading north out of Delhi on narrow, twisting Elk Creek Road (off Main Street), you'll pass through more wooded countryside before coming to the second major museum in Delaware County, Hanford Mills. Sitting beside a pond, Hanford is a group of weathered red buildings that operated as a "rural industrial complex" for well over 100 years. The site once provided area residents with everything from tools to feed; within its confines were a sawmill, gristmill, feed mill, woodworking shop, and hardware store. Between 1898 and 1927, the complex even generated the region's first electricity.

Today, Hanford Mills has been meticulously restored to look much as it did around the turn of the century. The toasty aroma of freshly cut wood fills the air as interpreters demonstrate everything from an enormous circular saw and early generator to a machine that cuts barrel tops and another that cuts broom handles. Over 20 vintage machines are demonstrated in all, while in the center of things churns a massive waterwheel surrounded by whirring gears and belts. Also onsite are a wagon house, smokehouse, icehouse, creamery, pig shed, and chicken coop.

Hanford Mills, junction of County Rds. 10 and 12, 607/278-5744 or 800/295-4992, www.hanfordmills.com, is open May–Oct., daily 10 A.M.–5 P.M. Admission is adults $6, children under 12 $3.

West Kortright Centre
Down the street from Hanford Mills is the West Kortright Centre, Turnpike Rd., 607/278-5454, www.wkc.org, an oasis for the arts. Housed in a handsome 1850s' Greek Revival church originally built by Scotch-Irish immigrants, the center is filled with rich stained-glass windows, polished wooden pews, and unusual kerosene chandeliers. From May through November, the center sponsors a wide array of special events ranging from jazz concerts and performance art to chicken barbecues and gallery exhibits. Many of its performers are well known; names from the past have included Dakota Staton, the Aztec Two-Step, Kenny Neal, and Ping Chong. The art gallery is open only sporadically, so be sure to call in advance.

To reach the center from Hanford Mills, take Elk Creek Road south to Turnpike Road and turn left.

WESTERN DELAWARE COUNTY
To East Sidney Lake
Route 14 leads northwest out of Delhi through hilly dairy country to the hamlets of **Treadwell** and **Franklin.** In Treadwell is **Barlow's General Store,** Main St., 607/829-8555, established in 1841. In Franklin is **Franklin Diner,** 83 Main St., 607/829-5424, offering a home-style breakfast and lunch Mon.–Fri., just breakfast on weekends; average main dish $6.

Beyond Franklin lies the **East Sidney Lake Recreational Area.** The lake features a sandy beach, boat docks, and picnic tables. Canoes can be rented and there's good fishing both on the lake (warm-water species) and below the dam (brown and brook trout). You can also walk out onto the dam for good views of the spillway and dam face.

Hamden and Walton
Route 10 west of Delhi leads through more hilly dairy country to the hamlet of Hamden, where a creaky **covered bridge** just north of Route 10 is usually lined with fly fishermen. Also on Route 10 near Hamden are the **Octagon Farm Market,** piled high with fresh produce, and **Hamden German Butchers,** selling first-rate homemade sausages and smoked meats. The **Robinson Brothers Auctions,** Rte. 10, 607/865-5253, take place in the brothers' barn most Thursdays. Viewing starts at 1 P.M., bidding at 6 P.M.

Beyond Hamden is the town of Walton, where the popular **Delaware County Fair,** 607/746-2281, takes place on the Walton Fairgrounds every August. An event now over 100 years old, the five-day fair features livestock shows and sales, tractor pulls, horse shows, a carousel, and a Ferris wheel. Plenty of local produce, homemade foods, and handicrafts are for sale.

The unusual **Octagon Bed and Breakfast,** Rte. 10, Walton, 607/865-7416, is housed in a historic brick octagon house built in 1855. There are four guestrooms with shared baths ($80–100 d).

Downsville and Vicinity

Five miles southeast of Walton off Route 206 lies **Bear Spring Mountain State Park,** 607/865-6989, featuring a lake, beach, bathhouses, boat rentals, hiking and equestrian trails, and 41 campsites. Call 800/456-CAMP to make campsite reservations; a basic site costs $12. Parking in summer and on weekends is $7.

Beyond the park is the rustic village of Downsville, at the western end of Pepacton Reservoir, near the dam. Here you'll find another **covered bridge,** this one a 174-foot span built in 1854. Canoes for paddling the East Branch of the Delaware can be rented at **Al's Sport Store,** Rte. 206 in the village, 607/363-7740, which also offers pick-up service.

Overlooking the Delaware is the spanking-clean **Downsville Motel,** Rte. 206, 607/363-7575 ($60–70 d). On Main Street, find the **Victorian Rose,** 607/363-7838, a lovely Victorian home turned B&B ($80 d). Open for lunch and dinner, the **Schoolhouse Inn and Restau-rant,** Main St., 607/363-7814, serves standard American fare in an old schoolhouse with original tin ceilings and oak floors. The former first-grade classroom is now a popular bar; average dinner entrée $13.

Nearby **Shinhopple** is home to the terrific **Peaceful Valley Bluegrass Festival,** Rte. 30, 607/746-2281, which takes place in mid-July. This is one of the top bluegrass festivals in the Northeast. It draws about 7,000 fans, many of whom camp at **Peaceful Valley Campground,** Rte. 30, 607/363-2211. The campground has 183 sites and is open April–Dec.; a basic site costs $16. It also offers canoe rentals and paddler shuttle service.

Deposit

At the far western edge of Delaware County along the West Branch of the Delaware is Deposit, a small village first known as an early lumbering town and then as a resort. Many fine old homes still line the streets. Housed in an 1868 Italianate bank on 2nd Street is the **Deposit Community Historical Society Museum,** 607/467-4422. Hours are May–Oct., Thursday and Sunday 2–4 P.M., and many Tuesdays 9 A.M.–noon, or by appointment.

At August's **Lumberjack Festival** in Riverside Park, 607/746-2281, you'll see all sorts of unusual events, including a beard-growing contest, cherry-picking contest, and open lumberjack competitions.

Central New York

Central New York is a jumbled mix of dying industrial cities, wooded hillsides, and wide pastoral vistas blanketed with farmers' fields. The land here is a gently rolling plateau, laced with enormous rivers—the Hudson, the Mohawk, the Susquehanna, and the Chenango. The Mohawk is named after the Mohawk Indians, an Iroquois tribe that has lived in upstate New York since before the arrival of the whites (see The Finger Lakes chapter Introduction).

Sophisticated Albany, the state capital, sits near the eastern edge of the region, just south of the confluence of the Hudson and Mohawk. The oldest city in New York, Albany offers an especially interesting collection of architectural sites, as well as the New York State Museum, one of the finest state museums in the country. North of Albany lie Troy and Schenectady, a pair of faded, relic-strewn industrial towns evocative of the not-so-distant past.

Through Albany and the adjoining Mohawk River Valley runs Route 20, America's longest highway. Once known as the Great Western Turnpike, from the 1780s to the 1820s, Route 20 was *the* major gateway to the West. Land-hungry settlers on their way to the Great Lakes Basin and elsewhere passed through here in droves.

With the completion of the Erie Canal in 1825, the Mohawk River Valley took on even greater importance. Hundreds of factories producing everything from velocipedes to baby food sprang up along its banks, employing thousands of Southern and Eastern European immigrants. The valley became the most densely populated area upstate.

Today, the valley is still home to a number of working factories, along with historic villages, Revolutionary War sites, and Erie Canal artifacts. The valley's largest city is Utica, site of the Children's Museum, the best of its kind upstate, and of the Munson-Williams-Proctor Institute, famed for its collection of American and European art.

long view of the Empire State Plaza by day

JAMES FENIMORE COOPER ON CENTRAL NEW YORK

Near the centre of the State of New-York lies an extensive district of country, whose surface is a succession of . . . mountains and valleys. It is among these hills that the Delaware takes its rise; and flowing from the limpid lakes and thousand springs of this region, the numerous sources of the Susquehanna meander through the valleys. . . . The mountains are generally arable to the tops, although instances are not wanting, where the sides are jutted with rocks, that aid greatly in giving to the country that romantic and picturesque character which it so eminently possesses. The vales are narrow, rich, and cultivated; with a stream uniformly winding through each.

James Fenimore Cooper,
The Pioneers

South of the Mohawk Valley lie Schoharie, Otsego, Madison, and Chenango Counties, sleepy lands of fertile farms, one-stoplight villages, lakes, and forests. In the center lies Cooperstown, site of the National Baseball Hall of Fame and former home to James Fenimore Cooper. Cooper set many of his novels in Central New York, accounting for the area's nickname, Leatherstocking Country. The term refers to the leather leggings worn by early Yankee settlers.

PRACTICALITIES

Recreation

Good **fishing** can be found throughout Leatherstocking Country, which is filled with clean lakes, rivers, and creeks. Otsego Lake is known for its lake trout, bass, and perch; Canadarago Lake for walleye and tiger muskie; Schoharie Creek for bass and walleye; Oneida Lake for lake pike. For more information, contact local tourist offices or contact the **Department of Environmental Conservation,** 518/402-9428.

Tour boats that ply the Hudson and the area's canals are docked in Albany and Troy. The 42- mile **Hudson-Mohawk Bikeway** runs between Albany and Rotterdam Junction.

Central New York has a plethora of uncrowded **state parks.** Most offer swimming, boating, fishing, camping, and easy hiking trails. For more information, contact local tourist offices or visit the New York State parks website: www.nysparks.com.

Transportation

The **Albany County Airport** is the oldest municipal airport in the United States, serviced by American Airlines, 800/433-7300; Continental, 800/525-0280; Delta, 800/221-1212; Northwest, 800/225-2525; United, 800/241-6522; and USAirways, 800/428-4322.

The **Oneida County Airport** (Utica-Rome) features flights by USAirways. Binghamton's **Link Field** is serviced by USAirways, Continental, and United.

Amtrak, 800/872-7245, provides train service to Albany-Rensselaer, Amsterdam, Utica, and Rome. **Adirondack–Pine Hill Trailways,** 518/436-9651 or 800/225-6815, and **Greyhound Bus Lines,** 800/231-2222, service the Capital District. Greyhound also provides bus service to Leatherstocking Country.

Emergencies

Throughout most of Central New York, dial 911 for emergencies. If not in service, dial "0" for the operator.

Hospitals in the area include **Albany Memorial Hospital,** 600 Northern Blvd., 518/471-3111; **Samaritan Hospital,** 2215 Burdett Ave., Troy, 518/271-3300; **Mary Imogene Bassett Hospital,** Atwell Rd., Cooperstown, 607/547-3355; **St. Elizabeth Hospital,** 2209 Greene St., Utica, 315/798-8111; and **Binghamton General Hospital,** 2042 Mitchell Ave., 607/762-2200.

Visitor Information

For general information on the Capital District—Albany, Troy, Schenectady—contact the **Albany County Convention and Visitors Bureau,** 25 Quackenbush Sq., Albany, NY 12207, 518/434-1217 or 800/258-3582, www.albany .org. For general information on the rest of

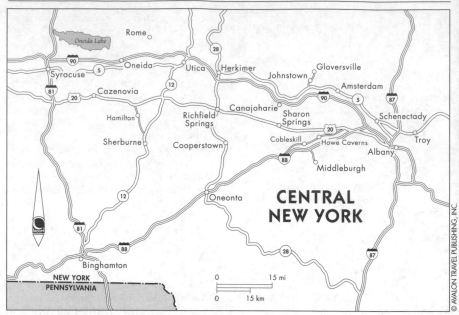

Central New York, contact **Cooperstown Chamber of Commerce,** 31 Chestnut St., Cooperstown, NY 13326, 607/547-9983, www.cooperstownchamber.org, or the local chambers and visitor centers listed below. For more information on any of the New York State parks or historic sites described below, visit the website: www.nysparks.com.

Albany

Albany may look like just another boring, midsize city pocked with a handful of lonely high rises and a half-deserted downtown, but beneath its apparently bland surface you'll find a surprisingly complex soul. Albany, as William Kennedy writes in *O Albany!,* is "as various as the American psyche itself, of which it was truly a crucible."

The oldest city in New York and one of the oldest in the nation, Albany is located at the head of the navigable portion of the Hudson River. Henry Hudson arrived in 1609, and by the mid-1600s the Dutch settlement of Fort Orange was a flourishing trading post.

Albany was an early home to writers Bret Harte, Herman Melville, and Henry James, whose grandfather William founded the family dynasty here. Presidents Martin Van Buren, Mil-

lard Fillmore, Grover Cleveland, Theodore Roosevelt, and Franklin Roosevelt all got their starts in the city, along with a number of less upstanding citizens. Most notorious of these was gangster Jack "Legs" Diamond, murdered in 1931 in a rooming house at 67 Dove Street. Albany is also home to a large branch of the State University of New York (SUNY).

As the state capital, Albany is dominated by the government. Come here at lunchtime when the legislature is in session and you'll see thousands of suited workers hurrying out for a sandwich and a few moments of sun. Though everyone seems harmless enough, this is a city notorious for political wheeling and dealing. When asked to explain Albany, an assemblywoman recently said, "Read Swift."

CENTRAL NEW YORK HIGHLIGHTS

The Capital District
New York State Museum, Albany
New York State Capitol Building, Albany
Schuyler Mansion, Albany
Historic Cherry Hill, Albany
Mansion Hill Inn, Albany
Miss Albany Diner, Albany
Jack's Oyster House, Albany
John Boyd Thatcher State Park, SW of Albany
Victorian storefronts, Troy
RiverSpark Heritage Trail
The Stockade, Schenectady

The Mohawk River Valley
Johnson Hall State Historic Site, Johnstown
Canajoharie Library and Art Gallery, Canajoharie
Herkimer Home, Little Falls
Herkimer Diamond Mines, Herkimer

Otsego County
Baseball Hall of Fame, Cooperstown
Farmers' Museum, Cooperstown
Fenimore House Museum, Cooperstown
Wood Bull Antiques, Cooperstown

Otesaga Hotel, Cooperstown
Inn at Cooperstown, Cooperstown
Petrified Creatures Museum of Natural History,
    Richfield Springs

Elsewhere in Central New York
Old resort hotels, Sharon Springs
Howe Caverns
Secret Caverns, near Howe Caverns
Iroquois Indian Museum, near Howe Caverns
Truck farms, Schoharie Valley
Munson-Williams-Proctor Institute, Utica
Fort Stanwix National Monument, Rome
The Mansion House, Oneida
Chittenango Falls, Chittenango
Cazenovia village
Antique stores, Madison to Bouckville
Earlville Opera House, Earlville

Binghamton
Roberson Museum and Science Center
The six Herschell carousels
Spiedie sandwiches
Clinton Street

HISTORY

Early Dutch Rule

In 1630 Dutchman Kiliaen Van Rensselaer bought 700,000 acres of land with Fort Orange at its center, establishing the patroonship of Rensselaerswyck. Under this Dutch system, a patroon was granted a sort of mini-kingdom in return for settling at least 50 people upon his land. Van Rensselaer brought over hundreds of settlers, and Rensselaerswyck soon grew into the most successful patroonship in the New World. As late as 1839 Van Rensselaer's descendants were still collecting rents from tenants.

Dutch rule ended in 1664, but Albany retained its Dutch character for the next 130 years. Banker Gorham A. Worth, visiting Albany in 1790, stated the town was "indeed Dutch, in all its moods and tenses; thoroughly and inveterately Dutch. The buildings were Dutch. . . . The

people were Dutch, the horses were Dutch, and even the dogs were Dutch."

The Boom Years

Around 1800 Albany began developing into a major transportation hub. The world's first successful steamboat run—Robert Fulton's *Clermont* in 1807—ended in Albany, and soon boats were chugging into the harbor daily.

The Erie Canal was completed in 1825, linking the Great Lakes to the Atlantic, and the city's population doubled in five years. Shortly thereafter came the railroads, as Albany blossomed into upstate New York's prime financial center and a major link between East and West. Cattleyards established in West Albany handled up to two million animals a year.

Large groups of Irish immigrants settled in Albany while building the Erie Canal, and thousands more Irish and Germans arrived with the coming of the Industrial Revolution.

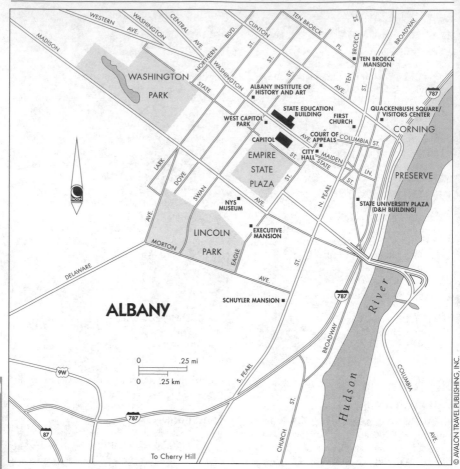

Soon factories manufacturing everything from checkers and dominoes to textiles and woolens lined the Hudson.

The Early 20th Century

Albany's prosperity continued through the first half of the 20th century. In the late 1930s, the city was the third largest express transfer and sixth largest mail transfer station in the United States. Nearly 150 passenger trains and 90 freight trains passed through daily, and the port handled the cargoes of 250 ocean-going vessels a year.

During this same period, Albany was promi-

nent in national politics. Theodore Roosevelt, Alfred Smith, and Franklin Roosevelt all ran for the U.S. presidency after serving as New York State governors.

Albany itself was tightly controlled by Democratic boss Dan O'Connell, who virtually ran the city from 1921 until his death in 1977 at age 91. Writes William Kennedy in *O Albany!*, "All of the Tammany tricks and traits were adapted to Albany by the Machine through the years: largesse to the poor; the establishment of a party organization more powerful than the local government; padded public payrolls . . . ;

control of the night world; open gambling. . . . In Albany, it was rumored, even the dead voted, early and often."

The Empire State Plaza

Albany fell on hard times in the 1950s when, like many other Northeastern cities, its manufacturing base began to decline and its downtown population moved to the suburbs. The city seemed well on its way to becoming a windswept slum, when in 1962 Gov. Nelson Rockefeller proposed building "the most spectacularly beautiful seat of government in the world"—the Nelson A. Rockefeller Empire State Plaza.

Legend has it Rockefeller conceived of the plaza during a visit from Princess Beatrix of the Netherlands in 1959: It humiliated him to drive royalty through the moldering capital. The plaza eventually cost at least $1 billion—an extraordinary sum for the time—displacing 3,600 households, many of them poor. All this caused much controversy at the time, but the plaza has been largely responsible for the rejuvenation of Albany's downtown.

GETTING AROUND
Orientation

Albany is an easy city to navigate. Traffic is usually light, and most visitor sights are located in or near downtown, which hugs the west bank of the Hudson. Unfortunately, I-787 runs right along the shoreline, depriving the city of its waterfront; however, a pedestrian bridge, **Hudson River Way,** which crosses over the highway, was opened in August 2002 and access to at least some of the shoreline is now possible.

Albany is centered on the Empire State Plaza and State Capitol Building, which sit perched side by side on a hill. From here, the downtown slopes eastward to the river. To the immediate west of the plaza are the residential neighborhoods of Central Square and Washington Park.

At the far western edge of Albany, near the airport, is Wolf Road and the town of Colonie, which function as the city's suburban center. Lots of shopping malls, hotels, and restaurants are located here.

Visitor Information

The best place to pick up information is at the **Albany Heritage Area Visitor Center,** 25 Quackenbush Sq. (at Broadway and Clinton Ave.), 518/434-0405 or 800/258-3582; open daily 10 A.M.–4 P.M. In the same complex is the **Albany County Convention and Visitors Bureau,** 518/434-1217 or 800/258-3582, www.albany.org, open Mon.–Fri. 9 A.M.–5 P.M. City Hall and the Empire State Plaza stock tourist brochures as well.

The **Times-Union Source Line,** 518/446-4000, is a 24-hour news, entertainment, sports, and business information line.

Tours

The **Albany Heritage Area Visitor Center,** 25 Quackenbush Sq. (Broadway and Clinton Ave.), 518/434-0405, offers guided trolley tours July–Sept. (call for rates and schedule), free walking-tour maps, and audio-tape guides. For a carriage tour of Albany, complete with two matched gray steeds, contact **Albany Carriage Service,** 518/465-5973.

One of Albany's foremost attractions is its architecture. A few highlights are mentioned below; for a thorough, self-guided architectural tour, pick up a copy of *Albany Architecture,* edited by Diana S. Waite (Mount Ida Press, 518/426-5935). The book outlines eight architectural tours and is available in most Albany bookstores.

Transportation

The best way to get around Albany is by car. Street parking is generally available or park in the giant underground lot located beneath the Empire State Plaza, off Madison Street between Eagle and Swan Streets.

SIGHTS
Empire State Plaza

Dominating downtown Albany is the Empire State Plaza, the extravagant brainchild of Nelson Rockefeller. An enormous marble platform sitting atop a hill, the plaza covers 98.5 acres and includes 11 buildings, among them the Legislature Building, Justice Building, four agency buildings,

The Empire State Plaza, conceived by Nelson Rockefeller, dominates downtown Albany.

COURTESY OF ALBANY COUNTY CONVENTION AND VISITORS BUREAU

CENTRAL NEW YORK

Corning Tower, and the Empire Center at the Egg—a round, whimsical performing arts center. Through the middle of the plaza knifes a long reflecting pool surrounded by modern sculpture.

Visitors to the plaza can relax by the reflecting pool, ascend to the free, 42nd-floor observation deck in the Corning Tower, and tour the plaza's fine art collection of 92 modern sculptures and paintings by the likes of Alexander Calder and David Smith. The place is a bit antiseptic, but quite interesting nonetheless.

The plaza is located between Eagle and Swan Streets, Madison Avenue and State Street. Free maps are available in the Visitors Assistance Office, Concourse level, 518/474-2418, at the north end of the plaza. The observation deck is open Mon.–Sun. 9 A.M.–2:30 P.M.

New York State Museum

On Madison Avenue at the southern end of the Empire State Plaza is the oldest and largest state museum in the country. Spread out over a maze of high-ceilinged rooms, it's packed full with life-size dioramas, sound and video shows, historical artifacts, and scientific specimens of all types. And it's all free of charge, 362

days a year (closed December 25, January 1, and Thanksgiving).

The museum is divided into three major exhibit areas: New York Metropolis, Adirondack Wilderness, and Upstate New York Native American Peoples. There are also exhibits on birds, minerals, and firefighting equipment, Discovery Place for children, and a well-stocked bookstore.

The Adirondack Wilderness exhibit is especially impressive. Here, in a vast darkened room, you hear the sounds of running water and birdsong before turning the corner to enter a "prehistoric wilderness." Other exhibits re-create a logging operation, a canoeing expedition, a blast furnace, and a black bear habitat.

The museum, 518/474-5877, www.nysm .nysed.gov, is open daily 9:30 A.M.–5 P.M.

New York State Capitol Building

On State Street at the northern end of the Empire State Plaza stands the stunning State Capitol Building. Begun in 1867, the castlelike edifice required 32 years and $25 million to complete—indeed, it was never entirely finished, as the original plans called for a dome and central rotunda. A clutch of architects, including Thomas Fuller, Henry Hobson Richardson, and Frederick Law Olmsted participated in the design, which explains its riotous hodgepodge of architectural styles.

Capitol tours lead visitors past the gold-leaf walls of the Senate Chamber and the enormous marble columns of the Assembly Chamber before culminating at the Richardson-designed "Million Dollar Staircase." Here 300 tiny faces carved by Italian stonecutters smile, glare, or stare at passersby. Seventy-seven of the faces are of such famous men as Abraham Lincoln and Walt Whitman, but most are anonymous, and each is different from the next. Free tours are offered daily at 10 A.M., noon, 2 P.M., and 3 P.M.; it's best to call ahead to reserve a spot, 518/474-2418.

Albany Institute of History and Art

One of the oldest museums in the United States, founded in 1791, the recently renovated institute is housed in an elegant beaux arts building and contains some wonderful gems, including many paintings by artists of the Hudson River School. Early works of American portraiture are also in the museum's collection, along with Dutch ce-

COURTESY OF ALBANY COUNTY CONVENTION AND VISITORS BUREAU

State Capitol Building, Albany

ramics, Albany-made silver, and New York–made furniture and pewter. Changing exhibits on the Hudson Valley and the Capital District are featured as well, while the Dutch Room offers a look at early Albany life.

The museum, 125 Albany Ave., 518/463-4478, www.albanyinstitute.org, is open Wed.–Sat. 10 A.M.–5 P.M., Sunday noon–5 P.M. Admission is adults $5, seniors and students $4, children 6–12 $2.50.

Albany Heritage Area Visitor Center

A good place to learn about Albany's history and culture is in this large, low-slung center, which contains many informative exhibits on everything from the city's ethnic heritage to its industrial past. Find here, for example, the tale of the billiard ball invented in Albany in 1868 in response to a lack of ivory.

Albany is part of the New York State Heritage Areas program, which are loosely delineated historic parks linked by a common theme. The Albany theme is transportation and business; the center publishes free walking-tour guides pinpointing relevant sites.

Also in the center are an attractive gift shop and the **Henry Hudson Planetarium,** with shows presented on Saturday only.

The center, 25 Quackenbush Sq. (Broadway and Clinton Ave.), 518/434-0405, is at the eastern edge of downtown, by I-797 and the Hudson. Open daily 10 A.M.–4 P.M., the center is free; planetarium shows cost adults $4.50, children under 12 and senior citizens $3.

Albany Center Galleries

One of Albany's foremost art galleries, the Albany Center Galleries has been the site of more than 100 major exhibitions since its opening in 1977, as well as numerous special events. Recently relocated, the galleries is now at 161 Washington Ave., in the public library building, 518/462-4775, www.albanycentergalleries.org; open Tues.–Thurs. noon–7 P.M., Sat.–Sun. noon–5 P.M.

Corning Preserve

This strange little oasis is stuck across the superhighway from the visitor center, by the very edge

A SHORT WALKING TOUR OF DOWNTOWN ALBANY

From the Albany Visitors Center at Quackenbush Square, walk two blocks to the corner of Clinton Avenue and North Pearl Street to view the sleek **Palace Theatre,** designed by noted movie palace architect John Eberson in 1929. A jewel of the RKO chain, built at a cost of $3 million, the Palace has housed the Albany Symphony Orchestra since 1931.

Cross Clinton Avenue to Clinton Square; the young Herman Melville lived in **No. 3 Clinton Square** when his first satirical sketches were published in the local *Albany Microscope.*

Next to the square, at North Pearl and Orange Streets, stands the graceful **First Church of Albany,** designed by famed Albany architect Philip Hooker in 1798. The church features the oldest pulpit and weathercock in America, as well as Tiffany stained-glass windows.

Two blocks south, at 79 North Pearl Street, stands the former **Kenmore Hotel,** now an office building. Designed in 1878 by Edward Ogden, the hotel was originally owned by Adam Blake, a wealthy African American who began his career as a waiter. The city's finest hotel for many years, the Kenmore hosted all the big bands of the 1920s, including Duke Ellington's and Benny Goodman's, and was a favorite hangout of gangster Legs Diamond.

Writes William Kennedy in *O Albany!* "Jack Burns . . . remembered Jack Diamond's presence: 'He had one section of the Rain-Bo Room. Nobody sat there but him and about six bodyguards and his girl, Kiki Roberts. Nobody ever gave him trouble. And he paid. And did he get service.'"

Heading west up **Columbia Street,** you'll pass a row of fine residences built between 1820 and the early 1900s. On the hill at Columbia and Lodge stands the handsome **Albany County Courthouse,** built in 1916.

Continue past the county courthouse and turn left on Eagle Street to reach the **New York State Court of Appeals.** Designed by Henry Rector in 1831, the structure features a fine domed rotunda and an even finer oak-paneled courtroom. Across the street from the courthouse is **Academy Park,** once home to Albany Academy, where Herman Melville and Henry James, Sr. attended school.

One block further south on Eagle Street is **City Hall,** Henry Hobson Richardson's stunning 1882 Romanesque work. The tower was built to store the city archives, and features a 60-bell carillon. You may be able to arrange a tour of the building by calling 518/434-0405.

City Hall provides a good view of the State Capitol and the 1912 **State Education Building.** The south side of the latter structure features 36 striking Corinthian columns—the longest colonnade in the United States.

Another block south of City Hall is **State Street,** an unusually wide thoroughfare dating back to Albany's days as a walled stockade. Most of the fort's churches and public buildings then stood in the middle of this street; today, it's lined with 17 banks in four blocks.

Walk down the State Street hill past the banks and **St. Peter's Episcopal Church** to Broadway. To your right stands the former **Delaware & Hudson Building and Albany** *Evening Journal* **Building,** a magnificent 660-foot-long structure with a lavish central tower. Designed in 1914 in the Flemish Gothic style, the building is considered architect Marcus Reynold's masterpiece. It now houses the administrative offices of the State University of New York.

Left of the State Street–Broadway intersection, at the corner of Maiden Lane, is yet another splendid building—the art deco **U.S. Post Office,** built in the 1930s. A frieze along the top recounts the story of the U.S. mail delivery system; inside you'll find a long ceiling mural covered with maps of the continents.

At the corner of Broadway and Columbia Street stands the former **Union Station,** built in 1900. Once an important transportation hub linking the New York Central to the Boston and Albany Railroad, the station is now the corporate headquarters of Norstar Bancorp.

of the Hudson River. More a park than a preserve, it offers a walking/biking trail, picnic tables, exercise stations, and sculptures by local artists. Special events are presented in summer. To reach the preserve, take the new pedestrian bridge, called **Hudson River Way,** at Broadway not far from the visitor center; note the lampposts, each of which tells about a different episode in Albany history. Or, head to the southern end of State University of New York (SUNY) Plaza and cross over on Hamilton or Pruyn Streets.

New York State Executive Mansion

One block south of the Empire State Plaza at 138 Eagle St. is the governor's mansion, open to the public by reserved tour only. An impressive Italianate building with a wraparound porch, the mansion dates to 1856, when it was constructed as a private residence. The state purchased the property in 1877, and each successive governor has put his stamp on it: Theodore Roosevelt built a gym, FDR sunk a pool, animal-lover Al Smith installed a zoo.

To arrange a tour of the mansion, call visitor services, Empire State Plaza, 518/473-7521. Tours are offered on Thursday afternoons only, Sept.–June; closed July–Aug.

Schuyler Mansion

Perched on a hill that once offered a great view of the Hudson is this gracious 1761 Georgian mansion. Now a State Historic Site, the home was built by Philip Schuyler, a leading Albany citizen who served as a general during the Revolutionary War. Daniel Webster once honored Schuyler as "second only to Washington in the services he performed for his country," but he was relieved of his duties and court martialed for ordering the evacuation of Fort Ticonderoga. A probable victim of political infighting, Schuyler was eventually acquitted, though he resigned his post.

The Schuyler mansion hosted all the major players of the day—Benjamin Franklin, Benedict Arnold, George Washington, Aaron Burr—and served as a prison for Gen. Burgoyne following the British surrender at Saratoga. Schuyler's daughter, Elizabeth, married Alexander Hamilton here.

The mansion, 32 Catherine St. at Elizabeth, 518/434-0834, is open April–Oct., Wed.–Sat. 10 A.M.–5 P.M., Sunday 1–5 P.M., or by appointment. Tours begin on the hour. Admission is adults $3, children $1.

Historic Cherry Hill

To the south of downtown Albany stands the homey, Colonial-era Cherry Hill. Built in 1787

COURTESY OF ALBANY COUNTY CONVENTION AND VISITORS BUREAU

Historic Cherry Hill, a Georgian-style home built in 1787 by Philip Van Rensselaer

THE BLACK WIDOW OF CHERRY HILL

The story of the Cherry Hill murder began in August 1826 when Jesse Strang, a man who'd feigned his own murder to abandon his family and flee to Albany, met Elsie Lansing Whipple at Bates' Tavern. Elsie, a relative of the Van Rensselaers, was 24 at the time, and unhappily married to engineer John Whipple. She'd already tried to poison her husband twice, to no effect.

Jesse was hired as a handyman at Cherry Hill, home of the Whipples. He and Elsie plunged into a secret love affair, passing notes in the halls and making love in the hayloft.

On May 27, Jesse bought a rifle, climbed into a shed next door to the mansion, and fatally shot John Whipple through the window. Elsie was downstairs placidly smoking a pipe.

Soon after the murder, Jesse's suspicious behav-ior led to his arrest. He confessed, but blamed Elsie for putting him up to it. Both were tried, but only Jesse was found guilty. Writes Louis C. Jones in *The Murder at Cherry Hill* (Cherry Hill Publications): "The Albany Establishment had closed ranks, however distasteful it may have been to do so, and saved one of their number from the disgrace of a public hanging."

Jesse was hanged on August 24, 1827—the last criminal in Albany publicly hanged. Between 30,000 and 40,000 people watched the grue-some event.

Afterward, Elsie moved to New York City, where she remarried. Her second husband died under mysterious circumstances; she then moved back upstate, and disappeared somewhere in the area of Onondaga.

by Philip and Mary Van Rensselaer, the house was home to five generations of the Van Rensse-laer family; the last member died in 1963.

The frugal Van Rensselaers had a hard time throwing anything away, so inside you'll find an odd assortment of furnishings from all five gen-erations. Among the highlights are early Dutch tiles, Empire chairs, a striking sleigh bed, turn-of-the-century swimming trunks, postcards from the 1920s, and a very early Castro convertible. An especially interesting room is the kitchen, equipped with both a Colonial-era wall oven and a freestanding gas stove. Miss Emily Rankin, the last Van Rensselaer to live in the house, ap-parently cooked with both but was partial to the wall oven, which reportedly baked first-rate bread.

Tours of the house, 523½ S. Pearl St., at 1st Ave., 518/434-4791, are offered July–Sept., Tues.–Sat. 10 A.M.–4 P.M., Sunday 1–4 P.M., with the last tour beginning at 3 P.M. Tours begin on the hour. Admission is adults $3.50, seniors $3, students $2, children 6–17 $1.

Lark Street

Two blocks west of the Empire State Plaza is 19th-century Lark Street. The bohemian hub of Albany, Lark Street is lined with an eclectic array of small shops, ethnic restaurants, and night-clubs. Most are located in the eight blocks be-tween Madison and Washington Avenues. Check out **Romeo's,** 299 Lark St., 518/434-4014, for unusual gifts and cards.

Lark Street sits on the edge of Central Square, a prosperous residential neighborhood notable for fine architecture. Some of the best examples stand along State Street between Lark Street and the Empire Plaza. In these two short blocks you'll find one opulent 19th-century home after another, many designed by Albany architects Charles Nichols, Albert Fuller, and Ernest Hoffman.

Washington Park and State Street

Continue another block west of Lark Street to Washington Park, a lush green oasis designed by Frederick Law Olmsted and Calvert Vaux in the 1870s. Carved throughout its 81 acres are curved roads, wooded glades, open meadows, and long, skinny Washington Lake. On its shores stands the Lake House, an extravagant terra cotta affair with pink terrazzo floors and wrought-iron chandeliers.

The opulence of State Street continues along the north side of the park. Highlights include No. 397, designed by Henry Hobson Richardson, and No. 441, the work of William Ross Proctor.

Ten Broeck Mansion

On the north side of Albany, in a neighborhood known as Arbor Hill, stands an imperial Federal-style home built for Abraham Ten Broeck and his wife Elizabeth Van Rensselaer in 1797–98. Ten Broeck served as a general in the Continental Army and later as state senator, judge, and mayor of Albany.

Now owned by the Albany County Historical Association, the mansion contains a fine collection of period furniture and showcases changing historic exhibits. In the basement hides a snug wine cellar that wasn't rediscovered until the 1970s. Its rare contents were sold for a whopping $42,000, and the proceeds used to restore the house.

The mansion, at 9 Ten Broeck Pl. between Ten Broeck and N. Swan Sts., 518/436-9826, www.tenbroeck.org, is open May–Dec., Thurs.–Fri. 10 A.M.–4 P.M., Sat.–Sun. 1–4 P.M. Admission is adults $3, children 50 cents.

The Big Dog

All along Broadway in northern Albany hulk old factory buildings dating back to the city's era of industrial activity. A highlight is the former **RTA Building,** 991 Broadway, at Loudenville Road. RTA was a distributor of RCA electrical appliances and on the building's roof sits a 25-foot-high, four-ton statue of Nipper, the symbol of the RCA-owned Victor Company. Nipper's head is cocked to the side and he wears a quizzical expression, as if to ask, what am I still doing here? The statue was built in Chicago about 1858 and shipped in five sections on railroad flat cars.

Shaker Settlement

On the western outskirts of Albany near the airport is America's first Shaker settlement, established in 1776. A religious sect founded in England in 1758, the Shakers later established 24 American communities from Maine to Florida (for more on the Shakers, see Columbia County in the Hudson Valley chapter).

In Albany eight sturdy, clean-lined Shaker buildings still stand, grouped around a crossroads. Seven are used by a geriatric nursing home, giving the place an off-limits feel. But

the splendid 1848 Meeting House has been converted into a visitor center. Inside you'll find a small exhibit, a gift shop offering Shaker crafts, and the large hall where the Shakers once held their meetings. The bleachers in back were set aside for the "World's People"—nonbelievers—who often came to the meetings to watch and listen to the Shakers' music. Today the hall is used for Shaker-related concerts, workshops, and crafts shows.

Free walking-tour maps of the settlement are available in the gift shop. Behind the Meeting House is a well-tended herb garden; down the road is the cemetery where the sect's founder, Mother Ann Lee, and 444 others are buried.

The settlement is located off Albany-Shaker Rd. (Rte. 151) near the junction of Watervliet-Shaker Rd. (Rte. 155), 518/456-7890. Hours are Tues.–Sat. 9:30 A.M.–4 P.M.

SPORTS AND RECREATION

Biking and Jogging

For 42 miles the **Hudson-Mohawk Bikeway** follows the Mohawk and Hudson Rivers, from Albany north to Rotterdam Junction. Maps are available at the Albany County Convention and Visitors Bureau. In Albany you can access the trail from the Corning Preserve.

Cruises

Dutch Apple Cruises, 137 Broadway, 518/463-0220, features sightseeing, dinner, and overnight cruises along the Hudson. Boats operate daily April–October.

Football

The **Albany Conquest,** 518/487-2222, one of the 34 teams in the pro football Arena Football League Two, play at the Pepsi Arena, 51 S. Pearl Street.

Indoor Sports

The spanking-clean, state-of-the-art **OTB Tele-Theater Racing and Sports Center,** 711 Central Ave., 518/438-0127, offers simulated indoor golf, batting cages, bowling, a basketball machine, dance floor, restaurant, and off-track wagering.

ACCOMMODATIONS

Motels

Many of Albany's motels are clustered on the western edge of the city, near the airport. Here you'll find a 97-room **Comfort Inn,** 866 Albany-Shaker Rd., 518/783-1216 or 800/274-9429 ($78–89 d); and the 116-room **Red Roof Inn,** 188 Wolf Rd., 518/459-1971 or 800/843-7663 ($66–86 d).

Closer to downtown is the 216-room **Albany Quality Inn,** 1-3 Watervliet Ave., 518/438-8431 or 800/221-2222, offering indoor and outdoor pools ($70–80 d, with breakfast included). Off I-787 is the **Ramada Inn Downtown,** 300 Broadway, 518/434-4111 or 800/333-1177, also equipped with an outdoor pool ($89 d).

Hotels

Near the airport is Albany's foremost hotel, the **Desmond,** 660 Albany-Shaker Rd., 518/869-8100, www.desmondhotels.com, a charming hotel-inn filled with period furnishings, artwork, and rich dark wood paneling. Many rooms feature balconies or private patios; two heated indoor pools and a health club are on-site ($130–170 d).

Inns and Bed-and-Breakfasts

One of the best—and only—places to stay in the heart of downtown is the **Mansion Hill Inn,** 115 Philip St., 518/465-2038, www.mansionhill.com, a friendly hostelry consisting of several historic buildings, a picturesque courtyard, and a first-rate restaurant. All the rooms are completely modernized, with queen-size beds, cable TV, and full private baths ($155–185 d, with breakfast).

Also a good choice is the neoclassical **State Street Mansion,** 518/462-6780, www.statestreetmansion.com, in the Central Square district. This elegant 1881 B&B offers 12 guest rooms, most with private bath ($95–165 d).

FOOD

Diners and Vendors

Just north of downtown reigns the yellow-and-maroon **Miss Albany Diner,** 893 Broadway, 518/465-9148, which dates back to 1941. Once

Renamed in 1986 in honor of William Kennedy's novel *Ironweed*, the Miss Albany Diner dates from 1941.

known as Lil's Diner, it was renamed after the filming of William Kennedy's novel *Ironweed* here in 1986. Average main dish $8.

During warm weather, **food vendors** set up shop in West Capitol Park beside the Capitol Building.

Historic Albany

A classic downtown Albany restaurant, frequented by legislators, is **Jack's Oyster House,** 42 State St., 518/465-8854. Specializing in seafood, it is said to be the oldest eatery in Albany. Run by the same family for generations, it features black tables, tiled floors, and big pane-glass windows. Reservations are highly recommended; average entrée $16.

Lark Street

Along this lively street are many small restaurants serving both lunch and dinner. For contemporary American fare, try **Justin's,** 301 Lark St., 518/436-7008, a lively spot partially housed in a historic building. Jazz is often featured on the weekends; average entrée $13. **Debbie's Kitchen,** 456 Madison Ave., near Lark, 518/463-3829, is known for its overstuffed sandwiches; average price $7.

Laid-back **El Loco,** 465 Madison Ave., at Lark, 518/436-1855, has been voted the city's best Mexican restaurant many years running. On the menu are traditional, Tex-Mex, and vegetarian dishes, and a wide selection of Mexican beers; average entrée $10.

Eclectic

A few blocks south of the Empire Plaza is the cozy 1861 **Mansion Hill Inn,** 115 Philip St., 518/465-2038, which serves new American-style fare ranging from pasta to leg of lamb. The restaurant focuses on dinner, but it also serves lunch several days a week; average entrée $18.

Quintessence, 11 New Scotland Ave., 518/434-8186, is a classy art deco diner where the fare ranges from Mexican to Italian. The eatery is open for breakfast, lunch, and dinner, and live blues is sometimes featured; average main dish $10.

French

Many regard **Nicole's Bistro at the Quackenbush House,** 25 Quackenbush Sq. (at Broadway and Clinton Ave., in the same complex that houses the Visitor Center), 518/465-1111, to be the best restaurant in Albany. Located in the city's oldest residence, dating back to the 1700s, it serves fine French cuisine in a cozy brick setting lined with black-and-white photographs. The prix fixe dinners start at a surprisingly reasonable $25; entrées cost $15–24.

Italian

One of the newer eateries in town is the popular **Buca di Beppo,** 44 Wolf Rd., 518/459-2822, serving "immigrant Southern Italian food" in a 1950s Little Italy setting; average entrée $15. The modern, upscale **Cafe Capriccio,** 49 Grand St., 518/465-0439, is a local favorite specializing in Northern Italian fare; average entrée $16. For a more old-fashioned dining experience, try the classic **Lombardo's,** 121 Madison Ave., 518/462-9180, frequented by politicians. It offers wall murals, tile floors, and traditional Italian dishes; average entrée $16.

SHOPPING

Albany is known for its shopping malls, many of which are located along Wolf Road near the airport. Largest is the glitzy **Colonie Center,** Wolf Rd. and Central Ave., Colonie, 518/459-9020, offering 120 upscale shops and an international food court. **Stuyvesant Plaza,** Western Ave. and Fuller Rd., 518/482-8986, is a smaller and more eclectic mall with a good bookstore and children's toy shop.

You'll find a number of antique shops along Central and Washington Avenues near their intersection one block north of Washington Park, and along Lake Street between Madison and Washington Avenues. Peppering Lark Street are clothing boutiques, jewelry stores, and gift shops. There are several vintage clothing stores on Quail Street just off Western Avenue.

ENTERTAINMENT

The city's best entertainment sources are the Thursday and Friday editions of the *Times-Union,* 518/454-5694, and *Metroland,* 518/463-2500, a free alternative weekly.

CENTRAL NEW YORK

Performing Arts

The **Empire State Performing Arts Center,** The Egg, Empire State Plaza, Madison Ave. and Swan St., 518/473-1845, www.theegg.org, is the capital's premier arts venue. It houses an 880-seat main theater and a 500-seat recital hall; both present a wide range of music, theater, and dance.

The professional **Capital Repertory Company,** 111 N. Pearl St., 518/445-7469, www.capitalrep.org, presents classical, contemporary, and world-premier works October–June. The company performs in the 258-seat Market Theater, formerly a grocery store.

The 1931, 2,800-seat **Palace Theatre,** 19 Clinton Ave., 518/465-4663, was once an opulent movie palace. Today, it's home to the Albany Symphony Orchestra, and host to touring rock acts and Broadway shows.

The tiny **Albany Civic Theater,** 235 2nd Ave., 518/462-1297, occupying a converted turn-of-the-century firehouse, presents four theater productions every year. Each runs but three weeks and tickets sell out fast.

Film

Spectrum Seven Theaters, 290 Delaware Ave., 518/449-8995, presents art, foreign, commercial, and independent films.

Clubs and Nightlife

Though much of downtown Albany shuts down at night, **Lark Street** is an exception. Here you'll find a good blues club, the **Lionheart Blues Cafe,** 258 Lark St., 518/436-9530; and **Justin's,** 301 Lark St., 518/436-7008, a popular restaurant and singles bar with weekend jazz.

Bogie's, 297 Ontario St., 518/482-4368, presents everything from funk and ska to rock and eclectic folk. The intimate **Valentine's,** 17 New Scotland Ave., 518/432-6572, is a top club for local rock. The **Lark Tavern,** 453 Madison Ave., 518/463-9779, hosts local rock, reggae, and "psycho-country" bands.

Another good blues spot is **Pauly's Hotel,** 337 Central Ave., 518/426-0828, which bills itself as Albany's oldest tavern. For a drink in a friendly neighborhood bar, step into **McCaffrey's,** 332 S. Allen St., at New Scotland Ave.,

518/435-9537, a long, creaky, hole-in-the-wall that dates back to 1901.

EVENTS

Albany celebrates its Dutch heritage with the **Tulip Festival** and **Pinksterfest,** 518/434-1217, held concurrently on the second weekend of May. Pinksterfest commemorates the day Fort Orange's African American slaves were freed by the Dutch. During the **Empire State Regatta,** held in June, scull and crew races take place on the Hudson River.

Throughout the summer, **free concerts** and other special events are staged at the Empire State Plaza, 518/474-2418. The **Park Playhouse,** 518/434-2035, presents free plays and other events at the Lake House in Washington Park in July and August.

In the northwestern suburbs of Albany is the **Pruyn House,** 207 Old Niskayuna Rd., Newtonville, 518/783-1435, a historic home with a grand old barn out back, the site of occasional summer jazz and classical events.

The fairgrounds in the nearby village of Altamont host some of the region's top special events. Among them are the **Old Songs Festival of Traditional Music and Dance** in June, the 100-year-old **Altamont Fair** in August, and the **Capital District Scottish Games** in early September. Call the Albany Convention and Visitors Bureau, 518/434-1217, for more information.

EXCURSIONS FROM ALBANY

Crailo State Historic Site

Directly across the Hudson from Albany in Rensselaer is the 1704 Crailo mansion. Home to the Van Rensselaer family until the mid-1800s, the house is now a museum focusing on the history of Dutch culture in the Hudson River Valley. Exhibits range from archaeological artifacts to a restored cellar kitchen. Surrounding the house is a riverside park where summertime concerts are held.

Crailo, 9 ½ Riverside Ave., 518/463-8738, is open April–Oct., Wed.–Sat. 10 A.M.–5 P.M. and

Sunday 1–5 P.M. Tours begin every half-hour. Admission is adults $3, children $1.

John Boyd Thatcher State Park

For terrific views of the Hudson and Mohawk Valleys and the Adirondacks, head 18 miles west of Albany to Thatcher State Park. Here you'll also find the most unusual **Indian Ladder Geologic Trail,** a half-mile-long ledge that is one of the richest fossil-bearing formations in the world. Other park features include an Olympic-size pool, hiking trails, playground, and picnic area. During the winter, heated comfort stations serve cross-country skiers.

The park, Rte. 157 off Rte. 85, 518/872-1237, is open daily year-round, but the geologic trail is only open May–Nov., weather permitting. Parking in summer is $7.

Rensselaerville

About 25 miles southwest of Albany is the charming one-street village of Rensselaerville, originally settled in the late 1700s by Connecti-cut families who arrived via Long Island. On the National Register of Historic Places, the village is filled with restored post-Colonial and Greek Empire homes, many built by Ephraim Russ (1784–1853), a highly talented carpenter-architect who once lived in the village.

On Main Street, you'll find lots of shops selling the handiwork of Valley craftspeople, including jewelers, fiber artists, glass-blowers and ceramists. Rensselaerville is also home to the **Rensselaerville Institute,** Rte. 85, 518/797-3783, which houses a small gallery and presents classical and jazz concerts during the summer. The gallery is open Mon.–Fri. 9 A.M.–5 P.M.

Bed-and-Breakfasts

About 15 minutes east of Albany is the **Gregory House,** Rte. 43, Averill Park, 518/674-3774, www.gregoryhouse.com, a gracious 150-year-old homestead with 12 nicely appointed guest rooms, an outdoor pool, and a first-rate gourmet restaurant. Rooms range $100–110 d.

Troy

At times, Troy feels like a Victorian ghost town. Enormous abandoned stores with big plate glass windows and faded gold lettering occupy downtown, while nearby residential neighborhoods feature elegant town- and row houses in various states of repair. The sidewalks are all but empty and traffic ridiculously light. No wonder they filmed *The Age of Innocence, The Bostonians,* and *Ironweed* here.

At other times, Troy just feels like a nice place to live, especially in recent years, since its waterfront has been revitalized with two enjoyable parks. People are friendly, rents low, and there's plenty of room to move about. The city sits on the east bank of the Hudson River, about 15 minutes north of Albany, and is home to three colleges (Rensselaer Polytechnic Institute, Russell Sage College, Hudson Valley Community College) and a prestigious private girls' school (the Emma Willard School).

History

From the mid-1800s through the early 1900s, Troy was a major industrial city that led the world in the manufacture of stoves and horseshoes, bells and brushes, and, especially, collars and shirts. A housewife tired of washing her husband's shirts invented the detachable collar here in 1825; Collar City, as Troy came to be known, once boasted 26 firms manufacturing over three million collars a year. Many of the factories were located along the Hudson just north of the city—their abandoned shells still stand today.

Always grittier and more industrialized than Albany, 19th-century Troy featured two distinct populations: the wealthy industrialists who built the lavish downtown, and the workers, many recent immigrants from Ireland, Germany, Italy, Poland, and French-speaking Canada. South Troy still harbors large Italian and Polish populations, while North Troy has historically been largely German. In more recent years, a large Latino population has taken root.

Troy's industrial fortunes were already beginning to decline by 1900, due to transportation

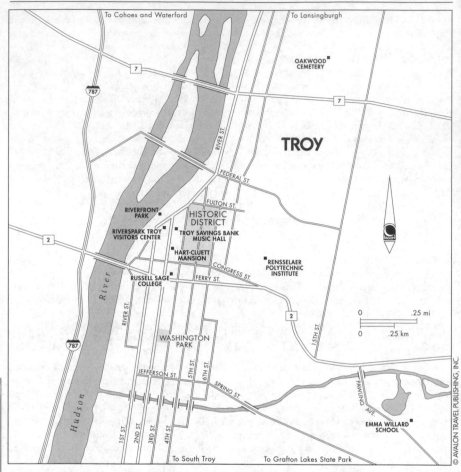

shifts and the rise of Pittsburgh's steel mills, but it wasn't until after WW II that the city really fell on hard times. Population dropped from a high of 76,000 to 54,000 today. Somehow, however, Troy managed to escape the scourge of urban renewal, and so retains its Victorian heart—making it a fun city to explore on a lazy summer's afternoon.

Orientation

Troy is a small and compact city with numbered streets running north-south and named streets running east-west. Most of the sights below are located in the downtown area and are easily accessed on foot.

Tours

Hudson-Mohawk Industrial Gateway, at the foot of Polk St., 518/274-5267, www.hudson-mohawkgateway.org, offers unusual tours several times a month that delve into the city's industrial and architectural past. The company's offices are housed in the imperial Burden Iron Works Building, which once featured a 60-foot-high waterwheel and produced most of the horseshoes used in America.

Visitor Information

The **Rensselaer Regional Chamber of Commerce,** 31 2nd St., Troy, NY 12180, 518/274-7020, www.renscochamber.com, is open Mon.–Fri. 8:30 A.M.–5 P.M. Pick up maps and brochures at the Troy RiverSpark Visitor Center, or visit the website: www.troyvisitorcenter.org.

SIGHTS

Troy RiverSpark Visitor Center

For a good introduction to Troy, stop by this first-rate center, where you'll find everything from an informative film to an electronic map that generates printed information. Most exhibits focus on the region's labor and industrial history, and include all sorts of interesting factual tidbits. Here you'll learn that the first all-woman labor union was formed in Troy in 1864, and that the first person to seriously study the geological sciences was lawyer Amos Eaton, later affiliated with the Rensselaer School (now Rensselaer Polytechnic Institute). Eaton began his scientific career while serving a life sentence for forgery—luckily for science, he was pardoned after four years.

RiverSpark is one of New York's State Heritage Areas—loosely delineated historic parks linked by a common theme. The area includes not just Troy, but also five smaller communities nearby; pick up a free driving-tour guide at the center.

The center, 251 River St., 518/270-8667, sits on the edge of Riverfront Park. Hours are June–Labor Day, Tues.–Sat. 11 A.M.–5 P.M.; call for off-season hours. Admission is free.

River Street Historic District

At 265 River St., the **Rensselaer County Council for the Arts** (RCCA Center), 518/273-0552, www.artscenteronline.org, houses a low-key gallery with temporary exhibits ranging from contemporary art to folk arts. Hours are Mon.–Fri. 9 A.M.–7 P.M., Saturday 9 A.M.–5 P.M., Sunday noon–4 P.M.; closed summer Sundays. Admission is free.

On River Street south of the RiverSpark Visitor Center is an attractive row of 19th-century storefronts restored and furnished with period signs and awnings for the 1992 filming of Martin Scorsese's *The Age of Innocence.* Troy townspeople liked the effect so much they decided to retain the signs and awnings, though some of the stores remain empty.

Near where 1st Street intersects with River Street is Troy's former **Banker's Row.** Most of the buildings here feature ornate, locally manufactured cast-iron storefronts.

Troy Savings Bank Music Hall

Just east of RiverSpark, at 32 2nd St., is this imposing 1871 building renowned for its acoustically perfect concert hall. The bank originally built the second-floor hall as a sort of gift for its shareholders. World-class musicians like Isaac Stern and Yo-Yo Ma have recorded here, and the hall hosts numerous annual events. For concert information, contact the box office, 7 State St., 518/273-0038, www.troymusichall.org.

Hart-Cluett Mansion

One block south of the Music Hall is the Rensselaer County Historical Society, housed in the elegant 1827 Hart-Cluett townhouse. The mansion is named after the prominent Troy families who once lived here and is filled with 19th-century furnishings by such well-known cabinetmakers such as Phyfe, Galusha, and Moore. The mansion, 59 2nd St., 518/272-7232, is open Tues.–Sat. 10 A.M.–4 P.M.; closed in winter. Admission is adults $4, seniors and students $3, children 6–12 $2.

Downtown Historic District

The heart of downtown Troy is located between 3rd and 5th, Fulton and Congress Streets. Strolling among the many 19th-century storefronts here, it's easy to imagine you're in the Victorian age—a man in a top hat or woman in hoop skirt could emerge at any moment.

One of the district's most impressive buildings is the **Frear Building,** at Fulton and 3rd Streets. Built around a courtyard topped with a skylight, the edifice was once home to Frear's Troy Cash Bazaar, a dry goods company that conducted a $1-million-a-year mail order business years before Sears Roebuck was born. Though the building now houses offices, the words Troy Cash Bazaar are still visible near the rooftop.

Russell Sage and Emma Willard

On the south side of Congress Street between 1st and 2nd Streets stands the lovely Russell Sage College, 518/244-2000, a cluster of ivy-covered buildings, former private homes, and courtyards. An all-women's college, the school was founded in 1906 by Margaret Olivia Slocum Sage, who was once a student at the Troy Female Seminary. The seminary was one of the country's first institutions of higher learning for women, founded in 1821 by Emma Willard. A statue honoring Willard stands on the Russell Sage campus on the 2nd Street side. The Emma Willard School, 235 Pawling Ave., now operates as a private high school for girls, and is known for its academic excellence. Among its graduates is Jane Fonda.

Across the street from the Emma Willard statue is the **Troy Public Library,** 518/274-7071. Built of white marble in the Italian Renaissance style, it holds an ornate interior adorned with gold leaf highlights, a coffered ceiling, and a Tiffany window bearing the words "Study as if you were to live forever and live as if you were to die tomorrow."

About a 15-minute walk south of the college is **Washington Park,** lined with a lovely collection of 19th-century town- and row houses. Some have been thoroughly renovated, others are rather dilapidated. Washington Park is one of the few private parks in the country—only residents possess keys to the iron-gated entrance.

The Junior Museum

Children will enjoy this cheery hideaway, filled with hands-on exhibits, live reptiles and fish, a children's art gallery, and a planetarium. Explore a log cabin and Iroquois longhouse, view temporary exhibits, attend special events. The museum, 105 Eighth St., 518/235-2120, www.juniormuseum.org, is open Wed.–Fri. 11 A.M.–4 P.M., Sat.–Sun. 10 A.M.–5 P.M. Admission is $5 per person, under two free.

Uncle Sam's Grave

One of Troy's odder claims to fame is the fact it was once home to Uncle Sam, a meatpacker whose full name was Sam Wilson. During the War of 1812, Wilson's firm was contracted to send meat to the troops. Shipped barrels were marked U.S., for United States, but Wilson's workers joked the initials stood for their boss, whom they'd nicknamed Uncle Sam. Later, when these workers enlisted in the army, the joke spread through the ranks, and soon the words Uncle Sam and United States became synonymous. The first cartoon figures, dressed in stars and stripes, appeared around 1830; the beard was added during the Civil War.

Sam Wilson himself lived a quiet life, dying in 1854 at the age of 88. He is buried in the **Oakwood Cemetery,** a hilly, tree-shaded retreat with great views of the city. Emma Willard and other prominent Trojans are also buried here. To reach the cemetery, 518/272-7520, take 2nd Street north to 101st Street, turn right, and watch for signs to the cemetery and grave. Hours are daily 9 A.M.–4:30 P.M.

RECREATION

The **Capt. J. P. Cruise Line,** 278 River St., 518/270-1901, offers sightseeing and dinner cruises aboard a re-created Mississippi paddleboat May–October. The boats are docked on Front Street.

ACCOMMODATIONS

Accommodation options in Troy are limited. Downtown you'll find a **Super 8,** 1 4th St., 518/274-8800 ($75–95 d); and a **Best Western,** 1800 6th Ave., 518/274-3210 ($74–85 d). In Averill Park, eight miles east of the city, is the **Gregory House,** a historic B&B with 12 guest rooms (see Excursions from Albany under Albany, above).

FOOD

Uncle Sam's Good Natural Products, 77 4th St., 518/271-7299, is a simple vegetarian deli where you can pick up a good salad or tofu burger; average main dish $6. Now under new management, the historic **Old 499 House,** 499 2nd

Ave., 518/238-0499, is a Troy institution, serving steak, seafood, sandwiches, and salads; average dinner entrée $14.

Several good restaurants, each quite different from the next, are located along the Hudson in Riverfront Park. The friendly **Troy Pub & Uncle Sam Brewery,** 417-419 River St., 518/273-2337, brews its own beer and soft drinks and serves a variety of American fare; average entrée $12. The high-ceilinged, brick-walled **River Street Cafe,** 429 River St., 518/273-2740, serves an eclectic array of international dishes ranging from Ho Chi Minh City Duck to Norwegian salmon. It's open for dinner only; average entrée $17.

ENTERTAINMENT

Performing Arts

The **Troy Savings Bank Music Hall,** 32 2nd St., hosts first-rate musicians from all over the world. From September to June, free noontime concerts take place on second Tuesdays. The box office, 518/273-0038, is located at 7 State Street.

The **New York State Theater Institute** offers professional regional theater. The box office, 518/274-3256, is at 37 1st St.

In Cohoes, to the north of Troy, is the **Cohoes Music Hall,** 58 Remsen St., 518/237-7999, a National Historic Landmark. Built in 1874, the 250-seat, second-story theater presents off-Broadway–style musicals September–May.

Nightlife

Thanks largely to its sizable student population, Troy possesses an active nightlife. Two popular music clubs are **Valenti's Pub,** 729 Pawling Ave., 518/283-6766, a good spot for local rock-and-roll; and the **Rolls Touring Co.,** 3rd Street at Broadway, 518/272-5453, a friendly pub with an eclectic booking policy. The **Troy Pub & Uncle Sam's Brewery,** 417 River St., 518/273-BEER, sometimes presents live rock, blues, or jazz on the weekends.

A popular local hangout in South Troy is the **South End Tavern,** 757 Burden Ave., 518/272-9661, a former speakeasy that once had separate entrances for men and women.

To find out about other clubs, or who's playing where, check *Metroland,* 518/463-2500, a free alternative weekly.

EVENTS

Free **Collar City Pops Concerts,** 518/274-7020, are held at the Riverfront Park bandshell July–August. Enjoy **music cruises** on board the Capt. J. P. paddleboat, 518/270-1901, June–September.

The two-day **Riverfront Arts Festival,** 518/273-0552, celebrates summer with free outdoor music and dance events, crafts and food vendors, roving performers, and sidewalk mural painting. The fest takes place in and around Riverfront Park in late June.

During the **Victorian Stroll,** 518/274-7020, held the first Sunday in December, the whole downtown is decked out for a Victorian Christmas. People dress in costume, and performers and musicians stroll the streets.

EXCURSIONS FROM TROY

Elsewhere in RiverSpark

From Troy, the 28-mile RiverSpark Heritage Trail winds past five communities and more than 40 significant industrial sites. Free trail maps are available in the RiverSpark Visitor Center.

In **Waterford,** the oldest incorporated village in the United States (1794), you'll find industrialists' mansions and the so-called **"Waterford Flight."** The village is located at the confluence of the Hudson and Mohawk Rivers, and the flight is a series of five lift locks that raise and lower boats from the Hudson (elevation 15.2 feet) to the Mohawk (elevation 184 feet).

Cohoes is a former company town still dominated by the old factory buildings of Harmony Mills, at one time the single largest producer of cotton cloth in America. The town centers around the 80-foot waterfalls that powered the mills and endless rows of interconnected red brick and stone buildings. Most are abandoned but are in excellent condition and so handsome, it's hard to believe they once housed dirty, clanking machinery.

Grafton Lakes State Park

About 12 miles southeast of Troy lies an idyllic, 2,357-acre outdoor recreation area, centered around four ponds and the Martin-Dunham Reservoir. Long Pond features a large sandy beach, a bathhouse, and rowboat rentals; hiking trails encircle several of the lakes. The park, Rte. 2, 518/279-1155, is open daily year-round; the beach is open Memorial Day–Labor Day. Parking in summer is $7.

Schenectady

The third city in the Albany-Troy-Schenectady triumvirate, poor Schenectady is not in the best of health. Since the late 1930s, its population has shrunk from about 96,000 to 65,000. One of the town's primary employers, the American Locomotive Company, went out of business in 1968; another, the General Electric Company, has shrunk from a high of 43,000 employees to a mere 8,000. The "City that Lights and Hauls the World" lights and hauls no more, and although a new urban development program was begun in 2000, it will be some time before its effects are felt.

Today Schenectady is best visited for its history. The oldest European settlement in the Mohawk Valley, the city boasts one of the largest and best collections of 18th-century buildings in New York—the historic Stockade. The visitor walking along this district's quiet, crooked streets, heavy with trees, will be transported back to a gentler age. Schenectady was also the site of one of the nation's first free African American communities and the country's first planned college campus.

Orientation

Schenectady spreads out like a fan from a bend in the Mohawk River. Major arteries are Nott, Union, and State (Route 5) Streets. I-890 runs along the west side of the city.

Information and Tours

The **Schenectady County Chamber of Commerce,** 306 State St., Schenectady, NY 12305, 518/372-5656, www.schenectadychamber.org, is open Mon.–Fri. 8 A.M.–4:30 P.M. Secure maps and brochures at the Schenectady Museum and the Schenectady County Historical Society Museum.

SIGHTS

Schenectady Museum and Planetarium

Like Albany and Troy, Schenectady is one of New York State's Heritage Areas—loosely designated historic parks linked by a common theme. The theme in Schenectady, as in Troy, is labor and industry.

Museum exhibits focus on early settlement, General Electric, and the American Locomotive Company. In 1935 General Electric produced more than one-half the world's electricity; at the peak of WW II American Locomotive employed 11,000 workers and produced the first M-7 "tank killer" in 19 days. The museum is also known for its science exhibits and 30-foot-high planetarium, and it holds a large costume collection.

The museum, 15 Nott Terrace Heights, off Nott Terrace, 518/382-7890, www.schenectady-museum.org, is open Tues.–Fri. 10 A.M.–4:30 P.M., Sat.–Sun. noon–5 P.M. Admission is adults $5, seniors $5, children 4–12 $3. Planetarium shows are held Sat.–Sun. only, and cost $1.50.

The Stockade

Along the banks of the Mohawk River, in the triangle formed by State and North College Streets, lies the Stockade. Settled in 1661 by Dutch merchants and fur traders, the outpost flourished until 1690, when a party of French-Canadians and their Indian allies burnt it to the ground, massacring most of the inhabitants and marching the rest off to Quebec.

Native Mohawks encouraged the Dutch to rebuild, and two years later the Stockade was flourishing once again. During the next two centuries all of Schenectady's most important families settled here, and today the residential district

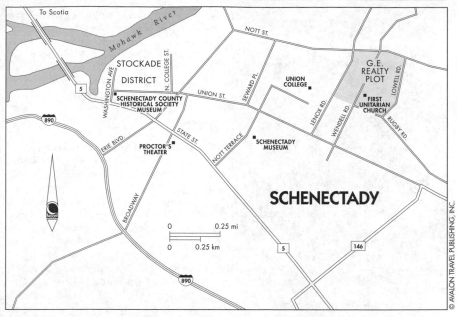

is a wonderful spot, filled with architectural landmarks of all styles and periods. The oldest are churches and graveyards dating back to the 1690s; the newest are homes built in the 1930s.

Plaques pinpointing some of the Stockade's more interesting sites are located throughout the district. Maps are available in the Schenectady County Historical Society Museum, located on the southern edge of the Stockade. For more information, visit the website: www.historicstockade.com.

Schenectady County Historical Society Museum

On display in this friendly, three-story museum is everything from antique dolls and guns to period costumes and furniture. Highlights include an elaborate dollhouse that once belonged to the family of Governor Yates, and the notebooks and letters of GE's electrical genius, Dr. Charles Steinmetz.

The museum, 32 Washington Ave., 518/374-0263, www.schist.org, is open Mon.–Fri. 1–5 P.M., and Saturday 9 A.M.–noon; closed some summer Saturdays. Admission is adults $2, children under 12 $1.

Proctor's Theater

Built in 1925, Proctor's may seem run-down on the outside, but inside, it's an architectural gem. A vaudeville palace on the National Register of Historic Places, it features an ornate auditorium complete with 2,700 seats and a 1931 Golub Mighty Wurlitzer Organ.

You can arrange free tours of the theater, 432 State St. near Broadway, by calling 518/382-3884 or 518/382-1083, www.proctors.org. Next door to the theater is the Proctor's Gift Centre, selling theater memorabilia.

Union College

The first planned college campus in America, Union College was designed in 1814 by classical landscape architect Joseph Jacques Ramee. Filled with broad lawns and giant elms, Union admitted only men until 1970.

At the center of the campus is the high-Gothic **Nott Memorial,** the only 16-sided building in the Northern Hemisphere. Nearby are **Jackson's Gardens,** beautifully landscaped formal gardens first planted in the early 1800s by mathematics professor Isaac Jackson.

The 1925 Proctor's Theater was once a vaudeville venue.

Union College, 518/388-6000, www.union.edu, is located between Lenox Rd., Seward Pl., Union Ave., and Nott and Union Streets. Parking is available in the lots at Nott Street and Seward Place.

GE Realty Plot

In the northeastern quadrant of the city bordered by Lowell, Lenox, and Rugby Roads and Nott Street, lies the GE Realty Plot, developed in 1899 as an exclusive residential enclave for top GE execs. The posh neighborhood is notable for its imposing upper-class homes laid out along wide, tree-lined streets. Structures es-

pecially worth seeing are the First Unitarian Society, 1221 Wendell Ave., designed by Edward Durrell Stone in 1962; and the Dr. Ernest Alexanderson House, 1132 Adams Street. Dr. Alexanderson was a prolific inventor, and the first home reception of a television program occurred in his house in 1927.

FOOD

In the Stockade find **Arthur's Food Market,** 35 N. Ferry St., 518/372-4141, selling sandwiches, desserts, and pizza. Located on the site of the 17th-century Old Public Market, Arthur's features an attractive patio with a handful of picnic tables; average main dish $7. For heaping platters of diner fare, try the modern **Blue Ribbon Diner,** 1801 State St., 518/393-2600, which is especially known for its cheesecake; average main dish $6.

Overlooking the Mohawk across from Schenectady is the **Glen Sanders Mansion,** 1 Glen Ave., Scotia, 518/374-7262. Housed in a historic stone home with original Dutch floors, the restaurant serves traditional American/continental fare for lunch and dinner; average dinner entrée $14.

ENTERTAINMENT

If possible, try to catch a show at the historic **Proctor's Theater,** 432 State St., 518/382-1083, which presents a wide range of events, including Broadway musicals, concerts, operas, dance troupes, and classic movies.

Well-known chamber music ensembles often perform at the **Union College Memorial Chapel,** Union College; call 518/388-6000 and ask for central scheduling.

The Mohawk River Valley

To the west of Albany lies the mighty Mohawk, flanked by river flatlands, aging industrial towns, and rolling hills. The river valley was first settled over 10,000 years ago by the Mohawk; the first European settlers, Dutch and German Palatines, arrived in the 1720s. During the Revolutionary War, the valley's loyalties were deeply divided between its many resident Tories and their allies the Mohawks, and the Colonial rebels.

The most scenic road through the valley is Route 5, supplemented by Route 5 S across the river to the south. Numerous bridges connect the two routes.

AMSTERDAM

Amsterdam (pop. 21,000) lies about 18 miles west of Schenectady on Route 5. By far the largest town between Schenectady and Utica, Amsterdam was once the center of a thriving carpet industry, and still manufactures clothing, toys, and electronic equipment.

In the scruffy downtown you'll find the **Guy Park State Historic Site,** built in 1766 by Sir William Johnson, British Superintendent of Indian Affairs, for his daughter Mary and her husband Guy Johnson. The site now houses the offices of the **Montgomery County Chamber of Commerce,** Guy Park, 366 West Main St., www.montgomerycountyny.com, 518/842-8200 or 800/743-7337, open Mon.–Fri. 8:30 A.M.–4:30 P.M., and some summer weekends.

School-age kids might enjoy a stop at the **Walter Elwood Museum,** housing youth-oriented exhibits on the Iroquois and the largest school museum in the state. The museum, 300 Guy Park Ave., 518/843-5151, is generally open Mon.–Fri. 8:30 A.M.–3:30 P.M., but closes at 1 P.M. on summer Fridays. Admission is free.

The Noteworthy Indian Museum

Housed in a snug historic building, this new museum is a welcome addition to the Mohawk Valley. Displaying over 60,000 artifacts ranging from clay pots and stone tools to beadwork and baskets, the museum tells the story of Native Americans in the valley from 12,000 years ago to the present. Poetry and paintings by contemporary artists are also featured; most of the museum's artifacts were collected by one man, Tom Constantino. The museum, Prospect and Church Sts., 518/843-4761, is open July–Aug., Tues.–Fri. 11 A.M.–5 P.M., Saturday 11 A.M.–4 P.M., and by appointment. Donations are welcomed.

FORT HUNTER

A few miles beyond Amsterdam on the southern shores of the Mohawk is the **Schoharie Crossing State Historic Site,** where the Erie Canal once crossed Schoharie Creek. The seven arches of the aqueduct that carried the canal across the creek were an engineering marvel in their day—they still stand, along with other historic canal structures. A small visitor center provides historical background; nearby is a three-mile hiking trail. The site, 129 Schoharie St. (Rte. 5 S), 518/829-7516, is open year-round dawn to dusk; the visitor center is open May–Oct., Wed.–Sat. 10 A.M.–5 P.M., Sunday 1–5 P.M. Admission is free.

AURIESVILLE

A few miles farther west on Route 5 S is an unexpected sight—the **National Shrine of the North American Martyrs,** spread over a shaded, parklike area seemingly located in the middle of nowhere. Welcome Pilgrims reads the sign over the entrance arch.

The National Shrine is dedicated to Father Isaac Joques and seven other Jesuit priests who were killed by the Mohawks in the 1640s. In 1930 the Catholic Church canonized the eight martyrs as the first saints of North America.

Auriesville was also the birthplace of the Blessed Kateri Tekakwitha, born in 1656 to a Christian Algonquin mother and a Mohawk chief. Orphaned at the age of three and baptized at 20, Tekakwitha was the first laywoman in

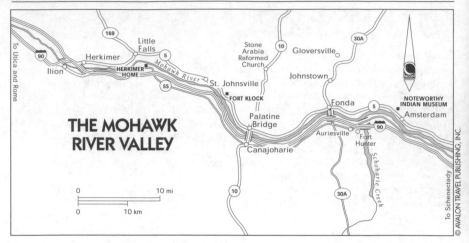

THE MOHAWK
RIVER VALLEY

© AVALON TRAVEL PUBLISHING, INC.

North America honored as "Blessed," and is said to have performed many miracles.

On an ordinary weekday, the National Shrine attracts but a handful of worshippers and curious visitors who stroll past a rustic open-air chapel, the Stations of the Cross, numerous statues, and the circular Coliseum Church. On Sunday, however, busloads of people fill the giant parking lot to attend masses and the priest-led Rosary, Stations, Eucharistic Procession, which winds past the Stations of the Cross beginning at 2:30 P.M.

The shrine, Rte. 5 S, at Noeltner Rd., 518/853-3033, is open daily May–Oct., Mon.–Sat. 10 A.M.–4 P.M., Sunday 9:30 A.M.–5 P.M. Services are Sunday at 9 and 10:30 A.M., noon, and 4 P.M.; weekdays at 11:30 A.M. and 4 P.M.

FONDA

To learn more about Kateri Tekakwitha, take the bridge over the Mohawk to Fonda and the **Kateri Tekakwitha Memorial Shrine.** Tekakwitha was baptized here in 1676, and it was here where she was later persecuted by her tribe for her Christian beliefs.

At the shrine is a snug wooden church with a peaked roof, built in the tradition of the Iroquois longhouse, and the **Mohawk-Caughnawaga Museum,** holding a sizable collection of Iroquois artifacts and modern art. Behind

both buildings is a vast lawn, peppered with the Stations of the Cross, a woodsy grove, and the only completely excavated Native American village in the United States. The excavation sounds more interesting than it actually is; there's not much to see here except a few stones.

The entire site is administered by the Franciscan friars, and a brother dressed in brown robes and sandals is usually on hand to answer any questions you might have. It all seems a bit incongruous and, for the non-Catholic at least, a rather disquieting mix of religion and history.

Both the church and the museum, Rte. 5, 518/853-3646, are open May–Oct., daily 10 A.M.–4 P.M. Admission is free.

JOHNSTOWN

If you detour north of Fonda on Route 30A, you'll come to the small town of Johnstown, founded in 1762 by Sir William Johnson, the British Superintendent of Indian Affairs. Sir Johnson had an unusually close relationship with the Iroquois; he was a good friend of Joseph Brandt, one of the most respected Mohawks of his day, and the husband of Molly Brant, Joseph's older sister, with whom he sired eight children. A contemporary once said of Molly, "She seldom imposed herself into the picture, but no one was in her presence without being aware of her."

Johnson's former home, the **Johnson Hall State Historic Site,** is now a meticulously restored museum, filled with Colonial artifacts and exhibits on the French and Indian War. An inviting park, perfect for picnicking, surrounds the house. It's located on Hall Ave., 518/762-8712, open May–Oct., Wed.–Sat. 10 A.M.–5 P.M., Sunday 1–5 P.M. Admission is adults $3, seniors $2, and children 6–12 $1.

Johnstown also contains the simple 1772 **Fulton County Courthouse,** N. William and E. Main Sts., the oldest courthouse in continuous use in the United States, open daily 9 A.M.–5 P.M. The **Johnson Historical Society Museum,** 17 N. William St., 518/762-7076, houses Johnson artifacts and a memorial related to women's rights leader Elizabeth Cady Stanton, who was born in Johnstown in 1815. Call for hours.

GLOVERSVILLE

Industrial history devotees will want to continue north on Route 30A to Gloversville, a sprawling and largely depressed town named for its number one industry—gloves. Together with Johnstown, Gloversville was once the glove-making capital of the world; a number of small factories here still produce them.

The best place to learn about the glove industry is the **Fulton County Historical Society & Museum,** housed in a creaky mansion on the edge of town. In 1800, it seems, there were over 170 glove manufacturers in the Gloversville area, most employing women who worked at home. After the invention of the sewing machine, nearly every kitchen contained a Singer upon which women worked when not caring for their children or cooking meals.

The museum also features exhibits on the creation of Great Sacandaga Lake, a huge, artificial lake just to the north of town within the confines of Adirondack Park. The museum, 237 Kingsboro Ave., 518/725-2203, is open Apr.–Nov., Tues.–Sat. noon–4 P.M., and July–Aug., Tues.–Sat. 10 A.M.–4 P.M. and Sunday noon–4 P.M. Admission is free.

You'll find a number of glove and leather outlets throughout the Johnstown-Gloverville area; watch for signs.

CANAJOHARIE

Back on Route 5 S on the south side of the Mohawk just west of Fonda is Canajoharie, Iroquois for "The Pot That Washes Itself." The name comes from the large geological pothole in Canajoharie Gorge, just south of the village, where water from a nearby waterfall churns and churns and churns. Both the pothole and the waterfall are now part of **Canajoharie Wintergreen Park and Gorge,** Wintergreen Park Rd., 518/673-5512, open Memorial Day–Labor Day, 9 A.M.–9:30 P.M.

During the early 1900s Canajoharie residents toiled in its prosperous food-packaging industries. Foremost among them was the Beech-Nut plant, packaging everything from bacon and peanut butter to chewing gum and candy. Today, Canajoharie still packages Beech-Nut baby foods and Life Savers candy.

The town's biggest visitor attraction is the **Canajoharie Library and Art Gallery,** billed as the "finest private gallery of any municipality of its size." This claim may be hard to prove but is probably close to true; the gallery houses a wonderful collection of 19th- and early 20th-century American paintings by the likes of Albert Bierstadt, Thomas Eakins, Gilbert Stuart, Winslow Homer, Andrew Wyeth, and Edward Hopper. The gallery, 2 Erie Blvd., 518/673-2314, www.clag.org, is open Mon.–Wed. and Friday 10 A.M.–4:45 P.M., Thursday 10 A.M.–8:30 P.M., Saturday 10 A.M.–1:30 P.M., and some Sundays. Admission is free.

PALATINE BRIDGE AND STONE ARABIA

Across the Mohawk from Canajoharie lies the blink-and-you'll-miss-it village of Palatine Bridge, the earliest European settlement in the Mohawk Valley. The village was established in 1723 by 60 Palatine families, many of whose descendants still live in the area.

Through the heart of Palatine Bridge runs

Route 10, leading to two lovely stone churches in the hamlet of Stone Arabia. The very fine **Stone Arabia Reformed Church,** erected in 1788, is built of light gray limestone, and features a domed wooden cupola up top. The 1792 **Stone Arabia Trinity Lutheran Church** stands on the site of the area's first log cabin. Behind the Reformed Church is a picturesque cemetery containing the remains of many Revolutionary War soldiers.

ST. JOHNSVILLE

West of Palatine Bridge is St. Johnsville, formerly a mill town producing felt shoes and underwear. Find here several handsome stone houses, including **Fort Klock,** a fortified homestead and fur trading post built by the Klock family in 1750. Although restored, the limestone house has never been altered from its original construction. Behind it stand an early 19th-century schoolhouse, blacksmith's shop, Dutch barn, and cheese house, all moved here from nearby. Fort Klock, Rte. 5, 518/568-7779, is open Memorial Day–mid-Oct., Tues.–Sun. 9 A.M.–5 P.M. Admission is adults $1, children under 10–15 50 cents.

LITTLE FALLS

Formerly awash in bicycle, velocipede, and tissue paper factories, this former Erie Canal mill town now features an appealing restored waterfront lined with shops, restaurants, and flowers. Little Falls is also home to **Lock 17,** which at 40 feet is one of highest lift locks in the world. Tankers and pleasure craft still pass through daily.

On Route 169 three miles southeast of Little Falls, across the Mohawk, stands the **Herkimer Home State Historic Site.** Once one of the grandest homes in all of the Mohawk Valley, the red-brick house was built by Gen. Nicholas Herkimer, who led the Colonial militia in the bloody Battle of Oriskany. Today costumed guides conduct guided tours, and you can attend such special events as a Colonial maple-sugaring bee. The house, 315/823-0398, is open May–Oct., Wed.–Sat. 10 A.M.–5 P.M., Sunday 1–5 P.M. Admission is free.

Accommodations and Food

The 1889 **Gansevoort House,** 42 W. Gansevoort St., 315/823-1833, is a cozy B&B equipped with fireplaces, music room, and book shop ($70–75 d). Also in town is a 56-room **Best Western,** 20 Albany St., 315/823-4954 ($75–85 d).

Along the historic waterfront is the **Canal Side Inn,** 395 S. Ann St., 315/823-1170, serving classic French cuisine, including several fish dishes and daily specials (average entrée $17, dinner only).

HERKIMER AND ENVIRONS

The seat of Herkimer County, Herkimer sprawls over a broad flat area at the mouth of West Canada Creek, a major Mohawk tributary. Once an important industrial and shipping center, the town is cut in two by a fat, ugly swatch of railroad tracks.

Along Main Street stand many striking historic buildings, the finest being the red-brick

© CHRISTIANE BIRD

Red-brick 1875 Herkimer County Courthouse was the site of the 1906 Gillette murder trial.

1875 **Herkimer County Courthouse** topped with a black-and-white wooden cupola. The courthouse was the site of the sensational Gillette murder trial of 1906, on which Theodore Dreiser based his famous novel, *An American Tragedy.*

Across the street from the courthouse looms the former Herkimer County Jail, where Gillette once awaited trial. Tours of the jail are offered by the **Herkimer County Historical Society,** which also runs a museum at 400 N. Main St., 315/866-6413. Museum exhibits focus on county history, dollhouses, and miniatures. The museum is open Mon.–Fri. 10 A.M.–4 P.M.; also open Saturday 10 A.M.–3 P.M. in July–Aug.; free admission. Jail tours offered daily, cost is $1 per person.

Herkimer Diamond Mines

Travel seven miles north of Herkimer on Route 28 and you'll come across a parched brown patch of earth where you can hunt for "diamonds." Actually brilliant quartz crystals, these 18-faceted rocks began forming a half-billion years ago when the area lay beneath the Devonian Sea. Water seeped into the pores of the rock beneath the sea's surface, evaporating millions of years later and leaving silica behind.

Visitors to the "mines" are equipped with hammers to break open the rocks, and the "diamonds" are easy to find. Also on-site is an extensive gift shop with a museum upstairs. The mines, Rte. 28, 315/891-7355 or 800/562-0897, www.herkimer-

diamond.com, are open April–Dec., daily 9 A.M.–5 P.M. Admission is adults $7.50, children 5–14 $6.50, under five free.

Remington Firearms Museum

Across the river from Herkimer is **Ilion,** site of the Remington Arms Factory since 1816. The plant was founded by Eliphalet Remington, Jr., who made his first rifle at his father's forge. The weapon proved to be of such high quality that friends and neighbors began placing orders, and soon Eliphalet built his own plant. Today the Remington Arms Factory is still Herkimer County's biggest employer.

Connected to the factory is the Remington Firearms Museum, 14 Hoefler Ave., showcasing both antique and modern firearms, including gold-plated double derringers and breech-loading rifles developed during the Civil War.

For more information on the museum and guided factory tours, call 315/895-3200.

Camping and Accommodations

Across from the Herkimer Diamond Mines is a **KOA** campground, Rte. 28, 315/891-7355 or 800/562-0897, offering campsites and cabins; open April–November. The cabins cost $42–49 per night and must be reserved in advance. If you'd rather stay at a motel, the **Herkimer Motel,** 100 Marginal Rd., 315/866-0490, is a good choice ($60–78 d).

Otsego County

One of the region's most prosperous counties, thanks largely to the many tourist attractions in Cooperstown, Otsego County is mostly back roads, tiny villages, and wooded hills and valleys. Two small lakes—Canadarago and Otsego—sit to the north, while to the south lies the county's only city, Oneonta, population about 14,000.

Visitor Information

The **Otsego County Chamber of Commerce,** 12 Carbon St., Oneonta, NY 13820, 607/432-4500 or 800/843-3394, www.cooperstown-otsego.com, is open Mon.–Fri. 9 A.M.–5 P.M. From June

through September the chamber operates **tourist information booths** on Rte. 20 in Cherry Valley and Richfield Springs, at the Unadillo Exit (Exit 11) off I-88, and on Rte. 7 in Colliersville.

COOPERSTOWN

Home to the National Baseball Hall of Fame and Museum, Cooperstown likes to think of itself as the most famous small town in America. It centers around a friendly, old-fashioned Main Street, and boasts a population of just 2,300. To the north are the still waters of Otsego Lake; to

HALLS OF FAME AND GLORY

From baseball players to boxers, dancers to feminists, jockeys to fly-fisherfolk, twirlers to fiddlers—it seems like everywhere you go in New York State, there's a Hall of Fame honoring the best of class, both famous and obscure. At the top of the list are such known institutions as the National Baseball Hall of Fame and Museum in Cooperstown, the National Soccer Hall of Fame in Oneonta, the National Women's Hall of Fame in Seneca Falls, and the National Museum of Racing and Hall of Fame in Saratoga Springs, not to mention the Catskill Fly Fishing Museum and Hall of Fame in Livingston Manor, the National Museum of Dance and Hall of Fame in Saratoga Springs, and the International Boxing Hall of Fame in Canastota.

But the list doesn't end there. Lovers of the obscure might want to check out the **Twirlers Hall of Fame** (baton twirlers, that is) located inside the Children's Museum in Utica (311 Main St., 315/724-6129), or the **American Maple Museum and Hall of Fame** in Croghan (Main St., 315/346-1107). The **North American Fiddlers Hall of Fame and Museum,** Comins Rd., Osceola, 315/599-7009, was created in 1976 by the New York State Old Tyme Fiddlers Association to honor "every fiddler who has ever made hearts light and happy with the fiddle's lilting music."

Said to be the oldest Hall of Fame in the country is the **Hall of Fame for Great Americans** at the Bronx Community College of the City of New York, University Ave. at W. 181st St., Bronx, 718/289-5161. Designed by Stanford White, the hall is actually a sweeping, semi-circular, indoor-outdoor colonnade, lined with bronze busts of 98 famous men and (a few) women. Perched above the Harlem and Hudson Rivers, the Neo-classical complex also offers stunning views.

According to state's tourism division, New York currently boasts 18 halls of fame, with three more on the way. For a complete list, call 800/CALL-NYS.

the south, east, and west, the rolling, forested hills of Leatherstocking Country.

Cooperstown was first settled in 1790 by William Cooper, father of James Fenimore, America's first internationally recognized author. The fiercely ambitious Cooper Sr. obtained the land through unscrupulous means during the confusion following the Revolutionary War, then immediately set about establishing himself as a grand gentleman. Within a decade he'd built the largest private home west of Albany, won widespread respect for his skill as a land developer, and established Cooperstown as the Otsego County seat. Later he became a county judge and a representative to the U.S. Congress.

James Fenimore Cooper wrote about Cooperstown in his novel *The Pioneers,* and set many of his Natty Bumppo tales on the shores of "The Glimmerglass"—Otsego Lake. After travels at sea and abroad, he settled down in his hometown and took over where his father had left off, playing lord of the manor. Cooper was buried in the town's Christ Church Cemetery in 1851.

In the late 1800s Cooperstown became home to the Clark family, who'd made a fortune in Singer Sewing Machines. Edward Clark, the family patriarch, built a miniature castle called Kingfisher Tower on Otsego Lake in 1876. In the late 1930s and '40s one of his descendants, Stephen C. Clark, established the town's three famous museums—the National Baseball Hall of Fame, the Farmers' Museum, and the Fenimore House Museum.

On a summer's day Cooperstown's population swells by the thousands. Tourists wearing baseball caps and T-shirts are everywhere, and parking can be a major problem. The best approach then is to park in one of the park-and-ride lots on Routes 80 and 28 and ride the free trolley into town. During the off-season, street parking is generally available.

Information

The **Cooperstown Chamber of Commerce,** 31 Chestnut St., off Main St., Cooperstown, NY 13326, 607/547-9983, www.cooperstownchamber.com, is open July–Aug., daily 9 A.M.–6 P.M.;

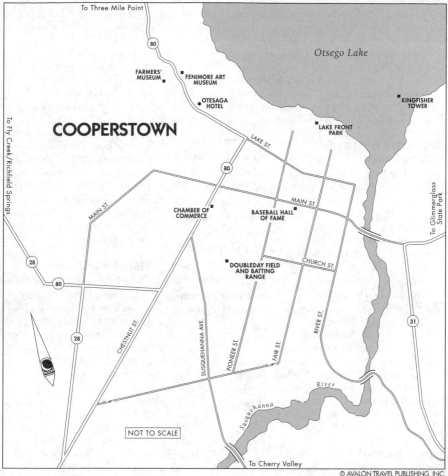

To Three Mile Point

Otsego Lake

COOPERSTOWN

To Fly Creek/Richfield Springs

FARMERS' MUSEUM

FENIMORE ART MUSEUM

OTESAGA HOTEL

KINGFISHER TOWER

LAKE FRONT PARK

LAKE ST.

MAIN ST.

CHAMBER OF COMMERCE

BASEBALL HALL OF FAME

DOUBLEDAY FIELD AND BATTING RANGE

CHURCH ST.

CHESTNUT ST.

SUSQUEHANNA AVE.

PIONEER ST.

FAIR ST.

RIVER ST.

To Glimmerglass State Park

River

Susquehann

NOT TO SCALE

To Cherry Valley

© AVALON TRAVEL PUBLISHING, INC.

June and Sept.–Oct., daily 10 A.M.–5 P.M.; call for off-season hours. A **visitor information kiosk** is located on Main Street near the flagpole. A helpful website is www.discovercooperstown.net.

National Baseball Hall of Fame and Museum

Established in 1939, this homage to America's favorite pastime is packed to the bursting point with displays covering every aspect of the sport, from famous ballparks and women's baseball to the World Series and the Negro League. Here you'll find lots of informative history, along with such memorabilia as Jackie Robinson's warm-up jacket, Hank Aaron's locker, the glove of Willie Mays, Yogi Berra's catcher's mitt, and that rarest of all baseball cards, the Honus Wagner 1909 T-206 tobacco card, recalled at the request of the nonsmoking ballplayer.

Occupying three floors and 50,000 square feet, the museum is divided into many specific exhibits—All-Star Games, Longest Games, Baseball Stamps, Youth Leagues. Study the floor plan before starting out. Also on-site are two gift shops and a theater screening short films. The average fan should allow for a half-day visit.

The museum, 25 Main St., 607/547-7200, www.baseballhalloffame.org, is open Memorial Day–Labor Day, daily 9 A.M.–9 P.M., Nov.–April, daily 9 A.M.–5 P.M. Admission is adults $9.50, seniors $8, children 6–14 $4. Combination tickets with the Farmer's Museum and Fenimore House Museum (see below) are also available.

Doubleday Field and Batting Range

Down Main Street from the Hall of Fame lies the oldest baseball diamond in the world, the site of the first official game in 1839. Originally built for 8,000 spectators and later expanded to accommodate 10,000, the field is now available for rent and is very popular among local groups.

Adjoining Doubleday Field is Doubleday Batting Range, where you can test your skills against a Tru-Pitch pitching machine, the same machine used by the major leagues. The machines throw 17 different kinds of pitches at varying speeds, and feature tennis balls for children and hard balls for older players.

Doubleday Field is open daily year-round; Doubleday Range, 607/547-5168, is open May–Oct., daily 10 A.M.–9 P.M.

Lake Front Park

Two blocks north of the Baseball Hall of Fame lies Otsego Lake, created during the last great Ice Age. Like many glacial lakes, Otsego is cool and deep, with steep banks and overhanging trees. Fed by springs, it is the source of the Susquehanna River, which flows south from here to Chesapeake Bay and the Atlantic Ocean.

Along the edge of the lake is Lake Front Park, a pleasant spot frequented by families. To one side is a statue called *Indian Hunter;* to the other, **Council Rock.** Once a meeting place for various Indian tribes, the rock was employed by Cooper in *The Deerslayer* as a rendezvous point for Deerslayer and his friend Chingachgook. "The rock

At the National Baseball Hall of Fame and Museum, you'll find lots of informative history and that rarest of all baseball cards, the Honus Wagner 1909 T-206 tobacco card, recalled at the request of the non-smoking ballplayer.

was not large," wrote Cooper, "being merely some five or six feet high, only half of which elevation rose above the lake. The incessant washing of the water for centuries had so rounded its summit, that it resembled a large beehive in shape. . . ." Today, a flight of stone steps leads down to a terrace overlooking the rock. Nearby are the headwaters of the Susquehanna River—here but a small stream.

From the park you can see the 65-foot-high **Kingfisher Tower** (completed 1907), designed in the style of a European castle by architect Henry Hardenbergh, who also designed the Plaza Hotel in New York City. Off-limits to the public, the castle can only be viewed from afar.

Elsewhere Downtown

The galleries of the **Cooperstown Art Association** lie diagonally across from the Baseball Hall of Fame. Founded in 1928, the association showcases a variety of work ranging from contemporary to traditional. The galleries, 22 Main St., 607/547-9777, are open Mon.–Sat. 11 A.M.–4 P.M., Sunday 1–4 P.M. Admission is free.

Flanking **Pioneer Street,** which intersects Main Street by the flagpole, are some of the oldest buildings in the village. Foremost among them is the dark, low-ceilinged **Smithy-Pioneer Gallery,** 55 Pioneer St., 607/547-8671, part of which was built about 1786 by William Cooper. Originally a storehouse, the building was later converted into a blacksmith's shop and now contains both historic artifacts and an art gallery. Hours are June–Sept., Tues.–Sat. 10 A.M.–5 P.M., Sunday noon–5 P.M. Admission is free.

Cooper's Town

Although the old Cooper family mansion was torn down long ago, Cooperstown still contains about 20 buildings that date back to James Fenimore's time. Most closely associated with Cooper is **Christ Church** on Fair Street, consecrated in 1810 on land donated by his father. In Cooper's fiction the church appears as "New St. Paul's"; the Cooper family plot is located in the cemetery behind the church.

For more Cooper-related sites, pick up a copy of *Cooper's Otsego County* by Hugh Cooke Mac-Dougall (New York State Historical Society). Though excessive in its praise of Cooper, who was hardly a noted stylist (Mark Twain once quipped that Cooper committed 114 literary offenses out of a possible 115), the book satisfactorily pinpoints places relating to Cooper's life and fiction.

Farmers' Museum

Just outside downtown Cooperstown is the second of its famous museums, composed of a dozen meticulously restored buildings dating back to before the Civil War. Run by the New York State Historical Association, this is not just another living history museum, but rather, a sort of granddaddy of them all; founded in 1943, it was the first open-air museum in New York State and one of the first in the country.

The museum is spread along one looping street, lined with a general store, blacksmith's shop, printing office, doctor's office, and druggist's shop. In the Main Barn near the entrance hang imaginative exhibits on early rural life; everywhere roam skillful guides in period dress, some demonstrating such arts as broom-making and open-hearth cooking. Sheep graze in the village common, fat cows wander a nearby hill.

One of the museum's odder exhibits is the 2,900-pound Cardiff Giant. Supposedly unearthed in nearby Cardiff in 1869 by the hitherto unassuming William Newell, the sleeping stone man with the mysterious smile soon drew visitors from all over the country. One Harvard professor claimed the Giant dated back to Phoenician times; Oliver Wendell Holmes drilled a hole behind his left ear to see if the brain was petrified. Only after Newell had raked in some tens of thousands of dollars was the statue proven to be a hoax.

The museum, Lake Rd. (Rte. 80), 607/547-1400, www.farmersmuseum.org, is open June–Sept., daily 10 A.M.–5 P.M.; Apr.–May and Oct.–Nov., Tues.–Sun. 10 A.M.–4 P.M. Admission is

adults $9, seniors $8, children 7–12 $4. Visit the excellent gift shop too.

Combination tickets with the Baseball Hall of Fame and Fenimore House Museum are also available.

Fenimore House Museum

Directly across the street from the Farmers' Museum is the third of Cooperstown's museum triumvirate. Also run by the New York State Historical Association, the Fenimore House holds the state's premier collection of folk art, fine art, and Native American art. Highlights include Thomas Cole's *Last of the Mohicans*, Gilbert Stuart's *Joseph Brandt*, a version of Edward Hicks's *Peaceable Kingdom*, and an eclectic collection of weathervanes, trade signs, cigar store Indians, and decoys.

New to the museum is a spacious $10-million wing built in 1995 to house the Eugene and Clare Thaw Collection of American Indian Art. Perhaps the most important privately owned collection of its kind, the collection includes about 700 works spanning 2,500 years of native North American culture. Among the many stunning items on display are a flowing Blackfoot headdress, a Lakota painted horsehide, and a brilliant blue Heiltsuk moon mask. Out back is an Iroquois hunting and fishing camp, where costumed interpreters demonstrate traditional skills and crafts.

The museum, Lake Rd. (Rte. 80), 607/547-1400, www.fenimorehousemuseum, is open June–Sept., daily 10 A.M.–5 P.M.; Apr.–May and Oct.–Nov., Tues.–Sun. 10 A.M.–4 P.M. Admission is adults $9, seniors $8, children 7–12 $4. Also onsite is the first-rate Fenimore Book Store. Combination tickets with the National Baseball Hall of Fame and Farmer's Museum are also available.

Glimmerglass State Park

At the northern end of Otsego Lake shimmers this peaceful oasis of green perched on rolling hills. Features include a swimming beach, plenty of hiking and biking trails, a playground, and a 39-site campground. The park, 607/547-8662, East Lake Rd., is accessible off County Road 31; for campground reservations, call 800/456-CAMP. A basic site costs $13.

In the heart of the park stands a grand,

neoclassical mansion known as **Hyde Hall.** Once home to the Clarke family, the building had fallen into serious disrepair but is now being restored. Tours, 607/547-5098, www.hydehall.org, are offered Memorial Day–Columbus Day, daily 10 A.M.–5 P.M.; cost is adults $7, seniors $6, and children 5–12 $4.

Breweries

Two breweries offering guided tours are in the Cooperstown area. Located on a farmstead is **Brewery Ommegang,** 656 County Road 33, 607/547-8184, the only brewery in the United States that brews all Belgian-style beers. Tours are offered daily noon–5 P.M., and cost adults $4, children free. **Cooperstown Brewing Company,** River St., in nearby Milford, 607/286-9330, creates products such as Nine Man Ale, Old Slugger, and Strike-Out Stout. Tours take place Mon.–Sat. 10 A.M.–6 P.M., Sunday noon–5 P.M.; cost is $2.50 adult.

Fly Creek

Two miles northwest of Cooperstown on Route 28/80 is tiny Fly Creek, home to the **Cooperstown Bat Company,** 518/547-2415. Long bats, short bats, old bats, new bats—they're all here at this factory-shop, where you can watch a bat being turned (July–Aug. only), take a look at collector bats, or buy a bat with your name on it.

Fly Creek also contains the **Fly Creek Cider Mill,** off Route 28/80, where apples are pressed in an 1856 wooden, water-powered cider mill. All original equipment is used. The mill, 607/547-9692, operates Memorial Day–Dec., daily 9 A.M.–6 P.M.

Shopping

Numerous shops selling everything from baseball memorabilia to clothing occupy Cooperstown and the surrounding area. The chamber of commerce publishes several helpful brochures.

Among the region's more unusual stores is **Wood Bull Antiques,** Rte. 28, 607/286-9021, a gigantic, four-story barn eight miles south of Cooperstown. According to the owners, the merchandise has been gathered from over 20 years of attic rummaging and close to 3,000 auctions.

Turn south from Route 28/80 at the one light in Fly Creek and bear right onto Christian Hill Road to reach the unusual **Waterwheel Woodworks,** 607/293-7703. Here, cabinetmakers Jim and Eileen McCormack produce handmade furniture one piece at a time using old-fashioned methods of wood joinery.

Sports and Recreation

Baseball: To catch a live game, baseball fans might want to head south on Route 28 to Oneonta to watch the Class A **Oneonta Tigers** (see below).

Swimming: You'll find good public beaches on Otsego Lake at **Glimmerglass State Park,** off County Road 31; **Three Mile Point,** off Route 80; and **Fairy Springs,** off County Road 31.

Camping and Motels

In addition to the campground at Glimmerglass State Park, camping options include the **Cooperstown Beaver Valley Campground,** Rte. 28 S, 607/293-7324, boasting three beaver ponds and a petting zoo (basic sites $28); and the **Cooperstown Shadow Brook Campground,** East Lake Rd., 607/264-8431 (basic sites $26–35). Both feature about 100 sites.

Cooperstown has a number of good, clean motels to choose from. In the heart of the village, overlooking Otsego Lake, is the 45-room **Lake Front Motel,** 10 Fair St., 607/547-9511, www.lakefrontmotelandrestaurant.com ($105–175 d in summer, $65–95 d in winter). Also on the lake is the 12-room **Hickory Grove Motel Inn,** Rte. 80, 607/547-9874 ($120 d in summer, $60–78 d off season), and the considerably larger **Lake 'N Pines Motel,** 7102 Rte. 80, 607/547-2790, offering everything from 35 standard rooms to five cottages, along with a swimming pool ($120–159 d in summer). Downtown, you'll find the 10-room **Baseball Town Motel,** 61 Main St., 607/547-2161 ($99 d in summer, $79 d off season). In nearby Fly Creek, try the **Major League Motor Inn,** Rte. 28/80, 607/547-2266 ($85 d in summer, $65 d off season).

Hotels and Inns

The 1902 **Otesaga Hotel and Restaurant,** 60 Lake St., 607/547-9931 or 800/348-6222, www

.otesaga.com, is a delicious grande dame of a hotel that's affiliated with Historic Hotels of America. Out front tower stately white columns; out back stretches a long, long porch with rocking chairs overlooking the lake. Facilities include a romantic ballroom with a 20-foot-high coffered ceiling, pool, tennis courts, and the first-rate Leatherstocking Golf Course. All 135 rooms are outfitted with period furnishings ($340 d with full breakfast and dinner).

The Otesaga also operates the luxurious **Coopers Inn,** Main and Chestnut Sts., built circa 1820. Reigning over its own little park in the heart of the downtown, the inn offers 20 handsomely decorated rooms and the use of all Otesaga facilities ($195 d with continental breakfast).

Meanwhile, the **Inn at Cooperstown,** 16 Chestnut St., 607/547-5756, www.innatcooperstown.com, is all that an inn should be—big, creaky, lined with a wide porch, and shaded with magnificent trees. All 17 guest rooms feature private baths and queen or double beds ($135–154 d, with breakfast). Also a good choice is the 1802 **Tunnicliff Inn,** 34-36 Pioneer St., 607/547-9611, offering 17 guest rooms, a restaurant, and a historic bar that's a favorite with the locals (see below) ($130–155 d in summer, $50–70 d in winter).

Bed-and-Breakfasts

The centrally located **Chestnut Street Guest House,** 79 Chestnut St., 607/547-5624, www.chestnut79.com, is a comfortable spot offering four attractive rooms, one completely outfitted in baseball memorabilia ($95–125 d). Just down the street is the **Landmark Inn,** 64 Chestnut St., 607/547-7225, www.landmark-bandb.com, an 1856 mansion with nine guest rooms and an elegant dining room ($135 d).

Food

Try the casual **Short Stop,** 65 Main St., 607/547-9609, for a simple breakfast, lunch, or early dinner. The **Doubleday Cafe,** 93 Main St., 607/547-5468, offers a nice variety of sandwiches and salads. Both are inexpensive, with most dishes under $10.

Reasonably priced lunches, and considerably more expensive dinners, are offered by the classy **Hawkeye Bar & Grill,** in the Otesaga Hotel, 60 Lake St., 607/547-9931. The fare is innovative American, and in warm weather, lakeside patio seating is available; average lunch entrée $10, average dinner entrée $20.

A variety of international dishes are served at the lovely lakeside **Blue Mingo Grill,** Sam Smith's Boatyard, Rte. 80, 607/547-7496. Lunch dishes include salads, grilled fish, and pizzas, while the dinner menu changes weekly and can include anything from Thai dishes to fresh lobster; average dinner entrée $19.

The **Hoffman Lane Bistro,** 2 Hoffman Ln., 607/547-7055, is a local favorite, serving everything from pastas and salads to grilled pork chops, tuna steaks, and chicken pot pies; average entrée $15.

Entertainment

An acclaimed opera festival takes place every July–Aug. at the **Glimmerglass Opera,** Rte. 80, a partially open-air theater by Otsego Lake. The box office is downtown at 18 Chestnut St., 607/547-2255, www.cooperstown.net/glimmerglass. Chamber music concerts, lectures, and plays take place regularly in **Hyde Hall,** 607/547-5098.

The basement **Taproom at the Tunnicliff Inn,** 34-36 Pioneer St., 607/547-9860, is a favorite local late-night hangout. The tables are carved with the initials of Cooperstown pilgrims, and beers on tap start at just $1.50. Also a local hang is the historic **Bold Dragoon,** 49 Pioneer St., 607/547-9800, which attracts a more raucous crowd.

For an elegant evening out, step into the Templeton Lounge of the **Otesaga,** 60 Lake St., 607/547-9931. Live music and dancing are offered nightly except Sunday, starting at 9 P.M.

CHERRY VALLEY

About 12 miles north of Cooperstown is the village of Cherry Valley, named for the wild cherries thriving in the surrounding countryside. Though now an unusually peaceful spot, Cherry Valley has endured a turbulent history.

During the Revolutionary War, Cherry Valley

was the site of a massacre perpetrated by 500 Tories and Mohawks under the command of Capt. Walter Butler and Chief Joseph Brandt. Thirty-two residents were killed and 70 taken prisoner, and the village burned to the ground.

After the war all but one of the prisoners returned to the valley to rebuild the town, soon the largest settlement southwest of the Mohawk. In 1800, the Great Western Turnpike—now Route 20—arrived, and by 1815 there were 15 taverns in the village and 62 more in the 52 miles between it and Albany. Sometimes as many as 40 wagons heading west spent the night in the village square, and Cherry Valley boasted its own marble works, iron foundries, tanneries, and distilleries.

Then came the Erie Canal in 1825, followed by the New York Central Railroad. Both diverted traffic away from the town, and by the early 1900s Cherry Valley was again a sleepy little village.

In the 1960s and '70s Cherry Valley was known for its thriving arts community. Allen Ginsberg once occupied a farm on the outskirts of town, and even today, in the fond words of one resident, the village attracts "the weirdos of the county."

Cherry Valley Museum

Much of the village's history is on view at the creaky, two-story Cherry Valley Museum, where artifacts range from inkwells and children's clothes to Civil War uniforms and an 1885 fire engine. A video tells the story of the massacre, and free walking/driving tour brochures to the village are available. The museum, 49 Main St., 607/264-3303, www.cherryvalleymuseum.org, is open May–Oct., daily 10 A.M.–5 P.M. Admission is adults $3, seniors $2.50, under 12 free.

Food

The elegant, chef-owned **Rose & Kettle,** 4 Lancaster St., 607/264-3078, serves contemporary European-American fare; average entrée $17. The tiny restaurant is open for dinner only Tues.–Sat.; closed in winter. A single rose adorns each table.

RICHFIELD SPRINGS

Travel a few miles west of Cherry Valley on Route 20 and you'll come to Richfield Springs, for-

merly known for its sulfur springs and grand old hotels. Evidence of these bygone days can still be seen in the bright white gazebo in the center of town and in the aging Victorian buildings along the main streets. The once-famous sulfur waters still flow from the fountain in **Spring Park** on Main Street, while to the south lies **Canadarago Lake,** a prime spot for walleye and tiger muskie. Off Route 28 on the west side of the lake is **Baker's Beach,** a public swimming area equipped with a lifeguard and changing areas; open June–Labor Day 11 A.M.–7 P.M.

Petrified Creatures Museum of Natural History

In the quirky Petrified Creatures Museum you'll see life-size dinosaurs painted purple, red, and green; listen to narrations about prehistoric life; and, best of all, dig for fossils. Like much of central New York State, the museum is located on land once covered by the Devonian Sea and sits on the edge of a "fossil pit." When the sea retreated, small creatures were left behind in the pits' primordial ooze; that ooze turned to limestone and the creatures to fossils. Forty-six different species have been found here, and fossils are so plentiful visitors are guaranteed to find at least one.

Established in 1934, the Petrified Creatures Museum, Rte. 20, 315/858-2868, is the oldest museum in central New York State. Hours are May 15–Sept. 15, daily 10 A.M.–6 P.M. Admission is adults $8, children 6–11 $4. Hammers and chisels for fossil hunting are provided; on sale in the jumbled adjoining gift shop find everything from shark teeth to butterfly-hatching kits.

Holy Trinity Russian Orthodox Monastery

About six miles north of Richfield Springs off Route 167 is a most surprising sight—the Holy Trinity Russian Orthodox Monastery. Established here shortly after the 1917 Russian Revolution, this is the largest Eastern Orthodox monastery on the continent.

Approaching from the south, you'll pass through a quiet region of farms and woodlands before suddenly spotting the magnificent group-

© CHRISTIANE BIRD

Jordanville's Holy Trinity Russian Orthodox Monastery is the largest Eastern Orthodox monastery in North America.

ing of golden domes and spires on your left. Inside the main chapel is a dizzying collection of icons, shimmering in dim light, while out back are gardens and a graveyard. Monks in long brown robes stroll the grounds.

Visitors are welcome at the monastery on Robinson Rd., Jordanville, 315/858-0940, but if you'd like to see the chapel's interior, make reservations in advance.

ONEONTA

Snuggled into hills at the southernmost end of Otsego County is the small city of Oneonta. Iroquois for Stony Place, Oneonta is home to Hartwick College, a branch of the State University of New York, and several interesting museums.

Among the latter is the **National Soccer Hall of Fame,** which traces the history of soccer in the United States from its 1860 beginnings to the

present. Housed in a large complex on a 61-acre campus, the hall begins with a Hall of Fame atrium and then goes on to two floors of exhibits. Historic photos, trophies, uniforms, and other memorabilia are on display, while out back are four well-used soccer fields. The museum, 18 Stadium Circle, off Brown St., off Rte. 205 (Exit 13 from I-88), 607/432-3351, www.soccerhall.org, is open June–Labor Day, daily 9 A.M.–7 P.M.; call for winter hours. Admission is adults $8, seniors $5.50, children under 12 $6.50.

Local history buffs and those interested in Native American culture will want to step into the recently renovated **Yager Museum at Hartwick College,** housing an excellent collection of over 20,000 artifacts. The museum, off Clinton St. near Anderson Hall, 607/431-4480, is open Wed.–Fri. 11 A.M.–4:30 P.M., Saturday noon–4:30 P.M., Sunday 1–4:30 P.M. Admission is free.

Sports and Recreation
Baseball: The Class A **Oneonta Tigers,** a farm team for Detroit, play ball at the old-time Damaschke Field, Neawha Park, 607/432-6326, June–Labor Day. The games draw large crowds, primarily tourists visiting Cooperstown.

Recreation: About seven miles north of the city is bucolic **Gilbert Lake State Park,** County Road 12 off Rte. 205, Laurens, 607/432-2114, which offers swimming, hiking, boating, camping, and a playground. Parking in summer is $7.

Camping, Accommodations, and Food
To reserve a campsite or cabin at the **Gilbert Lake State Park,** off Rte. 205, Laurens, call 800/456-CAMP; a basic site costs $13–15. A good motel in the area is the secluded **Redwood Motel,** Rte. 7, 607/432-1291 ($50–70 d).

One of Oneonta's more unusual hostelries is **Cathedral Farms Inn and Country Restaurant,** Rte. 205 (Exit 13 off I-88), 607/432-7483 or 800/327-6790, www.cathedralinn.com. Located on a former country estate, complete with peacocks and miniature horses, the inn offers 21 guest rooms and a first-rate restaurant specializing in fresh seafood, hand-cut beef, and homemade baked goods (average entrée $15, dinner only). The guest rooms are housed in the former servant's quarters; $135 d. Also affiliated with Cathedral Farms is **Sabatini's Little Italy,** Rte. 28, Southside, 607/432-3000, which serves classic Italian cuisine; average entrée $17.

Schoharie County

To the east of Cooperstown and southwest of Albany sits Schoharie County, a quiet haven of agricultural land centered around the fertile Schoharie Valley. During the Revolutionary period, the valley was a breadbasket for the colonies, producing much of its wheat; at the turn of the century, the valley's hop fields were among the richest in the world. Today the Schoharie Valley is known for its enormous truck farms producing wheat and corn, fruit and vegetables.

The **Schoharie County Chamber of Commerce,** P.O. Box 400, Schoharie, NY 12157, 518/295-7033 or 800/418-4748, www.schohariechamber.com.

SHARON SPRINGS

Heading into Schoharie County on Route 20 from Cherry Valley, you'll come to Sharon Springs, another village once known for its sulfur springs and grand old hotels. Most of the latter are located along Route 10, a delicious array of rambling old Victorians that until recently were in various states of abandonment. Now, however, Sharon Springs is being rediscovered—partly by its own residents, who have opened new shops and other establishments along Main Street.

At the heart of Sharon Springs is the 1847 **American Hotel,** which reopened for business in 2000 after a long hiatus, and the 1841 **Roseboro Hotel,** a grande dame of a 130-room establishment whose restaurant has reopened (see Accommodations and Food below). Also watch out for the striking white-and-turquoise **Imperial Baths,** 248 Main St., 518/284-2285 or 800/448-4314, www.adlerhotelspa.com, housed in the 1927 Adler Spa Hotel, a National Historic Landmark. Recently restored, the sulfur and mineral baths are open June–Labor Day, Sun.–Fri. 8 A.M.–4 P.M. Massages are also available.

Across the street from the Imperial Baths is the **Sharon Historical Museum and Schoolhouse,** Main St. (Rte. 10), 518/284-2350 or 518/284-2839, filled with historic photos, tintypes, and documents dating back to the 1850s. As the photos show, the surviving baths are nothing compared to the "water temples" that once filled the town. The museum, partially housed in an 1863 one-room schoolhouse, is open July–Aug. daily 1–4 P.M., June and September by appointment. Admission is free.

Food and Accommodations
The **American Hotel,** Main St., 518/284-2105, www.americanhotelny.com, offers nine comfortable guestrooms ($135 d, includes full breakfast) and a popular 65-seat restaurant. On the menu, which changes daily, is American fare ranging from filet mignon to grilled fish; average entrée $20.

The Roseboro, Main St., 518/284-2020, www.roseboro.com, is now open for dinner Wed.–Sun. and brunch on the weekends. On the menu is varied American fare; dinner entrées range $7–18.

Clausen Farms B&B Inn, Rte. 20, 518/284-2527, www.reu.com\clausen, a grand old Victorian homestead, offers 11 guest rooms, 80 acres laced with trails, a swimming pool, a restored bowling lane, 12 resident llamas, and—best of all—90-mile views of the Mohawk Valley ($110 d).

The **Brimstonia Cottage,** Main St., 518/284-2839, offers two cozy guest rooms complete with kitchenettes inside and splendid gardens for strolling outside ($110 d). Also in the area is the simple but comfortable **Sharon Springs Motel,** Rte. 20, 518/284-2114 ($79–95 d).

HOWE CAVERNS

By far the oldest—and most commercialized—tourist attraction in central New York is Howe Caverns, an extensive labyrinth of cathedral-like

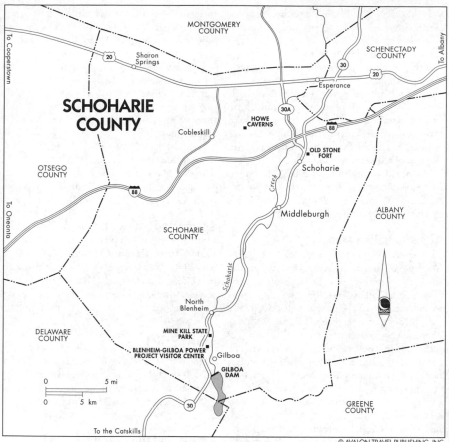

SCHOHARIE
COUNTY

To Cooperstown

MONTGOMERY
COUNTY

SCHENECTADY
COUNTY

To Albany

20 Sharon
Springs

30

Esperance

20

30A

HOWE
CAVERNS

88

Cobleskill

OLD STONE
FORT

OTSEGO
COUNTY

Schoharie

88

To Oneonta

ALBANY
COUNTY

Schoharie
County

Creek

Middleburgh

SCHOHARIE
COUNTY

North
Blenheim

Schoharie

DELAWARE
COUNTY

MINE KILL STATE
PARK

BLENHEIM-GILBOA POWER
PROJECT VISITOR CENTER

Gilboa

GILBOA
DAM

0   5 mi
0   5 km

30

GREENE
COUNTY

To the Catskills

© AVALON TRAVEL PUBLISHING, INC.

caves filled with shimmering stalactites, stalagmites, and flowstones. Through the caverns' center runs a small river, while at the far end laps a mysterious, quarter-mile-long lake.

Howe Caverns was discovered in 1842 by farmer Lester Howe. Finding a dark opening in a ledge, Howe tied a long rope to a sturdy tree and lowered himself inside. Each day he penetrated a bit deeper, until he'd explored nearly 1.5 miles of caves.

Word of Howe's discovery quickly spread, and before long he was conducting tours. Visitors paid 50 cents for a torturous eight-hour scramble underground. Later Howe lit the passageways

with gas, and in 1854 his daughter was married in one of the caves—a tradition that continues to this day. Over 350 weddings have to date taken place in the caverns.

A modern-day visit to the caves begins with an elevator ride descending down into the earth 156 feet. Tours proceed along paved walkways, where guides point out unusual rock formations lit by colored lights, then everybody climbs aboard for a boat ride on the lake. Temperatures below are always a steady 52°.

The caverns, Caverns Rd. off Rte. 7, 518/296-8990, www.howecaverns.com, are open daily 9 A.M.–6 P.M. Admission is adults $15, seniors

$12, children 7–12 $7. A gift shop and museum are on-site.

Caverns Creek Grist Mill

Less than a mile from Howe Caverns is a handsome gristmill, a working 1816 National Historic Landmark equipped with a 12-foot-high waterwheel and 1,400-pound millstone. The mill grinds wheat into flour for use in pancake mixes; one of the area's more unusual distinctions is the fact the first packaged pancake mix was concocted here in 1890.

The mill, Caverns Rd., 518/296-8448, is open Memorial Day–Labor Day, daily 11 A.M.–6 P.M. Admission is adults $4, children 2–12 $3. It's also possible to visit just the gift shop.

Iroquois Indian Museum

The newest addition to Caverns Road is the very fine Iroquois Indian Museum, designed in the shape of an Iroquois longhouse. Unlike most Native American exhibits, this museum pays as much attention to the present as it does to the past, through its remarkable collection of contemporary Native American art. You'll see artifacts such as ancient pottery and arrow points here, to be sure, but chances are what you'll remember best are the museum's exquisite watercolors, oils, clay figures, stone carvings, and baskets.

Largely run by the Iroquois and learned scholars, the museum features many special programs, including dance and crafts demonstrations, storytelling hours, and nature walks. Downstairs is a children's museum where young ones can play musical instruments or craft beaded bracelets; upstairs is an excellent bookstore.

The museum, Caverns Rd., 518/296-8949, www.iroquoismuseum.org, is open Apr.–Dec., Tues.–Sat. 10 A.M.–5 P.M., Sunday noon–5 P.M. Also open Monday in July and August; closed Jan.–March. Admission is adults $7, seniors and students 13–17 $5.50, children 5–12 $4.

Secret Caverns

Much less commercialized than Howe Caverns, the Secret Caverns provide an interesting contrast. Everything here has been left as natural as possible, allowing visitors to absorb the sights of this wondrous underworld without the distractions of megaphones, boat rides, and large tour groups. Even the descent is via natural means—stone steps rather than an elevator.

Like Howe Caverns, the Secret Caverns are filled with iridescent stalactites and stalagmites, illuminated along well-lit walkways under soaring ceilings. At the far end of the caves is a thundering 100-foot waterfall; everything else is eerily quiet.

The caverns, Caverns Rd., 518/296-8558, www.secretcaverns.com, are open June–Sept., daily 9 A.M.–6 P.M.; May and Oct., Sat.–Sun. 10 A.M.–4:30 P.M. Cost is adults $12, children 6–11 $5.

Accommodations and Food

On Howe Caverns property are the well-kept, 21-room **Howe Caverns Motel,** Caverns Rd., 518/296-8950, which was once air-conditioned by cool breezes from the caves ($100–110 d). A casual restaurant serving decent lunch and early dinner fare is attached to the motel; average main dish $9.

COBLESKILL

In the center of this small town is a pretty Historic District that houses the **Schoharie County Arts Council Gallery,** 589 Main St., 518/234-7380. Gallery hours are Mon–Fri. 9 A.M.–5 P.M., Saturday 10 A.M.–2 P.M.; admission is free.

Accommodations and Food

The 76-room **Best Western Inn of Cobleskill,** Campus Dr., off Rte. 7, 518/234-4321, offers an indoor pool and game room ($149–189 d). The 1802 **Bull's Head Inn,** 2 Park Pl., 518/234-3591, features open-hearth cooking, steaks, seafood, sandwiches, pasta, and over 70 kinds of beer. Live jazz and blues are often presented on the weekends; average dinner entrée $11.

SCHOHARIE

Just east of Cobleskill, in the quaint historic village of Schoharie, is the **Old Stone Fort.** The largest British raid in the area occurred here on October 17, 1780, when Col. John Johnson and Chief

Joseph Brant entered the valley and set fire to everything in sight. The valley was devastated, but the attackers failed to take stout Old Stone Fort.

Today, the restored fort serves as the centerpiece of the village. On display are war artifacts from the Revolution through WW II and period furnishings from historic Schoharie homes. Out back find a restored carriage shed, schoolhouse, two Colonial homes, and several barns.

The fort, N. Main St., 518/295-7192, is open May–Oct., Tues.–Sat. 10 A.M.–5 P.M., Sunday noon–5 P.M. Also open on Monday in July and August. Admission is adults $5, seniors $4.50, and students 5–18 $1.50.

Also in town is the small but unique **Easter Egg Museum,** Depot Ln., 518/295-8070 or 518/295-8696, where you'll find about 5,000 hand-painted Easter eggs. Open Palm Sunday–Easter Sunday daily noon–5 P.M.; July–Aug., Sat.–Sun. 1–5 P.M.

Food

Built in 1800, and remodeled in 1874, the **Schoharie Pharmacy & Soda Fountain,** Main St., 518/295-7300, boasts an antique soda fountain where you can order over 20 flavors of ice-cream sodas. For lunch or dinner in a historic setting, step into the 1870 **Parrott House,** Main St., 518/295-7111; average dinner entrée $12.

THE SCHOHARIE VALLEY

Traveling south of Schoharie on Route 30, you'll pass through the heart of the Schoharie Valley, spread out like a plush green carpet. Tractors and other farm vehicles move amongst endless cultivated fields, grazing cows, and **pick-your-own fruit farms.**

Visible from Route 30 near Middleburgh is **Vroman's Nose,** or Onistagraw—"Corn Mountain" to the Native Americans. The most prominent natural landmark in the Schoharie Valley, the outcropping resembles a nose and was named for an early settler. The summit of the Nose offers terrific views of the valley; a hiking trail leading to the top is accessible from a marked parking lot on West Middleburgh Road, off Route 30. The roundtrip hike takes about an hour.

Further south on Route 30 is North Blenheim, where the 232-foot **Blenheim Bridge** crosses Schoharie Creek. A National Historic Landmark, the bridge is believed to be the longest single-span two-lane covered wooden bridge in the United States. A plaque nearby remembers Tory William Beacraft, who was whipped to death by his neighbors after the Revolutionary War.

Blenheim-Gilboa Power Project Visitor Center

At the southern end of North Blenheim is the vast Blenheim-Gilboa Power Project and **Lansing Manor Museum.** Visitor center exhibits explain how the power plant produces 1.6 billion kilowatt hours of electricity a year by recycling water between the Blenheim and Gilboa reservoirs. Also featured are numerous hands-on science displays, computer games, historic exhibits, and a fossil collection. The Federal-style manor house—now owned by the power company—is furnished with handsome period antiques.

The center, Rte. 30, 518/827-6121 or 800/724-0309, is open daily 10 A.M.–5 P.M. The manor is open Memorial Day–Labor Day, Wed.–Sun. 10 A.M.–5 P.M. Tours of the power plant are available, but reservations *must* be made in advance. Free admission to everything.

Mine Kill State Park

Next door to the power project is Mine Kill State Park, Rte. 30, 518/827-6111, with 500 wooded acres overlooking the lower reservoir. The park features ball fields and game areas, an impressive three-pool complex, picnic areas, and nature trails. Parking fee Memorial Day–Labor Day is $7.

Petrified Forest

South of Gilboa, Route 30 skirts the Gilboa Dam and Schoharie Reservoir, part of the Catskill Reservoir system. Near the dam is Route 990v, leading to a small but amazing petrified forest consisting of stone stumps from now-extinct seed-bearing fern trees. Among the oldest types of trees known to humankind, these plants grew on the shores of New York's Devonian Sea about 365 million years ago. The stumps were uncovered by the New York Board of Water Supply in the 1920s.

Continue another half mile on Route 990v to reach a scenic overlook with great views of the reservoir.

Camping

Five miles south of Middleburgh lies **Max V. Shaul State Park,** Rte. 30, 518/827-4711, where 30 campsites are available. For reservations, call 800/456-CAMP; basic site cost is $13.

Oneida County

Compared to the other counties in Leatherstocking Country, Oneida County is positively crowded. Two large cities—Utica and Rome—are located here, along with Sherrill, the smallest city in New York State (pop. 3,200). The Mohawk River runs through the county as far west as Rome, while at its western edge lies whale-shaped Oneida Lake.

Visitor Information

The **Oneida County Information Center,** 315/724-7221 or 800/426-3132, www.oneidacountycvb.com, is located in Utica, off Exit 31 off the New York State Thruway (I-90). Hours are Mon.–Fri. 9 A.M.–5 P.M.

UTICA

Near the western end of the Mohawk River Valley lies Utica. Once an important industrial city, best known for its knitting mills, Utica lost much of its manufacturing base over the past few decades and now feels oddly arrested in time. Everywhere stand handsome but underutilized public buildings and abandoned red-brick factories.

Located at what was once for many miles the only ford across the Mohawk River, Utica was first settled by whites in the mid-1700s. In 1825 the Erie Canal brought prosperity to the town, along with new industries and immigrants. The first woolen mills opened in 1847, the first cotton mills in 1848, and the first firearm factories in the 1860s. Thousands of Irish and German immigrants began arriving in the mid-1800s; thousands of Poles and Italians came around the turn of the 20th century, and Utica still harbors a large Italian community. More recent arrivals have included refugees from Bosnia, Belarus, and Vietnam, and their presence is starting to bring new life to the city.

The heart of old Utica, where Main, Genesee, and Whitesboro Streets meet, is **Baggs Square,** named for Moses Baggs, who built a log tavern here in 1798. The square is lined with impressive turn-of-the-century buildings, as is Genesee Street itself, a main drag running virtually the entire length of the city. Three blocks south of Baggs Square is Bleecker Street, where Frank Woolworth opened his first five-and-dime in 1879; it was a failure.

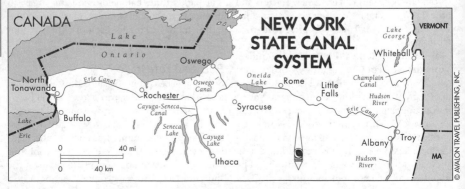

THE ERIE CANAL: PAST AND PRESENT

The Erie Canal was the making of New York City and New York State. With its completion in 1825 came an explosion of trade between the East and the Midwest. Shipping rates between Buffalo and New York City dropped 80–90 percent; by 1834, the canal's tolls had more than paid for the entire cost of its $7.7 million construction.

Pre-Erie Canal, New York City was the nation's fifth largest seaport, behind Boston, Baltimore, Philadelphia, and New Orleans. Fifteen years post-Erie Canal, New York was America's busiest port, moving tonnages greater than those of Boston, Baltimore, and New Orleans combined.

With the exception of Binghamton and Elmira, every major city in New York falls along the trade route established by the Erie Canal. And, even today, approximately 75 percent of the state's population still lives along the corridors created by the canals and the Hudson River.

Building the Canal

One of the first to envision the Erie Canal was a Geneva miller named Jesse Hawley. While languishing in debtor's prison in the early 1800s, Hawley wrote 14 newspaper essays promoting a cross-state canal. When President Jefferson first heard of the plan, he said, "It is a splendid project and may be executed a century hence . . . but it is little short of madness to think of it at this day." However, the essays came to the attention of politician DeWitt Clinton, who was swept into the governor's office in 1817 on a pro-canal platform.

Work on the canal began that very year. An engineering marvel of its day, the canal was built almost entirely by shovel and pick-ax, by men who had no engineering experience whatsoever. Over 25 percent of the canal builders were recent Irish immigrants earning 80 cents an hour. They started in Rome, where a light soil ensured rapid progress, and in 1819, the first 15-mile-long section opened up between Rome and Utica. It would take another six years, however, before the canal was completed, and many lost faith along the way. The project became known as "Clinton's Ditch" and "Clinton's Folly."

The work was grueling and often dangerous.

Close to 1,000 men died of malaria while running the canal through the Montezuma Swamp. Others died while constructing a flight of locks through the Niagara Escarpment—a solid wall of rock rising 565 feet above sea level.

Finally finished in 1825, the canal measured 363 miles long, 40 feet wide, and four feet deep. Alongside it ran a towpath for the mules and drivers who pulled the barges along before the advent of steam power.

The astonishing success of the Erie Canal sparked a canal-building craze, and between 1823 and 1828, several important lateral canals were opened up, including the Champlain, Oswego, and Cayuga-Seneca. The canals were enlarged three times over the years to accommodate larger boats. The completion of the enormous St. Lawrence Seaway in the 1950s, however, rendered New York's canal system all but obsolete.

Cruising the Canals Today

Today, less than 100 commercial barges a year ply the waters between Buffalo and Albany. The New York State Canal System primarily serves as a low-key, relatively unknown tourist attraction. It offers great potential to become much more than that, and the state has recently launched an extensive campaign to revitalize its canal front. As of yet, however, much of the canal remains scruffy and undeveloped. Its main attractions are the slow pace, the backside glimpses into an older, more industrialized America, and the farm-studded pastoral countryside.

Various boat companies operate excursions, or you can rent your own canoe or canal boat. Daily tour boats include the *Dutch Apple* in Albany, 518/463-0220, and **Lockport Lock and Erie Canal Cruises** in Lockport, 716/433-6155. Three-day cruises are offered out of the Syracuse area by **Mid-Lakes Navigation,** 315/685-8500 or 800/545-4318, a company that also rents canal boats. Canoes are available at the **Boat House, Canoe and Kayak Store** in Schenectady, 518/393-5711.

For more information on cruising the canal, contact the **New York State Canal Corporation,** P.O. Box 189, Albany, NY 12201-0189, 800/4-CANAL-4, www.canal.state.ny.us.

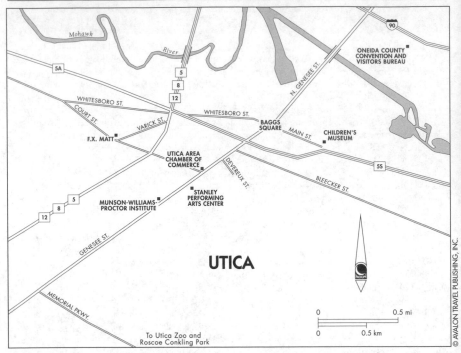

To Utica Zoo and
Roscoe Conkling Park

© AVALON TRAVEL PUBLISHING, INC.

Munson-Williams-Proctor Institute

This fine institute, housed in a streamlined Philip Johnson building filled with air and light, is part art museum, part art school, and part performing arts center. The museum's collection contains more than 5,000 works of art by the likes of Picasso, Dali, Pollock, Moore, and Burchfield. An institute highlight is the "Voyage of Life" series painted by Hudson River School artist Thomas Cole, depicting man's passage through the four stages of life—childhood, youth, manhood, and old age.

Next door to the art museum stands the **Fountain Elms,** an Italianate villa once home to the Proctor and Munson families. Now a museum, the mansion is still outfitted with its original furnishings, which include several enormous gilt-bronze chandeliers and two "slipper chairs" designed to help the ladies put on their high-button shoes.

The institute, 310 Genesee St., 315/797-0000, www.mwpi.edu, is open Tues–Sat. 10 A.M.–5 P.M., Sunday 1–5 P.M. Admission is free.

Saranac Brewery

Founded in 1888 by F. X. Matt, the Matt Brewing Company—makers of Saranac beer, among others—is now run by his grandson. When operating at full capacity, the plant can produce 2.4 million bottles of beer a day, most distributed within 200 miles of Utica.

Visitors to F. X. Matt are met by guides in costume dress who conduct one-hour tours through the plant. Stops include the brewhouse, where two enormous copper kettles hold 18,000 gallons of beer each; the temperature-controlled tanks, where the beer is fermented; and the bottling department, where the bottles are washed, filled, capped, and labeled. Visitors are then transported via trolley to a restored 1888 tavern where they're offered a mug of draft or root beer, compliments of the house.

The brewery, Court and Varick Sts., 315/732-0022 or 800/765-6288, www.saranac.com, offers tours hourly June–Aug., Mon.–Sat. 11 A.M.–4 P.M., Sunday 1–3 P.M.; and twice daily Sept.–May,

Mon.–Sat., when reservations are required. Cost is adults $3, children 6–12 $1.

Utica Zoo

This popular zoo is located at the southern end of the city, next door to **Roscoe Conkling Park,** designed by Frederick Law Olmsted. Residing here are about 300 species of mammals, birds, and reptiles, including the endangered Siberian tiger, golden lion tamarin, red panda, and bald eagle. The Children's Zoo holds barnyard animals and a petting area. Sea lion shows are presented every day but Tuesday, at noon and 3 P.M.

The zoo, Steele Hill Rd. at Memorial Pkwy., 315/738-0472, www.uticazoo.org, is open daily 10 A.M.–5 P.M. Admission is adults $4.50, children 2–12 $2.75; free in winter.

Children's Museum

Billed as the finest children's museum between New York City and Toronto, this lively institute holds a wide variety of imaginative exhibits and hands-on displays. Here, children can visit a Native American longhouse, examine dinosaur life of the Mesozoic era, find out what's under the "skin" of a new car, and experiment with laser light. Herd younger children to the Dino Den and play area.

The museum, 311 Main St. at Railroad St., 315/724-6129, www.museum4kids.net, is open Tues.–Sat. 10 A.M.–4:30 P.M., Sunday noon–4 P.M. Admission is $3.50 per person.

Accommodations

Downtown you'll find a **Best Western Motel Inn,** 175 N. Genesee St., 315/732-4121 ($89–129 d), and the sleek **Radisson Hotel,** 200 Genesee St., 315/797-8010, equipped with a pool, restaurant, and cocktail lounge with live entertainment on the weekends ($129 d, packages available).

The **Iris Stonehouse B&B,** 16 Derbyshire Pl., 315/732-6720 or 800/446-1456, is housed in a stone Tudor home with leaded glass windows. Featured are four guest rooms, two with private baths ($59–89 d).

Food

A number of Italian restaurants and pastry shops

are located along Bleecker Street. Among them is **Grimaldi's,** 428 Bleecker St., 315/732-7011, a cheery eatery that's one of the oldest and biggest restaurants in town; average dinner entrée $14.

The landmark **Devereux,** 37 Devereux St., 315/735-8628, offers hearty soups and overstuffed deli sandwiches, with live music on weekends; average sandwich $7. On the outskirts of town, find the Cape Cod–style **Hook, Line & Sinker,** 8471 Seneca Tpk., 607/732-3636, serving seafood, steak, and pasta; average entrée $18.

Entertainment

The city's premier performance venue is the **Stanley Performing Arts Center,** 259 Genesee St., 315/724-4000, originally built as a 2,945-seat movie theater in a "Mexican Baroque–style." Now on the National Register of Historic Places, the center presents an interesting mix of classical music, opera, and theater. The **Munson-Williams-Proctor Institute,** 310 Genesee St., 315/797-0000, features occasional jazz and blues artists, as well as classic movies.

Visitor Information

The **Utica Area Chamber of Commerce,** 520 Seneca St., Utica, NY 13502, 315/724-3151, www.mvchamber.org, is open Mon.–Fri. 8:30 A.M.–5 P.M.

ORISKANY BATTLEFIELD

Off Route 69 between Utica and Rome is the Oriskany Battlefield, the site of the bloodiest battle of the American Revolution. The battle took place during the siege of Fort Stanwix when 900 Continental troops, coming west to reinforce the fort, were ambushed by the British. Hundreds of soldiers on both sides were killed and the American general Herkimer fatally wounded. Subsequently the British general St. Leger, fearing yet more Colonial militiamen were about to arrive, abandoned the siege of Fort Stanwix and withdrew to Canada. Two months later, surrounded and cut off, British general Burgoyne surrendered his army at Saratoga—the turning point of the war.

On site at the battlefield, 315/768-7224, is a

small museum and 100-foot commemorative monument. National Park Service rangers offer guided tours. Hours are May–Oct., Wed.–Sat. 10 A.M.–4:45 P.M., Sunday 1–4:45 P.M. Admission is adults $3, children $1.

ROME

Rome must be the flattest city in all New York. Sitting athwart the basin of the upper Mohawk River, the city feels like a tiny windswept nub surrounded by a vast antediluvian plain. The fact that much of the downtown was destroyed during urban renewal doesn't help matters much either. Most of the city feels empty, depressed, forgotten.

Before white people arrived, Rome was an important Native American site known as De-O-Wain-Sta, or "The Lifting or Setting Down of Boat." The site marked the one-mile canoe portage between the upper end of the Mohawk River and Wood Creek, which linked the Great Lakes to the Atlantic Ocean. The English realized the strategic importance of the place and in 1758 built Fort Stanwix.

The Americans took over Fort Stanwix in 1776, and in 1777 successfully withstood a three-week siege waged by British general St. Leger. After the war, the settlement was renamed Rome in tribute to the "heroic defence of the Republic made here."

The digging of the Erie Canal began in Rome on July 4, 1817, and by mid-century the town was a bustling transportation center. Railroads followed the canals; then came the Rome Brass and Copper Company, attracting large numbers of Italian and Polish immigrants. By the 1930s Rome was processing one-tenth of all the copper mined in the United States. Today copper is still processed in Rome, though in much-diminished amounts.

Fort Stanwix National Monument

Dominating downtown Rome is its primary tourist attraction, the reconstructed Fort Stanwix. Built on a large parcel of land razed during urban renewal, the monument opened in 1976 to the tune of $7 million. It is said to be one of the most accurate reconstructed log-and-earth fortifications in the world.

Run by the National Park Service, the fort includes two long barracks, a guardhouse, officers' quarters, and various casemates, sentry boxes, and gun platforms. Surrounding the place is an ultra-neat wall built of pointy blond logs; at the entrance is a drawbridge. Costumed guides interpret military life; a small museum exhibits such artifacts as bullets, belt buckles, and game pieces.

The fort, 112 E. Park St., 315/336-2090, is open April–Dec., daily 9 A.M.–5 P.M., extended hours in summer. Admission is free.

Other Nearby Sites

Just north of Fort Stanwix is the **Rome Historical Society Museum,** a large, rambling, rather musty place where you can learn more about the city's history. Exhibits cover the Colonial period to Rome's recent industrial past; on-site is a well-stocked gift stop where you can pick up a free walking-tour guide to what remains of downtown. Most of Rome's finest buildings were erected in the mid to late 1800s and are located along nearby North Washington Street.

The museum, 200 Church St., 315/336-5870, is open year-round Tues.–Fri. 10 A.M.–5 P.M. and Saturday 10 A.M.–3 P.M. Admission is free.

Erie Canal Village

After touring Fort Stanwix, visitors usually head west a few miles on Erie Boulevard (Route 46/49 W) to Erie Canal Village. Built along the banks of the canal, on what was once a German neighborhood, the village re-creates the early *canawlers'*—or canal workers'—lives through a cluster of 19th-century buildings and mule-drawn packet boat rides.

In the village you'll find the 1858 Canal Store, packed with boat horns, tow ropes, and other essential provisions, and the 1869 Skull House, a gorgeous Italianate home built by wealthy cattleman Jacob Skull. The 1862 Verona Cheese Factory once churned out 60-pound rounds of cheddar cheese, while the 1862 Bennett's Tavern still serves cold draft or root beer, pretzels, and pickled eggs. Guides in period dress answer questions and drive mules pulling the packet boat *Independence* along a 1.5-mile stretch of canal. Rides last about 45 minutes.

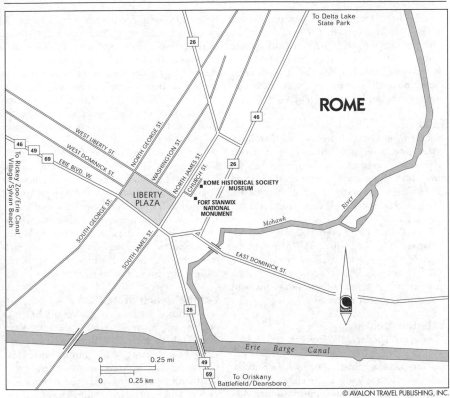

To Delta Lake
State Park

26

ROME

46

26

WEST LIBERTY ST
WEST DOMINICK ST
46
49
69
ERIE BLVD. W.
NORTH GEORGE ST.
WASHINGTON ST.
NORTH JAMES ST.
CHURCH ST.
To Rickey Zoo/Erie Canal
Village/Sylvan Beach

ROME HISTORICAL SOCIETY
MUSEUM

LIBERTY
PLAZA

FORT STANWIX
NATIONAL
MONUMENT

SOUTH GEORGE ST.

SOUTH JAMES ST.

Mohawk

River

EAST DOMINICK ST.

Moon

26

Erie Barge Canal

0   0.25 mi
0   0.25 km

49
69
To Oriskany
Battlefield/Deansboro

© AVALON TRAVEL PUBLISHING, INC.

CENTRAL NEW YORK

The village, Rts. 46/49W, 315/337-3999, www.eriecanalvillage.com, is open Memorial Day–Labor Day, Wed.–Sat. 10 A.M.–5 P.M., Sunday noon–5 P.M. Admission is adults $4, seniors $3, children 4–17 $3; boat rides cost $4, under three free.

Fort Rickey Children's Discovery Zoo

West of Erie Canal Village is a well-kept game farm housing creatures from bear and reindeer to donkeys and reptiles. Of special interest to young children is the large petting area filled with deer, sheep, and goats. Special daily events include pony rides and animal shows.

The zoo, Rte. 46/49 W, 315/336-1930, www.fortrickey.com, is open June–Sept., daily 10 A.M.–5:30 P.M., weather permitting. Admis-

sion is adults $8, seniors $6, children 2–16 $6, under two free.

Delta Lake State Park

About six miles northeast of Rome lies a peaceful 400-acre retreat centered around Lake Delta and its crescent-shaped beach. The park offers hiking, fishing, concession stands, boat launches, and campsites; good cross-country skiing in winter. The park, off Rte. 46, 315/337-4670, is open daily dawn–dusk; lifeguards are on duty Memorial Day–Labor Day; summer parking is $7. For campground reservations, call 800/456-CAMP; a basic site costs $14–16.

Accommodations

Downtown, the 104-room **Quality Inn,** 200

S. James St., 315/336-4300, features a pool, cable TV, and valet service ($79–99 d). On the outskirts of town, the 75-room **Paul Revere Lodge**, 7900 Turin Rd., 315/336-1776, www.thebeeches.com, features a pool, lawn games, room refrigerators, and the on-site restaurant Beeches (see below; $66 s $73–79 d).

Food

Not far from Fort Stanwix is East Dominick Street, once a veritable cornucopia of Italian restaurants. These are dying out now, but the street still features a few good pizza parlors and the family-owned **Savoy**, 255 E. Dominick St., 315/339-3166, specializing in pasta and seafood; average entrée $11.

As part of the Paul Revere Lodge (see above), **Beeches**, 7900 Turin Rd., 315/336-1700 or 800/765-7251, is housed in a historic stone building encircled by meadows and wooded groves. On the menu is traditional American fare; average dinner entrée $14.

Entertainment

The **Capitol Theatre**, 218 Liberty Plaza, 315/337-6453 or 315/337-6277, is a vintage 1928 theater featuring presenting dramas, musicals, the Syracuse Symphony, and recently released movies. The active **Rome Arts and Community Center**, 308 W. Bloomfield St., 315/336-1040, hosts everything from theater to jazz.

Visitor Information

The **Rome Chamber of Commerce**, 139 W. Dominick St., 315/337-1700, www.romechamber.com, is open Mon.–Fri. 9 A.M.–5 P.M.

WEST OF ROME

Sylvan Beach

About 15 miles due west of Rome, on the shores of Oneida Lake, is the Sylvan Beach resort.

Route 49 leading into the area is long, beautiful, and deliciously empty, lined with lime-green fields and rolling hills, but the waterfront itself is a crowded affair, packed with summer cottages, shops, and a four-mile beach. At one end lies the **Sylvan Beach Amusement Park**, Park Ave. off Main St. (Rte. 13), 315/762-5212, featuring over 20 rides. The park opens weekends April–June, and daily July–Labor Day. Admission free; ride fees vary.

Not far from the park is **Eddie's Restaurant**, 901 Main St., 315/762-4269, a local institution known for its spicy grilled ham sandwiches, hot dogs, fresh seafood, and Italian specialties. Opened in 1934 as a seasonal hot dog stand, Eddie's soon expanded into a full-service restaurant that attracted the likes of Nat "King" Cole, Frank Sinatra, and Duke Ellington. Sylvan Beach was a major resort at the time, hosting all the touring big bands. The average main dish is $8.

Verona Beach State Park

Just south of Sylvan Beach is Verona Beach, a place of two distinct personalities, split down the middle by Route 13. To the west is a long sandy beach, crowded in summer with vacationing families. To the east is a peaceful forest filled with white-tailed deer, wild turkeys, and a wide variety of birds, including hawks, herons, and osprey. The forest is clustered around a pond encircled by 16 miles of hiking trails.

The park, 315/762-4463, is open year-round. Lifeguards are on duty Memorial Day–Labor Day; summer parking is $7. To reserve one of the park's 100 campsites, call 800/456-CAMP; a basic site costs $13–15.

Vernon

Watch **harness racing** most evenings at 7:30 P.M., April–Nov., at **Vernon Downs**, off Rte. 31 (from I-90, take Exit 33), 315/829-2201, www.vernondowns.com.

Madison County

Rural Madison County is in the dead center of the state. Among its more unusual towns are Oneida, once home to the Utopian Oneida Community; and Chittenango, the birthplace of L. Frank Baum, author of *The Wizard of Oz*. Near the eastern edge of the county is Cazenovia, an attractive, tourist-oriented village overlooking Cazenovia Lake.

Visitor Information

Madison County Tourism, P.O. Box 1029, Morrisville, NY 13408, 315/684-7320 or 800/684-7320, www.madisontourism.com, is on Rte. 20 near South Street. Hours are Mon.–Fri. 8 A.M.–5 P.M.

ONEIDA

Perversely located in Madison rather than Oneida County is the town of Oneida, a gracious place filled with wide, shady streets and prosperous homes. Oneida was established in the mid-1800s when a Mr. Sands Higinbotham, who lived on the site, struck a deal with the railroad whereby it received free right of way across his property on the condition every passenger train stop for 10 minutes. The wily Higinbotham then built a refreshment stand and restaurant, and Oneida was born.

Along Route 46 just north of the city, and technically located in Oneida County, is the 35-acre Oneida Nation Territory. The Oneida are an Iroquois tribe that has lived in upstate New York since before the arrival of the whites (see the Finger Lakes chapter Introduction).

Cottage Lawn Museum

The best place to learn about Oneida's history is at Higinbotham's former home, now a muse-um operated by the Madison County Historical Society. Designed by Alexander Jackson Davis, the handsome Gothic Revival mansion showcases period furnishings, Erie Canal artifacts, and locally produced ceramics, glassware, and textiles.

The museum, 435 Main St., 315/363-4136, is open year-round, Mon.–Fri. 9 A.M.–4 P.M.; and June–Aug., Saturday 9 A.M.–4 P.M. Admission is $2 per person.

The Mansion House

The Oneida Community, a Utopian society that flourished in the mid-1800s, once occupied this large, red-brick Mansion House on the edge of town. Built around a central tower, the house is surrounded by a wide jade-green lawn and towering elms. Inside are over 300 rooms, many converted into apartments and guest rooms.

Tours are given by descendants of the Oneida Community who still live in the Mansion House. Most are single men and women in

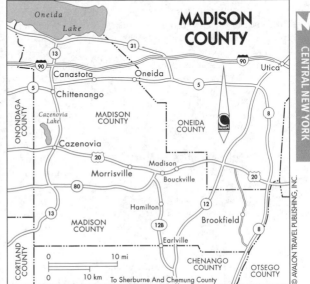

CENTRAL NEW YORK

© AVALON TRAVEL PUBLISHING, INC.

THE UTOPIAN ONEIDA COMMUNITY

Founded in 1848 by John Humphrey Noyes, the Oneida Community—a.k.a. the Perfectionists—believed that the second coming of Christ occurred in the year A.D. 70, meaning that the human race had been freed from sin, and personal perfection was possible. Men and women should work together to achieve that perfection, and relinquish all personal property. Marital vows should be abandoned in favor of "complex" marriages that allowed for several sexual partners.

When the Perfectionists first arrived in Oneida, they eked out a meager living by farming. However, they soon turned to more lucrative pursuits, such as selling canned fruits and vegetables, steel traps and chains, and finally the famed flatware still produced by Oneida, Ltd., today. All community members, men and women, shared equally in the work, taking turns at both menial and

managerial tasks. When not working, they improved their minds by reading the Bible and books about science, religion, and history.

In existence from 1848 to 1881, the Oneida Community was one of the longest-lived Utopian societies. At its zenith, it claimed about 300 members. In 1879, however, outside criticism—which had always been present—grew especially hostile, forcing Noyes to move to Canada. Here, he ruled from afar for about a year, but finally in 1881 the community disbanded. Property was distributed equally among all members, including the children, and the business incorporated.

Today, many descendants of the Oneida Community still live in Oneida; note the many mailboxes marked Noyes. A few live in the Mansion House, which was once home to the entire Community, and is now open to the public for guided tours, meals, and lodging.

their 70s who impart short anecdotes as they guide visitors through the Big Hall, Outer Library, Upper Sitting Room, Nursery Kitchen, Lounge, Dining Room, and History Room. A portrait of a stern-looking John Humphrey Noyes, the community's founder, hangs in one hallway; the History Room contains evocative photographs, letters, and ledgers. Everything is in mint condition.

Tours of the house, at 170 Kenwood Ave., 315/363-0745, www.oneidacommunity.org, are offered Wed.–Sat. at 10 A.M. and 2 P.M., Sun. at 2 P.M. Cost is $5 per person. To reach the house from downtown, take Route 5 east to Sherrill Road to Kenwood Avenue.

Oneida Silversmiths Factory Store
Just down the street from the Mansion House is the Oneida Factory Store, 606 Sherrill Rd., 315/361-3661, offering discounts in flatware, silver-plated serving items, crystal, and children's giftware. The store is in the Sherrill Shopping Center.

Shako:Wi Cultural Center
On Route 46 a few miles south of the city is an Oneida cultural center housing classrooms, a

gift shop stocked with books and handicrafts, and the Oneida Nation Museum. The museum features archaeological artifacts, photographic essays, silverwork by Oneida artist Richard Chrisjohn, and the collection of the late Bill Rockwell, Sr. Rockwell was one of the Oneida Nation's last traditional chiefs, and his collection includes traditional dress, beadwork, and woodwork.

The center, 5 Territory Rd. (Rte. 46), 315/829-8801, www.oneida-nation.net, is open daily 9 A.M.–5 P.M. Admission is free.

Turning Stone Casino
Off Route 365 about five miles northeast of the city is the big, glitzy Turning Stone Casino, the first legal casino in New York State, opened in 1993 and now one of upstate's biggest tourist attractions (a second casino opened on the St. Regis Mohawk Reservation in Akwesasne, near Canada, in 1999). Owned and operated by the Oneida Indian Nation of New York, the Turning Stone offers blackjack, craps, roulette, big six, baccarat, red dog, mini baccarat, acey deucey, and pai gow poker. Two traditional elements are missing, however—slot machines

(illegal in the state) and liquor. The Oneida decided alcohol had done enough damage to their people over the years.

Connected to the casino is an enormous bingo hall seating about 1,100. Games are played throughout the day, with doors opening at 10 A.M. Also on site is a 285-room hotel, upscale boutiques, an 18-hole golf course, and some of the fanciest restaurants in the region.

To reach the casino, on Rte. 365 in Verona, 315/361-7711, take Exit 33 directly from I-90; open 24 hours a day.

Accommodations and Food

Visitors interested in a meal or a room at the **Mansion House,** 170 Kenwood Ave., should call 315/361-3671. Meals are served family-style; rooms are simple but clean and adequate ($50–100 d). Also in the city is a 39-room **Super 8,** 215 Genesee St., 315/363-5168 or 800/800-8000 ($75–90 d).

Near the Turning Point Casino is **Joel's Front Yard Steak House,** Rts. 365 and 31, 315/363-5529. Outside stands an enormous mock steer, inside turns a working 1905 carousel with booths where you can have a drink while waiting for a table; average entrée $14.

CANASTOTA

Continuing west on Route 5 from Oneida, you'll come to the village of Canastota, notable for its well-preserved canal buildings along the old Erie Canal. One has been turned into the **Canal Town Museum,** 122 Canal St., 315/697-3451, which succinctly explains canal history. Hours are June–Aug., Mon.–Sat. 10 A.M.–4 P.M., Saturday 10 A.M.–1 P.M.; Apr.–May and Sept.–Oct., Tues.–Fri. 11 A.M.–3 P.M. Admission is free.

Canastota's other claim to fame is the **International Boxing Hall of Fame Museum,** founded in Canastota in 1984 largely because two major boxing champs—Carmen Basilio and Billy Backus—hailed from here. Most of the museum is housed in one large room. To one side are the robes of boxing greats and the fist casts of dozens of champs; to another, the Wall of Fame, inscribed with the names of all inductees. The fa-

mous purple trunks of Joe Louis are on display, along with Rocky Marciano's gloves and Mike Tyson's mouthpieces.

The museum, 1 Hall of Fame Dr., Exit 34 off I-88, 315/697-7095, www.ibhof.com, is open Mon.–Fri. 9 A.M.–5 P.M., Sat.–Sun. 9 A.M.–4 P.M. Admission is adults $4, seniors $3, youths 9–15 $3.

CHITTENANGO

A few miles west of Canastota is Chittenango, an old-fashioned village filled with boxy wooden homes and sturdy brick storefronts. Author L. Frank Baum was born here on May 15, 1856, the son of a maker of "fine barrels and butter firkins."

Chittenango honors its most famous native son with a pale **yellow brick road** that runs along the sidewalks of Genesee Street. Auntie Em's, Toto's, The Wizard's Printer read various signs. Oz souvenirs, including T-shirts, postcards, and baseball cards, are for sale in the **Chittenango Pharmacy,** 219 Genesee St., 315/687-7801, and **Burghard's Flower & Gift Shoppe,** 214 Genesee St., 315/687-7851.

Chittenango Landing Canal Boat Museum

This historic preservation site, where canal boats were once built and repaired, is an active archaeological project. Thus far, a three-bay dry dock has been excavated, along with a sunken canal boat. Also on-site are an interpretive center, restored sawmill, and blacksmith shop. The museum, 7010 Lakeport Rd., 315/687-3801, is open April–June, Sat.–Sun. 1–4 P.M.; July–Aug., daily 10 A.M.–4 P.M. Admission is adults $4, seniors $3, children under 12 $1, families $9.

The museum is part of the **Old Erie Canal Park,** 315/687-7821, a 36-mile linear park stretching between Rome and DeWitt. Through the park runs a hiking/biking trail used for cross-country skiing in winter.

Chittenango Falls State Park

On Route 13 about four miles south of downtown are Chittenango Falls, cascading for some 167 feet down, over, and under steplike rock ledges. Wider than most waterfalls, with streams that spread out like fans, the Chittenango Falls are among the most beautiful in the state. The park also offers hiking and nature trails, good fishing sites, and a 22-site campground.

The park, 315/655-9620, is open daily late April–late October. Parking in summer is $7. For camping reservations, call 800/456-CAMP; a basic site costs $13.

Food

Oz lovers will want to dine in **Auntie Em's Restaurant,** 262 Genesee St., 315/687-5704, all decked out in blue-checked curtains, *Wizard of Oz* posters, music scores from the 1939 movie, and little tin men hanging from the ceiling. The family-style eatery specializes in Auntie Em's homemade fare and is open for breakfast, lunch, and dinner; average main dish $7.

Events

The **Ozfest,** 315/687-3936, celebrates Baum's birthday with a parade, music, mimes, a crafts show, and an annual spaghetti dinner with Munchkins from the 1939 movie. The Munchkins are all in their seventies and eighties now, but a handful have arrived for this one-of-a-kind feast every year since 1988. The festival takes place on the weekend nearest May 15, Baum's birthday.

CAZENOVIA

Continuing south on Route 13, you'll come to Cazenovia, a favorite weekend getaway for Syracusans. Composed primarily of three country inns, Cazenovia sits on the edge of Cazenovia Lake, a four-mile swatch of deep blue rimmed with fine homes. The American Indians called the lake *Hod-way-gen-hen,* or Lake Where the Yellow Perch Swim.

Two of Cazenovia's inns, the Brae Loch and the Lincklaen House, occupy the heart of the village, surrounded by quaint, tourist-oriented shops. The third, the 1890 Brewster, is on a secluded drive by the lake.

Cazenovia was settled in 1793 by John Lincklaen, land agent for the Holland Land Company, which once controlled 3.3 million acres in western New York. In one of the greatest real estate promotions in U.S. history, the company sold plots of this land to settlers heading west on the Great Western Highway (Route 20). The main Holland Land Company office was actually located much farther west, in the town of Batavia, but Lincklaen opened a branch office here in hopes of catching settlers early. He named the town after the company's general agent in Philadelphia, Theophile Cazenove.

Lorenzo State Historic Site

"Situation suberb, fine land" were John Lincklaen's words when he first viewed Cazenovia; within a few years, he'd built himself an elegant Federal-style mansion. An educated man with an especially strong interest in the Italian Renaissance, Lincklaen named his new home Lorenzo in honor of the Medici.

Now a house museum open to the public, Lorenzo features an especially fine carriage house filled with dozens of horse-drawn vehicles. During the summer, carriage races are staged, just as they were back in the 19th century.

Lorenzo, 17 Rippleton Rd. (Rte. 13), south of Rte. 20, 315/655-3200, is open May–Oct., Wed.–Sun. 10 A.M.–5 P.M. Tours are every half-hour, with the last tour at 4:30 P.M. Admission is adults $3, seniors $2, children under 12 $1.

Accommodations and Food

If you'd like to stay overnight, the Scottish **Brae Loch,** 5 Albany St., 315/655-3431, www.braelochinn.com, offers 14 rooms nicely outfitted with antiques ($85–140 d). The 1835 **Lincklaen House,** 79 Albany St., 315/655-3461, www.cazenovia.com/Lincklaen, once a stagecoach stop, features 18 rooms and a complimentary afternoon tea ($99–195 d). The **Brewster Inn,** Ledyard Ave., 315/655-9232, www.cazenovia.com/brewsterinn.com, once the summer home of a wealthy financier, contains 17 rooms and is richly appointed with mahogany woodwork, antique furnishings, and Oriental rugs ($100–195 d). Less expensive digs are available at the 45-room **Cazenovia Motel,** 2392 Rte. 20 E, 315/655-9101 ($62–70 d).

For lunch, try the casual **Main Street Cafe,** 47

Albany St., 315/655-9765; average main dish $7. For dinner, head for one of the village's three famed inns, all of which are moderately priced (average entrée about $14). The Brae Loch serves fish, steak, and seafood, along with occasional Scottish specialties; average entrée $15. The Lincklaen House offers three menus—a tavern menu, casual fine dining menu, and fine dining menu—to suit all tastes and budgets. The Brewster Inn features classic American cuisine; average entrée $16.

MADISON TO BOUCKVILLE

In Cazenovia you'll again bump into Route 20, America's longest highway. Head east on the old route a few miles—through hilly, bucolic farmland—and between Bouckville and Madison you'll find an extraordinary number of **antique shops.** Over 100 dealers here comprise the largest grouping in the state. A guide to the shops, which specialize in everything from toys to furniture, is available in area tourist offices. The **Madison-Bouckville Antique Show,** 315/684-7320, held in mid-August, features over 1,000 dealers.

HAMILTON

From Route 20 just west of Bouckville, take Route 12B south through more fertile farmland to the town of Hamilton, home of **Colgate University.** The university, at Broad St. and Kendrick Ave., 315/228-1000, clusters around a peaceful quadrangle flanked by rectangular buildings built in early Georgian and neo-Gothic styles.

EARLVILLE

On Route 12B a few miles south of Hamilton is tiny, tree-lined Earlville, once a wealthy village on the Chenango Canal. In the center of the village is the 1892 **Earlville Opera House,** 16 E. Main St., 315/691-3550, www.earlvilleoperahouse.com, a rare, second-story theater. During the summer a wide variety of first-rate opera, theater, vaudeville, folk, jazz, and blues events

are staged in this National Historic Landmark, which also houses a small art gallery. Call for events information, gallery hours, and to arrange a tour of the opera house.

Surrounding the opera house are a number of shops and restaurants, often crowded with Colgate students and professors. For a welcome pint on a hot summer afternoon, step into the laid-back **Huff-Brau Tavern,** 4 W. Main St., 315/691-3300.

Nearby Recreation

Just south of Earlville in Chenango County is the 571-acre **Rogers Environmental Education Center.** In the main building are exhibits on local flora and fauna, including 350 mounted birds, while outside, five hiking trails wind around an observation tower. The center, 2721 Rte. 80 W, Sherburne, 607/674-4017, www.ascent.net/rogers, is open weekdays year round 8:30 A.M.–4:45 P.M., Saturday 1–4:45 P.M., and summer Sundays 1–4:45 P.M. Trails are open 24 hours a day; admission is free.

BROOKFIELD

If you detour east from Hamilton and Earlville to the Susquehanna hills near the village of Brookfield, you'll come to the 8,070-acre Baker Memorial Forest and the adjoining 3,346-acre Beaver Creek State Forest. The **Brookfield Trail System** runs through here, a network of 130 miles of horse trails. The trails, which also make for good hiking, lead through picturesque hill country peppered with large ponds and expansive valleys.

Good maps are essential for exploring the Brookfield Trail System; contact the Department of Environmental Conservation, Lands End Forest Division, Box 594, Rte. 80 W, Sherburne, NY 13460; 607/674-4036. The Rogers Environmental Center south of Earlville also often stocks maps. Someone usually rents horses in the Brookfield area, but as those someones change from year to year, your best bet is to inquire in the village.

CENTRAL NEW YORK

Binghamton and Vicinity

At the confluence of the Chenango and Susquehanna Rivers lies the flat, half-empty city of Binghamton, population 53,000. To its west, over the Chenango, lie Johnson City and Endicott; collectively, the area is known as the Triple Cities, or "Home of the Square Deal." And therein lies a tale.

Though not much more than a small town until the time of the Civil War, Binghamton exploded into a major metropolis with the coming of the Industrial Revolution. Dozens of factories sprang up along its rivers, employing thousands of immigrants, most from southern and eastern Europe.

Binghamton's first major industry was cigar making—until a permanent slump in sales caused by a general shift to cigarettes. In 1889 the first large-scale shoe factory was established in the city; by 1905, that one factory had expanded to 22. All were run by Endicott-Johnson, arguably the country's first paternalistic corporation.

Endicott-Johnson was responsible for building Binghamton's two sister cities. It also built the cities' parks, provided employee health benefits, instituted what may have been the nation's first eight-hour workday, and sponsored frequent company picnics and ball games. In return, E-J, as it was affectionately known, received fierce employee loyalty. Statues of George F. Johnson, the company's founder, stand everywhere.

In its heyday E-J employed more than 20,000 people. By 1966 that number had fallen to 10,154. Today all that's left is one small workboot division.

Until recently, the vacuum created by a shrinking Endicott-Johnson was filled by a growing IBM. First established here in the 1910s, the company eventually took over virtually all of Endicott. With IBM's downsizing around the turn of the 21st century, however, the Triple Cities are once again experiencing high unemployment. One-fourth of its population is now employed in the service industry; a major branch of the State University of New York is also located here.

> *Binghamton's culinary claim to fame is the spiedie, a sandwich made of marinated chunks of lean meat on a skewer served on Italian bread.*

Visitor Information

The **Broome County Chamber of Commerce,** 49 Court St., in the Metro Center, 2nd Fl., 607/772-8860 or 800/836-6740, www.binghamtoncvb.com, is stocked with an enormous number of brochures covering the entire region. The chamber is open Mon.–Fri. 8:30 A.M.–5 P.M.

SIGHTS

Downtown

Binghamton centers around **Courthouse Square,** located along Court Street between State and Exchange Streets. Here stand the neoclassical 1898 Broome County Courthouse, a Civil War Monument, and the beaux arts 1898 Old City Hall. This magnificent building with its elegant

the **1898 Broome County Courthouse,** on Binghamton's Courthouse Square

© CHRISTIANE BIRD

BINGHAMTON

NOT TO SCALE

© AVALON TRAVEL PUBLISHING, INC.

staircase and marble floors is now the **Grand Royale Hotel.** The polished brown desk in the lobby was once staffed by a police sergeant.

Along Riverside Drive at the southern tip of downtown is the confluence of the Susquehanna and Chenango Rivers, a ferocious brown cauldron of churning waters. The best way to get there is by car.

Roberson Museum and Science Center

Housed in both an elegant 1910 mansion and a modern building, this enjoyable complex contains art and history galleries, period rooms, a planetarium, a 300-seat theater, and a gift shop.

Exhibits range from a room devoted to native son Edwin Link, who developed the Link Flight Simulator, to displays on the region's folk art and varied ethnic heritage. There's also a science wing, a children's center with plenty of hands-on exhibits, and the **Binghamton Heritage Area Visitor Center.** The center publishes free walking- and driving-tour maps.

The Roberson also operates the **Kopernik Observatory** on Underwood Road in nearby Vestal. Equipped with three powerful telescopes, the observatory is open to the public most Friday nights March–Nov.; for schedule information, call the museum.

The museum, 30 Front St., 607/772-0660, www.roberson.org, is open Mon.–Sat. 10:30 A.M.–4:30 P.M., and Sunday noon–4:30 P.M. Admission is adults $6; seniors, students, and children 4–12 $4.

Discovery Center of the Southern Tier

Kids will also enjoy a visit to the Discovery Center, where they can "fly" a plane, crawl through a culvert, stand inside a bubble, or explore a wide variety of other hands-on exhibits. The center, 60 Morgan Rd., 607/773-8661, www.discoverycenter.org, is open July–Aug., Mon.–Sat. 10 A.M.–5 P.M., Sunday noon–5 P.M.; Sept.–June, Tues.–Fri. 10 A.M.–4 P.M., Saturday 10 A.M.–5 P.M., Sunday noon–5 P.M. Admission is $2, children under 2 free.

Clinton Street

If you drive north of the Roberson on Front Street about five long blocks, turn left, and head down Clinton about a mile, you'll come across a spread-out string of **antique stores.** One of the oldest and best known among them is the **Mad Hatter,** 284 Clinton St., 607/729-6036.

Also on Clinton St. are three **gold dome churches:** Sts. Cyril and Methodius at No. 148, St. Michael's at No. 280, and the Holy Spirit Byzantine at No. 360. These sanctuaries are a testament to the region's strong Eastern European heritage.

The Carousels

In each of the Triple Cities' six major parks is an elaborate woodcarved carousel, donated to the public by Endicott-Johnson founder George F. Johnson. The carousels, crowded with animals, operate at no charge for the price of "one piece of litter." As a young boy, Johnson didn't have the nickel fare needed for a carousel ride, and so promised himself that when he grew up and grew rich no one would ever be denied a ride.

All six carousels were manufactured in the early 1900s by the Allan Herschell Companies of North Tonawanda, NY. They're all designed in the "country fair" style and feature original Wurlitzer Band Organs.

The six carousels are located in Ross Park (Mor-

gan Rd.) and Recreation Park (Beethoven St.) in Binghamton; George W. Johnson Park (Oak Hill Ave.) and West Endicott Park (Page Ave.) in Endicott; C. Fred Johnson Park (C.F.J. Blvd.) in Johnson City; and Highland Park (Hooper Rd.) in Endwell. Hours of operation vary. For more information, call the Binghamton Visitor Center at 607/772-0660 or 607/772-8860.

Ross Park Zoo

The fifth-oldest zoo in the country, Ross Park is home to a wide variety of exotic creatures, including white tigers, snow leopards, spectacled bears, black swans, Siberian lynxes, Patagonian cavies, Japanese snow monkeys, and Rocky Mountain sheep. One of the zoo's finest exhibits is its 2.5-acre Wolf Woods where timber wolves and endangered red wolves roam free.

The zoo, 60 Morgan Rd., 607/724-5461, www.rossparkzoo.com, is open Apr.–Oct., daily 10 A.M.–5 P.M. Admission is adults $4.50, seniors and children 3–12 $3.

The zoo is located in Ross Park, 607/724-5461, where you'll also find the **Ross Park Carousel** and **Carousel Museum.** The museum holds a handful of historic exhibits; hours are the same as the zoo's. Admission is free.

Rod Serling Exhibit

Though born in Syracuse, *Twilight Zone* creator Rod Serling grew up in Binghamton, and a small exhibit honoring his memory can be found in the Forum, a performing arts center. The exhibit features quotes from Serling's childhood friends, pictures from his *Twilight Zone* days, and a 1960s-era TV set. Though the tribute is disappointingly meager, die-hard fans may want to stop by. The Forum, 236 Washington St., 607/778-2480, is open Mon.–Fri. 8 A.M.–4 P.M., and during performances.

Chenango Valley State Park

About 14 miles northeast of Binghamton lies the 1,071-acre Chenango Valley State Park. Here you'll find two glacial ponds, waterfalls, 18-hole golf course, hiking and nature trails, boat rentals, a bathing beach, a campground, good fishing sites, and a summertime schedule of special events. The park, Rte. 369, Chenango Forks, 607/648-5251, is open daily. Lifeguards are on duty Memorial Day–Labor Day; parking in summer is $7. To reserve one of the 216 campsites, call 800/456-CAMP; a basic site costs $13–15.

ACCOMMODATIONS

Budget travelers will find a number of motels along Front Street at the northern end of the city. Among them are a 65-room **Comfort Inn,** 1156 Front St., 607/722-5353 ($69–78 d), and the 98-room **Motel 6,** 1012 Front St., 607/771-0400 ($45–50 d). For families, the 106-room **Days Inn,** 1000 Front St., 607/724-3297, is a good choice, as it's equipped with a pool ($85–105 d).

The one-of-a-kind **Grand Royale Hotel,** 80 State St., 607/722-0000, Birmingham's former City Hall, has been divided into 60 guest rooms of varying shapes, sizes, and price ranges ($85–160 d). The modern **Best Western Binghamton Regency,** 225 Water St., 607/722-7575, offers 203 spacious guest rooms, an indoor pool, a business center, and several restaurants at surprisingly reasonable rates ($72–130 d).

FOOD

Binghamton's culinary claim to fame is the spiedie, a sandwich made of marinated chunks of lean meat on a skewer served on Italian bread. The tastiest and most authentic spiedies are available in the hole-in-wall **Sharkey's,** 56 Glenwood Ave., 607/729-9201; or at one of the **Lupo's** delis scattered around town.

A good spot for lunch or dinner is the cheery **Copper Cricket,** 266 Main St., 607/729-5620, offering dining on a closed-in front porch and a different menu daily; average dinner entrée $13. For first-rate contemporary fare in classy surroundings, try the **Landmark Bistro** in the Grand Royale Hotel, 80 State St., 607/722-9242; open Mon.–Fri., average lunch entrée $9. **Theo's,** 14 Main St., Johnson City, 607/797-0088, serves tasty soul food; average main dish $9.

Worth driving out of the way for is Sunday brunch at the **Silo,** Moran Rd., off Rte. 206 E,

Greene, 607/656-4377, housed in its namesake; the restaurant also serves a good dinner (average entrée $14). Though located in a sterile shopping mall, some of the best Thai food in the area is available at the **P.S. Restaurant,** 100 Rano Blvd., Giant Plaza, Vestal, 607/770-0056; average entrée $14.

ENTERTAINMENT

The city's top performance centers are the **Forum,** 236 Washington St., 607/772-2480; and the **Anderson Center for the Performing Arts,** State University of New York, Rte. 434 (Vestal Pkwy.), Vestal, 607/777-ARTS. The first presents a mix of classical music, opera, and theater; the second hosts everything from R&B to experimental theater.

The **Cider Mill Playhouse,** 2 S. Nanticoke Ave., 607/748-7363, is a cabaret-theater seating 300. The **Art Theatre,** 1204 Vestal Ave., 607/724-7900, is known for its art and foreign films.

The **Amsterdam,** 40 Willow St., Johnson City, 607/729-7717, is a laid-back tavern presenting live blues on the weekends. About 35 miles north of the city is the intimate **Night Eagle Cafe,** 15 LaFayette Pl., Oxford, 607/843-7378, hosting an eclectic array of music and cultural events.

The Class AA **Binghamton Mets** baseball team play at the Binghamton Municipal Baseball Park throughout the summer, 607/723-METS, www.bmets.com.

EVENTS

Multiethnic foods, dance, and music are the fare at the May **Two Rivers Ethnic Festival.** The **Otsiningo Pow Wow,** held on the site of an 18th-century Otsiningo Indian settlement, features dances, crafts, food, music, and storytelling. Come to the August **Spiedie Fest & Balloon Rally,** for hot-air balloons and that local culinary treat, the spiedie sandwich. At the September **Apple Festival,** you can sample 70-foot-long strudels and innumerable home-baked pies. For information on any of the above, inquire at the Broome County Chamber of Commerce, 607/772-8860.

CENTRAL NEW YORK

The North Country

Introduction

I am glad I shall never be young without wild country to be young in. Of what avail are forty freedoms without a blank spot on the map?

Aldo Leopold, 1945

Just exactly what or where the North Country is depends on who you ask. For some, it is everything that falls within Adirondack Park. For others, it is the country north of the Adirondacks, along the St. Lawrence River, bordering Canada. For still others, it is all 14 counties that lie above the Mohawk River. "The farther south you go," says Varick Chittenden, director of Traditional Arts in Upstate New York, Inc., "the bigger the North Country gets."

Close to one-third of New York State is a big, blank space on the map. Most of it is contained within Adirondack Park, a six-million-acre refuge that is an unusual mixture of public and private lands. Forty-three percent of the park is Forest Preserve that belongs to the people of New York.

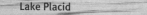

Lake Placid

COURTESY OF LAKE PLACID/ESSEX COUNTY VISITORS BUREAU.

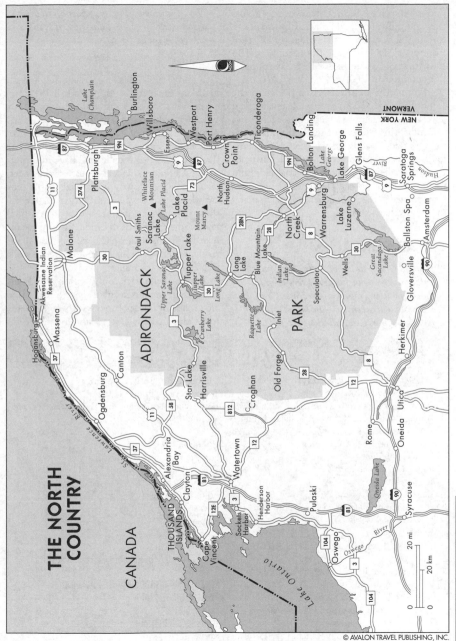

THE NORTH COUNTRY

CANADA

THOUSAND ISLANDS

ADIRONDACK

PARK

VERMONT

NEW YORK

© AVALON TRAVEL PUBLISHING, INC.

Fifty-seven percent is privately owned by industries and individuals, and devoted primarily to forestry, agriculture, and recreation. Within Adirondack Park live 130,000 people in 105 towns and villages, most of which have populations of less than 1,000.

Marking the southeastern entrance to the Adirondacks is Saratoga Springs, a small urban jewel best known for its superb horse racing and mineral springs. North of the Adirondacks lie the Thousand Islands, an evocative place-name for the insular flecks scattered up the St. Lawrence River. With the exception of a few small cities and resort towns, most of the Thousand Islands are as unpopulated as the Adirondacks, home to many more trees than people.

THE ADIRONDACKS

Few fully understand what the Adirondack wilderness really is. It is a mystery even to those who have crossed and recrossed it by boats along its avenues—the lakes; and on foot through its vast and silent recesses. . . .

Though the woodman may pass his lifetime in some section of the wilderness, it is still a mystery to him.

Verplanck Colvin, 1879

Two and a half times larger than Yellowstone National Park, Adirondack Park is the East's greatest wilderness. A vast and silent forest, it is filled with thousands of gleaming lakes and ponds, hundreds of rugged smoke-blue peaks, and endless miles of rushing rivers and streams that lead away from civilization back into time.

But Adirondack Park also bustles with cheery resort villages, scruffy industrial towns, and crowded recreational areas. During the region's short two-month summers, vacationers flock here by the thousands to canoe, fish, camp, and hike. During its endless harsh winters, year-round residents eke out livings through factory work, trapping, and logging.

Travelers who stick to the region's roads and villages will get a one-sided sense of the place. The roads offer superb views, to be sure, but roads also make it easy to underestimate the

NORTH COUNTRY HIGHLIGHTS

Saratoga Springs and Environs
Exploring downtown
The Saratoga Race Course in August
National Museum of Racing and Hall of Fame
Saratoga Spa State Park
Saratoga Performing Arts Center
Hattie's restaurant
Siro's restaurant and bar
Adelphi Hotel
Caffé Lena
Saratoga National Historic Park, Stillwater
Grant Cottage, Wilton
Cambridge village
"Grandma Moses Country," Washington County

Lake George and Southeastern Adirondacks
Hyde Collection, Glens Falls
Boating on Lake George
Hiking the mountains around Lake George
The village of Lake Luzerne
Rodeos at the Painted Pony Ranch, Lake Luzerne

Lamplight Inn B&B, Lake Luzerne
The Sagamore, Bolton Landing
Route 8 between Hague and Brandt Lake
Schroon Lake

Champlain Valley
Fort Ticonderoga, Ticonderoga
Crown Point State Historic Site, Crown Point
Westport village
Adirondack History Center, Elizabethtown
Deer's Head Inn, Elizabethtown
Essex village
Essex Inn, Essex
Ausable Chasm
Kent-Delord Museum House, Plattsburgh

High Peaks and Northern Adirondacks
Hiking, hiking, hiking
Jay village
Whiteface Mountain, Wilmington
Keene village

park's vast and haunting wildness. The only way to truly experience the Adirondacks is by canoe or foot.

As William Chapman White writes in *Adirondack Country,*

> *As a man tramps the woods to the lake he knows he will find pines and lilies, blue heron and golden shiners, shadows on the rocks and the glint of light on the wavelets, just as they were in the summer of 1354, as they will be in 2054 and beyond. He can stand on a rock by the shore and be in a past he could not have known, in a future he will never see. He can be part of time that was and time yet to come.*

The Land

Contrary to popular perception, the Adirondacks are not an extension of the Appalachian Mountains, but rather are part of the vast Canadian Shield. Nearly twice as old as the Appalachians, the Adirondacks are composed of Precambrian igneous and metamorphic rock thrust upward about 10 million years ago. Atop the summits is a bluish erosion-resistant bedrock that, at 1.2 million years old, is among the oldest exposed bedrock in the world.

Also contrary to popular perception, much of the Adirondacks is not mountainous. Most of the area lies between 1,000 and 2,000 feet above sea level, with the western and southern sections composed of gentle hills strewn with lakes, ponds, and streams. Most of the highest summits—known as the High Peaks—are in the northeastern section, around Lake Placid. Forty-two of the 46 High Peaks are over 4,000 feet; Mt. Marcy, at 5,344 feet, is the highest.

Throughout the Adirondacks run 1,200 miles of rivers fed by an estimated 30,000 miles of brooks and streams. Most significant among them are the Hudson—whose highest source is Lake Tear of the Clouds on Mt. Marcy—Raquette, Ausable, Sacandaga, Beaver, Oswegatchie, St. Regis, and Moose. The park also contains about 2,800 lakes and ponds, the largest of which are Lake George and Lake Champlain. Between Lake Champlain and the mountains runs the long and fertile Champlain Valley.

Route 73 from Keene to Lake Placid
Route 28 N from North Creek to Long Lake
Adirondack Park Visitor Centers, Newcomb and Paul Smiths
Lake Placid sports complexes
John Brown Farm State Historic Site, Lake Placid
Adirondak Loj, Lake Placid
Lake Placid Lodge, Lake Placid
Stevenson Memorial Cottage, Saranac Lake
Six Nations Indian Museum, Onchiota

Northwest Lakes and Central Adirondacks
Beth Joseph Synagogue, Tupper Lake
Canoeing the St. Regis Canoe Area
Wawbeek on Upper Saranac Lake
Long Lake village
Canoeing from Long Lake to Saranac Lake
Adirondack Hotel, Long Lake
A cruise on Blue Mountain Lake
Adirondack Museum, Blue Mountain Lake

Potter's Resort, Blue Mountain Lake
Hiking near Indian Lake
Rafting the Hudson River Gorge, North Creek
Raquette Lake Supply Co., Raquette Lake
Great Camp Sagamore, Raquette Lake

The Thousand Islands
H. Lee White Marine Museum, Oswego
Sackets Harbor village
Driving to Tibbetts Point, Cape Vincent
Clayton village
Antique Boat Museum, Clayton
Thousand Islands Inn, Clayton
Boldt Castle, Alexandria Bay
Fantasy Boat Tours, Alexandria Bay
Thousand Islands Park, Wellesley Island
Remington Art Museum, Ogdensburg
Traditional Arts in Upstate New York, Canton
Eisenhower Lock, Massena
Akwesasne Museum, Hogansburg

Flora and Fauna

The Adirondack forest supports over 70 different species of trees, most of which are in the spruce and fir, or beech, birch, and maple families. Generally speaking, the trees grow in five site categories: white pine, spruce swamp forest, mixed wood, hardwood, and upper spruce slope. White pines grow at the park's lowest elevations in the Champlain Valley, while spruce grows above 2,500 feet. In between, in ascending order, thrive the spruce swamp, mixed wood, and hardwood forests.

Woodland wildflowers such as dewdrops and lily-of-the-valley flourish in the lower Adirondacks, while on the peaks grow bright specks of alpine flora, mosses, lichens, and other hardy plants. Hundreds of species of shrubs, herbs, grasses, and ferns also abound. Several good guides to the park's flora and fauna are published by the Adirondack Mountain Club (see Hiking and Canoeing under Practicalities, below).

As for mammals, the Adirondacks are home to 55 species, including raccoon, porcupine, weasel, mink, otter, bobcat, fox, coyote, white-tailed deer, and black bear. The elusive moose and lynx have recently been reintroduced into the forest.

Birdlife in the park ranges from the very small—chickadees and nuthatches—to the very large—grouse and osprey. Two hundred and eighteen species have been spotted, including woodpeckers, hawks, warblers, kingbirds, flycatchers, ducks, peregrine falcons, and bald eagles. One of the most characteristic sounds of the Adirondacks is the haunting call of the loon.

In Adirondacks waters swim 86 species of fish, including trout, salmon, walleye, northern pike, and small- and large-mouth bass. The region also supports 35 species of reptiles and amphibians, and countless species of insects. Pesky blackflies thrive in the mountains from late May through June, and mosquitoes are plentiful throughout the summer.

Early History

Once the hunting grounds of Iroquois and Algonquin, the Adirondacks were largely overlooked by early white settlers. Military outposts went up along the shores of Lakes George and Champlain in the mid-1700s, but the rest of the region remained the haunt of hunters and trappers until well into the 1800s. Even logging proceeded slowly in the mountains, due to the difficulty of reaching the trees and getting them to market.

It wasn't until 1837 that New York State finally commissioned a natural history survey of the wilderness. Led by geologist and botanist Prof. Ebenezer Emmons, the party ventured into the High Peaks region and climbed Mt. Marcy. Accompanying Emmons was artist Charles Cromwell Ingham, whose paintings of the Adirondacks astonished the general public. Few realized that so great a wilderness remained in the Northeast.

By the 1840s, lumbermen had penetrated deep into the forest, and by the 1850s, New York was producing more lumber than any other state. Vacationers and enthusiasts were also beginning to discover the region. Most famous among them were the members of the Philosophers' Camp. Organized by William Stillman of Cambridge, Massachusetts, the camp included such eminent men as Ralph Waldo Emerson and Louis Agassiz, who came to hike, fish, canoe, botanize, talk, and write. The camp was first established at Follansby Pond near Long Lake in 1857 and later moved to Ampersand Pond near Saranac Lake.

After the Civil War, the Adirondacks began attracting many more vacationers, due largely to the 1869 publication of William H. H. Murray's *Adventures in the Wilderness.* Murray, a minister from Boston, both vividly described the wilderness and—more importantly—told readers how to get there. Within weeks after his book came out, the rush to the Adirondacks was on.

At first, vacationers stayed in the region's few large and rustic hotels, but soon it became fashionable to build private summer camps. In 1879, William West Durant created an architectural camp style that combined the features of a log cabin with those of a Swiss chalet. Wealthy families such as the Vanderbilts and Rockefellers embraced the style and built luxurious "great camps" that resembled self-contained villages. Many of these great camps still stand.

Verplanck Colvin and Adirondack Park

In 1872, years after explorers had discovered the sources of the Nile and various rivers out West, a

WILDERNESS GRIDLOCK AT ADIRONDACK PARK

The biggest ecological problem facing Adirondack Park today is not pollution, erosion, or even acid rain. It is overuse. "The park is being loved to death," says Ed Lynch, director of the Adirondack Park Visitor Interpretive Center in Paul Smiths.

Over 120,000 hikers enter the High Peaks region annually. One summer camp takes hundreds of campers each week on a hike up Ampersand Mountain, and as many as 200 people can be found atop Mt. Marcy on a fine summer day. Trees around Marcy Dam and Lake Colden bear the scars of ax marks, and the destruction of saplings by backpackers has caused certain campsites to be cordoned off. "People don't want to hear there's a problem," said Lynch, "but there is. . . . And this is not an area that can bounce back quickly if damaged."

Lynch and other park personnel urge hikers to shy away from the most famous summits—including Mt. Marcy, Ampersand, and Whiteface—

and tackle some of the lesser-known ones instead. Lynch especially recommends hiking outside the High Peaks region. Many other sections of the park also offer excellent trails up challenging peaks, and yet attract only a handful of hikers a year. Hamilton County, just south of the High Peaks, has several under-hiked mountains; among them are Owls Head Mountain near Long Lake and Snowy Mountain near Indian Lake. Many other less strenuous and all but overlooked trails can be found in the Northwest Lakes region.

Basic pamphlets describing hikes outside the High Peaks region are available through the Department of Environmental Conservation, 625 Broadway, Albany, NY 12233, 518/402-9428, www.dec.state.ny.us. Or, consult *An Adirondack Sampler: Day Hikes For All Seasons* by Bruce Wadsworth (Adirondack Mountain Club), or *Fifty Hikes in the Adirondacks* by Barbara McMartin (Back Country Publications).

---

young surveyor named Verplanck Colvin finally traced the Hudson River to its mysterious source. Starting in the Champlain Valley, he and his party hiked from peak to peak until reaching Mt. Marcy and what is now known as Lake Tear of the Clouds. "Far above the chilly water of Lake Avalanche," Colvin later reported to the state legislature, "at an elevation of 4,293 feet, is *Summit Water,* a minute unpretending tear of the clouds as it were—a lonely pool, shivering in the breezes of the mountains, and sending its limpid surplus through Feldspar Brook to the Opalescent River, the well-spring of the Hudson."

From that expedition on until 1900, Colvin surveyed the entire Adirondack region. Often financing his own expeditions, he sent back frequent reports to the state legislature, passionately arguing for the creation of a park to preserve the forest and its watershed.

Few listened at first, but as the century wore on, downstate New Yorkers began to worry about their water supply, and businesses about the build-up of silt in the New York Harbor. Protecting the forests would help solve both problems and create a giant "pleasuring-grounds for

the people." Largely because of the businessmen's influence, the idea took hold, and in 1885, the state passed an unprecedented bill establishing a 681,374-acre Adirondack Forest Preserve. This law, strengthened in 1892 and again in 1894, even went so far as to dictate that the preserve remain "forever wild," a phrase that has created considerable controversy ever since.

Modern Times

During the past 100 years, numerous land purchases by the state have increased the Adirondack Forest Preserve from its original 681,374 acres to its present 2.6 million acres. The park's Blue Line—a term derived from the color ink used in 1884 to delineate the park's boundaries on a map—now encompasses nearly six million acres, as opposed to its early 2.8 million acres.

With this growth has come conflict, exacerbated by increased tourism and a boom in second homes. The conflict has pitted conservationists concerned about the park's ecological future against those advocating varying forms of economic development.

The conflict reached one early crisis point in the

late 1960s, when the building of the Northway (I-87) opened up the region to yet more visitors. And so in 1968, Gov. Nelson Rockefeller appointed a state commission to study the future of the park. Among the commission's proposals was the establishment of an Adirondack Park Agency (APA) to encourage wise land-use planning.

Duly established in 1971, the APA has since instituted zoning laws for both the park's state *and* private lands. This has infuriated many residents, who feel that the state has no right to tell them what they can or cannot do with private property. Many also feel that the zoning laws, along with the original "forever wild" clause, are inhibiting economic growth in an area already suffering from out-migration and severe unemployment.

For the conservationists, of course, there is no real debate. In a world of ever-decreasing blank spots on the map, the park must be preserved.

It is a conflict unlikely to be resolved for decades to come.

PRACTICALITIES
When to Go
Winters in the North Country are long and harsh, and many tourist attractions don't open until mid-June, closing down again in September. Many lodges and motels close down as well, unless they're located near a ski resort.

During July and August the North Country's tourist season reaches its peak. Temperatures usually remain in the 70s and 80s during the day, and refreshingly cool in the evening. September, when the summer crowds disperse, is also an excellent time to visit; temperatures usually range from the 50s to the 70s.

If the weather is dry, the North Country's fall foliage season can be spectacular. The leaves usually peak in early October. For a fall foliage report, call 800/225-5697.

RECREATION
Hiking and Canoeing
With 2,000 miles of hiking trails, and canoe routes stretching 100 miles or more, the Adiron-

dacks is an outdoor lovers' paradise. Free, basic information on hiking trails, canoe routes, and tips for using the state's lands can be obtained by contacting the **Department of Environmental Conservation** (DEC), 625 Broadway, Albany, NY 12233; 518/402-9428, www.dec.state.ny.us.

Some of the DEC's brochures include enough information to actually embark on a hike or canoe trip, but many do not. The best source for more detailed information and maps—essential in many areas—is the **Adirondack Mountain Club,** 814 Coggins Rd., Lake George, NY 12845, 518/668-4447 or 800/395-8080, www.adk.org. The ADK maintains visitor information centers at Lake George and Lake Placid and runs the Adirondack Loj, a rustic lodge and campground at Lake Placid. The ADK also sponsors numerous workshops and outings, some of which are open to the general public. If you're interested in joining the ADK, the annual membership fee for an individual adult is $45.

Two of the best hiking guides for visitors new to the Adirondack region are the ADK's *An Adirondack Sampler: Day Hikes for All Seasons* by Bruce Wadsworth and *Fifty Hikes in the Adirondacks,* by Barbara McMartin (Backcountry Publications). Wadsworth's book focuses primarily on hikes for beginners, while McMartin's describes hikes of varying difficulty.

A number of day-hikes are sketched out below. These short descriptions should be supplemented with more detailed information from the ADK or other hiking guides.

Fishing
Among the many fish that swim the Adirondack waters are landlocked salmon, brook trout, lake trout, northern pike, pickerel, and small- and large-mouth bass. Meanwhile, the St. Lawrence River in the Thousand Islands offers some of the world's best bass and muskie fishing. The largest muskellunge ever caught in the region weighed over 69 pounds.

Fishing licenses are mandatory for everyone over age 16 and can be obtained in sporting goods stores, bait shops, and town offices. The DEC maintains fishing hotlines with information on good fishing spots: in the southeastern Adirondacks, call 518/623-3682; for the High Peaks and northwestern lakes, call 518/891-5413; for the Thousand Islands, call 800/248-4FUN.

North Country Guides and Outfitters

The guide is a firmly entrenched Adirondack institution. Traditionally thought of as a crusty, plaid-jacketed man wise in the ways of the woods, he's been around since the mid-19th century, when naive city folk coming up to explore the wilderness needed someone to help them find their way around and stay alive.

The Adirondack Guides' Association was formed in 1891 to help establish a uniform pay scale, and today hundreds of guides operate throughout the region. They're not as necessary as they once were, thanks to well-marked trails and detailed maps, but they can still guide you to out-of-the-way spots. Many also offer guided group trips, and rent or sell outdoor gear.

A number of guide companies and outfitters are listed by location below. For a more complete list, contact the **New York State Outdoor Guides Association,** 110 Main St., #150, Lake Placid, NY 12946, 866/4NYSOGA, www.nysoga.com. Or, check with the DEC, 518/402-9428, www.dec.state.ny.us.

Fishing guides are especially plentiful in the Thousand Islands region and are organized into associations. For more information, contact the chambers of commerce in Cape Vincent (315/654-2481), Clayton (315/686-3771 or 800/252-9806), and Alexandria Bay (315/482-9531 or 800/541-2110).

Camping and Accommodations

The DEC maintains 42 campgrounds and 500 island-based campsites within Adirondack Park. Some are listed below, but for a complete list, contact the DEC, 518/402-9428, www.dec.state.ny.us.

Campground reservations, highly recommended on summer weekends, can be made by calling 800/456-CAMP.

Saratoga Springs, Lake George, and Lake Placid offer a wide variety of accommodations. Elsewhere in the North Country, accommodations, though plentiful, tend to be limited to

motels and lodges. Some of these lodges can be quite luxurious and remote, and most offer meal plans.

Cottages that rent by the week are popular throughout the region. For more information, contact the regional tourism offices listed below.

In addition to the B&B registries listed in this book's introduction, several other registries operate in the North Country: the **Adirondack B&B Association,** P.O. Box 801, Lake George, NY 12845, www.adirondackbb.com; **B&B Adirondack Collection,** P.O. Box 814, Elizabethtown, NY 12932, 581/946-8323 or 888/222-9789, www.adirondackinns.com; and **Adirondack B&B Reservation Service,** website: www.adirondackbedbreakfast.com.

Eating

When traveling through the North Country, watch for signs advertising chicken barbecues, pig roasts, pancake breakfasts, and fish fries. These local fundraisers welcome outsiders and are cheap and delicious.

A specialty of the Thousand Islands region is the shore dinner. Offered by professional fishing guides as a traditional part of a fishing trip, the meal includes fresh fish, along with fatback sandwiches (fatback is similar to bacon, but is all fat), salad served with Thousand Islands dressing, corn on the cob, potatoes, French toast with maple syrup, and strong, dark "guide's coffee." Shore dinners sometimes are prepared during festivals or as community fundraisers.

Transportation

No major airports service the North Country. Most visitors fly to New York City, Albany, Syracuse, or Montreal, and then drive. The one commercial airport in Adirondack Park is just outside Saranac Lake. **USAirways,** 800/428-4322 flies into Watertown in the Thousand Islands area.

Amtrak, 800/872-7245, operates daily between New York and Montreal, with stops in Saratoga Springs, Glens Falls, Fort Ticonderoga, Port Henry, Westport, and Plattsburgh. The scenery along the way is spectacular.

Among bus companies, **Adirondack–Pine**

Hill Trailways, 800/225-6815, is the only one that provides service throughout the Adirondacks. **Greyhound,** 800/231-2222, www.greyhound.com, travels to Saratoga Springs, Glens Falls, Plattsburgh, and the Thousand Islands.

By far the best ways to explore the North Country are by car, canoe, and foot. The Adirondack North Country Association (ANCA), 22 St. Bernard St., Saranac Lake, NY 12983, 518/891-6200, publishes a good map that outlines scenic and historic driving routes; copies can be picked up for free in most tourism offices, or by writing the association and enclosing $2 for postage and handling.

Emergencies

In Saratoga, Washington, and Warren Counties, which include Lake George and Warrensburg, dial "911" for emergencies. Elsewhere in the North Country, "911" is just now being introduced; if not yet in effect, dial "0."

Hospitals in the region include the **Saratoga Hospital,** 211 Church St., Saratoga Springs, 518/587-3222; the **Champlain Valley Physicians Hospital,** 75 Beekman St., Plattsburgh, 518/561-2000; the **Adirondack Medical Center,** Church St., Lake Placid, 518/523-3311; the **Adirondack Medical Center,** Lake Colby Dr., Saranac Lake, 518/891-4141; and the **Samaritan**

Medical Center, 830 Washington St., Watertown, 315/785-4000.

Visitor Information

For general information about the Adirondacks, contact the **Adirondack Regional Tourism Council,** P.O. Box 2149, Plattsburgh, NY 12901, 518/846-8016 or 800/487-6867, www.adk.com. An Adirondacks **information booth** is located between Exits 17 and 18 off I-87 northbound, Glens Falls, 518/792-2730. Other helpful tourism-related websites include www.adirondacks.org and www.adirondack.net.

For general information on the Thousand Islands, contact the **Thousand Islands International Tourism Council,** 43373 Collins Landing Rd., Alexandria Bay, NY 13607, 315/482-2520 or 800/847-5263, www.visit1000islands.com. Open daily in summer, 8 A.M.–6 P.M., Mon.–Fri. 9 A.M.–5 P.M. in the off-season.

Saratoga Springs, Lake Placid, Lake George, Glens Falls, the Champlain Valley, and Alexandria Bay operate excellent tourist information centers. Those addresses and the addresses of smaller regional offices are listed under their respective sections.

Adirondack Life, 518/946-2191, is a glossy monthly with excellent articles on a wide variety of Adirondack topics. You'll find the publication at most area newsstands and general stores.

Saratoga Springs and Environs

Dukes and kooks, counts and no-accounts, stars and czars have added to the legend of Saratoga, where it isn't enough to stay the 30 days. Staying the 30 nights is the true test of stamina.

Joe Hirsch,
Daily Racing Form

For 11 months out of the year, Saratoga Springs is a charming Victorian town known for its first-rate arts scene, grand romantic architecture, sophisticated shops and restaurants, and therapeutic mineral springs. But on the 12th month, the town turns itself upside down with the buyers

and sellers of dreams. From dawn until dusk, and then from dusk until dawn, gossiping socialites mix with shrewd businesspeople mix with innocent tourists mix with breeders and trainers and grooms. And all for the love of the horse.

The Saratoga Race Course, built in 1864, is the oldest racetrack in America, and it has long represented the very best of what racing has to offer. Louisville may have its Kentucky Derby, Baltimore its Preakness, but it is to Saratoga that the serious cognoscenti come, every summer, for six weeks of exclusive racing. Attendance at the sprawling, Victorian-era grandstand—complete with striped awnings, clapboard siding, and gild-

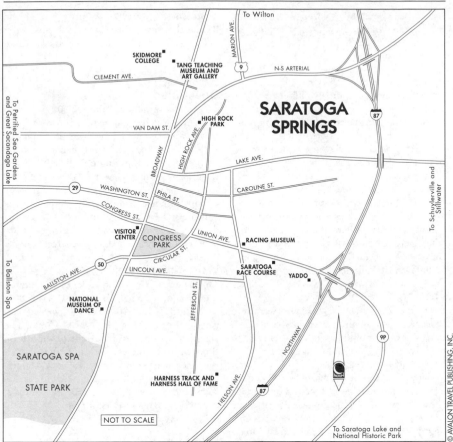

SARATOGA SPRINGS

ed cupolas—averages about 25,000 a day, or the equivalent of Saratoga's population year-round.

Even during nonracing season, Saratoga is an unusual place. The arts thrive at the Saratoga Performing Arts Center, Skidmore College, and Yaddo, a renowned artists' retreat; and harness racing takes place Jan.–Nov. at the Saratoga Raceway. The town also supports several fine museums, the regal Saratoga Spa State Park, and a plethora of good hotels and B&Bs. Surrounding Saratoga is lush, rolling countryside offering more cultural, historical, and scenic attractions. Best known among them is the Saratoga National Historic Park, where the 1777 battles that turned the course of the Revolutionary War were fought.

HISTORY

Early History

Saratoga Springs owes its existence to its mineral springs, first discovered by the Mohawk in the 14th century. In 1771, the Mohawk brought their ill friend Sir William Johnson to the "Medicine Spring of the Great Spirit." The waters helped ease the British Indian agent's suffering, and introduced the mineral springs to the white world.

In 1802, pioneer Gideon Putnam arrived in the area, bought the land around the present Congress Park, and built the three-story Union Hall, "the first commodious hotel erected at the springs for the accommodation of visitors." Other

THE NORTH COUNTRY

pioneers and hotels followed, and by the 1840s, the resort was known as a hot spot where high society met to partake of the waters and dally with games of chance.

Saratoga didn't really take off, however, until the 1860s, when prizefighter, gambler, and general roustabout John Morrisey built the Saratoga Race Course. The track was a near-instant success and was soon joined by elaborate gambling casinos and posh block-long hotels. Here fluttering socialites danced with hard-nosed gamblers beneath crystal chandeliers.

Saratoga regulars included prominent horsemen such as William R. Travers, financiers such as J. Pierpont Morgan, actresses such as Lillian Russell, and high rollers such as Diamond Jim Brady, who sometimes wore as many as 2,548 diamonds with his evening outfits. Ace reporter Nellie Bly of the New York *World* sent stories downstate about "Our Wickedest Summer Resort."

The 20th Century

But by the early 1900s, the wickedness seemed to be all but over. A reform movement closed down the casinos, some of the springs dried up due to excessive commercial pumping, and the fashionable crowd moved on.

Enter New York State, which in 1909 established a state reservation to preserve the largest cluster of springs. Within the next 25 years, the state transformed the reservation into Saratoga Spa State Park, building a hotel and two magnificent bathhouses. Saratoga's golden era of the spa began, with people coming from all over to take the cure—drinking mineral waters, taking baths, and exercising. The casinos, in full swing again, were this time under the control of gangsters such as Lucky Luciano and Dutch Schultz.

Saratoga suffered another decline after WW II as the public's interest in spa therapy declined and the casinos were shut down once again—this time for good. Only the race course mustered on, with races held every August without fail.

Then in the 1960s, Saratoga's many charms were discovered by a new generation. Old Victorian buildings were snatched up and renovated, and a new wave of socialites and vacationers moved in. Today, the town's most coveted social

event is Mrs. Mary Lou Whitney's Ball, held during the August meet, to which she invites 300 of her nearest-and-dearest racetrack friends.

GETTING ORIENTED

Orientation

Saratoga Springs (population 25,000) is a small and compact city centered on Broadway. The track lies to the east of downtown, off Union Avenue, while Saratoga Spa State Park is to the south, off South Broadway (Route 9). The Northway (I-87) passes within a few miles of the city.

All of the sites along Broadway lie within easy walking distance of each other. Both the track and the state park are about a mile from the downtown. Park downtown in the large free lots between Broadway and Circular Street.

Visitor Information

The **Saratoga County Chamber of Commerce,** 28 Clinton St., Saratoga Springs, NY 12866, 518/584-3255 or 800/526-8970, www.saratoga.org, is open Mon.–Fri. 9 A.M.–5 P.M. The chamber operates an **information booth** on Broadway near the entrance to Congress Park late June–Labor Day, daily 9 A.M.–5 P.M., with extended hours to 7 P.M. during racing season. Maps and brochures can also be picked up at the Heritage Area Visitors Center.

SIGHTS

Heritage Area Visitors Center

A good place to start a tour of Saratoga is in the visitor center at the Drink Hall, a 1915 trolley station later converted into a hall where mineral waters were sold. Back then, different waters were recommended for different times of the day: Hathorn in the morning, Coesa before dinner, and Geyser in the evening.

The beaux arts building with its Doric columns features two bas-relief murals out front. One depicts Sir William Johnson taking the cure at High Rock Spring. Another commemorates the surrender of British general Burgoyne during the Battle of Saratoga in 1777.

Inside the center, beneath a barrel-vaulted ceil-

SARATOGA'S MINERAL SPRINGS

Saratoga's springs gurgle up from ancient seas trapped in limestone layers that are sealed by a solid layer of shale. Through these layers runs a geological fault line which cracks the shale, allowing the water to escape to the surface. The limestone enriches the water with minerals, and carbon dioxide adds natural carbonation.

Most of the springs bubble up in Congress Park, High Rock Park, and the Saratoga Spa State Park. Some are marked by pavilions, others by fountains, and each has its own distinct taste. A complete guide to the springs and their supposed therapeutic values can be picked up at the Heritage Area Visitor Center.

Saratoga Spa State Park still offers mineral baths, as does the privately run **Crystal Spa,** 92 S. Broadway, 518/584-2556. The state's Lincoln bathhouse is utilitarian and very reasonably priced (see Saratoga Spa State Park); the Crystal Spa is more luxurious and expensive.

Two bottling companies continue to operate within the city: the world-famous **Saratoga Spring Water Company,** and the recently re-opened **Excelsior Springs Water Company.** The Saratoga Spring Company has been located on Geyser Road at the Route 50 entrance to Saratoga Spa State Park since 1872. Take the time to see its lovely Victorian gazebo, built in the late 1800s.

ing, are more romantic murals, exhibits on the history of Saratoga, and racks filled with tourism brochures. Saratoga is one of New York State's Heritage Areas—loosely designated historic districts linked by a common theme. The theme in Saratoga is the natural environment, and free walking-tour maps pinpointing the area's springs and other points of interest can be picked up here.

The center, 297 Broadway, at Congress St., 518/587-3241, is open May–Oct., daily 9 A.M.–4 P.M.; Nov.–April, Mon.–Sat. 9 A.M.–4 P.M. Admission is free.

Congress Park

Across the street from the visitor center lies Congress Park, a small jewel of a retreat filled with jade green lawns, graveled walkways, and flowering plants. In the center of things reigns the Italianate red-brick **Canfield Casino,** now home to the Museum of the Historical Society of Saratoga Springs; to one side is the **Trask Memorial.** Erected in 1915 by Katrina Trask in memory of her husband Spencer, a financier and leading advocate of the springs, the memorial is by Daniel Chester French, the sculptor of the Lincoln Memorial. Not far from the memorial rises the **Katrina Trask Gateway,** a dramatic granite staircase.

One of the oldest parks in the country, Congress Park dates back to 1792 when Nicholas Gilman, a member of the first U.S. Congress, "discovered" and named Congress Spring. Then along came Gideon Putnam, who in 1806 bought the swampland next to the spring, siphoned off some of its waters with a square wooden tube, and built Saratoga's first mineral water bathhouse.

In 1826, John Clarke drained the swamplands, built walkways and a Greek pavilion, and began bottling the waters. In 1876, Frederick Law Olmsted completely redesigned the park, replacing the old structures with high Victorian Gothic buildings.

The park is open daily dawn to dusk. Tours of the park, 518/587-3241, are offered in summer.

Canfield Casino

The lavish Canfield Casino was built by John Morrissey in 1870 as an adjunct to his new racetrack. One writer of the day described the place—nicknamed "Morrissey's Elegant Hell"—as having "gorgeously furnished toilet rooms, faro parlors and drawing rooms, carpeted with soft carpets and decorated with rich carvings and bronzes."

In 1894, Richard Canfield purchased the building and embellished it with more ostentatious touches, including stained-glass windows and a posh new dining parlor. Fabulous sums were won and lost in the casino's gaming rooms, and many "Monte Carlo suicides" are said to have been committed. Before the casino was shut down in 1907, Canfield purportedly netted the then-enormous profit of $2.5 million.

Today, the casino houses the **Museum of the Historical Society of Saratoga Springs.** Downstairs temporary exhibits focus on the history

The 1870 Canfield Casino, built by John Morrissey and once known as "Morrissey's Elegant Hell," today houses the Museum of the Historical Society of Saratoga Springs.

and culture of Saratoga. Upstairs are period rooms and an oddball collection of musty artifacts including Native American pottery, Egyptian spears, bullets from the Battles of Saratoga, and old gaming tables, cards, and chips.

The museum, in Congress Park, 518/584-6920, www.saratogahistory.org, is open Memorial Day–Labor Day, daily 10 A.M.–4 P.M.; call for off-season hours. Admission is $4 for adults, $3 for seniors and students, under 10 free.

Children's Museum at Saratoga

Kids under 10 years of age will appreciate a stop at this small museum, filled with interactive exhibits. Here youngsters can run a general store, blow giant bubbles, experiment with the laws of physics, and tumble about in a cheery play area. The museum, 69 Caroline St., 518/584-5540, www.childrensmuseumatsaratoga.org, is open July–Labor Day Mon.–Sat. 9:30 A.M.–4:30 P.M.; Tues.–Sun. in the off-season, call for hours. Admission is $4 per person, under 1 free.

Broadway

North of Congress Park begin the bustling blocks of downtown Broadway, lined with shops and restaurants that spill out onto the sidewalks in summer. Leafy trees spread their boughs, and inviting park benches beckon here and there.

At one time, Broadway was flanked with one grand hotel after another, some sporting balconies that stretched hundreds of feet. Today, only two of the smaller hotels remain: the 1840 Federal-style **Rip Van Dam,** No. 353, and the 1877 Victorian **Adelphi,** No. 365. The brown-and-yellow Adelphi is an especially gracious place, with a romantic period lobby and an expansive garden out back that's a good place for afternoon tea or a late-night drink.

Other buildings worth noting along Broadway include the 1916 Classic Revival **Adirondack Trust,** No. 473, adorned with Adirondack symbols and bronze Tiffany doors; and the 1910 beaux arts **post office,** No. 475. At Lake Avenue, across from the post office, is the 1871 Italian palazzo **city hall,** the birthplace of the American Banking Association and the American Bar Association.

High Rock Park

Along Maple Avenue one block east of where Broadway ends and North Broadway begins is narrow High Rock Park, a grassy area at the base of a bluff. In the park once bubbled the waters of the High Rock Spring to which the Mohawk brought the ill Sir William Johnson in 1771.

Today, the High Rock Spring is greatly diminished, but the waters of three other nearby springs are pumped into the park. Closest to the street is Governor Spring, highly carbonated and tasting of iron. Nearby is Peerless Spring, whose waters taste slightly salty. At the end of the block behind the textile mill is Old Red Spring, known for its high iron content. Its waters are said to help those with skin disorders and inflammation of the eyes.

East Side Historic District

Over 400 historic residences fill the east side of town between Lake and Union Avenues, Henry and Ludlow Streets. Many were built in the late 19th and early 20th centuries, and they cover a wide variety of architectural styles, including Victorian Gothic, Italianate, Second Empire, Queen Anne, and bungalow. Some are quite small and built close to the street. Others are mansion-size.

One street particularly worth strolling down is **Circular Drive.** At No. 20 stands the stunning 1873 **Batcheller Mansion Inn** built in a French Renaissance style.

Tang Teaching Museum and Art Gallery at Skidmore College

Saratoga's newest cultural attraction, opened in 2000, is a dynamic arts center hosting both contemporary art exhibits and cultural events. Donated to Skidmore College by Chinese-born American businessman Oscar Tang, whose daughter and wife are both Skidmore alumni, the museum was designed by acclaimed architect Antoine Predock. One recent exhibit featured the Sonnabend Collection, with works by Jasper Johns, Andy Warhol, and other contemporary masters. Other exhibits have focused on nontraditional media such as photography, video, and site-specific installations.

The museum, 815 N. Broadway, 518/580-8080, www.skidmore.edu/tang, is open Tues.–Sun. 11 A.M.–5 P.M.

Union Avenue

After Broadway, Union Avenue is Saratoga's other main drag. A wide boulevard leading east to the Saratoga Race Course, the avenue features some of the grandest Victorian architecture in town. Several of the buildings now operate as posh B&Bs that charge outrageous prices during the racing season; others hold offices, apartments, and condominiums. During the summer, Union Avenue, like the racecourse itself, is planted with thousands of white, purple, and pink impatiens.

National Museum of Racing and Hall of Fame

Even nonracing fans will want to step into this one-of-a-kind museum, filled with intriguing exhibitions on the history and mechanics of thoroughbred racing. Exhibits on the horse explain how all thoroughbreds can trace their origins back to one of three Arabian progenitors, and how at a full gallop, a horse takes in five gallons of air a second. Exhibits on racing champs tell the stories of Man o' War and Secretariat, Seattle Slew and Affirmed. Exhibits on Saratoga tell of the resort's gambling heyday, when it was

© CHRISTIANE BIRD

THE NORTH COUNTRY

Historic grand Victorian houses line Union Avenue, which leads east to the Saratoga Race Course.

frequented by Diamond Jim Brady, Lillian Russell, Lillie Langtry, and Florenz Ziegfeld.

The museum, 191 Union Ave., 518/584-0400, www.racingmuseum.org, is open Mon.–Sat. 10 A.M.–4:30 P.M. and Sunday noon–4:30 P.M., with extended hours during racing season. Admission is adults $7, seniors and students $5, children under 5 free. Throughout the summer, the museum also offers tours of the training track Wed.–Sun. at 8:30 A.M. Tickets cost $10.

Saratoga Race Course

The nation's oldest thoroughbred track comes to life every late July through early September. Most U.S. tracks present one weekly stakes race, featuring top-of-the-line horses; Saratoga has one every day. The meet's highlight is the Travers Stakes held on the fifth Saturday; other big events are the Whitney, the Alabama, and the prestigious Fasig-Tipton yearling sales.

Saratoga, filled with striped tents and bright flowers, remains one of the world's best tracks in which to get a close-up view of the horse-racing world. The thoroughbreds are walked through the crowd before being saddled in the paddock, and jockeys stop to talk and sign autographs between races.

Breakfast at the track is a Saratoga tradition.

Between 7 and 9:30 A.M., visitors can dine on steak and eggs in the clubhouse or munch donuts in the grandstand while watching the horses go through their morning workouts. Afterwards, tours of the backstretch are available at $10 per person.

The racecourse, 518/584-6200, www.nyra.com/saratoga, is located off Union Avenue, near its intersection with East Avenue.

Yaddo

Just east of the racetrack lies this artists' retreat, housed in a Victorian Gothic mansion that was once home to Spencer and Katrina Trask. Spencer Trask was a New York financier and philanthropist, Katrina a poet.

Artists come to Yaddo to get away from the noisy outside world and work in uninterrupted peace. About 4,000 writers, composers, and visual artists have worked here since the program began in 1926, including Flannery O'Connor, Saul Bellow, Leonard Bernstein, Langston Hughes, John Cheever, and Aaron Copland.

Though the house is off-limits to the general public, the landscaped grounds are not. Visitors are welcome to stroll through an Italian garden planted with over 100 varieties of roses, and a rock garden strewn with flower-

the starting gate at the Saratoga Race Course

RACING SEASON TIPS

Track Basics: The six-week meet runs from late July to early September; Tuesday is dark. The track opens at 11 A.M. weekdays, 10:30 A.M. weekends, and post time is 1 P.M. General admission is $2, admission to the clubhouse $5. No "abbreviated attire" is allowed in the clubhouse.

For general information during the meet, call the Saratoga Race Course at 518/584-6200. For ticket information, call 888/285-5961. For advance ticket sales, contact the New York Racing Association, Saratoga Reserved Seats, P.O. Box 030257, Elmont, NY 11003, 718/641-4700, ext. 4732, www.nyra.com.

Parking and Traffic: The New York Racing Association maintains large parking lots across from the track. Parking is also available in many private lots surrounding the track. If you're not planning to go to the track, avoid Union Avenue between noon and 1 P.M., and again around 5:30 P.M.

Seating: Most of the 6,688 reserved seats in the grandstand and clubhouse are sold by mail in January. However, about 1,000 grandstand seats go on sale ($4 each) every race day at the track's Union Avenue entrance. On weekdays, tickets are often available up until post time, but on weekends, they're gone by 10 or 11 A.M.

Many fans bring lawn chairs, blankets, and cooling perennials. Wistful marble statues stand here and there.

ers to the shady grounds behind the track, which are equipped with short-circuit TVs. Others watch the races on their feet, then retreat to benches near the betting windows.

How to Bet: Easy-to-follow instructions are printed inside the daily program, the *Post Parade,* available at the gate for $1.50. The minimum bet is $1.

After the Races: The most popular racetrack hangout is **Siro's,** 168 Lincoln Ave., 518/584-4030, adjacent to the track on the south side. A long bar is set up beneath a striped canvas tent, and live bands play from about 5:30 P.M. to 8:30 P.M.; the party then moves inside.

Polo Matches: Throughout August, world-class polo matches take place on Tuesday, Friday, and Sunday at the Saratoga Polo Field at Bloomfield and Denton Road. Most of the games begin at 6 P.M., call 518/584-8108 for more information, www.saratogapolo.com.

Accommodations: Most hotels and B&Bs double their prices during racing season, and many of the most popular places are booked solid at least eight months in advance. Even if you arrive at the last minute, however, you will find something. The chamber of commerce maintains an updated list of available rooms.

---

ing perennials. Wistful marble statues stand here and there.

The gardens, off Union Avenue between the racecourse and I-87, 518/584-0746, are open daily 8 A.M.–dusk.

Harness Track and Harness Hall of Fame

South of the main track stretches the half mile Saratoga Raceway, one of the country's foremost trotting tracks. Opened in 1941, the track features evening racing Jan.–Nov. with a short break in April. Some of the track's top races take place during the thoroughbred meet.

In the old horseman's building where the drivers once hung out is the Saratoga Harness Hall of Fame. On display are antique horseshoes, racing silks, high-wheel sulkies, and other memo-

rabilia. One exhibit honors Lady Suffolk, the "Old Grey Mare" of folk song fame who, in 1847, raced in Saratoga, 16 years before thoroughbred racing began.

The museum, 352 Jefferson St., off Nelson Ave., 518/587-4210, is open June–Sept., Thurs.–Sat. 10 A.M.–4 P.M.; call for off-season hours. Admission is free.

National Museum of Dance

South Broadway leads out of the downtown past the only museum in the country devoted exclusively to professional American dance—including ballet, modern dance, vaudeville, and tap. Housed in a low-slung building, the museum spreads out over four spacious halls filled with blown-up photographs and plaques. Temporary exhibits hang near the entrance, while

TV monitors screening famous performances are featured throughout. Overall, however, the museum is a surprisingly static affair that will appeal primarily to dance aficionados.

The museum, 99 S. Broadway (Rte. 9), 518/584-2225, is open Memorial Day–Dec., Tues.–Sun. 10 A.M.–5 P.M. Admission is adults $5, seniors and students $4, children under 12 $2.

Saratoga Spa State Park

More European than American in feel, remarkable Saratoga Spa State Park spreads out over 2,200 pristine acres, every one of which is meticulously planned. At one end is the Avenue of the Pines, flanked with towering green-black trees. At the other, Loop Road leads past a half-dozen mineral springs, all of which have a different taste, depending on their mineral content, making them fun to sample. In between are tennis courts, swimming pools, mineral baths, two golf courses, the Spa Little Theater, the Saratoga Performing Arts Center, and the **Gideon Putnam Hotel.** A grand Georgian affair built in the 1930s, the hotel features a marble-floored lobby and central hall, both worth a quick look-see.

Though no longer the drawing card they once were, the heart of the park remains its mineral baths. To the north of the park is the **Lincoln Bathhouse,** open July–Aug. daily 9 A.M.–4 P.M., and Wed.–Sun. the rest of the year. The place has an old-fashioned, institutional feel, with stark hallways, attendants dressed in white, and no-frills rooms and tubs, where clients relax in bubbling golden-brown waters, indulge in algae body wraps, and succumb to paraffin-wax and muscle-relief treatments; call 518/583-2880 for an appointment, treatments $20–70.

Near the center of the park lies the regal **Victoria Pool,** embellished with colored tiles, romantic archways, a bathhouse, and a small cafe. Even on the hottest days, the pool remains delightfully empty, partly because the park also boasts a second, larger pool—the **Peerless Pool,** adjoined with diving and wading pools. Fees at the Victoria are $6 adults, $3 children; fees at the Peerless are $3 adults, $1.50 children 5–12, plus a $5 vehicle use fee.

The park, off S. Broadway (Rte. 9) just south of downtown, 518/584-2000, is open daily year-round.

Petrified Sea Gardens

A sleeper of a Saratoga visitor attraction, the gardens feature a 500-million-year-old stromatolite reef clearly etched with fossils. Once at the bottom of the Cambrian Sea, the reef is strewn with wavy, pizza-size shapes that were made by cryptozoan colonies, odd-shaped glacial crevices, and potholes. Trails lead through the woods past petrified trees and mysterious erratics, or boulders left behind by receding glaciers. Also on-site is a re-created Native American medicine wheel, a homespun rock and mineral museum, and the "Iroquois Pine," a 295-year-old white pine reputedly the tallest white pine in the Northern Hemisphere.

The gardens, Petrified Gardens Rd., off Rte. 29 three miles west of downtown, 518/584-7102, are open June–Sept. 11 A.M.–5 P.M.; May and Oct.–Nov., Sat.–Sun. 11 A.M.–5 P.M. Admission is adults $3, seniors $2, children $1.50.

ACCOMMODATIONS

Motels

One of the best deals in town is the eight-room **Saratoga Lake Motel,** Box 236, Rte. 9P, 518/584-7438, www.saratogalakemotel.com, overlooking Saratoga Lake ($70 d May–July and Sept.; $90 d in racing season). Budget digs in downtown Saratoga include the 10-room **Spa Motel,** 73 Ballston Ave., 518/587-5280 or 518/584-6032 ($65–80 d; $90–110 d in racing season).

About a quarter mile from the racetrack is the 1890s **Kimberley Inn,** 184 S. Broadway, 518/584-9006, www.kimberleyinn.com, offering six newly renovated rooms, four with private baths and kitchenettes ($90–110 d; $150–175 d in racing season). The **Grand Union,** 92 S. Broadway, 518/584-9000, www.grandunionmotel.com, features 64 well-kept rooms, friendly service, and easy access to the Crystal Spa bathhouse ($65–80 d; $152–228 d in racing season).

Hotels

Good package rates are sometimes offered by the 150-room **Holiday Inn Saratoga,** 232

Broadway, 518/584-4550 (usually $109–140 d; $259–340 d in racing season). Ditto for the sleek 240-room **Saratoga Sheraton,** 534 Broadway, 518/584-4000 or 800/325-3535 (usually $100–200 d; $229–340 d in racing season).

The most romantic hostelry in town is the **Adelphi Hotel,** 365 Broadway, 518/587-4688, www.adelphihotel.com. Featured are an opulent lobby and 35 attractive guest rooms filled with antiques ($110–225 d; $185–430 d in racing season).

Located smack in the middle of well-manicured Saratoga Spa State Park is the Georgian Revival **Gideon Putnam Hotel & Conference Center,** off S. Broadway, 518/584-3000 or 800/732-1560, www.gideonputnam.com. Newly renovated, the hotel is a grand affair, offering 120 guestrooms and suites, a lobby ringed with historic paintings, a fine-dining restaurant, inviting bar, and easy access to the park's facilities ($150–260 d; $330–530 d in racing season).

Bed-and-Breakfasts

Downtown Saratoga has a plethora of Victorian-era B&Bs. One of the most spectacular is the Italianate **Batcheller Mansion Inn,** 20 Circular St., 518/584-7012 or 800/616-7012, www.batchellermansioninn.com, which offers nine spacious guest rooms ($150–295 d; $250–350 d in racing season). Equally unique is the 1901 Queen Anne **Union Gables,** 55 Union Ave., 518/584-1558, www.uniongables.com, all but surrounded by a wonderful wide porch. Each of the 10 guest rooms has a private bath and small refrigerator ($115–160 d; $265–290 d in racing season). The **Westchester House B&B,** 102 Lincoln Ave., 518/587-7613, www.westchesterbandb.com, dates back to 1886, when it was the "Family home of Almeron King, Master Carpenter." All of the rooms are air-conditioned and filled with antiques ($95–195 d; $225–295 d in racing season).

On the shores of Saratoga Lake is the inviting **Harren-Brook Inn,** 286 Rte. 9P, 518/583-4009, www.harrenbrookinn.com, run by two former schoolteachers with a good knowledge of the area. The nine guest rooms appear nicely appointed, while up front beckons a cozy sitting room, breezy porch, and small private beach. All

of the rooms have private baths, ceiling fans, and queen-sized beds; some have separate sitting rooms, and one features a Jacuzzi and king-size bed ($95–175 d; $150–195 d in racing season).

Numerous other B&Bs are located in and around Saratoga (see Excursions from Saratoga, below). For a complete list, contact the chamber of commerce.

FOOD

Saratoga is known for its many restaurants, which come in all styles and price ranges. Good breakfast and lunch spots are located downtown along Broadway, while more upscale restaurants line the side streets.

Bakeries and Diners

Mrs. London's, 464 Broadway, 518/581-1834, offers a mouth-watering selection of desserts, baked goods, and gourmet coffees; a great place for breakfast or an evening snack. The big and bustling **Saratoga Diner,** 133 S. Broadway, 518/584-9833, formerly known as the Spa City Diner, is the kind of comforting eatery that offers an extensive menu 24 hours a day. The family-owned **Shirley's Restaurant,** 74 West Ave., 518/584-4532, is a good spot for breakfast, lunch, and homemade pies.

American

Hattie's, 45 Phila St., 518/584-4790, has been a Saratoga institution since 1938. This is the place to go for tasty fried chicken, barbecued ribs, catfish, and sweet potato pie; average entrée $10.

Also an institution is the casual **Olde Bryan Inn,** 123 Maple Ave., 518/587-2990, housed in a rustic 1832 stone house. On the menu is everything from chili to seafood kebab, and up front is a big, comfortable bar; average entrée $13.

Lillian's, 408 Broadway, 518/587-7766, is outfitted with woodwork, brass, Tiffany-style lamps, and stained glass. The dependable menu includes lots of standard steak, chicken, and fish dishes, along with lighter fare; average entrée $14. Down the street is the Holmesian **Professor Moriarty's,** 430 Broadway, 518/587-5981, a classy bar/restaurant serving "plots" (appetizers), "crimes" (entrées), and "verdicts" (desserts); average entrée $15.

Sperry's, 30 ½ Caroline St., 518/584-9618, is an upscale bistro filled with memorabilia dating back to Saratoga's days as a fashionable spa. Specialties include delicious fresh fish, jambalaya, and homemade pasta; average entrée $18. **43 Phila Bistro,** 43 Phila St., 518/584-2720, is a sophisticated American-style bistro featuring dining by candlelight. On the menu is everything from Jamaican jerk chicken to dry-aged steak; average entrée $22.

The small and casually elegant **Eartha's Kitchen,** 60 Court St., 518/583-0602, serves delicious contemporary fare. The innovative menu changes frequently but always includes a grilled dish or two and much fish; average entrée $19.

Continental and French

Legendary **Siro's,** 168 Lincoln Ave., 518/584-4030, open only during racing season, boasts the best after-track bar scene, as well as the most exclusive restaurant in town. Featured are both innovative and traditional continental dishes; entrées range $25–38; reservations are essential.

An especially good time to visit the **Gideon Putnam Hotel,** Saratoga Spa State Park, off S. Broadway, 518/584-3000—open for breakfast, lunch, and dinner—is Sunday brunch. Expect an enormous buffet for about $16.

About four miles south of Saratoga is the excellent **Chez Sophie Bistro,** Rte. 9, Malta, 518/583-3538. Housed in an elegant old diner that's been completely remodeled, it serves an interesting selection of fish, chicken, meat, and duck dishes, all prepared with the freshest of ingredients; average entrée $19.

Italian, Mexican, and Indian

Good eats are to be had at three smaller restaurants, all of which offer entrées priced under $12. For fajitas, tostadas, and burritos, along with regional Mexican specialties on the weekends, try the **Mexican Connection,** 41 Nelson Ave., 518/584-4466. For curries, *biryanis,* and many vegetarian dishes, try **Little India,** 423 Broadway, 518/583-4151. For wood-fired pizza, pastas, creative salads, and Elvis memorabilia, try **Bruno's,** 237 Union Ave., 518/583-3333, across from the main track.

Waterfalls, an open kitchen, first-rate Italian food, and an extensive wine list attract an upscale crowd to **Chianti,** 208 S. Broadway, 518/580-0025; average entrée $22.

ENTERTAINMENT

Performing Arts

The **Saratoga Performing Arts Center** (SPAC), Saratoga Spa State Park, off S. Broadway (Rte. 9), 518/587-3330, www.spac.org, is an outdoor amphitheater with 5,000 seats below cover and more seats available on the surrounding lawns. The preeminent performing arts center of the North Country, SPAC presents the New York City Opera in June, the New York City Ballet in July, the Philadelphia Orchestra in August, and well-known rock, pop, and jazz stars throughout the summer. Picnicking before the concerts is a Saratoga tradition. Also at the center is the indoor, 500-seat Little Theater, where chamber music and drama are presented throughout the year.

The **Baroque Festival,** 165 Wilton Rd., Greenfield Center, 518/893-7527, takes place in July and August in an exquisite private music hall that seats only 110. Featured is baroque music played on period instruments, among them a handcrafted harpsichord played by director Robert Conant.

Clubs and Nightlife

Thanks largely to the presence of Skidmore College and the racetrack, Saratoga has a lively nighttime scene. **Caroline Street** is especially known for its many clubs and bars.

One of the biggest and best music spots in town is the three-clubs-in-one **Metro,** 17 Maple Ave., 518/584-9581. Downstairs is live rock or blues, upstairs is jazz, and out back is a pulsating disco room.

9 Maple Ave., 9 Maple Ave., 518/583-CLUB, is the place to go for serious jazz. **Desperate Annie's,** 12-14 Caroline St., 518/587-2455, a.k.a. DA's, is a popular college and local hangout, complete with pool table.

Caffé Lena, 45-47 Phila St., 518/583-0022, www.caffelena.com, is the oldest continuously run coffeehouse in America, founded in 1960 by Lena Spencer. Bob Dylan played here on his first tour of the East; Don McLean first played "American Pie" on the cafe's small stage. Lena is gone now, but her legacy continues through the cafe's lineup of top acoustic acts—Odetta, Jimmie Dale Gilmore, Tom Paxton, and others. Coffees and desserts are served.

The big and boisterous **Parting Glass,** 40-42 Lake Ave., 518/583-1916, presents first-rate Irish bands. On the menu are 170 beers and Guinness on tap, along with a wide selection of pub grub.

Lively **bar scenes** can be found at many restaurants, including Siro's, Sperry's, Professor Moriarty's, and the Olde Bryan Inn, all mentioned above. Behind the lobby of the **Adelphi Hotel,** 365 Broadway, 518/587-4688, lies a candlelit garden where drinks are served beneath the stars.

SHOPPING

Many **clothing boutiques** and **gift shops** pepper Broadway. Housed in the old Saratoga National Bank building is the **Lyrical Ballad Bookstore,** 7 Phila St., 518/584-8779, a packed-to-the-rafters antiquarian shop that stocks about 30,000 books. The rarest volumes are stored in the bank's old safe deposit vaults.

The **Regent Street Antique Center,** 153 Regent St., 518/584-0107, houses about 20 dealers.

EXCURSIONS FROM SARATOGA

Stillwater

The battles that turned the course of the American Revolution were fought about 12 miles southeast of Saratoga. The former battlefield is now part of **Saratoga National Historic Park.**

In October 1777, British general Burgoyne and his forces marched south from Canada to take control of the Hudson River. They planned to meet up with Col. Leger and his forces in Albany, and continue on to New York City to join up with Gen. Howe. Instead, just outside Saratoga, Gen. Burgoyne came upon the American forces, 9,000 strong. Led by Gen. Horatio Gates and Gen. Benedict Arnold, the Americans defeated the British in two fierce battles.

A tour of the park begins at the visitor center,

where you can pick up maps and watch an informative film. Beyond the center begins a nine-mile self-guided driving tour past strategic points equipped with audio recordings, plaques, and maps. Only a few bunkers remain, but the countryside is exceptionally lovely, especially in the late afternoon when the mists roll in from the nearby Hudson River.

The park, 648 Rte. 32, at Rte. 4, 518/664-9821, is open April–Nov., 9 A.M.–dusk, weather permitting; the visitor center is open daily 9 A.M.–5 P.M. Admission 9 A.M.–5 P.M. is $5 per car, $3 per hiker or biker.

Schuylerville

Continue north of the battlefield on Route 4 for about eight miles to reach Schuylerville, lined with worn white buildings and empty storefronts. Just south of the Route 32 intersection stands the recently restored **General Philip Schuyler House.** Also part of the Saratoga National Historic Battlefield, the house belonged to the Schuyler family who, pre-Revolution, ran a self-sufficient estate here that employed about 200 people. The house was burnt by Burgoyne during the Battles of Saratoga but was rebuilt that same year.

The house, Rte. 4, 518/664-9821, is open Memorial Day–Labor Day, Wed.–Sun. 10 A.M.–4 P.M. Admission is free.

Take Rte. 32 west of the Schuyler House about a half mile to reach the Saratoga Monument, a recently and beautifully restored gray obelisk on a hill. The third part of Saratoga National Historic Park, the monument features four niches honoring the battles' American leaders—Gen. Philip Schuyler, Gen. Horatio Gates, Col. Daniel Morgan, and Gen. Benedict Arnold. Statues stand in the first three niches, but the fourth stands deliberately empty. The monument is open Memorial Day–Labor Day, Wed.–Sun. 9:30 A.M.–4:30 P.M., and weekends in fall.

The wood-frame, Federal-style **Dovegate Inn,** 184 Broad St., 518/695-3699, www.dovegateinn.com, is a welcoming B&B offering three spacious guestrooms with private baths and air conditioning, a small restaurant, and a gift shop ($75–110 d, $125–145 d in racing season).

Ballston Spa

Before the Civil War, Ballston Spa outranked Saratoga as a fashionable resort and watering hole. After the war, however, the racetrack and casinos drew the crowds away, and Ballston Spa turned to knitting mills and tanneries. Today little evidence of any of these industries remains except at the **Brookside Saratoga County History Center.**

Housed in what was once a Georgian-styled resort hotel, the Brookside showcases exhibits on 19th-century spas, 20th-century amusement parks, the county's early African American settlers, and dairy farming. The center, 6 Charlton St., at Front St., 518/885-4000, www.brooksidemuseum.org, is open Tuesday noon–8 P.M., Wed.–Fri. 10 A.M.–4 P.M., Saturday noon–4 P.M. Admission is adults $2, children 5–18 $1.

Also in Ballston Spa is the **National Bottle Museum,** 76 Milton Ave. (Rte. 50), 518/885-7589. Although the place has the potential to be an eclectic delight, it's currently hard to appreciate, as most of its bottles—antique and handmade though they may be—are jumbled together without signage of any kind. Hours are June–Sept., daily 10 A.M.–4 P.M.; Oct.–May, Mon.–Fri. 10 A.M.–4 P.M. Admission is by donation.

Wilton

One of the oddest and most moving of house museums in all of New York State is **Grant Cottage,** perched on the hilltop in the middle of Mt. McGregor Correctional Facility. To get to the cottage, you must stop at a guard booth and enter a walled minimum-security complex topped with shiny barbed wire.

President Ulysses S. Grant came to Mt. McGregor in June of 1885 and spent the last six weeks of his life here, completing his memoirs. Afflicted with throat cancer, he was working frantically against time, trying to finish his book so that his family would have something to live on after he was gone. Grant had become bankrupt paying back the moneys he had urged his friends to invest in his son's company; the company went belly-up after his son's partner absconded with the funds.

In 1885, Mt. McGregor was home not to a

correctional facility but to the popular Hotel Balmoral, owned by Grant's friend Duncan McGregor. McGregor lent Grant his cottage both out of the goodness of his heart and because, as a shrewd businessman, he knew that if Grant died in the cottage, it would become a popular tourist attraction.

Die Grant did, and to this day, the house remains exactly as it was when he and his family left it. In one room are Grant's toothbrush, his nightshirts, and a half-empty bottle of medicinal cocaine and spring water. In another are the notes that Grant scribbled in pencil after he could no longer talk, and a bedspread stained with the wreaths brought by mourners. Most astonishing of all are the wreaths themselves, now over 100 years old and still in good, albeit dusty, condition.

Before his death, Grant—often sleeping as few as two hours a night—did succeed in finishing his memoirs. They are considered to be among the finest ever written by an American general and earned the family handsome royalties.

The cottage, off Ballard Road, Wilton, 518/587-8277 or 518/584-2000, is open Memorial Day–Labor Day, Wed.–Sun. 10 A.M.–4 P.M.; and Sept.-mid Oct., Sat.–Sun. 10 A.M.–4 P.M. Admission is adults $2.50, seniors $2, children 6–16 $1. To reach the cottage from Saratoga, take Route 9 north eight miles to Ballard Road and turn left.

Great Sacandaga Lake

About 20 miles west of Saratoga, inside Adirondack Park, is the largest manmade lake in New York, created in the 1920s for flood control purposes. Several parks line the lake's western shore, including **Northampton Beach Campground,** off Rte. 30, Northville, 518/863-6000, bordered by a large swimming beach. Parking in summer is $5 per vehicle. To reserve one of the 224 campsites, call 800/456-CAMP.

At the northern end of Great Sacandaga Lake lies **Northville,** a lively Adirondack town crowded with businesses and shops. Notable among them, the **Adirondack Country Store,** 252 N. Main St., 518/863-6056, housed in a creaky old farmhouse, sells regional crafts and books.

Northville marks the start of the famed 130-

mile **Northville-Placid Trail,** a favorite route among serious backpackers. And, if you happen to be in the Northville area on May 6, be sure and stop by the **Old Hubbell Factory Chimney** on 2nd Street. Every year, for some inexplicable reason, thousands of swifts arrive at their summer home on that date, flying in after wintering in South America.

Camping

Numerous good campgrounds ring Saratoga. Near Stillwater is the 362-site **Deer Run Campground,** off Rte. 67, Schaghticoke, 518/664-2804, overlooking the Valley of Peace; basic site rate is $30–32. Not far from the Grant Cottage is 272-site **Cold Brook Campsites,** 385 Gurn Springs Rd., Gansevoort, 518/584-8038; basic site rate is $20–22. Twelve miles north of Saratoga, in the foothills of the Adirondacks, is the 55-site **Rustic Barn Campsites,** 4757 Rte. 9 N, Corinth, 518/654-6588; a basic site costs $18–20.

Bed-and-Breakfasts

About seven miles from Saratoga stands the 1786 **Wayside Inn,** 104 Wilton Rd., Greenfield, 518/893-7249, www.waysidein.com, a rambling, low-ceilinged affair with wide floorboards and broad beams. The five guest rooms are comfortably fitted; next door is a laid-back performing arts and conference center ($85–115 d; $135–175 d in racing season). About five miles south of Ballston Spa is the **Olde Stone House Inn,** Box 451, Round Lake, 518/899-5048, www.oldestoneinn.com, an elegant 1820 cobblestone home surrounded by extensive grounds ($90–115 d; $130–170 d in racing season).

Washington County

Between Saratoga and Vermont, the Adirondack Mountains and the Green Mountains, lies a sliver of a county reaching north to Lake Champlain. Though often overlooked by travelers in the region, the countryside here is exceptionally lovely and quite different from elsewhere in the state. The hills are smaller, greener, and closer together; the villages, more genteel and picturesque. So it comes as no surprise to learn that this is **Grandma Moses Country.** The self-taught folk artist grew up near Eagle Bridge in southern Washington County, and painted the scenes she found around her. Her legacy is acknowledged by the many artists who live in the area, and by the vibrant arts scene flourishing along the New York–Vermont border.

Often overlooked by travelers, Washington County is exceptionally lovely and quite different from elsewhere in the state. The hills are smaller, greener, and closer together; the villages, more genteel and picturesque—it comes as no surprise to learn that this is Grandma Moses Country.

The historic moment supposedly occurred one evening in the mid-1890s when a Prof. Charles Watson Townsend, dining at the Hotel Cambridge, ordered ice cream with apple pie; a neighbor eating at the next table dubbed the concoction "pie à la mode." The professor ordered it by its new name during a subsequent visit to Delmonico's in New York City. The waiter had never heard of it and called for the manager, who declared in consternation, "Delmonico's never intends that any other restaurant shall get ahead of it. . . . Forthwith, pie à la mode will be featured on the menu every day." A *New York Sun* newspaperman, overhearing the conversation, reported it the next day, and before long, pie à la mode was a standard on menus across the country.

Completely renovated in 1999, the **Cambridge Hotel,** 4 W. Main St., 518/677-5626, still stands in the middle of town, where it is open for lunch, dinner, and accommodation for overnight guests

CAMBRIDGE

About 25 miles east of Saratoga Springs, Cambridge claims to be the birthplace of pie à la mode.

(see below). Elsewhere along the nicely restored, turn-of-the-century Main Street lie several art galleries, natural foods stores, and **Hubbard Hall,** 25 E. Main St., 518/677-2495. Originally a rural opera house, the 1878 hall now houses the co-operative **Valley Artisans Market,** 518/677-2765, on the ground floor, and a restored theater up above. A wide range of music, dance, and theater events take place throughout the year, including the popular **Music from Salem** classical series held on Fridays in summer.

New Skete Monastery

On a thickly wooded hilltop between Cambridge and Vermont stands the Eastern Orthodox New Skete Monastery. Home to 11 brothers, the monastery centers around a rough-hewn wooden chapel filled with icons painted by the monks. Nearby presides a more elaborate church.

The New Skete community's secular claim to fame, however, is—ahem—dogs. The monks began breeding and training German shepherds shortly after moving here in the 1960s, when it became apparent that they could not support themselves by farming. The business took off, especially after 1978, when one of the brothers wrote a best-selling, award-winning book, *How to Be Your Dog's Best Friend* (Little, Brown).

Though the kennels are off-limits to the public, you can stop into the chapel and a gift shop, stocked with the monks' homemade cheesecake, smoked meats, and various dog-related items. The nuns of New Skete run a similar gift shop five miles away on Ash Grove Road, off Chestnut Hill Road.

The shop and chapel, New Skete Road, off Chestnut Hill Road (Route 67) east of Cambridge, 518/677-3928, www.newskete.com, are open Tues.–Fri. 9 A.M.–noon and 2–4 P.M., Saturday 10 A.M.–4 P.M., and Sunday 2–4 P.M. The main church is open during Sunday morning services only. The New Skete Sisters also run a bake shop down the road at 343 Ash Grove Rd., 518/677-3810.

Accommodations and Food

The pride of Cambridge is the 1874 **Cambridge Hotel,** 4 W. Main St., 518/677-5623, www.cam-

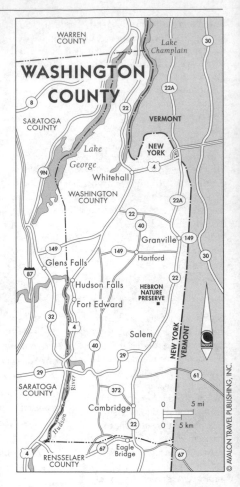

bridgehotel.com, which was renovated through the effort of dozens of area citizens. Downstairs you'll find a large, airy, Victoriana dining room that's open for lunch and dinner (dinner entrées $12–21). Upstairs are 16 modernized guest rooms, all equipped with private baths, air conditioning, and cable TV ($137–175 d in summer; about one third less off season).

EAGLE BRIDGE

The **homestead of Grandma Moses** (1860–1961) is still owned by her descendants, who operate the

Mount Nebo Gallery next door to their farm-house. For sale inside are paintings, prints, litho-graphs, posters, calendars, and greeting cards by Moses's great-grandson Will Moses. Also a self-taught artist, Will carries on in his great-grand-mother's tradition, painting farm and village scenes of a bygone era. "The kind of art I do appeals to middle America," Moses recently told a local paper. "It's mainstream art. I never went to New York, or got an agent. I prefer to be my own person."

The gallery, Grandma Moses Rd., 518/686-4334 or 800/328-6326, is a few miles south of Cambridge off Route 22 near the intersection of Route 67. Hours are Mon.–Fri. 9 A.M.–4 P.M., Saturday 10 A.M.–5 P.M., Sunday noon–5 P.M.

To view the largest public collection of paintings by Grandma Moses, as well as the one-room schoolhouse that she once attended, continue south on Route 22 to Route 7, then head east across the state line to the **Bennington Museum** in Bennington, Vermont. The museum, W. Main St., 802/447-1571, is about 18 miles from Eagle Bridge. Hours are June–Oct., daily 9 A.M.–6 P.M.; Nov.–May, daily 9 A.M.–5 P.M. Admission is adults $6, seniors and students $5, under 12 free.

NORTH TO SALEM

Intersecting Route 22 about four miles north of Cambridge is County Road 61, which heads east to the **Shushan Covered Bridge Museum,** 518/854-7220. Housed in an actual 1858 covered bridge that spans the Battenkill River, the muse-um features exhibits on local history. Next door to it lies the 1852 one-room schoolhouse. Hours are July 4–Labor Day, Wed.–Sun. 1–4 P.M.; Memorial Day–July 4 and Labor Day–Columbus Day weekends only, or by appointment. Dona-tions welcomed.

Another eight miles north on Route 22 will take you to Salem, a cozy New England–styled vil-lage rich with spreading maples and elms. At one end of town, housed in a 19th-century church, is the **Fort Salem Theatre,** E. Broadway, 518/854-9200, presenting summer stock June–Septem-ber. At the other end, **Steininger's,** Main St., 518/854-3830, a family-run candy kitchen, feels like a bit of Vienna transported west. "Each

chocolate, if it is made right, has its own story to tell—sometimes happy, sometimes sad, some-times romantic—but always beautiful," reads a quote from founder Frieda Steininger.

Hebron Nature Preserve

Along Route 22 about eight miles north of Salem spreads the 125-acre Hebron Nature Preserve, run by the Pember Museum in Granville. Fea-tured are eight nature trails that investigate vari-ous habitats. One trail leads to a large beaver dam, another through marshlands, a third through overgrown orchards and fields. Since all of the trails are under one mile in length, it's an especially good place for kids. The preserve is open year-round dawn to dusk; near the entrance are maps and a register. For more information, call the Pember Museum at 518/642-1515.

GRANVILLE

This sturdy town of red-brick buildings was set-tled first by Quakers from Vermont in 1781. Later, in the mid-1800s, it was famed for its col-ored slate quarries—producing maroon, green, and blue slate—worked primarily by people of Welsh descent. Granville today still sports slate roofs, slate chimneys, slate patios, slate sidewalks, and even slate business signs.

Pember Museum of Natural History

Housed in a striking Victorian mansion at the center of town, the Pember Museum is a sur-prisingly Old World place filled with elegant glass and wood exhibit cases. Preserved inside are hundreds upon hundreds of birds, insects, reptiles, and mammals, all collected by amateur naturalist Franklin Pember in the late 1800s.

Some of these species, such as the passenger pigeon and Carolina parakeet, are now extinct. Others, such as the South American possum and red kangaroo, come with their offspring in tow. Larger specimens, such as the Alaskan brown bear and brown pelican, almost burst out of their cases. Walk down the aisles here and you'll feel as if you're surrounded by a mag-ical, about-to-awaken menagerie.

The museum, 33 W. Main St. (Rte. 149),

518/642-1515, www.pembermuseum.com, is open Tues.–Fri. 1–5 P.M., Saturday 10 A.M.–3 P.M. Admission is adults $2.50, children $1.

Slate Valley Museum

To learn more about Granville's slate history, step into this brand-new museum, housed in a renovated 19th-century Dutch barn. Inside, memorabilia, tools, machinery, photography, and artwork date back to the days when Granville was known as the "Colored Slate Capital of the World." During the town's heyday around the turn of the century, 64 slate companies employing 3,000 men were located here.

At the heart of the collection is a powerful 25-foot mural depicting 13 men at work in a slate quarry. The mural was painted in 1939 by Woodstock artist Martha Levy for the federal Works Progress Administration.

The museum, 17 Water St., off Main St., 518/642-1417, www.slatemuseum.com, is open Tuesday and Fri.–Sat. 10 A.M.–4 P.M. General admission is $2.

Accommodations

About eight miles east of Granville is **Brown's Tavern Bed & Breakfast,** 8853 Rte. 40, S. Hart-

ford, 518/632-5904. The renovated 1802 tavern offers three simple but comfortable guest rooms with ceiling fans ($50–70 d).

WHITEHALL

At the head of Lake Champlain at the county's northern end lies Whitehall, the birthplace of the U.S. Navy. The first American fleet was built here in 1776 under the supervision of Benedict Arnold. Later, the village flourished as a trading center, thanks largely to the Champlain Barge Canal, which still operates between Lake Champlain and Troy.

Along the eastern edge of modern-day Whitehall runs a trim historic Main Street listed on the National Register of Historic Places. Nearby are pleasant waterfront parks and the **Skenesborough Museum,** housing models of the first U.S. Navy ships, along with canal and railroad exhibits. The museum also runs the **Heritage Area Visitors Center,** which is stocked with free walking-tour maps to the downtown.

The museum, off Rte. 4, 518/499-0716, is open June–Labor Day, Mon.–Sat. 10 A.M.–4 P.M., Sunday noon–4 P.M. Admission is free.

Lake George and Southeastern Adirondacks

Christened Lac du St. Sacrement in 1609 by Father Jogues, its European discoverer, Lake George lies in a deep fault valley the ends of which are blocked by glacial debris. Thirty-two magnificent miles long, the dark, spring-fed lake surrounds 225 islands. At the lake's southern end sprawls the busy tourist village of Lake George, but otherwise, much of the shoreline is crowded with dense pine.

As part of a strategic water route connecting Canada with New York City, Lake George played an important role in both the French and Indian War and the American Revolution. Between 1690 and 1760, the French and British fought four major battles along the shores of Lake George and nearby Lake Champlain. Fort Ticonderoga, at the foot of Lake George overlooking Lake Cham-

plain, and Fort William Henry, at the head of Lake George, date back to that period. During the Revolutionary War, the taking of Fort Ticonderoga from the British in 1775 marked the Americans' first major military victory.

Surrounding Lake George are the forested foothills of the Adirondacks, the summits of which offer glorious views of the lake below and the higher peaks farther north. To the west a smattering of small and lovely lakes, including Lake Luzerne, Schroon Lake, and Brandt Lake, offer similar distractions.

Visitor Information

Most of Lake George and the southeastern Adirondacks are in Warren County. The **Warren County Department of Tourism,** Municipal

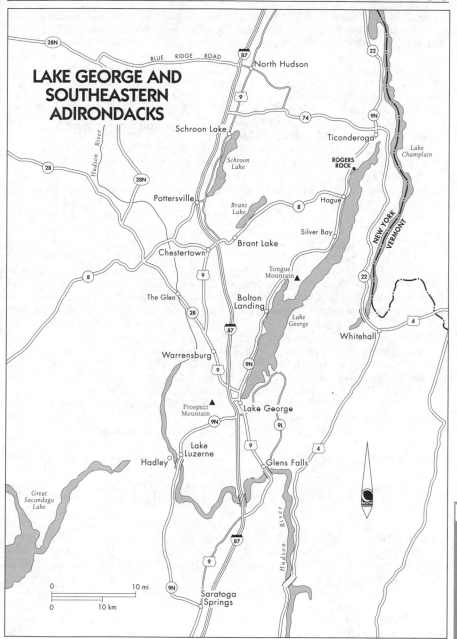

LAKE GEORGE AND SOUTHEASTERN ADIRONDACKS

28N

BLUE RIDGE ROAD

87 North Hudson

22

9

74

9N

Schroon Lake

Ticonderoga

Lake Champlain

Schroon Lake

ROGERS ROCK

28

28N

Hudson River

Pottersville

Brant Lake

8 Hague

Silver Bay

Chestertown

Brant Lake

NEW YORK

VERMONT

8

9

Tongue Mountain

22

The Glen

28

Bolton Landing

Lake George

87

Whitehall

4

Warrensburg

9

9N

Prospect Mountain

Lake George

9N

9L

Lake Luzerne

Hadley

9

4

Glens Falls

Great Sacandaga Lake

MOON

87

Hudson River

9

0   10 mi

9N

0   10 km

Saratoga Springs

© AVALON TRAVEL PUBLISHING, INC.

Center, 1340 Rte. 9, Lake George, NY 12845, 518/761-6366 or 800/365-1050, www.visit-lakegeorge.com, is open Mon.–Fri. 9 A.M.–5 P.M.

GLENS FALLS

Between Saratoga Springs and Lake George lies Glens Falls, a town of wide, empty downtown streets, peppered with handsome brick buildings. Nearby flows the Hudson River and a 60-foot-high waterfall that was responsible for turning the town into an early industrial center. First came lumbering and the manufacturing of lime and cement, followed by the paper, pulp-making, and insurance industries.

Hyde Collection

The main reason to stop in Glens Falls is to tour the first-class Hyde Collection, housed in a 1912 mansion styled as a Renaissance villa. Step inside this long, low-slung building, and you'll find yourself surrounded by palm trees, balconies, tile floors, fine antiques, and an important collection of Old Masters. Among them are works by Rembrandt, Rubens, El Greco, Botticelli, Tintoretto, Degas, Cézanne, van Gogh, and Picasso. American artists also are well represented, including Eakins, Homer, and Whistler.

The Hyde Collection was amassed by Louis Fiske and Charlotte Pruyn Hyde in the first half of the 20th century. Mrs. Hyde turned the family mansion into a museum in 1952, following her husband's death.

The museum, 161 Warren St., east of the Rte. 9 intersection, 518/792-1761, www.hyde-artmuseum.org, is open year-round Tues.–Sat. 10 A.M.–5 P.M., Sunday noon–5 P.M. Admission is free.

Chapman Historical Museum

Also worth a stop, especially for photography buffs, is the Chapman Museum, run by the Glens Falls–Queensbury Historical Association. Housed in an 1867 Victorian mansion, complete with several period rooms, the museum showcases an outstanding collection of photographs by Seneca Ray Stoddard. Stoddard, an artist, writer, cartographer, and surveyor, wrote numerous early guidebooks to the Adirondacks and captured the region's majesty through countless photographs.

The museum, 348 Glen St. (Rte. 9), at Bacon, 518/793-2826, www.chapmanmuseum.org, is open year-round Tues.–Sat. 10 A.M.–5 P.M. Admission is adults $2, seniors and students $1, under 12 free.

LAKE GEORGE VILLAGE

Everything at Lake George, from the House of Frankenstein wax museum to the Million Dollar Beach, seems to date back to the 1950s. Mom-and-pop motels, miniature golf courses, the Great Escape amusement park, the Magic Forest with its giant Uncle Sam statue looming out front—all cajole you back in time. Look at the place with one eye and it's a kitschy Americana theme park, with great appeal for kids. Look at it with another and it's a greedy tourist trap, sadly out of place in its majestic setting in the Adirondack foothills.

Lake George is basically a one-street town, with the majority of its souvenir shops and restaurants laid out along Canada Street (Route 9). Intersecting Canada Street at the lakefront, Beach Road leads to Fort William Henry and the **Million Dollar Beach,** which is much, *much* smaller and tamer than its name implies. Along the way are docks where boats and water-sports equipment can be rented. A small beach is also located in **Shepard Park,** at Canada and Montcalm Streets.

During the summer, Lake George village is packed with tourists—most of them families with surprisingly many kids in tow. After Labor Day, the place shuts down abruptly, to remain shuttered until Memorial Day of the following year.

Lake Excursions

Brave the hordes of tourists and take a cruise on Lake George. Though the boats are quite commercialized affairs, they do take you out into deep, dark blue waters framed with moody forests and peaks. Unfortunately, the annoying commentary en route tends to focus more on the rich and famous living in the area than on the lake itself, but it's easy to tune out the talk and just watch the untamed landscape slide by.

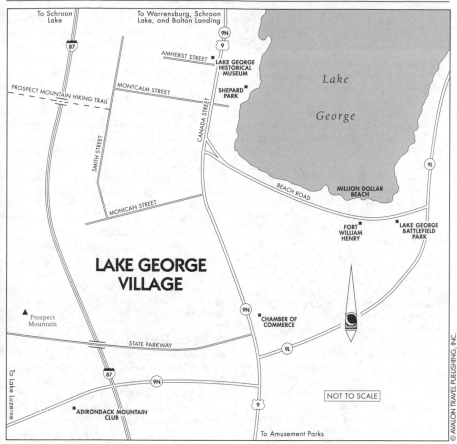

© AVALON TRAVEL PUBLISHING, INC.

Shoreline Cruises, 2 James St., 518/668-4644, offers day and evening cruises onboard an 85-foot, 250-passenger boat May–October. The **Lake George Steamboat Company,** Steel Pier, Beach Rd., 518/668-5777, offers sightseeing, dinner, and entertainment cruises onboard two 400-passenger and one 1,000-passenger reproduction steamships May–October. Basic one-hour cruises cost about $9 adults, $6 kids.

Fort William Henry

Across from the Lake George Steamboat Company dock stands a facsimile reconstruction of Fort William Henry. The museum on-site features French and Indian War artifacts, audiovisual presentations, life-size dioramas, and demonstrations of cannon and musket firings.

The original fort was built in 1756 by British general William Johnson, the man responsible for naming the lake—after King George III. In 1757, the fort was attacked by 1,600 French soldiers and 3,000 Indians—including the Onondaga, Seneca, Cayuga, Fox, Iowa, Miami, and Delaware—under the command of Gen. Montcalm. After a long siege, Montcalm arranged for a peaceful surrender. The Indians, however, ignored the agreement and attacked without warning, butchering the many men, women, and children who had taken refuge in the fort. James Fenimore Cooper based *The Last of the Mohicans* on the incident.

THE NORTH COUNTRY

THE SUNKEN TREASURE OF LAKE GEORGE

Beneath the waters of Lake George lie approximately 75 bateaux (flat-bottomed boats) that date back to the French and Indian War. The boats were part of a 260-vessel fleet deliberately scuttled by the British and the American colonists in 1758 to protect the craft from the French and Native Americans. The British returned to the lake in 1759 and raised close to 200 of the ships.

No one suspected that the remaining bateaux still existed until two teenage divers discovered them in 1960. That same year, three of the boats were raised from the lake, and one was put on exhibit at the Adirondack Museum in Blue Mountain Lake.

Beginning in 1987, a team of divers—now known as Bateaux Below, Inc.—began a survey of the seven sunken boats located off the Wiawaka Holiday House at the southern end of the lake. These boats were listed on the National Register of Historic Places in 1992 and are now a Shipwreck Preserve, open to divers Memorial Day–September.

In 1990, yet another ship was discovered—a 52-foot radeau (seven-sided battleship) named the *Land Tortoise*. Also part of the scuttled fleet, this fragile vessel is North America's oldest intact warship. It is off-limits to divers.

For a brochure on the Shipwreck Preserve, call the **Department of Environmental Conservation** at 518/402-9428.

The fort, though interesting enough as far as it goes, does not present much that's original. You might want to save your money for the more impressive and authentic Fort Ticonderoga, located at the northern end of Lake George overlooking Lake Champlain.

The fort, Beach Rd., 518/668-5471, www .fortwilliamhenry.com, is open May and Labor Day–Columbus Day, daily 10 A.M.–5 P.M.; Memorial Day–Labor Day, daily 9 A.M.–8 P.M. Admission is adults $10, children 3–11 $7.

Lake George Battlefield Park

In a small, hilly park behind the fort you'll find the largely unexcavated ruins of the original Fort William Henry, along with plaques explaining various aspects of the 1757 battle. Picnic tables throughout the park offer good views of the lake. The park is open May–Columbus Day.

Lake George Historical Museum

Housed in the Old Court House on Canada Street are three floors of exhibits on the history of Lake George. Of particular interest are the 1845 jail cells in the basement, an exhibit on lake shipwrecks, photos from the steamboat era, and an elaborate, doll-size wooden church carved by convicted murderer George Ouellet in 1881. After finishing his church, Ouellet sold it for a sizeable sum, hired a new lawyer to appeal his conviction, and was acquitted.

The museum, Canada and Amherst Sts., 518/668-5044, is open July–Aug., Fri.–Tues. 11 A.M.–4 P.M.; call for off-season hours. Admission is adults $3, children under 10 $1. The gift shop stocks a good collection of historic books and maps.

Prospect Mountain

For a terrific view of Lake George and the southeastern Adirondacks, drive up the Prospect Mountain State Parkway, which intersects with Route 9 just south of the village. The 5.5-mile drive leading up the 2,030-foot mountain offers 100-mile views of five states. Park your car near the top and board one of the "viewmobiles" that travel to the very crest of the mountain, where there are picnic tables, a fire tower, and the ruins of an old cable railroad.

An easy 1.6-mile hiking trail, marked with red blazes, also leads to the summit. To reach the trailhead from Lake George village, take Montcalm Street to Smith Street and turn south. The trail begins midway down the block, and follows the roadbed of the old cable railroad.

The parkway, 518/668-5198, is open June–Oct., daily 9 A.M.–5 P.M. Admission is $5 per vehicle.

Amusement Parks

Five miles south of the village looms the region's largest amusement park—the **Great Escape &**

Splashdown Kingdom, Rte. 9, 518/792-3500, offering over 125 rides, shows, and attractions, including the Steamin' Demon Loop Rollercoaster and the Black Cobra. Admission is adults $33, children under 48 inches $20, children under age 2 free.

Three miles south of the village, **Magic Forest,** Rte. 9, 518/668-2448, offers 20 rides for children and five for adults. Lots of animals are on the premises as well; during the daily "Diving Horse Act," a horse walks off a plank into a pool. General admission is adults $14, children $11.

One mile south of the village, **Water Slide World,** Rte. 9, 518/668-4407, includes a wave pool, water slides, bumper boats, hot tubs, and a "toddler lagoon." Admission is adults $24, children under 10 $21, seniors and toddlers $11.

All three parks open in June and close after Labor Day.

Adirondack Mountain Club (ADK)

Also to the south of Lake George village, near the intersection of Route 9 and Route 9 N, is an information center run by the Adirondack Mountain Club, a nonprofit organization dedicated to broadening the public's appreciation of the Adirondack wilderness. Stop here for information on hiking trails and camping areas. Various guidebooks for sale describe day-hikes, canoe routes, and backpacking trips; experts are on hand to answer questions.

The center, 814 Goggins Rd., off Rte. 9 N west of I-87, 518/668-4447, is open Mon.–Sat. 8:30 A.M.–5 P.M. To reach the center directly from I-87, take Exit 21.

Hiking Buck Mountain

On the southeastern shore of Lake George is Buck Mountain. A well-marked, 3.3-mile hiking trail leads to the summit and great views of Lake George, Lake Champlain, the Adirondacks, and Vermont's Green Mountains. To reach the trailhead, head east from the village to Route 9L. Turn left and continue for about seven miles until you see a turn for Pilot Knob and Kaatskill Bay. Follow this road about 3.5 miles to the trailhead, marked with a large sign and parking lot. The easy-to-moderate roundtrip hike takes about four hours.

Camping and Accommodations

To make reservations at the 68-site **Lake George Battleground State Campground,** off Beach Road, 518/668-3348, or the nearby 251-site **Hearthstone Point,** Rte. 9 N north of the village, 518/668-5193, call 800/456-CAMP. A basic site at both costs $14–16.

Dozens of small, moderately priced motels are located along Rts. 9 and 9 N. One of the friendliest and most reliable among them is the clean, family-run **Admiral Motel,** 401 Canada St., 518/668-2097, www.admiralmotel.com, complete with a heated outdoor pool ($90–105 d).

If you'd like to stay near the village but away from the madness, choose a hostelry on the lake's quiet east shore. A good option here is the classy **Dunham's Bay Lodge,** RR1, Box 1179, Rte. 9L, 518/656-9242, www.dunhamsbay.com ($175 d).

The upscale **Fort William Henry Motor Inn,** 50 Canada St., 518/668-3081, www.fortwilliam-henry.com, features two pools, three restaurants, and a concierge in season ($180–204 d; packages available in spring and fall).

Food

Fast food and sandwich shops are located all along Canada Street and Beach Road. Among them is the laid-back **Garrison Koom Cafe,** Beach Rd., 518/668-5281, serving burgers, sandwiches, and simple entrées. **Wagar's Soda Fountain & Candy Factory,** 327 Canada St., 518/668-3770, is a local institution where you can pick up everything from ice cream sundaes and sandwiches to Adirondack bear claws (nuts dipped in caramel and chocolate).

For more serious dining, try the airy, multi-level **Shoreline Restaurant,** 4 Kurosaka Ln., 518/668-2875, nicely situated overlooking a small marina. Menu selections range from fresh fish to chicken teriyaki. Sit out back on the deck and enjoy live entertainment in summer; average entrée $18. Also overlooking the water is the big, boisterous **Boardwalk,** foot of Amherst St., 518/668-5324, offering burgers and sandwiches at lunch, considerably more elaborate entrées at dinner (average price $18). **Montcalm South,** 1415 Rte. 9 at I-87 Exit 20, 518/793-6601, offers lots of seafood dishes and homemade breads, along with traditional American fare; average entrée $22.

Visitor Information

The **Lake George Chamber of Commerce,** Box 272, Lake George, NY 12845, 518/668-5755, www.lakegeorgechamber.com, is open year-round Mon.–Fri. 9 A.M.–5 P.M.; and July–Aug., daily 9 A.M.–5 P.M. You'll find it on Route 9 at the southern end of the village across from the Prospect Mountain State Highway.

LAKE LUZERNE

Take Route 9N out of Lake George village to reach Lake Luzerne, a quieter resort community about 10 miles away. Lake Luzerne traditionally has been known for its dude ranches, which is why you'll notice signs pointing to Big Hat Country along the way. Though the dude ranch business is not what it was once, the country's oldest weekly rodeo still takes place weekend nights throughout the summer at the **Painted Pony Ranch,** RD2, 703 Howe Rd., off Rte. 9 N, 518/696-2421. Guided trail rides are offered by **Bennett's Riding Stable,** along Route 9 N about five miles from I-87, 518/696-4444.

The trim village of Lake Luzerne, bounded by two rivers, consists of a few small streets crowded with Victorian homes. At the eastern end flows the Hudson River, where bubbling Rockwell Falls rushes downstream through a small park. At the western end, the Sacandaga River attracts whitewater rafters and canoeists. Rental equipment and guided whitewater raft trips down the Sacandaga's Class II and III waters are offered by the **Adirondack River Outfitters Adventures,** 518/696-5101 or 800/525-RAFT, in Lake Luzerne, and by **W.I.L.D./ W.A.T.E.R.S. Outdoor Center,** 518/494-7478 or 800/867-2335, in nearby Warrensburg.

Hudson River Recreation Area

Head north out of Lake Luzerne on scenic River Road about five miles to reach a 1,132-acre recreation area laced with short and easy hiking trails, many of which follow old logging roads. The Ferguson Brook Trail offers great views of the

The Sacandaga River is popular with whitewater rafters and canoeists.

Hudson River, while the Bear Slide Trail leads to frothy Buttermilk Falls.

A ranger is on duty at the gatehouse, off River Road, Memorial Day–Labor Day. For more information, call the Warren County Parks and Recreation Department at 518/623-2877.

Hiking Hadley Mountain

Although Hadley Mountain is only 2,700 feet high, it affords magnificent views from its summit. To the north loom the High Peaks, to the south are the Catskills and Great Sacandaga Lake, and to the east Lake George and the Green Mountains. The Adirondack Mountain Club considers the four-mile roundtrip hike to the summit easy to moderate in difficulty, about three hours roundtrip.

To reach the trailhead, take Route 9 N north of Lake Luzerne to Hadley and head north on Stony Creek Road. Continue three miles to Hadley Hill Road and turn left. Proceed slightly over four miles to Tower Road, turn right, and continue another 1.5 miles to the trailhead on the left, marked with a sign.

Camping and Accommodations

To make reservations at the 174-site **Luzerne State Campground,** Route 9 N south of the village, 518/696-2031, call 800/456-CAMP. A basic site costs $14.

The gracious **Lamplight Inn B&B,** 2129 Lake Ave., 518/696-5294 or 800/BNB-INNV, www.lamplightinn.com, is an award-winning 1890 hostelry featuring 10 bedrooms, fireplaces, 12-foot ceilings, and a wraparound porch. An addition offers five modern rooms equipped with Jacuzzis ($159–239 d in summer).

Between Lake George and Lake Luzerne the **Roaring Brook Ranch and Tennis Resort,** Luzerne Rd., 518/668-5767 or 800/88BROOK, www.roaringbrookresort.com, still operates as one of the oldest and best dude ranches in the area. Spread out over 500 acres, the well-kept resort includes 142 simple but comfortable rooms, 30-odd horses, five lighted tennis courts, three swimming pools, and saunas and fitness rooms (summer rates are $107–130 per person double occupancy, including riding, use of all facilities, breakfast and dinner; family rates available).

Food

In the heart of Lake Luzerne village is the charming **Papa's Ice Cream Parlor,** 2117 Main St., 518/696-3667, filled with old-fashioned milk bottles and picture postcards. On the menu are tasty sandwiches and ice cream treats; average sandwich $5. The **Waterhouse,** 85 Lake Ave., 518/696-3115, features traditional American fare and is known for its homemade pies; average entrée $15.

Events

The free, first-class **Lake Luzerne Chamber Music Festival,** 518/696-2771, featuring members of the Philadelphia Orchestra, takes place on Monday nights throughout the summer at the Luzerne Music Center, Lake Tour Rd., off Rte. 9N.

WARRENSBURG

On Route 9 a few miles northwest of Lake George village is the old mill town of Warrensburg. Founded in the early 1800s, Warrensburg boasts several attractive Victorian buildings downtown along Main Street (Route 9), as well as interesting restaurants and area accommodations. For the most part, however, the place is nondescript and extremely congested in summer.

Warrensburg is best known for its **antique shops,** most of which are located along Main Street.

Accommodations and Food

Perched on a hill surrounded by 176 woodsy acres is the friendly **Allynn's Butterfly B&B,** Rte. 28, 518/623-9390, www.allynsbutterfly-inn.com. The Federalist-style farmhouse offers four snug guest rooms and a sunroom where breakfast is served ($119–149 d).

A local institution, the Victorian **Merrill Magee House,** 2 Hudson St., 518/623-2449, www.merrillmageehouse.com, specializes in traditional American and Continental cuisine. To one side is an English-style tavern offering ales and stouts, to the other are several cozy dining rooms. Dinner dishes range from rack of lamb to grilled fish, and lunch is served as well; average dinner entrée $19. Also a B&B, the Merrill Magee features 10 modern rooms in a guesthouse out back ($115–135 d).

One of the finest restaurants in the area, specializing in innovative American dishes, is the rambling Civil War–era **Friend's Lake Inn,** Friends Lake Rd., 518/494-4751, www.friendslake.com, about 14 miles north of Warrensburg in historic Chestertown. The wine list alone runs about 25 pages long (full menu offered at dinner only, average entrée $23; bar and light lunch menu also offered in summer), while upstairs and out back are 16 lovely guest rooms, all equipped with queen size beds and private baths. Many of the rooms also have Jacuzzis and two have fireplaces ($275–425 d, including breakfast and dinner; B&B rates (breakfast only) $235–385).

Events

The **World's Largest Garage Sale,** 518/623-2161, boasting over 500 vendors, takes place on Main Street in downtown Warrensburg the first weekend in October.

BOLTON LANDING

Back along the shores of Lake George about 10 miles north of Lake George village sits Bolton Landing, another congested tourist town. During the summer the village traffic is bumper to bumper.

For many visitors, Bolton Landing's main attractions are its gift shops, most located along Main Street. Boats can be rented along the waterfront, while **Rodger's Memorial Park** and **Veteran's Park** offer small public beaches. The **Bolton Historical Museum,** Lakeshore Drive (Route 9 N), 518/644-9960, housed in a former Catholic church, includes an interesting collection of photographs by Seneca Ray Stoddard, along with an exhibit on sculptor David Smith, who once lived in the area (open July–Aug., Tues.–Sun. 11 A.M.–4 P.M., and some evenings 7–9 P.M.).

Isolated on its own private island at one end of the village reigns the storybook **Sagamore** hotel, Sagamore Rd., 518/644-9400. Originally built in 1883 and now listed on the National Register of Historic Places, the columned, gabled hotel remains a luxurious year-round resort. Features include four first-class restaurants, a full-service spa, tennis courts, playground, nearby golf course, and a sandy beach with great views of Lake George. Cruises of the lake are offered by the *Morgan,* a sleek wooden boat. The basic sightseeing cruise is free for guests; for nonguests, the cost is $15. Dinner cruises cost $55 per person.

Marcella Sembrich Opera Museum

From 1921 to 1935, Marcella Sembrich, a soprano who sang with the Metropolitan Opera, summered in Bolton Landing. In those days, the village was a favorite resort of opera stars, and Sembrich brought several students with her each year. Today, the diva's former studio still houses her sizeable collection of music, along with her costumes, furniture, and other memorabilia.

The museum, 4800 Lakeshore Dr., 518/644-9839, www.operamuseum.com, is open June 15–September 15, daily 10 A.M.–12:30 P.M. and 2–5:30 P.M. Admission is adults $2, under 12 free.

Accommodations

Across the street from the Sembrich Museum stands the homey **Hilltop Cottage B&B,** Lakeshore Dr., 518/644-2492, www.hilltopcottage.com, offering three guest rooms with shared baths and one guest cottage with a private bath ($80 d). Features of the family-oriented **Northward Ho,** Box 464, Lakeshore Dr., 518/644-2158, include 26 rooms, eight cottages, a private beach, pool, and playground ($68–83 d).

The **Sagamore** (see description above), Sagamore Rd., 518/644-9400, www.thesagamore.com, offers 100 luxurious rooms and suites in the historic main hotel ($159–269 d off-season; $359–518 d in summer), and 240 private lodges ($139–339 d off-season; $259–659 d in summer).

Food

The casual **Algonquin Restaurant,** Lakeshore Dr., 518/644-9442, built over the water, is a local favorite for both lunch and dinner. On the menu is everything from burgers to fresh fish; average entrée $16.

The Sagamore hotel, Sagamore Rd., 518/644-9400, offers four dining options. **Mr. Brown's Pub** serves sandwiches and salads ($9–18). **Club Grille** serves hamburgers and basic fare at lunch, top-of-the-line steaks and other grilled items at dinner (entrées $18–32). The **Sagamore Dining Room** specializes in innovative American cuisine served upscale buffet style. The *très* elegant **Trillium** offers superb gourmet fare (entrées $20–39).

NORTHERN LAKE GEORGE

Route 9 N continues north of Bolton Landing into much wilder countryside. At last the tourist centers are left behind as you veer away from the lakeshore, past the Tongue Mountain Range, and then return to it once again, passing the isolated resort communities of Sabbath Day Point, Silver Bay, and Hague.

Scenic **Route 8** heads west out of Hague to Brant Lake, about 10 miles away. En route lookouts offer great views of the High Peaks; in the fall, the surrounding Dixon Forest turns vivid hues of red, yellow, and orange. Mohawk legend describes this as the land of Broken Wing, a crippled brave who saved his village and is remembered every autumn by the turning of the leaves.

About two miles north of Hague on Route 9 N are the **Indian Kettles,** glacial potholes one to three feet in diameter and one to 12 inches deep. The white man's legend has it that the Indians once used the potholes for cooking.

Rogers Rock State Park

Just north of the Indian Kettles, Rogers Rock State Park offers a 321-site campground, boat launch, beach, and bathhouse, along with a 2.5-mile hiking trail that leads up 500 feet to Rogers Slide. At first, the trail winds mostly uphill and northerly, but then it flattens out to run along a ledge and open expanse. Keeping to the right at a fork just past the ledge will bring you to cliffs overlooking Lake George.

The park, Rte. 9 N, 518/585-6746, is open May–Labor Day. Parking is $7. For campground reservations, call 800/456-CAMP; a basic site costs $14.

Camping and Accommodations

Forty-eight of the islands dotting Lake George are available for camping, though accessible only by boat. For more information, write the Department of Environmental Conservation, Bureau of Recreation Operations, Warrensburg, NY 12885.

One of the last of the old lakeside hotels that once flourished in this region is the **Northern Lake George Resort,** Rte. 9 N, Silver Bay, 518/543-6528, www.northernlakegeorge.com. Built in 1896, when it was known as the Hotel Uncas, the hostelry has been altered over the years but still features an old-fashioned rustic lobby complete with stone fireplace and high ceilings. Also on-site are lakeside villas and motel rooms ($70–95 d).

SCHROON LAKE AND VICINITY

West of Lake George lies Schroon Lake, a quiet resort community with a laid-back Main Street and good-size public beach (off Route 9). During the summer, concerts are presented in the **Boat House Theater,** 518/532-7675, overlooking the lake, and one-hour narrated cruises are offered by

Schroon Lake Boat Tours, 518/532-7675. The area is also home to the **Seagle Music Colony,** Charley Hill Rd., 518/532-7875, a music retreat founded by concert baritone Oscar Seagle in 1915. The colony stages opera concerts and musical theater in July–early August.

Not far from the colony is the **Adirondack Rustics Gallery,** 739 Rte. 9., 518/532-0020, a rambling shop filled with the rustic furniture for which the Adirondacks is famous. Here you'll find tables, chairs, beds, and cupboards handmade from cedar, hickory, and other woods.

Pottersville

At the southern end of the lake lies Pottersville and the **Natural Stone Bridge and Caves.** Formed by the Ausable River, this geological park features odd-shaped rock formations, waterfalls, and potholes large enough to park a truck in. Tours of the area are self-guided, and good trout fishing abounds. A large rock shop on-site sells everything from petrified wood to geodes.

The bridge and caves, 535 Stone Bridge Rd., off Rte. 9, 518/494-2283, are open Memorial Day–Columbus Day, daily 9 A.M.–7 P.M. Admission is adults $9, children 6–12 $5.

Hiking Pharaoh Mountain

To the east of Schroon Lake rises Pharaoh Mountain, surrounded by the Pharaoh Lake Wilderness Area. The splendid views from the mountaintop—covered with open rock—take in nearby ponds and craggy hills, as well as the more distant High Peaks. The nine-mile roundtrip hike is of moderate difficulty and takes four to five hours.

To reach the trailhead, head north of Schroon Lake on Route 9 about two miles. Turn right onto Alder Meadow Road and continue 2.2 miles to a fork. Bear left on Crane Pond Road and travel 1.4 miles to a parking lot. Continue on the road on foot 1.9 miles to Crane Pond, where the trailhead begins at the end of another parking lot (parking is not permitted here).

Detour to North Hudson

On the edge of the High Peaks region about seven miles north of Schroon Lake village lies North Hudson, a tiny mountain hamlet surrounded by ponds and wilderness; year-round population is under 200.

Blue Ridge Road (Route 2) heads west out of North Hudson to skirt the southern edge of the High Peaks. The route runs alongside the Branch, which flows between Elk Lake and Schroon River; about three miles from the village cascade the lovely **Blue Ridge waterfalls.**

Camping and Accommodations

At the southern end of Schroon Lake lies the 72-site **Eagle Point Campground,** Rte. 9, 518/494-2220. For reservations, call 800/456-CAMP; a basic site costs $14.

The friendly **Schroon Lake Bed and Breakfast,** Rte. 9, 518/532-7042, www.schroonbb.com,

offers five comfortable guest rooms furnished with antiques ($115 d). Family-oriented **Wood's Lodge,** East St., 518/532-7529, centers around the queenly Victorian-era Lake House. Accommodations range from standard-size guest rooms, some with balconies ($105 d), to two-bedroom suites ($600–675/week) to five lakeside cabins ($505–535/week).

Tucked into the mountains north of North Hudson is the ultra-secluded **Elk Lake Lodge,** Elk Lake Rd., off Blue Ridge Rd., 518/532-7616. Situated on its own private lake surrounded by a 12,000-acre preserve, the main lodge (circa 1900) offers six rooms with private baths; on the lakefront are seven cottages ($110–150 per person, double occupancy, includes all meals).

Champlain Valley

In 1609, 11 years before the Pilgrims landed in Massachusetts, French explorer Samuel de Champlain "discovered" the long, thin, sparkling blue lake that now bears his name. Shortly after his arrival he killed two Iroquois with a single blast of his arquebus, thereby establishing the tenor of European–Native American relationships for centuries to come.

One hundred and ten miles long and 400 feet deep in spots, Lake Champlain is the largest freshwater lake in the United States after the Great Lakes. Encompassing 490 square miles, it stretches from New York north into Canada and east into Vermont. Even bigger than the lake itself is the basin in which it sits. On the New York side, that basin extends as far west as the Adirondack Mountains and as far south as Hudson Falls. About 25 percent of Adirondack Park lies within the Champlain Valley.

Compared to Lake George, the shores of Lake Champlain appear sparsely forested and surprisingly undeveloped. The countryside becomes especially magnificent north of Port Henry, where the raw jagged High Peaks of the Adirondacks rise to one side, the moody rounder peaks of Vermont's Green Mountains to the other.

Throughout the 19th and much of the 20th centuries, Lake Champlain supported numer-

ous iron ore and manufacturing plants, most of them along the shore. Many of these have closed in recent years, which helps account for the region's current high unemployment rate—upwards of 12 percent.

Away from the shore, the valley opens into rich farmland. Red barns, silver silos, and a patchwork of green fields spread out over one gentle slope after another. Dairy farming is especially big business here.

Visitor Information

Much of the Champlain Valley lies in Essex County. For general information, contact the **Lake Placid/Essex County Visitors Bureau,** Olympic Arena, 216 Main St., Lake Placid, NY 12946; 518/523-2445 or 800/447-5224, www.lakeplacid.com. Hours are daily 9 A.M.–5 P.M.; closed summer Sundays.

Near the Lake Champlain Bridge connecting New York with Vermont stands the **Lake Champlain Visitors Center,** 814 Bridge Rd., off Rts. 9 and 22, Crown Point, NY 12928, 518/597-4649 or 888/THE-LAKE, www.LakeChamplainRegion.com. Inside you'll find a multitude of brochures and several exhibits, including a good introductory video on the Adirondacks. Hours are Memorial Day–Columbus Day, daily

9 A.M.–4 P.M.; Columbus Day–Memorial Day, Mon.–Fri. 9 A.M.–4 P.M.

TICONDEROGA

Sandwiched in the two miles between Lake George and Lake Champlain lies Ticonderoga—the town and the fort. The town sits at the foot of Lake George; the fort overlooks Lake Champlain.

Visitor Information

The **Ticonderoga Area Chamber of Commerce,** 94 Montcalm St., Ticonderoga, NY 12883, 518/585-6619, www.ticonderogany.com, is open Mon.–Fri. 9 A.M.–4:30 P.M.

The Town

Sprawling, scruffy Ticonderoga centers around a historic downtown containing several interesting buildings. Among them is the **Heritage Museum,** Montcalm St. at Bicentennial Park, 518/585-2696, which houses displays on the area's industrial history. Traditionally, Ticonderoga has been known for its pencil and papermaking plants. The first commercial pencils—bearing the name Ticonderoga—were produced in the area in 1840; still operating in town is International Paper. (The museum is open July–Labor Day, daily 10 A.M.–4 P.M.; weekends in Sept.–Oct.; admission is by donation.)

The **Hancock House,** 3 Wicker St., at Moses Circle, 518/585-7868, is a replica of the house built for John Hancock in Boston. Originally home to the New York State Historical Association (now based in Cooperstown), the building currently houses a museum and library, with period rooms and exhibits on the area's social and civil history (open Wed.–Sat. 10 A.M.–4 P.M.; admission by donation).

Fort Ticonderoga

One of the Adirondacks' most popular visitor attractions, the meticulously restored Fort Ticonderoga sits within a shade-filled park. Originally built by the French in 1755, the fort bore the nickname "Key to a Continent." Strategically located along the Canada–New York waterway, Ticonderoga was attacked six times during the

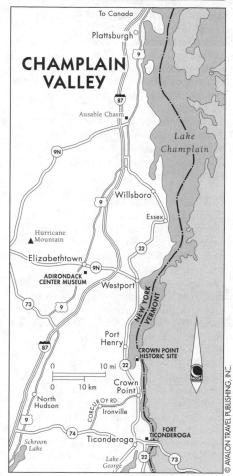

French and Indian and Revolutionary Wars. Three times it successfully held, and three times it fell. France, Great Britain, and the Americans all once held control.

Inside the fort are barracks, kitchens, bastions, stables, cannons, and artifacts pertaining to both wars. Among the more unusual items on display are a lock of George Washington's hair, a pocket watch once owned by Ethan Allen, and a rum horn given to Gen. Schuyler by Paul Revere. Throughout the summer, numerous special events are staged daily, including parades, cannon firings, and fife-and-drum musters.

Mount Defiance, also part of the complex, looms over the fort to the east. During the Revolutionary War, British general Burgoyne used the hill's vantage point to drive the Americans out of Fort Ticonderoga. Ancient cannons still perch on the hilltop.

The fort, on Fort Rd. (Rte. 74), 518/585-2821, is open May–Oct., daily 9 A.M.–5 P.M.; call for off-season hours. Admission is adults $12, seniors and students $10, children 7–12 $6, under 7 free.

Fort Ticonderoga Ferry

Continue east past the fort on Route 74 to reach a public boat ramp and dock for the sleepy Fort Ticonderoga Ferry, 802/897-7999, in operation in one form or another since the mid-1700s. From May through October, the flatbed ferry crosses whenever there's traffic to Shoreham, Vermont. The low-key journey only takes a few minutes and costs $7 per car with up to four passengers one-way, $12 roundtrip; $2 per bicycle and rider; or $1 per biped.

Camping, Motels, and Food

Six miles west of Ticonderoga lies the 72-site **Putnam Pond Campground,** off Rte. 74, 518/585-7280. For reservations, call 800/456-CAMP; a basic site costs $12. Standard motel rooms are offered by the six-room **Latchstring Motel,** 420 Montcalm St., 518/585-2875 or 800/562-5896 ($50–60 d); and the 39-room **Super 8 Motel,** Box 567, Rte. 9 N, 518/585-2617 ($80–90 d).

The **Hot Biscuit Diner,** 428 Montcalm St., 518/585-3483, is a good place for breakfast or lunch; average main dish $6. Housed in a former schoolhouse and open just for dinner is **Thatcher's Schoolhouse Restaurant,** Rte. 9 N, 518/585-4044, serving everything from sandwiches and burgers to steak and seafood ($5–15).

CROWN POINT

About eight miles north of Ticonderoga is the village of Crown Point, not to be confused with the Crown Point Historic Site a few miles farther

north. The village of Crown Point was once known for its iron industry, while at the Historic Site are the ruins of two forts.

Ironville

Hard though it is to believe today, the quiet, near-deserted area just west of Crown Point was once a major industrial center filled with dirty clanking machinery. A rich bed of iron ore was discovered here in the early 1800s, and throughout that century, the region teemed with mines, forges, and railroads. The high-quality ore attracted the U.S. Navy, intent on securing iron to build its first iron-clad warship, the Civil War–era *Monitor.*

Crown Point's industrial activity centered around the company town of Ironville, now a village so small it's all but disappeared. In its heyday, Ironville boasted a company store, company housing, and company script. Today, it's an exceptionally lovely hamlet with a strong New England feel; many of the area's early foremen originally hailed from there.

Behind a white picket fence in the middle of Ironville presides the **Penfield Homestead Museum.** This 1828 Federal-style building was once home to industrialist Allen Penfield, the first man to use electricity for industrial purposes (in 1831). Exhibits tell the story of Penfield's inventions and the area's industrial past. A collection of ancient machinery slumbers out back.

The museum, 708 Creek Rd., 518/597-3804, www.penfieldmuseum.com, is open mid-May–mid-Oct., Mon.–Sat. 10 A.M.–4 P.M., Sunday noon–4 P.M. Admission is adults $2, children $1. To reach Ironville from Ticonderoga, take Route 74 to Corduroy Road. From Crown Point, take Route 47 west, which becomes Ironville Road and then Corduroy Road.

Crown Point State Historic Site

North of Crown Point, a pudgy spit of land juts into Lake Champlain. Flat and windswept, with sweeping views of the north, the point once provided an ideal lookout spot. The French built Fort St. Frederic here in 1734, only to be conquered by the British in 1759, who in turn built Fort Crown Point.

The ruins of both forts still stand, near a visi-

© CHRISTIANE BIRD

Crown Point Historic Site is home to ruins of both French and British 18th-century forts.

tor center that provides historical background. Much of the area has not been fully excavated, but it has a lonely and haunting appeal.

The visitor center, Rte. 903, off Rtes. 9 N and 22 near the Champlain Bridge, 518/597-3666, is open May–Oct., Wed.–Mon. 9 A.M.–5 P.M.; the grounds are open 24 hours a day year-round. Admission to the visitor center is adults $2, children $1; the grounds are free.

Camping and B&B

Across from the Crown Point Historic Site is the 64-site **Crown Point Reservation State Campground,** off Rte. 22, 518/597-6303. For camping reservations, call 800/456-CAMP; a basic site costs $12.

Housed in an 1886 Victorian mansion is the **Crown Point Bed & Breakfast,** 32 Main St., 518/597-3651, www.crownpointbandb.com, offering six attractive guest rooms nicely furnished with antiques; $70–140 d.

PORT HENRY

On the mainland just north of the Crown Point Historic Site sprawls Port Henry, a large town of red-brick buildings spread over several steep hills. Like Crown Point, Port Henry was once known for its iron industry, which peaked here under the management of the Republic Steel Company during WW II. West of town hulks a giant 18-million-ton mountain of ore tailings that's visible for miles around. Locals hope that new refining techniques will enable the extraction of rare earth minerals from the pile.

Welcome to the Home of the Champ reads the sign at the town's entrance, while nearby stands a cheerful green serpent with a zigzagging tail. The **Champ** is a legendary monster who lives in the depths of Lake Champlain. Stories about him have circulated among the Iroquois for hundreds of years and among whites since 1609, when Samuel de Champlain reported seeing a 20-foot-long creature in the lake. Since then there have been over 300 reported sightings of the Champ, many of which have occurred near Port Henry.

Although there is no concrete proof that the Champ exists, the legislatures of both New York and Vermont have passed resolutions encouraging scientific inquiry into the depths of the lake. If *you* spot anything unusual, contact Champ Quest, P.O. Box 261, Vergennes, VT 05491.

THE NORTH COUNTRY

Events

Port Henry honors its mythical beast every August on **Champ Day,** 518/546-7261, with music, crafts, and food.

WESTPORT

Lying on a natural terrace above a deep bay, the tidy Victorian village of Westport has been a favorite stopping-off place since steamship days, when families traveling north on Lake Champlain debarked here to catch stagecoaches for points farther west. Later, Westport became a destination in its own right, as evidenced by the elegant homes along Route 22. Today, Westport remains one of the few villages in the Adirondacks that's accessible by rail; Amtrak travels through here on its way between New York and Montreal.

Westport is best known for its historic inns and the **Depot Theater,** Rte. 9, 518/962-4449, a restored 19th-century railway station, now a theater presenting professional summer stock daily June–September. Along the lakeshore is a busy marina where boats can be rented, and a public beach. Bordering Pleasant Street (Route 9 N) are a variety of shops, including the **Westport Trading Company,** 2 Pleasant St., 518/962-4801, which sells the work of over 100 area artists and artisans.

Accommodations

The clapboard **Westport Hotel,** 114 Pleasant St. (Rte. 9 N), 518/962-4501, www.thewestporthotel.com, dates back to 1876, the same year the railroad came to town. Inside are 10 guest rooms nicely outfitted in antiques; outside is an inviting wraparound porch ($35–50 with shared bath, $85 with private bath).

The stately 1875 **Inn on the Library Lawn,** 1 Washington St., 518/962-8666, www.innonthelibrarylawn.com, situated across the street from the town library, features 10 spacious guest rooms, a sitting room with a fireplace, and its own antique shop ($69–125 d, includes a gourmet breakfast). Also downtown is the fine Dutch Colonial **All Tucked Inn,** 53 S. Main St., 518/962-4400, www.alltuckedinn.com, which offers nine guest rooms and a glass-enclosed porch that overlooks the lake ($65–125 d).

Food

For casual dining at the marina, try the **Galley,** at the foot of Washington St., 518/962-4899. On the menu is eclectic international fare; live bands play on summer weekend nights (average entrée $12). The **Westport Hotel,** 114 Pleasant St. (Rte. 9 N), 518/962-4501, runs a cozy restaurant spread over several small rooms. It's open for breakfast and lunch; lunch entrées average $8.

ELIZABETHTOWN

About 10 miles west of Westport and Lake Champlain on Rte. 9 N lies Elizabethtown, the Essex County seat. Settled in 1791 by pioneers from Vermont, Elizabethtown was at first known for its lumber mills and later for its resort hotels. One of these, the 1808 **Deer's Head Inn,** still stands, one of the oldest operating inns in the Adirondacks.

In the center of town reigns the **Essex County Court House,** Court St. (Rte. 9 N), where the body of abolitionist John Brown lay in state on the way to burial in nearby North Elba (see Lake Placid). His wife and other members of the funeral entourage spent the night at the Deer's Head Inn while four young men from the village stood guard over the body. Today, the courthouse features a mural of Brown speaking in his own defense at his 1859 trial in West Virginia. Another mural depicts Samuel de Champlain firing his arquebus at the Iroquois.

Adirondack History Center

Housed in a big old schoolhouse on the edge of town, the laid-back Adirondack History Museum corrals an enormous hodgepodge of exhibits. A re-created log cabin kitchen and artifacts from an iron mine take up one floor; on another is an exhibit on the Iroquois and displays pertaining to the lumbering industry. A light-and-sound show offers some perspective on the French and Indian War, while Adirondack guideboats, early farm implements, antique bobsleds, and a roomful of dolls tell their stories of everyday life. Out back are a Colonial garden and a 1910 fire tower that once stood atop Adirondack Mountain.

The museum, Court St. (Rte. 9), 518/873-

6466, is open Memorial Day–Columbus Day, Mon.–Sat. 9 A.M.–5 P.M., Sunday 1–5 P.M. Admission is adults $3.50, seniors $2.50, youths 6–16 $1.50.

Accommodations and Food

Now more a restaurant than an inn, the recently renovated **Deer's Head Inn,** Court St., 518/873-9903, features a wide front porch, three dining rooms, and four simple but comfortable guest rooms ($60 d). The traditional American menu ranges from salads and sandwiches for lunch, to roast chicken and rack of lamb for dinner; average dinner entrée $14.

ESSEX

The loveliest village along the Lake Champlain shore is Essex. Filled with trim white buildings that date back to before the Civil War, the entire village is on the National Register of Historic Places. To the west rise the Adirondack's dramatic High Peaks; to the east sparkle the blue waters of the lake, offset by the dusk-blue mountains of Vermont.

Essex, founded in 1765 by Irishman William Gilliland, was one of the earliest European settlements on Lake Champlain. The community was destroyed completely during the American Revolution but soon rose again into a prosperous shipbuilding center and lake port. By 1850, Essex was one of the largest and busiest towns on the lake, with a population of 2,351.

Then came the Civil War, the opening of the West, and the building of the railroads, all of which drew commerce away from Lake Champlain. Essex's economy suffered and its population dwindled. There was little money for building; standing structures had to do. And so it remains today.

Essex centers around two parallel streets, Main and Elm, both just two blocks long. Excellent examples of Federal, Greek Revival, and Victorian architecture abound, while along the waterfront stretches **Maron Beggs Park** and a small marina.

The **Lake Champlain Ferries,** 802/864-9804, www.ferries.com, dock at the northern end of the village, crossing between Essex, New York and Charlotte, Vermont. The ferries depart throughout the year, taking 20 minutes one-way. One-way rate for a car and driver is $7.50, roundtrip $13.50; roundtrip rates for walk-on traffic are adults $3.50, children 6–12 $1. It's $2 per bicycle and rider.

Accommodations and Food

At the heart of Essex sits the 180-year-old **Essex Inn,** 16 Main St., 518/963-8821, www.theessexinn.com, a long and thin hostelry with an even longer and thinner two-tiered front porch. Breakfast, lunch, and dinner are served outside in warm weather (average dinner entrée $14), while inside are nine guest rooms ($85–135 d, includes full breakfast). The inn also contains a courtyard, clothing shop, and arts gallery; pick up free walking-tour brochures here.

The elegant **Stone House,** Church and Elm Sts., 518/963-7713, is a hospitable 1826 Federal-style home with four attractive guest rooms ($85–135 d).

NORTH TO AUSABLE CHASM

Continuing north of Essex on Route 22, you'll hug the lakeshore for a few glorious miles before heading inland to **Willsboro,** on the Bouquet River. Willsboro is a favorite spot among anglers thanks to its fish ladder at the Willsboro Dam. The ladder, off Route 22, allows landlocked salmon to ascend the river to spawning grounds farther upstream; you can watch the action from a viewing window.

Continue another eight miles north and you'll bump into the New York State Thruway (I-87), followed another five miles later by Ausable Chasm. After the serene back roads and peaceful vistas of Lake Champlain, this place comes as a shock. Ausable Chasm, one of the oldest tourist attractions in the United States, opened to the public in 1870; count on dozens of tour buses crowding the parking lot out front.

Carved out by the Ausable River over the past 500 million years, the Ausable Chasm's massive stone gorge stretches out over a mile and a half. Twenty to 50 feet wide, and 100–200 feet deep, it is filled with odd rock formations, caves, rapids, and waterfalls. A three-quarter-mile trail leads through the gorge to Table Rock, where rafts take

COURTESY OF LAKE PLACID/ESSEX COUNTY VISITORS BUREAU

Ausable Chasm

visitors the rest of the way. Buses at the end of the ride will shuttle you back to the parking lot.

The chasm, off Rte. 9, 518/834-7454 or 800/537-1211, www.ausablechasm.com, is open Memorial Day–Columbus Day, daily 9:30 A.M.–4:30 P.M. All-inclusive tickets are adults $24, children 5–11 $20.

Recreation and Camping

At the **Ausable Point State Park,** Rte. 9 at Lake Champlain, 518/561-7080, you'll find a beach, a bathhouse, good fishing spots, boat rentals, and a 123-site campground. For camping reservations, call 800/456-CAMP; a basic site costs $16.

PLATTSBURGH

The small industrial city of Plattsburgh (pop. 21,255) played an important role in both the American Revolution and the War of 1812. In 1776, the British won the Battle of Lake Champlain off Plattsburgh's shores. In 1814, the American Commodore Thomas MacDonough defeated a British fleet from Canada here by using an in-

tricate system of anchors and winches that enabled him to swivel his vessels completely around.

Historic Plattsburgh centers around **RiverWalk Park,** which runs along the banks of the Saranac River downtown. The park begins at Bridge Street and extends to the Champlain Monument at Cumberland Avenue. Addresses worth noting along the way include the 1830 **Trinity Episcopal Church** at Trinity Place; the 1917 **City Hall,** City Hall Place, designed by John Russell Pope; and the **Champlain Monument** itself, a gift to the city from France in 1909, commemorating the tercentenary of Samuel de Champlain's voyage.

Visitor Information

The **Plattsburgh–North Country Chamber of Commerce,** 7061 Rte. 9, Plattsburgh, NY 12901, 518/563-1000, www.goadirondack.com or www.northcountrychamber.com, is open year-round Mon.–Fri. 8:30 A.M.–5 P.M. A **visitor information center,** 800/487-6867, is located off I-87 heading south between Exits 41 and 40.

Kent-Delord Museum House

Across from the Champlain Monument stands the city's foremost visitor attraction, the Kent-Delord House. Built in 1797 and enlarged in 1811, the gracious house was commandeered by the British during the War of 1812. Home to three generations of the Delord family, the house contains nine period rooms furnished with antiques and an interesting collection of portraits. Of special interest is an exhibit on Fanny Delord Hall, a self-taught healer who in the late 1800s patented and marketed her own home remedy, Fanoline, "a healing, antiseptic and curative ointment, in cases of Eczema, Fever-sores, Catarrh, Salt-rheum, Piles, Sore Nipples, Burns, Blisters, Scratches, Corns, Sore Eyes, Chapped Hands and Lips."

The museum, 17 Cumberland Ave., 518/561-1035, is open Tues.–Sat., noon–4 P.M. and by appointment; closed January–February. Admission is adults $4, seniors and students $3, children under 12 $2.

Clinton County Historical Museum

To learn about Plattsburgh's history, visit the county museum, housed in a trim 1805 building

THE NORTH COUNTRY

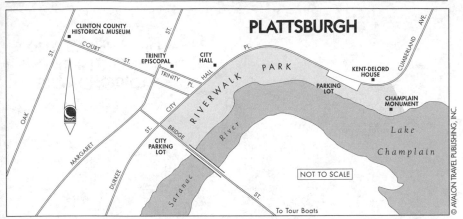

located two blocks from RiverWalk. On permanent display are a diorama on the battles of Lake Champlain, an exhibit on underwater archaeological discoveries, historic maps, and period furniture. Temporary exhibits highlight such North Country activities as iron mining and lumbering.

The museum, 48 Court St., at Oak, 518/561-0340, is open Tues.–Fri. noon–4 P.M.; call for Saturday hours. Admission is adults $4, seniors $3, children under 12 $2.

Camping and Motels

Just north of the city is **Cumberland Bay State Park,** Rte. 314, off Rte. 9, 518/563-5240, equipped with a 210-site campground. For reservations call 800/456-CAMP; a basic site costs $15. Various motels are located on the outskirts of town. One good choice is the clean, 500-room **Econo Lodge,** 528 Rte. 3, 518/561-1500 ($64–80 d).

Recreation

Captain Frank's, at the foot of Dock St., 518/561-8970, offers sightseeing, dinner, and entertainment cruises May–September.

The **Cumberland Bay State Park,** Rte. 314, off Rte. 9, 518/563-5240, encompasses a 2,700-foot-long beach. Parking in summer costs $7.

High Peaks and Northern Adirondacks

The term "High Peaks" generally refers to the heart of the Adirondacks, where 46 of the region's highest peaks can be found. Just west of the Champlain Valley, the High Peaks are loosely bounded by Elizabethtown to the east, Wilmington to the north, the Franklin County line to the west, and Newcomb to the south. At the center lies Lake Placid.

Many hikers come to the High Peaks region intent on climbing all 46 of its highest summits and thereby becoming a "46er." The tradition dates back to the early 1920s, when two young brothers, George and Robert Marshall, climbed to the top of Whiteface Mountain with their guide Herb Clark. Upon reaching the summit,

they made a pact to climb all the peaks in the park measuring 4,000 feet or more in height. Later, it turned out that some of the peaks on their list were under 4,000 feet, but no matter, a pattern had been set. Today, hikers come from all over the country to carry on the tradition.

To reach the High Peaks region from the Champlain Valley, take Route 9 N west from Ausable Chasm to Route 86, or Route 9 N west from Elizabethtown to Route 73. Both lead to Lake Placid. From the southeastern Adirondacks, Route 28 north of Warrensburg leads to Route 28 N, which skirts the southern edge of the High Peaks region before heading into the central Adirondacks.

THE NORTH COUNTRY

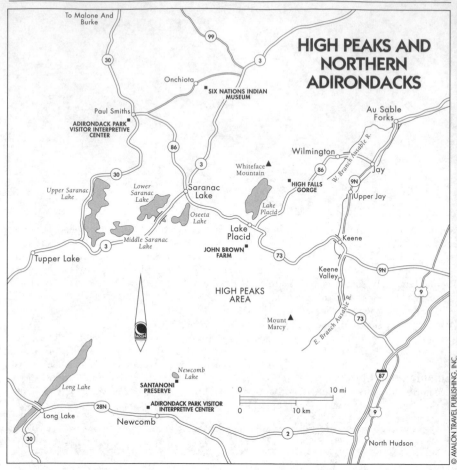

HIGH PEAKS AND NORTHERN ADIRONDACKS

To Malone And Burke

Onchiota

SIX NATIONS INDIAN MUSEUM

Paul Smiths

ADIRONDACK PARK VISITOR INTERPRETIVE CENTER

Au Sable Forks

Wilmington

Whiteface Mountain

HIGH FALLS GORGE

Jay

Upper Jay

Upper Saranac Lake

Lower Saranac Lake

Saranac Lake

Lake Placid

Oseeta Lake

Tupper Lake

Middle Saranac Lake

Lake Placid

JOHN BROWN FARM

Keene

Keene Valley

HIGH PEAKS AREA

Mount Marcy

Newcomb Lake

SANTANONI PRESERVE

Long Lake

ADIRONDACK PARK VISITOR INTERPRETIVE CENTER

Long Lake

Newcomb

North Hudson

W. Branch Ausable R.

E. Branch Ausable R.

0   10 mi

0   10 km

© AVALON TRAVEL PUBLISHING, INC.

Visitor Information

The **Lake Placid/Essex County Visitors Bureau,** Olympic Arena, 216 Main St., Lake Placid, NY 12946, 518/523-2445 or 800/447-5224, www.lakeplacid.com, is open daily 9 A.M.–5 P.M.; closed some Sundays. Also a useful site is www.WhitefaceRegion.com.

WEST ON ROUTES 9 N AND 86

Heading into the High Peaks region from Ausable Chasm on Route 9 N, you'll pass through **Au Sable Forks,** once home to illustrator Rockwell

Kent; and tiny **Jay,** beautifully situated on the East Branch of the Ausable River. In Jay are several old-fashioned country stores and the **Jay Craft Center,** Rte. 9 N, 518/946-7824, housing both a pottery studio and a gift shop. A few miles south in **Upper Jay** are a number of attractive **antique shops.**

From Jay, take Route 86 west to reach **Wilmington,** a small ski town huddled at the base of towering Whiteface Mountain. Adirondack Hospitality Since 1822, reads a sign.

Whiteface Mountain

The largest ski resort in New York, the state-owned Whiteface Mountain boasts 65 trails, nine chairlifts, and the highest vertical drop in the Northeast—3,216 feet. The mountain attracts expert skiers, but trails for intermediate and novice skiers are plentiful. Whiteface served as the downhill ski site for both the 1932 and 1980 Winter Olympics and is managed by the Olympic Regional Development Authority, based in Lake Placid.

During the summer, the mountain's peaks are accessible via the **Whiteface Mountain Cloudsplitter Gondola Ride** and the **Whiteface Mountain Memorial Highway.** The chairlift leads to Little Whiteface Peak, elevation 3,676 feet, while the highway leads to Whiteface Summit, elevation 4,867 feet. The highway ends at a lodge just below the actual summit, and from here you can either climb to the top via a stone staircase or take an elevator that rises through the center of the granite mountain. The summit affords superb views of the High Peaks to the south, Lake Champlain and the Green Mountains to the east, the St. Lawrence River and Canada to the north, and

COURTESY OF LAKE PLACID/ESSEX COUNTY VISITORS BUREAU

Lake Placid village and Whiteface Mountain

THE LEGEND OF WHITEFACE

There once was a young brave who wanted to win the hand of a beautiful Indian princess. The princess asked him to prove his love by bringing her the skin of the Great White Stag who roamed the region's highest peak.

Armed with two magic arrows an old chief had given him, the brave went to the mountain. For weeks, he hunted for the stag in vain. At last, late one evening, he found him standing in the mist at the top of the mountain. The brave deftly shot his two arrows. One pierced the stag's neck, the second his haunch; but when the brave rushed forward to claim his trophy, he couldn't reach him—the mountainside was too steep. The stag remained pinned to a ledge by the magic arrows, just out of reach.

When the brave awoke the next morning, the stag had disappeared, but the rock where he had hung had turned white. From then on, the Iroquois called the mountain Whiteface.

the Saranac Lake Valley to the west. Of the Adirondack's 46 High Peaks, only Whiteface is accessible by car.

Whiteface, 518/946-2223 or 800/462-6236 (events and snow conditions), is located off Route 86, www.whiteface.com. Peak-season lift tickets are adults $54, children 7–12 $34. Fees for the summer gondola ride, operating mid-June through mid-October, 9 A.M.–4 P.M., are adults $12, seniors and children 5–12 $8, families $35. To drive the toll road costs $8 for a car and driver, $4 for each additional passenger.

Santa's Workshop

Just before the entrance to the Whiteface Mountain Memorial Highway stands a cheery red-and-white cottage surrounded by flowers. Inside is a post office/gift shop where visitors can send letters postmarked the "North Pole," or buy T-shirts reading "I believe in Santa Claus." Out back, a cozy, kid-oriented theme park includes amusement-park rides, Santa's reindeer, and Santa's

THE NORTH COUNTRY

elves. Special events such as puppet shows and a Santa Claus Parade are presented daily.

The park, Rte. 431, off Rte. 86, 518/946-2211 or 800/488-9853, www.northpoleny.com, is open July 1–Columbus Day, Sat.–Wed. 9:30 A.M.–4:30 P.M., with limited activities weekdays in the spring and fall. Admission to the post office/gift shop is free; admission to the park is adults $15, children 3–17 $12, with reduced rates in the spring and fall.

High Falls Gorge

Five miles south of Wilmington is a deep and dramatic ravine, cut into the mountainside by the Ausable River, which drops over 700 feet here in the course of four waterfalls. Now developed into a tourist attraction, the area contains a self-guided network of bridges, paths, and steps leading past oddly shaped rock formations, rapids, and potholes. In a visitor center near the entrance are photography and mineral exhibits, and a gift shop selling Adirondack crafts.

The gorge, off Rte. 86, 518/946-2278, www.highfallsgorge.com, is open Memorial Day–Columbus Day, daily 9 A.M.–5 P.M. Admission is adults $7, children 4–11 $4.

Accommodations

Though best known as a restaurant, the **Hungry Trout**, Rte. 86, Wilmington, 518/946-2217 or 800/766-9137, www.hungrytrout.com, also offers 20 upscale motel rooms, a pool, and playground. Many of the rooms offer views of Whiteface Mountain ($69–159 d). The **Whiteface Chalet**, Springfield Rd., Wilmington, 518/946-2207 or 800/932-0859, www.whitefacechalet.com, is a small, modern hostelry centered on a cozy lounge and fireplace ($79–82 d).

Food

Stop into the **Country Bear,** Rte. 86, Wilmington, 518/946-2691, for a satisfying breakfast or lunch; average main dish $6. The **Hungry Trout,** Rte. 86, Wilmington, 518/946-2217, overlooking the churning white waters of the Ausable River, specializes in its namesake prepared a myriad of ways, along with continental fare; average entrée $19.

WEST ON ROUTES 9 N AND 73

Route 9 N leads northwest from Elizabethtown to **Keene,** the "Town of High Peaks." Completely surrounded by jagged mountaintops, Keene centers around one main street lined with white frame houses, white picket fences, and tourist-oriented shops. Most noticeable among them is **North Country Taxidermy & Adirondack Reflections,** Main St. (Rte. 73), 518/576-9549, sporting stuffed bears and wolves out front. The shop is stocks a wide array of gifts, including antlers—sold out of big bins—stuffed birds, mounted heads, leather goods, and bearskin rugs.

Route 9 N continues south of Keene to **Keene Valley,** another quiet mountain town with its share of souvenir shops. Among them is the rambling **Birch Store,** Rte. 73, 518/576-4561, selling a variety of gifts, books, and gourmet foods.

Route 73 climbs west out of Keene to Lake Placid. For much of the way, the route follows the riverbed of the wide Cascade Brook. En route you'll pass two sparkling lakes ringed with trees.

Hiking Hurricane Mountain

On the north side of Route 9 N, 6.8 miles west of Elizabethtown and 1.6 miles past Hurricane Road, a small parking area and sign point the way to Hurricane Mountain. The red-marked trail passes through a pretty coniferous forest before heading up to a ridge to the rocky summit pass. At the top await superb views of the Jay Range, the Green Mountains, Mt. Marcy, and Whiteface Mountain. The Adirondack Mountain Club lists the moderate-to-difficult hike as 5.3 miles roundtrip, averaging about four and a half hours.

Outfitters and Guides

Adirondack Alpine Adventures, Box 179, Rte. 73, Keene, NY 12942, 518/576-9881, www.alpineadventures.biz, offers rock- and ice-climbing guide service and instruction, as well as backcountry ski trips.

Accommodations

The historic **Bark Eater Inn,** Alstead Hill Rd., Keene, 518/576-2221, www.barkeater.com, centers around a sprawling, two-story farmhouse complete with stone fireplaces, wide floorboards, and seven guest rooms. Two snug annexes offer four more rooms, while a new log cabin reigns as the honeymoon suite. Surrounding the inn are miles of woodland that are perfect for horseback riding, hiking, and cross-country skiing. The inn also offers guided horseback-riding trips; most rooms $85–110 d, with breakfast, $315 d for the honeymoon suite.

The **Trail's End Family Inn,** Trail's End Rd., Keene Valley, 518/576-9860, www.trailsendinn .com, is a casual, laid-back hostelry with rooms of varying types. Some share baths, two are one- or two-room suites, and three are two-bedroom cottage that can accommodate up to six ($75–175 d, with breakfast). Housed in a lovely Italianate building is the **Key Valley Lodge,** Rte. 73, Keene Valley, 518/576-2003, www.keyvalleylodge.com, which also offers a variety of rooms, some of which share baths, some of which are suites. Guest rooms are furnished with antiques, while downstairs is a lounge with a fireplace and wraparound porch ($75–115 d, $135–155 for the suites; with breakfast).

Food

A Keene Valley landmark, the **Noon Mark Diner,** Main St. (Rte. 73), 518/576-4499, is the place to go for homemade donuts, soups, and bread, as well as chili, burgers, and simple dinners; average main dish $6.

NORTHWEST ON ROUTE 28 N

Scenic Route 28 N heads out of North Creek in the southeastern Adirondacks to skirt the southern edge of the High Peaks region. Along the way you'll pass one splendid lake and mountain vista after another; the ride is especially magnificent in the fall.

On the right about 13 miles northwest of Minerva (or two miles before Newcomb) stands the **Roosevelt Tablet,** a historical marker designating the spot where Theodore Roosevelt became president. Roosevelt had been hiking up Mt. Marcy and was eating lunch at Lake Tear of the Clouds when a messenger rushed up with the news that President McKinley—shot in an assassination attempt in Buffalo—had taken a turn for the worse. Roosevelt and his party fled the mountains by foot and carriage and arrived at this spot in the road when McKinley died.

Adirondack Park Visitor Interpretive Center

In the hamlet of Newcomb is the smaller of the Adirondack Park's two visitor centers; the larger one is in Paul Smiths. Both offer an excellent introduction to the park, with exhibits ranging from the region's logging history to local flora and fauna. Print out free information about trailhead locations and canoe routes at one of the computerized touch-screen stations, or follow one of the interpretive trails outside. In Newcomb, the trails lead out onto a peninsula in Rich Lake, past beaver ponds and old-growth hemlocks.

The center, Rte. 28 N, 518/582-2000, is open daily 9 A.M.–5 P.M. Admission is free.

Hiking to Camp Santanoni

On the shores of Newcomb Lake stands deserted Camp Santanoni, one of the old great camps, this one built in 1892 by Albany industrialist Robert Pruyn. Surrounded by the 12,000-acre Santanoni Preserve, the eerily empty camp built of massive logs includes a central lodge, boathouse, studio, and guest cottages. None of the deteriorating buildings are open to the public, and the only way in is to hike five miles along Santanoni Road.

The road is located on the north side of Route 28 N, about a mile east of the Adirondack Park Visitor Center. Near the camp's gatehouse is a parking area, while beyond stretch fields etched with stone fences. About a mile and a half in along the road is a deserted farmstead that once provided the great camp with all its provisions.

A yellow-marked trail runs north of the great camp along the eastern end of Newcomb Lake. Here you'll find several remote campsites with their own private beaches; campers are requested to sign in at the gatehouse entrance.

For more information, inquire at the Park Visitor Center or the Newcomb Town Offices, Rte. 28 N, 518/582-3211.

THE NORTH COUNTRY

LAKE PLACID

Twenty or so years ago, Lake Placid was a quiet mountain village best known to avid hikers and skiers and to those who had attended the 1932 Winter Olympics. All that changed in a heartbeat with the coming of the 1980 Winter Games, which put the place on the map.

Today, almost everyone who visits the Adirondacks visits Lake Placid, which centers around one long and sometimes very congested Main Street running alongside the lake. The village draws almost as many visitors because of its upscale shops and restaurants as it does for its lonely, mountainous countryside. Even the former Olympic sites, now managed by the Olympic Regional Development Authority, have become popular tourist attractions.

One of the more confusing things about Lake Placid is that it's not located on Lake Placid, but on Mirror Lake. Lake Placid, a much larger body of water, lies to the immediate north of the village.

> *One of the more confusing things about Lake Placid is that it's not located on Lake Placid, but on Mirror Lake.*

Olympic Center

At the entrance to the village stands the elongated Olympic Center, 216 Main St., 518/523-1655, www.orda.org, built for the 1932 Winter Olympics and renovated for the 1980 games. The center still houses four Olympic **ice-skating arenas,** one of which is open for public skating most of the year, along with the **Lake Placid/Essex County Visitors Bureau,** 518/523-2445, and the **Lake Placid Olympic Museum.** The museum houses exhibits and memorabilia from both Games; hours are Memorial Day–Columbus Day, daily 10 A.M.–4 P.M.; call for off season hours. Admission is adults $4, seniors $3, children 7–12 $2.

Around Mirror Lake

Main Street heads north of the Olympic Arena past about 100 shops, some of them one-of-a-kind, others—The Gap, Geoffrey Beene—ubiquitous chains. **With Pipe and Book,** 91 Main St., 518/523-9096, a village institution, sells used books, rare books, pipes, and tobacco.

THE NORTH COUNTRY

Olympic Center Ice Rink

At the end of Main Street lies Saranac Avenue, home to two top North Country shops. The **Adirondack North Country Craft Center,** 93 Saranac Ave., 518/523-2062, represents about 250 upstate artists and artisans working in both traditional and contemporary styles. The **Adirondack Store,** 109 Saranac Ave., 518/523-2646, sells everything from hand-knit sweaters to Winslow Homer prints.

A small **public beach** is situated south of the Olympic Center, on Parkside Dr., off Main Street. Just beyond the northern end of Mirror Lake lies Lake Placid and the **Lake Placid Marina,** Mirror Lake Dr., 518/523-9704, where one-hour lake cruises depart May–October.

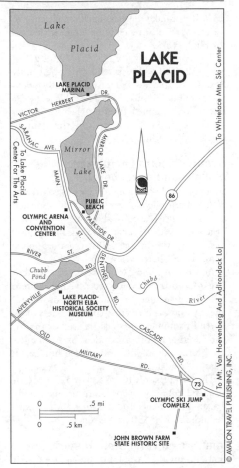

Lake Placid–North Elba Historical Society Museum

Now occupying the old Lake Placid railroad station, this eclectic local history museum houses antique sporting equipment as well as mementos of conductor Victor Herbert, who once summered on the lake. Especially interesting are the exhibits on the experimental colony for former slaves founded in 1849 by abolitionist John Brown (see below).

The museum, Averyville Rd., off Rte. 73, 518/523-1608, is open June–Sept., Tues.–Sun. 10 A.M.–4 P.M. Admission is free.

Hiking to Wanika Falls

Also on Averyville Road, 1.2 miles past the intersection with Old Military Road, is a blue-marked trail that leads to Wanika Falls. The day-long hike takes about seven hours over 13.4 miles, but the terrain is easy, and the waterfalls make the trip worthwhile. According to the Adirondack Mountain Club, the route leads through some of the finest forest in the region before ascending an old road leading to the Chubb River and the cascading falls, several hundred feet high. The trail is part of the much longer Northville-Placid Trail laid out by the Adirondack Mountain Club in 1922 and 1923.

Olympic Ski Jump Complex

If you approached Lake Placid from the east on Route 73, the first thing you undoubtedly noticed were the stark towers of the Olympic ski jumps, looming out of the landscape like giant misshapen thumbs. The site still serves as a training center and is open year-round, thanks to plastic mats, water ramps, and snow-making machines.

Upon entering the complex, stop first at the **freestyle aerial facility,** where—with any luck—you'll see athletes practicing their maneuvers by sailing over pools, off water-filled ramps. Next, visit the main lodge to view a photo exhibit on the history of ski jumping, and catch the chairlift to the 90-meter jump. If training is taking place here, you can watch from an observation deck. If not, take the glass-enclosed elevator to the top of the 120-meter jump for great views of the High Peaks.

The complex, off Rte. 73, 518/523-2202 or 800/462-6236, www.orda.org, is open daily May–Oct., 10 A.M.–4 P.M. An all-inclusive ticket costs adults $8, children 6–12 $5. Since the site is considerably more interesting when the athletes are at work, it's worth checking the training schedule in advance.

Olympic Sports Complex at Mount Van Hoevenberg

South of the ski-jumping complex rises Mt. Van Hoevenberg, the site of the Olympic bobsled and luge runs. The bobsled run measures 1,400 meters long with 16 curves. The luge run is 1,000 meters long with 15 curves. Passenger rides on the bobsleds are offered year-round.

Also on Mt. Van Hoevenberg, the excellent **Cross-Country Center** offers a 31-mile system of trails. In winter, the trails are groomed frequently and open to cross-country skiers of all levels. In summer, the trails are used by mountain bikers and horseback riders. Skis and bikes can be rented on-site, and guided horseback rides are available.

The complex, off Rte. 73, 518/523-4436 or 800/462-6236, www.orda.org, is open daily 9 A.M.–4 P.M. General admission is $5. The bobsled rides start at $30 per person.

John Brown Farm State Historic Site

In 1849, abolitionists John Brown and Gerrit Smith established a farming community for free blacks and escaped slaves in the Adirondacks. Each new farmer was given 40 acres to till, but since few came prepared to cope with the region's harsh climate, most left within a few years. Brown himself lived on the farm for several more years, in a trim cottage that has been nicely restored, and erected his own gravestone, as if in preparation for what was soon to come.

Brown was executed in Charlestown, Virginia, on December 2, 1859, following his seizure of the U.S. Arsenal at Harper's Ferry. His body was shipped north to New York City, where his coffin was exchanged for a new one so that he would not be buried in Southern property. At each stop along the way upstate, his entourage was greeted with sympathetic crowds and tolling bells. Today, a statue of Brown dressed in rough Adirondack clothes, with his arm around a young black boy, stands outside the house.

The farm, 2 John Brown Rd., off Rte. 73, 518/523-3900, is open May–Oct., Monday and Wed.–Sat. 10 A.M.–5 P.M., Sunday 1–5 P.M. Admission is adults $2, children $1.

Adirondak Loj

High in the mountains on the shores of Heart Lake is the retreat of the Adirondack Mountain Club (ADK), a nonprofit conservation, education, and recreation organization. Built in the 1920s, the classic lodge has accommodations for 46 people, along with a campground, information center, and trading post that sells camping supplies, maps, and outdoor guidebooks. During the summer, the lodge sponsors numerous seminars and workshops open to the general public; during the winter, skis and snowshoes can be rented here. Several trailheads begin at the Loj.

The Loj, Adirondak Loj Rd., off Rte. 73, 518/523-3441, www.adk.org, is eight miles south of Lake Placid. The Loj is open year-round; call for program schedule.

Hiking Mount Marcy

Mount Marcy, elevation 5,344 feet, is the highest mountain in the Adirondacks, and the one that draws the most hikers each year. More than 20,000 people make the seven-mile trek annually, and on a busy July weekend, as many as 200 people crowd at the summit. Things have certainly changed since that day in 1872, when Verplanck Colvin first hiked the mountain and discovered Lake Tear of the Clouds. "But how wild and desolate this spot!" he wrote. "It is possible that not even an Indian ever stood upon these shores. There is no mark of ax, no barked tree, nor blackened remnants of fire; not a severed twig or a human footprint. . . ."

Because of problems with over-use, park personnel urge hikers to shy away from Mt. Marcy and tackle lesser-known peaks instead. If, however, hike Mt. Marcy you must, one main trail begins at the Adirondak Loj. Known as the Van Hoevenberg Trail, it is marked in blue. Along the way you'll pass the Marcy Dam, Phelps Brooks, and Indian Falls. From the summit of Mt. Marcy, a 1.1-mile trail leads to Lake Tear of the Clouds, the source of the Hudson River.

Camping and Motels

The **Adirondak Loj,** Box 867, Adirondak Loj Rd., 518/523-3441, www.adk.org, offers four private rooms ($55 per person), four family rooms, and a large coed loft ($36–45 per person), along with a campground equipped with 13 lean-tos and 37 sites. You don't have to be an ADK member to stay here, but you must make reservations well in advance. Camping is also available at the 80-site **Whispering Pines,** Cascade Rd. (Rte. 73), 518/523-9322 or 800/437-9322, where a basic site costs $18–24.

Area motels include the 24-room **Alpine Air Motel,** 99 Saranac Ave., 518/523-9261 ($60–95 d), and a 61-room **Econo Lodge,** Box 527, Cascade Rd., 518/523-2817 ($75–98 d).

Inns and Lodges

The big, modern **Adirondack Inn,** 217 Main St. (Rte. 86), 518/523-2424 or 800/556-2424, www.adirondack-inn.com, offers 50 nicely appointed rooms and indoor and outdoor pools. Out front is a small lakefront beach ($109–169 d).

At the end of the village reigns the posh **Mirror Lake Inn Resort and Spa,** 5 Mirror Lake Dr., 518/523-2544, www.mirrorlakeinn.com, a grand Colonial-style structure that was rebuilt after a 1988 fire. Rooms at this AAA Four Diamond resort range from standard doubles to split-level suites, and come in a wide variety of prices. Also on-site are Averil Conwell Dining Room, bar, cozy lounges, spa, tennis courts, indoor and outdoor pools, and a private beach ($240–340 d for rooms, $420–650 d for suites).

Built in 1833, the inviting **Stagecoach Inn B&B,** 370 Old Military Rd., 518/523-9474, is playfully furnished with antiques and Adirondackiana. Five of the nine guest rooms have private baths and two have their own fireplaces ($75–105 d, with breakfast).

On the shores of Lake Placid lies secluded **Lake Placid Lodge,** Whiteface Inn Rd., 518/523-2700, www.thelakeplacidinn.com, an authentic old great camp complete with a stone fireplace and moose head. Now a member of the exclusive Relais & Chateaux group, the lodge boasts 22 very attractive guest rooms, 15 cabins, and a breezy porch overlooking the lake ($240–725 d).

Food

For sandwiches and baked goods, try the **Upper Crust Bakery & Cafe,** 215 Main St., 518/523-2269. For mouth-watering barbecue served inside or out, stop at **Tail o' the Pup,** Rte. 86, 518/891-5092, a classic roadside eatery located halfway between Lake Placid and Saranac Lake.

The **Charcoal Pit,** Rte. 86, near Cold Brook Plaza, 518/523-3050, offers an eclectic array of American, Greek, French, and Italian dishes; average entrée $16. On the lake across from the village is the **Boathouse,** 89 Lake Placid Club Dr., 518/523-4822, a large and comfortable blond-wood eatery with an outdoor dining deck. The menu ranges from salads and burgers to fresh fish and steak; average entrée $16.

One of the region's top restaurants, the elegant, candle-lit **Averil Conwell Dining Room** at the Mirror Lake Inn, 5 Mirror Lake Dr., 518/523-2544, specializes in an innovative fare that ranges from fresh pastas and seafood to steak and grilled duck (average entrée $24). Also on site is the freestanding **Cottage,** 5 Mirror Lake Dr., 518/523-2544, a sort of upscale pub built directly on the lake, where the menu is simpler but just as good (average entrée $14). A wide selection of wines and microbrews is also available here.

Entertainment and Events

The multipurpose **Lake Placid Center for the Arts,** 91 Saranac Ave., 518/523-2512, presents a wide range of music, dance, theater, film, and special events throughout the year. The 18-piece **Lake Placid Sinfonietta,** 518/523-2051, performs free concerts in the Mirror Lake bandshell Wednesday evenings, July–August.

Figure-skating, hockey games, and speed-skating events take place in the **Olympic Center Ice Arena,** 216 Main St., 518/523-1655, throughout the year. The **Lake Placid Horse Show** and **I Love New York Horse Show,** 518/523-2445, are held in July.

Outfitters, Guides, and Recreation

Canoes and other boats can be rented at **Jones Outfitters,** 331 Main St., 518/523-3468. Or, stop by **Captain Marney's,** 3 Victor Herbert Dr., 518/523-9746.

Bear Cub Adventure Tours, 30 Bear Cub Rd., 518/523-4339, offers canoe and kayak instruction and guided canoeing, fishing, backpacking, and hiking trips. For a scenic flight over the High Peaks, contact **Adirondack Flying Service,** Airport Rd., off Cascade Rd., 518/523-2473.

SARANAC LAKE

After the heavy tourist traffic of Lake Placid, Saranac Lake village comes as a relief. Saranac Lake, an unpretentious place with a busy downtown, caters to residents, not tourists.

Although classified as a village, Saranac Lake is a sizeable town (pop. 5,830), with stores, banks, a movie theater, churches, and supermarkets. Like Lake Placid, it is not located on the shores of its namesake, but on smaller Flower Lake, the body of water that you see downtown. The Saranac Lakes—Lower, Middle, and Upper—are farther west. Upper Saranac Lake is famous for its rustic Adirondack architecture, best glimpsed by boat.

Settled in 1819 by Jacob Smith Moody, Saranac Lake soon established itself as center for Adirondack guides. All of Moody's sons became guides, and their Uncle Martin once guided everyone from Pres. Grover Cleveland to Ralph Waldo Emerson.

In 1876, a Dr. Livingston Trudeau, suffering from tuberculosis, came to Saranac Lake to die. Instead, the fresh mountain air restored him, and in 1884 he opened the first outdoor sanatorium for the treatment of tuberculosis. By the

> *"The country is a kind of insane mixture of Scotland and a touch of Switzerland and a dash of America and a thought of the British Channel in the skies."*
>
> *Robert Louis Stevenson, describing upstate New York in a letter to John Addington Symonds, November 21, 1887*

early 1900s, the Trudeau Sanatorium was famed worldwide, with thousands flocking to "The City of the Sick" to take the cure.

The Trudeau Sanatorium closed in 1954, after antibiotics were developed, but its legacy lives on in the Trudeau Institute, a scientific research institute, and in "Doonesbury" cartoonist Garry Trudeau. Garry is the great-grandson of Dr. Livingston Trudeau.

Saranac Lake centers around Main Street and Flower Lake. The lively **Hotel Saranac**—a regional landmark run by students from Paul Smiths College—provides a good base from which to explore the area. A pleasant **public beach** is located on Lake Colby, just north of downtown.

Robert Louis Stevenson Memorial Cottage

Among the pioneer "lungers" who came to Saranac Lake to take the cure was Robert Louis Stevenson. In 1887, fresh from the success of his just-published *Dr. Jekyll and Mr. Hyde,* the author rented a cozy cottage on a hill within easy reach of Dr. Trudeau. While living here, Stevenson wrote some of his best essays and started his long tale, *The Master of Ballantrae.* "I was walking on the veranda of a small house outside the hamlet of Saranac. It was winter, the night was very dark, the air clean and cold and sweet with the purity of forests. For the making of a story, here were fine conditions," reads the quote by the door.

In the cottage today is a large collection of Stevenson memorabilia, including his ice skates, playing cards, letters to Henry James, autographed first editions, and the velvet jacket that he always wore while writing. On the mantelpiece are Stevenson's cigarette burns, which he left wherever he went.

The cottage, 11 Stevenson Ln., 518/891-1462, is open July–Sept., Tues.–Sun. 9:30 A.M.–noon and 1–4:30 P.M.; and by appointment. Admission is adults $5, children under 12 free.

Outfitters, Guides, and Recreation

For lovers of the outdoors, Saranac Lake is ideally situated between the High Peaks and the Northwest Lakes, which offer some of the best canoeing in the Northeast.

Recently relocated to Saranac Lake from Lake Clear is **St. Regis Canoe Outfitters,** 9 Dorsey St., 518/891-1838 or 888/775-2925, www.canoe-outfitters.com. This large and friendly operation, complete with a sprawling retail shop, rents and sells canoes, kayaks, and camping gear; provides instruction and trip-planning advice; and offers guided trips and shuttle services. Trips can be arranged for as short as one morning or as long as two weeks or more.

Adirondack Foothills, 518/359-7037, offers customized hiking, camping, canoeing, and fishing trips. **McDonnell's Adirondack Challenges,** 518/891-1176, offers much the same. **XTC Ranch,** Forest Home Rd., Lake Clear, 518/891-5684, is the place to go for horseback riding and for wagon and sleigh rides.

Accommodations

Downtown motels include the 69-room **Best Western Mountain Lake Inn,** 148 Lake Flower Ave. (Rte. 86), 518/891-1970 ($85–110 d); and the 20-room **Lakeside Motel,** 27 Lake Flower Ave. (Rte. 86), 518/891-4333 ($69–99 d).

The full-service **Hotel Saranac of Paul Smiths College,** 101 Main St., 518/891-2200 or 800/937-0211, www.paulsmiths.edu/hsaranac, is a snug brick hostelry built in 1927. Contained within are 92 small but comfortable rooms, and a lobby that's a replica of the foyer in the Danvanzati Palace in Florence, Italy ($95–195 d).

More secluded accommodations lie along the shores of Upper Saranac Lake, several miles northwest of the village (see Northwest Lakes and Tupper Lake, below).

Food

Like the Hotel Saranac in which it is housed, **A. P. Smiths',** 101 Main St., 518/891-2200, is run by eager students enrolled in Paul Smiths College's hotel management program. The restaurant serves contemporary American fare for lunch and dinner; average dinner entrée $14.

It might seem rather surprising to find a good Mexican restaurant in the heart of the Adirondacks, but nonetheless, here is the bright and cheery **Casa del Sol,** 154 Lake Flower Ave. (Rte. 86), 518/891-0977. In summer, dine on the outdoor patio; average entrée $11.

Entertainment and Nightlife

The **Pendragon Theatre,** 148 River St., 518/891-1854, presents professional regional theater November–January and June–September. On the docket are both classic and contemporary works.

A number of popular bars, many hosting local bands on the weekends, hug Main Street near the Hotel Saranac and along Broadway north of Main. Among them are the teeming indoor-outdoor **Water Hole,** 43 Main St., 518/891-9502; and the scruffy **Rusty Nail,** 90 Broadway, 518/891-9870. The **Boathouse Lounge** in the Hotel Saranac, 101 Main St., 518/891-2200, is a cozy, low-ceilinged bar/lounge that gets quite crowded on Saturday nights.

Events

Free jazz, blues, pop, and rock concerts are presented at the **Anderson Bandshell,** on Lake Flower Friday evenings in summer. The **Adirondack**

THE NORTH COUNTRY

NORTH COUNTRY CRAFTS

Rustic furniture, birchbark baskets, plaid woolen jackets, quilts, woodcarved decoys, bulky sweaters, balsam pillows, boats. . . .

Handcrafted items have always been part of the North Country scene. Over the past few decades, however, as the nation's love affair with mass-production has waned, there's been a true renaissance in the North Country arts. Hundreds of artists and artisans working in both traditional and more contemporary styles can now be found throughout the region. Most use local natural resources such as wood, pine cones, balsam fir needles, and locally raised wool to create their wares.

The region's long winters have contributed much to the strong folk art tradition. Confined to their homes for "11 months of snow, one of bad sledding," as some old-timers put it, people naturally turned to working with their hands. From the Mohawk came the art of basketmaking, from the French Canadians, woodcarving.

Perhaps most emblematic of the Adirondacks crafts is the traditional Adirondack guideboat, a specialized rowboat the light weight of which makes it easy to carry between lakes and rivers. Around the turn of the century, as many as 50 men were producing the handmade boats, each of which took about 300 hours to build and sold for around $50. To have a traditional guideboat built today costs about $7,000.

The most emblematic of Thousand Islands crafts is the decoy. Duck hunting has been popular in the region ever since the 1800s, when a market hunter could easily harvest 50–100 birds a day. Sleeping in tents the entire duck season, the hunters often turned to carving decoys at night, in between slugs of whiskey.

A good source for locating crafts shops and artisans' studios in the North Country today is the **Adirondack North Country Association** (ANCA), 20 St. Bernard St., Saranac Lake, NY 12983; 518/891-6200. A nonprofit organization, ANCA publishes a free "Craft Trails" map that's available at many tourism offices or by writing and enclosing an SASE.

Festival of American Music, takes place at various venues in July; local and national artists perform. Also in July is a juried **Craftfest.**

Mush into town for the **Saranac Lake International Dog Sled Races,** held in January. The largest **Winter Carnival,** in the Adirondacks—complete with an enormous ice palace—takes place in early February.

For more information on any of these events, contact the **Saranac Lake Chamber of Commerce,** 518/891-1990.

Shopping

The **Boat Shop/Adirondack Guideboats,** 9 Algonquin Ave., corner of Lake St. and Rte. 3, 518/891-3961, is an authentic boatbuilding shop that dates back to the 1930s. **Asplin Tree Farms,** Rte. 86, 518/891-5783 or 800/858-7336, one of the oldest and largest Christmas tree farms in the East, houses a popular gift shop. Their specialty is the traditional Adirondack balsam pillow filled with fragrant pine needles.

Visitor Information

The **Saranac Lake Area Chamber of Commerce,** 30 Main St., Saranac Lake, NY 12983, 518/891-1990 or 800/347-1992, is open year-round, Mon.–Fri. 8 A.M.–5 P.M. A **visitor information center,** Union Depot, is open July–Aug., Wed.–Sun. 10 A.M.–4 P.M.

PAUL SMITHS

About 10 miles northwest of Saranac Lake lies the hamlet of Paul Smiths, named after Appollos (Paul) Smith, a famed Adirondack guide who established one of the Adirondack's first hotels here in 1859. Charles Dickens once said of Smith, "he has no bad habits, and is, withal, the best rifle shot, paddler, and compounder of forest stews in the whole region." When Smith died in 1912, his funeral was the largest ever held in northern New York, drawing over 700 people.

The original Paul Smiths hotel has closed, but its spirit lives on through **Paul Smiths College,** Rts. 86 and 30, founded by the hotelier's son in the 1930s. The school is best known for its degrees in hotel management and the culinary arts.

Adirondack Park Visitor Interpretive Center

For an excellent introduction to the Adirondacks, step into this large and informative center, one of two run by the Adirondack Park (the second, smaller center is in Newcomb). Inside you'll find exhibits on everything from logging camps and Trudeau's Sanatorium to the region's problems with over-use and acid rain. Three different slides shows run continuously throughout the day, while information about trailhead locations and canoe routes is available on computerized touchscreen stations that provide free printouts. Out back are a butterfly house and interpretive trails leading through a 60-acre marsh.

The center, Rte. 30, 518/327-3000, is open daily 9 A.M.–5 P.M. Admission is free.

White Pine Camp

After years of deterioration, the great camp that served as Pres. Calvin Coolidge's summer White House in 1926 re-opened to the public in 1995. Still in the process of being restored, the 1907 camp overlooks Osgood Pond and contains about 20 asymmetrical buildings complete with soaring rooflines, unusual angles, and skylights. In the main cabin, changing exhibits explain the site's history and architecture, while among the surrounding outbuildings are a tennis house, indoor bowling alleys, and a Japanese teahouse.

The camp, 518/327-3030, is on White Pine Rd., a half mile east of the Rts. 86 and 30 intersection, www.whitepinecamp.com. Tours are offered July–Aug., Saturday at 10 A.M. and 1:30 P.M. Cost is adults $9, seniors $8, kids 5–15 $5.

Hiking St. Regis Mountain

To get a bird's-eye view of the region's many lakes and ponds, take Keese Mills Road, near the intersection of Routes 30 and 192. Drive 2.6 miles to a small sign that points the way to the left. Continue down a narrow paved road a half-mile to a large parking area and a trailhead leading up St. Regis Mountain. The hike up St. Regis is 4.9 miles roundtrip and takes about three and a

half hours. The hike is of moderate difficulty, except for a steep section near the summit.

ONCHIOTA

"Leaving 67 of the friendliest people in the Adirondacks (plus a couple of soreheads)" reads the sign at the northern end of Onchiota. Just who exactly those soreheads are, no one seems quite sure, but to meet the first variety, stop into the one-of-a-kind **Six Nations Indian Museum.**

From the outside, the museum looks much like an ordinary house. But move inside and you'll find yourself surrounded by a kaleidoscopic array of pictographs, paintings, basketwork, beadwork, quillwork, pottery, canoes, masks, drums, and lacrosse sticks—all very, very neatly arranged to cover virtually every square inch of wall and peaked wooden ceiling. The museum is the creation of one man, Ray Fadden, a Mohawk who drew most of the elaborate pictographs himself. The works tell traditional Iroquois tales through pictures rather than words.

Fadden, who spent much of his life as a schoolteacher, began fighting for the preservation of Iroquois culture as early as the 1940s. Back then hardly anyone listened, but Fadden never faltered and eventually was instrumental in the founding of numerous Iroquois heritage programs. Many of his former students are now major leaders in the Mohawk Nation.

Fadden still stops by the museum daily, but the place is run by his son and daughter-in-law. Visitors are warmly greeted at the door and conducted on personalized tours.

The museum, Buck Pond Campsite Rd., 518/891-2299, is open July–Labor Day, Tues.–Sun. 10 A.M.–5 P.M. Admission is adults $2, children $1. To reach Onchiota from Paul Smiths, take Route 86 east to County Roads 31 or 30 north (not to be confused with state Route 30, which leads to Malone). The museum is in the hamlet's center and is easy to find.

BURKE

Fans of Laura Ingalls Wilder might want to head north of Paul Smiths about 35 miles to the

Almanzo Wilder Homestead, located in farm country east of Malone. Wilder's husband, Almanzo Wilder, grew up here, and the author based her book *Farmer Boy* on his childhood. The trim, airy house has been carefully restored to reflect the book. Downstairs is the parlor where "Almanzo didn't mean to throw the blacking brush," and upstairs is his "soft, cold feather bed." In the kitchen are kerosene lamps, tallow candles, and a butter churn—all similar to the ones used by Almanzo—while out back is the red barn where he did his chores.

Wilder, who met her husband in South Dakota, never visited the Wilder homestead, but according to family members, the house was "as described in the book." In the entrance hall are photocopies of the sketches that Almanzo drew for Wilder, along with several of her letters.

The house, Burke Rd., off Rte. 11 east of Malone, 518/483-1207 or 866/438-FARM, www.almanzowilderfarm.com, is open June–Labor Day, Tues.–Sat. 11 A.M.–4 P.M., Sunday 1–4 P.M. Admission is adults $5, children 6–15 $2.50.

Northwest Lakes

The northwestern section of the Adirondacks is a sparsely populated area often overlooked by vacationers. Much of the land here is quite flat and covered with hundreds of lakes and ponds, along with endless unbroken forest. Though the region is primarily a canoer's paradise, it also has much to offer in the way of easy-to-moderate hikes.

ST. REGIS CANOE AREA

To the immediate west of Paul Smiths begins the St. Regis Canoe Area, a 20,000-acre region encompassing 58 lakes and ponds. Standing alone at the area's northern edge, and offering wide-angled views of the watery terrain, looms St. Regis Mountain.

Though St. Regis Canoe Outfitters, one of the area's largest outfitters, has recently moved its base of operations to Saranac Lake (see above), it still maintains an outpost at its original location in Lake Clear, 888/775-2925. To reach the outpost and several good boat launch sites, take Route 86 north from Saranac Lake to Route 186. Turn left and follow Route 186 west to its end and junction with Route 30. Continue straight ahead, past the junction, for 5.5 miles, crossing the Saranac Inn Golf Club. Just beyond the course, at a paved four-way intersection, turn right on Floodwood Road. Continue straight ahead 4.1 miles to the base.

Adirondack Fish Hatchery

Just south of the St. Regis Canoe Area you'll find a state fish hatchery filled with tens of thousands of salmon in varying stages of development. When grown, the salmon are used for stocking the Adirondack lakes. The hatchery, off Rte. 30, Saranac Inn, 518/891-3358, is open daily 9 A.M.–4 P.M. Admission is free.

Camping and Accommodations

Off Route 30 between the St. Regis Canoe Area and Tupper Lake village lie the secluded 355-site **Fish Creek Pond Campground,** 518/891-4560, and 290-site **Rollins Pond Campground,** 518/891-3239. For reservations at either, call 800/456-CAMP; basic sites cost $14–16.

Tucked into the woods near the fish hatchery is the **Sunday Pond B&B,** Rte. 30, Saranac Inn, 518/891-1531, www.sundaypond.com, a simple, Adirondack-style lodge with three guest rooms and a sleeping loft that's good for families ($75 d). Just west of the St. Regis Canoe Area is the classic **Lodge at Lake Clear,** RR1, Rts. 30 and 186, 518/891-1489, www.lodgeonlakeclear.com, you can choose among four guest rooms filled with Adirondackiana, two housekeeping chalets, and two suites complete with Jacuzzis ($149–259 d).

The region's most exclusive hostelry is **The Point,** Upper Saranac Lake, 518/891-5674 or 800/255-3530, www.thepointresort.com, an ultra-luxurious great camp once owned by the Rocke-

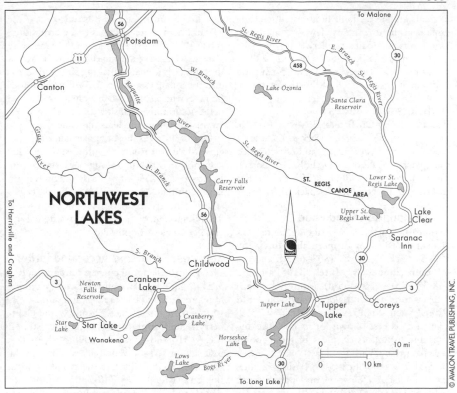

fellers. Now open to the public, the 11-guestroom Point features the absolute utmost in hedonistic delights—all for a mere daily rate of $1,200–2,300 d, which includes gourmet meals, wine and other beverages, and recreational activities.

Food

The snug **Lodge at Lake Clear,** Rts. 30 and 186, 518/891-1489, decorated with Adirondackiana, is renowned for its fine German cuisine. The menu changes nightly, but five or six entrées such as Wiener schnitzel or sauerbraten are always featured (the prix fixe dinner costs $30; reservations recommended).

TUPPER LAKE

Once a major industrial center, known for its lumbering, papermaking, and woodworking plants, Tupper Lake still harbors its share of smokestacks, especially along the lakefront. Meanwhile, the downtown remains small, tightly knit, and compact. Early 20th-century brick buildings house a police department, a bank, and various small businesses. Many of the street names bear evidence of the town's French-American heritage.

Historic Beth Joseph Synagogue

The oldest synagogue in the Adirondacks, Beth Joseph is an architectural gem, built in 1905 by Russian Jewish immigrants who had originally come to the region as peddlers. At its peak in the mid-1920s, the synagogue served about 35 families but was closed in 1959 due to a dwindling congregation. Now on the State Registry of Historic Buildings, the synagogue functions as a small museum. All fixtures and furnishings are

THE NORTH COUNTRY

original, and the vestibule houses an interesting exhibit on the town's early Jewish community. Downstairs is a small art gallery.

The synagogue, Lake St., 518/359-7229, is open July–Aug., Tues.–Fri. 11 A.M.–3 P.M., and Friday evening at 7 P.M. for Sabbath services.

Outfitters and Guides

Raquette River Outfitters, Box 652, Rte. 30, Tupper Lake, NY 12986, 518/359-3228, rents canoes, provides car shuttles, and offers guided canoe trips. **Cold River Ranch,** Rte. 3, Coreys, Tupper Lake, NY 12986, 518/359-7559, offers trail rides and overnight horsepack trips.

Accommodations and Food

Downtown you'll find several basic motels, including the 18-room **Tupper Lake Motel,** 259 Park St., 518/359-3381 ($58–68 d); and the 32-room **Shaheen's Motel,** 310 Park St., 518/359-3384 ($65–95 d). Midway between Tupper and Saranac Lakes sprawls the **Cold River Ranch,** Rte. 3, Coreys, 518/359-7559. The ranch is best known for its horsepacking trips but also offers six pleasant guest rooms ($38 per person, with breakfast).

Hidden in an idyllic woodsy setting six miles east of the village is **Wawbeek on Upper Saranac Lake,** 553 Panther Mountain Rd., off Rte. 30, 518/359-2656 or 800/953-2656, www.wawbeek.com. Once a private boy's camp, the Wawbeek centers around the regal turn-of-the-century Mountain House Lodge. Next door is a restaurant where innovative regional American dishes ranging from tuna to ostrich are served (average entrée $21). Also on-site are a modern guest annex, log-cabin cottages, tennis courts, and a private beach ($155–450 d).

Events

Lumberjacks strut their stuff during the two-day **Woodsmen's Field Days,** 518/359-3328, a major fest held in July.

CRANBERRY LAKE

Eleven miles square, with 55 miles of shoreline, Cranberry Lake remains one of the largest remote areas in New York State. Mostly state-owned, the lake has been virtually bypassed by civilization. Along Route 3 at the eastern end of Cranberry Lake sits a hamlet of the same name. To the west of the hamlet is a boat launching site, and to the east, the public **Cranberry Lake Campground.** Campers who prefer to rough it can row out to one of the 46 primitive tent sites designated with yellow markers along the lake's shoreline.

One of the area's most popular canoe trips begins at Inlet, off Route 3 southwest of the lake, and continues 16 miles along the **Oswegatchie River** to the lake itself. An easy hiking trail up **Bear Mountain** on the east side of the lake begins at the Cranberry Lake Campground. The hike is 3.6 miles roundtrip, takes about two hours, and offers good views of the lake.

Services, Food, and Accommodations

The creaky, stuffed-to-the-rafters **Emporium,** Rte. 3, 315/848-2140, can equip you with everything from groceries and bait to maps and canoes.

To reserve one of the 173 sites at the **Cranberry Lake Campground,** Long Pine Rd., off Rte. 3, 315/848-2315, call 800/456-CAMP. A basic site costs $14. If you'd prefer a motel, try the simple but comfortable **Cranberry Lake Lodge,** Box 632, Rte. 3, 315/848-3301, offering 23 rooms ($64–80 d) and a family-style restaurant (average main dish $8).

WEST ON ROUTE 3

From Cranberry Lake, Route 3 heads west through flat, woodsy, isolated countryside. Just over the St. Lawrence–Lewis County border, about 35 miles from Cranberry Lake, lies **Harrisville,** built on the banks of the Oswegatchie River. Dominating the main street is the sprawling **Scanlon's Bakery.** Whoa, Scanlon's Famous Bread, reads an enormous sign outside, while inside beckon racks of homemade bread, cookies, cinnamon rolls, donuts, and "old-fashioned buttermilk fried cakes." Scanlon's is also known for its Croghan bologna—a specialty of the area—and its homemade bean soup, served with all the bread you can eat.

If you head north of Harrisville on Route 812

about 50 miles, you'll come to the Thousand Islands. If you continue south about 14 miles along Route 812 towards Croghan, you'll come to the hamlet of Indian River and an astonishing outdoor **sculpture park.** Created by Veronica Terrillion, a folk artist now in her nineties, the park is alive with over 400 brightly painted statues of animals, people, and religious figures. Near the driveway poise several zebras, leopards, and a giraffe; in a small, lily-filled pond floats a boat transporting the figures of Terrillion's family.

Visitors are welcome to stop and take pictures of the park from the road, but please keep in mind that this is private property.

Central Adirondacks

Nestled into the center of Adirondack Park are more still blue lakes, encircled by densely packed forests and small- to moderate-size peaks. The climate here is not as harsh as it is farther north, and the landscape has a more human-size feel. Some sections of the Central Adirondacks, such as Indian Lake, attract only a handful of visitors; others, such as Old Forge, are disturbingly overrun.

LONG LAKE

Heading south from Tupper Lake on Route 30, you'll come to Long Lake, a 14-mile stretch of water that is really just an engorged section of the Raquette River. At the intersection of Routes 30 and 28 N presides the village of Long Lake, dominated by the creaky, rectangular **Adiron-** **dack Hotel,** an 1870s hostelry with wide verandas. Just across the Long Lake bridge from the hotel is a **public beach** and boat launch.

One of the region's most popular **canoe trips** begins at the Long Lake launch and heads north along the Raquette River through the High Peaks region. Past the High Peaks, paddlers can choose to either continue on the Raquette River to Tupper Lake or portage to Upper Saranac Lake. Either way, the trip covers about 40 miles and takes about four days.

Hiking Owls Head Mountain

At the southern end of Long Lake ascends the double-peaked Owls Head. The well-marked, 3.5-mile trail leading to the top is of moderate difficulty and takes about four hours to hike

© CHRISTIANE BIRD

Seaplanes offer sight-seeing excursions on Long Lake.

THE NORTH COUNTRY

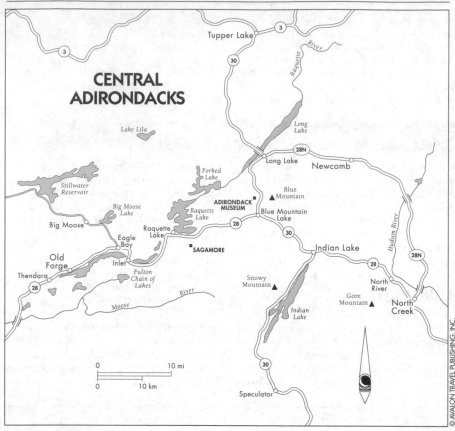

© AVALON TRAVEL PUBLISHING, INC.

roundtrip. Along the way you'll pass streams, valleys, a fire tower, Lake Eaton—a good place for a swim—and good views of the High Peaks.

To reach the trailhead, take Route 30 one mile north of Long Lake village to Endion Road and watch for signs.

Camping and Accommodations

Two miles north of the village is the 137-site **Lake Eaton Campground,** Rte. 30, 518/624-2641. Five miles west of Long Lake is the 80-site **Forked Lake Campground,** North Point Rd., off Rte. 30, 518/624-6646. For reservations at either, call 800/456-CAMP.

On the shores of the lake is the fourth-generation, family-run **Long View Lodge,** Deer-land Rd., Rts. 28 and 30, 518/624-2862, a comfortable, low-key place with 17 guest rooms, two cottages, and a private beach equipped with canoes and other boats ($65–80 d, breakfast included).

Though now better known for its restaurants than for its guest rooms, the **Adirondack Hotel,** Rte. 30, 518/624-4700 or 800/877-9247, www.adirondackhotel.com, still accommodates overnight visitors. The rooms, though spartan and well worn, are clean, and you can't beat the price ($45–75 d; the cheaper rooms share baths).

Food

The **Long Lake Diner,** Rte. 30, 518/624-3941, serves breakfast and lunch, along with a bar menu later in the day. The **Adirondack Hotel,** Rte. 30, 518/624-4700, includes a popular cafe that's open for breakfast, lunch, and a light dinner, and a more formal dining room that serves full-course dinners. In the lobby stands an enormous stuffed bear, and to one side is an inviting tap room (average dinner entrée $16).

Outfitters and Recreation

Boats and canoes can be rented at **Long Lake Marina,** Rte. 30, 518/624-2266, in the center of the village. **Adirondack Outfitters of Long Lake,** Rte. 30, 518/624-5998, also rents canoes, and sells outdoor gear. To take a scenic seaplane flight, contact **Helms Aero Service,** Rte. 30, 518/624-3931.

Shopping

You can't miss **Hoss's Country Corner,** Lake St., 518/624-2481, a big, square emporium built in the classic Adirondack style. Inside you'll find everything from groceries and clothing to handicrafts and a good selection of regional books.

BLUE MOUNTAIN LAKE

One of the loveliest lakes in all the Adirondacks is dark, spring-fed Blue Mountain Lake. Situated 1,800 feet above sea level, the isolated lake is sprinkled with small islands and flanked by towering Blue Mountain, a moody peak that the Iroquois once called "Hill of Storms." The lake, one of a chain of three, is stocked with bass, whitefish, and trout.

At the southern edge of the lake, along Routes 28 and 30, clusters the village of Blue Mountain Lake. Though home to only about 230 permanent residents, the village is a major cultural center, thanks to the presence of the renowned Adirondack Museum and the much smaller Adirondack Lakes Center for the Arts. A postage-stamp-size **public beach** is situated in the heart of the village, and several crafts galleries are located along Route 30. Among them is **Blue Mountain Designs,** Rte. 30, 518/352-7361, now over 25 years old.

A popular **canoe trip** starts at Blue Mountain Lake and heads west through Eagle and

Utowana Lakes to the .4-mile Bassett Carry. At the end of the portage flows the Marion River, which leads to Raquette Lake, which leads to the Fulton Chain of Lakes. Depending on how far you paddle, the trip can take anywhere from one to five days. A lean-to is situated on the north shore of Utowana Lake about a half mile above the dam.

Adirondack Museum

High on a slope overlooking Blue Mountain Lake presides the Adirondack Museum, a compact complex of 22 buildings that covers virtually every aspect of Adirondack life. By far the most important museum in the region, the complex has been described by the *New York Times* as "the best of its kind in the world."

Featured in the museum's two main buildings are first-rate exhibits on Adirondack history, natural science, culture, and art. Dioramas simulate scenes such as a logging camp, early Adirondack hotel, and hermit's cabin, while nearby are displays on fishing, trapping, and surveying. In one room is a Victorian hearse equipped with wheels for summer and runners for winter; in another, over 800 wooden miniatures carved by one man. Hanging in a central gallery are changing exhibits by artists such as Thomas Cole and Winslow Homer.

All around the main buildings, many smaller ones focus on specific themes. The Boat Building is packed with dozens of sleek wooden vessels; the Transportation Building, with 50 horse-drawn vehicles and a private railroad car. One cabin contains traditional Adirondack furniture; another, a rural schoolroom. At the Photo Belt, visitors sit down in front of a moving belt and watch historic photographs slide by.

The museum, Rte. 30, 518/352-7311, www .adkmuseum.org, is open Memorial Day–mid-October, daily 9:30 A.M.–5:30 P.M. Admission is adults $12, seniors $11, and children 7–16 $5. Also on-site is an inviting cafe and museum shop.

Adirondack Lakes Center for the Arts

This inviting two-story center presents both visual and performing arts. Exhibits in the past have covered everything from traditional quilts and Adirondack furniture to contemporary pottery and photography, while concerts have ranged from the Tokyo String Quartet to Aztec Two-Step. The center also features arts workshops, a film series, and a gift shop selling regional arts and crafts.

The center, Rte. 28, 518/352-7715, is open June–Nov., Mon.–Fri. 10 A.M.–4 P.M.; July–Aug., Mon.–Sat. 10 A.M.–4 P.M. Gallery admission is free. Evening events cost $4–16.

Hiking Blue Mountain

One of the best ways to get a good view of Blue Mountain Lake is to hike up brooding Blue Mountain, elevation 3,759 feet. Though quite steep in parts, the four-mile roundtrip hike is of moderate difficulty overall and takes about three hours. At the summit gleams the newly restored 1917 Blue Mountain Fire Tower, staffed with a ranger/guide on summer weekends. The trailhead and a well-marked hiking trail begin off Route 30, a half mile north of the Adirondack Museum.

Camping, Accommodations, and Food

Camping is available at the nearby 61-site **Lake Durant Campground,** Rte. 28, 518/352-7797. For reservations, call 800/456-CAMP; a basic site costs $12–14.

A mainstay in the Blue Mountain Lake

THE NORTHVILLE-PLACID TRAIL

L aid out by the Adirondack Mountain Club in 1922, the Northville-Placid Trail is a favorite among serious hikers and backpackers. Traversing over 133 miles of forest, it runs from Northville on Great Sacandaga Lake in the southern Adirondacks to Lake Placid in the High Peaks. It takes about 19 days to complete, and some sections are quite rugged and minimally maintained. Usage is low to moderate from Northville to Blue Mountain Lake, and heavy from Blue Mountain Lake to Lake Placid.

For a free brochure with basic information on the trail, contact the Department of Environmental Conservation. For maps and more detailed information, contact the Adirondack Mountain Club.

community—and its only public restaurant—is the Swiss chalet–styled **Potter's Resort,** Rte. 30, 518/352-7331, www.bluemountainlake.com. Guests can choose between cottages that rent by the week, and comfortable motel units ($80–90 d). Inside, the main lodge is a classic Adirondack dining room complete with moose and bear heads, stuffed beaver and deer. A wide and breezy deck overlooks the lake; on the menu is traditional American fare; average entrée $15.

Events

Paddle your kayak or canoe down to the **No-Octane Regatta,** 518/352-7311, held in late June. At the **Adirondacks Antique Show** in September, 50-odd vendors set up shop at the Adirondack Museum, 518/352-7311.

Outfitters and Recreation

Boats and canoes can be rented at the friendly, family-run **Blue Mountain Lake Boat Livery,** Rte. 28, 518/352-7351. Docked outside are two classic wooden launches that take visitors to isolated parts of the lake. The low-key **sightseeing tours** operate daily June–Sept., and cost adults $12, seniors $10, students and children over three $8. Reservations are recommended.

Blue Mountain Outfitters, Rte. 30, 518/352-7306 or 518/352-7675, rents canoes and kayaks, sells outdoor gear, and offers guided canoe trips.

INDIAN LAKE

Southeast of Blue Mountain Lake lounges long, skinny Indian Lake, named after Sabael Benedict, an Abenaki and the area's first settler. A hamlet of the same name clusters around the intersection of Routes 28 and 30 at the lake's northern end, while to the east stretches the Siamese Ponds Wilderness Area.

Siamese Ponds Wilderness Area

Covering an area of 112,000 acres, the Siamese Ponds region is roughly bounded by Route 28 to the north, Route 30 to the west and south, and Route 8 to the east. Often overlooked by vacationers, the area encompasses gentle mountains, dense forests, crystal-clear ponds, and rushing streams. In certain sections, you can hike all day without encountering another person.

Thirty-three miles of marked hiking trails—and many more unmarked ones—run through the wilderness, while scattered here and there are primitive tent sites and lean-tos. Major trailheads are located at the end of Big Brook Road (off Route 30 a half mile south of Indian Lake village); at Thirteenth Lake and the end of Old Farm Clearing Road (take Route 28 east to Thirteenth Lake Road); and on Route 8 about four miles west of Bakers Mills.

Hiking Chimney Mountain
One of the trails at the end of Big Brook Road leads up Chimney Mountain, named after its unusual central bulwark of layered gneiss, granite, and marble. The mountain is also known for its many crevices and caves. These should be explored by expert spelunkers only, but you might want to bring along a flashlight to shine down into the depths.

The roundtrip hike up and down Chimney Mountain covers three miles, takes two and a half hours, and is quite rugged in spots. From up top are good views of Kings Flow, Round Pond, and the High Peaks.

Hiking Snowy Mountain
The tallest of the southern Adirondacks, Snowy Mountain (elevation 3,899 feet) offers a long and challenging climb best suited for hikers in good condition. The hike to the summit—which offers excellent views of the surrounding lakes—is about seven miles roundtrip and takes about five hours. Steep sections are located near the trailhead and again near the top, while in between are rolling terrain and a sparkling brook that follows the trail for close to a mile. A complete description of the hike is outlined in Barbara McMartin's *Fifty Hikes in the Adirondacks*.

To reach the trailhead, take Route 30 south of the hamlet of Indian Lake 6.5 miles. Watch for a sign marking the trail on the right and a paved parking area on the left.

Rafting Trips
Whitewater rafting trips down the nearby Hudson River Gorge and Moose River are offered by the **Adventure Sports Rafting Co.,** 518/648-5812 or 800/441-RAFT, and **Adirondack Rafting Co.,** 518/523-1635 or 800/510-RAFT.

Camping and Accommodations
In general, camping is allowed anywhere in the **Siamese Wilderness Area,** 518/251-3933, as long as your campsite is at least 150 feet from roads, trails, streams, or ponds. At distances of less than 150 feet, you must look for designated campsites or lean-tos.

Overlooking Indian Lake is the clean and quiet **Point Breeze Motel,** Rte. 30, 518/648-5555 ($48–54 d).

For a list of area cottages that rent by the week, contact the Indian Lake Chamber of Commerce, 518/648-5112 or 800/328-LAKE, www.indi-an-lake.com.

NORTH CREEK
Off Route 28 midway between Indian Lake and Warrensburg in the southeastern Adirondacks lies North Creek, a small town wedged between mountains and the **Hudson River Gorge.** Towering over North Creek to the south is Gore Mountain; to the north flows the Hudson River and a 16-mile stretch of whitewater that's considered the finest rafting run in the east.

The Hudson River Gorge begins east of Indian Lake, just beyond the confluence of the Indian and Hudson Rivers. There, writes preservationist John M. Kauffmann in his book *Flow East,* "the Hudson drops ominously deeper between its dark forested shores. The gorge begins to yawn, and the cold, damp breeze, like the breath from a cave, sends a tingle along your spine."

During the spring, when the water runs high, the gorge should be tackled only by experts; the river offers near continuous Class III and IV rapids, and a number of deaths have occurred here over the years. In June, however, the run "is delightful," writes Kauffmann. "Then you can examine the water-worn rocks, undercut into weird grottos. Each niche at river's edge seems a Japanese garden of gnarled trees, shrubs, creeping vines and winking flowers."

Gore Mountain

The second-largest ski resort in New York State, Gore Mountain particularly attracts intermediate skiers. Featured are 44 trails, a vertical drop of 2,100 feet, and eight ski lifts, including the state's only gondola ride and a quad-chairlift. Like Whiteface, Gore is state-owned and managed by the Olympic Regional Development Authority. From July 4th to Columbus Day, the gondola ride operates to the summit, offering bird's-eye views of the countryside.

The mountain, Peaceful Valley Rd., 518/251-2411 or 800/342-1234 (snow info), www.gore-mountain.com, is located off Rte. 28. Peak-season lift tickets are about $40 for adults, $25 for children. The gondola ride costs adults $8, seniors and kids under 12 $5.

Barton Garnet Mines

On the back side of Gore Mountain lies Barton Mines, a sprawling operation that produces 90 percent of the world's industrial garnet; garnets are also New York State's stone. During the summer, visitors can tour the open-pit mines with guides who explain the area's geology and history. On-site you'll find a rock collection and mineral shop.

The mines, Barton Mines Rd., North River, 518/251-2706 or 518/251-2296, are just north of North Creek, off Rte. 28. Hours are July–Labor Day, Mon.–Sat. 9:30 A.M.–5 P.M., Sunday 11 A.M.–5 P.M.; Labor Day–Columbus Day, weekends only. Admission is adults $9.50, seniors $8, children $6; admission includes a season pass which allows for unlimited visits.

Outfitters and Guides

One of the oldest rafting outfitters in the state, the **Hudson River Rafting Company,** 1 Main St., North Creek, NY 12853, 518/251-3215, offers guided trips along the Hudson River Gorge and along the Moose, Black, and Sacandaga Rivers.

Accommodations and Food

Five miles south of North Creek, the **Black Mountain Motel,** Rte. 8, Johnsburg, 518/251-2800, offers 25 standard rooms, a pool, playground, and simple dining room ($47–65 d).

The **Copperfield Inn,** 224 Main St., 518/251-2500 or 800/424-9910, www.copperfield-inn.com, is an upscale motor lodge where you'll find 24 spacious rooms with plenty of amenities, a heated pool, health club, hot tub, and tennis courts ($180–230 d; packages available). Also on the premises is **Trappers Tavern,** serving casual meals like pizza and chili, and **Gardens,** a spiffy restaurant serving contemporary American dishes such as grilled tuna and rack of lamb (average entrée $16).

Events

The popular **Hudson River White Water Derby,** 518/251-2612, takes place the first weekend in May. Canoe and kayak races are featured.

RAQUETTE LAKE

Heading west of Blue Mountain Lake on Route 28 instead of east, you'll come to Raquette Lake. From the road, where it is only visible in glimpses, Raquette appears to be one of the smaller of the Adirondack lakes. In reality, it is the fourth largest, with 99 miles of waterfront.

It was on Raquette Lake that W. W. Durant built Camp Pine Knot, the first of the Adirondack great camps, in 1877. To create his retreat, Durant combined elements of the Adirondack log cabin and the Swiss chalet, a style that continues to predominate in the Adirondacks. Camp Pine Knot still stands near the lake, along with three other great camps—Camp Echo, Bluff Point, North Point—and the nearby Sagamore. Only the Sagamore is open to the public, but you can glimpse the other four by touring Raquette Lake by boat.

Alvah Dunning (1816–1902), a famed early guide, once lived at Raquette Lake. Dunning killed his first moose at the age of 11 and guided his first party at the age of 12. Forced to leave Piseco Lake after he outraged his neighbors by brutally beating his wife, Dunning spent much of his life railing against civilization and city people, "them city dudes with velvet suits and pop guns, that can't hit a deer when they see it and don't want it if they do hit it."

At the southwestern edge of Raquette Lake lies a hamlet of the same name, equipped with three marinas and little else. At the lake's southeastern edge stretches the **Golden Beach State Park,** Rte. 28, 315/354-4230, offering a swimming beach, hiking trails, boat rentals, 205-site campground, and good fishing spots. Parking in summer is $10–14. For camping reservations, call 800/456-CAMP; a basic site costs $12.

Great Camp Sagamore

A self-contained rustic village hidden deep in the woods, Sagamore was built by W. W. Durant in 1897 and sold to Alfred G. Vanderbilt, Sr. in 1901. Considered the prototypical great camp, Sagamore centers around a seemingly indestructible main lodge built of huge dark logs, while outbuildings house a dining hall, guest cottages, boathouse, horse barn, ice house, and bowling alley.

One of Sagamore's most interesting buildings is the casino playhouse, the walls of which are covered with animal "trophies" killed by generations of Vanderbilts. The camp was once known as the "headquarters of the gaming crowd," and the Vanderbilts entertained lavishly, inviting up everyone from Gary Cooper and Gene Tierney to Lord Mountbatten and Madame Chiang Kai-Shek.

Now a National Historic Site owned by the Sagamore Institute, Sagamore hosts numerous week-end and week-long learning vacations focusing on such subjects as woodcarving, storytelling, and folk music. You can also book a simple "Outdoor Weekend" with no classes or take a guided tour.

The camp, Sagamore Rd., 315/354-5311, www.sagamore.org, is located off Rte. 28 opposite Raquette Lake village. Tours are offered daily late June–Labor Day at 10 A.M. and 1 P.M.; call for fall hours Cost is adults $10, seniors and students $9, children ages 5–14 $3. Weekend rates, which include two nights' accommodations, classes, and all meals, are $225–350.

Outfitters and Recreation

Boats, canoes, and water-sports equipment can be rented at **Bird's Boat Livery,** Rte. 28, 315/354-4441; and the **Raquette Lake Marina,** off Rte. 28 in the village, 315/354-4361. Bird's also offers a **mail boat cruise** around the lake July–Aug., Mon.–Sat. at 10:15 A.M., and other boat trips by reservation. The mail boat cruises cost adults $8, children $6.

The **Raquette Lake Navigation Co.,** off Rte. 28 in the village, 315/354-5532, www.raquettelakenavigation.com, features lunch, dinner, sightseeing, and moonlight cruises aboard the

© CHRISTIANE BIRD

the main lodge at Great Camp Sagamore

150-passenger *W. W. Durant,* June–October. Call for schedule and fees.

Shopping

Inside the sprawling **Raquette Lake Supply Co.,** Main St., off Rte. 28, 315/354-4301, owned by the same family since the late 1800s, you'll find everything from a post office and laundromat to groceries and fishing supplies.

OLD FORGE AND THE FULTON CHAIN

After the relative solitude of Blue Mountain Lake, Indian Lake, and even Raquette Lake, Old Forge and much of the Fulton Chain come as a disheartening shock. The roads and hamlets here are surprisingly built up, and tourists slurping down ice cream cones seem to be everywhere.

Nestled in the western foothills of the Adirondacks, the Fulton Chain is a series of eight lakes, flanked by long ridges. None of the ridges reach over 600 feet high but they feature steep, glacier-created cliffs that drop dramatically down into the lakes. Excellent bird's-eye views can be had by hiking up Bald Mountain or by taking a ride up the McCauley Mountain chairlift.

Heading west from Raquette Lake on Route 28, you'll come first to Eighth and Seventh Lakes—the most pristine of the Fulton Chain—and to the attractive hamlet of **Inlet.** About two miles beyond Inlet is Big Moose Public Road (County Road 1), a wooded back lane that leads north four miles to Big Moose Lake. So far, so good. But then, about 10 miles beyond Inlet lies Old Forge, dominated by endless souvenir shops, motels, and the Enchanted Forest/Water Safari theme park. About a mile south of Old Forge is the village of Thendara.

One of the Adirondack's most famed and popular **canoe trips** begins in Old Forge and proceeds north through the Fulton Chain to Raquette Lake, Long Lake, and the Raquette River. Canoeists can then head to either Saranac or Tupper Lakes. The entire route is about 100 miles long, involves about nine miles of carry, and takes about six days. To canoe just the 18-mile-long Fulton Chain, from Old Forge to the Eighth Lake Campground, takes a full day and involves 1.7 miles of carry.

Detour to Big Moose Lake

Located off the beaten tourist track, Big Moose Lake is worth a detour, especially if you're looking for lunch (see Food, below). And, fans of

THE AMERICAN TRAGEDY THAT BECAME *AN AMERICAN TRAGEDY*

On July 11, 1906, a young man named Chester Gillette overturned a rowboat in the middle of Big Moose Lake, drowning—accidentally or deliberately?—his pregnant girlfriend Grace Brown. The case caught the attention of the entire nation, and became the basis for Theodore Dreiser's novel *An American Tragedy.* Dreiser stuck surprisingly close to the facts of the case. Like Gillette, his protagonist, Clyde Griffiths, grew up in a religious family that roamed the West; he traveled east to work in his uncle's skirt factory and was desperate to achieve the American Dream—no matter what it took.

Gillette was arrested the day after the drowning and incarcerated in the Herkimer County jail. Visitors lined up around the block to tour past his cell, and reporters flocked there from all over the country. Among those covering the case was ex-lawman Bat Masterson, who had become a sportswriter for the *New York Morning Telegraph.* Masterson was one of the few to question whether Gillette could receive a fair trial in Herkimer County—a charge that infuriated local officials.

Several buildings connected with the Gillette case still stand. In Cortland, south of Syracuse, is the rooming house where Chester lived while working at his uncle's factory. In Herkimer, in the Mohawk River Valley, stand the courthouse and jail in which he was tried and incarcerated. And the railroad station through which the couple passed just hours before the fateful event remains in Big Moose Lake.

Chester Gillette was found guilty of first-degree murder and was electrocuted at Auburn State Prison on March 30, 1907.

Theodore Dreiser's *An American Tragedy* will be *very* interested to learn that it was in the lake's South Bay that Chester Gillette drowned Grace Brown. Bear left on Big Moose Road upon reaching the lake, and you'll come to the old railroad station (now Big Moose Station restaurant) where Gillette and Brown alighted. Bear right and you'll reach the former site of the Hotel Glennmore, where the couple registered and rented their boat. The hotel is gone now, but several outbuildings remain.

Writes Dreiser: "The quiet, glassy, iridescent surface of this lake . . . seemed, not so much like water as oil—like molten glass that, of enormous bulk and weight, resting upon the substantial earth so very far below. And the lightness and freshness and intoxication of the gentle air blowing here and there, yet scarcely rippling the surface of the lake. And the softness and furry thickness of the tall pines about the shore. Everywhere pines—tall and spearlike. And above them the humped backs of the dark and distant Adirondacks beyond."

Arts Center/Old Forge
The oldest multiarts center in the Adirondacks, founded in the early 1950s, the Arts Center/Old Forge occupies a former boat storage barn. The main gallery focuses on changing art and photography exhibits, while in the Adirondack room are selected works—such as quilts and baskets—from the permanent collection. Film, concert, and lecture series are presented throughout the summer, along with crafts workshops, children's programs, and nature hikes.

The center, Rte. 28, Old Forge, 315/369-6411, is open Mon.–Sat. 10 A.M.–4 P.M., Sunday noon–4 P.M. Admission to the gallery is free. Events cost $5–12.

Hiking Bald Mountain
Four and a half miles east of Old Forge rises Bald Mountain, which offers superb views of the Fulton Chain for surprisingly little effort. From the well-marked parking lot at the foot of the mountain, the trail climbs only 400 feet in less than a mile: "If the climb were not too short to call a hike, or if you were not apt to meet hordes of other hikers, it could be one of the most satisfying treks in the Adirondacks," writes hiking guru Barbara Martin in *Fifty Hikes in the Adirondacks.*

To reach the trailhead, take Route 28 to Rondaxe Road and watch for signs.

Amusements and Recreation
About two miles south of Old Forge is **McCauley Mountain,** Old McCauley Rd., 315/369-3225, which functions as a small, 14-trail ski resort in winter. In summer, a chair lift leading to the summit operates July–Columbus Day.

The 60-acre **Enchanted Forest/Water Safari,** Rte. 28, Old Forge, 315/369-6145, contains traditional rides, water rides, theme areas such as Storybook Lane and Animal Lane, and daily circus shows. The park is open mid-June–Labor Day.

Old Forge Lake Cruises, Rte. 28, Old Forge, 315/369-6473, offers sightseeing and dinner cruises daily June–October.

The **Adirondack Scenic Railroad,** Rte. 28, Thendara, 315/369-6290 or 315/369-6472, offers one-hour rides along the Moose River aboard vintage open-window coaches. The railroad operates mid-June–October.

Outfitters and Guides
In Old Forge, boats and canoes can be rented at **Rivett's Boat Livery,** on the waterfront, 315/369-3123. **Adirondack River Outfitters,** 800/525-RAFT, conducts guided rafting trips down the Hudson, Moose, Black, and Sacandaga Rivers. **Tickner's Moose River Canoe Trips,** 315/369-6286, offers guided canoe and kayak trips, along with instruction, rentals, and sales.

Camping and Accommodations
In Inlet is the 120-site **Limekiln Lake State Campsite,** Rte. 28, 315/357-4401. For reservations, call 800/456-CAMP; a basic site costs $14. The homey **Cinnamon Bear,** Rte. 28, Inlet, 315/357-6013, is one of Inlet's few B&Bs; four simple guest rooms, some of which share baths ($80 d).

The expansive **Big Moose Inn,** Big Moose Rd., Big Moose Lake, Eagle Bay, 315/357-2042, www.bigmooseinn.com, sits by itself on the lakeshore, surrounded by pine. Inside you'll find

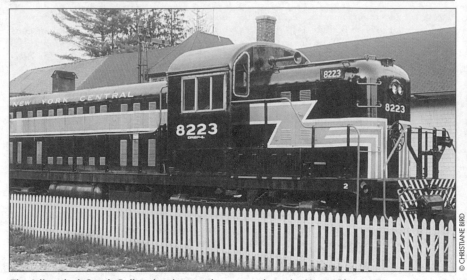

© CHRISTIANE BIRD

The Adirondack Scenic Railroad makes one-hour runs along the Moose River.

16 guest rooms, a central fireplace, restaurant, bar, and a comfortable lounge. Outside is a small beach equipped with canoes and other boats ($65–129 d; the less expensive rooms share baths).

The low-slung **Van Auken's Inne,** Forge St., Thendara, 315/369-3033, www.vanaukens-inne.com, with its l-o-n-g, two-tiered porch, contains 12 newly renovated guest rooms with private baths ($69–89 d). Some open out onto a breezy second-story balcony, while on the ground floor are a comfortable lobby, tap room, and restaurant (see below), all filled with antiques.

Among the many motels in Old Forge is the basic **Forge Motel,** Box 522, Rte. 28, 315/369-3313, which overlooks Old Forge Pond ($74–84 d). More upscale is the 52-room **Best Western Sunset,** Rte. 28, Old Forge, 315/369-6836, which offers an indoor pool, playground, and putting green ($89–189 d).

Food

Big Moose Station, Big Moose Rd., Big Moose Lake, Eagle Bay, 315/357-3525, in the old Adirondack Railroad station, serves tasty homemade diner fare for lunch and dinner. The soups are especially good, and almost everything is priced under $10.

Housed in its namesake, complete with soaring ceilings, exposed beams, and a waterwheel is the historic **Old Mill Restaurant,** Rte. 28, 315/369-3662, in Old Forge. On the menu are a multitude of traditional American favorites, including steak, pork chops, and shrimp and chicken dishes; average entrée $15.

In Thendara, the 1893 **Van Auken's Inne,** Forge St., off Rte. 28, 315/369-3033, serves contemporary American and continental cuisine. On the lunch menu are imaginative salads and sandwiches, while the dinner menu includes everything from grilled veal chops to fresh fish; average dinner entrée $16.

One of the top restaurants in the region is the elegant **Seventh Lake House,** Rte. 28, Inlet, 315/357-6028, renowned for its contemporary American cuisine and romantic setting on the lake, complete with big picture windows. Dishes range from pastas and fresh fish to steak and lamb (average entrée $18; dinner only).

Shopping

Old Forge Hardware, Rte. 28, Old Forge, 315/369-6100, bills itself as the "Adirondacks'

Most General Store." Inside, you'll find everything you could possibly need, from snowshoes and bird feeders to cookbooks and paperweights. **Moose River Trading Company,** Rte. 28, Thendara, 315/369-6091, stocks classic Adirondack gear.

Visitor Information

The **Town of Webb Tourist Information Center,** Main St., Old Forge, NY 13420, 315/369-6983, www.oldforgeny.com, is open Mon.–Sat. 8 A.M.–5 P.M. and Sunday 9 A.M.–5 P.M.; closed some Sundays in the off-season.

The Thousand Islands

Along the St. Lawrence River, at the northwest end of the state, stretches an area known as the Thousand Islands. In point of fact, there are 1,864 islands here, ranging in size from a few square feet to 22 miles long. Some support nothing more than a lone tree; one is home to Boldt Castle, a haunting Gothic presence near Alexandria Bay that is the region's premier visitor attraction.

Though the term "Thousand Islands" is often used to describe the large area reaching from Oswego in the south to Akwesasne in the north to Adirondack Park in the east, the islands themselves are clustered only in the center, between Cape Vincent and Alexandria Bay. Much of the rest of the region supports farms or endless unbroken acres of low-growing forest, rivers, and lakes. Several small industrialized cities flourish here as well, the largest of which is Watertown. Outside Watertown bustles Fort Drum, a 107,000-acre military training facility.

For the visitor, most of the Thousand Islands' attractions lie along the Seaway Trail, which hugs the shores of the St. Lawrence and Lake Ontario. From the trail, views of the river and its bypassing boat traffic are outstanding. Enormous tankers and cargo vessels slide by, on their way between the Atlantic Ocean and the Great Lakes. The 1959 completion of the St. Lawrence Seaway—a series of connecting channels and locks—turned the river into the longest navigable inland passage in the world. It stretches over 2,300 miles.

Because the Thousand Islands lie between the United States and Canada, the region attracts as many Canadian as it does American visitors. The Thousand Islands International Bridge (an extension of I-81) crosses over the St. Lawrence River near Alexandria Bay; the Seaway International Bridge spans the river near Massena.

History

Prior to the arrival of the whites, the Thousand Islands were inhabited by the Iroquois, who called the region *Manitonna,* or Garden of the Great Spirit. According to Iroquois legend, the islands were created by accident by the Great Spirit, who had promised all the tribes on earth a paradise if only they would stop quarrelling. The tribes promised and the Great Spirit delivered, only to have to retrieve his garden when the mortals broke their word. But as the Great Spirit was about to return to the sky, the garden slipped out of his grasp and crashed into the St. Lawrence River, breaking into a thousand pieces.

The first white man to enter the region was Jacques Cartier, who sailed down the St. Lawrence in 1635 and allegedly exclaimed, *"Les milles isles!"* The region maintained a close connection with France throughout the 1700s and early 1800s, when refugees fleeing France after Napoleon's reign settled near Cape Vincent. Among them were Napoleon's brother and sister, Joseph and Caroline Bonaparte.

The region also bore the brunt of much of the War of 1812. Fought between the United States and Britain, with the Americans hoping to drive the English out of North America once and for all, the war went largely unsupported by area residents. Many earned their livelihood by trading with England and Canada, and dubbed the three years' worth of battles "Mr. Madison's War." Handsome stone fortifications still stand in Sackets Harbor and Oswego, where major battles were fought, and historic War of 1812 plaques line the Seaway Trail.

The wealthy discovered the beauty of the Thousand Islands in the 1870s and soon built magnificent summer homes on private islands.

THE NORTH COUNTRY

THE SEAWAY TRAIL

The Seaway Trail is a 454-mile scenic highway that parallels New York's northern coastline along the St. Lawrence River, Lake Ontario, the Niagara River, and Lake Erie. Marked by green-and-white route markers, as well as brown-and-white War of 1812 signs, it forms the longest national recreational trail in the United States.

In the Thousand Islands region, the Seaway Trail runs from Oswego in the south to Akwesasne in the north along Routes 104, 3, 180, 12 E, and 37. More parks and beaches are located along this section of the trail than anywhere else in New York State. In total, the Thousand Islands region boasts 45 New York and Canadian state parks; two of the largest are Wellesley Island and Robert Moses.

Seaway Trail, Inc., 315/646-1000 or 800/SEA-WAY-T, www.seawaytrail.com, is headquartered at the corner of Main and Ray Streets in Sackets Harbor. Contact them for free information, or visit them on site. Their center houses nine rooms of exhibits dedicated to all aspects of the trail, including history, nature, and culture. Hours are May–Oct., daily 10 A.M.–5 P.M., and Nov.–April, Thurs.–Sun. 10 A.M.–5 P.M.

The Seaway Trail also publishes a free annual magazine, available in most regional tourism offices, and several helpful guides. Among them is *Seaway Trail Bicycling*, which outlines some of the region's excellent bike routes, and *Seaway Trail Lighthouses*.

Grand hotels went up on the shore as well, and huge steamboats plied the waters. All this opulence ended with the Depression, but evidence of it remains.

Information

For more information on the Thousand Islands, contact the **Thousand Islands International Tourism Council,** 43373 Collins Landing Rd., Alexandria Bay, NY 13607, 315/482-2520 or 800/847-5263, www.visit1000islands.com. Open daily in summer, 8 A.M.–6 P.M.; Mon.–Fri. 9 A.M.–5 P.M. in the off-season.

OSWEGO

At the southwestern end of the region, just north of the Finger Lakes, lies the small city of Oswego, population 19,195. Straddling the mouth of the Oswego River, overlooking Lake Ontario, Oswego operated as an important fort and trading post throughout the 1700s. During the American Revolution, Oswego served as a haven for Loyalists fleeing the Mohawk Valley, and remained in British hands until 1796. Named the first freshwater port in the United States in 1799, Oswego also played an important role in the War of 1812, protecting the supply route to the naval base at nearby Sackets Harbor.

Today, Oswego continues to function as a Great Lakes port and is a major sportfishing capital.

Fort Ontario State Historic Site

On the eastern edge of town, overlooking Lake Ontario, presides Fort Ontario. Originally built by the British in 1755, the site was attacked and rebuilt four times, with the present-day Fort Ontario constructed between 1839 and 1844.

During WW II, Fort Ontario served as a sort of emergency refugee center/internment camp for victims of the Nazi Holocaust. The only one of its kind for European refugees in the country, the center invited 874 Jews and 73 Catholics to relocate here, but upon arrival, the refugees were placed in a fenced-in compound and told not to leave. The shocked refugees were interned for a total of 18 months.

Today, Fort Ontario has been restored to its 1867–72 appearance. Costumed guides interpret the lives of the men and civilians who once lived here.

The fort, 1 E. 4th St., 315/343-4711, is open May–Oct., Mon.–Sat. 10 A.M.–4:30 P.M., Sunday 1–4:30 P.M. Admission is adults $3, children under 12 $2.

H. Lee White Marine Museum

Oswego's most delightful tourist attraction is the White Marine Museum, a sprawling, hodgepodge affair filled with everything from archaeological artifacts to mounted fish. One exhibit focuses on Lake Ontario shipwrecks, another on the city's

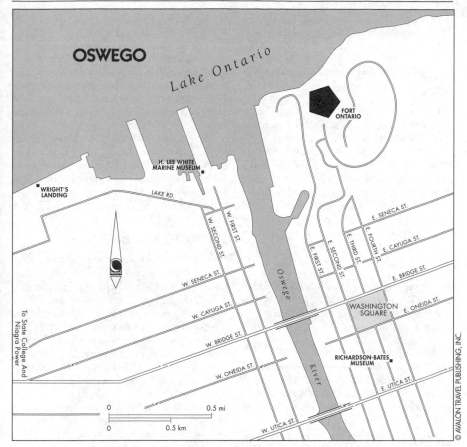

OSWEGO

Lake Ontario

FORT ONTARIO

H. LEE WHITE MARINE MUSEUM

WRIGHT'S LANDING

LAKE RD.

W. FIRST ST.

W. SECOND ST.

W. SENECA ST.

W. CAYUGA ST.

W. BRIDGE ST.

W. ONEIDA ST.

E. SENECA ST.

E. FOURTH ST.

E. THIRD ST.

E. CAYUGA ST.

E. SECOND ST.

E. FIRST ST.

E. BRIDGE ST.

WASHINGTON SQUARE

E. ONEIDA ST.

RICHARDSON-BATES MUSEUM

E. UTICA ST.

Oswego River

To State College And Niagra Power

MOON

0   0.5 mi
0   0.5 km

W. UTICA ST.

© AVALON TRAVEL PUBLISHING, INC.

once-thriving shipbuilding industry, a third on the legendary "monsters" of the lake, a fourth on the region's strong abolitionist history. Most everything in the museum has been donated, which gives it a casual and folksy appeal. Outside, a WW II tugboat and a derrick barge invite exploration.

The museum, at the foot of W. 1st St., 315/342-0480, www.hleewhitemarinemuseum.com, is open June and September, daily 1–5 P.M.; July–Aug., daily 10 A.M.–5 P.M. Admission is adults $2, children under 12 $1.

Richardson-Bates Museum

Built in the late 1860s, the Richardson-Bates house is a regal Italianate mansion still equipped with

95 percent of its original furnishings. The five plush period rooms downstairs are arranged according to photographs taken around 1890, while upstairs, succinct exhibits explain the history of Oswego County. The museum is run by the Oswego County Historical Society and contains about 13,000 artifacts, documents, and photographs.

The museum, 135 E. 3rd St., 315/343-1342, is open Tues.–Fri. 10 A.M.–5 P.M., Sat.–Sun. 1–5 P.M. Admission is adults $4, children $2.

Camping and Accommodations

On the lakeshore about 15 miles northeast of Oswego lies **Selkirk Shores State Park,** Rte. 3, 315/298-5737, equipped with a beach, hiking

THE NORTH COUNTRY

trails, and 148-site campground. For reservations, call 800/456-CAMP; a basic site costs $13–17. Area motels include a 44-room **Days Inn,** Rte. 104 E, 315/343-3136 ($60–74 d); and the 94-room **Best Western Captain's Quarters,** 26 E. 1st St., 315/342-4040 ($90–135 d).

Food

The ever popular **Rudy's,** Washington Blvd. on the lakeshore, a quarter-mile west of the State University of New York (SUNY) College at Oswego, 315/343-2671, specializes in fish and chips, and fried scallops and clams; average main dish $7. Overlooking the harbor downtown is **Admiral Woolsey's,** 1 E. 1st St., at the marina, 315/342-4433, offering a wide assortment of pastas, seafood dishes, and steaks; entrées are $12–23.

Events

One of the region's biggest celebrations is **Harborfest,** 315/343-FREE or 800/248-4FUN, held in late July; featured are tall ships, crafts, street entertainment, and fireworks.

Visitor Information

The **Oswego County Department of Promotion and Tourism,** 46 E. Bridge St., Oswego, NY 13126, 315/349-8322 or 800/248-4386, www.oswegocounty.com, is open Mon.–Fri. 9 A.M.–5 P.M.

EN ROUTE TO SACKETS HARBOR

The **Seaway Trail** (Route 104 to Route 3) heads north out of Oswego to Selkirk Shores State Park and the mouth of the Salmon River. Take a two-mile detour east on Route 13 along the river to reach the Salmon Capital of **Pulaski.** Almost everything here caters to anglers: Salmon Acres Motel, Portly Angler Lodge, Fish Inn Post, and Angler Parking—read the signs.

Continue another five miles east on Route 13 to reach Altmar and the **New York State Salmon River Fish Hatchery,** Rte. 22, 315/298-5051. Over 4.5 million fish are raised here each year, including chinook and coho salmon, and brown, rainbow, and steelhead trout. Self-guided tours take visitors past the incubation area, spawn house, and fish pens (open March–Nov., daily 9 A.M.–4 P.M.; admission is free).

From the mouth of the Salmon River, the Seaway Trail continues north along the shores of Lake Ontario. It bypasses several more parks and then bumps into deep blue **Henderson Harbor,** a perfectly shaped semicircle ringed with historic homes, vacation cottages, marinas, and ship-shape small boats.

About a mile southeast of Henderson Harbor is the hamlet of **Henderson,** where Confederate general Stonewall Jackson came for medical treatment for a stomach ailment before the Civil War. Part of his cure was to walk between the hamlet and the harbor daily.

SACKETS HARBOR

About 45 miles north of Oswego, or eight miles west of Watertown, lies picturesque Sackets Harbor. Built on a bluff overlooking Lake Ontario, Sackets Harbor is peppered with handsome limestone buildings that date back to the early 1800s. Though now primarily a resort village, Sackets Harbor remains for the most part undiscovered, which helps account for its charm.

During the War of 1812, Sackets Harbor dominated American naval and military activity. A large fleet was constructed in its shipyard and thousands of soldiers were housed in the barracks built on its shores. Heavy fighting between the British and American troops took place on the bluffs.

The former shipyard and adjoining battlefield is now Sackets Harbor's foremost visitor attraction, while the rebuilt barracks—situated a mile or two east of the village center—have been converted into apartments, restaurants, and a small inn. The battlefield is at the end of a short Main Street, lined with cheery shops, cafes, and historic buildings; more historic buildings flank quiet, tree-shaded Broad Street.

Sackets Harbor Battlefield State Historic Site

Hard though it is to believe today, the silent and all-but-deserted Sackets Harbor Battlefield was once the site of intense fighting between American and British troops. Monuments and plaques

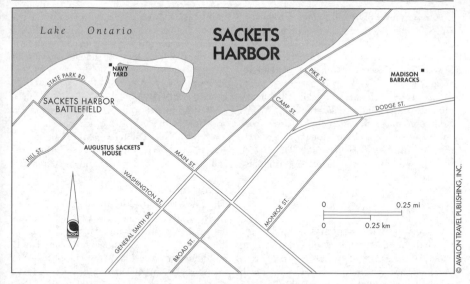

commemorating the events are strewn here and there, but for the most part, the battlefield remains an idyllic park, set atop a lush green bluff with glorious lake views. The **Battle of Sackets Harbor** is re-enacted here every July.

Adjoining the battlefield is the partially restored Navy Yard, enclosed by a white picket fence. Built in the 1850s to replace the thriving shipyard once situated here, the yard contains a restored commandant's house and a museum showcasing exhibits on the War of 1812.

The battlefield, foot of Main and Washington Sts., 315/646-3634, is open Memorial Day–Labor Day, Wed.–Sat. 10 A.M.–5 P.M., Sunday 1–5 P.M.; Labor Day–Columbus Day, Fri.–Sat. 10 A.M.–5 P.M., Sunday 1–5 P.M.; grounds open year round 8 A.M.–dusk. Admission is adults $1, children free.

Accommodations

At the Madison Barracks, 85 Worth Rd., the attractive **Old Stone Row Country Inn,** 123 Bartlett Rd., 315/646-1234 or 315/646-3374, features eight modern guest rooms complete with kitchenettes ($66–104 d). In the heart of the village, the three-story **Ontario Place Hotel,** 103 General Smith Dr., 315/646-8000, www.ontarioplacehotel.com, offers 28 spacious rooms and 10 suites equipped with Jacuzzis ($80–175 d).

Food

The **1812 Steak and Seafood Company,** 212 Main St., 315/646-2041, is known for its fresh seafood and all-you-can-eat crab-legs nights (average entrée $14). In the Madison Barracks, 85 Worth Rd., the **Barracks Inn,** 42 Madison Barracks, 315/646-2376, offers an imaginative menu and patio dining with great views of the lake; average entrée $13. Also in the Barracks is the **Trotting Bull,** 336 Brady Rd., 315/646-2333, serving both steaks and Mexican food; entrées range $12–20.

Visitor Information

Housed in the 1803 Augustus Sacket House, 301 W. Main St., Sackets Harbor, NY 13685, are the **Sackets Harbor Chamber of Commerce,** 315/646-1700; and the **Sackets Harbor Visitors Center,** 315/646-2321. Sackets Harbor is one of New York State's Heritage Areas—loosely designated historic districts linked by a common theme. The theme in Sackets Harbor is defense.

The chamber of commerce is open Mon.–Fri. 10 A.M.–5 P.M. The visitor center, containing three rooms of exhibits and a good introductory video, is open Memorial Day–Columbus Day, daily 10 A.M.–4 P.M. Admission is free.

One block away from the visitor center is the **Seaway Trail Discovery Center,** 401 Main St., at Ray St.

Visitors are welcome to explore the bucolic grounds of the **Madison Barracks,** 85 Worth Rd., 315/646-3374, which encompasses a vast parade ground, polo lawn, stone tower, officers row, and military burial ground. Pick up free walking-tour brochures in the management office just inside the main gate.

CAPE VINCENT

Situated on a windswept spit of land at the mouth of the St. Lawrence River is Cape Vincent, "home of the gamey black bass" ("gamey" as in "feisty"). Cape Vincent doesn't really have much to offer in the way of visitor attractions but is a pretty village to drive through, with a number of historic homes located along Broadway.

The area's first settlers were French, a fact celebrated every July on **French Heritage Day,** 315/654-2481. On Real Street once stood the "Cup and Saucer House," built in 1818 by Napoleon's chief of police, Count Real, in the hopes that the emperor could be rescued from the island of St. Helena. The building burned to the ground in 1867.

For more on the area, contact the **Cape Vincent Chamber of Commerce,** 175 N. James St., 315/654-2481, www.capevincent.org.

Sights

In the heart of the village, the **Cape Vincent Historical Museum,** James St., 315/654-4400 or 315/654-3094, showcases historical artifacts and a delightful collection of tiny figures created out of scrap metal by local farmer Richard Merchant (July–Aug., Mon.–Sat. 10 A.M.–4 P.M., Sunday noon–4 P.M.; off-season by appointment; admission is free). Not far from the museum the **Cape Vincent Aquarium,** Broadway, 315/654-2147, houses several hundred local fish (open May–Oct., daily 9 A.M.–5 P.M.; admission is free).

Worth driving out to is the 1854 **Tibbetts**

Point Lighthouse, several miles west of the village on the very tip of the cape. The lighthouse is not open for touring—it's now a youth hostel—but the drive along the shore road (Route 6) is outstanding.

Horne's Ferry

Cape Vincent is the only community left in New York State with a ferry to Canada crossing the St. Lawrence River. The ferry, 315/783-0638, operates hourly May–Oct., and the cost for a car and driver is $7. The crossing time is 10 minutes.

Accommodations

The **Tibbetts Point Lighthouse,** 33439 County Rte. 6, 315/654-3450, is a Hosteling International–American Youth Hostel offering 31 dormitory-style beds in single-sex rooms; family rooms also are available ($12/night for HI-AYH members, $15/night for nonmembers). Hostel accommodations are also available at the nearby HI-AYH **Kingston Hostel,** 613/531-8237, located on a Canadian island in the river; $18/night for members, $22 for nonmembers.

The boxy, brick **Roxy's Motel,** at Broadway and Market St., 315/654-2456, has operated continuously since 1894. Downstairs an old-fashioned restaurant and bar sport mounted fish and aging photographs of anglers with their catch; upstairs are 10 simple but adequate guest rooms ($50 d).

CLAYTON

One of the most interesting villages along the St. Lawrence, Clayton spreads along the riverfront, with lots of park benches ideal for watching the swift current slide by. The village contains four museums and the Thousand Islands Inn, where Thousand Islands salad dressing supposedly was invented. All along Riverside Drive stand sturdy brick storefronts, built in the late 1800s, while at the corner of Riverside Drive and Merrick Street reigns the **Simon Johnston House,** a clapboard Italianate home with a widow's walk and decorative eaves.

Settled in 1822, Clayton soon developed into a major shipbuilding center and steamboat port.

The St. Lawrence skiff, known for its sleekness and beauty, was first constructed here by Xavier Colon in 1868, and the 900-passenger *St. Lawrence,* the largest steamboat ever made, was built in the 1890s. During WW I, the Clayton shipyards produced submarine chasers and pontoon boats.

Tourists began frequenting Clayton in the late 1800s. Most came to fish and boat, and they stayed in huge wooden hotels—since burned down—along the waterfront. During Clayton's heyday, five express trains arrived here daily from New York City, and one hotel was equipped with a direct line to the New York Stock Exchange. Some vacationers even came during the winter, to ice-fish and watch the horse races run on the frozen St. Lawrence River.

Antique Boat Museum

Appropriately enough, Clayton has the finest collection of antique wooden boats in America. Among them are canoes, sailboats, launches, raceboats, runabouts, and, of course, the famed St. Lawrence skiff.

The gleaming boats, most built of highly polished woods and brass, are housed in a former lumberyard on the edge of town. There are over 150 vessels in all, spread out over eight buildings, along with a boatbuilding shop, almost 300

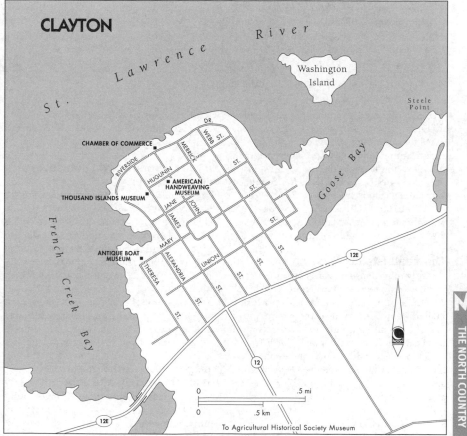

CLAYTON

St. Lawrence River

Washington Island

Steele Point

Goose Bay

French Creek Bay

CHAMBER OF COMMERCE

WEBB ST.
DR.
MERRICK
RIVERSIDE
HUGUNIN
AMERICAN HANDWEAVING MUSEUM
THOUSAND ISLANDS MUSEUM
JANE
JOHN
JAMES
MARY
ST.
ST.
ST.
ANTIQUE BOAT MUSEUM
ALEXANDRIA
THERESA
UNION
ST.
ST.
ST.
ST.
ST.
12E

MOON

12

0   .5 mi

0   .5 km

12E

To Agricultural Historical Society Museum

THE NORTH COUNTRY

The village of Clayton is surrounded by water on three sides.

COURTESY OF 1000 ISLANDS INTERNATIONAL TOURISM COUNCIL

inboard and outboard motors, and 12,000 nautical artifacts. The museum also contains extensive historical exhibits, including one on Clayton's rum-running days. During Prohibition, men smuggled liquor across the river from Canada on sleds, skates, and small boats honeycombed with hidden compartments.

The museum, 750 Mary St., 315/686-4104, www.abm.org, is open May–Oct., daily 9 A.M.–5 P.M. Admission is adults $6, children 5–17 $2.

Thousand Islands Museum

Recently moved into new digs on James Street is this eclectic museum devoted to local history. Among the exhibits here is the "Muskie Hall of Fame," devoted to the region's most prized fish, and an enormous collection of hand-carved decoys, a popular North Country folk art. According to the exhibit, one riverman claims to have carved over 1,000 decoys, another about 5,000. Also on site are re-created turn-of-the-century storefronts, including a general store, millinery shop, law office, and old country kitchen.

The museum, 312 James St., 315/686-5794, www.thousandislands.com/museum, is open May–Oct., daily 10 A.M.–4 P.M. Call for new admission prices.

American Handweaving Museum and Arts Center

Hand-woven North American textiles are the specialty of this small and low-key museum. Exhibits range from 18th-century lace collars and handkerchiefs to modern shawls and scarves. Adjoining the museum are classrooms where workshops are offered and a gift shop. Visitors are welcome to enroll in the workshops if space is available.

The museum, 314 John St., 315/686-4123, is open year round Mon.–Fri. 9 A.M.–4 P.M., and summer Sat.–Sun. 9 A.M.–4 P.M. Admission is by donation.

Northern New York Agricultural Historical Society Museum

On a quiet country lane about 12 miles southeast of Clayton sprawls an eight-building museum complex designed to "tell the story of agriculture in northern New York State." Spread out over 38 acres, the museum includes a 19th-century meetinghouse, farm kitchen, carriage house, ice house, one-room schoolhouse, lye store, and cheese factory where Yankee cheddar cheese was produced during the 1920s. Children will enjoy the many crafts demonstrations by guides in period dress.

The museum, Rte. 180, Stone Mills, 315/658-2353, is open June–Labor Day, daily 11 A.M.–4 P.M. Admission is adults $3, children free. To reach the museum from Clayton, take Route 12 south to Route 180 north.

Recreation
Uncle Sam Boat Tours, 604 Riverside Dr., 315/686-3511, offers three-hour cruises around Wesleyan Island (adults $15, children 6–12 $7.50), and also operates to Boldt's Castle out of Alexandria Bay (see Alexandria Bay, below).

Houseboat Rentals
Vacationing onboard houseboats is a popular activity in the Thousand Islands, and numerous houseboat rental companies once lined the St. Lawrence. Many still exist on the Canadian side, but insurance costs have forced most U.S. companies to close. The one exception is **Remar Houseboat Rental,** 510 Theresa St., 315/686-3579. No experience is necessary, and instruction is provided. Reservations should be made well in advance.

Camping and Accommodations
Campsites are available at 174-site **Cedar Point State Park,** Rte. 12 E, and at three island campgrounds accessible only by boat. For information, call 315/654-2522; for reservations, call 800/456-CAMP. A basic site costs $14.

Area motels include the 28-room **Bertrand's,** 229 James St., 315/686-3641 ($69 d); and the eight-room **Calumet Motel,** 617 Union St., 315/686-5201 ($50–60 d).

The 1897 **Thousand Islands Inn,** 355 Riverside Dr., 315/686-3030 or 800/544-4241, is the last of the great old hotels that once lined Clayton. Significantly smaller than it was in its heyday, it offers 14 modernized guest rooms, some overlooking the river ($69–100 d; packages available). Downstairs is a restaurant (see below).

Food
The **Harbor Inn,** 625 Mary St., 315/686-2293, serves a tasty diner-style breakfast (including homemade donuts) and lunch; in the evening, it becomes more formal, offering lots of seafood and scallop dishes; average dinner entrée $13. The **Koffee Kove,** 220 James St., 315/686-2472 is known for its chili and homemade breads.

Though the food at the **Riverside Cafe,** 506 Riverside Dr., 315/686-2940, is nothing special, it's one of the few restaurants in town that overlooks the water. On the menu is standard American and Italian fare; average entrée $12. **O'Brien's,** 226 Webb St., 315/686-3314, housed in a former gin mill, serves a wide variety of dishes ranging from pastas and chicken to steak and prime rib. Live bands often perform on the weekends; average entrée $14.

In the **Thousands Islands Inn,** 355 Riverside Dr., 315/686-3030, you'll find a comfortable, old-fashioned restaurant serving everything from fresh fish to pasta; average entrée $13. For sale are bottles of "Original Thousand Islands Salad Dressing," supposedly first created here in the early 1900s by one Sophia LaLonde.

Entertainment and Events
One of the region's most popular events is the resplendent **Antique Boat Show,** held every August for over 30 years. It is sponsored by the Antique Boat Museum, 315/686-4104.

Summer stock is presented at the **Clayton Opera House** July–August. **Free outdoor concerts** take place in Frink Park at the waterfront throughout the summer. The popular **Decoy and Wildlife Art Show,** attracting over 200 exhibitors, is held in the Clayton Arena in mid-July. For any of these events, call 315/686-3771.

Visitor Information
General information and free walking tours are available at the **Clayton Chamber of Commerce,** 510 Riverside Dr., Clayton, NY 13624, 315/686-3771 or 800/252-9806, www.1000islands-clayton.com. Hours are July–Sept., daily 9 A.M.–5 P.M.; Oct.–June, Mon.–Fri. 9 A.M.–4 P.M.

THE NORTH COUNTRY

THE PECULIAR STORIES OF THE THOUSAND ISLANDS

The 1,874 islands of the Thousand Islands laze in the deep blue St. Lawrence River like a "drunken doodle made by an addled cartographer," as one observer once said. Each and every one tells a story.

The largest of the islands is Wolfe Island. The smallest is Tom Thumb. The only artificial island, Longue View Island, was formed by filling in the area between two shoals. As the story goes, Longue View was created by a doting husband who wanted to build a summer home for his wife. When he couldn't find a single island that suited her, he had one built, and then added a luxurious mansion atop it. His wife then ran off with another man.

Devil's Oven on Devil's Island was the 1838 refuge of Canadian patriot Bill Johnston. After an abortive attempt to wrest Canada from the British empire, Johnston hid out in the cave for nearly a year before surrendering to the authorities. He was later pardoned and appointed a lighthouse keeper.

The Price is Right Island was given away in 1964 by Bill Cullen on *The Price is Right* TV game show. Deer Island is owned by the Skull and Bones Society of Yale University. Abbie Hoffman lived incognito—under the name Barry Freed—on Wellesley Island after jumping bail in 1974 on cocaine charges.

Florence Island, Arthur Godfrey's isle, was given to him as a gift by the 1000 Island Bridge Authority in return for free advertising. Godfrey sang the song "Florence on the St. Lawrence."

Grindstone Island was the site of the last existing one-room schoolhouse in New York State, in use up until 1989. Ash Island has its own private railroad line running from the boathouse to the main house on the cliff.

George Pullman of Pullman Car fame once owned Pullman Island and played frequent host to Pres. Ulysses S. Grant. Calumet Island was once the property of Charles Emery, president of the American Tobacco Company. Picton Island was owned by M. Heineman, originator of Buster Brown Shoes, and Oppawaka Island by J. H. Heinz of Heinz 57 fame.

ALEXANDRIA BAY

About 10 miles northeast of Clayton is Alexandria Bay, a busy tourist village that could be called the Lake George of the North. Here you'll find all sorts of '50s-era attractions, including miniature golf courses, junior speedways, kitschy souvenir shops, and mom-and-pop motels.

But for all its summertime hustle and bustle, Alexandria Bay has a permanent population of just 1,355 and a laid-back, downhome charm. The village centers around a snug waterfront, where a few narrow streets are crowded with tiny shops and restaurants. Teenagers strut their stuff in front of an amusement arcade, while twentysomethings exchange glances outside a boisterous bar. A white-haired woman wearing a pink apron, saddle shoes, and green socks sits on her stoop, watching the foot traffic go by.

Like Clayton, Alexandria Bay was a popular tourist resort and steamboat stop throughout the late 1800s and early 1900s. Millionaires built second homes on the islands across from the village, while hotels went up along the shore.

Evidence of those days can be found at the **Cornwall Brothers' Store,** foot of Market St., 315/482-4586. Originally owned by the town's founder, Azariah Walton, the building is now part museum, part re-created general store. Up front choose from a nice selection of penny candy, vintage postcards, handicrafts, and books; in back are historic photographs and artifacts.

From both ends of the village extend weathered piers at which excursion boats dock. Alexandria Bay is the main port for touring the Thousand Islands.

Boldt Castle

Looming over Heart Island, across from Alexandria Bay, is a gloomy, 127-room replica of a Rhineland castle. The castle was built by George Boldt, who came to the United States from Prussia in the 1860s. The son of poor parents, Boldt had tremendous industry and skill, and eventually became the most successful hotel magnate in the country. Both the Waldorf-Astoria in New York City and the Bellevue-Stratford in Philadelphia were his.

Boldt was deeply in love with his wife, Louise, and built the castle around the turn of the century as a symbol of his love for her. The castle was to be their summer home, and he employed the finest craftspeople, instructing them to embellish the building with hearts wherever they could. Boldt even had the island reshaped into the form of a heart.

Then in 1904, when the castle was 80 percent complete, Louise passed away. Boldt sent a telegram to the construction crew to stop work immediately, and never set foot on the island again. The castle was abandoned and allowed to deteriorate.

Finally, in 1977, the Thousand Islands Bridge Authority bought Boldt Castle, partially rehabilitated it, and introduced it to the tourist trade. Today, hundreds of visitors traipse through it daily, but all the activity in the world can't erase the castle's haunted and wildly romantic feel. All around are broken moldings, half-finished walls, and cold, echoing hallways.

In the former ballroom, exhibits explain the castle's history.

A free shuttle boat operates from the castle to the **Boldt Yacht House,** perched on a separate island nearby. Open to the public, the yacht house—completed before Louise's death—contains three original spit-and-polish boats and restored living quarters furnished with handsome antiques.

The castle, 315/482-2501 or 800/8-ISLAND, www.boldtcastle.com, is open mid-May through mid-October, daily 10 A.M.–6 P.M., with extended mid-summer hours. Admission is adults $4.75, children 6–12 $3, plus the cost of the boat ride over.

Excursion Boats

The only way to reach Boldt Island, as well as the other 1,800-plus islands in the St. Lawrence River, is by boat. And several boat companies offer tours.

Largest among them is **Uncle Sam's Boat Tours,** 315/482-2611 or 800/ALEXBAY, whose

aerial view of Boldt Castle, Heart Island

THE NORTH COUNTRY

huge replica paddleboats dock at the eastern end of James Street. Uncle Sam's features an hourly shuttle service to Boldt Castle that allows visitors to stay as long as they like, as well as various sightseeing and dining cruises. The shuttle costs adults $6.75, children 4–12 $4.25.

Empire Boat Tours, 4 Church St., 315/482-TOUR or 888/449-ALEX, also travel to Boldt Island, and offer various sightseeing and dining cruises. Boldt Island tickets cost adults $6, children $3.

If you'd prefer to rent your own motorboat or pontoon boat, stop into **O'Briens U-Drive,** 51 Walton St., 315/482-9548. Rentals are available by the hour, day, or week, and river maps and trip-planning advice are provided.

Wellesley Island State Park

To reach Wellesley Island and Wellesley Island State Park, you must travel over the **Thousand Islands International Bridge,** a slim suspension expanse that seems to lead straight up into the sky. Built in 1938, the bridge extends over five spans and stretches seven miles.

At the end of the first span lies the 2,636-acre state park, featuring hiking trails, swimming beaches, a campground, nine-hole golf course, playground, and great views of the river. Covering 600 acres of the park is the **Minna Anthony Common Nature Center,** which includes both a museum and a wildlife sanctuary laced with trails. In the museum are live fish and reptiles, mounted birds, and an observation beehive.

The park, 315/482-2722, can be reached by taking Exit 51 off I-81. The park is open year-round, and during the summer there's a $6 vehicle use fee. The nature center, 44927 Cross Island Rd., 315/482-2479, is open daily 8 A.M.–4:30 P.M., with extended hours in summer. Admission is free.

Thousand Islands Park

South of the state park, at the very tip of Wellesley Island, lies Thousand Islands Park, a quiet community filled with hundreds of wooden Victorian homes painted in luscious ice-cream pastels. Ornate carvings, shingled roofs, porches, turrets, and gables abound.

At one time, Thousand Islands Park was a private club that commanded an initiation fee of $100,000 and an annual fee of $10,000. Now on the National Register of Historic Places, the park is still largely privately owned but visitors are welcome. The community features its own movie theater, post office, library, and playground.

On the way to and from Thousand Islands Park, you'll pass by the smaller, scruffier community of **Fineview,** once home to a man who went by the name Barry Freed. During the late 1970s, Freed began a still-active—and quite effective—environmental organization called Save the River. Then in 1980, locals were astounded to discover that Barry Freed was actually activist Abbie Hoffman, on the lam from the FBI since 1974. Hoffman arranged a deal with the authorities and moved back into the national arena, only to commit suicide in 1989.

Camping and Accommodations

Campsites are available at the 80-site **Grass Point State Park,** Rte. 12 E, 315/686-4472; and the 429-site **Wellesley Island State Park,** Wellesley Island, 315/482-2722. For reservations, call 800/456-CAMP; basic sites cost $13–19, and cottages are also available.

Inexpensive area motels include the **Fitz-Inn Motel,** Box 381, Rte. 26, 315/482-2641 ($50–60 d); and the **Rock Lodge Motel,** Box 41, Rte. 12, 315/482-2191 ($50–80 d). **Capt. Thomson's,** 1 James St., next door to bustling Uncle Sam's Boat Tours, 315/482-9961 or 800/253-9229 (in NYS), www.capthomson.com, contains 68 standard rooms, some equipped with balconies overlooking the river ($90–170 d).

Featuring views of the river and Boldt Castle is the luxurious **Riveredge Resort Hotel,** 17 Holland St., 315/482-9917 or 800/ENJOY-US, www.riveredge.com. On-site are a health spa, indoor and outdoor pools, and two restaurants ($130–228 d).

The sleek **Bonnie Castle,** Box 219, Holland St., 315/482-4511 or 800/955-4511, www.bonniecastle.com, is the region's most extensive resort, equipped with 128 deluxe rooms and suites, a conference and entertainment complex, private beach and airport, swimming pools, tennis courts, nightclub, miniature golf courses, and restaurants ($120–185 d).

Food

Numerous casual restaurants stand along James and Market Streets downtown. Among them is the lively **Dockside Pub**, 17 Market St., 315/482-9849, serving sandwiches, soups, and pizza in a setting near the water; average main dish $8.

The historic **Admiral's Inn**, 20 James St., 315/482-2781, features a comfortable bar to one side, several cheery dining rooms to the other. Sandwiches and salads are offered at lunch, while dinner entrées include prime rib and fresh seafood; average entrée $14.

Overlooking the river at Fishers Landing, halfway between Alexandria Bay and Clayton, is **Foxy's Restaurant,** on the dock, 315/686-3781, a friendly, family-run Italian restaurant; average entrée $15.

Visitor Information

The **Alexandria Bay Chamber of Commerce,** 7 Market St., 315/482-9531 or 800/541-2110, www.alexbay.org, is open daily 9 A.M.–5 P.M., with extended hours in summer.

OGDENSBURG

The oldest settlement in northern New York, established in 1749, Ogdensburg is a busy port and industrial town at the juncture of the Oswegatchie and St. Lawrence Rivers. Along the St. Lawrence downtown runs the **Greenbelt Riverfront Park,** Riverside Dr., dotted with historical plaques that detail the War of 1812 Battle of Ogdensburg. A few blocks south of the park is the town's foremost visitor attraction—the Frederic Remington Art Museum.

Frederic Remington Art Museum

Artist Frederic Remington (1861–1909), best known for his paintings and bronzes of the American West, was born in the northernmost reaches of New York State. In his youth he made a total of 18 trips out West, collecting information and taking photographs that he would later use in his studio in New Rochelle, NY, to create his masterpieces. Remington never lived in Ogdensburg, but was born and is buried in nearby Canton. His wife moved to Ogdensburg after his death.

Housed in an imposing 1810 mansion, the Remington Art Museum contains the largest single Remington collection in the United States. On display are scores of oil paintings, watercolors, drawings, illustrations, and bronzes, including many small and relatively unknown gems. One room is filled with watercolors depicting the Adirondacks, another with a reproduction of Remington's studio. The most valuable Remingtons are kept in a locked gallery that is only open during guided tours, scheduled regularly throughout the day.

The museum, 303 Washington St., at State, 315/393-2425, www.remington-museum.org, is open May–Oct., Mon.–Sat. 10 A.M.–5 P.M., Sunday 1–5 P.M.; Nov.–April, Tues.–Sat. 11 A.M.–5 P.M. Admission is adults $6, students and seniors $4, children under 5 free.

CANTON

About 20 miles east of Ogdensburg lies Canton, Remington's birthplace. Settled by Vermonters in the early 1800s, Canton today is a busy small town (pop. 11,120), best known as the home of St. Lawrence University.

Traditional Arts in Upstate New York

Detour to Canton for the small but unusual Traditional Arts gallery, which focuses on the folk arts of the North Country. Exhibits in the past have highlighted such subjects as St. Lawrence River fishing arts, Mohawk tourist arts, quilts and quilting bees, and Old Order Amish crafts. Thoughtfully laid out displays offer plenty of background information and photographs.

The gallery is also a good place to find out about folk arts events. Storytelling still thrives in the North Country, and there are occasional traditional music concerts and dance fests. One of the region's biggest traditional celebrations is the Festival of North Country Folklife, held in nearby Massena.

The gallery, 2 W. Main St., 315/386-4289, is

open Tues.–Sat., 10 A.M.–4 P.M., or by appointment; closed Saturday in summer. Admission is by donation.

Silas Wright Museum

Now run by the St. Lawrence County Historical Association, this columned Greek Revival mansion once belonged to U.S. senator and New York governor Silas Wright. Regarded as an honest and intelligent man, Wright was so respected by his neighbors that he won his first election to the state senate in 1823 by 199 votes to one; legend has it that he himself cast the one dissenting vote. The first floor of the house has been restored to its 1830–50 period appearance, while upstairs are local history exhibits. St. Lawrence County is one of the largest and least populated counties east of the Mississippi.

The museum, 3 E. Main St., 315/386-8133, is open Tues.–Sat. noon–5 P.M. Admission is free.

MASSENA

The main reason to make a stop in the small industrial city of Massena is to get a good look at the giant **St. Lawrence Seaway,** which connects the Atlantic Ocean with the Great Lakes. The joint project of the United States and Canada, the Seaway can accommodate ships up to 730 feet long and 76 feet wide. The public works project was formally dedicated on June 26, 1959 by Queen Elizabeth II and Pres. Eisenhower.

Dwight D. Eisenhower Lock

Atop the long, spare Eisenhower Lock is a viewing deck from which you can watch ships being raised or lowered 42 feet as they pass through the Seaway. The process takes about 10 minutes and displaces 22 million gallons of water. Ships pass through regularly, except in the winter when the St. Lawrence freezes over, but the viewing deck is only open Memorial Day–Labor Day. Below the lock a small interpretive center, 315/769-2049, offers exhibits and a short film.

The lock is located on Barnhart Island Road, off Route 37.

Robert Moses State Park and Campground

Adjoining the Power Project, Robert Moses State Park, 315/769-8663, includes a swimming beach, bathhouse, boat rentals, picnic tables, playground, and great views of the river. The park also offers a 168-site campground; for reservations, call 800/456-CAMP. A basic site costs $13.

Events

The **Festival of North Country Folklife,** 315/769-3525, takes place every August in Robert Moses State Park. Featured are traditional music concerts, dancing, and storytelling, along with crafts and ethnic foods.

AKWESASNE

At the confluence of the St. Regis and St. Lawrence Rivers lies the St. Regis Indian Reservation, or *Akwesasne,* Where the Ruffed Grouse Drums. You'll see signs along Route 37: This Is Indian Land; Private Property; No FBI, IRS, Or Other Agencies. Gas stations selling tax-free gasoline, and mock tepees selling souvenirs strew the roadsides.

Akwesasne is home to about 6,000 Mohawk. The reservation straddles the St. Lawrence Seaway and the United States/Canadian border, and includes several islands.

In Hogansburg, about 10 miles east of Massena, is the large and well laid out **Akwesasne Museum,** housed in a big brown building that's also home to the Akwesasne Cultural Center and Library. The museum covers an entire floor and contains an outstanding collection of medicine masks, wampum belts, lacrosse sticks, carved cradle boards, water drums, Bibles written in the Mohawk language, beadwork, quillwork, modern artwork, historical photographs, and basketry.

Especially striking are the photograph and basket exhibits. The photographs date back to the 1920s and depict a prosperous, pre-Depression Mohawk community bustling with shiny cars, sturdy baby prams, women in white dresses, and men in hats. The basket exhibit contains everything from a wedding basket, which looks just like a cake, to a thimble basket.

The museum, Rte. 37, 518/358-2240 or 518/358-2461, is open year-round Mon.–Fri. 8:30 A.M.–4:30 P.M., and Saturday from fall to spring 11 A.M.–3 P.M. Suggested donation is adults $2, children 5–16 $1.

On Route 37 to the east of the museum is the **Akwesasne Mohawk Casino,** 518/358-2222, opened in spring 1999. The second licensed casino in New York State (the first is on Oneida land near Verona in central New York), the casino offers blackjack, craps, and roulette tables, and 1,100 video lottery terminals.

The Finger Lakes

Introduction

According to Iroquois legend, the Finger Lakes were created when the Great Spirit reached out to bless the land and left imprints of his hands behind. Six of his fingers became the major Finger Lakes—Skaneateles, Owasco, Cayuga, Seneca, Keuka, and Canandaigua. The other four became the Little Finger Lakes—Honeoye, Canadice, Hemlock, and Conesus.

Geologists tell it differently. They say the long, skinny parallel lakes formed from the steady progressive grinding of at least two Ice Age glaciers. As the glaciers receded, the lake-valleys filled with rivers that were backed by dams of glacial debris.

The Finger Lakes are a singular place. Depending on the weather, the water varies in hue from a deep sapphire blue to a moody gray,

while all around lie fertile farmlands heavy with fruit trees, buckwheat, and—especially—vineyards. You could spend a week here touring nothing but vineyards and still not see them all.

Along the lakes' southern edges, deep craggy gorges are sliced through the middle by silvery waterfalls. To the north, in the flat plain region south of Lake Ontario, preside hundreds of drumlins, gentle glacier-created hills.

But scenic beauty tells only half of the Finger Lakes story. Despite its somnolent air, the region has an important industrial, civil rights, and religious history. In Auburn stand the homes of abolitionists Harriet Tubman and William Seward; Seneca Falls hosted the first Women's Rights Convention; Rochester was once home to Frederick Douglass and Susan

Ontario Beach Park

B. Anthony; and in Palmyra is the Sacred Grove where Joseph Smith, founder of the Mormon religion, is said to have first seen the Angel Moroni. Equally surprising are the many seemingly off-the-beaten-track towns and villages filled with grand Italianate, Greek Revival, and Romanesque mansions—all financed by early industrial wealth.

HISTORY
The People of the Longhouse
When French explorers first arrived in the Finger Lakes area in the early 1600s, they found it occupied by a confederacy of five Indian nations. The French called the Indians "Iroquois"; the Indians called themselves "Haudenosaunee," or "People of the Longhouse."

The Mohawk Nation (Keepers of the Eastern Door) lived to the east of what is considered the Finger Lakes region, along Schoharie Creek and the Mohawk River Valley. The Seneca (Keepers of the Western Door) lived to the west, along the Genesee River. In the middle were the Onondaga (Keepers of the Council Fire), and it was on their territory the chiefs of the Five Nations met to establish policy and settle disputes. The two other "little brother" nations were the Cayuga, who resided between the Onondaga and the Seneca, and the Oneida, who lived between the Onondaga and the Mohawk. A sixth nation, the Tuscarora, joined the Iroquois confederacy in 1722.

During the Revolutionary War, all of the Iroquois except the Oneida sided with the British, as they had during the French and Indian War. Together with the Tories, they terrorized the pioneer villages and threatened the food supply of the Continental Army. In 1779, an angered General Washington sent Maj. Gen. John Sullivan into the region, ordering him to "lay waste all the settlements around so that the country may not only be overrun but destroyed." Sullivan punctiliously carried out his orders, annihilating 41 Iroquois settlements and burning countless fields and orchards. By the time he was done, the Iroquois nation was in ruins. Thousands fled to Canada; others were resettled onto reservations in 1784.

The Military Tract
After the Revolution, many of Sullivan's soldiers, impressed by the rich farmland, returned to the Finger Lakes, where they were given land in the "Military Tract" in lieu of payment. The tract, stretching roughly from Chittenango west to Geneva and from Ithaca north to Lake Ontario, covered some two million acres or one-sixteenth of present-day New York. The tract was divided into townships named by a surveyor with a love of the classics, hence the many Greek and Latin names remaining today: Ithaca, Ovid, Cato, Fabius, Manlius, Cicero, Dryden, Ulysses, Hector . . .

The region developed rapidly. Other settlers from New England and Pennsylvania arrived by the thousands, and by the early 1800s the woodlands of the Iroquois had become a busy agricultural region. Many communities sprang up on the sites of old Iroquois villages; many highways followed old Indian trails.

Prosperity and Reform
By 1825 the Erie Canal was completed, and the development of the Finger Lakes skyrocketed. Inland ports grew up all along the canal, and for 20 years, the area's rich farmland served as the breadbasket of the nation. When the Midwest took over that role, the Finger Lakes' farmers focused on fruit and dairy farming, shipping many of their goods east to New York City.

At the same time, the ports developed into major industrial centers. Extensive water power helped fuel the Industrial Revolution, and by the mid-1800s, factories manufacturing everything from pumps and woolens to glass and agricultural tools flourished throughout the Finger Lakes. Syracuse, Auburn, Seneca Falls, Elmira, and Rochester were among the largest manufacturing centers; smaller ones included Corning, Oswego, and Montour Falls.

Along with increasing prosperity came increasing social unrest. Upstate New York in the late 1820s, '30s, and '40s was rocked by one fiery religious movement after another. Sects and cults sprang up all over the region until it became known as the "burned-over district." Among the best-known movements were the Perfectionists, led by John Humphrey Noyes in

THE FINGER LAKES

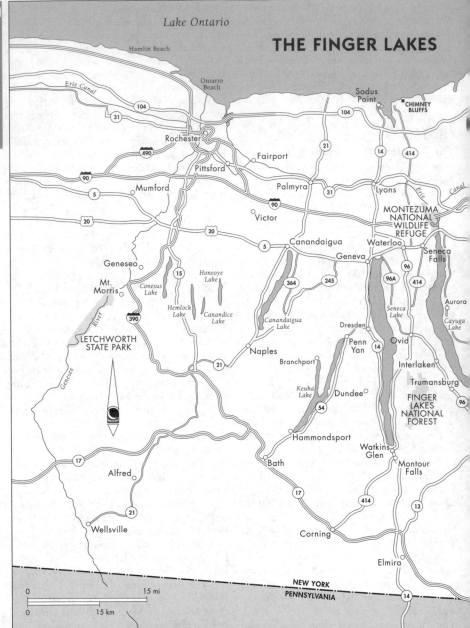

Lake Ontario

THE FINGER LAKES

Hamlin Beach

Ontario Beach

Erie Canal

104

31

104

Sodus Point

■ CHIMNEY BLUFFS

Rochester

490

21

14

414

Fairport

Pittsford

90

5

Mumford

Palmyra

31

Lyons

Erie Canal

20

90

Victor

MONTEZUMA NATIONAL WILDLIFE REFUGE

20

5

Canandaigua

Waterloo

Geneva

Seneca Falls

Geneseo

15

Honeoye Lake

364

245

96A

96

414

Mt. Morris

Conesus Lake

390

Hemlock Lake

Canandice Lake

Canandaigua Lake

Seneca Lake

Aurora

Cayuga Lake

Dresden

Penn Yan

14

Ovid

River

LETCHWORTH STATE PARK

Naples

21

Branchport

Interlaken

Trumansburg

96

Genesee

Keuka Lake

Dundee

FINGER LAKES NATIONAL FOREST

54

Hammondsport

Watkins Glen

17

Bath

Montour Falls

Alfred

17

414

13

21

Corning

Wellsville

Elmira

| 0 | | 15 mi |
| 0 | | 15 km |

NEW YORK

PENNSYLVANIA

14

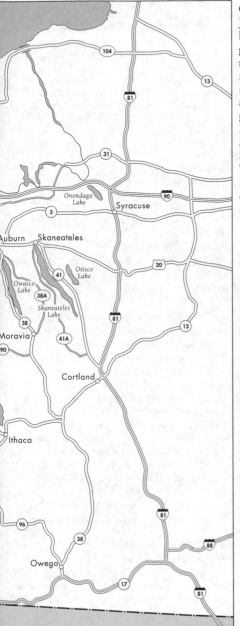

THE FINGER LAKES

Oneida to the east; the Mormons, founded by Joseph Smith in Palmyra; and the Spiritualists, led by the Fox sisters near Rochester. The religious fervor not only converted tens of thousands of citizens but also stimulated reform movements. Upstate became a hotbed for humanitarian causes, most notably the abolitionist and women's rights movements. Frederick Douglass and Susan B. Anthony worked in Rochester, Elizabeth Cady Stanton in Seneca Falls, Gerrit Smith in Peterboro and Skaneateles, and William Seward and later Harriet Tubman in Auburn. The first Women's Rights Convention convened in Seneca Falls in 1848, and one of the most dramatic rescues of a fugitive slave took place in Syracuse in 1851.

Modern Times

By the early 1900s, the dust settled. The Erie Canal declined in importance, thanks largely to the advent of the railroad; newer and larger factories opened up elsewhere, and the religious and reform movements lost fervor. The region's major cities remained important commercial centers, to be sure, but the rest of the land eased back into the sleepy agricultural state it is today.

PRACTICALITIES

Fishing

The Finger Lakes are known for great fishing. Lake trout, brown trout, small-mouth bass, large-mouth bass, and pickerel are especially prevalent. For more information, contact Finger Lakes Tourism (below) or any regional tourist office.

Transportation

The **Syracuse Hancock International Airport** and the **Greater Rochester International Airport** are serviced by Jet Blue, 800/JET-BLUE; American Airlines, 800/433-7300; Continental, 800/525-0280; Delta, 800/221-1212; United, 800/241-6522; and USAirways, 800/428-4322. USAirways also services the **Tompkins County Airport** (Ithaca) and the **Elmira-Corning Regional Airport.** A taxi ride from any of these airports to their respective downtowns costs $12–18.

FINGER LAKES HIGHLIGHTS

Syracuse and Environs
Erie Canal Museum and Heritage Area Visitor Center
Everson Museum of Art
Ste. Marie Among the Iroquois
Hotel Syracuse
Dinosaur Bar-B-Cue blues club
Skaneateles Lake Area
Sherwood Inn, Skaneateles
Cortland Country Museum Park, Cortland

Owasco Lake Area
Seward House, Auburn
Harriet Tubman Home, Auburn
Willard Memorial Chapel, Auburn
Fillmore Glen State Park, Moravia

Cayuga Lake Area
Heritage Area Visitor Center, Seneca Falls
Women's Rights National Historic Park, Seneca Falls

Elizabeth Cady Stanton House, Seneca Falls
Montezuma National Wildlife Refuge, Seneca Falls
Aurora village
Knapp Winery Restaurant, Romulus
Taughannock Falls State Park, Trumansburg
Taughannock Farms Inn, Trumansburg
Rongovian Embassy to the U.S.A. music club, Trumansburg

Ithaca
Ithaca Commons
Herbert Johnson Museum of Art, Cornell University
Greater Ithaca Art Trail
Cornell Lab of Ornithology and Sapsucker Woods
Buttermilk Falls State Park
Robert H. Treman State Park
Boating on Cayuga Lake
Moosewood restaurant

Amtrak, 800/872-7245, travels to Syracuse and Rochester. **Greyhound,** 800/231-2222; and **New York State Trailways,** 800/295-5555, provide bus service to various cities and towns throughout the region.

However, by far the best way to explore the Finger Lakes is by car.

Emergencies
Dial 911 for emergencies throughout the region. Hospitals include the **State University of New York Health Science Center,** 750 E. Adams St., Syracuse, 315/464-5540; the **Cayuga Medical Center,** 101 Dates Dr., Ithaca, 607/274-4011 or 607/274-4411 (emergency room); the **Arnot Ogden Medical Center,** 600 Roe Ave., Elmira, 607/737-4100 or 607/737-4194 (emergency room); and **Strong Memorial Hospital,** 601 Elmwood Ave., Rochester, 716/275-2100.

Accommodations and Food
The Finger Lakes feature a wide variety of restaurants and accommodations. Gourmet dining establishments can be found in all of the big cities, as well as some of the smaller towns, while simple

diners and family-style restaurants abound. Similarly, lodging options range from well-kept campgrounds and inexpensive motels to posh inns and B&Bs. Hotels operate only in the largest cities. Be aware, some businesses close during the winter.

In addition to the B&B registries listed in this book's On The Road chapter, several other registries also operate in the region. Among them are the **Finger Lakes B&B Association,** 315/536-1238 or 800/695-5590, www.flbba.org; the **B&B Network of Central New York** 315/498-6560 or 800/333-1604, www.cnylodging.com; the **B&B Association of Greater Ithaca,** 607/589-6073 or 800/806-4406, www.bbithaca.com; and the **Greater Rochester Area B&B,** 716/271-7872 or 800/724-6298, www.dartmouthhouse.com.

Visitor Information
Finger Lakes Tourism, 309 Lake St., Penn Yan, NY 14527, 315/536-7488 or 800/548-4386, www.fingerlakes.org, is a good central information source. Hours are year-round, Mon.–Fri. 8 A.M.–4:30 P.M. Most counties, cities, and towns also have their own specific visitor information centers; addresses follow in each section.

THE FINGER LAKES

Seneca Lake
Rose Hill Mansion, Geneva
Belhurst Castle restaurant and inn, Geneva
Chimney Bluffs, Sodus Point
Lodi Point State Marine Park, Lodi
Vineyards, near Lodi and Dundee
Finger Lakes National Forest, Hector
Watkins Glen State Park, Watkins Glen
Mark Twain's Study, Elmira
Harris Hill Soaring Center, Elmira
Corning Museum of Glass, Corning
Rockwell Museum, Corning

The Western Finger Lakes
Vineyards, Hammondsport
Glenn H. Curtiss Museum, Hammondsport
Caboose Motel, Avoca
Mennonite shops, in and near Penn Yan

Sonnenberg Gardens, Canandaigua
Ganondagan State Historic Site, Victor
Hill Cumorah Visitor Center and Pageant, Palmyra
Scenic Route 21 between Canandaigua and Naples
Grape pie, Naples
Letchworth Gorge and State Park

Rochester
Brown's Race and the Center at High Falls
Strong Museum
George Eastman House and International Museum
    of Photography
Monroe Avenue
Highland Park and Mount Hope Cemetery
Susan B. Anthony House
Ontario Beach Park and Seabreeze Amusement Park
Richardson's Canal House restaurant
Genesee Country Museum, Mumford

Syracuse

The main streets of Syracuse are oddly wide and flat, like fat gray rubber bands stretched out to their sides. It begs the question: who would lay out a city with so much empty space? The answer is simple. One street was once the Erie Canal (Erie Boulevard), another the Genesee Valley Turnpike (Genesee Street).

Like many towns in central New York, Syracuse boomed when the Erie Canal opened. But long before the canal, settlers were attracted to the area by its many salt springs—discovered first by the Onondaga Indians and later by French Father Simone LeMoyne in 1654. As early as 1797, the state took over the salt fields to obtain tax revenues on salt, then so valuable it was referred to as "white gold."

With the opening of the Erie Canal, the salt industry developed rapidly, reaching a high point of eight million bushels a year during the Civil War. Other Syracuse industries as well, including foundries, machine shops, and fac-

tories manufacturing agricultural tools, furniture, hardware, and candles. The Irish, who had arrived to dig the canal, remained to work the factories and were soon joined by large numbers of German immigrants.

After the Civil War, the salt industry declined, and other industries took over. Syracuse became known for its typewriters, ceramics, and Franklin cars, equipped with air-cooled engines. The Irish and Germans were joined by Italians, Poles, Russians, Ukrainians, and African Americans.

Today, Syracuse still supports a wide variety of peoples and industries, including the Niagara Mohawk Power Corporation, Bristol-Myers Squibb, and Syracuse University—perhaps best known for its 50,000-seat Carrier Dome arena, the only domed stadium on a college campus in the country. As the fourth largest city in the state (pop. about 165,000), Syracuse also has its share of serious urban ills, including a high

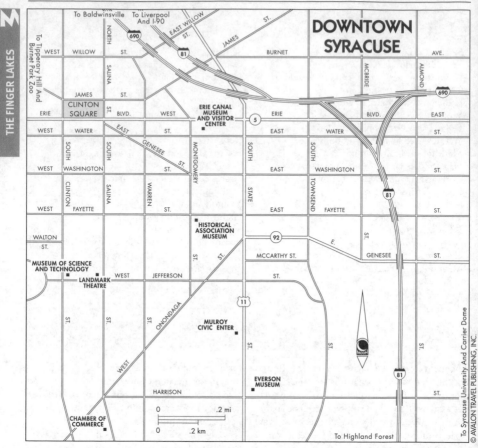

DOWNTOWN SYRACUSE

To Baldwinsville   To Liverpool And I-90

To Tipperary Hill And Burnet Park Zoo

WEST   WILLOW   ST.   NORTH   690   EAST WILLOW   ST.   JAMES   BURNET   ST.   AVE.   81   MCBRIDE   ALMOND   690

SALINA   ST.

ERIE   CLINTON SQUARE   BLVD.   WEST   ERIE CANAL MUSEUM AND VISITOR CENTER   5   ERIE   BLVD.   EAST   690

JAMES   ST.

WEST   WATER   EAST   ST.   EAST   WATER   ST.

GENESEE

WEST   WASHINGTON   SOUTH   SOUTH   ST.   MONTGOMERY   SOUTH   EAST   SOUTH   WASHINGTON   TOWNSEND   ST.

WEST   FAYETTE   CLINTON   SALINA   WARREN   ST.   STATE   EAST   FAYETTE   81   ST.

WALTON ST.   HISTORICAL ASSOCIATION MUSEUM   ST.   ST.   92   E.   ST.   GENESEE   ST.

MUSEUM OF SCIENCE AND TECHNOLOGY   MCCARTHY ST.

LANDMARK THEATRE   WEST   JEFFERSON   ST.

ST.   ST.   ST.   ONONDAGA   11

MULROY CIVIC ENTER   ST.   ST.   MOON   ST.   81

WEST   EVERSON MUSEUM   81

HARRISON   ST.

0   .2 mi
0   .2 km

CHAMBER OF COMMERCE

To Highland Forest

To Syracuse University And Carrier Dome

© AVALON TRAVEL PUBLISHING, INC.

THE FINGER LAKES

poverty and infant mortality rate, jammed court dockets, and a downtown struggling to stay alive.

Orientation

The heart of Syracuse is Clinton Square, where Erie Boulevard and Genesee Street meet. The main business district lies just south of the square and is dominated by Salina and Montgomery Streets. Syracuse University sits on a hill to the southeast, while to the northwest is Onondaga Lake. South of the city, the sovereign 7,300-acre Onondaga Reservation houses about 750 Native Americans. The Iroquois Confederacy's Grand Council of Chiefs still meets here every year, as it has for centuries.

I-90 runs east-west north of the downtown. I-81 runs north-south through the center of the city. The best way to explore Syracuse and environs is by car and foot; street parking is generally available. Sights downtown are within easy walking distance of each other.

Visitor Information

The **Syracuse Convention & Visitors Bureau,** 572 S. Salina St., at E. Adams St., Syracuse, NY 13202, 315/470-1910 or 800/234-4797, www .syracusecvb.org, is open Mon.–Fri., 8:30 A.M.– 5 P.M. Brochures and maps can also be picked up at the Heritage Area Visitor Center.

DOWNTOWN SIGHTS

Heritage Area Visitor Center and Erie Canal Museum

This long, low-slung 1850s building was once an Erie Canal weigh station for boats. Today, it's home to a visitor center, historical exhibits, a theater, a sculpture garden, and a 65-foot-long reconstructed canal boat. In the boat remain the original personal effects of some early passengers, including one heart-breaking letter from an Irishwoman who had just buried her husband at sea.

Syracuse is one of New York's Heritage Areas—loosely delineated historic districts linked by a common theme. The Syracuse theme is transportation, and business and capital. Free walking-tour brochures of relevant historic sites can be picked up in the visitor center at the Erie Canal Museum, 318 Erie Blvd., at Montgomery St., 315/471-0593, www.eriecanalmuseum.org. Hours are daily 10 A.M.–5 P.M. Admission is free.

West on Erie Boulevard

Heading west two blocks from the visitor center, you'll reach the heart of the city, **Clinton Square.** The former intersection of the Erie Canal and Genesee Valley Turnpike, in days past the square teemed with farmers' wagons, peddlers' carts, canal boats, excursion boats, hawkers, musicians, and organ grinders. Today, lots of free outdoor events are held here and in the winter, the square becomes a skating rink.

In the mid-1800s, Clinton Square evolved from a mere marketplace into a financial center. The four bank buildings along Salina Street—all on the National Register of Historic Places—hark back to those days. Note the four-sided, 100-foot clock tower on the 1867 Gridley Building (once the Onondaga Savings Bank); it was originally lit by gas jets.

At the western end of Clinton Square, near Clinton Street, stands the **Jerry Rescue Monument.** The monument commemorates William "Jerry" McHenry, born into slavery in North Carolina about 1812. Jerry successfully escaped to Syracuse, where he got a job in a cooper's shop making salt barrels. There he was discovered and arrested by federal marshals in 1851. A vigilante

Clinton Square was once the intersection of the Erie Canal and the Genesee Valley Turnpike.

abolitionist group headed by Gerrit Smith and Dr. Samuel J. May attacked the police station and rescued Jerry, who fled to Canada a few days later. Syracuse was subsequently denounced across the nation for its "lawless" citizenry.

One block further west on Erie Boulevard at Franklin Street reigns the stunning **Niagara Mohawk Power Corporation** building. Completed in 1932, the steel-and-black structure is a superb example of art deco architecture. The edifice is especially worth seeing at night, when lit by colored lights.

Museum of Automobile History

Three blocks north of Erie Boulevard is one of Syracuse's newer museums, the Museum of Automobile History, 321 N. Clinton St., at Herald Pl., 315/478-2277, www.autolit.com. On display are over 10,000 objects, including cars, motorcycles, trucks, antique license plates, horns, advertisements, and toys from the beginning of the automotive age on through the 1990s. Call for hours and admission fees.

Armory Square District

Head south on Franklin Street three blocks, and you'll find yourself in the Armory Square District, Syracuse's answer to Greenwich Village. At one end hulks the old Syracuse Armory, while all around are shops, cafes, and restaurants. The district centers around the junction of Franklin and Walton Streets. For more information on the district, contact 315/422-8284, www.armorysquare.com.

Rubenstein Museum of Science and Technology

The old Syracuse Armory now houses the MOST, a.k.a. the Rubenstein Museum of Science and Technology. The MOST moved into this location in 1992, finishing renovations in 1996.

The armory's former Riding Hall was cleared of sawdust to make way for exhibits on the earth, the human body, the environment, and the food web; the former Drill Hall showcases a 225-seat IMAX theater. Especially popular with kids are the old 1863 stables, now packed with hands-on exhibits, and the Silverman Planetarium.

The museum, 500 S. Franklin St., at W. Jefferson St., 315/425-9068, www.most.org, is open Tues.–Sun. 11 A.M.–5 P.M. Admission is adults $5, seniors and children 2–11 $4. IMAX shows also run Tues.–Sun.; a combination museum-IMAX ticket costs adults $9.75, seniors and children $7.75.

Landmark Theatre

One and a half blocks east of the MOST stands the 2,922-seat Landmark Theater, designed in 1928 by Thomas Lamb, a pre-eminent movie palace architect. The building's relatively sedate exterior does little to prepare you for its riotous interior—an ornate Indo-Persian fantasy bestrewn with gold carvings. Nearly destroyed by a wrecking ball in the 1970s, the Landmark is now a beloved local institution.

The lobby of the Landmark, 362 S. Salina St., at E. Jefferson St., 315/475-7979, www.landmarktheatre.org, is open Mon.–Fri. 10 A.M.–5 P.M. Arrange for a tour by calling in advance.

Onondaga Historical Association Museum

This fine county museum—one of the best in the state—covers virtually every aspect of Central New York's history, from the Onondaga Nation and early African American settlers to the Erie Canal and the salt industry. One display explores the 50 breweries that once operated in Syracuse, another the city's natural history. A plethora of historic maps, photographs, paintings, and artifacts are displayed.

The museum, 321 Montgomery St., between E. Jefferson and Fayette Streets, 315/428-1864, www.cnyhistory.org, is open Wed.–Fri. noon–4 P.M., and Saturday 11 A.M.–4 P.M. Admission is free.

> Settlers were attracted to the area by its many salt springs—discovered first by the Onondaga Indians. As early as 1797, the state took over the salt fields to obtain tax revenues on salt, then so valuable it was referred to as "white gold."

Everson Museum of Art

Housed in a sleek 1968 building designed by I. M. Pei, the Everson contains one of the world's largest collections of ceramics. Objects on exhibit range from ancient earth-colored Asian pots to modern rainbow-colored clay sculpture. The museum also displays small but fine collections of 18th-century American portraits, African and Latin American folk art, and contemporary photography. Temporary exhibits usually focus on one major American artist such as Winslow Homer, Ansel Adams, or Helen Frankenthaler.

The museum, 401 Harrison St., at State St., 315/474-6064, www.everson.org, is open Tues.–Fri. and Sunday noon–5 P.M., Saturday 10 A.M.–5 P.M. Suggested donation is $2.

Accommodations

The old-fashioned **Hotel Syracuse,** 500 S. Warren St., 315/422-5121 or 800/333-3333, www.hotelsyracuse.com, now affiliated with Radisson Plaza Hotels, is a grand affair sporting a chandelier-filled lobby, Stickley furniture, several restaurants, and a shopping arcade. The rooms are a bit small but comfortable ($99–125 d).

On the north side of downtown you'll find the 50-room **Econo Lodge,** 454 James St., 315/425-0015 ($55–80 d). Not far from Syracuse University stands **The Marx,** 701 E. Genesee St., 315/479-7000, a 285-room hostelry complete with a skyline restaurant, lounge, and indoor pool ($69–89 d).

Food

When in the Armory Square District, try **Pastabilities,** 311 S. Franklin St., 315/474-1153, for home-cooked Italian fare; average entrée $11. At the **Empire Brewing Company,** 120 Walton St., 315/475-2337, you can munch on hearty American fare while watching beer being brewed behind a glass wall; average entrée $12.

Significantly more upscale is the **Pascale Wine Bar & Restaurant,** 204 W. Fayette St., 315/471-3040, a historic townhouse serving imaginative French-American cuisine and Finger Lakes wines;

average entrée $16. The **Lemon Grass Grille,** 238 W. Jefferson St., 315/475-1111, specializes in Pacific Rim cuisine; average entrée $15.

Just north of Niagara Power reigns the **Dinosaur Bar-B-Cue,** 246 W. Willow St., 315/476-4937, a lively joint aswirl with murals of frolicking dinosaurs. The building is owned by bikers no less, and features live blues most nights, as well as a wide array of straightforward lunch and dinner dishes; average main dish $10.

In the Hotel Syracuse, 500 S. Warren St., 315/422-5121, is **Coach Mac's Sports Bar & Grill,** 315/422-5121, a local hangout operated by former football coach Dick MacPherson. Built to look like a tiny church, complete with a steeple and stained-glass windows, is **The Mission Restaurant,** 304 E. Onondaga St., 315/475-7344, serving Mexican and Caribbean fare, along with great margaritas; average entrée $14.

ELSEWHERE IN THE CITY

Rosamond Gifford Zoo at Burnet Park

The 36-acre Rosamond Gifford Zoo on the west side of town houses close to 1,000 animals and birds living in re-created natural habitats. The various inhabitants enjoy an arctic tundra, a tropical rain forest, an arid desert, and a region called the Wild North, where bears, red pandas, and bison roam free.

The zoo, 500 Burnet Park Dr., off S. Wilbur Ave., 315/435-8511, www.syracusezoo.org, is open daily 10 A.M.–4:30 P.M. Admission is adults $5, seniors $3, children 5–14 $2.

Tipperary Hill

Also west of downtown, at the juncture of West Fayette and West Genesee Streets, is the "Gateway to Tipperary Hill." As Syracuse's oldest Irish neighborhood, Tipperary Hill is best-known for its **upside-down traffic light** at the intersection of Tompkins and Lowell Streets—the only one in the country. When the stoplight was first installed, right-side-up, its lenses were immediately destroyed by irate citizens who did not want British red placed above Irish green. The city's fathers, realizing this was one battle they could never win, reversed the lenses to accommodate the neighborhood.

THE BREW MASTERS OF SYRACUSE

Syracuse has had a long and distinguished history in that most distinguished of arts, the brewing of beer. Before Prohibition, the city was the number one producer of hops in the nation, and the giant Anheuser-Busch has had a brewery in suburban Baldwinsville for more than 25 years.

Microbreweries are also flourishing in Syracuse. One of the oldest in the area is the **Middle Ages Brewing Company,** maker of the favorite Syracuse Pale Ale. Also well known is **Relyea Brewing,** which specializes in Erie Canal–themed brews such as Double Lock Lager. The **Empire Brewing Company** has its own restaurant in Armory Square (120 Walton St., 315/475-2337) where you can sample its products while watching beer being brewed behind a giant glass wall. Try a Skinny Atlas Light (named after nearby Skaneateles Lake) or a glass of Empire Brewing Stout. The **Syracuse Suds Factory** also has a restaurant in Armory Square (320 S. Clinton St., 315/471-AALE) and makes a specially brewed root beer, along with its alcoholic products.

In the heart of today's Tipperary Hill—now only about half Irish—stands the **Cashel House,** 224 Tompkins St., 315/472-4438, packed with all sorts of goods imported from Ireland. Across the street, **Coleman's Authentic Irish Pub** boasts both human- and leprechaun-size doors.

Salt Museum

To the north, in the suburb of Liverpool, lies lozenge-shaped Onondaga Lake, whose rich salt deposits first attracted settlers to the area. Unfortunately, the lake is now seriously polluted, but to one side stands a homespun museum equipped with an original "boiling block." Brine was once turned into salt here through boiling and solar evaporation. On display are battered antique iron kettles, wooden barrels, and other equipment, along with a fascinating collection of historic photographs.

The museum and lake belong to **Onondaga Lake Park,** which also offers bicycle rentals, a tram ride, a playground, and Ste. Marie Among the Iroquois—a second museum on the other side of the parkway.

The museum, Onondaga Lake Pkwy. (Rte. 370), 315/453-6715 or 315/453-6767, is open May–Sept., daily noon–6 P.M. Admission is free.

Ste. Marie Among the Iroquois

Much more elaborate than the Salt Museum, Ste. Marie Among the Iroquois re-creates the 17th-century world of the French Jesuits and Iroquois who once lived on the shores of Onondaga Lake. The exhibit begins indoors with displays on the Onondaga, then explores the meeting between the two cultures through artifacts, art, and historical documents.

Outdoors in a re-created French fort, costumed guides forge horseshoes, bake bread, and hollow out canoes. The French only lived in the area for 20 months. The Onondaga welcomed their presence, but the Mohawk did not, and in March 1658 the French withdrew. Their legacy lives on in the large community of Catholic Onondagas residing in Syracuse today.

The museum, Onondaga Lake Pkwy. (Rte. 370), 315/453-6767, is open June–Labor Day, Wed.–Sun 10 A.M.–5 P.M.; call for off-season

hours. Admission is adults $3.50, seniors $3, children 5–17 $1.50.

Accommodations

In a lovely residential neighborhood is the **Dickerson House on James,** 1504 James St., 315/423-4777 or 888/423-7777, www.dickensonhouse .com. This stately English Tudor B&B offers five attractive guest rooms filled with antiques, a small garden out back, and a guest kitchen generously stocked with snacks, beer, and wine ($110–135 d, including full breakfast).

In nearby Fayetteville, not far from the Stickley factory (see Excursions from Syracuse, below), find the comfortable **Craftsman Inn,** 7300 E. Genesee St., 315/637-8000, www.craftsman-inn.com, where all 90-odd rooms and suites are furnished in Arts and Crafts style, including much Stickley furniture ($91–185 d).

Many hotels and motels cluster east of downtown near Carrier Circle. Especially good rates are offered by the clean, comfortable, 54-room **John Milton Inn,** 6578 Thompson Rd., 315/463-8555 or 800/352-1061 ($37 d). More upscale digs can be found at the 149-room **Courtyard By Marriott,** 6415 Yorktown Circle, 315/432-0300 or 800/321-2211 ($114 d).

Food

Coleman's Authentic Irish Pub, 100 S. Lowell Ave., 315/476-1933, is a neighborhood institution featuring menus written in both Gaelic and English, and lots of hearty Irish fare; average entrée $11. For Old World German food, try **Weber's Grill,** 820 Danforth St., 315/472-0480, also a Syracuse institution, located just north of the downtown; average entrée $10.

Near Onondaga Lake Park at the **Ichiban Japanese Steakhouse,** 302 Old Liverpool Rd., 315/457-0000, dishes are prepared tableside on hibachis; average entrée $14.

SPORTS AND RECREATION

Amusement Parks: Song Mountain, Exit 14 off I-81 S or Exit 13 off I-81 N, Tully, 315/696-5711, offers a water slide, alpine slide, chairlift ride, miniature golf, and go-karts, June–Labor Day.

Cruises: **Mid-Lakes Navigation,** 315/685-8500 or 800/545-4318, offers excursion and dinner cruises on the Erie Canal. The boats leave from Dutchman's Landing off Route 370 north of Liverpool. The company also offers three-day canal cruises and has boats available for weekly rental.

Spectator Sports: Take in a Syracuse University football, basketball, or lacrosse game at the famed **Carrier Dome,** 900 Irving Ave., 315/443-4634. The AAA Syracuse Sky Chiefs, a farm team for the Toronto Blue Jays, play at P and C Stadium, Hiawatha Blvd. and Tex Simone Dr., 315/474-7833, July–September.

ENTERTAINMENT

Performing Arts

One of the more unusual arts organizations in town is the **Open Hand Theater,** 232 E. Onondaga St., 315/476-0466, featuring giant-sized puppets from around the world. Connected to the theater is an **International Mask and Puppet Museum,** 518 Prospect Ave., complete with hands-on activities; open Saturday 10 A.M.–4 P.M., closed July–Aug., or by appointment.

The **Syracuse Symphony Orchestra,** John II. Mulroy Civic Center, 411 Montgomery St., 315/424-8200, performs classical and popular music concerts Oct.–May.

The acclaimed **Syracuse Stage,** 820 Genesee St., 315/443-3275, presents a mix of classic and contemporary drama September–May. The Depression-era **Landmark Theatre,** 362 S. Salina St., 315/475-7979, hosts concerts, plays, dance troupes, and classic movies throughout the year.

Musicals, dramas, and comedies are featured year-round at the **Salt City Center for the Performing Arts,** 601 S. Crouse Ave., 315/474-1122. The Hotel Syracuse, 465 S. Salina St., 315/424-8210, has been hosting a **Famous Artists Series** for over 50 years. The series brings in great artists of the stage, concerts, and film, and presents Broadway productions.

Clubs and Nightlife

The best source for what's going on where is the *Syracuse New Times,* 315/422-7011, a free alternative newsweekly available throughout the city.

One of the liveliest music clubs in town is **Dinosaur Bar-B-Cue,** 246 W. Willow St., 315/476-4937, a friendly hole-in-the-wall joint filled with dinosaurs and blues paraphernalia, bikers and businesspeople. Live blues most nights.

A good club is which to hear local bands is **Shifty's,** 1401 Burnet Ave., 315/474-0048. On weekends, traditional Irish music fills the **Limerick Pub,** 134 Walton St., 315/475-1819. The **Happy Endings Coffeehouse,** 317 S. Clinton St., 315/475-1853, spotlights singer-songwriters, poets, and writers.

EVENTS

The **Syracuse Jazz Fest,** is the largest free jazz festival in the Northeast. The celebration runs for seven days in mid-June, and features a wide variety of jazz events, artists, and styles. In July, the city hosts a smaller but growing **Blues Festival.** In July and August, the Syracuse Pops and the Syracuse Orchestra play **free concerts** in the city's parks. Call 315/470-1910 for more information on any of these events.

One of the state's grandest parties is the **New York State Fair,** New York State Fairgrounds, 581 State Fair Blvd., off I-690 (Exit 7), 315/487-7711, featuring agricultural and livestock competitions, music and entertainment, amusement rides and games of chance, business and industrial exhibits, and talent competitions. The fair runs for 12 days, ending on Labor Day, and attracts about 850,000 people.

In November, the **Festival of Nations,** 315/470-1910, celebrates the traditions, song, and dance of 35 Native American groups.

EXCURSIONS FROM SYRACUSE

Beaver Lake Nature Center

This serene 560-acre nature preserve northwest of Syracuse offers 10 miles of well-marked trails and boardwalks, along with a 200-acre lake that's a favorite resting spot for migrating duck and geese. A visitor center displays exhibits on local flora and fauna.

The center, 8477 East Mud Lake Rd., off Rte.

370, Baldwinsville, 315/638-2519, is open daily 7 A.M.–dusk.

Highland Forest

Onondaga County's largest and oldest park is the 2,700-acre Highland Forest southeast of Syracuse. Spread out atop Arab Hill, the park offers great views of the surrounding countryside.

Adirondack-like in appearance, the forest is laced with four hiking trails ranging in length from less than a mile to eight miles. One-hour guided trail rides on horseback are offered April–Nov., and hay and sleigh rides on the weekends in fall and winter. Many visitors enjoy the park's excellent mountain biking and cross-country skiing.

Highland Forest, 315/683-5550, is located off Route 80 four miles southeast of Fabius; the drive from Syracuse takes about 30 minutes. The park is open year-round dawn to dusk.

Green Lakes State Park

About 10 miles due east of Syracuse, the 2,000-acre Green Lakes State Park contains two aquamarine glacial lakes. Facilities include a swimming beach, bathhouse, hiking and biking trails, playground, concession stand, campground, and 18-hole golf course. Boats can also be rented. Located at 7900 Green Lakes Rd., off Rte. 290, Fayetteville, 315/637-6111, the park is open daily dawn to dusk. Parking in summer is $6. For campground reservations, call 800/456-CAMP; a basic site costs $13–15.

Factory Tour

Ten miles southeast of Syracuse is **L. & J. G. Stickley,** Stickley Dr., Manlius, 315/682-5500 or 315/682-5441. The company leads free tours of its furniture factory every Tuesday at 10 A.M.

Camillus

Take Route 5 10 miles due west of Syracuse, and you end up in Camillus, an old Erie Canal town, now the site of 300-acre **Erie Canal Park,** 5750 DeVoe Rd., 315/488-3409 or 315/672-5110. The park features seven miles of navigable canal, 13 miles of hiking trails, a replica locktender's house, and the **Sims' Store Museum,** 109 East Way, filled with artifacts from the Erie Canal days. The park operates daily; the museum is open Saturday 9 A.M.–1 P.M.; boat rides are offered May.–Oct., Sunday 1–5 P.M., or bring your own boat.

Also in Camillus is the 1856 **Wilcox Octagon House,** 5420 W. Genesee St., 315/488-7800, one of the country's few remaining octagonal houses. Tours begin in the kitchen and wend their way up a circular staircase five stories to the cupola. The house is open on Sunday and holidays 1–5 P.M., or by appointment. Donations welcomed.

Skaneateles Lake Area

The farthest east of the Finger Lakes, deep blue Skaneateles (Scan-ee-AT-i-less) is also the highest (867 feet above sea level) and most beautiful. Fifteen miles long and one to two miles wide, the lake is surrounded by gentle rolling hills to the south and more majestic, near-mountainous ones to the north. Iroquois for "long lake," Skaneateles is spring fed, crystal clean, and clear. In the summer, its waters are specked with sailboats; in the winter, ice fishers build igloos.

The only real village on the lake is Skaneateles. Elsewhere along the shoreline preside handsome summer homes placed judicious distances apart.

SKANEATELES

Skaneateles the village spreads out along one long main street (Route 20) at the north end of the lake. Graceful 19th-century homes, white-columned public buildings, and trim brick storefronts are everywhere. Like Cazenovia for wealthy Rochesterians in Central New York, Skaneateles has been a favorite retreat among wealthy Syracusans for generations.

The first Europeans in Skaneateles were Moravian missionaries who visited an Onondaga village on this site in 1750. From 1843 to 1845, the village was the short-lived site of a Utopian community that advertised in the newspapers for followers and advocated communal property, nonviolence, easy divorce, and vegetarianism. Prior to the Civil War, Skaneateles served as the headquarters for abolitionist Gerrit Smith and was an important stop on the Underground Railroad.

Village Landmarks

In the center of the village is **Clift Park,** a waterfront refuge with a gazebo and wide-angled views of the lake. Docked at the end of a small pier are the two classic wooden boats of the **Mid-Lakes Navigation Co.,** 315/685-8500 or 800/545-4318. From May to September, the spit-and-polish vessels offer sightseeing, lunch, and dinner cruises of the lake. These same craft deliver the mail on Skaneateles Lake—a 100-plus-year-old tradition. Mailboat cruises are also available.

Across from the park stands the hospitable **Sherwood Inn,** a rambling, Colonial blue building that was once a stagecoach stop. The inn was established in 1807 by one Isaac Sherwood, a 300-pound man who began his career by delivering the mail on foot between Utica and Canandaigua, and ended it as the "stagecoach king."

Just down the street from the inn is **Krebs,** 53 W. Genesee St., a Finger Lakes institution dating back to 1899. For many years, Krebs reigned as the best restaurant in New York outside Manhattan, and diners flocked here from all over the state. At its peak in 1920, Krebs served 3,000 meals a day.

For more on the Sherwood Inn and Krebs, see below.

Skaneateles Historical Society Museum

To learn about the lake's history, step into this small local museum, housed in the former Skaneateles Creamery building. From 1899 to 1949, area farmers brought their milk here to be turned into buttermilk, cream, and butter. Displays include scale models of the boats that once sailed the lake, exhibits on dairy farming,

> *For many years, Krebs reigned as the best restaurant in New York outside Manhattan, and diners flocked here from all over the state. At its peak in 1920, Krebs served 3,000 meals a day.*

and information about the teasel, a plant resembling a thistle once used in woolen mills to raise a cloth's nap. For 120 years, Skaneateles was the teasel-growing capital of the United States.

The museum, 28 Hannum St., 315/685-1360, is open year-round, Friday 1–4 P.M.; and May–Sept., Thurs.–Sat. 1–4 P.M. Admission is free.

Scenic Drives

For spectacular views of the lake, drive down either Route 41 to the east or Route 41A to the west. Route 41A veers away from the shoreline at the southern end and leads to **New Hope Mills,** 315/497-0783, an operating 1823 flour mill. Here, grain is still ground with granite and burr stones operated by a 26-foot overshot waterwheel. Unbleached flours and grains are for sale. Hours are Mon.–Fri. 9 A.M.–4 P.M., Saturday 10 A.M.–2 P.M.

Accommodations

The upscale yet casual **Sherwood Inn,** 26 W. Genesee St., 315/685-3405, www.thesherwoodinn.com, includes a very popular restaurant serving traditional American fare (average entrée $15), a tavern with frequent live entertainment, and 20 attractive guest rooms, all decorated with antiques. Contributing to the inn's relaxed atmosphere are a big screened-in porch, an outdoor patio for summer dining, lots of fresh flowers, and a snug lounge ($95–170 d).

Near the heart of downtown is **The Gray House,** 47 Jordan St., 315/685-0131, a welcoming B&B housed in a spacious Victorian home, complete with a large parlor, two breezy porches, and gardens out back ($85–110 d).

A half mile east of downtown is the **Bird's Nest Motel,** 1601 E. Genesee St., 315/685-5641, with a pond, pool, nature trails, and nicely redone rooms and suites ($55–85 d).

On the outskirts of Skaneateles is the ultra-luxurious **Mirbeau Inn and Spa,** 851 W. Genesee St., 315/685-5006 or 877/MIRBEAU, www.mirbeau.com. An elegant, European-styled inn complete with wall frescoes, waterfalls, soft lighting, and spacious rooms, the Mirbeau offers a wide variety of spa treatments and getaway packages, as well as a serene restaurant serving innovative American cuisine; $165–365 d, four- and five-course prix fixe dinners $49–54 (a la carte also available).

Food

One of the oldest restaurants in the Finger Lakes (Franklin Roosevelt and Charles Lindbergh once ate here), **Krebs,** 53 W. Genesee St., 315/685-5714, is most famous for its seven-course continental dinners, but also serves lighter fare. Three basic entrées are served—chicken, lobster, and prime rib—along with homemade soups and baked goods. Out back is a formal garden (complete dinners $32–37; open May–Oct. dinner only), while upstairs is a low-ceilinged tavern where locals congregate.

The laid-back **Doug's Fish Fry,** 8 Jordan St., 315/685-3288, is a local favorite, renowned for its chowder, fried scallops, gumbo, and fish sandwiches. Tasty pancakes, soups, sandwiches, and, of course burgers can be found at **Johnny Angel's Heavenly Hamburgers,** 22 Jordan St., 315/685-0100. Average main dish at both, $8.

Rosalie's Cucina, 841 W. Genesee St., 315/685-2200, offers first-rate Italian fare, ranging from pizza and pasta to grilled lobster tails, in an adobe taverna; average entrée $16. For fresh Japanese food in a peaceful setting, step into **Kabuki,** 12 Genesee St., 315/685-7234; dinner entrées $7–20.

The **Sherwood Inn** and **Mirbeau** are also excellent dining choices (see Accommodations, above).

Events

Weekly **sailboat races** take place throughout the summer, while free **band concerts** are held on Friday evenings in Clift Park. **Polo games** are played in July and August at the Skaneateles Polo Club, West Lake and Andrews Roads, on Sunday at 3 P.M. The town's largest event is the **antique and classic boat show,** held in early July.

Visitor Information

For more information on the town, contact the **Skaneateles Chamber of Commerce,** P.O. Box 199, Skaneateles, NY 13152, 315/685-0552, www.skaneateles.com. You can pick up brochures at an information booth at 11 Jordan St. In summer, the **Skaneateles Historical Society,** 315/685-1360, often leads walking tours.

CORTLAND

About 12 miles from the southern tip of Skaneateles Lake sprawls the city of Cortland (pop. 19,800). Set in the midst of fertile farm country, Cortland was once a small industrial center, best known for its wire cloth, lingerie, and corset factories. Along Main Street between Tompkins Street and Clinton Avenue is a **National Historic District** of handsome homes and commercial buildings.

Cortland also claims literary fame. It was here that Chester Gillette, the real-life counterpart to character Clyde Griffiths in Theodore Dreiser's *An American Tragedy,* met Grace Brown. Writes Dreiser of Griffiths's arrival in his new hometown: "He found himself ambling on and on until suddenly he was . . . in touch with a wide and tree-shaded thoroughfare of residences, the houses of which, each and every one, appeared to possess more room space, lawn space, general ease and repose and dignity even than any with which he had ever been in contact. . . ." Gillette once worked in his uncle's Gillette Skirt Factory on the north side of town, and lived in the still-standing double house at No. 17½ E. Main Street.

Historic Sights

Perhaps one of the houses spotted by Gillette-Griffiths in his ramble was the castlelike **1890 House Museum,** built by wire manufacturer Chester F. Wickwire. Owned by the Wickwire family until 1974, the house now serves as an informal museum in the town's National Historic District. Inside are 30 rooms filled with parquet floors, stained-glass windows, ornate stenciling, and hand-carved woodwork. Above the top floor, a tower provides excellent views of the town, and out back stands a two-story carriage barn. Free walking-tour maps of Cortland's Historic District can be picked up here.

The house, 37 Tompkins St. (Rte. 13), 607/

756-7551, is open Tues.–Sun. 1–4 P.M. Admission is adults $3.50, seniors and students $2.50, children under 12 free.

Cortland Country Music Park Campground

Part campground, part country music mecca, this 18-acre site bills itself as the "great Nashville of the Northeast." During the summer, four or five concerts by such top performers as Roy Acuff and Kenny Rogers are staged, along with two-steppin' dance classes, square dances, and jamborees. The park offers live music by regional bands weekends year-round, and special events including Horseshoe Tournaments, an Old Timers Show, and a Festival of Bands.

Largely built by volunteers, the music park was started up in 1975 by a handful of country music fans. Centered around a low-slung Opry Barn, it is equipped with one of the largest dance floors in the Northeast, an outdoor stage, and a Hall of Fame Museum. In the museum, you'll find everything from a black-sequined dress formerly owned by Tammy Wynette to white boots once worn by Roy Acuff.

The music park, 1804 Truxton Rd. (Rte. 13), 607/753-0377, is one mile north of the I-88 intersection. The park is open daily year-round; call for the music schedule. The museum opens during events, or by appointment.

Shopping

It's worth traveling about eight miles south of Cortland to visit the **Book Barn of the Finger Lakes,** 198 North Rd., Dryden, 607/844-9365. The sprawling 1850s barn houses over 75,000 used, rare, and scholarly books. Located off Route 13 opposite the Tompkins-Cortland Community College, the bookstore is open Mon.–Sat. 10 A.M.–5:30 P.M., Sunday noon–5 P.M.

Owasco Lake Area

The smallest of the major Finger Lakes, Owasco is 12 miles long and 1.5 miles wide at its widest point. Iroquois for "the crossing," it lies 720 feet above sea level. For great views of Owasco, take Route 38 south, hugging the western shore, or Route 38A south, which travels high above the lake to the east. A few miles down, Route 38A bumps into Rockefeller Road, a shoreline route lined with 150-year-old camps and houses.

At the northern end of Owasco sits the city of Auburn, population 31,200. At the southern end are the village of Moravia, birthplace of President Millard Fillmore, the Fillmore Glen State Park, and miles of farm country.

AUBURN

For a small industrial city, Auburn been home to an unusually high number of remarkable men and women. Among them are Logan, or Tahgahjute, the Iroquois orator; Harriet Tubman, the African American leader; William H. Seward, the visionary statesman; Thomas Mott Osborne, the pioneer of prison reform; and Theodore W. Case, the inventor of sound film. Tributes to all can be found in the city.

Before the invasion of the whites, Auburn was a Cayuga Indian village established at the junction of two trails. Revolutionary War veteran Col. John Hardenbergh arrived in 1793 and built the area's first gristmill. By 1810, the budding village boasted 90 dwellings, 17 mills, and an incorporated library containing 200 books.

The opening of the Auburn State Prison in 1817 and the Auburn Theological Seminary in 1821 greatly stimulated growth, and by the mid-1800s, Auburn was thriving. It even entertained hopes of becoming the state capital. The impressive public buildings on Capitol Street and lavish private homes on State Street date back to those heady days.

Though Auburn is no longer the manufacturing center it once was, a number of factories still operate. Among them are a heating and air-conditioning manufacturer, electronics plant, bottle company, and roll factory.

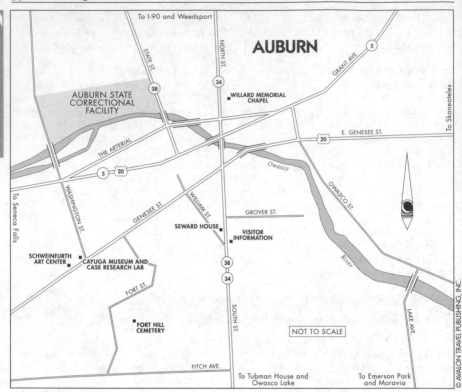

AUBURN

To I-90 and Weedsport

STATE ST.

NORTH ST.

GRANT AVE.

5

To Skaneateles

AUBURN STATE CORRECTIONAL FACILITY

38

34

WILLARD MEMORIAL CHAPEL

THE ARTERIAL

E. GENESEE ST.

20

5   20

Owasco

WASHINGTON ST.

WILLIAM ST.

GROVER ST.

OWASCO ST.

To Seneca Falls

GENESEE ST.

SEWARD HOUSE

VISITOR INFORMATION

River

MOON

SCHWEINFURTH ART CENTER

CAYUGA MUSEUM AND CASE RESEARCH LAB

38

34

FORT ST.

SOUTH ST.

LAKE AVE.

FORT HILL CEMETERY

NOT TO SCALE

FITCH AVE.

To Tubman House and Owasco Lake

To Emerson Park and Moravia

© AVALON TRAVEL PUBLISHING, INC.

Seward House

One of the most interesting house museums in New York is this stately 1816 Federal-style home shaded by leafy trees. The house belonged to William H. Seward, ardent abolitionist, New York governor, and U.S. senator, best remembered for purchasing Alaska from the Russians in 1857. Seward also served as Lincoln's secretary of state and was almost assassinated by a co-conspirator of John Wilkes Booth at the same time as the president.

Amazingly, almost everything in the Seward house is original. Inside you'll find not only Seward's furniture, but his grocery bills, top hats, pipe collection, snuff box collection, 10,000 books, political campaign buttons, tea from the Boston Tea Party, personal letters from Abraham Lincoln, and calling cards of former visitors Horace Greeley, Frederick Douglass, Millard Fill-

more, and Daniel Webster. In one hallway, floor to ceiling, hangs Seward's private picture collection of over 130 world leaders; in another, the couch upon which he died while taking a rest from writing his memoirs.

Seward first moved to Auburn for the love of Miss Frances Miller, whose father, Judge Elijah Miller, built the house. As a newly minted lawyer, Seward got a job in the judge's law firm, and proposed to his daughter. The ornery judge allowed the liaison on one condition: Seward could never take his daughter away from him. Seward agreed and—despite his enormous worldly success—lived under his father-in-law's thumb for the next 27 years.

The house, 33 South St., 315/252-1283, www.sewardhouse.org, is open July–Oct. 15, Tues.–Sat. 10 A.M.–4 P.M. and Sunday 1–4 P.M.; Oct. 15–June, Tues.–Sat. 1–4 P.M.; closed January.

Admission is adults $4, seniors $3.50, students $2, under 12 free.

Historic Districts

The Seward House is at the northern end of the **South Street Historic District,** which runs as far south as Metcalf Drive. Along this wide and shady boulevard, watch out for **No. 108,** an imposing 65-room mansion built in 1922 for Theodore W. Case, who brought sound film to the cinema. On **Grover Street,** which intersects South Street across from the Seward House, rests a peaceful enclave of brick-and-wooden homes built in the mid- to late 1800s.

Harriet Tubman Home

On the outskirts of Auburn, next door to the AME Zion Church, stands a two-story white home wrapped with a long front porch. Harriet Tubman, known as the "Moses of her people," settled here after the Civil War—her close friend and fellow abolitionist William Seward lived nearby.

Born a slave in Maryland in 1820 or 1821, Tubman escaped in 1849, fleeing first to Philadelphia and then to Canada. Yet as long as others remained in captivity, her freedom meant little to her. During the next dozen years, she risked 19 trips south, rescuing more than 300 slaves. She mostly traveled alone and at night. Her motto: "Keep going; children, if you are tired, keep going; if you are scared, keep going; if you are hungry, keep going; if you want to taste freedom, keep going."

A visit to Tubman's house begins in a homespun museum exhibiting displays on famous African American women and a first-rate video on Tubman's life. Afterward, Rev. Paul G. Carter of the AME Zion Church, or one of his family, leads visitors on a tour of the home. Few of Tubman's belongings remain, but the ones that do—including her bed and her Bible—are very evocative. The house also contains period pieces.

Tubman's home, 180 South St., 315/252-2081, www.harriettubmanhouse.com, is open June–Sept., Tues.–Fri. 10 A.M.–3 P.M., Saturday 10 A.M.–3 P.M.; call for winter hours. Admission is adults $5, seniors $3, children $2.

© CHRISTIANE BIRD

Fort Hill Cemetery

Harriet Tubman, William Seward, and numerous other Auburn notables are buried in the Fort Hill Cemetery, on a hill to the west side of State Street. Native Americans used the site as burial grounds as early as A.D. 1100; some archaeological artifacts found here now sit in the Cayuga Museum.

A large stone fortress-gate marks the cemetery entrance, while inside towers the 56-foot-high **Logan Monument.** Erected upon a mound believed to be an ancient Native American altar, the monument pays homage to Logan, or Tahgahjute, the famed Cayuga orator born near Auburn in 1727. Logan befriended the European settlers until 1774, when a group of marauding Englishmen massacred his entire family in the Ohio Valley. In retaliation, he scalped over 30 white men. Later that same year in Virginia, at a conference with the British, he gave one of the most moving speeches in early American history. "Logan never felt fear," he said. "He will not turn his heel to save his life. Who is there to mourn for Logan? Not one."

To reach the cemetery at 19 Fort St., 315/253-8132, take South Street to Fitch Avenue to Fort Street. It's open Mon.–Fri. 9 A.M.–4 P.M.

Cayuga Museum and Case Research Lab

Housed in a musty Greek Revival mansion that once belonged to the Willard and Case families, the Cayuga Museum is devoted to Cayuga County history. Exhibits cover early Native American culture, the Civil War, Auburn's industrial past, Millard Fillmore, and women's rights.

The most interesting part of the museum, however, stands behind the mansion proper, in a simple, low-slung building known as the Case Research Lab. Here in 1923, Theodore W. Case and E. I. Sponable invented the first commercially successful sound film, ushering in the movie era. Overlooked by historians for over 50 years, the lab was fully restored and opened to the public in 1994. Displays include the first sound camera and projector, original lab equipment, and Case's correspondence with Thomas Edison and Lee De Forest, a self-promoter who claimed *he* was the inventor of sound film.

The museum, 203 Genesee St., 315/253-8051, is open Tues.–Fri. 10 A.M.–5 P.M., Sat.–Sun. noon–5 P.M. Admission is free.

Schweinfurth Memorial Art Center

Behind the Cayuga Museum a modest art center features temporary exhibits by contemporary and classic artists. Shows range from fine art and photography to folk art and architecture. The center also houses a gift shop stocked with Auburn mementos and handicrafts from around the world.

The center, 205 Genesee St., 315/255-1553, is open Tues.–Sat. 10 A.M.–5 P.M., Sunday 1–5 P.M.; closed January. Admission is by donation.

Willard Memorial Chapel

The only complete Tiffany chapel known to exist, the Willard Memorial glows with the muted, bejeweled light of 15 windows handcrafted by the Tiffany Glass and Decorating Company. Louis C. Tiffany also designed the chapel's handsome oak furniture inlaid with mosaics, leaded-glass chandeliers, and gold-stenciled pulpit.

A visit to the chapel begins with a video on the chapel's history and the now-defunct Auburn Theological Seminary of which it was once a part. In July and August, free organ recitals are played in the chapel on Wednesday at noon.

The memorial, 17 Nelson St., 315/252-0339, is open Tues.–Fri. 10 A.M.–4 P.M., and July–Aug., Sat.–Sun. 1–5 P.M. Suggested donation is adults $2, children $1.

Auburn State Correctional Facility

Near the center of the city, along the arterial between State and Washington Streets, looms one of the area's foremost employers: the Auburn State Correctional Facility. Established in 1816, New York's oldest prison has had a long and grim history.

Auburn was the first facility to institute solitary cells: 3.5 by 7 by 7 feet, the smallest possible area in which a human could both lie down and stand up. Auburn also devised the shower bath punishment, in which prisoners endured cold water poured over them. Under the "silent system," prisoners were marched lock-step to fields and contract shops and forced to work all day without saying a word, then marched back again. Guards brandishing whips made sure no one spoke.

Despite, or perhaps because of, all this, visitors flocked from all over the country to tour the prison in the early years. Admission cost 12.5 cents until 1822, when the fee doubled to 25 cents to stem the over-enthusiastic tide.

In 1890 at Auburn the first person in the world—a murderer from Buffalo—was put to death in an electric chair. Others executed at Auburn before executions shifted in 1916 to Sing Sing included Leon Czolgosz, the assassin of President McKinley; and Chester Gillette, upon whose life Theodore Dreiser's *An American Tragedy* is based.

In 1913 state prisoner commissioner Thomas Mott Osborne brought relief to Auburn inmates. After serving undercover for a week, Osborne introduced the ideas of prisoner self-government and education. Riots in 1929 resulted in still more improvements and by the 1950s, the Auburn prison had been rebuilt. Today, it continues to function as a walled, maximum-security facility.

Emerson Park

On the south side of town, on the shores of Owasco Lake, Emerson Park offers a recreation area equipped with two bathing beaches, three launch sites, ball fields, and an especially large playground with a roller coaster, carousel, and kiddie rides. The park, Rte. 38A, 315/253-5611, opens May–September. Lifeguards are on duty July–Aug., and canoes and paddleboats can be rented.

Accommodations and Food

One mile south of Auburn you'll find the **Springside Inn,** 41 W. Lake Rd. (Rte. 38), 315/252-7247, www.springsideinn.com, a striking red Victorian with big white porches. Now under new ownership, the inn features both a popular restaurant serving American favorites such as steak, lobster, and duck (dinner only; entrées cost $9–20), and newly renovated guest rooms ($100–150 d).

The **Auburn Family Restaurant,** 161 Genesee St., 315/253-2274, is a homey spot, open for breakfast, lunch, and dinner. Just across from the Auburn prison find **Balloons,** 65 Washington St., 315/252-9761, a small steak house old enough to be an Auburn institution; average entrée $14. **Riordan's,** 10 E. Genesee St., 315/252-7175, is a bustling bistro and pub serving American fare; average entrée $15.

Motels in the area include the **Grant Motel,** 255 Grant Ave., 315/253-8447 ($42–52 d); and a **Day's Inn,** 37 William St., 315/252-7567 ($62–72 d).

Entertainment

The **Merry-Go-Round Playhouse,** 315/255-1785, in Emerson Park, presents musicals June–September. Free **Syracuse Symphony Auburn Concerts,** 800/724-3810, also take place in Emerson Park in summer.

About seven miles north of Auburn at the **Weedsport Speedway,** 1 Speedway Dr., off Rte. 31, Weedsport, 315/834-6606, stock cars and go-karts race April–September. On-site is a **Classic Car Museum.**

Visitor Information

The **Cayuga County Chamber of Commerce,** 36 South St., Box 675, Auburn, NY 13021, 315/252-7291, www.cayugacountychamber.org, is open year-round Mon.–Fri. 8:30 A.M.–5 P.M.

MORAVIA

Well off the beaten track, this small village boasts a number of handsome 19th-century buildings and the 1820s' **St. Matthew's Episcopal Church,** 14 Church Street. The sanctuary's interior is covered with elaborate oak carvings designed and executed in Oberammergau, Germany; to arrange a tour, call 315/497-1171.

Fillmore Glen State Park

Just south of the village lies the 857-acre Fillmore Glen State Park, centered around a deep and rugged ravine with five spectacular waterfalls. At the foot of the main falls is a geometric rock formation known as the Cowpens, and a popular swimming hole. Nearby await hiking trails, a campground, and a playground.

The park also contains a nondescript replica of the tiny log cabin in which Pres. Millard Fillmore was born. His actual birthplace lies about five miles east of the park. Fillmore grew up dirt poor and went to work at an early age; he later described his upbringing as "completely shut out from the enterprises of civilization and advancement."

The park, Rte. 38, 315/497-0130, is open year-round. Parking in summer is $6. For campground reservations, call 800/456-CAMP; a basic site costs $13.

Food

In Cascade just north of Moravia, visit **Zachary's on the Lake House,** Rte. 38, 315/497-1602, for fresh seafood, steak, and pizza on an open deck overlooking Owasco Lake. It's open for lunch and dinner; average dinner entrée $13.

Events

Fillmore Days 315/252-7291, held in late July, celebrates the birthday of the 13th president with food, crafts, entertainment, and a bathtub race down Main Street.

Cayuga Lake Area

The longest of the Finger Lakes, Cayuga stretches out for 38 moody miles, 381 feet above sea level. It varies in depth from a few feet to 435 feet, and supports a wide variety of marinelife. In shallow waters swim carp and large-mouth bass, in deeper ones, northern pike and lake trout.

Iroquois for "boat landing," Cayuga was named after the Iroquois nation that originally lived along and farmed its shores. The Cayugas were called Gue-u-gweh-o-no, or people of the muckland, exemplified by the once-enormous Montezuma Marsh at the northern end of the lake.

Today, just south of the marsh, sits Seneca Falls, the small industrial town where the first Women's Rights Convention met in 1848. Ithaca, a friendly cultural center home to Cornell University, Ithaca College, and craggy gorges with waterfalls higher than Niagara, anchors the southern end of the lake. Along the lake's western shores are a half-dozen first-rate wineries; on the eastern shores, the historic village of Aurora.

SENECA FALLS

Seneca Falls owes its early development to a series of waterfalls dropping over 50 feet. The first gristmill was built along the falls in 1795, and by the 1840s, the town supported dozens of water-powered factories. Many employed women worked 14-hour days for wages they had to turn over to their husbands. In 1840s America, women were not allowed to own money or property or to even serve as legal guardians of their own children.

Elizabeth Cady Stanton and her abolitionist husband Henry Stanton moved to Seneca Falls from Boston in 1847, a time when Seneca Falls was a major transportation hub and the Finger Lakes a center for the abolitionist movement.

Often home alone, caring for her children, Stanton felt isolated and overwhelmed by housework. She also noticed the worse plight of her poorer neighbors: "Alas! alas!," she wrote in her autobiography *Eighty Years and More,* "Who can measure the mountains of sorrow and suffering endured in unwelcome motherhood in the abodes of ignorance, poverty, and vice, where terror-stricken women and children are the victims of strong men frenzied with passion and intoxicating drink?"

On July 13, 1848, Stanton shared her discontent with four friends; then and there the group decided to convene a discussion on the status of women. They set a date for six days thence and published announcements in the local papers. About 300 people—men and women—showed up, a Declaration of Sentiments was issued, and the women deemed the convention a success. They were little prepared for the nationwide storm of outrage and ridicule that followed. Their lives, the town of Seneca Falls, and the nation would never be the same.

Orientation

Seneca Falls centers around Fall Street (Routes 5 and 20). Running parallel is the Seneca River and the Cayuga-Seneca Canal, which links Cayuga and Seneca Lakes. At the eastern end of town is the manmade Van Cleef Lake.

Heritage Area Visitor Center

For a good general introduction to Seneca Falls, stop into this first-rate center. The exhibits cover virtually every aspect of the town's history, from its Iroquois beginnings and early factory days to its women's history and ethnic heritage.

Seneca Falls is one of New York State's Heritage Areas—loosely designated historic districts linked by a common theme. The Seneca Falls theme is reform movements, but the center pays at least equal attention to the town's industrial past. Seneca Falls once held world fame for its knitting mills and pump factories, several of which still operate.

Don't leave the center without learning about the destruction of the city's once invaluable waterfalls. The falls were eliminated in 1915 to create the Cayuga-Seneca Canal and, by extension, Van Cleef Lake. The flooding destroyed over 150 buildings, and today, many foundations are still visible beneath the lake's clear waters.

The center, 115 Fall St., 315/568-6894, is

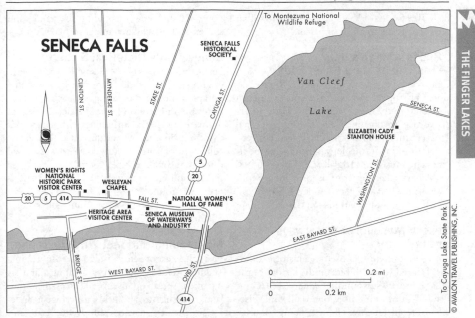

SENECA FALLS

To Montezuma National
Wildlife Refuge

SENECA FALLS
HISTORICAL
SOCIETY

Van Cleef

Lake

SENECA ST.

ELIZABETH CADY
STANTON HOUSE

CLINTON ST.

MYNDERSE ST.

STATE ST.

CAYUGA ST.

WASHINGTON ST.

WOMEN'S RIGHTS
NATIONAL
HISTORIC PARK
VISITOR CENTER

WESLEYAN
CHAPEL

5

20

FALL ST.

NATIONAL WOMEN'S
HALL OF FAME

20   5   414

HERITAGE AREA
VISITOR CENTER

SENECA MUSEUM
OF WATERWAYS
AND INDUSTRY

EAST BAYARD ST.

BRIDGE ST.

WEST BAYARD ST.

OVID ST.

0   0.2 mi

0   0.2 km

414

To Cayuga Lake State Park

© AVALON TRAVEL PUBLISHING, INC.

THE FINGER LAKES

open Mon.–Sat. 10 A.M.–4 P.M., Sunday noon–4 P.M. Admission is free.

Women's Rights National Historic Park

Down the street from the visitor center stand the ruins of the **Wesleyan Chapel,** 126 Fall St., where the historic 1848 convention took place. Alas, all that remains of the church today are two fragile brick walls and a piece of roof. The nearby 140-foot-long wall and fountain bears the Declaration of Sentiments: "We hold these truths to be self-evident; that all men and women are created equal. . . ."

Across the street from the chapel, in the spacious, two-story **Women's Rights Visitor Center,** you'll find exhibits on the convention, its leaders, and the times in which they lived. Other sections focus on such women's issues as employment, marriage, fashion, and sports. The exhibits are overly wordy, but there's lots of information here, along with free handouts and a good bookstore downstairs.

The center, 136 Fall St., 315/568-2991, is open daily 9 A.M.–5 P.M. Admission is adults $3, under 17 free.

Elizabeth Cady Stanton House

Also part of the Women's Rights National Historic Park, the Stanton house is about a mile from the visitor center on the other side of Van Cleef Lake. Stanton lived here with her husband and seven children from 1846 to 1862. During much of that time, she wrote extensively about women's rights.

Among the many reformers who frequented the Stanton home was Amelia Bloomer, the woman who popularized the pantaloons that bear her name. Though a resident of Seneca Falls, Bloomer did not sign the Declaration of Sentiments, believing it to be too radical.

Today, the airy Stanton home has been meticulously restored. Few furnishings remain, but everything is authentic, including the bronze cast of Stanton's hand clasping that of Susan B. Anthony's. Stanton met Anthony soon after the 1848 convention, and the women worked closely together throughout their lives.

Tours of the house, 32 Washington St., 315/568-2991, are offered Memorial Day–Sept.

THE FINGER LAKES

daily 10:15 A.M.–4:15 P.M. but it's best to call in advance. Tours cost $1 per person.

"This is woman's hour . . ." — The Life of Mary Baker Eddy

One block down from the Women's Rights National Historical Park stands a small museum dedicated to the life of Mary Baker Eddy. Interactive displays document the life of this original 19th-century woman who challenged conventional thinking in theology, science, and medicine. The museum, 118 Fall St., 315/568-6488, www.marybakereddy.com, is open June–Sept., Mon.–Sat. 9 A.M.–5 P.M., Sunday 1–5 P.M.; call for off-season hours. Admission is free.

Seneca Museum of Waterways and Industry

This new museum, housed in a historic building, is filled with exhibits on the history of the village and its surrounding waterways. A colorful 35-foot mural lines one wall, while elsewhere are antique fire engines, pumps, looms, and printing presses. One exhibit shows how the Erie Canal was built, another is a working lock model. Visitors are invited to record their thoughts on "Voices of the 20th Century," which films living history for future generations. The museum, 89 Fall St., 315/568-1510, www.senecamuseum.org, is open June–Sept., Tues.–Sat. 10 A.M.–5 P.M., afternoons in winter. Admission is free.

National Women's Hall of Fame

Also on Fall Street, the Women's Hall of Fame bills itself as "the only national membership organization devoted exclusively to the accomplishments of American women." True, but the hall is disappointingly static. Blown-up photos and plaques pay homage to everyone from painter Mary Cassatt to anthropologist Margaret Mead, but otherwise the hall only contains a few pick-up telephones with the taped words of famous women. Up front is a small gift shop.

The hall, 76 Fall St., 315/568-8060, www.great-women.org, is open May–Oct., Mon.–Sat. ˙:30 A.M.–5 P.M. and Sunday noon–4 P.M.; Nov.– ˙ril, Wed.–Sat. 10 A.M.–4 P.M. and Sunday

noon–4 P.M. Admission is adults $3, seniors and students $1.50, children under six free.

Seneca Falls Historical Society

Formerly known as the Mynderse/Partridge/Becker House, this historical museum is housed in a notable Queen Anne home, set back from the street behind an iron fence. Inside, 23 elegant rooms feature period furnishings, elaborate woodwork, and an extensive costume collection. A rare collection of 19th-century circus toys is strewn through the children's playroom.

The house, 55 Cayuga St., 315/568-8412, is open year-round Mon.–Fri. 9 A.M.–5 P.M.; July–Aug., Sat.–Sun. noon–4 P.M. Admission is adults $3 and families $7.

Montezuma National Wildlife Refuge

Five miles east of Seneca Falls is the Montezuma Wildlife Refuge, a haven for migrating and nesting birds. Spread out over 6,300 acres of swamplands, marshlands, and fields, the refuge includes a visitor center, nature trail, driving trail, and two observation towers. About 315 species of birds have been spotted in the refuge since it was established in 1937. Migrating waterfowl arrive by the tens of thousands in mid-April and early October. Late May to early June is a good time to spot warblers; in mid-September, the refuge fills with shorebirds and wading birds.

Before the turn of the century, Montezuma Marsh was many times its current size, stretching about 12 miles long and up to eight miles wide. The Erie Canal and Cayuga Lake dam projects greatly reduced its size.

The refuge, 3395 Rts. 5 and 20 E (Exits 40 or 41 off I-90), 315/568-5987, is open late April–November, daily dawn–dusk. Admission is free.

Cayuga Lake State Park

Three miles east of Seneca Falls lies the 190-acre Cayuga Lake State Park, offering a swimming beach, a bathhouse, hiking trails, a playground, and a 287-site campground. In the late 1700s, the park was part of a Cayuga Indian reservation, and in the late 1800s it was a resort area serviced by a train from Seneca Falls. The state park was established here in 1928.

The park, off Route 89, 315/568-5163, is open year-round. Parking in summer is $7. To reserve a campsite, call 800/456-CAMP; a basic site costs $13–15.

Accommodations

Several lovely B&Bs are in the heart of Seneca Falls. The 1855 **Hubbell House,** 42 Cayuga St., 315/568-9690, www.hubbellhousebb.com, built in the "Gothic cottage" style, overlooks Van Cleef Lake. Downstairs is a large double parlor, library, and dining room; upstairs are four guest rooms furnished with antiques ($85–105 d). The 1825 **Van Cleef Homestead B&B,** 86 Cayuga St., 315/568-2275, www.flare.net/vancleef, was built by Seneca Falls' first permanent resident, Lawrence Van Cleef. It's a Federal-style home offering three comfortable, air-conditioned guestrooms and a swimming pool ($80–99).

The **Guion House B&B,** 32 Cayuga St., 315/568-8129, is an 1876 Second Empire home with a huge front porch equipped with rocking chairs, a grand mahogany staircase leading to the second floor, and six nicely appointed rooms; call for room rates.

Food

There's something for everyone at the **Pump House,** 16 Rumsey St., 315/568-9109, which offers a wide variety of healthy dishes, including veggie and tuna wraps, along with steaks, pasta, and seafood; main dishes $6–14.

Events

The **Convention Days Celebration,** 800/732-1848, commemorating the first Women's Rights Convention, takes place on the weekend closest to July 19–20. Featured are concerts, dances, speeches, historical tours, food, kids' events, and a re-enactment of the signing of the Declaration of Sentiments.

Visitor Information

Seneca County Tourism, 1 DiPronio Dr., 315/539-1759 or 800/732-1848, www.visit-seneca.net, is open Mon.–Fri. 9 A.M.–5 P.M.

THE VINEYARDS OF THE FINGER LAKES

The hills of the Finger Lakes, covered with vineyards, glow pale green in spring, dust green in summer, red brown purple in fall. Ideal grape-growing conditions came about tens of thousands of years ago when the retreating glaciers deposited a layer of topsoil on shale beds above the lakes. The lakes in turn create a microclimate that moderates the region's temperatures.

In 1829 near Hammondsport, a Reverend Bostwick planted a few grapevines to make sacramental wine. His successful efforts were duly noted by his neighbors, and soon vineyards ringed the village. In 1860, 13 Hammondsport businesspeople banded together to form the country's first commercial winery—the Pleasant Valley Wine Company—and dozens of other entrepreneurs soon followed suit.

For many years, the Finger Lakes vineyards produced only native American Concord, Delaware, and Niagara grapes, used in the production of ho-hum sweet and table wines. About 25 years ago, however, several viticulturists began experimenting with the more complex European Vinifera grape, and today, excellent chardonnays, rieslings, seyval blancs, and sparkling wines are made throughout the region.

The Finger Lakes currently boasts close to 50 wineries, ranging in size from giant commercial Widmer's (in Naples) to small, family-run McGregor's (in Dundee). Most hug the shores of Cayuga, Seneca, or Keuka Lakes, and each lake has its own wine-growing association that publishes free maps and brochures, available throughout the region.

Most wineries are open May–Oct. Mon.–Sat. 10 A.M.–5 P.M., and Sunday noon–5 P.M., with more limited hours off-season. Tastings are usually free, but sometimes cost $1 or $1.50.

The best Finger Lakes wineries are described by geographic location throughout this chapter. For a complete list, contact the **New York Wine and Grape Foundation,** 315/536-7442, www.newyorkwines.org.

WATERLOO

A few miles west of Seneca Falls on Routes 5 and 20 is Waterloo, a surprisingly busy village filled with aging red-brick buildings and shady trees. As a plaque along Main Street attests, Waterloo claims to be the birthplace of Memorial Day. Originally known as Declaration Day, the event apparently first took place here on May 5, 1866, in honor of the Civil War dead. Flags flew at half-mast, businesses closed, and a solemn parade marched down Main Street. In 1966, the U.S. Congress and President Johnson officially recognized Waterloo as the birthplace of Memorial Day.

In the middle of town reigns the **Terwilliger Historical Museum.** Here you'll find a reconstructed Native American longhouse and village store, along with antique pianos, carriages, fire equipment, and a 1914 Waterloo mural. The museum, 31 E. Main St., 315/539-0533, is open July–Labor Day; call for schedule.

Food

On the west side of Waterloo is a honky-tonk strip where you'll find **Mac's,** 1166 Rts. 5 and 20, 315/539-3064, an old-fashioned drive-in complete with carhops. **Abigail's Restaurant,** 1978 Rts. 5 & 20, 315/539-9300, serves everything from veggie burgers for lunch (lunch Mon.–Thurs. only) to Italian dishes for dinner; average dinner entrée $11.

AURORA

Halfway down Cayuga's expansive eastern shore is picture-perfect Aurora, its houses laid out like beads on a string. Most date back to the mid-1800s; the entire village is on the National Register of Historic Places.

Called Deawendote, or Village of Constant Dawn, by the Cayuga, Aurora attracted its first white settlers in the late 1780s. Henry Wells founded Wells College here in 1868, and the school—a premier liberal arts college for women—remains a focal point of Main Street.

Also in Aurora is **MacKenzie-Childs,** 3260 N. Main St. (Rte. 90), 315/364-7123, a classy home furnishings design studio best known for its whimsical terra cotta pottery. The studio employs about 100 craftspeople, who design everything from glassware to lamps, and is housed on a 19th-century estate with great views of the lake. The retail store is open Mon.–Sat. 10 A.M.–5 P.M.; studio tours are often offered Mon.–Fri., call for details.

Accommodations and Food

In the center of Aurora presides the 1833 Federal-style **Aurora Inn,** Main St. (Rte. 90), currently closed for extensive renovations. Owned by Wells College, the inn is scheduled to reopen in 2003, with 10 guestrooms, two suites, a restaurant, and pub. To check on its status, contact Cayuga Tourism at 315/255-1658.

The **Restaurant at MacKenzie-Childs,** 3260 N. Main St. (Rte. 90), 315/364-7123, is open for lunch and weekend dinners, serving an eclectic American fare; average lunch entrée $11, dinner entrées range $17–26.

Entertainment

The charming, turn-of-the-century **Morgan Opera House,** Main St., 315/364-5437, offers musical and dramatic events May–September.

ROMULUS

Midway down the west side of the lake lies Romulus, known for its vineyards and wineries. Two of the best, only five miles apart, are the **Swedish Hill Vineyard,** 4565 Rte. 414, 315/549-8326; and the **Knapp Winery, Vineyards, and Restaurant,** 2770 County Rd. 128, 607/869-9271. Swedish Hill, a very large operation, produces about 30,000 cases of 25 different kinds of wines a year; Knapp is much smaller, but its wines are among the region's finest. Both wineries are open Mon.–Sat. 10 A.M.–5 P.M., and Sunday noon–5 P.M.

Food

The breezy **Knapp Winery Restaurant,** 607/869-9481, serves a first-rate lunch Thurs.–Mon. and dinner on the weekends; local produce is emphasized (average lunch entrée $8, average dinner entrée $18).

OVID

Heading south of Romulus on Route 96, you'll come to the hamlet of Ovid, astride a small ridge surrounded by farmland. In the heart of the village stand three red-brick Greek Revival buildings known as the **Three Bears** because of how they diminish progressively in size. The "Papa Bear" was once the county courthouse; "Mama Bear," the village library; and "Baby Bear," the county jail. Today, the buildings house county offices.

Camping and Accommodations

Off Route 89 overlooking Cayuga Lake is **Ridgewood Campground,** 6590 Cayuga Lake Rd., 607/869-9787, a good place for families, as it's equipped with a playground and miniature golf course. The campsites cost $14–21.

Nearby lies the **Driftwood Inn,** Rte. 89, Sheldrake-on-Cayuga, 607/532-4324, offering four guest rooms in the main house, two efficiency units, and two housekeeping cottages. Out front is a 260-foot-long waterfront equipped with small boats ($85–125 d).

The **Tillinghast Manor B&B,** 7246 S. Main St., 607/869-3584, is a palatial Victorian mansion with a square central tower, an inviting porch, and lots and lots of geraniums out front. All of the five spacious guest rooms feature king-size beds ($75–85 d).

INTERLAKEN

Closer to Cayuga than Seneca Lake, Interlaken, "land between the lakes," is an old-fashioned village with a few antique shops and a **Farmers Museum,** Main St., 607/532-4213 or 607/532-4642. Inside you'll find antique farm implements, including a dog-powered butter churn (open July–Aug., Thursday 2–4 P.M. and Saturday 10 A.M.–1 P.M., or by appointment; admission is free).

On the outskirts of Interlaken sprawls the family-owned **Lucas Vineyards,** 3862 County Rd. 150, 607/532-4825, featuring more great views of Cayuga Lake. At harvest time, grapes and juice are for sale along with wine.

TRUMANSBURG

Midway between Interlaken and Ithaca thunder **Taughannock Falls,** a skinny but dazzling 215-foot-long stream of water flanked on either side by towering stone walls. Just 10,000 years ago, the falls cascaded straight down into Cayuga Lake, but erosion has moved them almost a mile inland. Thirty feet higher than Niagara, Taughannock Falls are the highest straight falls east of the Rockies.

The falls are situated within the 783-acre **Taughannock Falls State Park,** which also offers lake swimming, fishing, boating, hiking, cross-country skiing, cabins, and a 76-site campground. Children will enjoy the park's imaginative playground, equipped with wooden towers and platforms.

The park, Rte. 89, 607/387-6739, is open year-round. Parking in summer is $6. For campground reservations, call 800/456-CAMP; a basic site costs $13.

Accommodations and Food

The friendly **Taughannock Farms Inn,** 2030 Gorge Rd., 607/387-7711, www.t-farms.com, is a large, rambling Victorian country inn overlooking the lake. Long a favorite among Finger Lakes residents, it includes both a relaxed restaurant serving traditional American cuisine (dinner only, average entrée $15) and 10 comfortable guest rooms, five of which are located in the main house, the rest in guest cottages ($95–235 d).

Entertainment and Events

One of the top music clubs in the region is the **Rongovian Embassy to the U.S.A.,** Rte. 96, 607/387-3334, a big, comfortable, laid-back joint with live jazz, rock, reggae, country, or blues most nights of the week.

In July and August, free jazz, Latin, folk, and rock concerts take place weekly in Taughannock Falls State Park, 607/387-6739.

THE FINGER LAKES

Ithaca

At the southern tip of Cayuga Lake lies Ithaca, a small, progressive university town whose population of 29,500 nearly doubles in size whenever its two colleges—Cornell University and Ithaca College—are in session. This is the kind of laid-back place where everyone wears Birkenstocks and reads Proust in outdoor cafes.

Ithaca was originally a Cayuga settlement that was destroyed during General Sullivan's ruthless 1779 campaign. The first white settlers arrived in 1788, but the town didn't really begin to grow until the opening of Cornell University in 1868.

For several years beginning in 1914, Ithaca was a center for the motion picture business. The Wharton Studios based itself here, and *Exploits of Elaine*, starring Lionel Barrymore and Pearl White; and *Patria*, starring Irene Castle, were both filmed in Ithaca. The region's unpredictable weather proved less than ideal for moviemaking, however, and in 1920 the industry moved West.

Ithaca also claims to be the birthplace of the sundae, supposedly first concocted here in 1891. "As the story goes," writes Arch Merrill in *Slim Fingers Beckon*, "an Ithaca preacher came into C. C. Platt's drugstore, weary and sweating after the Sunday morning service. He asked the druggist to fix a dish of ice cream and pour some syrup on it . . . and thus another American institution was born."

Orientation

Idyllically situated at the edge of Cayuga Lake, Ithaca is all but surrounded by steep hills and gorges. Three powerful waterfalls plunge right through the heart of the city.

The downtown is small, low-slung, and compact. In its flat center lies **Ithaca Commons,** a pedestrian mall spread out along State Street. Perched on a steep hill to the east is Cornell University. The roller-coaster streets surrounding Cornell are known as **Collegetown.** On another hill to the south sits Ithaca College.

The best way to explore Ithaca and environs is by foot and car. Street parking is generally available, but there are also two downtown municipal garages and several smaller lots.

Visitor Information and Tours

The **Ithaca/Tompkins County Convention & Visitors Bureau,** 904 East Shore Dr., near Stewart Park, Ithaca, NY 14850, 607/272-1313 or 800/284-8422, www.visitithaca.com, is open year-round, Mon.–Fri. 9 A.M.–5 P.M.; and June–Oct., Sat.–Sun. 9 A.M.–5 P.M. Brochures can also be picked up at the informal **Downtown Visitors' Center**—a booth in the lobby of the Clinton House, 116 N. Cayuga St., Ithaca Commons. Lobby hours are Mon.–Sat. 10 A.M.–6 P.M.

Also in the Clinton House is **Historic Ithaca and Tompkins County,** 607/273-6633, which publishes free walking-tour brochures of historic downtown sites. **Dire Wolf Natural History Tours,** 97 Genung Rd., 607/273-6316, specializes in guided tours of gardens, gorges, and woodlands.

The **Sagan Planet Walk,** 607/272-0600, www.sciencenter.org, was built in memory of astronomer Carl Sagan. It starts at the "sun" on the Commons in downtown Ithaca and continues on to visit nine "planets" along a three-quarter-mile route leading to the Sciencenter Museum. Visitors who get their "Passport to the Solar System" ($2) stamped along the way earn a free visit to the museum.

SIGHTS
Ithaca Commons

The pedestrian-only Commons runs along State Street between Aurora and Cayuga Streets and along Tioga Street between Seneca and State. European in feel, it's filled with fountains, trees, flowers, and benches, and is flanked with upscale shops and restaurants. On the south side, **Center Ithaca** holds two floors of stores surrounding a sky-lit atrium café. At the western end is **Clinton Hall,** 110 N. Cayuga St., also packed with shops and restaurants, and **Clinton House,** 116 N. Cayuga St., a historic hotel now housing various arts organizations.

Most of the buildings along the Commons were built between the 1860s and the 1930s.

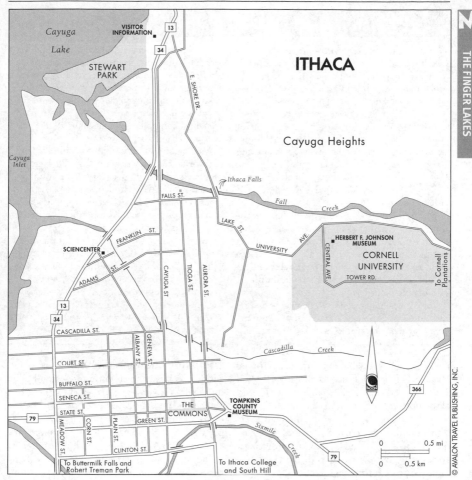

Note the handsome Italianate building at **No. 158 E. State St.,** and the art deco storefront at **No. 152 E. State Street.** Just beyond the Commons, at **No. 101 W. State St.,** glows a 1947 neon sign of a cocky chanticleer.

DeWitt Mall

One block north of the Commons, at the corner of Seneca and Cayuga Streets, is the DeWitt Mall. This former school building now contains about 20 shops, galleries, and restaurants, including the famed **Moosewood Restaurant.**

Among the galleries are the **Sola Art Gallery,** 607/272-6552, which specializes in the graphic arts (open Mon.–Sat. 10:30 A.M.–5:30 P.M.); and the **Upstairs Gallery,** 607/272-8614, exhibiting the work of area artists, many affiliated with Cornell or Ithaca College (open Tues.–Sat. 11 A.M.–3 P.M.).

Historic DeWitt Park

The oldest buildings in the city are located on or near DeWitt Park, a peaceful retreat at East Buffalo and North Cayuga Streets one block north of

BUYING AND SELLING WITH "ITHACA HOURS"

In Ithaca, they make their own money—a scrip called Ithaca Hours. The bills, which come in five denominations, are about the same size as U.S. dollars and are worth $10 an hour—the average wage in Tompkins County. They are used in a sort of barter system to exchange services. For example, a carpenter builds a cabinet for a neighbor for which he receives 10 bills. He sticks these in his wallet to use the next time he needs a participating member's expertise or the services of one of the 500 Ithaca businesses that accept Ithaca Hours.

In 1991 Ithaca resident Paul Glover developed Ithaca Hours. Lying in bed after a back injury, he envisioned a way to both improve the local economy and strengthen community ties. "The system expands the local money supply by making it easier for us to hire each other," he says. "It also makes it easier to start up new businesses—we extend loans without interest—and support local arts organizations."

In the beginning, about 90 people, including accountants, carpenters, and tutors, agreed to use the scrip as pay for their services. Today, that number has grown to several thousand residents and over 500 businesses, including fancy restaurants, a bowling alley, a medical center, and a used-car dealership. Glover publishes a newsletter online to keep subscribers up to date on who accepts the taxable scrip. He estimates that the equivalent of several million dollars in traditional money has exchanged hands so far.

Word of the program's success has spread around the world. Glover has mailed his Hometown Money Starter Kit to over 2,000 communities worldwide and has seen it adopted by groups in Argentina and Japan. He has been visited by Madame Mitterand of France and a top official from the People's Republic of China, and once sent a kit to Dr. Stephen Nzta, then a candidate for the presidency in Zaire. Glover is currently actively working with about 40 other communities to help them develop their own versions of Ithaca Hours.

To order a Hometown Money Starter Kit, send $25 to Hour Town, P.O. Box 365, Ithaca, NY 14851; 607/272-4330, www.ithacahours.com. Videos are also available for $15.

DeWitt Mall. Many buildings in this National Historic District date back to the early 1800s.

On the park's north side stands the 1817 **Old Courthouse,** thought to be the oldest Gothic Revival building in the state; and the **First Presbyterian Church,** designed by James Renwick, the architect of St. Patrick's Cathedral in New York City. On the east side is the Romanesque **First Baptist Church,** built in 1890.

Other Downtown Galleries

The eight-room **Asia House Gallery and Museum,** 118 S. Meadow St., 607/272-8850, specializes in the traditional fine arts, decorative arts, and antique folk arts of Asia (open Tues.–Fri. 11 A.M.–5 P.M., Saturday 11 A.M.–1 P.M.). **Handwork,** 102 W. State St., 607/273-9400, showcases the work of 25 local craftspeople (open Mon.–Sat. 10 A.M.–6 P.M., Sunday noon–5 P.M.).

To get a close-up look at artists at work, check out the **Greater Ithaca Art Trail,** website: www.arttrail.com.

Tompkins County Museum

Inside this large and recently renovated building you'll find a first-rate historical museum run by the DeWitt Historical Society. The society owns an impressive collection of over 20,000 objects, 3,000 books, and 100,000 photographs.

Permanent displays show the city's beginnings, its industries, and its surprising film history. Temporary exhibits focus on such subjects as folk arts, alternative medicine, Italian immigrants, and Finnish-American saunas.

The museum, 401 E. State St., at Seneca and Green Sts., 607/273-8284, is open Tues.–Sat. 11 A.M.–5 P.M. Admission is free.

The ScienCenter

Though the hands-on ScienCenter primarily appeals to young ones, adults can learn something here as well. Walk into a camera for a zoom-lens view of how it works. Draw your own picture on a "harmonograph." Measure the electrical current running through your body.

ON THE TRAIL OF ITHACA ART

A s befits a university town, Ithaca boasts more than its share of artists, about 60 of whom have banded together to offer a self-guided tour to their studios. On the tour, you can watch artists at work and/or buy their finished products. A wide variety of fields is represented, including painting, sculpture, photography, ceramics, wood carving, furniture, and stained glass. The artists put out a handsome brochure, available at tourism sites throughout the area, giving details on directions and hours. The trail is in especially fine form in October, when many of the artists conduct open houses, but operates all year. For more information, visit www.arttrail.com.

Watch a ball zigzag its way through an "audio-kinetic" sculpture.

The ScienCenter was largely created by volunteers, many of whom just happen to be Cornell scientists and engineers, which helps account for its homey yet high-tech feel. Out back an imaginative wooden playground filled with games teaches kids about physical principles such as gravity and heat.

The center, 601 1st St., at Franklin St., 607/272-0600, www.sciencenter.com, is open Tues.–Sat. 10 A.M.–5 P.M., and Sunday noon–5 P.M. Admission is adults $4.50, children 4–12 $3.50.

Ithaca Falls

At the corner of Falls and Lake Streets thunder Ithaca Falls, the last and greatest of the six waterfalls along the mile-long Fall Creek gorge. These "pulpit falls" are closely spaced rapids created by layers of resistant rock. To reach the site from Ithaca Commons—about a 20-minute walk—head north along Cayuga Street to Falls Street and turn right. To one side is a small grassy park and a wooded path that leads to a popular fishing hole.

Cornell University

High on a hill overlooking downtown Ithaca presides Cornell University, built around a long, lush green lined with ivy-covered build-

ings. The views from here are especially fine at twilight, when Cayuga's waters glow with the setting sun and the gorges begin a slow fade into black.

Cornell was founded in 1865 by Ezra Cornell and Andrew D. White, who vowed to establish an "institution where any person can find instruction in any study." In so doing, they challenged a number of long-standing mores. Their university was one of the first to be nonsectarian; to offer instruction to all qualified applicants, regardless of sex, race, or class; and to feature courses in everything from agriculture to the classics.

Traffic and information booths are located at each entrance to the central campus. Except in a few metered areas, parking is by permit only; purchase a permit at the traffic booths ($3 for four hours). Visitors to the Herbert F. Johnson Museum can park in metered spaces out front (two-hour limit).

Cornell students conduct free walking tours of the campus. The tours leave from the **Information and Referral Center,** Day Hall, Tower Road and East Avenue, 607/254-INFO, www.cornell.edu.

Herbert F. Johnson Museum of Art

At the northern end of the Cornell campus reigns the Johnson Museum of Art, housed in a striking modern building designed by I. M. Pei. The museum features especially strong collections of Asian and contemporary art but is also a teaching museum, containing a little bit of almost everything.

The Asian collection is situated on the fifth floor, where big picture windows open out onto 360-degree views of Cayuga Lake and the surrounding countryside. Among the many exquisite objects on display are funerary urns from the T'ang dynasty, silk paintings from 19th-century Japan, and bronze Buddhas from 15th-century Thailand.

The museum, Central Ave., 607/255-6464, www.museum.cornell.edu, is open Tues.–Sun. 10 A.M.–5 P.M. Admission is free.

Wilder Brain Collection

Those interested in the odd and macabre will want to step into Cornell's Uris Hall, East Avenue and Tower Road, and ride an elevator up to the second floor. In a small case to the rear of the building are the eight surviving stars of the Burt Green Wilder brain collection, which once numbered about 1,600 floating specimens.

Wilder was Cornell's first zoologist. He began assembling his collection in the late 1800s in the hopes of proving the size and shape of a person's brain were related to his or her race, sex, intelligence, and personality. Alas, his studies only disproved his theories, and in 1911, he rocked the scientific world by declaring that there was no difference between the brains of black and white men.

The pickled collection includes the extraordinarily large brain of criminal Edward Howard Ruloff, who was hanged in Binghamton on May 18, 1871. Ruloff allegedly killed his wife and daughter and was convicted of killing three men. He was also highly intelligent, and had published several scholarly papers despite his lack of formal education. His conviction caused a widespread sensation.

Burt Green Wilder's brain is also in the collection. Considerably smaller than Ruloff's, it sits yellowing in viscous formaldehyde. The creator has joined his creation.

Cornell University Plantations

Just north of the Cornell campus, a 2,800-acre oasis of green encompasses an arboretum, specialty gardens devoted to everything from wildflowers to poisonous plants, and nature trails winding through the Fall Creek gorge. Of special interest is an herb garden producing more than 800 herbs.

The plantations, 1 Plantations Rd., off Judd Falls Rd. and Rte. 366, 607/255-3020, are open year-round. Admission is free. Pick up maps in the gift shop. Descriptive brochures on the specialty gardens are on site.

Cornell Lab of Ornithology

At the eastern edge of the city lies a world-class center for the study, appreciation, and conservation of birds. Not everything is open to the public, but key attractions include 4.2 miles of trails through the Sapsucker Woods Sanctuary

and an observatory overlooking a waterfowl pond and bird-feeding garden.

The 220-acre **Sapsucker Woods** were named by bird artist Louis Agassiz Fuertes in 1901 after he spotted a pair of yellow-bellied sapsuckers—unusual for the region—nesting in the area. Sapsuckers continue to breed here each year.

Near the woods you'll find a visitor center where you can pick up maps and view paintings by Agassiz Fuertes. Also on site is the **Crows' Nest Birding Shop**—"the one stop for all your birding needs."

The visitor center, 159 Sapsucker Woods Rd., 607/254-BIRD, www.birds.cornell.edu, is open Mon.–Thurs. 8 A.M.–5 P.M., Friday 8 A.M.–4 P.M., and Saturday 10 A.M.–4 P.M. Woods and trails open 24 hours a day. Admission is free.

Buttermilk Falls State Park

Just south of downtown is Buttermilk Falls, plummeting more than 500 feet past 10 waterfalls, churning rapids, sculptured pools, and raggedy cliffs. Alongside the falls runs a trail leading up to spirelike Pinnacle Rock and Treman Lake. At the base of the falls are a natural swimming hole, ball fields, and a campground.

The park, Rte. 13, 607/273-5761, is open May–November. Parking in summer is $6. For campground reservations, call 800/456-CAMP. Basic campsites start at $13.

Robert H. Treman State Park

Five miles south of Ithaca lies Treman Park—1,025 acres of wild and rugged beauty. Near the entrance is Enfield Glen, a forested gorge traversed by a stone pathway and steps. The steps lead to 115-foot-high Lucifer Falls and a glorious vista stretching 1.5 miles down into a deep glen threaded by the Gorge Trail. The glen's cool environment supports a wide variety of ferns, mosses, and wildflowers, as well as trees and shrubs.

A three-story 1839 gristmill open to visitors, a natural swimming pool, and a campground are also on the grounds.

Off Route 13, 607/273-3440, the park is open April–November. Parking in summer is $6. For campground reservations, call 800/456-CAMP; a basic campsite costs $13.

SPORTS AND RECREATION

Circle Greenway: This 10-mile walk leads to many of Ithaca's foremost natural and urban attractions, including gorges, the waterfront, Cornell, and the Commons. A free map can be picked up at the Ithaca/Tompkins County Convention & Visitors Bureau.

Cruises and Charters: Cayuga Lake Cruises, 702 W. Buffalo St., 607/256-0898, offers dinner and Sunday brunch cruises aboard the M/V *Manhattan*. **Fin-Knapper Charters,** 607/277-2913, offers chartered fishing trips and natural history tours.

ACCOMMODATIONS

Motels

In the heart of downtown stands the comfortable, 58-room **Meadow Court Inn,** 529 S. Meadow St., 607/273-3885 or 800/852-4014 ($60 d).

Hotels and Inns

As the teaching hotel of Cornell's School of Hotel Administration, the **Statler,** 11 East Ave., Cornell University Campus, 607/257-2500 or 800/541-2501, www.statlerhotel.cornell.edu, is Ithaca's hotel of choice for visiting parents, academics, and travelers. The hotel features 132 guest rooms and two restaurants; guests have access to most of Cornell's facilities, including the gym, pool, tennis courts, and golf course ($105–155 d).

Far on the outskirts of town sits the luxurious **Rose Inn,** Rte. 34 N, 607/533-7905, www.roseinn.com, an 1850s Italianate mansion complete with a circular mahogany staircase, marble fireplaces, 15 guest rooms, and a dining room known for its gourmet dinners ($155–200 d, with breakfast). **La Tourelle,** 1550 Danby Rd. (Rte. 96B), 607/273-2734 or 800/765-1492, is a modern country inn built in the style of a European auberge ($99–109 d).

Bed-and-Breakfasts

One of Ithaca's most delightful hostelries is the **Buttermilk Falls B&B,** 110 E. Buttermilk Falls Rd., off Rte. 13 S, 607/272-6767, near the foot of the falls on the edge of town. The brick B&B dates back to 1820 and features spacious, antique-filled guest rooms—including one with a fireplace and double Jacuzzi—and very knowledgeable hosts ($95–265 d).

Also an excellent choice, located near Cornell and the downtown, is the **Peregrine House,** 140 College Ave., 607/272-0919, www.peregrinehouse.com. This cozy Victorian home offer nine comfortable guest rooms, all of which have been outfitted with modern amenities such as air conditioning and private baths ($79–109 d; call for off-season rates).

The **Log Country Inn B&B,** 607/589-4771, www.logtv.com, may sound rustic but it features soaring cathedral ceilings, fireplaces, a sauna, and five guestrooms equipped with all the amenities. Next door is a 7,000-acre forest perfect for hiking and cross-country skiing. Call for rates.

For more bed-and-breakfast suggestions, contact the Tompkins County Convention & Visitors Bureau or **Bed & Breakfast of Greater Ithaca,** 607/589-6073 or 800/806-4406, www.bbithaca.com.

FOOD

A number of casual eateries are located along Ithaca Commons. The 100 block of Aurora Street just off the Commons has one restaurant after another.

Natural Eats

Famed worldwide for its best-selling cookbooks and natural foods, the cooperatively owned **Moosewood,** 215 N. Cayuga St., DeWitt Mall, 607/273-9610, is a simple, casual place, crowded with rustic wooden tables. An outdoor dining area opens in the summer; average dinner entrée $11.

Historic Restaurants

Step into **Joe's Restaurant,** 602 W. Buffalo St., 607/273-2693, and you step into the 1950s: the place is outfitted with a Wurlitzer jukebox, an old Coke machine, and lots of neon. On the menu is tasty Italian fare; average entrée $11.

The Station, 806 W. Buffalo St., 607/272-2609, specializing in contemporary American food, occupies the beautifully restored Lehigh Railroad station; average entrée $16.

Bistros, Tapas, and Asian

Willow, 202 E. Falls St., 607/272-0656, is a local favorite, serving contemporary American fare; average entrée $17. **Just a Taste Wine and Tapas Restaurant & Bar,** 116 N. Aurora St., 607/277-WINE, serves 50 wines by the glass and an international menu. Outside is a lovely garden; average tapa $7. **Madeline's Restaurant and Bar,** North Aurora and East State Streets, on the Commons, 607/277-2253, offers excellent Asian cuisine from a variety of countries; average entrée $14. For the best Thai food in town, step into **The Thai Cuisine,** 501 S. Meadow St., 607/273-2031; average entrée $12.

Cajun and Soul

Hot spot **Maxie's Supper Club and Oyster Bar,** 635 W. State St., 607/272-4136, all done up in purples and reds, offers both spicy Cajun cuisine and stick-to-your-ribs Southern soul food. Everything's homemade at this family-run affair; average entrée $14.

ENTERTAINMENT

Performing Arts

The **Ithaca Performing Arts Center** is housed in the majestic State Theatre, 109 W. State St., 607/273-1037, a 1920s vaudeville house with 1,000 seats and a 2,500-square-foot dance floor. The center features a little of everything, including ballet, musicals, concerts, film, and dance.

Among the groups performing regularly in the city is the **Cayuga Chamber Orchestra,** 116 N. Cayuga St., 607/273-8981, the official orchestra of Ithaca. The **Ithaca Ballet,** 607/277-1967, performs both classical and contemporary works. The **Ithaca Opera Association,** 607/272-0168, presents two major operas every year.

The **Cornell Center for Theatre Arts,** 430 College Ave., 607/254-ARTS or 607/254-2700, stages six to 12 plays Sept.–May, along with the Cornell Dance Series and numerous

guest performers. Professional regional theater is staged by the acclaimed **Hangar Theatre,** Rte. 89, Cass Park, 607/273-8588, June–August. The **Kitchen Theater,** 607/273-4497, presents contemporary theater in the historic Clinton House.

Free concerts, 607/272-1313, ranging from classic jazz to 1950s rock take place on the Commons throughout the summer.

Clubs and Nightlife

Good club listings can be found in the Thursday edition of the *Ithaca Journal,* 607/272-2321, and in the *Ithaca Times,* 607/277-7000, a free alternative news weekly.

One of the best music clubs in the area is the **Rongovian Embassy** in nearby Trumansburg (see above). For serious jazz, check out the carriage house at the **Rose Inn,** Rte. 34 N, 607/533-7905, on a Friday or Saturday night.

Common Ground, 1230 Danby Rd., 607/273-1505, is the place to go for dance music. The **ABC Cafe,** 308 Stewart Ave., 607/277-4770, features folk, a weekly open mike, and jazz on Sunday.

EVENTS

The **Ithaca Farmers Market,** 607/273-7109, www.ithacamarket.com, selling crafts and home-baked goods as well as produce, takes place at Steamboat Landing, 535 3rd St., off Rte. 13, April–Dec., Saturday 9 A.M.–2 P.M. and Sunday 10 A.M.–2 P.M. A smaller version is held in De-Witt Park on Tuesday 9 A.M.–2 P.M.

The **Ithaca Festival,** complete with crafts, food, a parade, and entertainment, takes place the first weekend in June. In July and August, **free concerts** are presented Thursday at 7 P.M. on Ithaca Commons. For more info about these and other events, call 607/272-1313.

DETOUR TO OWEGO

Route 96B runs south of Ithaca to hook up with Route 96, an old stagecoach road that leads to Owego. Along the way you'll pass through farm country, much of it worn down and depressed.

Located on the Susquehanna River, five miles from the Pennsylvania border, Owego centers around a four-towered 1872 courthouse. Along the river runs Front Street, where historic brick buildings house snug shops and restaurants.

The town's most famous early citizens were Gen. Robert, who wrote Robert's Rules of Order in 1872, and Belva Lockwood, the first woman to run for the presidency—in 1884. To learn more about them, visit the **Tioga County Historical Society Museum,** 110 Front St., 607/687-2460, which also houses Native American artifacts, folk arts, and pioneer crafts. Hours are Tues.–Sat. 10 A.M.–4 P.M. Admission is free.

Also in town is the vintage **Tioga Scenic Railroad,** composed of early 1900s open-air cars that travel between Owego and Newark Valley. The trains leave from the original Owego Depot, a striking two-story wooden building containing railroad memorabilia and a large model train layout. Once in Newark Valley, passengers can board a shuttle to the 1840s **Bement-Billings Farmstead,** now inhabited by costumed guides.

The depot, 25 Delphine St., 607/687-6786, www.tiogascenicrailroad.com, is open year-round Mon.–Fri. 8 A.M.–4 P.M., and summer weekends. The trains operate July–October, weekends only; call for schedule and ticket prices.

Seneca Lake

At 36 miles long and 618 feet deep, Seneca Lake is one of the deepest bodies of water in the United States. She seldom freezes over and is renowned for her superb lake trout fishing. Given to sudden, capricious gusts of wind, she's the most mysterious of the Finger Lakes.

Ever since the days of the Native Americans, area residents have reported strange, dull rumblings coming from Seneca's depths. The sounds are usually heard at dusk in the late summer or early fall and are most distinct midway down the lake. The Native Americans believed the rumblings were the voice of an angry god; early settlers considered them omens of disaster; science attributes them to the popping of natural gas released from rock rifts at the bottom of the lake.

Whatever the cause, the dull rumbles—a sound much like gunfire—may have had some portent, for during WW II, a huge munitions depot and naval station was built along Seneca's eastern shore. The naval station is now long gone, but the 11,000-acre **Seneca Arms Depot** remains. Officially, it functions to "maintain and demilitarize ammunition," but the herd of snow-white deer that roam the grounds can't help but make you wonder. The deer can best be seen from Route 96A at dawn and dusk.

At the northern end of Seneca Lake lies Geneva, a historic town whose elegant South Main Street has been called "the most beautiful street in America." At the southern end is Watkins Glen, a rugged, 700-foot-deep gorge that's been turned into a natural theme park.

GENEVA

One of the larger towns in the region, Geneva is home to about 15,000 residents. Though overall a nondescript place, through its center runs the very elegant South Main Street, lined with leafy trees, stately homes, and Hobart and William Smith Colleges. Nurseries surrounding Geneva raise fruit trees, ornamental trees, and shrubs.

Geneva was once a major Seneca settlement known as Kanadesaga. During the French and Indian War, the British erected a fort here from which they and the Seneca conducted murderous raids—only to be massacred themselves during the 1779 Sullivan campaign.

Soon after the Revolution, settlers began to arrive. A visionary land agent laid out the town along a broad Main Street and a public green. This gave the place an air of dignity which, during the 1800s, attracted an usually large number of retired ministers and spinsters. Geneva soon earned the nickname "The Saints' Retreat and Old Maids' Paradise."

In 1847, the Medical College of Geneva College (now Hobart) received an application of admission from one Elizabeth Blackwell of Philadelphia. The students and deans, assuming it to be a joke, laughingly voted to admit her. A few weeks later, to everyone's amazement, Ms. Blackwell arrived, and in 1849, she graduated—the first woman ever granted a medical diploma in America.

Prouty-Chew Museum

The only South Main Street mansion open to the public is the Prouty-Chew. Built in the Federal style in 1829 by a Geneva attorney, the house was enlarged several times in the 1850s and 1870s, which accounts for its eclectic look. Now home to the Geneva Historical Society, the museum showcases changing exhibits on local history and art. Pick up free city walking- and driving-tour brochures here.

The house, 543 S. Main St., 315/789-5151, is open year-round Tues.–Fri. 9:30 A.M.–4:30 P.M., Saturday 1:30–4:30 P.M. Admission is free.

Rose Hill Mansion

Three miles east of downtown lies Geneva's foremost visitor attraction—the fine 1839 Rose Hill Mansion, built in the Greek Revival style with six Ionic columns out front. The mansion was once home to Robert Swan, an innovative farmer who installed the country's first large-scale drainage system. Tours of the house take visitors past a first-rate collection of Empire-style furnishings. Next door is the former carriage house; out front a long, emerald green lawn slopes down to Seneca Lake.

Located at Route 96A, 315/789-3848, Rose Hill Mansion is open May–Oct., Mon.–Sat. 10 A.M.–4 P.M., Sunday 1–5 P.M. Admission is adults $3, seniors and youths 10–18 $2.

Seneca Lake State Park

Also east of town, the popular Seneca State Park offers a marina, swimming beach, bathhouse, picnic tables, playground, and good onshore fishing spots. The park, Rts. 5 and 20, 315/789-2331, is open year-round. Parking in summer is $6.

Accommodations and Food

For dockside dining, try **Crow's Nest on Seneca**

Lake, 415 Boody's Hill Rd., off Rte. 96A near Rose Hill Mansion, 315/781-0600. On the menu are sandwiches and salads, seafood and beef; average dinner entrée $14.

The **Chanticleer Motor Lodge,** 473 Hamilton St., 315/789-7600 or 800/441-5227, offers standard motel rooms and a swimming pool ($50–60 d).

The extravagant, Romanesque **Belhurst Castle,** Lochland Rd. (Rte. 14 S), 315/781-0201, www.genevany.com, took 50 workers toiling six days a week four years to complete. Finished in 1889, it features everything from turrets to stained-glass windows. Inside is an upscale restaurant serving continental fare for both lunch and dinner (average lunch entrée $8, average dinner entrée $23), and about a dozen modernized guest rooms that vary greatly in size and price. Out front are formal gardens and a lakefront beach ($105–315 d, with breakfast). Also operated by Belhurst Castle is the lovely Georgian **Whitesprings Manor;** the same contact information and rates apply.

The luxurious, all-suite **Geneva-on-the-Lake,** 1001 Lochland Rd., 315/789-7190 or 800/3GENEVA, www.genevaonthelake.com, centers around a 1911 mansion built in the style of a 16th-century Italian villa. Each suite differs from the next, and outside extend 10 acres of formal gardens ($220–495 d, includes continental breakfast). The dining room, open to the public for lunch and dinner, serves first-rate continental fare using much fresh local produce (average dinner entrée $24).

Entertainment

The 1894 **Smith Opera House,** 82 Seneca St., 315/781-LIVE, offers a mix of theater, concerts, and film year-round. Tours of the house are available by appointment.

Visitor Information

The **Geneva Area Chamber of Commerce,** 1 Lakeside Dr., off Rts. 5 and 20, 315/789-1776, www.genevany.com, is east of downtown on the lakefront. Hours year-round are Mon.–Fri. 8 A.M.–4:30 P.M.; July–Labor Day, Sat.–Sun. 10 A.M.–4 P.M.

DETOUR TO SODUS POINT AND ENVIRONS

Worth a 30-mile detour north of Geneva on Route 14 is Sodus Point overlooking Lake Ontario. The village boasts some gorgeous views, an inviting public beach, and the handsome 1870 **Old Sodus Point Lighthouse and Maritime Museum,** 7606 N. Ontario St., 315/483-4936 (open May–Oct., Tues.–Sun. 10 A.M.–5 P.M.; admission is free).

The real reason to venture up here, however, are the **Chimney Bluffs.** Located on the eastern side of Sodus Bay, the bluffs rise 150 feet above the lake like some giant confectionery delight. All pinnacles, spires, and peaks, they're part of a glacier-created drumlin that has been eroded, carved, and shaped by water, wind, and snow. Atop some of the pinnacles sit lone trees; below them extends a stony beach.

Dozens of other drumlins (minus the pinnacles and peaks) can be found throughout this section of the Lake Ontario region. The only other places to view drumlins in North America are the areas bordering Lake Superior in Minnesota.

The Chimney Bluffs and its beach form part of the undeveloped Chimney Bluffs State Park. The park can be reached by taking Route 414 north to the end of Lake Bluff Road.

Alasa Farms

On your way to and from Sodus Point, you'll pass through serious farm country, heavy with rich black soil. Near the lake thrive apples, cherries, and peaches. Farther inland grow corn, wheat, potatoes, onion, and lettuce.

Off Route 14 just south of Sodus Point lies Alasa Farms. Once a 1,400-acre Shaker religious community, the site passed into private hands in the 1800s. Throughout the 1920s and 1930s, the farm raised everything from shorthorn cattle and hackney ponies to timberland and orchards, and today, it's still a 700-acre working farm. Visitors can opt for either a self-guided farm tour or an escorted tour of the Shaker Dwelling House.

The farm, 6450 Shaker Rd., Alton, 315/483-6321, is open June–Oct. by appointment.

Events

One of the region's foremost events is the **Sterling Renaissance Festival,** 315/947-5783, held in Sterling, near Fair Haven, about 25 miles west of Sodus Point. For seven weekends in July and August, the fest celebrates the Middle Ages with music, jousting, outdoor theater, crafts, and food.

SOUTH ON ROUTES 96A AND 414

From Rose Hill Mansion in Geneva, Route 96A heads south along the eastern shore of Seneca Lake past the Seneca Army Depot (see Seneca Lake Introduction). About 10 miles down is the 1,852-acre **Sampson State Park,** 315/585-6392, equipped with a marina, swimming beach, bathhouses, picnic area, playground, and 245-site campground. Parking in summer is $7. To reserve a campsite, call 800/456-CAMP; a basic site costs $15.

Below Sampson is Willard, where you'll bypass the enormous **Willard State Psychiatric Center.** Once one of the most advanced mental institutions in the world, Willard was named after a physician who fell dead while pleading the cause of the mentally ill before a legislative committee in Albany.

South of Willard, Route 96A veers inland to Ovid (see Cayuga Lake Area, above), where it hooks up with Route 414. Continue south on Route 414 to more small villages and one of the region's largest clusters of vineyards and wineries.

Lodi

Tidy Lodi hosts a farmers market in its village square June–September, Saturday 9 A.M.–noon. Two miles west of the village is the **Lodi Point State Marine Park,** off Route 136, a small park with a protected swimming area and pebble beach.

Just south of Lodi you'll find several excellent wineries. One of the newest is the **Lamoreaux Landing Wine Cellars,** 9224 Rte. 414, 607/582-6011, housed in a modern redwood building with great views of the lake.

Another mile or so down the road sprawls **Wagner Vineyards,** 9322 Rte. 414, 607/582-6450, centered around a weathered octagonal

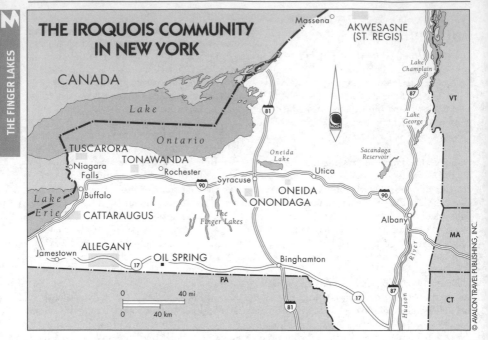

THE IROQUOIS COMMUNITY IN NEW YORK

building overlooking the lake. Established in 1979, Wagner now produces about 75,000 gallons a year. On the premises is the **Ginny Lee Cafe,** 607/582-6574, open for lunch only.

Finger Lakes National Forest

Between the southern ends of Seneca and Cayuga Lakes stands the Finger Lakes National Forest. The only real forest in the region, it supports evergreens, oaks, and maples, along with white-tailed deer, wild turkey, and grouse. Twelve miles long and five miles wide, the forest is laced with 25 miles of easy-to-moderate hiking trails. Near the entrance you'll find a visitor center where you can pick up maps. A small campground is available on a first-come, first-served basis for a small fee, and free camping is also allowed throughout the park.

The main entrance to the forest is Logan Road, 607/546-4470, off Route 414 south of Hector. Admission is free. The visitor center is open Mon.–Fri. 8 A.M.–4:30 P.M., and maps are available in the vestibule on weekends.

SOUTH ON ROUTE 14

From Geneva, Route 14 heads south along the western shore of Seneca Lake past two excellent wineries. **Fox Run Vineyards,** 670 Rte. 14, Penn Yan, 315/536-4616, is housed in an 1860s dairy barn with sweeping views of the lake. The **Anthony Road Wine Company,** 1225 Anthony Rd., Penn Yan, 800/559-2182, is not particularly scenic but produces a good seyval and riesling.

Dundee Wineries

More good wineries cluster near the lake's southern end. Among them is the **Hermann J. Wiemer Vineyard,** Rte. 14, Dundee, 607/243-7971, run by a foremost viticulturalist. Born on the Mosel River in Germany, Wiemer is especially famous for his rieslings.

Yet a few miles farther south is **Glenora Wine Cellars,** 5435 Rte. 14, Dundee, 607/243-5511. Established in 1977, Glenora now produces about 150,000 gallons a year and is best known for its

THE NATIVE AMERICAN CONFEDERACY OF SIX NATIONS

Before the arrival of whites, Algonquin and Iroquois tribes lived freely in New York. The Algonquin resided in the south and along the Hudson River Valley, while the Iroquois spread out across the north.

The Iroquois were actually a confederacy of five tribes—the Mohawk, the Oneida, the Onondaga, the Cayuga, and the Seneca—who had banded together around 1450 to end intertribal warfare. A sixth nation, the Tuscarora, joined the Confederacy in 1722.

The Iroquois survived through hunting, fishing, and the planting of the "Three Sisters"—corn, beans, and squash. Records were kept through storytelling and the weaving of elaborate wampum belts. Each of the Iroquois tribes was divided into matrilineal clans that took their names from birds and animals. The clans lived in longhouses comprised of 50–60 families, and all clan members were considered part of one family. Women selected the clan chiefs.

The men responsible for founding the Confederacy were a Huron now known as "The Peacemaker" and Hiawatha, an Onondaga chief. The two traveled from tribe to tribe for months, convincing their people to lay down their arms and embrace the Great Law of Peace. The Law gave equal voice to each of the tribes, guaranteed freedom of speech, set up a system for the impeachment of corrupt chiefs, and outlined an amendment procedure.

Sound remarkably familiar? It's because the Great Law served as one of the models for the U.S. Constitution. No firm textual evidence exists, but several framers of the Constitution met frequently with the Iroquois after the Revolution, and Benjamin Franklin in particular expressed a wish to use their system as a model. In 1988, Congress passed a resolution acknowledging this Native American contribution to the U.S. Constitution.

Today, approximately 40,000 Native Americans still live in New York State. About 35 percent reside on reservations, while the rest live in large urban areas, most notably Brooklyn. That metropolis has traditionally drawn an especially large number of Mohawk because of their sure-footed skill as high-rise steelworkers.

Eight Iroquois communities are located upstate, ranging in size from the 30,469-acre Allegany Reservation (Seneca) to the 5,700-acre Tuscarora Reservation. The state's only casinos are on Oneida territory about 20 miles east of Syracuse and in Mohawk territory near the Canada border.

---

sparkling wines. The winery offers panoramic views of the lake and presents first-rate **jazz concerts** every summer.

Also on site is the large, modern, and very comfortable **Inn at Glenora Wine Cellars,** 5435 Rte. 14, 607/243-9500, www.glenora.com, which features big picture windows overlooking the vineyards and spacious guestrooms complete with private balconies or patios ($130–235 d). Connected with the inn is an equally spacious restaurant and outdoor dining patio that serves tasty "regional fusion" specialties; average entrée $16.

WATKINS GLEN AND VICINITY

At the southern tip of Seneca Lake lies Watkins Glen, named for the astonishing gorge that rips right through its center. Near the entrance to the glen, now a state park, stand family-style eateries and plenty of souvenir shops.

Back in the 1950s and '60s, the main street of Watkins Glen and the steep roads surrounding it were the speedway of the American Grand Prix. During the races, as many as 75,000 spectators descended on the village, whose year-round population was—and is—under 3,000. Today, world-class auto races take place at the Watkins Glen International Race Track, four miles south of Watkins Glen.

Watkins Glen State Park

Created some 12,000 years ago during the last Ice Age, Watkins Glen is a wild and raggedy gorge flanked by high cliffs and strange, sculpted rock formations. Through its center rushes Glen

Creek, dropping some 700 feet in two miles over rapids, cascades, and 19 waterfalls.

Alongside the gorge runs the 1.5-mile Gorge Trail, made up of 832 stone steps, stone paths, and numerous bridges. The trail leads past tunnels, caves, and a natural stone bridge, all carved out of the sedimentary rock by Glen Creek. If you hike the trail on a fine summer's day, you'll have lots of company, but the gorge inspires awe nonetheless.

The park, off Rte. 14/414, 607/535-4511, is open May–Nov., daily 8 A.M.–dusk. In summer, parking is $6. Also in the park are campgrounds and an Olympic-size pool. For campground reservations, call 800/456-CAMP; a basic site costs $15–20.

Montour Falls

Route 14 leads south of Watkins Glen through narrow winding Pine Valley to Montour Falls, a small industrial community surrounded by seven glens. In the middle of town, flanked by buildings, is Chequagua Falls, plunging downward 165 feet into a deep pool. The falls are illuminated at night and near the top is a pedestrian bridge.

Along Genesee and Main Streets you'll find a handsome National Historic District composed of 24 brick buildings dating back to the 1850s. Among them is Memorial Library with Tiffany windows and the Greek Revival Village Hall.

Sports and Recreation

The **Seneca Grand Prix,** 2374 Rte. 414, 607/535-7981, features go-karts, a video games arcade, and miniature golf; open June–September.

World-class **auto racing** takes place June–Sept. at the Watkins Glen International Race Track, County Road 16, off Rte. 14/414 S, 607/535-2481.

From May to October, 50-minute **cruises** of Seneca Lake are offered every hour on the hour by **Captain Bill's Seneca Lake Cruises,** 1 ½ N. Franklin St., 607/535-4541. Captain Bill also runs dinner cruises.

Accommodations

One of the more idiosyncratic hostelries in the area is the **Seneca Lodge,** Rte. 329, off Rte. 14/414 at the south entrance to Watkins Glen State Park, 607/535-2014. A favorite haunt of bow-and-arrow hunters, the lodge centers on a restaurant and bar whose back wall, bristled with arrows, looks like the hide of a porcupine. As the tradition goes, the first bow-and-arrow hunter to shoot a deer each season shoots an arrow into the wall ($55–65 d).

More conventional digs can be found at the **Villager,** 106 E. 4th St., 607/535-7159, www .wgvillagermotel.com, which offers motel, hotel, and B&B style rooms that vary in price, with the motel rooms the cheapest ($60–90 d) and the B&B rooms, the most expensive ($110–140). Also on site is a heated swimming pool.

Food

Chef's Diner, Rte. 14, 607/535-9975, is a classic American eatery, now in its sixth decade. Come here for tasty pancakes or grilled cheese sandwiches.

Just west of the village you'll find **Castel Grisch Estate,** 3380 County Road 28, off Rte. 409, 607/535-9614, a winery that's also a German-style restaurant. Open for lunch during the week and brunch on Sunday. Outside is a deck overlooking the lake; main dishes cost $7–14.

Events

During the **Grand Prix Festival,** 607/535-4300, in early September, the 1948 American Grand Prix is reenacted in the streets of Watkins Glen.

Visitor Information

The **Schuyler County Chamber of Commerce,** 100 Franklin St., 607/535-4300 or 800/607-4552, www.schuylerny.com, is open Mon.–Fri. 9 A.M.–5 P.M., with extended hours in summer.

Elmira

Located on both sides of the Chemung River, a few miles north of the Pennsylvania border, Elmira is a hard city to figure. Some parts appear quite historic, with handsome stone and red-brick buildings; many other parts are crumbling, windswept, and seriously depressed.

Once the site of a Seneca village, Elmira was first overrun by whites in the 1780s. By the 1840s, the town was known for its lumbering and woolen mills, and by the 1860s, for its metal industries and furnaces producing some 22,000 tons of iron a year. Elmira also served as a major transportation center, sitting at the crossroads of the Erie Railroad, the Chemung River, and the Chemung and Junction Canals.

During the Civil War, the Union Army set up barracks in Elmira. In 1864, one of those barracks was turned into a prison camp for Confederate soldiers. The prison was poorly built and desperately overcrowded; thousands of prisoners died within a year.

Samuel Clemens, a.k.a. Mark Twain, spent over 20 summers in Elmira. His wife, Olivia Langdon, grew up in the area and Twain wrote many of his masterpieces—including *Tom Sawyer* and *The Adventures of Huckleberry Finn*—while staying at the Langdon family farm. Mark Twain's Study has since been moved onto the campus of Elmira College, which was one of the earliest colleges for women, founded in 1855.

Outside the city lies the National Soaring Center. Elmira has been known as the Soaring Capital of America ever since 1930, when the first National Soaring Contest took place here.

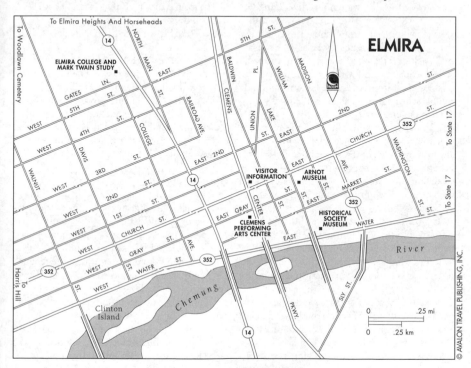

Orientation

Most of Elmira is north of the Chemung River. Exiting off Route 17 onto Route 352 W (Church St.) will take you into the heart of the city. Route 14 N runs past Elmira College and Woodlawn Cemetery (off West Woodlawn Avenue) to the suburban communities of **Elmira Heights** and **Horseheads**.

Visitor Information and Tours

The **Chemung County Chamber of Commerce,** 400 E. Church St., Elmira, NY 14901, 607/734-5137 or 800/627-5892, www.chemungchamber.org, is open year-round Mon.–Fri. 8:30 A.M.–5 P.M. In July and August, the chamber offers guided tours of Elmira's attractions onboard an open-air trolley; call for details.

DOWNTOWN SIGHTS

Mark Twain's Study

The story of Mark Twain and Olivia Langdon began in 1867 when Twain fell in love with her after viewing her portrait, shown to him by a friend as they were crossing the Atlantic. Upon arrival back in the United States, Twain immediately set up a meeting with Olivia. At first, she was not at all impressed. He was a rough-and-tumble self-made man; she was a refined young woman of good family.

But Twain was stubborn. For the next two years, he visited Elmira regularly, and eventually won over the entire Langdon family. In fact, near the end of his courtship, Olivia—who was sickly and delicate—was only allowed to visit with him for five minutes a day because she became so excited.

Twain's former study, modeled after a Mississippi steamboat pilot house, was built for him by his sister-in-law. Though it now looks rather forlorn, sitting by itself near a crossroads, Twain once described it as "the loveliest study you ever saw. It is octagonal in shape with a peaked roof, each space filled with a spacious window and it sits perched in complete isolation on the very top of an elevation that commands leagues of valleys and city and retreating ranges of blue hill."

Inside, the study is simple and functional—to one side a large greystone fireplace, to the other the door. A Remington Rand sits on a desk, a trunk inscribed with the name "Clemens" rests on the floor. Twain was one of the first writers to submit a typed manuscript to a publisher.

The study, Park Pl., Elmira College Campus, 607/735-1941, www.elmira.edu, is open June–Labor Day, Mon.–Sat. 9 A.M.–5 P.M., or by appointment. Admission is free.

Woodlawn Cemetery

Samuel Clemens is buried in the Langdon family plot, along with his wife, his father-in-law, and his son-in-law Ossip Gabrilowitsch, a noted Russian-born pianist. A 12-foot-high monument commemorates the two famous men.

Adjacent to the main cemetery is the **Woodlawn National Cemetery,** containing the graves of the 2,963 Confederate soldiers who died in the Elmira prison. Surrounding the Confederate graves are the graves of 322 Union soldiers.

The main cemetery, 1200 Walnut St., 607/732-0151, and the national cemetery, 1825 Davis St., 607/732-5411, are both open daily dawn–dusk.

Elmira Correctional Facility

Just north of the cemetery, at Davis Street and Bancroft Road, stands the grim Elmira Correctional Facility. The facility is built on the site of the Civil War prison camp and was originally a reformatory for first offenders between the ages of 16 and 30. Today, it houses a more general prison population.

Arnot Museum

In this restored neoclassical mansion built in 1833 hangs a fine collection of 17th- to 19th-century European and 19th- to 20th-century American paintings. At the heart of the collection are works acquired by Matthias Arnot in the late 1800s. Among them are paintings by Breughel, Daubigny, Rousseau, and Millet, hung floor to ceiling in the old salon style.

Behind the mansion a handsome modern wing houses both temporary exhibitions and rotating selections from the museum's Asian, Egyptian, and pre-Columbian collections. A gift shop sells work by regional artists and craftspeople.

The museum, 235 Lake St., at W. Gray, 607/734-3697, www.arnotartmuseum.org, is open Tues.–Sat. 10 A.M.–5 P.M., Sunday 1–5 P.M. Admission is adults $5, seniors $4, students $2.50; free to children under six and to everyone on Saturday–Sunday.

Chemung Valley History Museum

To learn more about Elmira'a history, stop into this small local history museum. Featured are exhibits on the Seneca, Mark Twain in Elmira, and the Civil War prison camp. The museum, 415 E. Water St., at Lake St., 607/734-4167, www.chemungvalleymuseum.org, is open Tues.–Sat. 10 A.M.–5 P.M., Sunday 1–5 P.M. Admission is free.

Near Westside

Roughly located between West Water and West 2nd Streets, College Avenue and Hoffman Street, the 20-block Near Westside is a National Historic District notable for its enormous collection of Victorian buildings. Among them you'll find homes built in the Federal, Greek Revival, Italianate, Second Empire, Queen Anne, stick, shingle, Colonial Revival, Craftsman, Tudor Revival, and even Prairie styles. The oldest homes date from the late 1820s, but most were built between 1850 and 1900.

The Near Westside Neighborhood Association, 353 Davis St., near W. 1st St., 607/733-4924, publishes free self-guided walking tours of the area. In summer, the association also offers guided tours.

NEARBY SIGHTS

Harris Hill Soaring Center and National Soaring Museum

A few miles west of Elmira rises Harris Hill, an idyllic, woodsy spot surrounded by other hills and valleys that produce good updrafts. Harris Hill has been attracting gliding and soaring aficionados since the 1910s.

Visitors to Harris Hill can take a sailplane ride aboard one of the delicate, insectlike vessels parked in the airfield's hangar. All the pilots are FAA certified, and the rides take about 20 min-

utes, soaring from air current to air current high above the countryside.

Just down from the airfield sits the National Soaring Museum, which chronicles the history of Harris Hill and flying in America. Of special interest are the museum's 12 antique gliders and sailplanes, and the simulated cockpit.

Located on Harris Hill Road, off Route 352, 607/734-0641, www.harrishillsoaring.org, Harris Hill offers sailplane rides daily June–Labor Day, and weekends April–May and September–October. The cost is $65 per person. The museum, 607/734-3128, www.soaringmuseum.org, stays open daily 10 A.M.–5 P.M. Admission is adults $6, seniors $5, students 6–17 $4.

Horseheads

Despite the intriguing name, Horseheads feels much like any other suburban village. Its moniker came about because in 1779, Gen. Sullivan and his men killed their worn-out and starving horses here. The first white settlers entering the valley in 1789 found the bleached skulls and named the place Horseheads. Appropriately enough, Horseheads's sister city is Bato-Machi, Japan. *Bato* means horseheads in Japanese.

Downtown, the only real visitor attraction is the **Horseheads Historical Museum,** 312 W. Broad St., 607/739-3938, operated by the Horseheads Historical Society. Inside you'll find the work of native son Eugene "Zim" Zimmerman, once a world-famous political cartoonist, and local history exhibits. Open Tuesday, Thursday, Saturday; call for hours. Admission is free.

Recently relocated to the outskirts of town from Geneseo, N.Y., is the non-profit **National Warplane Museum.** Run primarily by enthusiastic senior citizen volunteers, it is dedicated to the restoration and maintenance of flying-condition WW II and Korean War aircraft. The planes are spread out like hulking insects all around a small visitor center and hangar where someone is always busy repairing something. A highlight of the museum's collection is the "Fuddy Duddy"—a B-17 Flying Fortress, used during WW II.

One of the best times to visit the museum is during its Wings of Eagles Airshow, held the

THE FINGER LAKES

third weekend in August. Throughout the rest of the year, volunteers are always on hand to conduct personalized tours.

The museum, at the Elmira-Corning Airport (Exit 51 off Route 17), 617/739-8200, is open Mon.–Sat. 9 A.M.–5 P.M., Sunday 11 A.M.–5 P.M. Admission is adults $7, seniors $5.50, students 6–17 $4, families $18.

PRACTICALITIES

Camping

A few miles south of Elmira lies the **Newtown Battlefield Reservation,** where Gen. John Sullivan won a decisive battle over a large force of Iroquois and Tories on August 19, 1779. Situated on a hilltop with wide-angled views of the Chemung Valley, the former battlefield on Lowman Road off Route 17, 607/732-6067, is now a county park with hiking trails, a picnic area, and campgrounds.

Bed-and-Breakfasts

North of downtown presides the **Lindenwald Haus,** 1526 Grand Central Ave., 607/733-8753, a romantic Italianate mansion built in 1875. Surrounded by five acres, the inn features 18 spacious guest rooms, long creaky hallways, and

an airy living room that stretches most of the length of the house. Rocking chairs and braided rugs are everywhere ($65–95 d, with breakfast; the cheaper rooms share baths).

Food

Outside town stands the **Hill Top Inn,** 171 Jerusalem Hill Rd., off Rte. 17, 607/732-6728, offering panoramic views of Elmira and Pennsylvania. The Hill Top is an Irish restaurant that specializes in steak and seafood, and features outdoor dining in summer. It's usually open just for dinner, but this is subject to change (average entrée $16).

Pierce's 1894 Restaurant, 228 Oakwood Ave., Elmira Heights, 607/734-2022, is an elegant, award-winning restaurant especially known for its veal, Norwegian salmon, lamb dishes, and New York wines. All baking is done on the premises. Reservations are recommended; average entrée $19.

Entertainment

The **Clemens Performing Arts Center,** Clemens Center Pkwy. and Gray St., 607/734-8191, presents dance, music, and Broadway shows September–May. The Elmira Symphony and Choral Society are headquartered here.

Corning

Strange though it seems, Corning and its famed glass center is the third most popular tourist destination in New York State. This is undoubtedly largely due to a first-rate promotion and marketing campaign, and to Corning's strategic location more or less midway between New York City (the state's No. 1 destination) and Niagara Falls (No. 2). However, the Corning Museum of Glass *is* an impressive place, especially since its major 1999 expansion, and well worth braving the herds of tour buses to visit. You don't have to worry about long lines, either. Crowd control is down to a science here.

Corning, current population about 12,000, became a one-industry town not long after 1868, when the Flint Glass Company of Brooklyn re-

located here. The company chose Corning largely because of its strategic position on the Chemung River and Chemung Canal, which would allow for the easy delivery of raw materials.

In 1875, the company spread out along the waterfront and began to produce specialized types of glass, such as railway signal lenses and thermometer tubing. In 1880, the lightbulb division was developed in response to Edison's invention, and by the early 1930s, Corning was manufacturing 1,250,000 bulbs a day. In 1915, the company's research and development department invented Pyrex. In the early 1970s, a fiber optics division was established.

Today, about 6,000 Chemung County residents still work for Corning Incorporated. Many

THE FINGER LAKES

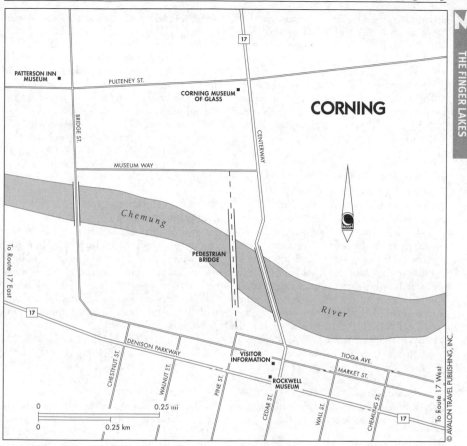

© AVALON TRAVEL PUBLISHING, INC.

others are involved in the tourism industry, servicing visitors who come to town to visit the Corning Museum of Glass.

Corning Museum of Glass

With its $62 million expansion and renovation now complete, the state-of-the-art Glass Museum sits surrounded by sleek corporate buildings on the north side of town. Its undulating walls are made of a blue-gray glass, while its new modern entrance is built of four giant panes of glass.

The museum is divided into several sections, some of which are entirely new. These include the Glass Innovation Center, which tells of the latest scientific advances in glassmaking, and the

Glass Sculpture Gallery, the largest of its kind in the world. Older, but renovated and still fascinating, is the heart of the institution, the museum building itself, which showcases more than 10,000 glass objects at a time, many dramatically displayed in darkened rooms with spotlights. The oldest objects date back to 1400 B.C., the newest to the 1990s. Among the many highlights are an iridescent vase from 10th-century Iran, an 11-foot-high Tiffany window from 1905, and a table-long glass boat cut by Baccarat in 1900.

Also on site is the Hot Glass Show, where visitors can observe the art of glassblowing up close, and the Steuben Factory, which houses skilled craftspeople at work. Visitors file by as artisans shape gobs of molten glass, cut them down to size, then polish and engrave them. This is the only place in the world where Steuben glass is made. Beyond the factory is an enormous gift shop.

The museum, 151 Centerway, off Rte. 17, 607/973-5371 or 800/732-6845, www.cmog.org, is open Sept.–June, daily 9 A.M.–5 P.M.; and July–Aug., daily 9 A.M.–8 P.M. Admission is adults $12, seniors $10, students 6–17 $6; family rates available.

Historic Market Street

After visiting the Glass Museum, most visitors stroll down a wide walkway that leads to Corning's historic downtown. This 19th-century district—once just another dying downtown—was extensively restored following Hurricane Agnes in 1972, when the street was all but destroyed by the flooding of the Chemung River.

Today, Market Street is brick sidewalks, locust trees, and one bustling shop or restaurant after another. At one end, you'll find contemporary glass studios with artisans at work: the **Vitrix Hot Glass Studio,** 77 W. Market St., 607/936-8707, and the **Noslo Glass Studio,** 89 W. Market St., 607/962-7886.

Heading east instead of west, you'll come to **Whitehouse Books,** 32 E. Market St., 607/962-BOOK, an independent bookshop offering new, used, and out-of-print books.

Rockwell Museum

Near the eastern end of Market St. presides the Rockwell Museum, which, contrary to the expectations of many visitors, has nothing to do with Norman Rockwell but everything to do with Western art. Collected by Corning denizen Robert F. Rockwell, this is said to be the most comprehensive assemblage of Western art in the East.

The museum occupies the restored Old City Hall and is nicely arranged around three themes—the Indian, the Landscape, and the Cowboy. Works by Frederic Remington, Charles M. Russell, and Albert Bierstadt hang from the walls, and Navajo rugs drape the stairwell. Exhibit cases contain Native American art and artifacts, while upstairs hangs an unrelated exhibit on de-

signer Frederick Carder, the co-founder of Steuben Glass.

After the crowds of the Corning Glass Center, the Rockwell Museum comes as a quiet relief. Rockwell was a passionate collector who once used the walls of his father's department store to exhibit his artwork, and the museum has an engaging, personal feel.

The museum, 111 Cedar St., 607/937-5386, www.rockwellmuseum.org, is open Mon.–Sat. 9 A.M.–5 P.M., Sunday 11 A.M.–5 P.M. Admission is adults $6.50, seniors $5.50, students 6–17 $4.50, families $20.

Benjamin Patterson Inn Museum Complex

A half mile north of Market Street is a complex of restored historic buildings peopled by guides in costume dress. Buildings include the Benjamin Patterson Inn, complete with a women's parlor, tap room, and ballroom; the De Monstoy Cabin, furnished as it would have been by early settlers; and an 1860s barn equipped with antique farm implements.

The complex, 59 W. Pulteney St., 607/937-5281, is open Mon.–Fri. 10 A.M.–4 P.M. Admission is adults $3, students 6–18 $1.

Accommodations

Across from the Patterson Inn Museum stands a 62-room **Comfort Inn,** 66 W. Pulteney St., 607/962-1515 ($80–112 d). More upscale is the177-room **Radisson Hotel,** 125 Denison St., 607/962-5000 ($89–148 d).

The handsome 1855 **Rosewood Inn,** 134 E. 1st St., 607/962-3253, www.rosewoodinn.com, offers seven guest rooms with private baths. Downstairs features an elegant parlor with a fireplace, where an afternoon tea is served ($120 d). Surrounded by fields and woods about midway between Elmira and Corning stands the **Rufus Tanner House,** 1016 Sagetown Rd., Pine City, 607/732-0213, www.rufustanner.com, a Greek Revival farmhouse turned bed-and-breakfast ($73–110 d).

Food

Visit **Jim's Texas Hots,** 8 W. Market St., 607/

936-1820, for ice cream and hot dogs, Texas-style. The airy, three-level **London Underground Cafe,** 69 E. Market St., 607/962-2345, serves first-rate gourmet salads and sandwiches, light entrées, and desserts. Families enjoy **Boomers,** 35 E. Market St., 607/962-6800, serving 99-cent kids' meals, homemade soups, salads, pastas, steak, and seafood; average dinner entrée $11.

The **Market Street Brewing Co.,** 63-65 W. Market St., 607/936-BEER, offers something for everyone, including rooftop and biergarten dining, dishes ranging from salads to steaks, a kids' menu, and, of course, fresh brews on tap; av-

erage entrée $15. At the casually elegant **Upstate Tuna Company,** 73 E. Market St., 607/936-TUNA, you can grill your own fresh meat, poultry, or fish over a large gas charcoal grill. Average entrée $16; open for dinner only.

Visitor Information

The **Corning Chamber of Commerce Visitors Center,** 1 Baron Steuben Pl., at Market St., Corning, NY 14830, 607/936-4686, www.corningny.com, is located in the heart of the downtown. Hours year-round are Mon.–Sat. 10 A.M.–6 P.M. and Sunday 11 A.M.–5 P.M.

Keuka Lake

Gentle, Y-shaped Keuka Lake is the only one of the Finger Lakes with an irregular outline. The name means canoe landing in Iroquois, and the lake sports over 70 miles of curving lakeshore, scalloped with coves and bays.

At the southern head of Keuka Lake lies Hammondsport, site of the nation's first winery, established in 1860. The small-town Penn Yan occupies the lake's northern tip. Several Mennonite communities are scattered throughout the Keuka Lake region. Driving south between Penn Yan and Dundee along Routes 14A or 11, or north of Penn Yan along Routes 14A, 374, and 27, you're bound to pass a horse-and-buggy or two clip-clopping down the road. Handwritten signs advertising Mennonite quilts, furniture, or produce for sale sometimes appear by the roadside, while more permanent shops are located near Penn Yan and Dundee.

HAMMONDSPORT

Nestled between steep, verdant hills and Keuka Lake, Hammondsport is a fetching Victorian village with a lively tourist trade. At its center lies the Village Square, anchored by a big, white Presbyterian Church. Shops and restaurants line Sheather Street, the main drag. Along the lakeshore are a sleepy park and two public beaches; the beach at the foot of Sheather Street is said to be the best. However, local viticulture draws

the most visitors. Tumbling down the surrounding hillsides are vineyard after vineyard, all supplying grapes for the area's nine wineries.

Glenn Hammond Curtiss, the pioneer aviator, was born in Hammondsport in 1878. Though not as well known as the Wright brothers, Curtiss made the world's first pre-announced flight on July 4, 1908, when he piloted his "June Bug" airplane over 5,090 feet

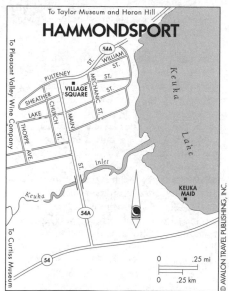

AMONG THE MENNONITES

A surprisingly large number of Mennonite and Amish Mennonite communities are scattered throughout the Finger Lakes and Western New York. Some were established generations ago, but many others were set up just over the past decade or so by people originally from Pennsylvania and Ohio, attracted to New York by its many recently abandoned family farms.

The Mennonite religion is a Protestant sect, founded by Dutch reformer Menno Simons in Switzerland in the 1500s. The Amish are the Mennonites' most conservative branch, established in Pennsylvania in the 18th century. Both groups shun modern society and technology, but the Amish are the most severe.

Throughout the region, you'll see traffic signs alerting you to horse and buggies, and you'll spot occasional plaques advertising handmade quilts, furniture, or baskets for sale. An especially large Amish population lives in Cattaraugus County in Western New York, while many Mennonites live in Yates, Schuyler, and Ontario Counties in the Finger Lakes. Local residents estimate that the Mennonite population in these last three counties—centered around Keuka Lake—has more than tripled in the past dozen years, to over 1,000.

Why do the Amish and Mennonites have success as farmers when others have failed is a topic for debate. Many believe that it has to do with the "plain people's" smaller-size farms and low labor costs. In Mennonite communities, everyone in the family, from young children to great-grandparents, contributes to the operation of the farm.

The Amish and Mennonites dislike having their pictures taken. Please respect their wishes.

just outside Hammondsport. Curtiss developed the U.S. Navy's first amphibian airplane, opened the first flying school in America, and established the Curtiss Aeroplane Company—all in Hammondsport. During WW I, the Curtiss company manufactured the popular Curtiss Jenny airplane which later became a favorite of barnstormers.

Pleasant Valley Wine Company Visitor Center

Even if the thought of touring wineries bores you to tears, you might want to stop into this center, one of the largest tourist attractions in the Finger Lakes. The Pleasant Valley Wine Company is the oldest continuous maker of wine in the United States, founded by a group of Hammondsport businessmen in 1860.

The visitor center features historic exhibits and an informative film, screened inside a 35,000-gallon former wine tank. A nearby working model train replicates the old Bath-Hammondsport Railroad, and a tasting bar offers products for sampling. Everything's very commercialized and the wine is only mediocre, but the place is interesting nonetheless. Winery tours are offered throughout the day.

The center, 8260 Pleasant Valley Rd. (County Rd. 88), 607/569-6111, is open April–Dec., daily 10 A.M.–5 P.M.; Jan.–March Tues.–Sat. 10 A.M.–4 P.M. Admission is free.

Wine and Grape Museum of Greyton H. Taylor

One of the odder tales in the chronicles of viticulture is that of the battle waged over the name Taylor. Walter S. Taylor, a grandson of the founder of the Taylor Wine Co., was kicked out of the company in 1970 after publicly attacking its "incompetence, greed, and jealousy." Subsequently, he and his father Greyton began their own winery high on Bully Hill.

In 1977, Coca-Cola bought the Taylor Wine Co. and sued Walter for using his family name on his own labels. The case went to court and Walter lost, only to become a local hero. "They have my name and heritage but they didn't get my goat!" he proclaimed and flamboyantly struck out the Taylor name on all his labels. "Branded For Life, by a man that shall remain nameless without Heritage" reads the bylines in his brochures.

The Taylor museum, adjacent to the **Bully Hill Vineyards,** tells little of this story. Instead, it focuses on antique wine-making equipment and the delicate, lyrical Bully Hill labels, all drawn by "Walter St. Bully." Also on site is the Bully Hill Restaurant, offering great views of the vineyards and lake (see Food, below).

The museum, 8843 Taylor Memorial Dr., off Rte. 54A, 607/868-4814, is open May–Oct., Mon.–Sat. 10 A.M.–4 P.M., Sunday noon–4 P.M. Admission is free.

Other Wineries

One of the region's top wineries is **Dr. Frank's Vinifera Wine Cellars,** 9749 Middle Rd., 607/868-4884. Dr. Frank, an immigrant from Ukraine who arrived in Hammondsport in 1962, was one of the first in the region to grow the European Vinifera grape. Today, his cellars are best known for their sparkling wines.

A few miles beyond Bully Hill is the **Heron Hill Winery,** 9249 Rte. 76, 607/868-4241, offering yet more superb views of the lake. Established in 1977, the 45-acre vineyard now produces about 30,000 gallons of wine a year.

Glenn H. Curtiss Museum

The cavernous hangars of the former Curtiss Aeroplane Company now contain a sprawling museum devoted to both Curtiss and the early history of aviation. About a dozen spiffy antique airplanes crowd the main hall, along with antique bicycles, motorcycles, propellers, and engines. Curtiss's first interest was the bicycle. One of his earliest planes, the Curtiss Pusher, looks just like a bike with double wings and wires attached.

A highlight of the museum is a replica of the famous "June Bug" airplane, built by volunteers in the mid-1970s. A Curtiss Jenny and delicate Curtiss Robin—resembling a giant grasshopper—stand nearby.

The museum, 8419 Rte. 54, 607/569-2160, www.linkny.com/curtissmuseum, is open May–Oct., Mon.–Sat. 9 A.M.–5 P.M., Sunday 11 A.M.–5 P.M.; call for off-season hours. Admission is adults $6, seniors $4, students $3, under 6 free.

Recreation

The **Keuka Maid Dinner Boat,** 607/569-2628, a 500-passenger vessel, offers lunch, brunch, and dinner tours May–Oct., Tuesday–Sunday. The boat docks in the village off Rte. 54A; reservations are recommended.

Accommodations

A good choice for families or anyone wanting a water view is the 17-room **Hammondsport Motel,** William St., 607/569-2600, which sits on the edge of the village by the lake ($63–70 d). The 30-room **Vinehurst Inn,** Rte. 54, 607/569-2300, features unusual spacious motel rooms with high ceilings ($64 d).

A pleasant place to stay in the heart of the village is the 1861 **Park Inn,** Village Square, 607/569-9387. The inn offers four small suites upstairs ($65–75 d), and a popular tavern downstairs.

About 15 miles away in the village of Avoca is the storybook **Caboose Motel,** 8620 Rte. 415, off Rte. 390, 607/566-2216. Here, you can sleep in snug, restored 1916 train cabooses outfitted with all the modern conveniences and kept in trim shape ($75 d). Also on the premises are more conventional motel rooms ($48 d).

Food

In addition to its mouth-watering ice cream treats, the cozy **Crooked Lake Ice Cream Parlor,** on the Village Square, 607/569-2751, serves a good breakfast and lunch. Also on the Village Square presides the Victorian **Park Inn Tavern,** 607/569-9387, open daily until midnight for lunch, dinner, and drinks; average dinner entrée $13.

The **Bully Hill Restaurant,** at Bully Hill Vineyards, 8834 Greyton H. Taylor Memorial Dr., 607/868-3490, offers first-rate salads, vegetarian pizzas, grilled chicken, and the like, all prepared with the freshest of ingredients. Open for lunch, and for dinner on the weekends; average lunch entrée $9.

Along the shores of Keuka Lake two miles north of Hammondsport, you'll find the popular **Three Birds Restaurant,** 144 W. Lake Rd., 607/868-3488, parts of which date back to 1890. Specialties range from bouillabaisse to medallions of veal. Dockside dining in summer is featured for both lunch and dinner; entrées cost $12–28.

A bit further north is the **Waterfront Restaurant,** 648 W. Lake Rd., Pulteney, 607/868-3455, where at least half the diners arrive by boat. Clambakes are featured throughout the summer, along with live entertainment. Seafood, pasta, and grilled meats are featured on the menu; average entrée $15.

NORTH ON ROUTE 54A

Route 54A heads north of Hammondsport into steep, vineyard-covered hills with great views of the lake. The route hugs the shoreline as far north as Branchport, then veers east to Penn Yan, located at the northern tip of the lake's longer prong.

Just east of Branchport is the **Keuka Lake State Park,** 3370 Pepper Rd., 315/536-3666, featuring a swimming beach, bathhouse, hiking trails, playground, campground, and good fishing sites. Parking in summer is $6. To reserve a campsite, call 800/456-CAMP.

Next you'll hit **Bluff Point,** a headland from which you can see both arms of the lake as well as, some say, seven counties and 10 lakes on a clear day. In the center of Bluff Point stands the **Garrett Memorial Chapel,** a lovely Gothic-style sanctuary built in memory of Charles Garrett, the son of a wealthy winemaker, who died of tuberculosis in his twenties. From Bluff Point south, between Keuka's arms, runs the eight-mile-long **Skyline Drive.**

PENN YAN

Named for its early Pennsylvanian and Yankee settlers, Penn Yan is an attractive small town (pop. 5,500). Its downtown centers on a historic Main Street, where you'll find **Belknap Hill Books,** 106 Main St., 315/536-1186, packed with over 20,000 out-of-print, used, and rare books.

On a windowless wall of **Birkett Mills,** 1 Main St., are mounted half of an enormous griddle and the words: "The annual Buckwheat Harvest Festival. Size of big griddle used to make world record pancake, Sept. 27, 1987. 28 feet, 1 inch." Birkett is the world's largest producer of buckwheat products and maintains a small retail shop in its offices at 163 Main St., 315/536-3311.

Oliver House Museum

This small local history museum, housed in a handsome brick building, is run by the Yates County Genealogical and Historical Society. One especially interesting exhibit pertains to Jemima Wilkinson, the 18th-century religious leader from Rhode Island who called herself the "Publick Universal Friend."

While in her early 20s, Wilkinson awoke from a severe fever one day to announce that she had been dead, her carnal existence had ended, and she was now reanimated by a Divine Spirit. Her mission was to be neither man nor woman but the Publick Universal Friend, brought back to life to save sinners from damnation.

An exceptionally beautiful woman, with brilliant black eyes and hair, Wilkinson preached celibacy and loyalty to her sect above all else. Despite her illiteracy and a strong accent difficult to understand, she gathered converts from all over New England, some of them quite wealthy. After being thrown out of several communities, she and her followers settled down in 1788 in the Finger Lakes, about eight miles west of Penn Yan. There, in a white clapboard house, Wilkinson held religious meetings attired in a silk purple robe, fine white dress, and man's shirt so that she appeared androgynous.

As more settlers came into the region, and Wilkinson's beauty began to fade, she lost much of her hold over her followers. After her death, the sect completely disintegrated, but the original Jemima Wilkinson House, now privately owned, still stands on Friend Road in Branchport.

The museum, 200 Main St., 315/536-7318, is open Mon.–Fri. 10 A.M.–4 P.M., Saturday by appointment. Admission is free.

Outlet Trail

Between Penn Yan and Dresden, along the Keuka Outlet connecting Keuka and Seneca Lakes, runs the Outlet Trail. Six miles in length, the trail follows an abandoned 1884 railroad track—an easy hike. Near the Penn Yan end are fitness stations, play areas, and foot bridges; along the way are waterfalls and the remains of early settlements. The best place to access the trail in Penn Yan is the boat launch at the corner of Water and Keuka Streets. Several plaques convey the trail's history, and there's plenty of parking here. A brochure describing the trail and its history can be picked up at the Penn Yan Chamber of Commerce.

Recreation

Auctions take place Saturday at 7 P.M. at **Hayes Auction Barn,** 1644 Rte. 14A, 315/536-8818.

The *Viking Spirit* **Cruise Ship,** 680 East Lake Rd., 315/536-7061, offers a daily cruises May–October.

Accommodations

Overlooking the lake just west of town stands the simple but adequate 17-room **Colonial Motel,** 175 W. Lake Rd., 315/536-3056 ($75–95 d). Also near the downtown is the considerably more stylish **Fox Inn,** 158 Main St., 315/536-3101 or 800/901-7997, www.fox-innbandb.com, an 1820s Greek Revival home with five cozy guest rooms and formal gardens out back ($105–135 d).

Situated on an 18-acre estate with great views of both Keuka and Seneca Lakes presides **Merritt Hill Manor,** 2756 Coates Rd., 315/536-7682, www.merritthillmanor.com, an 1822 country manor with five guest rooms ($110–125 d). Overlooking Keuka Lake is the Victorian **Keuka Overlook B&B,** 5777 Old Bath Rd., off Rte. 26, Dundee, 607/292-6877, www.keukaoverlook.com, offering four modernized guest rooms and a small winery ($85 d).

Food

Diner aficionados will want to stop into the squat, classic **Penn Yan Diner,** 131 E. Elm St., off Main St., 315/536-6004, which dates back to 1925. Meanwhile the simple **Millers' Essenhaus,** 1300 Rte. 14A, Benton Center, 315/531-8260, is a Mennonite restaurant serving such homemade specialties as barbecue sandwiches, split pea soup, and whoopie and shoofly pies; average entrée $11. The **Antique Inn,** 2940 Rte. 54A, 315/536-6576, is a casual family-style place serving basic pasta and seafood dishes; average entrée $12.

Shopping

Midway between Penn Yan and Dundee sprawls the **Windmill Farm and Market,** 315/536-3032, www.thewindmill.com, the oldest and biggest of several indoor/outdoor farm-and-crafts markets operating in the Finger Lakes. Every Saturday, May–Dec., 8 A.M.–4:30 P.M., about 200 local vendors set up shop in a large fairgrounds area off Rte. 14A. For sale are produce, flowers, furniture, crafts, wine, antiques, and homemade food. Many Mennonite families operate booths here.

A more permanent Mennonite store in Penn Yan is the **Quilt Room,** 1870 Hoyt Rd. (just north of the Windmill), 315/536-5964. In Dundee, you'll find **Martin's Bulk Foods,** 4898 John Green Rd., 607/243-8197, selling homemade pickles, pickled watermelon rinds, and other Mennonite specialties. Also in Dundee is the first-rate **McGregor Winery,** 5503 Dutch St., off Rte. 54, 607/292-3999, a family-run business perched on a bluff overlooking Keuka Lake.

Events

The **National Buckwheat Harvest Festival,** sponsored by the National Buckwheat Institute, takes place in late September. The **Yates County Fair,** takes over the Penn Yan fairgrounds in mid-July. On the Fourth of July and the Saturday before Labor Day, the shores of Keuka Lake glow with magical **Rings of Fire,** as in the days of the Seneca. The Seneca lit bonfires to celebrate the harvest; today the bonfires and highway flares celebrate the holidays. For information about any of these events, call the Yates County Chamber of Commerce, 315/536-3111.

Visitor Information

Just south of downtown is the **Yates County Chamber of Commerce,** 2375 Rte. 14A, Penn Yan, NY 14527, 315/536-3111 or 800/868-9283, www.yatesny.com. Hours are May–Dec., Mon.–Fri. 9 A.M.–5 P.M., Sunday 10 A.M.–5 P.M.; Jan.–April, Mon.–Fri. 8 A.M.–5 P.M. Also in town is **Finger Lakes Tourism,** 309 Lake St., Penn Yan, NY 14527, 315/536-7488 or 800/548-4386, www.fingerlakes.org, which represents the entire region. Hours are year-round Mon.–Fri. 8 A.M.–5 P.M.

Canandaigua Lake Area

The farthest west of the major Finger Lakes, Canandaigua is also the most commercialized. Rochester (pop. 235,000) is less than 30 miles away, and the lake has served as the city's summer playground since the late 1800s. At the northern end of the lake lies the historic city of Canandaigua, now largely a resort town. At the southern end rests the trim village of Naples.

Canandaigua is Iroquois for "The Chosen Place," and according to legend, the Seneca people were born at the south end of the lake, on South Hill. As the legend goes, the Creator caused the ground to open here, allowing the Seneca to climb out. All went well at first, until a giant serpent coiled itself around the base of the hill. Driven by an insatiable hunger, the snake picked off the Seneca one by one until at last a young warrior slew him with a magic arrow. The dying serpent writhed down the hill, disgorging the heads of its victims as he went; large rounded stones resembling human skulls have been found in the area. South Hill is now part of the Hi Tor Wildlife Management Area.

Also connected with the Seneca is tiny Squaw Island, located in the northern end of the lake. The Seneca people relate that many women and children escaped slaughter by hiding out here during General Sullivan's 1779 campaign.

CANANDAIGUA

The sprawling city of Canandaigua has a wide and expansive feel. Through its center runs busy Main Street, a four-lane thoroughfare lined with leafy trees and imposing Greek Revival buildings set back from the street. At the foot of Main extends the lake and City Pier. Tourist-oriented businesses dominate.

Following the Revolution, two New Englanders, Oliver Phelps and Nathaniel Gorham, purchased what is now Canandaigua, along with the rest of western New York, from the Native Americans. The first white settlers arrived in 1789, and shortly thereafter, the first land office in the United States was established near present-day Main

Street. Oliver Phelps then built the town around wide thoroughfares and a public square.

On November 11, 1794, the Seneca chiefs and Gen. Timothy Pickering met in Canandaigua to sign what was later known as the Pickering Treaty. A document of enormous significance, the treaty granted whites the right to settle the Great Lakes Basin. An original copy of the treaty can be found in the Ontario County Historical Society Museum.

Sonnenberg Gardens and Mansion

In the heart of the bustling downtown sits a serene 50-acre garden estate, composed of nine formal gardens, an arboretum, a *long* turn-of-the-century greenhouse, and a massive 1887 stone mansion. The Smithsonian Institution credited the place "one of the most magnificent late-Victorian gardens ever created in America."

Sonnenberg (German for "Sunny Hill") was once the summer home of Mary Clark and Frederick Ferris Thompson. Mr. Thompson, whose father helped to establish the Chase Bank, was co-founder of the First National City Bank of New York City.

The estate's nine gardens were created by Mrs. Thompson as a memorial after her husband's death in 1899. A classic Rose Garden features over 4,000 rose bushes, and the Japanese Garden took seven workers six months to create. The secluded Sub Rosa Garden contains statues of Zeus, Diana, and Apollo. The Blue & White Garden contains only blue and white flowers.

Visitors to Sonnenberg can wander freely—even the mansion is self-guided. Near the entrance is the inviting cafe, housed in one of the greenhouses.

The gardens, 151 Charlotte St., 585/394-4922, www.sonnenberg.org, are open June–Oct., daily 9:30 A.M.–5:30 P.M. Admission is adults $8, children 3–12 $3.

Granger Homestead and Carriage Museum

This 1816 Federal-style mansion once housed

THE FINGER LAKES

Gideon Granger, U.S. postmaster general under Presidents Jefferson and Madison. The home— "unrivalled in all the nation," Granger once boasted—is especially notable for its elaborate carved moldings and mantelpieces, and for its fine original furnishings.

Dark, towering trees surround the house. Out back is a carriage museum, packed with about 50 spit-and-polish coaches sporting carriages, sleighs, commercial wagons, and an undertaker's hearse.

The museum, 295 N. Main St., 585/394-1472, www.grangerhomestead.org, is open May–Oct., Tues.–Sun. 1–5 P.M. Admission is adults $5, seniors $4, students $1.

Ontario County Historical Society Museum

To learn more about the history of Canandaigua, step into this local museum, situated in a handsome brick building. On display is the original Six Nations' copy of the Pickering Treaty with the signatures of the famed Iroquois leaders Red Jacket, Cornplanter, Handsome Lake, Farmer's Brother, Little Beard, and Fish Carrier. Each signed with an X. The museum also features "life masks" of Abraham Lincoln (plaster-of-Paris masks taken from a mold of his face), a small children's discovery area, and temporary exhibits on various aspects of the county's past. Pick up walking-tour maps of the city.

632 The Finger Lakes

The museum, 55 N. Main St., 585/394-4975, is open Tues.–Sat. 10 A.M.–4:30 P.M. Admission is $2.

Ontario County Courthouse

Dominating downtown Canandaigua, and indeed much of the surrounding countryside, looms the bulbous dome of the Ontario County Courthouse. Hung in the two courtrooms of this 1858 Greek Revival structure is a marvelous collection of portraits. Among them are likenesses of Red Jacket and Susan B. Anthony, who was tried here in 1873 for voting in the national election in Rochester. She was found guilty and fined $100. A boulder on the courthouse grounds commemorates the Pickering Treaty, signed here in 1794.

The courthouse, 27 N. Main St., at Gorham, 585/396-4200, is open Mon.–Fri. 8:30 A.M.–5 P.M.

Kershaw Park

At the southern end of Main Street lies a busy, seven-acre lakefront park equipped with a small-craft launch area, volleyball courts, swimming beach, and picnic tables. The park is open Memorial Day–Labor Day, daily 9 A.M.–5 P.M. Adjoining the park is the **City Pier.**

Onanda Park

About eight miles south of Canandaigua on the west side of the lake lies the 80-acre Onanda Park, which features a wide, sandy swimming beach, ballparks, hiking trails, and shoreline fishing. *Onanda* is Iroquois for tall fir. The park, West Lake Rd., 585/394-0315, is open year-round dawn to dusk; lifeguards are on duty June–Labor Day. Parking in summer is $7 for nonresidents.

Shops and Galleries

Shopping is big business in Canandaigua, and the tourism office puts out a number of helpful brochures. An especially large number of shops cluster along South Main Street.

Three miles north of Canandaigua sprawls **Hanna Junction,** Rte. 21, 585/394-7740, an indoor/outdoor food-and-crafts market. Over 100 local vendors sell everything from fresh produce to handmade quilts April–Dec., every Thursday 10 A.M.–9 P.M.

THE FINGER LAKES TRAIL

Through the heart of the Finger Lakes runs a 557-mile main trail extending from the Pennsylvania–New York border in Allegany State Park to the Long Path in the Catskill Forest Preserve. Six branch trails and two loop trails that extend an additional 278 miles intersect the main trail. Most of the trailheads are marked with the yellow-and-green Finger Lakes Trail logo, and camping facilities are available along most sections.

The **Finger Lakes Trail Conference** publishes 45 maps that cover the entire trail system, along with several guide books. The individual maps cost about $1 each; a complete set is about $20. For a list of the maps and publications available, contact the Finger Lakes Trail Conference, 6111 Visitor Center Rd., Mt. Morris, NY 14510, 585/288-7191, www.fingerlakes.net/trailsystem.

Recreation

The *Canandaigua Lady,* 169 Lakeshore Dr., 585/394-5365, is a 150-passenger paddlewheel boat offering lunch, dinner, and moonlight cruises May–October. **Captain Gray's Boat Tours,** 585/394-5270, features one-hour narrated tours of the lake daily July–Labor Day, weekends May–Oct.; the boat leaves from behind the Inn on the Lake off Lakeshore Drive.

Seven miles northwest of Canandaigua lies the **Finger Lakes Race Track,** Rts. 332 and 96 (Exit 44 off I-90), 585/924-3232. Thoroughbred racing takes place here April–Nov., Friday–Tuesday.

Accommodations

A good choice for families is the 15-room **Kellogg's Pan-Tree Inn,** 130 Lakeshore Dr., 585/394-3909, located on the lakefront with easy access to a beach ($64–72 d). Adjoining the inn is the comfortable, relaxed **Kellog's Pan-Tree Inn Restaurant** that has been attracting families since 1924.

Also on the waterfront stands is the considerably more upscale **Canandaigua Inn on the Lake,** 770 S. Main St., 585/394-7800 or 800/228-2801, www.visitinnonthelake.com, the area's only full-service hotel. Among its features are 147 nicely appointed guest rooms, a pristine outdoor pool, saunas, and the airy, inviting Capri restaurant ($125–240 d).

The Canandaigua region is also home to many B&Bs. Among them is the snug, Colonial **Acorn Inn,** 4508 Rte. 64 S, Bristol Center, 585/229-2834, website: http://acorninnbb.com. Once a stagecoach stop, the inn now pampers guests with comfy canopy beds, luxurious private baths, and multicourse breakfasts ($120–185 d). Not too far away is the plush, 1810 **Morgan-Samuels B&B Inn,** 2920 Smith Rd., 585/394-9232, www.morgansamuelsinn.com, which offers six guest rooms, eight fireplaces, tennis courts, and gourmet breakfasts by candlelight ($125–235 d). High on a bluff overlooking Deep Run Cove stands the turn-of-the-century **Thendara Inn,** 4356 E. Lake Rd., 585/394-4868, containing five guest rooms furnished with antiques ($115–175 d) and a good restaurant (see below).

Food

For breakfast or lunch, try **Kellogg's Pan-Tree Inn Restaurant,** 130 Lakeshore Dr., 585/394-3909 (see Accommodations, above), where you can eat inside or out. Pancakes are served all day, all baked goods are homemade, and the place is famed locally for its creamed codfish; average main dish $8. **Koozina's,** 699 S. Main St., 585/396-0360, is a lively spot specializing in wood-fired pizza and pasta dishes; average entrée $9.

The Victorian **Thendara Inn,** 4356 E. Lake Rd., 585/394-4868, serves first-rate American cuisine, served in three period dining rooms with panoramic views of the lake; in summer, an outdoor patio is opened up (average dinner entrée $18; open for dinner only). Also at the inn is the more casual **Boathouse,** serving lighter fare for both lunch and dinner.

Nicole's at the Inn on the Lake, 770 S. Main St., 585/394-7800 (see Accommodations, above), offers great views of the lake and contemporary American fare. It's open for breakfast, lunch, and dinner; average dinner entrée $18.

Entertainment

During the summer, the Rochester Philharmonic Orchestra, 585/222-5000, performs every week-end at the **Finger Lakes Performing Arts Center,** Rte. 364 and Lincoln Hill Rd., an outdoor amphitheater. Rock, jazz, and pop music concerts are sometimes presented as well.

Visitor Information

The **Canandaigua Chamber of Commerce,** 113 S. Main St., near Phoenix St., Canandaigua, NY 14424, 585/394-4400, www.canandaigua .com/chamber, is open year-round Mon.–Fri. 9 A.M.–5 P.M.

VICTOR

About 10 miles northwest of Canandaigua sprawls the village of Victor, worth visiting because of the **Ganondagan State Historic Site.** During the 17th century, atop this grassy lime-green knoll, stood an important Seneca village and palisaded granary. The village was home to about 4,500 people; the granary stored hundreds of thousands of bushels of corn. All was destroyed in 1687 by a French army led by the governor of Canada. The French wished to eliminate the Seneca as competitors in the fur trade.

A visit to Ganondagan, which means "Town of Peace," begins with an interesting video that tells the story of the Seneca Nation and that of Jikohnsaseh, or Mother of Nations. Together with "The Peacemaker" and Hiawatha, Jikohnsaseh was instrumental in forging the Five Nations Confederacy; it was she who proposed that the Onondangan chief, who at first refused to join the confederacy, be appointed chairman of the Chiefs' Council. Jikohnsaseh once lived in the vicinity of Ganondagan and is believed to be buried nearby. No one searches for her grave, however, as a sign of respect.

Outside the visitor center begin three trails that lead over gentle terrain past informative plaques. The Trail of Peace relates important moments in Seneca history. The Earth of Our Mother Trail identifies plants important to the Seneca. The Granary Trail re-creates the day in 1687 Ganondagan was destroyed, through journal entries from the French forces.

To reach the site, 1488 Victor-Bloomfield Rd., 585/924-5848, www.ganandagan.org, from Rte.

332 heading north, turn left onto County Road 41 to Victor-Bloomfield Road. Trails stay open year-round 8 A.M.–sunset. The visitor center is open May 15–Oct., Tues.–Sun. 9 A.M.–5 P.M. Admission is free.

PALMYRA

About 15 miles due north of Canandaigua is Palmyra, an old Erie Canal town where Joseph Smith allegedly received, from the Angel Moroni, a set of gold tablets inscribed with the Book of Mormon. One of the largest outdoor pageants in the United States, the Mormon Hill Cumorah Pageant, celebrates that event every July.

Downtown Palmyra is small and compact, lined with sturdy brick buildings. At each corner of the intersection of Main Street and Route 21 stand four soaring churches—a fact that made it into *Ripley's Believe It or Not.* Just west of downtown is a graceful stone **Erie Canal Aqueduct,** off Route 31.

Downtown Palmyra holds four small museums, three of which are run by Historic Palmyra and open during the summer only. The fourth, the Grandin Building, is operated by the Mormon Church, as are the Joseph Smith Farm and Hill Cumorah Visitor Center on the outskirts of town.

Historic Palmyra

The **Alling Coverlet Museum** houses the largest collection of handwoven coverlets in the United States. Often referred to as the American tapestry, coverlets are ornate bed coverings made out of wool, cotton, or linen. Also in the museum, 122 Williams St., off Main, 315/597-6737, are quilts, miniature rugs, and a small gift shop. Hours are June–Sept. daily 1–4 P.M. Admission is free.

The nearby **Palmyra Historical Museum,** 132 Market St., 315/597-6981, occupies the former St. James Hotel. Exhibits here include 19th-century furniture, Erie Canal art and artifacts, children's toys, and lots of stern Victorian portraits.

Finally, the **William Phelps General Store,** 140 Market St., 315/597-6981, operated by the Phelps family from the 1860s until the 1940s, features the usual general store products downstairs and a most unusual series of unkempt

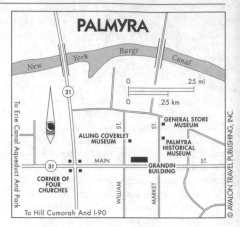

rooms upstairs. Miss Sybil Phelps, a village eccentric, lived here without electricity or plumbing until 1976. Residing with her were dozens of dogs and cats, who tore her once-lovely furniture to shreds. Dark stains still streak the walls and in the ceiling is a hole through which Miss Phelps once communed with her dead father.

Both the general store and Palmyra Historical Museum are open June–Sept., Tuesday, Wednesday, and Thursday 1–4 P.M. or be appointment. Admission is free.

Grandin Building

This handsome green-and-white building was once a printing business that published the first copies of the Book of Mormon in 1829–31. Exhibits explain how Joseph Smith found the gold tablets and translated them to a Palmyra schoolteacher, who wrote out the text in one long, unpunctuated sentence. An early copy of the Book of Mormon is here, along with hundreds of foreign editions, a reconstructed 19th-century press room, and portraits of early Mormons. A kindly and overly eager volunteer is usually on hand to answer any questions.

The museum, 217 E. Main St., 315/597-5982 or 315/597-5851, is open Mon.–Sat. 9 A.M.–5 P.M., Sunday 1–5 P.M. Admission is free.

Hill Cumorah Visitor Center

Although the Grandin Building provides some information, the best place to learn about the

THE MASSIVE HILL CUMORAH PAGEANT

The largest and oldest outdoor drama in America is the Hill Cumorah Pageant, staged just outside Palmyra every July since 1937. Likened by one critic to a "George Lucas techno-dazzler with the scope of a Cecil B. DeMille epic," the pageant tells the story of the Book of Mormon. The show includes a 37-foot-high erupting volcano, a 56-foot-long ship that's struck by lightning, and medieval battle scenes complete with swords and lances. The nativity scene is lit with a 5,000K carbon arc light—so bright that it required FAA clearance. A digital sound recording of the Mormon Tabernacle Choir provides the music. The pageant's cast numbers about 600 and the audience about 54,000 over a seven-night period.

The pageant is free and open to the general public. Many non-Mormons as well as Mormons attend, and although some proselytizing goes on, it's very low key. "Welcome to the Hill Cumorah Pageant, America's Witness for Christ" reads a sign over the entranceway; young people in medieval costume move excitedly through the crowd. They're eager to know where you're from and if you've ever attended before, but after handing out literature, they move on to greet other arriving guests.

The pageant doesn't begin until nightfall, but it's best to arrive by early evening to claim a seat and watch the pre-show activity. For more information, contact the Hill Cumorah Pageant, 315/597-5851, www.hillcumorah.com.

Mormon religion is this modern center, four miles south of the downtown. Most visitors are well-scrubbed Mormons straight from the heartland, but nonbelievers are welcome and are left more or less in peace to peruse the exhibits. A film provides a good introduction to Mormon history and beliefs, and exhibits tout the growth of the religion. There are currently about nine million Mormons worldwide, though only 1,500 live in upstate New York.

Behind the center stands Hill Cumorah, the drumlin where Joseph Smith supposedly found the gold tablets on September 22, 1827. It took him years to translate the tablets and after he was done, he reburied them. Atop Hill Cumorah today is a gold statue of the Angel Moroni.

The center, 603 Rte. 21, 315/597-5851, www.hillcumorah.com, is open Mon.–Sat. 9 A.M.–5 P.M., Sunday 1–5 P.M., with extended hours in summer. Admission is free.

Joseph Smith Farm and Sacred Grove

Born in Vermont in 1805, Joseph Smith first came to Palmyra with his family in 1815. The Smiths were farmers, and Joseph—described by one contemporary as a "quiet, low-speaking, un-laughing" boy—lived in this simple, white clapboard house until he was 22. He received his first vision in the Sacred Grove behind the house when he was only 14.

The farm, 29 Stafford Rd., 315/597-4383 or 315/597-5851, is open Mon.–Sat. 9 A.M.–5 P.M., Sunday 1–5 P.M., with extended hours in summer. Admission is free.

SOUTH ON ROUTES 364 AND 245

Heading south down Canandaigua's eastern shore, you'll pass through a series of picturesque valleys. Take County Road 1 off Route 364 to reach Rushville, a small village with several furniture shops. The **Loomis Barn,** 4942 Loomis Rd., 585/554-3154, is best known for its country and Shaker reproduction furniture. **Roses and Oak Ranch,** 4169 Ferguson's Corners Rd., 585/554-5409, specializes in Amish-crafted oak furniture.

At the southern end of the lake, Routes 364 and 245 skirt around South Hill and the **High Tor Wildlife Management Area.** Hiking trails traverse the preserve, which is also one of the few places left in New York where you can still spot bluebirds—the state bird. The main entrance to the area is off Route 245 between Middlesex and Naples; or, continue on Route 364 until it turns into West Avenue. For more information and maps, contact the Finger Lakes Trail Conference at 585/288-7191.

© CHRISTIANE BIRD

Mormon founder Joseph Smith lived in this Palmyra house until he was 22—and had his first vision in the Sacred Grove behind the house.

NAPLES

Just south of Canandaigua Lake, surrounded by hills, lies Naples, population 2,500. A tidy village with a brisk tourist trade, Naples centers around a historic **Old Town Square.** The **Brown House Gallery,** 107 N. Main St., 585/374-5129, houses the work of local artists. Open Mon.–Sat. 10 A.M.–5 P.M., Sunday 1–4 P.M.

Naples is one of the best places in the Finger Lakes to sample a sweet regional specialty— **grape pie.** The pies, made with dark grapes, are only available during the harvest season in fall.

Widmer Wine Cellars

One mile due north of the Old Town Square is Widmer's—one of the largest, oldest, and most commercialized wineries in the region. Tours start in a cool stone cellar filled with enormous oak vats, and end in a busy bottling plant that processes 300,000 cases of wine a year. Along the way, look for the hundreds of weathered oak barrels on a rooftop—these contain sherry that has been aging for half a century.

Widmer's has been producing Manischewitz, a kosher wine, since 1986. The wine is made in a separate winery equipped with all-stainless steel vats, and rabbis come down from Rochester to oversee the process.

The winery, 1 Lake Niagara Ln., off Rte. 21, 585/374-6311, www.widmer.com, is open daily for tours noon–4:00 P.M. Admission is free. Tours of the Manischewitz winery are offered on Thursday only.

Cumming Nature Center

About eight miles northwest of the village lies the 900-acre Cumming Nature Center. Owned by the Rochester Museum and Science Center, the preserve, a veritable outdoor museum, features six miles of themed trails leading through forests and wetlands. The Conservation Trail illustrates theories of forest management, while the Pioneer Trail, complete with a reconstructed homestead, teaches about the early settlers' lives. The Beaver Trail focuses on the principles of ecology, and the Iroquois Trail focuses on Native American life. Near the entrance is a visitor center.

The center, 6472 Gulick Rd., 585/374-6160, is open Wed.–Sun. 9 A.M.–4:30 P.M. Admission is adults $5, seniors and college students $3, children 5–18 $2.

Gannett Hill

Scenic Route 21 heads due north out of Naples to the highest point in Ontario County—Gannett Hill, 2,256 feet above sea level. Now part of Ontario County Park, the hill offers bird's-eye views of the surrounding countryside.

Food

Bob and Ruth's, 204 Main St., Old Town Square, 585/374-5122, is a village institution containing both a casual dining area and the more formal Vineyard Room. Specialties range from rotisserie chicken to Angus beef (average entrée $15). The historic 1895 **Naples Hotel Restaurant,** 111 S. Main St., 585/374-5630, specializes in traditional American fare; on Saturdays, live music is presented in the hotel's rathskeller downstairs (average entrée $13). Rooms can also be rented here ($75–100 d).

The Little Finger Lakes and Beyond

LITTLE FINGER LAKES

West of the six major Finger Lakes extend what are known as the little Finger Lakes: Honeoye (pronounced Honey-oy), Canadice, Hemlock, and Conesus. Honeoye sports a village of the same name at its northern end, and Conesus—closest to Rochester—is crowded with summer homes. Canadice and Hemlock, however, serve as reservoirs for Rochester and remain largely undeveloped. Set in deep, wooded valleys with no towns nearby, these are also the highest of the Finger Lakes—1,100 and 905 feet respectively.

At the southwestern end of Honeoye lies the largely undeveloped **Harriet Hollister Spenser State Park,** Canadice Hill Rd. (Rte. 37), no phone. Set on Canadice Hill, the park offers great views of the lake and—on a clear day—the Rochester skyline.

For other scenic views, travel the Canadice Lake Road down the eastern shore of Canadice Lake, or Ball Hill Road between Canadice and Hemlock Lakes.

LETCHWORTH STATE PARK

Along the Genesee River at the far western edge of the Finger Lakes plunges one of the most magnificent sights in the state: the 17-mile-long **Letchworth Gorge.** Dubbed the "Grand Canyon of the East," the gorge is flanked by dark gray cliffs rising nearly 600 feet. All around grows a dense, thicketed forest; through the center of

things sparkle three thundering waterfalls. The Seneca called the 107-foot-high Mid Falls *An-de-ka-ga-kwa* (the place where the sun lingers)—to take in the falls' extraordinary beauty.

Much of the Letchworth Gorge was purchased by industrialist William P. Letchworth in 1859. A conservationist and humanitarian, Letchworth bought the gorge both for his own personal use and to save the falls from becoming Rochester's hydroelectric plant. Before his death in 1910, he deeded the gorge to the people of New York to be used as a permanent park.

One main road runs through the park alongside the gorge, affording scenic views. At the southern end stand the Glen Iris Inn, which is a favorite luncheon spot, and the Letchworth Museum. Recreational facilities include 20 hiking trails ranging from one-half to seven miles in length, two swimming pools, 82 cabins, and a 270-site campground.

The park, 585/493-3600, can be entered from Mt. Morris (off Rte. 36), Portageville (off Rtes. 19A or 436), or Castile (off Rte. 19A); the Portageville entrances are closed in winter. Hours are daily 6 A.M.–11 P.M., and the vehicle use fee May–October is $6. For cabins or campsite reservations, call 800/456-CAMP; a basic site costs $18.

Glen Iris Inn

The creaky, yellow-and-white Glen Iris Inn, 585/493-2622, www.glenirisinn.com, sits in a large flat field overlooking Mid Falls. Once the home of William Letchworth, the Victorian mansion is now a modernized inn featuring 15 simple but comfortable guest rooms, a library with a good collection of regional books, and a gift shop ($75 d). The inn's bustling restaurant, flanked by picture windows, specializes in gourmet salads, seafood, and veal; open for breakfast, lunch, and dinner; average dinner entrée $18.

Letchworth Museum

Across from the Glen Iris is a rambling museum haphazardly packed with exhibits on the Seneca, William Letchworth, and the gorge's natural history. Note especially the exhibits relating to Mary Jemison, the "white woman of the Genesee."

The daughter of Irish immigrants, Jemison was taken prisoner by the Seneca at the age of 15 and lived the rest of her life among them. She married first a Delaware warrior and then, following his death, a Seneca chief; she bore seven children, and became a Seneca leader in her own right. Under the Big Tree Treaty of 1797, she was granted close to 18,000 acres along the Genesee River. Eventually, however, Jemison was moved to the Buffalo Creek Reservation with the rest of her people, where she died at the age of 91.

Letchworth moved Jemison's remains to the gorge in 1910 when her grave was in danger of being destroyed, and today, the **Mary Jemison Grave** stands on a hill behind the museum. Also on the hill is the **Council House** in which the last Iroquois council on the Genesee River was held on October 1, 1872. In attendance were the grandchildren of Red Jacket, Joseph Brant, Mary Jemison; and William Letchworth and Millard Fillmore.

The museum, 585/493-2760, is open May–Oct., daily 10 A.M.–5 P.M. Suggested donation is $1.

Nearby Accommodations and Food

Just south of the park is the 1870 **Genesee Falls Inn**, Rte. 436, Portageville, 585/493-2484, containing five cozy guest rooms, a Victorian-era dining room and taproom, and a coffee shop serving breakfast and lunch. Adjoining the inn is a modern motel unit with five additional rooms ($60–70 d).

See also Warsaw and Castille under Wyoming County in the chapter on Western New York.

GENESEO AND ENVIRONS

North of Letchworth are Cuylerville and Geneseo, newsworthy in the last decade because of the collapse of the Restof Salt Mine. The 18-square-mile rabbit-warren of chambers was once the largest salt mine in the Americas, but in 1994, a large section of its roof collapsed, and it closed. It's bleak and lonely country up here. Raggedy fields stretch out for miles, etched only occasionally with groves of dark-limbed trees.

In Cuylerville the informal **Tired Iron Tractor Museum**, Rte. 20A, 585/382-3110, displays a wide assortment of antique tractors. The museum is open July–Aug., daily 10 A.M.–6 P.M., June and September weekends only. Admission is adults $4, kids under 12 free.

Geneseo, a haven of culture, holds a flourishing branch of the State University of New York and a historic **Village Square,** bustling with shops and restaurants.

Rochester

Straddling the Genesee River gorge just south of Lake Ontario, presides Rochester (pop. 219,770). New York's third largest city, Rochester has traditionally been known for its behemoth high-tech industries—Eastman Kodak, Xerox, Bausch & Lomb. Many major educational and cultural institutions are based here as well, including the Eastman School of Music, Rochester Philharmonic, Strong Museum, and International Museum of Photography at the George Eastman House.

In the past, all this had added up to a prosperous and well-educated city that's been both highly admirable and, at times, a little bland. On one hand, it's been hard to beat Rochester's many fine museums, interesting restaurants, generous philanthropic spirit, and solid, friendly neighborhoods. On the other hand, the city has lacked a certain spark. No one has known this better than Rochesterians themselves; in the 1950s, Rochester newspaperman Curt Gerlig dubbed the city "Smugtown U.S.A.," and the name—in certain circles, at least—stuck.

But in more recent years, Rochester has been forced to reinvent itself. As its major employers have downsized to shadows of their former selves, laying off thousands upon thousands of workers, the city has lost its identity as a paternalistic company town to become one made up of many small firms. Rochester today is home to dozens of thriving but relatively unknown computer software, telecommunications, and medical equipment companies, and its population has learned to take nothing for granted. The areas around Rochester remain extremely prosperous, while its downtown suffers from common urban woes.

Rochester is a Midwestern city, with lots of solid brick buildings surrounded by a flat landscape. It was first established in 1803, but didn't really begin to grow until 1825 when the Erie Canal came to town. As America's first boomtown, Rochester's population increased 13-fold between 1825 and 1845.

Famous Rochesterians have included abolitionist Frederick Douglass, women's rights leader Susan B. Anthony, industrialist George Eastman, and musicians Cab Calloway, Mitch Miller, and Chuck Mangione. Native son Garth Fagan continues to live and headquarter his world-renowned dance troupe in the city today.

Orientation

Downtown Rochester is encircled by I-490, and is sometimes called the Inner Loop. Main Street runs east-west through the center of the downtown; Clinton Avenue runs north-south. Just west of South Street is the Genesee River.

Major thoroughfares fanning out from I-490 include East Avenue, Park Avenue, Monroe Avenue (Route 31), and Mt. Hope Avenue (Route 15). I-90 runs just south of the city. Lake Ontario lies about eight miles north of the heart of downtown.

The best way to explore Rochester is by car. You'll find several parking garages downtown, on or just off Main Street. Elsewhere in the city, street parking is generally available. Downtown sights are within walking distance of each other and the major museums in southeast Rochester.

Visitor Information and Tours

The **Greater Rochester Visitors Association,** 45 East Ave., Suite 400, Rochester, NY 14604, 585/546-3070 or 800/677-7282, www.visitrochester.com, is open year-round Mon.–Fri. 8:30 A.M.–5 P.M., Sunday 10 A.M.–3 P.M.; also summer Saturdays 9 A.M.–5 P.M. The association also operates a booth on the first floor of the Greater Rochester International Airport and runs an **Events Line** at 585/546-6810. You can pick up maps and brochures at the Heritage Area Visitor Center at Brown's Race as well.

Walking tours are offered periodically by the **Landmark Society of Western New York,** 585/546-7029, www.landmarksociety.org.

HISTORY
Early History

When the first white settlers arrived in the Rochester area in the late 1700s, they found a

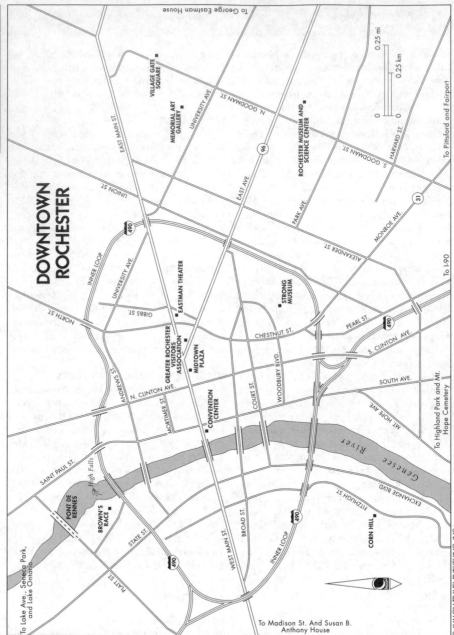

DOWNTOWN ROCHESTER

To George Eastman House

VILLAGE GATE SQUARE

MEMORIAL ART GALLERY

ROCHESTER MUSEUM AND SCIENCE CENTER

EAST MAIN ST.

UNIVERSITY AVE.

N. GOODMAN ST.

S. GOODMAN ST.

HARVARD ST.

EAST AVE.

PARK AVE.

MONROE AVE.

UNION ST.

490

96

31

INNER LOOP

UNIVERSITY AVE.

EASTMAN THEATER

STRONG MUSEUM

NORTH ST.

GIBBS ST.

ALEXANDER ST.

PEARL ST.

490

GREATER ROCHESTER VISITORS ASSOCIATION

MIDTOWN PLAZA

CHESTNUT ST.

S. CLINTON AVE.

ANDREWS ST.

N. CLINTON AVE.

MORTIMER ST.

COURT ST.

WOODBURY BLVD.

SOUTH AVE.

CONVENTION CENTER

MT. HOPE AVE.

To Highland Park and Mt. Hope Cemetery

To I-90

SAINT PAUL ST.

High Falls

PONT DE RENNES

BROWN'S RACE

Genesee River

EXCHANGE BLVD.

FITZHUGH ST.

STATE ST.

WEST MAIN ST.

BROAD ST.

INNER LOOP

490

490

CORN HILL

PLATT ST.

To Lake Ave., Seneca Park, and Lake Ontario

To Madison St. And Susan B. Anthony House

To Pittsford and Fairport

0.25 mi

0.25 km

0

N

rattlesnake-infested swamp and three tremendous Genesee River waterfalls. The settlers deemed braving the dangers of the swamp worth the rewards of the falls, and soon gristmills were operating all along the river banks. After the opening of the Erie Canal, the mills became so prosperous Rochester was dubbed the Flour Capital. When the grain industry moved westward, Rochester turned to other businesses, including horticulture, and renamed itself the Flower City.

During the mid-1800s, Rochester was a hotbed of social activism and radical thought. Frederick Douglass, the escaped slave and abolitionist, settled in Rochester in 1847 and published his newspaper, the *Northern Star,* here for 17 years. One of his close associates was Susan B. Anthony, who was arrested in 1872 for daring to vote in a national election.

Kodak and the 20th Century

In 1881, a quiet young bank clerk named George Eastman patented and produced the world's first rollable film—an invention that would change Rochester forever. By the turn of the century, Eastman Kodak was Rochester's largest employer, and Eastman a generous philanthropist. During his lifetime, he gave away over $100 million—about $1 billion in today's economy—mainly to schools, parks, the University of Rochester, and local hospitals. "I want to make Rochester the best city in which to live and work," he once said, and as far as many Rochesterians were concerned, he succeeded.

Like many other northeastern cities, Rochester fell on hard times in the 1960s. Factories closed, citizens fled the downtown, and racial tensions exploded in the riots of 1964. For the most part, however, things were never as bad in Rochester as they were elsewhere in the country. Eastman Kodak was still there, along with two new high-tech companies—Xerox and Bausch & Lomb.

Today, Eastman Kodak is still there. Although the company has downsized considerably—employing about 25,000 as compared to 60,200 in its 1982 heyday—it is still one of the city's largest employers. Rochester also generates about 40 percent of the state's exports of manufactured goods and has an unemployment rate well below the national average.

Rochester skyline

DOWNTOWN

At first, Rochester's downtown seems much like any other. Encircled by I-490, it centers around a Main Street flanked with a mix of historic buildings and modern glass-sheathed skyscrapers. At the corner of Main and Clinton Avenue sprawls the 1962 **Midtown Plaza,** the oldest downtown shopping mall in the country; at the corner of Main and South Avenue stand the **Rochester Riverside Convention Center** and the **Hyatt Hotel.** The graceful **Eastman Theatre,** with its rounded facade, is tucked onto Gibbs Street near Main, while the stunning art deco **Times Square Building** towers one block off Main at the intersection of Exchange Boulevard and Broad Street.

But walk a few blocks north of Main Street to Brown's Race, and you'll experience why this is no ordinary downtown. An enormous gaping gorge rips right through the heart of the city.

Brown's Race and the Center at High Falls

Brown's Race sits at the edge of wide, semi-circular High Falls—at 96 feet tall it is the highest of Rochester's three major waterfalls. Cupping the falls to both sides, but especially to the east, are jagged brown walls streaked with dull red. A **pedestrian bridge** crosses the river just south of the falls.

Brown's Race is made up of four interconnected brick buildings that once contained a series of water-powered mills. The word "race" refers to the diverted water- or raceways that once harnessed the power of the falls. After years of neglect, Brown's Race was extensively renovated in the early 1990s. It now features both a cluster of shops and restaurants and one of New York's **Heritage Area Visitor Centers**—loosely delineated historic districts united by a common theme. Officially, the theme in Rochester is the natural environment, but the center's many hands-on exhibits cover virtually every aspect of the city's history.

At dusk May–September, the center presents a free laser light show projected onto a 500-foot section of the gorge. The show tells the story of a Seneca spirit said to inhabit the river, and the tale of Sam Patch, a daredevil who lost his life going over the falls in 1829.

The center, 60 Brown's Race, at Platt St. and the Genesee River, 585/325-2030, is open Tues.–Sat. 10 A.M.–4 P.M., Sunday noon–4 P.M., with extended hours until 10 P.M. on summer Fridays and Saturdays when the laser light shows are presented. Admission is free.

Strong Museum

Up until the late 1990s, the Strong was one of the most unusual museums in all of New York State, specializing as it did in everyday American history and folk art. In it, you could find over a half million objects ranging from antique toys, dollhouses, and advertising memorabilia to weathervanes, political campaign buttons, and quilts.

Those objects are still there, but they've been relegated to the back rooms, as today's Strong has been reconstructed into a children's museum. The main exhibits now are: Sesame Street, Time Lab (with lots of hands-on history games), a kid-sized supermarket, a 1918 carousel, and a 1950s diner. The museum's founder, Margaret Woodbury Strong, is probably turning over in her grave.

Before her death in 1969, Margaret Woodbury Strong, the daughter of a wealthy family, had amassed more than 300,000 objects, some of which she began collecting as a child. Often, during her family's many trips abroad, she was given a large shopping bag at the start of each day and told she could shop until she filled it.

Strong's many passions included fans, parasols, Asian artifacts and art, dolls, dollhouses, miniatures, toys, marbles, canes, paperweights, glass, pottery, samplers, figurines, kitchen equipment, and costumes. Her doll collection, numbering 27,000, is especially impressive.

The museum, 1 Manhattan Square (corner of Chestnut and Woodbury Blvd.), 585/263-2700, www.strongmuseum.org, is open Mon.–Sat. 10 A.M.–5 P.M., Sunday noon–5 P.M. Admission is adults $6, children 2–17 $5.

Accommodations

Several large glass-sheathed hotels are located downtown. Though they cater mostly to business

COURTESY OF GREATER ROCHESTER VISITORS ASSOCIATION

Sesame Street at Strong Museum

In the heart of downtown, **Dinosaur Bar-B-Q,** 99 Court St., 585/325-7090, offers great ribs, Cajun and Cuban food, along with live blues on the weekends; average main dish $9. Romantic **Tapas 177,** 177 St. Paul St., 585/262-2090, is a very popular spot, serving an eclectic menu by candlelight, a wide variety of martinis, and live music on the weekends; average entrée $15.

Nestled into the East End entertainment district is the popular new **2 Vine,** 24 Winthrop St., 585/454-6020, serving lots of fresh seafood that's flown in daily, fresh local produce, and homemade pastries; it was voted "Best Restaurant" in a *City Newspaper* survey; average entrée $17. First-class **Edwards,** 35 S. Washington St., 585/423-0140, is renowned for its French-American cuisine, Edwardian decor, and impeccable service; average entrée $24.

SOUTHEAST ROCHESTER

The genteel southeastern quadrant of Rochester boasts three major museums, two minor ones, the University of Rochester, Mt. Hope Cemetery, and Highland Park. Through its center runs expansive **East Avenue,** peppered with stately mansions, gardens, and churches. Parallel to East Avenue runs **Park Avenue,** known for its classy boutiques, restaurants, and outdoor cafes. South of Park lies **Monroe Avenue,** a major commercial artery that's also one of the city's more eclectic neighborhoods. Many of the district's smaller residential streets got the names of colleges such as Dartmouth and Oxford.

Memorial Art Gallery

Connected with the University of Rochester, the Memorial Art Gallery is a small gem, containing a little bit of everything, from pre-Columbian sculpture and ancient Chinese ceramics to American folk art and late 20th-century painting. The gallery owns more than 9,500 objects in all, spanning 5,000 years; a dozen or so temporary exhibitions are staged each year.

In the center of the gallery, an enclosed, skylit sculpture garden features works by Henry Moore and Albert Paley, a known Rochesterian. To one

travelers, they often offer reasonably priced packages, especially on the weekends.

Connected to the Rochester Riverside Convention Center is the 15-story, 467-room **Four Points by Sheraton,** 120 E. Main St., 585/546-6400 or 888/596-6400 ($99–130 d). Across the street is the 26-story, 330-room **Hyatt Regency,** 125 E. Main St., 585/546-1234 or 800/233-1234 ($99–175 d). The **Crowne Plaza Rochester,** 70 State St., 585/546-3450 or 800/227-6963, is a 364-room luxury hotel on the Genesee River, complete with a large pool and fitness center ($89–134 d).

Food

For a quick and casual breakfast or lunch, visit the **food court** at the Midtown Plaza, Main St. and Clinton Ave., 585/454-2070. At Brown's Race, you'll find the **Triphammer Grill,** 585/262-2700, featuring lots of grilled fare, including steaks, seafood, and poultry, along with vegetarian dishes; average dinner entrée $15.

WEGMANS: THE MOST SUPER SUPERMARKET?

Not all grocery stores are created equal. No one knows that better than Wegmans, the Rochester-based supermarket chain whose stores have become tourist attractions.

Wegmans stores are *big*. Three times larger than the average supermarket, they contain pharmacies, dry cleaners, make-up counters, florists, cafes, pet centers, in-store play areas, video stores, and photo labs, not to mention fish departments carrying over 80 varieties of fish, produce departments stocked with 800 kinds of fruits and vegetables, cheese aisles with 250 cheeses (plus caviar), coffee departments with 50 types of beans, and bakeries producing fresh bread 'round the clock. The average Wegmans store has 30 checkout counters so no one has to wait in line more than a few minutes, and a dozen or so park benches for rest stops.

But that's not all. Piles of free recipes lie throughout the store, and there are daily food demonstra-tions by professional chefs. Shoppers choose from an endless array of takeout-prepared food—teriyaki beef kebabs, chicken cordon bleu, grilled sandwiches. Choices for eat-in include vegetable lo mein, fresh sauteed salmon, and Sunday brunch specialties served with chilled wine. Wegmans runs its own egg farm that produces 540,000 dozen eggs daily; they also fly in fresh lamb from Australia and fresh fish from New Zealand, Ecuador, and Hawaii.

Started up in 1916 with Walter and Jack Wegman delivering produce by horse and cart, Wegmans now boasts over 50 grocery stores. Most are located in upstate New York, with a handful in Pennsylvania. One of the largest in the Rochester area is **Marketplace Wegmans,** 650 Hylan Dr. (Exit 13 off I-390), 716/424-7255. For other locations, call 800/WEGMANS. Wegmans stores operate 24 hours a day.

side is Cutler's Restaurant, serving gourmet luncheons (average entrée $12).

The gallery, 500 University Ave., between Prince and Goodman Sts., 585/473-7720, www.rochester.edu/mag, is open Tues.–Fri. 10 A.M.–4 P.M., Saturday 10 A.M.–5 P.M., Sunday noon–5 P.M. Admission is adults $7, seniors and students $5, children 6–18 $2.

Woodside Mansion

One of the city's smaller museums, this 1839 Greek Revival–style home now serves as the headquarters for the Rochester Historical Society. Lots of fine architectural touches complement the inside, including a spiral staircase. Paintings, costumes, period furniture, toys, and historic photos are on display.

The museum, 485 East Ave., 585/271-2705, is open Mon.–Fri. noon–4 P.M., or by appointment. Admission is adults $2, seniors and students $1.50, children 12–16 $1, under 12 50 cents.

Rochester Museum and Science Center

Like many other top science museums, the Rochester Museum and Science Center (RMSC) houses plenty of fossils, dioramas, exhibits on flora and fauna, and prehistoric beasts. What makes the place really unusual, however, is **At the Western Door,** a powerful exhibit on the Seneca Nation.

The exhibit examines Seneca life from pre-European contact in the 1550s to the present. Separate sections, brimming with artifacts, focus on such subjects as the fur trade, the Iroquois Confederacy, the Sullivan campaign, and the sad history of broken treaties. As late as 1960, the Allegheny Senecas lost one-third of their reservation when it was flooded to create Kinzua Dam.

Also at the museum is the state-of-the-art **Strasenburgh Planetarium.** Sky shows happen daily.

The museum, 657 East Ave., 585/271-4320 or 585/741-1880 (taped info), www.rmsc.org, is open Mon.–Sat. 9 A.M.–5 P.M., and Sunday noon–5 P.M. Admission is adults $7, seniors $6, students 3–18 $5. The planetarium shows cost adults about $5, students $3.

George Eastman House

Just east of the RMSC is the grand 50-room Georgian mansion where Eastman Kodak founder George Eastman lived alone with his mother for much of his life. The house contains all the finest furnishings of its day, including Persian rugs, oil paintings, and carved mahogany furniture polished to a high gleam, but what makes the place interesting is Eastman himself. Born in 1854, Eastman left school at age 13 to help support his family. He worked first as a messenger boy earning $3 a week, then as an accountant at the Rochester Savings Bank. He began taking photographs at age 23 while on vacation and, annoyed with the hassle, began searching for an easier way to develop negatives. He spent three years experimenting in his mother's kitchen with gelatin emulsions. By 1880, George had invented a dry plate coating machine—the genesis of the Eastman Kodak Company.

Eastman's passions included music, fresh flowers, wild game hunting, and philanthropy. One year, he even gave a free camera to every child in America who was turning 13. Then, at age 78, suffering from an irreversible spinal disease, Eastman committed suicide in his bedroom. His suicide note read: "To my friends; My work is done—why wait?"

The **International Museum of Photography,** a long modern museum behind the mansion holds a fascinating collection of antique cameras and photographic equipment, along with two theaters, extensive archives, and four photography galleries. First-rate temporary exhibits by artists such as Ansel Adams and Henri Cartier-Bresson are presented here.

The house and museum, 900 East Ave., 585/271-3361, www.eastman.org, are open Tues.–Sat. 10 A.M.–5 P.M., Sunday 1–5 P.M. Admission is adults $8, seniors $6, students $5, kids 5–12 $3.

Stone-Tolan House Museum

Continuing to the far eastern end of East Avenue, you'll come to the oldest structure in Rochester, the 1792 Stone-Tolan House. A handsome, rustic building with wide floorboards, large fireplaces, and an orchard out back, the house was once both the Stone family home and a popular tavern (added onto the house in 1805). Somehow, in between serving customers, Orringh and Elizabeth Stone managed to raise nine children here.

The house, 2370 East Ave., near Clover St., 585/546-7029, www.landmarksociety.org, is owned by the Landmark Society of Western New York. Hours are March–Dec., Fri.–Sun. noon–4 P.M. Admission is adults $2, children 25 cents.

THE FINGER LAKES

George Eastman House

THE FINGER LAKES

Highland Park

In 1888, Frederick Law Olmsted designed Highland Park, a planned arboretum. One of the city's biggest celebrations—the **Lilac Festival**—takes place here every May, when the park's 1,200 lilac bushes bloom.

But lilacs are just the beginning. From early spring through late fall, Highland offers a riotous delight of fragrant Japanese maples, sweet-smelling magnolias, dazzling spring bulbs, delicate wildflowers, and 700 varieties of rhododendrons, azaleas, and mountain laurel. There's also a rock garden filled with dwarf evergreens and a pansy bed with 10,000 flowers planted in a different oval pattern each year.

In the center of the park reigns the 1911 **Lamberton Conservatory,** 180 Reservoir Avenue. Under the main dome grows a tropical forest, while other rooms contain orchid collections, banana trees, cacti, and house plants. Across from the conservatory is the 1898 **Frederick Douglass statue,** the first public statue erected to honor an African American.

Near Mt. Hope Avenue stands the Gothic-styled **Warner Castle.** Once the abode of a Rochester attorney and newspaper editor, the castle now houses the Garden Center of Rochester and a garden shop. Look in back to discover one of the park's loveliest secrets—a romantic sunken garden surrounded by wildflowers.

The park, 585/256-4950, is bounded by Mt. Hope, Highland, and Elm Avenues, and Goodman Street. South Avenue runs through the park. Open 24 hours a day.

Mount Hope Cemetery

From the corner of Mt. Hope and Elmwood Avenues extends the extravagant Mt. Hope Cemetery, a landscaped oasis of green strewn with knobby hills, ancient trees, marble tombs, and elaborate masoleums. One of the oldest cemeteries in the country, established in 1838, Mt. Hope contains the graves of every Rochesterian who was anyone, including Frederick Douglass and Susan B. Anthony.

An 1874 neo-Romanesque gatehouse marks the cemetery entrance, while just inside are a Gothic chapel and crematorium, and a white

Moorish gazebo. The Douglass grave is off East Avenue near the northern end of the cemetery; the Anthony grave is off Indian Trail Avenue at the far northern end.

Maps to the cemetery, 791 Mt. Hope Ave., are available at the Rochester Convention & Visitors Bureau. Friends of Mt. Hope Cemetery, 585/461-3494, www.fomh.org, offers guided walking tours on Saturday, spring–fall.

Monroe Avenue

This haven for students, artists, performers, and activists packs an eclectic array of neighborhood stores, "alternative" shops right out of the '60s, and ethnic restaurants. Most of the activity is centered between I-490 and Goodman Street.

Accommodations

In the museum district you'll find the quiet and comfortable **Days Inn Downtown,** 384 East Ave., 585/325-5010 or 800/329-7466, offering some of the lowest prices downtown ($79 d, includes continental breakfast). Nearby is the **Strathallan,** 550 East Ave., 585/461-5010, a newly renovated all-suite hotel with a spiffy solarium, health club, and rooftop bar. All of the 156 rooms are equipped with refrigerator and microwave, making it a good choice for families ($109–145 d).

One of the loveliest bed-and-breakfasts in Rochester is the **Dartmouth House,** 215 Dartmouth St., 585/271-7872 or 800/724-6298, www.dartmouthhouse.com, a spacious English Tudor home with a fireplace, window seats, very knowledgeable hosts, and three luxurious guest rooms equipped with private baths and phones. The B&B is within easy walking distance of the museums and many cafes and shops ($125 d).

Another good B&B choice is the Victorian **428 Mt. Vernon,** 428 Mt. Vernon Ave., 585/271-0792 or 800/836-3159, www.428mtvernon.com, located near the entrance to Highland Park. The seven antique-filled guest rooms are spacious and comfortable ($125 d).

Food

For a simple salad or tofu burger, step into the no-frills **Aladdin's Natural Eatery,** 646 Monroe

Ave., 585/442-5000. On Clinton Avenue, parallel to Monroe, is the **Highland Park Diner,** 960 S. Clinton Ave., 585/461-5040, a classic 1948 Orleans diner in the art deco style.

Back on Monroe Avenue, you'll find the **Olive Tree,** 165 Monroe Ave., 585/454-3510, serving a sort of imaginative "nouvelle Greek cuisine." Housed in a renovated 1864 brick storefront, the eatery uses fresh local ingredients and also serves Greek wines and beer; average entrée $16. Not far away is another good ethnic spot, the **Raj Mahal,** 324 Monroe Ave., 585/546-2315, known for its tandoori and vegetarian dishes, and fresh breads. Chefs prepare dishes behind a glass window while guests look on; average entrée $14.

ELSEWHERE IN THE CITY AND VICINITY

Corn Hill

Just south of downtown, between the Genesee River and Clarissa Street, lies Corn Hill, Rochester's oldest neighborhood. Once home to the city's wealthiest residents, Corn Hill fell into decline in the 1960s and 1970s but is now in the midst of a renaissance. Especially handsome residences stand along Atkinson Street, Plymouth Avenue, and South Fitzhugh Street.

In the heart of the neighborhood reigns the 1835 **Campbell-Whittlesey House Museum.** Once home to flour miller Benjamin Campbell, this elegant Greek Revival home boasts double parlors painted in 12 different tones and furniture decorated with gold stencils. Like many a Rochesterian, Campbell made a fortune after the opening of the Erie Canal and set about proving his wealth to his neighbors. Ironically, he soon overexpanded and was forced to sell his home.

One of the highlights of this house museum is a winsome musical instrument known as a grand harmonican. Composed of water glasses ground to different sizes, the instrument is played by running a wet finger around the glasses' rims.

Tours of the house, 123 S. Fitzhugh St., near Troup St., begin at the Landmark Society of Western New York headquarters, 133 S. Fitzhugh St., 585/546-7029, www.landmarksociety.org.

Hours are March–Dec., Fri.–Sun. noon–4 P.M. Admission is adults $2, children 25 cents.

Susan B. Anthony House

In a quiet, somewhat run-down neighborhood west of downtown stands the narrow red-brick home that once belonged to women's rights advocate Susan B. Anthony. Simply furnished in the style of the late 1800s, the house contains much Anthony memorabilia, including her typewriters, clothes, letters, photos, and stuffed Victorian furniture.

Anthony, born in Massachusetts in 1820, lived in this house from 1866 until her death in 1906. It was here she was arrested for voting in 1872, and here that she met and planned with fellow reformers Elizabeth Cady Stanton and Frederick Douglass. Anthony wrote her *History of Woman Suffrage* in the third-floor attic, a wonderful hideaway now once again strewn with her books and papers.

The house, 17 Madison St., off W. Main St., 585/235-6124, www.susanbanthonyhouse.org, is open Memorial Day–Labor Day, Tues.–Sun. 11 A.M.–5 P.M. Tours are on the hour and half hour, with the last one at 4 P.M. Winter hours are Wed.–Sun. 11 A.M.–4 P.M. Admission is adults $6, seniors $5, students and children $3.

Seneca Park and Zoo

North of the downtown, along the Genesee River, runs the long, skinny Seneca Park and Zoo. About 500 animals from nearly 200 species live in the zoo—black bears, polar bears, a Siberian tiger, white-tailed deer, reindeer, reptiles, and monkeys. Don't miss the aviary, where brightly colored tropical birds fly about free. Younger kids will enjoy the barnyard petting area and the touch table displaying turtle shells, snake skins, deer antlers, and the like.

The zoo, 2222 St. Paul St., a quarter mile north of Rte. 104, 585/266-6846, www.senecazoo.org, is open daily 10 A.M.–5 P.M. Admission is adults $5, seniors $4, children ages 3–11 $2.

Ontario Beach Park

When in downtown Rochester, it's easy to forget that Lake Ontario is less than 15 minutes away.

But indeed, north of the city along Lake Avenue, you'll soon find a land of wide open spaces, beaches, and parks.

Just before reaching the lake, you'll pass the 1822 **Charlotte-Genesee Lighthouse,** now a small museum with exhibits tracing the history of lighthouses and lake transportation. Originally, the lighthouse stood on the lakeshore, but sand deposits have moved it inland. The lighthouse, 70 Lighthouse St., at Lake Ave. and Latta Rd., 585/621-6179, is open May–Oct., Sat.–Sun. 1–5 P.M. Admission is adults $2, under 12 free.

On the shores of Lake Ontario runs the Ontario Beach Park, a half-mile-long sand beach with an aging art-deco bathhouse and a long, weathered fishing pier illuminated on summer nights. Around the turn of the century, the park was the "Coney Island of the West," attracting tens of thousands of Rochesterians to its elephant shows, water slides, and beachfront hotels. Harking back to those heady days is the park's still-operating 1905 **Dentzel menagerie carousel,** one of the oldest carousels in the United States. Stop by the locally famous **Abbotts Custard,** at the entrance to the park, selling a sweet, creamy ice cream.

The park, Lake and Beach Aves., 585/256-4950, is open daily year-round, but the carousel and Abbotts only in summer. Lifeguards are on duty June–Labor Day.

Seabreeze Amusement Park

From Ontario Beach Park, travel east about five miles along Lake Shore Boulevard to reach the Seabreeze Amusement Park. First established in 1879, the park now has 75 rides and attractions, including the Raging Rivers Water Park and the Jack Rabbit Roller Coaster. The 1920 Jack Rabbit is one of the few surviving all-wooden coasters.

Seabreeze, 4600 Culver Rd., 585/323-1900 or 800/395-2500, www.seabreeze.com, is open June–Labor Day daily noon–10 P.M.; weekends in May. General admission with two ride tickets is $7; an unlimited Ride & Slide pass is adults $17.50, children under 18 $13.50.

Accommodations

In Pittsford, to the immediate southeast of the city, is the modern **Brookwood Inn,** 800 Pittsford-Victor Rd., 585/248-9000 or 800/426-9995, www.hudsonhotels.com. On its premises are 108 large guest rooms, a heated indoor pool, and a sauna. Though nothing special to look at, it's a very clean and comfortable place ($89–129 d).

Also in Pittsford is **Oliver Loud's Inn,** 1474 Marsh Rd., 585/248-5200, a restored 1812 stagecoach inn on the canal, next to the renowned Richardson's Canal House (see Food, below). Rooms in this picturesque spot start at $110–120 s or d, including continental breakfast and a picnic basket.

Many of Rochester's motels are to the south of the city. In the suburb of Henrietta, you'll find a **Red Roof Inn,** 4820 W. Henrietta Rd., 585/359-1100, whose 108 rooms now come with recliners and lighted work desks ($69–79 d). Nearby stands a **Ramada Inn,** 800 Jefferson Rd., 585/475-9190 or 800/365-3065, offering 144 rooms and a full-service restaurant ($99 d).

Food

A number of landmark restaurants are located on the outskirts of the city. Foremost is **Richardson's Canal House,** 1474 Marsh Rd., Pittsford, 585/248-5000, a restored 1818 Erie Canal tavern with its own secluded garden. Elegant and highly acclaimed, the restaurant serves French country and American regional fare by candlelight; average entrée $24.

Also to the southeast is the picturesque **Spring House,** 3001 Monroe Ave., 585/586-2300, a former Erie Canal inn surrounded by a patio and gardens; average entrée $18. Due east, the **Daisy Flour Mill,** 1880 Blossom Rd., Penfield, 585/381-1880, serves American regional cuisine in an 1848 gristmill that's on the National Register of Historic Places. Live piano jazz is offered on the weekends; average entrée $18.

For great sushi and other Japanese favorites, try **Tokyo Japanese Restaurant,** 2930 W. Henrietta St., 585/424-4166; average entrée $16.

RECREATION

The 49-passenger *Sam Patch,* 250 Exchange Blvd., at the Genesee River, 585/262-5661, www.sampatch.org, a replica packet boat, offers sightseeing, lunch, and dinner cruises May–October. The 500-passenger *Spirit of Rochester,* 18 Petten St. Extension, Charlotte, 585/865-4930, sails for lunch, dinner, and moonlight cruises April–October.

ENTERTAINMENT

Classical Music, Opera, and Dance
The renowned **Rochester Philharmonic Orchestra,** 585/222-5000, performs at the Eastman Theatre October–May. One of the world's premier music schools, the **Eastman School of Music,** 26 Gibbs St., 585/274-1100, stages over 700 performances annually by students, faculty, and guest artists.

The **Garth Fagan Dance Company,** 50 Chestnut St., 585/454-3260, tours about 25 weeks a year but performs in Rochester one week each fall. The **Hochstein Music School Auditorium,** 50 N. Plymouth Ave., 585/454-4596, hosts the Rochester Chamber Orchestra, the Borinquen Dance Theatre, and classical music concerts.

Theater
Rochester's only resident professional theater, the **GeVa Theatre,** 75 Woodbury Blvd., at Clinton, 585/232-GEVA, stages nine productions annually. It's housed in a historic brick-and-limestone building that was once the Naval Armory. The **Downstairs Cabaret Theatre,** 585/325-4370, produces popular comedies and musicals.

The **Rochester Broadway Theatre League,** 585/325-7760, presents touring Broadway shows and concerts. Formerly known as the Pyramid Arts Center, the **Rochester Contemporary,** 137 East Ave., 585/461-2222, is the place to go for performance art and avant-garde theater.

Film
The **Little Theatres,** 240 East Ave., 585/232-3906, are three small film houses that screen excellent art, foreign, and independent films. Pay only $3 to view a second-run movie at **The Cinema,** 957 S. Clinton Ave., 585/271-1785. The **Visual Studies Workshop,** 31 Prince St., 585/442-8676, showcases contemporary photography, video, and independent film.

Music and Nightlife
The best music listings are published by *City Newspaper,* 585/244-3329, a free alternative weekly. One of the biggest and most active music clubs in the city is the **Water Street Music Hall,** 204 N. Water St., 585/325-5600. Regional and national acts play blues, rock, funk, and industrial.

The **Milestones Music Room,** 50 East Ave., 585/325-6490, brings in regional and occasionally national acts playing acoustic, blues, alternative, rock, and pop. The **California Brew Haus,** 402 W. Ridge Rd., 585/621-1480, presents a good dose of Southern rock. The **Centers at High Falls,** 60 Browns Race, 585/423-0000, is a restaurant, outdoor patio bar, and three nightclubs under one roof. The live music ranges from jazz to party bands.

Poetry and fiction readings are presented in various venues by **Writers & Books,** 585/473-2590.

EVENTS
The **Lilac Festival** takes place in Highland Park in mid-May. The **Monroe County Fair** takes place in late June. Lots of **free concerts** and other events are presented in Rochester's parks and public spaces throughout the summer. For more information on these and other events, call the Rochester Visitors Association at 585/546-3070.

EXCURSIONS FROM ROCHESTER
Hamlin Beach State Park
Off the Lake Ontario State Parkway about 20 miles west of Ontario State Park, the 1,223-acre Hamlin Beach State Park offers swimming beaches, hiking trails, nature trails, bike paths, a playground, and concession stands. One of the area's largest campgrounds is also located here.

The park, 585/964-2121, is open year-round. Lifeguards are on duty June–Labor Day. Parking in summer is $6. To reserve one of the campsites, call 800/456-CAMP; a basic site costs $15.

Genesee Country Village and Museum

Twenty miles southwest of Rochester, the world-class Genesee Country Village and Museum consists of 57 meticulously restored 19th-century buildings laid out around a village square. Among them are an early land office, two-story log cabin, fly tier's shop, octagonal house, Greek Revival mansion, Italianate mansion, bookshop, small-scale farm, blacksmith's shop, doctor's office, and pharmacy. Gravel walkways lead between the buildings; guides in period dress cook, spin, weave, and demonstrate other folk arts of the pre-industrial age.

Near the entrance are a Carriage Museum and a Gallery of Sporting Art, featuring works by such artists as Audubon and Remington. To the north is a 175-acre Nature Center, networked with three miles of hiking and nature trails.

The museum, 1410 Flint Hill Rd., off Rte. 36, Mumford, 585/538-6822, www.gcv.org, is open May–Oct., Tues.–Sun. 10 A.M.–4 P.M., with extended hours in July and August. A restaurant and cafeteria are on-site. Admission is adults $12.50, students and seniors $11, children ages 4–16 $7.

Genesee Country Village and Museum

COURTESY OF GREATER ROCHESTER VISITORS ASSOCIATION

Western New York

Western New York, reaching so far west that it almost borders Ohio, has a distinctively Midwestern feel. Like the heartland, the region wasn't settled until the early 1800s, and so lacks Eastern New York's Colonial history and even the Finger Lakes' post–Revolutionary War past. Most of the region's cities started as frontier boomtowns, and much of the countryside supports farmland.

Western New York's two largest cities are Buffalo and Niagara Falls, situated about 20 miles apart along the Niagara River, across from Canada. At Buffalo's southwestern edge lies Lake Erie, while north of Niagara Falls presides Lake Ontario, a favorite haunt of serious fisherfolk.

Buffalo is New York's second largest city. Seriously depressed following the decline of its steel industry in the 1970s, it still faces many economic difficulties, but has also rejuvenated itself to a surprising extent, with a renovated waterfront and theater district.

Niagara Falls has long been regarded as one of the world's great natural wonders. As far back as 1678, missionary Father

© CHRISTIANE BIRD

Niagara Falls

WESTERN NEW YORK

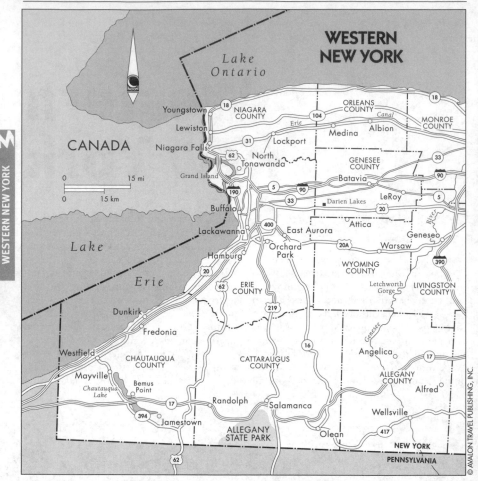

© AVALON TRAVEL PUBLISHING, INC.

Louis Hennepin wrote, "Betwixt the Lake Ontario and Erie, there is a vast and prodigious Cadence of Water. . . . The Universe does not afford its Parallel. . . . The Waters which fall from this horrible Precipice do foam and boyl after the most hideous manner imaginable, making an outrageous Noise, more terrible than that of Thunder."

To the east of Buffalo extends especially fertile farm country. To the south begin the dark, rolling foothills of the Allegheny Mountains. To the southwest lies Chautauqua Lake, a popular resort area that's also home to the famed Chautauqua Institute—a sort of cultural camp for adults.

PRACTICALITIES
Hiking

The southern half of Western New York is covered with state forests, through which run all-but-undiscovered hiking trails. Some are part of the Finger Lakes Trail network; most are not. A first-rate guide to hiking the area is *Fifty Hikes in Western New York* by William P. Ehling (Backcountry Publications). For more information on the Finger Lakes Trail, contact the **Finger Lakes Trail Conference,** 6111 Visitor Center Rd., Mt. Morris, NY 14510, 716/288-7191, www.fingerlakes.net/trailsystem. The conference publishes 45 sectional maps, all priced around $1.

Fishing

Fishing is big business in this part of the country, especially along Lake Ontario, which the state stocks with more than three million salmon and trout a year. For more information on fishing the Great Lakes, contact the visitor information centers listed below.

Chautauqua Lake is renowned for its giant muskies, as well as its walleye, bass, and panfish. The record muskie caught in the lake weighed 51 pounds, three ounces.

Transportation

Airlines that serve the **Greater Buffalo International Airport** include American Airlines, 800/433-7300; Continental Airlines, 800/525-0280; Delta Airlines, 800/221-1212; JetBlue, 800/JET-BLUE; Northwest Airlines, 800/225-2525; United Airlines, 800/241-6522; and US-Airways, 800/428-4322. USAirways also serves the **Jamestown Airport.**

WESTERN NEW YORK HIGHLIGHTS

Buffalo
Downtown architecture
Historic Allentown
Roosevelt Inaugural Site
Buffalo wings at the Anchor Bar
Albright-Knox Art Gallery
HallWalls Contemporary Arts Center
Buffalo and Erie County Historical Society Museum
Delaware Park and Forest Lawn Cemetery
Buffalo and Erie County Botanical Gardens
Erie Basin Marina
The grain elevators
Nietzche's music club
East Aurora village
Pedaling History Bicycle Museum, Orchard Park
Herschell Carousel Factory Museum, North Tonawanda
Old Man River restaurant, North Tonawanda

Niagara Falls
Niagara Reservation State Park, especially Prospect Point, Three Sister Islands, and the *Maid of the Mist*
Aquarium of Niagara Falls
The nighttime illumination of the Falls
Devil's Hole State Park
Castellani Art Museum
Artpark, Lewiston
Old Fort Niagara, Youngstown

Orleans, Genesee, and Wyoming Counties
Cobblestone architecture, Orleans County
Holland Land Office Museum, Batavia
Le Roy House and Jell-o Gallery, Le Roy
Iroquois National Wildlife Refuge, Alabama
Historic Wyoming Village
Hillside Inn, Wyoming Village
Architecture of Warsaw, Attica, and Arcade

Allegany and Cattaraugus Counties
Angelica village
The back roads and state forests of Allegany County
Wellsville Texas Hot restaurant, Wellsville
The village and crafts shops of Alfred
International Museum of Ceramic Art at Alfred
The Block Barn, Cuba
Seneca-Iroquois National Museum, Salamanca
Allegany State Park, Salamanca
Griffis Sculpture Park, Ashford Hollow
Amish farm country, near Randolph

Chautauqua County
Lucy-Desi Museum, Jamestown
Lucille Ball landmarks, Jamestown
Jamestown Audubon Nature Center, Jamestown
Bemus Point-Stow ferry
Hotel Lenhart, Bemus Point
Chautauqua Institution, Chautauqua
Historic Dunkirk Lighthouse, Dunkirk
Lily Dale Assembly, Cassadaga

A taxi ride from the airport to downtown Buffalo costs about $20; from the airport to Niagara Falls a taxi costs about $40. **ITA Buffalo Shuttle,** 716/633-8294 or 716/633-8318, provides service between the airport and Buffalo ($13) or Niagara Falls ($21). **Metro Bus and Rails,** 716/855-7211, provides local bus service.

Amtrak, 800/872-7245; **Greyhound,** 800/231-2222; and **New York Trailways,** 800/295-5555, all serve both Buffalo and Niagara Falls. Many smaller towns are serviced by Greyhound; **Coach USA,** 716/372-5500; and the **Chautauqua Area Regional Transit System,** 716/665-6466.

By far the best way to explore the region is by car.

Emergencies

Dial 911 for emergencies throughout the region. Area hospitals include **Buffalo General Hospital,** 100 High St., Buffalo, 716/859-5600; **Niagara Falls Memorial Hospital,** 621 10th St., 716/278-4000; **Genesee Memorial Hospital,** 127 North St., Batavia, 716/343-6030; **WCA Hospital,** 207 Foote Ave., Jamestown, 716/487-0141; and **Westfield Memorial Hospital,** 189 E. Main St., Westfield, 716/326-4921.

Visitor Information

For information about Buffalo, Niagara Falls, and the northern counties of Western New York, contact the **Buffalo Niagara Convention and Visitors Bureau,** 617 Main St., Buffalo, NY 14203, 716/-852-2356 or 800/BUFFALO; hours are Mon.–Fri. 8 A.M.–5 P.M. Their website is buffalocvb.com. For information on Allegany, Cattaraugus, and Chautauqua Counties, contact the county tourism offices listed throughout this chapter.

Buffalo

If ever there was a city of rabid sports fanatics, Buffalo is it. What other metropolis would build its two largest sports stadiums—Dunn Tire Park and the HSBC Arena—in the heart of the downtown, while sticking many of its cultural attractions several miles to the north?

If ever there was a city of strong ethnic persuasions, Buffalo is it. What other midsize city—Buffalo's population is only about 310,500—can boast the largest St. Patrick's Day Parade west of Manhattan (population eight million) and the largest Pulaski Day Parade east of Chicago (population three million)?

If ever there was a city of broad, tree-lined streets, expansive Victorian homes, and striking architectural landmarks, Buffalo is it. There aren't many places that have received the architectural stamp of approval from both *The New Yorker* critic Brendan Gill and architectural historian John D. Randall. Randall states that Buffalo has a wider range of American and European architectural forms than any other city in the world.

Visiting Buffalo is like visiting an overgrown small town. People talk to strangers here and point to recent civic improvements with enormous, and quite justified, pride. Nonetheless, the city has its share of urban problems, including a population exodus to more prosperous areas and rising crime rates.

HISTORY

Early History

Once the domain of the Iroquois, the Buffalo area was visited sporadically by French explorers in the 18th century. The French called the Niagara River *beau fleuve,* or beautiful river, which the English allegedly bastardized into "buffalo."

The city was laid out in 1803–04 by Joseph Ellicott, a land agent for the Holland Land Company. He modeled his plans after those of Washington, D.C., which his brother Maj. Andrew Ellicott had laid out. Niagara Square, like the White House, serves as a focal point from which major streets radiate.

Buffalo was incorporated in 1816 but didn't thrive until the Erie Canal was completed in 1825. The town stood at the transportation break between the Great Lakes and the canal, and soon warehouses sprang up all along the lakefront.

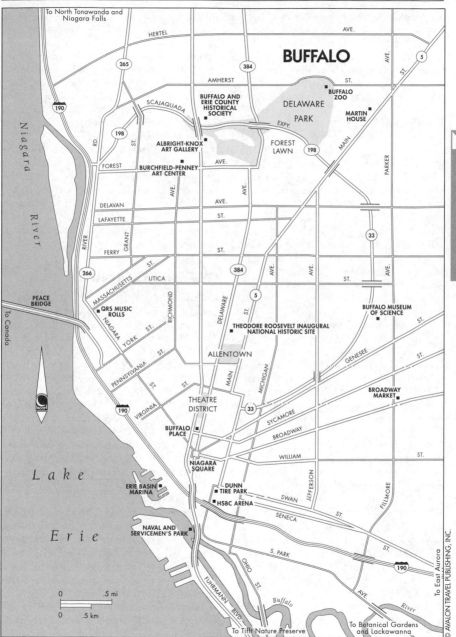

To North Tonawanda and
Niagara Falls

HERTEL   AVE.

BUFFALO

AMHERST   ST.

265   384

BUFFALO AND
ERIE COUNTY   DELAWARE   BUFFALO
HISTORICAL   ZOO
SOCIETY   PARK   MARTIN
SCAJAQUADA   HOUSE

190

198   ALBRIGHT-KNOX   FOREST
ART GALLERY   LAWN   198

FOREST   BURCHFIELD-PENNEY   MAIN
ART CENTER   AVE.

AVE.

RD.   AVE.   PARKER

DELAVAN   AVE.

LAFAYETTE   ST.

FERRY   ST.   33

266   UTICA
MASSACHUSETTS   384

PEACE   QRS MUSIC   5
BRIDGE   ROLLS   BUFFALO MUSEUM
OF SCIENCE

THEODORE ROOSEVELT INAUGURAL
NATIONAL HISTORIC SITE   GENESEE

ALLENTOWN

BROADWAY
MARKET

THEATRE
DISTRICT   33

SYCAMORE

BROADWAY

BUFFALO
PLACE   WILLIAM   ST.

NIAGARA
SQUARE

ERIE BASIN   DUNN
MARINA   TIRE PARK
HSBC ARENA   SWAN

Lake   SENECA

Erie   NAVAL AND
SERVICEMEN'S PARK   FILLMORE

190

S. PARK

0   .5 mi

0   .5 km   Buffalo   River

To Tifft Nature Preserve   To Botanical Gardens
and Lackawanna

Niagara

River

To Canada

MOON

To East Aurora

© AVALON TRAVEL PUBLISHING, INC.

WESTERN NEW YORK

Thousands of immigrants, most from Ireland and Germany, arrived.

Mrs. Frances Trollope, visiting the city in 1828, wrote: "All the buildings have the appearance of having been run up in a hurry, though everything has an air of great pretension; there are porticos, columns, domes and colonnades but all in wood."

The Rise of Industry

Buffalo's first iron foundry went up in 1826, and its first steam engine plant in 1829. By 1845, the city also boasted a stove factory, nail factory, cabinet factory, bell foundry, and numerous other plants producing such products as mirrors, picture frames, and bathtubs.

In the mid- to late 1800s, the rapid development of the railroads turned Buffalo into a major grain and livestock market. Eleven main railroad lines served five passenger and 14 freight terminals, with 300 passenger and 3,000 freight trains passing through daily. Today, Buffalo is still a major railroad center, handling more than 25,000 trains a year.

One of the railways, completed in 1873, connected Buffalo with the anthracite coal fields of Pennsylvania. That coal, together with Lake Superior iron ore and the newly developed Bessemer process, allowed for the large-scale production of steel. More immigrants, this time from Poland and Italy, poured in; the newly rich built lavish mansions along Delaware Avenue.

The Modern Era

By 1900, Buffalo was ready to show off its wealth and sophistication to the world. What better way to do so than to host the 1901 Pan-American Exposition? The exposition covered 350 acres, attracted eight million visitors, and featured everything from columned temples to the latest scientific inventions. The glamorous event was tragically marred, however, by the assassination of Pres. William McKinley, who was shot at the expo on September 6, 1901 by anarchist Leon Czolgosz.

Following the exposition, Buffalo continued to prosper. Blast furnaces went up along the Buffalo River, huge grain elevators along the harbor. But the McKinley assassination seemed to have

robbed the city of its earlier self-assurance. Trade routes shifted and Buffalo failed to fulfill its one-time promise to become a truly great city.

Buffalo reached its industrial zenith shortly after WW II. Relative prosperity continued, however, until the early 1970s, when newer, more efficient steel plants abroad caused a major shakedown of the steel industry. Buffalo's steel plants closed, the region's economy declined, and its population ebbed.

Enter the 1980s. Smaller manufacturing, finance, and advanced technology companies opened—and flourished. Then, in 1989, the U.S.-Canada Free Trade Agreement was signed and Buffalo became a major center for American companies looking to expand into Canada. Today, Buffalo owes much of its economic base to that agreement.

GETTING AROUND

Orientation

Buffalo is situated along the eastern shores of Lake Erie at the mouth of the wide Niagara River. Through the city's southern part runs the considerably narrower Buffalo River.

Downtown Buffalo centers around Niagara Square and Buffalo Place, a pedestrian-only thoroughfare along Main Street. Along the waterfront stretches Buffalo Harbor and a series of parks. The Peace Bridge leading to Canada is reached via I-190 north of downtown.

Immediately north of Buffalo lie the twin industrial cities of Tonawanda and North Tonawanda; to the south is the suburb of Lackawanna.

Transportation

The **MetroRail,** 716/855-7211, runs along Main Street from the Buffalo River to the University at Buffalo South Campus. The system is above ground and free along Buffalo Place (Main Street south of Tupper Street); below ground, the fare is $1.25. Tickets may be purchased from vending machines at all stations.

Most downtown sites are within walking distance of each other. The downtown area has an enormous number of parking lots. Elsewhere, street parking is usually available.

INFORMATION

Food

Thanks to its diverse population, Buffalo offers numerous inexpensive ethnic restaurants. A good guide to these spots is *The Cheap Gourmets' Dining Guide to the Niagara Frontier,* by Doug and Polly Smith, available in area bookstores.

The city is also the birthplace of two oddball specialties. One is Buffalo chicken wings—spicy wings served mild, moderate, or hot, with celery sticks and blue-cheese dressing. The other is beef-on-'weck sandwiches—thinly sliced roast beef piled high on fresh kimmelweck rolls sprinkled with pretzel salt and caraway seeds. The chicken wings were invented in 1964 in the Anchor Bar in Allentown by Teressa Bellissimo, mother of the late owner Dominic Bellissimo.

Visitor Information

The **Buffalo Visitor Center,** 617 Main St. (in the Market Arcade), run by the **Buffalo Niagara Convention and Visitors Bureau,** 716/852-0511 or 800/BUFFALO, www.buffalocvb.com, is open Mon.–Fri. 8 A.M.–5 P.M. Buffalo Place runs an **Events Hotline** at 716/854-4FUN.

Tours

Self-guided audio walking tours of historic Allentown, Delaware Avenue, downtown, and Main/North Pearl Streets can be picked up at the **Theodore Roosevelt Inaugural National Historic Site,** 641 Delaware Ave., 716/884-0095. The cost of each tape is $5, plus a $25 deposit, and cassette tape players can be rented.

Weekly architectural walking tours, bus tours, and trolley tours are offered May–October by the **Friends of the School of Architecture and Planning** at the University of Buffalo. Call 716/829-3542 for more information.

DOWNTOWN

Niagara Square

A good place to begin touring Buffalo is Niagara Square, which centers around the **McKinley Monument.** The monument honors Pres. William McKinley, who was assassinated in Buffalo while attending the 1901 Pan-American Exposition. Designed by architects Carrere and Hastings, the memorial consists of an obelisk surrounded by pools decorated with crouching lions.

Dominating Niagara Square is the monumental art deco **Buffalo City Hall,** erected in 1929. The hall's front entrance is lined with eight Corinthian columns three stories high, while inside are vast, vaulted ceilings covered with sculpted figures and paintings depicting local history. An **observation deck** on the 28th floor provides great views of the city, Niagara River, and Lake Erie. The deck, 716/851-5991, is open Mon.–Fri. 9 A.M.–4 P.M. Admission is free.

BLIZZARD-BLITZED BUFFALO

Buffalo has earned a reputation as the Blizzard Capital of the United States. This isn't entirely fair. There are snowier places—northern Michigan, for example—and most of Buffalo's snow falls south of the city proper, in the region's ski belt. Still, the Queen City of the Lakes does see more than its share of white stuff. Writes native son Verlyn Klinkenborg in *The Last Fine Time:*

"Snow begins as a rumor in Buffalo, New York. . . . The first flake appears and vanishes like a virtual particle in the mind of a physicist. . . . But suddenly, without seeming to begin, the sky is full of real particles falling so slowly that they appear to stand, wavering, in air. . . .

"By ten o'clock at night, the Niagara Frontier is shut tight. . . . The airport closed at seven o'clock. Transport has ground to a halt. The only thing open is the Niagara River, and that is not navigable in this season. Even indoors, you can hear the hush over Buffalo. You can feel the way the heavy snowfall changes a room, the way it redefines the interior, making the walls seem closer together, the roof heavier, the insulation thicker, as if the house had been built of logs and chinked with sphagnum moss, as if you might wake up in the morning and find the windswept tracks of lynx and snowshoe rabbit running down the middle of the street, as if the street itself were a frozen lake ringed by a forest of dark hemlock and spruce."

On Franklin Street just south of Niagara Square stands the 1870s' **Old County Hall,** where Pres. Grover Cleveland got his start, first as a lawyer and then as mayor of Buffalo. Designed in the high Victorian Gothic style, the building contains a lavish lobby done up in marble and bronze.

Church Street Architecture

Another block south, at the corner of Franklin and Church, stands the **Guarantee Building,** also known as the Prudential Building. Designed by Louis H. Sullivan in 1894, the 12-story terra cotta skyscraper is covered with elaborate ornamentation repeated on the elevators and mosaic ceilings indoors.

One block farther east, at the corner of Church and Pearl Streets, reigns **St. Paul's Episcopal Cathedral.** Designed by Richard Upjohn in the 1880s, the brown sandstone church features a front central tower topped with a tall, delicate spire.

Main Street and Buffalo Place

In the late 1970s, downtown Main Street—semi-abandoned for years thanks to urban flight—was transformed into a pedestrian thoroughfare named Buffalo Place. A sleek, above-ground section of the Metro Rail was built through its center, and slowly business began returning to the downtown.

Entering Buffalo Place from Church Street, you'll spot the **Ellicott Square Building,** 295 Main St., on the southeast corner. When completed in 1896, this block-wide edifice was the largest commercial office building in the world. Spanning Main Street south of the Ellicott is the enormous **Marine Midland Center.**

On the northwest corner of Main and Church stands the **Main Place Mall,** housing standard shops and a food court. Two long blocks north, at Huron Street, is the **Hyatt Regency Buffalo.** Originally an office building erected in 1893, the hotel features some of the finest murals in Buffalo. On the lobby's north wall is a scene depicting Buffalo harbor in the 1940s; the east wall shows the Seneca, headed by Red Jacket.

Theatre District

One block north of the Hyatt begins the restored Theatre District, a 20-block area extending west as far as Delaware Avenue and north to Tupper Street. About a half-dozen theaters and cabarets operate here, along with restaurants, galleries, and shops. Along Chippewa Street is the **Chippewa District,** known for its nightclubs.

Buffalo has an impressive theater history, which began in the mid-1800s, thanks to the traffic along the Erie Canal. Dozens of theaters catering to travelers sprang up almost overnight, and by the turn of the 20th century, Buffalo was one of the country's foremost drama centers. Actress Katherine Cornell, songwriter Harold Arlen, and choreographer Michael Bennett are among the many who've come out of Buffalo's performing arts scene.

The centerpiece of the district is **Shea's Performing Arts Center,** 646 Main St., 716/847-1410, www.shea.org, an opulent 1926 movie palace filled with marble and gilt. Saved at the last moment from the wrecker's ball in 1975, Shea's is now fully restored.

Buffalo has an impressive theater history, which began in the mid-1800s, thanks to the traffic along the Erie Canal. Dozens of theaters catering to travelers sprang up almost overnight, and by the turn of the 20th century, Buffalo was one of the country's foremost drama centers.

CEPA and Other Galleries

Across the street from the Shea Center is the CEPA Gallery, 617 Main St., 716/856-2717, www.cepa.buffnet.net, a first-rate exhibit space that focuses on photography, video, and film. Short for Center for Exploratory and Perceptual Art, CEPA is also a gathering spot for regional artists and a good place to go to find out about other arts events in town. Buffalo has a thriving alternative arts scene, with as many as a dozen small galleries—which tend to come and go—operating at one time. CEPA is usually open Mon.–Fri. 10 A.M.–5 P.M., Saturday noon–5 P.M., but call ahead.

Another gallery with a long track record is the renowned **HallWalls Contemporary Arts**

Center, 2495 Main St., 716/835-7362, which has been showcasing cutting-edge alternative art for over 20 years. It's open Tues.–Fri. 11 A.M.–6 P.M., Saturday 1–4 P.M. HallWalls is in the Tri-Main Building, which also houses numerous other arts organizations, galleries, and studios. Among them are the **Impact Artists Gallery,** 716/835-6817, and **Buffalo Arts Studio,** 716/833-4450.

To find out more about what's happening in the city arts-wise, pick up a copy of *ArtVoice,* 716/881-6604, a free biweekly publication.

Buffalo/Erie County Naval and Military Park

At the southern end of downtown, along the shores of Lake Erie, extends a six-acre maritime park dedicated to all branches of the armed forces. Most of the exhibits, however, have to do with the U.S. Navy; three decommissioned ships are berthed here.

Largest among them is the USS *Little Rock,* a 610-foot-long guided missile cruiser outfitted much the way it was in the 1960s when 1,400 men lived onboard. Next door slumbers the USS *Croaker,* a compact submarine that sank 11 Japanese vessels during WW II. Also seeing action in WW II was the USS *The Sullivans,* a destroyer named after five brothers from Waterloo, Iowa, who died in 1942 when a Japanese torpedo sank their ship. Shamrocks on the destroyer's smokestacks pay tribute to the brothers' Irish heritage.

Elsewhere in the park sit guided missiles, a PT boat, an Army M41 tank, and an Air Force F-101 Fighter Interceptor Jet. The Servicemen's Museum contains a good model ship collection.

The park, 1 Naval Park Cove, 716/847-1773, www.buffalonavalpark.org, is at the foot of Pearl and Main Streets. Hours are April–Oct., daily 10 A.M.–5 P.M., November Sat.–Sun. only; closed Dec.–Mar. Admission for adults is $6; seniors and students ages 6–16 pay $3.50.

Erie Basin Marina

Along Marina Drive north of the Naval Park is the Erie Basin Marina, where hundreds of pleasure boats dock. One side of the marina features

a pleasant park, while to the other several restaurants overlook Lake Erie. At the end of the dock is an observation tower, open May.–Oct., daily 8 A.M.–10 P.M.

Accommodations

A good downtown motel is the 61-room **Best Western Inn on the Avenue,** 510 Delaware Ave., 716/886-8333 or 800/528-1234 ($89–109 d). A good place for families is the 168-room **Holiday Inn Buffalo Downtown,** 620 Delaware Ave., 716/886-2121 or 800/HOLIDAY, which features a heated pool ($84–109 d).

Buffalo's finest hostelry is the 394-room **Hyatt Regency Buffalo,** 2 Fountain Plaza, at Main and Huron Streets, 716/856-1234 or 800/223-1234, housed in a lovely historic building equipped with a three-story glass atrium, indoor pool, and three restaurants ($99–199 d). The 468-room **Adams Mark Buffalo,** 120 Church St., 716/845-5100, offers a marble-floored lobby with a waterfall, rooms overlooking Lake Erie, and a big health club ($99–189 d). The lowest rates at both the Hyatt and the Adams Mark are usually available on the weekends.

Food

Near Niagara Square stands **Chef's,** 291 Seneca St., 716/856-9187, a Buffalo landmark specializing in Southern Italian fare; average entrée $14. A good place for a quick and simple lunch is the **Greenhouse Food Court,** Main Place Mall, 350 Main St., 716/855-1900.

Favorite restaurants in the Theatre District include the **Bijou Grille,** 643 Main St., 716/847-1512, a California-style bistro (average entrée $14), and **Hemingway's,** 492 Pearl St., 716/852-1937, a good place for a sandwich or burger (average main dish $9). The acclaimed **Coda,** 350 Pennsylvania Ave., 716/886-6647, housed in a converted grocery store, serves country French dishes from a menu that changes weekly; average entrée $19. For fine French fare, try **Rue Franklin,** 341 Franklin St., 716/852-4416, Buffalo's oldest—and some say best—French restaurant, housed in an elegant brick townhouse (average entrée $22; dinner only).

ALLENTOWN

Northwest of the Theatre District lies Allentown, the nation's second-largest historic district. The streets here are lined with one Victorian structure after another, with all styles represented. Many now house restaurants, art galleries, boutiques, and antique shops.

Allentown is roughly bounded by Main Street to the east, Edward Street to the south, North Street to the north, and Cottage and Pennsylvania Streets to the west. Through its center runs Allen and Virginia Streets, where the **Allentown National Preservation District Office,** 414 Virginia St., 716/881-1024, is located; hours are Mon.–Fri. 9 A.M.–5 P.M. Some visitor information can be picked up here, but for walking-tour brochures and audio tours, stop by the Roosevelt Inaugural Site (below).

Among the district's foremost architectural treasures are the typically middle-class **Tifft Houses,** Allen Street between Park and Irving Place; the extravagant **Williams-Butler Mansion,** 672 Delaware Ave.; and the **Wilcox Mansion,** now the Roosevelt Inaugural Site. Samuel Clemens, a.k.a. Mark Twain, once lived at 472 Delaware Ave., and F. Scott Fitzgerald spent part of his childhood at 29 Irving Place.

Theodore Roosevelt Inaugural National Historic Site

Theodore Roosevelt was formally inaugurated in the stately Wilcox Mansion in 1881 after the assassination of President McKinley. "It is a dreadful thing to come into the Presidency this way," wrote the pragmatic Roosevelt shortly after the event, "but it would be far worse to be morbid about it. Here is the task, and I have got to do it to the best of my ability; and that is all there is about it."

Once owned by a prominent lawyer named Ansley Wilcox, the 1838 house is now run by the National Park Service. The library where Roosevelt was sworn in has been fully restored; among the items on display throughout the house is the handkerchief that assassin Leon Czolgosz used to cover his handgun.

The house, 641 Delaware Ave., between

North and Allen Streets, 716/884-0095, is open Mon.–Fri. 9 A.M.–5 P.M., and Sat.–Sun. noon–5 P.M. Admission is adults $3, seniors $2, children 6–14 $1.

Accommodations

Built in the late 1800s, the **Lenox Hotel and Suites,** 140 North St., 716/884-1700, is well worn but a good value. On the premises are a restaurant and coin-operated laundry ($69–89 d).

Food

A famed Buffalo institution, the **Anchor Bar,** 1047 Main St., 716/886-8920, is the friendly Italian restaurant where Buffalo chicken wings were invented. Live jazz is often featured on the weekends; average entrée $12. Though not as well known, another neighborhood institution, the Greek-American **Towne Restaurant,** 186 Allen St., 716/884-5128, is a good place for breakfast and lunch (average main dish $8).

NORTH OF DOWNTOWN

Many of Buffalo's museums cluster together about four or five miles north of downtown, near Delaware Park. To get there take Delaware Avenue, a wide thoroughfare once lined with mansions, though only a few still stand.

Follow Delaware Avenue to Gates Circle and turn left on Chapin Parkway to reach Lincoln Parkway and Delaware Park. At the intersection of Chapin and Lincoln Parkway is the **William R. Heath House,** 72 Soldier's Pl., one of five houses in the city designed by Frank Lloyd Wright.

Albright-Knox Art Gallery

The centerpiece of Buffalo's art scene, this airy, low-slung museum is known around the world for its superb collection of contemporary art. The Albright-Knox was the first museum in the United States to purchase works by Picasso and Matisse, and the first anywhere to present a major exhibition of photography, in 1910.

All the major American and European artists of the past 50 years are well represented, including van Gogh, Gauguin, Pollock, Miró, and Mondrian. The museum also presents 10 first-rate temporary exhibits each year and houses a solid general collection that spans the history of art. The Gallery Shop includes an extensive selection of art books, and the Garden Restaurant serves gourmet sandwiches and salads.

The museum, 1285 Elmwood Ave., near Scajaquada Expressway, 716/882-8700, www.albrightknox.org, is open Tues.–Sat. 11 A.M.–5 P.M., Sunday noon–5 P.M., with extended hours during the summer. Admission is adults $5; students 13–18 and seniors $4.

Buffalo/Erie County Historical Society

Overlooking a small lake across from the Albright-Knox sits the only remaining permanent building from the 1901 Pan-American Exposition. Inspired by the Parthenon, the lovely structure once housed the New York State pavilion and is now home to the Buffalo and Erie County Historical Society Museum.

The museum features two unusual permanent exhibits. "Bflo. Made!" showcases virtually every product ever produced in the Buffalo region, from Pierce-Arrow cars and General Mills cereal to pacemakers and kazoos. "The People of Erie County" focuses on the area's vibrant ethnic history, from the Poles of the east side to the Irish of south Buffalo.

COURTESY OF BUFFALO/NIAGARA CONVENTION AND VISITORS BUREAU

Buffalo/Erie County Historical Society

The museum, 25 Nottingham Court, at Elmwood Avenue, 716/873-9644, is open Wed.–Sat. 10 A.M.–5 P.M., Sunday noon–5 P.M. Admission is adults $4, seniors $3, students $2.50, children 7–12 $1.50.

Burchfield-Penney Art Center

Also near the Albright-Knox is Buffalo State College, with jade green lawns and sturdy red-brick buildings. Signs point the way to Rockwell Hall and the third-floor Burchfield-Penney Art Center.

Spread out over four or five galleries, the center is a low-key affair dedicated primarily to Charles E. Burchfield, one of the finest watercolorists of the 20th century. Originally from Iowa, Burchfield spent most of his life living and teaching in Buffalo. He was fascinated by the Buffalo streets and by patterns of fire and sound, which he depicted in a mystical, expressionist style.

The center owns the world's largest collection of Burchfield works, exhibited on a rotating basis. Works by other contemporary Western New York artists are also exhibited.

The center, 1300 Elmwood Ave., 716/878-6011, is open Tues.–Sat. 10 A.M.–5 P.M., Sunday 1–5 P.M. Admission is free.

Art lovers might also be interested in visiting the **Charles Bruchfield Nature & Art Center** in nearby West Seneca, where Burchfield once lived. The center, 2201 Union Rd., 716/677-4843, offers an exhibition area, nature trails, a meditation garden, and a sculpture garden.

Delaware Park

Buffalo State College, the Albright-Knox, and the Buffalo and Erie County Historical Society all sit on the western edge of Delaware Park, a glorious, 350-acre expanse of green designed and laid out by Frederick Law Olmsted in the 1870s. Olmsted, who also designed Central Park in New York City, created an extensive park system throughout Buffalo that also includes Front, Martin Luther King, Jr., Cazenovia, and South Parks.

Near Lincoln Parkway on the park's west side lies Hoyt Lake and the regal **Delaware Park Casino,** 716/882-5920. Originally built as a boathouse and restaurant for the Pan-Am Expo, the building now houses a concessions stand that's open April–October, and an office where paddleboats can be rented.

Buffalo Zoological Gardens

In the heart of Delaware Park flourishes the city's most popular tourist attraction—the Buffalo Zoo. One of the oldest zoos in the country, founded around the turn of the century, the park is home to over 1,300 inhabitants. Among them are a rare white tiger, a one-horned Indian rhino, reticulated giraffes, and lowland gorillas. Highlights include "Habicat," where lions and tigers roam free; a tropical rain forest; an Asian forest; one of the largest reptile collections in the country; and—this is Buffalo, after all—a large herd of bison.

The zoo, 300 Parkside Ave., 716/837-3900, www.buffalo.zoo, is open daily 10 A.M.–5 P.M. Admission is adults $7, seniors $3, and children 2–14 $3.50.

Martin House

To the east of Delaware Park stands the 1904 Darwin D. Martin House, one of Frank Lloyd Wright's most important works. The long, horizontal building with its wide porches and few enclosed spaces is characteristic of the architect's early Prairie style.

Tours of the home, 175 Jewett Pkwy., at Summit, and the nearby Barton House (also designed by Wright), are offered Tues.–Thurs. and Sat.–Sunday. Call 716/856-3858 for exact hours. Tour price is adults $10, students $8.

Forest Lawn Cemetery

Abutting Delaware Park to the south extends expansive Forest Lawn Cemetery, the final resting place of Buffalo trappers, farmers, tradespeople, and statesmen since 1850. Near the entrance cluster small Iroquois graves and a tall monument honoring the famed Seneca orator Red Jacket, or "Sa-Co-Ye-Wat-Ha"—"he who keeps them awake." An all-too-prophetic quote on the memorial reads, "When I am gone and my warnings are no longer heeded, the craft and avarice of the white man will prevail. My heart fails me when I think of my people, so soon to be scattered and forgotten."

Beyond the Red Jacket memorial, the cemetery

spreads out over low hills networked with roadways. By the shores of the deep blue Mirror Lake stands the unusual Blocher monument, featuring life-size marble figures behind glass. President Millard Fillmore and Ely Parker, the Seneca brigadier-general, are also buried in Forest Lawn.

The cemetery, 1411 Delaware Ave., 716/885-1600, is open daily 8:30 A.M.–5 P.M. Free maps are available in the cemetery office, open Mon.–Sat. 9 A.M.–4 P.M., closed Sunday.

Food

Dozens of trendy eateries operate along Elmwood Avenue north of downtown. Among them is the new, stylish **Nektar,** 451 Elmwood Ave., 716/881-0829, a popular martini bar with an open grill serving light fare (average main dish $9). **Toro,** 492 Elmwood Ave., 716/886-9452, is the place to go for tasty *tapas* (average tapa $6), while **Ambrosia's Greek,** 467 Elmwood, 716/881-2196, serves savory Greek fare in a casual setting (average entrée $14).

Five-year winner of the local People's Choice award is **Hutch's,** 1375 Delaware Ave., near Gates Circle, 716/885-0074, a casual, bustling southwestern/Cajun bistro serving everything from rib-eye steak rubbed with garlic to grilled tuna; average entrée $14. **The Hourglass,** 981 Kenmore Ave., 716/877-8788, is a Buffalo institution, offering continental cuisine, homemade desserts, and an extensive wine menu; average entrée $22.

EAST OF DOWNTOWN

Buffalo Museum of Science

On the east side of Buffalo presides the four-story Buffalo Museum of Science, including exhibits on anthropology, astronomy, botany, geology, meteorology, and zoology. Children will love the hands-on exhibits in the Discovery Room, not to mention an exhibit called Dinosaurs and Co. Connected to the museum is Kellogg Observatory, open for viewings on Friday evenings, Sept.–May.

The museum, 1020 Humboldt Pkwy., at Utica Street, 716/896-5200, is open year-round Tues.–Sat. 10 A.M.–5 P.M., Sunday noon–5 P.M. Admission is adults $6; seniors, students, and children 3–17 pay $4.

Broadway Market

Though no longer the dynamic marketplace it once was, this Old World landmark, founded in 1888 in the heart of Buffalo's Polish neighborhood, still sells fresh ethnic foods. Over 40 vendors hawk everything from homemade soups and potato dumplings to chickens and pigs' heads. The market, 999 Broadway, near Fillmore, 716/893-0705, is open Mon.–Fri. 8 A.M.– 5 P.M., Saturday 7 A.M.–5 P.M.

Accommodations and Food

To the east, in the suburb of Clarence—known for its antique stores—is the acclaimed **Asa Ransom House**, 10529 Main St., 716/759-2315, www.asaransom.com. The 1853 inn features nine spacious guest rooms ($150–200 d, with breakfast) and an excellent restaurant serving American fare (average entrée $18; open for dinner Sun.–Thurs. only).

Heading toward the airport, you'll pass the extravagant **Salvatore's Italian Gardens,** 6461 Transit Rd., Cheektowaga, 716/683-7990, a sprawling, over-the-top Italian restaurant all done up in vibrant pastels (average entrée $19). Nearby is the popular **Polish Villa**, 2954 Union Rd., 716/683-9460, serving authentic ethnic fare; average entrée $10.

Adjacent to the glitzy new Galleria Mall and the Buffalo Airport is the **Four Points Sheraton,** 2040 Walden Ave., 716/681-2400 ($92–179 d). Another good airport choice is the **Sleep Inn and Suites–Buffalo Airport,** 100 Holtz Road Cheektowaga, 716/626-4000 ($89–99 d, with breakfast).

WEST OF DOWNTOWN

QRS Music Rolls

Established in 1900, QRS is the world's oldest and largest manufacturer of player piano rolls. In the 1920s, the company sold as many as 10 million rolls a year; today, that number is down to two to three hundred thousand, but thanks to enthusiastic hobbyists, is holding steady.

Tours of the low-key QRS factory begin with a short audiovisual presentation and then proceed to the factory floor. En route you'll learn that it once took an arranger eight hours to cut a master roll for a three-minute song, and that staff artist J. Lawrence Cook once wrote over 20,000 different arrangements. Today, no surprise, the songs are all cut by computer.

QRS, 1026 Niagara St., 716/885-4600, www .qrsmusic.com, offers tours Mon.–Fri. 10 A.M. and 2 P.M. Tickets are adults $2, children $1.

Accommodations and Food

Betty's Bed & Breakfast, 398 Jersey St., 716/ 881-0700, features two guest rooms, a skylight, a small garden, and very knowledgeable hosts who will go far out of their way to accommodate your every need. The handsome house dates back to the 1870s ($70 d).

Once the heart of Buffalo's Italian neighborhood, Grant Street near Delawan Avenue is still home to a number of traditional Italian shops and restaurants. **Guerccio's,** 250 Grant St., 716/ 882-7935, is an Old World food market. The **Italian Village,** 313 Grant St., 716/886-8285, offers all the traditional favorites and eppie rolls (fresh-cut dough wrapped around peppers, sausage, and cheese); average dinner entrée $11.

SOUTH OF DOWNTOWN

Buffalo and Erie County Botanical Gardens

In Frederick Law Olmsted's South Park reigns a pristine white conservatory, all domes, semicircular windows, and sheets of glass. Designed by the famed greenhouse architectural firm of Lord and Burnham in the 1890s, the conservatory is actually 12 small connected greenhouses. Each specializes in a different plant variety—bromeliads, orchids, cacti, fruit trees. In the center of things soars a pale green glass dome crowded with palms. Outside flourish acres of shrubs and flowering plants.

The conservatory, 2655 South Park Ave., at McKinley Parkway, 716/827-1584, www.buffalogardens.com, is open daily 9 A.M.–4 P.M.; Sat.–Sun. 9 A.M.–5 P.M. Donations welcomed.

Our Lady of Victory Basilica and National Shrine

Just south of the botanical gardens begins the suburb of Lackawanna. You'll find a fantastically elaborate Italian Renaissance church built in 1926, largely through the efforts of Father Nelson Baker, who also established several hospitals, schools, and other charitable institutions along Ridge Road. Two months after the cathedral was completed, Pope Pius XI declared it a Minor Basilica, making it the second church in the United States to be so honored.

The church, 767 Ridge Rd., at South Park Avenue, Lackawanna, 716/828-9444, is open daily 7:30 A.M.–7 P.M.

Steel Plant Museum

As hard as it is to believe today, quiet Lackawanna in the not-so-distant past was home to Bethlehem Steel, once the world's largest steel plant. During its heyday, the company employed more than 20,000 workers producing 6.5 million ingot tons annually. The 1,300-acre plant was located a few miles west of the Basilica, along Ridge Road near Lake Erie and Route 5.

Most of the plant is gone now, so to get a sense of the past you have to stop into the Lackawanna Public Library. On its lower level is a small museum honoring the area's former steel industry through historic photos, exhibits, and memorabilia.

The museum, 560 Ridge Rd., Lackawanna, 716/823-0630, is open Monday and Wednesday 1–9 P.M.; Tuesday and Thursday–Sat. 9 A.M.–5 P.M. Admission is free.

Tifft Nature Preserve

Near the city's harbor lies 264-acre Tifft Nature Preserve, administered by the Buffalo Museum of Science. Contained within are a 75-acre cattail marsh, a lake, several ponds, and five miles of easy hiking trails. Near the entrance a visitor center exhibits displays on local flora and fauna.

The preserve, 1200 Fuhrmann Blvd. (Rte. 5 S), 716/825-6397 or 716/896-5200, is open daily dawn–dusk. The visitor center is open Tues.–Sun. 9 A.M.–2 P.M., Saturday 9 A.M.–4 P.M., Sunday noon–4 P.M.

Grain Elevators

Walter Gropius, founder of the Bauhaus movement, once compared them to the monuments of ancient Egypt. Le Corbusier called them the "magnificent first fruits of a new age."

All along the Buffalo Harbor rise the giant grain elevators whose smooth facades inspired these architects of the early 20th century. First developed by Buffalo resident Joseph Dart in 1842, grain elevators helped turn the city into a major grain port. The elevators' innovative system of buckets and belts put Buffalo 20 years ahead of other ports that were still using manual laborers.

The earliest grain elevators were built of wood, but frequent fires soon led first to steel or tile construction, and then to concrete. In the early 1900s, a cylindrical concrete design became standard for grain elevators across the country.

Buffalo's grain elevators, some of which are still in use, are best viewed from the waterfront. Barring that, drive along Ohio Street, South Park Avenue, or Louisiana Street north of the Tifft Preserve near the mouth of the Buffalo River. The elevators rise up—mute, monolithic.

SPORTS AND RECREATION

Baseball: The **Buffalo Bisons,** 716/846-2000, a AAA team for the Cleveland Indians, play downtown at Dunn Tire Park, 275 Washington St., April–September. Tickets are generally available.

Cruises: The **Miss Buffalo Cruise Boats,** 716/856-6696, offer sightseeing tours of the Buffalo harbor, Lake Erie, and the Niagara River. The boats leave from the Erie Basin Marina June–September.

Football: The National Football League **Buffalo Bills** play at Ralph Wilson Stadium, 1 Bills Dr., Orchard Park, 716/649-0015, www.buffalobills.com, Sept.–January. Tickets are available for most games, especially if you order a few weeks in advance.

Hockey: The National Hockey League **Buffalo Sabres** play downtown at the HSBC Arena, at the foot of Main Street, 716/856-7300 or 716/855-4142, www.sabres.com, Sept.–April. Tickets are generally available.

Horse racing: Harness racing takes place

Wed.–Sat. at the **Buffalo Raceway,** Hamburg Fairgrounds, 5600 McKinley Pkwy., Hamburg, 716/649-1280.

Skiing: Delaware Park offers good cross-country skiing. For downhill, Buffalo residents usually head south to **Kissing Bridge,** Rte. 240, Glenwood, 716/592-4963; or to the **Holiday Valley Resort** in Ellicottville (see Cattaraugus County, below).

ENTERTAINMENT

Performing Arts

The renowned **Buffalo Philharmonic Orchestra** performs in the Kleinhans Music Hall, 370 Pennsylvania Ave., 716/885-5000. The hall, one of the nation's most acoustically perfect, was designed by Eliel and Eero Saarinen.

Shea's Performing Arts Center, 646 Main St., 716/847-1410, is a historic 1926 theater resembling a European opera house. Shows range from Broadway productions to opera and dance; the theater seats 3,100.

In nearby Lancaster stands turn-of-the-century **Lancaster Opera House,** 21 Central Ave., 716/683-1776. Performances include plays, musicals, and variety concerts.

Theater

In the Theatre District the 637-seat **Studio Arena Theatre,** 710 Main St., 716/856-5650, Buffalo's professional regional theater for over 25 years, presents both classic and contemporary drama.

More intimate Theatre District venues include the 100-seat **Alleyway Theatre,** 1 Curtain Up Alley, 716/852-2600, and the **Buffalo Ensemble Theatre at the New Phoenix,** 95 N. Johnson Park, 716/855-2225, which specializes in theatrical revivals and the classics.

Just west of the Theatre District is the **Ujima Theatre Company,** 545 Elmwood Ave., 716/883-0380, dedicated to the works of African Americans and Third World artists. The non-profit **African American Cultural Center,** 350 Masten Ave., near Utica Street, 716/884-2013, presents drama and other events in its Paul Robeson Theatre.

On D'Youville Square to the northwest of downtown reigns the **Kavinoky Theatre,** 320 Porter Ave., 716/881-7668, a beautifully restored 250-seat Victorian theater.

Clubs and Nightlife

The best sources for information about Buffalo's music and nightlife are the Friday edition of the *Buffalo News,* 716/849-4190; and *ArtVoice,* 716/881-6604, a free biweekly arts publication. An ever-shifting array of nightclubs operate in the **Chippewa District,** along Chippewa Street downtown. Lively, upscale bars can be found on **Elmwood Avenue** near Buffalo State College.

One of the oldest and best-known clubs in the city is laid-back **Nietszche's,** 248 Allen St., 716/886-8539, offering rock, country, reggae, blues, and folk. The **Continental,** 212 Franklin St., 716/855-3938, is the place to go for heavy metal. The **Anchor Bar** restaurant in Allentown (see Food, above) presents jazz on a regular basis. Folk music can be heard at **Metzger's Pub,** 4135 Seneca St., 716/674-9897.

A must stop for jazz fans is the **Colored Musicians Club,** 145 Broadway, 716/855-9383, a laid-back joint that was once the union local for black musicians.

EVENTS

Buffalo loves a festival. In mid-May, there's the **Hellenic Festival,** featuring Greek food, dance, and music. In early June the **Allentown Outdoor Art Festival** highlights work by over 400 artists and artisans. In mid-June the **Juneteenth Festival** takes place in Martin Luther King, Jr. Park.

The **Friendship Festival,** in early July commemorates almost 200 years of peace between the United States and Canada, with fireworks, food, and an extensive line-up of musical acts. One of the nation's largest outdoor food fests is the **Taste of Buffalo,** held on Buffalo Place in mid-July. The **Italian Heritage and Food Festival,** also in July, features food, games, rides, and entertainment. Poles celebrate their heritage during the August **Polish-American Arts Festival.**

For more information on any of these events, contact the Buffalo Convention and Visitors Bureau at 716/852-2356.

SOUTHERN EXCURSIONS

Orchard Park

Off a suburban street about 12 miles southwest of downtown Buffalo is **Pedaling History Bicycle Museum,** America's only all-bicycle museum and one of the few in the world. Over 200 bicycles are on display, including fat-tired streamliners, crude and heavy "bone shakers," impossibly high unicycles, courting tandems, and a floating marine cycle. First-rate historical exhibits explain how the bicycle was invented, and how the citizens of Victorian-era Boston once complained about the new craze, saying they could no longer control their horses for all the "racing bicyclists attired in black tights and long mustaches."

The museum, 3943 North Buffalo Rd. (Rte. 240/277), 716/662-3853, www.pedalinghistory.com, is open April–Jan. 15, Mon.–Sat. 11 A.M.–5 P.M., Sunday 1:30 P.M.–5 P.M.; Jan. 16–March, closed Tues.–Thurs. Admission is adults $6, seniors $5.40, children 7–15 $3.75.

Also in Orchard Park is **Ralph Wilson Stadium,** where the Buffalo Bills play (see Sports and Recreation, above).

East Aurora

Along Route 20A a few miles east of Orchard Park lies East Aurora, an idyllic village surrounded by hilly dairy country. East Aurora was once home to Pres. Millard Fillmore, and to Elbert Hubbard, a former soap salesman turned charismatic leader of the Arts and Crafts movement. "Conformists die, but heretics live forever," Hubbard was fond of saying. "Weep not peeling other people's onions."

Hubbard was the founder of an idealistic crafts community, the Roycrofters, whose **Roycroft Campus** still stands at the corner of Main and Grove Streets. Now a National Historic Landmark District, the 14-building complex still houses a number of artisans' workshops, along with gift shops, offices, a small museum, and the Roycroft Inn.

At the heart of the campus, **Roycroft Shops,** 31 S. Grove St., 716/655-0571, sells handmade items from around the world as well as crafts of Roycroft design. Out back is **Roycroft Potters,** 37 S. Grove St., 716/652-7422. Down the street is the small

Elbert Hubbard-Roycroft Museum, 363 Oakwood Ave., 716/652-4735, which documents the community's history. The museum is open June–Oct., Wednesday and Sat.–Sun. 2–4 P.M.

Another must-stop in East Aurora is **Vidler's 5 & 10,** 690-694 Main St., 716/652-0481. Out front flaps a spiffy red-and-white awning; inside are creaky wooden floors and display cases from the '20s selling old-fashioned *stuff,* including penny candy, wooden animals, marbles, magic cards, Buster Brown socks, mousetraps, lace, and ribbon. Almost everything costs under $1.

Two blocks off Main Street is the **Toy Town Museum,** 636 Girard Ave., 716/687-5151, www.toytownusa.com, a fascinating place for both children and adults. The museum documents the history of toys in the 20th century, along with children's games, stuffed animals, marionettes, music, and books. On display are one-of-a-kind toys, special exhibits, and the Fisher-Price Toy Collection. The toy company has been based in East Aurora since 1930. Museum hours are Mon.–Sat. 10 A.M.–4 P.M. Free admission.

© CHRISTIANE BIRD

In East Aurora, Vidler's carries a little bit of just about everything.

Also just off Main is the 1826 **Millard and Abigail Fillmore House,** 24 Shearer Ave., 716/652-8875, built by the future U.S. president with his own hands in 1826. Fillmore was then a young lawyer fresh off the farm. The house is open June–Oct., Wednesday and Sat.–Sun 2–4 P.M. Suggested donation is $3.

For more information on the village, visit www.eastaurorany.com.

Hamburg

Along Route 62, 15 minutes south of Buffalo, lies old-fashioned Hamburg—"the town that friendship built." This is supposedly where the hamburger was born, at the 1885 Erie County Fair. Vendor Frank Mensches had run out of the pork sausage he needed to make his specialty, a pork sausage sandwich. Hurrying to the local market, he picked up chopped meat instead, formed it into patties, and cooked it on his stove. The result was an instant success.

The Erie County Fair, 716/649-1280, still takes place in Hamburg in August.

Eden

As the self-proclaimed "Garden Spot of New York State," Eden, just south of Hamburg on Route 62, is a pristine small town surrounded by farm country. Not everything is agrarian here, however. Downtown stands the **Original American Kazoo Company: Museum, Gift Shop, Factory.** Established in 1916, the Original is now the only metal kazoo factory in the world. The company paid $5,000 for its first kazoo patent and still manufactures kazoos the way it always has, using die presses and sheet metal.

On display in the museum is a wooden kazoo, similar to its African prototype, and liquor-bottle–shaped kazoos made to celebrate the end of Prohibition. The record for the most kazoos ever played at one time was set in Rochester on January 2, 1986, when 54,500 kazoo-ists performed.

The company, 8703 S. Main St., near 1st Street, 716/992-3960, www.kazooco.com, is

> *Eden is the self-proclaimed "Garden Spot of New York State," and home to the only metal kazoo factory in the world.*

open Tues.–Sat. 10 A.M.–5 P.M., Sunday noon–5 P.M. Tours are given Tues.–Fri. 10 A.M.–3 P.M. Admission is free.

Camping and Accommodations

Two lakeside campgrounds are located south of East Aurora. To the southwest is **Colden Lakes,** 9504 Heath Rd., Colden, 716/941-5530, offering 120 campsites priced at $20–25. To the southeast is **Sleepy Hollow Lake,** Rts. 33 and 5, Sielh Rd., Akron, 585/542-4336, offering 200 campsites priced at $17–21.

A National Historic Landmark, the handsome 1905 **Roycroft Inn,** 40 S. Grove St., East Aurora, 716/652-5552, www.roycroftinn.com, is a one-of-a-kind place, filled with all original or re-production Roycroft furnishings—mostly heavy, beautifully designed pieces in oak. All 22 suites have at least one sleeping area, a sitting area, and a whirlpool tub, while the common rooms feature fireplaces, rich wood paneling, and Roycraft lamps. ($120–210 d).

Food

Not far from Rich Stadium in Orchard Park you'll find **Eckl's Beef & Weck Restaurant,** 4936 Ellicott Rd., 716/662-2262, a good spot to sample the local culinary invention; average dinner entrée $13.

In East Aurora the historic **Roycroft Inn** serves innovative American cuisine with a continental touch. Dinner entrées range from grilled tuna fillet to New York strip steak; average dinner entrée $19. Just outside town sprawls the **Old Orchard,** 2095 Blakely Rd., off Route 16, 716/652-4664, a historic farmhouse and former hunting lodge featuring large stone fireplaces and American/continental fare; average entrée $16.

BETWEEN BUFFALO AND NIAGARA FALLS

One way to reach Niagara Falls from Buffalo is to take Niagara Street north to River Road and the Robert Moses Parkway. The routes hug the shore of the Niagara River and, though highly industrialized in spots, offer an interesting back-side look at the region.

Grand Island

Just north of Buffalo begins Grand Island, the country's largest freshwater island. About five square miles larger than Manhattan, Grand Island was once seriously considered as a possible site for the United Nations. Earlier, in 1825, Maj. Mordecai Manual Noah founded Ararat on Grand Island as a refuge for persecuted Jews from Europe. He got as far as erecting a cornerstone for his new city, but the plan eventually failed due to lack of support.

Now primarily a suburban community, Grand Island hosts **Martin's Fantasy Island,** 2400 Grand Island Blvd., 716/773-7591, www.martinsfantasyisland.com, an 80-acre theme park with thrill rides, live entertainment, and a petting zoo. The park is open late June–Labor Day, daily 11:30 A.M.–8:30 P.M. Admission is adults $18, seniors $11, children under 48 inches $13. After 5 P.M., park entrance is $7 per person for everyone.

At the southern tip of the island lies **Beaver Island State Park,** 2136 W. Oakfield Rd., 716/773-3271, offering biking trails, a swimming beach, playground, and golf course. The park is open year-round; parking in summer is $6.

Herschell Carousel Factory Museum

In the sprawling industrial city of North Tonawanda, directly across the river from Grand Island, stands the old Herschell Carousel Factory. In its heyday in the 1920s and '30s, the plant produced over 50 carousels a year. Until 1928, all featured animals were carved entirely of wood; after 1928, the magical creatures were half-wood and half-aluminum.

Now both an informal museum and a workshop, the old factory contains a major exhibit on Allan Herschell, an expert woodcarver who was once the best-known carousel maker in the United States. Also on display are hand-carved animals dating back to the early 1900s, new carved animals in various states of completion, and historical exhibits. Out back spins a working 1916 carousel that adults as well as kids are invited to ride.

The museum, 180 Thompson St., off River Road, 716/693-1885, www.carouselmuseum.org, is open July–Aug., daily 11 A.M.–5 P.M.; April 1–June and Labor Day–Oct., Wed.–Sun. 1–5 P.M. Admission is adults $4, seniors $3, children 2–12 $2.

Camping and Food

Within easy reach of both Buffalo and Niagara Falls is the 587-site **Niagara Falls KOA,** 2570 Grand Island Blvd., 716/773-7583. A basic site costs $21.

The whimsical **Old Man River,** 375 Niagara St., Tonawanda, 716/693-5558, sports a whale on its roof and washing machine fountains; on the menu is everything from Sahlen's hot dogs, a Buffalo specialty, to sweet potato french fries. Almost as quirky, and serving a similar menu, is **Mississippi Mudds,** 313 Niagara St., Tonawanda, 716/694-0787.

Niagara Falls

The name Niagara Falls refers to both the city and the waterfalls. The city is a nondescript place, surrounded by endless industrial plants and humming electrical wires, but the falls . . . ah, well, the falls.

Oscar Wilde once called Niagara Falls "the second biggest disappointment in a young bride's life," but he must have been showing off that day, for despite the tourists, hoopla, and cliches, the falls are a sight to be seen. Stand in front of that white wall of water and you'll catch your breath. Guaranteed.

Located along the Niagara River between the United States and Canada, Niagara Falls are actually three falls in one: the American and Bridal Veil Falls on the New York side, and the even more spectacular Horseshoe Falls on the Ontario side. The thundering water is on its way from four of the Great Lakes—Superior, Michigan, Huron, and Erie—to the fifth, Ontario.

The falls began forming about 12,000 years ago at the end of the Ice Age. As the last glaciers melted away, huge torrents of water channeled along what is now the Niagara River, over the Niagara Escarpment. The water began eating away at the escarpment and the falls slowly moved upstream. Today, the falls cascade seven miles from their original location; carved out along as their path descends is the seven-mile canyon known as Niagara Gorge.

Five miles below the Falls squats massive Robert Moses Niagara Power Plant, providing electricity for much of the Northeast. The world's first commercial-scale, alternating current generator opened here in 1895. The alternating current technology made it practical to transmit power over long distances for the first time.

GETTING AROUND

Orientation

The city of Niagara Falls centers around its compact downtown dominated by the Niagara Falls Convention and Civic Center, 305 4th Street. The falls and their accompanying attractions are located on the western edge of the city in Niagara Reservation State Park. The park's major sights are within easy walking distance of each other; the same holds true downtown.

Across the river from the city of Niagara Falls, New York, is the city of Niagara Falls, Ontario. The two are connected by the Rainbow Bridge, off Robert Moses Parkway.

Tours

Gray Line of Niagara Falls, 716/694-3600, offers daily tours of both sides of Niagara. **Bedore Tours,** 716/285-7550, is a smaller company also offering tours. **Motherland Connextions Inc.,** 716/282-1028, offers African American heritage tours that concentrate on the region's underground railroad history (see the special topic, The Underground Railroad at the Niagara Frontier). **Rainbow Air,** 454 Main St., 716/284-2800, features helicopter tours over the falls.

a breathtaking 30-minute seasonal boat ride up close to one of the wonders of the world

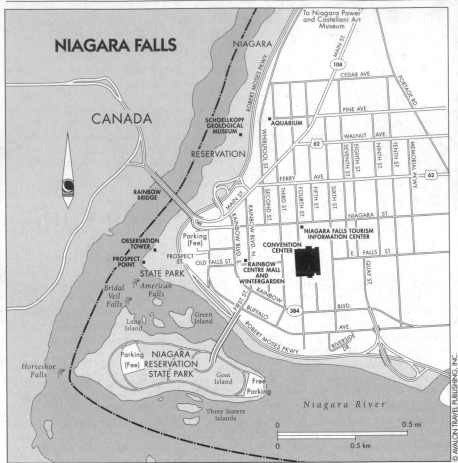

INFORMATION

The **Niagara Falls Official Information Center,** 4th and Niagara Streets, 716/284-2000, is open daily 9 A.M.–5 P.M., with extended hours in summer. The **Niagara Falls Convention & Visitors Bureau,** 310 4th St., Niagara Falls, NY 14303, 716/285-2400 or 800/421-5223, www.nfcvb.com, is open Mon.–Fri. 9 A.M.–5 P.M.

NIAGARA RESERVATION STATE PARK

In the mid-1800s the land surrounding Niagara Falls was privately owned and cluttered with factories and shacks. Visitors wishing to see the waterfalls had to pay owners a fee just to peek through a hole in a fence. Even so, the falls was a notorious tourist trap. Reported one traveler of the day, "I know of no place where one is so constantly pestered, where hackmen so incessantly worry you when you want to be at peace, where you are so dogged over every inch of ground you tread."

Enter artist Frederick Church, landscape architect Frederick Law Olmsted, and the "Free Niagara" movement, established around 1870. For 15 long years, the movement's proponents lobbied heavily to establish a park at the falls. The political opposition was enormous, but finally, in 1885, Gov. David Hill signed an appropriations bill that marked the beginning not only of Niagara Park but also of the entire New York State Park System.

Today, Niagara Reservation State Park is the oldest state park in the country. Designed by Olmsted, it receives about 12 million visitors a year.

There are two main entrances to the park, 716/278-1796, located just off Robert Moses Parkway. One is at Prospect Point, the other at Goat Island. General admission is free, but many of the attractions charge fees. Parking in summer is $5 at the Prospect Point and western Goat Island lots; the eastern Goat Island lot is free year-round.

Prospect Point

The best place to view the falls on the New York side is Prospect Point. The point sits at the edge of the American Falls' 1,000-foot brink, where you can look straight down into the foamy, turbulent waters. Rainbows often form in the cataract's mist.

Behind Prospect Point presides the **Visitor Center,** 716/278-1796, which offers a good introduction to the falls and the park's attractions. The film *Niagara Wonders* is screened here throughout the day, and there's also a snack bar and gift shop. Film tickets cost $2 for adults, $1 for children 6–12.

Departing from behind the center are **Viewmobiles,** which travel throughout the park April–October, weather permitting, stopping at all points of interest. Tickets cost $4.50 for adults, $3.50 for children 6–12, and you can board as often as you like.

Beyond the center stands the **Observation Tower,** featuring dramatic views from glass-enclosed elevators that rise 200 feet. Tickets cost 50 cents.

The tower's elevators also travel down to the foot of the Falls, where the *Maid of the Mist*

boats dock. Visitors here are provided with voluminous yellow slickers before being herded onto sturdy wooden vessels. The boats head straight into the bases of the falls, passing almost close enough to touch. Spray stings, the boats rock, and water thunders all around.

Still the best way to experience the falls, the *Maid of the Mist* has been a tourist attraction since 1846. The boats, 716/284-4233, www.maidofthemist.com, operate May–October. Tickets cost adults $8.50, children 6–12 $4.80, plus 50 cents for the elevator ride.

Goat Island

Upstream from Prospect Point, above the waterfalls, sits quiet Goat Island, a wooded flatland often overlooked by visitors. With the Bridal Veil and American Falls on one side and the Horseshoe Falls on the other, the island provides a very different view of the cataracts.

From Goat Island's western end descends the **Cave of the Winds Trip,** 716/278-1730, another excursion involving voluminous yellow slickers. This time, guides lead groups of visitors along soggy wooden walkways down to the base of Bridal Veil Falls. Tickets cost adults $6, children 6–12 $5.50; trips are offered Memorial Day–Oct., weather permitting.

Goat Island is flanked by several smaller islands, including the **Three Sisters Islands,** surrounded on all sides by swift, whitecapped waters. Step out onto these specks of land, and you'll feel as if you're part of the river itself and about to be swept over the curved edge of the falls.

Schoellkopf Geological Museum

Perched on the edge of Niagara Gorge, at the northern end of the park, is a museum dedicated to the geological history of the falls. As of this writing, the museum is closed for renovation but is scheduled to reopen for the 2003 season with plenty of multimedia shows, along with fossil and mineral exhibits. A footpath leads from the museum down deep into the gorge; explore on your own or take one of the guided walking tours led by the park's naturalists.

The museum, 716/278-1780, can be reached on foot via a path from Prospect Point, or by car via the Robert Moses Parkway. For more information on the tours, call 716/745-7848.

NIAGARA FALLS, ONTARIO, CANADA

Niagara's most spectacular cataract is Horseshoe Falls, best viewed from **Queen Victoria Park,** 905/356-2241, on the Canadian side. Though slightly shorter than American Falls—176 feet as opposed to 184—Horseshoe Falls boasts a much wider brink (2,200 feet) and handles about 90 percent of the river's volume of flow.

Queen Victoria Park can be reached via **Rainbow Bridge,** near Prospect Point. Proof of citizenship such as a passport or voter's registration card is required to cross the border. Once on the other side, a People Mover bus operates between all points of interest.

Considerably more built up than the American side, the Canadian side is also both more stylish and more commercial. Queen Victoria Park is beautifully landscaped, while along nearby Clinton Hill stands one kitsch museum after another: **Tussaud's Wax Works,** 905/374-6601; **Ripley's Believe It or Not,** 905/356-2238; **Guinness Museum of World Records,** 905/356-2299. A good restaurant offering buffet-style dining and superb views revolves atop the **Skylon Tower,** 5200 Robinson Rd., 905/356-2651.

A high point of a visit to the Canadian side is the **Journey Behind the Falls,** 905/354-1551. Out come the big yellow slickers again, followed by a walk *behind* Horseshoe Falls. The walk is open May–Dec., with limited access the rest of the year. Cost is adults $7 Canadian, children 6–12 $3.50 Canadian.

For more information, contact the **Niagara Falls, Canada Visitors and Convention Bureau,** 5433 Victoria Ave., Niagara Falls, Ontario, L2G 3LI, 800/56-FALLS. Hours are Mon.–Fri. 9 A.M.–5 P.M.

DOWNTOWN
Rainbow Centre Mall and Wintergarden
On Rainbow Boulevard opposite Prospect Point

begins the Rainbow Centre Factory Outlet Mall, housing the usual bargain shops. More interesting is the adjoining Wintergarden, a soaring atrium filled with over 7,000 tropical plants, waterfalls, and tables and chairs. The garden, 716/286-4940, is open daily 9 A.M.–9 P.M.

Aquarium of Niagara Falls
Directly across the Robert Moses Parkway from the Schoellkopf Museum in Niagara Park you'll find a first-rate aquarium with over 2,000 marine animals. Atlantic bottlenose dolphins, California sea lions, Peruvian penguins, electric eels, and many varieties of shark—blacktip reef shark, lemon shark, nurse shark, leopard shark—all call the aquarium home. Freshwater fish from the Great Lakes and exotic fish of the coral reefs also fin their way through the waters here. Various animal feedings are scheduled daily, and an observation deck provides good views of the gorge.

The aquarium, 701 Whirlpool St., at Niagara Falls Boulevard, 716/285-3575 or 800/500-4609, www.aquariumofniagara.org, is open daily 9 A.M.–5 P.M., with extended summer hours to 7 P.M. Admission is adults $6.50, children 4–12 $4.50.

Tourist Museums
In back of one of the town's souvenir shops, find the so-called **Daredevil Museum,** 303 Rainbow Blvd., 716/282-4046, actually a small, informal exhibit area. Here you'll learn about 63-year-old Annie Taylor, a schoolteacher who rode over Horseshoe Falls in a wooden barrel in 1901 and lived to tell the tale, and about the aerialists who challenged the Niagara Gorge on tightropes (open daily 9 A.M.–10 P.M., free). **Niagara's Wax Museum of History,** 303 Prospect St., 716/285-1271, tells similar stories through life-size wax figures (open daily 10 A.M.–11 P.M.; adults $5, children $2–3).

Accommodations
The cheapest beds in town are offered by **Hosteling International Niagara Falls,** 1101 Ferry Ave., 716/282-3700. Seven dormitories are equipped with bunk beds; rates are $14/night for members, $17/night for nonmembers.

Within easy walking distance of the falls is

the simple, 18-room **Coachman Motel,** 523 3rd St., 716/285-2295 ($55–109 d July–Aug.; $45–80 d off-season). Two blocks from the falls stands the **Quality Hotel and Suites,** 240 Rainbow Blvd., 716/282-1212, with 217 upscale motel rooms and an indoor pool ($89–169 d).

A good downtown B&B is the Victorian **Rainbow House B&B,** 423 Rainbow Blvd. S, 716/282-1135 or 800/724-3536, offering six guest rooms furnished with antiques ($80–95 d July–Aug.; $60–80 off season).

Housed in what was once the landmark Niagara Hotel is the 194-room **Travelodge,** 201 Rainbow Blvd., 716/285-9321, containing a grand lobby and modernized rooms overlooking the falls ($79–129 d July–Aug.; $59–79 off season). The attractive 400-room **Holiday Inn Select,** 3rd and Old Falls Sts., 716/285-3361, features indoor/outdoor pools and several restaurants ($89–159 d July–Aug.; $59–89 off season).

Food

Directly across from the Rainbow Bridge is the **Misty Dog Grill,** 716/285-0702, where you can order veggie dogs, turkey dogs, Sinatra ("your way") dogs, Russian dogs, German dogs . . . you get the idea; average dog under $3. Wedged between Niagara Park and the Rainbow Centre Mall is a **Hard Rock Cafe,** 333 Prospect Ave., 716/282-0007, offering classic American food and a souvenir shop; average main dish $10.

Overlooking the upper falls perches the Tudor-style **Red Coach Inn,** 2 Buffalo Ave., 716/282-1459, with leaded windows, stone fireplaces, and waiters in Olde English dress. The food ranges from omelettes to steak (average dinner entrée $14). The Old World **Polish Nook,** 2242 Cudaback Ave., 716/282-6712, offers traditional Polish cuisine.

Events and Entertainment

The American, Bridal Veil, and Horseshoe Falls are **illuminated** red, white, blue, green, and yellow for about three hours just after sunset throughout the year. During the summer, **free concerts** and other events are staged at E. Dent Lackey Plaza in the Niagara Falls Convention Center. From late November through early January, the **Festival of** **Lights** transforms the city into a fairy-tale land of colored lights; many special events are staged. For more information on any of these events, contact the Niagara Falls Convention and Visitors Bureau at 716/285-2400.

NORTH OF NIAGARA FALLS
Niagara Power Project Visitors' Center

Heading north of Niagara Falls on Robert Moses Parkway, you'll pass **Whirlpool State Park,** offering great views of a giant, swirling whirlpool, and **Devil's Hole State Park,** situated along the Niagara River's lower rapids. Both parks, 716/278-1770, feature hiking trails.

Directly north of the parks reigns the immense Niagara Power Project, one of the largest hydroelectric plants in the world. During the tourist season, about half of the Niagara River's water power (or 100,000 of 202,000 cubic feet) is diverted away from the falls for the production of electricity here and in Canada; at other times, that ratio rises to 75 percent.

The plant's newly renovated visitor center does a good job explaining the principles of hydroelectric power through hands-on exhibits and computer games. Also on display: exhibits on Niagara Falls, past and present, and films on energy-related subjects. Ascend to the observation deck for outstanding views of the Niagara Gorge.

The visitor center, 5777 Lewiston Rd., 716/285-3211, is open daily 9 A.M.–5 P.M. Admission is free.

Castellani Art Museum

Off Lewiston Road directly across from the Devil's Hole State Park runs University Drive, which leads to Niagara University and the Castellani Art Museum. Dedicated in 1990, the airy edifice houses over 3,000 artworks varying from the Hudson River School to contemporary sculpture.

The museum's first-rate Folk Arts Program sponsors continual exhibits, publications, artist demonstrations, and performances. Past exhibits have focused on such subjects as Polish-American Easter traditions, African American gospel traditions, and Halloween.

The museum, Senior Drive, off University

WESTERN NEW YORK

Drive, Niagara University, 716/286-8200, is open Wed.–Sat. 11 A.M.–5 P.M., Sunday 1–5 P.M. Admission is free.

Lewiston

Continue north of the power project about four miles to Lewiston, a historic 19th-century village. Among the many National Historic Landmarks here is a McDonald's restaurant, proudly ensconced in the 1824 Frontier House, 460 Center Street. One of the region's oldest and best

bakeries is **DiCamillo's,** 535 Center St., 716/754-2218, established in 1920. For more information on the historic area, stop into the **Historic Lewiston On the Water,** 850 Center St., 716/754-9500.

At the southern edge of town reposes the 200-acre **Artpark,** the only state park in the United States devoted to the visual and performing arts. During the summer, all sorts of events are staged, including storytelling, acrobatics, and theater and dance workshops. Other park features in-

THE UNDERGROUND RAILROAD
AT THE NIAGARA FRONTIER

Throughout the early to mid-1800s, the Niagara frontier served as the last stop on the Underground Railroad for slaves funneled north through New York City and Philadelphia. Though few records were kept, it is estimated that as many as 30,000 people may have passed through here on their way to Canada.

Seven "Stations," or sculptures, honoring those who helped the escaping slaves are displayed throughout the region. Conceived by artist Houston Conwill in 1988, the project was largely sponsored by the Castellani Art Museum in Niagara Falls.

Each of Conwill's sculptures is a tall, thin, bronze-and-copper "house" standing about six feet tall. At the top is an "attic" embossed with maps of the Underground Railroad and African symbols. At the base is a "cellar" with a door opening into a hiding place. On the door are notes taken from the cryptic correspondence once passed between stationmasters.

Information about the Stations of the Underground Railroad is available at the Castellani Art Museum, Niagara University, NY 14109; 716/286-8200. The Buffalo Niagara Convention and Visitors Bureau, 716/852-0511 or 888/228-3369, also publishes a free driving tour guide to underground railroad sites throughout the region. Four especially interesting sites are:

1) The **St. John's A.M.E. Church,** 917 Garden Ave., Niagara Falls. St. John's was one of the first African American churches founded in Niagara County. From its hillside site, the

fugitive slaves could see the beckoning lights of Canada and freedom.

2) The **Parliament Oak School,** 325 King St., Niagara-on-the-Lake, Canada. It was in this unassuming building that Canada's Act of 1793 was signed, guaranteeing freedom to slaves and their descendants. A quote from Harriet Tubman reads: "When I found I had crossed, there was such a glory over everything. I felt as if I was in Heaven. I am free and they shall be free. I shall bring them here."

3) The **First Presbyterian Church,** 505 Cayuga St., Lewiston. Abolitionist Josiah Tryon attended this white stucco church, built in the 1820s, and is buried in the graveyard next door. As the story goes, Josiah's wealthy brother Thomas Tryon had built a mansion along the Niagara River gorge north of Lewiston. The house was so isolated, however, that Thomas's wife refused to move into it, and Thomas allowed Josiah to hide fugitive slaves in his cellar.

4) The **Thomas Root Home,** 3106 Upper Mountain Rd., Pekin. Located midway between Niagara Falls and Lockport, the former Root home contains a trapdoor leading to a 5-by-10-foot cellar. Here "volumes bound in black," as the coded messages once read, spent the night before being driven to the border, hidden beneath piles of vegetables. The house is now privately owned, but the Station is set amidst a small row of pine trees accessible to the public.

clude hiking trails; good fishing spots; a 2,300-seat **Artpark Theater,** bringing in national acts; and a burial mound dating back over 2,000 years, to when the area was inhabited by the Hopewell Indians. Thirty feet long by 20 feet wide, the mound is listed on the National Register of Historic Places.

The park, 150 S. 4th St., 716/754-9000 or 800/659-7275, www.artpark.net, is open daily 8 A.M.–dusk. Parking in summer is $5. Some events are free; others require that you purchase a $5 daily activities ticket.

Youngstown

Even if you have no interest in military history, it's worth continuing a few miles north of Lewiston to Youngstown and **Old Fort Niagara.** Strategically located at the mouth of the Niagara River, where it controlled access to the Great Lakes, the fort is a strikingly handsome place with commanding views of Lake Ontario.

Fort Niagara was originally established by the French in 1726 and was occupied by American soldiers as late as the early 1900s. Its oldest standing structure is the 1726 French Castle, a rectangular stone edifice equipped with a bakery, guardhouse, living quarters, chapel, and trade room. Nearby plunges a well purportedly haunted by a headless ghost searching for its missing body part.

During the summer, the fort stages frequent daily events such as military musters and fife-and-drum drills. Surrounding the fort is **Fort Niagara State Park,** offering easy hiking trails and a swimming pool.

The fort, 716/745-7611, off Robert Moses Pkwy., is open daily 9 A.M.–4:30 P.M., with extended hours to dusk in summer. Admission is adults $7, children 6–12 $4.

Along Lake Ontario

East of Youngstown, the county spreads out past orchards and farmland, small harbors and good fishing spots. **Route 18** hugs the shoreline as it passes through the townships of Wilson, Newfane, and Somerset, all filled with unusual cobblestone homes. To visit the Cobblestone Museum in Childs, continue on Route 18 to Ontario County and head south on Route 98.

Route 104 east of Lewiston offers an equally scenic route, and an even greater allotment of cobblestone homes, and fruit farms.

Camping and Accommodations

Four miles east of Youngstown you'll find the 266-site **Four Mile Creek State Campground,** Lake Rd., off Route 18. For reservations, call 800/456-CAMP; basic rates are $13–17.

Near the entrance to Artpark stands the **Portage House,** 280 Portage Rd., Lewiston, 716/754-8295, offering 21 standard motel rooms ($68 d). The **Sunset House B&B,** 4228 Lower River Rd., 716/754-8598, features three guest rooms and a veranda overlooking the Niagara River ($90–95 d). The **Cameo Inn,** 4710 Lower River Rd., 716/745-3034, www.cameoinn.com, is a Queen Anne mansion containing three guest rooms and a riverside suite ($60–130 d).

Food

Six miles north of the Falls find **John's Flaming Hearth,** 1965 Military Rd., 716/297-1414, a local institution famed for its charcoal-broiled steak; average entrée $18.

In Lewiston is the **Apple Granny,** 433 Center St., 716/754-2028, a good spot for lunch, dinner, or a late-night snack (average main dish $8). The more upscale **Clarkson House,** 810 Center St., 716/754-4544, housed in an 1818 landmark, offers lobster, steak, and open-hearth cooking (average main dish $15).

EAST OF NIAGARA FALLS

Lockport

Head 25 minutes east of Niagara Falls via Route 31/270 to the Erie Canal town of Lockport, hometown of volleyball. As the story goes, the townspeople used a basketball for the game at first, but broken fingers soon led to the development of a lighter ball. Also said to be a Lockport invention is the fire hydrant—developed by a man whose factory later burned to the ground.

Two-hour cruises of the Erie Canal, highlighted by a trip through Locks 34 and 35, are offered by **Lockport Locks & Erie Canal Tours,**

716/693-3260. The canal boats dock at 210 Market St., off Main Street. Tickets are adults $12.50, children 5–12 $8.

Nearby, the **Lockport Canal Museum,** 80 Richmond Ave., at Locks 34 and 35, 716/635-6250, documents the area's canal history, with photos from 1812 to the present. The museum is open May–Oct., daily 9 A.M.–5 P.M.

Lockport Cave and Underground Boat Ride, 21 Main St., 716/438-0174, takes visitors through five flights of locks, industrial ruins, and a 2,430-foot-long tunnel that was blasted out of solid rock in the late 1850s. Tours offered daily May–Sept., 10 A.M.–8 P.M. Cost is adults $7.75, children $5.25.

Camping and Accommodations

Several small campgrounds and a long, long line of motels extend to the immediate east of downtown Niagara Falls along Niagara Falls Boulevard. Among the campgrounds are the 80-site **Niagara Falls Campground,** 2405 Niagara Falls Blvd., 716/731-3434, where a basic site costs $25. Among the motels is a 70-room **Quality Inn,** 7708 Niagara Falls Blvd., 716/283-0621 ($79–139 d July–Aug.; $50–75 off season).

Orleans County

East of Niagara County lies Orleans County, one of the flattest and quietest areas in the state. Agriculture is the number one industry here, and enormous truck farms raising fruits and vegetables spread out all along the highways and byways. Route 104, which cuts through the center of the county, is peppered with **pick-your-own farms.**

Albion, the county capital, and Medina, the main commercial center, are small historic villages along the Erie Canal. To the north lie Lake Ontario and Point Breeze, a harbor known for its world-class salmon fishing. Orleans County is also the best place in the state to learn about cobblestone architecture, a building style that is all but unique to New York.

Visitor Information

The **Orleans County Tourism Office,** 14016 Rte. 31 W, Albion, NY 14411, 585/589-3230 or 800/724-0314, www.orleansny.com, is open Mon.–Fri. 9 A.M.–5 P.M. The county runs a **fishing hotline** at 585/589-3220.

MEDINA

The main attraction in Medina is its wide, old-fashioned Main Street, flanked by mid–19th-century buildings. Many were built of a local red sandstone and still house thriving small businesses such as bakeries, variety stores, and clothing shops.

Along East Central Street just east of Main reigns **St. John's Episcopal Church,** once listed in Ripley's *Believe It or Not* as "the church in the middle of the street." At the north end of Main find the Erie Canal, and a boat basin in which the canal boats once turned around.

Nearby is the **Miss Apple Grove Inn,** W. Central St., 585/798-2323, serving everything from pasta to lobster; entrées are $8–15. Medina hosts the mellifluous **New York State Duck Calling Championship and Wildlife Festival,** 585/798-4287, every September. The event attracts hunters from all over the region.

ALBION

Farther east along the Erie Canal lies quiet Albion, centered around a 34-building **Historic Courthouse District,** Rte. 98 off Rte. 31. The handsome 1858 **Orleans County Courthouse,** Greek Revival in style, sports a silver dome visible for miles around and an old-fashioned courtroom crowded with polished wooden pews.

Another interesting stop is the elongated 1904 **Pullman Memorial Universalist Church,** E. Park St. and Rte. 98. The old English Gothic edifice was built by the manufacturer of railroad sleeping cars, George M. Pullman, who grew up in Albion before moving to Chicago and becoming a millionaire.

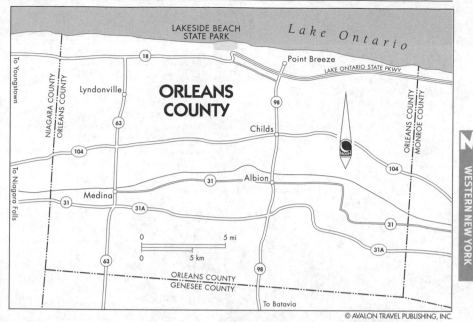

© AVALON TRAVEL PUBLISHING, INC.

CHILDS

Cobblestone Museum

The Cobblestone Museum is housed in the basement of one of the oldest (1834) and best preserved of New York's 25 cobblestone churches. Simple exhibits explain the masonry's history and technique, while upstairs is an intimate sanctuary lined with wood. Next door stand two more cobblestone buildings—an 1849 schoolhouse and an 1840 house filled with Victorian-era furnishings. Also on-site are reconstructed blacksmith and print shops.

The museum, 14393 Rte. 104, at Route 98, 585/589-9013, is open late June–Labor Day, Tues.–Sat. 11 A.M.–5 P.M., Sunday 1–5 P.M.; weekends in the fall. Admission is adults $3, children 6–12 $2.

Food

Across from the museum is one of the county's best restaurants, **Tillman's Village Inn,** Rts. 98 and 104, 585/589-9151. A former stagecoach stop, built in 1824, the inn serves various sand-

wiches and salads for lunch, and meat and fish entrées for dinner; average entrée $14.

Between Albion and Childs find the casual **Carlton Grill Station,** 1750 Oak Orchard Rd. (Rte. 98), Carlton Station, 585/682-4842, known for its tasty country-style cooking and fish fries; average main dish $8.

Continue about five miles north of Childs to reach **Brown's Berry Patch,** 14264 Rte. 18, just west of the intersection, 585/682-5569. A barn-size country store run by the same family since 1804, Brown's sells everything from raspberries and green beans to sandwiches and ice cream; out back you can pick your own berries and other fruits in season from the family farm. Open April–Nov. 1, daily 8 A.M.–8 P.M.

POINT BREEZE

On the shores of Lake Ontario, directly north of Childs, lies Point Breeze harbor centered around a busy marina. The **County Marine Park,** Rte. 98, is a good spot to launch a boat or have a picnic.

WESTERN NEW YORK

COBBLESTONE HOUSES

All across Western New York stand handsome houses built of smooth rounded stones small enough to hold in one hand. An ancient form of construction that dates back to Roman times, cobblestone masonry can be found in parts of England, Italy, and France. Of the approximately 1,000 cobblestone houses in North America, however, 800 are in Western and Central New York.

Cobblestone masonry in New York began after the construction of the Erie Canal. Masons from Ireland and England who had worked on the canal settled in the area, where they found abundant building materials on hand.

There are two kinds of cobblestone houses: those made of rough icelaid cobbles, and those made of polished waterlaid cobbles. The ice-laid variety can be found in the drumlin areas between Rochester and Syracuse. The water-laid variety—built of stones tumbled in the waters of Lake Ontario—are located west of Rochester.

Most of the cobblestone houses were built in a Greek Revival style between 1825 and 1860. Some featured meticulous patterns, such as herringbone or striped designs. Each mason had his own secret techniques and formula for mortar. By the late 1860s, however, cobblestone houses had become too expensive for the industrial age and the art died out.

A good concentration of cobblestone houses stands along Route 104 (Ridge Road) in Orleans and Monroe Counties. The Cobblestone Society, established to help preserve the houses, maintains a small Cobblestone Museum in Childs.

© CHRISTIANE BIRD

1834 cobblestone house

For easy hiking and biking, head a few miles west of Point Breeze to **Lakeside Beach State Park,** Lake Ontario State Pkwy., 585/682-5246. Campers can reserve a spot in the park's 274-site campground by calling 800/456-CAMP.

Genesee County

More flat, prosperous farmland fills the 500 square miles of Genesee County, located just south of Orleans County, midway between Buffalo and Rochester. According to the 1990 census, Genesee produces over $80 million of agricultural products each year. Dairy farming is the main occupation, with truck farming following close behind. Encircling the village of Elba stretches a rich, black muckland that yields the nation's second largest onion crop.

Genesee County's only city is Batavia, established in 1801 at the crossing of two Native American trails. To the county's northwest lies the Iroquois National Wildlife Center; to the southwest, Darien Lake, the state's largest "entertainment complex." Le Roy, a small town east of Batavia, is where Jell-O was invented.

Visitor Information

The **Genesee County Chamber of Commerce,** 210 E. Main St., Batavia, NY 14020, 585/343-7440 or 800/622-2686, www.geneseeny.com, is open year-round Mon.–Fri. 8:30 A.M.–5 P.M. In summer, the chamber operates a visitor information booth outside the Holland Land Office Museum, 131 W. Main St.; hours are daily 10 A.M.–7 P.M.

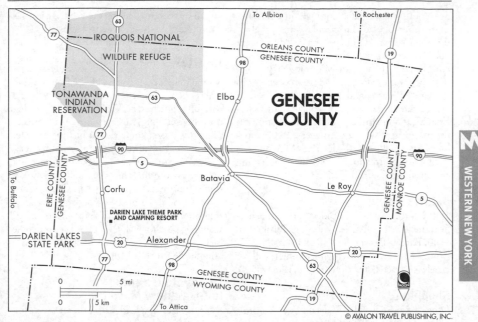

© AVALON TRAVEL PUBLISHING, INC.

BATAVIA

Once a lively industrial and trading center, Batavia received a near-fatal blow in the 1960s thanks to urban renewal. Dozens of downtown brick storefronts were razed and replaced by a soulless mall. The townspeople still haven't forgiven those involved, and the mall remains a target of great local resentment.

Batavia does have a few historic buildings left, most notably the striking Holland Land Office Museum and Richmond Memorial Library on Main Street, and the gracious homes along Ellicott Avenue.

The author John Gardner grew up in Batavia, and set his novel *Sunlight Dialogues* here. Those familiar with the city can recognize many of the streets and people he describes in the book.

Holland Land Office Museum

In the early 1800s, Western New York was divided into several enormous land tracts by investors eager to sell parcels to pioneers. The largest of these companies—surveying 3.3 million acres—was the Holland Land Company, composed of bankers from Amsterdam, Holland.

The business of selling the company's land was conducted in Batavia. Surveyor Joseph Ellicott built the company's first log-cabin office here in 1801 and a permanent stone office in 1815. Land sold for about $2 an acre.

Today, the Holland Land Company is a National Historic Landmark exhibiting prehistoric mastodon bones, Native American and pioneer artifacts, and early surgical instruments, among other things.

The museum, 131 W. Main St., 585/343-4727, www.hollandoffice.com, is open Mon.–Sat. 10 A.M.–4 P.M. Admission is free.

Old Batavia Cemetery

Along Harvester Avenue, off Main Street, lies the Old Batavia Cemetery, final resting place of Joseph Ellicott and other early pioneers. Of particular interest is the **Morgan Monument,** erected in 1880 by the National Christian Association Opposed to All Secret Societies.

The monument honors William Morgan, who

mysteriously disappeared one night in 1826 after threatening to reveal the secret laws and rituals of the Free Masons. His disappearance led to a great public outcry against secret societies and to the establishment of the Anti-Masonic Party. Anti-Masonry was the first third-party movement in the United States, and although short-lived, it helped launch the careers of William Lloyd Garrison and William Seward. The inscription on the monument—built with over 2,000 contributions from 26 states—describes Morgan as "a martyr to the freedom of writing, publishing and speaking the truth. . . ."

Batavia Downs

North of the city find the oldest parimutuel harness track in the United States. Established in 1940, Batavia Downs, 8315 Park Rd., 585/343-3750, offers evening racing in summer; call for details. To reach the track from I-90, take Exit 48.

Shopping

Oliver's Candies, 211 W. Main St., 585/343-5888, has been selling rich homemade chocolates and nut crunches since 1932.

Camping, Accommodations, and Food

Just outside town find the 175-site **Lei-Ti Campground,** 9979 Francis Rd., 585/343-8600, situated on a five-acre lake; a basic site costs $19. Not far away is the 175-room **Days Inn,** 200 Oak St., 585/343-1440, equipped with an outdoor pool ($79–89 d). The 76-room **Best Western,** 8204 Park Rd., 585/343-1000 or 800/631-0182, features a heated swimming pool and live entertainment ($69–114 d).

Miss Batavia, 566 E. Main St., 585/343-9786, a classic old-time diner, serves copious homemade fare; average main dish $8. **Sport of Kings,** 419 W. Main St., 585/343-1274, specializes in open-face souvlaki; average main dish $8. A popular racetrack hangout not far from the track is **Alex's Place,** 8322 Park Rd., 585/344-2999, serving steak, ribs, and shrimp; average entrée $14.

Events

The **Genesee County Fair,** 585/343-7440, takes place in mid-July. Nearby Elba honors the main-

stay of its economy during the **Elba Onion Festival,** 585/343-7440, in early August.

LE ROY

Several miles east of Batavia lies Le Roy, a surprisingly elegant, if somewhat run-down, town of fine old stone churches and Victorian homes. Through the center of things runs tree-lined Main Street.

Le Roy is best known as the birthplace of Jell-O, invented by a local carpenter named Pearl Bixby Wait in 1897. Wait lacked the means to market his product, however, and in 1899, he sold the formula to businessman Orota Woodward for $450. By 1906, Woodward had a $7 million enterprise on his hands; Wait was still working as a carpenter. Jell-O was later purchased by General Mills, but the plant continued operating in Le Roy until 1964.

Le Roy House and Jell-O Gallery Museum

Built in 1817 as a land office, the massive stone Le Roy House now serves as a local history museum featuring several period rooms, an exhibit on area pottery, and a gallery filled with memorabilia commemorating the wiggly dessert. On display are old packages, cookbooks, and advertisements dating back to the early 1900s. "Jell-O The Dainty Dessert" reads one ad from 1907; "When I'm eating Jell-O I wish I were a whale" reads another from 1952.

The museum also contains exhibits on Ingham University, an early school for women, in operation in Le Roy between 1837 and 1892. The university was founded by two sisters, Marietta and Emily Ingham, with money they had inherited from their mother.

The house and museum, 23 E. Main St., 585/768-7433, www.jellomuseum.com, are open May–Oct., Mon.–Fri. 10 A.M.–4 P.M., Sunday 1–4 P.M., or by appointment. Donations welcomed.

Food

The **D&R Depot,** 63 Lake St. (Rte. 19), 585/768-6270, housed in its 1901 namesake, serves all-homemade American fare; average main dish $9. The 1820s **Creekside Inn,** 1 Main St.,

585/768-9771, a Le Roy landmark, overlooks Oatka Creek; on the menu find American and continental dishes; average main dish $14. Along Route 5 between Batavia and Le Roy stands the **Red Osier Landmark,** Stafford, 585/343-6972, a casual but upscale steak and seafood restaurant acclaimed for its prime rib, carved tableside (average main dish $16; dinner only).

IROQUOIS NATIONAL WILDLIFE REFUGE

Once covered by a vast glacial lake, the Iroquois Refuge is now a 10,818-acre preserve of marshland, wooded swamp, wet meadows, pasture, and cropland. Tens of thousands of Canada geese and ducks stop over here during their spring migration, while others nest in the marshes throughout the summer. Muskrat, opossum, beaver, mink, cottontail rabbit, fox, and white-tailed deer also abound.

Near the entrance, a visitor center displays exhibits on local flora and fauna. Three nature trails run through the refuge, and four overlooks provide for wildlife observation.

The refuge, 1101 Casey Rd., off Route 63, Alabama, 585/948-5445, is open daily dawn–dusk. The visitor center is open year-round, Mon.–Fri. 7:30 A.M.–4 P.M., and mid-March–late May (migration season), Sat.–Sun. 9 A.M.–5 P.M. When the visitor center is closed, maps are available by the front door.

DARIEN LAKES

In the county's southwest corner find 1,846-acre **Darien Lakes State Park,** 10289 Harlow Rd., at Sumner Road, 585/547-9242, a quiet, wooded oasis centered around a large, lovely lake. The lake offers good fishing and a swimming beach, while nearby are 19 miles of hiking trails and a 150-site campground; for reservations, call 800/456-CAMP. Sites cost $15–20.

Kitty-corner to the park bustles the much noisier **Six Flags Darien Lake and Camping Resort.** Established in 1964 as a 164-acre campground, the park has since become an enormous entertainment complex. Featured are over 100 rides, shows, and attractions, including one of the world's top-10 wooden roller coasters and the nation's second-largest Ferris wheel. Other attractions include a water park, kids' amusement park, 2,000-site campground, and the Darien Lake Performing Arts Center, presenting nationally known rock and pop stars.

The theme park, Rte. 77 and Sumner Rd., Darien Center, 585/599-4641, is open daily July 1–Labor Day, 10:30 A.M.–10 P.M., and weekends in the spring and fall. All-day admission is adults $31, seniors $19, children under 48 inches $18, children under two free. A basic campsite for four costs $110 and includes park admission. On-site hotel accommodations costs $200/night and includes park admission for four.

WESTERN NEW YORK

Wyoming County

In Wyoming County, the flat farmland of Genesee County turns into a gentle sea of broad, rolling hills. Tucked into almost every valley are trim maroon barns topped with silvery silos, while all around graze cows. Especially **scenic roads,** bordered with patchwork fields, are Routes 78 and 39.

The county's key villages are Warsaw, Perry, Attica, and Arcade, all of which contain a number of striking architectural landmarks; most were built in the late 1800s and early 1900s.

Along the southeastern edge of the county

lies the famed **Letchworth Gorge,** also known as the Grand Canyon of the East (see The Little Finger Lakes and Beyond section in the Finger Lakes chapter). The park can be accessed from the villages of Castile and Portageville.

Visitor Information

The **Wyoming County Tourist Promotion Agency,** 30 N. Main St., Castile, NY 14427, 585/493-3190 or 800/839-3919, www.wyoming countyny.com, is open Mon.–Fri. 9 A.M.–5 P.M.

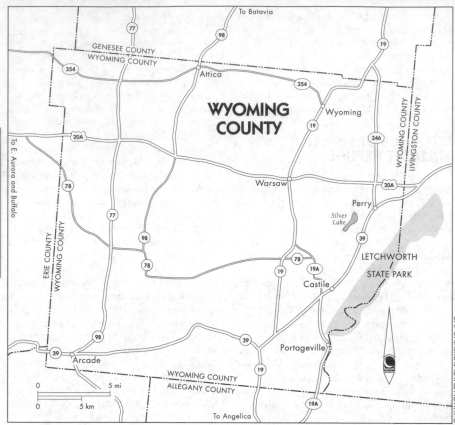

WYOMING VILLAGE

Wyoming village may be small, but it boasts over 70 buildings listed on the National Register of Historic Places. Equally unusual is the fact that its downtown is still lit with original gas streetlights.

Though first established in 1802, Wyoming didn't flourish until 1817, when Silas Newell founded Middlebury Academy here. The first institution of higher learning west of the Genesee River, the academy was a near overnight success, with as many as 200 students attending at one time. Most were the sons of wealthy Rochester and Buffalo businesspeople.

In the late 1800s, the village's cultural status was further enhanced by the presence of Mrs. Lydia Avery Coonley Ward. A devotee of the arts, Ward summered at Hillside, the family mansion on the edge of town, and brought many artists, intellectuals, and other leaders to visit. Among them were Susan B. Anthony, John Muir, and the Roosevelts.

Wyoming centers around a tidy **village green.** To one side presides the Greek Revival **Middlebury Academy,** 22 S. Academy St., 585/495-6582, now housing a small local history museum (open June–Sept., Tuesday 10 A.M.–4 P.M., Sunday 2–5 P.M.). Down the street stands a stately Edwardian **village hall,** donated to the town by Mrs. Ward.

On Route 19, three miles south of Wyoming, sprawls **The New Farm,** 585/237-2652, an indoor/outdoor farmers' market that operates

Apr.–Dec., Sat.–Sun. 8 A.M.–5 P.M. Local vendors sell everything from fresh produce to handmade quilts.

Accommodations

Mrs. Lydia Ward's old family mansion is now the wonderful **Hillside Inn,** 890 E. Bethany Rd., between Routes 19 and 20, 585/495-6800, an elegant yet homey Classic Revival mansion. Set amidst 48 acres of woodland, the inn offers 12 very spacious guest rooms ($80–175 d), an enormous front porch, fireplaces, whirlpools, and a restaurant serving innovative American fare (average dinner entrée $14).

WARSAW

Just south of Wyoming lies the stately town of Warsaw, the county seat. Set in the deep narrow valley of Oatka Creek, Warsaw owes much of its fine architecture to the salt boom of 1878–94. During those years, Warsaw was the nation's largest producer of table salt.

Striking architectural landmarks stand along West Buffalo, Liberty, Court, Park, and Main Streets. Buildings especially worth viewing include the large Queen Anne **Humphrey Mansion,** 230 W. Buffalo St., built in 1884 by one of the city's first bankers; and the simple white **Trinity Episcopal Church,** on West Buffalo Street in downtown, designed by architect Richard Upjohn in 1853.

Camping and Food

A good place for families is the 85-site **Dream Lake Campground,** 4391 Old Buffalo Rd., 585/786-5172, which offers swimming, boating, and miniature golf. A basic site costs $15–25.

In a rural setting south of the village is the **Old Heidelberg,** 3755 S. Main St. (Rte. 19), Warsaw, 585/786-5427, a first-rate German restaurant featuring such specialties as *sauerbraten* and *weisswurst;* average entrée $14.

PERRY

Situated in hilly terrain to the east of Warsaw is Perry. Once known for its textile mills, which attracted many Polish immigrants to the area, Perry still supports a small textile industry.

Perry sits on the edge of **Silver Lake,** regarded by some as the westernmost of the Finger Lakes. Along its shoreline twist narrow back roads lined with gingerbread cottages in varying states of repair.

In 1855–56, Silver Lake was allegedly inhabited by an eerie green-and-yellow sea serpent, in reality a mechanical creature built by local hotelier A. B. Walker to attract more tourists to the area. The hoax was successful at first, and the tourists poured in. Then in 1857, Walker's hotel burnt to the ground, and the remains of the beast were found in the ruins.

Food

The family-owned **Hole in the Wall,** 11 N. Main St., 585/237-3003, has been serving free meals to anyone in uniform since WW II. On the menu is everything from burgers to tenderloins—"quality food at Working Man's prices." **The Lumberyard,** 18 S. Federal St., off Route 39, 585/237-3160, is an upscale Perry landmark filled with antiques; on the menu is traditional American fare; average entrée $14.

CASTILE

Founded in 1808 at the confluence of the Genesee River and Wolf Creek, Castile was once home to a Dr. Cordelia Greene. One of the country's first women doctors, Greene opened a sanitarium for women here in the 1860s. The sanitarium was based on holistic healing methods, and among its many adherents was Susan B. Anthony.

The rambling sanitarium still stands on South Main Street across from the Cordelia Greene Library, 11 S. Main Street. The **Castile Historical Society Museum,** 17 E. Park Rd., 585/493-5370 or 585/493-2894, houses a small but interesting exhibit on the good doctor. Hours are Tuesday 9 A.M.–noon and 1–3 P.M. Admission is free.

ATTICA

West of Wyoming lies Attica, best known today as the home of the Attica Correctional Facility. Built in 1931 along Route 98 on the outskirts of town, the prison is surrounded by high massive walls, visible for miles.

Once a flourishing mill and railroad center, Attica is filled with mid-Victorian architecture, especially of the Second Empire style. Good examples stand downtown along Main and Market Streets. The **Attica Historical Museum,** 130 Main St., 585/591-2161, contains Victorian fashions and furnishings, and railroad memorabilia. Hours are Wednesday and Saturday 1–4 P.M. Admission is free.

Every August, the **Attica Rodeo,** 585/493-3190, comes to town. Rodeo circuit cowboys rate it one of the top rodeos in the east.

ARCADE

Tucked into the far southwestern corner of the county sits Arcade. Surrounded by fertile dairy country, Arcade was a major shipping center for cheese and other agricultural goods throughout the late 1800s and early 1900s. Rambling Victorian homes still stand along West Main Street.

Today, Arcade's main attraction is the orange-and-black **Arcade & Attica Steam Railroad,** whose vintage cars date back to 1915. Ninety-minute rides take passengers into the rural countryside, past fields and grazing cows, to the Curriers Station Stop. Entertainers keep things lively en route, while at Curriers is a small railroad museum.

The train leaves from the **Arcade & Attica Railroad Station,** 278 Main St., 585/492-3100, a turn-of-the-century depot with a double-pitched hipped roof. Excursions are offered June–Oct., Sat.–Sun.; and July–Aug., Wednesday and Friday. Call for exact schedule. Cost is adults $10, children 3–11 $7.

Allegany County

Allegany County is one of the least-known and most under-appreciated counties in New York State. Bordering Pennsylvania, in the foothills of the Allegheny Mountains, it has a reputation for being hicker than hick. And yet the countryside here is remarkably beautiful. One dark rolling hill leads into another, while up above climb towering cumulus clouds. Storms break out violently and unexpectedly, only to disappear again a half-hour later.

Allegany County is blanketed with 23 state forests, covering some 46,000 acres. It harbors the largest population of white-tailed deer and wild turkey in the state, along with a few black bears and much trout and bass. Hunting and fishing are big business here.

Allegany County has no cities and very little in the way of tourist "attractions." Instead, there are lots of scenic back roads and villages to explore, along with good hiking trails. The county is also known for its antiques. Small shops pepper the back roads, and auctions usually take place several times a week. Watch the *Wellsville Daily Reporter,* the *Olean Times Herald,* and especially the *Pennysaver* for announcements.

Driving through the countryside, you'll spot an occasional wildcat oil drill, its rusted head bobbing up and down. The first oil drill in the nation was set up in Allegany County in 1867, and by the mid 1930s, the county was producing about 5.4 million barrels a year. Today, Allegany's remaining oil field—part of the much greater field that centers in Pennsylvania—is all but impossible to access, but this is a poor county and dreams die hard.

Visitor Information

The **Allegany County Tourism Office,** Room 208, County Office Bldg., 7 Court St., Belmont, NY 14813, 716/268-9229 or 800/836-1869, www.co.allegany.ny.co, is open Mon.–Fri. 8 A.M.–4 P.M.

ANGELICA

At the county's center is the unusual village of Angelica. Founded in 1800 by Philip Church, a nephew of Alexander Hamilton, it's laid out around a large circular park lined with imposing churches and public buildings, most dating

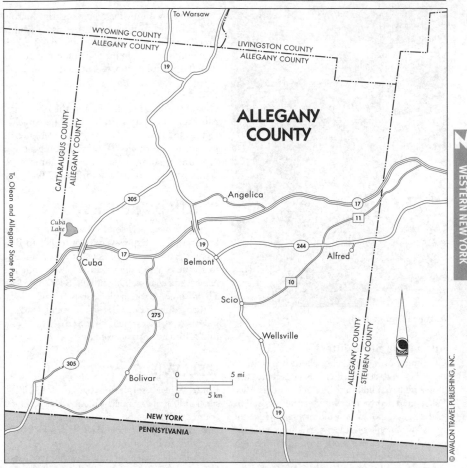

WESTERN NEW YORK

back to the 1800s. Intersecting the circle to either side extends wide, shady Main Street, flanked by roomy Victorian homes in various states of repair.

To one side of the park lies a small clay court where the ancient game of roque takes place on summer nights. Played on a hard surface and similar to croquet, roque originated in France centuries ago. At one time, it was popular throughout this part of the state, but today roque is only played in Angelica and in one other town in the United States—in Texas. Games in Angelica usually begin at dusk, and many of the players are old men, who take the game *very* seriously. Local legend even has it that once a player had a heart attack on the court, only to be pushed out of the way by his obsessed colleagues, who insisted that the game go on until the ambulance arrived.

Back in the 1800s, Angelica was a bustling railroad village and the county seat. Both enterprises moved out around the turn of the century, leaving Angelica to become a sleepy grande dame with a population under 1,000.

Along Main Street stand a half-dozen or so **antique stores.**

Open only during the maple sugaring season, mid-February to mid-April, the casual **Maple Tree Inn,** County Rd. 15A, 845/567-8181, is renowned throughout the region for its pancakes with fresh maple syrup, served all day long.

Events

One of the oldest county fairs in the state is the **Allegheny County Fair,** held on the Angelica Fairgrounds in late July. Angelica celebrates its past during **Heritage Days,** in mid-August. For more information on either event, contact the country tourism office at 845/268-9229.

SOUTH ON ROUTE 19

Route 19 meanders south of Angelica past the Southern Tier Expressway (Route 17) to Belmont, the county seat. Although there's not much to see here, you might want to check out the **Americana Manse,** 39 South St., 845/268-5130, a handsome Victorian house museum with local history exhibits; open by appointment.

South of Belmont is tiny **Scio,** where you might find an antique store or two.

Angelica Grange Hall

Allen Lake State Forest

Continue north of Angelica about five miles to reach the 2,420-acre Allen Lake State Forest, sitting atop a high, flat hill. In the forest's center is Allen Lake, encircled by four intersecting roads. The lake is a good spot for a picnic, or you can hike the roads, which offer great views. Hiking around the entire lake takes about about two and a half hours.

To reach the forest from Angelica, take Peavy Road north off County Road 16. Proceed about five miles to Vincent Hill Road and turn left, into the forest. Vincent Hill Road turns into Muckle Road, which leads to Allen Lake and a parking lot.

Accommodations and Food

The **Angelica Inn B&B,** 64 W. Main St., 585/466-3295, painted in pale greens and purples, offers seven attractive guest rooms and suites ($75–100 d). The **America House & Hotel,** 126 Main St., 845/466-7784, serves a good lunch throughout the week and dinner on the weekends (average dinner entrée $13).

WELLSVILLE

Route 19 heads south from Scio to Wellsville, a small industrial town that was once the hub of the county's oil industry. A large refinery operated here until 1957, but nowadays all that's left are a few wildcat drill sites.

Wellsville centers around an expansive Main Street frozen in the 1950s. Just down from an old art deco movie theater presides the family-run **Wellsville Texas Hot,** 132 N. Main St., 585/593-1400, a 1921 eatery marked with a green-striped awning and neon sign. Inside echoes a high-ceilinged hall lined with cozy booths that still have call-buttons for summoning the waitstaff. Specialties include meat loaf, chili, and, of course, Texas hots (hot dogs)—"famous for many, many miles."

Over the bridge on the south side of town lies a fine residential district built during the town's oil boom. Among the district's many mansions stands the resplendent **Pink House,**

W. 8th and Brooklyn Sts., whose owners once re-painted it every year with a secret-formula hue imported from Italy.

Events
The **Great Wellsville Balloon Rally,** 585/593-5080, featuring 50 hot-air balloons, takes place in mid-July.

ALFRED
Near the eastern edge of the county lies Alfred, a small village tucked into dark, wooded hills. Many of the buildings here are painted a sur-prising bright white, with orange terra cotta roofs reminiscent of the Mediterranean. The roofs are due to the rich clay soils surrounding the village, and to the presence of Alfred University since 1900, known for its College of Ceramics. The college has educated over one-third of all the ce-ramic engineers in the United States, along with an infinite number of fine artists.

Alfred University sits on a wooded hillside at the edge of the village, along Route 244. Of spe-cial interest to visitors are its International Mu-seum of Ceramic Art and Stull Observatory. The village itself is a small cluster of shops and busi-nesses, most oriented to the university's needs. The area immediately surrounding Alfred is known as Alfred Station.

Schein-Joseph International Museum of Ceramic Art at Alfred University
Currently housed in an arts center on campus, this small museum exhibits ceramics from the university's collection of over 8,000 pieces. Many of the pieces were produced in the Alfred area, but other national and international styles are also well represented.

The museum's current exhibit space only cov-ers 3,000 square feet, but plans are in the works to expand into a new $1-million, 20,000-square-foot facility. Ground for the new museum was broken in summer 2002.

The museum, Binns-Merrill Bldg., Alfred University Campus, 607/871-2421, www.ce-ramicsmuseum.alfred.edu, is open Tues.–Sun. 10 A.M.–5 P.M. Admission is free.

Stull Observatory
Billed as one of the finest teaching observatories in the Northeast, Stull is open to the public by appointment. The observatory boasts five major telescopes, the largest of which is a 32-inch New-tonian reflector. For more information, call 607/871-2208 during daytime hours.

Phillips Creek State Forest
Four miles west of Alfred along Route 244 ex-tends the rugged, 2,708-acre Phillips Creek State Forest, laced with trails that are especially popu-lar among cross-country skiers. The trailheads are located off a well-marked parking lot on Route 244.

A good choice for hikers is the Blue Trail, which makes an 8.6-mile loop through some of the thickest parts of the forest. The varied terrain includes gullies, creeks, and steep hills with ex-cellent views. The hike takes about four hours.

Accommodations and Food
Mostly catering to students and their parents is the aptly-named **College Inn,** Rte. 244, Alfred Station, 607/587-8107, which offers 30 upscale motel rooms ($55 d). The **Collegiate,** 7 N. Main St., 607/587-9293, is a village institution, serving breakfast all day, along with lunch and dinner.

Shopping
The **Canacadea Country Store,** 599 Rte. 244, Alfred Station, 607/587-8634, housed in an 1860s building with a tile roof, sells old-time toys, old-fashioned candy, baskets, and terra cotta and porcelain pottery. Along Route 244 are a number of small shops and studios selling the works of area potters.

CUBA
Near the western edge of the county lies Cuba, a low-key local resort that, thanks to Cuba Lake, is especially popular among fisherfolk. Built in 1858 as part of the Genesee Valley Canal Sys-tem, Cuba Lake was known for years as the world's largest manmade body of water.

Cuba centers around historic Genesee, Main, and South Streets. At 53 Genesee St. stands the tourist-oriented **Cuba Cheese Shoppe,** 585/968-3949, selling a large selection of New York–made cheeses, cheesecakes, and gourmet foods.

Along South Street between Grove Street and Stevens Avenue lies a Victorian-era **historic district.** At the south end of South Street, past the railroad tracks, reigns an unusual **Block Barn**—a long, rectangular, silver-gray structure with a multileveled red roof.

Cuba Lake itself is north of the downtown, off Route 305. Adjoining the lake is the Seneca Oil Spring, where the whites first saw petroleum in North America in 1627. The Seneca had already known about the oil for generations, and used to harvest it by spreading blankets on the surface of the water. The blankets absorbed the oil, which the Seneca then wrung out and used for medicinal purposes.

The Seneca Oil Spring, now part of the mile-square Oil Spring Reservation, is still owned by the Seneca Nation.

BOLIVAR

To learn more about the county's early oil history, head south to Bolivar and the **Pioneer Oil Museum of New York,** Main St., 585/268-9293. Inside you'll find historic photos, maps, and documents, along with tools and some pieces of heavy equipment used in the old days. The all-volunteer-run museum is open by appointment. Donations welcomed.

Cattaraugus County

The dark, rolling hills of Allegany County continue on into Cattaraugus County, home to magnificent Allegany State Park. Cattaraugus also has its share of meandering back roads, lost-in-time villages, and good hiking trails, but it is considerably more developed than Allegany County. Two small cities—Olean and Salamanca—and a popular ski resort—Ellicottville—are located here.

Abutting Allegany State Park to the north is the 30,469-acre Allegany Indian Reservation, the largest Native American reservation in the state. On the northern edge of the county, and spilling over into Erie and Chautauqua Counties, is the 21,680-acre Cattaraugus Indian Reservation. Both are home to the Seneca Nation.

In and around the villages of Randolph, Conewango, and Leon, as well as Cherry Creek in Chautauqua County, lives one of the oldest and most established Amish communities upstate; the Amish first arrived in the county from Ohio in 1949.

Visitor Information

The **Cattaraugus County Department of Economic Development, Planning and Tourism,** 303 Court St., Little Valley, NY 14755, 716/938-9111 or 800/331-0543, www.co.cattaraugus.ny.us, is open Mon.–Fri. 8 A.M.–5 P.M.

OLEAN

Alongside the broad main drag of downtown Olean runs an even broader swatch of scruffy railroad yards. The yards date back to the days when Olean was an important junction of the Erie and Pennsylvania Railroads, and a receiving depot for local oil refineries. The word "Olean" even comes from the Latin *oleum,* meaning oil.

Though no longer an oil town, Olean today is the county's largest manufacturing and shopping center. Several antique shops are located on Union Street. History buffs may want to stop into the **Bartlett House and Olean Point Museum,** 302 Laurens St., 716/376-5642 (open Wed.–Sun. 1–5 P.M.).

Along Route 417 a few miles west of downtown is **St. Bonaventure University,** a Franciscan institution chartered in 1875. In the middle of the trim, landscaped campus find the **Friedsam Memorial Library,** 585/375-2323, housing paintings by Rembrandt, Rubens, and Bellini, along with Chinese porcelain, rare books, and contemporary art. The li-

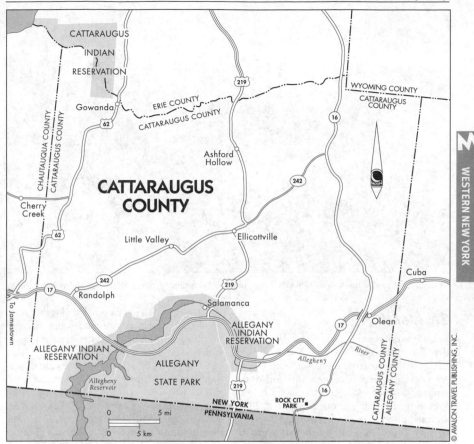

CATTARAUGUS
INDIAN
RESERVATION

219

WYOMING COUNTY
CATTARAUGUS
COUNTY

Gowanda

ERIE COUNTY

CATTARAUGUS COUNTY

62

16

CHAUTAUQUA COUNTY
CATTARAUGUS COUNTY

Ashford
Hollow

MOON

**CATTARAUGUS
COUNTY**

242

Cherry
Creek

62

Little Valley

Ellicottville

Cuba

242

219

17

Randolph

Salamanca

Olean

To Jamestown

ALLEGANY
INDIAN
RESERVATION

17

ALLEGANY INDIAN
RESERVATION

ALLEGANY

Allegheny

River

STATE PARK

Allegheny
Reservoir

219

NEW YORK
PENNSYLVANIA

ROCK CITY
PARK

16

CATTARAUGUS COUNTY
ALLEGANY COUNTY

0   5 mi

0   5 km

© AVALON TRAVEL PUBLISHING, INC.

WESTERN NEW YORK

brary is open Mon.–Fri. 8 A.M.–8 P.M., Saturday 10 A.M.–8 P.M., Sunday noon–8 P.M.

Rock City Park

This enormous outcropping of quartz conglomerate, formed some 320 million years ago, has attracted tourists since 1890. Once the bottom of a prehistoric ocean, it now sits on a hilltop, offering 35-mile views of the Allegheny Mountains.

Through the outcropping run "streets" and "alleys" created by erosion. Water and wind have sculpted many sections into odd shapes—the Tepee Rock, Monkey Face, the Half Sphinx. One area is believed to have been used as a shelter by the Seneca.

Rock City, 716/372-7790, is on Rock City Rd. (Rte. 16), 5.5 miles south of Olean. Hours are May–Oct., daily 9 A.M.–6 P.M. Admission is adults $4.50, children 6–12 $2.50.

Accommodations and Food

The 1889 **Old Library Restaurant and B&B,** 116-120 S. Union St., 716/372-2226, www.oldlibraryrestaurant.com, is a striking National Historic Landmark that houses both a lavish restaurant (average dinner entrée $16) and seven guest rooms across the street ($75–125 d).

Traditional American fare is featured at **Ho-Sta-Geh,** Rock City Rd. (Rte. 16), 716/372-0123, near Rock City; average entrée $12.

© CHRISTIANE BIRD

Rock City, formed some 320 million years ago, offers extraordinary views of the Allegheny Mountains.

SALAMANCA

In the heart of the thin, arc-shaped Allegany Indian Reservation lies Salamanca, the only city in the nation situated on a Native American reservation. The Seneca lease the land to the United States on a long-term basis; the current lease, signed in 1990, is due to expire in 2031, with an option to renew for another 40 years.

A few Seneca-run convenience store/gas stations flank the city's main thoroughfare, Broad Street, along with the fine Seneca-Iroquois National Museum and a high-stakes Seneca Bingo Parlor, 680 Broad St., 716/945-4080 or 877/860-5130. Otherwise, however, Salamanca looks like any other well-worn hinterlands town. South of the city extends the 65,000-acre Allegany State Park, the crowning jewel of southwestern New York.

Seneca-Iroquois National Museum

This thoughtful, well-laid-out museum covers the history of the Seneca Nation from prehistory to the present day. The exhibits cover a wide variety of subjects, from the Seneca's use of medicinal plants to contemporary Native American art. In one section is a life-size bark longhouse; in another, an explanation of the Iroquois clan system; in a third, a small theater where an informative slide show is presented.

Some of the most beautiful items in the museum are the white-and-purple wampum belts that the Iroquois wove to record significant events, laws, and treaties. "Great nations, like great men, should keep their words," reads a quote over the display. One wampum belt records the Treaty of 1794 negotiated between the Iroquois Confederacy and Timothy Pickering on behalf of George Washington. This treaty was broken as recently as 1964, when a section of the Allegany Reservation was confiscated to build the Kinzua Dam and Reservoir. The tribe still retains ownership of the land under the reservoir, but 130 Seneca were relocated against their will.

The museum, 794 Broad St. Extension, 716/945-1738, is open May–Nov., Thurs.–Tues. 9 A.M.–5 P.M., Sunday noon–5 P.M., closed Wednesday; Dec.–April, Mon.–Fri. 9 A.M.–5 P.M.; closed January. Admission is adults $4, seniors and students $3, children 7–13 $2. Near the entrance is a well-stocked gift shop selling handicrafts, postcards, and books.

Salamanca Rail Museum

At the eastern end of town stands a fully restored 1912 passenger depot housing exhibits on the Buffalo, Rochester, and Pittsburgh Railway. The high-ceilinged waiting room is still lined with rich red oak wainscoting, while to one side is a "Ladies Retiring Room" and an old-fashioned ticket office complete with telegraph keys. The exhibits tell the story of how the railroad built the city of Salamanca. One exhibit focuses on the early Seneca railroad workers, another on George Pullman of Pullman car fame.

The museum, 170 Main St., 716/945-3133, is open April–Dec., Mon.–Sat. 10 A.M.–5 P.M., and Sunday noon–5 P.M., but closed Mondays in April and Oct.–Dec.; closed Jan.–March. Admission is free.

ALLEGANY STATE PARK

The largest and wildest state park in New York, the Allegany stretches over mysterious, heavily wooded hills laced with 90 miles of hiking, biking, and horseback-riding trails. In the park's center lie two cobalt-blue lakes offering fishing, boating, and swimming in season. Camping, nature hikes, and kids' programs are featured year-round; bikes and rowboats can be rented.

The park's hiking trails range in difficulty from the easy 2.5-mile Three Sisters Hiking Trail in the Quaker Lake area to the rugged North Country Trail, which covers 18 miles before entering the Allegheny National Forest at the Pennsylvania border. An interesting moderate hike is the four-mile Bear Caves–Mt. Seneca Trail which passes by three small caves.

The park, Exit 17 or 18 off Rte. 17, 716/354-9121, is open daily year-round. Parking in summer is $6. To reserve a cabin or campsite, call 800/456-CAMP. A basic campsite costs $15.

Camping and Accommodations

Overlooking the Allegheny Reservoir about eight miles west of the park is **High Banks Campground,** Rte. 394, Steamburg, 716/354-4855 or 800/445-2267, owned and operated by the Seneca. Cabins and campsites are available and fees go toward tribal social service programs. Basic camping rates are $10–15.

Events

The mid-July **Keeper of the Western Door Pow Wow,** 716/945-2034, features traditional Native American arts, crafts, food, and dance.

Visitor Information

The **Salamanca Area Chamber of Commerce,** 716/945-2034, operates a tourist welcome center at 26 Main Street. Open Mon.–Fri. 9 A.M.–4:30 P.M.

ELLICOTTVILLE

After the quiet backcountry of much of Western New York, Ellicottville comes as a surprise. This is a bona fide resort village that's especially popular during the ski season. Downtown stand historic brick buildings housing upscale shops, restaurants, and bars. At the tree-shaded town square, find an imposing town hall and a turn-of-the-century gazebo.

Holiday Valley Resort

Ellicottville's main drawing card is Holiday Valley, a ski resort equipped with 52 slopes, 12 lifts, a ski school, snow-making capabilities, and on-slope accommodations. The mountain can't really compare with those of the Adirondacks, but it's a mecca for skiers living in the flatlands of Buffalo, Cleveland, and Toronto.

During the summer, Holiday Valley becomes a warm-weather resort. Features include an 18-hole golf course, a golf school, tennis courts, mountain biking, and a three-pool swimming complex.

Holiday Valley, 716/699-2345, www.holidayvalley.com, is off Route 219 a mile or two south of town.

Nannen Arboretum

Adjacent to the Cornell Cooperative Extension on the north side of the village lies the peaceful Nannen Arboretum, planted with over 250 species of rare trees and shrubs. The plants are arranged in small landscaped gardens such as the Japanese Stone Garden, the Cox Perennial Garden, and

WESTERN NEW YORK

the Lowe Herb Garden. To one side is a shallow reflective pool, spanned by a a Japanese-style bridge.

The arboretum, 28 Parkside Dr., off Rte. 219, 716/699-2377, www.cce.cornell.edu, is open dawn to dusk year-round. Admission is free.

McCarty Hill State Forest

West of the village reigns lovely McCarty Hill State Forest, filled with hardwoods, evergreens, and rugged hilltops with such odd names as Fish Hill, Poverty Hill, and Murder Hill. The summit of McCarty Hill itself offers good views of the surrounding rolling countryside and the ski slopes of Hidden Valley.

To reach the forest and a trail that leads to the summit, take Route 242 west to a dirt road named Whig Street. Turn left into the forest and continue to Hunger Hollow Road. Proceed about a mile to the intersection of Rock City Road, where you will see the white blazes of the Finger Lakes Trail. The trail leads to an old fire tower atop McCarty Hill before traveling farther east; to hike to the summit and back takes about two hours.

Accommodations

The handsome brick **New Ellicottville Inn,** 4-10 Washington St., 716/699-2373, www.ellicottvilleinn.com, contains 22 nicely appointed guest rooms furnished with rustic antiques ($99–159 d in summer, $125–155 d in winter). Downstairs is a popular restaurant serving traditional American fare (average entrée $16) and a lively bar/lounge.

The **Ilex Inn B&B,** 6416 E. Washington St., 716/699-2002, www.ilexinn.com, a renovated Victorian farmhouse, offers five modernized guest rooms, along with a cottage and suites, and a heated swimming pool ($75–155 d in summer; $125–225 d in winter).

Food

The casual **Balloons,** 30 Monroe St., 716/699-4162, features Tex-Mex food and country-and-western line dancing on the weekends; average main dish $9. The historic **Gin Mill,** 24 Washington St., 716/699-2530, housed in its namesake, serves especially good luncheon fare; average lunch entrée $8.

Also housed in its namesake is **The Barn,** 7 Monroe St., 716/699-4600, where traditional American favorites are featured; average entrée $15. **Dina's,** 15 Washington St., 315/699-5330, nicely laid out in an 1840 building, serves an eclectic mix of American, Italian, and Mexican fare; average entrée $14.

Events

During the summer, the Buffalo Philharmonic performs at Holiday Valley, and **free concerts** are presented at the village gazebo. The village's top chefs strut their stuff during the **Taste of Ellicottville,** 716/699-5046, in mid-August.

Visitor Information

The **Ellicottville Chamber of Commerce,** 9 W. Washington St., 716/699-5046, www.ellicotvilleny.com, is open Mon.–Fri. 8:30 A.M.–5 P.M., Saturday 10 A.M.–2 P.M.

ASHFORD HOLLOW

Head 10 miles north of Ellicottville to reach the magical **Griffis Sculpture Park,** perched on a hilltop with sweeping views of the valley below. Created by Buffalo artist Larry Griffis, the upper park is filled with whimsical 20-foot-high humanoid sculptures built of iron and steel. Some have middles as round and hollow as donuts, others are all lean, angular lines.

Surrounding the creatures is a pale green meadow, busy with rabbits and butterflies, while just below lies a still pond encircled with smaller sculptures of birds and wildlife. Roads and paths lead down through the woods to larger ponds and a second, less-interesting sculpture area showcasing the works of about 20 other artists.

The park, off Route 219, 716/267-2808 or 716/257-9344, is open May–Oct., 9 A.M.–dusk. Admission is adults $5, seniors and students $3, under 12 free.

RANDOLPH AND AMISH FARM COUNTRY

Named after a village in Vermont, bustling Randolph sits on an ancient city of the Mound

Builders, a prehistoric people who lived in upstate New York before the Iroquois. The town's main streets are flanked with handsome historic buildings.

From Randolph, Route 241 heads north into Conawango Valley and Amish farm country. Trim white homes complete with birdhouses, small gardens, and laundry lines abut the roads, while all around are rolling fields planted with corn and wheat. Black buggies sit in driveways, children dressed in somber blues and blacks play in a schoolyard, bonneted women in long dresses hang the morning wash out to dry.

Many of the Amish sell quilts, baskets, handmade furniture, birdhouses, baked goods, and maple syrup out of their front doors. Hand-printed signs advertising these wares are sometimes posted out front, while maps indicating the informal shops—which change frequently—are printed up each year. The maps are available or through the Cattaraugus County Department of Tourism. Shops can usually be found on Route 241 between Randolph and Conewango; on Pope Hill Road and North East Road off Route 241; along Route 62 between Conewango and Leon; along County Road 6 between Leon and Cherry Creek, and on West Road off County Road 6.

The occasional prosperous-looking Amish farm aside, this is poor country out here. Many family farms have been abandoned in recent years, and the villages are sad affairs, with shuttered shops and homes in disrepair.

Camping and Food
JJ's Pope Haven Campground, Rte. 241 and Pope Rd., Randolph, 716/358-4900, surrounded by Amish farmland, offers a playground, stocked pond, and swimming beach. A basic site costs $17.

For a casual breakfast, lunch, or dinner, stop into the **R&M Restaurant,** 265 Main St., Randolph, 716/358-5141. The restaurant is open 24 hours a day.

GOWANDA

Tucked away into the northern hills of the county find historic Gowanda, holding Victorian homes that date back to the days when the village was a stop along the **New York & Lake Erie Railroad.** The railroad still operates as a tourist attraction and features some of the steepest grades east of the Mississippi.

The railroad, 50 Commercial St., 716/532-5716, did not operate in the 2002 season, but may start up again in 2003; call for more information.

Accommodations
The **Tee Pee,** 14396 Four Mile Level Rd., 716/532-2168, is a four-guest room B&B on the Cattaraugus Indian reservation. The hosts offer tours of the reservation and of Amish country ($50 d).

Events
Featured at the mid-September **Fall Festival,** a major event held on the **Cattaraugus Indian Reservation,** Rte. 438, 716/938-9111, are traditional Iroquois arts, crafts, foods, and dancing. A **powwow** is also held in mid summer.

Chautauqua County

Chautauqua County has been a popular regional resort since the late 1800s, and it shows. Considerably more built up than most of Western New York, Chautauqua is a mix of old-fashioned resort villages, commercialized touristic attractions, homespun agricultural communities, and still-scenic back roads.

Chautauqua County centers on Chautauqua Lake, a 22-mile-long glacier lake 1,400 feet above sea level. Around the turn of the century, the lake was encircled with enormous hotels, while on its waters chugged a busy steamboat trade. Most famous of all the lake's attractions was and is the Chautauqua Institution, a National Historic Landmark that has been offering "learning vacations" since 1874.

The word Chautauqua is said to be Iroquois for "two moccasins fastened together," an apt description of the long, thin lake, indented in the middle. The Iroquois and later the French

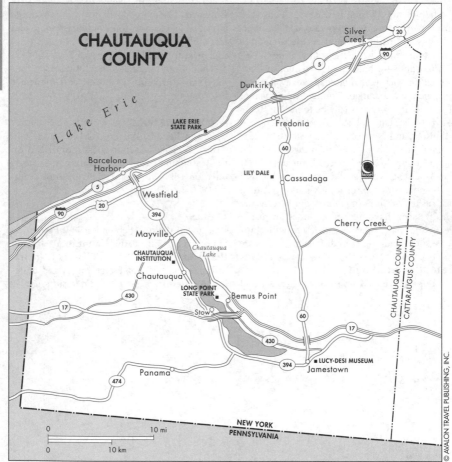

portaged their canoes between Chautauqua Lake and Lake Erie, located eight miles to the north. The old portage trail is now known as Portage Road, or Route 394.

Running along the shore of Lake Erie is the so-called **Grape Belt,** a five-mile-wide swatch of clay soil that's particularly well suited for growing grapes. In 1896, a Dr. Thomas Branwell Welch invented a way to preserve unfermented grape juice here, and Chautauqua proclaimed itself the "Grape Juice Capital" of the world. Welch's was headquartered in Westfield for years, and wineries prosper along the back roads.

Visitor Information

The **Chautauqua County Visitors Bureau,** Chautauqua Institution, Main Gate, off Rte. 394, Chautauqua, NY 14722, 716/357-4569 or 800/242-4569, www.tourchautauqua.com, is open daily. Summer hours are 9 A.M.–5 P.M.; call for winter hours.

JAMESTOWN

At the southeastern end of Chautauqua Lake lies Jamestown, a hilly city of red-brick industrial buildings, lavish Victorian homes, neat working-class neighborhoods, and a steadily declining number of abandoned storefronts. Once a leading furniture manufacturing center, Jamestown fell on hard times in the late 1900s, but is now in the midst of a comeback, thanks largely to several high-tech medical companies that have recently relocated here.

Founded by James Prendergast in 1811, Jamestown's earliest settlers included a number of skilled woodworkers who made furniture for the pioneers in the area. In the 1850s, Swedish cabinetmakers, attracted by the fledgling industry, began to arrive, and by the late 1800s, Jamestown was predominantly Swedish. The Swedes were joined by the Italians in the 1890s, and today, most of the city is still of Swedish or Italian descent.

Two famous Jamestown natives are naturalist Roger Tory Peterson and comedienne Lucille Ball. The band 10,000 Maniacs also hails from Jamestown.

Fenton History Center

Perched on a hilltop overlooking the compact downtown is an Italianate mansion built by Reuben Eaton Fenton, governor of New York from 1865 to 1869. Now home to the Fenton Historical Society, the house contains an interesting series of exhibits on Jamestown, Chautauqua Lake, and Lucille Ball.

The daughter of an electrical telephone lineman and a concert pianist, Lucille Ball was born in Jamestown in 1911. Her family encouraged her theatrical interests and at age 15, she took a bus to New York City and landed a job in the chorus of the Broadway musical *Stepping Stones.* She was fired shortly thereafter, perhaps because of her age, and during the next seven years suffered one disappointment after another. Her first big break didn't come until 1940, when she met Desi Arnaz during the filming of *Too Many Girls.*

Near the Ball exhibit are period rooms furnished as they would have been in Fenton's time, and rooms devoted to Jamestown's Swedish and Italian communities. The exhibits on Chautauqua Lake showcase photographs from the resort's Victorian heyday, as well as artifacts relating to ice harvesting and shipbuilding—two formerly prosperous industries along the lake.

The museum, 67 Washington St., 716/664-6256, www.fentonhistorycenter.org, is open Mon.–Sat. 10 A.M.–4 P.M. Admission is adults $3.50, children $2.50, free under 5. Pick up free self-guided walking tours of the city's historic districts in the gift shop.

Lucy-Desi Museum

More exhibits on the town's favorite daughter are housed in this museum, dedicated solely to Lucy and her husband. One panel features taped interviews with two of Lucy's childhood friends; another, an actor reading from Desi's autobiography. Excerpts from radio shows that Lucy and Desi were involved in are also featured, and a two-hour video of their TV shows runs continuously throughout the day. In addition, tapes of every single *I Love Lucy* episode are available for the watching, along with CD-ROMs of Lucy's scrapbook. About 2,000 items from Miss Ball's estate are showcased in all,

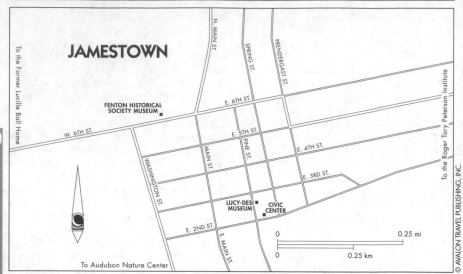

including costumes, gowns, photographs, letters, scripts, and awards.

The museum, 212 Pine St., 716/484-0800, www.lucy-desi.com, is open May–Oct., Mon.–Sat. 10 A.M.–5:30 P.M., Sunday 1–5 P.M.; Nov.–Apr., weekends only. Admission is adults $5, seniors and children $3.50, families $15. While in the museum, be sure to pick up a list of Lucy landmarks around town.

Lucille Ball Landmarks

Another small exhibit devoted to Lucille Ball is housed in the **Reg Lenna Civic Center Theater,** 116 E. 3rd St., 716/664-2465 or 716/484-7070 (box office), which contains a stunning blue-and-white domed ceiling, flanked by the muses. Lucy frequented the theater throughout her youth, often in the company of her grandfather, who was the first to urge her to perform. On display in the lobby are the comedienne's old dancing boots, top hat, favorite hair products (she was not a real redhead), and the like. The theater, which is housed in the same building as the Lucy-Desi Museum, is only open during performances, or by appointment.

Around the corner from the theater stands the **Lucille Ball Little Theatre,** 18 E. 2nd St.,

716/483-1095, where Lucy made her show business debut; and **Jones Bakery,** 209 Pine St., 716/484-1988, where she purchased her favorite Swedish rye. Even after finding fame and fortune, Ball continued to have the bread shipped to her in Hollywood, and it's still for sale in the family-run shop.

Ball's childhood home is in the suburbs at 59 W. 8th St., off Dunham Avenue, Celeron. The small, neat, private home is now painted a pale green with white trim. "Lucy Lane" reads the street sign on the corner.

For a much longer list of Lucy landmarks, make a stop at the Lucy-Desi Museum.

Roger Tory Peterson Institute

Off a cobblestone street at the edge of the city presides the Roger Tory Peterson Institute, a striking modern building built of fieldstone and wood. Though primarily a national center for the nature education of children, the institute also houses an art gallery, library, and gift shop. The gallery showcases paintings and artwork by Peterson and other naturalists.

The institute, 311 Curtis St., near Jamestown Community College, 716/665-2473, www.rtpi .org, is open Tues.–Sat. 10 A.M.–4 P.M. and Sunday 1–5 P.M. Admission is adults $3, seniors $2, students $1.

Jamestown Audubon Nature Center

In a valley formed by retreating glaciers lies a 600-acre wildlife sanctuary criss-crossed with five miles of trails. The trails lead past hardwood and coniferous forests, marshes, swamps, and ponds that are favorite stops for migrating birds. An especially large variety of plants grow in the sanctuary; over 400 species have been catalogued.

At the entrance to the park stands the Roger Tory Peterson Nature Building, where you can pick up self-guiding nature-trail booklets. Also in the center are exhibits by Roger Tory Peterson, a children's discovery center with hands-on displays, and 200 mounted birds, some of which are now extinct.

The nature building, 1600 Riverside Rd., 716/569-2345, is open Mon.–Sat. 10 A.M.–4:30 P.M., and Sunday 1–4:30 P.M.; the sanctuary is open daily dawn to dusk. To reach the nature center from Jamestown, take Route 60 south to Route 62 south. Proceed three miles to Riverside Road and turn left.

Accommodations and Food

At **Kaldi's Coffee House,** 106 E. Third St., 716/484-8904, you can order a Mrs. Grundy sandwich, named after Lucy and Ethel's road trip companion. Afterwards, stop at **Tastee Corners,** Southside Plaza on Foote Ave., 716/488-2669, all done up in neon lights, for a "bon-bon" sundae.

A more substantial meal can be had at the hearty **Ironstone,** 516 W. 4th St., 716/487-1516, serving traditional steak and seafood; average entrée $14. Romantic **MacDuff's,** 317 Pine St., 716/664-9414, is an upscale spot housed in an 1873 townhouse; average entrée $16.

In the heart of the city, find a 149-room **Holiday Inn,** 150 W. 4th St., 716/664-3400 ($89–99 d). On the outskirts is a 101-room **Comfort Inn,** 2800 N. Main St., 716/664-5920 ($69–109 d).

Events

Lucy-Desi Days, 716/484-0800, featuring young comics, a film fest, and other special events, takes place over Memorial Day weekend. Then, during the first week of August, there's **Lucy's Birthday Celebration.**

AROUND CHAUTAUQUA LAKE

From Jamestown, Route 430 heads north along the eastern shore of Chautauqua Lake, through one resort community after another. At the northern tip of the lake lies Mayville, the county seat, and Route 394, which circles back south along the lake's western shore. The Southern Tier Expressway (Route 17) crosses Chautauqua Lake just south of Bemus Point and Stow.

Bemus Point

Strung along the very edge of the waterfront is tiny Bemus Point, an old-fashioned resort village sprinkled with gift shops and restaurants. Through the heart of things runs Lakeshore Drive, lined with piers and boats on one side, cottages and vacationers lolling about on lounge chairs on the other.

Lakeshore Drive ends at the **Casino,** a recently remodeled building where special events are sometimes held during the summer. Out front docks the small, flat **Bemus Point–Stow Ferry,** which crosses Chautauqua Lake whenever there's a passenger. The ride takes about five minutes each way, and puts you in the middle of crisscrossing boats, some of which pass almost close enough to touch.

The best thing about Bemus Point is the creaky old **Hotel Lenhart,** 20-22 Lakeside Dr., 716/386-2715, a big, mustard-colored building with a long, long line of rockers out front. Though somewhat worn around the edges, the 1881 hostelry is a classic, owned by the same family for three generations.

Long Point State Park

Off Route 430 just north of Bemus Point, this busy state park and beach, 716/386-2722, is open Memorial Day–Labor Day, 9 A.M.–5 P.M. Lifeguards are on duty beginning in late June; parking is $5.

Midway Park

Immediately north of Long Point begins Midway Park, 716/386-3165, a family amusement park equipped with go-karts, bumper boats, miniature golf, an antique carousel, a roller rink, and an arcade. Along the shore are a swimming beach and paddleboat area. Hours are Memorial Day–Labor Day, Tues.–Sun. 1 P.M.–sunset. Admission, parking, and swimming are free; rides and attractions are individually priced.

Mayville

Historic Mayville is a pretty place, centered on the 1880s **Chautauqua County Courthouse** on Main Street. Docked not far away, on the pier in Lakeside Park, is the popular *Chautauqua Belle,* 716/753-2403, offering one-hour cruises of the lake June–August. The boat is a replica of a 19th-century paddlewheel steamship.

Chautauqua Institution

South of Mayville reigns the famed 856-acre Chautauqua Institution, a self-contained Victorian village-cum-learning camp for families and adults. Most vacationers live on the premises for a week or two at a time and take courses—often taught by renowned scholars—in everything from philosophy to film. Day visitors are welcome to tour the grounds, use the beaches, and attend many of the lectures, concerts, and other events.

Chautauqua is a peculiarly American institution, founded as a vacation school for Sunday school teachers in 1872. The idea of self-improvement in a pastoral setting caught on immediately, and soon mini- and traveling chautauquas advertising "pure, wholesome entertainment," found audiences all over the country. The Chautauqua movement, as it became known, pioneered many developments in adult education, including correspondence courses and the "great books" curricula.

These roots remain evident in Chautauqua today. The institution is a truly magnificent place, filled with palatial Victorian buildings and four

> *One of Chautauqua's highlights is the very fine 1881 Athenaeum Hotel. The hotel was wired for electricity by Thomas Alva Edison, and his table still stands by the one of the dining room windows. A shy man, Edison often escaped out the window to avoid admirers.*

wide white-sand beaches, but it retains a prim and proper Sunday school feel. Alcohol is not served in any of the institution's restaurants, and few four-letter words are heard.

One of Chautauqua's highlights is the very fine 1881 **Athenaeum Hotel,** once the largest wooden frame building in the country, and still open for overnight guests. The hotel was wired for electricity by Thomas Alva Edison, and his table still stands by the one of the dining room windows. A shy man, Edison often escaped out the window to avoid admirers.

Chautauqua, off Rte. 394, 716/357-6200 or 800/836-ARTS, www.chautauqua-inst.org, offers a variety of accommodations and vacation packages; call for a brochure. Day passes are $11, except on Sunday when entrance is free, and evening passes are $25. Tours are offered daily at 2 P.M. and 4 P.M. Chautauqua is open late June–August.

Panama Rocks Scenic Park

Detour eight miles southwest of Chautauqua Lake to reach the well-kept Panama Rocks Scenic Park. The park is similar to Rock City in Cattaraugus County, but is set in a forest rather than on a hilltop. Spread out over a half mile of quartz conglomerate, the park is laced with deep crevices, dark caves, 60-foot-high cliffs, and hiking trails.

The park, 1 Rock Hill Rd., off Rte. 474, 716/782-2845, www.panamarocks.com, is open May–Oct., daily 10 A.M.–5 P.M. Admission is adults $6, seniors $4, children 6–12 $3. The park is west of the only traffic light in Panama.

Camping and Accommodations

A few miles north of Bemus Point find the 120-site **Wildwood Acres Campground,** Brown Rd., off Rte. 430, 716/386-7037, where a basic site costs $15–20. Between Chautauqua and Stow, the 400-site **Camp Chautauqua,** Rte. 394, 716/789-3435, offers an indoor swimming pool, restaurant, tennis courts, dock sites, petting farm, and campsites priced at $25.

For budget travelers, the **Pine Hill Motel,** 3884 Park Way, at Woodlawn, Ashville, 716/789-3543, offers plain but quite adequate rooms ($50–85 d). **Webb's Year-Round Resort,** Rte. 394 S, Mayville, 716/753-2161, www.webbsworld.com, is a big, modern, family-oriented hostelry with its own marina, bowling alley, and goat-milk fudge factory ($99–139 d).

At the **Hotel Lenhart,** 20-22 Lakeside Dr., 716/386-2715, www.hotellenhart.com, the guest rooms are simply but comfortably furnished. Downstairs find an old-fashioned parlor and dining room serving traditional American fare ($120–160 d, includes breakfast and dinner; $55 d without meals).

Food

Most popular among Bemus Point eateries is the lively **Italian Fisherman,** 61 Lakeside Dr., Bemus Point, 716/386-7000. During the summer, its dining deck built out over the lake is always packed; average entrée $14.

If you'd like to eat at the **Athenaeum Hotel,** 716/357-4444, at the Chautauqua Institution, reservations are a must. The menu is prix-fixe at $32.50, and dinners feature two desserts. Also at the Chautauqua is the casual **Tally-Ho,** 716/357-3325, serving everything from burgers and salads to pasta and charbroiled steaks; main dishes cost $7–17.

ALONG LAKE ERIE

Westfield

Head north of Chautauqua Lake on Route 394 to reach Westfield, a town of solid brick storefronts and **antique shops.** Along Main Street (Route 20) alone are close to a dozen.

Downtown presides the **McClurg Museum,** an 1818 mansion that's now home to the Chautauqua County Historical Society. Inside are restored period rooms, Native American artifacts, early farm implements, and an exhibit on Grace Bedell. Grace was an 11-year-old Westfield girl who wrote to Abraham Lincoln during his 1860 campaign to suggest that he "would look a lot better" if he grew whiskers. Surprisingly, Lincoln followed her advice, and asked to meet her when his train stopped in Westfield the following year. A statue of Bedell and Lincoln stands across from the museum.

The museum, Rte. 394 and Main St., 716/326-2977, is open Tues.–Sat. 1–5 P.M. Admission is adults $1.50, children under 12 50 cents.

Head north on Route 394 to reach the beginning of the **Seaway Trail** (see the special topic, The Seaway Trail, in the Thousand Islands section of the North Country chapter), which starts at the Pennsylvania border, and the **Barcelona Harbor.** Here you'll find a marina and pier, and the 1829 **Barcelona Lighthouse.** Originally powered by natural gas, the graceful stone tower is now privately owned and off-limits to the public.

East to Dunkirk

The busy New York State Thruway (I-90), Route 5, and Route 20 all head east of Westfield to Dunkirk. Running closest to the shore is Route 5, also known as the Seaway Trail, which bypasses **Lake Erie State Park,** 716/792-9214. Situated on a bluff overlooking the lake, the park offers hiking trails, a campground, and a playground. Parking in summer is $6. For campground reservations, call 800/456-CAMP; a basic site costs $13–17.

Dunkirk itself is a low-key industrial city named after Dunkerque, France, whose harbor Dunkirk's own is said to resemble. The main visitor attraction is the **Historic Dunkirk Lighthouse and Veteran's Park Museum,** a well-kept site run almost entirely by volunteers. Guided tours take visitors through the old keeper's quarters, still furnished as they were in the 1940s, and up into the 95-foot-high 1875 tower. Elsewhere on the grounds are a museum dedicated to the armed forces, and dry-docked boats that kids are welcome to explore.

The lighthouse and museum, 1 Lighthouse Point Dr., off Rte. 15, 716/366-5050, www.netsync.net, is open July–Aug., Mon.–Tues. and Thurs.–Sat. 10 A.M.–4 P.M., with the last tour at 2:30 P.M.; April–June and Sept.–Dec., Mon.–Tues. and Thurs.–Sat. 10 A.M.–2 P.M. Admission is adults $5, children under 16 $2.

Fredonia

Just south of Dunkirk lies Fredonia, a pretty, historic town of red-brick buildings and tree-lined streets. The nation's first gas tank was sunk here in 1821, making it possible to light the entire village with gas lamps when the Marquis de Lafayette passed through on his 1825 tour.

Wineries

Many of the area's wineries are located on or just off of Route 20. Among the best known are the **Johnson Estate Winery,** Rte. 20 west of Westfield, 716/326-2191; **Woodbury Winery,** S. Roberts Rd., off Rte. 20 east of Dunkirk, 716/679-WINE; and **Merritt Estate Winery,** 2264 King Rd., off Rte. 20 near Silver Creek, 716/965-4800. All offer tastings and tours, and are open Mon.–Sat. 10 A.M.–5 P.M., Sunday 1–5 P.M.

Camping and Accommodations

When the Lake Erie State Park campground is full, head to the 116-site **Lake Erie–Westfield KOA,** 1 E. Lake Rd., Barcelona Harbor, 716/326-3573. Just south of Fredonia find a 132-room **Days Inn,** 10455 Bennett Rd., 716/673-1351 ($65–85 d).

Westfield's best-known hostelry is the handsome 1821 **William Seward Inn,** S. Portage Rd. (Rte. 394), 716/326-4151 or 800/338-4151, www.williamsewardinn.com. Featured are 12 antique-filled guest rooms of varying sizes, and gourmet breakfasts. Some of the rooms have Jacuzzis, and all have private baths ($70–185 d, with breakfast).

The 1868 Greek Revival **White Inn,** 52 E. Main St., Fredonia, 716/672-2103, www.whiteinn .com, is the region's oldest continuously operated hotel. Extensively renovated over the years, the inn offers 12 standard-sized rooms and 11 suites ($69–179 d, with breakfast). Downstairs is a very good restaurant (see below).

Food

A good place for lunch, dinner, or a cool drink on a hot day is the upscale **Dockside Cafe & Bar,** 30 Lake Shore Dr. E, Dunkirk, 716/366-8350, housed in the Ramada Inn, not far from the Dunkirk Lighthouse (average dinner entrée $15; seasonal).

One of the region's best restaurants is housed in the elegant **White Inn** (see Accommodations, above). A charter member of the prestigious Duncan Hines Family of Fine Restaurants, the restaurant specializes in innovative American and continental fare; average entrée $19. The **William Seward Inn** is also known for its gourmet dining; four-course prix-fixe dinners cost $45.

CASSADAGA

One of the more surprising offerings of Chautauqua County is the **Lily Dale Assembly,** a spiritual-development, natural-healing community that attracts mediums from all over the country. Throughout the summer, the assembly offers daily services, lectures, laying-on of hands, and sessions with clairvoyants.

Located on the forested shores of deep blue Lake Cassadaga, Lily Dale unofficially dates back to 1879 with the arrival of the Fox sisters of Rochester. The sisters had been communicating with the spirit world since 1849, when they awoke to sounds of a fight and a heavy body being dragged down the stairs. No humans appeared to be making the noises, and the sisters ascribed them to the spirit of a peddler who had been murdered in the house four years before.

Lily Dale centers around an 1883 auditorium where speakers and clairvoyants lecture and lead services daily. Events take place at the Healing Temple, Forest Temple, and Inspiration Stump, where mediums demonstrate their powers.

Overlooking the lake stands the wonderful **Maplewood Hotel,** a creaky, no-frills Victorian hostelry. Walk onto the wide front porch here and you're apt to hear groups of believers humming or worshipping together. "No readings, healing, circles or seances in this area please," reads a sign in the parlor.

Like Chautauqua, Lily Dale attracts both day and residential visitors. Day visitors are welcome to attend most of the daily lectures and to explore the grounds. Private readings can be arranged on the spot, but it's best to call ahead;

many of the most popular mediums are booked weeks in advance.

Lily Dale, 5 Melrose Park, off Rte. 60, Cassadaga, 716/595-8721 or 716/595-8722, offers a variety of accommodations and packages; rates at the Maplewood Hotel, 716/595-2505, are $42–63 d. Day fees are $7 for a 24-hour pass, $3.50 for an evening pass. Private readings cost $30–50. Lily Dale is open late June–August.

Resources

New York City
Quick-Reference Guide

Accommodations

The following accommodations are covered in the district sections listed.

UNDER $50

The Lower East Side
Bowery's Whitehouse

From Union Square to Gramercy Park
Gershwin (dorm rooms)

Chelsea and the Garment District
Chelsea Star (dorm rooms)

$50–100

Greenwich Village
Larchmont Hotel

From Union Square to Murray Hill
Carlton Arms; Hotel 17; Murray Hill Inn

Chelsea and the Garment District
Chelsea Star

Upper West Side
Malibu Studios; Riverside Tower Hotel

$100–150

Lower Manhattan
Cosmopolitan Hotel

Chinatown and the Lower East Side
Holiday Inn Downtown

SoHo and TriBeCa
Off-SoHo Suites

Greenwich Village
Washington Square Hotel

From Union Square to Murray Hill
Gershwin; Hotel Grand Union; Hotel 31

Chelsea and the Garment District
Chelsea Inn; Chelsea Lodge; Best Western Manhattan; Herald Square; Wolcott; Red Roof Inn

Midtown
Broadway Inn; Comfort Inn Manhattan; Habitat; Mayfair; Pickwick Arms; Park Savoy; Portland Square; Westpark

$150–250

Lower Manhattan
Holiday Inn Wall Street: Manhattan Seaport Suites

SoHo
Howard Johnson Express Inn-SoHo

From Union Square to Murray Hill
Carlton: Gramercy Park Hotel; Park Avenue South

Chelsea and the Garment District
Chelsea Hotel; Chelsea Savoy Hotel; Metro

Midtown
Days Inn Hotel Midtown; Fitzpatrick Manhattan; Edison; Mayfair; Roosevelt Hotel; Paramount

Central Park and the Upper West Side
Country Inn in the City; Excelsior; Hotel Beacon; Mayflower; On the Avenue

Brooklyn
New York Marriott Brooklyn (Downtown)

The Bronx
Le Refuge Inn

$250 and up

Lower Manhattan
Regent Wall Street; Ritz-Carlton New York Battery Park

SoHo
Mercer; SoHo Grand; TriBeCa Grand

From Union Square to Murray Hill
Morgans; Shelburne Murray Hill; W Union Square

Midtown
Algonquin; Drake Swissotel; Four Seasons; Gorham; Hotel Elysee; Mansfield; Plaza; Roger Smith; Royalton; St. Regis; Waldorf-Astoria

The Upper East Side
Barbizon; Carlyle; Franklin; Hotel Wales; Mark; Pierre

HOSTELS AND YMCAs

From Chelsea to the Garment District
Chelsea Center

Midtown
Vanderbilt YWCA

The Upper East Side
De Hirsch Residence at the 92nd Street Y

Central Park and the Upper West Side
Jazz on the Park; Hosteling International New York; West Side YMCA

Harlem and Upper Manhattan
Blue Rabbit International House; International House of New York; New York Uptown International House; Sugar Hill International House

BED-AND-BREAKFASTS

Upper East Side
East 93rd

Harlem
Urban Jem Guesthouse

Brooklyn
Angelique Bed & Breakfast (Carroll Gardens); Awaaba Mansion (Bedford-Stuyvesant); Awesome Bed & Breakfast (downtown); Bed & Breakfast on the Park (Prospect Park); Foy House Bed & Breakfast (Prospect Park)

Staten Island
Stanbrook Manor English Bed & Breakfast

Selected Restaurants

$. Inexpensive. Average meal under $15.
$$. Moderate. $15–30.
$$$. Expensive. $30–50.
$$$$. Very Expensive. Over $50.

AMERICAN

Lower Manhattan
$$ Bridge Cafe; Fraunces Tavern
$$$ Delmonico's

SoHo and TriBeCa
$ Moondance Diner
$$ Jerry's; Spring Street Natural
$$$ Cub Room; TriBeCa Grill; Zoe

The East Village
$ Angelika Kitchen (vegan); Kate's (vegetarian); Life Cafe; 7A
$$ Miracle Grill
$$–$$$ Five Points

Greenwich Village
$ Corner Bistro
$$ Anglers & Writers; Cornelia Street Cafe; Grange Hall
$$$ Gotham Bar and Grill; Old Homestead

From Union Square to Murray Hill
$$ Albuquerque Eats; America; Blue Smoke (barbecue)
$$–$$$ Black Duck
$$$ Gramercy Tavern; Mesa Grill

Chelsea and the Garment District
$-$$ Empire Diner; Chelsea Commons
$$-$$$ Alley's End; Keen's Steakhouse

Midtown
$ Carnegie Deli; Stage Deli
$$ Hourglass Tavern; Joe Allen; Virgil's Real BBQ; West Bank Cafe
$$–$$$ Rock City Cafe; Bryant Park Grill
$$$ Smith & Wollensky; Michael Jordan's—The Steakhouse New York; Sparks Steak House

The Upper East Side
$ Barking Dog Luncheonette
$$ Pig Heaven
$$–$$$ Sarabeth's Kitchen

Central Park and the Upper West Side
$ Barney Greengrass; Good Enough to Eat; Popover Cafe
$$ The Saloon
$$$ Boat House; Tavern on the Green

Brooklyn
$-$$ Junior's; Waterfront Ale House
$$-$$$ The Grocery; Max & Moritz; Rosewater
$$$ Gage & Tollner; Henry's End; Peter Luger's; River Cafe

Queens
$$$ Water's Edge

ASIAN

Chinatown, Little Italy, and the Lower East Side
numerous; see Chinatown Food section

The East Village
$ Mingala Burmese Restaurant
$$ Iso; Shabu Tatsu; Cyclo

SoHo and TriBeCa
$ Thai House Cafe
$$ Clay (Korean)
$$$ Nobu (Japanese)

Greenwich Village
$$ Japonica (sushi); Tangerine (Thai)

From Union Square to Murray Hill
$ Galaxy; Sam's Noodles
$$ Tatany (Japanese)
$$$ TanDa (fusion)

Chelsea and the Garment District
$$ Gam Mee Ok (Korean); Hangawi (Korean)

Midtown
$ Ollie's Noodle Shop
$$ Zen Palate (vegetarian)
$$$ Hatsuhana (Japanese); Shun Lee (Chinese); Sushisay (Japanese)

The Upper East Side
$ Baluchi (Asian/Indian); Sala Thai; Emo's (Korean)

Central Park and the Upper West Side
$ Broadway Cottage; Empire Szechuan Gourmet
$$ Jo-An (Japanese)

Brooklyn
$ Plan Eat Thailand; Red Hot Szechuan
$$ Cambodian

Queens
$-$$ Joe's Shanghai; Penang Cuisine Malaysia; Kum Gang San (Korean)

ECLECTIC/INTERNATIONAL

From Gramercy Park to Union Square
$$$ Union Square Cafe

Midtown
$$$$ Four Seasons

FRENCH/CONTINENTAL

Lower Manhattan
$$-$$$ Les Halles Downtown

Chinatown, Little Italy, and the Lower East Side
$$ Oliva

SoHo and TriBeCa
$$ La Jumelle; Lucky Strike
$$$ Balthazar; Le Pescadou; Odeon; Raoul's
$$$$ Danube; Chanterelle

The East Village
$$ Jules

Greenwich Village
$$ Florent, Pastis
$$$ Cafe Loup

From Union Square to Murray Hill
$$$ Les Halles; Park Bistro; Artisanal

Chelsea and the Garment District
$$$ Gascogne

Midtown
$ La Bonne Soupe
$$-$$$ Cafe Un, Deux, Trois; Chez Josephine
$$$$ La Cote Basque; Lutece

The Upper East Side
$$$ Le Bilboquet; Daniel

Central Park and the Upper West Side
$$$ Cafe des Artistes; Cafe Luxembourg

Brooklyn
$$ Patois; La Brunette
$$-$$$ Loulou

The Bronx
$$$ Le Refuge

INDIAN

The East Village
$$ Haveli; Mitali; various others on 6th Street

From Union Square to Murray Hill
$ Curry in a Hurry; Joy of India
$$ Mavalli Palace; Muriya

Midtown
$$$ Dawat; Nirvana

Queens
$-$$ Jackson Diner; Shaheen Sweets

ITALIAN

Lower Manhattan
$$-$$$ Ecco

Chinatown, Little Italy, and the Lower East Side
$-$$ Benito I; DaNico
$$$ Il Cortile; Taormina

The East Village
$$ Frank; John's; Lanza

Greenwich Village
$ Arturo's; John's
$$-$$$ Cent'Anni
$$$ Il Mulino

Chelsea and the Garment District
$$ Intermezzo
$$$ Da Umberto

Midtown
$-$$ Cucina & Co.
$$ Carmine's
$$$ Barbetta's; Trattoria dell'Arte

The Upper East Side
$-$$ Caffé Buon Gusto; Caffé Grazie
$$$ Paper Moon Milano

Central Park and the Upper West Side
$$ Isola; Meridiana

Harlem and Upper Manhattan
$ Patsy's Pizzeria
$$$ Rao's

Brooklyn
$ Patsy Grimaldi's; Totonno Pizzeria
$$ Gargiulo's
$$-$$$ Cucina; Queen; Al Di Lá

Queens
$ Manetta's
$$ Maducatis

The Bronx
$$ Dominick's; Mario's

LATIN/CARIBBEAN
SoHo and TriBeCa
$ Lupe's Kitchen
$$ Ideya

The East Village
$$ Boca Chica

Greenwich Village
$$ Caribe; Mi Cocina

From Union Square to Murray Hill
$$ Coffee Shop
$$$ Lola; Patria

Chelsea and the Garment District
$ La Chinita Linda; La Taza de Oro
$$ Blue Moon; Negril's; Rocking Horse Mexican
  Cafe; Bachue Cafe

Midtown
$$ Cabana Carioca; Ipanema
$$$ Bistro Latino

The Upper East Side
$$$ Rosa Mexicano

Central Park and the Upper West Side
$ Cafe con Leche; La Caridad (Cuban-Chinese)
$$ Gabriela's (Mexican)
$$$ Calle Ocho (Nuevo Latino)

Harlem and Upper Manhattan
$ Jamaican Hot Pot

Brooklyn
$ Vera Cruz

Queens
$-$$ Nostalgias (Bolivian); La Pequeña Colom-
  bia (Colombian); Tierras Colombianas
  (Colombian)

RUSSIAN
SoHo and TriBeCa
$$$ Pravda

Midtown
$$$-$$$$ Firebird

Brooklyn
$$$$ Primorski; Rasputin (both with enter-
  tainment included)

SEAFOOD
Lower Manhattan
$ Jeremy's Ale House

The East Village
$ Cucina di Pesce
$$-$$$ Pisces

From Union Square to Murray Hill
$$-$$$ Blue Water Grill

Midtown
$$$ Oyster Bar
$$$ Le Bernadin

Central Park and the Upper West Side
$$ Fish Restaurant

Brooklyn
$$ La Bouillabaisse; Lundy Brother's

The Bronx
$-$$ Johnny's Reef
$$ Crab Shanty

SOUTHERN/SOUL/CREOLE

The East Village
$-$$ Acme Bar & Grill; Great Jones Cafe

Greenwich Village
$-$$ Pink Teacup

SoHo
$-$$ Brother's Barbeque

From Union Square to Murray Hill
$-$$ Live Bait

Midtown
$$-$$$ B. Smith's

Central Park and the Upper West Side
$$ Shark Bar

Harlem and Upper Manhattan
$ M&G Diner; Miss Maude's Spoonbread Too;
  Miss Mamie's Spoonbread Too
$$ Sylvia's; Copeland's
$$-$$$ Sugar Hill Bistro

OTHER

The Lower East Side
$-$$ Katz's; Ratner's (both Jewish)
$$ Paladar (Cuban)

SoHo and TriBeCa
$$ Cafe Noir (French-Moroccan)

The East Village
$ Christine's (Polish); Odessa (Ukrainian); Second Ave. Deli; Veselka (Eastern European); Yaffa Cafe (eclectic)

$$ Time Cafe (eclectic); Two Boots (eclectic); Tsampa (Tibetan)
$$-$$$ First (eclectic)

Greenwich Village
$$ El Faro (Spanish); Gus' Place (Greek/Mediterranean)
$$-$$$ Meet (Mediterranean-American)

From Union Square to Murray Hill
$$ Turkish Kitchen

Chelsea and the Garment District
$ Bright Food Shop (Mexican-Asian)
$$$ Periyali (Greek)

Midtown
$-$$ Afghan Kebab House; Uncle Nick's (Greek)
$$ Taprobane (Sri Lankan)

The Upper East Side
$$ Mocca Restaurant (Hungarian); Persepolis (Persian)

Central Park and the Upper West Side
$$ Awash (Ethiopian); Cleopatra's Needle (Middle Eastern); World Cafe (eclectic)

Harlem and Upper Manhattan
$ Obaa Koryoe (West African)

Brooklyn
$ Cambodia Restaurant; Teresa's (Eastern European)
$$ Madiba (South African); Tripoli (Middle Eastern)

Queens
$$ Elias Corner (Greek fishhouse); Telly's Taverna (Greek); Uncle George's (Greek); Hemsin (Turkish); Blooms (Irish); Cafe Bar (Mediterranean)
$$$ Taverna Vraka (Greek)

Museums

New York is a city of museums. From the huge Metropolitan Museum of Art in Manhattan to the tiny Tibetan Museum in Staten Island, a person could spend weeks doing nothing but museum-hopping and still not be able to cover them all.

The city's most important museums are the Metropolitan Museum of Art, the Museum of Modern Art, and the American Museum of Natural History. Following not far behind are the Whitney, the Guggenheim, the Brooklyn Museum of Art, the Studio Museum in Harlem, the Cooper-Hewitt, the National Museum of the American Indian, and the Frick.

ART MUSEUMS

SoHo
Museum for African Art
New Museum of Contemporary Art

From Union Square to Murray Hill
Pierpont Morgan Library

Midtown
American Craft Museum
American Folk Art Museum
Dahesh Museum
International Center for Photography
(Museum of Modern Art: temporarily relocated
  to Queens)

The Upper East Side
Cooper-Hewitt
Frick
Guggenheim
Metropolitan Museum of Art
National Academy of Design
Neue Galerie
Whitney Museum of American Art

Harlem and Upper Manhattan
Cloisters
Studio Museum in Harlem

The Bronx
Bronx Museum of the Arts

Brooklyn
Brooklyn Museum of Art

Queens
American Museum of the Moving Image
Isamu Noguchi Garden Museum
Museum of Modern Art (temporary location)
Queens Museum of Art

CHILDREN'S MUSEUMS

SoHo
Children's Museum of the Arts

Central Park and the Upper West Side
Children's Museum of Manhattan

Brooklyn
Brooklyn Children's Museum

Staten Island
Staten Island Children's Museum

CULTURAL MUSEUMS

Lower Manhattan
National Museum of the American Indian
Museum of Jewish Heritage

Chinatown, Little Italy, and the Lower East Side
Museum of Chinese in the Americas

The East Village
Ukrainian Museum

Chelsea and the Garment District
Yeshiva University Museum (in the Center for
  Jewish History)

The Upper East Side
Asia Society
Jewish Museum
Museo del Barrio
Museum of the City of New York

Harlem and Upper Manhattan
Hispanic Society
International Salsa Museum

Staten Island
Tibetan Museum

HISTORICAL MUSEUMS
Lower Manhattan
Ellis Island Immigration Museum
South Street Seaport Museum
Skyscraper Museum

Chinatown, Little Italy, and the Lower East Side
Lower East Side Tenement Museum

The East Village
Merchant's House Museum

From Union Square to Murray Hill
Theodore Roosevelt's Birthplace

Central Park and the Upper West Side
New-York Historical Society

The Upper East Side
Mount Vernon Hotel Museum

Brooklyn
Brooklyn Historical Society

SCIENCE AND TECHNOLOGY MUSEUMS
Lower Manhattan
New York Unearthed

Midtown
Intrepid Sea-Air-Space Museum
Museum of Television and Radio

Central Park and the Upper West Side
American Museum of Natural History

Queens
New York Hall of Science

OTHER MUSEUMS
Lower Manhattan
New York City Police Museum

SoHo
New York City Fire Museum

Greenwich Village
Forbes Magazine Galleries

Central Park and the Upper West Side
Nicholas Roerich Museum

Harlem and Upper Manhattan
American Numismatic Society

Brooklyn
New York Transit Museum

Staten Island
Staten Island Institute of Arts and Sciences

Manhattan Shopping

DEPARTMENT STORES
Chelsea and the Garment District
Lord & Taylor
Macy's Herald Square

Midtown
Bergdorf Goodman's
Henri Bendel
H&M
Saks Fifth Avenue
Takashimaya

The Upper East Side
Barney's New York
Bloomingdale's

New York City Quick-Reference Guide

ANTIQUES AND FURNISHINGS

SoHo and TriBeCa
Portico Home
Moss
Wyeth
Urban Archaeology
various, esp. Lafayette and Wooster Streets

Greenwich Village
Old Japan, Inc.
Susan Parrish
Uplift Lighting
various, along Broadway

From Union Square to Murray Hill
ABC Carpet and Home

Chelsea and the Garment District
Chelsea Antiques Building
Garage
Markus Antiques

Midtown
Manhattan Arts & Antiques Center

The Upper East Side
Things Japanese (Japanese antiques)
Various other antique shops, especially Madison Avenue above 59th Street, and 60th Street between 2nd and 3rd Avenues

BOOKS, ETC.

The East Village
St. Marks Bookshop

Greenwich Village
Biography Bookshop
East West Books (Eastern/New Age philosophy)
Oscar Wilde Memorial Bookshop (gay books)
Shakespeare & Co.
Three Lives & Co.
Tower Books

Chelsea and the Garment District
Barnes & Noble

Books of Wonder (children's)
Revolution Books (radical)
Skyline Books (used)

From Union Square to Murray Hill
Barnes & Noble
Complete Traveller Bookstore
Forbidden Planet (science fiction)
Strand Book Store (eight miles of used books)

Midtown
Argosy
Barnes & Noble
Gotham Book Mart
Hagstrom Map and Travel Center
Mysterious Book Shop
Rand McNally Map & Travel Store
Rizzoli
Urban Center Books

The Upper East Side
Barnes & Noble
Kitchen Arts & Letters (cookbooks)

Central Park and the Upper West Side
Applause Theatre Books
Barnes & Noble
Gryphon
Murder Ink

Harlem and Upper Manhattan
various, Broadway near Columbia University

CAMERAS AND ELECTRONICS

Lower Manhattan
J&R

From Union Square to Murray Hill
The Wiz (other branches citywide)

CLOTHES

Lower Manhattan
Century 21 (discount; esp. menswear)

The Lower East Side

Forman's (discount women's designers)
various, along Orchard Street

SoHo and TriBeCa

Agnes B.
Alice Underground (vintage)
Amy Chan
Anna Sui
Canal Jean
Marc Jacobs
Betsey Johnson
Phat Farm
Prada
Stella Dallas (1940s-era)
What Comes Around Goes Around (vintage)
various, along Broadway, Spring and Prince
   Streets

The East Village

Love Saves the Day (vintage)
Screaming Mimi's (vintage)
Trash and Vaudeville

Greenwich Village

Andy's Chee-Pees (vintage)
Antique Boutique (vintage)
Cheap Jack's (vintage)
Patricia Field
Star Struck (vintage)
Urban Outfitters
various, Bleecker west of Sixth Ave.
shoe shoes along 8th St.

From Union Square to Murray Hill

Bebe's (women's wear)
Bolton's (discount designer wear)
Daffy's (discount designer wear)
Emporio Armani
various, Fifth Ave. between 14th and 23rd Sts.

Chelsea and the Garment District

J.J. Hat Center
Loehmann's
Reminiscence (vintage)
various, 34th Street between Fifth and Sixth
   Avenues

The Upper East Side

Issey Miyake
Levi Store
Niketown (sneakers)
Polo Ralph Lauren
Second Chance Consignment Shop
Tracey Tooker Hats
Yves St. Laurent
various, along Madison Ave.

Central Park and the Upper West Side

Laura Ashley
Off Broadway (secondhand)
various, along Columbus Ave.

CRAFTS AND GIFTS

Chinatown

Quong Yuen Shing
Pearl River Mart

SoHo and TriBeCa

Pop Shop (Keith Haring pop art)
various, along Broadway and West Broadway

The East Village

Alphabets
Howdy Do
Dinosaur Hill
various, along 9th Street

Chelsea and the Garment District

Abracadabra

Midtown

Coca-Cola Co.
Hammacher-Schlemmer

Harlem and Upper Manhattan

Mart 125

FLEA MARKETS/ OUTDOOR MARKETS

Chelsea and the Garment District
Annex Antique Fair and Flea Market
Chelsea Antiques Building
Garage

Central Park and the Upper West Side
P.S. 44

Harlem and Upper Manhattan
Malcolm Shabazz Harlem Market

HEALTH AND BEAUTY

The East Village
Kiehl's (natural beauty products)

Greenwich Village
Aphrodisia (herbs, oils)
Bigelow Chemists (pharmacy)

From Union Square to Murray Hill
Carapan (New Age spa)
La Casa de Vida Natural (Puerto Rican spa)

Midtown
Caswell-Massey (apothecary)
Elizabeth Arden (salon)
Georgette Klinger (salon)
Osaka Health Center (massage)

RECORD STORES

Lower Manhattan
J&R

The East Village
Fat Beats
Final Vinyl
Footlight Records
Sounds

Greenwich Village
Bleecker Bob's
Revolver Records
Tower Records

Chelsea and the Garment District
Academy Records & CDs
Jazz Record Center

Midtown
Colony Records (also sheet music)
Virgin Megastore

The Upper East Side
HMV
Metropolitan Opera Shop

Central Park and the Upper West Side
Gryphon Records
Tower Records

Harlem and Upper Manhattan
Rainbow Music Shop

TOYS AND GAMES

SoHo and TriBeCa
After the Rain

Greenwich Village
Chess Shop
Classic Toys
Game Show

From Union Square to Murray Hill
The Compleat Strategist

Midtown
F.A.O. Schwarz
Toys "R" Us

The Upper East Side
A Bear's Place
Big City Kite Company
Dollhouse Antics
Game Show

ONE-OF-A-KIND

Art Postcards: Untitled (both SoHo)
Art Supplies: Pearl Paint Co. (Chinatown)
Ballet Supplies: Ballet Company (The Upper West Side)
Botanicas: Botanica Altagracia (The Upper West Side); El Congo, Otto Chicas Rendon, Paco's (all Harlem and Upper Manhattan)
China: Fishs Eddy (From Union Square to Murray Hill)
Condoms: Condomania (Greenwich Village)
Cookware: Chinese American Trading Company (Chinatown), Broadway Panhandler (SoHo and TriBeCa)
Glassware: Lalique (The Upper East Side)
Jewelry: Cartier, Tiffany's (both Midtown)
Military Surplus: Kaufman Surplus (Midtown)
Musical Instruments: Matt Umanov Guitar Store (Greenwich Village); Manny's, Sam Ash, Steinway & Sons (all Midtown)
Posters: Chisholm Larsson Gallery (European travel posters; Chelsea and the Garment District); La Belle Époque (turn-of-the-century French posters; Upper West Side)
Science and Natural History: Evolution (SoHo); Star Magic (Greenwich Village and Upper East Side); Maxilla & Mandible (The Upper West Side)
Sewing Notions: various Garment District retailers
Sporting Goods: Paragon (From Union Square to Murray Hill)
Stationery: Kate's Paperie (SoHo); Jam Paper and Envelope (The East Village)

ETHNIC GOODS

Balinese: Mostly Bali (The East Village)
Chinese: Pearl River Mart (and others; Chinatown)
Guatemalan: Back from Guatemala (The East Village)
Indian: Little India Emporium (From Union Square to Murray Hill)
Italian: Rossi & Co. (and others; Little Italy)
Jewish: various, Essex Street, Rivington Street (The Lower East Side)
Native American: Common Ground (Greenwich Village)
Russian: Russian Arts (Greenwich Village)
Ukrainian: Surma (The East Village)

Suggested Reading

New York City

New York, city of writers, has been the subject of or setting for innumerable essays, biographies, memoirs, histories, guidebooks, poems, and novels. Here are but a few:

SPECIALTY GUIDES AND TRAVEL ESSAYS

Alleman, Richard. *The Movie Lover's Guide to New York.* In which hotel lobby did Douglas Fairbanks first woo Mary Pickford? Where was the movie *Ghostbusters* filmed? Alleman's well-written guide is packed with information on over 240 favorite movie sites.

Biondi, Joann, and James Haskins. *Black New York.* A long-overdue guide that begins with a short introduction to African American history in New York, then runs through various points of interest, including historic buildings, restaurants, music clubs, shops, and churches.

Federal Writers' Project. *The WPA Guide to New York City.* First published in 1939 and since reissued, the classic guidebook remains remarkably on target. It provides long and evocative descriptions of everything from Ebbets Field to the then-new Empire State Building.

Frank, Gerry. *Gerry Frank's Where to Find It, Buy It, Eat It in New York.* A monumental 600-plus-page reference manual on where to find everything from bridal gowns to massage therapists.

Freudenheim, Ellen, with Daniel P. Wiener. *Brooklyn: Where to Go, What to Do, How to Get There.* The first popular guidebook to Brooklyn since 1940 is filled with surprises. The authors explore over a dozen historic neighborhoods; listings and maps included.

Goldberger, Paul. *The City Observed: New York, A Guide to the Architecture of Manhattan.* The classic architectural guide to New York by the architecture critic for the *New York Times.* Provocative, informative, and very well written.

Leapman, Michael. *The Companion Guide to New York.* A first-rate, literate guide by a British writer who enjoys expounding on the New York character. The book concentrates on history and points of interest; practical listings are not provided.

Leeds, Mark. *Ethnic New York: A Complete Guide to the Many Faces and Cultures of New York.* An absorbing and detailed look at the multitude of ethnic neighborhoods—Asian, Italian, Arab, German, and more—that make up the five boroughs. Complete with extensive listings.

Letts, Vanessa. *Cadogan City Guides: New York.* Old Saybrook, CT: The Globe Pequot Press, 1993. A prize-winning British travel writer authors an informative and entertaining guide. Many off-the-beaten-track spots are covered.

Levine, Ed. *New York Eats.* A food shopper's delight, with separate chapters on baked goods, chocolates, cheeses, pasta, fish, meats, and more.

McDarrah, Fred, and Patrick J. McDarrah. *The Greenwich Village Guide.* A father and son teamed up to write this breezy, anecdotal walking guide to their neighborhood. Also included are sections on SoHo, TriBeCa, and the East Village.

Plump, Stephen. *The Streets Where They Lived: A Walking Guide to the Residences of Famous New Yorkers.* A succinct and entertaining guide to the former abodes of such celebrities as John Lennon, Edna St. Vincent Millay, Greta Garbo, James Dean, and Babe Ruth. Complete with short bios and maps.

Schwartzman, Paul, and Rob Polner. *New York Notorious.* Where was mob boss Albert Anastasia assassinated? Where did the Mayflower Madam set up shop? How did Nelson Rockefeller meet his untimely end? Two tabloid reporters tell all.

Simon, Kate. *New York Places and Pleasures.* An idiosyncratic guidebook by the well-known travel writer who grew up in the Bronx in the 1920s and lived much of her life in Manhattan.

Time Out Magazine Limited. *Time Out New York.* Written by the editors of *Time Out,* a London-based listings magazine that now has a New York edition, this hip, pithy guide does an especially good job of covering restaurants, bars, cafes, and music clubs.

Von Pressentin Wright, Carol. *Blue Guide New York.* One of the most in-depth guides around, the *Blue Guide* exhaustively covers all five boroughs, concentrating on history and architecture. Practical information is limited, and the prose is often dense and dull, but herein is buried a treasure trove of oddball facts.

White, Norval, and Elliot Willensky, eds. *AIA Guide to New York City.* The most important and entertaining book on New York architecture, organized as a series of walking tours.

Zagat, Eugene H. Jr., and Nina S. Zagat. *Zagat Survey: New York City Restaurants.* This classic, pocket-size guide bases its pithy entries on the reports of volunteer reviewers covering over 1,300 eateries. Many of the reviews are on target; others waffle to an embarrassing degree, or cater to a dull mainstream.

BIOGRAPHY, HISTORY, AND JOURNALISM

Allen, Irving Lewis. *The City in Slang: New York Life and Popular Speech.* A scholarly yet highly enjoyable look at words and phrases associated with New York. Among them: hot dog, rush hour, gold digger, shyster, smart aleck, pleasure hound, straphanger.

Asbury, Herbert. *The Gangs of New York.* A lively account of the gangsters of New York, from the Revolution to the 1920s.

Botkin, B.A., ed. *New York City Folklore.* Botkin edits an entertaining collection of "Legends, Tall Tales, Anecdotes, Stories, Sagas, Heroes and Characters, Customs, Traditions and Sayings" culled from other sources, including newspapers, guidebooks, biographies, children's songs, and literature.

Broyard, Anatole. *Kafka Was the Rage: A Greenwich Village Memoir.* Funny and perceptive, acerbic and reflective—Broyard reminisces on his youth in Greenwich Village just after WW II. Among his associates were Dwight McDonald, Delmore Schwarz, and Meyer Shapiro.

Burrows, Edwin G., and Mike Wallace. *Gotham: A History of New York City to 1898.* Published on the 100th anniversary of the Manhattan/Brooklyn merger, *Gotham* is a massive (1,000 pages plus) and fascinating work that chronicles everything from New York's Lenape Indian days to Teddy Roosevelt's reign as police chief. Despite its length, the book is an easy read.

Caro, Robert A. *The Power Broker: Robert Moses and the Fall of New York.* Much more than a biography, this Pulitzer Prize–winning tome tells the fascinating and often scandalous story behind the shaping of 20th-century New York. Though over 1,000 pages, the book is a compelling page-turner.

Christman, Henry M., ed. *Walt Whitman's New York: From Manhattan to Montauk.* Reprints of an engaging series of articles by Whitman that first appeared in the *Brooklyn Standard* in 1861. The poet spent the first 42 years of his life in the New York area.

Cohen, Barbara, Stephen Heller, and Seymour Chwast. *New York Observed: Artists and Writers Look at the City, 1650 to the Present.* Packed with excerpts and artwork ranging from Washington Irving to James Baldwin, Cecil Beaton to Diego Rivera, this oversize book offers a fine armchair view of New York.

Cohn, Nik. *The Heart of the World.* The writer who spawned *Saturday Night Fever* takes a wild and exuberant walk down the Great White Way. During his sojourn he meets pickpockets, transvestites, strippers, ex-politicians, and even an ordinary citizen or two.

Cole, William, ed. *Quotable New York.* Everyone from Charles Dickens to Malcolm X sums up the Big Apple in 100 words or less. "If you live in New York, even if you're Catholic, you're Jewish"—Lenny Bruce. "In New York it's not whether you win or lose—it's how you lay the blame"—Fran Lebowitz.

Darton, Eric. *Divided We Stand: A Biography of New York City's World Trade Center.* An insightful look at the architecture, politics, and history of the World Trade Center; written well before the September 11 attacks.

Dwyer, Jim. *Subway Lives.* A *New York Newsday* columnist takes a look at one of the Big Apple's most famous institutions by following the lives of seven typical New Yorkers through one composite day on the subway. Skillfully intertwined in the narrative is subway history, legend, and lore.

Friedman, Josh Alan. *Tales of Times Square.* A startling look at the seamy side of a now all-but-vanished Times Square. Strippers, porn brokers, pimps, hookers, and cops tell their stories; as one reviewer put it, "This book made me want to shower."

Hamill, Pete. *A Drinking Life: A Memoir.* The well-known New York journalist writes about a drinking life that began in immigrant Brooklyn

during WW II—when drinking was essential to being a man—and ended on a New Year's Eve 20 years ago. Along the way unfolds a bittersweet portrayal of a bygone New York.

Jackson, Kenneth T., ed. *The Great Metropolis: Poverty and Progress in New York City.* A lively, fun-to-read introduction to New York City history, compiled of articles first published in *American Heritage* magazine.

Jacobs, Jane. *The Death and Life of Great American Cities.* The classic and enormously influential 1961 study. Jacobs often disagreed with the influential urban planners of her day, and loved many of the things that make New York New York (teeming streets, small blocks, aging buildings).

Johnson, James Weldon. *Black Manhattan.* First published in 1930, this classic work paints one of the earliest portraits of the lives of African Americans in New York City. Much more than a history, the book also illuminates the Harlem Renaissance, of which Johnson was a part.

Johnson, Joyce. *Minor Characters.* A tender, lyrical account of Greenwich Village and the Beat Generation, written by an on-and-off lover of Jack Kerouac.

Kazin, Alfred. *A Walker in the City.* The perambulatory memoir of a distinguished literary critic who grew up in immigrant Brownsville. Kazin's sojourns into other neighborhoods and boroughs exposed him to new worlds.

Lewis, David Levering. *When Harlem Was in Vogue.* A brilliant, authoritative study of Harlem in the 1920s.

Liebling, A. J. *Back Where I Came From.* The *New Yorker* writer of the '30s and '40s pens a "love letter to the City of New York." Liebling reveled in the sights, sounds, smells, and—above all—speech and people of his hometown.

Lobas, Vladimir. *Taxi from Hell: Confessions of a Russian Hack.* He doesn't know how to drive, he doesn't speak English, and he doesn't know the city. Nonetheless, he lands a job as a New York City cab driver. The true story of an émigré Russian intellectual's first years in New York.

Magnum Photographers, with introduction by David Halberstam. *New York September 11.* A moving tribute to the city, its emergency workers, the World Trade Center, and the victims of the terrorist attack.

Manbeck, John B., ed. *The Neighborhoods of Brooklyn.* An informative look at New York City's most-populous borough, with much information about individual neighborhoods that's hard to find anywhere else.

Mitchell, Joseph. *Up in the Old Hotel.* A reprint of four classics penned by the deadpan *The New Yorker* chronicler of city life. "McSorley's Wonderful Salon," "Old Mr. Flood," "The Bottom of the Harbor," and "Joe Gould's Secret" are included.

Morris, Jan. *Manhattan '45.* The well-known travel writer imagines what Manhattan was like immediately after WW II.

Moscow, Henry. *The Street Book: An Encyclopedia of Manhattan's Street Names and Their Origins.* A meticulous street-by-street examination of the city, filled with odd surprises and delightful tidbits of history.

Sante, Luc. *Low Life.* A highly original and literate book that delves into the underbelly—opium dens, brothels, sweatshops—of old New York.

Simon, Kate. *Bronx Primitive: Portraits in a Childhood.* A rich, evocative, and startlingly frank coming-of-age story set in an immigrant Jewish neighborhood just after WW I.

Thomas, Piri. *Down These Mean Streets.* The edgy yet lyrical autobiographical account of a young Puerto Rican's search for identity in crime-ridden East Harlem.

Wakefield, Dan. *New York in the Fifties.* An evocative memoir of life in Greenwich Village in the pre-1960s bohemian heyday of Dorothy Day, Jack Kerouac, James Baldwin, Allen Ginsberg, Gay Talese, and Norman Mailer.

Wang, Harvey. *Harvey Wang's New York.* For a first-rate introduction to New York's extraordinary cast of characters, pick up this slim volume of portraits. Among those photographed are a pillow maker, mannequin maker, gravedigger, kosher butcher, and bowling alley mechanic.

White, E. B. *Essays of E. B. White.* The great *New Yorker* essayist, poet, and storyteller writes of New York and Florida, snow and pigs, railroads, and Will Strunk. Included is "Here Is New York," one of the most insightful essays on the city ever written.

FICTION

Auster, Paul. *New York Trilogy: City of Glass, Ghosts, the Locked Room.* Dark-humor, suspense, mind games, and film noir in a modern classic about New York City.

Baldwin, James. *Another Country.* A sprawling and disturbing novel, set largely in Greenwich Village and Harlem in the 1960s. Another Baldwin work that takes place in the city is *Go Tell It on the Mountain.*

Capote, Truman. *Breakfast at Tiffany's.* The moving story of a glamorous madcap adrift on the Upper East Side in the 1950s.

Crane, Stephen. *Maggie, A Girl of the Streets.* Crane's impressionistic, ground-breaking first novel—published at his own expense in 1893—was one of the first to make slum dwellers and social problems the subject of literature.

Doctorow, E. L. *Ragtime.* Rich white, Harlem black, immigrant Jew—Doctorow writes of three families whose lives converge in early 20th-century New York. A deft weaving of fictional characters and real people, including Emma Goldman and Stanford White.

Dreiser, Theodore. *Sister Carrie.* The classic novel of an innocent girl set adrift in a corrupt city, *Sister Carrie* begins in Chicago but comes to its harrowing conclusion in the bleak, heartless streets of New York.

Ellison, Ralph. *Invisible Man.* The classic 1952 novel follows a nameless protagonist from his home in the Deep South to the basements of Harlem. A masterpiece of African American literature that chronicles the effects of bigotry on victims and perpetrators alike.

Finney, Jack. *Time and Again.* A cult classic that time-travels back and forth between the present and the 1880s, when New York was little more than an overgrown small town.

Gaitskill, Mary. *Bad Behavior.* A fierce, original collection of stories about life in the bedrooms of the urban fringe.

Hijuelos, Oscar. *The Mambo Kings Play Songs of Love.* A rich and deeply resonant novel that recreates the world of immigrant Cuban musicians living in New York post–WW II.

James, Henry. *Washington Square.* One of James's shorter and more accessible novels, *Washington Square* is an engrossing tale of the manners and mores of upper-crust 19th-century New York.

Lopate, Philip, ed. *Writing New York.* A thought-provoking collection of short stories, essays, and poems about New York City.

McCarthy, Mary. *The Group.* One of America's foremost women-of-letters uses her acerbic wit to chronicle the lives of eight Vassar graduates living in New York in the '30s.

McInerney, Jay. *Bright Lights, Big City.* A young man immerses himself in the excesses of 1980s New York—the clubs, the drugs, the after-hour hot spots—until brought to an abrupt reckoning.

Morrison, Toni. *Jazz.* The Pulitzer Prize–winning author sets this novel in Harlem in 1926. This tale of passion, jealousy, murder, and redemption begins when a door-to-door salesman of beauty products shoots his lover.

Paley, Grace. *Enormous Changes at the Last Minute.* Quirky, funny, sad, combative, vulnerable Paley, who grew up in immigrant New York in the '20s and '30s, captures the soul of New York in one of her best collections of stories.

Parker, Dorothy. *The Portable Dorothy Parker.* Poems, stories, articles, and reviews by that most quotable of *New Yorker* writers.

Petry, Ann. *The Street.* Both a historical document and a novel, this bleak and poignant classic takes place in poverty-torn Harlem in the late 1940s.

Powell, Dawn. *The Wicked Pavilion.* A comic masterpiece set in the 1940s in a dingy yet fashionable cafe frequented by small-time hacks, hustlers, and poseurs. Among Powell's other novels set in New York is *Angels on Toast.*

Roth, Henry. *Call It Sleep.* A classic coming-of-age novel of immigrant life, first published in 1934 and set on the Lower East Side.

Thompson, Kay. *Eloise.* The heroine of this beloved children's book is a six-year-old who lives in the Plaza Hotel.

Wharton, Edith. *The Age of Innocence.* The first book written by a woman to win the Pulitzer Prize is a subtle, elegant portrait of desire and betrayal in moneyed Old New York. Among Wharton's other books set in the city are *The House of Mirth, A Backward Glance,* and *Old New York.*

Wolfe, Thomas. *The Bonfire of the Vanities.* The extravagant, hyperbolic tale of a greedy Wall Street bond trader who takes a wrong turn in the Bronx.

Zabor, Rafi. *The Bear Comes Home.* In this winner of the PEN–Faulkner Award, an intellectual sax-playing bear, well versed in literature, jazz and philosophy, fights to find his place in the world. A comic gem, with great insights into what it means to be an artist, set largely in New York City and Woodstock/Bearsville, New York.

Poetry

Among the many poets who have written extensively on New York City are Djuna Barnes, Hart Crane, Allen Ginsberg, Langston Hughes, Frank O'Hara and Walt Whitman.

New York State

A number of excellent regional presses, publishing everything from history to fiction, are located upstate. Foremost among them are the **Black Dome Press** (RR1, Box 422, Hensonville, NY 12439; 518/734-6357), **Purple Mountain Press** (P.O. Box E-3, Fleischmanns, NY 12430; 845/254-4062) in the Catskills, and **Heart of the Lakes Publishing** (P.O. Box 299, Interlaken, NY 14847; 607/532-4997) in the Finger Lakes. Their books are generally available in local bookstores.

SPECIALIZED GUIDES AND TRAVEL ESSAYS

Arbeiter, Jean, and Linda C. Cirino. *Permanent Addresses: A Guide to the Resting Places of Famous Americans.* More fascinating than the actual burial sites are the witty thumbnail sketches of the deceased. Includes sections on entertainers, presidents, social reformers, artists, sports figures, and more.

Berman, Eleanor. *Away for the Weekend: New York.* Though primarily aimed at New York

City folk, this well-written guide can be a good resource for out-of-towners as well. Berman offers 52 getaway suggestions for short trips in New York, New Jersey, and Connecticut.

Cantor, George. *Where the Old Roads Go: Driving the First Federal Highways of the Northeast.* In this sojourn along the first federal highways, Cantor takes readers to all sorts of out-of-the-way places, and includes plenty of background information.

Chase, Suzi Forbes. *The Hamptons Book: A Complete Guide.* An excellent source book for anyone planning to spend much time in the Hamptons. Included are extensive restaurant, lodging, entertainment, and shopping listings.

Folwell, Elizabeth. *The Adirondack Book: A Complete Guide.* An excellent resource for anyone planning to spend time in the Adirondacks, by the editor of *Adirondack Life* magazine. Includes extensive listings.

Harrison, Marina, and Lucy D. Rosenfeld. *Art on Site: Country Artwalks from Maine to Maryland.* This unique guide points the way to artists' studios, outdoor sculptures, eccentric gardens, and historic art sites. Over one-third of the destinations covered are in New York State.

Kauffman, Bill. *Country Towns of New York.* An interesting foray into small-town New York, covering both well-known destinations such as Cooperstown and more obscure ones such as Angelica.

Michaels, Joanne, and Mary-Margaret Barile. *The Hudson Valley and Catskill Mountains.* An excellent source of information on the Hudson Valley and Catskills. Organized according to county, with extensive listings.

Mulligan, Tim. *The Traveler's Guide to the Hudson River Valley.* An engaging, personalized guide offering a good mix of both practical and historical information.

Suggested Reading

Murray, William H. H. *Adventures in the Wilderness.* The 1869 guidebook that jump-started tourism in the Adirondacks is still a most readable classic (reissue).

Older, Anne, Peggy DiConza, and Susanne Dumbleton. *In & Around Albany, Schenectady and Troy.* An informative guide for anyone planning to spend time in the Capital District. Includes chapters on restaurants, shopping, sports, and recreation.

Schuman, Michael A. *52 New York Weekends.* A good sampler, with suggested outings in New York City, Long Island, and upstate.

Smith, Doug, and Polly Smith. *The Cheap Gourmets' Dining Guide to the Niagara Frontier.* An off-beat guide to some of the more unusual eateries in Western New York.

Steinbicker, Earl, ed. *Daytrips from New York: 100 One-Day Adventures from the Metropolitan Area.* An especially good guide for those wishing to explore the area by car. Detailed driving directions to area attractions provided, as well as maps.

Waite, Diana S., ed. *Albany Architecture.* Anyone interested in the state capital's extraordinary architecture will want to pick up this informative guide, complete with maps and photographs.

Webster, Harriet. *Favorite Short Trips in New York State.* Twenty-seven short trips from Long Island to Niagara Falls. Good tips for families traveling with children.

Williams, Deborah. *Country Roads of New York.* An engaging foray into upstate New York, organized according to day- or weekend-long drives.

Writers' Program of the Work Projects Administration. *New York: A Guide to the Empire State.* First published in 1940, this classic guidebook is packed full of intriguing historical tidbits on virtually every town upstate.

Reminick, Joan, ed. *Zagat Survey: Long Island Restaurants.* Good, pithy reviews, based on the reports of volunteer culinary reviewers.

OUTDOOR GUIDES

Anderson, Scott Edward. *Walks in Nature's Empire.* A guide to 35 of the Nature Conservancy's loveliest preserves, many of which are unknown to most New Yorkers.

Dyson, Katharine Delavan. *The Finger Lakes: A Complete Guide.* A succinct guide to attractions, restaurants, lodging, shopping, culture, history, and more.

Ehling, William P. *50 Hikes in Central New York.* Hikes in and around the Finger Lakes for both novice and experienced outdoorspeople. Detailed maps included.

Ehling, William P. *50 Hikes in Western New York.* Ehling explores one of the most underhiked regions of the state. Detailed maps are included.

Harrison, Marina, and Lucy D. Rosenfeld. *A Walker's Guidebook: Serendipitous Outings Near New York City.* Gentle meanderings through Long Island and the Hudson Valley. There is a special section for birdwatchers.

Kick, Peter, Barbara McMartin, and James M. Long. *50 Hikes in the Hudson Valley.* A triumvirate of experienced hikers recommend day-trips for both new and seasoned hikers in the Catskills and lower Hudson Valley. Detailed maps are included.

McMartin, Barbara. *50 Hikes in the Adirondacks.* The doyenne of New York's outdoor writers and an authority on the Adirondacks outlines the region's top trails. Detailed maps are included.

New York–New Jersey Trail Conference, Inc. *New York Walk Book.* Updated in 1998, this "hiker's Bible" reflects the many changes that have occurred in the region since the book was first published in 1923. Some of the old trails are gone, of course, but a surprising number of new areas have also opened up, thanks largely to the public acquisition of land. The book also features excellent sections on the history, geology, flora, and fauna of the regions immediately surrounding New York City.

Shea, Barbara. *Discover Long Island.* An excellent guide to Long Island's attractions, along with mini reviews of over 100 restaurants, written by a *Newsday* travel writer.

Wadsworth, Bruce. *An Adirondack Sampler: Day Hikes for All Seasons.* An excellent guide for beginning hikers and those new to the Adirondacks. Fifty hikes are recommended.

HISTORY, BIOGRAPHY, AND JOURNALISM

Adams, Arthur G. *The Catskills: An Illustrated Historical Guide with Gazetteer.* An informative history, with major sections on waterways, railroads, and famous hotels. The gazetteer, which sketches the histories of hundreds of towns, is especially interesting.

Brownell, Joseph W., and Patricia A. Wawrzaszek. *Adirondack Tragedy: The Gillette Murder Case of 1906.* The authors meticulously retrace the events of the Gillette case, upon which Theodore Dreiser based *An American Tragedy.* Historic photographs and documents are included.

Carmer, Carl. *The Hudson.* A personal, anecdotal history of the Hudson, first published in 1939. A folk historian who lived most of his life upstate, Carmer was the author of 32 books and the editor of 60 others.

Cuomo, Mario. *The New York Idea: An Experiment in Democracy.* At times the former governor's treatise on the state, published just prior to the 1994 gubernatorial election, reads suspiciously like a campaign speech, but there's valuable information here. Cuomo analyzes

certain aspects of New York's past and looks ahead to its future.

Ellis, David Maldwyn. *New York: City and State.* This concise, well-written volume offers an excellent introduction to the state's character and history.

Ellis, David M., et al. *A Short History of New York State.* Despite the title, an in-depth, scholarly look at the history of the Empire State. Well-written, but not aimed at those with a casual interest.

Evers, Alf. *The Catskills: From Wilderness to Woodstock.* The preeminent Catskills historian takes a comprehensive look at one of the state's most complex regions; an engaging read.

Graham, Frank Jr. *The Adirondack Park: A Political History.* This first-rate, well-written book covers both the general history of the park and its politics of land-use planning.

Hall, Bruce Edward. *Diamond Street: The Story of the Little Town with the Big Red Light District.* Surprising though it may seem, the sleepy town of Hudson, New York was once a notorious Red Light Capital known to sailors around the world. Hall chronicles the tale.

Jackson, Kenneth T. *Crabgrass Frontier: The Suburbanization of the United States.* An important study on the history of the suburb explores how New York City evolved and what its bedroom communities are like today.

James, Henry. *The American Scene.* In 1904, James—then over 60 and at the height of his fame—returned to America after decades spent in Europe. This book, both a travelogue and an essay on the American character, is the result. The four chapters on New York are especially fine.

Jamieson, Paul, ed. *The Adirondack Reader.* An excellent anthology whose writings span nearly

400 years of Adirondack history, natural history, and culture. Excerpts by everyone from Ralph Waldo Emerson to Joyce Carol Oates.

Jones, Louis C. *Murder at Cherry Hill: The Strang-Whipple Case, 1827.* The tale of an infamous murder involving one of Albany's leading families.

Kennedy, William. *O Albany!* The Pulitzer Prize winner of *Ironweed* takes a look at his hometown, that "improbable city of political wizards, fearless ethnics, spectacular aristocrats, splendid nobodies, and underrated scoundrels." Dense and hard to follow in spots.

Klinkenborg, Verlyn. *The Last Fine Time.* An evocative re-creation of Buffalo in the 1940s, as well as a succinct chronicling of America's ethnic and industrial history.

Lyons, Oren, and John Mohawk, eds. *Exiled in the Land of the Free: Democracy, Indian Nations, and the U.S. Constitution.* An intriguing account of the Native American influence on the framing of the Constitution.

Matthiessen, Peter. *Men's Lives: The Surfmen and Baymen of the South Fork.* The well-known travel and nature writer describes a vanishing way of life. Matthiessen grew up and continues to live on Long Island, where he has spent much time fishing with the men he writes about.

Merrill, Arch. *Slim Fingers Beckon.* A breezy, anecdotal history of the Finger Lakes, written by a folk historian and journalist. Merrill has written over 20 books on the Finger Lakes; this is one of his best.

Mountain Top Historical Society. *Kaaterskill: From the Catskill Mountain House to the Hudson River School.* Made famous by the painters of the Hudson River School, Kaaterskill Falls was once one of the most popular tourist destinations in America. This slim volume offers a good historical overview and information on hiking to the falls today.

Native American Services in New York State. *A Proud Heritage.* A brief but well-done introduction to the Iroquois and Algonquins in New York State, written and edited by Native American leaders and scholars.

Shoumatoff, Alex. *Westchester: Portrait of a County.* Though probably best-known for his writings on Brazil, Shoumatoff grew up in much more prosaic surroundings. Herewith, a lyrical ode to his roots.

Solomon, Nancy, with Paul Bentel. *On the Bay: Bay Houses and Maritime Culture on Long Island's Marshlands.* A folklorist documents the unique houses/shacks that fisherfolk have used as base camps for generations.

Stanton, Elizabeth Cady. *Eighty Years & More: Reminiscences 1815–1897.* In a powerful, absorbing autobiography, this early leader of the women's movement tells both her own story and that of all 19th-century American women. Stanton lived much of her life upstate and organized the first women's conference in Seneca Falls.

Thompson, Harold W. *New York State: Folktales, Legends and Ballads.* Though wordy at times, this classic is highly recommended for anyone interested in folk culture. It's full of wondrous tales about pioneers, "Injun-fighters," witches, whalers, canawlers (canal workers), mountaineers, lovers, and murderers.

Thompson, John H., ed. *Geography of New York State.* Though now 30 years out of date, this hefty volume remains the most comprehensive reference work on the state. Sixteen expert contributors cover New York's physical, historical, and economic geographies.

Van Zandt, Roland. *The Catskill Mountain House.* The story of the Catskills' most famous hotel is also the story of the rise and heartbreaking fall of the Catskills as a popular resort. Evocatively written; many historic photographs.

White, William Chapman. *Adirondack Country.* A comprehensive book on the region, written in the 1950s by a renowned journalist and essayist.

Wilson, Edmund. *Upstate: Records and Recollections of Northern New York.* One of the rare books that examines the character of upstate New York, where Wilson and his family summered for generations. The first third of the book, covering various aspects of New York history, is especially astute; the rest is diary entries.

Wilson, Edmund. *Apologies to the Iroquois.* A study of Iroquois culture, first published in 1960.

FICTION

Banks, Russell. *The Sweet Hereafter.* A horrific schoolbus accident in Sam Dent, NY results in the deaths of 14 children. Banks writes compassionately of how the small town responds and somehow moves beyond grief to redemption.

Conners, Bernard F. *Dancehall.* A mass paperback novel based on the murder of a young woman in Lake Placid, NY. The woman's remarkably well-preserved body surfaced from the intensely cold lake 20 years after her death.

Cooper, James Fenimore. *The Last of the Mohicans.* In knotty, unwieldy prose, Cooper's classic on the American frontier explores the friendship between two men—Hawkeye and Chingachgook—at odds with their own people.

Dobyns, Stephen. *Saratoga Hunting.* Low key detective Charlie Bradshaw, operating in the summer horse-racing capital of America, reopens two cases he thought he had solved 20 years earlier. The seventh of Dobyns's Charlie Bradshaw books.

Dreiser, Theodore. *An American Tragedy.* The classic book on the dark side of the American Dream, set largely in the Adirondacks and Central New York.

Edmonds, Walter Dumaux. *Drums Along the Mohawk.* Set in the Mohawk Valley during the Revolutionary War; later made into a movie of the same name starring Henry Fonda.

Ferber, Edna. *Saratoga Trunk.* Life in Saratoga Springs in the 1880s, as seen through the eyes of an ex-cowboy and his drop-dead gorgeous mistress.

Fitzgerald, F. Scott. *The Great Gatsby.* One of the finest works of 20th-century literature takes place largely on the north shore of Long Island.

Fox, Austin McC., ed. *The Legend of Sleepy Hollow and other selections from Washington Irving.* The first American literary writer of note tells the tales of the Headless Horseman galloping through Sleepy Hollow and Rip Van Winkle awakening from his 20-year sleep.

Gardner, John. *The Sunlight Dialogues.* A grand and complex portrait of America in the '60s, set in the small, agricultural town of Batavia, New York.

Kennedy, William. *Billy Phelan's Greatest Game.* The second, and arguably best, of Kennedy's triumvirate of novels set in underworld Albany chronicles the fall and redemption of a small-time hustler. The other two books in the cycle are *Legs* and *Ironweed.*

Oates, Joyce Carol. *Bellefleur.* The complex and opulent tale of six generations of Bellefleurs, a wealthy and notorious family who live in a region much like the Adirondacks. Other Oates novels set upstate are *A Bloodsmoor Romance* and *Mysteries of Winterthurn.*

Taylor, Robert Lewis. *Niagara.* A comic novel by a Pulitzer Prize–winning author, set in 19th-century Niagara Falls. A newspaperman is sent to the then-new resort to report on the escapades of its rich vacationers.

Zabor, Rafi. *The Bear Comes Home.* See Fiction under New York City, above.

Index

Children's Attractions

Animal Farm Petting Zoo: 298
Brooklyn Children's Museum: 233
Catskill Game Farm: 412–413
Children's Museum: 485
Children's Museum at Saratoga: 510
Children's Museum of Manhattan: 201
Children's Museum of the Arts: 105
Discovery Center of the Southern Tier: 496
Fort Rickey Children's Discovery Zoo: 487
Junior Museum: 460
Long Island Children's Museum: 293
Long Island Game Farm: 298
Muscoot Farm: 335
Staten Island Children's Museum: 254
Strong Museum: 642

see also amusement parks; wildlife refuges and zoos

Index

Museums and Galleries in New York City

M

Index

Index

Scenic Drives

State University of New York at New Paltz: 396–397
Statue of Liberty: 75–76
St. Augustus Church: 101
St. Bartholomew's Church: 166
St. Bonaventure University: 688–689
St. Demetrios Greek Orthodox Church: 240
Steel Plant Museum: 664
Steinway Piano Factory: 240
Ste. Marie Among the Iroquois: 590
Sterling Forest State Park: 352–353
Sterling Renaissance Festival: 615
Stevenson, Robert Louis: 548
St. George Hotel: 224
St. George's Episcopal Church: 136
St. George's Ukrainian Catholic Church: 114
Stillwater: 517
St. Irene's Greek Orthodox Church: 240
St. James: 275–276
St. James Church: 92
St. James Episcopal Church: 353
St. James General Store: 275
St. John's A.M.E. Church: 674
St. John's Episcopal Church (Medina): 676

State Parks

Allegany State Park: 691
Ausable Point State Park: 538
Bear Mountain State Park: 344–345
Bear Spring Mountain State Park: 441
Beaver Island State Park: 668
Buttermilk Falls State Park: 610
Catskill State Park: 390, 407
Caumsett State Historic Park: 274
Cayuga Lake State Park: 602–603
Chenango Valley State Park: 496–497
Chittenango Falls State Park: 491–492
Clarence Fahnestock State Park: 359
Darien Lakes State Park: 681
Delta Lake State Park: 487
Devil's Hole State Park: 673
Fillmore Glen State Park: 599
Fort Niagara State Park: 675
Gilbert Lake State Park: 477
Glimmerglass State Park: 473–474
Golden Beach State Park: 561
Grafton Lakes State Park: 462
Green Lakes State Park: 592
Hamlin Beach State Park: 649
Harriet Hollister Spenser State Park: 637
Harriman State Park: 343–344
Heckscher State Park: 297
Hither Hills State Park: 315
Hook Mountain State Park: 340
John Boyd Thatcher State Park: 457
Keuka Lake State Park: 628
Lake Erie State Park: 699
Lakeside Beach State Park: 678
Lake Superior State Park: 430
Lake Taghkanic State Park: 377
Letchworth State Park: 637–638
Lodi Point State Marine Park: 615
Long Point State Park: 697
Mills-Norrie State Park: 370
Mine Kill State Park: 481
Minnewaska State Park: 398
Montauk Downs State Park: 315
Montauk Point State Park: 315–316
Niagara Reservation State Park: 670–672
Nyack Beach State Park: 339
Orient Beach State Park: 287
Riverbank State Park: 215
Robert H. Treman State Park: 610
Robert Moses State Park: 293
Rockefeller State Park Preserve: 331
Rockland Lake State Park: 339
Rogers Rock State Park: 531
Sampson State Park: 615
Saratoga Spa State Park: 514
Selkirk Shores State Park: 567
Seneca Lake State Park: 614
Sterling Forest State Park: 352–353
Sunken Meadow State Park: 275
Taconic State Park: 378
Tallman Mountain State Park: 341
Taughannock Falls State Park: 605
Verona Beach State Park: 488
Walt Whitman Birthplace State Historic Park: 273
Watkins Glen State Park: 617–618
Wellesley Island State Park: 576
Whirlpool State Park: 673
Wildwood State Park: 279

Wildlife Refuges and Zoos

N Index

Acknowledgments

A heartfelt thanks to the many people who helped me put together this book, both in the current and earlier editions. Dozens of tourism officials made my job easier by providing me with background information and showing me around their corners of the state. Especially helpful were Mary Summers in Western New York, Beulah Decker in the Finger Lakes, Deb Taylor in Central New York, and the New York Convention and Visitors Bureau.

In New York City, I would particularly like to thank Kenneth Jackson of Columbia University, whose marvelous lectures on the history of New York City greatly influenced this book. A special thanks, too, to Robert Baron of the New York State Council on the Arts, who put me in touch with a string of folklorists working on un-usual projects across the state. Among them were Nancy Solomon, Janis Benincasa, Dan Ward, Varick Chittenden, Linda Norris, Peter Voorheis, Kate Koperski, Mary Zwolinski, Catherine Schwoeffermann, and Steve Zeitlin. In addition, I would like to thank historian Alf Evers; Tema Harnik of the Lower Hudson River Conference; Chuck Stead of Rockland County, and Deborah DeWan and the Erpf Catskill Cultural Center for information on environmental issues.

Finally, this book could not have been written without the support of my family and friends, and the staff at Avalon Travel Publishing. I am greatly indebted to my editors over the years for correcting my inconsistencies, tightening my prose, and shepherding this mammoth project through the editorial process.

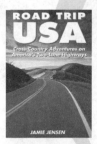

U.S.~ Metric Conversion

1 inch	=	2.54 centimeters (cm)
1 foot	=	.304 meters (m)
1 yard	=	0.914 meters
1 mile	=	1.6093 kilometers (km)
1 km	=	.6214 miles
1 fathom	=	1.8288 m
1 chain	=	20.1168 m
1 furlong	=	201.168 m
1 acre	=	.4047 hectares
1 sq km	=	100 hectares
1 sq mile	=	2.59 square km
1 ounce	=	28.35 grams
1 pound	=	.4536 kilograms
1 short ton	=	.90718 metric ton
1 short ton	=	2000 pounds
1 long ton	=	1.016 metric tons
1 long ton	=	2240 pounds
1 metric ton	=	1000 kilograms
1 quart	=	.94635 liters
1 US gallon	=	3.7854 liters
1 Imperial gallon	=	4.5459 liters
1 nautical mile	=	1.852 km

To compute celsius temperatures, subtract 32 from Fahrenheit and divide by 1.8. To go the other way, multiply celsius by 1.8 and add 32.

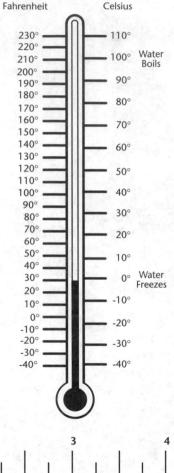